Footprint **New Zealand**

Darroch Donald
4th edition

*"New Zealand is not a small country
but a large village."*

Peter Jackson (Kiwi Film Director, *Lord of the Rings*)

New Zealand Highlights

See colour maps at back of book

❶ Experience history and culture combined at Waitangi – the **'birthplace of the nation'**, page 156.

❷ Find some relief at Kawakawa's **'Hundertwasser Public Toilets'**, perhaps the artiest in the world, page 158.

❸ Admire the vistas, have dinner, climb the mast, or even jump from Auckland's hypodermic **Sky Tower**, page 76.

❹ Be the first to see the sunrise from **East Cape**, page 326.

❺ Take the real 'underground' in the **'Lost World'** or the **'Haggas Honking Holes'** at **Waitomo**, page 224.

❻ Call in at the Devil's Home at the **Wai-o-tapu** Thermal Reserve, page 247.

❼ See some tremendous tectonics along the **Tongariro Crossing**, page 297.

❽ Bombard the senses at **Te Papa**, the nation's most celebrated museum, page 395.

❾ Find solitude at **Wharariki Beach** and feel guilty leaving footprints, page 464.

Tasman Sea

4

Contents

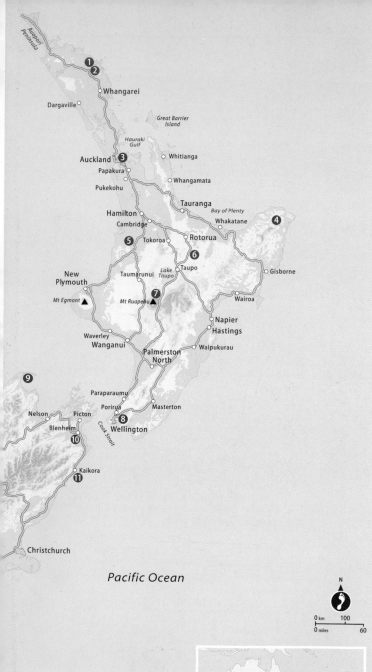

Auraori Peninsula

Whangarei

Dargaville

Great Barrier Island

Hauraki Gulf

Whitianga

Auckland ❸

Papakura

Whangamata

Pukekohu

Tauranga

Hamilton

Bay of Plenty

Cambridge

Whakatane

❹

Rotorua

Tokoroa

❺

❻

New Plymouth

Taumarunui

Lake Taupo

Taupo

Gisborne

Mt Egmont

Mt Ruapehu

❼

Wairoa

Napier

Hastings

Waverley

Wanganui

Waipukurau

Palmerston North

❾

Paraparaumu

Porirua

Masterton

Nelson

Picton

Cook Strait

Wellington

❽

Blenheim

❿

Kaikora

⓫

Christchurch

Pacific Ocean

N

0 km   100
0 miles   60

❿ See white, red
then a bit fuzzy,
touring the
**vineyards of
Marlborough**,
page 422.

⓫ It's no 'fluke'
spotting whales or
dolphins off the
Kaikoura Coast,
page 499.

⓬ Enter the realms
of Rohan or Edoras
(*Lord of the Rings*) in
the **Rangitata River
Valley**, page 480.

⓭ Go glacier
walking on **Franz
Josef** or **Fox**,
page 566.

⓮ Follow the
river to the **Rob
Roy Glacier**
near Wanaka,
page 641.

⓯ Visit the aptly
named **Paradise**
in the **Dart River
Valley**, page 625.

⓰ Admire the grace
of the albatross, or
the charm of a
penguin, on the
Otago Peninsula,
page 592.

⓱ Watch keas
dismantle your
hire car on
the majestic
Milford Road,
page 648.

⓲ Experience the
'sound of silence'
while kayaking
amidst dolphins on
Doubtful Sound,
page 659.

Bay of Plenty

Taupo & Ruapehu

Taranaki

East coast

Wanganui & Manawatu

Wellington

A boiling vent, aptly named 'The Champagne Pool', is just one of many colourful thermal features at the Wai-o-tapu Reserve near Rotorua.

Maori carving
The elaborate facial patterns, known as 'Moko', add to the fearsome look of a Maori warrior.

A foot in the door

Put Charles Darwin, Claude Monet and JRR Tolkien in a room with six bottles of vodka and some recreational drugs and, combined, they still could not come close to the concept of New Zealand. If nature had a design studio, full of her most surreal and stupendous ideas, on the mantelpiece would be New Zealand or, as the Maori call it, 'The Land of the Long White Cloud'.

The country is living proof that small can not only beautiful but also incredibly diverse and complex. The two main islands, North Island and South Island, are both quite different. North, which is far less mountainous, is home to more than two-thirds of New Zealanders, or 'Kiwis', who live life to the beat of a faster rhythm than their countrified neighbours to the south. For the tourist, North Island generally holds less aesthetic appeal than South Island, but few miss, or indeed forget, the expansive views across Auckland from its hypodermic Sky Tower; the dramatic displays of Maori culture in Northland; or the brooding and colourful thermal features in and around Rotorua.

South Island, however, is said to offer the 'true essence' of New Zealand. To travel through it is like a fun-filled lesson in geography and guarantees to have the digital camera running on overload. Vast empty beaches where you feel guilty leaving a single set of footprints; endless mountain ranges blanketed in snow and rainforest; pristine lakes, waterfalls and fiords; giant glaciers; vast limestone caves and arches; natural springs and fizzing hot pools. Whatever your intention, if you choose New Zealand, although it may seem at the end of the Earth it is certainly heaven upon it. It is like making an appointment with Doctor Nature and her able assistant nurse Adrenaline. And now is the time to 'take the cure'.

10 Kiwi collective

Despite its relatively infant history, New Zealand provides a fascinating cultural mêlée. Before the early European explorers paved the way for widespread colonial immigration, the native Maori had developed their own highly individual way of life. Despite the fact that, like any other displaced people, they have struggled to maintain this identity and culture, thankfully 'Maoritanga' (Maoridom) is enjoying something of a renaissance in modern day New Zealand. Maori issues are now taken very seriously within government and in legal circles, especially when it comes to land rights and the harvesting of natural resources. When it comes to tourism, however, the presentation of that native culture can be overly commercial.

If you can penetrate beneath the colourful veneer you will be exposed to a different world. Whether it is through a stay on a *marae*, a cultural performance, a *hangi* (feast), or simple friendship, learning about the traditional Maori lifestyle will enhance your visit and a provide a sense of hope that biculturalism has an optimistic future. You will also find that through the solid roots of Maoridom and colonialism a unique 'Kiwi' culture and identity is growing both strong and steadfast.

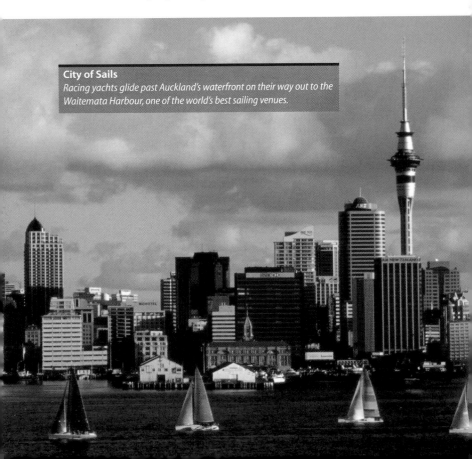

City of Sails
Racing yachts glide past Auckland's waterfront on their way out to the Waitemata Harbour, one of the world's best sailing venues.

Perfect isolation

New Zealand has a sound yet muted voice, seldom heard beyond Australasia. Its chronic struggle with anonymity within the developed nations has a good deal to do with its geographical position and size, and is both a blessing and a curse. The low population density means it lacks the many problems of overcrowding, and the diverse natural landscape is well suited to a healthy, outdoor lifestyle. It is also these ingredients that make it such an appealing place to live or visit.

Yet, stuck in the vast shadow of its charismatic neighbour, Australia, New Zealand struggles to be taken seriously on the world stage, or to assert much political or economic influence. Let's face it; no country wants to be seen as just a 'tourist playground' or that 'place full of sheep where *Lord of the Rings* was filmed'. But with continued good governance and sound environmental management New Zealand can, in its own way, be a world leader. It is very effective at leading by example and – to use an analogy – is a bit like the unassuming, popular local in the pub, who, when the religious arguments or international power grabs go horribly wrong and the inevitable fights break out, helps break it up, makes the foolhardy see sense and replaces the furniture.

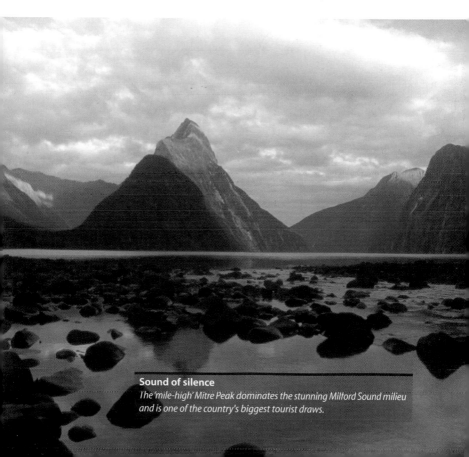

Sound of silence
The 'mile-high' Mitre Peak dominates the stunning Milford Sound milieu and is one of the country's biggest tourist draws.

1   *A fence near Wanaka decorated by underwear may seem an unusual sight, but such creative installations have become quite common.* ▶▶ *See page 628.*

2   *The vineyards of New Zealand often combine great wine with grandiose or 'statement' architecture, in this case Te Mata Estate, Hawkes Bay.* ▶▶ *See page 353.*

3   *The numerous lakes across the South Island provide a wealth of recreational opportunities, including kayaking, jet boating, fishing and windsurfing.* ▶▶ *See pages 24-25.*

4   *The cheeky kea is one of the most intelligent (and mischievous) birds on the planet. For them cars offer the ideal resource for complete and utter delinquency.* ▶▶ *See page 715.*

5   *Mount Cook National Park offers the rare opportunity to combine flightseeing with a glacier landing.* ▶▶ *See page 533.*

6   *A farmstay can be the perfect oppotunity to really experience New Zealand's rural life.* ▶▶ *See page 46.*

7   *The almost perfect volcanic peak of Mount Taranaki is one of New Zealand's most recognized mountains.* ▶▶ *See page 319.*

8   *One, two, three … bungeeee. The 134-m bungee at Nevis in Queenstown, is the country's highest.* ▶▶ *See page 616.*

9   *Christchurch is known for its English-style aesthetics and its fleet of lovingly restored trams that still rattle through the city centre streets.* ▶▶ *See page 472.*

10 *Rugby is the nation's principal sporting pastime. Two suburban teams come head to head in Auckland.* ▶▶ *See pages 28 and 107.*

11 *The famous signpost at the end of State Highway 1 in Bluff, South Island reminds you it's a very long way from anywhere.* ▶▶ *See page 669.*

12 *A parasail is launched from the shores of Lake Wanaka with the aid of a fast jet boat.* ▶▶ *See page 629.*

The bungee way of life

Outdoor activities are more than just a tourist attraction in New Zealand, they are a way of life. The national psyche seems to crave adventure and the environment is nothing short of a natural Disneyland. The sheer range of activities on offer is staggering, with a veritable smørgasbord of possibilities from sea kayaking, cruising or flightseeing to swimming with dolphins, whale watching or tandem skydiving. True, many of these activities can also be found elsewhere in the world, but in such wealth, to such a standard and surrounded by such scenic majesty – almost certainly not. Such is the average New Zealander's love of new and exciting feats of energetic entertainment, that they have become famous for creating their own bizarre and almost unimaginable pursuits. The methods and modes defy description here except to say that they consistently shift one's adrenaline pumps to overload. Where else in the world can you roll down a hill inside a clear plastic bubble, launch yourself by a bungee cord off the nation's tallest building, or fly at 120 kph strapped to little more than a stretcher with a microlight engine attached?

On a more sedate level are the endless opportunities for wilderness tramping (hiking). Many people come to New Zealand to experience some of the best walking on earth. It is no exaggeration to call New Zealand, and the South Island in particular, the walking capital of the world. Not only is the scenery awe-inspiring, but the range of options is vast. With 14 national parks offering everything from hour-long coastal walks to 10-day wilderness expeditions, you have choices of everything from easy-going strolls to once-in-a-lifetime challenges. Even the names are evocative Kepler, Dusky, Rees-Dart and Greenstone, to name just a few each blessed with its own range of extreme features from volcanoes and glaciers to lakes and waterfalls.

Wild world

Experiencing wildlife in New Zealand has been described as being as close to being on another planet as one can get. Millions of years of isolation have resulted in the evolution of a fascinating ark of unique species from the bizarre and whimsical kiwi to the prehistoric tuatara. With so few mammals in a country blanketed by native rainforest, it was the birds that dominated and, with no ground predators, many became flightless. Yet this biodiversity is now under siege and risks being lost forever. From the day that humans arrived, they placed an indelible footprint on the environment; the first step in an almost inevitable journey of destruction. Introduced animals and plants like the rat, the cat and the possum, together with unsustainable hunting and gathering methods, devastated native flora and fauna, many species becoming extinct or replaced. Today, for example, for every native plant there is one introduced and the iconic kiwi will almost certainly not be present in the wild anywhere except on offshore islands within another two decades. However, although it will never be the same again and is a mere echo of its former glory, modern-day New Zealand is still home to an incredible range of wildlife, most of which you will see nowhere else on earth. Your encounters will be many and memorable: from enchanting penguins to graceful albatrosses; cheeky keas to manic fantails, and rotund sea lions to breaching whales. Given the focus and fragility of its species, New Zealand is on the cutting edge of both conservation and ecotourism. As a visitor you will be able to experience both, working separately or in unison, and whether you love wildlife or are indifferent, you will be given a stark insight into our effect on the world and our place within it.

Left: The snow-capped ridgeline of Mount Sefton provides a dramatic backdrop for a tramper crossing the Mt Cook River. *Above:* Sorry, no entry, my beach! A gorgeously plump and belligerent Elephant Seal decides to rest up on a walkway on the Otago Peninsula.

River deep, mountain high
The Rob Roy glacier in Mount Aspiring National Park provides one of the best day walks in the South Island.

Essentials

Footprint features

Planning your trip

New Zealand is everything you have heard about it, and an awful lot more. If you can only go for two to three weeks, unless you stay put in one area, or visit just a few places, it is going to be an exercise in frustration. Three weeks is pushing it, six is better and eight weeks is about right, short of actual emigration. That said, providing you are selective with your itinerary and do enough research, New Zealand's size and infrastructure mean that you can cram a surprising amount in to a relatively short period of time without necessarily blowing your wig off.

If New Zealand presents an irresistible lure, you are probably a nature-friendly, active and independent person. Start planning well in advance. You will find full sight and activity listings throughout this book. The web is also a major source of information. It's a good idea to secure your own transport on arrival, or even before. New Zealand is small and relatively easy to get about, but independence is a major advantage. If you are in a group consider the many campervan options (see page 40). The country is well geared up for this type of travel.

You might also consider buying a car (see box, page 42). Second-hand cars are relatively cheap in New Zealand and, provided they're still in one piece, you can usually sell them again when you have completed your journey. If you cannot afford your own wheels, then both islands are well set up for coach travel (see page 38). Information on public transport can be found in the 'Ins and outs' and 'Listings' sections of each chapter and also on the websites for each town or region.

Where to go

Two weeks: North Island

You will almost certainly arrive in **Auckland** – the main international airport. Although the Auckland region has a lot to offer, only spend a day there, then move on quickly. Auckland is a great city – but a city nonetheless. It is modern and in many ways is not at all typical of New Zealand. Take a look from the top of the Sky Tower, stop by the Auckland Museum, and then head over to Devonport (including a walk to North Head) or one of the west coast beaches. Then the following day set off for Northland and the **Bay of Islands**, where there are numerous options for cruising the islands or dolphin watching. Don't miss Russell (the first significant European settlement) and Waitangi (where the Maori/Pakeha Treaty was signed). In the evening, the Maori performance at the Treaty grounds is recommended. The following day take a one-day trip to **Cape Reinga**, the northernmost tip of New Zealand. Then return to Auckland and dine in Ponsonby or Parnell. The next day head southwest, for a couple of days in the **Coromandel**. If you do not have your own transport consider the weekly cruise from Auckland with **360 Discovery Cruises**① *To8oo-888oo6, www.kawaukat.co.nz*, or an organized road tour with one of the Auckland-based operators like **Coromandel Explorer Tours**① *To9-8282753, www.coromandeltours.co.nz*. If you have your own transport in the 'Coro' don't miss Coromandel township (including the Driving Creek Railway), Colville, Cape Colville and Cathedral Cove. From Coromandel head to **Rotorua** for two days of volcanic scenery and a multitude of activities. From Rotorua head southwest to **Taupo**, being sure not to miss the Wai-o-tapu Thermal Reserve on the way. Make sure you see the Huka Falls and relax and enjoy a hot pool at De Brett's Thermal Resort. If the weather is fine the following day attempt 'The Tongariro Crossing', a full-day walk (moderate fitness required), or take a cruise on Lake Taupo, followed by a skydive from 12,000 ft, if your nerves can stand it. Alternatively from Taupo, get underground with a day trip to the **Waitomo Caves**. From Taupo take one of

⁛ Packing for New Zealand

New Zealand is a well-developed nation and anything you will need, from pharmaceuticals to camping gear, is readily available throughout the country. Given the favourable dollar rate if you are coming from Europe or North America, it might be better to travel light and buy as you go. Auckland can supply just about all your needs including quality maps and travel books. Backpackers, naturally, are advised to bring a good sleeping bag and a bed sheet. These are not always provided in hostels and certainly not available in the backcountry tramping huts. A good pair of boots and a large rucksack is a good idea if you are intending to hike. If you still own a film camera, as opposed to digital, bring film with you, it will be cheaper than buying it in New Zealand. Memory cards are readily available but best bought in duty free. Also remember also to bring an electrical adapterplug. Binoculars are recommended as are a sun hat, sunscreen and sunglasses.

two recommended routes south. Either head south on SH1, taking SH47 at Taurangi around the western side of the **Tongariro National Park**. If you can, take a scenic flight above the mountains from Whakapapa Village or drive up the Mountain Road from **Ohakune**. Stay in Ohakune. The next day travel to **Wellington** as early as possible. Alternatively, head southeast to **Napier** and the **Hawkes Bay**. Enjoy Napier itself or visit a winery or Cape Kidnappers and take some time to enjoy the view from Te Mata Peak in **Havelock North**. From Havelock head south through the **Wairarapa** stopping at Mount Bruce Wildlife Centre and, if you have time, take in the coast at Castlepoint. The following morning try to visit the remote **Cape Palliser**, the southernmost tip of the North Island. Once in **Wellington**, take a trip up the Cable Car, see the view from Mount Victoria and check out the Museum of Wellington City and Sea, and 'Te Papa' – New Zealand's multimillion dollar national museum. For lunch or dinner muse the menus on and around Courtney Place. The following day drive back to Auckland (nine hours) or head across early by ferry or plane for a week in the South Island.

Two weeks: South Island

By ferry or plane from Wellington, try to arrive in **Picton** early in the day so you can join one of the trips out into the **Marlborough Sounds** – either dolphin watching, kayaking or a half-day walk to Ship Cove. The following day drive to Blenheim and visit one or two of the vineyards before heading through Havelock, making your way to **Nelson**. Enjoy the rest of the day in Nelson then head off to Motueka via Mapua. The next day take a day-walk or kayak trip in the **Abel Tasman National Park**. Then continue to the west coast and **Franz Josef** stopping off at the Nelson Lakes National Park. In Franz Josef be sure to take a scenic flight around Mount Cook, or at the least a glacier walk on the Franz. The following day, drive from Franz Josef, stopping at Ship Creek and Haast to reach **Wanaka** by evening. The following day go canyoning, skydiving or for a walk up the Rob Roy Valley. Alternatively, take a scenic flight to Milford Sound. Head for **Queenstown** and spend the day deciding what to do. The bungee jump is an option as is the Shotover Jet and the views from the gondola. Spend another day visiting **Milford Sound** – it's best to bus in (to see Te Anau and the Milford Road) and fly out.

For the following three days there is an alternative: head directly to Christchurch or travel via Dunedin. For Christchurch drive from Queenstown to **Mount Cook** village. Spend the rest of the day taking in the scenery by foot, by bike or with a scenic flight. If you are up to it, climb up to the new Muller Hut for the night. The next day drive to Christchurch for a look at Tekapo and the McKenzie Country, arriving in **Christchurch**

❗ How big is your footprint?

Ultimately when it comes to being a responsible eco-tourist it is of course your own attitude that is crucial. Much of the **Environmental Code** advocated by the **DoC** is common sense. Over all, the entire concept can be summed up with two words: **respect** and **awareness**; and an age-old cliché: 'take nothing but pictures, leave nothing but footprints'. Given the unbelievable damage we humans have already inflicted on New Zealand's unique and ancient biodiversity, surely that attitude is not only poignant, but also demanded. Eco-tour operators are listed on page 63 and in the listings section of each relevant chapter.

The independent organization **New Zealand Royal Forest and Bird Society**, 90 Ghuznee St, Wellington, T04-385 7374, www.forest-bird.org.nz, produces an excellent quarterly magazine. The monthly *Wilderness Magazine* ($7) or bi-monthly *New Zealand Geographic* ($15), are also good, containing comprehensive outdoors and eco-activity information and are available in most newsagents and bookshops. For other magazines available in New Zealand see www.nzmagazineshop.co.nz.

late evening. Alternatively, you could spend the first two days in **Dunedin** and the Otago Peninsula with the following day in the **Catlins**. After a day in Christchurch, head for **Kaikoura** where you can take a whale-watching or dolphin-swimming excursion, leaving yourself enough time to catch the late ferry from **Picton** that night.

Three weeks: North Island

Add to the above these options. In Auckland try to get out on the **Hauraki Gulf**, visit **Tiritiri Matangi Island** (highly recommended), **Rangitoto** or **Great Barrier Island**. Spend some time exploring the Waitakeres and the west coast beaches. In the city visit Kelly Tarlton's Underwater and Antarctic Encounter and/or the Waterfront and the Maritime Museum. Adrenaline seekers should consider climbing the **Sky Towers** mast ('Vertigo') or the controlled bungee from the observation deck ('Sky Jump').

In Northland on the way to the Bay of Islands, don't miss the **Whangarei Heads** (Ocean Beach) and/or the **Tutakaka Coast**. While there consider diving the **Poor Knights Islands**. In the Bay of Islands consider a two-day kayak trip on and around the islands or walk to **Cape Brett**. Bruise your bum on the fast boat to the 'Hole in the Rock'. Heading north, take a peek at historic **Kerikeri** and the delights of the scenic coast road to Whangaroa. After visiting the Cape head southwest to the **Hokianga**. Just south of the Hokianga don't miss 'Tane Mahuta', the 1500-year-old kauri in the magnificent **Waipoua Forest**. Then learn more about the great trees at the **Kauri Museum** in Matakohe. Heading south from Auckland, spend a couple more days exploring the Coromandel. Go fishing from **Whitianga** or spend a day on **New Chums Beach**. Don't miss the Driving Creek Railway in Coromandel Township.

From Coromandel head to the Bay of Plenty. Spend a day enjoying one of the many activities in **Tauranga** or **Mount Maunganui**. There is plenty to detain you in the **Tongariro National Park** and you could also consider a kayaking trip down the Wanganui River in the neighbouring **Wanganui National Park**, before heading south to Wellington. North from Rotorua you can negotiate the **East Cape** via Whakatane. While in **Whakatane** visit the active volcano White Island or swim with dolphins. If you head west from Rotorua or Taupo, a day underground in the **Waitomo Caves** is recommended. If at all possible and you can afford it, try the **'Lost World'** trip, see page 229. From Waitomo you can follow the coast to **Taranaki** and spend some time around the mountain and the **Mount Egmont National Park** – arguably the most beautiful mountain in the country. From New Plymouth, which is a great town in itself, you could take in **Wanganui** and a trip on the Wanganui River before heading south to **Wellington**.

If you head west from Rotorua or Taupo, spend time in **Napier** and consider staying at **Lake Waikaremoana** in the Urewera National Park. Then, from Napier head south via **Havelock North** through the Wairarapa taking in Castlepoint, the Waiohine Gorge and **Cape Palliser**. From all these directions you will end up in Wellington and can spend more time in the city. For a superb day trip visit the wildlife paradise of **Kapiti Island**. From Wellington it is a nine-hour drive via SH1 back to Auckland, though the flight on a clear day – with Mount Taranaki on one side and Ruapehu on the other – is a delight.

Three weeks: South Island

Added to the above itinerary for the South Island, there are many additional excursions and activities. In Nelson and Marlborough consider an extra day or two in the Marlborough Sounds. Do part of the **Queen Charlotte Track**, or the lesser-known **Nydia Track**, a full-day cruise, a multi-day kayak trip from Havelock or **Picton**, or better still, spend a day or two getting to **French Pass**. From Nelson consider doing the **Abel Tasman Coast Walk** or a multi-day kayak trip. From Motueka, venture over Takaka Hill to **Golden Bay**. Visit the Pupu Springs, Farewell Spit and the beautiful **Wharariki Beach**. While in Golden Bay consider doing the **Heaphy Track** or exploring the northern sector of the Abel Tasman or Kahurangi national parks.

Returning to Motueka, head for the west coast via the Nelson Lakes National Park. Consider the **Angelus Hut Walk** in the Nelson Lakes then head to **Westport** via the Buller Gorge. From Westport venture north to **Karamea** and see the incredible karst scenery of the **Oparara Basin**. Walk part of the Heaphy Track coastal stretch. From Karamea head south down the west coast to **Franz Josef**, taking in the arts and crafts of **Hokitika**, the **white heron colony** near Whataroa and the secluded delights of **Okarito**. Then give yourself an extra two to three days around the Glacier Region. As well as the glaciers, take in **Lake Matheson** (at dawn or dusk) and the wild coastline.

Heading south to Haast, stop at **Munroe Beach** and Ship Creek. Spend at least two days around **Haast**, take a jet-boat trip and explore further south to **Jackson's Bay** and the **Cascade Saddle**. Having negotiated the Haast Pass to **Wanaka** spend some time enjoying the scenery and activities, particularly the local walks. From Wanaka head for **Queenstown** via the Cardrona Road and lose yourself in the incredible range of activities.

For a break from the chaos head north and explore the **Glenorchy/Paradise** areas (featured heavily in *Lord of the Rings*), **Arrowtown** or climb to the top of the **Remarkables**. From Queenstown drive to **Te Anau**, consider the Kepler, Routeburn or Milford Tracks (book well ahead) or a multi-day kayak trip on Milford or **Doubtful Sound**. Be sure to make the scenic drive to **Milford Sound** and give yourself an extra day there. Great day or half-day walks include **Key Summit** or **Lake Marian**. Just south of Te Anau, take in the stunning scenery and atmosphere of **Lake Manapouri** and Doubtful Sound. From Manapouri negotiate the Southern Scenic Route to **Dunedin**, and en route consider doing the **Humpridge Track**, visiting **Stewart Island** (to see the diurnal kiwi) and certainly give yourself three days exploring the **Catlins Coast**. Spend two to three days in Dunedin allowing at least one on the **Otago Peninsula**. Take a tour to see the **albatross colony** and the **yellow-eyed penguins**.

From Dunedin head north to Oamaru then inland to **Mount Cook** spending some time exploring the area and its activities. If you are fit spend a night up in the Mueller Hut. Via **Tekapo** and the McKenzie Country, then head to Christchurch giving yourself more time in the city. While in Christchurch spend a day exploring the **Banks Peninsula**. West of Christchurch consider the scenic drive to Mount Sunday and Mount Potts Station used for the set for Edoras in *Lord of the Rings*. North of Christchurch, as an adjunct to Kaikoura, head inland to enjoy a hot pool and perhaps a mountain bike ride in **Hanmer Springs**. From Hanmer Springs and Kaikoura enjoy the stunning coastal road that will deliver you back to **Picton** via the **vineyards** of Marlborough.

When to go

For travellers from the northern hemisphere spending Christmas Day on the beach, sunbathing while digesting a hearty barbecue, or seeing Santa parade around in shorts under cloudless skies, is really quite a bizarre experience. The summer or **high season**, from **November** to **March**, is of course the busiest time of year and at these times you'll be joining battalions of Kiwis also on holiday. Over Christmas and for the whole of January, almost the entire country heads to the beach or the mountains. Accommodation is at a premium and the roads to the major tourist destinations can be busy. But again, 'busy' roads in New Zealand, especially in the more remote parts of the South Island, equates to a car passing you every five or 10 minutes. In some parts of the country, you get so used to being alone that the sight of other cars can be a shock.

The months of late spring (**September/October**) or early autumn (**March/April**) are often recommended, as you are almost guaranteed accommodation and the weather is still pretty favourable. It is also cheaper. The winter or **low season** sits between **April/May** to **August/September**. During this period prices are often reduced with plenty of special deals, especially at weekends and mid-range establishments. Bear in mind that some places are closed in winter but generally speaking, tourism is a year-round affair in New Zealand. Also bear in mind that some places like Queenstown (the principal tourist destination in the South Island) are as busy in the winter months with skiing activities as they are with general activities in summer. Taking all the above into account, the best months to visit, unless you enjoy the tourist/holiday buzz, are **October/November** or **March/April**.

Climate → *For detailed weather information consult www.metservice.co.nz.*

New Zealand has what is called an 'ocean temperate' climate, which means that it is generally agreeable. As the country is fairly elongated and lying very much at a north to south angle, the weather varies greatly. The north and east of both islands are consistently a few degrees warmer than the south and west. Predictably, the warmest region of the country is generally Northland and the coldest Southland, but some inland areas of Otago and the east of the North Island also see higher temperatures. However, in recent years, there have been unusual weather patterns and plenty of inconsistencies. In 2006 for example a small flotilla of large icebergs came within 'flightseeing' distance of Southland and Otago. Once a rare phenomenon it may prove more common thanks to global warming and its effect on the Antarctic Ice Shelf. In summary, like any temperate climate you can rely on one thing – unpredictability.

In Auckland the winter (June to August) and summer (December to March) average temperatures are 8-15°C (48-59°F) and 14-23°C (57-74°F) respectively and in Dunedin 4-12°C (39-53°F) and 9-19°C (48-66°F) respectively. But this can be misleading: not too far inland from Dunedin, Alexandra is quite often the hottest spot in the country. When it comes to sunshine, various regions compete closely for the title of 'sunniest place'. For several years now it has been Nelson and Marlborough in the South Island. But next year it could just as easily be Napier on the relatively dry and sunny east coast of the North Island, or even Whakatane in the Bay of Plenty. Wellington and Auckland, too, boast a lot of sunshine with Auckland being far more humid. Wellingtonians also suffer from wind – quite severely too (thankfully not of the beans variety). The west coast and Fiordland in Southland also have their extremes of wind and rain. But having said that, the beauty of a place like New Zealand is that, even in winter, it doesn't rain for long periods. In summary, the weather is generally favourable here; you can swim in the sea, wear shorts in summer and will not be forced indoors for days on end. One other word of advice: thanks to ozone depletion, the sun in New Zealand is dangerous, so always wear a hat and the strongest possible sun block. Don't forget to slip, slap and slop. ▶▶ *See Health, page 54.*

Activities and tours

Birdwatching

Much of the wildlife in New Zealand is of the bird variety. Thanks to human intervention, the mainland is not the place it once was. However, there are still plenty of oppotunities to see the country's incredible birdlife first-hand. Offshore island reserves such as Tiritiri Matangi Island north of Auckland (see page 121) and Kapiti Island north of Wellington (see page 408), protect unique and endangered species that were wiped out from the mainland. The birds are naturally very tame allowing you to get up close.

DoC's Mount Bruce Wildlife Centre in the Wairarapa (see page 356), the Willowbank Wildlife Reserve in Christchurch (see page 480), or the penguin viewing tours and Albatross Centre on the Otago Peninsula (see page 592) are all recommended. The city zoos are also great places to see captive native wildlife at close range.

Perhaps the best and most comical of New Zealand's birds is the **takahe**, an ancient species that looks like a large prehistoric purple chicken. Only about 200 remain. Then of course there is the **kiwi** – that remarkable nocturnal bird with no wings, an awfully long beak and an ability to lay an egg the size of a small melon. There are many commercial nocturnal houses where you will get a good view of one, however, to see one in the wild you will either have to be exceptionally lucky or go on a specialist trip to Stewart Island (see page 672). Sadly, the kiwi is fast heading for extinction on the mainland.

Other species to look out for include New Zealand eagles, bush wrens, kokako and moa. For further information, see Background page 708.

★ **Head for ...**
North Island: Tiritiri Matangi Island, Kapiti Island, Mt Bruce Wildlife Centre; gannet colonies at Muriwai and Cape Kidnappers.
South Island: Farewell Spit (gannets), Kaikoura, Twizel (black stilts), Okarito Lagoon/Whataroa (white herons). Penguins can be spotted at Munroe Beach (Fiordland), Ship Creek (Fiordland), Oamaru, Stewart Island and the Otago Peninsula.

Contact
For specialist wildlife operators, see page 63.
Royal Forest and Bird Protection Society,
www.forestandbird.org.nz.

Bungee jumping

The strange practice of attaching a rubber band to your ankles and diving off a very high bridge has now become synonymous with a visit to New Zealand. The concept was developed by A J Hackett, who jumped from the Eiffel Tower in 1986 and from the Sky Tower in Auckland (see page 76) in 2000. Jumps vary from 'tasters' of 40 m (from a crane) to the 150 m 'parabungee' above Lake Wakatipu. Most are in Queenstown in the South Island, where you can do it from a bridge, high above a canyon, or even at night. Folk have jumped in tandem, in canoes, on bikes and, of course, butt naked. At $80-200, a jump is not cheap but it's a once-in-a-lifetime experience. AJ Hackett's mighty 134-m Nevis near Queenstown is recommended.

★ **Head for ...**
North Island: Auckland Sky Tower, Lake Taupo, Agrodome in Rotorua.
South Island: Queenstown, Hanmer Springs.

Caving

The underground world of the Waitomo Caves (see page 224) is a renowned playground. There are over 360 mapped caves, the longest of which is 14 km. Most have rivers which carve a wonderland of caverns, pools, waterfalls and rapids. These are negotiated with a headlamp, in a wetsuit, attached to a rubber ring. Added to that, there's a 300-m abseil into the 'Lost World' as well as the spectacle of glow-worms. There is a huge range of activities; almost all involve getting wet. Prices range from a 4-hr trip at $95 to a 7-hr trip at $355.

★ **Head for ...**
North Island: Waitmo Caves.

Contact
www.waitomo.com, http://tourism.
waitomo.govt.nz, www.waitomo.co.nz.

Cricket

Given the nation's colonial roots, cricket has long been a well-established spectator sport in New Zealand, with the national team, **The Blackcaps**, hosting visiting nations and touring overseas each summer. Cricket does not inspire quite the same fanatical following as rugby, but they share a healthy distain for their greatest foes – Australia. Test matches are held at the main provincial stadiums (see Rugby, page 28).

Fishing

New Zealand is fishing heaven. Noted as one of the best and most unspoilt **trout-fishing** venues in the world. All levels of experience are well catered for with numerous boat charters and guides from the relatively affordable $60 an hour to the all-mod-cons trips at around $150 an hour.

Fishing licences cost $18.50 for 24 hrs and $92 for a season and are available on-line from **New Zealand Fish and Game** (www.fishandgame.org.nz) and most fishing tackle outlets. May fishing related tourism operators also supply licences.

The warm Pacific waters that grace the North Island's shores attract a huge range of saltwater species from snapper to massive marlin, providing some superb sea and **big-game fishing**. And in New Zealand it's not just the preserve of the idle rich. Costs vary from the 3-hr novice trip to the highly organized but still affordable 3-day 'Hemingway' trips to catch that prize marlin. It's an unforgettable experience as you watch the seabirds, the occasional dolphin (sometimes even a whale) and the amazing flying fish erupting from the water, then suddenly the line from your rod and barrel-sized reel goes off like the wheels of a formula one car at the start of a race, and your jaw drops as you see a huge marlin sail out of the water at incredible speed, and the fight is on. It might sound like hard work, but you don't have to be the Incredible Hulk to do it. The cost of big game fishing varies between operators and depends on the vessel and the services on offer. Expect to pay between $1000 and $4000 a day for a full charter.

★ Head for ...
North Island: trout fishing in Lake Taupo, Tongariro River and Lake Rotorua; big-game fishing in Bay of Islands, Tutakaka Coast , Whitianga and Tauranga.
South Island: trout fishing in Wanaka (Otago) and Te Anau (Southland).

Flightseeing

For a real insight into what flying is all about, not to mention the stunning views, a flight in a **fixed-wing** aircraft or a **helicopter** is highly recommended. There are endless locations throughout the country and at around $100 for a 10- to 15-min flight in a helicopter or a 30-min flight in a small fixed-wing, it's well worth it. If you can only afford one flight, make it the helicopter flight around the glaciers and summit of Mt Cook. Most operate out of Franz Joseph or Fox glaciers. This 30-min trip ($250) on a clear day is truly breathtaking.

If you fancy having a go yourself, it's possible to fly a small training helicopter (accompanied and under close scrutiny, on a 30-min flight). This is one of the most exhilarating experiences of a lifetime (arguably even better than bungee jumping and tandem skydiving).

For a more sedate ride you could consider a trip by **hot-air balloon** which, although not so common and more expensive (around $285), is available in a number of locations. Or, for the full 'Biggles' experience, you can don the goggles and scarf and get strapped into a **biplane**.

★ Head for ...
North Island: spectacular flights include: the volcanoes of Tongariro National Park (from Taupo or Whakapapa); Mt Tarawera (from Rotorua); White Island (from Rotorua, Tauranga or Whakatane). The best places for hot-air ballooning are over Auckland, the Waikato (from Hamilton) and the east coast (from Napier and Caterton).
South Island: Fixed-wing: Kahurangi National Park (from Nelson or Picton), Kaikoura, Lake Tekapo, 'The Great Divide' and Mt Cook, Franz Josef, Glenorchy, Milford Sound (from Wanaka, Queenstown or Te Anau). Hot air balloon: over Canterbury (from Christchurch). Biplane: Gore and Wanaka.

Contact
There are numerous operators in Wanaka, Queenstown, Te Anau and Milford. www.flightseeing.co.nz, www.touristflightoperators.co.nz, www.airmilford.co.nz.

Fly-by-wire

Picture a metal hospital stretcher with a microlight engine on the back, suspended from a wire in a valley and flying like a pendulum, speeding through the air at up to 100 kph. Now imagine yourself strapped to this flimsy device, squealing like a school kid. This seemingly suicidal experience is available for at around $140 for 10 mins.

★ **Head for ...**
South Island: Queenstown.

Contact
www.flybywire-queenstown.co.nz.

Golf

New Zealand is blessed with hundreds of golf courses, from those that require a cute wedge shot to avoid sheep to others with well-manicured greens fit for an open championship. In Taupo and Rotorua you can even play on a steaming golf course; from little fumaroles on the fairways to bursts from the ground.

   Green fees vary from $35-200 and it's usually possible to hire clubs. If you go early and in the off season, it can be rare to even see another player. Attitudes to golfing etiquette are much less strict than in Europe or North America, so don't be surprised if you a group of Kiwi lads drop their trousers on the 18th tee to play a 'provisional', just accept it – it's tradition apparently.

★ **Head for ...**
North Island: Gulf Harbour in Auckland, Whangarei, Waitangi, Matauri Bay, Wairakei in Taupo and Wellington.
South Island: Millbrook in Otago.

Contact
www.nzgolf.org.nz, www.golfguide.co.nz, www.golfnewzealand.co.nz, www.golftours nz.com, www.nzgolf.net.

Horse trekking

The New Zealand landscape is ideal for horse trekking; there are a wealth of operators and horse riding is available throughout the country. All levels are well catered for and it will only cost around $40 for 2 hrs. Other equestrian options include thoroughbred stud tours in the Waikato (see page 232).

Contact
www.riding-holidays.com/new-zeland.html www.ridenz.com
International League for the Protection of Horses (ILHNZ), PO Box 10-368 Te Rapa, Hamilton, T07-849 0678, ilphnz@xtra.co.nz, publishes a very informative leaflet.

Jet boating

You have probably seen it. A red boat packed with tourists, all wearing the same 'well isn't this fun' expression, while thinking 'get me out of here now'. It is quite an unnerving experience whizzing down a river, heading straight at some rocks at insane speeds and closing your eyes in the face of inevitable death, only to open them again to find yourself still, remarkably, alive. Then, as a last hurrah, to be spun about in a 360° turn, just to make sure you are *completely* wet. Not all are adrenaline-pumping trips with some (especially in the North island) being more scenic affairs. Prices are reasonable, with a 30-min trip costing around $100.

★ **Head for ...**
North island: Rotorua, Moto River (from Opotiki), Wairakei Park, Whanganui River.
South Island: Glenorchy, Shotover River in Queenstown.

Contact
www.dartriver.co.nz, www.shotoverjet.com, www.hukajet.co.nz, www.riverjet.co.nz.

Kayaking

New Zealand is a renowned playground for kayaking whether on river, lake or sea – even fiord. For novices, kayaking just takes just a wee bit of time to get used to, but before you know it, you'll be off and paddling before you can say *'Deliverance'*. A word of warning – never share a canoe with a loved one. Within 5 mins there will be a major argument about technique, threats of violence and floods of tears. If you find it to your taste (the silence, the solitude and the scenery can be heart-warming) then consider a multi-day trip. The best of these are in the Bay of Islands (page 168), Abel Tasman National Park (page 460) and, most recommended, Fiordland (from Te Anau, page 652). Inland try Whanganui National Park (page 386). The coastal scenery is often best taken in by kayak and there are some great guides out there. You never know, you might even come across a friendly dolphin or fur seal. Costs again vary slightly but you can hire your own kayak for about $20 per hr; a 3-hr trip will cost about $100; a 4-day affair from $500.

★ **Head for ...**
North Island: Bay of Islands (from Paihia, Waitangi or Rawene), Whitianga, Lake Rotorua, Tauranga, Whanganui National Park.
South Island: Havelock and Picton, Abel Tasman National Park, Fiordland.

Contact
www.alpinekayaks.co.nz, www.seakayak nz.co.nz, www.abeltasmankayaks.co.nz, www.seakayaknewzealand.com, www.nzkayakschool.com.

Mountain biking

New Zealand is, as you might expect, a paradise for the avid mountain biker. With its wide range of magnificent landscapes, the country offers numerous tracks, both long and short and mainly through native bush or commercial forest. Bike hire is readily available and quite cheap, so give it a go. Whether you go down vertical rock faces and submerge yourself in mud pools, or stick to the straight and not-so-narrow, is up to you.

★ **Head for ...**
North Island: Whakarewarewa Forest Park, Rotorua, Taupo, Tongariro National Park (from Tongariro, Whakapapa or Ohakune), Wanganui and Wellington.
South Island: Picton, Christchurch, Hanmer Springs. Heli-biking from Wanaka or Queenstown.

Contact
www.mountainbike.co.nz, www.bike-nz.com, www.vorb.org.nz, www.planet bike.co.nz, www.bikenz.org.nz.
Cycle Touring Company New Zealand, Whangarei, T09-436 0033, www.cycle tours.co.nz, specializes in self-led cycling adventures on routes all over Northland from 2-9 days. Food and lodging included.

Mountaineering

It would take a lifetime or 6 to climb all the major peaks in New Zealand. Mt Cook at 3753 m is the country's highest. Although not especially high, the New Zealand peaks are spectacular, challenging and potentially dangerous. Many of the most accessible peaks are in the South Island, however Mt Taranaki in the North Island is the country's most-climbed mountain. To look at it on a clear day is to stand in awe. Its symmetry and isolation just beckons you up its precarious slopes.

If you are new to mountaineering, this is the perfect country in which to start. You are, after all, in Sir Edmund Hillary's back garden. Once you scale that first peak and feel the sense of achievement, you will almost certainly be hooked. If you are a novice seek advice and go well prepared; check the weather forecast and tell someone where you're going. Many tourist lives have been lost through sheer stupidity and over-confidence. There are numerous guided trips available especially around Taranaki and Mt Cook.

★ **Head for ...**
North Island: Mt Taranaki, Mt Ruapehu (from Whakapapa) Mt Hikurangi in Eastland.
South Island: Franz and Fox glaciers, Mt Aspiring, Nelson Lakes National Park, Wanaka and Queenstown.

Contact
NZ Alpine Club, Christchurch, T03-377 7595, www.alpineclub.org.nz. Specialist enquiries.
NZ Mountain Guides Association, www.nzmga.org.nz. Good source of information, contacts and weather reports.
Also useful are: www.alpinere creation.co.nz, www.adventure.co.nz and www.alpinismski.co.nz/aircraft.html

⦂ The 'other' PM

New Zealand has had some notable prime ministers that have, despite the size of the nation and its population, made their mark domestically and internationally. The charismatic Sir Robert Muldoon, who served as prime minister from 1975 to 1984, or the current PM and Labour party leader Helen Clarke who has been one of the world's most successful female heads of state. But there is another unofficial prime minister in New Zealand – a person whose every decision is scrutinized, debated, celebrated and often criticized equally if not more, than the country's political leaders. But the arena is not politics; it is sport and specifically rugby union – the country's 'national game'. Many Kiwis consider the role of head coach of national team the 'All Blacks' as the most important job in the land. But it is an extremely stressful position that carries with it as much risk as it does personal prestige. A national coach that steers his team to consistent success is a lauded national hero, but when he falls short on only a few occasions, he is inevitably sacked and can become a national disgrace almost overnight. Recent coaches that have suffered as a result of poor team performance include Laurie Mains and John Mitchell. See also box, page 371.

Essentials Activities and tours

Paraflying and tandem parapenting

What is the difference? One is done from the back of a speedboat over water, the other around hills and coastal slopes. It's basically a bit like glorified kite flying with you attached to the kite. Paraflying is the easier and more commercial of the 2 and is practised at many coastal resorts. You are strapped to a cradle below a special parachute and kept in the air by a speedboat. Parapenting (or paragliding) takes time to master. Like skydiving the novice is taken in tandem with an expert. It's great fun and will have you screaming like a banshee and gesticulating wildly to your highly amused compadres. A 10-min flight costs about $75

★ **Head for ...**
North Island: paraflying in the Bay of Islands and Mt Maunganui; parapenting at Te Mata Peak in Hawkes Bay.
South Island: Christchurch, Lake Wakatipu (Queenstown) and Lake Wanaka.

Contact
www.paraglidingnz.com
www.nelsonparagliding.co.nz,
www.skyout.co.nz,
www.extremeair.co.nz.

Rafting

This is another 'must do' activity. The rapids are graded from I to VI. Although the 45-min trips at about $95 are packed with adrenaline-pumping moments, the real experience only comes with a multi-day trip (4 days costs around $750). The 4-day trip down the wild and remote Motu in Eastland is New Zealand's best outdoor experiences. The trips are well organized and safe; most even do the campfire cooking for you. If the multi-day trip is beyond your budget or timeline then the best experience is the 45-min trip down the Kaituna Rapids near Rotorua (page 257). The highlight of this trip is the 7-m drop down the Okere Falls, the highest commercially rafted falls in the world.

★ **Head for ...**
North Island: Wairoa, Rangataiki, Mohaka and Kaituna rivers from Rotorua, Moto River (from Opotiki), Tongariro River (from Tokaanu and Turangi),
South Island: many regions have excellent opportunities. Queenstown is a good base.

Contact
www.nz-rafting.co.nz, www.raft.co.nz,
www.wetnwildrafting.co.nz,
www.whitewaterrafting.co.nz.

River sledging

This is the ludicrously simple but superb concept of rafting down a river on a bodyboard with little except a wet suit, flippers, a crash helmet and a PhD in lunacy. A 40-min dunking will cost you about $100.

★ **Head for ...**
North Island: Kaituna River in Rotorua, man-made falls of a dam in Hawera, Taranaki.
South Island: Wanaka.

Rock climbing

This exciting activity is on the increase in New Zealand.

★ **Head for ...**
North Island: Mt Eden Quarry (Auckland), locations near Taupo and Te Awamutu. Good climbing walls in Rotorua and Palmerston North.
South Island: main bases are Christchurch, Dunedin, Nelson and Wanaka. Most spectacular are Fiordland and Kahurangi National Park. Ice-climbing is spectacular on Franz Josef glacier. There are climbing walls in Twizel and Frankton near Queenstown.

Contact
www.climb.co.nz, www.alpine club.org.nz, www.mojozone.co.nz, www.wanakarock.co.nz

Rugby

Rugby is the most popular spectator sport in New Zealand, with the mighty **All Blacks** assuming an almost religious following. Every winter, the All Blacks host teams from abroad and tour overseas demanding huge respect if not a modicum of disguised fear. The All Blacks are, in essence, the crème de la crème of national talent derived from the Super Twelve tournament (which includes teams from New Zealand, Australia and South Africa) as well as the NPC, or National Provincial Cup, both of which precede the All Blacks test season.

With major matches staged at the high profile stadiums in Auckland (Eden Park); Wellington (The Westpac Stadium); Christchurch (Jade Stadium) and Carisbrook

(often dubbed the 'House of Pain') in Dunedin, it is often possible for visitors to go along and see what all the fuss is about – provided of course you can secure tickets.

Sailing

New Zealand, and Auckland in particular, is famous for sailing. Indeed, from 1995-2003 the Kiwis were the proud holders of the world's biggest sailing trophy – the America's Cup – and despite the loss are still considered not only the best sailors in the world but also the best designers and speed racers. Auckland is not called the 'City of Sails' for nothing. An estimated 1 in 4 of its inhabitants owns a recreational boat of some kind and this trend is echoed throughout the country.

At least a few hours out on the water are recommended but, if you can, try a multi-day trip. This will give you an insight into what sailing is all about. There are numerous opportunities to get out on the water in a proper yacht, though if you plan a longer trip there must be someone present with the relevant experience; 'tickets' and the Sir Peter Blakes of this world don't come cheap.

★ **Head for ...**
North Island: Hauraki Gulf and Bay of Islands.

Contact
Charter Link, Bayswater Marina, Auckland, T09-445 7114, www.charterlink.co.nz.
Charterbase, T09-426 4979, Auckland, www.charterbase.co.nz.
Sail Connections, PO Box 90961, 8 Madden St, Auckland, T09-358 0556, www.sailconnections.co.nz.

Scuba diving

New Zealand has some world-class diving venues with superb marine reserves all around the country. The Poor Knights is where most budding Jacques Cousteaus gravitate, for its combination of geology, marine life and water clarity. With up to 80 m of visibility you can go head to head with a huge grouper or clench your rubbers at the sight of a shark. There is also some fine wreck-diving available with the old navy frigates *Tui* and *Waikato* deliberately sunk for the benefit of divers off the east Northland coast. Another fine trip is the one to pay homage to the Greenpeace vessel *Rainbow Warrior* that was laid to rest off Matauri Bay; it was bombed in Auckland by French terrorists in 1985.

If you're not already qualified, local operators will often take you for a full or half-day first dive experience for around $200 including gear hire. If the thought of all that is too much you can also go snorkelling, which gives you a great insight into the wonders of the deep for minimum effort.

★ **Head for ...**
North Island: Poor Knights Islands, Hauraki Gulf, Whitianga, New Plymouth, Tutukaka Coast and Matauri Bay.
South Island: Marlborough Sounds, Fiordland.

Contact
www.scubadiving.co.nz, www.divenz.com, www.splash.co.nz, www.globaldive.net.

Shark encounters

While the vast majority of the human race still have nightmares at the mere suggestion of a fin surfacing above the water, it appears there is a lunatic fringe who actually wish to have a picnic with them. If you are one of these people and wish to encounter these fascinating creatures in their own habitat from the relative safety of a cage, you can do so in New Zealand. Sadly, thanks to commercial as opposed to recreational human activity, operators are finding it increasingly difficult to locate these ancient and toothy denizens of the deep. A 4-hr trip will cost about $200, prosthetic limbs extra.

★ **Head for ...**
North Island: Tutukaka and Napier.

Skiing and snowboarding

New Zealand is the principal southern hemisphere skiing and snowboarding venue and although it is of course seasonal (May-Aug), the slopes are highly accessible.

The average cost of hire for skis, boots and poles is around $35, snowboard and boots

$45. A lift pass will cost $35-80 per day, with concessions for students and children. Packages are available that include lift pass, equipment hire and one or more lessons. There may also be 'Lift and Ski Hire Packages' which cost from $75-100. A group lesson (2 hrs) will cost about $45 while a private lesson (1 hr) will cost about $75.

★ **Head for ...**
North Island: Tongariro National Park (from Whakapapa and Turoa).
South Island: Coronet Peak and the Remarkables near Queenstown, Cardrona and Treble Cone near Wanaka, Mt Hutt, Mt Potts and Porter Heightsnear Methvan, Arthur's Pass, Mt Lyford near Hanmer Springs.

Contact
www.nzski.com, www.snow.co.nz, www.brownbear.co.nz, www.nzsnow.com.

Surfing

New Zealand is a world-class surfing venue with an almost religious following, but is often overlooked by the surf set and so remains pretty uncommercial. You can get excellent and cheap tuition in many places (especially in Taranaki and Raglan). If you want a beginner's taste of what surfing is like, try boogie-boarding or bodysurfing. Boogie-boards are about half the size of a surfboard and made of compressed foam, and are cheap to buy or hire. With this and a pair of flippers you can then go pseudo-surfing and take out the difficult bit – standing up.

★ **Head for ...**
North Island: Eastland, Gisborne and Napier are the main places to head. Stent Road on Surf Highway 45, Manu Bay near Raglan and Piha, Shipwreck Bay near Kaitaia, Whangamata Bay, Matakana Island by Mt Manganui, Wanui Beach, Gisborne, Papatowai, Rakatoka Island.
South Island: Kaikoura, Colac Bay, Murdering Bay (near Dunedin).

Contact
www.surf.co.nz, www.surfingnz.co.nz, www.newzealandsurftours.com, www.surfingnz.com.

Tramping – it's no walk in the woods

If you have never been tramping before and intend to embark on one that involves a number of days, you need to be warned that it will be a challenge. A challenge not only to your physical, but also your mental self. Tramping is not walking the dog or even that long and congenial afternoon jaunt that is followed by 'oh wasn't that lovely, but I'm knackered now dear … can we go home for dinner?' Tramping is all about nature: nature's extremes, and your own. You can, and will, get extremely tired, hot, wet, thirsty, hungry and in New Zealand, bitten alive. But the rewards are immense. Not only will you experience nature at its best (or worst), your senses will be bombarded by all the immensity and richness that it offers, from stunning views, to the quiet chuckle of mountain streams – that you could swear are sometimes laughing at you. In many ways it is also a test. You are pitching yourself not against nature, but alongside it, and for many, this is a new and foreign experience, well out of their comfort zone. There will be no lattes, no email or McDonalds, no warm duvets or clean, flush toilets. There will be no hi-fi, no pubs, no dot-coms, stocks and shares, no fingernail polish or powder puff. You're going to get wet and you're going to smell. Again, although your companions may care, nature doesn't – that's natural. You're going to wake up tired because you were sharing a dorm with what sounded like a small family of warthogs (now that can't be natural!). Everyday you are out there, you are going to eat a meagre breakfast, put those wet boots on again, what feels like a small house on your back, and not for the first time, set off thinking 'what the hell am I doing here?' And again nature doesn't care. Instead, and only if you are receptive to it, somewhere along that track that day, nature will remind you exactly why you are there – or shouldn't be. There is also another welcoming and rare factor – appreciating the simple things in life. Once the day's walking is done and you have reached your shelter it is the simple things and simple cravings that really matter – a log fire for warmth or a cup of tea. And let's face it, almost all of us need to feel a lot more of that! So, in essence, you are either going to love it or hate it, but you are going to have to accept the challenge and take the risk to find out which. Above all, like any challenge or any risk, it is the best way to learn a bit more about yourself and others. One word of advice – travel light. I mean really light. Forget the butter, put your toothpaste in a film cartridge, anything to lighten the load, and in the South Island, don't forget to take lots of heavy duty insect repellent.

Tandem skydiving

Adrenaline aside, the beauty of taking the jump in New Zealand is the scenic factor. Once you have recovered from that falling feeling, the view of the land below hurtling towards you at 120 kph is unforgettable. There is some scant instruction before the actual jump but you are in very safe hands and you can come away with a DVD of the experience as well as a smile like 'Garfield'.

Jumps range in height from 9000-15,000 ft. The latter will give you about 40 seconds of free-fall. Jumps cost from $250 and the price increases the higher you go, but it is well worth it. Most commercial operators will not take first timers beyond 15,000 ft.

★ **Head for …**
North Island: Parakai and Taupo.
South Island: Wanaka, Queenstown and Te Anau.

Tramping

Even before the *National Geographic* proclaimed the Milford Track as 'the world's best walk', New Zealand could, without doubt, claim to be the tramping (or hiking) capital of the world. Not only is it one of the principal pastimes for many New Zealanders, it is also the reason many visitors come to the country. There is a vast network of routes and literally thousands of kilometres of track the length and breadth of the country, from the well-formed and trodden highway of the famed Milford Track, to the sporadic trail and markers of the lesser known Dusky Track. The range of habitats is immense, from remote coastlines and island traverses to rainforests, volcanic lakes and mountain peaks, with most penetrating national parks.

Other than the sheer scenic beauty and scope of opportunities in New Zealand, what makes tramping so popular is the ease of access and good condition of the tracks. Under the administration and advocacy of the Department of Conservation (DoC) all advertised tracks are clearly marked, well maintained and have designated campsites and huts offering clean water, basic accommodation, cooking facilities and toilets. Add to that the wealth of detailed information available, from route descriptions and access to up-to-date weather forecasts, it is little wonder that tramping is perhaps New Zealand's biggest and most uniquely precious tourist asset. Even safety is well managed, with the tracks classified by type and fitness required. Guided trips are available for the more inexperienced and an 'intentions sheet' system is used for major excursions. All this for as little as $6 per tent or nightly hut fees.

You are advised to consult the local DoC office before embarking on any of the major tramps regardless of experience and weather conditions and, if required, fill in an intentions sheet. Always make sure you are well prepared, equipped and of the required level of fitness. Unless you are experienced, tramping on the more remote and quieter tracks alone is not advisable.

The most famous track is, deservedly, the magnificent Milford Track, a 54-km 4-day trek that combines lake and mountain scenery. Also in the Te Waipounamu World Heritage Park is the Routeburn, Kepler, Dusky, Greenstone, Hollyford and the newest, the Hump Ridge Track. But these are only a few of the many tasty options.It would be easy just to recommend the likes of the Milford, Kepler and Abel Tasman, but a word of warning: many of the tracks are very busy and are now not so much tracks as public highways. The Milford, Kepler, Heaphy and Abel Tasman are considered the worst in this respect. Of course that does not mean that they should be avoided. They are still worth doing, and no less spectacular, but if you like a bit of solitude with your tramp, consider other options or at the very least go towards the start or the end of the tramping season (Oct-Apr). To give you some idea of how busy they are, the Milford now hosts about 10,000 trampers annually and the Abel Tasman up to 300 a day in mid-summer. This not only means a lot of company, it also means you must book accommodation sometimes weeks in advance.

Information, booking and safety

Hut fees vary depending on category and the services and facilities provided. The general fee range per person is as follows. **Great Walks Huts** (**GW**) $10-45 per night. GW huts have bunks with mattresses, basic cooking facilities, usually a log fire plus a clean water supply and long-drop toilets. **Serviced Huts** (**SV**) $10 (Serviced Alpine Huts $20-35) offering similar to more basic facilities to the above. **Standard Huts** (**ST**) $5. These are mere shelters with just water and toilets, some are very basic or just bivvies and are free of charge. Campsites associated with huts cost $15. An annual Hut Pass can be purchased for $90. All Great Walk Huts must be pre-booked, sometimes weeks in advance, and all huts (except those run by guided walk companies) operate on a first come first served basis. **Camping** is permitted at some huts ($15) or at designated campsites. DoC campsites come under 2 categories; 'serviced' which cost $8-12 and 'standard' which cost $3-10. Camping is free for children under 5.

Tramping track classifications

All DoC managed and maintained walks from 5-min boardwalks to mountain traverses have a classification, as follows:

Path Easy Generally low-lying and well formed. Suitable for all ages and levels of fitness. No walking boots required.
Walking Track Easy and well formed. Can involve short or steady climbs. Suitable for all ages and the reasonably fit. Shoes are okay, but proper walking boots preferable.
Tramping Track Requires relevant skill and experience. Generally continuous track but may be vague in parts. Expect a full range of topographies up to scrambling. Suitable for people of average fitness. Walking boots required.
Route Requires a high degree of skill and route-finding experience. The track may only have markers as guidance. A high level of fitness and equipment (including maps) is required.

★ **Head for ...**
The most popular tramps come under the heading of New Zealand's (DoC) 'Great Walks'. **North Island**: 'Great Walks' include the **Tongariro Northern Circuit** in the Tongariro National Park (including the volcanic delights of the Tongariro Crossing) and the beautiful circum-navigation of **Lake Waikaremoana** in the Te Urewera National Park.
South Island: 'Great Walks' include the highly popular bays and estuary crossings of the **Abel Tasman Coast Track** in the Abel Tasman National Park, the beautiful coastal stretches of the **Heaphy Track** in the Kahurangi National Park and the muddy delights of the **Rakiura Track** on Stewart Island (the newest of the country's 14 national parks). Quieter and still spectacular tramps in the South Island include the **Travers-Sabine** in the Nelson Lakes, **Rees-Dart-Cascade Saddle** between Glenorchy and Wanaka and the stunning, but difficult, **Dusky Track** in Fiordland.

Contact
VICs and DoC field centres stock excellent leaflets for each track ($1), maps and can provide up to date track and weather reports as required. For detailed information about all the major tramping tracks and 'Great Walks', accommodation bookings and other information, contact the local DoC Field Centre or visit the website www.doc.govt.nz.

Walking

The walking opportunities are endless. New Zealand is a walker's paradise and most VICs or regional DoC offices compile lists of the most notable long and short walks in each region. There is everything from coastal or bush walks to historical trails. Multi-day walks enter the realm of tramping, the New Zealand term for hiking. The country is world-famous for this, offering some of the best tramping trails in the world (see box, page 30).

★ **Head for ...**
Recommended 1-day walks are:
North Island: Tongariro Crossing (best accessed from Taupo) and the Tarawera Falls walk near Rotorua.
South Island: there are simply too many to list or recommend, but you should at least try the coastal walk at Wharariki Beach. Glacier walking on Fox, Franz Josef, or Rob Roy.

Whale watching and swimming with dolphines

The New Zealand coast is world famous for its rich variety of marine mammals. Pods of dolphin can regularly be seen, from the large, common bottlenose to the tiny and endangered Hector's dolphin. New Zealand is also on the main whale migration routes, making it relatively easy to encounter them. Just off Kaikoura on the South Island's northeast coast a deep coastal trench attracts whales close to the shore, making it one of the world's best whale-watching spots. Huge pods of dolphin frolic in the surf and seem to delight in investigating any clumsy human who ventures into the water. Encounter success rates are high and operators offer a refund, or another trip, if the whales/dolphins do not turn up. A 2½-hr whale-watching trip costs around $130, $60 for children. A 2-hr dolphin-swimming experience (30 mins in the water) will cost around $130, $120 for children (spectators half price). Dolphins can be seen year-round, however summer is the best time if you want to swim with them. The endangered Hector's dolphin can also be viewed from Curio Bay in the Catlins, Southland and around Banks Peninsula in Canterbury.

⁞ Lord of the Rings locations

For a detailed account see Ian Brodie's *The Lord of the Rings Location Guide*, $30, which even provides GPS references, www.harpercollins.co.nz.

1 **Matamata** This was the setting for Hobbiton and the Shire. Not much remains of the set but there are still a few hobbit holes, paths and even the tree where Bilbo held his birthday party. See page 232.

2 **Tongariro National Park** Scenes depicting Mordor were filmed here with Mount Tongariro featuring as Mount Doom. The Whakapapa ski area on Mount Ruapehu was where the battle of the Last Alliance was filmed. See page 293.

3 **Wellington City** This was the base for the production of the films and many of the studio sets were created here. Mount Victoria was used for the scene where the Hobbits race to the ferry with the Nazgul in hot pursuit, hiding under tree roots as they go. See page 392.

4 **West of Christchurch** Mount Sunday and Mount Potts were used for the set of Edoras and Meduseld, King Thoden's grand hall in the realm of Rohan. Rocky outcrops at the Poolburn Reservoir near Alexandra provided the perfect backdrop for the realm of Rohan. A number of tours are available. See box, page 480.

5 **Queenstown** Skippers Canyon was used for the Ford of Bruinen with Arwen fleeing the Nazgul. Deer Park Heights was used for the scene of the refugees escaping Rohan. The Remarkables ski field was used as Dimrill Dale. Twelve Mile Delta became the Ighilien Camp. A number of tours are available, including a flightseeing 'Trilogy Tour'. See page 619.

6 **Arrowtown and Glenorchy** A number of locations were used in the area including Kawarau River and Chard Farm which became Anduin and the site of the Pillars of the Kings. The Arrow River became the Ford of Bruinen where Arwen and Frodo escaped from the charging Nazgul. See pages 624-625.

★ **Head for ...**
North Island: Bay of Islands, Whakatane. Tauranga, Bay of Plenty.
South Island: dolphin swimming in the Marlborough Sounds (from Picton), Akaroa, Kaikoura, Punakaiki, the Catlins Coast. Seal swimming at Abel Tasman.

Contact
www.whaledolphintrust.org.nz, www.dolphin safari.co.nz, www.whales.co.nz.

Wine tours

New Zealand produces some excellent wine. For details, see Eating and drinking, page 48.
North Island: Waitakeres, Hawke's Bay
South Island: Blenheim, Nelson, Queenstown

Zorbing

Last and by no means least is zorbing. This is a most bizarre concept that could only be the creation of incredible Kiwi ingenuity. Described as a 'bi-spherical momentous experience', it involves climbing into a clear plastic bubble and rolling down a hill. Sadly, the organized venture involves a short hill that takes about 10 seconds to roll down and relieves you of about $45 – a bit of a rip-off. But what you could do with your own zorb blows the mind. Incidentally, you can also do a wet run – joined inside the bubble by a bucket of water.

★ **Head for ...**
North island: Agrodome in Rotorua.

⁞ Osama Bin Beetle

In these paranoiac days of terrorist threats, 'Al Qaeda' and 'homeland security' it is all too easy to focus the concept of personal and national security on purely human issues. On the home shores, the 'front-line' of this security is, of course, customs and visa regulations. It is in essence, about keeping what is perceived or proved to be 'bad' from getting in. But in real terms, traditionally and consistently, throughout the centuries of intercontinental human travel, it is not the threat that we humans pose to each other, but a nation's 'biosecurity' and the deliberate or indirect introduction of non-native plant and animal species that has the greatest long-term impact. This 'Osama Bin Beetle' effect is something in which New Zealand is particularly well versed and is in no small part due to the vulnerability of its unique ecosystem and its tragic history of extinctions. Many of the numerous current conservation wars are being fought as a direct cause of such carelessly deliberate or accidental invasions. Some are high-profile and highly visible, like the brush-tailed possum, but many others are low-profile invasions in the form of seeds, algae or insects. Over one in three plants are now non-native, countless native species have been lost and many other are threatened. So sure, be wary not to wear those 'well-heeled' shoes on the plane, but also be aware that Auckland airport sniffer dogs are trained to be far more partial to a mouldy piece of fruit.

Taking a tour

Although New Zealand is very much the domain of the independent traveller there are a number of specialist tour operators. As you might expect most of these are either eco- or activity-based. The **New Zealand Tourism Board** has detailed operator listings on its website, www.purenz.com. Other tour operators are listed in the Activities and tours sections throughout the book. ▸▸ *See also Discount travel agents page 37, and Tour operators page 61.*

Responsible tourism

For the vast majority of tourists it is New Zealand's environment and nature that are its greatest attraction. Yet regardless of your interest or your intention, the moment you set foot in New Zealand you are by definition an **eco-tourist**. Be aware that although your hosts may not demand it, the environment does. There is no doubt whatsoever that the environment is the biggest and brightest jewel in the tourism crown and a resource that is not only precious but requires considerable protection.

Yet one could argue that environmentalism and tourism are a contradiction in terms. Surely what makes New Zealand so special, so attractive, is the very lack of humanity and its areas of virtually inaccessible wilderness. There is no doubt this is true, but thankfully, the New Zealand psyche is such that it seems to successfully marry tourism and environmentalism and bestow upon the union a blessing that has so far resulted in a congenial, if naturally imperfect relationship. So good in fact, that the country has earned the reputation as one of the best eco-tourism destinations in the world. Part of this success is due to the vast area that is protected as forest parks, national parks, nature and marine reserves – almost a quarter of the entire country – all coming under the committed, yet under-resourced advocacy and administration of the **Department of Conservation (DoC)**, www.doc.govt.nz.

Before you arrive you can avail yourself of a wealth of information on its excellent website, www.doc.govt.nz, and throughout your travels you will find dedicated information centres and field stations in all cities, major provincial towns and national parks. If you intend to go walking or to embark on a longer tramp then you will find DoC invaluable; its system of huts and campsites is an essential part of the experience.

Given the country's natural resources New Zealand, not surprisingly, is on the cutting edge of eco-tourism. The sheer choice and quality of activities, let alone the location in which they can be experienced, are superb from whale watching at Kaikoura or tramping in Fiordland to exploring the island sanctuaries of Kapiti or Tiritiri Matangi. New Zealand is one of very few countries where you can see rare or endangered species (especially birds) at close hand and in solitude. For many this is a new and welcome experience and in deep contrast to the constraints of a being in a busy hide or being surrounded by an orgy of twitchers all falling over each other to compare the size of their telescopes.

Getting there

Airport information → *For airlines see Auckland, page 108.*

There are six airports in the country which handle international flights, but Auckland is the principal international airport. Wellington, Palmerston North and Hamilton in the North Island and Christchurch, Dunedin and Queenstown in the South Island also receive regular flights from eastern Australia.

For information on negotiating Auckland International Airport, see page 71, or visit the website www.auckland-airport.co.nz. Other airports' websites include: **Wellington**, www.wellington-airport.co.nz, and **Christchurch**, www.christchurch-airport.co.nz.

Buying a ticket

There are now enormous numbers of high-street phone and internet outlets for buying your plane ticket. This can make life confusing but the competition does mean that dogged work can be rewarded with a very good deal. Fares will depend on the season, with prices much higher during December to January unless booked well in advance. Mid-year tends to see the cheapest fares. **Air New Zealand**, www.airnewzealand.com, is New Zealand's main international airline and flies from a considerable number of capitals and major cities. **Qantas**, www.qantas.com.au, also offers regular flights via New Zealand en route to or from Australia. Other airlines worth looking at are **Emirates**, www.emirates.com and **Cathay Pacific**, www.cathaypacific.co.nz.

The internet is the best way of finding a bargain ticket, but can be frustrating unless you just want a straight return or single fare to a single destination. If you are considering a multi-destination journey it is worth checking with two or three agents in person. **One-way** flight tickets are not necessarily much more expensive than half a return fare. If you are contemplating a lengthy trip and are undecided about further plans, or like the idea of being unconstrained, then a single fare could be for you. Note that immigration officials can get very suspicious of visitors arriving on one-way tickets, especially on short-term visas. Anyone without long-term residency on a one-way ticket will need to show proof of substantial funds – enough for a stay and onward flight. Discuss this with your local New Zealand Embassy or High Commission before deciding on a one-way ticket. **Round-the-World** (RTW) tickets can be a real bargain if you stick to the most popular routes, sometimes working out even cheaper than a return fare. RTWs start at around £900 (€1328) or US$2000, depending on the season.

When trying to find the best deal, make sure you check the route, journey duration, stopovers, departure and arrival times, restrictions and cancellation fees. Many cheap flights are sold by small agencies; most are honest and reliable, but there are some risks involved when buying tickets at rock-bottom prices. Do not pay too much money in advance and check with the airline directly to confirm your reservation.

From Europe

The main route, and the cheapest, is usually via Heathrow or Frankfurt and the USA (Los Angeles), though fares will also be quoted via other US cities and Asia. Either route usually takes from 20 to 30 hours including stops. There are no non-stop routes, so it's worth checking out what stopovers are on offer: this can be a good opportunity to see Kuala Lumpur or LA. A 30-hour journey, only stopping in airports to refuel is, in a word, gruelling and not recommended. Increased security at US airports has also become a factor in recent years and many travellers express derision at being treated as if guilty until proven innocent and are rarely afforded a smile and basic civility, especially at Los Angeles airport (LAX). Stopovers of a few nights do not usually increase the cost of the ticket substantially. The cheapest return flights, off-season, will be around £700 (€1032), rising to at least £1000 (€1475) around Christmas. Mainstream carriers include **Air New Zealand** and **Qantas** (west via the USA); and **Singapore Airlines**, www.singapore air.com, or **Thai Air**, www.thaiair.com (east via Asia)

From Australia

As you might expect there is a huge choice and much competition with trans-Tasman flights. Traditionally most flights used to go from Cairns, Brisbane, Sydney and Melbourne to Auckland but now many of the cheaper flights can actually be secured to Wellington, Christchurch and Queenstown. Other destinations include Palmerston North, Hamilton and Dunedin. The New Zealand based **Freedom Air**, www.freedom air.co.nz, service to Dunedin is cheap (as low as NZ$500 return) but with only a few flights a week they must be booked well in advance. Flights and especially ski packages to Queenstown can also be cheaper and have been heavily promoted in recent years, but conditions usually apply, giving you limited flexibility. At any given time there are usually special deals on offer from the major players like **Qantas** (JetStar), **Freedom Air** and **Air New Zealand** so shop around. Prices range from AUS$500-750 return. Use the listings in this book, the web, your local travel agent and the national newspapers. From Australia you are likely to be interested in 'open-jaw' tickets that will allow you to fly in to one city and depart from another. This will almost certainly be more expensive and, given the many restrictions and conditions imposed, they are often hard to secure at a good price. Always be careful to check the conditions of the cheaper 'temporary' deals with regard to your minimum or maximum allowed length of stay, cancellations, refunds etc. The flight time between Sydney and Auckland is three hours, Melbourne three hours and 45 minutes.

From the Americas

There are direct **Air New Zealand** and **Qantas** flights from Los Angeles (LAX) to Auckland. Sadly, one of the cheapest carriers, **United**, succumbed to recent financial strains and has had to cut services to New Zealand, but still retains Australia. The cost of a standard return in the low season from LAX starts from around US$1050, from New York from US$1500 and Chicago from US$1450. In the high season add about US$800 to the standard fare. **Air Canada**, www.aircanada.com, and **United**, www.united.com connect with **Alliance** partners at LAX from Vancouver, Toronto and Montreal. Prices range from CAN$1750-2700. **Singapore Airlines**, www.singapore air.com flies direct to Auckland daily from LAX stopping in Singapore. There are also direct flights from Buenos Aires to Auckland with **Aerolineas Argentinas**, www.aerolineas.com.ar, flying out of New York and Miami. The flight time between LAX and Auckland is around 12½ hours.

Departure tax

On leaving New Zealand there is a departure tax of $20-25 depending on which airport you leave from. This is not included in your ticket price.

Discount travel agents

Australia

Flight Centres, 82 Elizabeth St, Sydney, T133133, www.flightcentre.com.au, with branches in other main cities.
STA Travel, 855 George St, Sydney, T02-92121255; and 240 Flinders St, Melbourne, T03-96547266, www.statravel.com.au.
Travel.com.au, 80 Clarence St, Sydney, T1300-130482, www.travel.com.au.

North America

Air Brokers International, 323 Geary St, Suite 4111, San Francisco, CA 94102, T1800-8833273, www.airbrokers.com. Consolidator and specialist in RTW and Circle Pacific tickets.
Discount Airfares Worldwide On-Line, www.etn.nl. Discount agent links.
STA Travel, T1800-7814040, www.sta travel.com. Discount/youth travel company.
Trailfinders, T1300-780212, www.trail finders.com. Popular and well-established.

Travel CUTS, 187 College St, Toronto, ON, M5T 1P7, T1888-3592887, www.travel cuts.com. Specialists in student discount fares, IDs and other travel services.
Travelocity, www.travelocity.com. Online consolidator.

UK and Ireland

Austravel, T0870-1662130, www aus travel.com. Specialists in Australasian travel itineraries and discounts.
Ebookers, www.ebookers.com. Comprehensive travel booking website.
Expedia, www.expedia.com. Online travel site, with lots of background information.
STA Travel, 6 Wrights Lane, London, T0871-2300040, www.statravel.co.uk. Specialists in student discount fares and IDs.
Trailfinders, 194 Kensington High St, London W8 6FT, T0845-0585858, www.trail finders.com. Excellent tailor-made itineraries.
Usit Campus, 19 Aston Quay, Dublin 2, T01-6021904/6778117, www.usit.ie. Student/ youth specialists in Ireland.

Getting around

Public transport in all its forms (except rail) is generally both good and efficient. All the main cities and provincial towns can be reached easily by air or by road. Although standard fares, especially air tickets, can be expensive there are a vast number of discount passes and special seasonal deals available, aimed particularly at the young, independent traveller. Although it is entirely possible to negotiate the country by public transport, for sheer convenience you are advised to get your own set of wheels. Many of the country's delights are only to be seen off the beaten track and are certainly a long walk from the nearest bus stop. You will also free yourself of organized schedules. Long-term vehicle hire or temporary purchase is generally viable (especially if the costs are shared) and whether you go the way of a standard vehicle or campervan, you will find the country is well geared up for this mode of travel. Having said that, petrol costs are expensive and need to be taken into account.

Domestic air travel in New Zealand is in an almost constant state of flux due to the highly competitive nature of air travel in general and especially within Australasia. Currently **Air New Zealand** and **Qantas Link** are the principal domestic air carriers providing services between Auckland, Christchurch and Wellington and most regional centres. Thankfully, the relative lack of competition has not adversely affected prices. On the contrary, bookings made well in advance over the web with **Air New Zealand** or **Qantas** can see you flying from Auckland to Christchurch for as little as $100.

Worse still is the state of rail travel. In 2002, **TranzRail** closed all domestic routes except the Auckland/Wellington (**Northerner**), the Christchurch to Greymouth (**Tranz-Alpine**) and the Christchurch to Picton (**TranzCoastal**). Again only time will tell whether these survive. It seems that even in New Zealand, modern society is becoming so obsessed with speed and the increased pace of life that trains are just too slow.

⚡ Travelling times and distances from Auckland

	Distance	Car	Bus/Coach	Train	Air
Wellington	647 km	8 hrs	9 hrs	10 hrs	1 hr
Christchurch	1000 km	2 days	2 days	2 days	1 hr
Dunedin	1358 km	2-4 days	2-4 days	3 days	2 hrs
Queenstown	1484 km	2-4 days	2-4 days	-	2½ hrs
Bay of Islands	241 km	3 hrs	4 hrs	-	50 mins
Rotorua	235 km	2 hrs	3 hrs	4 hrs	45 mins

Air

As well as the principal international airports of Auckland, Wellington and Christchurch, New Zealand has many smaller provincial town airports that are mainly well served. **Air New Zealand Link** ① T0800-737000, www.airnewzealand.co.nz, and **Qantas** ① T0800-808767, www.qantas.co.nz, also offer a number of domestic services but exist on a lesser footing. Both are highly professional and efficient and you will rarely have problems with delays or service.

Apart from the major domestic operators there are many smaller companies with scheduled services. These include: **Great Barrier Airlines** (Great Barrier, Coromandel and Northland), **SoundsAir** (offering a viable alternative to the ferry between the North and South Islands) and **Southern Air** (between Invercargill and Stewart Island). All these companies are listed in the relevant sections. Note that flying anywhere in New Zealand is, on a clear day, a scenic delight and often well worth the expense.

Discount fares If you can, book domestic flights well in advance on the internet or through a travel agent. Most discounted fares can only be purchased in New Zealand and are subject to 12.5% GST (tax). There are always a number of dynamic deal schemes available that will make considerable savings depending on season and availability. For more information ask your travel agent or see the website, www.air newzealand.co.nz. Student and backpacker discounts of up to 50% are available on some domestic flights on presentation of an ISIC, YHA, VIP or BBH card. Conditions and rates vary, so research and book well in advance.

Bus

National bus travel in New Zealand is well organized and the networks and daily schedules are good. Numerous shuttle companies service the South Island and there are also many local operators and independent companies that provide shuttles to accommodation establishments, attractions and activities. These are listed in the Transport sections of the main travelling text.

The main bus companies are **Intercity**, www.intercitycoach.co.nz, and **Newmans**, www.newmanscoach.co.nz. They often operate in partnership. For information and reservations call the following regional centres: Auckland T09-623 1504; Rotorua T07-348 0999; Wellington T04-385 0512; and Christchurch T03-365 1114. Intercity operates in both the North and South Islands, while Newmans operate throughout the North Island, except in Northland where **Northliner Express**, T09-307 5873, www.north liner.co.nz, co-operates with Intercity. The latest coach company is **Nakedbus.com**, which uses the same model of low overheads and internet-only booking service that the cheap airlines do. It has managed to undercut the long-established companies.

Other companies in the North Island are: **Coromandel Explorer Tours**, T07-866 3506, www.coromandeltours.co.nz, a small company that recently began offering services around Coromandel; and **White Star**, T06-7583338, who serves the route

⁞ Combination travel passes

The **New Zealand Travel Pass**, T0800-339966, www.travelpass.co.nz, offers a two-in-one pass, combining unlimited coach travel and one ferry crossing (five days $387, 15 days $845); or a three-in-one option adding either the Tranz Coastal or TranzAlpine train journey (five days $489; 15 days, $904).

TranzScenic offers the **Scenic Rail Pass**, T04-495 0775/T0800-277 482, www.tranzscenic.co.nz, which combines travelling by train with the inter-island ferry crossing (seven-day South Island pass $249, child $150; seven-day South Island pass with ferry $289/$199; seven-day all services, $289/$189; seven-day all services with ferry, $329/$210).

between New Plymouth and Wellington, taking in Wanganui and Palmerston North. For luxury sightseeing tours throughout New Zealand contact **Great Sights**, T0800-028 7913, www.greatsights.co.nz. ▸▸ *For Backpacker buses and coach tours, see page 61.*

Concession fares All the bus companies offer a variety of concessions. With **Intercity** and **Newmans** infants less than two years travel free and children less than 12 years travel at 33%. Travellers over the age of 60 years travel at 20%, backpackers (YHA, VIP, BBH, Nomads cardholders) and students at 15%. There are 'super' fares of 25% and 'supersaver' fares of 50%, but these should be pre-booked. Intercity and Newmans also operate a **Club Free-Way Card**, similar to Frequent Flyers, which accrues points that can later be redeemed for discounts or free tickets. Membership costs $15. Newmans also offers attractive discounts but these tend to be more limiting in both timetable and destination. Economy fare cancellations must be made up to two hours in advance to avoid a loss of 50% on the ticket price.

Bus passes The **Intercity Flexi-pass and Travelpass** offers flexible travel and travel in combination with ferry and rail; valid for 12 months. **Intercity Countrywide bus passes** offer a choice of three 'hop-on/hop-off' routes throughout both the North and South Islands. An Auckland to Christchurch (or reverse) trip costs from $565 and two Auckland and back deals (or Christchurch and back) from $585 and $729. Valid for three months. **Intercity North and South Island bus passes** offer a wide range of fixed-route options covering one or both islands and the main tourism centres including Rotorua, the Bay of Islands and Wellington in the North island and Nelson, Christchurch, Queenstown and Milford in the South. Consult the website for details, www.intercity.coach.co.nz.

Essentials Getting around

Campervans → *See also Car, below.*

New Zealand is well geared up for campervan hire and travel and there's an accompanying glut of reputable international companies. Being a fairly compact country it is certainly a viable way to explore with complete independence. Although hire and petrol costs may seem excessive, once you subtract the inevitable costs of accommodation, provided you are not alone and can share those costs, it can work out cheaper in the long run. You will find that motorcamps are available even in the more remote places and a powered site will cost $15-30 per night. Note that lay-by parking is illegal and best avoided, but if you are lost or stuck, you will rarely be confronted. Again, like car rental rates, campervan rates vary and are seasonal. Costs are rated on a sliding scale according to model, season and length of hire. The average daily charge for a basic two-berth/six-berth for hire over 28 days, including insurance is $195/295 in the high season and $75/120 in the low season. Although there are fewer risks involved with campervan hire, the same general rules apply as with car hire. You generally get what you pay for but shop around and check the small print. The average campervan works out at about 14-16 litres per 100 km in petrol costs. Diesel is generally cheaper than petrol but at present more harmful to the environment.

The most popular rental firms are **Britz** ① *To800-831900/To9-275 9090, www.britz.co.nz*; **Maui** ① *To800-8008 0009/To9-2753013, www.maui-rentals.com*; and **Kea Campers** ① *To800-520052/To9-441 7833, www.keacampers.com*. For more unconventional vehicles, **Spaceships** ① *31 Beach Rd, Auckland, To800-SPACE SHIPS, To9-309 8777, www.spaceships.tv*, which offers Toyota People Movers or campervan hybrids complete with DVD and double bed from $49 per day off season and $109 peak, with 24-hour road assistance. Motorhomes can be booked through **Maui Motorhome Rentals & Car Hire** ① *To800-8008 0009/To9-275 301, www.maui.co.nz*.

Car

Other than a campervan this is by far the best way to see New Zealand. Petrol is expensive (around $1.50 per litre or $6 per gallon), but it will give you the flexibility and freedom needed to reach the more remote and beautiful places. Outside the cities traffic congestion and parking is rarely a problem. In many remote areas, especially in the South Island, the roads are single track and unsealed, so a little more driving skill is required. Generally, keep the speeds and gears low while on these roads. Also, in most rural areas, you will almost certainly encounter livestock of all shapes and sizes along the road verges, so be careful. At night you should of course take extra care and though there are very few mammals in New Zealand, one thing you will encounter is the cat-sized and brush-tailed possum. But with 70 million of the little critters denuding the countryside of its native vegetation and the ruination of native wildlife, no one will mind the occasional road kill.

Rules and regulations In New Zealand you drive on the left (though most Aucklanders drive where they like). The 'give way to the right' rule applies except when turning left; ie the oncoming car has right of way. This will seem rather strange for the UK driver who, if unaware of this rule, will end up on the receiving end of much abuse. Make sure you familiarize yourself with the rules before setting out (*NZ Road Code* booklets are available from AA offices).

The accident rate in New Zealand is high, so be extra vigilant. The speed limit on the open road is 100 kph and in built-up areas it is 50 kph. Police patrol cars and speed cameras are omnipresent so if you speed you will almost certainly be caught. A valid driving licence from your own country or an international licence is required to get behind the wheel in New Zealand and certainly must be produced if you rent a vehicle.

Parking In the cities parking can be very expensive. Do not risk parking in restricted areas or exceeding your time allotment on meters. Alas, in the major towns it feels like there is a traffic warden round every corner and up every tree. Most meters take gold and silver coins so take a supply. Also, it is very important to note that you must park with the flow of traffic, never against it; failing to do so will result in a fine. Finally, never leave or hide valuables in your car and lock it at all times.

Motoring organizations The **New Zealand Automobile Association (AA)** ⓘ *99 Albert St, City, Auckland, T09-966 8800/T0800-500555, www.aa.co.nz; breakdowns, T0800-500222*, is the principal motoring organization in New Zealand. It has offices in most provincial towns. It also provides a great range of maps and travelling information as well as the usual member benefits. If you have bought a vehicle and intend to travel extensively throughout New Zealand, the basic annual membership fee of around $80 (which provides the basic breakdown assistance) is recommended. If you intend travelling down the west coast and to Fiordland and to a lesser extent Southland in the South Island, breakdown cover is highly recommended. Members of equivalent motoring organizations in other countries may qualify for reciprocal benefits.

Car hire Almost all the major companies (like **Avis**, **Budget** and **Hertz**) are represented in New Zealand and you will find offices at airports as well as the major airports, cities and provincial towns (listed in the Directory sections throughout the guide). There are also many local operators, which you can support as opposed to the big corporates, but if you intend to travel extensively you are advised to stick with one of the major companies as they generally offer better cars, have more extensive networks as well as sound insurance and accident coverage. You must be over 21 and have a valid driver's licence to hire a vehicle; insurance premiums for the under 25s can be high. Small, older and, typically, Japanese cars (1600 cc) start at about $55 per day but rates vary

Essentials Getting around

Buying a car

Having a set of wheels to see New Zealand is highly recommended. Given the fact that second-hand cars are cheap and readily available it is worth some serious thought. Even on a low budget it's possible to buy a car, share running costs then resell on leaving. Auckland is a good place to buy but choose carefully.

Buying procedure and legalities

Automobile Association membership costs around $80 per annum. It covers emergency breakdown service or towing to the nearest garage. You also get free maps, information and insurance discounts. **Auckland AA**, T09-966 8800/T0800-500555; breakdown, T0800-500222.

→ **Change of ownership** The buyer and seller must fill in a MR13A, which can be obtained and submitted at any New Zealand post office, $9.20.

→ **Credit check** Have the car's legalities checked before purchase. AA Auto Report on the web ($25) or T0800-500333. Quote chassis and licence plate numbers.

→ **Highway/Road Code** There are a few subtle differences in New Zealand road rules (right of way while turning right is a prime example). You are advised to familiarize yourself with the *NZ Road Code* booklet available from the AA centres or major bookshops, $15.

→ **Insurance** Not compulsory but Third Party is highly recommended. The AA offer good rates along with breakdown membership.

→ **Licence** A current international or accepted driver's licence is essential.

→ **Registration** Registration can be gained with legal ownership and a valid WOF certificate for six months (about $112) or 12 ($217).

→ **Vehicle inspections** The AA does a thorough inspection as do a number of companies found under 'Vehicle Inspection Services' in the *Yellow Pages*; cost $120 (members $95). It is highly recommended, T0800-500333, www.nzaa.co.nz/ www.carinspections.co.nz.

→ **WOF (Warrant of Fitness)** All cars need a safety certificate to be legally on the road and to obtain registration. Most garages and specialist 'drive-in/drive-out' Vehicle Testing Stations (VTS) do a WOF test which if passed will last six months (see 'Warrant of Fitness' in the *Yellow Pages*). It costs about $45. If you buy a car with a WOF make sure it is not more than 28 days old.

Where to buy a car

There are a number of auto magazines available at newsagents but the major daily newspapers (*New Zealand Herald*, Wednesday and Saturday) and the auctions are also recommended. Backpacker noticeboards and the hot new website 'Trade Me' www.trade me.co.nz are also worth a look.

→ **Backpacker car markets** There are car markets at 20 East Street, Auckland, T09-377 7761; and 33 Battersea Street, Christ-church, T03-377 3177. The website, www.backpackerscarmarket.co.nz, is a good place to look and for re-sale, but be sure to have a full vehicle inspection done before purchase.

→ **Car auctions** Turners Car Auctions, corner of Penrose and Leonard Roads, Penrose, www.turn ers.co.nz. **Hammer Auctions**, corner of Neilson and Alfred streets, Onehunga, T09-579 2344, www.hammer auctions.co.nz. Check the websites for viewing and category auction days.

→ **Car fairs** Ellerslie Racecourse, Greenlane, www.car fair.co.nz, Sunday 0900-1200; **Manakau Car Market**, Manakau City Centre Car Park, Sunday 0900-1300.

depending on season, kilometres covered and the length of time you have the car (getting cheaper the longer you rent it). A medium-sized 2000 cc car will cost around $80 per day with unlimited kilometres. Without unlimited kilometres you are looking at around $0.30 per kilometre.

There are of course cheaper deals out there (up to 50%) but not without risk and you will also find that many companies advertise rates below $50 a day but do not include insurance and mileage costs. You can also rent a vehicle in one of the major cities (Auckland being the cheapest) and drop it off at another. This will almost certainly involve a drop-off fee of around $150-175 but may be worth it for the convenience. In the summer high season, if you are returning to Auckland, it is worth bargaining since many operators have a glut of cars needing to be driven back north.

Overall, the choice is vast so you are advised to shop around, but beware of cowboy operators and always read the small print before you sign. Some of the cheaper companies have an insurance excess of $750 even on minor repairs, so be careful. Always go over the car with a company representative and get them to acknowledge and list any dents or scratches that you see on the vehicle. Also if you have a camera take a few pics of your own and at the same time they do. This may avoid considerable frustration trying to prove you were not to blame. If you do not have a credit card you may have to leave a substantial cash deposit of between $500 and $1,000. Although it comes at extra cost, a 'Collision Waiver' can often be secured, which means you do not automatically lose this deposit in the event of an accident. Note also you may not be covered on certain roads. You will certainly not be covered if you venture onto any of the 'sand highways' on the coast, like Ninety Mile Beach.

There are a few motorcycle rental firms in Auckland and although not cheap, it can be a superb way to see the country, especially in the South Island.

Car-pooling An option worth considering if funds are restrictive is sharing travel costs by car-pooling, ride-sharing and lift-sharing. The website, www.carshare.co.nz, is a free resource that encourages people to network with other like-minded travellers, organize their travel plans together and, of course, save money by sharing travel costs.

Cycling

Touring New Zealand by bike is highly recommended and becoming increasingly popular, especially in the South Island. Although it is not exactly flat, it is 'topographically manageable'. Cycle hire companies are listed in the Transport section of each town. Other companies are listed under Specialist activity tours on page 63.

Ferry

Other than a few small harbour-crossing vehicle ferries and the short trip to Stewart Island from Bluff in Southland, the main focus of ferry travel is of course the inter-island services across Cook Strait. The two ports are Wellington at the southern tip of the North Island and Picton in the beautiful Marlborough Sounds on the South Island.

There are currently two services: the **Interislander**① *Wellington Railway Station, T0800-802802/T04-498 3302, www.interislandliner.co.nz*; and the smaller of the two companies **Bluebridge**① *T0800-844844/T04-4716188, www.bluebridgeco.nz*.

Generally speaking, all vessels have plenty of deck access with good views. For amenities go for the Interislander's 'Kaitaki' and for more traditional ferry experience go for the **Bluebridge**. For details on the inter-island crossing, see box page 410; for Stewart Island services, see page 672.

Hitching is still quite heavily practised in New Zealand but not entirely safe. As ever, it is not advised for those travelling alone, especially women. If you do decide to take the risk, keep to the main highways and don't hitch at night. The usual common sense rules apply and if in doubt, don't. Another good tip is never take off a rucksack and put that or a bag in the car first. For the opportunist thief this can be like Christmas; as they speed off with your gear, you will be left standing there like a proper Charlie.

Train

The rail network in New Zealand is in a seemingly incessant state of flux and has struggled to maintain anything other than a core network between its main population centres. However, that said, the trains in themselves are pretty comfortable, the service is good and the stunning scenery will soon take your mind off things. Within the **North Island** there is a daily service between Auckland and Wellington known as the **'Overlander'**. Within the **South Island**, the daily services between Picton and Christchurch (the **'TranzCoastal'**) and Christchurch to Greymouth (the **'TranzAlpine'**), are both world-class journeys. Also, designed specifically as a tourist attraction, the **Taieri Gorge Railway** runs from Christchurch to Middlemarch and back.

All fares are of a single class, but prices range greatly from 'standard' to 'super saver' so check carefully what you are entitled to and what deals you can secure. Reservations and timetables from the Auckland or Wellington railway station information centres, accredited Visitor Information Centres (I-Sites) or travel agents throughout New Zealand: **TranzScenic** ① *To800-872467/To4-495 0775, www.tranzscenic.co.nz, 0700-2200*. For further information on TranzScenic's 'Scenic Rail Pass', see box, page 39.

Maps

Detailed urban and rural maps are readily available throughout New Zealand. **Wises**, www.wises.co.nz, produces a range of handbooks and fold-out city maps; its provincial town maps for both the North and South Islands are invaluable and are stocked in most large bookshops. Most information centres provide free leaflet maps and the coverage is generally excellent. The **Department of Conservation** (DoC) offices (see page 34) are very well stocked with national park and rural maps. For really detailed maps the **Land Information New Zealand** offices can provide for all your needs. **Mapworld** ① *To800-MAPWORLD, www.mapworld.co.nz*, in Christchurch is an excellent outlet and also stocks complete CD-ROMs of all New Zealand national, regional and town maps. In the UK, **Stanfords** ① *12-14 Long Acre, Covent Garden, London, WC2E 9LP, To20-7836 1321, www.stanfords.co.uk; also 29 Corn St, Bristol, and 39 Spring Gardens, Manchester*, has a good choice and is recommended.

Sleeping

Besides actually getting there, accommodation in New Zealand will be your biggest expense. There is a wealth of choice and, though you will rarely end up without a bed for the night, you are advised to book ahead during the high season. At present the New Zealand Tourist Board are heavily plugging homestay/farmstay options. You are advised to try this at least for a few nights to encounter real Kiwi hospitality and general Kiwi life.

Visitor Information Centres (I-Sites) are a great help with accommodation and generally stock all the highly illustrated leaflets. They can also offer plenty of good advice regarding the range of options and sort out bookings. The web is also a major source of information with almost all reputable establishments now having at least an email address. There are also many books available including the *AA Accommodation Guides*, www.aaguides.co.nz; *Jason's Motels and Motor Lodges Guide*, www.jasons.co.nz; *The New Zealand Bed and Breakfast Guide*, www.bnb.co.nz; and *Friars B&B*

Hotel price codes

Prices are based on a double room (usually with en suite bathroom) during high season. Cheaper rooms are often available with shared bathrooms. Many places, especially hotel chains, offer low season and weekend specials. **Prices are in New Zealand dollars.**

LL	$250 and over
L	$175-249
AL	$120-174
A	$80-119
B	$50-79
C	$25-49
D	under $25

Guide, www.friars.co.nz; as well as numerous motorcamps, motels, campsites and backpacker guides (most of which are free).

Hotels

Hotels in New Zealand can generally be listed under one of four categories:

Large luxury hotels There are a surprising number of large, modern and luxurious (four- to five-star) hotels in the major cities, particularly in Auckland. There are so many luxury rooms and apartment blocks in the city centre it's amazing they can all survive. These major hotels tend to be part of major international or trans-Tasman chains and the prices range from $250-500 per night. As you would expect, all rooms are equipped with the latest technology including laptop plug-in ports and Sky TV. They also have restaurants and leisure facilities including swimming pools, spa pools and gyms.

Standard chain hotels These range in age and quality and include names such as **Quality Hotels, Novotel** and **Copthorne Hotels**. Found in all major cities and the larger provincial towns, their standard prices are $175-300 but they have regular weekend or off-season deals. Most have restaurants and facilities such as a heated pool.

Boutique hotels These vary in size and price but tend to be modern and of a luxurious standard. The smaller, more intimate boutique hotels are overtaking the major chains in popularity. On average double rooms here can cost anything from $175-400.

Traditional pub and budget hotels Many of the rural towns have kept the traditional wooden hotels. Don't be fooled, however; some of these may look grand from the outside, but often the interior doesn't match up. However, a basic cheap and comfortable room can still be found here generally. Beware of the bars in many of these places, unless you're quick on the draw – or know the age of the All Black fly-half that scored in the last minute of the Bledisloe 27 years ago at exactly 1500. Also note that prices are often dropped at weekends and during the off-season.

Lodges and B&Bs

There are a growing number of luxury **lodges** throughout the country and most sell themselves on their location or classic 'bush setting' as much as their architecture, sumptuous rooms, facilities and cuisine. Prices tend to be high, ranging from $200 to a mind-bending $2600 per night (which equates to almost eight months in a well-equipped campsite). **B&Bs** are not as common in New Zealand as they are in Europe, but can still be found in most places. They vary greatly in style, size and quality and can be anything from a basic double room with shared bathroom and a couple of boiled eggs for breakfast to a luxurious en suite or self-contained unit with the full breakfast. Again prices vary, with the standard cost being as little as $75-100. Some of the more luxurious, however, are extortionate. When looking at prices bear in mind a full breakfast costs at least $15 in a café or restaurant. Many lodges and B&Bs also offer evening meals. The average Kiwi B&B has still got a long way to go, but you will find most hosts to be very congenial and helpful folk.

Homestays and farmstays

Generally speaking if an establishment advertises itself as a homestay it will deliberately lack the privacy of the standard B&B and you are encouraged to mix with your hosts. The idea is that you get an insight into Kiwi life, but it may or may not be for you depending on your preferences and personality. Other than that they are very similar to B&Bs, with breakfasts as standard and an evening meal often being optional.

Farmstays of course give you the added agricultural and rural edge, and are generally recommended. Accommodation can take many forms from being in-house with your hosts or fully self-contained, and breakfasts and evening meals are often optional. You may find yourself helping to round up sheep or milking a cow and if you have kids (farmstays usually welcome them) they will be wonderfully occupied for hours.

Both homestays and farmstays tend to charge the same, or slightly lower, rates as B&Bs. **New Zealand Farm Holidays** ① *T09-412 9649, www.nzfarmholidays.co.nz*, based near Auckland, produces a helpful free catalogue listing about 300 establishments. For farmstay options in Southland (considered the hub of agriculture in New Zealand) contact the very helpful **Western Southland Farm Hosting Group** ① *T03-225 8608, www.farmhost.co.nz*. Visitor Information Centres (I-Sites) can help you find homestays or farmstays and the New Zealand Tourist Board website, www.purenz.com, also has a detailed list. If you're interested in working on a farm, **Farm Helpers (FHiNZ)** ① *16 Aspen Way, Palmerston North, T06-355 0448, www.fhinz.co.nz*, has a very useful website. A booklet listing over 190 associate farms is also available on line for $25.

Motels

Motels are the preferred option of the average Kiwi holidaymaker. They are everywhere and reproducing furtively. They vary greatly, from the awful, stained 1950s love shacks to the new and luxurious condos with bubbly spa pool. There is usually a range of rooms available and almost all have at least a shower, kitchen facilities and a TV – though whether it actually works and has Sky TV (or doubles as a plant pot) depends on the price. Most are clean and comfortable and well appointed, while in others you may find yourself trying to sleep next to the main road. Prices vary from studio units at about $70-90, one-bedroom units from $80-100 and suites accommodating families and groups for an additional charge for each adult. Many of the bigger and better establishments have a restaurant and a swimming pool. Many also make the most of the country's thermal features and have spas, sometimes even in your room.

Hostels

New Zealand is well served with hostels and budget accommodation establishments. Naturally, they vary greatly in age, design, location and quality. Some enjoy a busy atmosphere in the centre of town while others provide a quiet haven of sanctity in the country. They also have a range of types of beds on offer, with many having separate double and single rooms as well as the traditional dormitory. Dorms are usually single sex but sometimes optionally mixed. Camping facilities within the grounds are also common. Generally, hostels are good places to meet other travellers, managers are usually very knowledgeable and helpful; pick-ups are often free. Bikes, kayaks or other activity gear can often be hired at low cost or are free to use. Wherever you stay you will have access to equipped kitchens, a laundry, games or TV room, plenty of local information and, of course, phones and the internet. Prices vary little for a dorm bed, from $16-20 depending on season. Single rooms and doubles tend to be around $55, or about $25 per adult. In the high season and especially over Christmas through to March you are advised to pre-book everywhere at least three days in advance.

YHAs

The **Youth Hostel Association NZ** ① To800-278299/T03-3799970, www.yha.co.nz, is part of a worldwide organization with over 4500 hostels in 60 countries. There are about 63 establishments throughout New Zealand; the vast majority are associates as opposed to YHA owned and operated. Being part of a large organization, most are on a par if not better than the independent backpacker hostels. They all offer very much the same in standard of accommodation and facilities. They are also to be congratulated on their intensive eco-friendly policies with recycling not only provided in most hostels, but actively and enthusiastically embraced.

YHAs are only open to members but you can join in your home country (if YHA exists) or in New Zealand for an annual fee of $40 ($30 for renewals). Non-members can also stay at hostels for an additional charge of $3 per night if you wish accruing a stamp for their Downunder Card system. With 15 stamps you get a full one year membership. YHA membership cards are very handy even if you do not intend to stay consistently at YHA hostels. They entitle you to a number of discounts, including up to 30% off air and bus travel. There are a number of associate YHA hostels where no membership card is required but where members get a small discount. Pick up the YHA *Accommodation and Hostel Guide* at any major VIC (I-Site).

Backpacker organizations

There are 3 other major backpacking membership organizations in New Zealand which provide hostel listings and discounts, including a dollar off each night's stay and reductions on transport and activities. **Budget Backpacker Hostels Ltd (BBH)**, T03-379 3014, www.backpack.co.nz, has around 350 member establishments that must meet certain minimum quality criteria. These are listed in its *Blue Book* (free from VICs) along with handy descriptions, contact details and location maps of each hostel.

If you choose, you can purchase a BBH Club Card ($40, with $20 free phone card) that guarantees the listed prices. Recommended.
Nomads, T(61)02-9299 7710, www.nomads world.com, based in Australia. Offers the same kind of deal but with far fewer hostels (Auckland, Rotorua, Wellington and Christchurch) for an annual membership of AU$34.
VIP Group, PO Box 60177, Titirangi, Auckland, T09-816 8903, www.vip.co.nz. About 100 New Zealand establishments are members. Annual membership fee is $39.

Motorcamps and cabins

New Zealand's fairly compact size and quality road network lends itself to road touring. Given that so many visitors and Kiwis take the campervan or camping option, New Zealand is very well served with quality motorcamps and campsites. In fact, it is hailed as one of the best in the world. Motorcamps can be found almost everywhere and not necessarily just in towns. The hub of many a remote beach, headland or bay is often the great Kiwi motorcamp. The quality and age does of course vary. Some are modern and well equipped while others are basic. Almost all motorcamps are equipped with laundry facilities and a few will charge a small fee ($0.20-1) for hot showers. Prices are generally very reasonable and range from $9-16 per person (child half price) for non-powered sites. Powered sites are often the same price or less than $5 more.

Most motorcamps have a range of cabins from dog kennels to well-appointed alpine-type huts. They vary in price staring with a 'standard cabin' with little more than a bed and electric socket for a mere $35 to a better facilitated cabin for up to $60 per night (for two) with an additional charge of $12-15 per person after that.

The **Top Ten** chain of motorcamps, which has almost 50 camps nationwide, though up to $3 more expensive per night, is generally highly recommended. If you stick to the Top Ten affiliates you will also find yourself consistently bumping into the same people, which can be great or, conversely, an utter nightmare.

Essentials Sleeping

DoC campsites and huts

The **Department of Conservation**, www.doc.govt.nz, has over 100 basic campsites all over the country with many being in prime locations. They tend to provide clean running water, toilet facilities and BBQ areas, but rarely allow open fires. The national parks in particular are all excellently facilitated with comfortable well-equipped huts. There is usually a nightly fee of $2-10. Fees for huts are anything from $5-40 per night depending on category and location. If you plan to use DoC campsites and huts you are advised to research their locations, fee structures, rules and regulations and book well in advance.

Holiday homes and cottages (baches)

This is one accommodation option very often overlooked by visitors. The country has a wealth of holiday homes and baches (seaside huts, cottages or mansions), which are available for rent throughout the year. While in summer they will most probably be frequented by the owners, in the off season you can sometimes find a real bargain. The best place to look is in the national newspapers, travel or house rental sections. The regional VICs can also often be of assistance. Most operate on a minimum weekend or week stay basis and costs vary depending on quality and location. If you are travelling with a family or group, this option is well worth looking into.

Eating and drinking

Food

Budget-permitting you are in for a treat. The quality of food in New Zealand is superb. Although there are many types of traditional cuisine and restaurants in evidence, the principal style is 'Pacific Rim'. It dips into the culinary heritage of many of the cultures of the Oceania region, with inspiration and influences from Thailand, Malaysia, Indonesia, Polynesia, Japan and Vietnam as well as further afield like Europe. For dishes that have a distinctly Kiwi edge look out for the lamb (arguably the best in the world), pork, venison and freshwater fish like salmon and eel. Despite its reputation as perhaps the best trout-fishing country in the world, you cannot buy trout commercially. Although this is a shame, it does provide the added incentive to go and catch your own; many restaurants will be happy to cook it for you.

As you might expect there is a heavy emphasis on fine seafood. The choice is vast with many warm-water fish like snapper, kingfish, hoki, hapuka and orange roughie. Catching these yourself and cooking them on a BBQ fresh off the boat will provide a memorable culinary experience. Other seafood delights include crayfish (the South Pacific equivalent to the lobster), oysters (the best being from Bluff in the South Island), paua (abalone), scallops and the famous green-lipped mussels. These mussels are very substantial, delicious and should not be missed. They are also relatively cheap and readily available. There are also some treats in store from below the ground. The kumara (sweet potato) will shed a whole new light on the humble 'spud', while many of the international vegetables like asparagus and broccoli come cheap (especially while in season) and are always fresh. From the tree the fruit of choice is of course the succulent kiwi fruit or 'Chinese gooseberry' which although not exclusively grown in New Zealand is deservedly celebrated. Other fine fruits include feijoa and tamarillo. The celebrated dessert in New Zealand is the pavlova; a sort of mountainous cake made of meringue and whipped cream. For a real traditional feast try a Maori *hangi* (see box, page 50). Prepared properly and without ketchup you will be amazed at just how good and different fish, meat and vegetables can taste when cooked underground.

If you intend to do your own cooking, supermarkets offer a wide choice of fare. The main chains are **Big Fresh, Woolworths** and **New World,** with **Pac-n-Save** and **Countdown** being marginally cheaper. One bonus of supermarket shopping are the

Restaurant price codes

All the places listed are recommended as offering relatively good value, quality and standards of service within their respective price category. Some are also noted for having particularly pleasant or unusual surrounds.

Prices are in New Zealand dollars. Eateries are divided into three categories:

¶¶¶	$25 and over for a main course
¶¶	$18-24 for a main course
¶	under $18 for a main course

current deals offering $0.04 a litre off petrol at selected fuel companies for every $40 or more spent. For fresh fruit and vegetables, stick to the numerous roadside or wholesale fruit markets where the difference in price and quality can be astonishing.

Drink

Other than **L&P** (a fairly unremarkable soft drink hailing from Paeroa) New Zealand lacks a national drink. If there is one, it is the highly sub-standard and over-rated beer called **Lion Red**. This and a number of other equally watery relations are drunk not so much by the pint as the jug, and are all backed by a very 'Kiwi-bloke' image, which is regularly promoted with less-than-PC advertising. Rest assured, however, that all the main internationally well-known bottled beers are available, as are some good foreign tap ales like Caffrey's and Kilkenny. Depending on the pub and how it is kept and poured, you can also get a good Guinness.

Beer and lager is usually sold by the 'handle', the 'glass' (pint) or the 'jug' (up to three pints). Half-pints come in a 12-fl oz (350 ml) glass. Rarely is a pint a proper imperial pint, it's usually just under. Drinks generally cost $6-7 for a pint, about $4-5 for a jug of Lion Red and up to $7 for a double shot. Alcohol is much cheaper in rural pubs and RSAs (Retired Servicemen's Associations), where you can usually get yourself signed in. The minimum drinking age has just been reduced from 21 to 18. Liquor shops (off licences) are everywhere and alcohol can generally (in most places) be bought seven days a week. There is a thriving coffee culture almost everywhere in the main towns and cities, so you will not go without your daily caffeine fix.

New Zealand wine

New Zealand's rich diversity of climates and soil types has borne an equally rich array of wines and after over a century of development the country now boasts many of internationally recognized standards. Wine is produced the length and breadth of the country but the Hawkes Bay and Nelson/Marlborough areas are the principal wine producing regions. New Zealand Sauvignon Blanc is rated throughout the world as one of the best, but there is growing recognition for its Chardonnay, Pinot Noir, Methode Traditionelle sparkling wine, Riesling, Cabernet Sauvignon and Merlot. Fruit wines, including the unusual 'kiwi fruit wine', are also evident. The choice is vast and whether a connoisseur or a novice you are advised to experiment. If you can, visit one of the many vineyards that offer tastings and cellar sales. For more information about New Zealand wines refer to www.nzwine.com or www.winesnewzealand.co.nz. See also the *Footprint Wine Guide to the World*.

Eating out

There are eateries to suit every taste and budget from the ubiquitous fast-food joints to world-class seafood restaurants. Auckland and Wellington (which has more cafés and restaurants per capita than New York) are particularly rich in choice with a vast selection of cafés, café-bars, brasseries and specialist international restaurants giving added

⦂ The hangi

Pronounced 'hungi', this is the traditional Maori and Pacific Island feast or method of cooking. To the uninitiated, the concept of cooking your dinner in the ground may seem a bit odd, but it is actually incredibly efficient and produces a certain taste and texture in the food that is extraordinarily good. Hangis were designed for the masses and were as much a social occasion as anything else. Traditionally the men would light a large fire and place river stones in the embers. While the stones are heating a pit is dug in the earth. Then the stones are placed in the pit and sacking placed upon them (before sacking it was suitably fashioned plant material). Then, presumably, the boys went off for a beer while the good ladies of the tribe prepared the meat. Nowadays this includes chicken, wild pig and lamb, but was formerly moa, pigeon and seafood. Vegetables are added too, particularly the traditional sweet potato, *kumara*. Once cleaned and plucked the smaller items are wrapped in leaves (now foil) and the whole lot placed in a basket (traditionally woven leaves from the flax plant, now wire-mesh) and then the whole affair is covered with earth. Then the ladies join the men for beer and a chat. Meanwhile, the steam slowly cooks the food and the flavours are sealed in. Then a couple of hours later it is all dug up *et voilá* – it's 'pig-out' time. The succulence and smoked flavours of the food are gorgeous.

Although due to modern-day health and safety requirements it is not really possible to sample a proper *hangi*, the commercial offerings by the Maori tourist concerns can still be very tasty and well worth the experience. Rotorua is the principal venue (see page 254). If you ever have the opportunity of a real one, do not pass it up.

puff to the celebrated 'Pacific Rim'. There is often a fine line between cafés and restaurants. **Cafés** perhaps provide a more informal atmosphere with an emphasis on a broader range of cheaper light meals during the day, happily simmering on into the night with more substantial dishes. They also almost always serve coffee, breakfast or brunch, are licensed (or at the very least BYO) and often provide outdoor seating. **Restaurants** are similar with few expecting formal attire. You can find upmarket, snooty eateries if you wish, but they will not provide the celebrated, laid-back, food-centred focus of the vast majority. Many of the top hotels, motels and lodges are open to non-residents and provide fine dining at affordable prices. Most cities and major towns have at least one Irish or old English-style pub offering 'pub-grub' from the 'Full-Monty' breakfast and Irish stew to good old fish and chips – all for under $18. **Vegetarians** are generally well catered for in the main centres and provincial towns, while the more remote corners of New Zealand still offer the 'half cow on the barbie'. Ask for a vegetarian dish in a South Island backcountry station and you'll most probably be shown the door.

Eating out in New Zealand is generally good value, especially for those visitors revelling in the more than favourable dollar exchange rates. Even backpackers on a strict budget should be able to treat themselves occasionally. The vast majority of eateries fall into the 'mid-range' bracket ($18-25 for a main).

Most cafés open for breakfast between 0700 and 0900 and stay open until at least 1700, and often until late into the evening or the early hours. This usually applies seven days a week with special Sunday brunch hours provided. Most mid-range restaurants open their doors daily for lunch (often 1100-1400) and dinner (from 1800). The more exclusive establishments usually open for dinner from about 1800, with some (especially in winter) only opening some weekday evenings and at weekends.

Most cities are blessed with numerous venues hosting first-class concerts and shows. Theatre, orchestral concerts, ballet, dance, comedy, rock and jazz are all well represented. Many international rock stars now include at least one gig in Auckland in their itinerary. On a smaller scale you will find a vibrant nightlife in New Zealand cities and major provincial towns. Although not necessarily world class, the nightclubs, cabarets, pubs and local rock concerts will certainly have you 'shaking your pants'. There's even Country and Western and line dancing. New Zealand boasts two large, modern, 24-hour casinos in Christchurch and Wellington. **Ticketek** are the national administrators for information and ticketing and a full listing of shows and events can be sourced from their website, www.ticketek.co.nz or www.nzlive.com.

Pubs, bars and clubs

The pub scene has come on in leaps and bounds over the last decade with new establishments opening up almost everywhere. Before the 1990s the vast majority of pubs in New Zealand were the archetypal male bastions – establishments where ashtrays were built into the tables, pictures of the local hairy rugby team adorned the walls and the average Saturday night consisted of a good argument about sport, a band playing Deep Purple's *Smoke on the Water*, followed by a fight, copious wall-to-wall vomiting and a failed attempt to get home. Of course such places still exist, but generally speaking pubs and bars are now a much more refined and classy affair yet still retain that congenial and laid-back 'traditional pub' atmosphere. Now you can enjoy a good beer and conversation over an open fire in winter or under the sun in summer. New Zealand has also caught on to the 'Irish pub' fad and although some are gimmicky, others are very good, offering fine surroundings and beer to match. Many drinking establishments are also now attached to restaurants and cafés with outdoor seating. If you really must sample the old-fashioned Kiwi pub you will find them often in the hotels or main streets of the rural towns. While not all bad, do not walk round in a pair of pink shorts, or without knowing what an 'All Black' is.

In December 2004 it became illegal to smoke in all pubs, restaurants and cafés in New Zealand, though many still provide segregated (legal) areas outside.

Pubs and bars are generally open from 1100-2230 with many having an extended licence to 2400 and sometimes even 0300 at weekends.

Festivals and events

There are a huge range of events and festivals held throughout the year, ranging from the bizarre **Great Naked Tunnel Run** in Fiordland (see page 655) to the huge, spectacular **Opera in the Park** in Auckland. One of the more obscure events is the **Wildfoods Festival** on the South Island's west coast, an extravaganza of gourmet 'bush tucker' based on natural (or highly unusual) food resources from the land and sea. The many regional and provincial town **Food, Arts and Wine Festivals** are usually held in summer and provide a fitting and lively celebration of the country's wealth of creations. There are also many traditional (if a little commercial) **Maori cultural performances** in the main centres and particularly in Rotorua.

New Zealand hosted the UK and Ireland **Lions Tour** in 2005. Despite all the pre-tour hype resulting from the English team's success at the Rugby World Cup in Australia 2003 and the Welsh Grand Slam of the Six Nations Tournament in 2005, the tour proved something of a disappointed for the Lions, with convincing victories for the All Blacks in all three test matches. Now, looking almost certain to take the 2007 Rugby World Cup convincingly and scheduled to host the 2011 Rugby World Cup it seems the nation is once more on a roll.

Local VICs have listings of events and the NZTB website, www.purenz.com or www.nzlive.com both have detailed nationwide events listings. Regional and city events are listed in the relevant sections.

Shopping

Although on first acquaintance you might be forgiven for thinking it is all fluffy sheep or rugby jerseys, shopping in New Zealand can be a rewarding and interesting experience. For a country so sparsely populated there is a surprising wealth of quality goods on sale, from international designer label clothing to traditional arts and crafts.

Arts and crafts
Beyond the international and the kitsch, New Zealand arts and crafts consist of a vast array of South Pacific, Maori and contemporary Kiwi styles and influences. Much of the art is very colourful, reflecting the beautiful bright blues and greens of the environment, while two-dimensional works are often beautifully carved panels, figures, bowls and furniture made of native woods like kauri and rimu.

Pottery and ceramics abound. There are Maori pendants (*tiki*) carved from whale bone and greenstone (*pounamu*). These have been made and worn by the Maori for centuries and often depict sacred animals or spirits. If you buy one, it is customary to offer it as a gift. They are also often associated with *mana* (power or standing) and fertility. There are many cheap and nasty versions on sale, especially in the city souvenir shops, so if you want quality, look in specialist arts and craft or museum shops. Almost everywhere you will also see the stunning hues of the abalone shell (or *paua*). The *paua* is harvested naturally under strict controls and the shells are utilized as a by-product. You can buy the best quality half shells polished and varnished for about $25 or choose from the many jewellery pieces created or inlaid with colourful fragments.

Also proving popular are possum fur products. Though not quite in the same league as wool it can make an eminently fetching pair of cosy gloves with matching furry hat. One enterprising outlet in the South Island has even gone so far as to venture into the rather up and down business of possum fur nipple warmer production.

Clothing
On the clothing front look out for the famous red or blue plaid Kiwi 'swandrie'. It's a sort of thick woollen shirt/jacket and offers the best protection from the cold. You will also see the world-famous All Black rugby jerseys all over the place. Although the real thing is now made by Adidas (in a much less appealing synthetic material) the 'Canterbury' rugby tops have to be the best cotton-made tops in the world and last for years. Make sure the one you buy is made by the Canterbury Clothing Company (CCC). It has a factory shop in Christchurch (see page 489) and anothe branch in Auckland (see page 105). For modern fashion look out for some award-winning Kiwi labels, like Zambesi, NomD, Karen Walker and World.

Essentials A to Z

Accident & emergency

For police, fire or ambulance: T111. Make sure you obtain police/medical reports required for insurance claims. For legal advice contact the **Citizen's Advice Bureau** in Auckland, T0800-367222.

Children

For families and travellers with children you will generally find New Zealand very child friendly and replete with all the usual concessions for travel and activities. With so many outdoor activities safety is a natural concern, but this is nothing common sense can't take care of. If your child does not speak English, always make sure they are carrying some kind of identification.

There are a few hotels that will not accept children especially some of the 'higher end' boutique B&Bs or lodges. Check in advance.

A good resource is **Kids Friendly New Zealand**, www.kidsfriendlynz.com. Also, in Queenstown/Wanaka look out for the independent magazine *Kidz Go*, www.kidz go.co.nz, available from the VIC (I-Site) .

Customs & duty free

Customs

New Zealand's environment and highly unique biodiversity has been decimated by unwelcome and non-native wildlife and vegetation. Not surprisingly it has imposed strict bio-security laws. Be extra vigilant about not carrying any fruit, animal or plant matter of any kind without prior permission. Heavy fines are imposed on those who flout the rules. The New Zealand Customs Service website, www.customs.govt.nz, provides comprehensive advice for travellers including details of restricted items. The usual rules and regulations are also in force regarding pets or any live animals, drugs and firearms.

Duty free

Apart from your personal effects and as long as you are over 17 years of age you are allowed the following importation

concessions: 200 cigarettes or 250 g of tobacco or 50 cigars, or a mix of all three weighing no more than 250 g; 4½ litres of wine or beer and one 1125 ml bottle of spirits, liqueur or other libation. Goods up to a total combined value of NZ$700 are duty- and tax-free. New Zealand duty-free liquor is some of the cheapest in the world.

Disabled travellers

Most public facilities are well geared up for wheelchairs, however older accommodation establishments and some public transport systems (especially rural buses) are not so well organized. It is a requirement by law to have disabled facilities in new buildings. The larger airlines like **Air New Zealand** and **Qantas** are well equipped. Disabled travellers usually receive discounts on travel fares and some admission charges. Parking concessions are also available for the disabled and temporary cards can be issued on production of a mobility card or medical certificate.

For more information within New Zealand contact: **Enable**, T0800-171981/T06-952 0011, www.enable.co.nz; and **New Zealand Disability Resource Centre**, 14 Erson Av, PO Box 24-042 Royal Oak, Auckland, T09-625 8069, www.disabilityresource.org.nz. **Accessible Kiwi Tours Ltd**, T07-315 6988, www.toursnz.com, is a specialist tour company acting specifically for the disabled, based in Opotiki in the Bay of Plenty.

Electricity

The New Zealand supply is 230/240 volts (50 hertz). Plugs are either 2- or 3-pronged with flat pins. North American appliances require both an adapter and a transformer; UK an adaptor only; Australian appliances are the same. Adapters and transformers are widely available at hardware stores or the airport.

Embassies and consulates

For further information on visas and immigration, page 63. See also www.mfat.govt.nz.

Foreign consulates in New Zealand

Auckland

Australia 7th floor, 188 Quay St, City, T09-921 8800. **Canada** 9th floor, 48 Emily Pl, City, T09-309 3690. **Denmark** 7th floor Harbour View Blg, 152 Quay St, City T09-537 3099. **Germany** 6th floor, 52 Symonds St, City, T09-913 3674. **Ireland** 7th floor, Citibank Blg, 23 Customs St East, City, T09-977 2252. **Japan** Level 12, ASB Bank Centre, 135 Albert St, City, T09-303 4106. **Korea** Level 10, Sofrana House, 396 Queen St, T09-379 0818. **Netherlands** Level 1, 57 Symonds St, City, T09-379 5399. **Sweden** 13th floor, 13 O'Connell St, City, T09-373 5332. **UK** IAG House, 151 Queen St, City, T09-303 2973. **USA** Level 3, Citibank Centre, 23 Customs St East, T09-303 2724.

Wellington

Australia 72 Hobson St, T04-473 6411, **Canada** Level 11, 125 The Terrace, City, T04-473 9577, www.voyage.gc.ca. **France** 42 Manners St, T04-384 2555. **Germany** 90 Hobson St, T04-473 6063. **UK** 44 Hill St, Wellington, T04-924 2888, www.bri tain.org.nz. **USA** 29 Fitzherbert Terr, Thorndon, T04-462 6000.

New Zealand embassies abroad

See also www.nzembassy.com.
Australia High Commission Commonwealth Av, Canberra, ACT 2600, T+61-(0)2-6270 4211. **Consulate General** Level 10, 55 Hunter St, Sydney, PO Box 365, NSW 2001, T+61-(0)2-8265 2000.
Canada High Commission Suite 727, 99 Bank St, Ottowa, Ont K1P 6G3, T+1-613-238 5991. **Consulate General** Suite 1200, 888 Dunsmuir St, Vancouver, BC, V6C 3K4, T+1-604-684 7388.
France Embassy 7 Rue Leonard de Vinci, 75116, Paris, T+33-01-45 01 43 43.
Germany Embassy Friedrichstrasse 60, 10117, Berlin, T+49-30-206210.
Netherlands Embassy Eisenhowerlaan 77n, 2517KK, The Hague, T+31-70-346 9324.
UK High Commission New Zealand House, 80 Haymarket, London SW1Y 4TQ, T+44-(0)20-7930 8422.
USA Embassy Observatory Circle NW, Washington DC, 20008, T+1-202-328 4800.

Consulate General 2425 Olympic Blvd, Suite 600E, Santa Monica, CA 90404, T+1-310-566 6555/T+1-310-460 4424.

Gay & lesbian travellers

Homosexuality is generally well accepted in New Zealand and indeed in some parts it is flourishing. Auckland has a thriving gay and transvestite community heavily focused around the Ponsonby and Karangahape Road (K'Road) areas, where there are many gay and gay-friendly clubs, cafés and pubs. There are also a number of specialist publications and independent groups, see the Auckland chapter, page 101. Each Feb Auckland hosts the popular 'Hero Parade' – the national gay event of the year. The festival involves a street parade and entertainment in the Ponsonby area. Although not quite on the scale of the world famous Sydney 'Mardi Gras', it is enjoyed by thousands, both gay and straight. How could one, for example, possibly resist 'Drag Aeorobics with Buffy and Bimbo' (www.buffyandbimbo.com)?
New Zealand Gay and Lesbian Tourism Association (GALTA) PO Box 638, Queenstown, T021-762796, www.gay pages.co.nz, provides information on gay and lesbian New Zealand.

Useful websites include www.pink pagesnet.com, www.gaynewzealand.com and www.gaytravelnet.com/nz.

Publications to look out for in the main centres include the long-established *Gay Express*, www.gayexpress.co.nz.

Health

The standards of public and private medical care are generally high, but unless you have a genuine accident it is important to note that these services are not free. Health insurance is recommended. A standard trip to the doctor will cost around $40 with prescription charges on top of that. Dentists and hospital services are expensive.

Safety precautions

Other than the occasional crazed driver, there are few dangerous creatures in New Zealand. An exception is the **Katipo Spider**. Small and black, about 25 mm from leg tip to leg tip, it is found on beaches, under stones and in driftwood throughout the North Island and parts of the South. It is not uncommon and can be fatal, with agonizing pain around the bite. Antivenin is readily available in hospitals.

Although not poisonous, the dreaded **sandfly** is found everywhere, but particularly common in the wetter and coastal areas of Fiordland. These black, pinhead sized 'flying fangs' can annoy you beyond belief. There are numerous environmentally friendly available such as: *Shoo*, *Botanica* and *Repel*.

Giardia is a water-borne bacterial parasite on the increase in New Zealand which, if allowed to enter your system, will cause wall-to-wall vomiting, diarrhoea and rapid weight loss. Don't drink water from lakes, ponds or rivers without boiling it first.

The **sun** is dangerous and you should take care. Ozone depletion is heavy in the more southern latitudes and the incidence of melanomas and skin cancer is above average. Burn times, especially in summer, are greatly reduced so get yourself a silly hat and wear lots of sun block.

New Zealand's **weather**, especially at higher elevations, is changeable and can be deadly. If you are tramping, or going 'bush' make sure you are properly clothed, take maps, a first-aid kit and a compass. Above all inform somebody of your intentions.

Volcanic eruptions and **earthquakes** are a rare but exciting factor and can prove fatal. In the event of an earthquake, stand in a doorway, get under a table and if you are in the open, get indoors or keep away from loose rock formations and trees. Apparently, all the major existing volcanoes in New Zealand are well 'overdue'.

Should you come across any **injured wildlife** call the nearest DoC office and try to ensure the animal is taken to one of the few local wildlife rehabilitators. Provided the animal is not on the 'Don't touch' list (ask DoC) and you use common sense, capture the animal and put it in a dark, fully-enclosed box with some ventilation holes. Then find out the location of the nearest rehabilitator and take it there yourself. If in doubt, leave it alone. If you come across a **whale stranding** or an obviously sick seal on the beach call DoC immediately or, in the South Island, **Marine Watch**, T02-535 8909.

Insurance

Although New Zealand honours its reputation as clean and green it has a dark side and crime rates are high, especially when it comes to theft – for which tourists are an obvious target. Full travel insurance is advised, but at the very least get medical insurance and coverage for expensive personal effects. The **New Zealand Accident Compensation Scheme** covers visitors to New Zealand for personal injury by accident. Benefits include some emergency medical expenses, but do not include loss of earnings.

There are a wide variety of policies to choose from, so shop around. Always read the small print carefully. Check that the policy covers the activities you intend or may end up doing. Also check exactly what your medical cover includes, ie ambulance, helicopter rescue or emergency flights back home. Also check the payment protocol. You may have to cough up first (literally) before the insurance company reimburses you. Dig out all the receipts for expensive personal effects like jewellery or cameras. Take photos of these items and note down all serial numbers. It will also almost certainly be necessary to extend the premium and pay more to cover individual items worth more than NZ$500. In recent years there have been a number of high profile cases of tourists trying to rip off their insurers. New Zealand police are pretty savvy to such fraud especially in the main centres so be extra vigilant with paperwork and when a genuine crime has occurred report it immediately, preferably with an independent witness.

Insurance companies
In North America
Young travellers can try the **International Student Insurance Service** (**ISIS**), available through **STA Travel**, (USA) T1-800-7814040, www.statravel.com. Other companies include: **Access America**, T1-800-7296021, www.access america.com; **Travel Assistance International**, T1-800-8212828, www.travelassistance.com; **Travel Insurance Services**, T1-800-9371387, www.travelinsure.com; and **Travel Guard**, T1-800-8264919, www.travelguard.com.

STA Travel, www.statravel.co.uk, offer good-value policies. Other companies that specialize in travel for those under 26 include: Columbus, T0870-033 9988, www.columbusdirect.com; Direct Line, T0845-246 8704, www.directline.com; and the Flexicover Group, T0870-990 9292, www.flexicover.co.uk. Some companies will not cover people over 65 years old, or may charge higher premiums. Specific policies for older travellers are offered by Saga, T0800-559 3231, www.saga.co.uk.

Internet

New Zealand had one of the highest per capita internet access rates in the developed world. Internet cafés and terminals are everywhere and if you are amongst the many who start walking funny or dribbling if you do not get your daily 'email-inbox-fix' you should be fine. As well as internet cafés, libraries and VICs are a good bet, they charge standard rates of $6-12 per hr. Due to growing competition, rates are getting cheaper, with rates as little as $3 per, but you are advised to shop around.

Language

English is of course the principal language spoken in New Zealand. Maori is the traditional. See also page 707 and Glossary of Maori words on page 722.

Laundry

Most towns, villages and accommodation establishments have launderettes. They tend to operate with $1 or $2 coins. A full wash and dry will cost about $6.

Media

Although not blessed with the same choice as countries like the UK, the **newspapers** in New Zealand are pretty good, featuring fairly comprehensive and factual sections on local, national and international news as well as sport, business and travel. The main dailies are the *New Zealand Herald*, www.nzherald.co.nz (Auckland and upper North Island), the *Dominion* (Wellington and lower North Island)

and the *Press* (Christchurch and central South Island). The *Sunday Star Times* is available nationally. The website www.nzstuff.co.nz, is good for national and regional news.

National **magazines** of interest include *North and South*, which covers a wide range of traditional and contemporary issues; *New Zealand Geographic*, the quality New Zealand version of the great US national icon; *New Zealand Wilderness*, a glossy outdoor activity magazine; and *New Zealand Outside*, a similar effort. These are readily available at bookshops.

Although New Zealand radio is quite good, **television** is a shocker; the 4 principal terrestrial channels have little to offer. Except for good news and current affairs programmes you are bombarded with the usual UK or US soaps or gameshows. Most New Zealanders have now subscribed to Sky TV. Perhaps most aggravating of all is the advertising. It is not unusual to get the same advert every 10 mins for days.

Money

The New Zealand currency is the dollar ($), divided into 100 cents (c). Coins come in denominations of 5c, 10c, 20c, 50c, $1 and $2. Notes come in $5, $10, $20, $50 and $100 denominations.

Exchange rates (July 2007)
US$1 = NZ$1.34; UK£1 = NZ$2.70; €1 = NZ$1.83; AUS $1 = NZ$1.12.

Traveller's cheques (TCs)
The safest way to carry money is in TCs. These are available for a small commission from all major banks. American Express (Amex), Visa and Thomas Cook cheques are widely accepted. Most banks do not charge for changing TCs and usually offer the best exchange rates. Keep a record of your cheque numbers and keep the cheques you have cashed separate from the cheques themselves, so that you can get a full refund of all uncashed cheques. It is best to bring NZ$ cheques to avoid extra exchange costs.

Credit cards, ATMs and EFTPOS
All the major credit cards (Visa, MasterCard, Amex, JCB and Diners) are widely accepted. Most hotels, shops and petrol stations use EFTPOS (Electronic Funds Transfer at Point

⁞ The 'Trade Me' phenomenon

Need something important? A roof rack or a rucksack perhaps? How about something uniquely Kiwi, such as a rugby ball signed by all the (now deceased) members of Wharethewhakaawee Rugby Football Club? Or how about something utterly useless (yet strangely appealing) like a luminescent dog coat, a Cliff Richard fridge magnet, or a set of edible underpants?

Perhaps nowhere else on earth can our innate retail demon be satisfied more than by logging on to the nation's best known e-commerce phenomenon and auction site 'Trade Me', www.trademe.co.nz. Created in 1999 by Kiwi university dropout and IT entrepreneur Sam Morgan (before E-bay could muscle in on the New Zealand market) it became an instant and over-whelming success. In 2006 it was such a marketable entity Sam sold it for a cool $700 million, making him one of New Zealand's richest and youngest multimillionaires.

One million Kiwis use the site daily, while 50,000 are online at any one time. Incredibly Trade Me currently takes up over 50% of total net traffic in New Zealand. It is so popular that, like I-pods or mobile phones, one could argue it is actually altering or indeed 'creating' new social behaviours in its wake. Sam is now one of the most revered and influential people in New Zealand (along with the Prime Minister, coach of the All Blacks) and Trade Me regularly causes ripples across the land.

Here are just a few examples. In 2006 an enterprising young lady ran on to the pitch 'with hardly a stich on' during a televised All Blacks rugby match, then tried to sell her generously sized bra on Trade Me. Sadly for her, the $4000 bid never materialized, but went on to become something of a national celebrity. Then there was the occasion Tana Umanga, former captain of the All Blacks, hit a fellow player in a nightclub with a ladies handbag, breaking a mobile phone in the process. Said bag and phone then went on to accrue $22,800 for its owner on Trade Me.

Other notable sales included the country of Australia for a rather pricey $200,045,000 (withdrawn by Trade Me administration), a rug made of cat fur, and an amputated leg (withdrawn by administration and quickly added to the list of 'prohibited items').

of Sale), meaning you don't have to carry lots of cash. It is best suited to those who have a bank account in New Zealand, but credit cards can be used with the relevant pin number. If you intend to stay in New Zealand for a while you may be able to open an account with one of the major banks and secure an EFTPOS/ATM card and PIN. ATMs are readily available in almost all towns and though they accept non-host bank cards, it's best to stick to your own bank's ATMs so you do not incur hidden fees. Credit cards can of course be used and some banks are linked to foreign savings accounts and cards by such networks as **Cirrus** and **Plus**.

Banks

Almost all towns and villages have at least one of the major bank branches. The main banks are the **Bank of New Zealand**, the **National Bank of New Zealand**, the **ASB Bank**, **Post Bank** and **Countrywide Bank**, with other trans-Tasman banks, like **Westpac Trust** and **ANZ** also in evidence. Bank opening hours are Mon-Fri 0900-1630 with some city branches opening on Sat until 1230. Exchange offices like **Thomas Cook**, **Travelex** and **American Express** tend to have longer opening hours, sometimes staying open until 2100 in the cities.

If you need money quickly or in an emergency the best way is to have it wired to you via any major bank with **Western Union** (NZ) T1800-325 6000, www.westernunion.com; or via **Thomas Cook** and **Moneygram** (NZ) T0800-872893, www.thomascook.com. The transfer can take less than an hour or up to a week depending how much is being transferred and how much you are willing to pay ($30-80). Charges are on a sliding scale; it will cost proportionately less to wire out more money. Most postshops can assist with money transfers.

Cost of living/travelling

If you are visiting from the UK or the US you will be pleasantly surprised at how far a pound or a US dollar will go. Those travelling from Europe will find things generally cheaper, though beer costs about the same. For accommodation and restaurants, see pages 45 and 49. Petrol is expensive at around $1.50 per litre ($6 per gallon). Many organized activities are also expensive.

The minimum budget required, if staying in hostels or campsites, cooking for yourself, not drinking much and travelling relatively slowly is about $75 per person per day, but this isn't going to be much fun. Going on the occasional tour, travelling faster and eating out occasionally will raise this to a more realistic $100-120. Those staying in modest B&Bs, hotels and motels as couples, eating out most nights and taking a few tours will need to budget for $200-300 per person per day. Costs in the major cities will be 20-50% higher. Non-hostelling single travellers should budget on spending around 60-70% of what a couple would spend. Despite the highly favourable exchange rates, you will find that money still evaporates just as quickly and mysteriously as anywhere else, so it is wise to budget before your arrival.

See also student travellers, page 59, for discounts available.

Opening hours

Most government offices are open 0830-1630. Weekday business hours are usually 0900-1700. Most retail outlets close at 1730 and in the larger towns many are also open at the weekend. The modern malls open daily with at least one late shopping night a week, usually Thu or Fri. Also, in the main centres, the larger supermarket chains are open in the evenings. Almost every town and village has the iconic Kiwi corner 'dairy' which are often open until 2000 and sometimes until 2300. Petrol (gas) stations are open until about 2300 with some open 24 hours; many now sell a substantial range of supermarket type items.

Post

Post offices (most often called 'Post Shops') are generally open Mon-Fri 0900-1700, Sat 0900-1230. Within New Zealand standard (local) post costs $0.45 for medium letters and postcards (2-3 days); $0.90 for airmail (fast post) to domestic centres (1-2 days); $1.50 for airmail letters to Australia and $2 for standard overseas airmail letters to Europe, North America, East Asia, Australia and South Pacific. Domestic mail takes 1-2 days, perhaps longer in rural areas. When sending any cards or letters overseas be sure to use the free blue 'Air economy' stickers. Books of stamps are readily available as are pre-paid envelopes and a range of purpose-built cardboard boxes. Average international delivery times vary depending on the day of the week posted, but a standard letter to the UK can take as few as 4 days (scheduled 6-12 days). North America is scheduled 4-12 days and Australia and the South Pacific 3-8 days. For details see www.nzpost.co.nz.

Poste Restante

Mail can be sent to 'Post Restante', CPO (Chief Post Office) in the main centres, where it will be held for up to 30 days. If you are being sent any mail make sure the sender marks your surname in capitals and underlines it. The principal pick-up points are:
Auckland Wellesley St Post Shop, Bledisloe St, T09-3796714, Mon-Fri 0730-1730).
Christchurch Cathedral Square Post Shop, Cathedral Sq, T03-3775411, Mon-Fri 0800-1800, Sat 1000-1600.
Dunedin Dunedin Post Shop, 243 Princess St, T03-4773518, Mon-Fri 0830-1730.
Nelson Nelson Post Shop, corner of Trafalgar and Halifax sts, T03-5467818, Mon-Fri 0745-1700, Sat 0930-1230.

Queenstown Main Post Office, 15-19 Camp St, T03-4227670, Mon-Fri 0830-1800, Sat 0900-1600.
Wellington 43 Manners St, T04-473 5922, Mon-Fri 0800-1730, Sat 1000-1330.

Public holidays

If you are a tourist, public holidays can be an inconvenience since shops and banks close and cohorts of Kiwis join you. School holidays are particularly bad with Jan and Feb being the worst months. During these times you should book accommodation and activities well ahead. Bear in mind this also applies to the winter season at the major ski resorts like Tongariro, Wanaka and Queenstown.

Jan 1-2 New Year; Feb 6 Waitangi Day; Good Fri; Easter Mon; Apr 25 Anzac Day; 1st Mon in Jun Queen's Birthday; 4th Mon in Oct Labour Day; Dec 25 Christmas Day; Dec 26 Boxing Day.

Anniversary Day varies between the provinces: Jan 17 Southland; Jan 22 Wellington; Jan 29 Auckland; Feb 1 Nelson.

Safety

Despite appearances or what you may have heard, New Zealand has its fair share of crime. There are over 1 million registered firearms in New Zealand, one in four of the population and many are in the hands of the poor, the drug gangs, the mad and the bad. Tourists are rarely targeted for anything other than petty crime but you still need to be careful. Theft, especially in Auckland, is rife and tourist accommodation establishments are not exempt. Cars and their contents are also regularly targeted. Do not relax your guard; keep money safe and out of sight. Keep your vehicle locked at all times and put valuables in the boot (trunk). It may sound ridiculous but you also need to be wary of other tourists. Having suitable insurance cover is also wise. Urban New Zealand has its fair share of rapes, some brutal, so women should be just as vigilant as they need be in the more populous and notorious nations.

Drink driving and speeding laws are very strict in New Zealand: do not even think about driving while under the influence, and keep

your speed down. Thanks to the heavy road toll (though some say its principally a major source of government revenue) speed cameras and patrol cars are omnipresent. Drug laws are also strict so don't get caught in possession. One other thing: if you do get lumped with speeding or parking tickets, as tempting as it may be, it is far less hassle to pay it off and not consider 'doing a runner'. After all, you may well want to return one day!

Smoking

In Dec 2004, it became illegal to smoke in bars, restaurants and the work place, except in segregated sections, is provided. Smoking is not allowed on any public transport.

Student travellers

If you are a student (and can prove it) you will enjoy discounts on public transport and specialist tourist travel, tourist attractions and tourist-based activities throughout New Zealand. There are also some savings to be made on insurance, restaurants, shopping and accommodation. However, if you are backpacking note that the main discounts are best secured through the affiliation and membership of one or more of the specific backpacker chains (ie YHA, BBH, Nomad or VIP). See Backpacker organizations, page 47.

The International Student Identity Card (ISIC), www.isiccard.com, is the most widely accepted form of ID and far more effective and hassle-free than an institution-specific identity card. ISIC cards are also available from STA travel, www.statravel.co.uk. The International Student Travel Confederation (ISTC), www.isic.org, is the principal administrator of the scheme. Consult their website for specific contacts within your own country. For information on student visas, see Visas and immigration, page 63.

Taxes

There is a 12.5% GST (Goods and Services Tax) placed on almost every bought item in New Zealand. Prices quoted almost always include GST, but on bigger quotes or services it pays to check.

Telephone

Within New Zealand there are 5 area codes: Auckland and Northland **09**; Bay of Plenty, Coromandel, Taupo, Ruapehu and Waikato **07**; Eastland, Hawkes Bay, Wanganui and Taranaki **06**; Wellington **04**; South Island **03**. All telephone numbers in this book include the area code.

   Telecom payphones are found throughout the country and are colour coded. Although there are both coin (blue) and credit card (yellow) booths available, the vast majority are 'phone-card only' so you are advised to stock up. Cards come in $5, $10, $20 and $50 and are available from many retail outlets, visitor information offices and hostels. Unless you want to see just how fast digital numbers can disappear on screen, do not use these Telecom cards for anything other than domestic calls within New Zealand.

   There is a wealth of cheap international calling cards and call centres available. One of the best is **E Phone**, www.eph.co.nz, a calling card that accesses the net through an 0800 number. The cards vary in price from $10-$50 and can be bought from many retail outlets (look for the E Phone flag signs outside the shops). They can be used from any landline telephone. Voice instructions will tell you what to do and how much credit you have available before each call.

   Local non-business calls are free from standard telephones in New Zealand, so it is not too offensive to ask to use a host's or friend's domestic (non-business) telephone. 0800 or occasionally 0508 precede toll-free calls. Try to avoid 0900 numbers as they are usually very expensive. The 2 major **mobile** service providers are **Telecom**, www.telecom.co.nz and **Vodaphone** , www.vodaphone.co.nz.

Time

New Zealand Standard Time (NZST) is 12 hrs ahead of GMT. So at 1200 in New Zealand it is 1000 in Sydney, 0900 in Japan, 1900 yesterday in New York or 2400 in the UK. Allow for daylight saving: from the 1st Sun in Oct to the 3rd Sun in Mar the clock goes forward 1 hr.

Tipping

Tipping in New Zealand is at the customer's discretion. In a good restaurant you should leave a tip of 10-15% if you are satisfied with the service, but the bill may include a service charge. Tipping is appreciated in pubs and bars and taxi drivers also expect some sort of tip; on a longer journey 10% is fine. As in most other counties, hotel porters, bellboys, waiters and waitresses should all be tipped to supplement their meagre wages.

Toilets

Public toilets are readily available and very rarely are you charged for the privilege.

Tourist information

The official New Zealand Visitor Information Network is made up of around 100 accredited **Visitor Information Centres** (**VICs**) nationally known as I-Sites.

   National I-Sites are based in Auckland and Christchurch as well as the main tourist centres, like Rotorua and Queenstown. Open 7 days a week, they provide a comprehensive information service including accommodation bookings and domestic airline, bus and train ticketing.

Phone facts

Emergency	111
New Zealand country code	+54
International access code	00
National operator	010
International operator	0170
National directory enquiries	018
International directory enquiries	017

Souvenir shops and occasionally other retail outlets, currency exchange and cafés are often attached.

Regional I-Sites are found throughout the country and there may be more than one in each region. They provide a general information booking service usually 7 days a week and there is also a huge amount of free material.

Local I-Sites can be found almost anywhere, providing local information as well as assistance in accommodation and transport bookings. They are open at least 5 days a week, but are subject to varying seasonal and weekend hours.

Useful websites
Accommodation and transport
www.aatravel.co.nz Useful general New Zealand travel and sleeping information. www.auckland-airport.co.nz and www.christchurch-airport.co.nz Worth a quick look before you enter the country. www.backpack.co.nz Comprehensive guide to hostels in New Zealand. www.intercitycoach.co.nz Intercity bus information and additional news about fare concessions and package deals. www.interislander.co.nz and www.bluebridge.co.nz The principal websites for the inter-islander ferry services. www.jasons.co.nz Useful information on transport, accommodation and activities. www.orbitz.com Good general travel site with broad information and competitive airfares for New Zealand. www.travel-library.com Detailed general travel site packed with good tips on buying flight tickets. www.tranzscenic.co.nz Provides all your rail information needs. www.travelplanner.co.nz Useful visitor information and good links. www.yha.org.nz One of the principal backpacker travel organizations.

Photography
www.andrisapse.co.nz and www.craigpotton.co.nz Some of the best photographers, photographs and pictorial references of New Zealand. www.darrochdonald.com The author's website with comprehensive photographic coverage of New Zealand.

General information
www.destination-nz.com Useful tourist/visitor based sites with good links. www.doc.govt.nz The invaluable website of the Department of Conservation provides detailed information on national parks, tramping and short walks. www.ecotours.co.nz Good site outlining reputable eco-tours throughout the country. www.mapworld.co.nz Best map supplier in New Zealand including CD-ROMS. www.newzealandvacations.co.nz and www.nzcity.co.nz Regional news and a superb weather satellite picture. www.nzembassy.com Lists all the overseas New Zealand embassies and some other useful immigration links. www.nzherald.co.nz Excellent website of the Upper North Island's main daily newspaper, with national and international news, as well as sport, weather and travel. www.purenz.com Official website of the New Zealand Tourism Board packed with useful information, listings and contacts. www.searchnz.co.nz One of the country's best national search engines. www.tourism.net.nz Directory of tourism and travel companies. www.trademe.co.nz New Zealand's version of Ebay has over 1 million members and around 50,000 on-line at any one time. www.yellowpages.co.nz Useful for any national telephone and address listings.

History and culture
Comprehensive sites worth looking at include: **www.maori.org.nz**, **www.nzhistory.net.nz**, **www.nz live.com** and **www.teara.govt.nz**

Tour operators

In the UK
Australian Pacific Touring (UK), T020-88797444, www.aptouring.co.uk. Escorted tours or fully independent packages. **Explore Worldwide**, T0870-3334002, www.exploreworldwide.co.uk. Special interest trips such as cycling, walking or family holidays. **High Places**, T0114 275 7500, www.high places.co.uk. Specialists in mountain trekking and adventure travel. **Kuoni Worldwide**, T01306741111, www.kuoni.co.uk. Tailor-made itineraries.

Travelmood, 214 Edgware Rd, London, W2 1DH; also at 1 Brunswick Court, Bridge St, Leeds, LS2 7QU; and 16 Reform St, Dundee, DD1 1RG, T0871-226 6151, www.travel mood.com. 21 years' experience as a top travel specialist offering tailor-made trips to the Far East and adventure and activity travel in Asia.

In North America

Abercrombie and Kent, T1-800-5547016, www.abercrombiekent.com. Well-established US company offering a diverse range of luxury guided trips of 9-13 days, with other longer trips in combination with Australia.
Newmans South Pacific Vacations, T1-800-342 1956, www.newmansvacations.com. Lots of tours or fully independent itineraries.
Swain Tours, T1-800-22-SWAIN, www.swain tours.com. Tailor-made or group tours of around 16 days, from approximately $3000.
Tauck, T1-800-788 7885, www.tauck.com. Australia and New Zealand combos, or a 9-day NZ tour taking in the best of Auckland, Rotorua, Queenstown and Milford from $3000.

In New Zealand
Backpacker bus companies
The principal backpacker bus companies offer good value flexible routes and options.
Bottom Bus, T03-434 7370, www.bottom bus.co.nz. Runs along the Southern Scenic Route between Dunedin and Milford Sound.
Contiki, 1st floor, 15-17 Day St, Newton, Auckland, T0800-CONTIKI/T09-300 1601, www.contiki.com;
Flying Kiwi, T0800-693296, www.flying kiwi.com. Eco/activity-orientated.
Kiwi Experience, T09-366 9830, www.kiwiexperience.com.
Magic Travellers, T09-358 5600, www.magicbus.co.nz.
Stray, 31 Beach Rd, Auckland City, T09-309 8772, www.straytravel.co.nz.

Coach tours
Great Sights, 180 Quay St, Auckland, T0800-744487/ T09-306 7633, www.great sights.co.nz. A wide range of tours throughout the country, from day city tours to 2-11 day excursions as well as a 3 to 12-day hop-on/ hop-off option.

Guthreys Tours, T0800-732528/
T09-302 2645, www.guthreys.co.nz.
Tours from Auckland to Rotorua, Taupo,
Waitomo and Bay of Islands a speciality.
Scenic Pacific Tours, T0800-500388/T03-
359 3999, www.scenicpacific.co.nz. Well-
established company offering de luxe (yet
good value) coach trips with the emphasis
on activities as much as sightseeing.
Thrifty Tours, T09-359 8380, www.thrifty
tours.co.nz. Budget-conscious tours with
flexibility. Range of options from 2-16 days
in both islands. Thrifty specials to Waitomo,
Rotorua and the Bay of Islands.

Eco-tourism operators
Adventure South, PO Box 33, 153 Christ-
church, T03-942 1222, www.advsouth.co.nz.
Eco-based 5-23 day cycling and hiking trips.
Catlins Wildlife Trackers, Papatowai, Owaka,
Southland, T/F03-415 8613, www.catlins-
ecotours.co.nz. Eco-tours and conservation
holidays in New Zealand.
Elm Toursim, Elm Lodge Backpackers,
Dunedin, Otago, T03-454 4121/T0800-
356563, www.elmwildlifetours.co.nz.
Award-winning company offering excellent
nature tours of the Otago Peninsula, Catlins
and Southern Scenic Route.
Heritage Expeditions, 53B Montreal St,
Christchurch, Canterbury, T03-365 3500,
www.heritage-expeditions.com. Guided
birdwatching trips and expeditions in New
Zealand, Sub-Antarctic Islands and Antarctica.
Kiwi Wildlife Tours, 346 Cowan Bay Rd,
Warkworth, Auckland, T09-422 6868,
www.kiwi-wildlife.co.nz. 1- to 20-day guided
birdwatching trips locally and nationally.
Miranda Shorebird Centre, 283 East
Coast Rd, Pokeno, Tiritiri Matangi Island,
Auckland, T09-232 2781, www.miranda-
shorebird.org.nz. Specialist wader field
centre on internationally significant site,
accommodation available.

Nature safaris
Hiking New Zealand, T0800-697232 /
T03-384 3706, www.hikingnewzealand.com.
Popular, with a wide range of trips to suit all
fitness levels, including the Great Walks as
well as some 'off the beaten track' adventures.
Manu Tours New Zealand, 106 Ocean
Beach Rd, Tairua, T07-864 7475, www.nz
birding.co.nz. Great for avid 'twitchers'

with a national hunt to see as many
endemics as possible in 17 days.
Nature Quest New Zealand, Dunedin,
T03- 489 8444, www.naturequest.co.nz.
South Island based company offering
guided trips or independent custom
designed itineraries.

Specialist activity tours
Active Earth, T0800-201040, www.active
earthnewzealand.com. Good guided activity
tours of the North Island, from 5-10 days.
New Zealand Pedaltours Ltd, PO Box 37-
575, Parnell, Auckland, T0800-302 0968/T09-
585 1338, www.pedaltours.co.nz. Specialist
cycle tours and eco-tours, from $595.
Ridenz.com, T0800-413369, www.ride
nz.com. Selected riding holidays with
operators in both islands.

Vaccinations

There are no vaccinations required to enter
New Zealand but as with any country, you
are advised to get a tetanus injection or
ensure that your boosters are up to date.
See also Health, page 54.

Visas and immigration

For embassies and consulates, see page 53.
Visa information is also available from New
Zealand Immigration Service (NZIS), Private
Bag, Wellesley St, Auckland, T0508-558855/
T09-914 4100, www.immigration.govt.nz.
   All visitors must have a passport valid for 3
months beyond the date you intend to leave
the country. Australian citizens or holders of
an Australian returning resident visa can stay
in New Zealand indefinitely. UK citizens do not
need a visa and are automatically issued with
a 6-month visitor permit on arrival. All visitors
making an application for a visitor permit
require: (a) a passport that is valid for at least
3 months after your departure from New
Zealand; (b) an onward or return ticket to a
country you have permission to enter; (c)
sufficient money to support yourself during
your stay (approximately NZ$1000 per
month). The sufficient funds factor can be
waived if you have a friend or relative in New
Zealand (citizen) who agrees to sponsor you
by guaranteeing to support you financially
during your stay. If you have to apply for a

visitor visa you can do so at your nearest
New Zealand Embassy or by downloading
the relevant forms from the website.

Longer stays and work visas
It is illegal to work on a visitor permit. Non-
residents (with the exception of Australian
citizens) must obtain a **work visa** which
allows you to enter the country, then a **work
permit** which allows you to work upon
arrival. Applications for both are best made
well before arrival. The NZIS website has
details and application forms to download.
An exception to this rule is the **working
holiday visa** which is available for those
aged 18-30 from a number of countries
(including Canada, Japan, Ireland, Germany,
France and the UK) and entitles you to work
for 12 months; conditions apply. See also
Working in New Zealand, below. **Student
visas** come under a separate category.
You can also get extensions on your visitor
permit for up to 9 months but you must
meet certain criteria. For detailed
information contact the NZIS direct.

For a **residence visa** an application must
be made from your own country. It involves a
points system relating to factors such as age,
education and occupation. The target number
required fluctuates depending on the
perceived demand for immigrants and,
to a degree, politics. For details, consult the
'Migration' section on the website or contact
the NZIS direct. Be warned – you will need
endless supplies of patience. Once a residence
visa is secured you can apply for **citizenship**
after 3 years' residency in New Zealand.

Weights and measures

The metric system is used throughout.
Distances are in kilometres, petrol is in litres.
Ask for a pint in a pub, however, and you
will not be looked at in a funny way.

Women travellers

There are few specific problems that
especially affect women or single female
travellers in New Zealand. Here equality rules
both the landscape and the roost. You are,
after all, in the country that afforded women
the vote well before they did in the USA and
UK. Traditionally, beyond the male-initiated

inter-tribal killing and rampant moa killing,
Maori women were and are held in high
esteem. However, that said, the country is
not immune to the usual crime and social
problems so all the normal common-sense
levels of vigilance and precaution should be
adopted; see Safety, page 59.
Bushwise Women, T(61)2-6684 0178,
www.bushwise.co.nz. For trips especially
designed for women.

Working in New Zealand

See also Visas and immigration, page 63.
If you are coming from Europe (especially the
UK) or North America and plan to find casual
work in New Zealand to pay your way around
the country, think again. Given the favourable
exchange rates you are far better securing
casual work in your own country and saving,
rather than doing so in New Zealand. Time
will be short enough with so much to see and
do. However, if you are desperate, backpackers
can occasionally work for their keep at some
vineyards, orchards and farmstays (see page
46). Given the ever-increasing development of
tourism in Queenstown you are just about
guaranteed to find a job in both the summer
and winter high seasons. One organization
that will help you locate these is **Farm
Helpers (FhiNZ)**, 16 Aspen Way, Palmerston
North, T0800- 327681/T06-355 0448,
www.fhinz.co.nz. Its website is a fine place to
start and a booklet listing over 190 associate
farms is also available on line for $25.

Other useful contacts include: **Seek**,
T0508- 733569, www.nzjobs.co.nz, which is
a recruitment specialist based in Auckland;
and the excellent website www.seasonal
work.co.nz, which offers job listings and a
host of other information. Do not expect
to be paid premium hourly rates. The
minimum is around NZ$10.

There is also an option of working voluntarily
through **Willing Workers on Organic Farms
(WWOOF)** PO Box 1172, Nelson, T03-544
9890, www.wwoof.co.nz. Reports of this
network are good and as a member ($30
joining fee) you can get free comfortable
accommodation in return for a few hours
of daily work. You receive a comprehensive
booklet with operator listings upon receipt
of membership.

North Island

Auckland

❚ Footprint features

Introduction

With a population of one and a quarter million, Auckland is Polynesia's largest city and by far the biggest in New Zealand. In fact, it's home to almost a third of the total population. For the vast majority of visitors, Auckland will be their arrival point and their first introduction to the country. Many will treat it only as a gateway to better things, but they may be pleasantly surprised by what it has to offer.

Thanks to its spacious suburban sprawl, Auckland covers more than 500 sq km – twice that of London and close to that of Los Angeles – but because the city is built on an isthmus and constantly fragmented by coastline, you are never far from water. The sea pervades almost every aspect of Auckland life, from recreation to cuisine. Aucklanders own more recreational boats per capita than any other city in the world, earning it the affectionate nicknames of 'City of Sails' and 'Nautical Capital of the South Pacific'.

Most sailing is done in Auckland's backyard: the beautiful aquatic playground and island-studded waters of the Hauraki Gulf is one of the most beautiful sailing venues in the world. As well as sailing, you can go fishing, swimming or surfing, all within minutes of the city centre and, in some places, have the beach to yourself. The city also boasts some impressive man-made attractions such as the stunning 360° views from the hypodermic Sky Tower, and its bustling city centre streets and trendy suburbs are home to a thousand world-class restaurants.

★ Don't miss ...

1 **Sky Tower** Climb the mast, take in the 360° views, dine in the revolving restaurant, or bungee from 192 m, page 76.

2 **Auckland Museum** Get acquainted with Kiwi history, wildlife and culture, page 81.

3 **Devonport** Take a cruise across Auckland Harbour to this historic suburb. Muse in the galleries, enjoy a glass of wine in one of the restaurants, or walk to take in the views from North Head, page 83.

4 **Mount Victoria** Watch the sunrise from the summit of the city's volcanic cone, page 83.

5 **Café culture** Order a flat white and soak up the atmosphere in Ponsonby, K'Road or Parnell, pages 96-98.

6 **West coast beaches** Experience the solitude of the wild west, page 116.

7 **Hauraki Islands** Take a trip to the stunning islands by ferry, yacht or launch, page 120.

8 **Tiritiri Matangi Island** Mix with rare and endangered species, page 121.

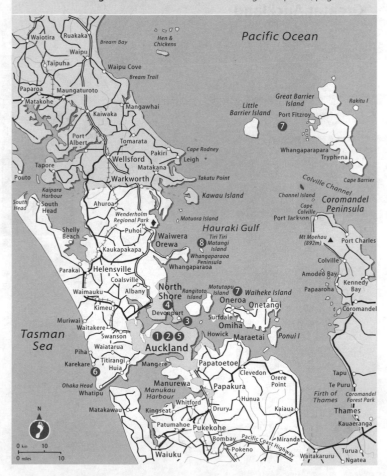

Auckland

→ *Colour map 1, C4 Population: 1,320,000*

Auckland has been labelled a Polynesian city but in reality it enjoys a cosmopolitan make-up of Pacific, European, Asian and indigenous Maori. Modern Auckland is the fusion of four cities: North Shore, an expanding, predominantly European and contemporary area with attractive beaches and quiet modern suburbs, north of the bridge; Auckland City itself, the heart and hub, with its central business district around Queen Street growing ever skywards, together with the waterfront and its happening inner city suburbs; Waitakere, to the west, a mix of low and high income suburbs dominated by the bush-clad Waitakere Ranges; and Manakau to the south, with its lively low-income suburbs of predominantly Maori and Pacific Island citizens. All combine to create a huge multi-ethnic sprawl of modern humanity, in which, naturally, it is very easy to get lost. ▸▸ *For Sleeping, Eating and other listings, see pages 89-111.*

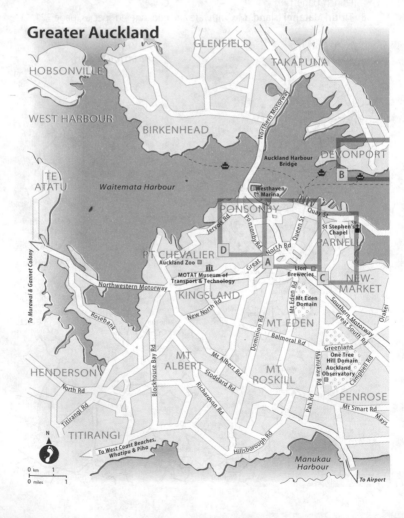

Greater Auckland

Ins and outs

Getting there

Airport information Most visitors arrive by air (see page 35). **Auckland International Airport (AKL)** ① *20 km south of centre, T09-275 0789, www.auckland-airport.co.nz*, is a relatively small, modern and friendly gateway to the nation. On the ground floor there is an **Airport I-Site Information Centre**, T09-256 8535, open from 0500 until the last flight, which provides transport details, baggage storage and can help book hotels. The hospitality ambassadors (smiley folk in bright blue jackets) or customer service officers (red jackets and splendid hats) can also offer assistance. Airport facilities include shops, food outlets, mailboxes, internet, crêche, free showers (towel hire from the Airways Florist shop on the ground floor) and telephones. Phone cards are sold at the information kiosk and most major outlets on the ground floor. There are also day rooms for hire that contain a bed, desk, TV, coffee, tea and shower facilities, from $30 for four hours (tickets at Airways Florist). Showers are free. ▸▸ *For airline offices, see page 108.*

⁑ Related maps
A Auckland centre, p78.
B Devonport, p83.
C Parnell &
* Newmarket, p93.*
D Ponsonby, p87.

Transport from the airport The **Airbus,** T0508-247287, www.airbus.co.nz, is a cheap option leaving the airport every 20-30 minutes from 0600-2200 (from the city 0435-2250), $15, child $6 one way; backpacker concessions available. Taxis wait outside the terminal and charge about $40 to the centre. The **Super Shuttle,** T0800-748885, www.supershuttle.co.nz, provides a door-to-door service from $23 one way. The main car rental operators are represented at both international and domestic terminals. The domestic terminal is only a short distance from the international and free transit shuttles operate between both terminals every 20 minutes from 0600-2230.

To get to the city by car from the airport, take the main exit road (George Bolt Memorial Drive) to the intersection with SH20. Follow signs for Auckland City and take the motorway to Queenstown Road exit. Turn right into Queenstown Road and continue straight ahead, through the roundabout into Pah Road which becomes Manukau Road (SH12). Follow Manukau Road and turn right at the traffic lights (before Newmarket) into Alpers Avenue. At the end of Alpers Avenue, turn right into Gillies Avenue then almost immediately left to join SH1 motorway. The last exit to the city centre is Nelson Street.

Getting around

Bikes, scooters and motorcycles These are a brave option in Auckland, given the way people drive. Unless you are an experienced city cyclist, it's safest to stick to walking, buses or a car. However, outside the city centre and major suburbs, bike and motorcycle touring can be a joy. ➤➤ *For rental companies, see Transport, page 110.*

Bus Public transport is a major bone of contention in Auckland as traffic congestion clogs the city's roads and pollutes the air. Although adequate for the average visitor, it is generally poor and improvements are not happening fast enough. Most central and suburban buses stop at the **Britomart Transport Centre** (**BBT**), centrally located between Customs and Quay streets near the waterfront (bottom of Queen Street). Information can be obtained from the terminal itself or all major tourist information offices and by contacting **MAXX,** T09-366 6400/T0800-103080, www.rideline.co.nz. This website also offers a convenient journey planner.

The principal suburban carrier is **Stagecoach,** www.stagecoach.co.nz, which offers a 'Discovery Pass' allowing unlimited travel on bus, ferry and train for $14, or $39 for seven days. The excellent **Auckland City Loop 'Link' bus** is an ideal way to get about the city centre and charges a flat fare of $1.50 for each journey. ➤➤ *For further details, see Transport, page 109.*

Car Most of the major sights and attractions are centrally located and can be accessed on foot or by bus or ferry. For longer stays a car is recommended due to the urban sprawl. Car ownership per capita in Auckland is one of the highest in the world and you will quickly see that Auckland is not only a 'City of Sails' but also a 'City of Wheels'; driving can be hazardous and rush hour is best avoided. Metered and multi-storey parking costs up to $6 an hour and traffic wardens are omnipresent. There are more car rental companies than you could shake a gear stick at, ranging from fully insured, nearly-new cars, to dodgy looking rent-a-dents. ➤➤ *For car rental companies, see Transport, page 109.*

Ferry and water taxi Almost all ferries depart from the historic **Ferry Building** on the waterfront, at Quay Street. A limited commuter service to some waterside suburbs has been developed, but the vast majority of ferry traffic is tourist-based and operated by **Fullers** ① *T09-367 9111, www.fullers.co.nz.* There are many excellent island or harbour locations, trips and tours to choose from. Fares are generally very reasonable.

Taxi All Auckland taxi drivers are required to belong to a registered taxi company. This sets certain standards, but that is no guarantee of good English or not being taken via 'the scenic route'. Meters are usually based on time, not distance, so it often pays to get an estimate first. Typical rates are around $2.50 base charge and then about $2 per kilometre. Taxis are widely available and can be flagged down, ordered by phone or picked up at numerous city centre ranks. ▸▸ *For taxi companies, see Transport, page 110.*

Train Auckland has a scant suburban rail network operating out of the Britomart Terminal between Customs and Quay streets near the waterfront. For local suburban rail information contact **MAXX**, T09-366 6400, www.maxx.co.nz. The Auckland to Wellington 'Overlander' service is operated by **TranzScenic**, T04 495 0775/T0800-872467, www.tranzscenic.co.nz, which also runs from the Britomart Terminal. Further information about routes and timetables can be obtained from VICs and the terminal itself. Reservations can be made at all mainstream travel agents.

Tourist information

There are Visitor Information Centres (VICs/I-Sites) at both airport terminals; **International Airport Terminal**, T09-256 8535; **Domestic Terminal**, T09-256 8480. There are two main VICs in the CBD: **Atrium** ⓘ *Skycity, corner Victoria and Federal sts, T09-367 6009/T0800-AUCKLAND, www.aucklandnz.com, daily 0800-2000*; and the quieter **Viaduct Harbour** ⓘ *next to the Maritime Museum, corner Quay and Hobson sts, T09-367 6009, Oct-Mar Mon-Fri 0830-1800, Sat-Sun 0900-1700; Apr-Sep 0900-1700*. If you venture north across the bridge, there are VICs at **North Shore** ⓘ *49 Hurstmere Rd, Takapuna, T09-486 8670, www.northshorenz.com, Mon-Fri 0830-1700, Sat-Sun 1000-1500*, or **Devonport** ⓘ *3 Victoria Rd, T09-446 0677, www.north shorenz.com, daily 0830-1700*. All information centres provide piles of free leaflets and many can help book accommodation. Don't miss the readily available *Auckland A to Z, Auckland What's On, I-Tag Visitors Guide, TNT Magazine* and the *Backpackers' News* – all excellent, up-to-the-minute publications. The *New Zealand Herald* is the main Auckland and North Island daily, www.nzherald.co.nz. For all things environmental and ecological, including nature walks, get yourself to the **Department of Conservation** (DoC) ⓘ *Information Centre, Ferry Building, Quay St, T09-379 6467, www.doc.govt.nz, Mon- Fri 0930-1730, Sat 1000-1500, Sun closed*, on the waterfront.

Maps Perhaps your first purchase in Auckland should be a map. All your needs can be met in that department right in the centre of the city. The **Auckland Map Centre** ⓘ *National Bank Building, 209 Queen St, T09-309 7725*, has a fine selection of national and local maps of varying scale, as does **Speciality Maps** ⓘ *Albert St*, and **Whitcoulls** ⓘ *corner of Queen and Victoria sts*. Whitcoulls also has a comprehensive national travel guide sections, as does **Borders** ⓘ *291 Queen St*.

Various free tourist handouts have some colourful maps of the city, but if you are serious get the *Wises Auckland Compact Handi Map Book* ($25), or at the very least the foldout version ($15). Other than that, you will probably quickly find yourself slipping into the local habit of using the Sky Tower as the seemingly omnipresent beacon, and the main volcanic cones and the harbour as guidance and orientation.

Orientation

The heart of the city centre is the **CBD** (Central Business District) and the main drag of **Queen Street**. On either side, the jungle of high-rises gives way occasionally to older buildings like the **Auckland Art Gallery** and the green inner city sanctuaries of **Albert Park** and **The Domain**, with its crowning glory, the **Auckland Museum**. Immediately to the north, the **Waitamata Harbour** calls a halt to the concrete, and ferries and sails take over on the **waterfront** where the historic **Ferry Building** looks almost out of place compared to the ugly, modern tower blocks that back it.

Along the waterfront is the yachting focal point of the **Viaduct Basin**, the former **America's Cup Village** and the **Maritime Museum**. Across the Harbour Bridge is the

48 hours in Auckland

Many visitors to Auckland allow too little time. Although not entirely representative of the country and, in many ways, just a modern city like any other, Auckland has a lot to offer. If you only have 48 hours in the city, forget jet lag – you don't have time.

Once you have found your hotel, and provided the weather is fine, head straight for the **Sky Tower** and its all-encompassing view. From the main observation deck you can see the vast sprawl of the city and pinpoint various sights to visit. Note that despite its seemingly endless suburban sprawl, wherever you are in Auckland you are never far from the sea. Looking out to the Hauraki Gulf and its islands, you can instantly see why one in four Aucklanders own a boat. Adrenaline junkies might like to consider climbing up the mast of the tower or better still taking the plunge from above the observation deck. At 192 m, this is New Zealand's highest 'controlled' bungee jump – welcome to adrenaline country.

Once back down to earth, head to the former **America's Cup Village** on the waterfront and have lunch in one of the many, mainly upmarket, restaurants (**Cin Cin** in the Ferry Building, **Euro** on Princess Wharf and **Kermadec** overlooking the America's Cup Village are recommended). Then, from the Ferry Building, catch a ferry to **Devonport** and take a leisurely walk east to **North Head** from where you will get a memorable view back towards the city centre. Once back in the heart of Devonport, enjoy a coffee or glass of wine in one of its street-side cafés. If you still have some energy

walk to the top of **Mount Victoria** for more good views. Back in Auckland, indulge in some retail therapy on **Queen Street** and **Victoria Park Market**.

In the evening relax with a stroll along **Ponsonby Road**. Muse at the huge range of cafés and restaurants and decide which best suits you for dinner (see page 97, for suggestions).

The following morning (preferably before sunrise and with your own wheels) grab a picnic lunch and a flask of coffee and head west of Auckland to Scenic Drive and the **Waitakere Ranges**. Stop to watch the sunrise over the city then take a look in the **Arataki Visitor Centre** (open from 0900, free). Choose which of the **west coast beaches** you prefer.

After lunch head back to Auckland and visit the **Auckland Museum** in the Domain where you will get a fine introduction to Maori culture and New Zealand wildlife. Lovers of art should consider a trip to the **Auckland Art Gallery** (city centre), while more action can be found with the sharks and penguins at **Kelly Tarlton's Underwater World** and **Antarctic Adventure** near Mission Bay. In the evening, watch the sunset from the summit of Mount Eden before heading to a local café or restaurant.

Those without independent transport should consider a day-cruise to **Waiheke** or **Rangitoto Island**. Lovers of wildlife should not miss a day-visit to **Tiritiri Matangi Island**. If you have a week in Auckland seriously consider spending two or three days on **Great Barrier Island**.

huge expanse of **North Shore City**, while closer, and immediately across the **Waitamata Harbour**, is the small and attractive suburb of **Devonport**, with its village feel. It boasts the volcanic cones of **Mount Victoria** and **North Head**, both of which offer great views. Around the corner are the relatively calm and safe **beaches** of the North Shore, stretching to the **Whangaparaoa Peninsula** and the edge of the city, 40 km away.

East of the Whangaparaoa Peninsula is the **Hauraki Gulf**, with its glistening waters and magical islands playing host to swarms of yachties. To the north, just off the Whangaparaoa Peninsula, is **Tiritiri Matangi Island**, an open bird sanctuary. Beyond Tiri is the small but mountainous **Little Barrier Island**. East again, in the far distance, is **Great Barrier Island**, Auckland's beautiful getaway. Closer, is the most obvious and famous island, **Rangitoto**, with its classic volcanic cone and green botanical blanket, guarding the entrance to the harbour. Next to Rangitoto are **Browns** and **Motuihe islands** and, behind them, **Waiheke**, the Gulf's most visited and populous island.

Back on the mainland, the eastern suburbs of **Mission Bay** and **St Heliers** stretch towards the distant Asian enclave of **Howick**. These seaside suburbs attract many visitors and Aucklanders, most of whom follow the waterside **Tamaki Drive** to soak up the sun on the beaches or bathe in the shallow bays.

Dominating the southern horizon are two of the most well-known volcanic mounts in the city, **Mount Eden** and **One Tree Hill**. South from these impressive landmarks, the low-income suburbs of South Auckland spread unceasingly to the southern city limits of the **Bombay Hills**. Within these suburbs are the **Auckland Botanical Gardens**. Thankfully, nature has called a halt to city expansion to the west in the impressive form of the bush-clad **Waitakere Ranges**. The lower-income suburb streets of **Henderson** and **Glendene** give way to the expensive dwellings of **Titirangi**. The inner western suburbs host the **Auckland Zoo** and **Museum of Transport and Technology** (**MOTAT**), both of which border the pleasant lakeside park of Western Springs.

Finally, the best place to find your bearings is the observation decks of the amazing **Sky Tower**, especially on a clear day.

Background

According to Maori legend, when Maui (founder of New Zealand/Aotearoa) fished up the North Island, his efforts to subdue his catch created the islands of the Hauraki (the scales) and the bays and the beaches of the Isthmus (the wounds). Maori gods of the Ocean and Wind further shaped and modified the geography and created the warm moist climate. It was the gods of the resident giant, Mataaho, who created the volcanoes (legend has it he was cold) with their most recent piece of central heating being Rangitoto Island, which guards the mouth of the Waitamata Harbour.

The first Maoris to settle in the area were thought to be moa hunters (moa being the once numerous, but now extinct, flightless New Zealand bird) before AD 1000. But later, from the 12th to 14th centuries, further migrations and *waka* (Maori canoes) brought first the Nga-Oho and later the Nga-Tai and Nga-Marama tribes. The latter, led by the ambitious Kiwi Tamaki, ruled for some time, taking up residence in *pa* (Maori settlements, often fortified) on almost every volcano in the district, including a main *pa* on what is now named One Tree Hill. But his reign did not last and, after a brutal conflict with other *hapu* (sub tribes), particularly the Ngati-Whatua from the Kaipara district to the north, he succumbed. This, together with an epidemic of smallpox brought by the early Europeans, meant the area became relatively unpopulated.

All this changed in 1820, with the first official visit by *Pakeha* (white Europeans), which in the form of the Reverends Samuel Marsden and John Gare Butler, two missionaries who were keen to expand their teachings beyond the Bay of Islands. From that point more organized integration and low-key European settlement began. But it was not until 20 years later, in 1840, on the signing of the Treaty of Waitangi, that New Zealand's Lieutenant Governor, Captain William Hobson, bought a 3000-acre 'pie shaped' part of the isthmus from the Ngati-Whatua for £55 and a few blankets. He called this area Auckland, after George Eden second Baron Auckland, then governor general of India, probably in return for giving him command of *HMS Rattlesnake* in which Hobson first visited New Zealand in 1837. Hobson's intention was to create a new capital of New Zealand, the original settlements of the Bay of Islands, particularly Russell, having a distinctly unsavoury and disobedient population.

And so, for a short time, Auckland became the capital and the focus for the invading pioneers. One such pioneer, a Scots medic called Logan Campbell, took full advantage of Hobson's acquisition for the Crown and, in the first years of its existence, took almost total control of half the fast expanding 'pie'. He became mayor of the settlement and the so-called 'Father of Auckland'.

The rapidly growing demand for more land created great conflict with the Maori, contributing in part to the New Zealand Land Wars of the 1860s. Presumably, the Maori were beginning to realize that, in exchange for a few quid and some basic goods, they were fast losing '*mana*' (presence, standing, integrity or honour) as well as their indigenous and rightful control.

Thanks to the Land Wars, and the discovery of gold elsewhere in Otago and in the nearby Coromandel, Auckland floundered a little. To add insult to injury, in 1865 Auckland lost its status as capital to Wellington and with it the seat of government.

However, towards the end of the 1800s, thanks to its fertile soils and climate and the brief but explosive 'Kauri' years – when there was widespread deforestation of the Kauri tree – Auckland's fortunes changed and the 'squashed pie' rapidly became the 'full bakery'. The rate at which Auckland continued to develop during the 20th century was astonishing. The irresistible combination of geography, climate, industry, agriculture and business opportunities has seen the population explode, creating the thriving cosmopolitan city we see today.

City centre

Sky Tower, Sky City and the Casino
① *Corner of Victoria and Federal sts, T0800-759 2489, www.skycityauckland.co.nz. Restaurant bookings, T09-363 6000. Theatre information and bookings, Tiketek T09-307 5000. Observation levels open Sun-Thu 0830-2300, Fri-Sat 0830-2400, $25, child $8 (backpackers $15). Restaurant open lunch 1000-1500, dinner from 1730, weekend brunch 1000-1500; minimum charge $25, T09-363 6000.*

For many Aucklanders in the early 1990s, the prospect of a casino and a futuristic 328-m **Sky Tower** smack bang in the city centre made them quake in their jangles (sandals). Construction began in 1994, on the corner of Victoria and Federal streets; for the following 32 months, Aucklanders watched with disbelief and awe as Sky City sprouted its great hypodermic into the heavens. It was naturally the talk of the town, finally opening in 1997 in a hail of publicity. No one at the time denied the unbelievable imagination, construction, technology and logistics it took to create, but many criticized the tower, saying it was too futuristic and a blot on the landscape. But Aucklanders have grown to love it – perhaps because it really is like a beacon. It's an awesome sight and, unless you hate heights, you just have to go up it.

The Sky Tower has four **viewing decks** and a revolving **restaurant**. The lift takes a mere 40 seconds to reach the main observation deck, where you can walk around the full 360°, taking in the stunning views, while being educated by an audio guide. There is also a **'live weather feed'** and touch-screen computers. If you would like a coffee, go down one level to the lower observation deck. Conversely, if you would like to check that 'weather feed' in person and feel the wind in your hair go up to the outdoor observation deck above the restaurant. If you are brave and have a few dollars more, why not shoot another few storeys up to the **sky deck**, the highest available observation point. If you really think you are brave you can stand on glass panels in the

● The highest bungee jumped in New Zealand was by A J Hackett himself from the 192-m
● Sky Tower in 1998.

Sky Tower – some statistics

The Sky Tower was opened in 1997 and took two years and eight months to build. At 328 m tall it is the tallest man-made structure in the southern hemisphere and 23 m taller than the AMP Tower in Sydney. The tower's shaft measures 12 m in diameter and its foundations reach 15 m into the earth. It houses the highest weather station, post box and restaurant in the southern hemisphere. The restaurant completes a 360° revolution every 60 seconds. It is designed to withstand a 8.0 earthquake and 200 kph winds.

Such winds would only create a 1-m sway of the entire structure. During construction, the tower was kept absolutely vertical using complex telemetry including three global satellite-positioning systems. There are 1257 steps to the Sky Deck. The fastest recorded ascent during the annual 'Sky Tower Vertical Challenge' is five minutes, 57 seconds. In 1998, AJ Hackett made a 192-m bungee jump from the main observation deck, the highest jump ever attempted from a ground structure.

main observation deck and look down – a most disconcerting experience. Or at night, enjoy a meal in the **Orbit** revolving restaurant. The food is great, if you can keep it down long enough to enjoy it.

In the last two years the great tower has become, perhaps inevitably, the focus for some typical Kiwi, lunatic activities. It was really only a matter of time before the tourist entrepreneurs would find some way for tourists to jump off it or climb out upon its mast or pergola and now, alas, with the safety inspectors clearly satisfied, you can do both. The controlled bungee is known as the 'Sky Jump', and the mast climb 'Vertigo'. ▸▸ *For further details see Activities and tours, page 105.*

Sky City claims to be Auckland's largest multi-faceted entertainment and leisure destination. The **main casino** provides all kinds of gambling and gaming options, restaurants, bars and live entertainment 24 hours a day; it has seen the ruin of many. Even if you are not a gambler it is well worth a look. The **Alto Casino and Bar** is a more intimate and sophisticated experience with a more rigorous dress code – one for the real wheelers and dealers. **Sky City Theatre** is a 700-seat, state-of-the-art entertainment venue, staging national and international events and productions. As well as the Orbit restaurant there are five other eateries offering everything from Pacific Rim to Chinese, traditional buffet or café-style options. Ample car parking is provided in a seemingly endless rabbit warren below the complex.

The waterfront and America's Cup Village

The once sandy beaches of the waterfront have now become cliffs of glass and concrete as the city has grown relentlessly outwards and upwards over the last 150 years. Radiating from the historic **Ferry Building**, built in 1912, the waterfront is the place where the city of concrete becomes the 'City of Sails' and where the locals would say it takes on its proper and distinct character. The waterfront has always been a focus of major activity. In the early years it was the point where exhausted immigrants first disembarked to begin a new life in a new land. Later, the immigrant ships gave way to the fleets of log-laden scows bringing kauri to the timber mills. Today, recreation has taken over, as modern ferries come and go and lines of expensive yachts rock gently together at the **Westhaven Marina**, the largest in the southern hemisphere.

The waterfront has seen perhaps the most rapid development of all, centred around the **Viaduct Basin** – until recently the hallowed home of the America's Cup Village. Even before New Zealand took the cup from the USA's tight grasp in 1995, the Viaduct Basin was a stopover point for the Whitbread Round the World Race (also

Sleeping

Albert Park
  Backpackers **1** *C4*
Ascott
  Metropolis **10** *C4*
Aspen House **5** *B5*
Auckland Central
  Backpackers **2** *C3*
Auckland City
  YHA **3** *E3*
Bond Street
  Lodge **20** *F2*
Cintra
  Apartments **4** *E4*
Columbia **15** *E4*
Elliott St
  Apartments **21** *C3*
Freemans B&B **7** *D1*
Heritage **8** *B3*
Hilton & White
  Restaurant **18** *A3*
Princeton
  Backpackers **17** *D4*
Quay West **12** *B3*
Quest Auckland **13** *D3*
Sebel **14** *A3*
Sky City Grand **16** *C3*
Surf & Snow **22** *C3*

Eating

Cin Cin **4** *A4*
Euro **6** *A3*
Food hall on Atrium
  on Elliot **8** *C3*
French Café **9** *D4*
Gallery Café **10** *D4*
Harbourside Seafood
  Bar & Grill **4** *A4*
Joy Bong **3** *F1*
Kermadec **11** *A3*
Mecca **2** *C4*

Mexican Café **16** *C3*
Middle East Café **41** *C3*
O'Connell Street
  Bistro **29** *B4*
Orbit & Observatory
  (Sky Tower) **5** *C3*
Rakinos **13** *C4*
Sake Bar Rikka **14** *C1*
Seamart Deli
  & Café **15** *B2*
Soul **1** *A3*
Toto **17** *C2*
Verona **18** *E2*
Vertigo at Mercure
  Hotel **7** *A4*
Vulcan **19** *B4*
White Lady **20** *B4*
Wildfire
  Churrascaria **21** *A3*

Bars & clubs

Belgian Beer
  Café **22** *B4*
Blend &
  Club 4:20 **35** *E1*
Danny Doolans **12** *A3*
Deschlers **27** *C4*
Dispensary **28** *C3*
Empire **30** *B2*
Float **34** *A3*
Galbraith's Ale
  House **45** *F2*
Loaded Hog **37** *A3*
London **38** *C3*
Minus 5 **23** *A3*
Muddy Farmer **42** *B3*
Papa Jack's Voodoo
  Lounge **43** *B4*

Link bus route - - -

won by New Zealand in 1994) and the place has become an aquatic stadium of profound celebration. New Zealanders are proud of their yachting heritage and, even outside the fierce competition of the yachting trophy wars, this is reflected on the waters of the Viaduct Basin. Much debate has raged, since the somewhat embarrassing loss of the America's Cup in February 2003, as to what will become of the Viaduct Basin and the site of the former syndicate headquarters, but five years on it still seems to maintain much of its social and aesthetic allure.

New Zealand National Maritime Museum

ⓘ *Corner of Quay and Hobson sts, on the waterfront and within easy walking distance of the centre or Britomart Transport Centre, To800-725897/To9-373 0800, www.nz maritime.org; daily 0900-1800, winter 0900-1700; $16, child $7. 'Ted Ashby Heritage Cruise' (1½ hrs) in summer Tue, Thu, Sat, Sun at 1200 and 1400, $15, child $7; museum extra. Museum and Heritage Cruise: $24, child $12, concessions available.*

Even if you are a committed landlubber and have little interest in actually sailing, the New Zealand National Maritime Museum (Te Huiteananui-a-Tangaroa) is a wonderful museum and well worth a visit. On the waterfront at the entry to the America's Cup Village, it depicts a very important aspect of New Zealand's history and, more importantly perhaps, the particularly maritime flavour of the 'City of Sails'. The museum is well laid out, chronologically, so that you begin with the replicas and a high video presentation of early Maori, Polynesian arrivals before moving on to European maritime history, including immigration. Here, in the replicated living quarters of an early immigrant ship, complete with moving floor and appropriate creaking noises, you cannot help sympathizing deeply with the brave souls who made the journey.

Moving on, you emerge into the galleries of New Zealand's proud yachting history, including the stories of New Zealand's participation and triumphs in the Louis Vuitton Cup, the Whitbread Round the World Yacht Race and, of course, the much-lauded America's Cup. Much of this story is the personal resumé of the late Sir Peter Blake, New Zealand's most famous sailing son who was so tragically murdered in the Amazon in 2002; and more recently Russell Coutts, considered by many – after his lucrative move from Team New Zealand to skipper the Swiss challenge Alinghi in 2003 – the 'Judas' of Kiwi yacht racing. Naturally, though now almost like a shrine for mourning, there is also an exhibit and replica of the America's Cup itself. During its proud stay between there 1995 and 2001 the original was housed in the New Zealand Royal Yacht Squadron Headquarters at the Westhaven Marina, but for the past few years, of course, it is languishing somewhere in Switzerland.

The museum also houses the scenic and relaxed **Big Boat Café** as well as a maritime shop with nautical gifts and memorabilia. If you are trying to trace your roots, you can search the computer immigration records and passenger arrivals in 'The Immigrants' section of the museum.

A number of excellent cruises are available from the museum, including the popular 'Ted Ashby Heritage Cruise', aboard the 57-ft traditionally built scow *Ted Ashby*, and weekend excursions aboard the unfortunately named but nonetheless charming *SS Puke* – 'The loveliest Little Steamboat Around'. All the vessels are beautiful replicas or originals and it is an ideal opportunity to get out on to the water.

The Domain → To get to the Domain, see Auckland Museum, below.

ⓘ *To9-379 2020, Winter Gardens and Fernz Fernery, 0900-1730, free.*

The Domain is one of Auckland's less obvious volcanic cones and New Zealand's oldest park. Originally another enclave and early Maori *pa*, it was formally put aside as a reserve by Governor Hobson in 1840. Within its spacious grounds are a number of historic features including the **Bledisloe** and **Robert Burns Memorial statues** and its crowning glory, the **Auckland Museum** and **War Memorial** (see below). Other points of interest include the **Winter Garden** and **Fernz Fernery** where you can take in

the scents of various blooms or study the 300 species of fern on display. The Formal
Garden within the Domain was once the site of the Auckland Acclimatisation Society
where exotic trees, birds and fish were kept before being released to wreak havoc on
indigenous species. The park also has a number of quiet inner city bush walks, some
with alluring names such as 'lovers walk', which would fool you into the belief you are
far from the city, were it not for occasional glimpse of the Sky Tower through the
branches. If you get hungry during your wanderings then the **Domain kiosk** (daily
1000-1500) by the duck pond serves basic snacks and refreshments.

Auckland Museum (Te Papa Whakahiku)

ⓘ T0800-256873, www.aucklandmuseum.com, daily 1000-1700, $5 donation. Maori
performance Jan-Mar 1100, 1200, 1330, 1430; Apr-Dec 1100, 1200, 1330; $15, child $7.50.
Guided tours daily 1030, $10, child $5. Most city tour buses stop at the museum, as does
the Link bus from the CBD. The museum is also on the 'Coast to Coast' walkway.

The Auckland Museum, an impressive edifice that crowns the spacious surroundings
of the Auckland Domain, houses some wonderful treasures, displayed with flair and
imagination. Its most important collection is that of Maori *taonga* (treasures) and
Pacific artefacts which, combined, is the largest such collection in the world. Other
special attractions include an award-winning Children's Discovery Centre, Social and
Settlement History Sections, Natural History Galleries, and 'Scars on the Heart', the
story of New Zealanders at war, from the Maori Land Wars in the late 1800s to the
campaigns in Gallipoli and Crete in the two world wars of the 20th century. The
museum also houses a major national **War Memorial** and hosts the traditional dawn
gathering of veterans on Remembrance (Anzac) Day on the forecourt. The most recent
addition to the building is 'The Dome' described as a four-storey suspended bowl,
clad in Fijian Kauri that hangs over the auditorium and events centre, crowned in
copper and glass. This and its surrounding infrastructure increased the footprint of
the museum by 60% and it certainly forms a striking first impression from the
museum's south entrance.

If you are short of time make sure you see the **Maori Court**, a fascinating
collection of pieces from woven baskets to lethal hand weapons carved from bone or
greenstone, all centred round the huge 25-m Te Toki a Tipiri war canoe (*waka*) and a
beautifully carved meeting house (*hotunui*). The authentic Maori concert held three to
four times daily by the **Manaia**, performance group is also worth seeing.

In the **Natural History Galleries** pay particular attention to the 'Human Impacts'
section, which will give you a frightening reality check of how New Zealand has been
systematically raped of the vast majority of its once huge indigenous biodiversity
from the first day man set foot on the shores of this unspoilt paradise. The **Children's
Discovery Centre** is a 'sensory learning feast' that you and the kids might find it hard
to drag yourselves away from. There are computers, games and plenty of things to
jump on, look through, poke or prod. The museum café is on the ground floor, and
there is a well-stocked museum shop.

Auckland Art Gallery (Toi-O-Tamaki)

ⓘ Based in 2 separate galleries: Main Building and New Gallery Building, T09-379 1349,
www.aucklandartgallery.co.nz, daily 1000-1700, free, $7 for temporary exhibitions;
guided tours at 1400. Both galleries are in close proximity and within easy walking
distance from Queen St. The 'Link' bus stops right outside the gallery every 10-20 mins.

The Auckland Art Gallery is essentially two buildings: one in Kitchener Street and the
other on the corner of Wellesley Street and Lorne Street in the city centre. They
combine to form the largest and most comprehensive collection of art in the country.
The first building and **Old Gallery** (Kitchener Street) is over 100 years old and,
although it has undergone major reconstruction and has added extensions over the
years, it retains its French Renaissance revival charm.

Auckland City centre

The gallery spaces within its walls display exhibitions from the permanent collections. These include small collections of some of the better known international masters, particularly 17th-century pieces, but it is the New Zealand works by **Charles Goldie** and **Gottfried Lindauer** that are of particular interest. Goldie and Lindauer were early European settlers who specialized in oil landscapes and portraits of Maori elders in the 18th and 19th centuries. The works of Goldie are impressive to say the least, with their almost Pre-Raphaelite detail bringing the portraits to life, particularly the detail of the *moko* (Maori facial tattoos). However, one has to be a little wary of the romanticism of the depictions of Maori life as seen through early European eyes: the warrior savages being civilized by those who think they know better.

The **New Gallery**, which opened in 1995, is nearby on Wellesley Street. It houses mainly temporary exhibitions that explore new art, new ideas and media. The **Colin McCahon room**, which displays the works of this more contemporary and hugely respected New Zealand artist, demonstrates the often very conceptual nature of these more modern works. The installations vary from the fascinating to the ridiculous.

Albert Park

Behind the art gallery, Albert Park is the informal lunchtime escape for city suits and university students. The park was formerly another Maori *pa* and later, during the Second World War, the site of concrete bunkers. These sites and the park as a whole have now thankfully been replaced by manicured flowerbeds, statues, a floral clock and old spider-like fig trees. It's a great place to bring a sandwich, escape the noise and look up at the Sky Tower. On the park's western fringe, housed in a small cottage, is the **Bruce Wilkinson Collection** ① *daily 1000-1600*, which houses ornate clocks and ornaments. Worth a look if only to remind you that it is time to move on.

North shore

North Shore City, or the North Shore, as it is better known, is most famous for the miles of coastline and pretty bays that fringe its quiet eastern suburbs. Many British immigrants reside north of the bridge and in summer you will find them on one of the many sheltered beaches enjoying the sun and aquatic delights they never could back home. The commercial centre of the North Shore is **Takapuna**, with its attractive range of modern shops, popular restaurants and bars; but it is **Devonport** with its history, city views and village feel that deservedly attracts most tourists.

Ins and outs

Getting there Devonport is 12 km from the city centre across the Harbour Bridge. By car, take the Takapuna off ramp, turn right on Lake Road and just keep going. Alternatively, take Bus 813 from the BBT. The North Shore can also be accessed by boat, **Fullers Ferry** ① *Ferry Building, Quay St, T09-367 9111, www.fullers.co.nz, Mon-Thu every 30 mins 0615-2030, then hourly until 2300, Fri-Sun every 30 mins 0610-0030, last sailing 0100; $9 return, child $4.40*.

The **Devonport Explorer Tour** ① *T09-357 6366, www.devonporttours.co.nz, daily, every hour 1000-1500, 2 hrs, $30*, is a combination of ferry, bus and walking which is personally guided and includes North Head and Mount Victoria. It also offers a tour option with a buffet lunch at McHughs of Cheltenham (departs 1100, from $50) and a dinner option at the Watermark Restaurant (departs 1800, from $65).

Devonport VIC (I-Site) ① *3 Victoria St, T09-446 0677, www.northshorenz.com, daily 0800-1700*, is almost next door to the historic Esplanade Hotel. The centre and its friendly staff will provide information on historic sights, the best short walks and places to stay.

Devonport, Mount Victoria and North Head

The heart of North Shore City is in **Devonport**. This is the area's oldest and most popular settlement, lying on the shores of its southernmost edge. Devonport's greatest asset is the fact that it is so near yet so far from the city centre, creating a distinct village feel. A 10-minute ferry ride from the city centre, or a 12-km drive across the Harbour Bridge, brings you immediately to the heart of this historic and picturesque little suburb. Victorian villas, craft shops, pavement cafés and pleasant short walks all lie in wait, dominated by its two volcanoes, Mount Victoria and North Head, both of which offer great views. For a longer stay try one of its many quaint bed and breakfast hideaways.

According to Maori tradition the great ancestral canoe, Tainui, rested here on its coastal explorations in or around the 14th century, before both Mount Victoria and North Head were, not surprisingly, settled by the Maori and used as *pa*. A village called Flagstaff on the western side of Mount Victoria was one of Auckland's earliest European settlements before land sales expanded in all directions to eventually form the suburb and naval base called Devonport – after its namesake in southwest Devon, England.

If time is short your best bet is to take the short walk to **North Head** which guards the entrance to Waitamata harbour. Follow the shore east along the pohutukawa-lined King Edward Parade from where you can enjoy the view of the harbour, alive with all manner of craft, from jet skis to huge supply ships. From there you can climb up and all around North Head and enjoy the commanding views back across the city and the Hauraki Gulf. The warren of underground tunnels and bunkers built amidst the hysteria of various potential invasions during both world wars provide added interest.

From North Head climb down to **Cheltenham Beach**, a popular swimming and sunbathing spot in summer and one that gives the most surreal and almost surreal view of the volcanic island of **Rangitoto**. It is a particular delight at sunrise. On your return to the village, if you are feeling energetic, try to include a climb to the summit of **Mount Victoria**. Equally stunning views of the city can be had from here; its slopes retain the remnants of the Maori *pa*. From there you can wander to Victoria Road for lunch or some shopping before catching a ferry back to the city.

The **Naval Museum** ⓘ *Spring St, T09-445 5186, daily 1000-1630, free; 1-hr tours of the naval base Sat-Sun 1300 and 1430, book ahead*, is best left to those with a specific interest. The low-key **Devonport Museum** ⓘ *31a Vauxhall Rd, T09-445 2661, Sat-Sun 1400-1600, free*, in the Cambria Reserve, is small but still worth a look.

Devonport

Sleeping
Esplanade Hotel 3
Jasmine Cottage 2
Peace & Plenty Inn 4
Villa Cambria 5

Eating
Manuka 1
Monsoon 2
Watermark 4

To Auckland — To Waiheke

0 metres 300
0 yards 300

Auckland North shore

Devonport is famous for its resident artists and there are a number of quality galleries. **Art of this World** ① *Queen's Parade, across the road from the wharf, T09-446 0926*, is the best, but the **Flagstaff** ① *Victoria Rd, T09-445 1142*, and **Art by the Sea** ① *King Edward Parade, T09-445 6665*, are also worth a look.

The **Devonport Arts Festival** is held every March. Shopping in the village is a delight and there are a number of interesting craft shops, but you may be hard pressed to drag yourself away from the two excellent second-hand bookshops: **Evergreen Books** and the **Hard to Find (But Worth The Effort)** at 15 and 81A Victoria Road respectively.

City East

Kelly Tarlton's Antarctic Encounter and Underwater World

① *23 Tamaki Drive, T09-528 0603, www.kellytarltons.co.nz, daily 0900-1800, $28, child $14. Explorer Bus departs hourly from the Ferry Building, Quay St, while Stagecoach buses depart regularly from Commerce St, $2.40. Taxi $16 one way. Or it is a scenic 6-km walk along the waterfront and Tamaki Drive.*

A 10-minute drive east of the city centre along Tamaki Drive is Kelly Tarlton's Antarctic Encounter and Underwater World. The development is housed within the walls of Auckland City's old disused sewage holding tanks beneath the car park and Tamaki Drive itself. It is a fascinating concept, and typical of the imagination, ingenuity and determination of New Zealand's most famous and best-loved diver, treasure hunter and undersea explorer, Kelly Tarlton, the founder and driving force behind the project. Sadly Kelly died just seven months after it opened.

The attraction is divided into two main parts. The **Antarctic Encounter,** takes you through a range of informative displays relating the story of early Antarctic exploration, including the triumphs and tragedies of Shackleton, Amundsen and Scott. Before you enter a replica of Captain Scott's 1911 hut in the Antarctic, you are primed by a weather update from the modern-day base. The barely imaginable sub-zero temperatures, wind speeds and familiar words of 'snowing today' make the famous and tragic story of Scott's last expedition in 1910 all the more poignant. The replica hut is an impressive representation, complete with piano. From there you board a snow cat which takes you through the equally impressive **Penguin Encounter**. A running commentary describes the huge king and smaller, more genteel, gentoo penguins in their carefully maintained natural conditions. Such is the standard of the facility and the care of the birds that they breed happily and if you are lucky you will see, at close range, the huge and hilarious down-covered chicks. On the freezing snow they stand upright and dozing in their tatty attire, as if waiting in a queue for a much-needed new fur coat.

After more information about Antarctica and a 'Conservation Corridor', you enter the original **Underwater World**. This is a world-class live exhibit for which Kelly Tarlton pioneered the concept of viewing sea life through fibreglass tunnels. It is a strange mix of distance and intimacy as you walk beneath huge stingrays and sharks gliding gracefully and menacingly above your head. Smaller tanks contain a host of other species from beautiful sea horses to ugly moray eels and the highly poisonous scorpion fish. Open rock pools provide a tremendous learning experience for kids. For the more adventurous there are opportunities to dive with sharks from $175.

Tamaki Drive, Mission Bay and St Heliers

On a sunny afternoon, especially at the weekend, there is almost no better place to be in central Auckland than somewhere along Tamaki Drive. All along its 9-km length it is both a buzz of activity and a haven of relaxation. Round every corner the view of Rangitoto and yachts plying the harbour predominate. You will see people roller-blading, walking, jogging and cycling, leaving the road to the vintage cars and city posers. Bike and rollerblade hire is readily available along the route for $8-12 per hour.

If you have time, take the short walk up the hill to the **M J Savage Memorial Park**, from where the view of the harbour mouth and Rangitoto is wonderful. This is a rather elegant memorial to the nation's first Labour prime minister. It was here, at Bastion Point, where one of the most serious recent altercations occurred between Maori and *Pakeha* in the late 1970s. The matter, as ever, concerning land ownership and sale, was eventually settled after a 17-month stand-off between police and the local Nga-Whatua, whose fine *marae* (sacred courtyard) sits on the southern edge of the park. There are many fine cafés and restaurants along Tamaki, and in **Mission Bay** and **St Heliers**, from which to sit back and watch the sun set before perhaps taking in a movie at the art deco **Berkley Cinema** ① *Mission Bay, T09-521 9222*. **Achilles Point**, at the very end of Tamaki Drive, with its secluded beach, is a favourite spot for lovebirds and naturist bathers, and has wonderful views over the gulf and back towards the city.

Parnell and Newmarket → *See map page 93.*

Trendy Parnell, 2 km east of the city centre, was once a rather run-down suburb, but in recent years it has undergone a dramatic transformation which has seen it almost overtake Devonport and Ponsonby in the popularity and fashion stakes. It has the same 'village within a city' feel as Devonport, with tiny brick-paved lanes and boutique style outlets, and boasts some of Auckland's finest galleries, shops and restaurants.

At the top of Parnell Rise is the recently finished **Auckland Cathedral of the Holy Trinity** ① *T09-303 9500, www.holy-trinity.org.nz, Mon-Fri 1000-1600, Sat and Sun 1300-1700, free,* whose angular structure is aesthetically interesting but nothing compared to the beautiful stained-glass windows and 29-ton organ within. Guided tours and an audio-visual display are both available. The older **Cathedral of St Mary** ① *same opening hours,* which now rests in its big sister's shadow, is one of the largest wooden churches in the world and its wonderfully peaceful interior is a delight. The stained-glass windows are beautiful, as is the entire wooden construction. There is usually a volunteer guide on hand who will proudly explain the 110-year history and show you pictures of how the grand old building was moved to its present site from across the road in 1984. The café (daily from 0700) on the cathedral forecourt has some great food and is an excellent place to sit and admire its unusual architecture.

Around the corner in Ayr Street you will find **Kinder House** ① *2 Ayr St, T09-379 4008, Tue-Sun 1100-1500, $4,* a recently renovated, two-storey building originally built in 1856 as the home of pioneer churchman and artist John Kinder. It displays some of his art works. A little further down Ayr Street is **Ewelme Cottage** ① *14 Ayr St, T09-379 0202, Wed-Sun 1030-1200 and 1300-1630, $7.50 (joint ticket with Highwic House in Newmarket),* built in 1863 as the Auckland home of the family of Archdeacon Vicesimus Lush. It was altered in 1882 but has remained largely unchanged and contains a collection of colonial furniture and household effects.

Back towards the harbour in Judges Bay is the very cute **St Stephen's Chapel**, one of a number of examples designed by Frederick Thatcher, the favourite architect of the former prominent missionary bishop, George Selwyn. It was one of Auckland's first churches. Although it is not generally open to the public you can have a peek in the window. Access to the park is off Gladstone and Judges Bay Roads. **Parnell Rose Gardens** nearby are a charming escape with rows of scented varieties.

South of the cathedral, Parnell merges into the more modern commercial centre and suburb of **Newmarket** (www.newmarket.net.nz) which is best known for its shops, restaurants, cafés and entertainment (see pages 96 and 100). Historians may be interested in the grand **Highwic House** ① *40 Gillies Av, T09-524 5729, Wed-Sun 1030-1200 and 1300-1630, $7.50,* the former home (in the 1860s) of 'colonial gentleman of property' Alfred Buckland. For lovers of beer, the **Lion Breweries** ① *380 Khyber Pass Rd, T09-358 8366, www.lionzone.co.nz, daily tours, 1 hr 50 mins with 20 mins sampling time, $15, child $7.50, bookings essential,* offers an interesting tour, but more for an appreciation of the quantity and technology rather than the quality of the product.

Auckland City East

Further east beyond the rather seedy suburb of Panmure is Howick, the largest Asian enclave in Auckland. The suburb is a concrete jungle but it has a pleasant centre with some interesting shops. The biggest attraction in these parts is the award-winning **Howick Historical Village** ⓘ *Bells Rd, Lloyd Elsmore Park, Pakuranga, T09-576 9506, www.fencible.org.nz, daily 1000-1600, $13, child $7; Howick and Eastern buses run a regularly from the city centre, T09-366 6400.* This is a fine example of a restored 'Fencible settlement'. Fencibles were pensioned British soldiers re-enlisted to defend the sites against the Maori and the French in the early years of Auckland settlement and expansion. The village is a 'living museum' where staff in period clothing entertains. The **Homestead Café**, with its suitably historic theme, is also on site.

City West

Ponsonby and Herne Bay

Although offering little in the way of conventional tourist attractions, a wander round Ponsonby and Herne Bay does present an example of upmarket Auckland living and culture. For the last two decades the back streets of both postcodes have steadily developed as the reserve of the well-off, as rows of renovated villas and designer homes attest. But, of course, in Ponsonby any elitism is challenged by Ponsonby's main drag, which is itself as cosmopolitan and up beat as it ever has been. There you can be well-off, well-on, or a little out of order, it matters not.

Auckland Zoo

ⓘ *T09-360 3819, www.aucklandzoo.co.nz, daily 0930-1730, $18, child $9, 5 mins' drive from the centre; from the Great Western Motorway take the Western Springs off ramp and follow signs, free car parking. Or take Explorer Bus or Bus 045 from the city centre.*

Set in pleasant parkland next to Western Springs and 6 km west of the city centre is New Zealand's premier wild animal collection. It has kept pace with the more conservation-minded function of zoos and is worth a visit. The zoo claims to be leading the way in the breeding of native species including **kiwi** and **tuatara** – both of which are on display. All the old favourites are also there – elephants (sometimes taken on walkabout around the zoo), giraffes, hippos, tigers and orang-utans.

Auckland Zoo has gradually developed some imaginative themed exhibits with sponsorship from corporate New Zealand. The huge walk-through aviary, alive with the song of native bird life, is a must-see, as is the 'Newstalk ZB Rainforest' where you feel more captive than the obscenely laid-back spider monkeys. More recent additions include 'Pridelands', the spacious home of the giraffe, lion and zebra with its adjoining 'Hippo River' and a new state-of-the-art seal and penguin exhibit. 'KidZone' provides the usual touchy-feelies with rabbits and other assorted furry friends.

Museum of Transport, Technology and Social History

ⓘ *T09-815 5800, www.motat.org.nz, daily 1000-1700, $14, child $7. By car, follow the Western Springs Motorway, taking the Western Springs turning; or take Bus 045 from Customs St in the city centre, every 15 mins, 30-min journey.*

The Museum of Transport, Technology and Social History (MOTAT) is on the Great North Road, 4 km west of the city next to the attractive parklands of Western Springs and near the Auckland Zoo. It was opened in 1967 and is sadly showing its age. A mish-mash of tired-looking buildings over two sites houses many and varied exhibits, from vintage cars, fire engines and motorcycles to telephone boxes and printing presses. It is in great need of a major revamp, but trainspotters, and those looking for somewhere else to take the kids on a rainy day, may find it worth a visit.

The second site, the **Sir Keith Park Memorial Site** (named after New Zealand's most famous war time aviator) concerns all things to do with aviation, rail and the military, including a restored flying boat. The sites are connected by a tramline, which passes Western Springs Park and stops at the zoo on the way.

Ponsonby

Sleeping 🛌
Abaco on Jervois **1** *B2*

Brown Kiwi
  Backpackers **2** *B2*
Colonial Cottage **3** *B1*
Great Ponsonby B&B **4** *C1*

Eating 🍴
Andiamo **1** *B1*
Atlas Power Café **3** *B2*
Atomic Café **4** *D2*

Café Cezanne **6** *B2*
Chandelier **29** *D2*
Dizengoff **7** *C2*
Empress Garden **8** *A1*
GPK **11** *C2*
Lord Ponsonby's Deli **13** *B2*
Open Late Café **16** *D2*
Ponsonby Fresh Fish
  & Chip Co **17** *D2*

Ponsonby Pies **18** *D2*
Prego **19** *C2*
Rocco **24** *D3*
Shahi Café **2** *B2*
SPQR **22** *D2*
Vinnies **25** *B1*

Link Bus Route - - -

City South

Mount Eden

At 196 m Mount Eden, the closest volcano to the city centre, provides a spectacular view and the vast, almost surreal crater gets your imagination running wild as you picture it 'going off'. The best time to come here is at dawn, especially on misty winter mornings, when it can be a photographer's delight, and you can avoid the coach-loads of visitors.

At the southern base of Mount Eden, **Eden Gardens** ⓘ *24 Omana Av, T09-638 8395, daily 0900-1630, $5, child free, concessions available, café 1000-1600,* is a great place for lovers of all things green that grow. It is an all-seasons garden with a fine variety of flowering shrubs and New Zealand natives. Mount Eden village itself is worth a look, boasting some interesting shops and a number of fine cafés and restaurants. Mount Eden is a long walk from the city centre, and given the climb you might be better off taking Bus 274 or 275 from the BBT in the CBD.

Cornwall Park and One Tree Hill

ⓘ *Cornwall Park Visitor Centre, T09-630 8485, www.cornwallpark.co.nz, 1000-1600, free. Café and free 'points of interest' trail leaflet available.*

Just to the south of Mount Eden, and 5 km south of the Sky Tower, is Cornwall Park, a great escape from the hustle and bustle of city life, as the hordes of joggers and picnic-carrying locals will testify. It is famous not only for its crowning glory, the monument and the tree, but also the well-preserved remains of Maori *pa* on and around the summit. Kiwi Tamaki, the great chief of the Nga Marama, lived here during the mid-18th century with his thousands of *whanau* (family) and followers, attracted by the rich pickings of the region's coast and its fertile soils. His claim to the region ended after being routed by sub-tribes from the north and his people being decimated by a smallpox epidemic introduced by the Europeans. Around the summit, if you look carefully, you will see the grass-covered terraces on which sat dwellings and the 'kumara pits' scattered beside them. With the land essentially vacant when the first European settlers arrived, it was the Scot, Logan Campbell, the most powerful and well-known of the new capital's residents, who eventually took ownership. Shortly before his arrival, a single Totara tree stood proudly on the summit. This had already given rise to the hill's Maori name, *Te-Totara-a-Ahua*, meaning 'Hill of the single Totara'. This tree was rudely cut down in 1852 by early settlers and it was Campbell who planted several trees in its place, including the lonesome pine you could see until its demise in 2001. The prosperous Campbell, mayor and 'Father of Auckland', donated his estate (now the park) to the people of New Zealand to commemorate the visit in 1901 of the heirs to the throne, the Duke and Duchess of Cornwall – hence the name.

At the base of the hill is a visitor centre in **Huia Lodge**, Campbell's original gatekeeper's house. It houses some interesting displays and a video surrounding the natural and human history of the park. Across the road is the simple and faithfully restored **Acacia Cottage** ⓘ *dawn till dusk, free,* in which Campbell himself lived, though the building itself originally stood in the city centre and was relocated here in the 1920s.

Also within the park boundary at its southern end is the **Auckland Observatory** ⓘ *T09-624 1246, www.stardome.org.nz, times and events vary; standard viewing session with show $14, child $7. To get there by car: from SH1 take the Greenlane off ramp, the main entrance to the park is off Green Lane West. By Bus: 302, 305 or 312 depart regularly from the city centre.* This is the official home of Auckland's star gazers, and also contains the **Stardome Planetarium**, a cosmic multimedia experience played out on the ceiling for the general public. Outdoor telescope viewing sessions and special events are also held, depending on what the weather and the heavens are up to. You can even 'adopt a star', an interesting concept that will probably have you trying to find it again, for the rest of your life.

Rainbow's End

ⓘ *Near the Manukau Shopping complex, corner of Great South and Wiri Station Rd, Manukau, T09-262 2030, www.rainbowsend.co.nz, daily 1000-1700. All day unlimited rides $40, children $30. By car, head south and take the Manukau off ramp from SH1, it is a further 500 m. Buses 327, 347, 447, 457, 467, 487 or 497 from the city centre.*

Rainbow's End is advertised as '23 acres of fun'. It's New Zealand's largest theme park and has rides and attractions with such alluring and stomach-churning names as the 'Corkscrew Rollercoaster', 'Goldrush' and the mighty (18-storey) 'Fear Fall'. Along with these are old favourites like dodgems, go-karts, bumper boats, mini golf and an interactive games arcade. Even small kids and cowardly parents are catered for in the more sedate 'Land Castle'.

Auckland Botanical Gardens

ⓘ *T09-267 1457, daily 0800-dusk, free. Visitor Centre: Mon-Fri 0900-1600, Sat and Sun 1000-1600; café 0830-1630. By car, head south, take the Manurewa off ramp from SH1, turn left into Hill Rd. Stagecoach buses (Papakura, Pukekohe or Drury) leave from the BBT every 15 mins; alight in Great South Rd, Manurewa, just before Hill Rd.*

In Manurewa, 20 minutes south of the city centre, are the Auckland Botanical Gardens. Since planting first began in 1974 an extensive 64-ha, 10,000-plant collection has sprouted, consisting mostly of New Zealand natives. There is also an ornamental lake, a nature trail and a handsome and wonderfully fragrant display of New Zealand-bred roses. The gardens also have an interpretative visitor centre, an attractive café and a library. The annual Ellerslie Flower Show, which is the southern hemisphere's most illustrious gardening and horticultural event, was recently relocated here from the Ellerslie Showground, and usually takes place during the last week of November.

Otara Market

ⓘ *T09-274 0830, every Sat 0600-1100. By car, head south and take the Otara off ramp from SH1. Buses 487/497 from the BBT, 1 hr.*

The southern suburbs are the poorest part of the city. They can be dangerous and are not a place to stray, especially at night. However, they are definitely the place to experience the atmosphere of urban Maori or Pacific Island living. The Otara Market, held every Saturday morning in the Otara town centre car park, 18 km south of the city centre, is ideal for this and is thought to be the largest Maori and Polynesian market in the world. Like most street markets there is always a lot of nonsense for sale but some of the clothes, fabrics and certainly the fruit and vegetables are weird, wonderful and reasonably priced. Try some yams or *taro* – a type of vegetable and traditional staple diet for many native Polynesians.

⊖ Sleeping

As you might expect of the country's largest city and principal arrival point, Auckland is not short of accommodation. Most of the major hotels are to be found in the city centre, particularly on the waterfront or on either side of Queen St. There are also hundreds of B&Bs and homestays available, but these tend to be concentrated in the better-known suburbs like Parnell and Ponsonby. Further afield, in the surrounding countryside, farmstays are becoming increasingly popular (see Essentials, page 46, for further details). Contact **New Zealand Farm Holidays**, T09-412 9649, www.nzfarm holidays.co.nz, for a list of those nearby. There are lots of motels throughout the city, mostly in the suburbs of Greenlane and in Manukau and Mangere, the latter 2 being near the airport. Self-catering can be readily found in all types of accommodation, but the city centre plays host to a number of plush apartment buildings, most at the higher range of the market. If you are travelling alone and intend to stay longer than a few days, a flatshare is undoubtedly the best and cheapest option; check the Sat listings in the *New Zealand Herald*, but start hunting early. With New Zealand being such a huge backpacker destination, there are many hostels, from the awful to the plush, rowdy to the sedate. They, too, are mostly in the city centre or the more happening suburbs like Parnell. The popular and professional **YHA**, www.yha.co.nz, has 2 hostels in Auckland and many more throughout the country. There aren't many motorcamps in Auckland and most campsites are where they should be, amidst the beauty of the surrounding countryside parks and on the many islands of the Hauraki Gulf. The main VICs will help you find what you are looking for and provide a booking service (see page 73).

Campsites
Auckland Regional Parks Campsites, T09-3662000. There are 22 regional parks in and around Auckland and 39 basic facility vehicle and backpack campsites. From $5-$10 per night. DoC also have many regional campsites and administer almost all the Hauraki Island campsites. For information contact **DoC**, T09-379 6479.

Motels
There are lots of motels on Kirkbride Rd and McKenzie Rd in Mangere, near the airport. There are also a huge number on Great South Rd; they are similar in style and price and include the following:
AL Oak Tree Lodge, (104), T09-524 2211, www.oaktree.co.nz.
A Ascot Star Motel, (92), T09-520 4833, www.ascotstar.co.nz.
A Greenlane Manor, (353), T09-571 2167, www.greenlanemanor.co.nz.

Motorcamps
All the following are in the **B-D** price range.
Avondale Motor Park, 46 Bollard Av, Avondale, T09-828 7228, www.auckland motorpark.co.nz. 15 mins from the centre, with all the usual facilities plus a gaggle of friendly ducks. Close to the metro train station.

Manukau Top Ten Holiday Park, 902 Great South Rd, Manukau City, T09-266 8016, www.manukautop10.co.nz. Handy for the airport or for those heading south.
North Shore Motels and Top Ten Holiday Park, 52 Northcote Rd, Takapuna, T09-418 2578, www.nsmotels.co.nz. The most popular holiday park in the city offering lodges, motel and cabin accommodation as well as the usual reliable Top Ten motorcamp facilities. 5 mins to the beach.
Remuera Motor Lodge and Inner City Camping Ground, 16 Minto Rd, Remuera, T09-524 5126, remlodge@ihug.co.nz. The only traditional-style motorcamp near the centre. Quiet bush setting, standard facilities.

Self-catering
Many other types of accommodation also offer self-catering. The following are in the city centre and are recommended.
L Quest Auckland, 62 Queen St, T09-300 2500, www.questapartments.com.au. New in 2006.
AL Cintra Apartments, 3 Whitaker Pl, T09-379 6288, www.cintra.co.nz.
AL Elliott St Apartments, corner of Elliott and Wellesley sts, T09-308 9334, www.esapts.co.nz.

City centre *p76, map p78*

L Ascott Metropolis, 1 Courthouse Lane, T09-300 8800, www.the-ascott.com. Marketed as 'the definitive' luxury hotel in Auckland. It is a well-positioned all-suite hotel with all trimmings, and offers a range of rooms from the de luxe to the premier. The recreation area is worth a look in itself.
L Heritage Hotel, 35 Hobson St, T09-379 8553, www.heritagehotels.co.nz. With more rooms than any other hotel in the country, the Heritage is more like a village complex. It offers a wide range of luxury and standard en suite options, most of which have great views. The indoor and outdoor recreation areas are fantastic.
L Hilton Hotel, Princes Wharf, 147 Quay St, T09-978 2000, www.hilton.com. Making its mark during the America's Cup, the Hilton

● *For an explanation of the Sleeping and Eating price codes used in this guide, see the inside*
● *front cover. Other relevant information is provided in the Essentials chapter, pages 44-51.*
Note that prices are given in New Zealand dollars.

sits in an enviable position on Princes Wharf, overlooking the harbour on both sides, and only a short stroll from the city centre. Contemporary, luxury and boutique in style the accommodation and service is naturally first class, but for many it is the in-house restaurant, **White**, which really exceeds expectations. Classy yet informal it offers memorable views across the harbour. In-house health and beauty spa.

L Quay West, 8 Albert St, T09-309 6000/T0800 937373, www.mirvachotels.com.au. Standard well-established, 5-star option in the CBD. Rooms are spacious and exquisite, the views even better; the Roman pool and spa are so cute you will probably spend most of your stay there. Facilities include internet and a reputable in-house bar and restaurant offering contemporary New Zealand cuisine. Off-street parking.

L The Sebel, corner of Hobson St and Customs St West, T09-978 4000, www.mirac hotels.com.au. Ideally situated overlooking the Viaduct Basin and former America's Cup Village. It offers high standards of suite-style accommodation and service.

L Sky City Grand Hotel, corner of Victoria and Federal sts, T09-363 6000, www.skycity auckland.co.nz. One of the newest 5-star offerings, right in the heart of the city and very handy for facilities within the Sky City complex. It offers an impressive marriage of luxurious quality and modern style with elegant standard or executive suites and premium self-contained rooms, all with the usual 5-star features. In-house facilities include a heated lap pool, gym, health and beauty spa, sauna and a rather noisy sun deck.

AL-A Columbia Hotel, 15 Whitaker Pl, T09-963 8600, www.columbiahotel.co.nz. Modern multi-storey with an almost minimalist retro feel. 1- to 2-bedroom units and budget studios, some with internet port and all with en suite, Sky TV. Very clean, good facilities, and within a short walk of Queen St.

AL-A Freemans B&B, 65 Wellington St, T09-376 5046, www.freemansbandb.co.nz. Better known for its location than anything else. B&B and self-contained options within walking distance of the centre.

B-C Aspen House, 62 Emily Pl, T09-379 6633, www.aspenhouse.co.nz. A no-nonsense cheaper hotel, well placed, comfortable and clean. Standard or connecting rooms with TV.

Some rooms are small which is reflected in the price. Wireless internet, free breakfast and undercover parking $10 per night.

B-D Surf and Snow, corner of Victoria St and Albert St, T09-363 8889, www.surfand snow.co.nz. A new hostel set in a historic building with high ceilings and polished floors. Good, modern facilities, spotless standard or en-suite singles/doubles and dorms. Good location and the service is pretty polished too.

C Auckland City YHA, corner of City Rd and Liverpool St, T09-309 2802, yhaauck@ yha.org.nz. One of 2 YHAs in Auckland, the other is just around the corner, at 5 Turner St, T09-302 8200. Both are reliable with modern and clean facilities, good kitchen, pleasant friendly atmosphere, in-house bistro. 4- and 5-star Qualmark ratings respectively.

C-D Albert Park Backpackers, 27-31 Victoria St East, T09-309 0336, www.albertpark.co.nz. A long-established, smaller slightly quieter version of the ACB, below.

C-D Auckland Central Backpackers (ACB), corner of Queen St and Darby St, T09-358 4877, www.acb.co.nz. The busiest and most high-profile of the central backpacker hostels, with simple clean accommodation, 24-hr reception, security, café, bar, internet and a travel shop attached. The travel shop staff are very knowledgeable and helpful. There's always a buzz of activity and it's the perfect starting point for socialites.

C-D Princeton Backpackers, 30 Symonds St, T09-963 8300/T0508-237833, www.auckland backpackers.co.nz. Modern, centrally located multi-storey with a range of good-value en suite units (with kitchenette) sleeping up to 4, perfect for couples and small groups looking for a bit of privacy. Well facilitated with a tidy internet/TV lounge, restaurant and café on site. No off-street parking.

North shore p82, see map p83

LL-L Peace and Plenty Inn, 6 Flagstaff Terr, Devonport, T09-445 2925, www.peace andplenty.co.nz. A top B&B on the waterfront offering luxury accommodation and fine food. 7 beautifully presented individually decorated rooms with every attention to detail.

L-AL Emerald Inn, 16 The Promenade, Takapuna, T09-488 3500, www.emerald-inn.co.nz. Wide range of options with suites, units, a cottage and villas, close to the beach and all amenities.

L-AL Esplanade Hotel, 1 Victoria Rd, Devonport, T09-445 1291, www.esplanade hotel.co.nz. One of Auckland's oldest hotels, dominating the promenade with fine views of the harbour. Due to its position (15 mins from the city centre by car, or a 10-min ferry ride from the CBD) it's a good place to get away from the centre and enjoy Devonport's 'village within a city' atmosphere. All rooms are en suite, with the spacious 'harbour view' suites being the most sought after. Sky TV and wireless internet. Classy in-house restaurant with an open fire in winter adds to the charm. Tariff includes breakfast.

L-AL The Spencer on Byron, 9-17 Byron Av, Takapuna, T09-916 6111, www.spencer byron.co.nz. The highest building on the North Shore so it is never short of good views. Overall a reliable option close to the 'Shore's' major centre and a pleasant alternative to the city centre (8 km).

L-AL Villa Cambria, 71 Vauxhall Rd, Devonport, T09-445 7899, www.villa cambria.co.nz. Victorian villa with all mod cons in a quiet location in Devonport village. Has a great self-contained 'loft' and several fresh, tastefully decorated en suites with a mix of antique and Asian features, all with plenty of privacy. Fine breakfast. Limited off-street parking and internet.

A Jasmine Cottage, 20 Buchanan St, Devonport, T09-445 8825, www.photo album.co.nz/jasmine. Lovely courtyard cottage in quiet garden setting, queen en suite with tea and coffee making facilities. Exceptional hosts.

City East *p84, map p93*

LL-AL Devereux Boutique Hotel, 267 Remuera Rd, Remuera, T09-524 5044, www.devereux.co.nz. A quality hotel set in a sprawling historic villa near Remuera and Newmarket, with earning a solid reputation with 4-star rating. 12 stylish suites. Breakfast included.

L Aachen House, 39 Market Rd, Remuera, T09-520 2329, www.aachenhouse.co.nz. Well-regarded boutique hotel in an Edwardian mansion full of antiques. Not everyone's cup of tea, but the rooms are spacious with en suite bathroom, and the beds themselves are magnificent. Fine in-house cuisine.

L Seaview Heights, 23a Glover Rd, St Heliers, T09-575 8159, www.seaview.co.nz. 2 well-appointed suites with great views towards the harbour and Rangitoto.

L St George's Bay Lodge, 43 St George's Bay Rd, Parnell (close to Parnell Rd), T09-303 1050, www.stgeorge.co.nz. Elegant Victorian villa in a quiet street and tastefully renovated and decorated. 3-mins from Parnell village.

AL Ascot Parnell, 4/32 St Stephens Av, Parnell, T09-309 9012, www.ascotparnell.com. A historic and characterful house with huge rooms. Terrific breakfast included.

AL Chalet Chevron, 14 Brighton Rd, Parnell, T09-309 0290, www.chaletchevron.co.nz. Older style 3-storey residence with plenty of character and a gracious homely feel. Double and single rooms available all with private bathrooms. Generous breakfast included. Broadband internet.

AL-A Off Broadway Newmarket Motel, 11 Alpers Av, Newmarket, T09-529 3550, www.off-broadway.co.nz. Modern, reliable motel with stylish studios or suites with spa, within walking distance of Newmarket shops and restaurants.

A Parnell Inn, 320 Parnell Rd, Parnell, T09-358 0642, www.parnellinn.co.nz. 16 clean and comfortable executive and standard studio units, 3 with kitchenettes. Right on Parnell Rd but still quiet. Licensed café.

A Parnell Village Motor Lodge, 2 St Stephens Av, Parnell, T09-377 1463, www.parnellmotorlodge.co.nz. Good-value long-established option perfectly situated in the heart of Parnell Village and just a short bus ride from the CBD. 2-storey residence offering standard studios and Edwardian or modern apartment style studios. Off-street parking. Plenty of restaurants nearby.

C-D City Garden Lodge, 25 St George's Bay Rd, Parnell, T09-302 0880, www.citygarden lodge.co.nz. A huge mansion of a place with wooden floors and Kauri staircase. Clean, comfortable and friendly with all the necessary facilities. Emphasis is on offering a quiet location in which to escape the city pace or recover from your arduous travels.

C-D Lantana Lodge, 60 St George's Bay Rd, Parnell, T09-373 4546. A quiet but smaller option with various room types and free internet. Clients are well looked after.

Parnell & Newmarket

Sleeping

Ascot Parnell **2**
Chalet Chevron **5**
City Garden Lodge **6**
Devereux Boutique **12**
Lantana Lodge **7**
Off Broadway
  Newmarket Motel **13**
Parnell Inn **8**
Parnell Village
  Motor Lodge **9**
St George's Bay
  Lodge **11**

Eating

Antoine's **1**
Burger Fuel **19**
Cibo **2**
Iguacu **3**
Java Room **4**
Karin Japanese **5**
Kenzie **16**
La Bocca **6**
Lava **18**
Mikano **7**
Oh Calcutta **8**
Portofino **10**
Rikka **11**
Rosehip **15**
Trinity **13**
Verve **14**
White Lady **9**

Bars & clubs

Claddagh **17**
Penny Black **22**

Link Bus Route ---

City West *p86, map p87*

LL-AL Hastings Hall, 99 Western Springs Rd, T09-845 8550, www.hastingshall.co.nz. Classic, spacious historic villa with a fine range of rooms and suites (most en suite) sumptuously decorated with much love and attention to detail. Sky TV, internet, pool, spa and all the trimmings. Close to Western Springs park and the zoo.

L Waitakere Park Lodge, 573 Scenic Drive, Waitaura, T09-814 9622, www.waitakere estate.co.nz. Off the beaten track, set in 80 acres of bush at the base of the Waitakere Ranges. Close to the vineyards and west coast beaches. 17 suites with bush and city views. A la carte restaurant.

AL Great Ponsonby B&B, 30 Ponsonby Terr, Ponsonby, T09-376 5989, www.ponsonby bnb.co.nz. Undoubtedly one of the best in the city, this B&B is a restored villa in a quiet location only a short stroll to the 'funky' Ponsonby Rd. Range of tastefully decorated en suite rooms and studios with a colourful Pacific influence. Enthusiastic, knowledgeable owners and a friendly dog and cat. Sky TV.

A Abaco on Jervois, 59 Jervois Rd, Ponsonby, T09-376 0119, www.abaco.co.nz. Recently fully renovated, comfortable and conveniently situated for Ponsonby and the city centre. Within walking distance of 30 restaurants. Spa rooms available. Internet, off-street parking.

A Colonial Cottage, 35 Clarence St, Ponsonby, T09-3602820. Olde worlde charm in an old Kauri villa. Alternative health specialists and organic emphasis.

C-D Brown Kiwi Backpackers, 7 Prosford St, Ponsonby, T09-378 0191, www.brown kiwi.co.nz. The best backpacker hostel west of the city. Good reputation and full of character. Close to Ponsonby Rd and link bus service.

City South *p88*

L Jet Inn, 63 Westney Rd, Mangere, T09-2754100, www.jetinn.co.nz. 3 km from the airport, 16 km from the city. Modern and well facilitated. Ideal for a pre/post-flight sleep.

A Bavaria Guest House, 83 Valley Rd, Mt Eden, T09-6389641, bavaria@extra.co.nz. Spacious and comfortable with 11 suites, nice deck and garden. German spoken.

A Hotel Grand Chancellor, corner of Ascot and Kirkbride Rds, Airport Oaks, T09-275 7029, www.grandhotelsinternational.com. A safe bet if you need to be near the airport. All the trimmings, such as a pool and restaurant.

B Bond Street Lodge, 77 Bond St, Kingsland, T09-846 4585, www.bondstlodge.co.nz. Modern 3-storey budget accommodation on the fringe of the city centre and in the fast developing suburb of Kingsland. A fine alternative to the CBD and only 5 mins' walk from Eden Park. Tidy rooms (with internet ports), shared bathrooms and kitchen. Spacious lounge. Off-street parking.

C-D Oaklands Lodge Backpackers, 5a Oaklands Rd, Mt Eden, T09-638 6545, info@oaklands.co.nz. A good budget choice on the fringe of the CBD, Victorian villa with a relaxed atmosphere and a tempting short walk to the summit of Mt Eden.

🍴 Eating

When it comes to eating, Auckland is said to be on a par with New York and London. With almost 1000 restaurants in the city it is not surprising to learn that 'dining out' is New Zealand's 3rd biggest retail spend. Note that restaurants and cafés are essentially the same thing, with the latter perhaps just being a bit more casual. The cafés listed separately below are some of the traditional favourites; those particularly noted for their character, ambience and/or coffee.

The city centre offers waterside dining indoors and out, with spacious brasseries,

intimate silver service, or romantic balconies overlooking the viaduct and harbour. Elsewhere, in High St and Vulcan Lane, you can find a more casual setting in the many streetside cafés. Many of the pub also offer a decent meal for a reasonable price (see Bars and clubs, below). To the west of the city centre, Ponsonby (Ponsonby Rd) has for years managed to hold on to its reputation as the culinary heart of the city, with Parnell coming a close second. Service is generally good and refreshingly friendly. Tipping is not essential but appreciated. BYO means bring your own (bottle).

City centre p76, map p78

Cin Cin, Ferry Building, 99 Quay St, T09-307 6966, www.cincin.co.nz Mon-Fri from 1100, Sat-Sun from 0930, Fri-Sat until 0300. Established as one of Auckland's top restaurants for years, Cin Cin has changed hands a number of times. With its location right next to the ferry docks it is very much a happening place, serving Pacific cuisine to the highest standard. The service here is outstanding, as is the wine list. Licensed, outdoor dining available.

Euro, Shed 22, Princes Wharf, Quay St, T09-309 9866, daily for lunch and dinner, brunch Sat-Sun from 1030. A waterfront restaurant designed to capture the sailing crowd, with a boast of being the 'best of the best'. It has a very luxurious clean-feel interior with a large mesmerizing clock projected onto the wall, and offers new and imaginative cuisine in the revered Pacific Rim style. Licensed, outdoor dining available.

Harbourside Seafood Bar and Grill, 1st floor, Ferry Building, T09-307 0556, daily from 1130, licensed. Located right above Cin Cin, it is advertised in all the tourist publications and seems to live up to all the praise. This is a good opportunity to try New Zealand snapper or green-lipped mussels.

Kermadec, 1st floor, Viaduct Quay Building, corner of Lower Hobson St and Quay St, T09-309 0412, www.kermadec.co.nz Mon-Fri for lunch and dinner. Perhaps the best restaurant in town, and arguably the best seafood venue. Here you can tickle your taste buds with the many delights of the Pacific Ocean as well as more traditional fare. There are 2 private rooms in a Japanese-style decor that contain small ponds. Don't miss the seafood platter. Licensed and BYO.

Orbit Restaurant, Sky Tower, corner Victoria St and Federal St, T09-3636000, daily 1730-2200, Sat-Sun 1000-1200, licensed. Over two thirds of the way up the Sky Tower, this restaurant has the best view of any in the city, if not the entire hemisphere. The restaurant itself revolves, though sadly at a sedate speed. Although the food is not as good as the view, it is comprehensive in selection and has a good reputation. The Observatory is the other option in the Sky Tower and offers buffet-style fare. Open for dinner daily and lunch Thu-Sun.

White, Hilton Hotel, Princes Wharf, 147 Quay St, T09-978 2020, www.white restaurant.co.nz, from 1830. Since the America's Cup, White has earned a reputation that now places it amongst the very best of Auckland's offerings. There is no doubt the views across the water and classy atmosphere have as much to do with that as the food and the service. **Bellini**, the hotel's self-styled cocktail bar, is an added attraction.

Wildfire Churrascaria, Princes Wharf, Quay St, T09-353 7595, www.wildfire restaurant.co.nz daily from 1130. Wildfire has reinvented itself as a 'Brazilian BBQ' restaurant focusing on South American-style skewered meats generously dished out by Churrasco waiters' on a set menu. It's an interesting concept and if half a cow isn't your thing then fear not, à la carte comes to the rescue with seafood and vegetarian options. There's live Brazilian music at weekends. Licensed, outdoor dining available.

The French Café, 210 Symonds St, T09-377 1911, www.thefrenchcafe.co.nz, lunch, Fri, dinner Tue-Sat, licensed. Well-established favourite that has stood the test of time. Fine starters available as main courses, excellent fresh fish dishes.

Joy Bong, 531 Karangahape Rd, T09-377 2218, daily from 1700, licensed. Once part of the notoriously competitive Ponsonby restaurant family this relocated Thai restaurant known affectionately as the 'bong' continues to enjoy a solid reputation. Good value.

O'Connell Street Bistro, 3 O'Connell St, T09-377 1884, dinner daily, lunch Tue-Fri, licensed. An intimate, tiny venue serving fine examples of Pacific Rim with a legendary wine list. Express menu for theatre-goers.

Sake Bar Rikka, 19 Drake St, Victoria Park Market, T09-377 8239, lunch and diner Tue-Sun, licensed. Some say Sake is now past its best but it remains for now one of the best Japanese restaurants in town. Fine seasonal dishes in a wood-beamed warehouse, in character with the Victoria Park Market.

Seamart Deli and Cafe, corner of Fanshawe St and Market Pl, T09-302 8989, lunch and dinner daily from 1100, licensed. Being attached to one of the main fresh seafood outlets in town you cannot really go wrong. Great chowder and smoked fish.

Soul, Viaduct Harbour, T09-356 7249, daily for lunch and dinner. Much to the chagrin of the local competition, owner and chef Judith Tabron ensured that Soul was the place to be during the America's Cup and its reputation lives on. Doubtless, the open-air decks overlooking the harbour had much to do with that, but the food is also excellent and affordable. Fish is recommended.

Toto, 53 Nelson St, T09-302 2665. Lunch, Mon-Fri, dinner daily. Licensed, outdoor dining and private rooms available. Lavishly decorated Italian-style restaurant offering some of the finest Italian food in the city.

Vertigo, top floor, **Mercure Hotel**, 8 Customs St, T09-302 9424, daily breakfast, lunch and dinner, licensed. A bit more down-to-earth than the **Orbit** restaurant in the Sky Tower, but still an impressive view and good modern dishes to go with it.

Food Hall on Atrium on Elliot, Elliot St. A convenient, cheap daytime venue.

Mexican Café, 67 Victoria St West, T09-373 2311, Mon-Fri 1200-1430, 1700-late, Sat-Sun 1700-late. A favourite cheap and cheerful café that has been around for years (no mean feat in Auckland), so it must be good.

Middle East Café, 23a Wellesley St, T09-379 4843, daily 1200-2100. For many years this tiny café has become a sanctuary for office workers and shoppers eager to absorb its cosy ambience, brimming character and legendary 'shawarmas' (strips of lamb in bread packet with a delightful garlic and tomato dip). All sorts of quirky Middle Eastern artefacts adorn the walls. It's hard to imagine you're still in Auckland.

White Lady, corner of Queen St and Short-land St, open all night. Believe it or not this is a caravan that looks more like a train, which seems to appear from nowhere each night, towed by an old tractor. Within its battered walls are 2 battered-looking gentlemen, serving various items of battered food, which taste amazing (as do most things at 0300). It's the best 'post-drink munchies' venue in the city and is open until the sun rises.

Cafés

Gallery Café, 1st floor, Auckland Art Gallery, corner of Wellesley St East and Kitchener St, T09-377 9603. A great café, even without all the in-house artworks.

Mecca, Chancery Mall, Chancery Lane, CBD, T09-356 7028, daily 0700-late. A new café/restaurant/bar worth a mention due to its

location in the heart of the new Chancery Centre – a haven for fashion shops and designer labels. Decent coffee, attractive menu and a good spot for people-watching.

Rakinos, 1st floor, 35 High St, T09-358 3535. Hard to find but worth it. Great coffee and traditional café fare.

Verona, 169 Karangahape Rd, T09-307 0508. Perhaps The K'Rd's favourite café, colourful in character and clientele.

Vulcan, Vulcan Lane, T09-377 9899. Unpretentious old favourite.

North shore p82, map p83

Killarney Street Brasserie, 2 Killarney St, Takapuna, T09-489 9409, Mon-Fri 1130-late, Sat-Sun 1030-late, licensed. Extensive menu selection with servings to match.

Manuka, 49 Victoria Rd, Devonport, T09-445 7732, Mon-Fri 1100-late, Sat-Sun 0900-late, licensed. The pick of the bunch in Devonport with its much-loved wood-fired pizzas and laid-back atmosphere.

Monsoon, 71 Victoria Rd, T09-4454263, daily dinner. Reliable, value Thai/Malaysian option offering both eat-in and takeaway.

Watermark, 33 King Edward Parade, T09-4460622, dinner daily from 1800, Sun for brunch. A risky concept outside the centre, Watermark offers buffet dinners at a set price of $26. The Sun brunch is also popular at $16. Seems to be working and quite classy too.

City East p84, map p93

Antoine's, 333 Parnell Rd, Parnell, T09-379 8756, dinner Mon-Sat, lunch Mon-Fri, licensed. Parnell's best and on a par with anything in the city. French cuisine with some firm favourites with the regulars – the duck is exquisite. Very professional.

Cibo, 91 St Georges Bay Rd, T09-303 9660, lunch Mon-Fri, dinner Mon-Sat. A long established favourite located in-of all things-an old chocolate factory. There is no doubting the class here, the smooth service or culinary talents of lauded chef Kate Fay. Good wine list and great outdoor seating.

Hammerheads, 19 Tamaki Drive, Orakei, T09-521 4400, daily 1130-2200, www.hammerheads.co.nz, licensed. A tourist favourite. Right next to Kelly Tarlton's Underwater World, with decent seafood and fine harbour views.

Mikano, 1 Solent St, Mechanics Bay, T09-309 9514, Mon-Fri 1130-late, Sat 1730-late, Sun 1000-late, licensed. A bit out the way, next to the helicopter base and container wharves, but with a great view across the harbour and serving a very high standard of mainly Asian-inspired fare. Well worth the trip. Has maintained a good reputation for years.

Iguacu, 269 Parnell Rd, Parnell, T09 358 4804, www.iguacu.co.nz, Mon-Fri 1100-0100, Sat-Sun 1000-0100. Licensed. Parnell's 'place to be seen', especially with the younger set. Not for the casually dressed or happily single female, but still immensely popular. Menu from snack-size to feast. Top breakfast spot.

Java Room, 317 Parnell Rd, Parnell, T09-366 1606, dinner Mon-Sat 1800-late, licensed and BYO. Fine selection of Asian and Pacific Rim cuisine at affordable prices.

Karin Japanese, 237 Parnell Rd, Parnell, T09-356 7101, daily lunch 1200-1400, dinner 1800-2200. Parnell's Japanese offering with all the traditional favourites and prices.

Lava, 425 Tamaki Drive, St Heliers, T09-575 9969, daily for lunch and dinner and for the inevitable beach view breakfast and brunches on Sun, licensed. Formerly 'Halo' and 'Saints', this is yet another reinvention upon this particular patch of the waterfront. The removal from the ecclesiastical labels may be a cardinal sin but the fare remains heavenly.

Oh Calcutta, 151 Parnell Rd, Parnell, T09-3779090. Up against stiff opposition in the city, Oh Calcutta consistently ranks as one of the finest in all departments from food quality to ambience and service. Right in the heart of the Parnell restaurant strip.

Rikka, 73 Davis Cres, Newmarket, T09-522 5277, daily 1200-1500, 1800-2400, licensed. An offshoot of the city centre branch and no less popular. Fantastic interior. The Tenshin section of the menu is more expensive but highly recommended if you are new to Japanese food.

Tonino's, 35 Tamaki Drive, T09-528 8935, daily lunch and dinner, licensed and BYO. A good value Italian choice in Mission Bay, with generous pasta dishes and standard pizza choices. Dine-in or takeaway.

Burger Fuel, 164 Parnell Rd, T09-377 3345. One of several in a chain fast reproducing around the city which is a sure sign that their generous range of burgers from half-cow to veggie are going down exceptionally well.

La Bocca, 251 Parnell Rd, Parnell, T09-375 0083, dinner Mon-Sat 1800-late (summer only), licensed. A fine laid-back Italian café especially noted for its seafood.

Portofino, 156 Parnell Rd, Parnell, T09-373 3740, daily for lunch and dinner, licensed and BYO. Long-standing favourite, reliable and affordable, again, Italian style.

Verve, 311 Parnell Rd, Parnell, T09 379 2860, daily from 0730, dinner Tue-Sat, licensed. A great 'all rounder' in every way both day and night. Always busy and a top breakfast spot.

White Lady, corner of Broadway and Remuera Rd, Newmarket, open all night. The sister of the infamous **White Lady** in the city centre. It sees its fair share of loonies in the wee hours trying to read the extensive menu, but the stalwart owners remain in control.

Cafés

Café Jazz, 563 Remuera Rd, Remuera, T09-5240356. A good place to go if you're in Remuera and need a coffee or lunch.

Kenzie, 17a Remuera Rd, T09-522 2647. Good 'chill over a coffee and watch the world go by' establishment on the edge of busy Broadway.

Rosehip, 82 Gladstone, Parnell, T09-369 1182. A bit pricey, but remains a popular haunt, well-situated next to the rose gardens and away from busy Parnell Rd. Good coffee.

Trinity, 107 Parnell Rd, Parnell, T09-300 3042. Prompt no-nonsense service and a good hearty breakfast. Fine coffee.

City West *p86, map p87*

Prego, 226 Ponsonby Rd, Ponsonby, T09-376 3095, lunch and dinner daily, licensed. A favourite with the locals who know they will get good food and good service. Italian-style menu. Great wood-fired pizza and fish.

Andiamo, 194 Jervois Rd, Herne Bay, T09-3787811, Mon-Fri from 1130-late, Sat-Sun from 1000-late, licensed. Always busy, with a particularly fine all-day breakfast selection.

Chandelier, 152 Ponsonby Rd, T09-360 9315. Sited next to the infamous **SPQR** (see cafés, below), the Chandelier restaurant and lounge bar is predictably and marvellously over the top with Italian-inspired decor and food to draw in a mainly avant-garde clientele. Quite an experience.

GPK, 262 Ponsonby Rd, Ponsonby, T09-360 1113, Mon-Fri 1100-late, Sat-Sun 0900-late, licensed. One of Auckland's most successful restaurants, with another branch in Mt Eden. Always busy with a lively atmosphere. The bar is as popular as the menu.

The Hunting Lodge, Waikoukou Valley Rd, Waimauku, T09-411 8259, lunch and dinner Wed-Sun (daily in summer). Licensed. Plugged as Auckland's top countryside restaurant, serving traditional fare like beef and lamb and set in the heart of vineyard country. Popular after a day's wine tasting.

Rocco, 23 Ponsonby Rd, Ponsonby, T09-360 6262, Mon-Fri from 1200-late and Sun from 1800. Enjoys a reputation for consistently good Spanish and Italian inspired dishes with a specialization in game and seafood. Cosy private dining upstairs.

Vinnies, 166 Jervois Rd, Herne Bay, T09-376 5597, daily from 1830, licensed. This is considered to be one of Auckland's finest, now under the care of ex-Hilton (White Restaurant) executive chef, Geoff Scott. A special menu is available allowing you to sample a wide variety of dishes. Professional in style, quality and presentation. Book ahead.

Dizengoff, 256 Ponsonby Rd, Ponsonby, T09-360 0108, daily 0700-1700, unlicensed. A fine counter service operation offering takeaway or sit-in items that attract a wide-ranging clientele, making it a great spot for people-watching. Light food with a Jewish influence. The breakfasts (especially the salmon and eggs on toast) are delicious.

Empress Garden, 227 Jervois Rd, Herne Bay, T09-376 5550, lunch and dinner daily, licensed. One of the city's oldest and most popular Chinese restaurants set out of the way in suburban Herne Bay. The Peking duck comes highly recommended. Good value.

Lord Ponsonby's Deli, 267 Ponsonby Rd, Ponsonby, T09-3765260. A fine deli, ideal for picnic takeaways.

Ponsonby Fresh Fish and Chip Co, 127 Ponsonby Rd, Ponsonby, T09-378 7885, daily 1100-2130. A Ponsonby institution. Although the portions have gradually decreased in size, the quality has pretty much stayed the same. Try the local Pacific fish. Always busy, and it is takeaway only, so expect to place an order then return about 20 mins later. Good vegetarian burgers.

Ponsonby Pies, 288 Ponsonby Rd, Ponsonby, T09-361 3685, daily 0900-1700. You must not leave Auckland without trying a

'Ponsonby Pie'. This is the base for an operation that distributes the famous pies to food outlets citywide. The fillings are fresh, imaginative and for $3 you can't go wrong.

Shahi Café, 26 Jervois Rd, Ponsonby, T09-378 8896, daily, lunch 1200-1400, dinner from 1800-late, licensed and BYO. The 3rd Shahi venue. Small, romantic and intimate.

Cafés

Atlas Power Café, 285 Ponsonby Rd, Ponsonby, T09-3601295. A predominantly gay venue serving great coffee.

Atomic Café, 121 Ponsonby Rd, Ponsonby, T09-3764954. A Ponsonby favourite serving good coffee in lively, pleasant surroundings.

Café Cezanne, 296 Ponsonby Rd, Ponsonby, T09-3763338. Very popular with students and backpackers. Good hearty fare with the classic Ponsonby atmosphere.

Open Late Café, 134a Ponsonby Rd, Ponsonby, T09-03764466, Sun-Wed 1830-0200, Thu till 0300, Fri-Sat till 0400. A reliable old favourite, not so much for its food as its hours. The place to go if you have got carried away after a long night out and want some café-style fare. Service could be better though.

SPQR, 150 Ponsonby Rd, Ponsonby, T09-360 1710, Mon-Fri 1100-late, Sat-Sun 1000-late, licensed. One of the oldest and trendiest places in Ponsonby, a favourite with many for food and beverages and deservingly so. More mince than a butcher's dog and a very high posing quotient to boot – daahling.

City South p88

Roasted Addiqtion, 487 New North Rd, Kingsland, T09-815 0913. Mon 0700-1600, Tue-Fri 0700-2200, Sat-Sun 0800-1700 Increasingly popular both for its fine coffee, music and highly imaginative evening menu.

Sitar Indian Restaurant, 397 Mount Eden Rd, Mt Eden, T09-630 0321, dinner Tue-Sun from 1730, lunch Tue-Fri 1200-1400, licensed and BYO. The most popular Indian restaurant south of the city centre.

Crucial Traders, 473 New North Rd, Kingsland, T09-846 3288. Laid-back café favourite for those tired of the Ponsonby scene.

Frazers, 434 Mount Eden Rd, Mt Eden, T09-630 6825. A popular spot for locals, students and backpackers. Good selection of cheap light meals and fine coffee.

● Pubs, bars and clubs

Sadly, when it comes to good pubs, Auckland is really not in the same league as most other cities of its size. Only in the last decade has the city, and New Zealand as a whole, woken up to the fact that the 'ashtray built into the table, rugby boys and jugs of insipid beer until you're sick' establishments were not everybody's 'pint of ale'. However, whether you are an ardent trendsetter, an avid Guinness drinker or cocktail specialist it can still perhaps provide a pub that will suit your needs. With the arrival of the new millennium you can at least find most things, from gay venues, quiet intellectual establishments and, on occasions, even good beer. Pubs are well distributed around the city but are concentrated mainly in the city centre and the trendy suburbs of Parnell, Newmarket and Ponsonby, with the occasional desirable establishment lying further afield. Centred in High St and Vulcan Lane are a number of Auckland's top spots.

Most nightclubs in Auckland are based in the city centre on Queen St, Vulcan Lane, High St and Karangahape Rd (or K' Rd – noted especially for its gay and transvestite scene). Some venues in Ponsonby and Parnell, although not considered clubs, also remain open well into the wee hours with less emphasis on actual dancing. For the most up-to-date information surrounding venues and gigs refer to the free *Auckland Grove Guide*, available from the VIC, www.grooveguide.co.nz. Most of the clubs are open nightly, warming up towards the end of the week before going off at the weekend. Venues usually have a cover charge of about $5-15, and drinks will be at least $6. Dress codes often apply. Pubs vary greatly with their attempts at last orders, but generally speaking the solid drinking stops from midnight to 0300, and from then on it's clubbing till dawn.

City centre *p76, map p78*

Pubs and bars
Belgian Beer Café (Occidental), 6-8 Vulcan Lane, T09-300 6226. With Queen St clubs and a number of major backpacker hostels nearby, this bar rages well into the night; popular by day and serves a fine lunch.

Tries hard to push the Euro feel with favourable results.

Danny Doolans, on the Viaduct Basin, T09-358 2554. Considered by many to be the best Irish pub in the city. Goes off like a rocket at weekends. Particularly good for live music.

Deschlers, 17 High St, T09-379 6811. Also close to Queen St, this is a cocktail lounge with lounge lizard music. A big favourite at the weekend with trendy young things with wandering eyes.

Dispensary, corner of Victoria St West and Hobson St, T09-309 2118. Although this 24-hr pub and its decor are nothing spectacular, this can be a very interesting establishment in the wee hours when all the others are shut. From about 0300 the place fills with real party animals and clocked-off bar persons, all with a story to tell.

The Empire, corner of Nelson and Victoria sts, T09-373 4389, www.theempire.co.nz. A fine-looking establishment and a real party spot at weekends, offering live music at night and a fine espresso by day in its either frantic or peaceful courtyard.

Float, Shed 9, Princess Wharf, T09-307 1344, www.float.co.nz. Trendy bar that is cold and clinically decked out. It is designed to host a weekly TV sports programme, and with the cleverly designed fold-away stands of seating can also house a big crowd while presenting live sporting events on a big screen. Definitely for the trendy or sports orientated.

The Loaded Hog, on the Viaduct Basin, T09-366 6491. The Viaduct Basin, which acted as the yacht base for both the Whitbread and 2 America's Cup regattas, is right outside its doors. Due to its location it has always been popular and is frequented mainly by the well-to-do and trendy both day and night. Its huge interior and interesting agricultural and sailing theme decor is worth a look. It also brews its own beer and serves good food.

Minus 5, Princess Wharf, T09-377 6702, www.minus5.co.nz. An extraordinary concept in trendy cocktail bars Minus 5 is one of 2 in the country (the other is in Queenstown) that takes 'cool' to the literal level with a bar made of ice. The decor (all of it bar the bottles) is all fashioned from ice and include some impressive sculptures. Obviously it is not a place to linger too long and it is touted more as a one-off experience rather than a regular with a pool table. No locals here propping up the bar – though the thought is highly amusing. Tours last about 30 mins and come replete with a loan of cosy jackets and gloves. Entry from $27 (includes one drink). **The Muddy Farmer**, 14 Wyndham St, T09-336 1265. Similar in size, popularity and decor as the **Loaded Hog** and **Danny Doolans** but not so well placed. The bar is great but the beer is expensive. **Soul**, T09-356 7249, on the Viaduct Basin. With its outdoor seating, this was the perfect place to see and be seen during the most recent America's Cup.

Clubs

On K' Rd, although most of the clubs are essentially gay orientated, they are very welcoming and popular with all comers. **Blend**, 324 K' Rd; **Club 4:20** (upstairs); and **Rising Sun** at 373 K' Rd, are popular spots and the dance music can be excellent especially if you go around 2400. Later on, as it gets busy, don't be surprised (or indeed offended) if a very large Pacific Island gentleman called Dina, in the most amazing scarlet number, high heels and a huge fruit filled hat, gives you a cheeky squirt with his large water pistol – it's all done in the best possible taste.

For more traditional options, head down to the bottom of Queen St and join the queues outside venues around Princess and Viaduct Wharf High St and Vulcan Lane. **Khuja Lounge**, 536 Queen St, is a popular options. Khuja Lounge has Latino, hip-hop and funk from DJs and live percussionists. **Papa Jack's Voodoo Lounge**, Vulcan Lane, is another busy venue with a large bar playing mixed dance music and rock.

North shore *p82, map p83*

The North Shore has its fair share of pubs and there are a number of favourites that certainly deserve to lure locals and visitors across the bridge. **The Northcote Tavern**, 37 Queen St, Northcote (almost immediately across the bridge), T09-480 7707. Very popular with locals, who flood in after work before disappearing into the vast suburbs of the shore city. It has 2 very relaxed contrasting

public and lounge bars, the latter with a fine Scots theme. Great Guinness. **Puhoi Hotel and Tavern**, just north of Orewa, 40 km north of the city, in the tiny settlement of Puhoi, T09-422 0812. More an experience than a watering hole. Very popular in summer and a favourite haunt of bikers on Sun afternoons. Basic, but richly decorated with a historic interior and interesting clientele. **Speakers Corner English Ale House**, 7 Anzac Rd, Browns Bay, T09-479 6060. Next to the beach and hugely popular for its range of fine, mainly British beers and good pub grub which is available daily from 1100.

City East *p84, map p93*

There are a number of bars nestled in among the cafés and shops of Parnell Rd, which are, along with those in Ponsonby, considered to be the trendiest drinking spots in the city. **The Claddagh**, 372 Broadway, T09-522 4410. Despite the ever-growing competition, this remains one of the most popular Irish pubs in the city. Opened in 1997 by the much-loved Noel and Margaret, originally from Limerick (and essentially the founders of Irish bars in Auckland) it is a wonderful homely Irish pub and a favourite haunt of Irish and Scottish immigrants. Throughout the day it is quiet and welcoming, but as the evening draws in and the locals start to arrive, it gets busier and busier, till eventually (especially at weekends) it is jumping to the sound of Irish music late into the night. Serves a fine pint of Guinness. **Iguacu**, 269 Parnell Rd, T09-3584985. The old favourite and the kick-off venue for others. From there just follow the designer clothing and the clickity-clack of high heels. **The Penny Black**, corner of Khyber Pass Rd and Broadway, T09-529 0050. An old favourite and one of a number of pubs in Newmarket, near Parnell.

City West *p86, map p87*

The main drinking venue west of the city centre is Ponsonby, which is similar to Parnell. Here trendy young things parade up and down the pavements and in and out of the many cafés and bars which fringe them. **Garage Bar**, 152 Ponsonby Rd, T09-378 8237. Ideal if you want to escape to a more intimate surrounding.

City South *p88*

Galbraith's Ale House, 2 Mount Eden Rd, Mt Eden, T09-379 3557. Used to be the old Grafton library and is perhaps the only notable pub south of the city centre. Within its grand exterior a fine range of foreign and home-brewed ales are available (at slightly elevated prices) as is a fine menu. Further south of here beyond Mt Eden and into the depths of South Auckland the pubs are not generally recommended.

🍸 Entertainment

The after-sunset scene in Auckland has improved greatly in recent years and now boasts some fine venues for dancing, comedy or huge outdoor summer events in the Auckland Domain; check out Infoline, T09-367 1077, the *New Zealand Herald*, www.nzherald.co.nz, or www.events auckland.com and www.nzlive.com. The free publication *What's Happening* is also a very useful guide, again available from information centres. For gigs and clubbing look out for *The Fix* magazine. For up-to-the-minute information and comment tune in to BFM's gig guide on the radio or net, www.95bfm.co.nz. The Edge, T0800-843334/T09-3075060, www.the-edge.co.nz, is a conglomerate of Auckland's main venues offering the top international performance events. It combines the Aotea Centre, The Civic, the Auckland Town Hall, and Aotea Square. The regularly updated event schedule leaflets is available from all the main information centres.

Cinemas

There are many cinema complexes throughout the city. New Zealand often receives films before Europe due to film distribution arrangements. For a daily guide to all venues and films consult the *New Zealand Herald* entertainment section, especially in the weekend edition. Admission is around $10, cheap nights are usually Tue.
Academy, 44 Lorne St, T09-373 2761, www.academy-cinema.co.nz. Specialist films.
Force Entertainment Centre, 291-297 Queen St, T09-915 2222. Has 12 screens.
Rialto, 169 Broadway, Newmarket, T09-369 2417.
Village Sky City Cinemas, 291 Queen St, T09-979 2400.

Comedy clubs

There is a healthy comedy scene in Auckland, and stand-up New Zealand humour (on stage) can be very similar to that found in the US and Europe. See the *New Zealand Herald* weekend edition for details. There is also an Annual Comedy Festival held in late Apr at various venues throughout the city. The main venues for comedy are: Classic Comedy and Bar, 321 Queen St, T09-373 4321; The Classic, 321 Queen St, T09-373 4321, www.covert theatre.com; and Silo Theatre, Lower Grays Av, T09-366 0339, www.silotheatre.co.nz.

Gay and lesbian

The Auckland gay scene is kept up to date with the *Express Magazine* ($2.50) which can be bought from the magazine outlets Magazzino (see Shopping, page 103). This publication and the local gossip can also be sought at the Pride Centre, T09-302 0590, www.pride.org.nz, or in the predominantly gay cafés and clubs. The main club venues are listed above in the clubbing section.
Useful websites: www.gaysainz.net.nz, www.gaynz.com, www.gaytravel.net.nz/ nz/auckland, and www.pride.org.nz.

Music venues

Auckland is well served with local, national and international gigs and venues. Most major concerts take place (usually just for one night in New Zealand) at the Aotea Centre, Western Springs, North Shore Events Centre or Ericsson Stadium. Although New Zealand is isolated, it's not unusual to hear Robbie Williams, Coldplay or to find oneself throwing one's knickers at an ageing Tom Jones. The traditional local music venues are described below. The best bet for schedules is the *New Zealand Herald*, www.nzherald.co.nz.

General and Irish folk and rock

The Claddagh, 372 Broadway, Newmarket, T09-522 4410. 'Diddly dee' jam session Mon nights, regular bands most others.
Danny Doolans, 204 Quay St, T09-358 2554.
Devonport Folk Music Club, The Bunker, Mt Victoria, Devonport, T09-445 2227. Mon night.

Jazz and Rhythm'n'Blues

Iguacu, 269 Parnell Rd, Parnell, T09-358 4804.
London Bar, corner of Wellesley and Queen sts, T09-373 3684, Fri-Sat.

Rock

Galatos, 17 Galatos St, T09-303 1928, Wed-Sat.
King's Arms, 59 France St, Newton, T09-373 3240.
Masonic Tavern, 29 King Edward Parade, Devonport, T09-445 0485, every Fri night.
Rose and Crown, 69 Customs St West.

Theatres

For listings see the entertainment section of the *New Zealand Herald*, particularly at the weekend. Tickets can be booked through **Tiketek**, T09-307 5000. For further information contact **Auckland Theatre Company**, T09-309 0390, www.atc.co.nz.
Bruce Mason Theatre, corner of Hurstmere Rd and the Promenade, Takapuna, North Shore, T09-488 2940.
The Herald Theatre, Aotea Sq, Queen St, T09-309 2677.
Maidment Theatre, corner of Princess St and Alfred St, at the university, T09-308 2383.
Silo Theatre, Lower Grays Av, T09-366 0339, www.silotheatre.co.nz. 'Off-the-wall' theatre.
Sky City Theatre, Sky City, corner of Victoria and Federal sts, T09-912 6000/ T0800-759 2489, www.skycity.co.nz.

✪ Festivals and events

Some of the most popular national events include the free 'Opera' and 'Christmas in the Park'. Both are held annually in the Auckland Domain over the Christmas period (dates vary) and can attract up to 100,000 people. For details see www.eventsauckland.com, www.aucklandnz.com and www.nzlive.com.
Jan Sky City Starlight Symphony (last week). A free open-air event held annually (sometimes with a different name) in the Auckland Domain, attracts over 300,000. Auckland Anniversary Weekend Sailing Regatta held on the Waitemata Harbour.
Feb NZ Golf Open (1st week). Hero Festival, see www.hero.org.nz. New Zealand's oldest and biggest gay-fest. Not quite in the same league as Sydney's Mardis Gras but colourful and entertaining none the less with events like 'drag aerobics with Buffy and Bimbo' and 'wigs on the waterfront'. Mission Bay Jazz and Blues Streetfest (1st Sat), www.jazz andbluesstreetfest.com. Devonport Food and Wine Festival (3rd week), T09-353 4026, www.devonportwinefestival.co.nz.
Mar Pacifika Festival (2nd week), www.aucklandcity.govt.nz/pasifika. New Zealand's largest Pacific culture festival with food, arts, crafts and music performances. Round the Bays Fun Run, www.roundthe bays.co.nz, a charitable event that attracts over 7000 competitors. AK08 Festival (2nd week), www.aucklandfestival.co.nz, since its inception in 2004, this multifarious arts event has promised an impressive line up of international stars as well as local artists.
Mar-Apr Royal Easter Show, www.royaleastershow.co.nz.
Apr Waiheke Jazz Festival (see page 127). Sky Tower Vertical Challenge, competitors from 10 years old and up, race up and down the Sky Tower with mixed results. Rally of New Zealand, part of the world series; 25 stages start and finish in the city.
Jun New Zealand Boat Show, www.the newzealandboatshow.co.nz.
Jul Auckland International Film Festival (1st week), www.enzedff.co.nz.
Oct New Zealand Fashion Week, an increasingly high profile event and the annual showcase for established and up and coming designers. Plenty of hype, pretension, vacuous models and mass back-stabbings offstage.
Nov Ellerslie Flower Show (last week), the biggest horticultural event in the southern hemisphere, usually held at the Auckland Botanical Gardens.
Dec Christmas in the Park (4th week), a popular and free precursor to the Starlight Symphony, again held in the Auckland Domain and hugely popular.

If you fancy some serious retail therapy then Auckland should not disappoint. And given the currency exchange rates, if you are coming from Europe or the US, you are in for a treat. Whatever you're after, Auckland has it all. The most popular shopping spots are to be found in the city centre, and also in Parnell and Newmarket to the east, and Ponsonby to the west. Most major suburbs have the ubiquitous mall that provides both quality and quantity.

If you are looking for products specific to New Zealand, whet your appetite by visiting the **New Zealand Trade Centre**, 26 Albert St, City, T09-366 6879. Although you cannot actually buy things here, it will give you an insight into what is available. The *Official Auckland Shopping Guide* and individual leaflets are available from VICs, and there are even a few specialist shopping tours available.

Art
There are plenty of quality art galleries in the city, and if you are serious about buying or viewing get the detailed *Auckland Gallery Guide* or the *Auckland Art Precinct Map* from the main VICs and allow a full day. Many Auckland artists reside in the western suburbs in and around Titirangi and the Waitakeres. The VIC can supply the relevant brochures should you wish to investigate in detail. Pacific and especially New Zealand art is unique, appealing and colourful – reflecting the very nature of New Zealand itself. The best gallery venues are Parnell (ask about the **Parnell Arts Trail**), Devonport, Titirangi and the city centre. Some quality original artwork is also available on the 2nd floor of the Auckland International Airport at cheaper prices.

Books
Borders, 291-297 Queen St, T09-309 3377, open until 2200, dwarfs the largest of the more traditional stores like **Dymocks**, 246 Queen St, T09-379 9919, or **Whitcoulls**, 210 Queen St, T09-356 5400. These majors should meet all your traditional needs, along with **Paper Plus** and **Books and More**, which also have smaller outlets in most major suburbs and shopping malls. For smaller, more personal outlets try:

Auckland Map Centre, National Bank Building, 209 Queen St, City, T09-309 7725.
The Children's Bookshop, corner of Jervois and St Mary Rds, Ponsonby, T09-376 7283. Travel books and maps.
Hard to Find (But Worth the Effort), 171 The Mall, T09-634 4340. Has a delightful rabbit warren-like interior and is (hard to find your way out) an experience in itself.
Magazzino outlets at 123 Ponsonby Rd, T09-376 6933, and at 6 Morrow St, Newmarket, T09-524 0604. Magazines.
Unity Bookshop, 19 High St, Auckland City, T09-307 0731.
The Woman's Bookshop, 105 Ponsonby Rd, Ponsonby, T09-376 4399.

Camping and tramping gear
Although there is a good selection of camping and tramping clothes, boots and equipment to be found in Auckland and New Zealand, there does not seem to be the range or the quality available in Europe or the US. However, the best places to try are:
Bivouac Outdoor, 210 Queen St, City, T09-366 1966, and 300 Broadway, Newmarket, T09-529 2298.
Doyles, 66 Hobson St, CBD, T09-377 6998. Good value.
Kathmandu, 151 Queen St, City, T09-309 4615, and 200 Victoria St West, City, T09-377 7560.
Tent Town, 399 New North Rd, Kingsland, T09-846 1076.

Clothing
Most of the leading international brands and labels can be found in the city centre especially in the new **Chancery Mall** on Chancery Lane (off High St, CBD). O'Connell and **High St** in the CBD are also famous for designer fashions – look out for Feline, Tanya Carlson, World, Karen Walker, and Morrison Hotel. Newmarket and Ponsonby are also other favourite spots. There are specialist boutiques on Ponsonby Rd including **Sabine**, **Wallace Rose** and **State of Grace**. The best factory shops are in the **Dressmart** outlets in suburban Onehunga. For listings get hold of a copy of the *Auckland Fashion Guide* from the VIC. To source a comprehensive list

of clothing stores and other shops in Newmarket visit www.newmarket.net.nz.
Atrium on Elliot, Queen St, T09-358 3052.
Barkers, Queen St, T0800-808700. Menswear.
Country Clothing, Queen St, T09-366 3940.
George Harrison, Atrium on Elliott, T09-366 7788. Menswear.
Kate Sylvester, High St CBD and Newmarket, T09-524 8872. Womenswear.
Little Brother, 5 High St, T09-377 6536. Menswear.
Rodd and Gun throughout the city, T09-522 0607. Menswear.
Saks, 254 Broadway, Newmarket, T09-520 7630. Menswear.
Zambesi, T09-377 7220, outlets throughout the city.
Zebrano, Newmarket, T09-523 2500. Womenswear.

Gifts, jewellery and souvenirs

Auckland city centre has souvenir shops everywhere packed with everything from cute furry kiwis in All Black shirts to the omnipresent bone or greenstone Maori pendants – which, traditionally you are supposed to buy for someone else, not yourself. Parnell and K' Rd are also recommended. But, the more discerning buyer should wait to see the smaller more provincial souvenir shops which tend to offer more specialist, unique stock. If you like the look of Kauri or other wood crafts and are heading for Northland wait and buy there, it may well be better quality and also cheaper.
Aotea New Zealand Souvenirs, Lower Albert St, City, T09-379 5022.
Artisanz, Victoria Park Market, Victoria Park, City, T09-303 1116.
Craftworld, T09-831 0277, 15 mins from the city centre, in West Auckland in **Westgate Shopping Centre**, Fernhill Drive, Massey. One of the largest craft shops.
The Elephant House, 237 Parnell Rd, Parnell, T09-309 8740. One of the best craft shops.
Great Kiwi Yarns, 107 Queen St, T09-308 9013. For original knitwear.
The Great New Zealand Shop, Downtown Shopping Centre, Queen St, T09-377 3009. For the classic Kiwi souvenirs.
NZ Fine Jewellery, 239 Queen St, City, T09-307 2053. For quality New Zealand jewellery.
Touch the Earth, Downtown Shopping Centre, Queen St, T09-366 4474.

United Tongan Church, about 1 km down Richmond Rd, off Ponsonby Rd. On Sat mornings the original Tapa Cloths for sale are occasionally displayed outside. They are reasonably priced, light, easy to pack and interestingly original.

Markets

The most famous market in Auckland is the **Victoria Park Market**, opposite Victoria Park, just a few mins' walk west of the city centre., www.victoria-park-market.co.nz. It provides 7 days a week shopping with a variety of outlets from shops to stalls that expand into the car park on Sat. There are a wide variety of products with a market theme, a number of good cafés, a food hall and a pub, all in pleasant surroundings.

K'Rd (Karangahape Rd), at the southern-most end of Queen St, is an excellent area for unusual shops, particularly Polynesian clothing and craft items. The Sat morning market on the bridge over the motorway can also produce the odd unusual bargain.

If you would prefer a less commercial, raw Polynesian feel then an excursion to the **Otara Market** in the rather dodgy suburb of Otara in South Auckland is interesting and good for a wander (see page 89).

Photography

Digital camera equipment and film is readily available throughout the city, but for specialist equipment try **Camera and Camera**, 162 Queen St, City, T09-303 1879.
PCL, 86 Parnell Rd, Parnell, T09-309 8090.
The Photo Warehouse, 154 Queen St, City, T09-309 0715.

Shopping malls

Downtown Shopping Centre, 11-19 Customs St, City, T09-978 5265.
Manukau Shopping Centre, corner of Great South Rd and Wiri Station Rd, Manukau City, T09-978 5300. The largest shopping centre in New Zealand.
The Plaza Pakuranga, Main Highway, Pakuranga, T09-572 0264.
St Luke's Shopping Centre, 80 St Luke's Rd, Mt Albert, T09-978 6000.
Shore City Galleria, corner of Lake Rd and Como St, Takapuna, T09-978 6300.
West City Shopping Centre, Catherine St, Henderson, T09-978 6700.

Sports

Quality sports stores can be found throughout the city and suburbs, but in this land of rugby and for that world-famous sporting souvenir – the All Blacks Jersey – head no further than:

The Rialto Centre, 165 Broadway, Newmarket, T09 520 0766.

Maritime Museum Shop on the waterfront, page 80. For all things nautical, and for the America's Cup souvenir and clothing range.

▲ Activities and tours

Bridge climb

For anyone who has been to Sydney and seen the Sydney Harbour Bridge, let alone made the ascent of that world famous 'Bridge Climb', the mere sight of Auckland's equivalent will bring about a wry smile if not the full 'paah'. However, this is Auckland, not Sydney, and besides, the views are still amazing. Night trips can also be arranged.

Harbour Bridge Experience (Bridge Climb), Westhaven Reserve, T09-361 2000, www.ajhackett.com. 1½ hrs from $65. Bridge climb and bungee combo from $140.

Bungee jumping and sky walking

There are 2 opportunities for bungee jumping in New Zealand's largest city, both highly unique and perhaps – given the nation's obsession with the sport – inevitable.

A J Hackett, T09-3612000/T0800-462 8649, www.ajhackett.com. The newest jump opportunity, from the Harbour Bridge, from $85, child (10-15) $85. Spectators can do the 'express climb' to the jump platform for $15, Bungee and bridge climb combo, from $140. Owned and operated by the undisputed leaders in the field, it may not be the highest or the best, but it is still a lot of fun.

Sky Jump, T0800-759586, www.skyjump.co.nz, from $195 (maximum weight 125 kg). This is the original and much talked about jump from just above the restaurant of the Sky Tower. But there is a 'catch' (thankfully, or sadly, depending how you look at it). Given the incredible jump height of 192 m, not to mention all that nasty hard concrete and people watching you below, it is not possible to jump conventionally with an elastic cord attached to the ankles and to do the 'yoyo' bit. Obviously if you did, in this scenario, you would probably end up like Garfield the ginger cat plastered against somebody's office window. So be advised, watch what is involved first and note that it is a cable-controlled

descent in the horizontal, not vertical, position. That said, at 20 seconds and 75 kph it is should still get the adrenaline pumping. **Sky Screamer**, based next to Atrium on Elliot on Victoria St, www.reversebungy.com. From $35 (2nd launch $15) is certainly aptly named and is your chance to be strapped into a seat and launched at high speed heavenwards (in a sort of reverse bungee), having left your stomach and your Sunday-best expletives behind. Spectating is almost as good as taking part.

Sky Walk, T0800-759586, www.sky walk.co.nz. The latest Sky Tower adventure – and yet another opportunity to soil the proverbial pants – in essence, involves walking around the tower's pergola (or ring) on a 1-m walkway with 192-m drop and nothing but thin air on either side. An overhead safety tether travels above. Not for the fainthearted. From $110 .

Vertigo, T09-368 1917/T0800-483784, www.4vertigo.com. This is the exciting opportunity to climb inside the mast of t he Sky Tower to the 'crows nest' – at 300 m, the highest publicly accessible, man-made platform in the southern hemisphere. The view on a clear day is simply unforgettable. 2 hrs from $145, child $75 (14 or over), Recommended.

Canyoning

Although Wanaka is generally considered the country's canyoning capital, the streams and waterfalls of the Waitakere Ranges west of the city and the Coromandel Peninsula provide some exciting opportunities.

Awol Adventures, T0800-462965, www.awol adventures.co.nz. Half- or full- day trips, with overnight excursions, from $135.

Canyonz, T0800-422696, www.canyonz.co.nz. 3-hr excursions with beach visit from $175 and an extended 5-hr trip to Coromandel from $225.

See www.climb.co.nz or www.indoor climbing.co.nz for details. Auckland has plenty of opportunities, both indoors and outside. **Mt Eden Quarry** offers excellent climbing on basalt rock cliffs.

Extreme Edge, www.extremeedge.co.nz. One of the largest indoor rock climbing walls in New Zealand.

University of Auckland Recreation Centre, 17 Symonds St, T373 7599 ext 87888, www.auckland.ac.nz/recreation. Has a cutting edge indoor climbing wall.

Cruises

A cruise around the inner harbour, or better still, out into the Hauraki Gulf, gives you the opportunity to experience Auckland's 'other-and-far-more-attractive-half' and is highly recommended. Once out there you will see why Auckland is considered such a yachties' heaven. The waterfront and Viaduct Basin is the place to 'cruise shop'.

360-Discovery (Kawau Kat) Cruises, T0800-888006, www.360discovery.co.nz, or ask at the VIC. A range of harbour cruise options as well as day trips to Kawau Island and the Coromandel Peninsula.

Dolphin and Whale Safari, T09-357 6032/ T0800-397567, www.dolphinsafari.co.nz. Trips depart from the Viaduct Harbour daily at 0930 (year round) with an additional summer sailing at1600, cost $140, child $100. 6-hr whale- and dolphin-watching trips are often in conjunction with university research projects, so there is no shortage of knowledge. Although there is reputedly a 90% success rate, the Hauraki is not generally as productive as many other sites around New Zealand like the Bay of Islands, Whakatane or the great sea mammal capital, Kaikoura. What is guaranteed, however, is stunning scenery and an entertaining day-long cruise.

Fullers, Fullers Cruise Centre, Ferry Building, waterfront, T09-367 9111, www.fullers.co.nz. The main operator offering everything from a 2-hr harbour cruise (taking in the Viaduct Basin, Devonport, the Harbour Bridge etc) from $31, child $16, to island transportation and stop-overs (see Hauraki Islands, page 120). The day trip to Tiritiri Matangi Bird Sanctuary is particularly recommended.

Ocean Rafting, Viaduct Basin, T0800-801193, www.oceanrafting.co.nz.

Offering the 'fast' cruise option on board a rigid inflatable with trips ranging from a 30-min whirl around the inner harbour from $35, child $15, to a 2-hr trip round the outer islands, from $130, child $70.

Golf

Auckland, like much of New Zealand, is a golfer's heaven. Green fees are very reasonable ($35-50). Club hire is available at most courses. Mid-range, reasonably quiet and scenic courses include **Hauapi**, Riverhead, West Auckland, T09-412 8809; **Murawai**, west coast beaches, T09-411 8454; and **South Head**, West Auckland, Kaipara Heads, T09-420 2838; the latter is a good 45-min drive, but the course is a delight.

For more expensive, high-profile courses try: **Formosa**, Beachlands, South Auckland, T09-536 5895; **Gulf Harbour**, Whangaparaoa Peninsula, T09-428 1380, www.gulf-harbour. co.nz; or **Titirangi**, West Auckland, T09-827 5749.

Hang-gliding

Aqua Air, T0508-438 4444, www.get high.co.nz. Conventional tandem hang-gliding from $120, but also the rather novel concept of water take-off and landings.

Horse trekking and stud visits

Horse trekking operations are generally focused on the west coast beaches particularly around Murawai or Parakai.
South Kaipara Horse Treks, T09-420 2835, www.horserides.co.nz. Half or full day and overnight from $75.
Tasman Rides, T09-420 8603, www.tas manrides.co.nz. 1-4 hrs from $30.

Hot air ballooning

Although Christchurch and the Canterbury Plains is considered 'ballooning central' in New Zealand Auckland can still offer some fine city and harbourscapes during the 1-hr standard dawn runs, from $280 for 2.
Balloon Expeditions, T09-416 8590, www.balloonexpeditions.co.nz.
Balloon Safaris, T09-415 8289, www.balloonsafaris.co.nz.

Kayaking

Canoe and Kayak Company, T09-473 0036, www.canoeandkayak.co.nz. Based on the north shore beaches, offering river and coastal adventures from $49. There's even eminently attractive 'Paddle to the Pub' option, from $59.

Fergs Kayaks, 12 Tamaki Drive, T09- 529 2230, www.fergskayaks.co.nz. From $75, departs at 0900 or 1600, 6-7 hrs. Based in the city itself, long established and owned by Olympic champion Ian Ferguson. A range of trips on offer including the deservedly popular day or night guided trips to Rangitoto Island. Independent hire available.

Given Auckland's proximity to Waiheke Island (page 122) and the beautiful, varied coastline it is no surprise to find several operators based there, including the following who offer a range of half- to full-day or overnight guided trips from $75-240. Independent hire also available. Try **Kayak Company**, T09-372 2112, www.thekayak company.co.nz, or **Ross Adventures**, T09-372 5550, www.kayakwaiheke.co.nz.

Leisure centres

Village on Broadway Cinemas, Broadway, Newmarket, T09-520 0806. Olympic pools and fitness centre, next to the cinema complex.

Quad biking and 4WD

It would be rude not to have a quad bike operator and some 4WD adventures somewhere around the city and the west coast beaches and forest trails lend themselves to the pursuit.

4 Track Adventures, Woodhill Forest, T0800-487225, www.4trackadventures.co.nz. Half- to full-day trips covering 15-55 km, from $125.

Extreme 4WD Adventures, Helensville, T0800-493238/T09-420 3050, www.extreme 4wd.co.nz. Self-drive, $75 for 2 hrs.

Rugby

Eden Park Stadium, Reimers Av, Kingsland, T02-9815 5551, www.edenpark.co.nz. New Zealand's largest stadium, hosting up to 48,000 spectators for major rugby and cricket matches.

Sailing

Naturally, there are many opportunities to experience the Hauraki in the best possible way – by sail. Options range from catamarans to racing yachts. The VIC has full listings. 2 of the most popular vessels are the racing yachts of SailNZ and the tall ship Soren Larsen.

SailNZ, T09-359 5987, www.sailnz.co.nz, offers cruises and match races between authentic America's Cup racing yachts, the NZL 40 and NZL 41. A basic, yet exhilarating 2-hr sailing trip costs from $135, child $110; the full-on race between the 2, during which you have the opportunity to participate, costs $195, child $175. There are also all-inclusive sailing trips to the Bay of Islands with one offering 'the ultimate coastal maxi adventure' with a 2-night excursion on board the Lion New Zealand, once owned by Sir Peter Blake. Given the location and the history, this is the ideal opportunity to indulge.

Soren Larsen, T09-411 8755, www.soren larsen.co.nz. This vessel has been gracing the gulf for a number of years and starred in the TV hit series The Onedin Line. There are a number of multi-day sailing options where you can take the helm or help raise sails, or simply kick back and watch. 5-night voyages to the Bay of Islands from $480.

Skiing and snowboarding

Snowplanet, Small Rd, Silverdale, T09-427 0044, www.snowplanet.co.nz, daily 1000-2200. Indoor skiing, snowboarding and air-boarding (a high-tech air filled bodyboard for snow), 1hr from $29 child $24, day-pass $49 child $44. Lessons available. Also has a neat café overlooking the slope.

Surfing

The best surfing is on the west coast beaches. The Piha breaks are internationally renowned. **Surf and Beach Tours**, T09-832 9622, www.newzealandsurftours.co.nz. A reputable outfit offering surfing trips and lessons to the west coast beaches from $99

Swimming

Birkenhead on the Shore, T09-418 3560; **Olympic Pool**, Newmarket, 77 Broadway, T09-522 4414; the **Tepid Baths**, Viaduct Basin, 100 Customs St West, T09-379 4745 and the thermal complexes at Parakai and Waiwera.

Tour operators

There are many coach tours to key locations including the Bay of Islands, Waitomo and Rotorua, ranging from simple day tours to activity and accommodation packages. Shop around and compare prices. The VIC has full details. Good local tour companies include:

Auckland Wine Tasting Tours, T09-630 1540, www.winetrailtours.co.nz. Explore the ever-increasing range of vineyards and vintages springing up around the region, from $175 (includes lunch).

Bush and Beach, T09-837 4130/ T0800-423 224, www.bushandbeach.co.nz. Specializing in insightful and flexible eco-trips to the west coast beaches and Waitakeres, from $110.

Coromandel Explorer Tours, T07-866 3506, www.coromandeltours.co.nz. For those short of time, or without their own wheels. Day tours of the peninsula (0800-1930) from $220, 2 days from $380, 4 days from $400 (excluding accommodation). Recommended.

Geo Tours, T09-525 3991, www.geotours .co.nz. Ideal opportunity to join a geological/ natural history-based tour in a region and city dominated by volcanic features. Half-day from $90, full day from $120 (2-day Rotorua tour from $410).

Potiki Adventures, T09-845 5932, www.potikiadventures.co.nz. Excellent Maori-themed adventure tours, with a range of fixed or custom activities from hiking to Marae stays. Their 'Auckland Orientation Trip' (8 hrs from $145) is a fine introduction to the city, region and country from the Maori perspective. Recommended.

Walking

The best walking opportunities in the region are to be found at the **Wiatakeres** and **west coast beaches**, see the relevant areas for details. Regional parks and islands like **Rangitoto** and **Tiritiri Matangi** also offer excellent walking opportunities. See Hauraki Islands section page 120, or consult the VIC.

Arataki Information Centre, Scenic Drive, Titirangi, T09-366 2000, is a fine place to gather information before a walk.

⊖ Transport

Air

Air New Zealand flies regularly to most provincial centres including **Wellington** (10 daily, 1 hr, $100-240), and **Christchurch** (18 daily, 1 hr 20 mins, $80-190). Tickets are best secured in advance on the internet.

Domestic airline offices

Air New Zealand, corner of Customs and Queen St, City, T09-357 3000/T0800-737000, www.airnewzealand.co.nz.

Great Barrier Airlines, Auckland International Airport (Domestic Terminal), T09-275 9120/T0800-900600.

Great Barrier Express, Auckland International Airport (Domestic Terminal), T0800-900600/T09-275 9120, www.greatbarrierairlines.co.nz.

Mountain Air, T0800-222123/T09-256 7025, www.mountainair.co.nz.

International airline offices

Aerolineas Argentinas, 15th floor ASB Centre, 135 Albert St, T09-379 3675.

American Airlines, 191 Queen St, City, T0800-887999.

Air Canada, Level 5, 120 Albert St, City, T09-969 7470.

Air Pacific, Sofrana House, 396 Queen St, T09-379 2404, www.airpacific.com.

Air Vanuatu, 2nd floor, West Plaza Building, corner Customs and Albert St, City, T03-733435, www.airvanuatu.com.

British Airways, T09-966 9777, www.ba.com.

Cathay Pacific, 11th floor, National Bank Tower, 205 Queen St, T09-379 0861.

Freedom Air, T0800-600500.

Garuda Indonesia, Westpac Trust Tower, 120 Albert St, T09-366 1862, www.garuda-indonesia.com.

Japan Airlines, Westpac Trust Tower, 120 Albert St, T09-379 9906.

Korean Airlines, 120 Albert St, City, T09-9142000, www.koreanair.com.

Lufthansa Airlines, T09-303 1529.

Malaysia Airlines, 120 Albert St, T09-373 2741.

Polynesian Airlines, Samoa House, 283 K'Rd, City, T09-262 4197.

Qantas Airlines, 191 Queen St, City, T0800-808767/T09-357 8900.

Singapore Airlines, West Plaza Building, corner of Albert and Fanshawe sts, City, T0800-750760, www.singaporeair.co.nz.

Bicycle

Adventure Cycles, 1 Laurie Av, Parnell, T09-309 5566, www.adventure-auckland.co.nz/advcychm. For bike hire. Great service with a free helmet provided, lock, tool kit and water bottle, plus maps and tips. Prices range from about $35 a day to $200 a month. Also offers a 50% buy-back for up to 6 months, which equates to the rental rate for 1 month when an inexpensive bike is purchased, and is a good deal.

Bus

Local

MAXX, T09-366 6400, www.maxx.co.nz. Has a detailed telephone information service on all major local city transport carriers routes, prices and connections with ferry services.
Stagecoach, T09-366 6400, www.stage coach.co.nz. Publishes an *Auckland Busabout Guide*, available from the bus terminal and all major VICs, showing routes and departure points for the main city attractions. Fares are on a staged system 1-8 and range between $1.30-7.50. They offer a 'Discovery Pass' allowing unlimited travel on board bus/ferry/train for $14; 7-day $39.

'City Circuit' is an environmentally friendly electric red bus providing a free service around the immediate city centre every 10 mins, daily 0800-1800.

The Auckland City Loop 'Link' is a good way to get around the city centre. Each journey costs $1.50 and buses run every 10 mins on weekdays 0600-1900, every 15 mins evenings and weekends 0700-1800. You will feel like a sardine at rush hour. The route (which goes both ways) runs from the city centre (Britomart)-Quay Park-Parnell-Newmarket-Hospital-University-AUT-Library-Myers Park-K'Rd-Ponsonby-Victoria Park-Casino/Sky City-Mid Queen St-Britomart. For further details and information, see the website: www.stagecoach.co.nz/citycircuit.

The Double Decker 'Explorer', T0800-439756, www.explorerbus.co.nz, bus has all day sightseeing with commentary; $30 day pass, $15 for 1hr ride.

Long distance

The 2 main players providing standard coach travel from Auckland to destinations throughout New Zealand day and night are: Intercity Coach Lines, T09-623 1503, www.intercitycoach.co.nz; and Newman's, www.newmanscoach.co.nz. All coaches arrive/depart from the Sky City Coach Terminal, 102 Hobson St, City (round the corner from the Sky Tower), T09-638 5700, Mon-Fri 0700-2200, Sat-Sun 0700-2000. Northliner Express, T09-3075873, www.northliner.co.nz, offers a valued service to a number of North Island destinations, especially Northland. Concession fares apply. Buses arrive and depart from the Northliner Travel Centre, HSBC Building (opposite the Ferry Building), 172 Quay St.

Car

For those interested in buying a car or campervan, see Essentials, page 42.

If you own a car and have been drinking, there is a wonderful service in Auckland called Dial-a-Driver, T0800-800000/T09-828 6398. A sober employee drives you and your car to your chosen destination while another driver follows in a company car. The drivers are generally friendly and immensely stoic.

Car hire

Take time to find a good deal through the main VICs. A new, fully insured car without mileage costs from around $75 a day.

For a cheap, no nonsense deal, try Scotties (see below) Ask about the 'buy-back deals' and drop-off arrangements with its sister operation in Christchurch.
A2B Rentals, 11 Stanley St, City, T0800-222929, www.a2brentals.co.nz .
Action Rent-a-Car, 30 Grayson Av, T09-277 4422, www.action-rent-a-car.co.nz. Free pick-up, 24-hr service.
Affordable Rental Cars and Vans, 48 Carr Rd, Mt Roskill, T0800-454443/ T09-630 1567, www.car-rental.co.nz.
Alternative Rental Cars, 115 Beach Rd, City, T09-373 3822, www.hireacar.co.nz.
Apex Rental Cars, 39 Beach Rd, City/ 30 Rennie Drive, Airport, T09-257 0292/ T0800-500660, www.apexrentals.co.nz.
Avis, 17/19 Nelson St, City, T09-379 2650.

Big Save Car Rentals, 39-43 The Strand, Parnell, T0800-422771.
Budget Rent A Car, 163 Beach Rd, City, T09-976 2270, www.budget.co.nz.
Hertz, 154 Victoria St, T09-3676360.
Rent-a-Dent, 45 Union St, City, T09-309 0066.
Scotties, 27 New North Rd, Eden Terr, T09-303 3912.
Thrifty Car Rental, Airport, T09-366 0562/ T0800-737070, www.thrifty.co.nz.

Campervan hire

Adventure Campervans, 2 Beach Rd, Otahuhu, T09-276 7100/T0800-123555, www.nzmotorhomes.co.nz.
Backpacker Campervan Rentals, 36 Richard Pearse Drive, Mangere (3 km from Auckland Airport) T09-275 0200/ T0800-422267, www.backpackercamper vans.com. Offices in Wellington, Christchurch and Queenstown.
Britz Motorhomes, 36 Richard Pearse Drive, Mangere, T09-255 0620/T0800-831900, www.britz.com. Offices in Wellington, Christchurch and Queenstown.
Kea Campers, 36 Hillside Rd, T0800-520052/ T09-4417833, www.keacampers.com. Offices throughout the country.
KiwiKombis, 96 Uxbridge Rd, Howick, T09-533 9335, www.kiwikombis.com. The iconic if slow old favourite.
Maui Motorhomes, 36 Richard Pearse Drive, Mangere, T09-255 0620/T0800-651080, www.maui-rentals.com.
Spaceships, 31 Beach Rd, CBD, T09-309 8777, www.spaceships.tv. 'Kick-ass'

campervans at the top end of the scale, equipped with everything you might need.
Tui Campers, 142 Robertson Rd, Mangere East, T03-359 7410, www.tuicampers.co.nz.

Ferry

For further information about ferry services, contact the VIC.
Fullers, ground floor of the Ferry Building, T09-367 9111/T09-3676892, www.fullers.co.nz. The main ferry company.
Rubens Water Taxi, Viaduct Basin, T09-422 8881/T0800-111616, www.water taxi.co.nz. Not quite as popular as in Sydney Harbour, but these are a good way of zipping over to the North Shore or the eastern suburbs.

Scooter and motorcycle

NZ Motorcycle Rentals and Tours, 35 Crummer Rd, Ponsonby, T09-360 7940, www.nzbike.com. An award-winning national company. It hires out a range of bikes from the 50 cc sensible sewing machines to the 1100 cc scary monsters, all at reasonable rates.

Taxi

Alert Taxis, T09-309 2000.
Auckland Taxi Co-op, T09-300 3000.
Citicabs, T09-300 1111.
Corporate Cabs, T09-377 0773.
Discount Taxis, T09-529 1000.

◐ Directory

Banks

There are numerous outlets along Queen St and within the CBD. **American Express Currency Exchange**, 105 Queen St, City; also at NZ Cup Village, Quay St, City; and 67-69 Symonds St, City. **ANZ Banking Group**, 126 and 268 Queen and Victoria St, T04-472 7123/ T0800-269296, www.anz.co.nz. **ASB Bank Ltd**, corner of Queen and Wellesley sts, T0800-803804/ T09-306 3011, www.asbbank.co.nz. **Bank of New Zealand**, 80 Queen St, T09-375 1300/T0800-240000, www.bnz.co.nz.

National Bank of New Zealand, 205 Queen St, T09-359 9826/ T0800-181818, www.nationalbank.co.nz. **Travelex**, 32 and 157 Queen St, T0800-4401100. **Westpac Trust**, 79 Queen St, T09-302 4200/T0800-400600, www.westpac.co.nz.

Disabled facilities

Auckland Disabilities Resource Centre, 14 Erson Av, Royal Oak, T09-6258069, www.disabilityresource.org.nz.
Enable, T0800-362253, www.enable.co.nz.

Embassies and consulates

Australia 7th floor, 188 Quay St, City, T09-921 8800. **Canada** 9th floor, 48 Emily Pl, City, T09-309 3690. **Denmark** 7th floor Harbour View Building, 152 Quay St, City, T09-537 3099. **Germany** 6th floor, 52 Symonds St, City, T09-913 3674. **Ireland** 7th floor, Citibank Blg, 23 Customs St East, City, T09-977 2252. **Japan** Level 12, ASB Bank Centre, 135 Albert St, City, T09-303 4106. **Korea** Level 10, Sofrana House, 396 Queen St, T09-379 0818. **Netherlands** Level 1, 57 Symonds St, City, T09-379 5399. **Sweden** 13th floor, 13 O'Connell St, City, T09-373 5332. **UK** IAG House, 151 Queen St, City, T09-303 2973. **USA** Level 3, Citibank Centre, 23 Customs St East, T09-303 2724.

Gay and lesbian

Express Magazine available from outlets of **Maggazzino** (see Shopping, page 103). **Pride**, T09-302 0590, www.pride.org.nz.

Internet

Readily available in the CBD including: **Auckland City Library**, 44-46 Lorne St, City, T09-377 0209. **CyberDatez**, 320 Queen St, City, T09-3770320. **Cyber Max Café**, Level 1, 291 Queen St, City, T09-9792468. **Net Zone**, 4 Fort St, City, T09-3773906.

Laundry

Clean Green Laundromat, 18 Fort St, T09-358 4370, Mon-Sat 0900-2000.

Left luggage

Auckland International Airport, T09-275 6467, daily 0600-2300. **Downtown Bus Terminal**, corner of Quay St and Albert St, Mon-Fri 0700-1900, Sat-Sun 0700-1800. **Sky City Bus Terminal**, Hobson St, daily 0700-2200.

Libraries

Central City Library, 44-46 Lorne St, City, T09-377 0209, Mon-Thu 0930-2000, Fri 0930-2100, Sat 1000-1600, Sun 1300-1700.

Medical services

Accident and medical centres

Ponsonby Accident and Emergency, 202 Ponsonby Rd, T09-376 5555. **Shorecare**, 209 Shakespeare Rd, Takapuna, T09-486 7777. **Westcare**, 57-75 Lincoln Rd, Henderson, T09-836 6000. **White Cross St Lukes**, 52 St Lukes Rd, St Lukes, T09-815 3111.

Hospitals

Auckland Hospital, Park Rd, Grafton, T09-367 0000. **Greenlane Hospital**, Greenlane Rd West, Greenlane, T09-367 0000. **Middlemore Hospital**, Hospital Rd, Otahuhu, T09-276 0000. **North Shore Hospital**, Shakespeare Rd, Takapuna, T09-486 8930. **Waitakere Hospital**, Lincoln Rd, Henderson, T09-839 0000.

Police

Emergency Dial 111. Main police station is at the corner of Cook and Vincent sts, City, T09-302 6400.

Post offices

Main post office and post restante, Wellesley St West, City, T09-379 6714, Mon-Fri 0730-1730. Additional branches at 23 Customs St, T09-302 1059; 167 Victoria St West, T09-367 9617; and **Downtown Shopping Centre**, Queen St, T09-309 6343.

Supermarkets

There are **Night Owl** or **Star** 24-hr grocery stores on Queen St and the waterfront. **Foodtown**, 76 Quay St. **New World**, 2 College Hill, City (near Victoria Park on the Link bus route), daily until 2400.

Travel agents

Auckland Central Travel, corner of Queen and Darby sts, City, T09-358 4877, www.acb. co.nz, Mon-Fri 0800-1800, Sat-Sun 0800-1700. Backpacker-friendly adventure travel shop, free information and discounted rates on rentals, rail, coaches, ferries, tours. **Backpackers World Travel**, 23 Victoria St East, City, T09-368 1742. **STA Travel**, 267 and Level 10 220 Queen St, City, T0508-782872/T09-309 0458.

North of Auckland → Colour map 1, 4A

The Kaipara Harbour, with a combined coastal length that exceeds 3200 km, is one of the biggest natural harbours in the world. It was of huge economic significance in the Kauri logging and export days of the mid- to late-1800s, with the ports of Helensville to the south and Dargaville to the north being of particular importance. Some 40 km north of the city centre (but a mere stone's throw from the northern edge of it) is the Hibiscus Coast – a coastline dominated by the 3-km beach adjacent to the main town, Orewa. Around Orewa there are the more sheltered bays of the Whangaparaoa Peninsula to the south and the Wenderholm Regional Park and Puhoi River to the north. ▶▶ See Sleeping, Eating and other listings, pages 113-114.

Ins and outs

Getting there Ritchies, T09-833 6053, www.ritchies.co.nz, from Auckland BBT, Monday to Saturday. **Stagecoach**, T09-366 6400, www.maxx.co.nz, offers a regular daily service to and from Orewa and the Whangaparaoa Peninsula from Auckland. By car, take SH16 off the Great Western Motorway in the city.

Tourist information Hibiscus Coast VIC (I-Site) ① *on the main drag, 214a Hibiscus Coast Highway (HCH), next to Orewa Beach Holiday Park, T09-426 0076, www.orewa-beach.co.nz, Mon-Sat 0900-1700, Sun 1000-1600,* can fill you in on what local activities are available and where to stay. Book accommodation well ahead in summer.

Southern Kaipara, Helensville and Parakai

The **VIC (I-Site)** ① *27 Commercial Rd, T09-420 8060, www.helensville.co.nz, Mon-Fri 1000-1700, Sat 1000-1400,* will help with activity and accommodation bookings.

Looking at Helensville today, it is hard to imagine it as a bustling port; these days it is a rather dull place, with little to attract you except perhaps a reminder of yesteryear in the **Pioneer Museum** ① *Commercial St, T09-420 7881, Wed, Sat-Sun 1300-1530 or by arrangement, $5, children free.* Most other sights and activities are water-based.

Nearby, **Parakai** is famous for its hot pools at **Aquatic Park Parakai Springs** ① *150 Parkhurst Rd, T09-420 8998, www.parakaisprings.co.nz, $15, child $8, daily 1000-2200.* A long soak is particularly welcome after a horse trek on the beach.

Hibiscus Coast and the Whangaparaoa Peninsula

Whangaparaoa Peninsula At the ever-expanding northern fringe of Auckland City is the Whangaparaoa Peninsula. It is essentially a rather unexciting enclave for the northern Auckland suburbanites. However, the scenery is good and there are some attractions worth considering. **Snowplanet** ① *Small Rd, Silverdale, T09-427 0044 www.snowplanet.co.nz, daily 1000-2200, 1 hr from $29, child $24, day-pass $49, child $44,* is a new snow-sports facility offering indoor skiing, snowboarding and air-boarding (a high-tech air-filled bodyboard). Lessons are also available, and there's a café overlooking the slope. Elsewhere, kids and rail buffs might enjoy a visit to the **Whangaparaoa Narrow Gauge Steam Railway** ① *400 Whangaparaoa Rd, Stanmore Bay, T09-424 5018, www.rail.co.nz, Sep-Jun Sat 1200-1300, Sun 1000-1700), $6.*

There's also the **Gulf Harbour** ① *www.gulf-harbour.co.nz,* with its posh marina village and international standard golf course. In 2006 it hosted the New Zealand Open Golf Tournament, but if you have ventured this far out and left your golf clubs at home, then you would be better off heading for the **Shakespeare Regional Park**. Here, beyond Gulf Harbour, you will encounter fine views, a few walks and the occasional quiet beach. Alternatively, if your timing is right, take the Fuller's ferry from the Gulf Harbour Marina to the beautiful open bird sanctuary of **Tiritiri Matangi Island** (see page 121).

Orewa   Although the coastal resort of Orewa is not essentially part of Auckland City it
has, with the recent motorway and ever-encroaching housing developments, become
a satellite town. But Orewa is still a staunchly independent community. It boasts a
fine beach which lures the city slickers and visitors in increasingly healthy numbers in
summer, but otherwise there is not a great deal on offer, except perhaps a coffee and
snack before heading north. The focus of the town is **Hillary Square**, which boasts a
statue of the great man himself. Sir Edmund Hillary is New Zealand's best-known
explorer and climber, the first to conquer Mount Everest.

Orewa to Warkworth   At the northern end of Orewa you will pass the scenic **Red
Beach** before winding your way to **Waiwera Thermal Spa Resort** ⓘ *21 Main Rd,
T09 427 8800, www.waiwera.co.nz, Sun-Thu 0900-2200, Fri-Sat 0900-2230, $22,
child $11, family $53*. It's a small resort built around natural hot springs, where you
can laze about in a purpose-built resort that has large pools, spas and water slides for
the kids, and even a separate covered pool where you can take in a movie –
presumably to emerge afterwards looking like a walnut. Their new and well-facilitated
spa complex 'Infinity' offers all the usual body treatments with a private spa costing
around $30 per hour, and massage from $55 for 30 minutes.

About 1 km north of Waiwera is **Wenderholm Regional Park**. This is one of the
region's most handsome regional parks, sited on a sand spit deposited by the Puhoi
River and now grassed over and dominated by beautiful large pohutukawa trees. The
beach is often wild and windswept and offers a wonderful view of the small offshore
islands and the mountainous Little Barrier Island to the north. The park has some
excellent walking tracks ranging from 20 minutes to 2½ hours. There is a choice of
coastal walks, or the more challenging headland walks, where you may see, or hear,
the fluid song of the tui and clattering wings of the keruru or native pigeon. If history is
your preference, the park's administration block is dominated by the 1860s colonial
homestead, **Couldrey House** ⓘ *T09-366 2000, Sat-Sun only 1300-1600; bus 895
terminates here on Sun in summer*.

The small and picturesque village of **Puhoi** is just off SH1, 5 km north of Wenderholm.
It has an intriguing history as a Catholic Bohemian settlement established in 1863.
Although most of the memories are focused in the **Puhoi Historical Society Museum**
ⓘ *in the former convent school, www.puhoihistoricalsociety.org.nz, open Christmas to
Easter, over weekends and during school holidays 1300-1600, donation*, much of the
story is evident in the historic **Puhoi Tavern**. It is a fascinating little pub full of historic
clutter and characters. Provided no one is playing pool you can read all about the early
settlers and sympathize with their desperate cause. It is a depressing and unhappy
story of a seemingly never-ending struggle with the land, hunger and desperation.
Despite the awful stories the pub is very appealing and on the second Friday of each
month a local Bohemian band play their toe-tapping tunes. On a fine summer Sunday
afternoon the river can be a fine place to be, as you gently wind your way downstream to
Wenderholm Regional Park in a canoe or Canadian kayak.

◉ Sleeping

Helensville and Parakai *p112*
A **Kaipara House B&B**, corner of SH16 and
Parkhurst Rd, Helensville, T09-420 7462,
kaiparah@ihug.co.nz. 3 spacious rooms with
thermal baths, and a separate summerhouse.
A **Malolo House**, 110 Commercial Rd,
Helensville, T09-420 7262, malolo@xtra.co.nz.
Comfortable villa-style B&B and backpacker
accommodation. Centrally located.

C-D **Point of View**, Te Makiri, Helensville,
T09-420 7331, www.pointofview.co.nz.
Pleasant and alternative backpacker
farmstay run by local poet/songwriter.

Campsites
D **Parakai Hot Pools**, Parkhurst Rd, Parakai,
T09-420 8998. Basic caravan and campsites,
standard facilities. Reduced entry to the pools.

LL The Gulf Harbour Lodge, 164 Harbour Village Drive, Gulf Harbour, Whangaparaoa Peninsula, T07-428 1118, www.gulfharbour lodge.com. One of the main luxury options in the area with the added bonus of free access to the **Gulf Harbour Country Club** facilities. Cheaper weekend rates.

L-AL Moontide Lodge, 19 Ocean View Rd, Hatfields Beach, T09-426 2374, moontde@ nznet.gen.nz. An excellent B&B set on the cliffs above Hatfields Beach, north of Orewa. It offers beautifully appointed rooms with great views and decks. Fine breakfasts and dinner on request. German and French spoken.

A Coach Trail Villas and Beach Cottages, 1 Waiwera Rd, Waiwera, T09-426 4792, www.kiwistay.co.nz. Offers comfortable accommodation in villa or self-contained waterfront cottages within walking distance of the hot pools, should you need to hang yourself out to dry overnight in Waiwera.

A Waves, corner of Hibiscus Coast Highway and Kohu St, T09-427 0888, www.waves.co.nz. Modern small hotel option close to the beach.

C-D Marco Polo Tourist Lodge, 2D Hammond Av, Hatfields Beach, Orewa, T09-426 8455, www.marcopolo.co.nz. Comfortable backpacker hostel with full range of room types, a relaxing garden and palm tree-painted bedroom walls.

C-D Pillows Travellers' Lodge, 412 Hibiscus Coast Highway, Orewa, T09-426 6338, pillows.lodge@xtra.co.nz. Another budget option with value double en suites with TV.

Motels

Motels dominate the northern end of Orewa and almost all of them can be found on either side of the main drag – the Hibiscus Coast Highway.

A Anchor Lodge Motel, 436, T0800-000426, www.anchorlodge.co.nz.

A Beachcomber Motel, 246, T09-426 5973, www.beachcombermotel.co.nz.

A Hibiscus Palms Motel, 416, T09-426 4904, www.hibiscuspalms.co.nz.

Motorcamps

Orewa Beach Holiday Park, 265 Hibiscus Coast Highway, T09-426 5832. 4-star facilities including camp kitchen.

🍴 Eating

Helensville and Parakai *p112*

🍴 **McNutts Farm and Café**, 11 km north of Parakai, 914 South Head Rd, South Head, T09-420 2853, www.macnut.co.nz. A good alternative, in combination with a macadamia nut orchard tour ($3). Congenial and friendly.

🍴🍴 **Ginger Crunch Station Café**, 2 Railway Rd, T09-420 9133, Wed-Sun 0900-1500. Based at the historic rail station and-as the name suggests-a purveyor of fine Ginger Crunch as well as all day breakfasts, light meals, home made baking and good coffee.

Hibiscus Coast and Whangaparaoa Peninsula *p112*

There are numerous small cafés and takeaways in Orewa.

🍴 **Muldoon's Irish Bar**, Unit 8/9 Westpac Plaza Moana Av, T09-427 8000. Small, family oriented pub with a good good.

🍴 **The Sahara Café**, 336 Hibiscus Coast Highway, right on the waterfront, T09-426 8828, daily. Offers quality, convenience and a hearty all-day breakfast.

🍴 **Walnut Cottage Café**, Orewa House, 498 Hibiscus Coast Highway, T09-427 5570, Mon-Thu 0930-1630, Fri-Sun 0930-1800. BYO and licensed. Situated in some very congenial grounds.

⛰ Activities and tours

Helensville and Parakai *p112*

Several tours leave from Helensville to link up with others in Dargaville, see page 186.

Kaipara Fishing Charters, T0800-000070, bookings@kaiparafishing.co.nz.

South Kaipara Horse Treks, T09-420 2835, www.horserides.co.nz.

Tasman Rides, T09-420 8603, www.tasmanrides.co.nz.

Taylor Made Tours, T09-4391576, www.taylor madetours.co.nz. Great range of options from touring on water and land, with some quad biking on remote beaches, from $55.

Hibiscus Coast and Whangaparaoa Peninsula *p112*

Puhoi River Canoe Hire, 84 Puhoi Valley Rd, T09-422 0891, www.puhoirivercanoes. $40 for the full river adventure or $20 per hr.

West of Auckland → Colour map 7 A1

From the centre of the city the Great Western Motorway straddles the inner inlets of the Waitemata Harbour before taking you to the western suburbs of Auckland. From these western fringes of the city, the Waitakere Ranges rise to form a huge area of bush with an extensive network of walking tracks. These seemingly endless hills then eventually reach the sea and the wild west coast beaches that offer a huge contrast to the quiet Pacific beaches of the Hauraki Gulf. ▸▸ *For Sleeping, Eating and other listings see page 117-118.*

Ins and outs

Getting there Public transport to the Waitakeres and especially the west coast beaches is limited. Hiring a car or taking an organized tour are your best options. Alternatively **TranzMetro**, www.transmetro.co.nz, has a rail service from the city to Henderson and Waitakere; a workable option if you hire a bike. From Titirangi village it is a 27-km ride to Whatipu. **Piha Surf Shuttles**, T09-627 2644, www.surfshuttle.co.nz, offers a daily service to Piha (taking in Karekare) departing the city at 0830 and returning at 1600, from $30 one way, $50 return. For Muriwai, take Helensville (**Ritchies**) buses 069 and 067 to Waimauku and flag down a car from there. **Bush and Beach**, T09-575 1458, www.bushandbeach.co.nz, includes Muriwai in its tours, see Auckland Activities and tours page 108.

Waitakere City

West Auckland, or Waitakere City, is made up of a number of diverse suburbs. Te Atatu, Swanson, Henderson, New Lynn and Glendene are relatively low-income areas of little note, except for being home to the 'Westie', a peculiar type of Aucklander who dresses predominantly in black, loves rock 'n' roll, does not believe in hair salons, and simply loves anything on wheels that goes fast, burns rubber and makes lots of noise. The **Great Western Motorway** pays homage to this almost nightly, with nearly every dawn presenting a trail of abandoned vehicles that never made it home.

Further west and south is **Titirangi** where, on the slopes of the ranges around **Scenic Drive**, the more well-to-do citizens enjoy their secluded, often beautiful, bush dwellings with wonderful views across the city. Titirangi, 'the gateway to the Waitakeres', is a very pleasant little village that is worth a visit in itself, with a number of pleasant cafés, interesting shops and a good art gallery, **Lopdell House** ① *corner of Titirangi and South Titirangi Rds, T09-817 8087, www.lopdell.org.nz, daily 1000-1630, free.* Overall, Waitakere City is most famous for its liberal attitudes, art, vineyards and orchards and its spectacularly wild unspoilt bush and beaches. It has, as a result, proclaimed itself Auckland's 'Eco-City' with the **Kumeu** area being known as the 'Gannet and Grape district'.

The Waitakeres

The 'Waitaks', as they are affectionately known, are one of the region's biggest and most attractive regional parks, offering a 200-km network of walking tracks, many of which hide such scenic delights as large kauri trees, waterfalls and large dams. Before embarking on any activities in the area, visit the **Arataki Information Centre** ① *on the hill at the southern end of Scenic Drive, 6 km from Titirangi, T09-817 0089/ T09-817 0077, www.arc.govt.nz/arc/auckland-regional-parks/arataki, daily 0900-1700 (1600 in winter).* It is a newly renovated centre that provides a vast amount of information, interesting interpretative displays, an audio-visual display, nature trail, education centre and, dominating the scene, an impressive Maori *pou* (carving), which lost its rather impressive 'manhood' a few years ago (though another was duly carved, and the glint in his little paua shell eye restored). From here make sure you take detailed advice on walks and buy the relevant maps. The Waitakeres have seen their fair share of lost trampers over the years. Don't forget to pick up the *Welcome Out West*, *Art Out West*, *Artists' and Artisans' Trail* and *Accommodation Out West* leaflets, as well as numerous walking maps and options from the centre, all free.

Sights The 28-km **scenic drive** is the best way to get an impression of the area as it winds along the eastern fringe of the Waitakeres, offering stunning views across the city both by day and by night. One of the best views can be seen from the garden of **Hellaby House** ① *515 Scenic Drive, gardens daily 1300-1600, Sun, 1100-1700, free*, just below the TV masts. Its elderly owner, Rose, who loved the Waitakeres with a passion, donated Hellaby House to the city; given the view from her backyard this is not surprising.

West Auckland is one of the best-known wine-producing areas of the country, containing nearly 20 **wineries** with such famous names as Corbans, Coopers Creek, Matua Valley, Nobilo and Babich. The northern areas of Waitakere City host most of these, especially in the Kumeu area. Most wineries offer tastings. **Soljans** ① *SH16, Kumeu, T09-412 5858, www.soljans.co.nz, daily 0900-1730, shop and café*, is recommended. Copies of the official *Wine Trail* and *Wineries of Auckland* leaflets can be found at the **Kumeu and District VIC (I-Site)** ① *Main Rd, Huapai, T09-412 9886, www.kumeudistrict.co.nz*, and main city VICs. ▸▸ *See Activities and tours, page 118.*

One of the most unusual attractions in the area is the **Watercare Rain Forest Express** ① *T09-302 8028, www.watercare.co.nz, $25 (twilight $28), child $12 ($14), regular trips on Sun 1400, 'glow-worm special' 1800 in summer, booking essential*, a fascinating and fun 2½-hour trip on the small gauge railway train that still plies the numerous lines and tunnels to service and maintain the local dams. **Bush and Beach** run tours, see page 118.

Wild west coast beaches ⊜⦿ ▸▸ *pp117-118.*

Whatipu
If you are looking for solitude and a real sense of wilderness, without doubt one of the best places to go in the region is Whatipu. Situated 45 km from the city centre, at the southernmost tip of the Waitakere Ranges, its huge expanse of sand in part forms the narrow mouth of the **Manukau Harbour**. At the terminus of the winding, unsealed road, past the picturesque little settlements of **Huia** and **Little Huia**, is a small cluster of buildings that make up **Whatipu Lodge**. The lodge is the last sign of habitation and chance of accommodation before you head north along the 6-km-long beach that stretches all the way to Karekare. If you can pull yourself away from the sound of the surf, head inland across the 700 acres of sand dune and wetland. Hidden in the undulations of dune grasses and cabbage trees are extensive wetlands that are home to noisy paradise shelduck, delicate pied stilts and elegant black swans. At the foot of the bush-clad hills are the remains of the **Parahara Railway** that once hauled huge kauri from Karekare in the 1870s. A boiler and a small tunnel still remain, even though the sand has long swallowed the tracks.

If you are on foot you can head north to Piha. Just before the road falls down the hill to Whatipu, take the Donald McLean Road up to the summit of **Mount Donald McLean**. The summit itself is a short 10-minute walk from the road end, and the view across the Waitakeres, the harbour and back across to the tiny Sky Tower is magnificent.

Karekare
Like most of the west coast beaches, the bush-clad hills of the Waitakeres fall dramatically into the sea and form a natural amphitheatre of vegetation and cliff, with the beach as its stage, the wind its song and the surf its applause.

There are a number of short walks and tracks around Karekare, some of which head inland or south to join the extensive Waitakere network. For long inland excursions, make sure you carry a map and supplies. The short walk up the Taraire Track to **Karekare Falls** is worthwhile, especially if you intend to swim in the pool beneath it. Another is the **Colman's Track** from the end of Watchmans Road, where the path creeps up the hill at the northern point of Karekare beach and terminates with a magnificent view. Looking south you can see well past Karekare beach to the huge expanse of Whatipu beach beyond, as well as the tiny, inaccessible Mercer Bay, immediately below and north. If you are feeling energetic, keep going along the track which follows the coast to meet Te Ahahu Road eventually, at Piha.

Piha

It is very hard to spend the day at Piha beach without contemplating packing it all in to live here. Piha has been luring dreamers and surfers for years and is, along with Muriwai, one of the west coast's most popular beaches. And as you climb down the windy road you will quickly realize that, for a few lucky souls, the dream has become reality. Although it can be very busy in summer, it still retains a distinctly isolated charm perhaps due to the lack of public transport. When you get fed up with sunbathing, swimming or trying to hold on to your surfboard in the fierce surf, there are two things you must do. The first and most obvious is to climb **Lion Rock** (a strenuous 30-minute walk), the guardian of the beach that looks with menace out to the ocean; from the summit you can look down on the surfers bobbing about in search of the perfect wave. The other thing to do, especially in a wild winter storm or at sunset, is to take the **Tasman Lookout Track** at the south end of the beach to **The Gap**. Here you can sit and watch in awe at the power of the breakers as they pound and crash into the narrow gap.

There is also an interesting, if less dramatic, walk at the northern end of Piha Beach, which leads to the isolated and beautiful **White's Beach**. If you have time, also try to see the **Kitekite Falls** from the Kitekite Track down Glen Esk Road behind the main camping ground. If you swim at Piha you can do so in relative safety, but always stay between the flags and in sight of the lifesavers. Piha has been the watery grave for many shore fishermen and uninitiated swimmers. If you get into trouble, raise an arm and keep it aloft – you will be in an inflatable rescue boat before you know it.

Muriwai

Muriwai, 15 km north of Piha and 45 km west of the city centre, is the west coast's most visited beach. On summer weekends it plays host to locals and visitors, who nestle down in the black sands to soak up the sun, surf, fish, play, or look over the **gannet colony**. These angry-looking birds have taken up residence on the flat rock outcrops at its southern end to breed, forming a small seabird city. It is a delight in spring, when the stomachs of the fluffy white chicks being kept full by the comings and goings of their bad-tempered parents. Muriwai boasts the only major North Island colony, after Cape Kidnappers on the east coast, near Napier.

Muriwai is well-serviced for locals and tourists and boasts a fine golf course (T09-411 8454). If Muriwai beach is too busy for you then try **Maori Bay**, another favourite surf spot just south of Muriwai, reached via Waitea Road. If you find the huge stretch of beach a bit daunting, a good way to explore is on horseback; try **Muriwai Beach Homestay and Horse Riding** (see Sleeping, below).

● Sleeping

For local B&B and farmstay options contact the **Arataki Information Centre**, T09-817 0089, or consult the free *Staying Out West* leaflet available from all VICs.

The Waitakeres *p115*
C Aio Wira, T09-810 9396, www.airwira.org.nz. A peaceful simple retreat set in 4 ha of mature native bush.

B-D Whatipu Lodge, T09-811 8860, whatipu lodge@xtra.co.nz. Book a cabin or a tent site which will give you plenty of time to explore before heading back to the city the next day.

Piha *p117*

AL Piha Lodge, 117 Piha Rd, T09-812 8595, www.pihalodge.co.nz. Award winner with 2 self-contained units. Large pool and spa.
A Piha Cottage, T/F09-812 8514, www.piha cottage.co.nz. A secluded self-contained cottage in quiet bush surroundings.

Motorcamps
B-D Piha Domain Motor Camp,
T09-812 8815. In the heart of the village, tent sites and cosy huts, camp kitchen. Bookings advisable.

Muriwai *p117*
B Muriwai Beach Homestay and Horse Riding, 781 Muriwai Rd, T09-411 7111, www.farmstayauckland.co.nz. Offers the choice of queen, twin or single in a country setting only 2 km from the beach. Base for horse trekking, about $70 for 2 hrs.

Motorcamps
B-D Muriwai Beach Motor Camp,
T09-411 5309. Powered and non-powered sites and camp kitchen, but no cabins.

❶ Eating

Piha *p117*
The **RSA**, T09-812 8138, across the river from the motorcamp, and **Surf Club**, 23 Marine Parade, T09-812 8896, at the southern end of the beach, offer great value meals, but you will have to ask a member to sign you in. Opening times vary.

Other than that there are the usual sad-looking pies to be had at the general store near the motorcamp, or burgers and the ubiquitous fish and chips at the burger bar, next to the Surf Club (summer only).

Muriwai *p117*
The **Waterfront** general store serves light meals and refreshments.
▼▼▼-▼▼ Hunting Lodge, Waikoukou Valley Rd, T09-411 8259, www.thehuntinglodge.co.nz,

open for lunch and dinner Wed-Sun. A more upmarket option.
▼ Wuz's Café, 185 Motutara Rd, Muriwai Beach T09-411 8624. Open daily for breakfast, lunch and dinner.

▲ Activities and tours

The Waitakeres *p115*
Canyoning
Although Wanaka is generally considered the country's canyoning capital, the streams and waterfalls of the Waitakere Ranges west of the city provide some exciting opportunities and are a worthwhile trip.
Awol Adventures, T0800-462965, www.awoladventures.co.nz. Half- to full-day trips with the added option of night and overnight excursions, from $155.
Canyonz, T0800-422696, www.canyonz. co.nz. Full-day excursions with beach visit from $175

Tour operators
Bush and Beach, T09-575 1458/T0800-423224, www.bushandbeach.co.nz. A well-established company that opens up the Waitakeres and west coast beaches to those visitors without their own transport. Their Waitakere Rainforest and black sand beaches trip is a memorable half-day option taking in the Waitakeres and west coast beaches from $110, full-day extended trip $155.
Potiki Adventures, T09-845 5932, www.potikiadventures.co.nz. Excellent Maori-themed adventure tours, with a range of fixed or custom activities from hiking to marae stays. Their 'Auckland Orientation Trip' (8 hrs from $145) is a fine introduction to the city, region and country from the Maori perspective and includes the west coast beaches. Recommended.

Wine tours
Auckland Wine Trail Tours, T09-630 1540, www.winetrailtours.co.nz. Excellent half- and full-day tours concentrating on vineyards, or a combination of vineyards and general sights in the Wiatakeres, from $95.
NZWinePro, T09-575 1958, www.nzwine pro.co.nz. Offers one of the best wine tour packages available (half or full-day from $129).

South of Auckland → Colour map 2, B1

With so much to see elsewhere and usually limited time to do so, there is little to attract the international visitor to South Auckland. However, if you have ample time or want to take an alternative route to the Coromandel Peninsula, the scenic coast road via Miranda is recommended. Along the way the Shorebird Centre and Miranda Hot Pools on the shores of the Firth of Thames can make an interesting and soothing stop. Within the city itself Rainbow Springs is a fine place to take the kids, while Montgomerie Farm in Clevedon offers a traditional farm show and can be combined with a walk in the Hunua Ranges Regional Park. ▶▶ *For Sleeping, Eating and other listings, see page 120.*

Sights

Once you leave the city southbound through the **Manukau City** and **Franklin District** the SH1 climbs over the Bombay Hills then falls to meet the Waikato River towards Hamilton. The **Franklin VIC (I-Site)** ① *Mill Rd, Bombay, T09-236 0670, www.tourism franklin. co.nz*, can recommend excursions or detours in the area.

If you are heading to the Coromandel Peninsula, the best way is to follow the **Pacific Coast Highway** via **Howick** and **Whitford**. The route is generally well marked (with the Pacific Coast Highway logo) and has a number of interesting stops on the way. Just before you hit the coast proper you pass the **Omana Regional Park**. This small park offers outstanding views of the gulf across to Waiheke and a pleasant beach with a rock platform that provides safe and shallow swimming at high tide and is ideal for kids.

Further south and inland again, is the farming town of **Clevedon**, home to **Auckland's Polo Club**, T09-292 8556, which has games on Sundays in the summer. There are also a number of cafés in which to grab a cup of tea. Nearby, **Montgomerie Farm** ① *Pioneer Rd, T09-292 8724*, offers traditional sheep-shearing demonstrations (1100 and 1430), and lamb-feeding for the kids (in spring); horse trekking is also available. South of Clevedon (but a diversion off the Pacific Coast Highway) is **Hunua**, on the edge of the **Hunua Ranges Regional Park**. These bush-clad ranges contain the watersheds for a number of dams that supply Auckland with most of its water. Although the park and the ranges are not in the same league as the Waitakeres west of Auckland, there are a number of interesting walks – the best of which is an all-day hike that takes in the Wairoa River, Cossey's Dam and the 30-m **Hunua Falls**. For information visit the **Hunua Ranges Park Visitor Centre** ① *Hunua, T09-366 2000, daily 0800-1630*, or the **Clevedon Information Centre** ① *Clevedon Gallery, 9 North Rd, T09-292 8660*.

Back on the Pacific Coast Highway east of Clevedon you will hit the coast again. It is a very pleasant drive framed by pohutukawa trees and an area famous for its bird life. Christened the **Seabird Coast**, it is well worth stopping at the **Miranda Shorebird Centre** ① *Pokeno, T/F09-232 2781, www.miranda-shorebird.org.nz, daily, 0900-1700*, home of the **Miranda Naturalists' Trust**. The Firth of Thames offers an internationally important habitat and stopover point for thousands of migrating wading birds. The 'target' birds at Miranda (for study not shooting) are the native wrybill – a strange little wader with a crooked beak designed for specialist feeding – and the rare New Zealand dotterel. Both join the near 60 other transitory species that stop over for a short time in spring and autumn to refuel for migration. The godwit, a medium-sized wader that breeds in Alaska, makes the journey to spend the southern hemisphere winter in New Zealand. Recent studies suggest that they do this journey non-stop, in a week. They fly at 4000-6000 m and reach speeds of 60-70 kph. Just a few kilometres south of the Shorebird Centre are the **Miranda Hot Pools** ① *T07-867 3055, Mon-Thu 0800-2100, Fri-Sun 0800-2230 all year, $12, child $6*. Private spas are also available.

🕐 Sleeping

South of Auckland *p119*

LL Umoya Lodge, Mount Rataroa, Pokeno, T09-232 7636, www.umoyalodge.co.nz. Stunning, luxury lodge in an elevated position overlooking the coast. Spacious suite and self-contained lodge. Superb in-house cuisine.

L The Inverness Estate, Ness Valley Rd, Clevedon, T09-292 8710, www.inverness.co.nz. Luxury accommodation in a country setting with fine food and its own estate wine.

A The Miranda Holiday Park, 595 Front Miranda Rd, T09-867 3205, mirandaholiday park@extra.co.nz. Wonderful facilities including its own hot pools. Recommended.

C-D Miranda Shorebird Centre, T09-232 2781. Bunk, single/double room and self-contained accommodation available from $13-40. Great value, offers a fine roost.

Camping

Omana Regional Park, T09-303 1530. The region's campsite.

🍴 Eating

South of Auckland *p119*

🍴 **Kaiaua Fishery**, T09-232 2776. Fish and chip shop on East Coast Rd in Kaiaua, north of Miranda, has a great reputation.

🍴 **Bayview Hotel**, Kaiaua, T09-232 2717, daily from 1700. Offers takeaways and snacks as well as a restaurant serving mainly seafood.

Hauraki Islands → *Colour map 2, A2*

The Hauraki Gulf is famed for its picturesque islands, which range in size from the 179-ha Motuihe to the 93-sq-km Waiheke. There is significant contrast in their use and character as well as their geography. Close to the city Waiheke is by far the most populated, so much so that it is often labelled 'just another suburb' of Auckland. Famed for its vineyards and blessed with a number of fine beaches, it has for decades been a favourite and convenient escape from the city for both residents and visitors. Perhaps most obvious among the island family is Rangitoto with its atypical volcanic cone that dominates the horizon and although now fully clad in bush reveals some fascinating lava flows upon closer inspection. Second largest in the group is Great Barrier, which is 90 km from the city, offering a true island escape and some superb scenery, walks and beaches. Two other islands in the Hauraki are the world-renowned wildlife reserves of Tiritiri Matangi near the Whangaparaoa Peninsula on the city's northern fringe, and the mountainous Little Barrier, which can be seen on a clear day to the north. Tiri is the most accessible and offers visitors an insight in to what New Zealand used to be like, with abundant bird life and such enchanting avian odysseys as the takahe and spotted kiwi. Little Barrier is home to a few precious and well-looked after kakapo – a large flightless parrot that with less than 100 remaining is one of the rarest birds in the world.

Ins and outs

Getting there To Rangitoto, **Fullers**, T09-367 9111, www.fullers.co.nz, runs ferries from the Ferry Building on Quay Street, daily at 0915, 1215 and 1315, $21, child $11. It also offers a ferry/tour package with the 'Rangitoto Explorer' – a carriage pulled by a tractor that winds its way around the island, with an interesting commentary, $50, child $26. Booking is essential for all trips. Take plenty of water, sun block and a hat – the black scoria can emanate terrific heat. **Fullers** also runs a ferry to Motuihe at weekends in conjunction with the Rangitoto ferry. Additional sailings in summer, $20, child $10.

To Tiritiri Matangi, **360-Discovery (Kawau Kat)**, T0800-888006, www.360discovery. co.nz, runs a service from Auckland from Pier 3 (next to the Ferry Building) Wednesday to Sunday at 0900, $59, child $28; or the same ferry from Z Pier, Gulf Harbour on the Whangaparaoa Peninsula, 45 minutes later, $35, child $17. Trips return by 1645.

Rangitoto Island

Rangitoto seems to dominate your views of the Hauraki Gulf from almost every vantage point in the city, so it is only a matter of time before its classically shaped cone lures you across the water to take a closer look. Rangitoto first emerged from the sea in a series of eruptions about 600 years ago, when Maori were known to be inhabiting the area. One Maori myth suggests that the eruption occurred after a casual dispute between the gods of fire and volcanoes, but many years later science put it all down to being the latest of the many eruptions to take place in the area over the millennia. It is only a 30-minute journey by ferry to take a closer look and to enjoy one of the island's walks.

Most of these walks culminate at the summit from where there is a 360° view of the gulf and the city and you can peer down into its bush-clad crater. The vegetation of the island is of international importance with the recent botanical blanket boasting 200 species of native tree (the most prolific and famous being its pohutukawa) and flowering plants, 40 kinds of fern, some orchids and, of course, many lichens. All this is interspersed with the ankle-breaking mounds of loose laval scoria.

There are a number of **walking** options, all neatly presented in DoC's guide to the island – available from the DoC office in the Ferry Building. If you have time and want to get away from the crowds that immediately make for the summit (two hours), follow the tracks from the wharf to the summit via McKenzie Bay. It can take six hours but gives you a great feel for the island and its plant life, and provides great sea-level views.

Motutapu Island – the contrasting island connected to Rangitoto by a short causeway – has a few interesting Maori archaeological sites but is best visited as part of the extensive winter replanting programmes that are taking place in conjunction with DoC. As you can see from Rangitoto, Motutapu needs it.

Tiritiri Matangi Island

Even if you are not particularly interested in wildlife 'Tiri' (as it is affectionately known) is well worth a visit. This jewel in the Hauraki is one of the few 'open bird sanctuaries' in New Zealand and has become an internationally famous conservation success story. Situated 4 km off the Whangaparaoa Peninsula, north of the city centre, the 220-ha island was originally leased for farming from 1855 to 1971, during which time the native forest was reduced to 6% of its former glory. Thankfully, the island was recognized by the New Zealand Wildlife Service (now DoC) as having great potential as a wildlife sanctuary. A nursery was set up in 1983 and from 1984 volunteers became involved in planting over 250,000 trees and shrubs, and the island is now 70% regenerated. A vital poison drop rid the island of rats making it predator free and ready for the arrival of most of its current avian residents. Now Tiri has become the safe haven for numerous rare and endangered species including the famous takahe, little spotted **kiwi**, **kokako**, whitehead, saddleback, North Island robin, kakariki, stitchbird and brown teal. Being an open sanctuary, members of the public can visit and experience what New Zealand used to be like, with the bush alive with the sound of birdsong. The **takahe** – those big friendly purple chickens with red beaks – are perhaps the most famous of its current tenants. These amazing, almost prehistoric birds, were thought to be extinct until a small group was rediscovered in the wild Fiordlands of the South Island. Since then a successful breeding programme has increased numbers and, given there are only about 200 of these birds left in the world, seeing them is an unforgettable experience.

The island has a numerous and varied network of **walks** on which you are almost certain to 'encounter' takahe and other species. The coastal scenery and sea views are magnificent. Do not miss the little blue penguin boxes near the wharf or the 'Wattle Track'. Kiwi are nocturnal so don't expect to see one unless you stay at the bunkhouse overnight. Ray and Barbara are excellent hosts, as are the highly committed volunteers of **Supporters of Tiritiri Matangi** ① T09-479 4490, *www.tiritirimatangi.org.nz*. Contact them for details of volunteer work. A guided tour costs $6. There is a souvenir shop on the island, but no food, so take a packed lunch. Snacks are available on the ferry.

Other islands in the Hauraki

Motuihe

This small unusually shaped island of 179 ha lies between Motutapu and Waiheke. There is archaeological evidence that suggests the island was inhabited and used extensively by Maori before it was purchased and farmed by European pioneer W H Fairburn in 1839. Ownership changed hands again a few times before the Crown finally bought it in 1872 and used it as a quarantine station. This station would be used as a prisoner of war camp in the First World War (prisoners included the infamous German Captain Felix von Lucker), an emergency hospital during the influenza epidemic in 1918, and a naval training base in the Second World War. In 1967, when the Hauraki Gulf Marine Park was established, the island came under the control of the Auckland City Council. Today, although the island is still farmed and is a DoC reserve, it is essentially a recreation venue, popular for swimming, fishing and escaping the city. There are a number of walks of up to three hours taking in a number of geological formations, archaeological sites, and the graves of those who died during the influenza epidemic. For detailed information about Motuihe and the ongoing conservation projects being undertaken refer to the website www.motuihe.org.nz.

Little Barrier Island

On a clear day it is just possible to see the mountainous bush-clad peaks that make up Little Barrier Island from the city. Little Barrier lies 90 km north of Auckland and 18 km west of her big sister, Great Barrier. This island is a plant and wildlife reserve of international value and significance. Being predator-free, it is sanctuary to a host of native birdlife, such as black petrel, cooks petrel and brown teal (all endangered). Other unusual inhabitants include the tuatara (a prehistoric native reptile), rare skinks and New Zealand's only bat (and native mammal) – the short-tailed bat. There are also 350 species of native plant on the island. But perhaps the most famous inhabitants are the **kakapo**. These flightless heavyweights (up to 3.5 kg) are the rarest parrot, and one of the most endangered birds, in the world. At present only 62 known individuals remain in captivity or on protected off-shore islands around New Zealand.

Waiheke Island → *Colour map 2, A2*

At 93 sq km, Waiheke is the largest island in the gulf and, only 20 km from the city (a 35-minute ferry ride), it is also the most visited and heavily populated. It has plenty of beaches, activities, easy access, fine restaurants and accommodation, but if you are looking for a real 'island experience' then you are far better going to Great Barrier. The main village and focus of attention on Waiheke is Oneroa at the western end of the island, just a short walk from the Matiatia Wharf. From Oneroa east, the settlements generally fade after Palm Beach and Onetangi, until the occasional holiday home and residential property gives way to farmland. ►► *See Sleeping, Eating and other listings, pages 125-127.*

Ins and outs

Getting there Fullers, T09-367 9119, offers a passenger-only service from the Auckland Ferry Building every two hours Monday to Friday 0520-2345, Saturday 0630-2345, Sunday 0700-2130; $28.50, child $15.60. There is also a service from Halfmoon Bay in the eastern suburbs and a number of tour packages (see page 127). **Pine Harbour Ferries**, T09-536 4725, www.pineharbour.co.nz, runs a fast (20 minutes) passenger service at weekends from the Beachlands Marina, $25, child $15 return with onward services to Auckland city centre (20 minutes), $20, child $10 return. Passenger and car ferries are also run by **Sealink**, T09-300 5900/T0800-732546, www.sealink.co.nz, a less salubrious service that runs almost hourly daily from Halfmoon Bay to Kennedy's Point, 0600-1830, $125 family car only, passengers $28.50. Bookings essential.

Getting around **Fullers**, T09-369 79111, offers a four-route service to and from the main Matiatia wharf and connects with all ferries. **Route One** runs to and from Onetangi taking in Oneroa, Blackpool, Surfdale and Ostend. **Route Two** goes from the wharf to Oneroa, Little Oneroa, Hauraki Store, Palm Beach and Ostend to Rocky Bay and back. **Route Three** runs from the wharf to Oneroa, Blackpool, Surfdale, Hauraki store, Palm Beach, Ostend, Onetangi to Rocky Bay and back. **Route Four** runs to Oneroa, Surfdale, Ostend to Onetangi and back. Tickets and $10 day passes available on the bus. 'Bus and Boat' specials are often available.

Waiheke Island

Sleeping
Boatshed **10**
Connells Bay Cottage & Sculpture Park **1**
Delamore Lodge **2**
Glass House **9**
Glenora Estate **4**
Hekerua Lodge Backpackers **5**
Kennedy Point Vineyard Guesthouse **6**

Le Chalet Waiheke Apartments **3**
Midway Motel **7**
Miro **8**
Onetangi Beachfront Apartments **12**
Onetangi Road Vineyard **13**
Palm Beach Lodge **14**
Punga Lodge **15**
Seadream Holiday Apartments **16**
Waiheke Island Resort **19**

Waiheke Island Hostel **20**
Whakanewha Regional Park **22**

Eating
Harbour Masters & Bar **2**
Mudbrick Vineyard **3**
Nourish Café **5**
Stonyridge **4**
Te Whau **1**
Vino Vino **8**

① *2 Korora Rd, in front of the Artworks Complex, Oneroa, T09-372 1234, Mon-Sat 0900-1700, Sun 0930-1600, www.waiheke nz.com, www.tourismwaiheke.co.nz and www.gotowaiheke.co.nz, left luggage $2.* Other than the island map ($1), publications to look out for are the *Gulf News*, www.waiheke gulfnews.co.nz, $1.50 (Thursday), the free *Gulf Islander*, the *Waiheke Marketplace* and the annual *Island Time – A Visitors Guide to Waiheke*. For walks, *Waiheke Island Walkways* is comprehensive; for vineyard details ask for the *Waiheke Island of Wine*.

Background

Waiheke was first settled by the Maori in AD 1200 and over the centuries tribes settled or were ousted by others, with the last bloody invasion coming from the notorious Bay of Islands-based *Hongi Hika* in the 1820s. European settlement began shortly after missionary Samuel Marsden established a mission near Matiatia in 1818. Sadly, like the rest of the region, Waiheke was cleared of its kauri by the first European settlers before livestock were introduced to create the bare rolling hills we see today. As the population of Auckland steadily grew so did the island's popularity as a holiday destination and by the 1960s clusters of baches (Kiwi beach holiday homes) were joined by an increasing number of permanents who were looking for that quiet 'alternative' lifestyle. So much so that the island was cruelly called 'Cadbury Island' (after the chocolate bars) – because you had to be either a 'fruit' or a 'nut' to live there.

Oneroa and around

Near the wharf and sandwiched between the popular Oneroa Bay and Blackpool beaches is the main settlement of Oneroa – a well-known creative haunt. Waiheke has been home to arty types for years and boasts some well-known artists, poets and writers, including the internationally renowned Zinni Douglas, Barbara Bailey and ceramist Hilary Kerrod. The VIC can provide information about art outlets and studios.

Situated just behind the VIC, the **Artworks Complex** is a small conglomerate with a cinema, a library, restaurant and the **Whittakers Musical Museum** ① *T09-372 5573, www.musical-museum.org, closed Tue, $3; entry and performance $12.50, child $5,* which displays over 100 musical instruments dating back 500 years, and which has live (1½-hour) performances at 1300.

Vineyards

Within a few kilometres of Oneroa are two fine examples of Waiheke's other claim to fame: vineyards. **Peninsula Estate** ① *52a Korora Rd, T09-372 7866, www.peninsula estate.co.nz,* offers free tastings and tours by prior arrangement; daily 1100-1430. **Mudbrick Vineyard** ① *2 km west of Oneroa, Church Bay Rd, T09-372 9050, www.mud brick.co.nz,* is open daily 1030-1700 in summer; see also Eating, page 126. Although their reign is now threatened, traditionally the two most famous vineyards on Waiheke are **Goldwater Estate** ① *18 Causeway Rd, Putiki Bay, T09-372 7493, www.goldwater wine.com, visits by appointment,* and, heading east, **Stonyridge Vineyard** ① *80 Onetangi Rd, T09-372 8822, www.stonyridge.co.nz, tastings daily 0900-1700, tours at weekends at 1130, $10.* There is also a fine café, which produces one of the world's most sought-after Cabernets-Larose. South of Onetangi is **Te Whau Vineyard** ① *218 Te Whau Drive, Rocky Bay, T09-372 7191, www.tewhau.com,* one of the newest on the island and noted for its fine labels, superb views and a classy café. You can visit the vineyards on the island on an organized tour (see page 127).

Onetangi and around

Within walking distance east of Oneroa along **Oneroa Bay** and up through the pleasant reserves and back roads is the next 'community', **Palm Beach** (two hours), with its small collection of houses and lovely sandy beach, which has a secluded spot for naturists. There is also a **General Store** that offers bike, boogie board and snorkelling gear hire.

From Palm Beach it is about 3 km to **Onetangi**, the site of Waiheke's longest and perhaps most popular beach. The Onetangi Beach Store hires out equipment for watersports. The **Waiheke Island Historic Village and Museum** ① *165 Onetangi Rd, T09-372 5168, Mon, Wed, Sat-Sun (daily during school holidays) 1200-1600, free,* is overlooked by a 700-year-old Maori *pa* and has cottages and a small museum exhibiting collections of farm machines, engines and assorted bric-a-brac. Also close by on Waiheke Road is the Forest and Bird Society's **Nature Reserve** which may, if you are lucky, produce the odd tui or native pigeon amidst its native tree plantations.

South of Oneroa
South of Oneroa are the scattered settlements of **Blackpool**, **Surfdale**, **Ostend** and **Omiha**, with little in the way of sights. Ostend has a Saturday morning market, while Omiha boasts the **Whakanewa Regional Park** – a pleasant scenic spot with camping.

Further afield
East of Onetangi, the habitation diminishes and farmland, the odd vineyard and secluded bay takes over. If you have time the **Stony Batter Reserve**, on the islands northeast headland, is worth a visit (1½-hour walk from the delightful **Cactus Bay**). It consists of an underground complex linked by a series of tunnels which, like others in Auckland, were built in the Second World War in fear of foreign invasion.

At the far south eastern corner of the island amidst some of its most stunning views is The **Connells Bay Sculpture Park** ① *Cowes Bay Rd, T09-372 8957, bookings only (mid Oct-mid April).* A stunning private collection of installations by some of New Zealand's best-known sculpture artists, all in a sublime garden setting with great views. There is no café but you are welcome to take a picnic. Recommended.

***

● Sleeping

Given its popularity and proximity to the city, Waiheke is very well served with lodging, but in recent years the focus seems to be mainly on vineyard accommodation luring couples or honeymooners. **Fullers**, Ferry Building on Quay St, T09-336 79111, www.fullers.co.nz, provides packages with accommodation included. **Waiheke Unlimited**, T09-372 7776, www.waihekeunlimited.co.nz, also acts as an agent for self-contained accommodation. There are also a number of lodges, motels, hostels and over 100 B&Bs to choose from, many with the ever-inviting 4-poster beds.

Oneroa and around *p124, map p123*
LL Boatshed, corner of Tawa and Huia sts, Little Oneroa, T09-372 3242, www.boat shed.co.nz. Neat architecture incorporates modern individual boatshed-style units and an elevated 'lighthouse' all luxuriously decked out for clients' comfort and relaxation. Expensive but certainly different.
LL Delamore Lodge, 83 Delamore Drive, Owhanake Bay, west of Oneroa, T09-372 7372, www.delamorelodge.com. 4 stunning luxury suites with private patios and panoramic views

of the Hauraki Gulf. A fine example of how well luxury and architecture can combine.
L Glenora Estate, 160 Nick Johnstone Drive, Church Bay, T09-372 5082, www.glenora estate.co.nz. Nestled within 3 ha of land, this 17th-century style farmhouse and barn offers wonderful en suite rooms – ideal for couples.
AL-A Punga Lodge, 223 Ocean View Rd, Little Oneroa, T09-372 6675, www.ki-wi.co.nz/ punga.htm. Comfortable but conventional self-contained or B&B units in garden and bush.
A Le Chalet Waiheke Apartments, 14 Tawa St, Oneroa, T09-372 7510. Self-contained apartments with decks and fine views in a quiet bush setting, further out from the beach.
A Seadream Holiday Apartments, 35 Waikare Rd, Oneroa, T09-372 8991, www.seadream .co.nz. Close to the beach, 2 well-appointed units, a studio and a larger unit with lounge.
B-D Hekerua Lodge Backpackers, 11 Hekerua Rd, Little Oneroa, T09-3728990, www.hekerualodge.co.nz. Describes itself as an oasis of tranquillity, offering fine doubles (1 en suite) twins, singles and dorms, an unusual pool and spa, all surrounded by native bush. Bike hire, internet.

Onetangi and around *p124, map p123*

L Palm Beach Lodge, 23 Tiri View Rd, Palm
Beach, T09-372 7763, www.waiheke.co.nz/
palmbch.htm. Spacious Mediterranean-
style suites with fine views.
L-AL Waiheke Island Resort, 4 Bay Rd,
Palm Beach, T09-372 0011, www.waiheke
resort.co.nz. One of Waiheke's better-known
luxury establishments with a wide range of
options from villa and chalet accommodation
for up to130 people. Fine restaurant and
swimming pool. Good venue for socialites.
L-A Miro, Browns Rd, Onetangi, T09-
372 7854. Vineyard based self-contained
Tuscan-style villa. A cheaper homestay-
style double is also available.
AL Onetangi Beachfront Apartments,
27 The Strand, Onetangi, T09-372 7051,
www.onetangi.co.nz. Self-contained luxury
apartments, 9 refurbished and 6 standard
units. BBQs, spas, sauna and free use of kayaks.
AL Onetangi Road Vineyard, 82 Onetangi
Rd, T09-372 1014. Offers a self-contained
set-up for 2 in a private vineyard cottage.
C-D Waiheke Island Hostel, 419 Seaview Rd,
Onetangi, T09-372 8971, www.waiheke
hostel.co.nz. Newly refurbished and friendly,
offering a cheaper option with plenty of
choice including en suite doubles, family
and twin bunk rooms with fine views, Sky TV
lounge, BBQ and mountain bikes available.

South of Oneroa *p125, map p123*
LL The Glass House, 33 Okoka Rd,
Rocky Bay, T09-372 3173, www.theglass
house.co.nz. The Glass House provides
modern, luxury accommodation with an
outstanding level of quality. As the names
suggests, walls of glass predominate with
a spacious, mainly open- plan interior
decorated in contemporary minimalist
style. The 3 classy suites command
exceptional views across the Hauraki Gulf.
One, the aptly named 'lookout suite', also
incorporates its own freestanding bathtub
and private deck. Outdoor hot tub and
swimming pool. Artworks are displayed
in a rotating exhibition in conjunction
with a reputable Auckland gallery. The
in-house restaurant offers excellent
4-course dinners. Massage, yoga and
beauty treatments are also available.
At the time of going to press The Glass
House was undergoing renovations.

AL Kennedy Point Vineyard Guesthouse,
44 Donald Bruce Rd, Ostend, T09-372
5600, www.kennedypointvineyard.com.
Well-appointed suites in a vineyard retreat.
A The Midway Motel, 1 Whakarite Rd, Ostend,
T09-372 8023, www.waihekemotel.co.nz.
Has small and large units, an indoor heated
pool, spa and spa room suites.

Campsites
Whakanewha Regional Park, T09-366 2000.
If you have a tent, you can have your own
110-ha retreat with fine views for $10.

Further afield *p125*
LL Connells Bay, Cowes Bay Rd, T09-372
8957, www.connellsbay.co.nz. A charming
100-year-old, luxury self-contained guest
cottage just metres from the beach on a
25-ha property featuring the classy sculpture
park (see page 125). Minimum 2-night stay.

⑦ Eating

Oneroa and around *p124, map p123*
Mudbrick Restaurant, attached to the
vineyard, T09-372 9050, www.mudbrick.co.nz,
daily, bookings essential. Great set menus
including a bistro degustation from $95,
à la carte and, of course, a fine wine list.
Harbour Masters Restaurant and Bar,
Matiatia, west of Oneroa, T09-372 2950.
Just a short stroll to the wharf, this is a
convenient option for an evening meal or
extended lunch for those with a ferry to catch.
Vino Vino Restaurant, 3/153 Ocean View
Rd, Oneroa, T09-372 9888, www.vinovino.
co.nz. Mediterranean fare in relaxed surrounds
overlooking the bay. Try the mussels.
Waiheke Resort Restaurant, near Palm
Beach, T09-372 7897. Outdoor decks with
fine views across the Gulf. Bookings essential.

South of Oneroa *p125, map p123*
Nourish Café, 3 Belgium St, Ostend,
T09-372 3557. Recommended for fresh
light meals, snacks and good coffee.
  The following vineyards are recommended.
Stonyridge, 80 Onetangi Rd, Ostend,
T09-372 8822, open weekends 1130-1700,
and Thu-Sun in summer.
Te Whau, Te Whau Point, T09-372 7191,
weekends 1100-1630, and Wed-Mon
1100-1700 in summer.

❶ Bars, pubs and clubs

Oneroa and around *p124, map p123*

Harbour Master's Restaurant and Bar, Matiatia, a short walk from the wharf, T09-372 2950, www.harbourmasters.co.nz. Reputedly where it all happens, especially when bands visit from the mainland.

❷ Entertainment

Oneroa and around *p124, map p123*
Live music
Live music can be heard on summer weekends, at a number of low-key eating venues.
Artworld Complex, Oneroa (behind the VIC), T09-372 2496. Cinema decked out with comfy sofas donated by residents, which after a day wine tasting results in inevitable soporifics.
Lazy Lounge Café 139 Oceanview Rd, Oneroa, T09-372 5132, www.thelazylounge.co.nz.
Vino Vino, 3/153 Ocean View Rd, Oneroa, T09-372 9888, www.vinovino.co.nz.

❋ Festivals and events

Waiheke Island *p122, map p123*
Feb Waiheke Wine Festival, www.waihekewine.co.nz. Very popular.
Mar/Apr Waiheke Jazz Festival, (Easter) www.waihekejazz.co.nz. Hugely popular, attracting national and international artists.

⛰ Activities and tours

Waiheke Island *p122, map p123*
Ananda Tours, 20 Seaview Rd, Ostend, T09-372 7530, www.anadatours.co.nz. The most expensive, offering art, eco and scenic tours.
Flying Carpet Sailing, 104 Wharf Rd, Ostend, T09-3725621, www.flyingcarpet.co.nz. A pleasant 6½-hr day cruise including lunch on a spacious catamaran, $125. 2-hr trip Fri/Sat/Sun from $65, 3-hr dinner cruise Fri/Sat $95.
Fullers, T09-3679111, www.fullers.co.nz. Offers a number of tour packages inclusive of ferry fare: the Island Explorer Tour ticket (departing at 1000) includes an all-day bus pass, from $42, child $21; the **Vineyard Tour** (departs 1100) takes in 3 of the island's best, plus an all-day bus pass for $90.
The Kayak Company, T09-372 2112, www.thekayakcompany.co.nz. Offers similar trips, 2 hrs to full day, from $45-120.

Out-There Surf, 21 Belgium St, Ostend, T09-372 6528. Hires out dive gear, surfboards and body boards.
Ross Adventures Sea Kayaking, Matiatia, T09-372 5550, www.kayakwaiheke.co.nz. Half- (4 hrs), full- or multi-day trips, from $70.
Skydive Waiheke, T09-372 4541, www.skydivewaiheke.co.nz. Safe and highly professional. Tandems with superb views of the city and pick-ups from the wharf.
Windsurfing Waiheke, 60 Ostend Rd, T09- 372 6275, www.windsurfing-waiheke.co.nz. For something a little more demanding, 2 hrs from $45 (independent hire available).

Vineyard tours
Waiheke Island Adventures Ltd, T09-372 6127, www.waihekeislandadventures.com. A local operator offering a more personal service and flexible itineraries.

⊖ Transport

Waiheke Island *p122, map p123*
Bicycle hire
Available at the Matiatia Wharf, T09-372 7937, from around $25 per day.

Car hire
Waiheke Auto Rentals, T09-372 8998, www.waihekerentals.co.nz. Operates a fleet of cars, station wagons, 4WDs, sports cars and a minibus from $50 per day.
Waiheke Rental Cars, T09-372 8635, www.waihekerentalcars.co.nz. Rent cars (from $50 a day), minibuses, jeeps, motorbikes and scooters (from $40 a day).

Taxi
Quality Cabs, T09-372 7000.
Waiheke Tuk Tuk, T09-372 6127, www.waihekeislandadventures.com.

❶ Directory

Waiheke Island *p122, map p123*
Oneroa has banks with 24-hr ATMs, a post office, chemist, grocery shops, petrol station and a number of cafés and bars. Internet access is available at most backpacker hostels and the **Lazy Lounge Cafebar**, 139 Oceanview Rd (centre of the village), T09-372 5132.

Great Barrier Island → *Colour map 2, A2*

Unlike Waiheke, Great Barrier (or the 'Barrier') has not yet been spoilt by the influences of the city and still offers the visitor a true island adventure. The ferry to the Barrier is a joint island service that at first is packed with commuters and visitors before it empties dramatically at Waiheke and you are left amongst the Barrier locals, the fishing rods and rucksacks of the occasional intrepid backpacker. The bar on the boat suddenly takes a hammering and the conversation turns to local Barrier gossip, kingfish and snapper. The orange glow of the city gradually fades behind Rangitoto and you begin to feel a welcome isolation close in. Great Barrier is the second largest island in the gulf and lies almost 90 km northeast of Auckland. It used to be part of what is now the Coromandel Peninsula and in a way shares the same isolated, under-developed feel, with rugged hills, numerous bays and beautiful quiet beaches. The Barrier is 'possum free' so a precious habitat for some rare and endangered species – the brown teal and New Zealand's largest skink, the cheveron – being the most notable. For those out to do some diving, fishing, tramping, surfing, sailing and relaxing it is unsurpassed in the region. ▶▶ *For Sleeping, Eating and other listings, see pages 132-134.*

Ins and outs

Getting there by air The main airfield is at Claris in the centre east of the island about 17 km from Tryphena's Shoal Bay Wharf. Another airfield is at Okiwi, north of Claris. **Great Barrier Airlines**, offices at the Auckland Domestic Terminal (and at the airfield on the Barrier at Claris), T09-275 9120, T0800-900600, www.greatbarrierairlines.co.nz, is the main carrier; it offers an efficient service to the island from Auckland and North Shore airports, as well as connecting flights to the Coromandel (Whitianga) and Whangarei in Northland. There are two to four flights daily 0745, 1015, 1500 and 1600 and 1800 from Auckland, returning 0900, 1300, 1600 and 1700 from Claris, with extra flights in summer on demand. A standard return costs around $180, child $100 and a single $89, child $49. Fly-Boat option cost $139. Surfboards $35 return, bikes $35. These prices are cheap considering the scenic extravaganza on offer. **Mountain Air's Great Barrier Express**, T0800-222123, www.mountainair.co.nz, offers a similar service. Both airlines offer pick-up/drop-off shuttle services throughout the island (see Getting around, below) and a 'fly and boat' package for about $140 (highly recommended).

Getting there by sea Ferry services access the island mainly at Tryphena but also Whangaparapara and Port Fitzroy. **Fullers**, T09-367 9111, www.fullers.co.nz, offers regular passenger ferry services from the city (two hours), from $105, child $50 return; book ahead. **Sealink** (Subritzky Shipping), T0800-732546/T09-300 5900, www.sea link.co.nz, offers a vehicle and passenger service on the *MV Sealink*, from Wynyard Wharf in Auckland. Sailings daily except Saturday (three hours); extra sailings in summer. Vehicle $410 return, passenger $105, child $72 return. Fly/boat options from $147.

Getting around A network of roads (mostly unsealed) connects the main settlements. Public transport around the island is well organized. **Great Barrier Airlines** (GBA) and **Mountain Air** provide shuttles to and from the airport. A swarm of vehicles will meet you at Tryphena Wharf (Shoal Bay) or Claris Airport. Many hotels provide pick-ups but, if you have not yet booked, the taxis/shuttles will take you to the VIC in Tryphena or beyond. Hitching is generally safe – don't be surprised if you find yourself on a quad bike or steamroller. **Great Barrier Travel** runs a daily service around the main centres and meets incoming aircraft 0800-1520. A one-way fare to Tryphena costs $12; hop-on/hop-off passes available. Other transport operators include **Mike Newman** in Port Fitzroy T09-429 0052 and **GBI Transfer and Shuttles**, T09-429 0062. ▶▶ *See Transport, page 134.*

0033/T09-367 6009, www.greatbarrier.co.nz, daily 0900-1700. Also useful is www.great
barrierisland.co.nz. Take detailed maps if you intend to explore the island's wild interior.
Free handouts are available from the **Fullers** information centre and DoC offices at the
Ferry Building in Auckland, or the **DoC** ① *Port Fitzroy, T09-429 0044, www.doc.govt.nz,
Mon-Fri 0800-1630*, or the VIC in Claris. The DoC leaflets are detailed and informative.

Background

The Maori name for Great Barrier is *Aotea* meaning 'White Cloud' or 'Clear Day'. Before
the Europeans arrived, over 12,000 Maori were settled on the island; that population
has all but disappeared with only a few descendants of the first tribes still remaining.
Captain Cook renamed the island during his 1769 voyage (along with its more
mountainous sister, Little Barrier). 'Great Barrier' was an obvious name for the island's
placement between open ocean and the inner gulf. The European history was initially
centred on the kauri industry and for a while it prospered. Once cleared, attentions
turned to the mineral deposits of gold, silver and copper, which did not prove very
productive. The plunder above and below ground complete, the sea became the focus,
with a thriving whaling station being set up in Whangaparapara (the remnants of which
still remain). Now, 100 years on with the kauri, minerals, whales and human population
depleted, the island has been left to the alternative, almost self-sufficient lifestylers –
people who thankfully are much more conservation-minded. The DoC now owns and
administers over half of the island. The current permanent population of the island
juggles around 1000 but increases dramatically with visitors in the summer months.

Sights

Great Barrier is an activities destination, from lounging on the beach to multi-day
tramps in the huge **Great Barrier Forest**, which is where you will find the most notable
'sights', both natural and historical. There are numerous walks or tramps and the best
source of information on these is the DoC office in Port Fitzroy. The *Essential Guide to
Great Barrier* highlights the best walks and routes. Most tramps start or finish from
various access points on the road between Port Fitzroy and Whangaparapara. The most
popular starting point is Port Fitzroy, where supplies and information can be gathered at
the wonderfully stocked general store and DoC office.

Tryphena and the south

Tryphena is the main arrival point (by sea) and centre of population on Great Barrier. It
is split into three areas or bays: **Shoal Bay** where the wharf is, **Pa Beach** and **Mulberry
Grove**. In Pa Beach and Mulberry Grove you will find most of what you need petrol to
accommodation. Most shops are in the Stonewall Complex in the heart of Tryphena.

About 4 km north, **Needle Rock** (270 m) is a fine place to start exploring the island.
It is a rough 20-minute scramble to the summit, which offers a great view back to
Tryphena and the Coromandel to the south and all that awaits you to the north.

Medlands Beach is perhaps the most popular beach, especially with surfies, but
it is also a fine place to swim, fish, sunbathe or take a walk around the headlands.

Around Claris

North of Claris is a crossroads. Head directly north for about 3 km, and you will arrive
at the access point for the **Kaitoke Hot Springs** – a flat, easy one-hour walk past the
Kaitoke Swamp to a series of pools in which you can relieve tired limbs.

Some 2 km along and south of the Whangaparapara Road on the Te Ahumata
track, the concrete foundations are all that remain of the **Orville Stamping Battery** that
once crushed quartz from the Te Ahumata gold field. From Whangaparapara Harbour, it

Aiguilles Island

SS Wairarapa

Miners Head

▲ Tataweka
(526m)

Rangiwhakaea Bay

Ahuriri Point

Bird Rocks

SS Wairarapa
Walkway

Waikaro Point

Katherine Bay

Whangapoua
Beach

SS Wairarapa
Graves

Whangapoua Estuary

Okokewa Island
(Green Island)

13

Komahunga Bay
(Mona Bay)

Port Abercrombie

8   Okiwi

Nelson Island
(Peter Island)

DOC Office 3 6

Haratataunga Beach

Haratauaga - Okiwi Track

Port Fitzroy

Windy
Canyon Walk

Kaikoura Island
(Selwyn Island)

Palmers Track

Haratataunga Rd

Kauri Dam

Mt Hobson
(Hirakimata 621m)

DOC Kaiarara
Hut

Opakau
Island

Peach Tree Track

Tramline Track

Great Barrier
Forest

Grey Rd

Awana
Bay

Rangiahua
Island
(Flat Island)

Forest Rd

Palmers
Beach

Mahuki Island
(Anvil Island)

Junction
Islands

Kaitoke
Hot Springs

Kaitoke
Creek

Whangaparapara Rd

Whangaparapara

7

Orville
Stamping
Battery 4

Claris +

Whangara Island
(Cliff Island)

Whangaparapara
Whaling Station

Blind Bay Rd

3 5
1

Pitokuku
Island

Whangaparapara Bay

Okupu

5

Blind
Bay

Memory Rock

11

10

Needle Rock
(270m)

12 1

Tryphena

7 17
Fullers
Office 2

Store 1
2
15

Shag Point

Shoal Bay
Wharf

14

Cape Barrier Rd

To Auckland ▶

16

is still possible to see the remains of the Barrier's old **whaling station**. The oceans around the Barrier were the killing fields for thousands of whales from the 1950s before operations thankfully ceased in the 1960s.

Heading east from the Claris crossroads, cross the river and continue up around the headland to **Palmers Beach** with its shroud of pohutukawa trees falling chaotically to the beach. This is a fine beach but access is not easy. The far more accessible **Awana Bay** is also a fine spot, popular for surfing.

Port Fitzroy and the north

The path to **Windy Canyon Lookout** starts at the Palmers Track entrance on the summit (330 m) of Whangapoua Hill/Aotea Road (15 minutes). It then climbs 100 m through Windy Canyon to the central ridge and offers good views of the Okiwi Basin and Kaitoke. The Palmers Track then follows the ridge and climbs steeply to the summit of Mount Hobson (three hours one way). At 621 m, **Mount Hobson (Hirakimata)** is the island's highest point. On a clear day its 360° view of the island and beyond is unsurpassed. The summit is the principal nesting site for the rare black petrel. Only about 4500 remain and they are only found on Great and Little Barrier Islands. They spend most of their life out at sea and are nocturnal on land, so don't expect to see any. They also nest in burrows so make sure you keep to the paths. From the summit the track splits – The Kaiarara track offering a route west to **Port Fitzroy** (with some fine remains of kauri dams on the way) or south via the Peach Tree Track that ends at the Kaitoke hot springs. The well preserved remains of a **kauri dam** can be seen along the Kaiarara Track. Kauri dams were used by loggers to drive large numbers of kauri downstream, allowing access to remote areas of bush. The lower one at Kaiarara was one of the largest driving dams to be built in New Zealand and is one of its best examples.

The SS Wairarapa was one of many ships wrecked on the island and certainly the most tragic, with the loss of 130 lives. It ran ashore near Miner's Head in 1894. The 30-minute walk along Whangapoua Beach to Tapuwai Point from the road end takes you to one of two graveyard sites on the island – the other being at Onepoto Beach at Katherine Bay on the west coast.

Rakitu Island
(Arid Island)

Whakatautuna Point

N

0 km 2
0 miles 2

Medlands
Beach

Windy Hill
(361m)

Rosalie
Bay Rd

Vol Ruahine
(402m)

Cape Barrier

Sleeping
Earthsong Lodge **2**
Fitzroy House **3**
Foromor Lodge **5**
Great Barrier Lodge **7**
High Tide & Green Grass **8**
Medlands Beach
　Backpackers & Motel **10**
Medlands Beach Bach **11**
Oasis Lodge **12**
Orama Christian
　Community **13**
Pigeon's Lodge **14**
Pohutukawa Lodge **15**
Stray Possum Lodge **16**
Tipi & Bob's
　Waterfront Lodge **17**

Eating
Angsana Thai **5**
Barrier Oasis **1**
Claris Texas Café **3**
Cruisy Café & Bakery **7**
Curragh Irish Pub **2**
Great Barrier Island Sports
　& Social Club **4**
Port Fitzroy Boating Club **6**

The **Whangapoua Estuary** is a top spot for wildlife and is home to many interesting coastal and wetland species including spotless crake, banded rail and brown teal. If you spot a brown teal – a rather nondescript little brown duck – consider yourself very lucky as there are only 1200 left in the world. Great Barrier is home to 80% of these.

⛺ Sleeping

Great Barrier is remote and basic, with no mains power, street lights, reticulated water supply or extensive road network. However, when it comes to accommodation you can either enjoy that simplicity or be utterly spoilt. Book well in advance in summer. The best bet is to contact the island's VIC, or check out www.greatbarrier.co.nz and www.great barrierisland.co.nz. **Fullers**, Ferry Building, Auckland, T09-367 9111, www.fullers.co.nz, offers accommodation packages and advice from its office on the mainland. **Island Accommodation**, T09-429 0995, www.island accommodation.co.nz, is the local agent.

Tryphena and the south *p129, map p130*
LL Earthsong Lodge, 38 Medland Rd, Tryphena, T09-429 0030, www.earthsong lodge.co.nz. A popular 5-star luxury option overlooking Tryphena Harbour. The fine cuisine is reflected in the price.
LL Foromor Lodge, Medlands Beach, T09-429 0335. A 'helicopter arrival'-type venue on a fine beachfront location at Medlands. 2 double en-suites. Meals and activities included.
LL Oasis Lodge, Tryphena, T09-429 0021, www.barrieroasis.co.nz. Set in a vineyard, this is an old favourite. Luxury and cheaper cottage options available, meals included.
L-AL Tipi and Bob's Waterfront Lodge, Puriri Bay Rd, Tryphena, T09-429 0550, www.water frontlodge.co.nz. An old favourite with 6 tidy self-contained units, close to amenities.
AL Pigeon's Lodge, 179 Shoal Bay Rd, Tryphena, T09-429 0437, www.pigeons lodge.co.nz. A fine B&B with rooms with bathrooms and set in quiet bush.
A Medlands Beach Bach, T021-367771, www.greatbarrier.co.nz. Mid-range self-contained option and one of the original beach baches set right on the surf beach.
A-D Medlands Beach Backpackers and Motel, T09-429 0320, www.medlands beach.com. Budget accommodation for couples and families. Chalet and villa as well as a traditional 4-bunk lodge. It is remote so stock up with food. Surfies' favourite.

A-D Pohutukawa Lodge, Pa Beach, Tryphena, T09-4290211, www.currachirishpub.co.nz. Close to shops, restaurants and the pubs. B&B en suites and backpacker accommodation.
A-D Stray Possum Lodge, 64 Cape Barrier Rd, Tryphena, T09-429 0109, www.straypossum .co.nz. Excellent backpacker hostel near the wharf, offering dorms, doubles, self-contained chalets and camping in a lovely bush setting. Bar, Sky TV, internet and pizza café. Friendly management and staff. Tours available, bikes, boogie boards and wet suits for hire.

Around Claris *p129, map p130*
A Great Barrier Lodge, Whangaparapara, T09-429 0488, www.greatbarrierlodge.com. Accommodation is in cottages in the grounds and, being out of the way, just about all you need is available. Car, bike and equipment hire, licensed bar and restaurant. Close to the hot pools.

Port Fitzroy and the north
p131, map p130
AL Fitzroy House, T09-429 0091, www.fitz royhouse.co.nz. Self-contained cottage in a wonderful setting with heaps of activities. Tramp and Sail package available.
A Orama Christian Community, near Port Fitzroy, T09-429 0063, www.orama.org.nz. Self-contained flats and cottage, guestroom, cabin and bunkroom, in a very scenic spot. Has its own library, shop and laundry.
A-C High Tide and Green Grass, 2 Mabey Rd, Okiwi, T09-429 0190. Solar powered house set in 5 ha of pasture and bush offering isolation and peace, backpacker lodge available.

Camping
There are 6 DoC campsites and 1 DoC hut available (The Whangaparapara hut having burnt to the ground recently). Bookings are advised and current charges (average $6) are available on enquiry at the main DoC office is in Port Fitzroy, T09-429 0044. The campsites are at Akapoua Bay (Port Fitzroy), Whangaparapara, Medlands, Whangapoua,

Harataonga and Awana. For convenience Akapoua Bay is advised, and the best of the more secluded campgrounds is Harataonga; there is also a guest lodge sleeping 8. The Kaiarara Hut, T09-429 0044, $10, has 24 bunks, a wood stove, toilet and cold water.

Private campgrounds are also available at Great Barrier Island Campground, Puriri Bay, Tryphena, T09-429 0184, $10; Orama Christian Community $10, (see above); and Mickey's, Awana Valley, T09-429 0170, probably the most entertaining camping venue on the island and all for under $10.

① Eating

There are very few restaurants on the Barrier; most are attached to hotels, many of which offer excellent cuisine. Food can be bought in Tryphena at: Stonewall Village Store, T09-429 0451; The Outpost, T09-429 0610, and Mulberry Grove Store and Café, 1 Mulberry Grove, T09-429 0909; in Whangaparapara at The Claris Store, T09-429 0852, and Great Barrier Lodge, T09-429 0488; and at Port Fitzroy General Store, T09-429 0056.

Tryphena and the south *p129, map p130*
♥♥♥ **Barrier Oasis**, Stonewall, Tryphena, T09-429 0021. Top quality cuisine for guests and visitors, lunch and dinner. Booking essential.
♥♥ **Curragh Irish Pub**, Stonewall Complex, Tryphena, T09-429 0211. Good pub food with a wicked seafood chowder.
♥♥ **Earthsong Lodge**, Tryphena, T09-429 0030. Excellent French cuisine. Bookings essential.
♥ **Cruisy Café and Bakery**, Stonewall Village, Tryphena. Home-made sandwiches and snacks.
♥ **Stray Possum Lodge**, Tryphena. Pizza.
♥ **Tipi and Bob's**, Tryphena, T09-429 0550. Menu includes fish and chips and takeaways.

Around Claris *p129, map p130*
♥♥ **Angsana Thai Restaurant**, 63 Gray Rd, Claris, T09-429 0292. Excellent Thai and Kiwi cuisine, vegetarian dishes. Bookings advised.
♥♥ **Claris Texas Café**, Claris, T09-429 0811, daily 0800-1600. Fine food all day and from 1800 Thu-Sun. Best coffee on the island.
♥♥ **Great Barrier Lodge**, Whangaparapara, T09-429 0488. Restaurant and bar.
♥ **Great Barrier Island Sports and Social Club**, Claris, T09-429 0260. Open Wed/Fri/Sat. Good value bar meals and takeaways.

♥ **Port Fitzroy Boating Club**, T09-429 0072, Thu-Sat from 1600, from 1000 in summer.

① Pubs, bars and clubs

Great Barrier Island *p128, map p130*
In summer the bays are alive with the sound of clinking gin bottles and laughter from the yachts and expensive launches. On the mainland there are 2 fine places to drink:
Curragh Irish Pub, at the Pohutukawa Lodge, T09-429 0211. Live entertainment with an unusual Kiwi/Irish flavour.
The Stray Possum Lodge, T09-429 0109. Has a delightful little bar, where the occasional wild party sometimes ensues.

⊛ Festivals and events

Great Barrier Island *p128, map p130*
The Barrier Island Sports and Social Club in Claris hosts a monthly market (last Sat).
May Great Barrier Island Seafood Celebration. The main and increasingly popular annual festival on the Barrier. Visit www.seafoodgreatbarrier.com for details.

▲ Activities and tours

Great Barrier Island *p128, map p130*
Boat hire
GBI Adventure Rentals, Mulberry Grove, Tryphena, T09-429 0062, www.greatbarrier island.co.nz. A wonderland awaits you.

Fishing
The VIC has information on local charters. Some of the best land-based spots are Lighthouse Point (Shoal Bay, Tryphena), Cape Barrier, Shag Point, 'Shark Alley' (south headlands of Medlands Beach) and Harataonga.

Golf
Claris Golf Club, T09-429 0420. The Barrier has a golf course, but mind the pukekos.

Kayaking
The Barrier is a sea kayaking paradise. Circumnavigation of the island takes about 5 days and is an awesome trip needing careful planning and local help.
Aotea Kayaks, T09-429 0664, trips from $30.

Fitzroy House Outdoor Centre,
T09-429 0091. Hire only.
Great Barrier Lodge, T09-429 0488.
Independent hire costs about $45 a day.

Mountain biking

This is a great way to explore the island;
both airlines and ferry operators are bicycle-
friendly. For environmental reasons most
tracks are off limits, but a fine track that is
accessible is the DoC forest 4WD track off
Whangaparapara Rd. Companies include:
GBI Hire, Claris, T09-429 0471; **Great Barrier
Lodge**, Whangaparapara, T09-429 0488; and
Paradise Cycles, Tryphena, T09-429 0303.

Scuba diving

The waters around the Barrier are wonderfully
clear. Great diving can be found all around the
island, but preferred spots are Tryphena Harbour,
around Port Fitzroy and off Harataonga Bay.
Great Barrier Lodge, Whangaparapara,
T09-429 0488. Refills available.
Hooked on Barrier, 89 Hector Sanderson
Rd, Claris, T09-429 0740. Also offers refills.
Mobile Dive Centre, Tryphena Wharf,
T09-429 0654. Dive gear for hire.

Swimming

Swimming (especially for kids) is best kept
to sheltered west coast bays, but the big
eastern beaches are fine for adults if you are
vigilant. Take flippers and a boogie board.

Surfing

The best spots are Medlands, Kaitoke,
Palmers and Awana Bays.

Tour operators

Barrier Tour Co, T09-429 0222, www.gbi
nz.com/tours. Small-group guided tours.
Discover Great Barrier, T021-420935,
www.discovergreatbarrier.co.nz. Also
offers tours for small groups.

Walking/tramping

1 day From the start of Palmers Track at the
top of Okiwi Hill take a look at Windy Canyon
before continuing to the summit of Mt
Hobson. From there take the Peach Tree Track
directly to the hot springs with pick-up again
from Whangaparapara Rd. The Harataonga –
Okiwi Track (5 hrs) and Rosalie Bay Rd end
to Claris (5 hrs) are also fine walks.

2 days Follow the route above, but from
Mt Hobson, check out the kauri dam remains
before continuing along the track and staying
the night at the Kaiarara Hut (see Sleeping).
The next day take the Forest Rd and Tramline
Tracks to finish your tramp in style at the
Kaitoke Hot Springs. Arrange a pick-up from
the Whangaparapara Rd access point.

⊖ Transport

Great Barrier Island *p128, map p130*
Bus **Great Barrier Travel**, T0800-426832/
T09-429 0474, runs a bus from Tryphena to the
main centres 5 times daily in summer. Day pass
($39), 5-day pass ($59), hop-on/hop-off.

Car hire Petrol and diesel available at
Tryphena (Mulberry Grove), Claris, Port Fitzroy
and Whangaparapara. **Gas**: refills at Claris
Motors, **Port Fitzroy Store** and 428 Shoal
Bay Rd, Tryphena.
Aotea Rental Cars, T09-429 0474.
GBI Rental Cars, Mulberry Grove, Tryphena,
T09-4290062, full range including mokes.
Great Barrier Lodge, Whangaparapara,
T09-429 0488. All companies offer a range of
vehicles from hatchbacks to mokes, from $55.
Medlands Rentals, Kaitoke, T09-429 0861,
www.medlandsrentals.co.nz.

Taxi The typical fare from Tryphena to
Claris is around $12. **Great Barrier Travel**
(see Bus, above), offers transfers on demand.

⊕ Directory

Great Barrier Island *p128, map p130*
Banks There are no banks but EFTPOS is
available in most shops, cafés, hotels and
restaurants. **Internet** Claris Texas Cafe, daily
0800-1600, T09-429 0811. **Laundry** Claris
Fuel and Laundromat, T094-290075. **Medical
services** Health Centre, Claris, T09-429 0356.
Pharmacy: Claris, T09-429 0006. **Police**
Claris, T09-429 0343. **Post office** Outpost,
Tryphena (Stonewall Complex), T09-429
0610. Port Fitzroy Store, T09-429 0056. You
can even send a message by pigeon at
the **Pigeon Post**, Claris, T09-429 0242. **Public
toilets** Shoal Bay, Whangaparapara, Port
Fitzroy Wharves, Mulberry Grove and Pa Beach
Tryphena, Medlands, Claris and the Airfield.
Telephone Available at main centres.

Footprint features

Introduction

Northland is often called the 'birthplace of the nation' and 'the 'winterless north'. The region is rich in history, has a fine climate and boasts some of the most stunning coastal scenery in the country. It was here that the first Maori set foot in New Zealand, about AD 1000, followed by the first European settlers over 800 years later. It was also here, in the Bay of Islands in 1840, that the Treaty of Waitangi was signed – the document that launched the relationship between two deeply contrasting peoples. This relationship is reflected in the calms and the storms of unsettled ocean currents that unite uneasily at New Zealand's northernmost point, North Cape. Lost in time in the Waipoua Forest, making all that human history seem like yesterday, stands one of the few remaining 'ancient' kauri trees: the centuries-old 'Tane Mahuta'.

All in all, for the modern day visitor, although the fine weather label does not always hold true, Northland must feature as one of the most aesthetically and historically interesting regions to visit in New Zealand. Most of what it has to offer is signposted and detailed as the aptly named and celebrated 'Twin Coast Discovery'.

★ Don't miss ...

1 **Ocean Beach** Watch the sunrise on the beach then synchronize watches at the Clock Museum in Whangarei Town Basin, page 150.

2 **Old Russell Road** Explore the Northland Coast, page 151.

3 **Poor Knights Islands** Head out to sea on a fishing or scuba diving trip from Tutukaka, page 155.

4 **Waitangi National Reserve** Discover the 'Birth of the Nation', page 158.

5 **Bay of Islands** Have a go at one of the many activities on offer in this beautiful bay, including swimming with dolphins, kayaking, sailing, big game fishing or taking a fast jet boat ride, page 167.

6 **Cape Reinga** Visit the northernmost tip of New Zealand where the Tasman Sea meets the Pacific Ocean, page 176.

7 **Waipoua Kauri Forest Park** Stand in awe below the massive 1500-year-old kauri tree 'Tane Mahuta', page 182.

8 **Te Kopuru** Check out the bizarre garden decorations at 51 Norton Street, near Dargaville, page 184.

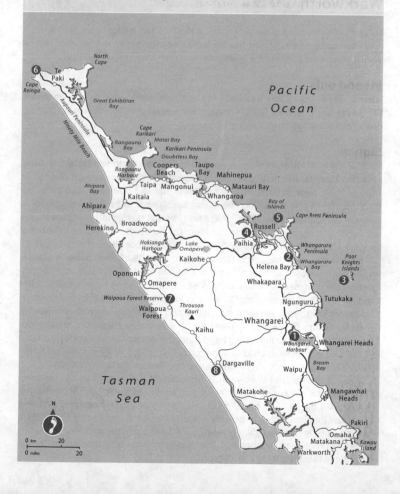

Northland Introduction

Warkworth and Kowhai Coast

→ *Colour map 1, C4*

Although not geographically within Northland, Warkworth is for most a starting point and a gateway to the region. Most travellers, in their haste to reach Whangarei or the Bay of Islands (on SH1), miss it out altogether, while others stop for lunch or a coffee by the river before taking the slower and more scenic route north, along the Kowhai Coast, via the vineyards of Matakana, then on to the scenic coastal settlements of Leigh, Mangawhai and Waipu. Whatever your intention, Warkworth and the pleasant coastal bays, peninsulas and islands to its east, are certainly worthy of a stop. When it comes to tourism and its associate services, the district is developing at a phenomenal rate.

The Kowhai Coast extends from Wenderholm Regional Park, just north of Waiwera, to Pakiri Beach and contains three regional parks, Kawau Bay, including Kawau Island, the Marine Reserve at Goat Island and over 26 accessible beaches popular for boating, fishing, diving and walking. ►► *For Sleeping and Eating and other listings, see pages 143-145.*

Warkworth ●●●● ►► pp143-145.

Although of some historic significance as a former kauri-milling town, Warkworth is now essentially a farming and tourism service centre set in the heart of Rodney District and on the banks of the Mahurangi River, 70 km north of Auckland.

Ins and outs

Intercity, T09-623 1503, and **Northliner**, T09-438 3206, buses arrive outside **Warkworth VIC (I-Site)** ① *1 Baxter St, T09-425 9081, www.warkworth-information.co.nz, Mon-Sat 0830-1730, Sun 0900-1500.*

Sights

Much of the local history is nicely presented in the **Warkworth and District Museum** within the **Parry Kauri Park** ① *Tudor Collins Drive, on the southern outskirts of the town, T09-425 7093, www.museum.orcon.net.nz daily, summer 0900-1600, winter 0900-1530, $6, child $1.* The museum falls under the shadow of two impressive 600- to 800-year-old kauri trees (the tallest on the east coast of Northland), and explores, in a number of carefully recreated rooms, the life of the early pioneers and the influence of the great kauri industry upon them. There is also a small but pleasant nature trail.

Four kilometres south, and in stark contrast, is the **Warkworth Satellite Station**, which is the Telecom NZ national base for international satellite communications. Although the unmanned visitor centre has now closed, the two huge satellite dishes may lure still you off the main road for a closer look. Back on SH1 again, and less than 1 km further south, you can get back to nature and all things sweet and communal at the **Honey Centre** ① *Perry Rd, T09-425 8003, www.honeycentre.co.nz, daily 0900-1700, free.* It provides an interesting insight into the industry and a close-up look at a resident hive, and provides an ideal opportunity to buy a tub of the golden stuff for the kids to spread gratuitously all around the hire car. There is also a café on site.

About 4 km north of Warkworth is **Sheepworld** ① *T09-425 7444, www.sheep worldfarm.co.nz, daily 0900-1700, shows at 1100 and 1400, $9 (with show $17.50), child $5/$8.* If the foot falls heavy on the accelerator at the very prospect of such a place, then just hold off. It is actually quite entertaining and worthy of the stop. Although chasing them is rightly frowned upon, you are allowed to feed the lambs and get involved in some shearing. The souvenir shop more than caters for the remainder of your visit; there's also a café.

⦂ Wallabies abroad

In the sporting arena Australians are often called Wallabies and New Zealanders, of course, Kiwis. But when it comes to the influence of playing home or away, this story – quite literally – takes the biscuit. In the late 1800s the then-governor of New Zealand, Sir George Grey (a man not impartial to owning the odd pet), shipped, along with several zebra, antelope and kookaburras, a group of South Australian tammar wallabies to his privately owned Kawau Island, near Auckland. Although the antelope and zebra soon perished, the wallabies survived, indeed thrived, munching there way through the islands native vegetation and reaching pest proportions. The Department of Conservation would quietly love to have seen their total eradication, were it not so controversial. This was further exacerbated given the fact that the wallabies had become a tourist attraction, and were proving popular with day visitors from which they sought considerable camaraderie especially when eating. Ironically, meanwhile, in Australia, that specific genetic strain of tammar wallaby had become extinct. Now, remarkably rediscovered, it is hoped a small group of the Kiwi wallabies can be shipped back to South Australia to resurrect the species.

But it doesn't end there. In recent decades another unrelated group of wallabies were released near the South Island town of Waimate. They also reached pest proportions, except there, they are now hunted and even used as the filling of a local butcher's pie. And when it comes to sport, most Kiwis wish Wallabies were regularly reduced to the fillings of meat pies.

A further 3 km north is the **Dome State Forest**, which provides a number of walks ranging from 40 minutes to three hours. The best walk takes 1½ hours and involves climbing to the Dome Summit from where you can spot the Auckland Sky Tower on a clear day. All the walks start at the top of the **Dome Café**, which is open daily.

To the east of Warkworth, on the scenic Mahurangi Peninsula, are the popular coastal holiday venues of **Snells Beach** (with the **Salty Dog Tavern**, see page 144), **Algies Bay** and **Martins Bay**, the latter having the best beach, and **Sandspit**, from where the ferry departs to **Kawau Island** (see below).

Short river trips by steamboat ($15) and self-guided or guided tours of the Matakana vineyards are also on offer from Warkworth; contact the VIC for information.

Kawau Island 🛏 » pp143-145.

Kawau Island is a popular holiday resort 8 km off the coast on the Mahurangi Peninsula. In summer its sheltered bays are almost more popular than terra firma, as yachties from far and wide drop anchor to enjoy the surroundings, fish, swim, dive or party long into the wee small hours. In pre-European times the island was the headquarters of Maori raiders who made numerous attacks on surrounding tribes from their villages and *pa*.

Ins and outs

Getting there A seasonal cruise run by **360 Discovery** ① T09-307 8005/T0800-888006, www.360discovery.co.nz, departs from the Auckland waterfront on Saturdays at 0900, arriving back at 1650, $69, child $15 (lunch available). **Matata Cruises** ① T021-960910, www.kawau-bay-cruises.co.nz, offers a daily cruise from

Sandspit at 1000 and 1400, $30. Water taxis also operate from Sandspit; contact **Ruben's Water Taxi** ① *To800-111616/To9-422 8881, www.watertaxi.co.nz.* There is no public transport to Sandspit from Warkworth. For a taxi call To9-425 0000.

Around the island

European ownership dates back to 1837 when the island became the focus for mining activities – first manganese, then copper – with operations ceasing in 1869. There are still remnants of copper mines a short walk from the wharf. In 1862 Sir George Grey, in his second term as Governor of New Zealand, purchased the island for a mere £3500 and began a 26-year stay in Bon Accord Harbour, where he created perhaps the biggest modern day tourist draw, the **Mansion House** ① *To9-422 8882, daily 1000-1530, $4, child $2.* Grey was fascinated by botany and zoology, developing a small collection of exotic animals and plants and also using the island as an acclimatization centre. He even had a pair of zebra brought from Africa to pull his carriage, which resulted in their death shortly after. Sadly, George was also blissfully unaware of the monumental environmental damage he was unleashing on the increasingly threatened New Zealand native wildlife and vegetation. To this day the odd wallaby hops through the bush, accompanied by the laughing of the Australian kookaburra (see box, page 139).

In 1967, 79 years after Sir George Grey went home to England, the island became part of the **Hauraki Maritime Park**. Some 176 ha were put aside as public domain, the Mansion House turned from guesthouse to museum and the rest of the island went to farmers and the wallabies.

North of Warkworth ⊜⦿ ↠ *pp143-145.*

Matakana and around

Blink and you may miss Matakana, 8 km north of Warkworth on the main Warkworth to Leigh Road, but the surrounding countryside is increasingly famous for its **vineyards**. **Heron's Flight Vineyard** ① *49 Sharp's Rd, To9-422 7915, www.heronsflight.co.nz, daily 1000-1800; tours and tastings available, café on site*, is one of a number producing a fine nationally recognized merchandise. Others include: **Ascension** ① *To9-422 9601, www.ascensionvineyard.co.nz;* **Hyperion** ① *To9-422 9375, www.hyperion-wines.co.nz;* **Matakana Estate** ① *To9-425 8446;* **Ransom** ① *To9-425 8862;* **Mahurangi Estate** ① *To9-425 0306, www.mahurangi.com;* and a few scattering of other labels around Mahurangi. The VIC (I-Site) in Warkworth, see page 138, can provide details.

Also of interest is the **Morris and James Country Pottery and Café** ① *Tongue Farm Rd, To9-422 7116, 1000-1700; café daily 0830-late, winter Thu-Fri until late.* It uses clay sourced from the Matakana River to produce a wonderful array of terracotta pots and tiles that have become famous throughout the country. There are free weekday pottery tours and the café serves delicious food and local wines in a relaxed garden setting.

Tawharanui

If you have time, do not miss the biggest countryside and northernmost coastal park in the region, Tawharanui (pronounced 'Ta-fara-nui'). It takes some getting to via Takatu Road just north of Matakana, but is well worth the effort. Even before you reach the park you are afforded spectacular views of Kawau Island and beyond. Being so isolated, it is quieter than most other parks and offers beaches, walks and scenery unrivalled in many other eastern coastal parks. A haven for native birds, you are almost sure to see noisy paradise shelduck, together with pied stilts and variable oystercatchers. Plans are afoot to turn Tawharanui into a 'mainland island' protected with predator-free fences: an exciting prospect. The two main beaches are ideal for relaxing or swimming and look out across Omaha Bay to Leigh. Extended walks out to the headland offer even better views. Permits are available for camping.

Leigh and the Goat Island Marine Reserve

The original name for Leigh was Little Omaha – common sense given its position on the west of Omaha Cove, 13 km from Matakana. However, to avoid confusion with its sister settlement of Big Omaha, slightly inland, the name was changed to Leigh. Why 'Leigh' remains a mystery. Whatever, Leigh is a small fishing community the nature of which is best summed up by its rather mundane street names like 'Wonderview', 'Barrierview', 'Grandview' and, yes, even 'Seaview'.

Matheson's Beach is 1 km to the west of the village and is a popular spot in summer for all beach and aquatic pursuits, but by far the main focus of attention lies 4 km north of Leigh, around **Goat Island** and its associate **marine reserve**. Although the island itself, 300 m offshore, is fairly nondescript, the waters that surround it are very special. In 1975, these waters were established as New Zealand's first marine reserve. Treated essentially like any reserve on land, the entire aquatic flora and fauna is fully protected, and no angling or shell fishing is allowed. Basically, nothing can be taken except photographs and scientific samples. The result is an astonishing abundance of marine life that brings hordes of divers to the area all year round. The added allure is that you do not need to be Jacques Cousteau to enjoy it. From the shore, swimmers and snorkellers can (particularly in summer) find themselves surrounded by shoals of inquisitive fish looking for an easy meal. In the early days it was possible to feed the fish, but it quickly became obvious a diet of cheese slices and crisps was not conducive to their good health. Indeed a sign just before the beach now states: 'Do not feed the fish, it can make them sick'.

Dive gear can be hired from **Goat Island Dive** ① *142a Pakiri Rd beside the Sawmill Café, T0800-348369, www.goatislanddive.co.nz.*

On the surface, the glass-bottom boat **Aquador** ① *T09-422 6334, www.glass bottomboat.co.nz,* offers a number of trips around the island lasting up to 45 minutes ($20), with a commentary and good views of the fish and abundant marine life below. Trips are weather dependent and can be subject to seasonal schedules.

Pakiri

The main road north of Leigh splits in to a series of metalled roads that begin to give the first raw impressions of rural Northland life. About 10 km north of Leigh is the very pleasant and fairly isolated beach at Pakiri. Pakiri is also one of the best bases for horse trekking in the North Island. **Pakiri Beach Horse Treks** ① *Taurere Park, Rahuikiri Rd, Pakiri Beach, T09-422 6275, www.horseride-nz.co.nz,* is a popular outfit offering a huge range of trekking options from one-hour to seven-day safaris and twilight rides. It also provides a range of basic or more comfortable homestay accommodation and a café.

Mangawhai Heads

From Pakiri the metalled roads wind their way up to Mangawhai, a short distance from the sweeping coast and beaches of the Jellicoe Channel. Slightly inland the rather exposed **Spectacle** and **Tomorata Lakes** play host to local water-skiers and jet-skiers. The best spot at which to access the beach and coastal views is at **Te Arai Point**, just north of Spectacle Lake. There is little in the way of habitation here, which adds to the peace and isolation. North along the beach from Te Arai there is a wildlife refuge that takes in the impressive sand spit of the **Mangawhai Harbour**, but this is best accessed just south of Mangawhai village on Bull Road (off Black Swamp Road).

Some 10 km north of Te Arai is **Mangawhai**, a small farming village which offers a limited range of motel and motorcamp accommodation. Mangawhai Heads, a short distance to the north of the village, is basically a scattering of holiday houses frequented by the wealthy in summer. The beaches around both villages are popular with surfers and beach-goers, and 'The Heads', as it is better known, is also a good base for deep-sea and game fishing.

There is no information centre in Mangawhai but there is an information booth next to the main drag, Molesworth Drive, near the golf club. The website, www.mangawhai heads.co.nz, is also useful. Here you can see the various accommodation options and local activities available. The leaflet *Magical Mangawhai* is comprehensive and available from regional tourist offices, local shops and motor parks.

Waipu and around ⊜🖉🅦 ›› *pp143-145.*

North of Mangawhai the road negotiates the headland and falls to the beautiful shoreline settlements of Lang's Beach and Waipu Cove at the southern end of Bream Bay, before turning inland to the proudly Scottish enclave of Waipu.

Background
Waipu was founded in 1853 by a party of 120 Scottish settlers who were part of a group of 400 that originally left their homelands under the resolute leadership of the Reverend Norman McLeod. They did so in desperation during the terrible Highland Clearances, which resulted in mass migrations in the early 1800s. Their first stop was Nova Scotia but after a series of bad winters and crop failures they left for the new colonies in Australia and then New Zealand onboard sailing ships they skilfully built themselves. With their resettlement a relative success, word was sent to Nova Scotia and a further 850 followed to settle the area. Hints of the ethnic origins are all around the village with street names like Braemar Lane, Argyll Street and Caledonian Park. Also, in the village square is the grand war memorial monument which is made of Aberdeen Granite and was shipped especially from Scotland in 1914 to commemorate the 60th anniversary of the town's founding.

Sights
The small community is very proud of its Scottish heritage and no visit to Waipu would be complete without a look inside the **Waipu Museum and Heritage Centre** ① *T09-432 0746, www.waipumuseum.com, 0930-1600, $5, child $2*, with its large Nova Scotian flag outside – a flag that combines the ancient Scottish Saltire and Lion Rampant designs. Inside the museum, walls are decked with photographs, and faces of early immigrants look down on cases full of personal effects from spectacles to spinning wheels. Logbooks listing the immigrant arrivals and the ships on which they arrived are being continuously updated. It is little wonder that many Nova Scotians come to Waipu to trace their ancestors and at times find family heirlooms amongst the treasured pieces. There has been so much interest over the years that the new heritage centre was added to house more modern resources with which the public can now trace their lineage. The staff in the museum are very knowledgeable.

Every New Year's Day since 1871 the **Waipu Highland Games** – the largest and longest-running in the southern hemisphere – gets into full swing with highland dancers, pipe bands and kilted, caber-tossing men, who descend on the village from far and wide. ›› *See Festivals and events, page 145.*

The **Old Waipu Firehouse Art Gallery** ① *in the old Waipu fire station on West End St, T09-432 0797, www.artistsnz.com, daily*, is worth a look with some fine examples of local art at affordable prices. On the eastern edge of Waipu adjacent to Johnston Port Road is the **Waipu Wildlife Refuge**, where you can see a variety of native shorebirds in an easily accessible area situated around the mouth of the Ruakaka River.

The **Waipu Caves**, 13 km to the west of Waipu (via Shoemaker Road), offer a great opportunity to see glow-worms through a 200-m passage, part of an extensive limestone cave system. The cave has free access, so caution is advised. Going alone is not recommended and do not enter without a torch and appropriate footwear. A map giving directions is available in the museum and the cave is signposted from Waipu

Caves Road. If you would prefer to see the sights above ground using the four-legged option, or take a guided tour of the cave, **North River Horse Treks**, T09-432 0565/ T0800-743-344, can oblige. Again, take appropriate clothing, a swimsuit and a torch.

North of Waipu and back on SH1 you follow the edge of Bream Bay (the beach is best accessed at Uretiti 6 km north of Waipu) before turning inland towards Whangarei. At the northern end of Bream Bay and the entrance to Whangarei Harbour is the unsightly **Marsden Oil Refinery** ① *T09-432 8194, daily 1000-1700*. This is where all of New Zealand's crude oil is imported. Sadly, even with all the best technology in the world, the refinery and its tanker traffic poses a significant threat to Northland's pristine coastline and remains a potential environmental disaster. However, see if the **visitor centre** at the refinery can persuade you otherwise.

● Sleeping

Warkworth and around *p138*
Warkworth offers plenty of country B&B options. The VIC (I-Site), www.warkworth-information.co.nz, has full listings.
LL Uhuru Lodge, 390 Pukapuka Rd, Mahurangi West, T09-422 0585, www.uhurulodge.co.nz. A spectacular, spacious house in farm and bush setting over a private bay. Superb pool.
L Saltings B&B, 1210 Sandspit Rd, T09-425 9670, www.saltings.co.nz. Luxury B&B with classy suites and rooms and self-catering accommodation in a fine vineyard setting.
A Central Motel, 24 Neville St, Warkworth, T/F09-425 8645, www.centralmotel.co.nz. Basic and affordable option.
A Willow Lodge B&B, 541 Woodcocks Rd, T/F09-425 7676. Tidy self-contained units 3 mins from the town in a quiet setting, friendly, knowledgeable hosts.
A-D Sheepworld Caravan Park and Backpackers, SH1 (4 km north of Warkworth), T09-425 9962, www.sheepworldcaravan park.co.nz. Next to the sheep farm, with full facilities including café and spa pool.

Kawau Island *p139*
There is a wide range of options in the satellite coastal villages. The VIC (I-Site) in Warkworth has extensive listings and will arrange bookings, see Warkworth, above.
A Coppercabanas Cedar Lodge, Smelting House Bay, T09-4228700, www.copper cabanas.co.nz. Self-contained waterfront units.

A-D Kawau Lodge , North Cove, T09-422 8831, www.kawaulodge.co.nz. 4-star lodge in a tranquil location. Recommended.

Matakana *p140*
Camping permits are available for Tawharanui.
LL The Castle Matakana, 378 Whitmore Rd, T09-422 9288, www.the-castle.co.nz. Fine country living, food and wine in a modern designer home with rural and sea views. 3 tastefully decorated luxury guest rooms including the sumptuous 'Tower Suite' all replete with contemporary NZ artworks.
LL Sandpiper Lodge, Takatu Rd Peninsula, T09-422 7256, www.sandpiperlodge.co.nz. Near the beautiful Tawharanui Regional Park. Very classy. Pool and restaurant attached.
B Matakana House Motel, 975 Matakana Rd, T09-422 7497, www.matakana house.co.nz. Mid-range and very tidy.

Leigh and Goat Island *p141*
LL-L Tera del Mar, 140 Rodney Rd, Leigh, T09-422 6090, www.teradelmar.co.nz. A rambling Victorian villa offering all mod cons. One room has a 4-poster bed and open fire.
A-C Leigh Sawmill Café Accommodation, 142 Pakiri Rd, Leigh, T09-422 6019, www.leighsawmillcafe.co.nz. A more affordable option in the village offering tidy rooms with en suite bath and also bunks.
C-D Goat Island Campground, Goat Island Rd, Leigh, T09-422 6185. Budget option with powered camping sites, may close in winter.

Northland Warkworth & Kowhai Coast Listings

● *For an explanation of the Sleeping and Eating price codes used in this guide, see the inside*
● *front cover. Other relevant information is provided in the Essentials chapter, pages 44-51.*
Note that prices are given in New Zealand dollars.

C-D Whangateau Holiday Park, 559 Leigh Rd, Whangateau, T09-422 6305. On the beachfront and friendly.

Pakiri p141
AL Miller's Ark, just north of Pakiri, T09-431 5266, www.pakiriretreat.co.nz. A rather intriguing homestay or self-contained option.
A-D Pakiri Holiday Park, on the beach, T09-422 6199, www.pakiriholidaypark.co.nz. Some decent cabins, luxury cottages, camp kitchen and kayak hire.

Mangawhai Heads p141
AL Mangawhai Lodge, 4 Heather St, T09-4315311, www.seaviewlodge.co.nz. Best B&B in the area and good value.
A Hidden Valley Chalets, corner of Te Arai Point and Mangawhai Rd, (15 km off SH1), T09-431 5332, www.hiddenvalley.co.nz. Good self- contained chalets, peaceful area. Outdoor spa.
A Milestone Cottages, Moir Point Rd, Mangawhai, T09-431 4018, www.milestone cottages.net.nz. An award-winning self-contained option, near the beach. Pool, kayaks.
B-D Coastal Cow Backpackers, 299 Molesworth Drive, T09-431 5246. The best budget backpacker option in the area, cosy, spotlessly clean and run by enthusiasts with an obvious fondness for all things bovine.

Motorcamps
B-D Mangawhai Heads Motor Camp, Mangawhai Heads Rd, T09-431 4675.
B-D Riverside Holiday Park, Black Swamp Rd, Mangawhai, T09-431 4825. Close to the beach and the sand spit wildlife refuge.

Waipu and around p142
There are a number of good B&Bs and lodges in the area mainly in Waipu Cove or Lang Beach to the south of Waipu village.
L Royal Palm Lodge, 19 Highland Lass Pl, Lang's Beach, T09-432 0120, www.royalpalm lodge.co.nz. A modern villa with a range of well-appointed rooms and en suite baths, a spa and excellent cuisine.
A Flower Haven B&B, 53 St Ann Rd, Waipu Cove, T09-432 0421, www.flowerhaven.co.nz. Self-contained apartment with sea views and close to the beach.
A Hinterland Fold Farmstay, McLeods Rd, Waipu, T09-432 0304, www.hinterlandfold.

co.nz. Of particular note, it has a good value self-contained studio on a stud farm for 'heelan' coos'.
A Stone House B&B, Cove Rd, Waipu, T09-432 0432, www.stonehousewaipu.co.nz. Self-contained 2-bedroom stone cottage, self-contained cabin and budget 'loft'-style accommodation, all a short stroll to the beach. Recommended.

Motels
A Waipu Clansman Motel, 30 Cove Rd, Waipu, T09-432 0424. Standard facilities.
A Waipu Cove Resort, 891 Cove Rd, T09-432 0348. By the beach.
A-D Waipu Cove Cottages and Camping Ground, Cove Rd, T09-432 0851, covecottages@xtra.co.nz. Tidy and popular.
C-D Waipu Wanderers Backpackers, 25 St Mary's Rd, T09-432 0532, www.waipu.co.nz/waipuwanderers. Small, cosy and conveniently located.

● Eating

Warkworth p138
Sandpiper Lodge, T09-422 7256 (see Sleeping above), is the best option for fine dining. Bookings essential.
Millstream Bar and Grill Theatre, 15-17 Elizabeth, T09-422 2292, daily. A la carte menu and boutique theatre showing recent releases.
Warkworth Pizza Company, Neville St, T09-425 7373 daily 1100-1500, 1700-late. A local favourite.
Salty Dog Tavern, Snells Beach, T09-425 5588. An old English-style pub with good beer and pub grub, just like back home.

Cafés
Duck's Crossing Café, Riverview Plaza, T09-425 9940, daily 0730-1630.
Queens St Corner Café, opposite the VIC, T09-425 8749, daily.

Leigh and Goat Island p141
Sawmill Café, 142 Pakiri Rd, T09-422 6019. Summer daily, 0930-late; winter Thu-Sun late. The place to go for fresh light meals, good coffee and occasional live music.
Leigh Fish and Chips, Cumberland St, T09-422 6035, daily 1100-2230 (later on weekends). Given the fishy nature of the village it would be rude not to sample these delights.

Mangawhai Heads *p141*
🍴 **Naja Garden Café**, Molesworth Drive, T09-431 4111, daily 0830-1700, dinner Thu-Sat in winter. Licensed. Modern food, all-day breakfast.
🍴 **Sail Rock Café**, 12 Wood St, T09-431 4051, daily in summer. A la carte plus a range of pizzas and café lunches, bar and BYO.
🍴 **Karvana Cafe**, 7 Wood St, T09-431 5587. Good for a quick coffee, or a nice cool beer.

Waipu and around *p142*
🍴 **Clansman Motel and Restaurant**, 30 Cove Rd, Waipu, T09-432 0424.
🍴 **Pizza Barn and Bar**, 3 Cove Rd, Waipu, T09-432 1011.

🍴 **Food45**, 45 The Centre, T09-432 0254, daily in summer.

⚫ Festivals and events

Waipu and around *p142*
1 Jan Highland Games, www.highland games.co.nz. For details contact the Waipu Caledonian Society, T09 432 0746.

⚫ Directory

Warkworth *p138*
Internet At the library next to the VIC, Mon-Thu 0900-1700, Fri 0900-2000, Sat 0900-1200.

Whangarei and around

→ *Colour map 1, B4 Population: 45,000*
Given the obvious allure of the Bay of Islands to the north, with its promise of stunning scenery and a whole host of activities, few visitors pay much attention to Northland's largest town. However, if you do choose to linger here a while, you will find that it actually has quite a lot to offer – not only in aesthetics (just take a look at the Town Basin) but also in some lesser-known gems only a short drive away. One such pearl is Ocean Beach at Whangarei Heads – the perfect place to sit just after a storm or watch the sun rise. ➻ *For Sleeping, Eating and other listings, see pages 151-155.*

Ins and outs

Getting there **Onerahi airport**, T09-437 0666, is 9 km west of the city and is linked to the city centre by shuttle bus, $10. The district is serviced by **Air New Zealand Link**, T0800-737000/T132476, www.airnewzealand.co.nz. **Great Barrier Airlines**, I09-275 9120, www.greatbarrierairlines.co.nz, also run a Friday and Sunday service from Whangarei to Claris (on Great Barrier Island) from $189 return.

The **bus station** is in Rose Street, T09-438 2653, downtown Whangarei, but they can also stop at the VIC at the southern approach to town. **Intercity**, T09-438 2653, and **Northliner**, T09-438 3206, has a daily coach service to and from Auckland and destinations further north. If you are arriving by car, take extra care on the stretch of road from Waipu to Whangarei.

Getting around Whangarei has a fairly comprehensive bus service. Timetables are available from the VIC or **Infoline**, T09-438 4639/T09-438 6005; the standard city fare is $2. **Kiwi Carlton**, T09-438 2299, provides a 24-hour taxi service. There is no public transport for getting to Whangarei Heads (page 150), but cycling is an option. You can hire a bike from **Town Basin Hire**, Jetty One, T09-437 2509, $25 a day.

Tourist information The main **VIC (I-site)** ⓘ *Tarewa Park, 92 Otaika Rd, T09-438 1079, www.whangareinz.org.nz, Mon-Fri, 0830-1700, weekends 0930-1630, extended hours in summer,* is just as you come into the town (northbound). The staff are very friendly and helpful and there is a café attached. The new toilets are also worth a sneaky muse. The regional **DoC office** ⓘ *Ka Ka St, T09-430 2133, www.doc.govt.nz,* can provide a useful pamphlet called *Whangarei District Walks*; also available from the VIC.

Related map
A Whangarei centre, p148.

Mt Parahaki
(241m)

Memorial Dr

To Abbey Caves & 17

Patiki St

Dundas Rd

Punga Grove Av 11

Kohe St

Jessie St

Bahama Pl

Memorial Dr

Panorama Dr

Riverside Dr

Kauri Pl

Tanekaha Dr

To Airport & 4 16 3

Waioneone Creek

Lime Burners Creek

N

| 0 metres | 300 |
| 0 yards | 300 |

Sleeping
Alpha Motel & Holiday Park **5**
Avenue Heights Motel **7**
Bunkdown Lodge **1**
Channel Vista **4**
Cherry Court Motor Lodge **2**
Cheviot Park Motor Lodge **3**
Graelyn Villa **14**
Kamo Springs Caravan Park **13**
Kingswood Motor Inn **10**
Little Earth Lodge **17**
Lodge Bordeaux **18**
Lupton Lodge **9**
Mulryan's **12**
Pohutukawa Lodge **6**
Settlers **8**
Totaranui B&B **16**
Whangarei Falls Backpackers
 & Holiday Park **15**
Whangarei Manaakitanga YHA **11**
Whangarei Top Ten Holiday Park **19**

Eating
A Deco **2**
Adriatic Fisheries **1**
Topsail Café **3**

Northland Whangarei & around

Background

True to the area's tradition it was a Scot, William Carruth, who was the first to buy a block of land from the Maori in 1839 and settle at the mouth of the Hatea River. He was quickly joined by other settlers and before long a small community developed. Like so many other Northland communities they quickly focused their activities on kauri timber milling and, for a short while, prospered. But after Kororareka (Russell) in the Bay of Islands was sacked in 1845 by the notorious Maori chief Hone Heke, most of the local European settlers fled south to Auckland for safety, only to venture north again a few years later. With these disruptive beginnings initial progress was slow, until the quest for Kauri gum in the 1850s; the building of a shipyard in the 1860s finally brought prosperity and a rapid expansion to the area. It was not until the 1930s that both road and rail links with Auckland were completed, but by then the busy port had already put Whangarei on the map as the main commercial centre and capital of the north.

Sights

A good place to start your tour of Whangarei's sights is with a fine view of the city and the harbour itself. **Mount Parahaki** on Memorial Drive (off Riverside Drive) is 241 m high and was once the site of New Zealand's largest Maori *pa*. Today it is crowned with a war memorial and a rather tacky red cross that glows at night. You can also walk up Parahaki (one hour) via the **Mair Park**, a peaceful park of native bush and well-marked trails. There is an old gold mine and remnants of Maori fortifications within it.

The jewel in Whangarei's scenic crown is the congenial **Town Basin**, where expensive nautical hardware bobs and squeaks on the glistening waters of the marina. The Basin is an award-winning waterfront development which houses a number of interesting attractions including the Claphams Clocks Museum, art galleries, craft shops and a café and restaurant. There is also a small **information booth** ① T09-438 1315, beside Clapham's Clocks Museum to help you find your way around.

Without doubt the best attraction, other than the atmosphere of the Basin itself, is **Clapham's Clock Museum** ① T09-438 3993, www.claphamsclocks.com, daily 0900-1700, $8, child $4, a highly entertaining and ever-growing collection of timepieces from all around the world. The best thing to do is to take a guided tour, otherwise the collection, which is the biggest in the southern hemisphere, is a bit daunting.

There are two good art galleries at the Basin. The historic colonial **Reyburn House** ① Tue-Fri 1000-1600, Sat-Sun 1300-1600, (the oldest in Whangarei), features displays of local art. West of the Town Basin, in the peaceful and pleasant **Cafler Park and Rose Gardens**, is the small modern **Whangarei Art Museum** ① Water St, T09-430 7240,

Whangarei centre

Sleeping 😴
Kingsgate **1**

Eating 🍴
Bob **1**
Caffeine Espresso
Café **10**

Dickens Inn **2**
Gybe **8**
Killer Prawn **3**
Mokaba **9**

Mondos Café **7**
Reva's on the Waterfront **4**
Water Street Brasserie **6**

The Poor Knights Islands

The Poor Knights Islands, lying 24 km off Tutukaka, are the remnants of a large volcano, which erupted over 10 million years ago. The islands themselves provide a predator-free refuge for land animals like tuatara, native lizards, giant weta, flax snails, giant centipedes and a wide variety of rare seabirds. They are also home to several species of distinctive plants, including the Poor Knights lily, found only on 'The Knights' and the Hen and Chicken islands off Whangarei Heads. But it is the marine reserve, and the wonderful spectacle below the water, for which the islands are most famous. A rich habitat of caves, arches, tunnels and sheer cliffs attract a wide variety of marine life from sharks to black coral. Sponge gardens, kelp forests and gorgonian fields are inhabited by a myriad of fish, shellfish, urchins, anemones and even tame groupers, which welcome divers with their distinctively vacuous look. All this combined with the exceptional water clarity make 'The Knights' one of the top dive venues in the world.

www.whangareiartmuseum.co.nz, *Tue-Fri 1000-1630, Sat-Sun 1200-1630, donation*, which shows the best of local art past and present and also hosts touring national exhibitions. A short walk will take you to the **Fernery, Conservatory and Cacti House**. ① *T09-438 4879, daily 1000-1600, free*. The Fernery houses New Zealand's largest collection of ferns, while the Conservatory is filled with ever-changing displays of flowers. Near the park on Rust Avenue is the **Forum North Cultural Complex** (see Entertainment, page 154).

On the outskirts of town at the end of Selwyn Avenue is the celebrated creative haven of the **Northland Craft Trust** (**Craft Quarry**) ① *daily 1000-1600, free*. It's an impressive collective of working artists and crafts people producing an array of works from pottery and lithographs to traditional Maori carvings – worth a visit.

Further west and 6 km out of town, in the suburb of Maunu, is the **Whangarei Museum, Clarke Homestead** and **Kiwi House** ① *T09-438 9630, www.whangarei museum.org.nz, daily 1000-1600, $5, $8 all sites*. It is an indoor/outdoor complex with a colonial farming block and homestead and a modern building housing a number of significant Taonga or Maori treasures, including kiwi feather capes and a musket that belonged to the great northern warrior Hone Heke. The display is deliberately indigenous in content and perspective. 'Live Days' are held regularly during the summer with special events like bullock riding, vintage car displays and horse-drawn carriages. The Kiwi House is one of the better examples in the country with exhibits of native flora and live kiwi. Note that there is usually only one. This is deliberate as kiwi are solitary birds and fiercely territorial.

Next to the museum is the **Whangarei Native Bird Recovery Centre** ① *T09-438 1457*. Although not freely open to visitors you may be allowed to visit by prior arrangement and for a donation. This charity has the main centre in the north for wild bird rehabilitation and an excellent and successful kiwi egg incubation facility. To the south of the city on SH1 is the **Paper Mill** ① *T09-438 2652, Mon-Sat 1000-1500, donation; small charge to make paper*. This tourist attraction is growing in popularity and deservedly so. It gives the visitor an insight into traditional craft papermaking using recycled materials in an historical setting, and you can even try to make some yourself. Just 1 km further south is the **Longview Winery** ① *T09-438 7227, www.long viewwines.co.nz, Mon-Sat 0830-1800 in summer, 0830-1730 in winter*, a 30-year-old estate producing popular and award-winning wines.

To the north of the city on Ngunguru Road, Tikipunga, are the slightly over-rated 23-m **Whangarei Falls**, which are worth a peek if you are passing. (Perhaps a better way to experience them is to abseil down them with **Northland Outdoors**, T09-430 3474.) The **AH Reed Memorial Kauri Park** on Whareora Road is the pick of the local parks with some fine examples of native Kauri trees up to 3 m in diameter and 500 years old. They are impressive, but nothing compared to the 1500-year-old Tane Mahuta on the west coast (see page 182), which in turn is nothing, compared to some monsters that once were. The park has short walks and tracks and a very pleasant waterfall thrown in for good measure.

Although they are hard to find and a bit out of town, the **Abbey Caves** are worth a visit. If you take a right off Memorial Drive (up Mount Parahaki) on to Old Parua Bay Road and on to Abbey Caves Road you will, with a little difficulty, find a DoC sign next to the road. Provided you have adequate footwear, a torch and are not alone (or have kids in tow), then follow the footpath and signs past the weird and wonderful limestone foundations that lead to the caves. Do not venture too far into the caves without a guide. If you are brave, switch off your torch and amidst the sound of trickling water, enjoy the small galaxy of glow-worms above. It is easy to get lost in and around the caves so the best option is to join a guided tour from **Bunkdown Lodge**, T09-438 8886, $25 (see Sleeping, page 151).

Whangarei Heads

Ocean Beach is one of Northland's best: it's quiet, beautiful and, in a raging easterly wind, a place where the senses are bombarded with nature at its best. On the way you will begin to notice the prevalence of evocative Scots place names like McLeod's and Urquart's Bay and street names like McDonald Road – all family names of the 'overspill' Scots settlers from the Bream Bay and Waipu enclaves. Above these quiet communities and scenic bays are the towering peaks of **Mount Manaia**, the base of which can be accessed from the car park next to the Manaia Club. It is an excellent, but steep walk through native bush that takes about three hours return. You cannot climb to the peak summits themselves – they are *tapu* (sacred and off limits) – steeped in Maori legend. Other fine coastal walks are to **Peach Cove** (three hours) and **Smugglers Cove** (one hour) both reachable from **Urquart's Bay**.

If you only do one thing in the Whangarei district, then make sure it's a trip to watch the sunrise at Ocean Beach, 35 km west of the city.

Tutukaka Coast

Tutukaka is on the loop road that also takes in Ngunguru and Matapouri before turning inland again back to SH1 and Whangarei. By car from the city suburb of Tikipunga, take the Ngunguru Road past Whangarei Falls. On the outskirts of the city in Glenbervie the roads become lined by drystone walls giving the area a distinctly British countryside feel (no doubt a legacy of the early settlers) before New Zealand bush takes over once again and you hit the coast at Ngunguru.

Even if fishing and scuba diving did not exist, the Tutukaka coastline would still deserve to be one of the finest coastal venues in Northland. But its rugged scenic bays are best known throughout New Zealand and beyond as the gateway and safe harbour to some of the best **deep-sea fishing** and **diving** in the world. The **Poor Knights Islands** (see box, page 149), which lie 25 km offshore, are internationally significant both above and below the waterline, with a wide range of wildlife and vegetation. Here the nutrient-rich currents meet in water of unusually high clarity to create a showcase of marine life much of which is seen nowhere else in the country. Although landing is forbidden without a permit, the islands themselves are home to rare terrestrial species, like the prehistoric tuatara, a reptile that has changed little in 60 million years. Most activity in the area takes place from Tutukaka with its large sheltered marina while the village of **Ngunguru**, 5 km before it, has most of the visitor and resident amenities.

Most people take SH1 to the Bay of Islands, though a far more interesting route is via the Old Russell Road which leaves SH1 for the coast at Whakapara, about 28 km north of Whangarei. Here you are entering a mobile phone free zone, on roads with more animals than cars, and on which the children (predominantly Maori) do not mind walking in the rain. Welcome to rural Northland and the simple spirit of the north. After simply enjoying the countryside and its atmosphere you reach the coast at **Helena Bay** which, along with Whananaki and Mimiwhangata to the south and the Whangaruru Peninsula to the north, offers remote and beautiful coastal scenery.

From Whangaruru the road passes the neck of the beautiful **Cape Brett Peninsula**, offering great walking in equally stunning coastal scenery, before turning inland and slowly negotiating its way to Russell. If you intend to reach Paihia you can get the vehicular ferry at Okaito to Opua (last ferry 2050, except Friday 2150).

● Sleeping

Whangarei *p145, maps p146 and p148*
Whangarei has a wide variety of places to stay and pre-booking is generally not essential, although it's recommended in summer.
LL-L Lodge Bordeaux, 361 Western Hills Drive, T09-438 0404, www.lodgebordeaux .co.nz. Classy 5-star lodge motel conveniently located close to the CBD. 15 well-appointed suites, fast internet, pool and spas.
AL Avenue Heights Motel, 355 Western Hills Drive (SH1), T09-438 2737, www.avenue heights.co.nz. New motel, conveniently located, with 10 tidy luxury units.
AL Channel Vista, 254 Beach Rd, Onerahi, T09-436 5529, channelvista@igrin.co.nz. 2 fully self-contained and traditional bedrooms with great harbour views.
AL Kingsgate Hotel, 9 Riverside Drive, T09-438 0284, www.kingsgatewhangarei.co.nz. Well-established hotel overlooking the marina and Town Basin. Modern rooms with standard 3-star facilities. In-house bar/restaurant offers à la carte and buffet-style dining. Indoor pool, spa pool and sauna. Off-street parking.
AL-A Graelyn Villa, 166 Kiripaka Rd, T09-437 7532, www.graelynvilla.co.nz. Nicely restored villa, comfortable and homely.
AL-A Lupton Lodge, 555 Ngunguru Rd, Glenbervie, T09-437 2989, www.truenz.co.nz/ luptonhouse. Traditional Kiwi villa in peaceful surrounds. Friendly owners. En suite or shared bathroom, pool.
A Cherry Court Motor Lodge, 35 Otaika Rd, T09-438 3128, www.cherrycourt.co.nz. Swimming pool, laundry and licensed restaurant nearby.
A Cheviot Park Motor Lodge, corner of Cheviot St and Western Hills Drive,

T09-438 2341, www.cheviot-park.co.nz. Modern and friendly.
A Kingswood Motor Inn, 260 Kamo Rd, T09-437 5779, 5 mins' north of the city centre, disabled facilities, laundry, spa.
A Mulryan's, Crane Rd, Kamo, T09-435 0945, info@mulryans.co.nz. Comfortable B&B style accommodation in a restored kauri villa. Quiet country setting and a great breakfast.
A Pohutukawa Lodge, 362 Western Hills Drive, T09-430 8634, www.pohutukawa lodge.co.nz. Modern studios, some with spas.
A Settlers Hotel, Hatea Drive, T09-438 2699/ T0800-666662, www.settlershotel.co.nz. In a nice setting overlooking the river and within walking distance of the Town Basin. Bedrooms with en suite bath, laundry, pool and private spas, licensed à la carte restaurant.
C-D Bunkdown Lodge, 23 Otaika Rd, T09 438 8886, bunkdown@ihug.co.nz. Large, modern, more like a B&B and even has a bath. Very helpful, friendly hosts who have an information centre attached. In-house tours to Abbey Caves $40 and strong links with local activity operators. Popular so book ahead. Recommended.
C-D Little Earth Lodge, 85 Abbey Caves Rd (6 km from town centre), T09-430 6562, www.littleearthlodge.co.nz. Small, purpose-built and well-facilitated in peaceful rural setting and close to Abbey Caves. Full range of rooms, classy and clean replete with Balinese decor. Recommended.
C-D Whangarei Falls Backpackers and Holiday Park, Ngunguru Rd, Tikipunga, T0800-227222/T09-437 0609. A great backpacker hostel that doubles as a

motorcamp. It contains all the usual mod cons plus a pool, spa and TV room.

C-D Whangarei Manaakitanga YHA, 52 Punga Grove Av, T09-438 8954. Set in peaceful surroundings and spacious grounds overlooking the harbour and Tower Basin, 5-min walk from the town centre. Dorms and doubles with all the usual facilities. Dive trips to the Poor Knights Islands can be arranged as well as guided walks to Abbey Caves.

Motorcamps and campsites
A-D Whangarei Top Ten Holiday Park, 24 Mair St, T09-437 6856, whangareiholiday@ actrix.co.nz. This is the best of the bunch.
B-D Alpha Motel and Holiday Park, 34 Tarewa Rd, T09-438 6600.
B-D Kamo Springs Caravan Park, 55 Great North Rd, T09-435 1208.

Whangarei Heads *p150*
There is little in the way of accommodation at the heads beyond McLeod's Bay but the small communities of Parua Bay just before it, and Pataua and Taiharuru a few kilometres north, have a number of options.
A Tide Song, Taiharuru Estuary, Beasley Rd, T09-436 1959, www.tidesong.co.nz. Self-contained in a bush and seaside setting.
A Totaranui B&B, 205 Owhiwa Rd, (20 km east), T09-436 5166, www.totaranui.co.nz. Laid-back, good value B&B/homestay set in an elevated position in the bush. 2 cosy en suite doubles, and good views across the harbour. Friendly hosts are a dab hand at making fresh homemade bread. Generous breakfast.

Motorcamps and campsites
A-D Treasure Island Trailer Park, Pataua South, T09-436 2390, www.treasureisland nz.co.nz. Motorcamp with a beachfront campsite, camp kitchen.

Tutukaka Coast *p150*
AL Oceans Hotel, Marina Drive, Tutukaka, T0508-623267, www.oceanshotel.co.nz. Modern resort-style hotel with a nautical theme. Rooms or suites available, in-house à la carte restaurant not surprisingly with a seafood edge, local activity bookings and all the usual bells and whistles.
AL Poor Knights Lodge, Tutukaka, T09-434 4405, www.poorknightslodge.co.nz. 2 nicely appointed suites with decks overlooking the bay, internet, dinner on request. Dive and fishing trips arranged.
AL Waipouri Lodge, Tutukaka, T09-434 3696, mckillop@extra.co.nz. Self-contained 3-bedroom home.
A Bluewater Cottages, T09-434 3423, www.bluewaterparadise.co.nz. Halfway between Tutukaka and Matapouri (35 km from Whangarei), smart cottage-style accommodation, with memorable sea views.
A Dreamstay, Sandy Bay, T09-434 3059, www.bed-and-breakfast.co.nz/dreamstay. B&B, homestay or self-contained options.
A Malibu Mals Divestay, Tutukaka Block Rd, Kowharewa Bay, T09-434 3450, www.mali bumals.co.nz. Self-contained units or B&B.
A Pacific Rendezvous Motel, Tutukaka, T09-434 3847, www.oceanresort.co.nz. The most celebrated motel in the area with great views across the Tutukaka Harbour.
A Pukepoto Orchards, 521 Ngunguru Rd, Glenbervie, T09-437 5433, www.bed-and-breakfast.co.nz/pukepoto. Self-contained units in garden setting.
A The Sands Motel, Whangaumu Bay, Tutukaka, T09-434 3747, sandsmotel@ xtra.co.nz. Spacious self-contained units.

Motorcamps and campsites
B-D Ngunguru Holiday Park and Backpackers, Papaka Rd, Ngunguru (5 km before Tutukaka), T09-434 3851, water.edge@ xtra.co.nz. Standard cabins and facilities with shared facilities for backpackers, water's edge with kayak and bike hire.
B-D Tutukaka Holiday Park, T09-434 3938, www.tutukakaholidaypark.co.nz. Fairly new park opposite the marina, 6 cabins, powered and non-powered sites, standard facilities.

Whangarei to the Bay of Islands *p151*
Accommodation is basic and sparse with the exception of a few luxurious retreats.
LL-AL Moureeses Bay, Whananaki North, T09-623 1353, info@moureesesbay.co.nz. A peaceful, classy barn-style self-contained house with modern fittings and facilities, just a stone's throw from the beach.
L-A Robin's Nest, Oakura, T09-4336035, www.robinsnest.co.nz. Another tidy self-contained option close to all the activity operators in the village.
C-D Farm Backpackers and Homestay, near Whangaruru, T09-433 6894, www.the

farm.co.nz. Comfortable and friendly, with a warm welcome, but perhaps the biggest attraction are the activities, including horse trekking, use of quad and mountain bikes and even yacht racing. Recommended.

Motorcamps and campsites
There are basic motorcamps mainly at Oakura (just north of Helena Bay).
C-D Oakura Motels and Caravan Park, Oakura Bay, T09-433 6803. Beachside camps with units, cabins, powered or non-powered sites.
C-D Whangaruru Beachfront Camp, Whangaruru, T09-433 6806. An alternative.
D Mimiwhangata Bay and Coastal Park, bookings can be made through the **Tarewa Park Visitor Centre**, T09-430 2133. DoC's relatively cheap facilities with a self-contained lodge, cottage, beach house (book well in advance) and a campsite.

Basic DoC camping facilities are also available at Whananaki and Whangaruru; contact DoC, T09-430 2007.

❶ Eating

Whangarei *p145, maps p146 and p148*
In addition to the eateries listed below, there is a supermarket, **Pak-n-Save** on Walton St Plaza, T09-438 1488, Mon-Fri 0830-2000, Sat and Sun 0830-1900.
♥♥♥ A Deco, 70 Kamo Rd, T09-459 4957. As the name suggests, an art deco property housing an award-winning restaurant said by many to be the best in Northland. Imaginative and beautifully presented Pacific Rim cuisine. Good wine list.
♥♥♥ Gybe Restaurant and Bar, Quayside Town Basin, opposite Reva's, T09-459 7438. The seafood menu of this nautical restaurant is worth a look.
♥♥♥ Killer Prawn, 28 Bank St, T09-4303333, www.killerprawn.co.nz. A swish and busy restaurant/bar considered the best eatery in town, offering a wide selection of traditional and specialist seafood options. Try the namesake 'Killer Prawn' – a small pond of seafood in which to bathe your taste buds.
♥♥♥ Mokaba, Quayside Town Basin, T09-436 5706, daily. The newest of the good eateries, Mokaba's is making its mark with its imaginative international cuisine, ice

cream and a fine cup of coffee. Live music most weekends, licensed.
♥♥♥ Reva's on the Waterfront, Quayside Town Basin, T09-438 8969. International cuisine in pleasant surroundings, great pizza, licensed. Live music.
♥♥♥ Topsail Café, 1st floor, Onerahi Yacht Club, Beach Rd, Onerahi, T09-436 0529, Mon-Sat from 1800, Sun brunch 1000-1500. Serves continental-style cuisine and is a local seafood favourite.
♥♥♥ Water Street Brasserie, 24 Water St, T09-438 7464, Tue-Sat, BYO. Fine traditional cuisine in modern surroundings.
♥♥ Bob, 29 Bank St, T09-4380881. Laid back, popular café and a favourite for breakfast.
♥♥ Caffeine Espresso Café, 4 Water St, T09-438 1116. Arguably the best café in the city centre.
♥♥ Dickens Inn, corner of Cameron and Quality sts, T09-430 0406, www.dickens inn.co.nz. One of Whangarei's most popular pubs. Pub-style cuisine, breakfast, lunch, dinner and snacks, children's menu.
♥♥ Mondos Café, 14 Quayside, Town Basin, T09-430 0467. One of the best cafés in the city set overlooking the quay, ideal for lunch or a light snack.
♥ Adriatic Fisheries, Kensington, 91 Kamo Rd, T09-437 3874. Best fish and chippy in town.

Whangarei Heads *p150*
If you want to cook for yourself, the **Taurikura General Store**, just west of Ocean Beach, is a traditional and interesting place to stock up, also has a café in summer. You can also get supplies at the supermarket in the **Onerahi Shopping Centre**.
♥♥ Flames International Hotel, Waverley St, Onerhai, T09-436 2107.

Tutukaka Coast *p150*
♥♥♥ Knights Restaurant (Oceans Tutukaka), Marina Rd, Tutukaka, T0508-623267, daily, licensed. Resort restaurant with a nautical theme and a seafood edge.
♥♥ Marina Pizzeria, Tutukaka T09-434 3166. Quality pizzas.
♥♥ Schnappa Rock Cafe, Marina Rd, Tutukaka, T09-434 3774, daily til late. Café bar that forms the main focus for the Tutukaka community and occasional live bands.

⑥ Pubs, bars and clubs

Whangarei *p145, maps p146 and p148*
There are a number of trendy bars and
nightclubs in Whangarei. **The Killer Prawn**
and the **Bacio Bar**, on Bank St, are the local
places to be seen. While the **Frings Brauhaus**,
104 Dent St, is a microbrewery bar with a fine
beer garden. For the full 'shake of the pants'
try **Heaven** or **Danger Danger** on Vine St, and
Rynoz, Cameron St, all of which are pretty
lively but, as you would expect, have that small
town atmosphere. **Dickens Inn**, on Cameron
St, is better for something a little quieter.

⑥ Entertainment

Whangarei *p145, maps p146 and p148*
The main cinema is the **Sky City Cinemas**,
James St, T09-438 8550. The **Forum North
Cultural Complex**, Rust Av, T09-438 3815, is
a well-equipped space and one of the best in
the country for cultural and performing arts.

▲ Activities and tours

Whangarei *p145, maps p146 and p148*
Bush safaris
The Bushwacka Experience, Highway 14,
Maungatapere, T09-434 7724. Thrilling
trips in a 4WD, BBQ and abseiling. Daily
4-hr trip $85, 2-hr $55. Recommended.
Green Gecko Tours, 53 Kauika Rd, T09-
437 75328. Reputable natural and human
history day tours with an enthusiastic and
very knowledgeable ex-DoC officer.

Cruises and kayaking
Bream Bay Charters, Whangarei Harbour,
Ruakaka, T09-432 7484.
Town Basin Hire, Jetty One, Riverside Drive,
Town Basin, T09-437 2509, hires out bikes,
rollerblades and leisure craft including kayaks.

Cycling
Cycle Touring Company New Zealand,
100 Church St, Whangarei, T09-436 0033,
www.cycletours.co.nz. Self-guided cycling
adventures on routes all over Northland from
2-9 days. Accommodation and food included.

Dolphin, seabird and whale watching
Although viewing success rates are far lower
than Kaikoura in the South Island, sightings of

a number of whale species are possible.
Dolphin trips are also better catered for in
the Bay of Islands but if time is short and you
do not intend to head north, **Bream Bay
Charters**, see Cruises above, offers trips locally.

Fishing
The harbour and more especially the
Tutukaka Coast offers excellent sea fishing.
Big game fishing charters are available at
Tutukaka with record catches in summer.
Bream Bay Charters, Ruakaka, T09-432
7484, offers good trips locally.

Scenic flights and skydiving
Northland Districts Aero Club, Onerahi
Airport, T09-436 0890. Also offers tandem
sky diving, 10,000 ft, from $225.
Tower Aviation, Onerahi Airport,
T09-436 0886. Expensive but spectacular.

Scuba diving
See also Tutukaka Coast, below.
Dive Connection, 140 Lower Cameron St,
T09-430 0818, www.diveconnection.co.nz.
Offers full dive courses.
Dive HQ, 41 Clyde St, T09-438 1075,
www.divenow.co.nz.
Knight Diver Tours, 30 Heads Rd,
T0800-766756, www.poorknights.co.nz.
Pacific Highway Charters, T09-437 3632,
www.divenz.co.nz.

Tutukaka Coast *p150*
Adventure sports
Jet-skiing, mountain biking, kayaking
and surfing available from:
Ngunguru Holiday Park, T/F09-434 3851.
Tutukayax, Marina Beach, T09-437 7442.
Water Sport Hire, 14 Kopipi Cres, Ngunguru,
T09-434 3475.

Cruising
Cave Rider, T0800-288882/T09-434 3867,
www.caverider.co.nz. High speed 2½-hr jet
boat trips to the Poor Knights Islands taking
in what is reputed to be the biggest sea cave
in the world, Riko Riko, from $90, child $45.

Fishing
Fishing is not allowed in the marine reserve of
the Poor Knights but the surrounding ocean
has some of the best deep-sea fishing in the
world, with numerous species like shark and

marlin. The 'big game' season runs Dec-Apr. A day trip costs at least $200 a head. Most companies are based in Tutukaka:

Delray Sports fishing Charters, T/F09-434 3028, delray@igrin.co.nz.
Lady Jess Charters, T09-434 3758.
Whangarei Deep Sea Anglers Club, T09-43 43818.

Golf
Whangarei has some fine golf courses, including: Northland Golf Club, Pipiwai Rd, Kamo, T09-435 0042; The Pines, Parua Bay, T09-436 2246; Sherwood Park, Millington Rd, Maunu, T09-434 6900; and Whangarei Golf Club, Denby Cres, T09-437 0740, the best.

Horse treks
Whananaki Trail Rides, Whananaki, T09-433 8299, www.hostrekin.co.nz. Trekking in local kauri forests and on the beach, from $35 (free camping and budget accommodation).

Rugby
The ITM Stadium in the city is the venue for local and provincial games as well as international test matches.

Scuba diving
Tutukaka is the main dive base with companies offering personalized tours and equipment hire. Most boats leave for the Poor Knights Islands about 0830 and return at 1600. As well as the Poor Knights, wreck dives are also available to the sunken navy frigate *Tui* just offshore from Tutukaka, and the *Waikato*, another warship sunk in 2000. A 2-dive trip costs about $175-200 including full gear hire. Tuition, snorkelling and kayaks are also available for the novice.
Dive Tutukaka, T09-434 3867, www.diving.co.nz. The main dive company, now internationally recognized, runs a very professional outfit from its base on the marina. It offers over 10 'world-class' site dives with names as 'The Labyrinth' and 'Maomao Arch' as well as dive courses, snorkelling, kayak, and whale- and dolphin-watching activities. Full day from $175. Recommended.

Skateboarding
The Skateboard Park, William Fraser Memorial Park, Riverside Drive, has a modern 1500-sq-m facility.

Swimming
Whangarei Aquatics, Ewing Rd (near the Town Basin), T09-438 7957, daily $4 Olympic-size outdoor pool and a large indoor heated pool, spas and sauna.

Walking
One of the best walks in the area is at Tutukaka Head. To reach the car park take the 'right of way' sign right off Matapouri Rd, 400 m past the marina turning. It is marked private but actually it isn't. From there, the track goes over the headland before falling to a small beach and a series of small rock stacks. After negotiating the stacks (beware at high tide), climb the hill to the light beacon (2 km; 1 hr return), from where there are magnificent views along the coast. A few kilometres north of Tutukaka, before the road turns inland again, are a number of small settlements and attractive bays and beaches. Matapouri and Whale Bay, 1 km to the north, are worth a stop.

Whangarei to the Bay of Islands *p151*
Oakura Bay Cruises, Oakura Bay (just north of Helena Bay), T09-433 6877.

● Transport

Whangarei *p145, maps p146 and p148*
Car hire
Avis, 14 Hannah St, T09-438 2929.
Budget, 22 Maunu Rd, T09-438 7292.
Rent-a-Cheapy, 69 Otaika Rd, T09-438 7373.

● Directory

Whangarei *p145, maps p146 and p148*
Banks Most major branches can be found on Bank St (funnily enough).
Internet Available at the library (see below); the VIC; JJ's Internet, 46 John St, T09-430 8387, Mon-Fri 0900-1800, Sat-Sun 0930-1700, $3 per hr; and Klosenet, 34 John St, T09-438 8111, Mon-Sat 1000-2100, Sun 1100-1800. **Library** The library is on Rust Av, T09-430 7260. **Medical services** Primecare, 12 Kensington Av, T09-437 1988. 0830-2200. **Post office** 16-20 Rathbone St, T09-430 2761. Open Mon-Fri 0830-1700, Sat 0900-1300.

Bay of Islands → *Colour map 1, B4*

Paihia is the main launching point for the Bay of Islands; if you arrive here by road you may be disappointed because all you can see is one very little island just offshore. However, what you will certainly see are plenty of 'no vacancy' signs, boats (including a ferry that crosses the bay to the small village of Russell) and ticket offices. But don't worry, they are out there – all 150 of them. The Bay of Islands is one of the major tourist draws in the country, offering the visitor numerous water-based activities and superb coastal scenery. The area is also of huge historic significance in that it is the site of the first European settlement and the signing of the Treaty of Waitangi – the document that began the uneasy 'voyage' of New Zealand's bicultural society. While the islands themselves are the main attraction, most are uninhabited and you can only stay at designated campsites. Most visitors stay on the mainland and take cruises to the islands. You can also explore them by kayak, yacht or sailing boat; go big game fishing for marlin or shark; dive amidst shoals of blue maomao; swim with the dolphins; bask in the sun; or jump out of a plane. ▸▸ *For Sleeping, Eating and other listings, see pages 163-170.*

Ins and outs

Getting there The **Bay of Islands airport** (also known as Kerikeri airport) is located just outside of Kerikeri. Flights to/from Auckland take around 40 minutes via **Air New Zealand Link**, T0800-737000. **Paihia Taxis and Tours**, T09-402 7506, and **Kerikeri Taxi Shuttle Service**, T09-407 9515, operate a shuttle service between Paihia and Kerikeri via the airport, $10 one way. There are car hire companies at the airport and in town.

Northliner, T09-402 7857, and **Intercity**, T09-623 1503, run regular daily coach services to the Bay of Islands from Auckland and all major points on the SH1. The journey from Auckland takes about four hours. They also link with the **West Coaster** service to Omapere and Dargaville, T09-913 6100/T09-402 8989. In Paihia all buses arrive outside the Maritime Building on the wharf. Book at the VIC (I-Site) on the waterfront. Most people, however, arrive at Paihia by car on the SH1 from Whangarei. A more scenic route is along Old Russell Road will bring you in 'the back door' via Russell.

Russell is served by two ferry services: one is a passenger-only service running directly from Paihia, the other is a vehicle ferry operating from the wharf at Opua, 9 km to the south (see page 159 for details).

Tourist information and orientation Paihia is the main resort town in the Bay. Its focus is on the waterfront where the vast majority of activities on or around the islands and Bay of Islands Maritime and Historic Park can be booked and boarded. For the best of land-based attractions you are far better off heading across the water to Russell or the short distance north to the Waitangi National Reserve, possible diversions along the way include the collection of fierce looking Maori *pou* (carvings) and the 1917 sailing ship the *Tui* along the way. The **tourist office** ① *Marsden Rd, T09-402 7345, www.north land.org.nz, www.paihia.co.nz, daily 0800-2000 (reduced hours in winter)*, is on the waterfront by the wharf. Look out for the useful *Northland Visitors Guide*, free.

Paihia and Waitangi 🏨🍴🎭☀️⛺🚌🍸 ▸▸ *pp163-170.*

Paihia was the site of New Zealand's first church and missionary centre, but unless you have an inexplicable fetish for motels there is little in the way of sights, with the town acting primarily as an accommodation and amenity centre for tourists.

Paihia & Waitangi

Huia Creek Walkway
To Mt Bledisloe
Whare Runanga
WAITANGI
Visitor Centre & Treaty House
Waitangi National Reserve
War Canoe
Waitangi River
Hobson Beach

Bay of Islands

Woolworths Supermarket
Te Ti Bay
Motumaire Island

To Russell

Taylor Island

Te Kemara Av
Te Karuwha Pai
Tau Henare Dr

Marsden Rd
Davis Creek
Moana Av
Bayview Rd
Selwyn Rd
Discount 4 Supermarket
Williams Rd
Joyces Rd
Upr School Rd
School Rd
Wallace La
PAIHIA
Fullers/Kings Booking Office

Marsden Rd
Kings Rd
Bedggood Cl
McMurray Rd
Greys La
Seaview Rd
Sullivans Rd
Binnie St
Panorama Av
Panorama St
Tohitapau Rd
Veronica St
Courts

Motuarahi Island

Haumi River

To Keri Keri Airport
To Omata Estate Vineyard, Kawakawa Whangarei & Auckland Opua Ferry

0 metres 300
0 yards 300

Sleeping
Abri Apartments **1**
Admirals View Motel **14**
Allegra House **13**
Aloha Garden Resort Motel **2**
Bay Adventurer & Bay
 View Apartments **11**

Bay Cabinz **3**
Bay of Islands Lodge **20**
Beachcomber Resort **4**
Captain Bob's **12**
Copthorne Hotel
 & Resort Bay of Islands **6**
Dolphin Motel **7**
Haruru Falls Resort
 Panorama **18**
Kingsgate Bay of Islands **19**
Mousetrap **9**

Paihia Beach Resort & Spa **10**
Peppertree Lodge **17**
Pipi Patch & Bar **11**
Saltwater Lodge **11**
Twin Pines **8**
Waiora **5**

Eating 🍴
Bistro 40 **1**
Café Over the Bay **2**
Only Seafood **1**

Ruffino's **6**
Swiss Café & Grill **3**
Stonegrill at Paihia
 Pacific Hotel **4**
Sugarboat **5**
Waikokopu Café **7**

Bars & clubs 🍸
Beachhouse **8**
Lighthouse Tavern **9**

Waitangi is a short walk north of Paihia and is a pleasant contrast. It's a site of celebrated national heritage as the Treaty of Waitangi was signed here in 1840 at the Treaty House, which is now a national museum and visitor centre for the Waitangi National Reserve.

Waitangi Visitor Centre and Treaty House

ⓘ T09-402 7437, www.waitangi.net.nz, daily 0900-1700. $12 ($22 including tour).

A little further along, across the bridge, is Waitangi and the very impressive Waitangi Visitor Centre and Treaty House set in the **Waitangi National Reserve**. This is the heart of New Zealand's historical beginnings. The haunting sound of piped Maori song leads you into the visitor centre where your first stop should be the audio-visual display before taking the pleasant walk around the reserve. It's well done but does give you a rather politically correct outline of events that led to the signing of the Treaty of Waitangi in 1840 and the significance of the document right up to the present day (see page 697). The main focus of the reserve is the beautifully restored **Treaty House**. It was built in 1833-1834 and was once the home of British resident, James Busby, who played a crucial role in the lead-up to the treaty signing. The house is full of detailed and informative displays that help clarify the quite confusing series of events surrounding the creation of the treaty. Near the Treaty House the reserve boasts perhaps the most visited **Whare Runanga** (Maori meeting house) in the country. To call this, or any *whare*, merely 'a house' is rather an understatement. They are essentially artworks, with all the meaning, soul and effort therein and the Whare Runanga at Waitangi is a fine example.

In front of the Treaty House and Whare Runanga is a spacious lawn overlooking the bay to Russell. From the lawn it is a short walk down to the shore where the **war canoe** *Ngatokimatawhaorua*, is housed. This impressive 35-m-long craft is named after the canoe in which Kupe, the great Maori ancestor and navigator, discovered Aotearoa (New Zealand), and was commissioned along with the Whare Runanga as a centennial project commemorating the signing of the treaty. The *Ngatokimatawhaorua* continued to be launched every year as part of the high profile **Waitangi Day** commemoration ceremonies hosted on and around the national reserve. However, in recent years, after attracting protesters, Waitangi Day was scrapped and there was a call for a more progressive and low-key 'New Zealand Day'.

There are daily half-hour *kappa haka* **Maori performances** at 1030, 1130, 1330 and 1430, $12, child $5 (excludes entry). A recent addition to the Waitangi experience is the **Culture North Treaty of Waitangi Night Show** ⓘ T09-402 5990, www.culturenorth. co.nz, $50 all-inclusive, free pick-up, which is staged most evenings and is highly recommended. It is genuine and so far lacking in the commercialism so rife in other tourist areas. This is the one 'must-do' beyond the islands themselves.

The **Huia Creek Walkway**, which begins near the Treaty House, is an easy walk (two hours) through the reserve to the unremarkable **Haruru Falls**, taking in a fine example of mangrove habitat on the way.

Running adjacent to the reserve is the **Waitangi Golf Course**, which along with **Mount Bledisloe**, 3 km away, commands fine views across the bay.

Around Paihia

You might think it ridiculous to recommend a public convenience as a major attraction but if you have time, visit the **Kawakawa 'Hundertwasser' Public Toilets** in the centre of Kawakawa, 17 km south of Paihia. This marvellous and colourful creation of local artist Friedrich Hundertwasser who died in 2000, is now something of an icon and a monument. South of Kawakawa the **Kawiti Glow Worm Caves** ⓘ T09-404 0583/ T09-403 7887, daily 0830-1630, $10, child $5, tours hourly on the hour, are also well worth a visit. Local Maori guides give a very interesting and genuine tour that provides insight into their natural and human history.

Russell 🏠⚡❀ ›› pp163-170.

About 2 km across the bay from Paihia, still on the mainland, is the contrasting settlement of Russell which enjoys a village feel and a rich history that eludes its frenetic, tourism-based neighbour. With the advent of the first European settlement, Kororareka quickly grew to be the base for whalers, sealers and escaped convicts and earned the sordid and notorious reputation as 'the hellhole of the Pacific'. The earliest missionaries tried their best to quell the unholy mob with mixed results. When the Treaty of Waitangi was signed in 1840, although it was the largest European settlement in New Zealand, William Hobson, the then governor, decided it was not a good marketing ploy to give it capital status and instead bought land in what is now Auckland. To make matters worse, the treaty was seen by local Maori as a fraud and not as beneficial as was promised, with financial benefits in particular failing to materialize. Their scorn (led by the infamous chief Hone Heke) was focused on the Flagstaff near Russell, which proudly flew the Union Jack. Heke and his men duly cut it down, not once but four times, the last felling causing a major battle in which Kororareka was sacked and the first Maori Wars began. Once relative peace returned the authorities decided to make a new beginning and lose the notorious label, calling it Russell.

Today Russell, along with Kerikeri (also in the Bay of Islands), is flaunted as the most historic village in New Zealand and, although it bustles with transitory tourists in the summer and is inundated at New Year, it manages admirably to maintain a sedate and close community feel, which if you stay, can warm the heart.

Northland Bay of Islands

Russell

To **5** **10** & Tapeka Point Reserve (1km)

Flagstaff Hill

Tapeka Rd

Flagstaff Rd

Wellington St
Kent St
Queen St
Prospect St
The Strand
York St
Church St
James St
Long Beach Rd

Kororareka Bay

To Paihia

Fullers/ Bradley's

Russell Mini Tours

Cass St
Chapel St
Supermarket

Beresford St

To Long Beach

6

Baker St
Ashby St
Hazard St
St Pious

Russell Museum

Anglican Church
DoC Visitor Centre
Robertson St

Bay of Islands

Pompallier

Matauwhi Rd

Blind Rd

Omata Estate Vineyard & Opua Car Ferry (11 km)

8 **7**

Hope Av
Florence Av

Matauwhi Bay

N

0 metres 400
0 yards 400

Sleeping 🛏
Arcadia Lodge **1**
Duke of Marlborough & Restaurant **2**
Eagles Nest **5**
Orongo Bay Homestead **11**

Ounuwhao Harding House **7**
Pukeko Cottage B&B & Backpackers **8**
Pukematu Lodge **10**
Russell Top Ten Holiday Park **6**
Triton Suites **3**

Eating ❶
Birdie Num Nums **1**
Gables **4**
Kamakura **3**
York St Café **2**

Ins and outs

Getting there Russell can be reached by **passenger ferry** ① *Paihia Wharf, Oct-Mar every 30 mins 0720-2230, less in winter, $5, child $2.50*; or there is a **vehicle ferry** ① *every 10 mins from Opua, 9 km south of Paihia, daily 0650-2200, car and driver $9, campervan $15, passenger $2 one way*. Most of the Paihia-based tours pick up in Russell on their way out to the islands. For more information contact the VICs.

Tourist information There is no official tourist centre in Russell but the offices for **Bradley's** ① *at the end of the wharf, T09-403 8020, 0730-1700*, and **Fuller's** ① *Cass St, T09-403 7866, daily 0730-1700*, can provide some information on excursions. For information on walks, consult the **DoC Bay of Island's Area Visitor Centre** ① *The Strand, T09-403 9005, russellvc@doc.govt.nz, daily summer 0700-1700, winter 0900-1630.* ▸▸ *For further details, see Activities and tours, page 167.*

Sights

For a detailed historic indulgence head for the **Russell Museum** ① *corner of Pitt and York sts, T09-403 7701, daily, Jan 1000-1700, Feb-Dec 1000-1600, $5, child $0.50.* It has an interesting collection of early settler relics and, having being built to commemorate the bicentenary of Captain Cook's visit in 1769, features a host of information about the explorer including a very impressive 1:5 scale model of Cook's ship *The Endeavour*.

A short distance south along the shore from the museum is **Pompallier** ① *T09-403 9015, daily 1000-1700, $7.50, child $3.50.* This historic 1842 dwelling was originally set up by the early missionaries as a printing works. It later served as a tannery and a private home before becoming a small museum in 1990. On the corner of Church Street and Robertson Street is the 1836 **Anglican Church** which was one of the few buildings to survive the 1840s sacking and Maori war (bar a few visible musket ball holes) and remains the oldest church in New Zealand. For a grand view it is worth the steep climb to **Flagstaff Hill** (*Maiki*). Parts of the current pole were erected in the late 1850s over a decade after Hone Heke's attempts at clear felling. One kilometre north, the earth terraces of the ancient *pa* on the **Tapeka Point Reserve** make a pleasant walk.

Long Beach, 1 km behind the village, is also a pleasant spot and a fine venue on a hot summer's day. If the history of Russell is of particular interest the *Heritage Trails* leaflet from the DoC visitor centre is useful or you might like to join the excellent Maori guided tour on offer with **Fernz Eco Tours** ① *T09-403 7887, www.fernzecotours.co.nz, half or full-day from $125.* **Russell Mini Tours** ① *T09-403 8044, 3 tours daily from 1000, $19, 1 hr,* also offers local tours and depart from outside the Fuller's Office on Cass Street.

Cape Brett Walk

This is one of the finest walks in Northland following the ridge of Cape Brett to the lighthouse and DoC Cape Brett Hut. With a clear view across the Bay of Islands it provides some spectacular coastal scenery. The well-formed track starts near Rawhiti, 29 km from Russell in Oke Bay (secure parking is available at **Hartwells**, Kaimaramara Bay, end of Rawhiti Road, T09-403 7248). It will take an entire day (about eight hours) to walk the 20 km to the Hut though if you cannot face the return journey, book a water taxi back to Rawhiti from just below the hut with **Kiwi Eco Tours** ① *T09-403 8823, www.kiwiecotours.co.nz, $30.*

To attempt the walk and stay in the hut you must first pay a hut fee of $10 and a track fee of $30 at the DoC visitor Centre in Russell. You can also post the fee to the centre (PO Box 134, The Strand, Russell). You will then be given a code for the door lock. Essential maps and all the relevant information are available from there. Basic camping is available near the start of the track in Rawhiti, T09-403 7044. The track is on Maori Trust land so stick to the rules.

Perhaps the best way to tackle the walk is with the reputable **Cape Brett Walkways** ① *T09-403 8823, www.capebrettwalks.co.nz,* which offers a number of attractive alternatives for doing the walk either way, in a day, including transport from Russell and Paihia or from Rawhiti inclusive of track fees. Contact them direct for the latest fees and itineraries for guided or self-guided tour options.

● *The original name for Russell was Kororareka, which derived (so legend has it) from the utterings of a wounded Maori chief who, after being given some penguin soup, said "Ka-reka-te-korora" (how sweet is the penguin).*

Kerikeri ▣⬤⬤⬤⬤⬤ ►► *pp163-170.*

You have never tasted a mandarin until you have been to Kerikeri. Travelling north from Paihia the rolling hills give way to corridors of windbreaks that hide the laden trees of citrus, grape and kiwifruit for which the area is famous. The word *keri* means 'dig', and it was here, in pleasant little 'Dig Dig', that the first plough cut into New Zealand soil in 1820. Along with Russell, Kerikeri is rich in Maori and early European history with the Kerikeri Basin, 2 km northeast of the present town, being the nucleus of New Zealand's first European colonization.

Ins and outs

Getting there and around Kerikeri is 22 km north of Paihia just off SH1. The **Bay of Islands airport** is located just outside Kerikeri (see page 156). Both **Intercity** and **Northliner** coaches stop in the centre of town on Cobham Road. Several tour shuttles can get you to Kerikeri for the day including **Kerikeri Tours**, T09-407 9904, from $18 one way. **Paihia Taxis and Tours**, T09-402 7506, and **Kerikeri Taxi Shuttle Service**, T09-407 9515, also operate a shuttle from $12 one way providing drop-off or pick-up to and from the airport along the way.

Tourist information The independent **Kerikeri Visitor Centre** ① *library complex, Cobham Rd, T09-407 9297, www.kerikeri.co.nz, Mon-Fri 0900-1700, Sat 1000-1200* can provide general local information. The **DoC information office** ① *34 Landing Rd, T09-407 8474,* can provide advice on walks in the Puketi Forest.

Sights

For a sense of history and atmosphere head straight for the **Kerikeri Basin** past the main commercial centre. There the road falls to meet the babbling Kerikeri River and the dominant and attractive **Stone Store** ① *daily 1000-1700, $3.50.* This was New Zealand's first stone building and was completed in 1835. It was used by the first Anglican bishop George Selwyn as a library in the early 1840s and later as an ammunition store during conflicts between Ngapuhi chief Hone Heke, before assuming its intended purpose as a general mission store. Today it is neatly laid out as testimony to that function with a museum on its top floor.

Almost immediately next door is the two-storey Kemp House or **Mission House** ① *daily 1000-1700, $5, combined entry with Stone Store $7.50, children free.* This is the oldest surviving building in New Zealand (at the very young age of 179). It was established by pioneer missionary Samuel Marsden on land offered to him by the great local Maori warlord Hongi Hika, who accepted 48 felling axes for the land and also offered Marsden and his staff protection from invading tribes. In 1832 it became the home of catechist-blacksmith, James Kemp, and his family – generations of whom lived in the house until 1974, when it was passed over to the nation as an historic site. The house is now packed with Kemp family relics.

Overlooking both buildings is the more ancient **Kororipo Pa** which was chief Hongi Hika's more basic domain (until, not surprisingly, he had a European-style house built nearby in the 1820s).

A short stroll across the river is **Rewa's Village** ① *T09-407 6454, daily, $3, child $0.50.* This is an authentic recreation of a pre-European Maori fishing settlement, or *kainga*, named after Hongi Hika's successor. With its very basic ponga tree fern-trunk huts and shelters you can only wonder what the early Maori must have thought of the Euro-architecture of the time.

The **Kerikeri Basin** offers a number of pleasant short walks along the river, the most notable of which takes in the 27-m **Rainbow Falls** (also accessible 3 km north from Waipapa Road; leaflet available from DoC). Another fine short walk is to **Ake Ake Point and Pa**, accessible from the pretty Opito Bay, 20 km east of the city.

As well as its fruit, Kerikeri is also famous for its **arts and crafts**. The free leaflet *Kerikeri Art and Craft Trail* lists a number of venues, the best of which is **Origin Art and Craft Co-op** ① *SH10, T09-407 1133, daily 1000-1700*. It has a wide range of works on display and for sale from pottery to stained glass. Well worth a visit is **'Kaleidoscopes'** ① *256 Waipara Rd, T09-407 4415*. The **Kauri Workshop** ① *just as you come in to town on Kerikeri Rd, T09-407 9196*, has a quality range of kauri and other native wood products. From there you can take a stroll next door to the **Makana Chocolate Factory** ① *T09-407 6800, daily 0900-1730*, where you can watch the stuff being made while wondering why all the employees are not the size of small houses. If natural beauty and skin products are your thing then you can't get more natural than the terrific range on offer from **Living Nature** ① *Bulls Gorge Kerikeri turning on SH10, T09-407 7895, www.livingnature.com, 0900-1800*. Beauticians and therapists are available on site.

On an ecological theme is the excellent **Aroha Island Ecological Centre** ① *Kurapari Rd, 12 km east of the town, T09-407 5243, kiwi@aroha.net.nz (see Sleeping below), daily but may be closed 1 month in winter*. Aroha Island and the neighbouring **Rangitane Scenic Reserve** are important remnant habitats of the brown kiwi. The island is kept predator-free and therefore offers a small but valuable sanctuary for a few birds. Alas, with the kiwi being nocturnal, daytime visitors will only be able to see interpretative material in the visitor centre. However, if you stay overnight you may get the opportunity to see, and certainly hear, the birds after dark on a guided tour.

Kerikeri to Kaitaia

Provided you have your own transport, the roads that branch off SH1 to the coast north of Kerikeri offer stunning coastal scenery and some secluded beaches that are well worth visiting. About 15 km north of Kerikeri the road loops to the coast taking in the small settlements and peaceful hideaways of **Matauri Bay**, **Te Ngaire**, **Wainui**, **Mahinepua** and **Tauranga Bay** before rejoining SH1 again near Whangaroa. From there you meet the sweeping shores of **Doubtless Bay** with its mainly retirement communities of **Mangonui**, **Coopers Beach** and **Cable Bay**, before cutting across the picturesque **Karikari Peninsula** on your way to the last significant northern outpost and predominantly Maori enclave of **Kaitaia**.

Matauri Bay ◉▲ » *pp163-170.*

The views above Matauri Bay are stunning, with the numerous **Cavalli Islands** offering a sight that almost surpasses that of the Bay of Islands. Captain Cook named the islands after travalli (a species of fish) bought by Cook from local Maori. The **Samuel Marsden Memorial Church** in Matauri Bay commemorates New Zealand's pioneer missionary who first preached the gospel in the Bay of Islands on Christmas Day 1814.

The area remains a top venue for **deep-sea fishing** and **scuba diving**. Matauri Bay has always been a popular holiday spot, but assumed additional national fame when the wreck of the Greenpeace vessel *Rainbow Warrior* was laid to rest off the Cavallis in 1987. The famous flagship was bombed by French secret service through a ludicrous act of terrorism in Auckland in 1985. The idea was to prevent her leading a protest flotilla to the French nuclear test grounds on the Pacific atoll of Mururoa. Her sunken hull, 3 km offshore, provides the poignant home to a myriad of sea creatures while an impressive memorial on the hill overlooking the islands near the beach pays tribute to the ship, her crew (one of which was killed) and the continuing cause for a nuclear-free region. The incident sparked an international outcry and New Zealanders are in no hurry to forget, or forgive. There is an echo of Maori history, spirit and support in the Bay with the *waka* (war canoe) *Mataatua II* located near the campground. The history of this legendary canoe led to the local tribe, the Ngati Kura, offering the remains and the *mana* of the modern day *Rainbow Warrior* a final resting place.

North to Whangaroa

From Matauri Bay the road follows the coast to the picturesque bays and settlements of **Te Ngaire** and **Wainui**. A branch road, just past Wainui, will take you to **Mahinepua Bay**, which provides a classic touch of seclusion, scenery and the only campsite (DoC). From there the road climbs again, offering fine views inland at Radar Heights (an old radar station), before temporarily leaving the coast towards Tauranga Bay and Whangaroa.

● Sleeping

Paihia *p156, map p157*

Paihia is well-served with accommodation to suit all budgets. There are motels all over town, most are centrally located, as well as numerous backpacker hostels. King St is the main focus and is home to the most modern, lively hostels. With so much competition in these parts all of them have to maintain good standards so you can't go far wrong. There are also a number of self-contained options.

Despite a wealth of beds, remember that the Bay of Islands is also the favoured holiday spot for hundreds of New Zealanders. It is essential to book ahead in summer, especially over Christmas. If you are looking for peace and quiet you would be better staying across the water in Russell where you will find the best lodges and B&Bs.

LL Bay of Islands Lodge, SH11, Port Opua, T09-402 6075, www.bayofislandslodge.co.nz. Luxurious 5-star cedar-clad lodge set in an elevated position and amidst private bush, commanding views across Opua Bay. There are 4 spacious well-appointed rooms with all the bells and whistles and to top it all, a small infinity swimming pool.

L-AL Abri Apartments, 10 Bayview Rd, T09-402 8003, www.abri-accom.co.nz. 2 delightful modern stand-alone self-contained studio apartments. Peaceful location.

L-AL Allegra House, 39 Bayview Rd, T09-402 7932, www.allegra.co.nz. Conveniently located in the heart of Paihia with fine views across the bay to Russell and beyond, this modern home offers the choice of conventional B&B accommodation or a

spacious self-contained apartment with an extra en suite if required. There are 2 B&B rooms that can accommodate single, twin or double. Both have TV, tea and coffee making facilities and a fridge. Owners are fluent in both German and French. Internet and off-street parking. Minimum 2-night stay.

L-AL Beachcomber Resort, T09-402 7434, www.beachcomber-resort.co.nz. A slightly ageing yet popular hotel resort with New Zealanders, at the southern end of town. Studios and family suites. Right next to the beach. Fine buffet breakfast.

L-AL Kingsgate Hotel Bay of Islands, Marsden Rd, T09-402 7416, www.millenniumhotels.com. Central and reliable with views directly across the bay.

L-AL Paihia Beach Resort and Spa, 116 Marsden Rd, T0800-870111/T09-402 0111, www.paihiabeach.co.nz. Studios and suites with good views, spa facilities and treatment rooms on site.

L-AL Waiora, 52 Puketona Rd (northern end of town), T09-402 6601, www.waiora-valley.co.nz. A fine peaceful option, 4-star with in-house health spa.

L-A Aloha Garden Resort Motel, 32-36 Seaview Rd, T09-402 7540, www.aloha.co.nz. At the top of the range, has a good reputation.

AL Copthorne Hotel and Resort Bay of Islands, Tau Henare Drive, T09-402 7411, www.copthornebayofislands.co.nz. The most high-profile hotel located right on the waterfront and within the Waitangi Reserve. Modern, recently refurbished rooms with standard facilities. There is an in-house café/

Northland **Bay of Islands** Listings

● For an explanation of the Sleeping and Eating price codes used in this guide, see the inside ● front cover. Other relevant information is provided in the Essentials chapter, pages 44-51. Note that prices are tive in New Zealand dollars.

restaurant, and the independent **Waikokopu Café** only a few mins' away in the reserve grounds is also recommended. Large and unusual outdoor pools and spas. Spacious grounds and only a short stroll from the Waitangi Reserve and Waitangi Golf Course.

A Admirals View Motel, 2 McMurray Rd, T0800-247234, www.admiralsview lodge.co.nz. 5-star rated accommodation with cheaper and popular garden studios.

A Bay Cabinz, 32-34 School Rd, T09-402 8534, www.baycabinz.co.nz. Cosy cedar cabins sleeping 1-4.

A Dolphin Motel, 69 Williams Rd, T09-402 8170, www.paihiamotel.co.nz. Mid-range option, quiet location, plus private spa pool.

A-D Bay Adventurer and Bay View Apartments, 28 Kings Rd, T09-4025162, www.bayadventurer.co.nz. One of the most recent backpacker additions. An award-winner that marries both self-contained apartments with modern standard backpacker facilities. Pool, spa, internet and off-street parking.

B-D The Pipi Patch, 18 Kings Rd, T0800-462396/T09-358 4877, www.pipi-patch.co.nz. Great selection of value options from bunks to doubles. There's a popular bar attached, which for travellers is the main focus and meeting venue in town, as well as the haunt of a few good-value locals. Off-street parking.

B-D Saltwater Lodge, 14 Kings Rd, T09-402 7075/T0800-002266, www.saltwaterlodge. co.nz. The most popular and the busiest hostel with an impressive range of facilities, as you might expect from its rare 5-star rating. Immaculately clean, very tidy rooms and bathrooms, from dorm to double, incredible kitchens, sky TV, internet, gym, kayak and bike hire and even disabled facilities. Off-street parking. Recommended.

C-D Captain Bob's, 44 Davis Cres, T09-402 8668, capnbobs@xtra.co.nz. A perfectly adequate hostel, away from the Kings Rd hype.

C-D Mousetrap, 11 Kings Rd, T09-402 8182, www.mousetrap.co.nz. A quieter hostel and very arty.

C-D Peppertree Lodge, 15 Kings Rd, T09-402 6122, www.peppertree.co.nz. Again a quieter hostel, with free bike and kayak hire.

Motorcamps and campsites
L-D Haruru Falls Resort Panorama, 6 km northwest of Paihia on the Old Wharf Rd T0800-757525, www.harurufalls.co.nz.

Has powered sites and camping facilities as well as motel units and a pool. The Haruru Falls are directly in view.

A-D Twin Pines, a short walk up the hill, T09-402 7322, www.twinpines.co.nz. Fairly unremarkable but with a pub, restaurant and camp kitchen.

Russell *p159, map p159*
Russell has the widest selection of B&Bs north of Whangarei.

LL Eagles Nest, 60 Tapeka Rd, T09-403 8333, www.eaglesnest.co.nz. One of the best lodges in the country. Impressive architecture, sumptuous beautifully appointed suites and self-contained villas, pool, spa, superb cuisine and just about everything a body needs.

L Pukematu Lodge, Flagstaff Hill, T/F09-4038500, www.pukematulodge.co.nz. Perched high on the hill this modern B&B offers spectacular views across to the Waitangi Reserve and Paihia. The hosts (one of which is of local Maori descent and the village policeman) go the extra mile to make sure you stay is memorable and enjoyable. The cosy, stylish suites furnished in recycled rimu wood, offer plenty of privacy and a huge deck provides the perfect venue for a generous breakfast. Evening meals including a Maori *hangi* BBQ are available on request. In-house tours of the village with plenty of fascinating historical and personal insight. Credit cards welcome. Recommended.

L-AL The Duke of Marlborough, T09-403 7829, www.theduke.co.nz. Right on the waterfront and oozing all the gracious charm its 150-year location deserves, 'The Duke', as it is affectionately known, offers some welcome relief from the tourist hype of Paihia. The recently refurbished modern rooms perhaps deflect from the establishment's historic charm, but there is no denying the quality, with some affording fine bay views and a large bath or spa. The cosy bar and à la carte restaurant offers a fine place to relax. When you're here, it's difficult to believe, the village was once called the 'Hell Hole of the Pacific'. Continental breakfast included, cooked breakfast extra.

L-AL Orongo Bay Homestead, Aucks Rd, T09-403 7675, www.thehomestead.co.nz. Beautiful rooms in what used to be New Zealand's first American Consulate (1860).

Organic gourmet dinners can be arranged, boom in advance. Recommended.

L-AL Ounuwhao Harding House, Matauwhi Bay, T09-403 7310, www.bay-of-islands.co.nz/ ounuwhao. A good B&B or self-contained option in historic surrounds.

L-AL Triton Suites, 7 Wellington St, T09-403 8067, www.tritonsuites.co.nz. Very flash boutique motel units in the centre of the village.

A Arcadia Lodge, 10 Florence Av, Matauwhi Bay, T09-403 7756, www.arcadialodge.co.nz. Lovingly restored, historic Tudor house with 3 characterful, spacious suites, great breakfast.

B-D Pukeko Cottage B&B and Backpackers, 14 Brind Rd, T09-403 8498, www.pukeko cottagebackpackers.co.nz (book well ahead). Small and cosy.

C-D Wainui Lodge, 92D Te Wahapu Rd, T09-403 8278, stoken@xtra.co.nz. Backpacker hostel in an idyllic rural waterfront location between Okaito (3 km) and Russell (5 km). 2 doubles and dorms, and a fine relaxed atmosphere.

Motorcamps and campsites
A-D Russell Top Ten Holiday Park, Long Beach Rd, T09-403 7826, www.russelltop10 .co.nz. Range of motels, flats, cabins and backpacker rooms. Reliable and fairly modern.

Kerikeri p161
Accommodation in Kerikeri is plentiful and generally less expensive than Paihia. Although not as busy, you are still advised to book ahead, especially at Christmas and in Jan. Hostels also tend to fill up Apr-Aug due to the fruit-harvesting season.

LL Sommerfields, Inlet Rd, T/F09-407 9889, www.sommerfields.co.nz. Luxury, modern B&B accommodation set in 2 ha just outside Kerikeri.

LL-L The Summerhouse B&B, 424 Kerikeri Rd, T09-407 4294, www.thesummer house.co.nz. A deservingly popular B&B set in a 1-ha citrus orchard, only 2 mins from Kerikeri. Contemporary New Zealand art complements a choice of 2 modern en suites, or a self-contained suite with its own private entrance. Legendary breakfast.

L Buddha Lodge, 1608 E State Highway 10, T09-407 7780, www.buddhalodge.co.nz. Another countryside retreat with some fine organic cooking.

L Kerikeri Village Inn, 165 Kerikeri Rd, T09-407 4666, www.kerikerivillageinn.co.nz. New B&B in a contemporary Santa Fe-style house. Fine views and sumptuous breakfast.

A Kauri Park Motel, 512 Kerikeri Rd, T/F09-407 7629, www.kauripark.co.nz. Relatively new and set in sub-tropical garden setting. Large nicely appointed units, some with private spa.

B Aroha Island Ecological Centre, Kurapari Rd, T09-407 5243. Cottage-style lodge (sleeps 5), B&B, campervans and campsites. Kayaks available, kiwi-watching at night.

B-D Pagoda Lodge, 81 Pa Rd, T09-407 8617, www.pagoda.co.nz. Unusual property once the domain of an eccentric Scotsman with an obsession with all things Asian. Self-contained units under main pagoda building, boathouse and luxury tents. Not exactly typically kiwi, but all very unique, comfortable and a nice change. Kayak and bike hire.

C-D Hone Heke Lodge Backpackers, 65 Hone Heke Rd, T/F09-407 8170, www.hone heke.co.nz. Named after the 'William Wallace-Braveheart-of local Maori history, offering dorms, twins and doubles, some with en suite bath, tent sites.

C-D Kerikeri YHA, 144 Kerikeri Rd, T09-407 9391, www.yha.org.nz. Set in large forested grounds. Double, twin and family rooms, self-contained cottage, campsites.

Motorcamps and campsites
There are also campsites at **Hone Heke Lodge Backpackers** and **Kerikeri YHA** (above).
B-D Kerikeri Top Ten Holiday Park, Aranga Rd, T09-407 9326. Modern motorcamp, centrally located next to the river.

Matauri Bay p162
The area, like the Bay of Islands, is very popular so book in advance.

LL Cavalli Beach House, Mahinepua Rd, T09-405 1049, www.cavallibeachhouse.com. Luxurious accommodation in a fine setting and an unusual beachfront house. Fine cuisine.

LL Huntaway Lodge, Te Ngaire Bay, 4 km north of Matauri Bay, T09-405 1611, www.huntawaylodge.com. Exclusive lodge in a superb setting overlooking the ocean and 3 secluded beaches: Te Ngaere, Piapia and Wainui. There are 3 modern, tastefully decorated guestrooms. Cuisine is a speciality here with a first-class 3-course dinner for $90. Breakfast included in the tariff. Activities such as fishing, diving, golf, sightseeing and sailing can be arranged and there is free use of kayaks.

Motorcamps and campsites
C-D Matauri Bay Holiday Park, T09-405 0525. Tight on the beach in the shadow of the *Rainbow Warrior* memorial hill (which sadly affects the view). All the usual facilities for camping and campervans but no units.

North to Whangaroa *p163*
Tauranga Bay hosts a scattering of options. **A-B Tauranga Bay Motel**, T09-405 0222. Basic with 6 units, 100 m from the beach. **B-D Tauranga Bay Holiday Park**, T09-405 0436, www.taurangabay.co.nz. New self-contained beachside log cabins. Many come here to join **Northland Sea Kayaking**, T09-405 0381, a popular sea kayaking outfit offering $80 day trips with an extra $20 for accommodation. It can provide shuttle pick-ups from the main bus route at Kaeo.

⊙ Eating

Paihia and Waitangi *p156, map p157*
As you would expect, there are plenty of choices in Paihia, most serving fresh local fish and seafood. The **Discount 4** supermarket is on Williams Rd while **Woolworths**, with all mod cons, is more of a trek at the northern end of town (500 m west of the roundabout) on the Puketona (KeriKeri) Rd, daily 0700-2200.
♔ Sugarboat, Waitangi Bridge, T09-402 7018, www.sugarboat.co.nz. Mediterranean dishes with Pacific Rim influence on board a retired tallship, with bar.
♔ Bistro 40, 40 Marsden Rd, T09-402 7444 , lunch from 1200, dinner from 1800, licensed. Together with **Only Seafood**, below, the best seafood in town.
♔ Only Seafood, 40 Marsden Rd, T09-402 6066, daily from 1700, licensed. See **Bistro 40** above.
♔ Stonegrill Restaurant, in the **Paihia Pacific**, 27 King's Rd, T09-402 8221. Also reliable with good à la carte menu.
♔ Swiss Café and Grill, Marsden Rd, T09-402 6701, licensed. Good for traditional European fare.

Cafés
Café over the Bay, right on the waterfront, T09-402 8147, breakfast from 0800. Has a nice healthy variety of snacks, good coffee and a small deck overlooking all the action.
Ruffino's, 39 William's Rd, T09-402 7964, daily from 1730, licensed. Good if you're just looking for a pizza snack in a central location.
Waikokopu Café, Waitangi National Reserve, T09-402 6275, daily 0900-1700. BYO and licensed. Undoubtedly one of the best places for daytime eating with pleasant surroundings and a highly imaginative menu including the sumptuous 'Whalers Breakfast'.

Russell *p159, map p159*
There are some good restaurants along the waterfront (Strand). The supermarket is centrally located on Cass St, daily 0800-1900.
♔♔♔ Duke of Marlborough Hotel (see Sleeping, page 164), open for lunch and dinner. For a bit of tradition the restaurant here is an old favourite, with a great atmosphere and outdoor seating overlooking the bay.
♔♔♔ Gables, T09-403 7670, www.gables restaurant.co.nz. On the waterfront. Romantic atmosphere, fine Mediterranean cuisine and a good wine list, but it's a tad on the expensive side.
♔♔♔ Kamakura, waterfront (Strand), T09-403 7771, www.kamakura.co.nz. One of the area's best restaurants, it's worth a muse of the menu.
♔♔♔ Omata Estate Vineyard, Aucks Rd (halfway between Opua and Russell), T09-403 8007, www.omata.co.nz, closed Mon. Some of the best eating in the region can be had at this congenial place over-looking the vines and the bay. A great place to be on a summer's day. Expensive lunch and dinner but worth it. Booking essential.
♔♔ York St Café, York St, T09-403 7360, daily 1000-2100. Great pizzas, seafood and breakfasts. Licensed.
♔ Birdie Num Nums, 2 Cass St, T09-403 7754. If none of the options above appeal then there is always this fish and chippie.

Kerikeri *p161*
The New World **supermarket** is on Kerikeri Rd in the town centre. Keri Pies are widely available – try one of Northland's finest here.
♔♔ The Black Olive, Main Rd, T09-4079693, Tue-Sun 1700 till late. BYO. Fantastic pizza. Sit in or take away.

¶¶ **Landing**, Kerikeri Basin, T09-4078479, daily 0900-2100. In a great setting across the road from the stone store. English pub-style lunch and fine dining in the evening. Beautiful on a sunny day. Sometimes has live music.

¶ **Café Cinema**, Hobson Av, T09-4079121. Offers a $22 'movie and meal deal' most nights which is good given the quality of the food (Dutch influenced). The cinema also has lots of character. Recommended.

¶ **Café Jerusalem**, Cobblestone Mall, T09-4071001, Mon-Fri 1100-2300, Sat 1500-2300. Cheap Middle Eastern food, sit-in or take away. Vegetarian snacks.

¶ **Kerikeri Club**, Cobham Rd, T09-407 8585. Mon-Sat 1300-2200, Sun 1500-2200. Cheap food and lots of it, in the local RSA, bridge and tennis club.

⊙ Pubs, bars and clubs

Paihia p156, map p157
The best pubs in town are along Kings Rd amidst all the backpacker establishments.
Beachhouse, next door to Saltwater Lodge. The place to be.
Lighthouse Tavern, upstairs in the Paihia Mall. Once the bars close, all clubbing (almost literally) takes place here. Not recommended.
Pipi Patch Backpackers, 18 Kings Rd. Most popular with the younger crowd.

Kerikeri p161
Citrus Bar, Kerikeri Rd, T09-407 1050. The main focus for a lively social evening in Kerikeri.

⊛ Festivals and events

Paihia and Waitangi p156, map p157
Feb Waitangi Day, New Zealand's 'national day' held at the Waitangi Reserve. The most genuine display of Maori culture and largest gathering in the country.
Aug Jazz and Blues Festival, T09-404 1063, www.jazz-blues.co.nz. A popular 3-day event attracting over 50 acts that include street performances in both Paihia and Russell.
Sep Taste Bay of Islands Festival. Over 30 winemakers and brewers gather together at the Copthorne Hotel and Resort near Paihia to offer the very best regional fare.

Russell p159, map p159
May Country Rock Festival, www.country-rock.co.nz. In its 9th year, the Country Rock Festival is held in various locations in Paihia and Russell. It's a fairly low-key but entertaining event hosting mainly New Zealand based acts.
Aug See Jazz and Blues Festival, above.

▲ Activities and tours

Paihia and Waitangi p156, map p157
The minute you arrive in Paihia you are under pressure to book, book, book and buy, buy, buy. Competition is fierce as the huge range of tour and activity operators vie for your attention and dollar. The booking offices open daily 0700-2130, until 1830 in winter. The best thing to do is to take your time and to take advice from the unbiased VIC before venturing into the 'booking mall' on the waterfront to be mauled by the sales sharks. It is better not to book ahead as you will lose much freedom of choice. The 2 main players are:
Fullers, T09-402 7421, www.fullers-bay-of-islands.co.nz (not the same company as the ferry operators in Auckland); and
Kings, T09-402 8288, www.kings-tours.co.nz. Both offer similar tours around the islands with Cape Brett's famous 'Hole in the Rock' being the main highlight. Trips generally involve combinations of activities from simple sightseeing to island stops, lunch cruises and swimming with dolphins.

Boomnetting
Cling on for dear life to a large net slung alongside a cruise boat. The boat stops if dolphins are spotted in the hope that they venture near. Part of a 6-hr cruise trip including the 'Hole in the Rock'.
Kings, see above, offers a complete trip for $95, child $50.

Cruising
A huge choice, again in combination with sightseeing, dolphin encounters and the 'Hole in the Rock' – a massive natural arch in a rock outcrop at the very tip of Cape Brett through which the cruise boats navigate the ocean swell. Trips range from 3 hrs ($70, child $35) to 6 hrs ($125, child $50). Some cruise options take in a stop on Urupukapuka Island, a favourite haunt of Zane Grey (www.zane

Northland Bay of Islands Listings

grey.co.nz), the famous American author and big-game fisherman. The bay at Otehei is beautiful, spoilt only perhaps by the rather gimmicky yellow submarine *Nautilus* in which you can venture under the water; $10. If you wish to stay on the island to take in the atmosphere, sights, archaeological walks (see DoC leaflet) and would prefer to pick up a later ferry, there is the basic **Zane Grey Lodge**, T09-403 7009, or **DoC campsites**. The **Zane Grey restaurant** in front of the lodge will see you right for a decent meal.

See also under Sailing, below.

Fullers (see above) offers a day-long Island 'Escape' package for $45, child $22.50, departs 0830. Also very popular (especially in high swell) is the bone-crunching, high speed 'Hole in the Rock' trips in the rather lewd sounding **Excitor**, T09-402 7020. Several trips daily, 1½ hrs, $72. There is an informative commentary and stops on the way and both are just as fast.

Mac Attack, T09-402 8180, offers 'Hole in the Rock trips' as above. The 'Mac', however, does pride itself on actually threading its way through the Hole, but given the heavy swell this is never guaranteed. You can take a camera but you will probably return with blurred pictures of the posterior of the person in front. And forget wearing specs unless fitted with automatic wipers.

The Rock, T0800-762527, www.rockthe boat.co.nz. For the more traditional, holistic approach, The Rock offers an excellent 24-hr cruise on board its own purpose-built craft, from $148. It is proving deservedly popular offering a whole host of activities from snorkelling to dolphin watching. The vessel itself is comfortable and well-kitted out with shared (twin or quad) or private cabins, bar and dining area. Meals are inclusive and the experience is a lot of fun. The layout also lets you be as social or as private as you like.

R Tucker Thompson, T09-402 8430, www.tucker.co.nz. For a more traditional approach, try polishing your best hook and exploring the bay aboard this tall ship. It's a popular and laid-back cruise with island stopover, BBQ lunch and some memorable swing diving from the yardarm, from $110.

Dolphin watching

The Bay of Islands is a top spot for dolphins, orca and the occasional migratory whale and there is much debate about the impact of tourist activities on the creatures, though the jury is still very much out. Only 3 companies are allowed actively to approach the dolphins, and all offer a similar experience of observation and encounter, including a scenic trip around the islands and the 'Hole in the Rock'. Limited numbers are allowed in the water at a time, so it can be slow and frustrating, but the animals come first. All 3 companies have high success rates and will take you out again the following day for free if you don't find any dolphins.

Dolphin Discoveries, T09-402 8234, www.dolphinz.co.nz, offer 2 trips daily at 0900 and 1300, a 'Discover the Bay' sightseeing/watching trip for $72, child $39, and dolphin swimming trips $105, child $65.

Dolphin Encounters (Fullers), T09-402 7421, www.fullers-bay-of-islands.co.nz, Oct-Apr, depart daily at 0800, returning at 1200 and 1230-1630; May-Sep, 0800-1200, $105, child $53. Trip with stop at Urupukapuka Island, Oct-Apr, daily at 0800-1730.

Fishing

The Bay and the upper Northland Coast is the best sea angling and big-game fishing venue in the country and one of the best in the world. A trip can be just about affordable for the average Joe at $250-350 a day. It is a very exciting experience, especially if you are 'in the chair' when you hook a big one. There are numerous reputable charter boats operating from Paihia and Russell. Contact the Paihia VIC for details. For beginners and standard sea-fishing options (including diving) try: **Captain Bucko's**, T09-402 7788, www.captainbucko.co.nz. From $95 (4 hrs).

Golf

Waitangi Golf Club, Tau Henare Drive, T09-402 7713. Above the Treaty Grounds in Waitangi and overlooking the bay. When it comes to aesthetics this has to be one of the finest courses in the country. Visitors welcome.

Kayaking

Bay Beach Hire, on the waterfront opposite Kings Rd, T09-402 6078, www.baybeach hire.co.nz. Offers freedom hire of single and double kayaks and guided trips. The popular sunset trip costs from $55.

Coastal Kayakers, T09-402 8105, www.coastal kayakers.co.nz, offers half- or full-day guided trips (some up river to Harufu Falls) and also the excellent 3-day experience. 3 days on a remote bay with a kayak to explore the islands can be a great adventure, and is a fine chance to encounter dolphins. All equipment and food provided. Half-day trip $55, full day $75, multi day $130-480; independent hire available for $40 per day. Sea Kayak Adventures, T09-402 8596, www.seakayakingadventuresnz.com. Offers an excellent service, trips at around $170 per day, occasional specials for backpackers. All equipment and food provided.

Parasailing and jet skiing
Flying Kiwi Parasail, T09-402 6078, www.parasail-nz.co.nz. A far more sedate option to the tandem skydive which operates along the foreshore in Paihia; 600 ft from $70, 1000 ft from $85. Jet ski hire, T09-402 8118 (Oct-Apr).

Quad biking and horse trekking
Bush-n-Bike Adventures, T09-404 1142, www.bushnbike.co.nz. 1½-hr horse treks (suitable for all levels, from $55) or quad biking (from $75) over farmland, through bush and along the Tirohanga River Valley 15 km south of Paihia. Courtesy pick-ups. Good wet weather activity.

Sailing
There are numerous independent sailing charters and options in the bay, contact the Paihia VIC for advice and details. A day on the water will cost about $75-125. See also under Cruising, above.
Bay of Islands Sailing (*Gungha II*), T0800 478900, www.bayofislandssailing.co.nz. Departing Paihia and Russell daily, the $85 trip features fresh snacks and lunch, snorkel gear, kayaks and fresh lunch.
Carino, T09-402 8040, bayofislandssailing@ xtra.co.nz. Dolphin trips under sail.
Ecocruz, T0800-432627, www.ecocruz.co.nz. Excellent 3-day trip around the islands on the 72ft ocean-going yacht *Manawanui*. The focus is on native marine wildlife with the aid of the 'bathyscope', with more traditional activities thrown in, including kayaking, snorkelling and fishing. Recommended.

Great Escape Yacht Charters, Opua, T09-402 7143, www.greatescape.co.nz Hire your own yacht, from $100 per day
Gungha, T0800-478900, www.bayofislands sailing.co.nz. Fast and modern.
Phantom, T0800-224421. Fast and modern.
SailNZ, T0800-724569, www.sailnew zealand.co.nz.

Scenic flights and skydiving
BOI Sky-Hi Tandem Skydive Ltd, T0800-427 593, www.nzskydive.co.nz. The customary 'But, but, but… what if' here in the Bay of Islands is based at the airport and all perfectly safe. Standard jumps of 6000-12,000 ft from a good value $185-$260.
Salt Air, T09-4028338, www.saltair.co.nz. A range of spectacular fixed wing and helicopter scenic flights from a 30-min local jaunt to a top-of-the-range flight to Cape Reinga and back, with a stop and some 4WD. Expensive at $365, but worth it.

Scuba diving
The bay is a fine dive venue and trips are also available for the Greenpeace 'Rainbow Warrior Wreck Dive'. See also Captain Buckos under Fishing.
Dive North, T09-402 7079, www.divenorth. co.nz, specializes in *Rainbow Warrior* trips.
Paihia Dive, T09-402 7551, www.divenz.com, has a very tidy purpose-built launch and offers a 2-dive trip with all gear from around $200.

Tours
Paihia acts as base for a number of full-day coach trips to the far north and Cape Reinga. The trips vary a little but usually entail a number of stops to view kauri in the Puketi Forest, the lighthouse at the cape and a dune surfing experience, whereby you throw yourself down huge sand dunes on a boogie board. Fullers and Kings (see page 167) offer the trip for around $100, as do the following:
Awesome Adventures, T09-402 6985, www.awesomenz.co.nz. Recommended.
Dune Rider, T09-402 8681, www.dune rider.co.nz. A hefty 'go-anywhere' vehicle.
Northern Exposure, T0800-573875.
Paihia Duck (usually parked on the waterfront like some cartoon monster), T09-402 8681, www.paihiaduck.co.nz. Offers short tours of the local area in an amphibious vehicle contact, 1½ hrs from $55.

One of the best coastal walks in the North Island is nearby in the very scenic form of the Cape Brett Walk (see Russell, page 160). Recommended.

Adventure Puketi, T09-401 9095, www.adventure-puketi.co.nz. Informative half- or full-day walks in the Puketi Forest and Manganinganinga Kauri Reserve with Ian Candy, a local resident who has immersed himself in its innate natural wonders for over 40 years, $90-$150.

Cape Brett Walkways, T09-403 8823, www.capebrettwalks.co.nz. Packages for the Cape Brett and other walks in the region.

Water Taxis

One of the best way to see the islands is to create your own itinerary of stops or overnight stays. Water taxi companies offering affordable rates and flexible schedules, include:

Kiwi Ecotours Water Taxis, T09-403 8823, www.kiwiecotours.co.nz and **Paihia Islands Shuttles**, T09-402 7678, www.islandshuttle.co.nz.

Kerikeri *p161*
Eco-tours

Aroha Island Ecological Centre, PO Box 541, Kerkeri, T09-407 5243, www.aroha. net.nz. Peaceful island where overnight visitors can see the North Island Brown Kiwi in its natural surroundings. Activities include walking, kayaking and workshops.

Horse trekking

Lakeside Horse Treks, T09-407 9422. $35 per hr.

Scenic flights

Quantum Aviation, Kerikeri, T09-407 7333. Offers flights both scenic and aerobatic.

Fruit picking

If you intend to find work in the orchards of Kerikeri, the hostels will provide advice and occasionally transport.

Walking

For details on camping and walks contact DoC in Kerikeri, T09-4078474.

As well as the attractive short walks along the river from the Basin reserve, further afield (northwest of Kerikeri) the **Puketi** and **Omahuta forests** can be accessed between Waipapa and Kapiro on SH1. These forests contain a number of impressive Kauri trees linked by a boardwalk. A brief stop here is usually included on the agenda for most of the Cape Reinga coach tours from Paihia. **Adventure Puketi**, T09-401 9095, www.adventure-puketi.co.nz, offers informative half- or full-day walks.

Matauri Bay *p162*
Golf

Kauri Cliffs Golf Course, Kauri Cliffs, Matauri Bay Rd, T09-405 1900, www.kauricliffs.com. One of the most scenic golf courses in the country, but expensive at over $200 a round.

Scuba diving

The *Rainbow Warrior* is a well-known and popular wreck. A number of companies offer trips from Whangarei, Tutukaka and Paihia (see pages 162 and 169). **Matauri Bay Charters**, Matauri Bay Holiday Park, T/F09-405 0525. The local company.

⊖ Transport

Paihia *p156, map p157*
Bicycle hire

Bay Beach Hire, T09-402 6078, at the southern end of the beach opposite Kings Rd. Bikes from $35 per day.

Taxi

Haruru Cabs, T09-402 6292, or **Paihia Cabs**, T09-402 5948.

⊕ Directory

Paihia *p156, map p157*
Internet Internet and cheap overseas calls available at **Boots Off**, Selwyn Rd, T09-402 6632, or the **Waterfront Booking Centre** (Awesome Adventures). **Post office** 2 Williams Rd, Paihia, T09-402 7800, Mon-Fri 0800-1730, Sat 0800-1400. **Medical services** Selwyn Rd, T09-402 8407.

Kerikeri *p161*
Internet Kerikeri Computers, 88 Kerikeri Rd (0900-1700).

Whangaroa Harbour and Doubtless Bay → Colour map 1, B3

Although most visitors are by now a little drunk on bays and coastal scenery, Whangaroa Harbour and the wide sweep of Doubtless Bay add that last little tipple of pleasant aesthetics before the sandy mass of the Aupouri Peninsula and Cape Reinga heralds the end of the nation's terra firma – next stop Hawaii. The small settlement of Whangaroa is best known for its sea fishing; while Mangonui (to the transitory visitor anyway) is known for its fish and chips. Completing the arc of Doubtless Bay, is the Karikari Peninsula, a wonderfully quiet spot with some memorable and deserted beaches on which to proudly make a solitary line of footprints. ▸▸ For Sleeping, Eating and other listings, see pages 172-173.

Whangaroa ⊜⑦▲ ▸▸ p172-173.

Whangaroa, on the eastern shoreline of the Whangaroa Harbour, has more the feel of an inland lake than a coastal settlement due to the hills and the subsequent hidden narrow harbour entrance. It is a modern-day base for a number of deep-sea fishing charter companies and boasts the historic claim as the site where the sailing ship *Boyd* was sunk after a *Pakeha*/Maori disagreement in 1809. A small **gallery** based in the well-stocked general store will enlighten you. Whangaroa was also home to the first **Wesleyan Mission**, which was established in 1823, and is where the infamous Maori chief Hone Heke died in 1828. The settlement is dominated by the almost globular volcanic plug, **St Paul**, which provides a great view. It is a short but stiff climb best accessed from the top of Old Hospital Road.

Mangonui and around ⊜⑦▲ ▸▸ p172-173.

Although historically noted as a port for whaling ships and kauri export, today the congenial waterfront community of Mangonui is most famous for its fish and chips. Once you've tasted them you'll no doubt agree that this is a change for the better.

Ins and outs

All the main Doubtless Bay settlements are serviced by **Northliner** or **Intercity** coaches, which stop in Mangonui. There is an independent **VIC (ISite)** ① *waterfront, Mangonui, T09-406 2046, www.doubtlessbay.co.nz, daily 0930-1700 (winter hours vary).* The free *Doubtless Bay Visitors Directory* has a host of local information. Internet is available next door at **Mangonui Stationers** ① *T09-406 0233, Mon-Sat 0830-1700.*

Sights

Just beyond Mangonui are the small beachfront settlements of **Coopers Beach** and **Cable Bay** (a former terminus for ocean cable). This is the habitat of the rich retiree, but the beaches themselves and the view across **Doubtless Bay** make up for the real estate. Thankfully, history also comes to the rescue a little further along the coast at **Taipa**, the spot where Maori legend proclaims Kupe, the discoverer of Aotearoa, first landed. Now his honourable footprints are followed by the bucket and spade brigade, who descend in their hundreds in summer. The 1840s **Butler House, Gardens and Whaling Museum** ① *Butler Point, towards HiHi, T09-406 0006, www.butlerpoint.co.nz, $12, child $2, phone ahead,* is worth a visit if you are interested in the local history.

Karikari Peninsula ⊜⦿ ⟫ p172-173.

The temptation is to miss the Karikari Peninsula and head straight for Kaitaia or the cape but, if you have time, visit the area; its isolated and remote beaches have considerable appeal. This T-shaped peninsula separates Doubtless Bay and the mangrove swamps of **Rangaunu Harbour**, with the broad empty sweep of **Karikari Bay** to the north. This bay is a natural danger zone for whale strandings. The last, in 1995, involved over 100 beached pilot whales. **Whatuwhiwhi** is the main settlement on the peninsula and is serviced by a shop, service station, takeaway and the **Whatuwhiwhi Top Ten Holiday Park**, itself is worthy of investigation for its fine location near the beach. There is a popular DoC campsite and coastal walkway at Maitai Bay. Rock-fishing here is said to be excellent. Karikari Beach can be accessed from a number of marked points along the way. Also of note on the peninsula is the **Karikari Estate vineyard** ① *based at the Carrington Club (see Sleeping, page 173)*, *T09-408 7222, www.carringtonclub.co.nz*, the country's most northerly. It is open for tastings and only complements the place as an ideal spot for a 'special' lunch or luxury stay.

⊜ Sleeping

Whangaroa *p171*
LL Butterfly Bay, T09-405 0681, www.butter flybay.co.nz. Luxurious self-contained hideaway with its own beach. Fine seafood.
L Kingfish Lodge, T09-405 0164, www.kingfishlodge.co.nz. This is a famous, 50-year-old establishment that is a favourite isolated haven for sea anglers and only accessible by boat. Has 12 fully serviced en suites, silver service cuisine, gym, sauna and a well-stocked bar (also open to visitors).
AL-D Sunseeker Lodge, Old Hospital Rd, T/F09-4050496, www.sunseekerlodge.co.nz. Peaceful, friendly backpacker accommodation with 2 motel units and doubles. Internet.
A Whangaroa Motel, Church St, T/F09-4050222. Self-contained units with views across the water.
B-D Kahoe Farms Hostel, SH10, Whangaroa, T/F09-405 1804, www.kahoefarms.co.nz. Small, delightful backpacker hostel on a working farm offering a fine relaxing base. Spotless doubles, twins and dorms, kayak hire and sublime homemade pizza. Buses stop outside.

Motorcamps and campsites
B-D Whangaroa Harbour Motor Camp, Whangaroa Rd, T09-405 0306, dyleewhangaroa@xtra.co.nz. Usual facilities. Arranges dive and fishing trips and charters.

Mangonui and around *p171*
LL-L Coopers Beachfront Suites, 18 Bayside Drive, Coopers Beach, T09-406 1018, www.coopersbeach.net 2 luxury self-contained suites in a quiet location, with great sea views.
AL Carneval, 360 SH10, Cable Bay, T09-406 1012, www.carneval.co.nz. Perched on a hill overlooking Doubtless Bay this modern B&B provides a fine base to just kick back and relax, or to explore the Aupouri Peninsula to Cape Reinga. Fresh en suites with contemporary decor offering either garden or ocean views. The Swiss-German owners have created a fine marriage of European and Kiwi hospitality and as a former chef Roly can ensure some memorable cuisine. A sauna and log burning fire add to the appeal. Organized trips to Cape Reinga and a range of other aquatic based activities can be arranged.

⬤ *For an explanation of the Sleeping and Eating price codes used in this guide, see the inside*
⬤ *front cover. Other relevant information is provided in the Essentials chapter, pages 44-51.*
Note that prices are tive in New Zealand dollars.

AL Waterfront Motel Apartments, Waterfront, Mangonui, T09-406 0347, www.mangonuiwaterfront.co.nz. Lovely themed, self-contained apartments ideal for couples and conveniently located in the heart of the village. The Waterfront Café is so close you can smell the coffee.
A Mangonui Motel, 1 Colonel Mould Drive, T/F09-406 0346, www.mangonuimotel.co.nz. Set in a peaceful location 1 min from the village with good views across the bay, 6 self-contained units.
A-C Old Oak Inn, Waterfront Rd, Mangonui, T09-406 0665. Characterful historic kauri hotel with good value, clean doubles and backpacker accommodation. A café, bar and licensed restaurant are also attached.

Motorcamps and campsites
B-C HiHi Beach Holiday Camp, HiHi Beach Rd, HiHi, off SH10, 7 km south of Mangonui, T/F09-406 0307. Peaceful beachfront location.

Karikari Peninsula *p172*
LL-A Carrington Club, Maitai Bay Rd, T09-408 7222, www.carringtonclub.co.nz. Luxurious modern lodge or villa option and a host of activities including horse riding, its own 18-hole golf course, vineyard and private beach. The restaurant is also excellent.
A Reef Lodge Motel, Rangiputa Beach, T09-408 7100, www.reeflodgemotel.co.nz. Self-contained 1 or 2 bedroom studios and conventional units next to the beach, well off the beaten track, spa pool.
A White Sands Motor Lodge, Rangiputa Beach, T09-408 7080. Modern units and 1 studio in a beachside location, on site store.

Motorcamps and campsites
A-C Whatuwhiwhi Top Ten Holiday Park, Whatuwhiwhi Rd, T09-408 7202. Offers a peaceful holiday location next to the beach.
    There's also a popular DoC campsite located at Maitai Bay.

🍴 Eating

Whangaroa *p171*
🍴 **Marlin Hotel**, T09-405 0347. Provides some rather unremarkable fare.

🍴 **Whangaroa Big Game Fish Club**, across the road, T09-405 0399. Has a restaurant and pleasant veranda bar, winter hours are limited.

Mangonui and around *p171*
There are a number of cafés scattered along the waterfront offering fine local seafood.
🍴 **Old Oak Inn** (see Sleeping page 173). Good for breakfast, lunch or dinner.
🍴 **Waterfront Café**, Beachfront Rd, T09-406 0850, daily 0830-late. A good bet.
🍴 **Mangonui Fish and Chip Shop**, just north of the village on Beach Rd, T09-406 0478, 0800-2100. Everything revolves around the delights of this popular licensed chippy.

Karikari Peninsula *p172*
🍴 **Carrington Club Restaurant**, Maitai Bay Rd, T09-408 7222, www.carringtonclub.com. It is a bit of a drive to this luxury resort on the Karikari Peninsula, but the food, wine and scenery are worth it. Bookings advised.

🔺 Activities and tours

Whangaroa *p171*
Fishing
There are a number of fishing charters available from the marina beside the Whangaroa Big Game Fish Club, T09-405 0347, and quality, good-value trips aboard the yacht Snow Cloud, T09-405 1663, from $90 a day (minimum 2).

Mangonui and around *p171*
Many of the Paihia-based Cape tour operators also pass through Mangonui and bookings can be made direct, or through the VICs (I-Sites) in Paihia or Mangonui.
A-Z Diving, T09-408 3336, www.atoz diving.co.nz. Local and *Rainbow Warrior* wreck dives from $135.
Paradise Connection, T/F09-408 7055, www.paradisenz.co.nz offers the local Cape Reinga day excursion, and its sister operation 4x4 Exclusive Tours, takes the personalized approach with day or multi-day tours to the cape and other local attractions.

Aupouri Peninsula → *Colour map 1, B3 Population: 5000*

The Aupouri Peninsula forms the northernmost tip of New Zealand and satisfies that strange human desire to reach the very end of everything. Like some long sandy pier, people naturally gravitate and rush as if late for an appointment for an obligatory photo with the lighthouse and a signpost to famous cities with distances that bend the mind. And to further satisfy that sense of 'okay, what now?' an organized trip is made truly memorable with a blast down Ninety Mile Beach on the peninsula's western flank. It is, in fact, less than 90 miles and nearer to 90 km. Clearly, whoever first measured it was northbound and in a bit of a rush. ⟫ *For Sleeping, Eating, and other listings, see pages 176-177.*

Kaitaia 🛏🍴❄🏔🎭 ⟫ *pp176-177.*

Kaitaia is the main rural service centre for the Far North. It is predominantly Maori with an interesting smattering of Dalmatian blood – mainly Croats who came during the kauri gum boom years of the late 1800s. For the tourist it provides a gateway to the Aupouri Peninsula, with its famous, uninterrupted sweep of **Ninety Mile Beach** to **Cape Reinga** and **North Cape**, the northernmost tip of New Zealand.

Ins and outs

Kaitaia airport ① *6 km north*, is served daily by **Air New Zealand Link**, T0800-737000. **Northliner** and **Intercity** coaches drop off outside the **Far North VIC (I-Site)** ① *lighthouse, Jaycee Park, South Rd, T09-408 0879, kaitaia@i-site.org, daily 0830-1700.*

Sights

The **Far North Regional Museum** ① *next to the VIC, T09-408 1403, Mon-Fri 1000-1700, $4*, is worth a peek. Although hardly outstanding it is well laid out and proudly boasts a number of important exhibits and Maori *Taonga* including the Kaitaia Carving (one of the earliest Maori carvings in existence) and a very impressive 1500 kg anchor left by de Surville in 1769. Other collections include some interesting Moa remains and the far more modern remnants from the wreck of the *Rainbow Warrior*. There is also the regulation collection of kauri gum and digging items that feature heavily in every museum in Northland. The **Okahu Estate** ① *corner of Okahu Rd and the Ahipara/Kaitaia highway, 3½ km from Kaitaia, T09-408 2066, www.okahuestate.co.nz, 1000-1700 (closed winter weekends)*, is one of New Zealand's northernmost wineries. It is in pleasant surrounds and offers free tastings. Tucked somewhat uncomfortably behind the modernity of KFC is the **Tuku Wairau Centre** ① *237a Commerce St, T09-408 4884, home of Tall Tale Tours*. Here you can immerse yourself in all things Maori with *marae* tours where you learn and partake in traditional protocol (two hours from $35), and bush walks, where you can learn about traditional plant remedies (from $35). If you are feeling creative you can also try your hand at bone carving or flax weaving (both $45).

Further field **Gumdiggers Park** ① *Heath Rd, off SH1, 13 km north of Awanui, T09-406 7166, www.gumdiggerspark.co.nz, daily 0930-1730, from $5, child $2*, is well worth a look. The result of a local John Johnson's passion to recreate a little piece of family history, it is a faithful representation of a gumdigger's village around 1900 and depicts what must have been a hard and basic existence. A lot less impressive and far more commercial is the **Ancient Kauri Kingdom** ① *Awanui, 8 km north of Kaitaia, T09-406 7172, www.ancientkauri.co.nz, daily, free*, which lures in the coach loads with its range of kauri furniture and crafts. The shop is perhaps worth a muse but what makes a stop here really worthwhile is the impressive 50-tonne log centrepiece, the old kauri logs drying in the car park, and the date scones in the café.

⁝ The souls departing

The northern tip of New Zealand is steeped in Maori legend and tradition. The name Reinga means 'Place of Leaping' and it is here, according to Maori lore, that the souls of the dead depart Aotearoa to the after-life. After travelling up the west coast to Spirits Bay, the dead are believed to descend the slopes of the headland to the roots of an old, lone pohutukawa tree, before falling into the sea. From there they are said to re-emerge on Ohaua, the highest point of the Three Kings Islands, where, still within view of Aotearoa, they bid their last farewell, before returning to the lands of their ancestors – Hawaiki.

North to the cape ⊜✈ ↦ pp176-177.

Human nature being what it is, one is naturally drawn up the Aupouri Peninsula to reach the northernmost tip of New Zealand. The peninsula itself, which is bounded by **Ninety Mile Beach** to the west and **Great Exhibition Bay** and the **Rangaunu Bay and Harbour** to the east, used to be covered in kauri forest, but today mainly consists of extensive dune systems and swamps, interspersed with commercial forestry. Although the windswept dunes that back Ninety Mile Beach cannot fail to impress, it is the white silica sands of **Kokota** – the huge sand spit on the Parengarenga Harbour – that stands out the most. This remote peninsula offers one of the best coastal walks in the country and in spring and autumn is alive with flocks of migratory wading birds. The highest point south of the cape is the 236-m **Mount Camel** near Houhora, which stands out like a sore thumb. Sadly, access is some distance from the north and to enjoy its view is a major hike. From Houhora you pass the village of **Pukenui** before winding your way towards the remote and highly spiritual lands and landscapes of the cape itself with **Cape Reinga** to the west and **North Cape** – the true northernmost point, to the east.

Ins and outs

Getting there With your own wheels it will take about 1½ hours to reach the cape from Kaitaia. The road is sealed all the way to the cape but watch your speed – many a budding rally driver in their Maui campervan has come to grief along this stretch. Although Ninety Mile Beach is classified as a highway, you are not advised to take anything other than a 4WD vehicle onto the sand. For those in rental cars (which are not insured on the sand) who cannot resist the temptation to do so, be warned: it will probably all end in tears. If you are short of time the best way to see the peninsula is to join the many coach tours from Paihia, Mangonui or Kaitaia. ↦ See Activities and tours, page 167.

Pukenui and further north

Pukenui is the last major settlement on the way to the cape, so it may pay to grab some petrol or a coffee at the café and general store, or on your return quench your thirst at New Zealand's northernmost pub the **Houhoura Tavern**. Sharkophobes should not enter – there are very gruesome pictures on the wall. About 25 km north of Pukenui you reach the small Maori enclave of **Te Kao**. This is the best place to park up and access the **Kokota Sand Spit**. The forestry gate is about 1 km up the road but vehicular access is forbidden. Ensure you have maps and a compass since the myriad forestry roads to reach the sand spit and bluff are difficult to negotiate. Eventually you will emerge, preferably on the beach to the west. From there walk north to the sand bluff and dunes which are wild, remote and stunning. Allow eight hours.

From Te Kao the road passes through the basic motorcamp at Waitiki Landing before entering the huge **Te Paki Station and Recreation Reserve** towards North Cape, Cape Reinga and the lighthouse. This reserve has a total area of 23,000 ha and contains some of the most extraordinary landforms in New Zealand. The Maori call this area *Te Hiku o te Ika* (tail of the fish) from the legend that tells how the giant fish (North Island) was pulled from the sea by Maui from his canoe (South Island). Geology posits a more prosaic theory. The rocks that form the cape were formed 60 million years ago and later separated from the mainland. Then around two million years ago sand moved northwards from Kaitaia forming a huge tombolo and the peninsula we see today. The area supports a wide variety of coastal scenery from cliffs to wide sweeping beaches. There is a great network walks in the area (information from DoC) but access may be denied, or permission required, T09-409 7831. Local Maori own almost a quarter of the land, and areas around North Cape are particularly sacred. The tip of North Cape, the northernmost point of New Zealand, is a scientific reserve with limited access.

For most visitors, sadly, the visit to this amazing area will be all too brief and revolve around Cape Reinga and the **lighthouse**. The views from the hill above the lighthouse are stunning and in stormy weather you can see the Tasman Sea and Pacific in an uneasy union, and as far as the Three Kings Islands, 57 km offshore. The northland coastline has claimed over 140 vessels and many lives since 1808, with the majority falling foul around the cape. The lighthouse was built in 1941 and contains the lens from the original lighthouse built on Motuopao Island to the south. Beside the lighthouse is the obligatory multi-destination signpost for that vital memento.

● Sleeping

Kaitaia *p174*
LL Taharangi Marie Lodge, 700 Sandhills Rd, Ninety Mile Beach, T09-406 7462, www.90mile.co.nz. In perfect isolation among the sand dunes of Ninety Mile Beach with a heavenly outdoor spa. Fine base for explorations further north.
L Okahu Vineyard Cottage, corner of Okahu and Pukepoto Rds, T09-408 2066, www.okahuestate.co.nz. Very cosy 3-bedroom cottage amongst the vines.
A Sierra Court Motor Lodge, 65 North Rd, T09-408 1461, sierracourt.kaitaia@xtra.co.nz. Basic but comfortable 1-2 bedroom units.
A Wayfarer Motel, 231 Commerce St, T09-408 2600, www.wayfarermotel.co.nz. Centrally located.
C-D Main Street Lodge Backpackers, 235 Commerce St, T09-408 1275, www.tall-tale.co.nz. Maori-operated and recently revamped with en suite rooms and the opportunity of a great cultural experience.

Cape Reinga *p176*
The accommodation north of Kaitaia is fairly basic, with Houhoura, Pukenui and Waitiki Landing offering the best base (the latter being the last available beds before the cape).

A Houhora Chalets Motor Lodge, corner of Far North and Houhoura Heads Rd, T09-409 8860, www.chalets@xtra.co.nz. A-frame units near the Wagener Museum.
A-D Pukenui Lodge Motel and Youth Hostel, SH1, 42 km north of Kaitaia and 68 km south of Cape Reinga, Pukenui, T09-409 8837, www.pukenuilodge.co.nz. Tidy self-contained motel units with satellite TV and backpacker accommodation in a former post office store overlooking the Houhora Harbour. Spa and bike hire. Organized trips to the cape and Ninety Mile Beach. Small supermarket opposite. Standard 2-bedroom motel studios, twin double and shared budget hostel rooms.

Motorcamps and campsites
B-D Pukenui Holiday Camp, Lamb Rd, T09-409 8803. Better facilities than the very basic, but more scenic Houhora equivalent.
B-D Waitiki Landing, SH1, only 20 km from the Cape, T09-409 7508. Tent sites, bunks and cabins. Restaurant on site.

There are DoC campsites, T09-408 6014 at Rarawa on the east coast just south of Te Kao; at Kapowairua next to the beautiful Spirits Bay; and at Tapotupotu Bay, near the cape.

Eating

Kaitaia *p174*

Beachcomber Restaurant, The Plaza, 222 Commerce St, T09-4082 010. Mon-Fri 1100-1430, Mon-Sat 1700-late.

Bluehouse, 14 Commerce St, T09-408 4935, daily from 0700. Arguably the best café with traditional Kiwi fare and good coffee.

Bushman's Hut Steak House, corner of Bank St and Puckey Av, T09-408 4320, Tue-Sun 1700-2100. Live music and good value.

Cape Reinga *p176*

The café in Pukenui and the restaurant at Waitiki Landing are your only hope.

Festivals and events

Kaitaia *p174*

Mar **Te Houtaewa Challenge**, www.new zealand-marathon.co.nz, is a gruelling 60-km run up Ninety Mile Beach with added 5-person relay, 42-km marathon, 21-km half marathon and a leisurely 6-km walk for the lazy. The **Festival of Maori arts and crafts** runs in parallel with the Te Houtaewa Challenge.

Activities and tours

Kaitaia *p174*

A number of quality day trips leave Kaitaia for the Cape Reinga/Ninety Mile Beach circuit. They are really good value and generally offer more time at the cape and various other stops than their distant counterparts operating out of Paihia. All stop at the Ancient Kauri Kingdom or Gumdiggers Park, the cape and the Te Paki Stream sand dunes (for dune surfing) before running almost the entire length of Ninety Mile Beach. Note that tours run in either direction depending on tides. For other activities see Ahipara, page 181.

Cape Reinga Adventures, T09-4098445, www.packorpaddle.co.nz. Offers a range of activity packages including kayaking, fishing, horse trekking and 4WD adventures around the peninsula. The full moon kayaking is particularly recommended, half or full day from $85, full moon $150, overnight $190.

Far North Outback Adventures, T09-408 0927, www.farnorthtours.co.nz. Offers a more personalized luxury 4WD tour of the

cape. Flexible itinerary, friendly, great food and great value, from $400.

Harrison's Cape Runner, 123 North Rd, Kaitaia, T09-408 1033, capetours@xtra.co.nz. Leaves daily at 0900, returning about 1700, $45, child $25, lunch included. Harrison's also operates a more personalized '4x4 Reef Runner' tour, which takes in a half-day of 4WD driving, spectacular views and sand tobogganing. Twin tour discounts apply.

Sand Safaris, 221 Commerce St, T09-408 1778/10800-869090, www.sandsafaris.co.nz. A full-day tour with all the usual stops and activities including the Gumdiggers Park (see page 174). Departs daily 0900, returning 1700, $60, child $30 (includes entry to the park).

Tall Tale Tours, based at the Tuku Wairua Centre, 237a Commerce St, T09-408 4884, www.tall-tale.co.nz. Offers a unique Maori cultural package including a visit to a *marae* where you learn about stories, myths and legends, 2 hrs, $35. You can also try flax weaving or bone carving (from $45).

Shooting

If all that sand does not appeal, you might try your hand with a .22 rifle at the **Far North Indoor Shooting Gallery**, Hillcrest Rd, T09-408 0097/T027-2869154.

Scenic flight

Blue Sky Scenics, Kaitaia Airport, T09-406 7320. Scenic flights over the cape.

Surfing

At the southern end of 90 Mile Beach, the long left-hand break at **Shipwreck Bay** is one of the best in the country, if a little fickle. On the plus side, it's usually uncrowded, and so far north that the water is considerably warmer than the rest of the country.

Walking

For details about local walking and mountain biking routes consult the *Kaitaia Area Walks* leaflet, available from the VIC (I-Site), $1.

Directory

Kaitaia *p174*

Internet VIC (I-Site) or Hackers Internet Café, 84 Commerce St, Kaitaia, T09-4084999. Mon-Wed 0900-2100, Thu-Sat 0900-late, Sun 1000-2100. The VIC (I-Site) is cheaper.

South to the Hokianga Harbour

→ *Colour map 1, B2*

With the vast majority of visitors joining organized trips to the cape from the Bay of Islands, most miss out on the western side of Northland; but if you have your own transport it is well worth heading back south via SH12 and the Hokianga, Waipoua Forest and Dargaville. Other than the palpable sense of being well off the beaten track, the attraction and highlights are the dunescapes of the Hokianga Harbour opposite Opononi and, further south in the Waipoua Forest, with its mighty and ancient kauri trees. Sadly, very few of these giants remain to make a mockery of our human longevity, but you can get a true sense of their former glory, if not their sad fate, at the excellent Kauri Museum, before SH12 rejoins SH1 to Auckland. ►► *For Sleeping, Eating and other listings, see pages 180-181.*

Ahipara and around ⊜🌀🏃‍♂️▲ ►► *pp180-181.*

Ahipara forms the southern extremity of Ninety Mile Beach and is 14 km west of Kaitaia. Formerly a 2000-strong gum-digging community it is now a shadow of its former self but still a scenic spot offering a number of beach-based activities. The VIC (I-Site) in Kaitaia will provide all the relevant information (see page 174). The website www.ahipara.co.nz, is also useful. The hill at the far end of town has fine views up Ninety Mile Beach.

South to Rawene

From Ahipara the road turns south to **Herekino,** through Broadwood and **Kohukohu** to **Narrows Landing** on the **Hokianga Harbour**. There you meet the ferry to **Rawene** and the heart of Hokianga. This road is fairly tortuous and once again the familiar Northland Mobile-Phone-No-Service-Zone country sights apply. There is little of interest on the road itself but two venues in the area are of particular note. First is the **Golden Stairs Walkway** on the southern shore of the mouth of the **Whangape Harbour**. If you can muster the courage and tackle the sealed route to the little settlement of Pawarenga, this walk is well worth it. The mouth of the Whangape Harbour is like a small fjord and out of character with the other larger harbours along the west Northland coast. The walk is fairly short but steep and culminates at the northern tip of the vast and wild beach. From here you could continue down the beach to Mitimiti, where there is a fine and remote backpacker hostel (see below). The following day could be spent exploring the coast before being dropped off at the end of the Golden Stairs Walkway again, from where you negotiate the return to retrieve your car. Be sure to secure all belongings out of sight and lock the car.

The second venue is actually **Mitimiti** and the wild **Warawara Forest**, which is the second largest kauri forest in New Zealand, still containing some whoppers. The 41-km road to get to Mitimiti from Narrows Landing is quite arduous but worth the drive simply for the views and remote nature of the Northland countryside, not to mention the broad stretch of coast and wild beach at its terminus. If you stay at the **Manaia Hostel** at Mitimiti you can just about have 50 km of beach to yourself for fishing, walking or (careful) swimming. The Maori owner of the hostel will happily take you for a tour of the beach, and while doing so give you a fascinating insight into the area's Maori history. The **Tree House** is another fine youth hostel located near the Narrows Landing Ferry. ►► *See Sleeping, page 180.*

Rawene and Kaikohe

Rawene is essentially the gateway to the heart of Hokianga from the north, but has a heart of its own that seems strangely broken. The **Rawene Ferry** ① T09 405 2602, daily 0730-1930, light vehicles $14, foot/car passengers $2), runs across the inlet. Even in the earliest years of Maori and European settlement, when a large sawmill and shipyard was established in the area, Rawene saw its fair share of conflicts, both internally and externally. However, these days it is a relatively quiet place with lots of potential. There is little to hold the visitor, except the laid-back **Boatshed Café and Gallery** ① T09-405 7728, and the historic 1868 **Clendon House** ① T09-405 7874, Nov Apr 1000 1600, $2, both on the waterfront. Clendon House is the former residence of James Clendon, a local dignitary who was, amongst other things, the former Hokianga district magistrate.

To the east of Rawene and 14 km north of the small settlement **Taheke** (off SH12) is one of Northland's newest natural tourist attractions, though at almost three million years old, new is hardly an apt description. The **Wairere Boulders** ① McDonnell Rd, Horeke, T09-401 9935, www.wairereboulders.co.nz, daily, $10, child $5, can loosely be described as a valley of ancient basalt rocks formed by ancient pyroclastic flows that have since eroded and become stacked upon one another, creating a strange geological labyrinth, or 'stream of rocks'. A well-formed path with boardwalks winds through the conglomerate to give the best views. Allow three hours.

Just south of Rawene you join the SH12 to Opononi and Omapere and all points south to Dargaville. East of here is the small town of **Kaikohe** just before SH1. **Kaikohe Hill** offers a good view, perhaps followed by a soak in the wooden hot tubs of the **Ngawha Springs Waiariki Pools** ① southeast of town, daily 0700-1930, $3. The springs are said to cure some rheumatic, lumbago, arthritic and skin conditions. The old Maori warrior Hone Heke recognized the remedial power of the springs, bringing his wounded here for treatment after the British assault on his fortified Ohaeawai pa.

Opononi and Omapere 🖐️🍴▲ ➡ pp180-181.

These two converging waterfront villages are the main resorts in the Hokianga. The villages and the harbour entrance are dominated by the impressive bare sand dunes that grace its northern shore. They rise to a height of 100 m and at sunset glow with an orange radiance. It was here in the Hokianga Harbour, in the 10th century, that the great Polynesian explorer Kupe first set foot in Aotearoa (New Zealand) from his homeland of Hawaiki. After a short stay he went home again leaving a small group behind. Although Kupe himself never returned his ancestors did and it was christened Hokianganui-a-Kupe meaning 'the place of Kupe's great return'. The area is also known as Te Kohanga o Te Tai Tokerau or 'the nest of the northern tribes'. Indeed, it remains the centre point from which most Northland Maori trace their ancestry. Both Opononi and Omapere were somewhat insignificant until the appearance of a solitary wild dolphin in 1955. Opo, as she was christened, won the hearts of the nation and subsequently put little Opononi on the map.

Ins and outs

Intercity runs a service through Omapere from the south (Tuesday, Thursday and Sunday) to Paihia and returning south from Paihia (Monday, Wednesday and Friday). **West Coaster** links with the latter and also offers a service from Paihia to Auckland, T09-913 6100/T09-402 8989. All buses stop at the **VIC (I-Site)** ① on the main road (SH12) roughly halfway between the two communities, T09-405 8869, www.hokianga tourism.org.nz, which can provide transport bookings, information and internet.

Sights

Most activity in Opononi and Omapere revolves around the two hotels, particularly the **Omapere Tourist Hotel** with its deck over looking the harbour and mountainous sand dune. Supposing you do nothing else, a meal, a coffee or a cold beer here is memorable especially at sunset.

The small **Omapere Museum** ① *0930-1630, free*, housed above the information centre, has some interesting historical stories, pictures and items, of which the original and highly entertaining 'Tally Ho' video about Opo the dolphin stands out.

For a fine coast walk head for the southern edge of Omapere and the **Arai-Te-Uru** headlands. The tip of the headland supported a signal station that for many years used to help ships negotiate the tricky harbour entrance. The headland offers a great view across to the sand spit (North Head) or *Niua* to give it its Maori name. The **Ocean Beach track** takes you down to the rocky coast below, where a blowhole and cave can be explored (turn left and watch the tide). The **Coastal Walkway** also starts here and winds its way round to the remote and beautiful beaches to the south. **Pakia Hill** at the southern end of Omapere also offers spectacular views of the harbour and the dunes. The **Labyrinth Woodworks and the Amazing Maize Maze** ① *along Waiotemarama Gorge Rd next to the Kauri Forest Walk, T09-405 4581, www.nzanity.co.nz*, is worth a look and has all sorts of other puzzles to baffle the brain. The **Kauri Forest Walk** is a pleasant 10-minute amble that takes in a waterfall, or you can go the full hog with a six-hour hike up to Mount Haturu. Back in the centre of Omapere the *Mamaku*, SH12, is the rather cute-looking local **craft co-operative**, T09-405 8662, set up in 1979, selling fine wood, fibre, glass works and bone carvings.

● Sleeping

Ahipara and South to Rawene *p178*

L Beachfront, 14 Kotare St, Ahipara, T/F09-4094007, www.beachfront.net.nz. Tidy, beachside self-contained accommodation promising 'surf views from every pillow'. Hosts also operate a fishing charter boat.

L-A Ahipara Bay Motel, Reefview Rd, T/F09-409 4888, www.ahipara.co.nz. New motel overlooking the end of Ninety Mile Beach, with standard and luxury units, restaurant and bar. Also offers its own quad bike hire, horse trekking and Cape Tours.

AL Beach Abode, 11 Korora St, Ahipara, T/F09-409 4070, www.beachabode.co.nz. Wide range of modern self-contained accommodation options.

AL Shipwreck Lodge, 70 Foreshore Rd, Ahipara, T09-409 4929, www.shipwreck lodge.co.nz. Modern B&B in a superb beachside location. 3 lovely suites.

B-D Manaia Hostel, West Coast Rd, T09-409 5347, mitimiti@xtra.co.nz. Great budget self-catered accommodation, 2 twins and a double, in a truly remote Northland location. Internet. Beach and forest adventure activities and outings. Recommended.

B-D Tree House, 168 West Coast Rd, Kohukohu, T09-405 5855, www.tree house.co.nz. Remote gem located off the beaten track and alongside the Hokianga Harbour. Set in 7 ha of bush and orchards it offers basic but characterful cabins, dorms and a retired house-bus that serves as a double and/or single. Sheltered camping available with one powered site, 100 m from the main building. Limited food supplies. Cabins, shared dorms and a house-bus 6 km south of Kohukohu and 2 km west of the Hokianga car ferry. No public transport available.

B-D Tui Inn, Herekino, T09-409 3883, www.tuiinn.co.nz. Comfortable budget lodging south of Kaitaia. Something a little different. Relaxing friendly atmosphere and activities like horse trekking, diving or fishing at relatively low cost. Grant and Tangi are terrific hosts and you are ensured of a memorable stay. There are 10 beds, 2 van sites and 2 campsites. Recommended.

Motorcamps and campsites

A Ahipara Motor Camp and Backpackers, 168 Takahe St, T09-409 4864, www.ahipara motorcamp.co.nz. For campervans, tents or backpackers. Camp kitchen.

Rawene *p179*

A Hokianga Blue, T09-405 7675, www.hokiangablue.co.nz. Modern, tidy studio accommodation with en suite and deck overlooking the harbour. In-house kayak adventures are an added attraction.

A Old Lane's Store Homestay, 9 Clendon Esplanade, T09-405 7554. Pleasant self-contained lodging in an historic villa, just past Clendon House and not far from the café.

B Masonic Hotel, Parnell St, T09-405 7822. Simple, affordable accommodation and food.

B-D Rawene Motor Camp, 1 Marmot St, T09-405 7720. Small but adequate with camping and campervan sites. Swimming pool.

Opononi and Omapere *p179*

AL Hokianga Haven, 226 SH12, Omapere, T09-405 8285, www.hokiangahaven.co.nz. A fine beachside B&B, with a cosy guestroom. Friendly art-oriented hosts, dogs and a hammock. Recommended.

A Copthorne Hotel and Motel, SH12, Omapere, T09-405 8737, www.omapere.co.nz. A fine spot right next to the beach and the wharf. Well-equipped units are available, as are powered sites and campsites. Heated pool, nice lawns, restaurant and bar.

B-D Globe Trekkers, SH12, Omapere, T/F09-405 8183, www.globetrekkerslodge.com. Small, friendly beachside outfit with a range of rooms, tent sites and organized activities.

C-D House of Harmony, SH12, Opononi, T09-405 8778, www.houseofharmony.co.nz. Small and friendly backpacker hostel.

C-D Okopako Wilderness Farm, 140 Mountain Rd (1½ km off SH12), South Hokianga (5 km south of Opononi), T09-405 8815. YHA affiliate. Spacious lodge with doubles, twin and family rooms and on-site caravans. Open-plan living area with open fire. Farm activities and horse trekking. Magic Bus drops off at the door. Pick-ups from Opononi.

● Eating

Ahipara and around *p178*

¶¶ Bayview Restaurant, at the Ahipara Bay Motel (see Sleeping, page 180), daily from 0600, Fri-Sat 1900, Sun 1600.

¶ Waterline Café, on the waterfront in Kohukohu, T09-405 5552, Tue-Thu 0930-1630, Fri-Sat 0930-late, Sun 0930-1600.

¶ Boatshed Café, Clendon Esplanade, T09-405 7728, daily 0830-1630. A welcome stop before or after the ferry crossing. Varied selection of light snacks, good coffee and harbour views. Colourful arts and crafts from local artisans adorn the walls and spaces with some available for purchase.

Opononi and Omapere *p179*

Four Square supermarket in Opononi. **¶¶-¶¶ Copthorne Hotel** (see Sleeping, above) has a good restaurant offering the traditional New Zealand fare.

¶ The Opo Beach Takeaway, next to the Opononi Hotel, T09-405 8065, daily 1000-2100. Great fish and chips.

▲▲ Activities and tours

Ahipara *p178*

Adventure Centre, 15 Takahe St, T09-409 2055, www.ahipara.co.nz/adventurecentre. For a whole host of activities ranging from horse trekking to sand tobogganing.

Tua Tua Tours, Ahipara Rd, T0800-494288, www.tuatuatours.co.nz. Guided quad bike tours, lots of fun, 3 hrs $145, 1½ hrs $80.

Wildcat Fishing Charters, T09-409 2055.

Rawene *p179*

Hokianga Blue Kayaks, T09-409 2055, www.hokiangablue.co.nz. Half- to 3-day sea kayaking adventures, guided or freedom hire from $65-495. An ideal opportunity to explore the harbour and sand spit.

Opononi and Omapere *p179*

Alma 80 Scow, T09-405 7704, www.hokianga cruises.co.nz. Cruises on the Hokianga aboard a 78-ft kauri ship. Fishing also available.

Footprints Waipoua, T09-405 8737. Maori guided trips to the Waipoua forest in association with the Copthorne Hotel. The 4-hr 'Twilight Encounter' is recommended, offering a unique insight in to the natural world of the giant kauri at dusk, from $65.

Hokianga Express Charters, T09-405 8872. Trips to the dunes to explore or go sand-boarding ($20). Also fishing and dive trips.

Northland Coast to Coast Tours, T09-405 9460. Tours throughout the Hokianga.

Okopako Horse Treks, Mountain Rd, T09-405 8815. 2 hrs from $45.

Kauri Coast → *Colour map 1, B3*

Just south of Omapere you bid farewell to the coast and the Hokianga and enter 'kauri country'. Waipoua, Mataraua and Waima forests make up the largest remaining tract of native forest in Northland, and the Waipoua and Trounson Kauri forests contain 300 species of tree including the great kauri with two of the finest examples and living monuments to these magnificent and awe inspiring trees. The mighty kauri forests used to blanket much of the upper North Island but, thanks to the activities of man, those forests have been plundered and raped and remain a mere suggestion of their former selves. The Waipoua Forest is home to the largest remaining individuals, including the much-loved and ancient Tane Mahuta or 'Lord of the Forest'. For lovers of life and for those who have a healthy respect for nature, to visit this great tree is something of a pilgrimage. For those who have never really thought about it, it is a fine place to start. ▸▸ *For Sleeping, Eating and other listings, see pages 185-186.*

South of Omapere ● ▸▸ *pp185-186.*

Waipoua Kauri Forest and around

The 15,000-ha Waipoua Forest includes the 9105-ha Waipoua Sanctuary of which 2639 ha contain mature kauri trees. The original block of forest was bought from the local Maori chiefs for $4400 in 1876 and, although the original intention was to use the land for 'settlement purposes', most of the forest was reserved for government forestry purposes in 1906. Thankfully, due to much local and national pressure, which came to a head in 1952 with a 70,000-strong petition, the forest is now safely under the administration of DoC. The 20-km drive through the forest is appealing in itself, with roadside kauri and umbrella-like ponga ferns giving you just a hint of what Northland and much of the entire country used to be like.

Walking tracks at the northern end of the forest, immediately next to the highway, give access to the two largest known kauri specimens, **Tane Mahuta**, or 'Lord of the Forest' and **Te Matua Ngahere**, the 'Father of the Forest'. Tane Mahuta can be reached within five minutes and is an awesome sight, with a trunk height of 17.7 m, girth of 13.8 m and total height of 51½ m. It is estimated to be over 1500 years old. Two kilometres south of Tane Mahuta is a car park where you pay a $2 security fee (such is the level of car theft from the most destructive of New Zealand's introduced mammals – the human). From here, there are a number of short or long walks. Te Matua Ngahere, the second largest tree, can be reached in about 20 minutes, while the **Four Sisters**, a stand of four trees growing together like a huge botanical oil rig, are only 100 m from the car park. The Yakas Track is 6 km in length and takes in another monster, the **Yakas Kauri**, before emerging at the visitor centre. A lookout point, 1½ km from the park's southern boundary, is worth a look on the one-hour trek from the visitor centre.

The **Waipoua Forest Visitor Centre** (DoC) ① *off SH12 towards the southern end of the park. T09-439 3011, www.doc.govt.nz, daily 0900-1700*, contains an interesting museum and can provide all walking or sundry information.

Trounson Kauri Park and Kaihu

There is also a smaller but impressive kauri forest in the 450-ha **Trounson Kauri Reserve**, which is 17 km south of Waipoua. The road is signposted about 40 km north of Dargaville and goes through Donelly's Crossing, which has everything bar the saloon and stagecoach. A 'tipi' site is available, and facilities include hot showers and a communal cookhouse ($7); powered sites are also available. In summer at night there are **guided tours** ① *T09-439 0621, Oct-May, $20, child $12, see Kauri*

Coast Top Ten Holiday Park, Sleeping, page 185, to hear the kiwis. The forest has a healthy population of North Island browns because of its isolation from other predator-rich forests by a sea of farmland. The camp (T09 439 2011) is closed in winter.

Just south of Trounson is the settlement of **Kaihu**. The Nelson's **Kaihu Kauri** (0900-1700 Monday to Saturday) is a good quality retail outlet for quality kauri crafts.

Kai Iwi Lakes

About 30 km south of Waipoua and 10 km towards the coast is the aquatic summer playground of the Kai Iwi Lakes. This is a favourite Northland holiday spot for those wanting to enjoy the combination of endless beach and surf, together with the more sedate inland waters of the three main lakes – **Kaiiwi**, **Taharoa** and **Waikere**. Here, mainly in summer, you can enjoy sailing, windsurfing, water skiing, jet skiing and fishing. Lacking much cover and being so close to the beach, bear in mind the lakes can be a little exposed at times.

Dargaville and around ⊜❼▲❻ ➤➤ *pp185-186.*

Dargaville, located on the banks of the **Wairoa River** (the Kaipara Harbour's largest and longest tributary) has become a shadow of its former self, due to the exhaustion of the kauri forests. It was founded in 1872 by Irish timber merchant Joseph Dargaville, when the district was already the enclave of a large group of Dalmatian settlers. Kauri timber was the name of the game and for many years Dargaville was an important export centre. The rivers north of the bustling port were choked with kauri being worked downstream, and it was from here that much of Northland's kauri was shipped to Australia and elsewhere. With the myriad tributaries of the Northern **Kaipara Harbour** inundating the region, access in those days was only possible by boat from the port and timber-milling town of Helensville, on the south of Kaipara Harbour, north of Auckland.

Today Dargaville is a main service centre for the farms with their barren fields on which the great kauri once stood, and the river nearby transports little except ducks. The region as a whole is also known as the 'Kumara Capital' of the country producing the best of this sweet potato introduced by the early Polynesian navigators.

Ins and outs

Intercity and **Mainline**, T09-278 8070, www.maincoachline.co.nz have connecting services to Auckland (from $39). **West Coaster** runs an Auckland to Paihia service and back. Buses stop on Kaipa Street. Information and ticketing is available from the **Kauri Coast VIC (I-Site)** ① *67-69 Normanby St, T09-439 8360, www.kauricoast.co.nz, daily in summer 0830-18000, winter 0830-1700, Sat-Sun 1000-1600*.

Sights

Although generally considered as the principal gateway to the Kauri Coast, and an important supply or overnight stop on the developing and popular Twin Coast Highway, there are some significant things to see in Dargaville. A number of tour operators and local activities are also based here. The information centre has put together an **Historic River Walk**, with an interesting free leaflet; it is 5 km and takes about an hour. One of the highlights is the **Dargaville Museum** ① *T09-439 7555, daily 0900-1600, $5*, which bears the remnants and relates the sorry tales of the many ships wrecked trying to negotiate the notorious Kaipara Bar. It also has a collection of Maori *taonga* and pioneer exhibits and, at 84 kg, the largest piece of kauri gum in the world (just a few grams more than a similar piece in the Kauri Museum at Matakohe).

The useful *Kauri Coast* brochure from the VIC (I-Site) details the various attractions including galleries and outlets at which to see kauri and other native woods being crafted, on display or for sale. This is your best chance to buy quality kauri products at competitive prices. One 'working' studio, the **Woodturners Kauri Gallery** ① *4 Murdoch St, T09-439 4975, www.thewoodturnersstudio.co.nz, daily*, is run by Rick Taylor, who has been turning and chipping away at kauri for over 26 years.

It is worthwhile taking a look at the coast near Dargaville and the ridiculously long **Ripiro Beach** – if only to see what 104 km of almost uninterrupted sand looks like. It is accessible at a number of places, the best serviced being **Baylys Beach**, 14 km west of Dargaville. But if you fancy a look at the local countryside (and the locals) followed by a truly remote walk to the disused 1884 **Kaipara Lighthouse** and the seemingly endless sand dunes of the **Kaipara Heads**, then take the road to the tiny outpost village of **Poutu**. It is a strangely disconcerting 69 km south from Dargaville and gives an inkling of the staggering length of the Kaipara Harbour's shoreline; at 3000 km it is one of the longest natural harbour coastlines in the world.

Before you leave Dargaville or if you have only an hour or so then head to the rather seedy village of **Te Kopuru** (12 km southwest) and take a look at what must be one of the most interesting and bizarrely decorated gardens on the planet. Located at **51 Norton Street** and round the corner in Wilson Street, it puts a whole new meaning to the words 'buoy' and 'ballcocks', and makes Barbara Cartland's collection of earrings look tedious. One can only shudder at what the bathroom must look like.

If you are not on a tour or cannot be bothered with the 69 km to the Kaipara Heads and the remote walk to the Kaipara Lighthouse then there are three interesting peaks to conquer in the vicinity, all of which offer interesting views of the vast Kaipara Harbour. **Mount Tutamoe** is a four- to five-hour walk; the 221-m **Mangaraho Rock** (11 km south of Dargaville) is 45 minutes around base and 30 minutes to summit; and the very knobbly **Toka Toka Peak** (17 km south) is a 20-minute walk. For directions and more information call at the VIC.

Matakohe and the Kauri Museum ●●🕖 ⇢ *pp185-186.*

The village of Matakohe, 45 km south of Dargaville, is the home of the **Kauri Museum**. The museum is one of the finest in the country and provides a fitting finale to the Twin Coast Discovery Highway before the SH12 meets the main SH1 at Brynderwyn and heads back south to Auckland. The museum is on SH12, 26 km from SH1 at Brynderwyn, which is 114 km north of Auckland. All major coach companies that take the Twin Coast Discovery Highway stop at the museum.

Sights

The **Kauri Museum** ① *Church Rd, T09-431 7417, www.kauri-museum.com, daily Nov-Apr 0830-1730; May-Oct 0900-1700, $15, child $3*, houses a number of highly imaginative displays that offer a detailed insight into the natural history of the kauri and man's exploitation and love affair with the great tree. Starting in the Volunteer Hall one cannot fail to be impressed with the 22½-m section of the Balderston kauri, a local specimen that was killed by lightening. It is a massive example but a relative youngster. On the wall at its base this is dramatically highlighted with life-size circumference outlines of larger recorded trees. The largest outline, depicting a tree that once grew in the Coromandel, has a diameter of 8½ m, which makes the Balderston slice seem like a piece of cress and even dwarfs Tane Mahuta. Around the edges of the hall there are some exquisite examples of kauri furniture and finely crafted models of some of the many kauri scows that used to ply the Kaipara Harbour.

Next to the Volunteer Hall is the **Steam Sawmill**. This is a good working mock-up which takes you through the complex and ingenious methods used to cut the huge logs. Additional displays in the **Smith Wing** outline examples of wood types and ages, the extraction of kauri gum and include some monstrous moving equipment and saws that show what a task it was get the tree from bush to mill. That effort and detail is cleverly and subtly highlighted right down to a bead of sweat from a mannequin's nose.

Other wings of the museum display mock-up pioneer family rooms, machines hall, chainsaw displays, fine kauri furniture, timber panels and carvings. Downstairs is the world's best kauri gum display with some fine (and some not so fine) carvings, busts and ornaments, all carefully fashioned from the tree's resin or sap. This 'amber' (its other name) is of varying ages, some of it hundreds of thousands of years old. Within the museum grounds there are some nicely restored examples of kauri buildings, including the 1867 Pioneer Church and 1909 Post Office. A well-stocked souvenir shop offers a great opportunity to purchase some finely crafted pieces of kauri including some 'Swamp Kauri' pieces, which are tens of thousands of years old.

The museum is well worth a visit and stands as a wonderful tribute to man's imagination and sheer hard work in the extraction and use of the kauri. If there has to be some criticism it is that there is not enough to echo the fact that man's love affair with this great native tree has been an incredibly damaging and unsustainable affair.

● Sleeping

Waipoua Kauri Forest and around *p182*
LL Waipoua Lodge, SH12, T/F09-439 0422, www.waipaualodge.co.nz. 5-star luxury in a former wool shed and stables. Restaurant attached for in-house cuisine.
A Solitaire Homestay, SH12, 6 km north of the forest, T09-405 4891, solitairehomestay@ xtra.co.nz. Comfortable B&B in traditional kauri villa. En suite rooms and standard doubles.
B-D Kaihu Farm Backpackers, Kaihu, 20 km south of Waipoua, bus stops outside, T09-439 4004. Backpacker rooms and twin/double.

Motorcamps and campsites
A-D Kauri Coast Top Ten Holiday Park, Trounson Park Rd, Kaihu, T09-439 0621. Powered sites and cabins in a very pleasant site next to the river. Clean, modern and quite homely. Guided night tours to Trounson Kauri Reserve in summer to hear kiwi (if you're lucky) but certainly to see glow-worms and native eels, $20. Recommended.
C-D Waipoua DoC, Waipoua, T09-439 0605. Cabins for 2-4 available. Hot and cold showers and some with cooking facilities. Campsites and campervan sites.

Kai Iwi Lakes *p183*
A Country Cottage, Kai Iwi Lakes Rd, T09-439 0303. 2 self-contained cottages near the lakes. Also has jet skis for hire.
A Hilltop Studio, SH12, T09-439 6351, rwatt@igrin.co.nz. Single self-contained

unit in bush setting, about 10 km from the lakes.
AL Willowdale B&B, 115 Kai Iwi Rd, T09-439 4645, www.willowdale.co.nz. Peaceful homestead near the lakes, with B&B rooms and self-contained cottage. Meals by arrangement.

Campsites
Basic facilities available at **Pine Beach** on the shores of **Taharoa**, and **Promenade Point**, $6, T09-439 8360. Book at the Dargaville VIC (I-Site), see page 183.

Dargaville and around *p183*
L Kauri House Lodge, Bowen St, Dargaville, T09-439 8082. Spacious kauri-built house with comfortable rooms with en suite bath.
L Lighthouse Lodge, Pouto Point, T09-439 5150, www.lighthouse-lodge.co.nz. A remote and luxurious hideaway at the very end of the northern Kaipara Peninsula at Kaipara Heads, a long drive and most probably not a 1-night stay, but worth the journey. Fishing trips and quad bikes.
AL-A Awakino Point Boutique Motel, Awakino Point, Dargaville, T/F09-439 7870, www.awakinopoint.co.nz. Quiet, comfortable and central.
A Parkview Motel, 36 Carrington St, Doraville, T09-439 8339, www.parkviewdargaville.co.nz. Pool spa and children's play area.
B Bayly's Beach B&B, Bayly's Coast Rd, T09-439 7157, mlkdh@win.co.nz. Cosy, rural self-contained cottage, 1 km from the beach.

C-D **Greenhouse Backpackers**, 13 Portland St, Dargaville, T09-439 6342. Former primary school with spacious dorms, units ideal for couples.

Motorcamps and campsites
B-D **Baylys Beach Holiday Park**, 22 Seaview Rd, Baylys Beach, T/F09-439 6349, www.baylysbeach.co.nz. Small and functional near the beach. Also offers quad bike hire.
B-D **Dargaville Campervan Park and Cabins**, 18 Gladstone St, T/F09-439 8479, dargavilleholidaypark@xtra.co.nz. Central location opposite Woolworths, usual facilities including camp kitchen and internet.

Matakohe p184
A **Matakohe House**, Church Rd, T09-431 7091, www.matakohehouse.co.nz. 50 m from the museum. Comfortable modern double and twin rooms. Communal lounge, evening meals. Café and art gallery next door. Overall convenience and good value.
C-D **Old Post Office Guest House**, corner SH12 and Oakleigh, Paparoa, 6 km east of the museum, T/F09-431 6444. Homestead with Old World character and charm, with one room an ex-prison cell. Backpackers welcome.

Motorcamps and campsites
C-D **Matakohe Top Ten Motor Camp**, 350 m from the museum, T/F09-431 6431, www.matakohetop10.co.nz. Fairly modern, tent sites, camp kitchen and fast internet.

❼ Eating

Dargaville and around p183
In Dargaville itself there is not a huge selection beyond the usual takeaways. **Woolworths** is on Victoria St, T09-439 3935, daily 0700-2200.
♥♥ **Blah, Blah, Blah Café and Bar**, 101 Victoria St, T09-439 6300. Breakfast, blah blah, blah.
♥♥ **Funky Fish Café**, 34 Seaview Rd, Baylys Beach, T09-439 8883, daily 1100-late. The best place in the area and becoming fairly legendary. Well worth the drive.
♥♥ **New Asian Restaurant**, 73 Victoria St, T09-439 8388, daily 1100-2200. Palatable local Chinese.
♥♥ **Steakhouse and Bar**, corner of Victoria and Gladstone sts, T09-439 8460, daily. Good family venue.

Matakohe p184
♥♥ **Matakohe House**, 50 m from the museum, doubles as a café offering quiches, pasta, teas and fine coffee. Smorgasbord on Sat.
♥♥ **Sahara**, corner of Franklin Rd and SH12, 7 km from Matakohe in the historic former BNZ bank, T09-431 6833, Wed-Sun from 1100. Tidy restaurant and bar with friendly hosts.

▲▲ Activities and tours

Dargaville and around p183
There is a range of options available including scenic beach excursions by 6WD coach or 4WD along Ripiro Beach, from $55, child $25. Harbour cruises onboard the *Kaipara Kat*, quad bike tours and fishing are additional options.
Kaipara Cruises, T0800-466793, link to Helensville on the Southern Kaipara Harbour just north of Auckland.
Pete's Safari Tours, T09-439 0515, www.pete safari.co.nz. 2-hr sightseeing tours or day-long fishing trips on the remote beaches. Transport from Dargaville.
Taylor Made Tours, T09-439 1576, www.kaiparaaction.co.nz.

❶ Directory

Dargaville and around p183
Internet Internet at the VIC (I-Site) or Kauri Computers, 79 Victoria St, Mon-Fri 0900-1730, Sat 0900-1230. **Police** T09-439 3400. **Post Office** 80 Victoria St, T09-439 6051, Mon-Fri 0800-1700.

Coromandel Peninsula

⁛ Footprint features

Introduction

In many ways the Coromandel Peninsula is like a compact and easily accessible mix of Northland and Great Barrier Island. It offers varied and spectacular coastal scenery, rugged mountain bush and a relaxed lifestyle, which together make it the main attraction on the Pacific Coast Highway.

The west coast, bounded by the Firth of Thames, is the most undeveloped side of the peninsula. It has a ragged coastline of islands and pebble beaches, lined with some of the best examples of pohutukawa trees in the country. For three weeks in December the olive evergreen leaves that crown the gnarled trunks, flower in a radiant mantle of crimson, earning them the label of New Zealand's Christmas tree.

In contrast, the east coast is a plenitude of beautiful bays and sandy beaches, with Cathedral Cove and Hot Water Beach being two of the most celebrated in New Zealand. Here you will find most of the development, activity and population, from the transitory tourist in the holiday townships of Whitianga and Whangamata to the rich retiree in the rather sterile resorts of Matarangi and Pauanui.

Between the two coasts a dominating backbone of bush-clad mountains make up the Coromandel Forest Park, with its wealth of walks and historic logging and mining remains. In summary, if you have the time, put the 'Coro' firmly on the travelling agenda.

★ Don't miss ...

1 **Coromandel Forest Park** Explore the old kauri dams then spend a night in the DoC Pinnacles Hut in the heart of the park, pages 191 and 193.
2 **Coromandel Township** Chill out in the laid-back town and take a ride on the unique Driving Creek Railway, page 194.
3 **Castle Rock** Climb up to see the views across the peninsula, page 195.
4 **Cape Colville** Stop for supplies in the Colville General store, before setting off to explore the Pohutukawa Coast, page 195.
5 **New Chums Beach** Go swimming or take a stroll along the beautiful beach near Whangapoua, page 196.
6 **Whitianga** Head out on a boat for some sea fishing or kayaking, or try bone carving in the town centre, page 201.
7 **Cathedral Cove** Be the first to see the sunrise and lay the day's first footprints in the sand, page 202.

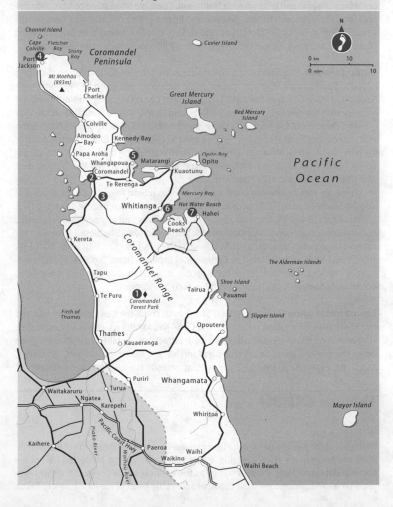

Coromandel Peninsula Introduction

Thames to Coromandel

→ *Colour map 2, B2 Population: 10,000*

From Thames, the SH25 negotiates a seemingly endless number of headlands and a string of small coastal communities before climbing inland towards the township of Coromandel – the main focus of the peninsula's west coast. After numerous tricky bends, this latter section of road offers a welcome relief and some stunning vistas of what the Coromandel is all about with its numerous bays, small offshore islands and bush-clad mountain ranges, not to mention the occasional smug-looking bovine, happily chewing the cud. ⟫ *For Sleeping, Eating and other listings, see pages 192-193.*

Ins and outs

Getting there Air Coromandel and **Great Barrier Airlines**, To800-900-600, www.air coromandel.co.nz, operate a twice-daily service to and from Auckland (around $100, child $65), for Whitianga and Matarangi. There are also scheduled flights to and from Great Barrier Island and Whangarei in Northland. There are often some combination fly/boat/bus packages with **Fullers**, **Sealink** and **Intercity**. You can also visit Coromandel Township on a day-cruise (from $82, child $41) from Auckland Tuesday, Thursday, Friday and Saturday with **360 Discovery**, To800-888006, www.360discovery.co.nz.

Getting around The Coromandel Peninsula is the premier destination on the North Island's 'Pacific Coast Highway' tourist route that links Auckland to the north, with Napier and Hawkes Bay to the east. Like the 'Twin Coast Discovery' in Northland, the route is well signposted, with free leaflets and maps readily available at all VICs (I-Sites). Throughout the peninsula there is a combination of sealed roads (linking the main towns) and unsealed roads (linking west to east and the further up the north of the peninsula), which results in difficult and time-consuming driving. All the roads are scenic but very windy and are often affected after heavy rain. The best way to deal with this is to relax and take your time.

There are regular **Intercity** offers coach services to and from the Coromandel; it is also a feature of their Wellington or Rotorua North Island Pass schedule. The VIC (I-Site) in Thames act as agents, To7-868 7251. A number of bus tour companies offer shuttle, personalized or specialist tour options, including: **Go Kiwi Shuttles**, To7-866 0336/To800-446549, www.go-kiwi.co.nz, Auckland to Thames from $27, Whitianga from $48, shuttle plus tours and charter; and **Coromandel Explorer Tours**, To7-866 3506/To800-028687, www.coromandeltours.co.nz, day-tour from $220, two-day from $380 (plus accommodation), four-day from $400 (plus accommodation).

Tourist information There are VICs (I-Sites) throughout the Coromandel for free and comprehensive information on all that 'the Coro' has to offer as well as places to stay. They also book travel and sell tickets for local attractions. Details of the VICs are given under the relevant town. You'll find them in Thames, Coromandel Town, Whitianga, Tairua, Whangamata and Waihi. The principal website is www.thecoromandel.com.

Thames ⊜⦿⊜⦿ ⟫ *pp192-193.*

→ *Colour map 2, B2*

Thames is at the western base of the Coromandel Peninsula at the mouth of the Waihou River and fringe of the Hauraki Plains. Behind the town rise the bush-clad hills of the **Coromandel Forest Park**. Thames serves as the gateway to the peninsula, either north to Coromandel town and the west coast, or across the heart of the forest park to Tairua and the east coast. Thames is the largest town on the Coromandel and was one of the largest towns in New Zealand during the peak of the kauri logging and gold mining eras of the late 1800s, though you would not guess it now. Other than essential services there is little in the town to hold the tourist back, except perhaps a few historic buildings and the old **Gold Mine and Stamper Battery**. On its doorstep, the **Kauaeranga Valley**, the main access point to the Coromandel Forest Park, is well worth a visit.

Ins and outs

Tourist information Most of the town's amenities are on Pollen Street, which runs the length of the town from south to north. The **VIC (I-Site) and bus terminal** ① *206 Pollen St, T07-868 7284, www.thamesinfo.co.nz, Mon-Fri 0830-1700, Sat-Sun 0900-1600*, provides free street maps. The DoC office is at the **Kauaeranga Valley Visitor Centre** ① *T07-867 9080, www.doc.govt.nz, daily 0800-1600*.

Sights

Perhaps the best place to start and to get your bearings is the **War Memorial Monument Lookout** on Waiotahi Creek Road, at the northern end of the town. From there you can get a fine view of the town and across the Hauraki Plains and Firth of Thames. Also at the northern end of town, on Pollen Street, is the **Thames Gold Mine and Stamper Battery** ① *T/F07-868 8514, www.goldmine-experience.co.nz, daily 1000-1600, $10, child $4*. It offers regular 45-minute tours which take in the impressive ore-crushing stamper, various horizontal tunnels and a small-gauge railway all with an informative commentary about the process and history of gold mining along the way. You can try your hand (and your luck) at gold panning.

Along the same mining and mineral theme, the **Thames School of Mines and Mineralogical Museum** ① *corner of Brown and Cochrane sts, T07-868 6227, Wed-Sun 1100-1600, $3.50, child free*, has a varied and interesting collection of rocks and minerals from around the world. Given the significance of the area for both kauri logging and gold mining the small **Thames Historical Museum** ① *corner of Pollen and Cochrane sts, T07-868 8509, daily 1300-1600, $4, child $2*, is worth a peek.

Other places of interest that may (or may not) tickle your fancy include: the **Matatoki Cheese Farm** ① *Wainui Rd, off SH26, 7 km south of Thames, T07-868 1284, www.matatokicheese.co.nz, daily 1000-1630 (Sun in winter), from $2*; the very leggy inhabitants of the **Piako Ostrich Farm** ① *311 Piako Rd, Turua, south off SH25, T07-867 5326, www.ostrichfarm.co.nz, $5, child $3.50, tours daily*, or the wonderfully aromatic products on sale at the **Eco People and Natural Soap Factory** ① *corner of Grey and Pollen sts, T07-868 3830*.

There are also a number of notable gardens, walks and art and craft galleries in the area including: **Lyndell and Rapaura Gardens**; the **Twin Souls and Mahara Garden Pottery**; the sculpture park and the **Maori craft gallery** (Te Whare Whakairo) and the **Historic Grahamstown Trail**. Details of these can be obtained from the VIC (I-Site).

Coromandel Forest Park (Kauaeranga Valley)

▶▶ *pp192-193*.

→ *Colour map 2, B2*

The Coromandel Forest was, in the late 1800s, one of the most extensive kauri logging areas in the North Island. At the head of the **Kauaeranga Valley**, there is a fine **DoC Kauaeranga Visitor Centre** ① *13 km east of Thames, T07-867 9080*, set in a very pleasant recreation area, accessed via Parawai Road at the southern end of town. A fascinating audio-visual display gives you an insight into the life and times of the early pioneer loggers. (If you do not have your own wheels the **Sunkist Lodge**, see Sleeping page 193, in Thames offers a shuttle service to the park; from $25 return,

To7-868 8808.) From here there are a number of fine walks spread through the forest park. These vary from a few hours to a few days, taking in some of the best scenery the park has to offer and a few remnants of the old logging days, including the impressive **Dancing Creek Dam**. The **Kauaeranga Kauri Trail** (leaflet from the Visitor Centre) is the most popular walk taking trampers to the interesting Pinnacles rock formation.

Thames Coast and north to Coromandel Town

>> *pp192-193.*

The coast road to Coromandel township is scenic but very windy and quite dangerous, so take your time. On the way, the **Rapaura Watergardens** ① *6 km up the Tapu-Coroglen Rd, To7-868 4821, www.rapaurawatergardens.co.nz, 0900-1700, $10, child $4*, are worth a look, with numerous paths and lots of 'Monet-like' lily ponds. After your explorations you can enjoy a cuppa and a snack in the **Koru Café**, or even stay the night in the self-catering lodge or cottage.

Just east of the gardens, a little further up the road and along a fairly steep track, is the impressive **'Square Kauri'** estimated to be over 1000 years old. Ask at the gardens for detailed directions. While on the Tapu-Coroglen Road (on the right, about 2 km before the gardens) it is worth stopping to see the quirky work of sculptor Heather Stevens at the **Mahara Garden Pottery**, To7-868 4817. Another pleasant garden with the added attraction of butterflies is the **Butterfly and Orchid Garden** ① *3 km north of Thames, To7-868 8080, www.butterfly.co.nz, daily summer 1000-1600, winter 1100-1500, from $10, child $5, café and shop*. If you haven't seen a Monarch yet, this may be your chance.

Just north of Kereta the SH25 climbs, turns inland and at the crest of the hill, offers a magnificent view of the northern part of the Coromandel Peninsula.

● Sleeping

Thames *p190*
There are also some pleasant B&Bs out of town and ideally placed near the forest park in the Kauaeranga Valley.
AL Cotswold Cottage, Maramarahi Rd, T/F07-868 6306, www.cotswoldcottage.co.nz. A restored villa set in spacious grounds with a range of rooms. Local cuisine a speciality.
AL Grafton Cottage, 304 Grafton Rd, T07-868 9971, www.graftoncottage.co.nz. 5 very smart chalets with fine views, B&B or self-contained. Pool and spa.
AL-A Coastal Resorts, 608 Tararu Rd, T07-868 6843, www.coastalresorts.co.nz. Overlooking the Firth of Thames, just north of the town offering self-contained chalets, spa and Sky TV.
AL-C Brian Boru Hotel, 200 Richmond St, T07-868 6523, brianboru@xtra.co.nz. The best hotel option, established in 1868, provides affordable, traditional hotel and standard motel-style accommodation, double spas.

A Brookby Motel, 102 Redwood Lane, T/F07-868 6663, www.brookbymotel.co.nz. A newly renovated motel option with Sky TV and just a short walk from the town centre.
A Huia Lodge, 589 Kauaeranga Valley Rd, T07-868 6557, www.thames-info.co.nz/huialodge. 2 units with en suite.
A Tuscany on Thames, corner of Jellicoe Crescent and Banks St, T07-868 5099, www.tuscanyonthames.co.nz. Spotless motel units with double spa baths.
B-D Dickson Holiday Park, 3 km north of Thames, T07-868 7308, www.dickson park.co.nz. Pleasant streamside rooms with shared facilities and en suite bathrooms with TV, plus all the usual facilities. The 3-hr return 'Home of the Butterfly and Orchid gardens' and 'Rocky's Goldmine Trail' begin from here.
C-D Gateway Backpackers, 209 Mackay St, T07-868 6339, gateway@wave.co.nz. Near the VIC (I-Site) and bus stop this is a handy, homely option with all room types, the usual

facilities and a peaceful garden. Also offers daily shuttles to the Kauaeranga Forest Park.
C-D Sunkist Lodge, 506 Brown St, T07 868 8808, www.sunkistbackpackers.com. Well-established and friendly alternative, housed in one of the oldest buildings in the town. 4-star rating with spacious doubles, twins and dorms, large well-equipped lounge and kitchen, 24-hr Internet, travel desk, organized BBQs and regular shuttles to the Coromandel Forest Park from $25 (return).
C-D Thames Central Backpackers, 330 Pollen St, T07-868 5330, www.thamescentral backpackers.com. Cheap, comfortable and renovated hostel right on the main drag and within walking distance of the bus terminal.

Motorcamps and campsites
B-D Miranda Holiday Park, Front Miranda Rd, 30 km west of Thames, T07-867 3205, www.mirandaholidaypark.co.nz. Although some distance from Thames this is an excellent motorpark with above average facilities, plus the added attraction of its own hot pool. Recommended to get your visit to the Coromandel off to a good start.

Coromandel Forest Park *p191*
There is a DoC campsite near the visitor centre and 7 others located throughout the park ($7, child $2).
D Pinnacles Hut, on the park track, T07-867 9080. Run by DoC, a fine place to stay; beds (80) must be booked in advance, $15.

Thames Coast and north to Coromandel Town *p192*
If you are beginning to feel dizzy trying to negotiate all the bends in the road, this stretch of coast has some fine accommodation in which to recover. It is also a good place to base yourself to explore the peninsula.
AL Te Puru Coast View Lodge, 468 Thames Coast Rd, Te Puru, T07-868 2326, tepuru-lodge@xtra.co.nz. A boutique Mediterranean-style getaway with excellent views and fine in-house cuisine.

A-D Te Mata Lodge, off Te Mata Creek Rd, 20 km north of Thames, T07-868 4834, www.tematalodge.co.nz. Self-contained cottages, cabins and campsites in the valley, yet within walking distance of the coast.

Motorcamps and campsites
C-D Tapu Motor Camp, 18 km north of Thames, T07-8684837. Popular but fairly basic beach/riverside location.

❼ Eating

Thames *p190*
Thames has yet to produce a truly reputable restaurant so don't expect a food fest.
❢❢ **Food For Thought**, 574 Pollen St, T07-868 6065. Mon-Fri 0730-1530. Good value.
❢❢ **Kaveetas Indian Cuisine**, 518 Pollen St, T07-868 7049. Standard Indian with the added attraction of some good veggie dishes.
❢❢ **Old Thames Restaurant**, 705 Pollen St, T07-868 7207. Good value with a loyal local following, day and evening menus. Licensed.
❢❢ **Sola Café**, 720b Pollen St, T07-868 8781, Tue-Sun 0900-1600 and 1800-2100 Wed-Sat. New and already perhaps the most popular café in town with good vegetarian options and the best coffee.

❸ Transport

Thames *p190*
Bicycle hire Paki Paki Bike Shop, Goldfields Shopping Centre, T07-867 9026.
Car hire Saunders Motors, 201 Pollen St, T07-868 8398, or Ultimate, 400 Pollen St, T07-868 6440. **Taxi** Thames Gold Cabs, T07-868 6037.

❹ Directory

Thames *p190*
Internet Available at the VIC (I-Site), 206 Pollen St, T07-868 7284. **Laundry** World-Wide-Wash, 742 Pollen St, T07-868 7912. Mon-Fri 0830-2100, Sat-Sun 1000-2100.

● For an explanation of the Sleeping and Eating price codes used in this guide, see the inside
● front cover. Other relevant information is provided in the Essentials chapter, pages 44-51.
Note that prices are tive in New Zealand dollars.

Coromandel Town and around

→ *Colour map2, A2 Population: 2000*

Coromandel Town has a wonderful bohemian village feel and a warm atmosphere. The locals, many of whom are artists, are friendly and contented souls who walk about with a knowing smile, as if they are well aware they have come to the 'right' place. It is refreshingly free from the drearily ubiquitous high-street chains or rows of unsightly advertising hoardings, and only a lamp-post opposite the road junction as you arrive in the heart of the town bears any signs or place names. The village, and indeed the whole peninsula, derives its name from the visit, in 1820, by HMS Coromandel, which called in to load kauri spars. Again, gold and kauri in the late 1800s were the attraction, and some old buildings remain, though sadly not the beautiful native bush that once cloaked the hills. Just north of the town one of New Zealand's most famous potters, Barry Brickell, has created – along with many fine works from his kiln – a quirky Driving Creek Railway. ▸▸ *For Sleeping, Eating, and other listings, see pages 196-198.*

Ins and outs

Tourist information VIC (I-Site) ⓘ *355 Kapanga Rd, T07-866 8598, www.coromandel town.co.nz, Mon-Sat 0900-1700, Sun 1000-1300 (extended summer hours)*. In keeping with the village the staff are very friendly and helpful. The same office also provides DoC information and internet facilities.

Sights

The **Coromandel Mining and Historic Museum** ⓘ *841 Rings Rd, T07-866 7251, daily in peak season 1000-1600, winter Sat-Sun 1330-1600, $2, child $0.50*, is a fairly small affair but provides a worthy insight into the rapacious days of gold mining, when the town had three times the population it does now. The 100-year-old operational **Coromandel Gold Stamper Battery** ⓘ *410 Buffalo Rd, T07-866 7933, daily, summer 1000-1700, tours $6, child $3, gold panning $5*, is set in very pleasant surrounds with a waterwheel and stream in which you can try your hand at gold panning.

The **Driving Creek Railway** ⓘ *T07-866 8703, www.drivingcreekrailway.co.nz, trains run daily at 1015, 1400, also 1245 and 1515 in summer, $20, child $11, family $50*, created by Kiwi sculptor Barry Bricknell, is well worth the visit. Barry has lived in Coromandel for years and his artistic creations, open-air studio and railway line all ooze character and charm. Building began on the narrow-gauge railway in 1975 as a means of transporting clay to the kilns at the base of the hill. Now 25 years on, the line winds its way almost 2 km up the hill through regenerating bush to the expansive views from the ridge-top terminus (New Zealand's 'Eiffel Tower'). It is a delight and a construction of budget engineering genius, together with artistic creativity and environmental sensitivity. Tunnels and embankments built of empty wine bottles (the fuel of the railway builders), together with some of Barry's evocative – and at times quite erotic – sculptures, decorate the route. There is an entertaining and informative commentary along the way with the occasional stop (one of which is to see some impressive creepy-crawlies). There are plans to build a predator-free bush area and museum near the present base terminus, which is housed in the old brickworks (where all the bricks used along the railway were made). As it stands this area, the kilns and the shop are all fascinating.

The one-hour short walk at **Long Bay Scenic Reserve**, west of Coromandel, is very pleasant, taking in bush and beach (for the beach turn right to Tucks Bay on reaching the road). It begins at the end of Long Bay Road and is accessed at the **Long Bay Motor Camp**. The view from the short walk to the **Tokatea Lookout**, at the crest of the hill, up Kennedy Bay Road (via Driving Creek Road) is well worth it.

Don't miss the **craft shops** along Coromandel's main street. The **Weta Design**
Store ① *46 Kapanga Rd, www.wetadesign.co.nz*, is particularly good. The VIC (I-Site)
and the free *Coromandel Craft Trail* leaflet will point the way to others.

South on the 309 road → *Colour map 2, A2*
The old 309 road, which starts just south of Coromandel Town, winds its way 22 km to
Whitianga and has a number of fine attractions along the way. The other route to
Whitianga is along the SH25.

The first stop on the 309, 4½ km from Coromandel, is the charming **Waiau**
Waterworks ① *T07-866 7191, www.waiauwaterworks.co.nz, daily 0900-1700, closed*
in winter, $10, child $5, which is a garden full of fascinating whimsical water
sculptures and gadgets. Like the Driving Creek Railway, it is Kiwi ingenuity and
imagination at its wonderfully eccentric best. Great for kids.

A short distance up the road from the waterworks there is a track on the left that
takes you a further 2 km to the start of the Castle Rock Walk (standard cars will be
fine). The aptly named **Castle Rock** (490 m) is a very knobbly-looking volcanic plug
that commands a wonderful view of the northern end of the peninsula. It is a stiff
climb and one to two hours return depending how fit you are. Take suitable footwear
as the track is more like a stream in winter, but the view is worth the effort.

Just over 7 km up the 309 are the **Waiau Falls**. It is a 15-minute walk to a very
pleasant glade where the falls crash over a rock face. Less than a kilometre further up
the road is the **Kauri Grove**, a stand of ancient kauri, some of the very few left alone
and protected, and all the more impressive for it. The walk takes about 20 minutes.
From here you can return to Coromandel Town or carry on to Whitianga.

North to Colville and the Cape → *Colour map 2, A2*
North of Coromandel Town, the Colville Road rejoins the coast at **Papa Aroha** (Land of
Love) and **Amodeo Bay**. From these charming bays you will be able to feast your eyes
once again on Mount Moehau and what is called the **Pohutukawa Cape**. These
wonderfully old and gnarled *pohutas* that grace the shoreline are some of the best
examples in the country, and in December flower in a gorgeous crimson mantle. From
this point you are entering perhaps the most remote and scenic area of the Coromandel
Peninsula with an atmosphere all of its own. The beach at **Waitete Bay**, 5 km north of
Amodeo Bay, is a cracker and a favourite haunt in summer. From here the road climbs
over the hill and falls again to the historic settlement of **Colville**, with its amazingly
well-stocked **general store** ① *T07-866 6805, Mon-Thu 0830-1700, Fri 0830-1800, Sat*
0900-1700, Sun 0930-1700. Next door, the **Colville Café** is a great place for a snack.

Just north of Colville you can cross the peninsula northeast on the Port Charles Road
to Port Charles or back down southeast to Kennedy Bay, then back to Coromandel. **Port**
Charles is the northernmost settlement on the east side of the peninsula and has a
great bay and beach. **Kennedy Bay** is less well endowed than Port Charles in both
scenery and amenities, but gives the passer-by an insight into real peninsula life. Note
the St Paul's Anglican Church, which must have a very small congregation.

The **Port Jackson Road**, which heads north of Colville, is an absolute delight with
the Moehau Range looming on your right and pebble beaches to the left. The road itself
becomes almost completely shrouded by huge gnarled pohutukawa trees. About 13 km
north of Colville you reach the small Te Hope Stream and the beginning of the Mount
Moehau Track (temporarily closed). **Mount Moehau** is 893 m and the highest peak
anywhere near Auckland. Indeed, on a clear day the Moehau range is visible from the
city. Mount Moehau is a superb climb, but somewhat frustrating, because the last few
hundred metres to the summit (and what must be incredible views) is sacred to the
Maori and out of bounds. So if you do make the climb, show suitable respect and settle
for nearly reaching the top. The first 2 km of the walk, which follows the river, are still
superb with numerous clear pools (sadly swimming is prohibited) and small waterfalls

to enjoy. The track, before it starts to make a serious ascent, is a delight and you are almost certain to see native wood pigeon and hear tui. At the time of going to press the track was closed due to the potential spread of a fungus that is killing the native and eminently appealing Archey's frog (see box, page 201).

After negotiating numerous idyllic pebble bays, the road eventually climbs round the northern tip of the cape and falls steeply to **Port Jackson** and **Fletcher Bay**, where the road ends. From here you can enjoy great views of Great Barrier Island, seemingly only a stone's throw away across the Colville Channel. Fletcher Bay marks the beginning of the popular **Coromandel Walkway**, which connects Fletcher Bay with Stony Bay and effectively the east coast road and all points south; information about the walkway is available at the VIC (I-Site). There are two tracks about 7 km in length and they take about three hours one way. The steeper of the two tracks offers better views and also doubles as a fine mountain biking route.

SH25 to Whitianga

From Coromandel Town the SH25 winds its way east, over the ranges, offering fine views, before descending steeply to Te Rerenga and Whangapoua Harbour. **Whangapoua village**, 4 km north of the junction at Te Rerenga, is essentially a conglomeration of holiday homes and baches that come alive in the summer months. A 30-minute walk north from the road end in Whangapoua is **New Chums Beach**, which is one of the best beaches in the Coromandel. The fact that you cannot drive there and have to negotiate the headland by foot seems to protect its beauty, enhance its character and make it a truly magical place. Even in bad weather it is worth the walk.

Back on SH25, heading east, is the sterile real estate settlement of **Matarangi**, which is saved only by its sweeping beach and great golf course. About 6 km further on at the end of the beach is **Kuaotunu**, a pleasant spot, especially for swimming. Kuaotunu also acts as the gateway to **Opito Bay** via the scenic and intriguingly named Black Jack Road. Opito has a lovely beach with magnificent views across to the Mercury Islands and numerous other small Islands. In summer this is a great spot to escape the crowds. (Yeah – who does own that house at the end of the beach?)

● Sleeping

Coromandel Town *p194*
There is a good range of accommodation in and around Coromandel Town, mainly in the form of B&Bs, motels, motorcamps and backpacker hostels. The VIC (I-Site) has comprehensive information about B&Bs. In summer you are advised to book ahead everywhere.
LL-L Buffalo Lodge, 860 Buffalo Rd, T/F07-866 8960, www.buffalolodge.co.nz, closed May-Sep. Tasteful, 5-star luxury in a bush setting with sweeping views. Fine cuisine.
L-AL Karamana Homestead, 84 Whanga-poua Rd, T07-866 7138, www.karamana homestead.com. A 1872 semi-rural kauri villa with French, Victorian and colonial themed rooms and a separate cottage for more privacy. Plenty of antiques, fine food and luxury. Afternoon Devonshire teas a speciality ($15).
L-D Anchor Lodge Resort, 448 Wharf Rd, T07-866 7992, www.anchorlodge

coromandel.co.nz. A modern motel in the heart of town and very tidy, offering 14 luxury units, pool, spa, 24-hr internet, off-street parking and also backpacker rooms.
AL-A Coromandel Colonial Cottages, 1737 Rings Rd, T/F07-866 8857, www.coromandel_ colonial_cottages.co.nz. Self-contained cottage-style motel units with large grounds and a swimming pool.
AL-A Coromandel Court Motel, 365 Kapanga Rd, T07-866 8403, www.coro mandelcourtmotel.co.nz. Fairly new, well-equipped and very central, behind the VIC.
AL-A The Green House B&B, 505 Tiki Rd, Coromandel, T07-866 7303, www.thegreen housebandb.co.nz. Tidy B&B with 2 en suite rooms. The friendly hosts volunteer at the VIC so they are very well informed.
AL-A Pottery Lane Cottage, 15 Pottery Lane, T07-866 7171, r&bmartin@xtra.co.nz. 2 good-value, self-contained cottages in a peaceful

garden setting and within a short stroll from the village centre. The first has a separate double and twin room while the second is smaller and open-plan. Both have plenty of character and are tastefully decorated in the classic cottage-style. Off-street parking.

A Jacaranda Lodge, 3195 Tiki Rd, SH25, T07-866 8002, www.jacarandalodge.co.nz. Big farmstay with 6 rooms (2 en suite), just south of the village. Home-grown produce adds to the appeal.

A Te Kouma Harbour Farmstay, SH25, T07-866 8747, www.tekouma.co.nz. If you are looking for a farmstay, although it is some distance back towards Thames, then this offers great value self-contained cottages and a whole host of activities beyond mere animal patting. Recommended.

A-D Tidewater Tourist Park, 270 Tiki Rd, T07-866 8888, www.tidewater.co.nz. Offers backpacker accommodation. Sauna and camp kitchen.

C-D Coromandel Town Backpackers, 732 Rings Rd, T07-866 8327. Small, central and handy for all amenities. Attractive, double rooms and off-street parking.

C-D Lion's Den Backpackers, 126 Te Tiki St, T07-866 8157. Small, homely, with friendly owners who can offer lots of sound advice about exploring the region. The house-truck is a novel option for couples. Located just a short walk from the village centre and excellent homemade pancakes.

C-D Tui Lodge, 60 Whangapoua Rd, T07-866 8237. A bit further out, but has a good range of accommodation with en suite bathrooms, a sauna, tent sites and free bike hire.

Motorcamps and campsites
A-D Coromandel Holiday Park, 636 Rings Rd, T07-866 8830. Central and has good facilities and modern cabins.
B-D Long Bay Motor Camp, 3200 Long Bay Rd, to the west of town, T07-866 8720.
C-D Shelly Beach Top Ten Motels and Holiday Park, Colville Rd, T07-866 8988. North of town on the beach. Usual facilities including camp kitchen.

A-D Anglers Lodge, Amodeo Bay, T07-866 8584, www.anglers.co.nz. Offers excellent motel units and a campsite, with swimming pool, spa, shop, kayak hire and charter boat (water taxi), all on site.

A-D Colville Farm, 2140 Colville Rd, T07-866 6820, www.colvillefarmholidays.co.nz. The peninsula's northernmost backpacker hostel and campsite offering shared accommodation, bush lodges and tent sites on a working farm. Horse trekking.

B Pohutukawa Coast Chalets, near Papa Aroha, just north of Coromandel, T07-866 8379. Comfortable, good value, self-contained 'A Frame' cabins, some of which have fine views. Discounts for 5 days or more.

C-D Fletcher Bay Backpackers, T07-866 6172, js.lourie@xtra.co.nz. The northernmost backpacker hostel, offering a remote but welcome overnight stop if you have done the Coromandel Walkway.

C-D Mahaudra Centre, T07-866 6851, www.mahamudra.org.nz. Popular Buddhist retreat with a fine range of accommodation from shared to separate rooms and cabins. Meditation courses available.

Motorcamps and campsites
The DoC operates 5 campsites with basic facilities at Fantail Bay, Port Jackson, Fletcher, Stony and Waikawau Bays. For information and availability, T0800-455466. $7, child $2. Bookings are essential at Waikawau Bay in summer, T07-866 1106/T07-8679080.

C-D Papa Aroha Holiday Park, Papa Aroha, T07-866 8818, www.papaaroha.co.nz. A good place to camp or park up with the van. Motel units, cabins, chalets fishing charters/trips (from $80 for 1 hr), water taxi service, boat and kayak hire.

SH25 to Whitianga p196
L-AL Kuaotunu Bay Lodge, SH25, Kuaotunu, T07-866 4396, www.kuaotunubay.co.nz. A great purpose-built lodge a stone's throw from the beach with twin/ double or self-contained unit with a good reputation, owned by long-term and friendly residents.

Coromandel Peninsula Coromandel Town & around Listings

● *For an explanation of the Sleeping and Eating price codes used in this guide, see the inside*
● *front cover. Other relevant information is provided in the Essentials chapter, pages 44-51.*
Note that prices are tive in New Zealand dollars.

A **Drift In B&B**, 16 Gray's Av, T/F07-866 4321. A good value B&B with great views.

A **Kaeppeli's**, 40 Gray Av, Kuaotuna, T07-866 2445, www.kaeppelis.co.nz. B&B run by a Kiwi/Swiss family and chef. Renowned for its cuisine.

B-D **Black Jack Lodge, Chalet and Backpackers**, 201 SH25, at the river mouth, eastern end of Kuaotunu Beach, T07-866 2988, www.black-jack.co.nz. Modern, beachside backpacker hostel with lodge and chalet options, tidy en suite doubles and dorms. Camping available. Free use of kayaks and bike hire.

Motorcamps and campsites

There is a campsite is at Whangapoua (Hamiora), T07-866 7183, and a general store that can also assist in organizing bach rentals, T07-866 8274.

There are 2 holiday parks at Kuaotunu (and a well-stocked store), including B-D **Kuaotunu Motor Camp**, T07-866 5628, www.kuaotunumotorcamp.co.nz.

⊙ Eating

Coromandel Town *p194*
The main eateries are on Kapanga Rd.

₦ **Coro Smoking Co**, 70 Tiki Rd, T07-866 8793, daily 0800-1800. No, not the Coro's answer to anti-smoking legislation but instead the perfect place to smoke your own catch of the day or choose from a range of fresh, locally caught seafood.

₦ **Peppertree Restaurant and Bar**, T07-866 8211, daily from 0900. Award-winning fine dining with a lunch and mainly seafood dinner menu. It has a pleasant interior, bar and outdoor eating area. On summer evenings book in advance.

₦ **Success Café**, T07-866 7100. Fine light meals on offer during the day (includes good-value cooked breakfasts) and a more comprehensive menu in the evening year round. Again seafood is the speciality (try the mussels or lamb). Licensed and BYO.

₦ **Umu Restaurant and Café**, 22 Wharf Rd (opposite the BNZ), T07-866 8618, daily 0930-late. Good pizza and vegetarian options.

₦ **Coromandel Takeaway**, 24 Wharf Rd (opposite the BNZ), T07-866 8438, daily from 1100-2100. Fish and chips.

North to Colville and the Cape *p195*

₦ **Colville Store and Café**, daily 0930-1600, Fri-Sun 1800-2000. This well-stocked place will more than do, considering the location.

▲ Activities and tours

Coromandel Town *p194*
Activity operators seem to come and go in Coromandel and you are advised to call in at the VIC (I-Site) for the latest listings.

Argo Tours, T07-866 7667. Tours to mining sites, wetas and tame eels, from $55.

Papa Aroha, T/F07-866 8818, papa.aroha@xtra.co.nz. Fishing or scenic tours (around $60 for 3 hr); also hires out kayaks.

Snapper Safaris, T07-866 7667. Offers fishing and scenic cruising, from $35 (departs from the Town Wharf daily 0700, 1230 and 1600). Book at the VIC.

Strongman Coaches, T07-866 8175, www.coromandeldiscoverytours.co.nz. For those who enjoy walking, Strongman offers a 6-pack shuttle service to the Coromandel Coastal Walkway (far north between Fletcher Bay and Stony Bay 3-4 hrs, for a manly $90.

White Star (Colville), T07-866 6820. Horse trekking.

⊖ Transport

Coromandel Town *p194*
Bicycle hire
Bikes are available from **Tide Water Tourist Park**, 270 Tiki Rd, T07-866 8888.

Bus
Intercity runs a service to and from **Thames** and a daily service to **Whitianga** stopping in the town centre. For information and tickets contact the VIC (I-Site).

⊕ Directory

Coromandel Town *p194*
Internet VIC (I-Site), 355 Kapanga Rd, T07-866 8598; also at **Star and Garter Saloon Bar**, 5 Kapanga Rd, T07-866 8503.

Whitianga and the east coast

→ *Colour map 2, A2 Population: 3000*

Whitianga is a very popular holiday town on the shores of beautiful Mercury Bay, which was given its planetary name by Captain Cook during a spot of astronomy on his brief visit in 1769. 'Whiti' (pronounced 'fitty') – as it is affectionately known – has much to offer, including a number of fine beaches within walking distance of the town. It also acts as a convenient short-cut access point, across the narrow Whitianga Harbour entrance and Ferry Landing, to two fine smaller resorts – Cooks Beach and Hahei. Although there is an abundance of leisure activities to choose from, Whiti is perhaps most famous as a sea- and big-game fishing base and, like the Bay of Islands, a trip on the water is highly recommended. In summer and especially at Christmas and New Year, Whiti's growing resident population increases dramatically, resulting in excellent tourist services and amenities year round. ▸▸ For Sleeping, Eating and other listings, see pages 203-208.

Ins and outs

Getting there and around Whitianga airport is 3 km south of the town and is serviced from Auckland by **Air Coromandel/Great Barrier Airlines**, T09-275 9120, from $99 one way. **Intercity** buses drop off and pick up outside the VIC (I-Site) in the centre of town and service the local area. Other smaller shuttle companies operate to and from Auckland, Hamilton or Rotorua and tour around the peninsula (see also page 190). **Go Kiwi**, T0800-446549, www.go-kiwi.co.nz, offers shuttles from Auckland (from $54) and some recommended tour options. Contact the VIC (I-Site) for operators offering a full-day hop-on/hop-off service from Ferry Landing to Cooks Beach, Cathedral Cove, Hahei and Hot Water Beach. All buses can be booked at the VIC (I-Site).

The passenger-only ferry to Ferry Landing takes five minutes and operates continuously in summer 0730-2300, less frequently in winter; $2, child $1. The ferry to Pauanui, T027-497 0316, leaves from Tairua Wharf on Wharf Road, hourly in summer and every two hours in winter 0900-1700, $6 return. Good-value cruises are also offered in summer. Tairua is the main gateway to Alderman, Shoe, Slipper and Mayor Islands. Opoutere can be reached by bus from Whangamata, T07-865 8613.

Tourist information 'Whiti' VIC (I-Site) ⓘ *66 Albert St, centre of town, T07-866 5555, www.whitianga.co.nz, daily 0900-1800, Sat Sun 0900-1600,* can provide information about the many fine craft shops around Whitianga. **Tairua VIC (I-Site)** ⓘ *Main St, T/F07-864 7575, info.tairua@xtra.co.nz, summer daily 0930-1600, winter, 1000-1400,* can assist with finding accommodation or book water-based activities or island trips. **Whangamata VIC (I-Site)** ⓘ *616 Port Rd, T07-865 8340, www.whangamatainfo.co.nz, Mon-Sat 0900-1700, Sun 1000-1600.* **Waihi VIC (I-Site)** ⓘ *Upper Seddon St, T07-863 6715, www.waihi.org.nz, daily 0900-1700 in summer, 0900-1630 in winter.* Ask for the very useful *Discover Waihi* brochure.

Sights

The **Mercury Bay Museum** ⓘ *on the Esplanade, daily summer 1000-1600, Tue, Thu, Sun winter, $5, child $0.50,* is fairly small, but does a good job of showcasing the area's rich human history which goes back over 1000 years, when Maori explorer Kupe made landfall here. Cook's visit is also documented. The main waterfront beach is called **Buffalo Beach**, named after *HMS Buffalo* which was wrecked here in 1840. It is a fine beach but gets a little hectic in summer. **Flaxmill Bay**, across the water just beyond Ferry Landing, and better still **Lonely Bay**, at the eastern base of the Shakespeare Cliff Scenic Reserve, are often a better bet.

Even if you do not intend to go as far as Cooks Beach and Hahei, the short ferry ride across to **Ferry Landing** is worthwhile. The wharf itself was built in 1837 and, though it is one of the oldest in New Zealand, is less than attractive with its concrete coating. However there is a nice café and a number of fine **coastal walks** nearby. Immediately to the right of the wharf is the Whitianga Rock Walk (20 minutes) which takes in a Maori *pa* and offers a great view back over Whiti. The Maramaratotara Bay Walk (40 minutes) joins the Rock Walk and also has good views. A little further down the road, opposite the **Flaxmill Bay Resort**, is the access point to the **Shakespeare Cliff Scenic Reserve**. Climb the path to the right then cross the hill to the viewpoint where you are rewarded with a wonderful view across the bay.

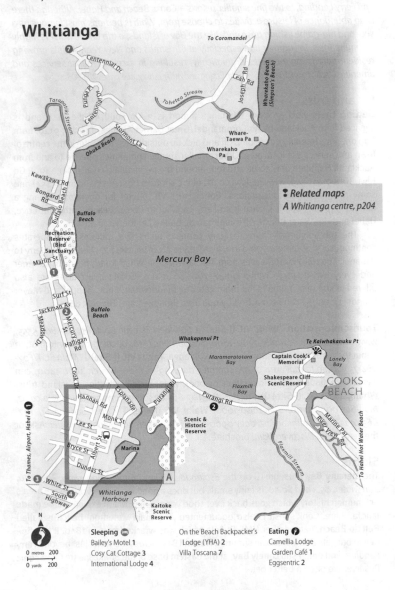

Whitianga

Related maps
A *Whitianga centre, p204*

Sleeping 🛏
Bailey's Motel **1**
Cosy Cat Cottage **3**
International Lodge **4**

On the Beach Backpacker's
Lodge (YHA) **2**
Villa Toscana **7**

Eating 🍴
Camellia Lodge
Garden Café **1**
Eggsentric **2**

0 metres 200
0 yards 200

Archey's frog

In just about every realm of New Zealand's fascinating and unique natural history you encounter the unusual and the endangered, and when it comes to the nation's few amphibians there is no exception.

In the damp nooks and crannies of the Coromandel Ranges and the Waikato, lives an enchanting character called Archey's frog – or *Leiopelma archeyi*, as he is heartily known at official engagements. But this is no ordinary frog, or at least not the green hand-sized variety that clears his throat and gives you a furtive wink before jumping in to the garden pond. No, for a start little Archibald is small (about 31-37 mm in length) and would certainly not win any beauty contests. He is also very old, having been around for over 200 million years, and is one of the most primitive frogs in the world.

He is one of four native species and three non-native species present in the country; his remaining number ranges at worst in the 100s and at best in the 1000s. He is a simple animal, terrestrial, found in dense, moist broadleaf forest under damp rocks and plants and has little contact with the wider world – a bit like the average politician really. And the similarity doesn't end there; he too is currently classed as 'threatened'. But alas – and in all seriousness – for poor Archey things are particularly bad and, like many frog species around the world (and ultimately ourselves), the future does not auger well. In recent years, DoC surveys have revealed a drastic decline in numbers due to the deadly frog-killer Chytrid fungus – a virulent disease that affects their highly sensitive skin. Once contracted the disease either suffocates them, or causes death by the absorption of toxins. As yet it is unknown which.

Sadly, as with just about everything that has ravaged New Zealand's fragile ecology since man's arrival, the fungal disease is an introduced natural phenomenon. In essence it spread from overseas on the back (literally) of other non-native frogs brought into the country.

As you may be aware, frogs are very sensitive to ecological changes and are considered barometers to the health of the ecosystem. Populations have been decreasing globally since the 1980s and New Zealand is now beginning to follow the global trend. It is all very tragic (and so typical), but what can we do to help? Well, people can spread the fungus by collecting and releasing introduced frogs, so DoC are asking the public to stop doing this (not that you probably have a stray frogs about your person) and to refrain from even entering some known habitats within the Coromandel (which are well advertised). You are also asked to report and sick or dead frogs to DoC if you encounter any, and note the exact location. Sickness symptoms include 'no escape response, slow movement, no attempt to right itself once flipped onto its back, wasting (a thin frog), abnormal eyes or skin, deformities, or finding frogs in an unusual place, such as in direct sun and away from water'. In essence – and with a loud clearing of the throat and a furtive wink – just like a 'healthy politician' really!

Whiti has a couple of excellent **bone carving studios,** which offer the opportunity to carve your own bone pendant – traditionally from whale bone but now typically from beef bone. **Bay Carving** ① *next to the museum on the Esplanade, T07-866 4021, www.dreamland.co.nz/baycarving, 0900-1600, evenings by appointment,* is very well equipped and provides expert tuition ($40-80). You choose your own design then test your skills. The other company that offers all-day tuition is the **Bone Carving Studio** ⓘ *6B Bryce St, T07-866 2158, www.carving.co.nz*, which offers more comprehensive full-day courses from $80 and acts as a showpiece for the professional trade.

East coast 🏠🚲▲ ⇉ *pp203-208.*

Hahei, Cooks Beach and Hot Water Beach → *Colour map 2, A3*

Hahei is a wonderful little unspoiled coastal settlement, 35 km by road from Whitianga. A shorter route is via the ferry from Whitianga. Both Hahei and Cooks Beach have wonderful beaches in their own right, especially **Hahei Beach** that looks over a wealth of islands and rock outcrops. But the real jewel in the region's crown, indeed perhaps for the whole peninsula, is the amazing **Cathedral Cove**, which guards the **Te Whanganui-A-Hei Marine Reserve**; watching the sunrise here is an unforgettable experience. Access is by boat or a half-hour walk. The track starts from a glorious lookout point just north of Hahei on Grange Road. Tracts of native bush and pine have to be negotiated before the path falls, almost literally, to the beach. It is actually two beaches connected by a natural rock arch (negotiable at low tide). There are sandstone pinnacles on both beaches, with the highest pinnacle, Sail Rock, on the western beach. Although the beach can get very busy it offers great sunbathing, swimming and scenery, and it is very difficult to drag yourself away.

About 15 km south of Hahei is **Hot Water Beach** where you can dig a hole in the sand to access natural hot water. You can only do this for about two hours each side of low tide. Once filled, you can settle in to read a book or watch the surfers doing what you can't. The beach in itself is very pleasant, but be warned: it is also very dangerous with notorious rips. The **Hot Water Beach Store** hires out spades for $5. Once suitably boiled or if you did not time the tides right, then pop your head into the **Moko Art Gallery** ⓘ *24 Pye Pl*, just opposite the main car park. The arts and crafts are reasonably priced, very Kiwi and top class.

Tairua and Pauanui → *Colour map 2, B3*

Only the Tairua Harbour and a resulting 20-km road trip separate these deeply contrasting communities. **Tairua**, which was settled as a milling and farming town, is the older, smaller and more accessible of the two, situated on SH25. **Pauanui**, in contrast, is full of expensive holiday and retirement homes with fussy gardens, 4WDs and luxury watercraft. It's a place where men wear polyester shorts and knee-length nylon socks with fawn-coloured dress shoes, and the women sport the latest clinical blue-rinse hairdo. Not exactly the haunt of the happy-go-lucky traveller. Perhaps the best thing about the two towns is the setting and the memorable view from **Paku Hill** which dominates the harbour entrance. It can be accessed from the end of Tirinui Crescent off Paku Drive.

Opoutere

Opoutere is one of the Coromandel's best-kept secrets. It has a quiet and magical atmosphere with gorgeous sweeping white-sand **Ocean Beach**, guarded by the Wharekawa Harbour and a narrow tract of forest. At the tip of the sand spit is the **Wharekawa Wildlife Refuge**, where oystercatchers and rare New Zealand dotterel breed in summer. Special care should be taken not to enter this area and disturb the birds (dogs are strictly forbidden). The beach can be accessed from the car park around the corner from the **Opoutere Youth Hostel** (YHA), see page 205. While you are in the area it is also well worth your while visiting the unusual artworks of Guity and David Evelyn at the **Topadahil Studios** ⓘ *Opoutere Rd, T07-865 7266*.

Whangamata

Whangamata is a very popular holiday spot and the main **surfing** venue on the Coromandel. Well-serviced with luxury and budget accommodation, eateries and mainly water-based activities, it acts as a magnet to youngsters, especially at New Year. There are a number of good short coastal walks, while south of the town the **Wentworth and Parakiwai valleys** offer longer walks taking in remnants of the gold mining years and waterfalls. The often busy beach at Whangamata is over 4 km long, while the quieter **Whiritoa Beach** and lagoon, 12 km south of Whangamata, also offers a lovely bush walk, heading north. There is a quality **art and crafts trail** in the area (see VIC for details) and, like Tairua, Whangamata is also a base for trips to the outer islands, including **Mayor Island**. Before you leave Whangamata (from the north) be sure to duck in to **Whangamata Traders** ① *114 Port Rd*, where the copious and multifarious second-hand and antique goods are an attraction in themselves.

Waihi

Although gold mining once flourished all around the Coromandel, Waihi was in many ways the capital of operations, with 1200 mines producing half of the country's gold. The scale of operations earned Waihi the reputation as the most famous mining town in New Zealand. The town itself, although well-serviced, is nothing remarkable, but it boasts a heart of gold and seems to retain a sort of Wild West feel.

The most impressive evidence of the town's mining history is the enormous **Martha Mine** ① *Waihi Gold Mining Company, Barry Rd, T07-863 9880, www.martha mine.co.nz, guided tours most weekdays from $6*, which sits like a huge, but strangely discrete bomb crater right in the centre of town. The Martha Mine was one of the originals that reopened after a brief redundancy in the mid-1900s and is reputed to currently produce over NZ$1 million of gold and silver a week. Today, from a lookout behind the VIC, you can watch huge earth-moving trucks relentlessly winding their way in and out of the massive terraced hole.

The very reasonable admission charge aside, the **Waihi Arts Centre and Museum** ① *54 Kenny St, T07-863 8386, www.waihi.co.nz/arts/museum, Mon-Fri 1000-1600, Sat-Sun 1330-1600, $3, child $1*, is well worth a look. It displays an array of mining memorabilia and interesting working models, including a miniature stamping battery. Inevitably you leave a lot wiser about the incredible systems and network of tunnels that insidiously lies beneath your feet.

Nearby, the Ohinemuri River winds its dramatic way west, through the **Karangahake Gorge**, where there are a number of interesting walks and mining relics (DoC leaflet available from the VIC). A vintage steam train, the **Goldfields Railway** ① *T07-863 9020, www.waihirail.co.nz, trains leave from Wrigley St, daily at 1100, 1230, 1400, $15 return, child $8; café at Waikino station, daily 1000-1600*, runs 6.5 km (30 minutes) into the gorge from Waihi to **Waikino**.

There are also two wineries in the area, two golf courses and a generous collection of gardens, including the pretty **Waihi Waterlily Gardens** ① *Pukekauri Rd, T07-863 8267, daily in summer 1000-1600, $6*. If you want to go to the beach, head for the popular surfers' hangout at **Waihi Beach**, 11 km to the east. A pleasant 45-minute coastal walk at the northern end of the beach will take you to the very pretty **Orokawa Bay**.

Sleeping

Whitianga *p199, maps p200 and p204*
There is a huge range of accommodation in Whitianga to suit all tastes and budgets. The VIC has all the information and can pre-book, which is highly recommended in summer.

LL Villa Toscana, Ohuka Park, T07-866 2293, www.villatoscana.co.nz. A superb Italian-style villa set in an elevated position on 2 ha of native bush near the town. Enormous, fully self-contained designer suite has, not surprisingly, a distinct Italian feel, with 2 bedrooms, its own entrance and a deck that commands memorable views across the bay, replete with spa pool. In-house gourmet Italian cuisine (dinner $180), a legendary breakfast and an extensive personal wine cellar adds to the appeal.

LL-AL Villa Di Lusso, 5 Victoria St, T07-866 4397, www.traveloptions.co.nz. New luxury apartment option over-looking the estuary and marina.

L Silenco Lodge, T07-866 0304, gavin@enternet.co.nz. Out of town and set in 14 acres of bush. More affordable but still at the luxury end – spa, log fire, the works.

L-A Bailey's Motel, 66 Buffalo Beach Rd, T07-866 5500, www.baileysmotel.co.nz. At the mid to higher end of the market but comfortable, on the beachfront and close to town.

AL-C International Lodge, 4 White St, T07-866 0544, www.internationallodge.co.nz. New purpose-built lodge aimed at the 'flashpacker' market, offering 12 tidy, spacious rooms, some en suite. Free internet.

B Cosy Cat Cottage, 41 South Highway, T07-866 4488, www.cosycat.co.nz. A tidy cottage with a distinctly feline theme offering both B&B en suite rooms and a separate self-contained option. No dogs allowed!

C-D Cat's Pyjamas, 12 Albert St, T07-866 4663, www.cats-pyjamas.co.nz. The smallest of 3 back-packers in Whiti and a fine one to boot. Well-located right in the heart of town with all the usual choice of rooms (some en suite), as well as a cosy lounge with open fire.

C-D On the Beach Backpacker's Lodge (YHA), 46 Buffalo Beach Rd, T07-866 5380, www.coromandelbackpackers.co.nz. Overlooking the bay, standard and en suite doubles and dorms. Bike and kayak hire.

Motorcamps and campsites

Given the rapacious development that has happened in recent years, the town is surprisingly short of motor park facilities.

B-D Mercury Bay Motor Camp, 121 Albert St, T07-866 5579. Long-established, family orientated, the most convenient to the town centre. Camp kitchen.

Whitianga centre

School Rd • Eyre St • Springbok Av • Hannan Rd • Albert St • Esplanade • Mercury Bay • Library • Purangi Rd • FERRY LANDING • Wharf • Whitby Av • Simpson Pl • Kenneth Av • Mill St • Mercury Bay Museum • Passenger Ferry • Monk St • Bone Carving Studio • Cook Dr • Lee St • Cinema • Scenic & Historic Reserve • Coghill St • Blacksmith • Mary St • Isabella St • Campbell St • Supermarket • Bryce St • Owen St • Victoria St • Marina • Annette Pl • Whitianga Harbour • Dundas St

N
0 metres 200
0 yards 200

Sleeping
Cat's Pyjamas **3**
Mercury Bay Motor Camp **4**
Villa Di Lusso **1**

Eating
Café Nina **2**
Fireplace & Bar **5**
Salt **6**

Smitty's Bar & Grill **7**
Snapper Jacks **8**

Hahei *p202*

LL-AL Island View Villas , 11 Christine Terr,
T07-866 3247, view@paradise.net.nz. On the
hill on the southern end of the village, the
range of self-contained units and rooms are
immaculate and the views unforgettable.
Swimming pool and spa. Recommended.

AL Spellbound B&B, 77 Grange Rd, T07-866
3543, www.spellboundhahei.co.nz. At the
northern end of the village, with equally
good views as Island View Villas, above.
2 king/twin rooms and 1 queen, all en suites.

AL-A The Church, 87 Beach Rd, T07-866
3533, www.thechurchhahei.co.nz. As
the name suggests this accommodation/
restaurant combination is set in and around
a former village church. Accommodation
takes the form of attached wooden studio
units, separate studio or self-contained
cottages surrounding the church (restaurant)
and surrounded by private gardens. 2 of the
self-contained cottages have an open fire
adding to the cosy ambience. The licensed,
à la carte restaurant is a local favourite.

A-D Hahei Holiday Resort, Harsant Av, T07-
866 3889, www.haheiholidays.co.nz. Right
on the beach is this fine and spacious facility
with self-contained (beachfront) lodges and
backpacker accommodation. Camp kitchen.

A-D Tatahi Lodge, Grange Rd, T07-866
3992, www.dreamland.co.nz/tatahilodge.
Excellent motel and backpacker hostel
with 5 units and modern facilities, a short
stroll from the beach.

Hot Water Beach *p202*

L Hot Water Beach B&B, 48 Pye Pl, T07-
866 3991, www.hotwaterbedandbreak
fast.co.nz. Modern home looking right
across Hot Water Beach, with spa.

A Auntie Dawn's Place, 15 Radar Rd,
T07-866 3707, www.auntiedawn.co.nz.
A cheaper and friendly option with a couple
of self-contained flats and in-house B&B.

Tairua and Pauanui *p202*

LL Puka Park Lodge, Pauanui Beach, T07-
864 8088, www.pukapark.co.nz. Reputed to
provide the most luxurious accommodation
on the peninsula. Fine private bush chalets
with a restaurant and bar in the main lodge
house. Spa, pool and organized activities.

LL-D Slipper Island Resort, T021-776977,
www.slipper.co.nz. An opportunity to escape
the mainland to a private island with lodge,
self-contained chalets, tent sites and activities.

L Delicate, T07-864 8142, www.delli
cote.co.nz. An attractive, peaceful homestay
lodge set amidst an organic orchard and
gardens in the Rewarewa Valley. 3 very
attractive rooms with en-suites, guest
lounge. In-house cuisine. Recommended.

AL-A Pacific Harbour Lodge, Main Rd,
T07-864 8581, www.pacificharbour.co.nz.
One of the best motels, centrally
located with a good restaurant.

AL-A Pauanui Pines Motor Lodge,
174 Vista Paku, Pauanui Beach, T07-864
8086, www.pauanuipines.co.nz. A fine
award-winning motel in Pauanui.

C-D Pinnacles Backpackers, 305 Main
Rd, T07-864 8446, flying.dutchman.bp@
xtra.co.nz. A reputable alternative that
also offers tent sites.

C-D Tairua Beachhouse Backpackers,
342A Main Rd, T07-864 8313, Tairua
backpackers@xtra.co.nz. Centrally located
with spa and internet.

Opoutere *p202*

B-D Opoutere Youth Hostel (YHA),
T07-865 9072. A fine, peaceful place to
stay with great facilities, short walks nearby,
and a lovely view across the harbour.
Considered the best backpacker hostel in
the region. Recommended.

Whangamata *p203*

Consult the VIC (I-Site) and book in
advance in summer and New Year.

LL Brenton Lodge, 1 Brenton Pl, T/F07-865
8400, www.brentonlodge.co.nz. A gorgeous
bijou country retreat with 2 romantic
cottages, 1 en suite and lots of pampering.

LL Bushland Park Lodge, 444 Wentworth
Valley Rd, T07-865 7468, www.bushlandpark
lodge.co.nz. Another fine establishment in a
lovely location, European in style, emphasis
on health and a quality restaurant attached.

AL-A Palm Pacific Resort, 413 Port Rd,
T07-865 9211, www.palmpacificresort.co.nz.
A large modern motel in the centre of town
with tidy de luxe and standard units,
restaurant, pool, spas and sauna.

AL-A Pipinui Motel, 805 Martyn Rd, T07-
865 6796, www.pipinuimotel.co.nz. A new
motel set away from the main road and,
accordingly, quieter than the larger resorts.

There is a basic DoC campsite at Wentworth Valley, Wentworth Valley Rd ($7), T07-865 7032.
B-D Settlers Motor Camp Park, 101 Leander Rd, T07-865 8181. Usual facilities including camp kitchen.

Waihi p203

Waihi and Waihi Beach, 11 km to the east, are well-serviced with the full range of accommodation options.
A Goose Farm Cottage, Owahara Falls, Karangahake Gorge, T07-863 7944. Popular with honeymooners, self-contained, pretty.
A Sea Air Motel and Motor Park, Emerton Rd, Waihi Beach, T07-863 5655, www.sea-air.co.nz. Relatively new standard motel.
A Trout and Chicken B&B, 2 km from town, 9137 SH2, Waihi, T07-863 6964, www.trout andchicken.co.nz. Peaceful, modern B&B and self-contained studio set in an organic blueberry orchard.
B Chez Nous B&B, 41 Seddon St, T07-863 7538. Central and good value.

Motorcamps and campsites

A-D Waihi Beach Top Ten Holiday Park, 15 Main Beach Rd, Waihi Beach, T07-863 5504, www.waihibeach.com. Has some fine beachside cabins and sheltered campsites.
B-D Athenree Hot Springs and Holiday Park, Athenree Rd, T07-863 5600, www.athe nreehotsprings.co.nz. A little further field and offers all the usual with the added attraction of the natural (public) hot springs.
B-D Waihi Motor Camp, 6 Waitete Rd, T07-863 7654. Newly developed with chalets, log cabins, tent sites and camp kitchen. Good value.

● Eating

Whitianga p199, maps p200 and p204

Whiti is well-served with fine eating establishments; most offer a variety of fresh seafood; the best are along the Esplanade.
Café Nina, behind the VIC (I-Site) at 20 Victoria St, T07-866 5440, from 0800 and 1730 for dinner. The finest café in town. Small and bustling, it covers a great range of healthy and imaginative dishes.
Camellia Lodge Garden Café, corner of Golf Rd and South Highway, T07-866 2253,

daily 1000-1530. A bit out of town but worth the trip for lunch, it is set in a lovely garden.
Fireplace Restaurant and Bar, T07-866 4828, Wed-Sun for dinner. On the Esplanade, aesthetically the best with a lovely fire. Pizza and lamb a speciality.
Salt Restaurant, 1 Blacksmith Lane, T07-866 5818, daily from 1100. Overlooking the marina with good outdoor seating. Specializes in Pacific Rim and Thai cuisine.
Eggsentric Café and Restaurant, Purangi Rd, Flaxmill Bay (1 km east of Ferry Landing), T07-866 0307, daily for lunch and dinner Tue-Sun (closed in Aug). Without doubt the most colourful place around and at times the liveliest, whose artistic and multi-talented owners put on organized and often impromptu musical performances and poetry readings. Licensed and BYO.
Snapper Jacks, Albert St, T07-866 5482, daily from 1100. Reputedly the best fish and chips in town.
Smitty's Bar and Grill, 37 Albert St, T07-866 4647. For decent pub grub this is a good bet.

Hahei p202

The Church, 87 Beach Rd, T07-866 3797, www.thechurchhahei.co.nz, Thu-Tue. The talents of Swiss chef Andy Schuerch are extremely popular.
Café Luna, nearby at 1 Grange Rd, T07-866 3016, daily in summer from 0900 until late, reduced hours in winter. Great breakfast, $16.

Tairua and Pauanui p202

Puka Park Lodge (see Sleeping, page 205), bookings advised. The area's fine dining option.
Colenso Country Café, SH25, 12 mins north of Tairua, T07-866 3725, 1000-1700. A top spot for partaking in fine food.
Shells Restaurant, Main Rd, Tairua, T07-864 8811, Tue-Sat. Convenient for dinner.
Out of the Blue Café, Main Rd, Tairua, T07-864 8987, 0800-1600. Serves good coffee, imaginative lunches and snacks, and a fine breakfast.

Whangamata p203

Nickel Strausse, at Bushland Park Lodge (see Sleeping, page 205). Cosy, fine dining.
Oceanas, 328 Ocean Rd, T07-865 7157. Very 'fresh', a little more upmarket and the

place to head for those who like
seafood and Pacific Rim cuisine.
♥ Vibes Café, 638 Port Rd, T07-865 7121
Light lunches and the best coffee in town.

Waihi *p203*
¶¶ Chambers Wine Bar and Restaurant,
22 Haszard St, T07-863 7474, 1100-late.
Housed in the old 1904 Council Chambers
building, offering a mix of Mediterranean
and Antipodean dishes.
¶¶ Ti Tree Café, 14 Hazard St, T07-
863 7649. A local favourite.
¶¶ Waitete Orchard Café, Waitete Rd,
off SH2, T07-863 8980, daily 0830-1730.
Great lunch venue with organic flair,
fruit wines and ice cream.
¶¶-¶ The Porch, 23 Wilson Rd, T07-863
1330, daily lunch and dinner. Funky, South
Pacific-style café bar with cosy open fire.

▲ Activities and tours

Whitianga *p199, maps p200 and p204*
Cruising, fishing and scuba diving
There are numerous charters of all shapes
and sizes offering a wide range of trips from
fishing and diving to speedboat cruising out
into Mercury Bay and beyond. Bare in mind
that most coastal fishing charters charge
per boat rather than per person, so group
bookings are best, or be prepared to join
others. The best bet for fishing is to call at
the VIC (I-Site) and ask who is going out
on any particular day.
   The stunning coastal explorations
with **Hahei Explorer** is also well worth
considering (see Hahei page 208).
Cathedral Cove Dive, T07-866 3955,
www.hahei.co.nz/diving. Offers trips for
certified divers to the Te Whanganui-A-Hei
Marine Reserve off Cathedral Cove. The
scenery above water is equally stunning.
Cave Cruzer, T0800-427893/T025-866744,
www.cavecruzer.co.nz. The *Cave Cruzer* is a
rigid inflatable that can take you on a range of
tours around the bay from 1-3 hrs ($40-90),
taking in the main coastal sights including a
stop at Cathedral Cove and an evening trip
with a spot of cross Maori live music from $65.
Alternatives include older sailing vessels and
glass-bottomed boats to luxury speedboats.
The VIC can assist with the details.

Seafaris Glass Bottom Boat, T07-867 1962,
www.glassbottomboatwhitianga.co.nz. 2-hr
eco-tours to Cathedral Cove and around
with underwater viewing and snorkelling,
from $75, child $40.

Golf
Whitianga has a fine golf course located
about 4 km south of town, T07-866 5479.
Matarangi, north of Whitianga, is also an
excellent course, T07-866 5394.

Horse treks
Rangihau Ranch, Rangihau Rd, Coroglen,
T07-866 3875. Conventional treks.
Twin Oaks Riding Ranch, 9 km north
of Whitianga, T07-866 5388, www.twin
oaksridingranch.co.nz. Treks depart daily at
1000 and 1400 and 1800, 2 hrs from $35.

Kayaking/windsurfing/watersports
The coast, with its eroding sandstone
scenery and pohutukawa trees is ideal for
sea kayaking, and a trip in calm conditions
is highly recommended.
Banana Boat, T07-866 5617. If you want
to make a complete and utter Charlie of
yourself you should have a go on the 'Whiti
Banana Boat'. This is a large inflatable yellow
'phallus' that blats around the bay at high
speed, with you desperately trying to hold
on, is actually a great laugh. There are a
number of trip options including the 'Hell
Bender', the 'Thrill' and 'Kiddies Ride'.
Ask at the VIC for details.
Cathedral Cove Sea Kayakings, T07-866
3877, www.seakayaktours.co.nz. Based in
Hahei, offers kayak hire and half- or full-day
kayak trips at $75 with all equipment
provided. Courtesy transport to/from
Whitianga Ferry. Recommended.
Seafari, T07-866 0677. Windsurfing tuition.

Ropes course
High Zone, south of Whitianga near the 309
Rd turning, T07-866 2113, www.highzone.
co.nz. 'Hang around' like a chimp with their
14-m adventure ropes course. From $10-60.

Hahei *p202*
A trip here can combine with your own
explorations of Cathedral Cove by foot, perhaps
followed by some swimming and sunbathing.

Hahei Explorer Tours, T07-866 3910, haheiexplorer@paradise.net.nz. If you want to experience Cathedral Cove from the water, this is an excellent trip. Daily scenic trips on board a nippy inflatable cost $59, child $35, for 1 hr. The tour also takes in caves and a blowhole not accessible by foot.

Tairua and Pauanui *p202*

There are a number of attractive water-based activities operating mainly out of Tairua, a fine surf beach at Pauanui and the popular *Broken Hills Recreation Area walks* (leaflet from VIC (I-Site).
Dive Tairua, Tairua, T07-864 8054, www.dive tairua.co.nz. Good-value dive trips to the Alderman Islands, courses and lodging. Also offers independent kayak hire from $20 per hour, or $60 per day.
Pine Treks, T07-864 7078. Horse trekking, suitable for beginners.

Whangamata *p203*

Whangamata VIC can book the numerous water-based trips and activities on offer.
Kiwi Dundee Adventures, T07-865 8809, www.kiwidundee.co.nz. A well-established operator offering an extensive and imaginative range of eco-tours from 1-5 days, taking in natural sights and gold mining remnants, from $200.

Surfing

Whangamata's oldest surf shop **Saltwater**, 505 Port Rd, T07-865 8666 and the

Whangamata Surf School, T07-865 6879, are the focus for the latest surfers' gossip and board hire.

Waihi *p203*
Surfing
Learn to Surf, T07-863 4587. The local outfit providing the very entertaining opportunity of learning to stand on a surf board for more than 3 nanoseconds.

⊖ Transport

Whitianga *p199, maps p200 and p204*
Bicycle hire
Bike Man,15 Coghill St, Whitianga, T07-866 0745, from $35 per day.

Taxi and shuttles
Mercury Bay Taxis, Whitianga, T09-866 4141. Go Kiwi Shuttles, T0800-446549/ T07-866 0336, www.go- kiwi.co.nz, offers tours and shuttles to Hahei and Hot Water Beach from $35.

⊕ Directory

Whitianga *p199, maps p200 and p204*
Internet Bartley Graphics, 706 Port Rd, Whangamata, T07-865 8832. **Inter Earth**, Shop 14, Blacksmith Lane, Whitianga, T07-866 5991, Mon-Fri 0900-1700, Sat 1000-1600 (extended hours in summer).

The Waikato

⁝ Footprint features

Introduction

The Waikato is one of the country's richest agricultural areas, where the eponymous river – the longest in the country – snakes its way through a landscape of green rolling hills and fields. The Waikato, the homeland of the Tainui people – one of the largest tribes in the land – is rich in Maori history, as well as being home to the current Maori queen and head of state. The first Maori king was elected here in 1858 and the subsequent formation of the Maori King Movement, in direct opposition to rule under the British monarchy, led to much bloodshed. After almost a year of fierce battles and confrontation the British finally quashed the Kingites, who fled to southern Waikato, which is now also known as King Country. Today, peace reigns, but the memory lives on.

Waikato also boasts New Zealand's fourth largest city, Hamilton, which despite being an unremarkable commercial centre, is increasingly seen as an alternative base to Auckland. Although not a major tourist destination, the Waikato is a region with considerable diversity from the famous surf beaches on its coast to the jewel in the crown of the King Country, the Waitomo District – a wonderland of limestone caves and subterranean activities that deservedly make it one of the North Island's premier tourist attractions. Also of note, since the abiding success of the film *Lord of the Rings*, is the small agricultural town of Matamata, where local farmland was used to create the set of 'Hobbiton', home of Frodo and friends. Although very little remains, it is still the first stop on the 'tour of homage' for *Lord of the Rings* fanatics.

★ Don't miss ...

1 **Raglan** Dream about VW Beetles and 'left-hand breaks' with the surfies in this laid-back seaside resort, page 220.
2 **Kiwi House** Encounter a kiwi, a kea or a kokako at Otorohanga's famous bird park, page 224.
3 **Waitomo Village** Hug an angora rabbit or see the highly entertaining agricultural show at Woodlyn Park, page 224.
4 **Waitomo caves** Head underground in style with the Haggas Honking Holes or descend 100 m into the awe-inspiring Lost World, pages 224 and 229.
5 **Kawhia** Take the back roads from Waitomo to this intriguing coastal village, stopping at the misty Marokopa Falls on the way, page 227.
6 **Mount Te Aroha** Climb the mountain for a spectacular 360° view, then take a well-earned relaxing dip in a hot pool in the Te Aroha Domain, page 231.

The Waikato Introduction

Hamilton and Waikato North

→ *Colour map 2, B2 Population: 120,000*

Perched on the serpentine banks of the famous Waikato River, 129 km south of Auckland, Hamilton is the main service centre for the rich fertile agricultural region of the Waikato. Being so close to the major tourist destinations of Auckland and Rotorua, the city struggles to attract visitors for any length of time as it has few major attractions. It is, however, ideally located for explorations around the Waikato Region and can be used as base for exploring the North Island. Hamilton is also a university town and plays host to some major national events including the annual National Agricultural Field Days in June and the colourful Balloon over Waikato in April. Visitors stopping briefly in the city can enjoy a ride down the Waikato on the MV Waipa Delta paddleboat and visit the celebrated museum, gardens and 'Free-flight Aviary' of Hamilton Zoo. ►► *For Sleeping, Eating and other listings, see pages 215-218.*

Ins and outs

Getting there and around

Air Hamilton has a busy international **airport**① *15 km south of the city, T07-848 9027, www.hamiltonairport.co.nz.* **Freedom Air**, To800-600500, www.freedomair.com, flies regularly from eastern Australia; **Air New Zealand**, To800-737000/T07-839 9835, www.airnewzealand.co.nz, services all the major domestic destinations. A shuttle into the city costs about $12, T07-843 7778.

Road Hamilton is on the SH1 and is well serviced north and south by **Intercity** and **Newmans**, To9-913 6200. There are also buses from Auckland, Northland, Rotorua and New Plymouth with **Northliner**, To9-438 3206, **Pavlovich**, To9-302 2645 and **Dalroy's**, To6-759 0197/To508-465622, www.dalroytours.co.nz. For internet fares throughout the North Island try **Nakedbus.com**. All buses arrive and depart from the **Transport Centre** ① *corner of Bryce and Anglesea sts, T07-834 3457/T07-839 3580, Mon-Thu 0715-1730, Fri 0715-1845, Sat 0900-1645, Sun 0900-1845.* It has a café, internet and also is home to the VIC (I-Site). For information on local bus services, contact **Busit**, To800-4287 5463, www.busit.co.nz.

Both SH1 and the main Auckland to Wellington trunk rail line run through the heart of the Waikato. An alternative route south is SH27, which branches off SH1 just south of Auckland at the Bombay Hills and also accesses Waikato East. SH27 passes through Matamata before rejoining SH1 again at Tirau. The principal signposted touring route is called the 'Thermal Explorer Highway', from Auckland via Hamilton, Rotorua and Taupo to Napier. A free touring map is available from all major VICs, www.thermalnz.co.nz.

Train Hamilton is on the main trunk 'Overlander' rail line with services daily to Auckland, Wellington, Rotorua and Tauranga, To800-872467, www.tranzscenic.co.nz. The **train station** is on Fraser Street, in Frankton.

Tourist information and orientation

Hamilton VIC (I-Site) ① *Hamilton Transport Centre, corner of Bryce and Anglesea sts, T07-839 3580, www.visithamilton.co.nz, www.waikatonz.co.nz, Mon-Thu 0715-1730, Fri 0715-1845, Sat 0900-1645, Sun 0930-1845.* **DoC** ① *5 Northway St, T07-838 3363.* For information regarding the Waikato North region, contact **Huntly VIC (I-Site)** ① *next to the river on 160 Great South Rd, SH1, Huntly, T07-828 6406, Mon-Fri 0900-1700, Sat-Sun 0900-1500.*

Background

The earliest recorded settlers in the Hamilton area were Maori from the Tainui *waka* (canoe) that settled on the banks of the river. At that time, the Waikato River was the major means of communication, transportation and trade with other settled areas. In the 1860s the first Europeans began to settle, during the Land Wars and the notorious '*raupatu*' or land confiscations. A military outpost was established in Hamilton East and existed for a number of years before communications and relations improved and agriculture developed. In 1867 the road was opened to Auckland, followed 10 years later by the railway. From that point on settlement began in earnest and the city developed as a major agricultural service centre. The town was named in honour of Captain John Charles Fane Hamilton, the commander of *HMS Esk*, who was killed while leading the naval brigade at the Battle of Gate *pa* near Tauranga in 1864.

Hamilton 🍴🍷🏠🛏️❄️⭐️📷🏧🛍️ ⇝ *pp215-218.*

The modern **Waikato Museum of Art and History** ⓘ *1 Grantham St, (south end of Victoria St), T07-838 6606, www.waikatomuseum.org.nz, daily 1000-1630, $2; special exhibitions $12, child $6,* overlooks the river. It presents a wide-ranging programme of both permanent and temporary exhibitions, including a balance of contemporary and historical art of regional significance and national importance. The history of Hamilton is explored with a particularly impressive collection of Tainui Maori *taonga* (treasures). The highlight of the collection has to be the beautiful, carved and decorated *waka*, 'Te Wainika', given to the museum in 1973 by Te Arikinui Dame Te Atairangikaahu, the Maori Queen. There is also an adjunct science and technology centre, which offers all the usual whizz-bang earthquake simulation stuff. It's great for little kids and big kids alike. There is also a fine café/restaurant, selling interesting fare such as ostrich antipasto and kangaroo loin, amongst other things. **Arts Post Galleries** ⓘ *120 Victoria St, T07-838 6928, daily 1000-1630,* runs in conjunction with the museum and focuses on existing and emerging local artists with three exhibition spaces.

While near the river it is worth taking a stroll to soak up the almost English atmosphere, with its rowboats and pleasant gardens. On the eastern bank, just across from the museum, is the historic paddleboat, **MV Waipa Delta** ⓘ *T0800-472335, www.waipadelta.co.nz,* the original of which first plied the Waikato in 1876. It now runs various cruises: lunch cruise ($45), coffee cruise ($20) and dinner cruise ($59).

Just south of the city centre and east of Cobham Bridge are the celebrated **Hamilton Gardens** ⓘ *T07-856 3200, 0730-sunset, visitor centre 1000-1600, free.* These are a conglomerate of Japanese, Chinese and English flower gardens, mixed with numerous smaller and more traditional themed displays. The gardens also have a popular café/restaurant. The VIC (I-Site) has a free and comprehensive *Heritage Trail* leaflet, another outlining *Hamilton's Walkways* and the *Waikato Vintage Wine Trail.*

Hamilton Zoo ⓘ *T07-838 6720, www.hamiltonzoo.co.nz, daily 0900-1700, extended hours in Jan, $10, child $5,* is 8 km from the city centre (take the SH23 Raglan Road, turn right onto Newcastle Road, then go straight ahead down Brymer). Modern and progressive in its outlook, the zoo not only acts as a major attraction, but also attempts to mix a considerable collection of native New Zealand species with others important to international conservation breeding programmes. The highlight is the 3800-sq-m, walk-through 'free-flight aviary', which houses 10 species of indigenous, rare and endangered New Zealand birds within a native bush setting. Other attractions include the Sumatran tigers, and the 'Waikato Wetlands' and 'Out of Africa' exhibits. The latest edition is Mototo the white rhino, who has won many hearts, although not quite as many as the very grumpy Kune pig in the centre of the park.

⁞ Te Kooti

Te Kooti – or Rikirangi Te Turuki – (1830-1893) could arguably be considered the William Wallace (*Braveheart*) of Maoridom. Although the battles were less bloody and his death far less gruesome, his resolve and integrity (or *mana*) was certainly on a par with the great Scot.

Born near Gisborne, of a good family but of no particular chiefly rank, he was given a sound education at the Waerenga-a-hika Mission School before becoming a horse-breaker and later, a seaman on a small schooner trading the east coast of the North Island. During the Maori uprising and siege of Waerenga-a-hika in 1865, Te Kooti actually supported the *pakeha*, but was accused of supplying the Hauhau Maori rebels with ammunition and intelligence regarding the positions of colonial Government troops.

Without trial and after being essentially set up by a local *pakeha*-allied Maori chief, he was exiled to the Chatham Islands with a group of Hauhau rebels in 1866. Te Kooti had constantly protested his innocence, but his claims were ignored. During his two years on the Chathams Te Kooti studied the New Testament and, after claiming he had experienced a Divine revelation, established the tenets of his own 'Ringatu' faith. Convinced that the government had no intention of releasing him, Te Kooti and a small group of other exiles captured a ship and forced the crew to take them back to the east coast of the North Island. Now a fugitive and considered dangerous, he was immediately pursued by government forces. Again, after writing to the government and claiming his innocence, his protestations were ignored. Given little choice, Te Kooti had to fight and, gathering considerable support, he did so with a vengeance.

In a fierce battle at Matawhero against a large force commanded by Colonel Whitmore, he and his men killed 33 Europeans and 37 allied Maori. Still outnumbered and closely pursued he retreated to the Urewera Forest. Ropata Wahawaha, who was a Maori chief allied to Whitmore, executed 120 of Te Kooti's men. For the following three years Te Kooti was relentlessly pursued and harried not only by government forces, but also European colonials and allied Maori tribes. When battles ensued Te Kooti fought with courage or always managed cleverly to elude his enemies. In 1872 he sought refuge in the Waikato where the Maori 'King Movement' had been established by fellow Maori rebels. There he spent much time peacefully, still proclaiming his original innocence as well as consolidating and spreading the word of his Ringatu religion.

Te Kooti was finally pardoned in 1883 and died back on the east coast, 10 years later – a free man. To this day his Ringatu religion lives on in the Bay of Plenty and his memory in the hearts of all Maori.

Waikato North

Ngaruawahia → *Colour map 2, B1*

Nineteen kilometres north of Hamilton, Ngaruawahia is the Maori capital of New Zealand. It is home to the Maori Queen, Te Atairangikaahu (first queen and sixth person to hold office), and one of the best and most significant *maraes* in the country: the **Turangawaewae marae**, beside the river on River Road, and only open once a year in March, during the annual regatta, when a number of *waka* (canoes) are displayed on the river. (The town is located where the Waipa meets the mighty Waikato.)

Another point of interest in Ngaruawahia is the **Mahinarangi House**, built in 1929. It is beautifully carved both inside and out, with the royal coat of arms on the giant doors, entitled 'Te Paki O Matariki', announcing the hope of peace and calm between Maori and *pakeha*. Next door is the Queen's official residence. Ngaruawahia also has a number of good walks including the **Hakarimata Walkways** and **Taupiri Mountain**, the site of the Waikato's most sacred burial ground. If you fancy a well-deserved hot soak after your walk or explorations of the town you might like to head 23 km west to the **Waingaro Hot Springs** ① *T07-825 4761, 0900-2130, $8,* featuring large thermal mineral pools and spas. Motor park accommodation is also available.

Huntly and around

With its power station and the slow-moving muddy waters of the Waikato, Huntly is not a pretty place. The underground coal reserves are the largest in New Zealand and the power station produces 20 per cent of the country's needs. However, the new **National Coal Museum** ① *26 Harlock St, T07-828 8128,* displaying local and national mining history, may tempt you to linger.

In direct contrast to the man-made gloom of Huntly are the numerous lakes and wetlands that surround the town. These are popular for water sports and birdwatching. For a detailed description of the lakes and walks ask for the DoC leaflet *Waikato Wetlands* at the Huntly VIC or DoC in Hamilton. If you have kids and can bear it, **Candyland** ① *75 Henry Rd, 15 mins southeast of Huntly in Taupiri, T07-824 6818, www.candyland .co.nz, daily 1000-1700,* is the largest sweet shop in New Zealand. Candy making shows are offered on weekends at 1030 and 1300, adult $8, child $5.

> ⁞ *The SH1, both north and south of Huntly, is a notorious accident black spot, so drive with care.*

Te Kauwhata → *Colour map 2, B2*

The main attraction in this mainly grape-growing area is the **Rangiriri Battle Site Heritage Centre** ① *T07-826 3663, 0900-1700, free,* which sits just off the SH1 next to the Rangiriri Hotel (a congenial, old-fashioned country pub that offers a fine pub lunch). Although the place seems to function more as a roadside café than anything else, there is some memorabilia and an information office where you can arrange to see an audio-visual display. The battle that took place in Rangiriri in 1863 was one of the bloodiest of the Maori Land Wars and involved a small group of Maori who made a brave stand against the numerically superior British forces. The remains of the redoubts from which they fought still survive, as does the cemetery. There are also two **vineyards** here: Cooks Landing ① *Paddy's Rd, T07-826 0004, www.cookslanding.co.nz,* with a café, restaurant, wine-tasting tours and direct sales daily; and Rongopai Wines ① *55 Te Kauwhata Rd, T07-826 3981, www.rongopaiwines.co.nz, tasting and sales Mon-Fri.*

◉ Sleeping

Hamilton *p212, map p216*
Hamilton has plenty of mid-range options and it is not usually necessary to pre-book. Ulster St, just north of the city centre, is the main motel drag and there is certainly plenty of choice. But there are not many B&Bs in Hamilton. The VIC (I-Site) has full listings.
LL-L Novotel Tainui Hotel, 7 Alma St, T07-838 1366, www.accorhotels.co.nz. The city's best located hotel is great value for money. Standard 4-star facilities. Some rooms have views across the river. The inhouse café/restaurant offers indoor and outdoor à la

carte dining, again with pleasant views. Spa and sauna. Secure, valet parking.
L Narrows Landing, 431 Airport Rd, Tamahere, T07-858 4001, www.thenarrows landing.co.nz. Near the airport, offers self-contained accommodation, with country views and a fine restaurant attached.
L-A Ambassador Motor Inn, 86 Ulster St, T07-839 5111, www.silveroaks.co.nz. A short walk from the river, with a restaurant attached.
L-A Barclay Motel, 280 Ulster St, T07-838 2475, www.barclay.co.nz. All mod cons including spa facilities.

L-A Chloe's, 181 Ulster St, T07-839 3410, www.chloes.co.nz. Has a restaurant adjacent. **L-A Sails Motel**, 272 Ulster St, T07-838 2733, www.sails-motorinn.co.nz. Spa facilities.

AL-A Ventura Inn and Suites, 23 Clarence St, T07-838 0110, www.venturainns.co.nz. One of Hamilton's newest hotels in a quiet position, on the fringe of the CBD. Standard rooms, de luxe studios (king-sized bed and

Hamilton

N

0 metres 200
0 yards 200

Sleeping
Ambassador Motor Inn **2**
Barclay Motel **11**
Cedar Lodge **3**
Chloe's **4**
Eagles Nest Backpackers **6**
Hamilton City
  Holiday Park **13**

Hamilton East
  Motor Camp **9**
J's Backpackers **12**
Narrows Landing **1**
Novotel Tainui **8**
Sails Motel **10**
Ventura Inn & Suites **5**

Eating
Bank Bar & Brasserie **1**
Barzurk Pizza Bar **3**
Iguana **11**
Museum Café/Restaurant **2**
Sahara Tent Café & Bar **4**
Scott's Epicurean **5**
Tables on the River **6**

spa) and standard suites (king-sized bed, pull-out sofa and kitchenette) available. No in-house restaurant, but some of the city's best are within a short stroll.

Bars & clubs 🌀
Biddy Mulligan's **7**
Fox & Hounds **8**
Loaded Hog **9**
Outback, Loft & Diggers **10**

B Cedar Lodge, 174 Ulster St, T07-839 5569, www.cedarlodge.co.nz. One of the cheapest on Ulster St.

C-D Eagles Nest Backpackers, 937 Victoria St, T07-838 2704 A relatively new establishment that seems to enjoy a good reputation. Centrally located and spotless.

C-D J's Backpackers, 8 Grey St, T07-856 8934, www.Jsbackpackers.co.nz. A long established suburban offering with comfortable dorms, twins and doubles. Also organizes trips.

Motorcamps and campsites
There are 2 basic motorcamps with camping facilities in East Hamilton, 3 km from town:
C-D Hamilton City Holiday Park, 14 Ruakura Rd, T07-855 8255, www.hamiltoncityholidaypark.co.nz.
C-D Hamilton East Motor Camp, 61 Cameron Rd, T07-856 6220. Camp kitchen.

🍴 Eating

Hamilton *p212, map p216*
Hamilton boasts an amazing number of café/restaurants (mainly along the southern end of Victoria St), all trying to outdo each other in interior design, theme and cuisine.
🍴🍴 **The Bank Bar and Brasserie**, corner of Hood and Victoria sts, further south, T07-839 4740, Sun-Thu 1100-2300, Fri-Sat 1100-0300. A local favourite, especially with the suits at lunchtime and trend-setters at night. Generous servings.
🍴🍴 **Iguana**, Victoria St, T07-834 2280, www.iguana.net.nz, Mon-Wed 1000-late, Thu-Sun 1000-0300. A well-established, spacious favourite, with a wide-ranging mainly Pacific Rim menu and excellent gourmet pizza. The bar is popular which adds to the establishment's lively atmosphere.
🍴🍴 **Tables on the River**, 12 Alma St, T07-839 6555, Mon-Fri from 1130, Sat from 1730. A regional award winner overlooking the river. International and traditional Kiwi fare.
🍴 **Café Alma**, in the **Novotel Tainui Hotel**, see Sleeping page 215.)
🍴🍴 **Museum Café/Restaurant**, Grantham St, T07-839 7209, daily from 1030, Tue-Sat dinner from 1800. You can't go far wrong here, with an eclectic menu. Jazz on Thu.
🍴 **The Sahara Tent Café and Bar**, 254 Victoria St, T07-834 0409. A Middle Eastern-style eatery, which is worth seeing, never mind eating in.

¶ **Scott's Epicurean**, 181 Victoria St, T07-839 6680. A funky little café with a highly imaginative lunch/brunch menu. ¶ **Barzurk Pizza Bar**, 250 Victoria St, T07-834 2363, daily, 1200-late. Recommended for gourmet pizza.

❶ Pubs, bars and clubs

Hamilton *p212, map p216*
With so many trendy bars and restaurants Hamilton enjoys a lively and friendly social scene and if you mingle with the locals it will probably be a long and interesting night.

For a traditional Irish pub with live bands at the weekend **Biddy Mulligan's**, 742 Victoria St, T07-834 0306, is a good bet. Another favourite is the **Fox and Hounds**, corner Victoria and Alama sts. **The Bank**, corner of Hood St, or the **Loaded Hog**, 27 Hood St, are the places for trendsetters to be, particularly at weekends, when you can rip your tights and shake your pants to dance music.

For more traditional Kiwi pub atmosphere and for younger crowds, try **Outback**, **Loft** or **Diggers Bar**, all on Hood St.

❷ Entertainment

Hamilton *p212, map p216*
Casino
Hamilton has succumbed and now has its own casino, the main focus within the flash **Sky City Hamilton Riverside Entertainment Centre**, 346 Victoria St, T07-834 4900, www.skycityhamilton.co.nz, daily 1100-0300. Minimum age 20, smart casual dress.

Theatres
For information and bookings contact the VIC (I-Site) or **Theatre Services**, T07-838 6600. **The Founders**, 221 Tristram St, T07-838 6603. Opera, ballet/dance and musicals. **Meteor**, 1 Victoria St, T07-838 6603. The smallest. Drama, dance, bands and comedy. **Westpac Community Theatre**, 59 Clarence St, T07-838 6603. Drama, ballet/dance, concerts, musicals and comedy.

❸ Festivals and events

Hamilton *p212, map p216*
Mar Ngaruawahia Maori Regatta, 12 km north of Hamilton. Held annually for over 100 years, the regatta celebrates Maori culture. Replicas of *waka* are rowed by Maori in native dress, attracting 30,000 people. **Jun** Fieldays Agricultural Show, www.fieldays.co.nz. Held middle weekend.

❹ Shopping

Hamilton *p212, map p216*
Shopping centres include: **Hamilton Central Shopping Centre**; **Westfield Shopping Centre**, corner of Hukanui and Comries Rd, Chartwell,; **Downtown Plaza**; and **Centreplace Shopping Centre**. **Crow's Nest Books**, Worley Pl. A good second-hand bookshop. **New Zealand World**, 24 Garden Pl. For New Zealand souvenirs. **R&R Sports**, 943 Victoria St, T0800-777767/ T07-839 3755. Has a wide range of outdoor equipment for sale and hire including skis, hiking boots, wetsuits, surfboards and kayaks.

❺ Activities and tours

Hamilton *p212, map p216*
The Waikato countryside lends itself to hot-air ballooning and indeed hosts the high profile **Balloons Over Waikato Festival** every Apr. **Kiwi Balloon Company**, T021-623595, www.kiwiballooncompany.co.nz. The main operator in the region, with flights from $275.

❻ Transport

Hamilton *p212, map p216*
Bicycle hire R&R Sports (see Shopping) or Bike Barn, corner of Ulster and Liverpool sts, T07-838 0575. **Car hire** Rent-A-Dent and First Choice, 383 Anglesea St, T07-839 1049. Waikato Car Rentals, Brooklyn Rd, T07-855 0094. **Taxi** Hamilton Taxi Society, T07-847 7477, T0800-477477.

❼ Directory

Hamilton *p212, map p216*
Banks The main banks are found on Victoria St, most offer foreign exchange. **Internet** Numerous locations. Also the VIC (I-Site) and the library on Garden Pl. **Medical services** Victoria Central Medical Clinic, 750 Victoria St, T07-834 0333. **Post office** 36 Bryce St, T07-838 2233, Mon-Fri 0800-1700, Sat 0900-1400.

Waikato Coast

..*ith the well-advertised attractions of Waitomo and its caves, the Waikato Coas. seldom features very high on the average travelling agenda. Indeed, after some unique subterranean adventures most simply pass through the Waikato on their way south, or east to the capital of all things thermal – Rotorua. But for those with more time, who wish to ride a world-class 'left-hand break', or who simply wish to get off the beaten track, then the Waikato Coast offers some pleasant surprises. The small laid-back coastal village of Raglan, 50 km west of Hamilton, offers a palpable sense of relaxation, not to mention plenty of the aforementioned and near legendary surf breaks. Further south, a diversion off SH1 to the remote coastal village of Kawhia, and back via the Marakopa Falls to Waitomo, can be a relaxing, scenic and often solitary highlight.* ▸▸ For Sleeping, Eating and other listings, see pages 220-222.*

Ins and outs

Getting there and around The drive to Kawhia from anywhere is quite arduous but scenic. If you are peckish be sure to stop for a homemade pie at the **Oparau petrol station** (T07-871 0683, 0600-2200). Raglan is 48 km from Hamilton. The commuter-orientated **Hamilton Busit**, T07-847 5343/T0800-4287 5463, offers daily services (three times daily Monday to Friday, twice daily at weekends) to Raglan, departing from Hamilton Transport Centre for $12 return (first at 0930). In Raglan, buses stop at the VIC. For a taxi in Raglan, T07-825 0506.

Tourist information The **Kawhia Museum** ⓘ T07-871 0161, www.kingcountry.co.nz, www.kawhia.co.nz, operates as a VIC. The **Raglan VIC** ⓘ 4 Wallis St, T07-825 0556, daily 0900-1700, www.raglan.net.nz, www.raglan.org.nz, is small but highly efficient.

Kawhia → *Colour map 2, B1*

Outside the summer influx of mainly domestic holidaymakers, when the population almost triples, Kawhia (pronounced 'Kafia') is a sleepy, fairly unremarkable, coastal village on the shores of the Kawhia Harbour southwest of Hamilton. But perhaps due to its remote location and nature's rich pickings, Kawhia seems in no hurry to announce itself as anything more spectacular, and has the contented atmosphere of a place entirely happy with its lot. And it would seem that this has always been the case. Kawhia (which actually translates as 'place of abundance') was home to the Tainui people who first arrived here some 750 years ago. So happy were they with the place and its natural provision, that it took them over 300 years before heading inland to settle other parts of the Waikato. Even then, it was only through inter-tribal disputes, which ironically were over the abundant fishing grounds.

Most of Kawhia's points of interest are on the shoreline in the town and extending around to the harbour entrance and **Ocean Beach**. This is the most popular beach with summer visitors and it is best accessed through the Tainui Kawhia Forest Track southwest of the town centre. Ocean Beach boasts the **Puia Hot Springs** (a far less commercial echo of Hot Water Beach in Coromandel). Here, too, you can dig your own 'spa bath' in the sand, but it's difficult to know where exactly to do this, especially in the off-season. It is perhaps best to join a local tour to access the best spots (see page 222). Back in town if you want to immerse yourself in Kawhia's interesting history and learn more about the Tainui landing, the small **Kawhia Museum** ⓘ T07-871 0161, www.kawhia.co.nz, Oct-Apr Wed-Sun 1200-1600, or by appointment, free, which sits next to the wharf, will proudly oblige. The *Best of the West* Heritage leaflet will pinpoint and explain specific sites.

When the Tainui people first made landfall they tied their canoe to a pohutukawa tree and named it **Tangi-te-Korowhiti**. Although the specific tree is not marked, it is one of a small grove at the northern end of Kaora Street. What is marked is the site of its burial with two stones – **Hani** and **Puna** – which can be seen behind the **Maketu marae** about 500 m south of the landing site (ask for permission at the *marae* to see them).

Raglan → *Colour map 2, B1*

Raglan is the Waikato's main seaside resort and is internationally renowned for its fine surfing. So when you arrive in the heart of the village, with its palm trees and laid-back cafés, don't be surprised if you end up being sandwiched in a queue or sharing your lunch table with a colourful length of fibreglass with 'Ride 'em Baby', 'The Big Phallus' or 'No Fear' written on it. In Raglan these strange, almost religious objects seem to make up half the population. The village itself is on the quiet Raglan Harbour with all the surf action on beaches a short drive away heading west. One of those beaches – Manu Bay – has apparently one of the best left-hand breaks in the world.

The main attractions around Raglan are its beaches, the most convenient and safest for swimming being **Te Kopua**, which borders the Raglan campground. Access is via the camp access road west, or across the footbridge at the end of Bow Street in the centre of the village. All the main surf beaches are west of town. **Ocean Beach** is the first and as well as surfing, it is also popular for swimming and the view across the 'Raglan Bar' (harbour entrance). Access is off Wainui Reserve Road via a walking track. Surf lifesavers operate in summer and, as always, you must swim between the flags. The next beach is **Manu Bay**, with its famous left-hand break, the best spot to surf or spectate. Further still is **Whale Bay**, which is a great spot for both surfers and the uninitiated, but it can only be accessed over rocks.

For wild coastal scenery **Ruapuke Beach** is popular but remote. Follow the old coast road (taking in the impressive **Te Toto Gorge** on the way), then follow Ruapuke Beach Road and walk from there. Other beaches near the town that are safe and child-friendly include **Cox's Bay** (accessible from Bayview Road and Daisy Street or the walkway along Government Road) and **Puriri Park** (Aro Aro Bay) at the end of Wallis Street.

If you are interested in local history the small **Raglan and District Museum** ① *22 Kaitoke St, T07-825 7195, weekends 1300-1530, donation*, has mainly European material. Further afield on SH23 are the aptly named 55-m **Bridal Veil Falls**, which are a bit of a trek but worth it, particularly after heavy rain. If the 756-m summit of **Mount Karioi** beckons it is best accessed from Te Toto Gorge, 12 km southwest (see above). There are fine views from the top; allow six hours. It is known by the Maori as 'the sleeping lady', the reason for which is obvious if you study its outline.

● Sleeping

Kawhia *p219*
B Blue Chook Inn, Jervois St, T07-871 0778. A congenial little place with 2 self-contained units and a 3-bedroom villa.
B Kawhia Motel, corner of Jervois and Tainui sts, T07-871 0865. Basic but central.

Motorcamps and campsites
B-D Kawhia Beachside S-Cape, 225 Pouewe St, as you come into town, T07-871 0727, www.kawhiabeachside scape.co.nz. The usual range of motorcamp accommodation including a self-contained

cottage and backpacker facilities. Bike and kayak hire. Good camp kitchen.
B-D Kawhia Camp Ground, 73 Moke St, T07-871 0863, www.kawhiacampingground.co.nz. Reputable and popular motor/camping ground, it has cabins as well as powered, non-powered sites and internet access. Also offers 4WD trips to the hot springs.

Raglan *p220*
Raglan has plenty of options with many self-contained and pitched at the quiet retreat/weekend getaway market. Ask at the

VIC or visit www.raglan.net.nz. Note
that the surf school and horse trekking
operators offer accommodation packages.
LL-L Solitude Lodge, 349 Wainui Rd,
T07-825 8045, www.solitude.co.nz. Stands
out for both character and sheer peace and
quiet. Perfect for romantic couples.
LL-AL Magic Mountain, T07-825 6892.
Farmstay option, 30 mins from the village,
with in-house horse trekking (see Activities
and tours, page 222).
LL-AL Ocean House and Bach, Whale Bay,
T03-442 8697, www.oceanhouse.co.nz.
Ideal for keen surfers, this tasteful modern
eco-oriented lodge and bach is in the perfect
position overlooking Raglan's famous surf
break. The lodge is fully self-contained,
while the bach has motel unit facilitation.
L Rohi Mahu, 26 Rose St, T07-8256831,
www.rohimanu.co.nz. One of the better
luxury B&Bs in retro-open plan style with 2
rooms. As well as the class accommodation
there are in-house holistic health treatments
and chef hosted dinners available for
4 or more from $100 per person.
AL-C Solscape, 7 km west of the village
centre at 611 Wainui Rd, T07-825 8268,
www.solscape.co.nz. If you're looking for
something completely different this really
is the only place to stay in Raglan. The
owners have gone to great pains to
relocate and renovate an array of railway
wagons as colourful accommodation
units from dorm to self-contained. Smaller
cabooses (cabin houses) and a choice of
3 fully self-contained cottages (2 with
open fires) are also available. The entire
property enjoys views across the bay
and there is also a veritable menagerie
of animals on site including a couple of
ex-wild Kaimanawa horses, saved from
the bullet in central North Island in the late
1990s. Good value and recommended.
A-B Raglan Sunset Motel, 7 Bankart St,
T07-825 0050, www.raglansunsetmotel.co.nz.
Popular modern motel in the heart of the
village and close to the beach, with studios
and family units, some with spa. Pleasant and
peaceful alfresco area adds to the appeal.
B Harbour View Hotel, 14 Bow St, T07-825
8010. A traditional Kiwi hotel in the centre
of town, worth mentioning because it is
nicely renovated, cheap, clean and has
a good restaurant attached.

B-D Raglan Kopua Holiday Park,
Marine Parade, T07-825 8283, www.raglan
holidaypark.co.nz. Almost on an island
of its own, with a beach and linked to
the village by a short bridge.
**C-D Raglan Backpackers and Waterfront
Lodge**, 6 We Nira St, T07-825 0515,
www.raglanbackpackers.co.nz. The main
backpacker hostel in the village is quite
small but purpose-built and well situated.
Popular of course with the surfing set.
Kayak and bike hire. Recommended.

❼ Eating

Kawhia *p219*
❛❛ **Annie's Café**, T07-871 0198. Wed-
Sun 1000- 1600 and Fri, Sat 1800-late.
Traditional fare.
❛❛-❛ **Kawhia Hotel**, Powewe St,
T07-871 0700. Basic meals.
❛ **Kawhia Fisheries**, on the wharf.
The best bet, serving fish and chips.

Raglan *p220*
Four Square supermarket, 16-18 Bow St,
Mon-Fri 0730-1700, Sat-Sun 0730-1600.
❛❛ **Aqua Velvet**, 17 Bow St, T07-825
8588, Thu-Tue 0800-1500, dinner Fri-
Sat from 1800. A flash and rather retro
addition to Raglan's culinary scene. Live
music at weekends.
❛❛ **Tongue and Grove Café**, 9 Bow St,
T07-8250 027, daily 0830-late. One of the
most popular and affordable eateries
in town. Good size value breakfasts.
❛❛ **Verandabah**, Harbour View Hotel (see
Sleeping), T07-825 8010. Standard pub fare.
❛❛ **Vinnies**, 7 Wainui Rd, T07-825 7273,
1000-late, Sat-Sun from 0800-1100. Popular,
traditional cuisine with a seafood edge.
❛ **Raglan Fresh Fish and Takeaways**,
35 Bow St. Good fish and chips, but service
not so great unless you are a local or are
attached to a surfboard.

❽ Festivals and events

Kawhia *p219*
1 Jan Whaleboat Racing Regatta. Held
since 1910, the annual New Year's Day
regatta sees whaleboats dating back to
the 19th century racing alongside replicas
of the 5-oared craft.

▲ Activities and tours

Kawhia *p219*
Kawhia Cultural Cruises and Tours, T07-871 0324, $35, child $20. Offers 2½-hr cultural cruises around the harbour, one with 'hangi'-style meal, from $50. Other options include horse trekking and sea kayaking.
Sand Rover Tour, operates out of the Kawhia Camping Ground, T07-871 0863, www.kawhiacampingground.co.nz. The friendly and enthusiastic 4WD tour includes fishing and a picnic at the Te Puia Hot Springs.

Raglan *p220*
There are several fishing and harbour cruise charters. In summer you can try paragliding, kayaking and kitesurfing. Ask at the VIC.
Gag Raglan, 9a Bow St, T07-825 8702, www.gagraglan.com. State-of-the-art surf shop, surfboard hire and conditions reports.

Magic Mountain, 30-min drive south of Raglan, T07-825 6892, www.magic mountain.co.nz. Horse treks in great scenery, including the Bridal Veil Falls. Day trips from $80. Cosy farmstay accommodation (**AL**) also on offer.
Raglan Harbour Cruises, T07-825 8960, from $20. Trips to see the unusual Pancake Rock formations (no description necessary!).
Raglan Surfing School, T07-825 7873, www.raglansurfingschool.co.nz. 2-3 hr lesson costs around $89. It also offers independent board rentals and accommodation packages.

❶ Directory

Raglan *p220*
Internet   At the Tongue and Groove Café, the library and the video shop, which are all on Bow St. **Police** Nero St, T07-825 8200.

Waikato South

Heading south, beyond the gentle meanderings of the Waikato River and the uninspiring urban vistas of Hamilton, the rest of the Waikato is typical of the North Island countryside with deliciously green, gently rolling hills replete with plump and contented dairy cows. However, in these parts, perhaps more than anywhere else in the country, looks are deceiving since beneath the hooves and the haystacks exists a very different world more suited to the stuff of mystical dreams and wild adventures. As Rotorua is to bubbly mud or Kaikoura is to whales, then southern Waikato and Waitomo is to subterranean caves, rivers and glow-worms. There is easy access to a labyrinth of incredible limestone caves and underground river systems and to all the unique activities that go with them. Where else for example can you abseil 100 m into the 'Lost World' or float through the 'Haggas Honking Holes'? ▶▶ For Sleeping, Eating and other listings, see pages 227-229.

Ins and outs

Getting there Intercity, T09-638 5700, www.intercitycoach.co.nz, **Nakedbus.com** and **Pavlovich**, T09-302 2645/T0800-759999, www.pavlovichexpress.co.nz, are among the many bus companies that run a regular service north and south to Te Awamutu, Otorohanga, Te Kuiti and Waitomo from Hamilton. **Hodgson Motors**, Ohaupo Road, T0800-4287 5463, offers a regular service to and from Hamilton to Te Awamutu for $5.50 one way. **Perry's Buses**, Te Kuiti, T07-876 7570, is the local bus company serving Waitomo to the coast. It does a weekday coastal run between Kawhia and Te Kuiti, via Waitomo, $10 one way. Otorohonga and Te Kuiti are also on the main Auckland to Wellington rail line, T0800-872467. For transport to the **Waitomo Caves**, see page 224.

Information Otorohanga VIC (I-Site) ① *on the main SH3 drag at 21 Maniapoto St, T07-873 8951, www.otorohanga.co.nz, Mon-Fri 0900-1730, Sat-Sun 1000-1600,* can provide internet access. **Te Kuiti VIC (I-Site)** ① *Rora St in the centre of town, T07-878 8077, daily 0900-1700 (reduced hours in winter)* and **Te Awamutu VIC (I-Site)** ① *1 Gorst*

Te Awamutu → *Colour map 2, B2*

Te Awamutu is in the heart of Waikato dairy farming country and the Waipa District, which also takes in Cambridge to the east. It is most famous for its **Rose Gardens** ① *Gorst Av, across the road from the VIC*. The gardens contain hundreds of varieties with such alluring names as 'Disco Dancer', 'Sexy Rexy' and 'Big Daddy' and are nurtured to be at their smelly best for the **Rose and Cultural Festival** held during the first two weeks of November. Local activities worth looking at here include rock climbing, with the region offering some of the North Island's best. Quad biking and horse trekking are other reliable options.

The **Te Awamutu District Museum** ① *135 Roche St, To7-871 4326, www.ta museum.org.nz, Mon-Fri 1000-1600, Sat 1000-1300, Sun 1300-1600, free*, is a bizarre leap of time, culture and theme, with some fine examples of local Maori *taonga* mixed with a celebration of the town's two best-loved sons – Neil and Tim Finn, of the rock bands *Split Enz* and *Crowded House*. Somehow, it seems a bit like running a video of Freddie Mercury strutting his stuff next to the original Crown Jewels in the Tower of London, but such is the dilemma faced by the New Zealand small town museum.

You can hang around – literally – at the **Wharepapa Rockfields**, about 20 km southeast of the town. The crags include the 'Froggatt Edge', which is considered the best sport-climbing crag in the North Island, with over 115 climbs. The VIC (I-Site) will give you information and directions to the fields, as will 'base', **Bryce's Wharepapa Outdoor Centre** ① *1424 Owairaka Valley Rd, To7-872 2533, www.climb.co.nz*, and the aptly named **Boulderfield Café**

There are numerous walks around Te Awamutu, and the town also acts as the gateway to the **Pirongia Forest Park**. Dominated by the 959-m Mount Pirongia, the park offers some fine long and short walks, including the seven-hour summit track, which rewards you with great views. Again the VIC (I-Site) will provide directions and information (which is best described in the *Go Bush* leaflets or DoC's own *Pirongia Forest Park*). Alternatively, pay a visit to the home of the **DB Clydesdale Team** ① *To7-871 9711, www.clydesdales.co.nz*, an impressive team of Clydesdale horses. The well-groomed team used to appear regularly on TV to promote a national brewer. In the advert they would charge around some picturesque riverbed at the behest of their fictional owners, an annoyingly good-looking couple, who called everybody 'mate' and seemed to do nothing but pat each other on the back, mend fences and drink beer. Thankfully for the average South Islander or Kiwi ruralite, this urban-created marketing image, presented as the Kiwi archetype, is as transparent as it is wrong.

Otorohanga → *Colour map 2, C2*

The small agricultural service town of 'Oto', as it is better known, is so close to Waitomo with its famous caves that it struggles to attract anything other than occasional passing tourist. However, it does fancy itself as the gateway to the caves and boasts one of the best kiwi houses and displays of native New Zealand birds in the country. If you happen to be in Oto on the second Saturday in March you may catch the **Great Kiwiana Festival**, when the streets are decked with flower baskets and the gumboot-clad locals have fun celebrating anything and everything 'kiwi'.

Before heading off to Waitomo or making a beeline for the kiwi house it is worth looking at the **Kiwiana Displays** at various points along the main street. They are very well presented and chronicle a range of kiwi icons, heritage and heroes from Sir Edmund Hillary to rugby and Pavlova. The VIC (I-Site) has a locations leaflet which comes with a quiz. Recommended.

Established in 1971, the **Otorohanga Kiwi House and Native Bird Park** ⓘ *Alex Telfer Drive, T07-873 7391, www.kiwihouse.org.nz, daily 0900-1630, $15, child $4,* is one of the oldest native bird and reptile parks in the country, housing over 50 species, including three of the four known species of kiwi. It maintains the delicate balance of visitor attraction and conservation activity, attracting thousands of people each year, yet behind the scenes, successfully breeding more than 65 kiwi since 1975. The park's main attraction is the unique double nocturnal house where you are almost certain to see a kiwi going about its fascinating and comical hunt for food. They locate grubs using the sensitive nostrils right at the tip of their long beaks. Back outside, once your eyes have readjusted to daylight, you can go on to see a number of raptors, waterfowl and reptiles, including the prehistoric tuatara and cheeky native parrot, the kea. The walk culminates with a large walk-in aviary where other rare birds can be spotted. Throughout the park there are also some fine examples of native trees.

Te Kuiti → *Colour map 2, C2*

Te Kuiti is fairly unremarkable but is often used as a base for the Waitomo Caves, 19 km to the north. It is a small provincial town known as the sheep-shearing capital of New Zealand (witness the rather grotesque statue at the southern end of town). For a number of years it was home and refuge to the rebellious east coast Maori chief Te Kooti who built the highly aesthetic **Te Tokanganui-o-noho marae** at the south end of Rora Street. Also on Rora Street is the new and magnificent **Te Kuititanga-o-nga-Whakaaro Millennium Pavilion**, which is next to the railway, near the VIC (I-Site). Its carvings and stained and sandblasted window designs are great works of art. The big event of the year is the annual **Te Kuiti Muster** in April when the town celebrates its reputation with sheep-shearing championships, the 'bloated sheep race' and street celebrations. There are some fine gardens in the area, outlined in the free *King Country Gardens* leaflet available from the VIC (see page 222).

Waitomo and the caves 🖮🅹▲ » *pp227-229.*

→ *Colour map 2, C2*

The district of Waitomo ('wai' water and 'tomo' hole), with its underground wonderworld of limestone caves, is the region's (and one of the North Island's) biggest tourist attractions. Above ground, the typical farmland and the tourist village itself almost completely belie what is hidden below. Although only the geologically trained eye would suspect it, there is an astonishing network of over 360 recorded caves in the area, the longest over 14 km. If you don't mind getting wet, you should promise yourself that you will try at least one of the amazing underground activities, beyond the highly commercial tour of Glow-worm Cave. Wherever you go, it is pretty unforgettable.

Ins and outs

Getting there To get to the Waitomo Caves by bus, the **Waitomo Shuttle**, T07-873 8214, $10 one way, operates a regular service from 0900-1730, between Otorohanga's bus depot, train station, motels, backpacker hostels, motorparks and Waitomo. The **Waitomo Wanderer**, T07-873 6108/T0508-926337, www.waitomotours.co.nz, $40 ($68 return), runs a daily service from Rotorua. It departs Rotorua at 0745 and arrives in Waitomo at 1000, departing Waitomo again at 1545. **Intercity, Newmans,** T07-873 8951, **Pavlovich,** T0800-759999, www.pavlovichexpress.co.nz and **Great Sights,** T0800-744 487, all offer highly commercial day trips to the Glow-worm Cave from Auckland and Rotorua; shop around for the best deal. **Magic Traveller Buses** and **Kiwi Experience** (see Essentials, page 62) allow more flexibility than the day-trip option. The best idea is to get to Otorohanga on a standard Intercity bus and get to Waitomo independently from there. If coming by car, note there is no fuel available in Waitomo Village.

878 7640, www.waitomo.org.nz and www.waitomo-museum.co.nz, daily 0845-1930,
(reduced hours in winter) $5, child free, is at the heart of operations in the small tourist
village of Waitomo. Almost all the above-ground attractions, below-ground activity
operators, booking offices and tourist amenities are within walking distance. Although
compact it can be confusing, so the best bet is to absorb the information at the VIC
(I-Site) and take your time. There are numerous and often very similar activities on offer.
Let the staff book on your behalf, or go to the relevant tour operator for more
information. There is a village store attached to the **Waitomo Adventure** (Luminosa)
booking office (next to the VIC/I-Site), that sells limited supplies. The VIC (I-Site) has
stamps, internet access and currency exchange. There is also an ATM outside.

Sights

Glow-worm Cave ① *39 Waitomo Caves Rd, 8 km, To7-878 8227, www.waitomo
caves.co.nz, tours every 30 mins 0900-1700, arrive early, $33, child $14, cave combo
ticket (Glow-worm and Aranui) $50, child $23*, is Waitomo's biggest attraction, but it is
also the most commercial. During the day, lines of buses park outside and group after
group are herded underground. The caves were first extensively explored in 1887 by a
local Maori, Tane Tinorau, and English surveyor, Fred Mace. Further explorations
eventually led to the opening of the cave to tourists in 1889. They now attract almost
250,000 visitors annually. Although the cave remains impressive, you cannot help
feeling that you're on some Steven Spielberg film set, about to sit on Santa's knee and
ask him for an extension to your MasterCard. Having said that, the highlight of the
45-minute tour – the silent, almost religious homage to see the glow-worm galaxy by
boat – is incredible and well worth it, especially if you have never seen these amazing
insect larvae before. The cave also has the obligatory shop and café attached.

Aranui Cave ① *3 km west of Glow-worm Cave near the Ruakuri Scenic Reserve, tours
are hourly 1000-1500 and limited to groups of 20, $30, child $14; cave combo ticket
(Aranui and Glow-worm), $50, child $23; book at Glow-worm Cave or the VIC*, offers a
far more realistic and sedate experience. Its discovery, by Maori hunter Ruruku Aranui,
happened by accident in 1910. While out pig hunting, Rukuru's quarry disappeared into
the small entrance, followed enthusiastically by his dog. After a year of explorations and
amidst much excitement, the caves were opened to tourists in 1911. Whilst underground,
with effective lighting, the colour and variety of the stalactites and stalagmites, and the
sound of a thousand drips of water, you can let your imagination run wild and emerge
satisfied that you have experienced a real limestone cave.

Sights and activities above ground A fine insight into the area can be found at the
Museum of Caves ① *VIC (I-Site), To7-878 7640, www.waitomo-museum.co.nz, daily
0830-1700, 1730 in summer, $5, child, free entry with some activities*. Considered the
best limestone cave museum in the world, it offers interesting and highly informative
displays about cave formation, the history surrounding the local caves and the natural
history, including the spectacular and intriguing glow-worms. If you are claustrophobic
and shudder at the very thought of going underground then there is also an audio-
visual display and even a fake cave to crawl through.

The **Waitomo Walkway** (three hours return), begins opposite Glow-worm Cave and
follows the Waitomo Stream, taking in a number of limestone features before
arriving at the **Ruakuri Scenic Reserve**. This reserve encompasses a short walk that is
hailed as one of New Zealand's best. Although it does not deserve quite that billing, it
is well worth it, with a circular track taking in interesting caves and natural limestone
bridges, hidden amongst lush, native bush. At night, just before the path crosses the
stream, you can see a small 'scintilla' of glow-worms. These are the only glow-worms
you'll see around here for free, so take a torch.

The Waikato · Waikato South

❗ The formation of limestone caves (karst)

Limestone is a fossil rock made from the layered remains of countless marine animals. The limestone around Waitomo was therefore formerly the seabed, formed about 30 million years ago. Over the millennia these layers have been raised by the action of the earth's plates. In some places the limestone is over 200 m thick. Through its gradual uprising the limestone bends and buckles creating a network of cracks and joints. As rainwater drains into these cracks it mixes with small amounts of carbon dioxide in the air and soil forming a weak acid. This acid slowly dissolves the limestone and the cracks and joints widen. Over time small streams flow through converging cracks and eventually form underground caves.

Once these caves are created, the same acidic water seeps from the cave walls or drips from the roof, leaving a minute deposit of limestone crystal. Slowly these deposits form stalactites, stalagmites and various other cave features. The size and rate of their formation depends on the rate of flow. Stalactites form from the drips falling from the ceiling of the cave and stalagmites grow up as the drips fall to the floor. When the two join, pillars are formed; when they spiral around they are called helictites.

Various minerals in the soil like iron oxide can add colouration to the formations. The growth rates of caves and limestone features vary considerably according on topography, vegetation, and of course the weather. It is also important to realize that, like everything else, the caves have a 'lifespan', eventually collapsing to form gorges, holes or arches. The 'Lost World' near Waitomo is a fine example of part of a cave system that collapsed in on itself. These caves are also home to a unique range of plants and animals of which the New Zealand glow-worm is the most spectacular example.

Another popular walk is the **Opapaka Pa Walk**, which takes about 45 minutes return and is 1 km east of Waitomo. The view is memorable and there are also some interesting interpretation points explaining about the *pa* and the medicinal uses Maori made of surrounding flora.

Woodlyn Park ⓘ *To7-878 6666, www.woodlynpark.co.nz, shows are staged on demand, book first, $20, child $12*, is the above-ground entertainment 'must see' in Waitomo, if not the region. Like the Driving Creek railway in the Coromandel it is a typical example of Kiwi imagination, ingenuity and that simple 'can-do' mentality. The 'show', hosted by ex-shearer Barry Woods or staff, is an informative, interactive (and at times comical) interpretation of old and modern-day Kiwi country life, and is very hard to describe. It involves a clever pig, a not so clever pig, an axe, a homemade ingenious computer, dogs, sheep, a 'kiwi bear' and a pair of underpants. Enough said – you'll just have to go and see for yourself. As the visitor book says – 'look out Bill Gates'. Also on the grounds Barry has built a large tyre-lined pond on which you can blat about in a jet boat for $55 and as for accommodation, don't even go there!

About 500 m north, down Waitomo Valley Road from Woodlyn Park, in Waitomo Village, is the **Shearing Shed** ⓘ *To7-878 8371, shows daily at 1245, free, shop daily 0900-1630*, where cute Angora bunnies are cuddled to within an inch of their little lives and then given a short back and sides so that their highly-prized fur can be used for knitting. Still on the animal theme, the **Altura Garden and Wildlife Park** ⓘ *4 km south of Waitomo village on Fullerton Rd, To7-878 5278/To800-361291, daily summer 1000-1700, $12, child $5*, provides a diversion if you have kids or wish to stay above ground. There is a wide range of animals on display, with all the regulars including emus and horses. Horse trekking is available from $40 for half an hour to $60 for 1½ hours.

The **Marokopa Road**, which winds its way to Te Anga and the small coastal town of Marokopa, before heading north to Kawhia, is a long but pleasant trip with a number of worthwhile stops on the way. If you have your own wheels the first stop should be the slight diversion to see the impressive view looking back towards Waitomo from 3 km down Waipuna Road. The road is on the left, 11 km from Waitomo. Once back on the main road sit back and enjoy the scenery until you reach the **Mangapohue Natural Bridge Scenic Reserve**. Here a short streamside walk (10 minutes) will take you to an impressive natural limestone arch, complete with unusual stalagmites. This arch was once part of a large cave and it is hard to imagine that the rather inconspicuous little stream essentially created it all. About 5 km further on are the **Piripiri Caves**, accessed by a short but stiff climb up a boardwalk. These caves are in stark contrast to the well-lit, tourist-friendly offerings in Waitomo. They are dark and forbidding, and the path into them is steep and quite dangerous. If you are alone do not venture far and take a torch.

A little further on and about 35 km from Waitomo are the beautiful 32-m **Marokopa Falls**, which have to rate as amongst the best in the North Island, though due to their remote location they are not well known. A 15-minute walks descends to a lookout. If you go beyond the lookout to take photos prepare to get very muddy. From the falls it is a short distance to the small settlement of **Te Anga** where there is a tavern for lunch.

From Te Anga you have the choice of a very scenic road heading north to Kawhia or carrying on to the coast and **Marakopa**, a small, remote fishing village with black-sand beaches. From Marakopa you can to drive to **Awakino**, another small coastal settlement, on the main SH3 New Plymouth road, but it is long, unsealed and fairly arduous.

● Sleeping

Te Awamutu p223

Te Awamutu and the southern Waikato is considered the farmstay capital of New Zealand and there are over 500 B&Bs and farmstay beds in the area. It is therefore a great place to experience New Zealand rural life, see Essentials, page 46. The VIC has listings of these and some modern local motels.
B-D Road Runner Motel and Holiday Park, 141 Bond Rd, T07-871 7420.

Otorohanga p223

Accommodation in is limited; ask at the VIC.
A Palm Court Motel, corner of Clarke and Maniapoto sts (SH3), T0800-686764, T07-873 7122. Modern, clean and comfortable.
C-D Oto-Kiwi Backpackers, 1 Sangro Cres, T07-873 6022, http://otokiwibakpak.tripod.com/home.html. Has a good reputation. Facilities include campsites and internet. Also offers farm tours and trips, including to the caves and back and some in-house fun with a karaoke studio.

Motorcamps and campsites
D Otorohanga Holiday Park, 12 Huiputea Drive, T07-873 7253. Full range of facilities including a camp kitchen.

Te Kuiti p224

The VIC lists local B&Bs and farmstays.
C-D Casara Mesa Backpackers, Mangarino Rd, T07-878 6697, casara@xtra.co.nz. Comfortable with good en suite doubles as well as the usual share options. Breakfasts, transport and bike hire available.

Motorcamps and campsites
C-D Te Kuiti Camp Ground, Hinerangi St, T07-878 8966, www.tewaka.com.

Waitomo and the caves p224

There is a wide range of accommodation in Waitomo Village, but in summer pre-booking is essential.
AL-A Waitomo Express and Hobbit Motel, 1177 Waitomo Valley Rd, T07-878 6666, www.woodlynpark.co.nz. If it is the unusual you are looking for, look no further than Barry Woods at Woodlyn Park (1 km down Waitomo Valley Rd) and his converted train carriage, hobbit motel, or ex-WWII aircraft accommodation.
AL-D Waitomo Caves Hotel, T07-878 8240, www.waitomocaveshotel.co.nz. On the hill overlooking the village this historic, if somewhat staid, hotel offers a wide range

of comfortable standard, en suite or family rooms and has a restaurant attached.

A Abseil Inn B&B, 709 Waitomo Caves Rd, T07-878 7815. The aptly named Abseil Inn is up an 'exciting' driveway within walking (or climbing) distance of all amenities. Tidy, clean and classy decor. En suite double and queen rooms. Recommended.

A Te Tiro, 970 Caves-Te Anga Rd, T07-878 6328, www.waitomocavesnz.com. 2 modern self-contained timber frame cottages (sleeping 1-5) in the picturesque hills 10 km west of Waitomo. Good value.

A-B Caves Motor Inn, T07-873 8109, on SH3 (728), just south of Waitomo Caves turning. Fine motel choice with a good restaurant.

B-D Juno Hall Backpackers, T07-878 7649, www.junowaitomo.co.nz. This is a great log-cabin style hostel 1 km from the village, with a pool and log fire. Courtesy van.

B-D Kiwi Paka YHA, behind the VIC and Tavern, T07-878 3395, waitomo@kiwipaka-yha.co.nz. The best backpacker hostel with an emphasis on providing quality budget accommodation rather than bunks and dorms. There is a full range of rooms and some separate chalets on offer, from double to shared, some with en suite. Facilities are above average with a fine in-house pizzeria and café. Recommended.

Motorcamps and campsites

A-D Waitomo Caves Top Ten Holiday Park, T07-878 7639, www.waitomopark.co.nz. A modern, convenient and very friendly motorcamp right in the heart of the village. Spacious, great facilities including internet, pool and spa. Possibly the best showers of any park in the country. Recommended.

Waitomo to Kawhia p227

B-C Marokopa camping ground, Marokopa, T07-876 7444. Basic campsite with cottages, backpacker cabins, powered sites, a very basic shop, good showers and a small café.

❶ Eating

Te Awamutu p223

🍴 **Rose and Thorn Cafe**, 32 Arawata St, T07-871 8761. Locally recommended.

🍴-🍴 **Ngaroto Nurseries Café**, 208 Ngaroto Rd, 5 km north of town, T07-871 5668. Provides a pleasant rural lunch or coffee option.

Otorohanga p223

🍴-🍴 **Be'Guinness Bar and Brasserie**, Maniapoto St, T07-873 8010, open daily. Generous pub grub.

🍴-🍴 **Regent Café and Bar**, Maniapoto St, next to the library, T07-873 7370, Sun-Thu 0630-1700, Fri-Sat 0630-2100. The most popular venue in a limited selection.

Te Kuiti p224

There are numerous rather forgettable cafés and eateries on Rora St and the best bet is:

🍴 **Riverside Lodge Café Bar and Restaurant**, east down King St, then turn right before the bridge, T07-878 8027, Tue-Sun 1230-late.

Waitomo and the caves p224

There is a village store next door to Waitomo Luminosa, open until 1900, but you are advised to stock up before arriving.

🍴 **Caves Motor Inn**, 8 km east of Waitomo Village (see Sleeping). Good value for dinner.

🍴 **Roselands Restaurant**, 3 km from Waitomo Village up Fullerton Rd, T07-878 7611, daily in summer 1100-1400. The best place for lunch, specializing in hearty BBQs and salads in a lovely garden setting.

🍴 **Waitomo Caves Hotel** (see Sleeping, page 227). Decent traditional à la carte traditional cuisine.

🍴 **Waitomo Tavern**, near the VIC, T07-878 8448. The place for cheap and basic pub grub and a pint with the locals.

Cafés

🍴-🍴 **Morepork Café**, at the Kiwi Paka YHA (see Sleeping, above). The best-value evening meal in town (especially pizza).

There are 3 other cafés in Waitomo run by the operators: the Waitomo Adventures' **Cavelands**, village centre; Legendary Black Water Rafting Company's **Long Black**, 2 km east, which does a fine breakfast for around $12; and **Glow-worm Caves Café**, just west of the village. All are open daily from 0800-1730 (later in summer).

▲ Activities and tours

Te Awamutu p223

Castle Rock Adventures, 1250 Owairaka Valley Rd, T0800-225462, www.castlerock adventure.co.nz. Full day of climbing tuition for $200 per person, half-day $150.

It also offers abseiling from $50, self-guided mountain bike hire for $35 half-day, $50 full-day. Modern well-facilitated shared or private accommodation from $25-80. It's a fine operation and well worth considering. **Pirongia Horse Treks and ATV Tours**, T07-871 9960.

Waitomo and the caves *p224*
There is a wide range of choice and competition is fierce; research the options carefully and take your time. Whatever activity or operator you choose, it will usually be money well spent. Note that there are also price reductions for combinations with some also offering free museum entry. A combination of trips that offer value for money and a high level of safety and professionalism is the Lost World Epic followed by the Haggas Honking Holes.
Black Abyss, Legendary Black Water Rafting Company, 5 hrs, 2½ hrs underground, $175. Price includes museum, showers, soup and bagels. This is one of the more adventurous trips, involving a 30-m abseil.
Black Labyrinth, Legendary Black Water Rafting Company, 3 hrs, 1 hr underground, $90. Price includes museum entry, showers, soup and bagels. This trip involves floating down a subterranean river by a waterfall, the cave formations and glow-worms.
Blackwater Rafting, Rap, Raft 'n' Rock, 4½ hrs, 1½ hrs underground, $125 (includes free museum entry). 27-m (80 ft) abseil into a cave, then a float through a river system with a great display of glow-worms.
Haggas Honking Holes, Waitomo Adventures, $165, 4 hrs, 2 hrs underground. With a name like that who can resist? Slightly more full on, this trip involves an abseil, rock climbing and an intimate encounter with a waterfall, as well lots of crawling and scenery.
Lost World Epic, Waitomo Adventures, dinner included, $355, 7 hrs, 5 hrs underground. If you can afford it and are fit enough this has to be one of the best and most unusual full-day activity trips in the country. It involves an exciting descent into a gaping hole and is followed by the exhilarating and highly entertaining 3-hr negotiation of the cave system and underground river. It involves walking, climbing, swimming, wading, jumping and even racing, with the final stage a quiet reflection on the trip

under a galaxy of glow-worms, before emerging, like some intrepid latter-day explorer, at the river entrance. If you can splash out, it's a once-in-a-lifetime trip.
Spellbound, 2-3 hrs, 2 hrs underground, $40, child $20 (includes museum entry). Mainly eco-based adventure for those who want to remain dry, with a trip into a cave system.
St Benedict's Cavern, Waitomo Adventures, $120, 3½ hrs, 1½ hrs underground. This cave was discovered in 1962 but was only opened commercially in 2003. It is said to be the prettiest cave in the region and had parts of it christened 'The Hobbit Holes' long before *Lord of the Rings* was filmed in New Zealand. Your exploration of the cave will involve 2 abseils and a flying fox. Great fun.
Tumu Tumu Toobing, Waitomo Adventures, $95, 4 hrs, about 2 hrs underground. This trip, along with the Haggas Honking Holes, is ideal if you are limited for time. The least strenuous of Waitomo Adventures' tours, it involves a highly entertaining walk, swim and float down an underwater stream with glow-worms and interesting rock formations.

Tour operators
Altura Garden and Wildlife Park Horse Treks, 4 km south of Waitomo village on Fullerton Rd, T07-878 5278/T0800-361291, from $40 for 30 mins to $60 for 1½ hrs (includes park entry) from $40-85, half-day.
Caveworld, 277 Te Anga Rd, T07-878 6577/ T0800-228386, www.caveworld.co.nz. Offers its own range of options such as the exclusive 'Baby Grand' and also a night glow abseil.
Legendary Black Water Rafting Company, 2 km east of Waitomo VIC, T0800-228464, T07-878 6219, www.waitomo.com/ www.blackwaterrafting.co.nz.
Rap, Raft 'n' Rock, T07-873 9149/T0800-228372, www.caveraft.com. Rock climbing and accommodation also available.
Spellbound, 277 Te Anga Rd, T07-878 7621, www.waitomospellbound.co.nz. Run by the founders of the **Legendary Black Water Rafting Company**.
Waitomo Adventures Ltd, next to the VIC , T0800-924866, T07-878 7788, www.waitomo.co.nz/www.waitomowalk.com.
Waitomo Big Red 4x4, T07-878 8393. The local quad bike adventure company. Trips to suit all ages and experience; $99 for 2 hrs. Cave combo options.

Waikato East

The English-looking countryside of the eastern Waikato is among the most l crative areas in New Zealand; over the decades, many a fortune has been secured through its fertile soils. However, other than the hot pools in Te Aroha or horse studs surrounding the pleasant town of Cambridge, there was always a paucity of major tourist attractions, until, that is, a character called 'Frodo' arrived. In 1999 at the behest of Lord of the Rings film director Peter Jackson, location researchers scoured the area for a plot of land that suited the universal image of Tolkien's 'Hobbiton'. Near the quiet agricultural service town of Matamata, a discreet plot was secured and it proved to be the perfect setting for one of the most complex sets created for the film trilogy. Despite the fact almost nothing remains bar a few pieces of hardwood, it seems the film's bandwagon came careering down th hill here as much as anywhere in the nation and the much hyped 'Tour to Hobbiton' are proving that the Waikato soil can line pockets in other ways. ►► *For Sleeping, Eating and other listings, see pages 233-234.*

Ins and outs

Getting there **Busit Services,** T0800-4287 5463, links Hamilton and Thames (via Paeroa) most days, arriving at Thames VIC ((I-Site). **Intercity,** T09-913 6100, offers services to Matamata from Hamilton or Tauranga stopping outside the Matamata VIC (I-Site). Most of the main bus operators heading north or south on SH1 stop in Cambridge. For local bus information and services to/from Hamilton contact **Busit** or **Cambridge Travel Lines,** T07-827 7363.

Tourist information **Paeroa VIC (I-Site)** ① *17 Belmont Rd, T07-862 8636, www.pae roa.org.nz, Mon-Fri 0900-1700, Sat-Sun 0930-1430.* **Te Aroha VIC (I-Site)** ① *in the original Te Aroha Hot Springs Domain, ticket office at 102 Whitaker St, T07-884 8052, www.tearoha-info.co.nz, Mon-Fri 0930-1700, Sat-Sun 0930-1600.* The enthusiastic, friendly but under-resourced staff will provide all your local information needs including maps and advice about accommodation. **Matamata VIC (I-Site)** ① *45 Broadway, T07-888 7260, www.matamatanz.co.nz.co.nz, Mon-Fri 0830-1700, Sat-Sun 1000-1500,* can assist with transport and accommodation enquiries or bookings, has internet facilities and also acts as agents for the 'Hobbiton' tour. **Cambridge VIC (I-Site)** ① *corner of Queen and Victoria sts, T07-8233456, www.cambridge.co.nz, Mon-Fri 0900-1700, Sat-Sun 1000-1600,* takes travel bookings and offers bike hire. Don't leave without the free *Cambridge Welcomes You* booklet. **Tirau VIC (I-Site)** ① *next to the Big Sheep in the Big Dog, T07-883 1202, www.tirauinfo.co.nz, daily 0900-1700,* and **Tokoroa VIC (I-Site)** ① *SH1, T07-886 8872, www.southwaikatonz.com,* can both can assist with enquiries, bookings and details about local walks and attractions.

Paeroa → *Colour map 2, B2*

Poor Paeroa. It's neither here nor there – and that seems to be its problem. People are always rushing through on their way to the Coromandel or the Bay of Plenty and rarely stop. And if they do, it is only very briefly, to get their photograph taken beside a huge plastic bottle of 'Lemon and Paeroa' (L&P), which is New Zealand's only national soft drink. Although not made in Paeroa, the spring water, which is mixed with lemon juice to create the drink, was discovered here in 1900 and made the place famous. This old, once thriving port has little to offer, but don't write the place off entirely. Of late this iconic aberration has inexplicably reproduced and is now supported by another 5.4 m specimen at the **L&P Café and Bar** ① *corner of SH2 and Seymour St, T07-862 7773, www.cafeandbar.co.nz.* The added attraction here of course is the opportunity to grab

a light lunch, an ice cream or a coffee. Of more substance (just) is the **Paeroa Museum**
① *37 Belmont Rd, Mon-Fri 1030-1500*, which does its best with displays about local history, bone china collections and some Maori artefacts. For view junkies, **Primrose Hill,** near the town centre, offers great views back across the Hauraki Plains – which, alas for poor Paeroa, are flat and boring! If you are in Paeroa on the third Sunday in February you will find the place pumping with the motorcycle extravaganza '**Battle of the Streets**'. This increasingly popular annual event attracts bikers from far and wide, but if the notorious gangs turn up, the event can end up being very aptly named. Luckily this does not coincide with the other major event in the same month – the **Pipe Band Tattoo** – the result would be Mad Max meets Braveheart.

Te Aroha → *Colour map 2, B2*

In 1875 Te Aroha was little more than a single house in the shadow of the mountain, occupied by Irish pioneer Charlie Lipsey, and subsequently known as 'Lipseytown'. With the discovery of gold nearby in 1880 the settlement expanded, but only temporarily, as the mining returns proved relatively poor. Later, with the discovery of the hot soda water geyser, the Hot Springs Domain were born and today this remains the jewel in the crown of this mainly agricultural service town. Incidentally, Mount Te Aroha in Maori means 'Mountain of Love', and comes from the story of a Bay of Plenty Maori chief who once made those utterings in relief after getting lost and seeing the glorious views south, homewards towards his *pa*.

There are two major attractions in Te Aroha, **Mount Te Aroha** and the **Hot Springs Domain**. As far as activity goes the two could hardly be more opposite, but the four- to five-hour return climb up the 952-m summit can be rewarded with a dip in the pools, providing the perfect marriage of the two. The mountain path is accessed at the rear of the Domain. The Whakapipi or **Bald Spur Lookout** about halfway up is easily reached after about 45 minutes and offers a fine view west. But, if you can, carry on to the summit and take in the spectacular 360° view, north across the Coromandel and south to the Bay of Plenty. For track information see the *Te Aroha Mountain Tracks* leaflet from the VIC (I-Site). There is also a popular 12-km mountain bike track (circuit) adjacent to the springs. It's an all-weather surface with hard and easy options, but there remains one major drawback: as yet there is no bike hire outlet in town. However, the YHA offers free bike hire to its guests.

On your return by foot or pedal you can fall straight into the **Te Aroha Mineral Pools**① *near the track entrance, T07-884 8717, www.tearohapools.co.nz, daily 1000-2200, $10-15, private pools available.* The pools, which were originally created in the late 1800s, are the world's only naturally flowing hot soda spa pools.

The **Wyborn Leisure Pools**① *T07-884 4498, daily 1100-1900, $6, child $3,* are just a short distance further on. They offer hot and cold outdoor pools and more modern bathhouses. Behind the pools is the **Mokena Geyser,** which is one of very few soda water geysers in the world. Named after the Maori chief and benefactor of the land on which the Domain now stands, the geyser shoots 3-m high about every half-hour.

Also on the Domain is the **Te Aroha Museum** ① *T07-884 4427, Sat-Sun 1300-1600, donation.* Housed in the original bathhouse (which was once said to be possibly the most attractive building in the country and 'the sanatorium of New Zealand'), it now contains some interesting displays on the mining and agricultural development of the town. Oh, and two rather pretty toilets. Also of considerable historical interest, but not housed in the museum, is the 1712 Queen Anne pipe organ in **St Mark's Church**① *T07-884 8052.* The town has a fairly unremarkable arts and crafts trail, and a gardens and heritage trail; ask for leaflets at the VIC (I-Site). For a pleasant easy grade short walk there is the wildlife-rich **Howarth Memorial Wetlands Walk,** on the banks of the Waihou River. The VIC (I-Site) can give you directions and a leaflet.

Matamata lies in the heart of Waikato's rich and fertile agricultural landscape and is the epitome of affluent rural Kiwi life. Large ranches and spacious farmsteads would seem to suggest that the domestic and export agricultural worth of New Zealand is alive and well. Although it is pleasant enough, there was never a great deal here to attract the tourist – that is until a film about a little hobbit called Frodo came along.

Long before *Lord of the Rings* hit the world's movie screens, a small plot of private farmland close to Matamata was being transformed into the magical village of **Hobbiton** ① *Rings Scenic Tours depart the VIC at 0930, 1045, 1200 1315, 1430 and 1545, T07-888 6838, www.hobbitontours.com, from $50, child $25*, home to two of the film's key characters Frodo and Sam. It was felt that the surrounding countryside (which looks something akin to England's rural landscapes) was perfect for portraying 'The Shire' and the plot itself the ideal place to create the unique subterranean homes and busy gardens of Tolkien's Hobbiton. Although there has been a lot of hype about the set and with Hobbiton tours up and running, you must be under no illusions as to what remains. As with all the 'Rings' sets throughout the country there were strict conditions in place to ensure almost all trace of the sets were removed. So now, in essence, a trip to Peter Jackson's Hobbiton is more an exercise in the imagination than reality – and an expensive one at that. There are some remnants, the highlight being an over-grown 'Hobbit Hole' with a plywood frontage but that is essentially it. So for 'Rings' fanatics the $50 for the two-hour tour may seem worth it, but for the average person it is highly debatable. For kids in particular it could prove a real disappointment. Until something credible or more meaningful is recreated at the former set, for most people the sign declaring Matamata as 'Hobbiton', across the road from the VIC (I-Site) is itself more of an attraction.

Elsewhere in Matamata a few of the old, low-key attractions remain. The historic and well-armoured landmark **Firth Tower**, on Tower Road, was built in 1882 by Yorkshireman Josiah Firth, and is the town's other main attraction. Why exactly it was so well fortified and therefore cost so much to build, is a matter of debate. The tower is the centrepiece of the **historical museum** ① *T07-888 8369, daily 1000-1600, $5, child $1*, which explains the intriguing history.

About 6 km from Matamata, the **Opal Hot Springs** ① *T07-888 8198*, are a popular spot, and compete with Te Aroha's Domain, with a pool complex of mineral and private spa pools. Back in town if you have an interest in pigeons **Keola Lofts** ① *428 Hinuera Rd, T07-888 1728, daily 1000-1600*, is a lively presentation about them.

Cambridge → *Colour map 2, B2*

Also on the Waikato River, 20 km south east of Hamilton on SH1, is the pleasant country town of Cambridge, a popular spot to stop at while heading south to Taupo or beyond. Recognized nationally as a centre for thoroughbred horse studs, antiques, arts and crafts, and known locally as 'the town of trees', Cambridge has a distinctly English feel.

The VIC (I-Site) has some excellent leaflets outlining the numerous antique, art and craft outlets in the town. The most famous is the **Cambridge Country Store** ① *92 Victoria St, T07-827 8715, Mon-Sat 0830-1630, Sun 0900-1600*, which is housed in an old church. It has a wide range of crafts including native New Zealand wood pieces, ceramics, knitwear, Maori carvings, wine and food. The **All Saint's Café** attached serves fresh snacks and home baking. For horse and pony fanatics the **Cambridge Thoroughbred Lodge** ① *SH1, Karapiro, 6 km south of the town, T07-827 8118, www.cambridgethoroughbredlodge.co.nz, daily 1000-1500, shows at 1030 Tue-Sun, afternoon by arrangement, $12, child $5*, puts on an entertaining hour-long 'New Zealand Horse Magic Show' where a range of horse breeds are shown and perform to order with much horsey humour and audience participation. For a more thorough equestrian insight you might like to consider a 'Thoroughbred Stud Tour'

with the very vamperian sounding **Barry Lee Bloodstock Ltd** ① *T07-827 5910,*
www.barrylee.co.nz, book at the VIC. The tour costs $120 for up to four people and
lasts an hour taking in four studs, so it's good value.

The small **Cambridge Museum** ① *Victoria St, Mon-Sat 1000-1600, Sun 1000-
1400,* is housed in the old courthouse. There are a number of good walks in and around
Cambridge. For a short walk, the **Te Koutu Lake** on Albert Street is very picturesque,
while the tramp up **Maungatautari Mountain** (at the terminus of Maungatautari and
Hicks Road, off SH1, a few kilometres south of town) is a more strenuous affair rewarded
with fine views of the river and beyond. The mountain is also a very important spot for
native wildlife after the creation of 'Warrenheip' – an ecological 'island' of native bush,
fenced off and cleared of introduced predators before being left to regenerate and
being restocked with native birds, including kiwi. For more information, contact the
Maunga Trust ① *T07-823 7455, www.maungatrust.org.*

Tirau → *Colour map 2, B2*

Tirau is at the junction of SH1 and SH27 – the two main routes south – making it a
popular coffee stop. The highlight of the town is not hard to miss and comes in the
form of a giant corrugated iron sheep and a dog on the Main Road. Its popularity has
led to the creation of other **corrugated iron art** by local artist Steven Clothier. The
sheep houses the **Big Sheep Wool Gallery** ① *T07-883 1954,* which sells an array of
New Zealand-made woolly products and kitsch sheep souvenirs. There is a range of
other tourist-orientated shops on Main Street selling various New Zealand products.

Putaruru and Tokoroa → *Colour map 2, B-C3*

Tokoroa is a major forestry base and takes its name from a Maori chief who was killed
during the Maori Land Wars of the mid 1800s. The main attraction here (other than the
toilet or a coffee) are the various walks and mountain biking tracks in the surrounding
forest. **Hatupatu Rock** is an interesting place steeped in Maori legend. In Putaruru the
Timber Museum ① *3 km south of the village on SH1, T07-883 7621, daily 0900-1600,
$8, child $3,* is the main draw. It has a steam engine and some ancient native logs.

● Sleeping

Te Aroha *p231*
Accommodation is fairly limited in Te Aroha.
AL Aroha Mountain Lodge, 5 Boundary St
T07-884 8134, www.arohamountainlodge
.co.nz. A lodge-style B&B with 6 luxury
en suite rooms or the charming fully self-
contained Miners Cottage with 3 double
rooms all right next to the spas and
starting point for the mountain walks.
B Te Aroha Motel, 108 Whitaker St,
T07-884 9417. The town's lone motel.
B-D Te Aroha Holiday Park and Backpackers,
217 Stanley Rd, T07-884 9567. Basic facilities.
C-D Te Aroha YHA Hostel, Miro St, T07-
884 8739. Friendly 12-bed hostel where
cooking is a speciality. Free bikes.

Matamata *p232*
B-D Lazy Tramper, 282 Old Kaimai Rd St,
T07-543 3185, www.thelazytramper.co.nz.

New tidy, rural-based backpacker hostel set
in a former schoolhouse, large living area
with open fire, well-equipped kitchens and
all the usual room configurations.

Cambridge *p232*
LL Maungatautari Lodge, 844 Maungatautari Rd (6 km south of Cambridge, 3 km off
SH1), T07-827 2220, www.malodge.com.
New, purpose-built boutique hotel on a
working farm and thoroughbred breeding
operation in the heart of the Waikato. A
choice of suites or individually decorated villas
with 5-star facilities. Extensive gardens and a
swimming pool. In-house restaurant offers
innovative and contemporary Kiwi cuisine
with an organic edge. Horse riding, massage
and beauty therapies also available.
L Houseboat, T07-827 2195, www.house
boatescape.co.nz. For something different

consider a self-drive houseboat, from $600 for 2 nights excluding fuel.

L Thornton House B&B, 2 Thornton Rd, T07-827 7567, www.thorntonhouse.co.nz. A very tastefully renovated historic 1902 villa with 2 well-appointed rooms. Central.

A Bubble Lodge Homestay, 64 Cowley Drive, T07-823 4046, www.bubble lodge.co.nz. Intriguingly named and good-value operation in suburban Cambridge, with modern tasteful decor, run by a friendly, cat-crazy couple.

A Cambridge Mews, 20 Hamilton Rd, T07-8277166, www.cambridgemews.co.nz. Perhaps the best motel in town.

A No1 Motels on Victoria, 87-89 Victoria St, T07-823 1467, www.no1motels.co.nz. New and affordable centrally located motel.

Motorcamps and campsites
B-D Cambridge Motor Park, 32 Scott St, T07-827 5649. Only 1 km from town. Camp kitchen.

Tokoroa *p233*
B-D Tokoroa Motor Camp and Backpackers, 22 Sloss Rd, T07-886 6642. If you are looking to park up for the night this is your best bet.

❼ Eating

Te Aroha *p231*
❢❢ Ironique Café and Bar, 159 Whitaker St, T07-884 8489, daily from 1000. This place stands out for its traditional à la carte menu, light lunches and good coffee.

Matamata *p232*
❢❢ Workmans Café and Bar, 52 Broadway, T07-888 5498. The best place in Hobbiton, open for breakfast, lunch and dinner Tue-Sun.

Cambridge *p232*
❢❢ Souter House, 19 Victoria St, T07-827 3610, www.souterhouse.co.nz. Tue-Sat. Long-established accommodation and restaurant combo; a good choice for dinner.
❢❢-❢ Frans Café, 62 Victoria St, T07-827 3946, Mon-Sat. Worth trying for lunch or dinner.

Tirau *p233*
❢❢ Loose Goose, 7 Main Rd, T07-883 1515, closed Tue. More impressive on the outside than inside but still a good choice.
❢❢ Oxford Landing, Main Rd, T07-883 1534.
❢❢-❢ Alley Cats, Main Rd, T07-883 1107. Standard café fare.

▲▲ Activities and tours

Cambridge *p232*
The Boatshed Café, on the shores of Lake Karapiro, south on SH1 then right on Gorton Rd and right again on Amber, T07-827 8286, www.theboatshed.net.nz. Offers kayak hire, 3 hrs from $20.

❶ Directory

Te Aroha *p231*
Internet Te Aroha Library, Rewi St, T07-889 5689.

Cambridge *p232*
Internet All Saints Café, 92 Victoria St.

Bay of Plenty

⁛ Footprint features

Introduction

When Captain James Cook explored this particular stretch of the country's coast in the 18th century he christened it the Bay of Plenty. Back then a mere stretch of the legs on terra firma was no doubt enough to attain such a label. But now, for us modern-day navigators, the obvious question remains – so, is it?

Well, if statistics are anything to go by the answer is categorically yes. By population, the Bay of Plenty is the North Island's fastest-growing region, with the real estate figures of Tauranga now generally accepted as being a barometer to the health of the national economy. The region is also the most visited tourist destination in the North Island and is where the very idea of New Zealand tourism began.

Rotorua, or 'Roto-Vegas' as it is known, is the thermal and volcanic capital of New Zealand, with geysers, hot pools and vents of bubbling mud. The city also has a rich and fascinating human history. Tauranga – along with its close neighbour Mount Maunganui – is another tourist hot spot and considered the capital of the region. Its sunny climate and beaches as well as its proximity to Coromandel and Auckland, attract visitors by the bus load. Even the cruise ships have started visiting this busy port. The outlying towns, too, get their turn on the tourist merry-go-round. Proud Whakatane offers not only a lovely coast and congenial atmosphere but also its own distinct attractions. One minute you can be swimming with dolphins, the next reeling in a marlin, and the next staring down the steaming barrel of White Island's volcanic crater.

★ Don't miss ...

1 **Tarawera Falls** Follow the track along the Tarawera River to Lake Tarawera for one of the best walks in the region (if not the North Island), page 247.

2 **Tamaki Twilight Cultural Tour** Experience Māori culture with singing, dancing and a *hangi*, page 247.

3 **Wai-O-Tapu** Take in the incredible thermal reserves around Rotorua and listen to the gentle fizzing of the 'Champagne Pool' or the therapeutic melody of bubbling mud, page 247.

4 **Agrodome Complex** Do the tourist thing and check out the 'Sheep-Shearing and Sheep Dog Show', page 249.

5 **Rainbow Springs** Eye up the trout and the huge, octogenarian eels at this freshwater spring, page 250.

6 **Activities** Go cruising or fishing on Lake Rotorua or Rotoiti; raft the Okere Falls; try whitewater sledging; go mountain biking in the Whakarewarewa Forest Park; or try out the infamous 'luge', page 255.

7 **White Island** Visit this active volcano or take a trip dolphin watching from the congenial seaside town of Whakatane, page 269.

Bay of Plenty Introduction

Rotorua → *Colour map 2, C3 Population: 70,000*

Rotorua – alias 'Sulphur City' – can sometimes be smelled before it's seen, though they say you get used to it. Of all the places in the Bay of Plenty, nature has indeed given Rotorua 'plenty'. The natural thermal wonders first attracted the Maori in the 14th century and later the Europeans, though nature has not always been so kind. The violent eruption of the Tarawera volcano in 1886 led to the loss of 150 lives.

Rotorua is deserving of its 'most visited' tourist status. The city and the region probably offer more unusual sights and activities than anywhere else in New Zealand. And although, like Taupo, it is particularly famous for its thermal and volcanic features, lakes and fishing, the region offers a multitude of other activities. Here you can join in a Maori concert or gorge yourself at a Maori hangi (feast), throw yourself down a 7-m waterfall in a raft, jump out of planes, bike, walk or shop till you drop. ▶▶ *For Sleeping, Eating and other listings, see pages 251-258.*

Ins and outs

Getting there
Air Rotorua airport ① *10 km from the town centre, on the eastern shores of Lake Rotorua, T07-345 6176, www.rotorua-airport.co.nz*, is served by **Air New Zealand Link**, T0800-737000, www.airnewzealand.co.nz, with daily flights from Auckland, Wellington and other principal domestic centres. **Qantas**, T0800-808767, www.qantas.co.nz, also offers a daily service from Christchurch and Queenstown. **Super Shuttle**, T07-345 7790, and the main taxi companies provide transfers to and from the airport; shuttle $15 one way, taxi $20. The international airport in Hamilton (see page 212) runs a shuttle service that connects with **Pavlovich**, T09-620 5490/T0800-759999.

Road Rotorua is reached via SH5, which branches off SH1 at Tirua from the north and Taupo from the south. It is a major destination on the signposted 'Thermal Explorer Highway' tourist route. **Intercity, Newman's** T09-348 0999, and **Pavlovich**, T09- 620 5490/T0800-759999, buses service Rotorua daily and stop outside the VIC (I-Site) on Fenton Street. The **Waitomo Wanderer**, T03-437 0753/T0508-926337, www.waitomo tours.co.nz, runs a daily service between Waitomo and Rotorua, departing Rotorua at 0745, $40, $68 return, two hours, see page 224. **Nakedbus.com** also runs a service between Rotorua and Taupo from $19. There is a specialist **travel centre** ① *T07-348 5179, www.rotorua.nz.com*, within the VIC (I-Site), which handles enquiries and bookings.

Getting around
Around town **Baybus**, T0800-422 9287, www.baybus.co.nz are the principal local bus company, the main stop being on Pukuatua Street. Several local shuttles vie for business in providing daily transportation to the Tamaki Maori Village, Waimangu Volcanic Valley, Waiotapu Thermal Wonderland and Waikite Valley Thermal Pools, with scheduled and flexible non-scheduled pick-ups and drop-offs available, from around $25 return. The **Geyser Link**, T0800-0004321, www.gyserlink.co.nz, leaves for most major attractions several times daily and the fare usually includes entry. Contact the VIC (I-Site) for other local operators. For a taxi, call T07-348 1111. ▶▶ *For specific tour buses, see Activities and tours, page 257.*

Tourist information
Tourism Rotorua Travel and Information ① *1167 Fenton St, T07-348 5179/T0800- 768678, www.rotoruanz.com, daily 0800-1800*, is one of the oldest and busiest

tourist offices in the country. It is the principal base for all local information, as well as the bus arrival and departure point. The in-house travel centre administers local and national bus, coach, air and rail ticketing. There is a currency exchange office (0800-1730), toilets, showers, a shop, a café and even a hot thermal footbath outside. Information is also available from the **DoC** ① *99 Sala St, T07-349 7400, www.doc. govt.nz. Mon-Fri, 0800-1600.*

Rotorua

Related maps
A Rotorua detail, p241.

Sleeping		
Anns Volcanic **2**	Kingsgate **8**	The Springs **25**
Ascot on Fenton **3**	Kiwi Paka **7**	Wylie Court **14**
Bel Aire Motel **4**	Quality Geyserland **9**	
Cosy Cottage **5**	Regal Palms **6**	
Four Canoes **17**	Rob Roy Motor Inn **10**	
Funky Green Voyager **1**	Robertson House **24**	
Geneva Motor Lodge **23**	Rotorua Thermal	
Grand Tiara Rotorua **12**	Holiday Park **11**	
	Silver Fern **13**	

Background

Ohinemutu on the shores of Lake Rotorua and Whakarewarewa to the south of the present city were first settled by Maori from the Arawa Canoe around the 14th century. These early Maori were quick to utilize the many benefits offered by the local thermal activity and for almost four centuries they thrived happily and peace reigned. Then, in 1823, the Te Arawa were invaded by the Ngapuhi chief Hongi Hika from Northland. Despite the fact that Hika's warriors were armed with European muskets the Te Arawa, determined to defend their little piece of paradise, put up a valiant fight, inflicting heavy losses on the intruders.

By the 1840s the first missions had been established on the shores of Lake Rotorua and Lake Tarawera. However, their sanctity was soon disrupted by more inter-tribal warfare, this time from the Waikato Maori to the west. During the Waikato campaigns and Maori King Movements of the New Zealand Wars, the Te Arawa elected to side with the New Zealand government and, in 1864, a force of east coast Ngati Porou attempted to cross Arawa lands to assist the Waikato tribes, only to be repelled by the Te Arawa and sent packing. This led to further reprisals from the Waikato tribes, which were subsequently repelled with government assistance. It was not until the end of the New Zealand Wars that any substantial European settlement began. With the obvious attraction of both the aesthetic and therapeutic qualities of the thermal waters of the region, the population rapidly expanded and tourism flourished. With the eruption of Mount Tarawera in 1886, settlement was temporarily halted, but as confidence returned so did the tourists and, now over a century on, that attraction and popularity continues.

Sights

Lake Rotorua

Lake Rotorua is the largest of the 17 lakes in the Rotorua thermal region, covering an area of 89 sq km and sitting at a height of 279 m above sea level. It is, as you might expect, a flooded volcanic crater. A feature of many of the launch trips based on the city's lakefront is the bush-clad nature reserve of **Mokoia Island**, scene of the classic love story of the Arawa princess Hinemoa and her suitor Tutanekai. But Mokoia was also the site for far less romantic encounters. During the invasion of Hongi Hika's warriors in 1823, the Arawa *pa* on Mokoia was sacked, but having sustained such heavy losses, the invaders could not hold what they had temporarily conquered. Today the lake is a top venue for recreational activities including boating, water skiing and, above all, trout fishing. ▸▸ *See Activities and tours, page 255.*

On the northern shores of the lake are the **Hamurana Gardens** ① *733 Hamurana Rd*, where the largest spring in the North Island erupts with a beautiful clarity and a volume of over one million gallons (four million litres) an hour. The gardens also feature a tract of giant redwoods. Although the gardens are no longer an official tourist attraction the river and spring is worth seeing if you are in the area.

Ohinemutu

Situated on the lakefront within the city, and reached via narrow streets lined with steaming drains, is the former Maori settlement and thermal area of Ohinemutu. The focal point of the village is the **Tamatekapua marae**, a beautifully carved *whare-runanga* (meeting house), erected in 1939. It is often used as the focus for Maori events and performances and, despite its fairly modern renovation, still contains carvings from the 1800s. It was named after the head of the original Arawa canoe which first made landfall in the Bay of Plenty in the 14th century.

Just opposite the *marae* is the Tudor-style **St Faith's Church** ① *daily 0800-1700, free*, built in 1910. Its interior pillars, beams, rafters and pews are beautifully carved with Maori designs, and on a sandblasted window overlooking the lake a 'Maori Christ' is portrayed, dressed in a *korowai* (chief's cloak). Buried in the graveyard are many notable members of the Arawa tribe, among them the only European to be admitted to full chieftainship, the colonial force officer Captain Gilbert Mair (1843-1923). He twice saved the Arawa from inter-tribal attacks. It is interesting to note that the graves are built above ground to protect them from the thermal activity and intense heat. Had they been buried in the conventional style they would have been cooked before the last sod of earth had been replaced. At the entrance of the churchyard is a four-gabled canopy under which a bust of Queen Victoria used to sit. It was presented to the Arawa in 1870 by Prince Albert, the first member of the British royal family to visit New Zealand. The bust recently disappeared in mysterious circumstances. All around the village you can see quite intense thermal activity, that was enjoyed and utilized by the first Maori settlers. There is still a boiling pool near the church that is frequently used for boiling eggs and cooking meat – and perhaps the occasional member of the British monarchy.

Government Gardens and Rotorua Museum of Art and History
① *T07-349 4350, www.rotoruamuseum.co.nz, daily, summer 0900-2000, winter 0930-1700, $11, child $5. Guided tours daily at 1100 and 1400. Shop and a café on site.*

Rotorua detail

N

0 metres 200
0 yards 200

Sleeping 😴
Ambassador
  Thermal Motel **1** A2

Base Backpackers **6** C2
Central Backpackers **3** B2
Crash Palace **4** C2
Eaton Hall **5** C2
Millennium Rotorua, Nikau
  Restaurant & Zazu Bar **8** C3
Princes Gate **9** B2
Royal Lakeside
  Novotel **10** A2
Treks Backpackers **2** B1

Eating 🍴
Bistro 1284 **1** C1
Blue Baths **8** B3
Fat Dog **2** A2
Freos **3** A2
Lewisham's **6** A2
Lovely India **7** A2
Pig & Whistle **9** B2
Relish **5** A2
Rendezvous **10** C1

Robert Harris Coffee
  House **11** C2
Zambique **12** A2
Zanelli's **13** B1

Bars & clubs 🍸
Fuze **15** A2
Hennessey's **4** B2
Lava **14** B1

Just west of Ohinemutu and fringing Lake Rotorua are the elegant and beautifully maintained **Government Gardens**. They form a stark and attractive setting for the museum, with the well-manicured bowling greens and croquet lawns, ponds and scented roses, creating a distinctly Edwardian, colonial atmosphere.

The **Rotorua Museum of Art and History** itself is housed in the once-famous **Bath House**. Built in 1908, it was designed along the lines of the European spas and attracted hundreds of clients the world over who hoped to take advantage of the thermal waters' therapeutic and curative powers. At the time the soothing waters were thought to be a cure for any ailments, as diverse as anxiety and even obesity. Its popularity for 'taking the cure', together with the added volcanic features and attractions surrounding the city, made the Bath House the focus of the New Zealand government's first major investment in the new concept of tourism. In one wing of the museum you can see some of the original baths, changing rooms and equipment, together with photographs. Given the rich local Maori history it is not surprising to find a superb collection of Te Arawa *taonga* (treasures) which contrast interestingly with collections of modern artworks by local Maori artists. There are also displays that feature the great Tarawera eruption of 1886 as well as touring exhibitions and more modern dynamic offerings. Not to be missed is the excellent audio-visual display entitled *Rotorua Stories*. It screens every 20 minutes and is a 15-minute introduction to the great historical legends and stories of the area. It comes complete with shuddering pews during the fascinating account and depiction of the Tarawera eruption.

A short distance from the museum are the **Blue Baths** (Blueys) ① *T07-350 2119, daily, 1000-1600 in winter, pools open till 1900 in summer, from $9, child $6*. Built in the Spanish Mission style during the Great Depression of 1933, the pools soon flourished as one of the major social and recreational venues in the city, and were one of the first public baths to offer 'mixed' bathing. Due to competition and social change, the Blueys' were closed in 1982. However, still much loved, they were restored and re-opened in 1999 as functional hot pools, museum and tearooms. There is an entertaining video presentation relating the story of the pools, and the museum displays are imaginatively set in the former male and female changing room cubicles.

Behind the Blue Baths is the highly popular **Polynesian Spa complex** ① *T07-348 1328, www.polynesianspa.co.nz, daily 0800-2300, $15, child $4*. Rain or shine this is a Rotorua 'must do' and, although often very busy, it is a delight. There is a luxury spa complex and hot springs and pools, private spa pools, a family spa, shop and café. A range of massage treatments are also available. If you cannot afford the luxury spa then the therapeutic adult hot springs will not be a disappointment. Until recently the main baths, which range in temperature from 33°C to 43°C, were set outside in timber-style tubs overlooking the lake and although they still remain a new complex has recently been added to address the ever-increasing visitor numbers. Progress aside, it is a great place to ease the aches and pains of your active tourist pursuits and to mix with the locals, though the omnipresent tour groups can make it all very chaotic. The best times to go are at lunch and dinnertime when the tour buses are elsewhere.

Whakarewarewa/Te Puia

① *3 km south of the city, along Fenton St (just head for the steam), T07-348 9047, www.tepuia.com, summer daily 0800-1800, winter 0800-100, $28, child $14, guided tours depart hourly. Maori concerts 1015, 1215, 1515, tour and concert $35, child $17.50. Mai-Ora evening performance and feast 1515, 1815, $85, child $50. General admission and Mai-Ora $101, child $57.50. There is a shop and a café on site.*

'Whaka' (pronounced 'Fuckka') is the most famous and historic of the region's thermal reserves. The entire complex has recently undergone a face-lift and been re-branded under the banner of **Te Puia**, which relates to the former fortified 'pa' that protected the resident tribe. With the new name and, naturally, the new prices, it claims to be New Zealand's premier Maori cultural centre and is certainly the most commercial. The complex includes the Rotowhio Marae, the Mai Ora Village (a replica of the former Te Arawa Maori settlement) and the modern and thriving Maori Arts and Crafts Institute. The complex also hosts a number of natural thermal attractions. The star attraction is the much-celebrated Pohutu, the country's largest geyser, but as well as the great spout there are also boiling pools, silica terraces and, of course, the obligatory bubbling mud.

On entering you have the option of self-guided or Maori-guided tour (recommended) around the reserve. A series of paths branch out from the main visitor block and take in a strictly 'showpiece' nocturnal kiwi house before passing the large and at times, fairly inert Ngamokaiakoko ('Leaping Frog') mud pool, before the path delivers you at the geyser formations. There used to be around 60 geysers in Whaka, but now there are essentially two. The famed **Pohutu** or 'Big Splash' goes off like a broken water hydrant 10 to 25 times a day (more recently for days on end), to a height of over 30 m, while the more impotent Prince of Wales (sorry Charles) geyser nearby, is less spectacular.

The tracks then negotiate the small mud pools and volcanic features of the valley before arriving back near the entrance and the **Rotowhio Marae**. There are many features in this functional *marae*, including a banquet and weaving house and a *waka* (canoe). The *marae* also hosts daily **cultural performances** that feature a traditional *powhiri* (welcome), demonstration of the *taiaha* (warrior's weapon), *haka* (posture dance), *poi* (women's dance) and a range of traditional Maori songs. A longer performance entitled 'Mai-Ora' in the evenings also includes a *hangi* (feast). There is a deliberate element of interactivity with visitors, but it is generally well balanced and if you're feeling shy you won't be forced to join in.

The **Maori Arts and Crafts Institute** was established in 1963 to ensure that the traditional artist aspects of Maori culture are not lost. A viewing platform allows visitors to see students at work in the woodcarving studio before taking them through galleries and display areas where pieces of completed work can be seen and are for sale.

Whakarewarewa Forest Park

On the southern outskirts of Rotorua is the recreational playground of the Whakarewarewa Forest Park, well known for its excellent walking and mountain biking opportunities. The best way to choose from those opportunities is to visit the **Fletcher Challenge Information Centre** ① *Long Mile Rd, off Tarawera Rd, just off SH30 heading east, T07-350 0110, Mon-Fri 0830-1730, Sat-Sun 1000-1600*. It has a number of interesting interpretative displays as well as all track information and colour-coded track maps. The walks range from 20 minutes to eight hours, with the shortest taking in a tract of giant **Californian Redwoods** (along Long Mile Road) and the longest taking in the shores of the Blue and Green lakes. ▸▸ *See Activities and tours, page 257.*

Kuirua Park

If you arrive in the city from SH4 north, the steam that issues from the thermal features in Kuirua Park will be your first sight and smell (if not taste) of the city's volcanic activity. The park is 25 ha, with gardens linked by tracks to a number of low-key thermal pools and features, as well as the cutely named 'Toot and Whistle' miniature steam railway, which is perfect for kids. There is also a miniature golf course and the city's **Aquatic Centre** ① *0600-2100*. While in the vicinity of Kuirua take a short drive down Tarawera Road. On the left heading south, you will see two fenced-off sections that are billowing steam. These were – believe it or not – former properties until 1998, when new boiling springs literally erupted in the driveway. Under a system of government volcanic damage compensation the families were forced to move and the land given back to nature.

If you want a great view of the city and surrounding area, then **Mount Ngongotaha** to the west of the city is easily accessible by car. From SH5 heading north, take Clayton Road at the crossroads with the Old Taupo Road. After about 3 km Mountain Road is signposted off Clayton to the right. The **Aorangi Peak Restaurant** is near the summit.

Around Rotorua

To Tauranga

Okere Falls

Skyline Skyrides

Hamurana Gardens

Okere Hamurana Rd

Oturoa Rd

To Waitomo, Hamilton, & Auckland

6

Lake Rotorua

33

Hell's Gate & Waiora Spa

3

4

Lake Rotokawau

Agrodome

5

9

Mokoia Island

30

Lake Rotokawa

Paradise Valley Ventures

Rainbow Springs
Skyline Skyrides

7 Kawaha Point

8

Kiwi Encounter

Mt Ngongotaha

Paradise Valley Rd

Paradise Valley Springs

Pukehangi Rd

Rotorua

A

Lynmore

Fletcher Challenge Information Centre

Whakarewarewa/ Te Puia

Lake Okareka

Whakarewarewa Forest Park

Blue Lake

1

2 **2**

Te Wairoa Buried Village

Green Lake

Tamaki Maori Village

Related maps
A Rotorua, p239.

Waimangu Rd

5

N

0 Km 1
0 miles 1

Sleeping
Accolades Boutique **4**
Ariki Lodge **9**
Blue Lake Holiday Park **1**
Duxton Okawa Bay **3**
Hamurana Country Estate **6**
Kawaha Point Lodge **8**
Lake Tarawera Lodge **2**
Peppers On The Point **7**
Solitaire Lodge **5**

Eating
Landings Café **2**

Waikite Thermal Pools

Waikite Valley Rd

Lake Opouri

Mud Pools

Lady Knox Geyser
(Erupts at 1015 daily)

Wai-O-Tapu

To Orakei Korako, Wairakei & Taupo

Bay of Plenty Rotorua

Bay of Plenty Rotorua

Around Rotorua ⊟ ⊩ *pp251-258.*

Blue and Green lakes → *Colour map 2 ,C3*

Southeast of the city, off SH30, Mount Tarawera Road takes you to some of the most celebrated lakes of the Rotorua region. The road runs adjacent to the Whakarewarewa Forest Park, before arriving at the Blue and Green lakes. **Blue Lake** (Tikitapu) has a very cheery atmosphere and is good for boating and swimming, with a very pleasant walking track that circumnavigates its shores, while **Green Lake** (Rotokakahi) is *tapu* (sacred) and off limits to all recreational activities.

Buried Village

Past the Blue and Green lakes, the road enters the Te Wairoa Valley, home of the Buried Village. Prior to the 1886 eruption, the Te Wairoa Valley was the focus for Maori-guided tourist trips to see the pink and white terraces at the foot of Mount Tarawera. The sudden and violent eruption of Tarawera on the evening of 10 June 1886 was witnessed by the tourists staying at the village hotel. Sadly for them and many of the settlers, this sight of the mountain was their last. Much of the area, including the village and its hotel, was laid waste with a blanket of rock and ash falls. Interestingly it was the Maori *whare* (houses) that fared better due to their stronger construction and steeply sloping roofs. There is a small and fascinating **museum** ① T07-362 8287, *www.buriedvillage.co.nz, daily 0900-1730, $25, child $7,* which relates the sorry tale, complete with everyday items excavated from the ash almost a century later. Of particular interest is the treatment of the poor Maori elder who, hours before the eruption, made the prediction that it was about to blow. After the interior displays of the museum, a pleasant walk takes you around the remains of some of the original buildings. To complete the main walk you have the option of a 10-minute extension on a new boardwalk above the 80-m **Te Wairoa Falls** that offers views across the lake. You can take a guided or a self-guided tour of the village. There's a shop and café on site – not to mention the occasional ghost.

Lake Tarawera → *Colour map 2, C3*

Lake Tarawera is almost the same size as Lake Rotorua and lies at the slightly higher elevation of 315 m. With a shoreline that is sparsely populated and almost entirely rimmed with bush, the lake has a pleasant atmosphere, dominated by the slopes of the jagged volcanic ridge of Mount Tarawera on its western shore. The lake has been altered in both shape and depth by Tarawera's eruptions over the centuries.

It was on Lake Tarawera on 31 May 1886 that two separate boat loads of tourists, on their way to see the then world-famous Pink and White Terraces (since obliterated), caught sight of a fully-manned *waka* (war canoe) in the mists. Both the Maori and the *pakeha* knew there was no such *waka* in the region and, due to the fact it was seen by so many independent eyewitnesses, it was taken as a bad omen. Just 11 days later Tarawera erupted and the whole area was laid waste with the loss of 150 lives. Today the lake is an almost deceptive picture of serenity and is the venue for fishing and other water-based recreational activities. **Hot Water Beach** on its southern edge is a popular spot where thermal activity creates an area of warm water, which is pleasant for bathing.

There are three DoC campsites and numerous walking opportunities around Lake Tarawera, including the excellent **Tarawera Falls Track**. The best way to visit the beach and to take in the atmosphere and learn more of the area's diverse and, at times, violent history, is on one of the three tours available, see Activities and tours, page 256, for details. The **Landing Café**, T07-362 8502, opposite the jetty, just off Lake Tarawera Road, is a fine place for a meal or snack.

Mount Tarawera

Standing at 1111 m, with a 6-km converging gash of craters, is the dormant volcano Mount Tarawera. In looks it is very different to the highly classic snow-capped cones of Ngauruhoe and Ruapehu in central North Island. It is essentially a conglomerate of three mountains: **Wahanga** to the north, **Ruawahia** in the centre and **Tarawera** to the south. All were naturally very different in appearance prior to their eruption in 1886.

A number of scenic helicopter flights and 4WD tours provide the opportunity to see its colourful interior, but generally speaking it is hard to access independently and is on Maori Reserve Land. Indeed, there is no public transport for miles around and independent access is actively discouraged. Guided tours by 4WD are available with **Mount Tarawera NZ Ltd**, see page 257. For mountain activity operators, see page 255.

Tarawera Falls

① *To access the forest you need a permit, obtainable from the Fletcher Challenge Forests Redwood Grove Visitor Centre, Long Mile Rd, Rotorua, T07-346 2082; or from the Kawerau VIC, Filter Photography Shop, Tawarewa Court Mall, Kawarau, T07-323 7550. The permit costs $2 and is valid for 2 weeks. They will give you directions on how to access the forest itself and negotiate the unsealed tracks to the falls car park.*

The Tarawera Falls and walkway are set in the heart of the **Tarawera Forest**, where the Tarawera River flows from the eastern shores of Lake Tarawera and northern slopes of Mount Tarawera. The falls are remote and hard to access, but this is part of their charm, and the effort is definitely worthwhile. The walkway, complete with waterfalls, a disappearing river, beautiful native bush and swimming holes, has to rate as one of the North Island's best short to medium walkways. The falls are of particular interest because the river first disappears underground before reappearing from a sheer cliff face. The track can be tackled either from above or below the falls.

There are three or four ways to get there. By car it is a 70-km drive (one way) from Rotorua via SH30 and the forestry township of Kawerau. Although the roads through the forest are very straight, do not go fast, and keep your headlights on at all times. Once you reach the falls car park it is a 10-minute walk to the base of the falls past the crystal-clear waters of the river. From the falls the track then zig-zags up behind them, through native bush with huge ponga ferns before arriving at the point where the river disappears underground. Then you can continue past a series of other beautiful falls and a swimming hole before emerging at the head of Lake Tarawera. The walk to the lake is about 4 km (2½ hours one way). You can also access the track via the Eastern Okaitania Walkway, but in total this involves an enjoyable two-day tramp. The falls are also part of the agenda on the recommended full-day tour with **Te Kiri Treks**, T07-345 5016 (see Activities and tours, page 258). You may also be able to negotiate being dropped off and picked up by charter boat from Lake Tarawera (see page 256).

Tamaki Maori Village

About 10 km south of Whakarewarewa, on SH5, Tamaki Maori Village is an award-winning complex that was created by **Tamaki Tours** ① *T07-349 2999, www.maori culture.co.nz, daily 0900-1600*, one of the original creators of the Maori concert and *hangi* experience. The village is a faithful recreation of Maori buildings, custom and lifestyle prior to European settlement. It also houses an **art gallery**, specializing in Maori art. There is a daily concert performance at 1230. Perhaps the best way to see the village is to join the 'Twilight Concert and Tour', from $92 (see page 257). Alternatively, **Tamaki Tours** offers an hourly shuttle from the city.

Wai-O-Tapu

① *29 km south of Rotorua off SH5, not to be confused with Waimangu Thermal Valley 4 km before it, T07-366 6333, www.geyserland.co.nz, daily 0830-1700, $25, child $8.50. Dave's Shuttles offers a daily and regular service from Rotorua (VIC at 0925), $20* *return, T027-246 7451. Geyser Link Shuttles, T0800-000 4321, also offers transport from Rotorua (VIC at 0930) for $20-25, half-day tour along with te Puia from $85.*

Wai-O-Tapu is, without doubt, the best thermal park in the region, with an almost surreal and colourful range of volcanic features, from mud pools and silica terraces to the famous and beautiful 'Champagne Pool'. If you can, time your arrival with the daily 1015 eruption of the **Lady Knox Geyser**, which is signposted on the Wai-O-Tapu Loop Road (off SH5).

Just before the geyser, again on the Loop Road, are a number or globulous mud pools that are separate from the park itself. These, too, are worth a peek. The thermal park proper is at the southern end of the Loop Road. The full self-guided walk around the park will take about two hours. Along the first section of track there are a number of features including steaming caverns, mud pools and cavernous holes, with evocative names like **Devil's Home** (very photogenic), the **Devil's Ink Pots** and **Thunder Crater**. The track then arrives at a lookout across the aptly named **Artist's Palette**, a multi-coloured silica field. It really is a wonderful sight to behold with pastel shades of yellow, green and blue, fading in and out of swathes of billowing white steam. A boardwalk takes you across the silica fields, where you can either go on to investigate a silica waterfall, some 'alum cliffs', 'frying pan flat' and some colourful lakes, or (more likely) get entirely engrossed with the **Champagne Pool**. This is hard to describe, but essentially is a bright orange-edged, steaming, fizzing pool of about 60 m in diameter. Without doubt it is the highlight of the park and certainly rates as a 10 out of 10 on the 'awesometer'. What you are looking at is in fact a 62-m-deep flooded volcanic vent, the base of which boils the water to a surface temperature of around 74°C. Hot stuff. From the Champagne Pool it is a short meander past more steaming, gurgling crevasses and a pastel green lake, before returning to the visitor centre, shop and café.

Kerosene Creek

Between the Waiotapu and Waimangu Thermal Reserves is the dormant 'volcanoette' **Rainbow Mountain**, which although commanding a fine view from the summit requires a 4WD and considerable guile to get there. Far less stressful is a visit to the natural hot waters of **Kerosene Creek** that emanates from the lakes at its base. DO NOT swim in the lakes. It is not a good idea to do so as a rather sad-looking white cross with dishevelled flowers would suggest. Instead, go past the lakes down Old Waiotapu Road (signposted off SH5) to the marked Kerosene Creek parking area. The rest is all towels and 'Oooohh that's good'. One word of warning however: you will very probably not be alone, especially in summer, and the car park is often hit by thieves, so do not leave valuables in the car and make sure you lock it.

Waimangu Volcanic Valley

ⓘ *26 km south of Rotorua, off SH5, T07-366 6137, www.waimangu.com, daily 0830-1645. There is a walk-only or walk and cruise option from $28, child $7.50. There is also a full-day Waimangu round-trip tour with road transport, a visit to the Buried Village, a cruise on Lake Tarawera, and an easy 3.6-km walk with lunch, from $255. Dave's Shuttles offers a daily regular service from Rotorua (outside VIC from 0925) $20 return T027-246 7451.*

The volcanic features in the Waimangu Volcanic Valley are all very recent and were created as a result of the 1886 eruption of Tarawera. Lake Rotomahana is essentially a water-filled crater which, before the eruption, was once the site of the famed pink and white silica terraces. Sadly, both of the terraces were completely obliterated by the eruption, but what were created in their place were the lake and a number of new volcanic features around it. These include the **Waimangu Cauldron** – the world's largest boiling lake – the **Inferno Crater Lake** that rises and falls up to 10 m a month, steaming cliffs, and numerous boiling springs and steaming fumaroles. At the turn of the last century the now inactive **Waimangu Geyser** used to be the largest in the world, spouting water to a staggering 500 m. The park is self-guided and you can see it partly on foot and partly by boat but there are a number of options.

The **Waikite Thermal Pools** ① *between Waimangu and Wai-O-Tapu, from SH5 turn west onto Waikite Valley Rd at Waiotapu Tavern, the pools are about 4 km on the right, T07-333 1861, www.hotpools.co.nz, daily 1000-2130, $8, child $4*, consist of large family and adult hot pools in a country setting. Ideal for family picnics. Private pools and camping are also available.

Hell's Gate and the Waiora Spa → *Colour map 2, C3*

① *15 km from Rotorua, SH30, Tikitere, T07-345 3151, www.hellsgate.co.nz, daily 0900-2030, $25, child $10. Park entry, mud bath and spa from $80, child $30. Private mud bath and spa from $100. Massage 1 hr, $130. Hell's Gate offers a complimentary shuttle for its combo and massage packages. Geyser Link Shuttles, To800-000 4321, also offers shuttle services from Rotorua VIC at 0930, from $20.*

If you can ignore the very saucy looking, scantily clad couple daubing each other in mud on all the promotional material, the aptly-named Hell's Gate thermal reserve and Waiora Spa, will not disappoint. It is not the most colourful of the reserves, but certainly one of the most active, and a thoroughly steamy affair. The 10 ha are set on two levels separated by a tract of bush, yet subtly connected by a warm thermal stream, complete with steaming waterfall. The pools of bubbly mud and water on the lower levels, with such evocative names as 'Sodom and Gomorrah' and 'The Inferno', hiss with menace and are quite scary, reaching temperatures well over that required to boil your potatoes.

The upper level of the reserve is much of the same, with steaming lakes and myriad tiny steaming vents, scattered with features including mini mud volcanoes and cauldrons of boiling water. Best of all is the **Devil's Cauldron**, a small pit that is home to a lively globular mud pool which makes the most wonderfully disgusting noises. Thankfully the entire reserve is connected with a boardwalk, from which, for obvious reasons, you are encouraged not to stray.

With all that mineral rich bubbly mud about it would seem rude not to create a **mud spa** and this is indeed Hells Gate's latest venture. There are a number of attractive options from massage or sulphur spas, to the wonderfully messy and therapeutic mud facials, scrubs and (best of all) private mud baths. After all that, the small shop and café, which are also on site, seem a little mundane.

Agrodome complex

① *10 km north of Rotorua on SH5, T07-357 1050, www.agrodome.co.nz, www.zorb.com, daily 0830-1700. Shows at 0930, 1100 and 1430, $22, child $11 (farm tour $5 extra). Try to attend the busiest show: mid-morning or mid-afternoon.*

The Agrodome complex is one of the principal tourist draws on the Rotorua circuit, and deservedly so. It has a wide array of attractions from the full-on **bungee jump** to some more sedate farm activities. The focus of the complex and its principal feature attraction is the **sheep show**. If the very thought of such an event leaves you cold, then think again: it is highly entertaining. This ovine spectacular features over 19 breeds of sheep – all of which are highly domesticated, wonderfully tame and very co-operative. Before the show starts the 'stars' are available for copious stroking and perhaps an autograph if you're lucky. The actual animal show is very informative, entertaining and professional. There is much audience participation and the opportunity to bottle-feed the lambs. As for the audience, well, they are almost as entertaining as they attempt to video and photograph the entire proceedings.

Surrounding the Agrodome there are a scattering of sundry attractions including a **woollen mill** and a **chocolate factory**. Activities abound including a **farm tour** (optional extension to the sheep show, combo $28, child $13), Freefall Extreme ($45), helicopter rides (from $69-665) and jet boats ($40 child $30), as well as the 'Swoop' and 'Zorbing'. The **Swoop** is a glorified swing, where you are strapped into a harness then dropped from a height of 40 m. Apparently somewhere on the way down you reach over 130 kph, with a G-force of three, which, roughly translated, means your kidneys seek an unexpected and rapid exit out of your back passage. However, it all seems to go down very well ($40, child $30). **Zorbing** is described as a 'biospherical monumentous disturbance' and is the unique New Zealand invention of rolling down a hill in a large clear plastic bubble. It can, if you so wish, be filled, with a bucket or six of water. It is highly entertaining but a bit of a rip-off as the entire episode lasts about 10 seconds and costs $45. **Freefall Extreme** is the latest thriller and involves a lot of wind and a very fetching suit, all in order to simulate a freefall experience from about 5 m. It is fun but the real thing is far better, so long as you have a nice chappy with a parachute on your back. Once flush with adrenaline you can sample the souvenir shop and café on site.

Trout Springs and Kiwi Encounter

The Rotorua region is rich in freshwater springs, the streams from which are home to thousands of brown and rainbow trout. Trout are not native to New Zealand and were introduced to the region in the 1800s. Some of these springs have been developed into tourist resorts where you can observe both wild and captive trout above and below the water or feed the swirling masses. Some streams are also home to the unbelievably huge native New Zealand eels.

The largest and most popular springs resort is **Rainbow Springs** ① *5 km from the city centre on SH5 north, T07-350 0440, www.rainbowsprings.co.nz, 0800-2100 (later in summer), $25, child $13.50.* Here the attraction of the trout is combined with other wildlife treats, including some very tame native birds in a free-flight aviary. The underwater viewing area is particularly popular and a fine reminder of what fish should look like as opposed to piled up on a platter in a fish shop or supermarket counter with that 'Oh my God' expression on their faces. There are also fluffy farm animals for the kids to stroke and regular guided tours of the park, farm animal shows and a café on site.

There are also the smaller but quite charming **Paradise Valley Springs** ① *11 km from the city along Claydon Rd, which is straight on at the Koutu Corner intersection as you head north out of the city on the Old Taupo Rd, T07-348 9667, www.paradise valley.co.nz, daily 0800-dusk, $23, children $11.50.* This attraction is very similar to Rainbow Springs with the same features (and added lions), but provided there are no coach tours, it enjoys a quieter, more congenial atmosphere. There is also a small bottling plant which utilizes the pure spring water. The **Geyser Link**, T0800-000 4321, offers regular shuttle services from $20.

Opposite the Rainbow Springs complex is the new **Kiwi Encounter complex** ① *T07-350 0440, www.kiwiencounter.co.nz, 1000-1700, $26.50, child $16.50.* As the name suggests the attraction comes in the form of that truly enigmatic creature and national icon, the kiwi. There are of course a number of well-established tourist operations that display kiwi throughout New Zealand and some fine ones too, but this is undoubtedly one of the best. Here, right from the outset they seem to strike a fine balance between pleasing people and making money but not doing so to the detriment or exploitation of the birds themselves. All the display material is impressive enough, but it is the fact that it is a working hatchery that holds eminent appeal. You will certainly see live kiwi and be bemused at their hilarious natural antics, ie scuttling about like old men in big fur coats with their hands firmly in their pockets, or fussing about for food like a short-sighted old seamstress rummaging in a box of buttons. Surely if any animal should have evolved supporting a pair of bifocal spectacles, this is it. But that aside, the experience is only augmented by a view through to the husbandry area where you can see staff tending to incubating eggs, or, if you are very lucky, chicks (November to March). Needless to say the latter is a sight that would render a very large, menacing looking gentleman astride a Harley Davidson to a tearful dribbling mess.

Skyline Skyrides

ⓘ *T07-347 0027, www.skylineskyrides.co.nz, daily 0900-late. Gondola $22, child $10; gondola and 2 luge rides $35, child $17; gondola and 5 luge rides $39.*

If you are physically able, everyone who visits Rotorua should call into the Skyline Skyrides to take a ride up the mountain in the gondolas and have a go on the infamous luge, which basically involves throwing yourself down a concrete course on a plastic tray with wheels and primitive brakes. Sounds mad? It is, and apparently keeps the casualty department of Rotorua Hospital very well attended. However, don't let that deter since, like anything, a little daring it is utterly addictive and a lot of fun. Perhaps part of its appeal is the fact that once down, and if still alive, you can then hitch a ride on a secondary chairlift to repeat the operation time and again. You are given brief instructions, a plastic helmet and a chance to try the 'family' course first, just to get the hang of it. This is very slow – so much so that you can have a conversation with complete strangers, if not tea and cakes on the way down – and once completed you can attempt the main course with its savage turns and precipitous jumps. As well as the luge and scenic gondola there is also a Sky Swing that will reputedly fly you (and two others) through the air at 120 kph, from $30. Other more conventional activity options include helicopter trips, mountain biking and then once the adrenaline has settled there is always the scenic restaurant, with its memorable views across the city and the lake.

Whirinaki Forest Park

ⓘ *60 km southwest of Rotorua on SH38, T07-3661080. For detailed information of how to access this excellent forest park contact DoC in Rotorua, or better still call in at the DoC field centre on the main road in Murupara, at the northern edge of the park.*

Whirinaki Forest Park is one of New Zealand's finest remaining podocarp forests, aptly described by one famous botanist as a 'dinosaur forest'. The park is off the beaten track but that is part of its charm. There are a number of excellent **walking tracks** taking in the diverse remote forest landscape with giant trees, waterfalls, river valleys and lagoons. There are DoC campsites and huts within the park to allow longer multi-day tramps. For organized walking tours within Whirinaki, see Activities and tours, page 258.

● Sleeping

Rotorua *p238, maps p239 and p241*
There are over 12,000 tourist beds in Rotorua, so the choice is huge. Many of the main hotel chains are here and there are lots of motels on either side of Fenton St, between the centre of town and Whakarewarewa. Pre-booking is advised throughout the year. Whatever you do and wherever you end up, make sure there is an accessible hot pool in-house or nearby.

Hotels and B&Bs
LL-AL Grand Tiara Rotorua, corner of Fenton and Sala sts, T07-349 5200, www.grandhotelsinternational.com. Recently renovated, this is one of Rotorua's best and most expensive. Close to Te Puia (Whakarewarewa) thermal reserve, it has a pool, spas, gym, café, excellent cuisine specializing in Japanese and seafood and even an Irish pub attached. Maori concert and feasts nightly.

LL-AL Royal Lakeside Novotel, lake end of Tutanekai St, T07-346 3888, www.accor hotels.co.nz. In the heart of town, near Lake Rotorua and Government Gardens. Good reputation with in-house spas, and a popular restaurant and bar. It also offers one of the best hotel Maori concerts and *hangis*.

AL Millennium Rotorua, corner of Eruera and Hinemaru sts, T07-347 1234, www.millenniumrotorua.co.nz. Popular chain hotel just metres from the Polynesian Spa (discounts to guests). The modern rooms and suites have plenty of style with marble floored bathrooms and residential-style decor, Sky TV and internet access. The fine in-house bar and restaurant, **Nikau**, is considered one of the city's best. Although the Polynesian Spa is the best place to go, there is a spa and fitness centre on site, with massage, beauty and body treatments.

AL Quality Hotel Geyserland, 424 Fenton St, T07-348 2039, geyserland@silveroaks.co.nz. Famed for its location overlooking the Whakarewarewa (Te Puia) Thermal Reserve. You can literally hear the Pohutu geyser going off and look down on a pool of bubbling mud. Recently refurbished (though from the outside you wouldn't guess) it has all the usual facilities and in-house hot pools.

AL-A Kingsgate Hotel, Fenton St, T07-348 0199, www.kingsgaterotorua.co.nz. Recently refurbished, comfortable, no-nonsense option with good facilities including brasserie, pool, spa and gym. Offers its own Maori performance and banquet.

AL-A The Princes Gate, 1057 Arawa St, T07-348 1179, www.princesgate.co.nz. Conveniently located between the city centre and Government Gardens, the 1897 Princes Gate advertises itself as one of the country's leading boutique hotels. Whether it actually honours that heady claim is inevitably debatable, but there is no denying its character. There is a wide range of rooms, some fully self-contained, and replete with 4-poster beds and (a rarity these days) a proper bath. An elegant in-house bar/restaurant, sauna and the obligatory private thermal pools all add to the hotels appeal.

A-B Eaton Hall, 1255 Hinemaru St, T07-347 0366, www.eatonhallbnb.cjb.net. Good value, comfortable B&B, close to the Polynesian Spa.

A-B Robertson House, 70 Pererika St, T07-343 7559, www.robertsonhouse.co.nz. Lovingly restored colonial villa with plenty of character in a quiet location. 4 tidy, spacious en suites (twin and double) with standard facilities. A good mid-range B&B option.

A-B The Springs, 16 Devon St, T07-348 9922, www.thesprings.co.nz. Purpose-built luxury B&B in a quiet central location. 4 attractive en suites, off-street parking.

Motels

There are almost 100 motels in Rotorua, most on Fenton St, so the choice is vast. Most are modern and very much the same and, given the fierce competition, you will rarely be let down. The best bet is to take a drive down Fenton and literally take your pick. The following are just a few of the most recommended or well-situated.

AL Four Canoes, 273 Fenton St, T07-348 9184/T0800-422663, www.fourcanoes.com.

Hotel/motel that uses the Maori theme and an evening Maori performance and *hangi* to attract custom. Wide range of suites with spa pools and a buffet restaurant.

AL Silver Fern, 326 Fenton St, T07-346 3849, www.silverfernmotorinn.co.nz. Hailed as one of the city's best. Range of suites with spa pools.

AL-A Ambassador Thermal Motel, corner of Whakaue and Hinemaru sts, T07-347 9581, www.ambassrotorua.co.nz. Ideal waterfront location close to the Polynesian Spa.

AL-A Geneva Motor Lodge, 299 Fenton St, T07-348 6033/T0800-333002, www.geneva motorlodge.co.nz. 14 tidy suites and 2 units with spas and spa pool.

AL-A Regal Palms, 350 Fenton St, T07-350 3232/T0800-743000, www.regalpalmsml.co.nz. The Regal is one Rotorua's newest motels and is certainly one of the best. Very classy decor and attention to detail throughout, which goes well beyond what you might expect from a motel, even with its 5-star rating. Superior and executive suites and apartments all with spa. Facilities also include a sauna, internet and guest lounge and bar.

AL-A Wylie Court, 345 Fenton St, T07-347 7879, www.wyliecourt.co.nz. 36 suites, with pool and a restaurant. Free wireless internet

A Ascot on Fenton, 247 Fenton St, T07-348 7712, www.ascotmotel.co.nz. Spas in all units.

A Bel Aire Motel, 257 Fenton St, T07-348 6076. Older and good value.

B Anns Volcanic, 107 Malfroy Rd, T07-347 1007, www.rotoruamotel.co.nz. Offers good rates and a first rate personable service.

B Rob Roy Motor Inn, 291 Fenton St, T07-348 0584, www.robroymotel.co.nz. Offers good rates and has a thermal mineral pool.

Hostels

B-D Base Backpackers, 1140 Hinemoa St, T07-350 2040, www.basebackpackers.com. Centred around the 20-m climbing wall complex, this new, spacious multi-level facility provides tidy modern rooms from 4-8 dorm to doubles with en suite bathroom, a café, large games room, good kitchen facilities, internet access and a bar overlooking the climbing action. It also features a female only area. The only drawback is the lack of off-street parking.

B-D Funky Green Voyager, 4 Union St, T07-346 1754. One of the city's smallest and best backpacker hostel. Well-established and eco-friendly offering 4 doubles, 8 twins and dorms. Good kitchen facilities, plenty of local information and close to the supermarket. Parking a bonus.

B-D Kiwi Paka, 60 Tarewa Rd, T07-347 0931, www.kiwipaka-yha.co.nz. A deservingly popular establishment, with a fine range of dorm, unit, motel, campervan and campsite options. The staff are on the ball and the amenities are excellent. There's a large kitchen and sitting room, a bar and café and a thermal pool. Activities arranged. It is a bit out of town but most operators provide pick-ups.

B-D Treks Backpackers, 1278 Haupapa St, T07-349 4088, www.treks.co.nz. A fine establishment and the newest addition to Rotorua's competitive scene. Carefully considered in layout and design, well facilitated (with a glorious kitchen and living area and en suite doubles) and run by caring staff, it is undoubtedly a fine choice. Prides itself in individual attention so more mature travellers and couples are well looked after and the loud party crowds discouraged. Local activities are personally researched so there is lots of sound advice that will only enhance your visit to the region. Recommended.

C-D Central Backpackers, 1076 Pukuatua St, T07-349 3285. A congenial, friendly and more historic establishment that is deservedly growing in popularity. Beds not bunks, single rooms, an in-house spa and off-street parking.

C-D Crash Palace, 1271 Hinemaru St, T07-348 8842, www.crashpalace.co.nz. Head here for the quieter more homely treatment.

Motorcamps and campsites

B-D Cosy Cottage, 67 Whittaker Rd, T07-348 3793. An excellent motorcamp just north of the city centre, almost lakeside. It is one of the only motorcamps in the world that can boast a 'naturally heated' campsite. It has a wide range of cabins, good amenities and spa pools.

B-D Rotorua Thermal Holiday Park, Old Taupo Rd, T07-3463140, www.rotorua thermal.co.nz. Well-maintained, spacious and sheltered motorpark with a wide range of accommodation options from standard self-contained units to standard and en suite log cabins, powered and non-powered sites. There is a good camp kitchen for self-caterers, a comfortable TV lounge, internet, small shop, a fine licensed café and free hot pools on site. Within walking distance of the Whakarewarewa (Te Puia) Thermal Reserve.

Rotorua and the surrounding area is exceptionally well endowed when it comes to luxurious rural lodges, boutique hotels and B&Bs. Most are lakeside and offer peace and quiet with all the usual 5-star mod cons. The VIC in Rotorua has full listings.

LL Accolades Boutique Hotel, 31 Flemington Pl, Brunswick, T07-345 5033, www.accolades-boutique-hotel.co.nz. A stunning 5-star property in a quiet rural location. Spacious, exuding class and commanding fine views across Lake Rotorua. Excellent facilities and exceptional hosts. Recommended.

LL Hamurana Country Estate, 415 Hamurana Rd, Ngongotaha, T07-332 2222, www.hcestate.co.nz. Luxurious mansion, recently fully refurbished, with 12 luxury en suites, the best of which overlook Lake Rotorua. Beautifully appointed and well regarded for its cuisine.

LL Peppers On The Point, 214 Kawaha Point Rd, Rotorua, T07-348 4868, www.onthe point.co.nz. Beautifully refurbished, spacious 1930's lodge set in an elevated position overlooking Lake Rotorua. Sumptuous, tasteful interior design incorporating 7 en suites with spa. In-house fine dining, health treatments and a gym. Pure class.

LL Solitaire Lodge, Lake Tarawera, T07-362 8208, www.solitairelodge.co.nz. Highly celebrated hideaway on the shores of Lake Tarawera. Excellent service, fine attention to detail in the Kiwi-faceted decor, and a great range of facilities. A choice of 9 spacious, luxurious suites, some with spa, private decks and lake views. Of added appeal is the cuisine at the in-house restaurant and a collection of art showcasing some stunning original artworks by, amongst others, celebrated New Zealand wildlife artist Raymond Ching. Various charter boats and fishing guides are available from the lodge.

L Duxton Okawa Bay, SH33, Mourea, Lake Rotoiti, T07-362 4599, www.duxton.com. A good mid-luxury hotel option out of town, in an idyllic lakeside setting. Full amenities including restaurant and private beach.

L Kawaha Point Lodge, 171 Kawaha Point Rd, lakeside, T07-346 3602, www.kawaha lodge.co.nz. Classy kauri lodge with 8 en suite double or twins, 2 with spa baths, garden with pool.

AL Lake Tarawera Lodge, Te Mu Rd, Lake Tarawera, T07-362 8754, www.lake tarawera.co.nz. Beautiful location. 6 self-contained country-style cottages, 6-roomed Mission House and campsite. Very popular with the fishing fraternity, trips arranged.

AL-A Ariki Lodge, 2 Manuariki Av, Ngongotaha, T07-357 5532. Spacious, well-appointed and lakeside, Ariki offers a good mid-range option north of the city.

Motorcamps and campsites
B-D Blue Lake Holiday Park, on the banks of Blue Lake on Tarawera Rd, T07-362 8120. If you are looking for a quiet country spot look no further. There is a beach across the road for swimming, kayak hire and a lovely walk around the lake.

● Eating

Rotorua *p238, maps p239 and p241*
There are more than 50 restaurants in Rotorua offering a wide range of cuisine to suit all budgets. Most of them are on or around Tutanekai St towards the lake. You should also consider sampling one of the many Maori *hangis* available. Few of them are truly authentic, having neither the time nor the health and safety go-ahead to dig earth pits and cook the food underground, they will still give you just a taste of how good a Maori *hangi* can be (for options see page 247).

₦₦₦ Lewisham's Café and Restaurant, 1099 Tutanekai St, T07-3481786, daily 0930-2200. Has a good reputation, offering traditional European dishes with a definite Austrian edge. The venison and wiener schnitzel are recommended.

₦₦₦ Nikau Restaurant, in the Millennium Rotorua hotel (see Sleeping, page 251), T07-347 1234. A good reputation for traditional European and Kiwi-style fine dining without being too formal. The bar, **Zazu**, is also popular.

₦₦₦ The Rendezvous, 1282 Hinemoa St, T07-348 9273, daily from 1800. A popular award-winning restaurant offering fine Pacific Rim dishes in very congenial surroundings. There is venison, quail and even emu on the menu.

₦₦₦ Zanelli's, 1243 Amohia St, T07-348 4908, Tue-Sun from 1730. Touted as the best Italian restaurant.

₦₦ Freos, lake end of Tutanekai St, T07-346 0976, daily from 0830. A busy little café/restaurant that offers traditional Kiwi fare and has a loyal following.

₦₦ Landings Café, Spencer Rd, Lake Tarawera, T07-362 8502, daily from 0900. Book for dinner. A fine, affordable and friendly spot with a distinctive Scots flavour.

₦₦ Lovely India, 1123 Tutaneaki St, T07-348 4088, daily from 1130. Perhaps the best Indian eatery in the city and good value.

₦₦ The Pig and Whistle, corner of Haupapa and Tutanekai sts, T07-347 3025, daily 1130-2130. Great pub food washed down with their own brews.

₦₦ Relish, 1149 Tutanekai St, T07-343 9195. Usually busy with a fine atmosphere and locally recommended for pizza.

₦₦ Zambique, Tutanekai St, T07-349 2140, Mon-Sat from 0800-late. Well known for its creative modern dishes and good coffee.

₦ Bistro 1284, 1284 Eruera St, T07-364 1284. Tue-Sat from 1800, booking advised. Congenial little place causing something of a stir locally having won the city's best restaurant award 4 years running. Crispy skinned chicken with smoked mushroom sausages is the signature dish with lamb another speciality. Recommended.

₦ Blue Baths, Government Gardens, T07-350 2119, daily 1000-1600. Afternoon teas and traditional Kiwi fare in historic tearooms.

₦ Fat Dog, 1161 Arawa St, T07-347 7586. Mon-Fri 0900-late, Sat-Sun 0800-late. Consistently rated as the best café in town, always busy and friendly with a mixed clientele. Imaginative blackboard menu.

₦ Robert Harris Coffee House, 227 Tutanekai St, daily from 0730. An old faithful, with the usual reliable snacks and breakfast.

● Pubs, bars and clubs

Rotorua *p238, maps p239 and p241*
Fuze, 1122 Tutaneaki St, T07-349 6306. New bar/restaurant/club in the heart of the action that attracts a slightly older crowd.

Hennessey's, 1206 Tutanekai St, T07-343 7901. Popular Irish pub. Good beer and live music.

Lava Bar, at the Hot Rock Backpackers, 118 Arawa St, T07-347 9469. Especially popular with travellers and a younger crowd.

Pig and Whistle, corner of Haupapa and Tutanekai sts, T07-347 3025. Nicely decorated, brews its own ales and has a congenial atmosphere. It also has bands on weekends. **Zazu Bar**, in the Millennium Rotorua hotel (see Sleeping, page 251), T07-347 1234. The classy place where the locals are apparently secretly hanging out. Happy hours on Fri at 1930 and Sat at 1730 are especially popular.

⊛ Festivals and events

Rotorua *p238, maps p239 and p241*
Jan Opera in the Pa, world-class opera amidst the geothermal splendour of the Rotowhio Marae. **Wild Moa**, Rotorua's premiere multi-sport event, www.wildmoa.co.nz.
Feb Lakeside 2006, annual concert and entertainment in the soundshell by the lake.
Mar International Two-Day Walk (3rd week), 10-, 20- and 30-km walks through Rotorua forests and city.
Apr Rotorua Marathon (last week), 42-km run around Lake Rotorua.
May Cateye Moonride, www.moon ride.co.nz, a night time mountain biking event held in the Whakarewarewa Forest Park (unfortunately lights are allowed). **Rotorua Tagged Trout Fishing Contest** (3rd week), catch the tagged trout in Lake Rotorua and become a rich fisher-person.
Jun Targa Rally of Rotorua, www.rally rotorua.co.nz, the largest annual sporting event in the area.
Oct New Zealand Trout Festival, marks the opening of the Rotorua lakes season.
Nov International Trout Tournament, 3-day tournament with major prizes attracting anglers worldwide.
Dec New Year's Eve Mardi Gras, wild shenanigans down at the waterfront.

O Shopping

Rotorua *p238, maps p239 and p241*
As you might expect, there are lots of souvenir shops in Rotorua. Most are on Fenton St.
Maori Arts and Crafts Institute, at the Whakarewarewa Thermal Reserve, SH5, is worth looking at for Maori Art.
The Map and Track Shop, 6 Tarawera Rd, T07-345 9333. The best place for maps.
Outdoorsman Headquarters, 6 Tarawera Rd, T07-345 9333. Outdoor/camping equipment.
The Souvenir Centre, 1231 Fenton St. One of the better ones.

▲ Activities and tours

Rotorua *p238, maps p239 and p241*
In New Zealand, only Queenstown – the reputed activity capital of the world – can claim to have more activities than steamy Rotorua. As the country's second most-visited tourist destination 'Roto Vegas' can certainly satisfy just about everyone, from adrenaline junkies keen to fly upside down in a bi-plane or raft down a waterfall, to those in search of some therapy in the form of a delightfully messy mud bath or a soothing mineral spa.

But before parting with any cash take a long hard look in the VIC to see the vast range on offer and ask about the various combo deals that can save both time and money.

Agrodome
Agrodome complex, just north of Rotorua on SH5, T07-357 1050, www.agrodome.co.nz. Offers a wealth of activities including bungee jumping, jet boating, 'The Swoop', 'Free Fall' and the infamous Zorb (see page 249).

Climbing
The Wall, 1140 Hinemoa St, T07-350 1400, www.basebackpackers.com, daily. An impressive 20 m climbing wall. For $20 you will get some instruction with all the gear.

Eco-tours
Nature Connection, based in the city, T07-347 1705, www.natureconnection.co.nz. Offers a range of excellent fully-guided, fully-equipped half- to full-day trips to local sights and the Whirinaki Forest Park, from $100.
Whirinaki Rainforest Guided Walks, T07-377 2363, www.rainforest-treks.co.nz. Offers 1- to 3-day fully-catered treks led by professional Maori guides, starting at Rotorua and Taupo. The 3-day trek includes 2 nights at a safari-style camp in the rainforest, complete with hot showers. Prices range from $155 for the 1-day eco-cultural walk, from $285 for 1-day privately guided walk; from $745 for the 3-day Rainforest Trek.

Fishing
As you might expect there are numerous guided and self-guided charters that mainly operate on Lake Rotorua or Lake Tarawera. Reputable charters include:

Clearwater (Lake Tarawera), T07-362 8590, www.clearwater.co.nz. Luxury launch.

Ernie Scudder, T07-332 3488, www.trout fly.co.nz. Big Ern' offers a great trip on the *Silver Hilton*, from $80 per hr, special day rate of $500. Great fun and recommended.

Rotorua Trout Safaris, T07-362 0016, www.wildtrout.co.nz.

Stillwater, T07-345 4044, www.trout catch.co.nz. Prices start at about $85 per hr.

4WD and quad bikes

Off Road NZ, 193 Amoore Rd (off SH5 north), T07-332 5748, www.offroadnz.co.nz. A range of thrills and spills in a range of 4WD vehicles and buggies. From their base near the city you can go uphill and down dale (including a monstrous 15-m 'luge' drop) and through some very large mud pools. There is also clay bird shooting and archery available. Guided tours (you drive) daily 0900-1700, from $80.

Golf

Arikikapakapa Course, Rotorua Golf Club, at the southern end of Fenton St, T07-348 4051. The best in the area.

Government Gardens, T07-3489126. Has a range and a short 9-hole course.

Health treatments and spas

There are an increasing number of health treatment facilities in addition to the busy, high-profile spas and thermal reserves.

QE Spa, Whakaue St, T07-348 0189, www.qehealth.co.nz. Mon-Fri 0800-2200, Sat-Sun 1400-2200. Massage from $50, mud bath from $45. Recommended.

Jet-boating

Kawarau Jet, City Lakefront, Memorial Drive, T07-343 7600/T0800-529272, www.nzjet boat.co.nz. Fast jet boat trips to the Manupirua Hot Springs or Mokoia Island, from $64.There are also self-drive speedboats available for hire – but alas, a lot slower.

Horse trekking

Paradise Valley Ventures, 679 Paradise Valley Rd, T07-348 3300, www.paradisetreks .co.nz. Horse trekking (1 hr, $60) 15 mins from the city in typical North Island rural setting.

Peka Horse Treks, SH30, T07-3461755. Ideally situated close to Whakarewarewa Forest Park, good forest trails, 1 hr from $50.

Kayaking and waka experience

Adventure Kayaking, T07-348 9451, www.adventurekayaking.co.nz. Extensive range of half- or full-day tours to a number of lakes and rivers in the region, as well as fishing trips and twilight paddles, from $110. Independent hire available from $40 per day.

Go Kayaking, T07-362 4222. Offers similar trips with more emphasis on teaching the beginner; from $75. Independent hire also available from $40 per day.

'Hoe Waka', T0800-463925, www.mana adventures.co.nz. One of only 2 commercial operations in New Zealand that provides the opportunity to paddle a *waka* (Maori war canoe). Naturally the experience is augmented with lots of Maori tradition and interactive protocols. Lake Rotorua experience 45 mins from $45, 2-hr trip from $70, 4 hrs from $120 (weather permitting).

Kaituna Kayaks, T07-362 4486/T0800-465292, www.kaitunakayaks.com. Half-day from $130. Full-day course $240, 2-day from $300. Recommended for river kayaking and some very good professional tuition.

Mana Adventures, T07-343 6404. Set up by a well-known and popular Maori operator. Trips involve a 5-hr excursion to Makoia Island on Lake Rotorua, from $95, with an overnight (camping) option from $135.

Lake Tarawera tours

See Lake Tarawera, page 246.

Lake Tarawera Launch Cruises (MV Reremoana), operates from the jetty just off Lake Tarawera Rd, T07-362 8502. A charming little launch which offers a 2-hr 'Eruption Trail' cruise, daily at 1100 with a 30-min stopover to visit the shores of Lake Rotomahana – the former site of the 'pink and white terraces', $30, child $15. A 45-min scenic cruise leaves on demand until dusk, $20, child $11 and trips to Hot Water Beach from $438, child $23.

Lake Tarawera Water Taxis, Boatshed Bay, T07-362 8080, The most flexible company offering free pick-ups from town with lake cruises (3 hrs, $48) or shuttle services to Hot Water Beach on demand.

Maori concerts and hangis

A trip to Rotorua is not complete without the Maori cultural experience of a concert and/or *hangi* (feast). There are numerous options, some good some not so good. The major hotels almost all offer *hangis* and concerts, but these tend to be less grand affairs than the above and very commercial. A hotel *hangi* and concert will cost you $65-90. The following are recommended:

Mai Ora, based at Whakarewarewa (Te Puia), T07-349 9047, www.tepuia.co.nz. Fine cultural performances with entertaining interaction and an all-you can eat *hangi*, from $85, child $50 (see page 242). Expect up to 100 people.

Matariki Hangi and Concert, at the Royal Lakeside Novotel, T07-346 3888. Daily at 1830, one of the best on offer, from $60.

Mitai, based at Rainbow Springs off SH5, T07-343 9132, www.mitai.co.nz. The performance is said to be raw and authentic incorporating a short bush walk and *hangi* (90-100 people), $85 including transport.

Tamaki Tours Marae Experience, T07-3492999, www.maoriculture.co.nz. Daily twilight *marae* tour, performance and *hangi* with some audience participation; from $92. Expect around 100 people. Pick-ups from your accommodation are provided.

World of the Maori (Rotoiti Tours), T07-348 8969 (book at the VIC). Daily 'Magic of the Maori' performance takes place at the Rakeiao Marae on the shores of Lake Rotoiti (20-min drive) but is well worth the trip and caters for smaller groups, from $75, children $37.50.

Others include: **Grand Tiara**, T07-349 5200; **Sudima Lake Plaza**, T07-348 1174; and **Kingsgate**, T07-348 0199.

Mountain biking

Whakarewarewa Forest Park is just one of many popular and challenging venues for mountain biking around Rotorua, with over 30 km of trails (see page 243). For track and operator information, contact T07-346 1717, www.bikerotorua.co.nz.

Planet Bike, T07-346 1717, www.planet bike.co.nz. Offers organized trips. Try the kayak and bike combo trips from $90. Independent bike hire also available, from $35 for 2 hrs, $55 per-day.

Rafting and whitewater sledging

Whitewater sledging is the new and exciting concept of doing all you do in a raft, on a Grade V river except alone on a type of 'head-first' water toboggan.

Kaitiaki Adventures, T07-357 2236/T0800-338736, www.sledge-it.com. Sledging and

rafting trips, with the opportunity to learn about Maori culture on the way, from $99.

Kaituna Cascades, T07-343 4199/T0800-KAITUNA, www.kaitunacascades.co.nz. Good outfit offering similar trips to **Raftabout**, below, ranging from $72 (45 mins) to $385. You get a photo of the drop down the falls.

Raftabout, T07-343 9500/T0800-RAFT ABOUT, www.raftabout.co.nz. Consistently receives good reviews as a very professional, safe and experienced company that offers a range of whitewater rafting on the Kaituna, Rangitaiki Wairoa rivers from its purpose-built riverside base. The most popular and recommended trip is the 45-min blast down a stretch of the Kaituna (located between Lake Rotorua and Lake Rotoiti) which negotiates 14 falls. The largest of these is the famous and highly entertaining 7-m drop down the Okere Falls – the highest commercial rafted falls in the world. Trips start at $89 and there are various combo packages with everything from skydiving to the infamous luge.

River Rats, T07-345 6543/T0800-333900, www.riverrats.co.nz. A similar company offering a wider range of multi-activity adventure packages that include jet boating, bungee jumping, 4WD, luge, bikes and more. Also offers a more sedate rafting trip aimed at families and kids, starting at the Aniwhenua Falls before negotiating a gorge with a few gentle grade 2 falls.

Sledgeabout, T07-343 9500, www.raft about.co.nz. A new and exhilarating sledging option on the rapids of the lower Kaituna Gorge, from $99.

Wet-n-Wild, T07-348 3191/T0800-462 7238, www.wetnwildrafting.co.nz. Reputable company offering all the local trips but also specializing in multi-day trips on the Motu and Mohaka rivers. From $85.

Sightseeing tours

There are a wealth of independent operators and the VIC offers reductions and package deals. For eco-tours, see page 255.

Eight Beating Hearts, T07-349 0972, www.8beatinghearts.co.nz. A new Maori-operated tour company, offering the genuine and fun Maori perspective through a range of interactive adventure and discovery tours. Some include overnight stays.

Mount Tarawera NZ Ltd, T07-349 3714, www.mt-tarawera.co.nz. One of the few operators licensed to take tours on to the mountain to see the dramatic Tarawera craters (or 'gash') left by the violent eruption of 1886. The sight leaves you in no doubt about the ferocity of the explosion. There's a wide range of options including a guided full-day eco-tour from $149, a fly/drive option from $390 and heli-biking from $610. **Rotorua Duck Tours**, T07-345 6522, www.ducktours.co.nz. The amphibious yellow duck shuttles the camera-toting masses to Kuirua Park and the Lakefront followed by 'splash-down' at Sulphur Point, Lake Okareka and the Blue Lake. It is of course highly commercial but the combination of its novelty, the scenery and the entertaining commentary make it worthwhile. Tours last 90 mins and depart from the VIC, from $68. **Te Kiri Treks**, T07-345 5016, www.tekiri.co.nz. A Maori-operated company that provides an excellent day out in a 4WD, taking in Ohinemutu, Whakarewarewa, Waiotapu, Tarawera and a few secret spots along the way. Lunch is provided in a beautiful self-built bush camp. All for $120. Good value, entertaining and recommended.

Scenic flights

Most scenic flight operators are based at either the airport, Whakarewarewa, the Lake Rotorua waterfront near the town centre (float planes) or at the Agrodome. Flights range from city and Mt Tarawera fly-overs to extended trips to the volcanically active White Island in the Bay of Plenty. **Volcanic Air Safaris**, based at the airport and the waterfront, T07-348 9984/T0800-800848, www.volcanicair.co.nz. Has a fleet of fixed-wing and float plane aircraft as well as helicopters that take in all the local sights and go as far as White Island from $60-795.

Skyline skyrides

Accessed by a scenic gondola there are a number of activities available on the slopes of Mt Ngongotaha. These include the infamous luge, a flying fox, flight simulator and helicopter trips, T07-347 0027.

Tandem skydiving

NZone, operates from the airport, T07-345 7520. Highly professional, with jumps daily, depending on weather conditions. From 9500 ft for $245 (15,000 ft, $395).

Walking

DoC/VIC has information on the wealth of opportunities in the region, which range from a short walk around **Government Gardens** and the waterfront, to the **Tarawera summit** climb (see page 250), the 20-min to 8-hr walks through the **Whakarewarewa Forest Park** (see page 243), and the superb **Tarawera Falls** walk (see page 247). Other excellent walking tracks are to be found around Lake Okataina in the **Lake Okataina Scenic Reserve**; these are best accessed from SH30 at Ruato (Lake Rotoiti) or Lake Okareka (Tarawera Falls Rd). The **Okere Falls** walk (30 mins) is accessed from SH30 east and then SH33 (16 km) and worth the trip, while a great view can be had from the summit of **Rainbow Mountain** (2 hrs) which is accessed off SH5, 26 km south of Rotorua. A little further afield is the **Whirinaki Forest**, which is lauded as having an almost prehistoric appearance. **Walk About Rotorua**, T07-348 9480. Offers transport and guided walks. 2-hr walks around town include Government Gardens and Ohinemutu and there is an interesting commentary along the way; tours depart from the VIC at 0900 and 1300, $25, child $10.

⊖ Transport

Rotorua p238, maps p239 and p241
Airline offices Air NZ, corner of Fenton and Hinemoa sts, T07-343 1100. **Bicycle hire** Planet Bike, 30 Clouston, T07-346 1717, 2 hrs $35, full-day from $55; Rotorua Cycle Centre, 1111 Hinemoa St, T07-348 6588. **Car hire** Budget, Fenton St, T07-348 8127; Rent-A-Dent, 14 Ti St, T07-349 3993.

❶ Directory

Rotorua p238, maps p239 and p241
Banks All major branches on Hinemoa St. Money exchange: Travelex, VIC, T07-348 0640, T0800-200232, daily 0830-1800. **Internet** Numerous outlets including: Contact Cyber Café, corner of Pukuatua and Fenton sts, T07-348 9440; Cyber World, 1174 Haupapa St, T07-348 0088. **Medical services** Lakes Prime Care, 1165 Tutanekai St, T07-348 1000, 0800-2200 (also 24 hr duty doctor). **Police** Fenton St, T07-348 0099. **Post office** 1189 Hinernoa St. Mon-Fri 0730-1700, Sat 0830-1600, Sun 1000-1500 (Post Restante).

Tauranga → Colour map 2, B3. Population 66,000

Tauranga has enjoyed tremendous growth in recent years. So much so that it is used as a barometer of the general state of the economy and national real estate prices. As well as its thriving commercial and business centre, busy port (the name means 'sheltered anchorage') and rich horticultural farmland, it seems Tauranga is also proving the ideal place in which to enjoy the archetypal Kiwi lifestyle. With the combination of location, climate, attractive beaches and the many associated activities, as well as its proximity to the delights of Rotorua, it has much to offer both the native and the tourist. Dominating the scene is the harbour and the volcanic dome of Mount Maunganui to the north, which guards its precarious entrance. Nowadays there are almost as many cruise liners as there are merchant ships, and the town's tourist allure seems almost set to overtake its popularity with the locals.
▸▸ *For Sleeping, Eating and other listings, see pages 263-268.*

Ins and outs

Getting there

Tauranga, 210 km southeast of Auckland and 83 km north of Rotorua, is a major destination on the Pacific Coast Highway, which connects Auckland with Napier in the Hawke's Bay region. **Tauranga airport** ① *4 km east of the city centre*, is served daily by **Air New Zealand Link**, T0800-737000. A taxi to the centre costs about $15, T07-575 4054 or T07-578 6086.

  Intercity and **Newman's** buses operate daily services from most North Island destinations arriving at the VICs (I-Sites) in the city and Mount Maunganui; both handle bookings and ticketing. **Nakedbus.com**, offers cheap internet deals, and **Go Kiwi Shuttles**, T07-866 0336/T0800-446549, www.go-kiwi.co.nz, offers regular services from Auckland via Thames, Whitianga and Rotorua. **Supa-Travel**, T07-571 0583, is a local company offering a daily service from Auckland (connecting with **Northliner** and **Pavlovich** services to Northland). It also runs from both Tauranga and Mount Maunganui VICs (I-Sites). **Call-A-Bus**, T0800-100550, www.bus.co.nz, offers a similar daily mini-bus service from Auckland airport, $55 one way.

Getting around

Tauranga city centre is fairly compact and easily negotiable by foot. **Bayline Coaches** (Bay Hopper), T07-578 3113/T0800-422 9287, is the local suburban bus company operating regular daily services to Mount Maunganui and east as far as Opotiki. Buses depart from the corner of Wharf and Willow Streets beside the VIC (I-Site); day pass $6. **Te Puke Bus Services**, T07-573 6949, serves Te Puke via Papamoa, and departs from Wharf Street. For car rental and taxi companies, see Directory, page 268. **Bay Ferries**, Southern Pontoon, Coronation Wharf, The Strand, T0800-337791 www.bayferries.co.nz, connects Tauranga with Mount Maunganui and offers eight sailings daily 0720-1910, $4.50 one way.

Tourist information

Tauranga VIC (I-Site) ① *95 Willow St, T07-578 8103, www.bayofplentynz.com or www.tauranga.govt.nz, Mon-Fri 0830-1730, Sat-Sun 0900-1700.* For quick reference be sure to avail yourself of the free *What's to See and Do* leaflet. DoC information is also available here. **Mount Maunganui VIC (I-Site)** ① *Salisbury Av, T07-575 5099, Mon-Fri 0900-1700, Sat-Sun 0900-1600, closed weekends in winter.*

Background

The shores were already quite heavily settled by the Maori by the time Captain James Cook passed the area on his circumnavigation of New Zealand in 1769. The earliest

Tauranga orientation

Related maps
A Tauranga centre, p264.
B Mount Maunganui, p262.

Sleeping
Ambassador Motor Inn **1**
Beach Front Villas **13**
Beach House Motel **10**
Bell Lodge **3**
Cosy Corner
  Motor Camp **4**
Fantail Lodge & Villas **15**

Just the Ducks Nuts
  Backpackers **5**
Matahui Lodge **9**
Ridge Country
  Retreat **8**
Silver Birch Holiday
  Park **7**

Top Ten Papamoa
  Beach Holiday Resort **12**

Eating
Bluebiyou **3**
Mills Reef Winery **1**
Somerset Cottage **2**

European settlement took the form of flax traders and missionaries of 'The Elms', which was established on the Te Papa Peninsula in 1834. Due to inter-tribal warfare this mission was temporarily abandoned before enjoying resurgence from 1838. With the gathering momentum of the Maori King Movement in the Waikato region in the early 1860s the government set about blocking supply routes from outlying areas of the east coast. Troops were dispatched and redoubts built on the Te Papa Peninsula. With such a build-up of forces it was perhaps inevitable that conflict would ensue, and the first major battle with the Ngaiterangi Maori occurred at Gate Pa in April 1864. This proved to be one of the most significant Maori land wars in the country. As a result of the conflict and government victory, over 20,000 ha of land were confiscated and a military presence remained to secure the peace. From this point, as road access improved, settlement grew steadily. In recent years, with the development of the port and the attractions of the 'lifestyle' element, the population has experienced a boom.

Sights

The main historical attraction in Tauranga is the **Elms Mission House** ① *T07-577 9772, www.theelms.org.nz, Wed, Sat, Sun 1400-1600, $5*, set amidst pleasant grounds on Mission Street on the Te Papa Peninsula, on the site of the original mission. Nearby in **Robbins Park** on Cliff Road on the eastern side of the peninsula are the remnants of the **Monmouth Redoubt** ① *daily 0900-1800*, built by government forces during the New Zealand Wars. There are gardens and a begonia house. At the base of the hill, at the southern end of Dive Crescent, is the **Te Awanui Waka**, a replica Maori war canoe. **Gate Pa Church** on Cameron Road, south of the city centre, marks the spot of the Battle of Gate Pa in 1864. Tauranga's perpetual growth seems set to reach the fine arts with the creation of a chic new **art gallery** ① *corner of Willow and Wharf sts, www.art gallery.org.nz*, due to open in late 2007. Ask at the VIC (I-Site) for details.

As well as the obvious attraction of **'the Mount'** (see below), there are a number of superb **beaches** in the area, most stretching from Mount Maunganui east to Papamoa. Not surprisingly the climate also lends itself to wine making and there are a scattering of excellent **vineyards** including the lauded **Morton Estate Main Road Katikati** ① *T0800-667866, www.mortonestatewines.co.nz*. The cellar door is open daily and there is a restaurant and bar open Wednesday to Sunday for lunch and dinner, T07-552 0620.

Excursions

Although perhaps a bit far for a special return trip from Tauranga, if you are heading north (or south) anyway the small village of **Katikati** is worth a brief stop. It is known for its quality historical murals (there are now 23) that grace the sides of buildings along the main street and throughout the village. They are really quite good and portray the social history of the area. For more information visit the website, www.katikati.co.nz, or ask at the VIC (I-Site) for more information. Also worth a look are the **Katikati Bird Gardens** ① *25 km north of Tauranga and 7 km south of Katikati, signposted off SH2, T07-549 0912, www.birdgardens.co.nz, daily Sep-Apr 1000-1630, $9, child $4*. Set in 4 ha of attractive gardens there are over 50 species on show both native and non-native, with the undeniable 'stars' (as ever) being the 'cheeky kea' – a native alpine parrot imbued with considerable intelligence and delinquent tendencies.

Mount Maunganui ●🔧📷▲ ➤ *pp263-268.*

Six kilometres north of Rautanga and dominated by 'the Mount', the town of Mount Maunganui is graced by golden beaches and maintains an irresistible appeal. In winter the streets and beaches are almost empty, but in summer and particularly over the New Year, the town is a tourist battleground with the Mount crowned with an army of view junkies and the beach with battalions of soporific sunbathers. Mount Maunganui itself (known as 'Mauao' or 'The Mount') is 232 m high and dominates the coastal horizon at the narrow entrance to Tauranga Harbour. Not surprisingly, perhaps, its sheer presence has resulted in it becoming the physical focal point of culture and heritage in the region.

Sights

Once an island and an almost impregnable Maori *pa*, the Mount now serves as an obvious tourist attraction and a landmark for ships negotiating the harbour's treacherous entrance. There is a network of pathways which criss-cross the Mount, offering a range of pleasant walks to suit all levels of fitness. The summit climb, which is best accessed from the south of the motorcamp, takes about 45 minutes one way and, as you might expect, is rewarded with a memorable view. The 3½-km base track walk is a less demanding option and also offers some memorable views.

Mount Maunganui

Sleeping
Belle Mer Apartments 7
Calais Mount Resort 5
Mission Belle Motel 2
Mount Backpackers 3

Mt Maunganui B&B
 & Chalet 1
Mount Maunganui
 Domain Motor Camp 4
Oceanside Twin Towers 8
Pacific Coast Backpackers 6

Eating
Astrolabe 1
Bombay Brasserie 2
Boost 6
Main St Café 4
Mount Mellick 7

From the narrow neck of the Mount, **Ocean Beach** begins a stretch of sand that sweeps, almost uninterrupted, east to the cape. Just offshore from Ocean Beach are the two small islands **Moturiki** and **Motuotau**. Moturiki can be reached from the shore, has a blowhole and is a popular spot for fishing, while Motuotau is important for its wildlife. Other than the Mount and the beaches the town's major attraction are the **Mount Maunganui Hot Salt Water Pools** ① *at the base of the mount, Adams Av, T07-575 0868, Mon-Sat 0600-2200, Sun 0800-2200, from $6, child $3*. Here, therapeutic salt water is heated to 39°C in a number of large communal and private pools. The perfect après-pool activity is to then sample an deliciously creamy ice cream from **Copenhagen Cones** across the road.

Even if you cannot stay up on a board for more than a nanosecond or have never tried surfing, the **Mount Surf Shop and Museum** ① *139 Totara St, T07-927 7234, $5, daily 1000-1500*, is worth a look if only to see the huge collection of boards on display and the intriguing 'shrine' to Malibu surfing guru 'Da Cat'.

● Sleeping

There is plenty of choice in Tauranga itself and Mt Maunganui, but it's best to book ahead in mid-summer when the area is hugely popular with Kiwi holidaymakers. Most of the region's luxury lodges and B&Bs are northwest of the city towards Katikati.

Tauranga *p259, maps p260 and p264*
LL Fantail Lodge and Villas, 117 Rea Rd, 35 km north of Tauranga, near the small village of Katikati, T07-549 1581, www.fantail lodge.co.nz. This popular country lodge estate offers a fine base from which to explore the Bay of Plenty and the Coromandel Peninsula. Set in beautiful rural surroundings it offers luxury suites and self-contained garden villas. Additional features include a reputable European-influenced guest restaurant, an in-house spa complex and informative and entertaining eco-tours of the region.
LL Matahui Lodge, 187 Matahui Rd, T07-571 8121, www.matahui-lodge.co.nz. A stunning property in a tranquil spot overlooking Tauranga's Inner Harbour and Matakana Island. All the facilities and comforts you might expect and friendly hosts with a passion for fine food and wine. Dinner by arrangement.
LL Ridge Country Retreat, 300 Rocky Cutting Rd, Welcome Bay, T07-542 1301, www.rcr.co.nz. Beautifully appointed suites and an overall emphasis on health and beauty with a full range of in-house therapies on offer. You simply won't want to leave.
LL-L The Sebel Trinity Wharf, 51 Dive Cres, T07-577 8700, www.mirvachotels.com.au. The newest hotel in the city – and an impressive one at that – built over 3 former piers at Trinity Wharf. As such, the beautifully appointed suites offer excellent views across the harbour and you will have access to all the usual bells and whistles.
L-AL Hotel on Devonport, Devonport Towers, 72 Devonport Rd, T07-578 2668, www.hotelondevonport.net.nz. Quality boutique hotel with all the bells and whistles right in the heart of town. Designed with business people in mind but still a fine convenient place to indulge yourself.
L-AL Puriri Park Boutique Hotel, 32 Cameron Rd, T07-577 1480, www.puriri park.co.nz. Well-established and facilitated centrally located hotel. Modern self-contained suites. Good weekend and winter specials.
AL Durham Motor Inn, corner of Cameron Rd and Harrington St, T07-577 9691. One of the better motels in the city centre. 20 clean modern units, pool and spas.
AL-A Beach House Motel, 224 Papamoa Beach Rd, T07-572 1424, www.beachhouse motel.co.nz. Modern, award-winning and unusual beachside motel in Papamoa with 18 luxury units, spa, Sky TV.
AL-A Harbour City Motor Inn, 50 Wharf St, T07-571 1435, www.taurangaharbourcity .co.nz. One of the city's newest upper-range motels, ideally located in the heart of Tauranga. The most striking thing about this motel is its stylish design and the attention to detail. Modern features and an almost minimalist aspect to the decor make it look and feel more like an Auckland boutique hotel than a provincial motel. Both studio and 2-bedroom units have spa baths. General facilities also include Sky TV and secure parking.

A Ambassador Motor Inn, 9 Fifteenth Av, T07-578 5665, www.ambassador-motorinn.co.nz. Modern 4-star rated motel at the estuary end of the avenue. Wide range of units, spa and heated pool.
A Beach Front Villas, 535 Papamoa Beach Rd, T07-572 0816, www.papamoabeach.co.nz. Although a few miles from Tauranga in Papamoa, this complex and the villas are on the beachfront and are recommended.
B Strand Motel, 27 The Strand, T07-578 5807, www.strandmotel.co.nz. Comfortable, basic, budget motel located close to all amenities.
B-D Bell Lodge, 39 Bell St, SH2 North (Waihi Rd), T07-578 6344, www.bell-lodge.co.nz. Very smart purpose-built complex located 4 km the city, in park surroundings. Large kitchen and comfortable en suite rooms or dorms, open fire, tent sites and off-street parking. Free pick-ups and free trips to 'The Mount'.
B-D Harbourside Central Backpackers, 105 The Strand, T07-5794066, www.backpacktauranga.co.nz. New and large hostel right in the heart of the action popular with socialites and fruit pickers who have benefited from the in-house job-finding service. Double and twin with shared bathrooms or en suites and dorms some with harbour views. Good rooftop garden, free bike hire.
C-D Tauranga YHA, 171 Elizabeth St, T07-578 5064, yhatour@yha.org.nz. Well-established hostel in a quiet, central location. Friendly and comfortable with twin, double (one en suite), dorm and camping options.
D Just the Ducks Nuts Backpackers, 6 Vale St, T07-576 1366, www.justtheducksnuts.co.nz. Small, but with a name like that

Tauranga centre

Sleeping
Durham Motor Inn **3**
Harbour City Motor Inn **4**
Harbourside Central Backpackers **8**
Hotel on Devonport **2**
Puriri Park Boutique **1**
Sebel Trinity Wharf **7**
Strand Motel **5**
Tauranga YHA **6**

Eating
Collar & Thai **2**
Harbourside **3**
Mediterraneo Café **5**
Shiraz Café **4**
Wharf Street **1**

Bars & clubs
Buddha Lounge **10**
Cornerstone **8**
Grumpy Mole **9**
Harrington's **11**

Bay of Plenty Tauranga Listings

an inevitably popular, laid-back hostel located about 2km from the city centre with the usual facilities including a log fire and free bike hire.

Motorcamps and campsites

A-D Top Ten Papamoa Beach Holiday Resort, 535 Papamoa Beach Rd, T07-572 0816, www.papamoabeach.co.nz. A fine beachfront camp with a wide range of options and facilities.

B-D Silver Birch Holiday Park, 101 Turret Rd, SH2, T07-578 4603, www.silverbirch.co.nz. Harbourside location, en-suite or basic cabins some with kitchen facilities. Tent sites with camp kitchen.

Mount Maunganui p261, map p262

Mt Maunganui is becoming increasingly popular as a true resort-style holiday location and is beginning to have that mini-Gold Coast feel to it. So, apartment blocks predominate, all promising the usual modern amenities, ocean views and of course, location, location, location … The VIC has full listings.

LL-AL Belle Mer Apartments, 53 Marine Parade, T07-575 0011/T0800-100235, www.bellemer.co.nz. Again, well located, sitting just opposite the beach and within walking distance of shops and hot pools the 3-storey block offers luxury 2-3 bedroom apartments most with sea views and all with spas, fully equipped kitchen, Sky TV and private balcony.

LL-AL Calais Mount Resort, 6 Adams Av, T07-575 3805, www.calais.co.nz. Again, close to all amenities and modern, but with the added attraction of free hot pool tickets.

LL-AL Oceanside Twin Towers, 1 Maunganui Rd, T07-575 5371, www.oceanside.co.nz. Luxury apartments with all the standard amenities, commanding the finest views and just opposite the hot water pools.

AL Mission Belle Motel, corner of Victoria Rd and Pacific Av, T07-575 2578, www.mission bellemotel.co.nz. Modern, luxury Spanish-style motel in the heart of town.

B Mt Maunganui B&B and Chalet, 463 Maunganui Rd, T07-575 4013, www.mount bednbreakfast.co.nz. Has stood the test of time surrounded by reproducing apartment blocks, so they are doing something right. Refurbished and centrally located, 5 rooms with shared bathrooms, with breakfast, all good value. A new separate chalet sleeps 6.

C-D Mount Backpackers, 87 Maunganui Rd, T07-575 0860, www.mountbackpackers.co.nz. Smaller, more centrally located backpacker hostel. Assistance finding seasonal work.

C-D Pacific Coast Backpackers, 432 Maunganui Rd, T07-574 9601, www.pacific coastlodge.co.nz. Lively with excellent range of comfortable doubles, singles and bunks. Wide range of activities organized, often with price reductions. Recycling policy.

Motorcamps and campsites

C-D Cosy Corner Motor Camp, 40 Oceanbeach Rd, T07-575 5899. A quiet camp, further along the beach.

C-D Mount Maunganui Domain Motor Camp, Adams Av, T07-575 4471. Ideally located at the base of the Mount and next to both the beach and the hot pools, but charges accordingly and relies too much on that fact to the detriment of its facilities.

🍴 Eating

Tauranga p259, maps p260 and p264

Tauranga has a fine selection of restaurants and cafés to suit all tastes and budgets. Most are on or around the Strand overlooking the harbour. Pick up the free and comprehensive *Dine Out* guide from the VIC (I-Site).

🍴 **The Bluebiyou**, 559 Papamoa Beach Rd (city east), T07-572 209, daily from 1100. Right next to the beach in Papamoa. Great if you want to get away from the city.

🍴 **Harbourside Restaurant**, T0800-721714, www.harbourside-tga.co.nz, 1130-late. Enjoys a loyal following and the reputation as Tauranga's best restaurant. Located as much on the water as beside it, at the southern end of the Strand, it offers an excellent and imaginative all-day blackboard and à la carte menu, with an emphasis on local seafood.

🍴 **Mills Reef Winery and Restaurant**, 143 Moffat Rd (city west), T07-576 8800, daily from 1000. Another out-of-town option for lunch and dinner is this renowned (but expensive) restaurant, specializing in seafood and fish delights. Live music on Sun.

🍴 **Somerset Cottage Restaurant**, away from the city centre, at 30 Bethlehem Rd (city west), T07-576 6889. A small, congenial place serving a classic range of international cuisine to suit a wide range of tastes. Fine reputation and an excellent wine list. Bookings essential.

¶¶ **Collar and Thai**, Goddards Centre, 21 Devonport Rd, T07-577 6655, Mon-Fri 1130-1400, Mon-Sun 1730-late. For Thai food you can't go wrong here, good value.

¶¶ **Wharf Street Restaurant**, Upstairs 8 Wharf St, T07-578 8322, daily, open till late. Another award-winner with a wide-ranging menu including vegetarian. Once again seafood dominates. Fine harbour views.

¶ **Mediterraneo Cafe**, 62 Devonport Rd, T07-577 0487. New café proving popular with the locals for a good vibe, coffee or value breakfast.

¶ **Shiraz Café**, 12 Wharf St, T07-577 0059. Mon-Sat from 1100. A great range of lunchtime snacks (try a shwarma or falafel) and value breakfast.

Mount Maunganui *p261, map p262*

¶¶ **Astrolabe** (not named after a space ship, but a shipwreck), 82 Maunganui Rd, T07-574 8155. The combination restaurant, bar and café facilities here are to be recommended. It offers breakfast, lunch and dinner with a range of fine and imaginative traditional dishes. Live bands often play at weekends.

¶¶ **Bombay Brasserie**, 77 Maunganui Rd (almost directly opposite Astrolabe), T07-575 2539, daily from 1800. An excellent, affordable Indian restaurant that seems to be getting the thumbs up from discerning British curry aficionados.

¶¶ **Boost**, below the Twin Towers on Adams Av, T07-574 3360, daily. Modern and trendy, and a safe bet for gourmet and vegetarian pizzas and also serves a fine coffee. Takeaways available.

¶¶ **Mount Mellick**, 317 Maunganui Rd, T07-574 0047, daily 0900-2200. Irish pub good for traditional European fare with an all-day roast on Sun, live music Fri-Sat.

¶ **Main St Café**, just south of the roundabout at 262 Maunganui Rd, from 0700. Locals head here for a good, cheap breakfast.

◑ Pubs, bars and clubs

Tauranga *p259, maps p260 and p264*
Cornerstone, The Strand. Has a distinctly European feel and is a popular spot,

especially on sunny evenings when the clientele spills out on to the street.
Grumpy Mole, 41 The Strand, T07-571 1222. Also popular, this entertainment venue has a 'hump-day' every week, whatever that may be.

Clubs
Buddha Lounge, 61B The Strand, T07-928 1216, Thu-Sat until 0300. Reputed to be the best place to go in the wee hours.
Harrington's, 10 Harrington St, T07-578 5427. Thu-Sat till 0500. The most commercial club attracting mainly a young crowd.

⊛ Festivals and events

Tauranga *p259, maps p260 and p264*
Jan Brightstone Blues Brews and Barbecues, outdoor performances with national and international celebrities, mixed with boutique brewery products and BBQs, www.blues brews.co.nz. **Port of Tauranga Half-Iron Man**, hailed as the country's premier event of its kind, attracting more than 1000 national and Australian competitors, www.halfironman.co.nz.
Mar Tauranga Food and Wine Festival, a celebration of local and national food and wine.
Apr Montana National Jazz Festival, considered (after Waiheke Auckland perhaps) to be the country's premier jazz event, performed in the Baycourt Theatre, bars and cafés, refer to www.jazz.net.nz.
Nov Garden and Arts Festival, a biannual event held over a weekend early in the month. It alternates between a **Garden festival** where regional gardens are opened to the public, and an **Arts festival**, where visual art exhibitions are staged throughout the city.

▲ Activities and tours

Tauranga and Mount Maunganui *p259 and p261, maps p260, p264 and p262*
Abseiling and climbing
Rock House, 9 Triton Av (opposite the Mount Action Centre), in Mt Maunganui, T07-572 4920, www.therockhouse.co.nz, Tue-Fri 1200-late, Sat-Sun 1000-1800, $14, child $10. A rock wall that's proving very popular. Instruction provided.

Cruising and sailing
Blue Ocean Charters, Corporation Wharf, Tauranga, T07-578 9685, www.blueocean

charters.co.nz. Offers a wide range of half-day, full-day or evening, scenic harbour, island and fishing trips from $70.
South Sea Sailing Company, T07-579 6376, www.southseasailing.com. Offers day and multi-day eco-cruises aboard its luxury catamaran and is licensed to offer dolphin watching and swimming. Day trips from $100.

Dolphin watching
Butler's Swim with the Dolphins, Tauranga, T07-578 3197, www.swimwith dolphins.co.nz, $120, child $90. With over 15 years experience of providing dolphin watching and swimming eco-trips on its 18-m sailing ship *Galaxsea*. Departs daily for an all-day trip at 0900 from the port at Tauranga and 0930 from Mt Maunganui. All gear provided, take your own lunch.
Dolphin Seafaris, Coronation Pier, The Strand, T0800-3268747, www.nzdolphin.com. Offers a similar 3- to 4-hr trip, $120, child $90.

Fishing
There are numerous fishing charters (including big game) available and the VIC has full listings and prices.
Blue Ocean Charters, Wharf St, Tauranga, T07-578 9685, www.blueoceancharters.co.nz. Wide range of opportunities including diving, dolphin watching and fishing, from $70.
Tauranga Marine Charters, T07-552 6283. Mt Maunganui-based operator with lots of local knowledge.

4WD and quad biking
U-Drive (Longridge Park), Te Puke, T07-533 1818, www.adventure4wd.co.nz, from $85, child $39. One of the region's best 4WD activity operators and is based at the Longridge Park complex in Te Puke. It has over 3 km of track and a wide range of vehicles. Suitable for all levels.

Golf
Available at **Mount Maunganui Club**, Fairway Av, T07-575 4487; and **Tauranga Golf Club**, Cameron Rd, T07-578 8465.

Helicopter flights
There are a number of helicopter companies ranging from the conventional to the iconic.
Aerius, Te Puke, T07-533 1290, www.aer ius.co.nz. Flights in a cute little red number.

Kiwikopters, Tauranga airport, T07-572 4077, www.kiwicopters.co.nz. For the iconic Bell 47s (a la M.A.S.H IV series) that has its own MASH medical camp to land in.
Volcanic Air Safaris , Tauranga airport, T07-575 2266, www.volcanicair.co.nz. Conventional helicopter flights.

Horse trekking
Briar's, 22A Otimi St, Te Puke, T07-533 2582, www.briarshorsetrek.co.nz. Beach and coastal rides offering memorable views, from $55, 3hr $100.
World of Horses, SH2 between Tauranga and Katikati (14 km), T07-548 0404. Offers not only horse trekking but also display, corral, show stables and a café.

Jet boating and jet skiing
Longridge Park, Te Puke, T07-533 1515. Offers thrilling jet-boat ride amongst its many attractions, $85, child $39.

Kayaking
Oceanix, Mt Maunganui, T0800-335800, www.oceanix.co.nz. Offers a range of excursions that take in very different environments from New Zealand's largest port and the Maunganui Heads to the McLaren Falls Park. Sunset and moonlight trips are also an option, from $85.
Waimarino Adventure Park, Bethlehem, Tauranga, T07-576 4233, www.wai marino.com. Also offers a range of guided and self-guided day trips on Tauranga Harbour and local rivers with one taking in a glowworm canyon, from $90.

Mountain biking
Oropi Grove, 3 km up Oropi Rd from SH28, accessed off Joyce Rd (off Pyes Pa Rd), Tauranga, T07-577 3055. Considered the best track in the area.

Parasailing and kite surfing
Big Sky Parasail, Salisbury Wharf, Mt Maunganui, T0800-244759. 'The lift of a lifetime' around the celebrated Mount.
Kite Surfing New Zealand, Tauranga, T07-570 1947, www.kitesurfingnz.com. One-on-one lessons from $90.

Rafting

The **Wairoa**, **Kaituna** and **Rangitaiki** rivers near Tauranga are major venues for white-water rafting. For operators, see page 257.

Scenic flights and flight simulator

Flight Experience, Tauranga airport, Dakota Way, T07-574 3737, www.flightexperience .co.nz, from $95, 2hr $295. If taking the controls of a commercial airliner has always been a fantasy then it can become a little closer to reality with this authentic take-off and landing flight simulator.

Island Air Charters, Hangar 1, at the airport, T0800-545455. Will take you for local flights, or further afield to White Island, Slipper Island, Rotorua and the Coromandel. White Island from 1hr, $120.

Tauranga Aero Club, Aerodrome Rd, T07-575 3210. Similar flights to **Island Air Charters**.

Scuba diving

The 2 main operators in the city offer dive and snorkelling tours around Mt Maunganui and to local wrecks and Mayor Island.

Dive HQ, 213 Cameron Rd, T07-578 4050, www.divehqtauranga.co.nz.

Dive Tauranga, 50 Cross Rd, Tauranga, T07-571 5286, www.diveunderwater.com.

Sightseeing and wine tours

The VIC (I-Site) has a full listing of local day trip operators in the area.

Tasting Tours, Ohauiti, Tauranga, T07-544 1383, www.tastingtours.co.nz. An entertaining day of beer and wine tasting with lunch at the very congenial **Mills Reef Vineyard Restaurant**, from $130.

Surfing

Matakana Island is a short boat trip (or long paddle) from Mt Manganui and offers some of the most pristine tubes in the country. The island doesn't break as often as some of its east coast counterparts and scoring the right combination of wind and tide is tricky, but once you've sampled a Makatana tube you'll be wanting more.

Tandem skydiving

Tauranga Tandem Skydiving, at the airport, T07-576 7990, freefall@xtra.co.nz.

Thermal pools

There are numerous hot pools in the area, with the most popular being the **Mount Maunganui Hot Pools** (see page 263). There are also hot springs at: **Athenree**, Athenree Rd, north of Tauranga, on SH2, T07-863 5600, daily 0900-1700. **Fernland Spa Mineral Hot Pools**, 250 Cambridge Rd (SH29), Tauranga, T07-578 3081, daily 1000-2200.

Walking

The *Tauranga Walkways* booklet is free from the VIC and outlines a number of local walks. The walks around **Mt Maunganui** and to its summit are worthy of being the main walking attraction, but the **McLaren Falls Park** (about 10 km south of the city on SH29, T07-543 1099, Wed-Sun), and the **Rerekawau Falls (Kaiate Falls)** tracks (signposted from Welcome Bay Road) have other pleasant short walking opportunities. In McLaren Falls Park there are also some interesting animals including very hairy Tibetan yaks. The **Kaimai Ranges**, just to the west of the city, also offer numerous longer and more strenuous walks.

⊖ Transport

Tauranga *p259, maps p260 and p264*
Bicycle hire Hedgehog Tauranga, T07-578 7554. **Car hire** Avis, 325 Cameron Rd, T0800-655111; Budget, Intercity Building, Dive Cres, T07-578 5156; Rent-A-Dent, 19 Fifteenth Av, T07-578 1772; Rite Price Rentals, 25 Totara St, Mt Maunganui, T07-575 2726. **Taxi** Taxi Cabs, T07-575 4054; Tauranga Mount Taxis, T07-578 6086.

❶ Directory

Tauranga *p259, maps p260 and p264*
Banks Major branches and ATMs in the city centre. **Internet** Cyberzone, 1/75 Grey St; Gateway, Shop 18, Goddard Centre, Devonport Rd, T07-571 1112; Maunganui Library, Maunganui Rd; Mount Internet, 87 Maunganui Rd, T07-575 0860. 0900-2000; Tauranga Library, Willow St. **Medical services** Baycare, 10th St, T07-578 8000. 1700-0800; Hospital, Cameron Rd, T07-579 8000. **Post office** 17 Grey St, T07-577 9911, Mon-Fri 0830-1700, Sat 0900-1600, Sun 1000-1500.

Whakatane and Opotiki → *Colour map 2, B4*

Whakatane is the principal town in the eastern Bay of Plenty, at the mouth of the Whakatane River. It has a vibrant atmosphere that is often lacking in many New Zealand towns of the same size. There is just something about it – something that can warm the heart. Opotiki, 60 km southeast of Whakatane, near the mouths of the Waioeka and Utara rivers, is a small seaside town with some fine beaches and, like Whakatane, is rich in Maori history, with settlement taking place before the great migrations of the 14th century. It was the base of the Hauhau – a semi-religious sect of Maori rebels who were fierce enemies of the early Pakeha. ⤭ *For Sleeping, Eating and other listings, see pages 270-272.*

Ins and outs

Getting there and around **Whakatane airport**① *just northwest of the town off SH2,* is served by **Air New Zealand Link**, To800-737000. The airport shuttle will get you into town for about $14, To7-307 0070. For taxis use the same number or To800-421829. **Intercity** buses run to Whakatane from around the country; the VIC (I-Site) acts as a booking agent. The Bay of Plenty company **Bay Bus**, To800-368267, runs from Tauranga daily except Sunday, and from Opotiki on Monday and Wednesday. You can connect with the East Cape and Opotiki shuttle from Whakatane. For shuttle buses going around the East Cape (SH35), see page 326.

Tourist information **Whakatane VIC (I-Site)** ① *corner of Quay Drive and Kakahoroa Drive (east of the centre),* To7-308 6058, www.whakatane.com, *Mon-Fri 0830-1830, Sat 0900-1700 (reduced hours in winter),* also has DoC information. **Opotiki VIC (I-Site)** ① *corner of St John and Elliot sts,* To7-315 3031, www.opotikinz.com, *daily 0800-1700.* The **DoC** ① To7-315 1001, is an adjunct to this office. The free booklet *Opotiki and East Cape Free Holiday Guide* is a must for anyone touring the area.

Background

Whakatane has a rich Maori history going back to 1150 when the Polynesian explorer Toi-te-Hauatahi landed and was reputed to have settled. Later, in the mid-14th century, the ancestral canoe, Mataatua, captained by one Chief Toroa, is believed to have also landed. Due to the New Zealand Wars in the 1860s there was not any major European settlement founded until later in the century, and more especially in the early 1900s, when land drainage opened up the land for farming.

The name Whakatane means 'to act like a man', and it came about after the heroic acts of Wairaka, the high-spirited daughter of Toroa. When the *waka* landed at the rivermouth, the men came ashore to investigate. As was the case in those days, the women were instructed to stay in the canoe, but they were so busy nattering away they didn't notice the canoe drifting. This left them in a bit of a predicament as the oars were *tapu* (out of bounds) to the womenfolk. However, young Wairaka, the spirited daughter of the chief, took up the oars and, rowing furiously for the safety of the shore, proclaimed; *'Ka Whakatane au I ahau'* which roughly translated means 'we must now play the part of men'. A very beautiful and evocative statue of Wairaka now stands on a rock at the harbour entrance – a reminder to us all of her heroism.

Whakatane

The major attraction of Whakatane is as a gateway to visit the active volcano **White Island**, which can, on a clear day, be seen 50 km offshore, steaming away merrily. The other major activities are swimming with dolphins, fishing and, to a lesser extent, walking in the **Urewera National Park, Whirinaki Forest Park** and **Tarawera Falls** areas. The town also enjoys some of the highest annual sunshine hours in the country.

If you have your own transport, perhaps the best thing to do first is to get your bearings. To do this take Hillcrest Road south from the centre of town and the road over the hill west towards Ohope Beach. At the crest of the hill turn left and follow the signs to the **Kohi Point Scenic Reserve**. At the headland (which was the *pa* site of the first Maori settlers) you will get a grand view of the town, the coast and White Island. From here you can also embark on a number of short or long scenic coastal walks.

The island close to shore is **Moutohora Island**, also known as **Whale Island** (it does indeed look like a whale from the side). Moutohora is another less active volcano which has some hot springs and a number of historic *pa* sites. It is privately owned and a wildlife refuge administered by DoC. Although generally off limits, DoC does offer occasional guided tours in the summer months; contact the VIC (I-Site) for details.

Back in the town centre another natural feature is the **Pohaturoa**, a large rock outcrop located at the corner of the Strand and Commerce Street. For some six centuries this was used by the Maori as a meeting place and was also where the local Ngati Awa tribe signed the Treaty of Waitangi in the 1840s. While the summit was used as a sacred place for the bones of early chiefs, the newborns were given a form of baptism and dedicated to the gods in a stream at its foot. More local information can be gleaned at the **Whakatane District Museum and Gallery** ⓘ *Boon St, T07-306 0505, Mon-Fri 1000-1630, Sat-Sun 1100-1500, donation*. It has As well as a wealth of historical displays and a fine dynamic gallery space, it houses a collection of over 20,000 photographs.

No trip to Whakatane would be complete without a short drive west along to the harbour entrance to see the gorgeous, svelte sculpture of **Wairaka** – a fine tribute to the town's roots and womanhood. There is also an interesting **mural** on the wall at the corner of the Strand and the Quay. It depicts a bi-cultural scene of Maori and *Pakeha* (whites). If you look closely you will see the head of Captain Cook has been defaced a number of times. This is a reflection of some strong feelings that still exist in the area regarding bicultural and land issues. The Tuhoe Iwi, whose lands lie to the south of Whakatane, are well known for their particularly staunch stand.

Ohope

Just 8 km over the hill from Whakatane, heading east, is the 11-km-long sandspit called **Ohope Beach**, guarding the entrance to the Ohiwa Harbour. Principally a beach resort, it is a fine place to while away a few hours in the sun, swimming, sunbathing or just watching White Island billow with steam in the distance.

Opotiki

The **Hukutaia Domain** is about 6 km from the town and signposted to the left after the Waioeka Bridge. It is a hectare of bush with many New Zealand native trees, including a historic 2000-year-old puriri tree called 'Taketakerau', with a girth of about 22 m and a height over 23 m. The hollow in this tree was used by the local Iwi to store the preserved bones of their dead, in an elaborate ritual and as protection from enemy desecration. Also of historical interest is the **Church Of Hinoa** (St Stephen's Anglican Church) at the north end of Church Street. It was originally built for the Church Missionary Society and the Reverend Karl Volkner, who first arrived in 1859. Sadly, given local bad feeling towards the *Pakeha*, he was considered a government spy and killed by Hauhau emissaries in 1865. There naturally followed much unrest in the region.

🛏 Sleeping

Whakatane *p269*

AL Motuhora Rise B&B, 2 Motuhora Rise (off Waiewe) St, T07-307 0224, jtspell@xtra.co.nz. Fine B&B on the outskirts of town. En suites, open fire and spa. Dinners on request.

AL-A Barringtons Motor Lodge, 34 Landing Rd, T0800-830130, T07-308 4273, www.barringtonsmotorlodge.co.nz. Modern units, some with spa and disabled facilities.

AL-A Pacific Coast Motel, 41 Landing Rd, T07-308 0100, www.pacificcoastwhakatane.co.nz. A modern option with luxury 1-bedroom or studio units, and spa.

AL-A White Island Rendezvous, 15 Strand East, T0800-242299, T07-308 9588, www.whiteisland.co.nz. Part of the **Pee Jay White Island** tour operation. Modern waterfront motel with a full range of units from standard to de luxe with spa, a fully self-contained apartment and cottage. Sky TV and internet ports. Café open 0630-1700.

A Briar Rose, 54 Waiewe St, T07-308 0314. Charming cottage in bush setting close to town. Double, single and studio en suite. Good value.

A Clifton Manor Motel and B&B, 5 Clifton Rd, T07-307 2145. B&B in a spacious home and self-contained units within walking distance of town centre. Pool.

B Nau Mai Motel, 61 Landing Rd, T07-308 6422. Budget motel option, central.

B-D Karibu Backpackers, 13 Landing Rd, T07-307 8276, www.karibubackpackers.co.nz. Friendly no-nonsense suburban house hostel in central location. Tent sites. Bus drop-offs right outside, off-street parking, free bike use.

B-D Lloyds Lodge Backpackers, 10 Domain Rd, T07-307 8005, www.lloydslodge.com. A small, friendly option in a centrally located 1930's villa. Owned by a Maori couple who add a memorable cultural aspect to your stay. Doubles and dorms, off-street parking.

C-D Whakatane Holiday Park, McGarvey Rd, T07-308 8694. Basic but next to the river.

Ohope p270

There are numerous motels on the waterfront.

LL-AL Beachpoint Resort, 5 West End, waterfront, T0800-232247, www.beach point.co.nz. Smart modern apartments and pool over-looking the beach.

A The Ocean View, 18 West End, waterfront, T07-312 5665, www.oceanviewmotel.co.nz. 2 units without the 'resort' feel, quiet, wireless broadband.

A Surfs Reach, 52 West End, waterfront, T07-312 4159, www.surfsreachmotels.co.nz.

A-B Jody's on the Beach, 31 West End, waterfront, T07-312 4616.

A-B The Rafters, 261A Pohutukawa Av, T07-312 4856, the_rafters ohope@xtra.co.nz. Single unit with sea views and full cooking facilities. Good value.

Motorcamps

C-D Ohope Beach Top Ten, 367 Harbour Rd T07-312 4480, www.ohopebeach.co.nz. A good motorcamp in a quiet spot at the west end, right on the beach.

Opotiki p270

There are many motels, farmstays, B&Bs and backpacker hostels in Opotiki.

AL Capeview Cottage, 167 Tablelands Rd via SH35, T07-315 7877, www.cape view.co.nz. Peaceful, modern cottage B&B in country setting cottage, 5 km from town.

C-D Central Oasis Backpackers, 30 King St, T07-315 5165, centraloasis@hotmail.com. A small traditional cottage in the heart of town with doubles, twins and dorm. Free use of body boards and bikes and will assist with East Cape transport bookings.

C-D Opotiki Beach Backpackers, Appleton Rd, T07-315 5117, hangout@paradise.net.nz. A small beachside backpacker hostel 5 km west of the town enjoying a good reputation with doubles, twins, singles and dorms. Free use of body boards and kayaks. Pick-ups from town. Closed Jun-Aug. Recommended.

Motorcamps

C-D Opotiki Holiday Park, Potts Av, T07-315 6050. The only motorcamp within the town – basic but adequate.

● Eating

Whakatane p269

There is a decent choice of eateries, and all are pretty affordable. The **New World** super-market is on Kakahora Drive, daily 0800-2000.

♥ The Wharf Shed, Strand East, T07-308 5698, daily from 1100. A fine restaurant with an imaginative, mainly seafood menu.

♥ Where Else Inn, 62 Strand, T07-308 6721. Good, reliable, traditional TexMex dishes.

♥-♥ The Bean, 76 Strand. Head here for a snack, and a global range of quality beans.

♥-♥ Global, Commerce St, T07-308 9000.

♥-♥ Ground Zero Café, 163 The Strand T07-308 8548, daily 0800-1700. Free internet.

Ohope p270

♥ Pier 5, Fisherman's Wharf, T07-312 4015. Has the best seafood and harbour views.

♥ Vanilla, 19 Main Rd, T07-312 5292. Best place for choice and coffee.

The **New World** supermarket is at the western end of Bridge St as you head out of town. ¶ **Hot Bread Shop Café**, on the main road through town opposite the **Eastland Pacific Motel**, T07-315 6795, daily 0500-1700. Wide selection of light meals, good coffee. Internet.

◑ Pubs, bars and clubs

Whakatane *p269*
The Craic, in the **Whakatane Hotel**. A superb small, cosy Irish pub.

▲ Activities and tours

Whakatane *p269*
Dolphin watching
The bay is rich with playful dolphin. Encounters with pods of over 1000 are not uncommon. **Dolphins Down Under**, Green Wharf, T0800-354 7737, www.dolphinsdownunder .co.nz. Offers a weather-dependent, 5-hr trip to White Island with dolphin swimming and snorkelling from $135, or a 3-hr dolphin swimming trip from $100, child $75. If a pod of dolphins is found (highly likely) you can either observe or get in the water. Several trips daily in summer. Booking essential. **Whales and Dolphins**, 96 The Strand, T07-308 2001, www.whalesanddolphinwatch.co.nz. Offer similar trips at 0730, 0930 and 1230, from $130 (swim), $95 watch only.

Horse trekking
Tui Glen Farm, 2 km from Kawerau (25 min-drive from Whakatane), www.tuiglen.net.nz, T07-323 6457. 1 hr from $35, beach rides $70.

Hot pools
Awakeri Hot Springs, 16 km away, just off SH30 to Rotorua southwest of the town, T07-304 9117, $5. The nearest hot pools to Whakatane. Basic but relaxing, with a motorpark and camping available.

Jet boating
Kiwi Jet Tours, T07-3070663, www.kiwijet boattours.com. Quality 20-min trips down the Rangitaiki taking in the 'Weeping Gorge', $50.

Scuba diving and snorkelling
Dolphin Down Under (see also Dolphin-watching). Dive trips and snorkelling.

Dive White (Island), 186 Strand, T0800-348394, www.divewhite.co.nz. The principal operator in the area offering dive trips and snorkel trips off White Island from $180 (snorkel), $225 dive (gear included).

Tours to White Island and scenic flights
Air Discovery, based at Whakatane airport, T07-308 7760, www.airdiscovery.co.nz. Offers fixed-wing trips from 55-min White Island trip ($189) to 2 hr trip taking in White Island and Mt Tarawera ($349) and hands-on-flying where you briefly take the controls during a 20-min flight from $99. **Pee Jays**, 15 Strand East, T07-308 9588, T0800-733529, www.whiteisland.co.nz. Highly commercial operator which offers a 5-to 6-hr volcano trip leaving at 0830. Lunch and refreshments provided. It will often deviate off schedule if dolphins are spotted, $150. Bookings essential. **Vulcan Helicopters**, Whakatane airport, T0800-804354, www.vulcanheli.co.nz. 3-hr tour, 1 hr on the island, from $395.

Ohope *p270*
Ohiwa Harbour Tours, Ohope, T07-308 7837, ohiwaharbourtours@xtra.co.nz. A local eco-tour that encompasses a trip by road to take in natural and human historical facts, followed by a 2½-hr cruise on the wildlife rich Ohiwa Harbour. Light refreshments are provided, but take your own food. 3 hrs, $60. Recommended.

Opotiki *p270*
Motu River Jet Boat Tours, T07-325 2735, www.motujet.co.nz. The main operator for the remote Motu River. 2 hrs, $85, child $50. **Wet 'n' Wild**, T07-348 3191, www.wetnwild rafting.co.nz. Offers one of the North Island's best wilderness rafting expeditions, the multi-day trip down the remote Motu River. Provided the river levels are good, this is an unforgettable experience that will cost around $700. Recommended.

◑ Directory

Whakatane *p269*
Internet Available at the VIC. Wireless access at **Ground Zero Café**, 163 The Strand T07-308 8548, daily 0800-1700. **Post office** corner of Commerce St and The Strand, Mon-Fri 0830-1700, Sat 0900-1200.

Taupo and Ruapehu

‡ Footprint features

Introduction

From space, Lake Taupo, the largest lake in New Zealand, looks like a large bullet-hole shot through the heart of the North Island. This is perhaps fitting given that its placid waters, now world famous for trout fishing, mask a frightening heritage of volcanoes and thermal activity – one that is the trademark of the Taupo and Ruapehu region. Here are the remains of the largest volcanic eruption in the last 5000 years.

Now, during its dormancy, Lake Taupo is home to a bustling tourist town, Taupo, renowned not only for its fishing, but a host of other activities from rafting and mountain biking to tandem skydiving; you can even fly a helicopter here. But what is of added appeal in this popular volcanic hotspot is that after exerting yourself, all the aches and pains can be soothed away in the town's popular and wonderfully relaxing hot pools.

Evidence of ancient and ongoing volcanic activity is apparent throughout the region, but nowhere more so than in the Tongariro National Park. Steeped in Maori legend and spirituality, New Zealand's oldest national park boasts the still active volcanoes of Ngauruhoe and Ruapehu – the North Island's highest peak, which erupted in spectacular fashion as recently as 1996. When the mountains are in a less aggressive mood the park provides excellent skiing, tramping and walking opportunities, including the great Tongariro Crossing, a walk full of volcanic wonder and considered one of the best day-hikes in the country.

★ Don't miss ...

1 **Mount Tauhara** Take in the spectacular view from the summit, page 280.
2 **Wairakei Park** Visit the 'Craters of the Moon', the Volcanic Activity Centre and the thunderous Huka Falls, page 280.
3 **Orakei Korako Thermal Reserve** Enjoy some peace, quiet and relaxation, page 283.
4 **Lake Taupo** Cruise, sail or fish for trout on this huge flooded caldera. Or take a different view from 9000 ft at 200 kph with an instructor (and parachute) strapped to your back, page 288.
5 **Golf** Play a round or two on one of Taupo's first-class 'steaming' golf courses, page 289.
6 **Tongariro National Park** Hike the memorable 'Tongariro Crossing' – one of the best day-walks in the country. Then indulge in a relaxing soak in the Taupo Hot Springs, page 297.
7 **Ruapehu Crater Lake** Climb up the lake from the Whakapapa ski-field – then ski back down, page 299. Cross your fingers she doesn't blow.

Taupo and around → *Colour map 3, A4 Population: 20,000*

For those heading south, Taupo is really the first place that begins to satisfy the imagination in terms of what New Zealand is 'supposed' to look like: wide open spaces with snow-capped mountains and clear blue lakes. As you come over the hill into the town on a clear day, the scene hits you like the first sip of a fine wine, with the huge expanse of Lake Taupo dwarfing the distant snow-tipped volcanoes of the Tongariro National Park. Take a while to enjoy it from the roadside lookout above the town before merging into the picture in the sure knowledge that it gets even better from here.

Because of its position in the centre of the North Island, Taupo is the commercial headquarters for the central districts of Taupo and Ruapehu, as well as a major tourist resort. The town is very pleasant, busy, friendly and well set out, nestled close to the source of the Waikato River (the longest in the country), and lies on the northernmost bank of the huge lake, once a mighty volcanic crater. The region has a multitude of activities to enjoy. Fishing is, of course, the main attraction, but you can also try the more adrenaline-pumping pursuits of bungee jumping and tandem skydiving, as well as mountain biking, golf, sailing and walking. One of the latest activities is the fairly unique and mind-bending opportunity to take the controls of a helicopter. Beyond the town and its lake, the glorious mountain peaks of the Tongariro National Park provide an irresistible lure with that omnipresent edge of fear that maybe, just maybe, another volcanic eruption will strike. ▶▶ For Sleeping, Eating and other listings, see pages 284-292.

Ins and outs

Getting there

Air Taupo airport ① *just off SH1, 8 km south of the town, T07-378 7771, www.taupo airport.co.nz,* receives direct daily flights from Auckland and Wellington with **Air New Zealand Link,** T0800-737000, www.airnewzealand.co.nz, with connections from the South Island. Shuttles and taxis usually meet incoming flights at the airport. **Taupo Taxis,** T07-378 5100, operates an airport shuttle service from $18. Shuttles can also be booked with **Taupo Top Cabs,** T07-378 9250.

Road Taupo is on the SH1, 280 km south of Auckland and 80 km from Rotorua; it is a major stop on the tourist 'Thermal Explorer Highway'. By bus Taupo is served daily by **Newman's, Intercity** and **Nakedbus.com,** which arrive and depart from the **Travel Centre** ① *16 Gascoigne St, T07-378 9032,* and **Pavlovich,** T0800-759999, www.pav lovichexpress.co.nz, which stop outside the VIC (I-Site).

Turangi is well served by both **Newman's, Intercity** and **Nakedbus.com** which stop near the VIC (I-Site) on the corner of Ngawaka Road and Ohuanga Street. The VIC (I-Site) also acts as bus ticketing agents.

Getting around

Tongariro Expeditions, T07-377 0435, www.thetongarirocrossing.co.nz, offers daily services via Turangi to Tongariro Crossing in summer, or Whakapapa in winter. **Alpine Scenic Tours,** T07-892 3716/T0800-872258, www.alpinescenictours.co.nz, also runs between Turangi and Taupo, with additional services to Tongariro National Park and Whakapapa daily in summer. See Tongariro National Park, page 293, for details.

The colourful and entertaining **Hot Bus,** T07-377 1967, www.thehotbus.co.nz, is a hop-on/hop-off service that links most major attractions including the hot pools, Huka Falls and the Craters of the Moon, with an hourly service 1000-1600, $4 per person per 'hop-on', $7 return, $10 day pass.

www.tongarirocrossing.com, offers a Tongariro Crossing shuttle service at 0600, 0730 and 0900 from $35. For taxis, hike hire and car rental see Transport, page 292.

Tourist information

Taupo VIC (I-Site) ① *30 Tongariro St, SH1, T07-376 0027, www.laketauponz.co.nz, daily 0830-1700*, has all the usual information and a good range of maps. It also handles DoC enquiries and offers specialist information available on the Tongariro Crossing (see box page 297) with up-to date weather forecasts.

Turangi VIC (I-Site) ① *Ngawaka Pl, just off SH1, T07-386 8999, www.laketaupo nz.com, www.ruapehunz.com, daily 0830-1730*, sells fishing licences ($18.50 for 24 hours) and provides information about where to catch the 'big ones'. Internet is available and there is a wealth of information on other activities in the Kaimanawa Forest Park and Tongariro National Park. Hut bookings and ski passes can also be arranged. All the local DoC information is held at the VIC (I-Site).

Background

Prior to European settlement Taupo was called *Tapuaeharuru*, meaning 'resounding footsteps', and was allegedly named by a Maori chief, who thought the ground felt hollow. The main *pa* site and fortified village was near the lake outlet – the Waikato River. In 1868 an Armed Constabulary force established a garrison on the site of the present township to assist in the national campaign to rout the Maori rebel leader Te Kooti. By the late 1800s the area's thermal activity was already beginning to attract visitors and the land was bought from the Maori and trout introduced into the lake. From that point, it seems, Taupo's destiny was sealed and the tourism trade flourished.

Sights

Taupo's natural sights are mostly outside the town itself (see below and Tongariro National Park, page 293). The most immediate and dominant sight in town is of course the huge expanse of **Lake Taupo** itself – 619 sq km. On a calm day it can be mirror-like, disturbed only by the wakes of boats and ducks. But it wasn't always like this and the origin of the lake itself will make you quake in your walking boots: Lake Taupo is in fact the tranquil remains of one the biggest volcanic eruptions the planet has created in the last 5000 years. The latest occurred in AD 186 spewing out over 30 cu km of debris at up to 900 kph (about 30 times more than Mount St Helens spewed out).

The now placid waters are famous for copious trout and are the domain of the serious angler. The lake is used for numerous other water-based activities including sailing, cruising, windsurfing and waterskiing. Most of the longer cruises take in the remarkable **Maori rock carvings** (a huge face complete with *moko* or tattoos), which can only be seen from the water and adorn an entire rock face in Mine Bay, 8 km southwest across the lake. Although remarkable, they were only created in recent years, which does somewhat dampen the excitement. For cruising and other lake activities, see Activities and tours, page 288.

Near the very tacky oriental-style trout statue is the **Taupo Museum and Art Gallery** ① *Story Pl, T07-376 0414, daily 1030-1630, donation $5*. There are some interesting photos and artworks that focus on the early days of the region, and a gallery that features regular exhibitions. Just a little further west the **Waikato River**

● *There was so much ash after the last volcanic eruption that the effects were seen as far*
● *afield as China and Rome.*

Taupo

Related map
A Taupo centre, p285.

To Reporoa

Broadlands Rd

Tauhara Rd

Elizabeth St

John St

Terence St

Brice St

Cumberland St

Matai St

Miro St

Manuka St

Taharepa Rd

Hinemoa Av

Hinekura Av

Gillies Av

Tamatea Rd

Koha Rd

Taupo View Rd

Kapua Pl

Crown Rd

Invergarry Rd

Anna Pl

Arthur Cres

Kiddle Dr

Glengarry Pl

MacDonell St

Henry Hill Rd

Hildon Pl

Taharepa Rd

Sunset St

Tawa St

Kotare St

Puriri St

Liston Av

Rahui Rd

Waihora St

Rokino Rd

Avanui St

Ngamotu Rd

Taupo Hot Springs 3

Ngauruhoe St

Kurupae Rd

Murray St

McCauley St

Crowther Terr

Waipahihi Av

Bearchman Gr

Armstrong Gr

State Highway No 5

Arrowsmith Av

To Napier & Mount Tauhara

Fairview Terr

Harvey St

Wall St

Shepherd Rd

Te Heuheu St

Fairmont Rd

Chesham Av

Norfolk Rd

Korimako Rd

Lowry Pl

Lake Terr (State Highway No 1)

Waipahihi Bay

Ingle Av

Pipi St

Bernard St

Tremaine Av

Gradwell St

Regents Pl

Kensington Pl

Two Mile Bay

Hawai St

Matuku St

Paata St

Kereru St

Frederick St

Richmond Av

Anchorage Resort Motel 1

Mapou Rd

Tobin Pl

Ward Pl

Rainbow Point

Oregon Dr

Rainbow Cres

Charles

Grace Cres

To Turangi & Airport

N

0 metres 200
0 yards 200

Taupo and Ruapehu Taupo & around

Sleeping
Anchorage Resort Motel 1
Berkenhoff Lodge 2
De Brett's Thermal Resort 5
Essence (Moana Landing) 8
Huka Lodge 12
Lakeland 6
Lake Taupo Lodge 10
Lake Taupo Top Ten
 Holiday Park 7
Orakei Korako Resort 11
Rainbow Lodge
 Backpackers 9
Terraces & Restaurant 3
Wairakei Resort 4

Eating
Ploughmans Pub 1

begins its 425-km journey to the Tasman Sea and winds its merry way north behind the town towards **Wairakei Park** (see below).

On a cliff edge, carved out over the millennia by the river, is the headquarters for **Taupo Bungee** ① *202 Spa Rd, T0800-888408, www.taupobungy.co.nz*, which might be your first opportunity to get an elastic band tied to your ankles before throwing yourself over a 45 m cliff. Masochistic adrenaline junkies will be delighted to hear that the ones in the South Island are at least twice this height. A jump in Taupo will cost from $99, which includes a video and some photos with which to terrify the folks back home.

The **AC Baths** ① *top of Spa Rd, T07-377 3600 www.taupovenues.co.nz/ac baths.asp, daily 0600-2100, $6.50, child $2.50*, is one of two large thermal pool complexes in Taupo. Here you can soak away all your troubles in a range of recently renovated outdoor, indoor and private spa pools while the kids do their thing on the hydro-slide. Next door, the **Taupo Events Centre** ① *T07-376 0340, www.taupoevents centre.co.nz*, hosts major sporting tournaments, exhibitions and trade shows. It also has a quality 12-m **climbing wall**, see Activities and tours, page 288.

The other thermal complex is the excellent and recently refurbished **Taupo Hot Springs** ① *next to De Brett's just off SH5 (which heads west from SH1, along the lake front at the southern edge of town), T07-377 6502, www.taupohotsprings.com, daily 0730-2130, $12, child $4*. This is the better of the two complexes with all the usual facilities including a massage and beauty treatment centre, hydro-slides and private pools. It's a fine place to relax and mix with the locals, as well as the occasional visiting celebrity, including by all accounts former Xena Warrior Princess 'aka' Lucy Lawless. **Hot Bus**, T07-377 1967, offers a return shuttle to the pools for $20 including entry.

To the east of town looms the dormant volcano **Mount Tauhara** (1088 m). Not only is it a grand site, but also a great walk with superb views that make the three-hour return trip well worth it. The track, which is about one-third grazing paddock to two-thirds native bush, begins from the bottom of Mountain Road, 5 km from Taupo on the Napier SH5 Road. Do not be fooled by the immediate summit in view, which is a false summit. The track enters the bush-filled crater to the true summit beyond it. Adequate footwear and patience are required.

Wairakei Park 🏊⛰ ↠ *pp284-292.*

Huka Falls
① *Signposted from the SH1, accessed via the Huka Falls Rd, www.hukafalls.com. There is an information kiosk in the car park at the falls.*

No visit to Taupo would be complete without a muse of utter fear and trepidation at the mighty Huka Falls. In the heart of the Wairakei Park north of the town, these falls are arguably the most spectacular in the country. From a sedate steady flow roughly 100 m across, the waters of the Waikato River are forced through a cleft of solid rock only 15 m wide, before falling 7 m into a cauldron of aquatic chaos and foam. From the car park a bridge crosses the rapids before joining a walkway down to the waterfall where, depending on the flow (regulated at Lake Taupo for electricity generation), the falls can be up to 11 m in height with a staggering volume of 220,000 litres per second. Believe it or not some utter lunatics have attempted the ultimate adrenaline buzz of 'riding' the Huka by canoe. The last time it was attempted, in 1994, two canoeists went down. One made it in about 60 seconds. The other disappeared in the torrent and reappeared minus canoe, and life, 40 minutes later.

The **walking tracks** that lead both north and south along the river from here are worthy of a trek on foot or mountain bike. Just up river is the exclusive retreat of **Huka Lodge** (see Sleeping, page 284), an exorbitant luxury pad that hosts the filthy rich and visiting dignitaries.

Honey Hive
ⓘ *T07-3748553, daily 0900-1700, free.*

Carrying along the Huka Falls Loop Road (north) you can take a small diversion to admire the view looking back at the falls, before passing **Helistar Helicopters** (see page 289) and arriving at the Honey Hive. For honey monsters this is the 'place to bee' with some interesting interpretative displays, a working glass-fronted hive and the **Beez Kneez Café**. There is also a shop where you can purchase a tub of Manuka honey, the most delectable toast spread on earth.

Volcanic Activity Centre
ⓘ *T07-374 8375, www.volcanoes.co.nz, daily 1000-1700, $8, child $4. The fascinating website provides the latest status reports on national earthquakes and eruptions.*

Wairakei Park

To Rotorua

To Auckland

Palmer Mill Rd

Aratiatia Rd

Aratiatia Rapids

Rapids Jet

Aratiatia Rapids Lookout

Dam

Rapid Rd

View Rd

Wairakei Thermal Valley

Wairakei Village

Geothermal Power House

Prawn Park

Waikato River

Wairakei Terraces

NZ Woodcraft

Huka Jet

African Queen Riverboat

Borefield Lookout

Wairakei Golf Course

Volcanic Activity Centre

Aratiatia Rd

Wairakei Golf Club

Honey Hive

Craters of the Moon

Taupo Horse Treks

Helistar Helicopters

Huka Falls Lookout

Huka Falls

Rakanui Rd

Aratiatia Rd

Reid's Farm

Centennial Dr

Broadlands Rd

Huka Falls Rd

Spa Rd

County Av

Taupo Golf Club

AC Baths & Events Centre

Taupo Bungee

Tauhara Rd

Spa Rd

Taupo

A

N

0 metres 500
0 yards 500

Sleeping 🛏
Huka Lodge **1**
Wairakei Resort **2**

Taupo and Ruapehu Taupo & around

The next attraction along the road is the Volcanic Activity Centre and its geological delights. It's well worth a peek, if only to get an inkling of the scale and magnitude of the natural powers that lie beneath your feet. The Taupo district is in the heart of one of the most active volcanic zones in the world, the details of which are well presented in the centre. There are models and displays, all with appropriate shaking and rumbling noises.

Prawn Park

ⓘ *To7-374 8474, www.prawnfarm.co.nz, daily 0900-1700, $9, child $2.50. Tours leave daily 1100-1600, every 30 mins.*

Carrying along Huka Falls Road you pass **NZ Woodcraft** (a glorified native wood souvenir workshop) before reaching the road end and the riverbank. Here you will find Prawn Park. Hailed as the world's only geothermal prawn farm, you can join an informative tour (to meet 'em), see the prawns crassly anthropomorphized (greet 'em), before you are encouraged to tuck into a few (and eat 'em), in the **Prawn Farm Restaurant**. After all that you can perhaps understand why their star captive was called 'Grumpy' – apparently the largest prawn in captivity. Prawnless meals are also available in the restaurant for those of a sensitive disposition.

Jet-boat river trips

Alongside Prawn Park are the headquarters of **Huka Jet** ⓘ *To7-374 8572, www.huka jet.co.nz*, offering an adrenaline filled trip to view the base of the Huka Falls with the obligatory 360° spins, from $89, child $49. Trips depart daily every half hour from 0830 to 1730 or on demand.

Craters of the Moon Volcanic Reserve

ⓘ *Daily, free but offer a donation.*

Back on SH1 and almost directly across it, you can access the Craters of the Moon Volcanic Reserve. This is a very steamy affair somewhat akin to taking a stroll through a smouldering bush fire. From almost every conceivable crack and crater along the 50-minute walk, steam quietly billows into the air, with only the faintest hiss giving you an indication of the forces that lie below. The track is easy going, with most of it made up of boardwalk. The reserve and the car park are staffed by friendly thermo-volunteers selling thermo-souvenirs and they will kindly keep a hot eye on your car.

Wairakei Golf Course

Heading north again up SH1 you pass the Wairakei Golf Course to the left. This is a superb course of international quality and, as far as golf courses go, very cheap and easy to access (if not easy to play). If you just happen to be there in August or September it is also one of the best places in New Zealand to see **tui**, the native bird, which features in the course logo. If you go to the trees behind the clubhouse you can often see large flocks of them feeding amongst the flowering branches in an almost hyper feeding frenzy. Their call is one of the most unusual and entertaining in the avian world, with an inconceivable range of whistles, clicks and knocking noises, most of which are beyond the human audible frequency range.

Wairakei Terraces

ⓘ *SH1, 7 km north of Taupo, To7-378 0913, www.wairakeiterraces.co.nz, 0900-1700, $18, child $9; cultural performances with a traditional* hangi *(feast) are also held Wed-Sat at 1800 subject to bookings, from $75, child $37.50.*

The latest of the region's thermal attractions, the terraces complex in Wairakei takes a historical and cultural look back in time when the Pink and White terraces, destroyed during the great Tarawera eruption of 1886, were the region's, and one of the world's, most famous volcanic features. As usual there is lots of steam and boiling water, Maori carvings and a very welcome therapeutic footbath.

Aratiatia Rapids

To complete a convenient circuit back into town you can continue up SH1 and on to SH5 for about 2 km, before turning right, following the signs to Aratiatia. This will take you to a dam on the Waikato that tempers the flow of the Aratiatia rapids, a similar gorge to the Huka Falls, but more jagged. The dam gates are opened at 1000, 1200 and 1400 daily in winter (plus 1600 in summer); all openings depend on water levels. You can see the rapids from a viewpoint just beside the dam or from a hilltop lookout about 1 km further up the road. From here it is a short drive back into Taupo via the Taupo Golf Club on Spa Road. **Rapids Jet** ① *To7-378 5828, www.rapidsjet.com, 4 trips daily, from $85, child $45*, is at the base of the falls on Rapids Road. It's an entertaining trip beginning with a spin upstream to the base of the controlled rapids and power station, then downstream through a series of rapids with plenty of 360° spins along the way. Recommended.

Orakei Korako Thermal Reserve

① *Head north from Taupo on SH1 for 27 km, turn right onto Tutukau Rd for 13 km, then left on to Orakei Korako Rd, To7-378 3131, www.orakeikorako.co.nz, 0830-1630 (hours vary according to demand), $26, child $8.*

About 40 km north of Taupo is one of the least visited, but best thermal parks in the country. Even without the thermal park, this tranquil lakeside spot, formed by another dam on the Waikato, offers the visitor sanctuary from the hustle and bustle of Taupo and its busy tourist attractions. From the lakeside visitor centre and **Geyserland Resort Lodge** only plumes of steam and a strange colourful silica terrace across the water give any indication of the numerous interesting volcanic features awaiting you. Once delivered at the terraces by boat you are free to roam the self-guided tracks of the reserve. There is a bit of everything here including colourful algae-covered silica terraces, boiling pools, geysers and lots of bubbling mud. Added to that, a short boat trip takes you to the fascinating **Ruatapu Cave** which descends into the earth, with the warm **Waiwhakaata Pool** (Pool of Mirrors) at its base. Apparently, if you put your left hand in the pool and make a secret wish, it will come true. The cave itself is about 40 m deep and from its depths you can look heavenwards towards its gaping entrance and the daylight, shrouded by fronds of silhouetted silver fern. You can stay as long as you like in the reserve before re-boarding the boat back to the visitor centre. If you have any questions about the reserve ask local guide Chris, an entertaining 'geyser' of considerable knowledge.

Pureora Forest Park

This little-known forest park to the west of Taupo offers a number of easy short walks as well as the more demanding climb to the summit of **Mount Pureora** (1165 m). The park is also the focus for the successful reintroduction of the **kokako**, a native bird with a beautiful haunting song. Most of the main park sights can be taken in on a scenic drive that starts from Kakaho Road, south of the intersection of SH32 and Poihipi Road, to emerge again at Mangakino. For maps and more information see the Taupo VIC (I-Site), see page 277.

Turangi and Tokaanu ●●●▲ ⤷ *pp284-292.*

→ *Colour map 3, A3 Population: 4000.*

① *SH1, 50 km south of Taupo, 4 km inland from the southeastern edge of Lake Taupo.*

Turangi is a small, pleasant village, world famous for trout fishing on the scenic Tongariro River that flows past the eastern edge of the village before quietly spilling into the huge expanses of the lake. The village is well served with accommodation and amenities and is often used as a base for exploring the Tongariro National Park.

The village would not be content without proudly displaying some live trout somewhere and the **Tongariro National Trout Centre** ① *3 km south of Turangi on SH1, T07-386 8085, daily 1000-1600, free,* tries hard. Although there is some way to go before it could be called a major attraction, you can at least see a trout hatchery in operation, huge swirling shoals of adult fish in a large pool and some others in an underwater viewing area. There is also an interpretive centre where you can learn about their interesting life cycle.

The neighbouring village of Tokaanu, 5 km to the west along SH41, also provides accommodation, amenities, and basic **thermal pools** ① *Mangaroa St, T07-386 8575, 1000-2100, $8,* as well as fishing and boat access to Lake Taupo.

● Sleeping

Taupo *p276, maps p278 and p285*
There is a wealth of motels with the best being the 'lake view' options on or around Lake Terrace and the waterfront. The cheaper options tend to be a bit 'time warped' and are in the town's western suburbs. There are also many luxury lodges, B&Bs, homestays and farmstays available, mainly around town and in Acacia Bay to the east of Taupo. For full details contact the VIC (I-Site).
LL Essence (Moana Landing), 110 Lake Terr, Lake Taupo, T0275-424202/T0800-377362, www.essencenz.com. Ultra modern and chic, fully self-contained apartment right on the lakefront south of the town centre.
LL Huka Lodge, Huka Falls Rd, T07-378 5791, www.hukalodge.com. Luxury at its most lucrative, in quiet seclusion beside the river. Mingle with heads of state and visiting stars. Watch your money evaporate.
LL Lake Taupo Lodge, 41 Mapara Rd, Acacia Bay, T07-378 7386, www.laketaupo lodge.co.nz. Another top establishment offering total luxury in 4 suites with dining room, reading gallery, open fire. Includes exquisite cuisine.
L Terraces Hotel, (formerly Debretts Hotel) Napier-Taupo Highway, T07-378 7080, www.terraceshotel.co.nz. First established in 1889 this renovated hotel on the edge of the town has 18 rooms, 2 studio suites, bar and restaurant that combined offer both class and character. The added attraction of course is the Hot Springs and Spa Resort only a short stroll away.
L-AL Caboose Taupo, 100-102 Lake Terr, T07-376 0116, www.taupo.caboose.co.nz. A luxury establishment with a 'colonial African' theme. The lodge, which sits on the waterfront overlooking the lake, offers log cabin-style architecture with an attractive

range of suites ranging from the basic motel-style units named 'Train Compartments' to the intriguingly named 'Warthog Hollow' or executive suite, that sleeps 1-6. In-house facilities include spas, pool, and a restaurant/ bar that includes ostrich on the menu as well as the usual contemporary New Zealand fare. The 'safari staff' can arrange local activities with fishing 'safaris' a speciality.
L-AL Quest Taupo (Aspen Villas), 9-11 Tui St, T07-378 7487, www.questtaupo.co.nz. Immaculate 5-star fully self-contained units with spa 50 m from the lakefront.
AL Lakeland, 282 Lake Terr, Two Mile Bay, T07-378 3893, www.lakeland.co.nz. Mid-to upper-range comfort next to the lake. Restaurant and bar, spas and pool.
AL-A Tui Oaks, corner of Lake Terr and Tui St, T07-378 8305, www.tuioaks.co.nz. One of the best motels in the upper range, great views across the lake. Pool, restaurant and bar.
A Anchorage Resort Motel, Lake Front, Two Mile Bay, T07-378 5542, www.taupo motel.co.nz. Good facilities including pool, spas and gym.
A Ascot, 70 Rifle Range Rd, T07-377 2474, www.ascotattaupo.co.nz. Comfortable modern motel within walking distance of town.
A Catelli's Motel, 23-27 Rifle Range Rd, T07-378 4477, www.catellis.co.nz.

Backpacker hostels
C-D Action Downunder YHA Hostel, 56 Kaimanawa St, T07-378 3311, www.yha.co.nz. A very tidy 86-bed YHA associate with great modern rooms and facilities including family and double en suites with personal computer and internet – a rare find. Off-street parking, impressive kitchen facilities, outdoor big-screen movies, spa, gym and bike hire. All in all one of the best YHAs in the North Island.

C-D Berkenhoff Lodge, 75 Scannell St, T07-378 4909. Slightly out of the centre but has a fine 'rambling house' atmosphere and is friendly and well kept. An added attraction is the basic in-house bar (locally popular), café, spa and free bikes.

C-D Rainbow Lodge Backpackers, 99 Titiraupenga St, T07-378 5754, www.rainbowlodge.co.nz. Well established, popular and congenial backpacker hostel run by one of the longest-serving managers in the game. Good dorms and excellent doubles. Recommended.

C-D Tiki Lodge, 104 Tuwharetoa St, T07-377 4545, www.tikilodge.co.nz. A modern purpose-built hostel in the heart of town. Excellent facilities include spacious double en suites, spa, internet and off-street parking. The excellent staff will ensure you have a comfortable stay, but it is 'Denday', the pathologically laid-back cat, who is testimony to how congenial this place can really be. Here is a cat who could sleep for New Zealand. Recommended.

C-D Urban Retreat, 65 Heuheu St, T07-378 6124, www.taupourbanretreat.co.nz. New, purpose-built party-oriented hostel right in the heart of town. Full range of rooms centered around a happening social area and bar that is the focus for early evening action before heading out on to the town. Good facilities throughout. A great place to meet others and be social, but not if you intend to catch up on some sleep and gather your thoughts.

Motorcamps and campsites

A-D De Brett's Thermal Resort, Napier/Taupo Highway (SH5), T07-378 8559, www.debrettsresort.co.nz. A well-facilitated 5-star motorpark located right opposite the best hot pools complex in the town. Standard and self-contained cabins, studio and family units and lodges. Powered and non-powered sites, camp kitchen and TV lounge. Concession rates to thermal pools are an added incentive. Recommended.

B-D Lake Taupo Top Ten Holiday Park, 28 Centennial Drive, T07-378 6860. An adequate if not overly spacious alternative, closer to town and opposite the newly renovated AC Thermal Baths.

Campsites

Reid's Farm, next to the river on the Huka Falls Rd. Offers controversial free camping just outside Taupo but it does get busy and can attract less than desirable neighbours.

Wairakei Park *p280, map p281*

LL-L Wairakei Resort, 7 km north of town on SH1 and right in the heart of all the Wairakei Park attractions, T07-374 8021, www.wairakei.co.nz. One of the few conventional-style hotel resorts in the area, and right in the heart of all the Wairakei Park attractions. It is well appointed and laid out with good facilities especially for the sporty, with tennis, golf and squash, plus a spa, pool and sauna in which to relax after all the activity.

Taupo centre

Lake Taupo

0 metres 200
0 yards 200

Sleeping
Action Downunder YHA Hostel **1**
Ascot **9**
Caboose Taupo **2**
Catelli's Motel **3**
Quest Taupo (Aspen Villas) **8**
Tiki Lodge **5**
Tui Oaks **7**
Urban Retreat **6**

Eating
Bach **1**
Burbury **7**
Lotus Thai **3**
Max Café **8**
Mr India **5**
Mulligan's **4**
Pimento's **12**
Plateau **2**
Replete Café **6**
Villino **9**

Bars & clubs
Finn MacCauls **11**
Jolly Good Fellows **13**

Orakei Korako Thermal Reserve *p283*
B Orakei Korako Resort, 494 Orakei Korako
Rd, T07-378 3131, www.orakeikorako.co.nz.
Log cabin-style accommodation across
the lake from the thermal reserve. Quiet,
comfortable with modern motel-style units
and backpacker facilities. Spa pool on the
deck overlooking the lake and reserve.

Turangi and Tokaanu *p283*
LL River Birches, T07-386 0445, www.river
birches.co.nz. Very classy boutique fishing
lodge with 3 sumptuous en suites. Breakfast
included, 3-course dinner available for $65.
Geared up for anglers, but recommended
for any discerning traveller.
LL Tongariro Lodge, Grace Rd, T07-386 7946,
www.tongarirolodge.co.nz. Fine lodge on the
banks of the river. Range of very luxurious
chalets, some with kitchen facilities. Again,
geared up for anglers with its own resident
fishing guides. Restaurant and bar.
AL-A Anglers Paradise Resort, corner of
SH41and Ohuanga Rd, T07-386 8980,
www.anglersparadise.nz. Well-appointed
motel with swimming pool and spas.
A-B Creel Lodge Motel, 183-187 Taupahi Rd,
T07-386 8081, www.creel.co.nz. Popular due
to its position backing on to the Tongariro
River, peaceful atmosphere and good value.
A-B Parklands Motorlodge, corner of SH1
and Arahori St, T07-386 7515, www.parklands
motorlodge.co.nz. Modern and comfortable,
close to the Rafting Centre. Pool, spa, sauna,
restaurant and bar, activities organized.
B-D Bellbird Lodge, 3 Rangipoia Pl, T07-
386 8281, www.bellbird.co.nz. Smaller of
the budget options with distinctly homely
feel. Doubles, share, no singles. Transport
arranged to Tongariro Crossing.
B-D Extreme Backpackers, 26 Ngawaka Pl,
T07-386 8949, www.extremebackpackers.co.nz.
Very tidy lodge-style accommodation with
private and shared accommodation. Café
with open fire, climbing-wall, open fire
and internet. Recommended.
B-D Riverstone Backpackers, 222 Tautahanga
Rd, T07-386 7004, www.riverstoneback
packers.co.nz. 'Purpose-renovated boutique'
backpacker hostel, 4 mins from the town
centre. Standard room types with shared or
private bath. Spacious and well facilitated, with
indoor and outdoor log fires that add to a
relaxed and cosy atmosphere. Equipment hire.

Motorcamps and campsites
C-D Club Habitat, Ohuanga Rd, T07-386 7492,
clubhabitat@xtra.co.nz. Large motel, motorcamp, backpacker hostel and campsite with
good facilities. Restaurant, bar, sauna and spa.

❼ Eating

Taupo *p276, maps p278 and p285*
There is a wide selection of restaurants, cafés
and brasseries in Taupo, most are in the many
motels and in the heart of town, around the
waterfront. If you have been looking forward
to sampling a big fat juicy trout, you will be
disappointed. Under the conservation act it is
illegal to buy or sell trout. However, if you have
had a successful fishing trip most restaurants
will be delighted to cook your catch for you.
There is a plethora of mid-range eateries
along the waterfront and Robert St, all
claiming to have the best menus and views.

There are 2 supermarkets: **New World**,
247 Old Taupo Rd, T07-349 7720; and
Pak-N-Save, Ruapehu St, T07-377 1155.
♥♥♥ Caboose Restaurant, Caboose Taupo,
(see page 284) 100 Lake Terr, T07-376 0116.
Everything short of the full water buffalo.
♥♥♥ Reflections in the Lake, Tui Oaks Hotel
(see page 284), T07-378 8305. A pleasant
candlelit affair overlooking the lake.
♥♥ The Bach Restaurant, 2 Pataka Rd, Lake
Terr (out of the centre), T07-378 7856, summer
daily 1200-1400 and from 1800; winter
Mon-Fri from 1800 and Sat-Sun 1200-1400.
A deserving award-winner with lake views
and the best pizza in town. Set menu $68.
♥♥ The Lotus Thai Restaurant,
137 Tongariro St, T07-376 9497, daily
1200-2100, closed Tue. Good Thai fare.
♥♥ Mr India, 30 Tuwharetoa, T07-377 1969,
Mon-Sat 1100-1430 for lunch and from
1730 for dinner. Reliable Indian option.
♥♥ Pimento's, 17 Tamamutu St, T07-377
4549, from 1800 (closed Tue). A firm
local favourite offering an imaginative
Pacific Rim menu and tidy aesthetics.
♥♥ Plateau, 64 Tuwharetoa St, T07-377 2425,
daily from 1130. If you are looking for a good
traditional beef or lamb dish look no further.
An imaginative menu and congenial
surroundings including a great open fire.
♥♥ Terraces Hotel Restaurant, Napier-Taupo
Highway, T07-378 7080, www.terraces
hotel.co.nz. Historic hotel with a classy

restaurant. A fine option and a good evening out especially when combined with a visit to the Hot Springs and Spa, a short stroll away.

Villino Restaurant, 45 Horomatangi St, T07-377 4478, www.villino.co.nz, daily. Popular, especially for Sun brunch. Bistro and à la carte menu with a mix of European and Pacific Rim dishes. Try the classic New Zealand venison and kumara.

Burbury, 42 Roberts St. An old favourite, with a good waterfront location. Always busy and offers a fine selection of quick snacks, breakfasts and bottomless cups of coffee.

Max Café, Roberts St, open 24 hrs. Good value and choice when all the others are shut.

Mulligan's, 17 Tongariro St, T07-376 9100. Decent pub grub in quiet surroundings.

The Ploughmans Pub, 43 Charles Cres, T07-377 3422. A pleasant and peaceful English-style pub just off SH1 heading south out of town offering good pub grub.

Replete Café, 45 Heu Heu St, T07-378 0606. Considered one of the best cafés and daytime eating establishments.

Turangi and Tokaanu p283

Though you can't buy trout in New Zealand, most eateries will cook your catch for you.

Angler's Café, in the Angler's Paradise Resort, T07-386 8980, daily from 1800. Good food at affordable prices.

Brew House Bar and Restaurant, in the Club Habitat Complex, 25 Ohuanga Rd, T07-386 7492, daily 0700-2100. Offers good pub grub to wash down with its microbrewery ales. Breakfasts are also good.

Parklands Motorlodge (see Sleeping, page 286). Good, reasonably-priced food.

Red Crater Cafe, at the Extreme Backpackers, 26 Ngawaka Place. Good value and has an open fire.

Valentino's, in the town centre, T07-386 8821, from 1830. A popular Italian joint.

❶ Pubs, bars and clubs

Taupo p276, maps p278 and p285
Most of the action emanates from Tongariro and Tuwharetoa sts (waterfront) and their connecting blocks in the heart of town, which is where the best pubs are to be found.

Finn MacCauls, Tuwharetoa St, T07-378 6165. This pseudo Irish offering is a good venue and has bands at the weekends.

Fine lake views and a congenial atmosphere.

Mulligan's, 17 Tongariro St, T07-376 9100. A fine establishment with a relaxed atmosphere and the best place to mix with both locals and travellers. It tends to go off like a rocket towards the end of the evening especially at weekends when the occasional red or yellow cards are presented to anyone in imminent danger of making a Charlie of themselves.

Ploughmans, Charles Cres, T07-377 3422, at the southern edge of the town. Good for a quiet pint and traditional pub food.

❸ Festivals and events

Taupo p276, maps p278 and p285
Feb The biennial **Lake Taupo Arts Festival** (1st and 2nd weeks) swings into action, attracting local and national artists and exhibitions. the street performances are excellent, T07-377 1200, www.taupo fest.co.nz. **Great Lake Relay**, taking place almost immediately after the arts festival, is a 160-km relay around the lake, www.relay.co.nz.
Mar **Ironman New Zealand** (1st week), attracts the obscenely fit from all over New Zealand, who compete in a 1-day triathlon event, www.ironman.co.nz. **Tongariro Mountain Classic**, combines a gruelling 50-km cycle and 26-km run over Mt Tongariro, followed by a manic 23 km kayak down the Tongariro River. Perhaps it's the $20,000 worth of prizes that provides the motivation, but one can only watch in awe and amazement.
Apr **Lake Taupo International Trout Fishing Tournament** (around the 3rd week).
Aug **Taupo half-marathon** (1st week in Aug), the masochists return once again. This event sees all ages, shapes and sizes running (or crawling) around the lake.
Oct **Powerade Day-Night Thriller**, not to be out-done, diligent mountain bikers from far and wide descend on the town for 12-hr 5-person lap race that apparently finishes after dark.
Nov **Great Lake Cycle Challenge** (late Nov), T07-378 1546. At least this event finishes before sunset.
Dec The town's demanding schedule of events and legendary assault on the average physical constitution comes to a tumultuous end when locals gather by the lakeside for hearty renditions of Christmas carols.

O Shopping

Taupo *p276, maps p278 and p285*
Kura, 47A Heu Heu St, T07-377 4068. For interesting New Zealand art and crafts.

▲ Activities and tours

Taupo *p276, maps p278 and p285*
Bungee jumping
Taupo Bungee, just off Spa Rd, T07-377 1135, www.taupobungy.com. From $100 (tandem $160) for a 45-m jump.

Charter boats
As you might expect there are numerous boat charters plying the lake. The marina office in Taupo, at the Boat Harbour, along Storey Place, has all the information.
Chris Jolly Outdoors, T07-378 0623, www.chrisjolly.co.nz (see Cruising, below).
Sailing Centre, 75 Kurupae Rd, 2 Mile Bay, T07-378 3299, www.sailingcentre.co.nz.
Taupo Launchmen's Association, T07-378 3444.

Climbing
Events Centre Climbing Wall, corner of Spa Rd and AC Baths Av, T07-376 0350. Mon-Fri 1700-2100, Sat-Sun 1200-2100. Excellent climbing-wall, from $8-13.
Rock and Ropes, based at the fun park Crazy Catz between Rotorua and Taupo on the SH5, T07-374 8111, T0800-244508, www.rockn ropes.co.nz. A challenging low and high ropes course with a giant 15-m swing, which combined offers a fine alternative to more traditional activities especially if dependent on fine weather. The 'Giant Swing' costs $15, 'Three Challenge' $40, and half-day from $65.
Wilderness Escapes, T07-378 3413, www.wildernessescapes.co.nz. Reputable local operator offering a wide and successful range of activities including abseiling, climbing, hiking, kayaking and caving. Half-, full- or multi-day options. Climbing and abseiling half- or full-day from $85-$210.

Cruising
There are numerous opportunities to cruise the lake in all types of craft from the sedate to the ridiculous. Most day trips leave regularly from the Boat Harbour on Storey Place. Almost all take in the 10-m Maori rock carvings at Mine Bay, 8 km southwest of the town (only accessible by boat or kayak) .
The Barbary, T07-378 3444. A fine 50-ft ocean-going yacht that was (apparently) once owned by Errol Flynn. Daily at 1030 and 1400 and 1700; 2½ hrs $30, child $10.
Cruise Cat Scenic Cruises, Chris Jolly Outdoors, T07-378 0623, www.chrisjolly .co.nz. Mon-Sat 1030-1200, Sun 1030-1230, 1½ hrs trips to see the Maori rock carvings and the picturesque Whakaipo Bay. $35, child $16 (Sun Brunch Cruise from $53, child $34).
Ernest Kemp, T07-378 3444. A small and delightfully cute replica steamboat that leaves from the Boat Harbour daily at 1030 and 1400 (1700 in summer). Again it takes in the Maori rock carvings – be it all very slowly. $30, child $12.
Purefun, T0800-867272, www.purefun.co.nz. A fast rigid inflatable that was used for official duties during the Americas Cup in Auckland. It's an entertaining and informative trip that will, depending on the lake conditions, have you holding on like a rollercoaster and up-close enough to the carvings to get the obligatory photo, from $50. Departs daily at 1530. Recommended.

Fishing
As you might expect there is a wealth of operators desperately wanting to make a living doing what they love the most and perfectly willing to take you out to try to catch a 'monster trout'. Guides charge from $60 per hr for up to 2 people with a full day costing anything from $250 per head. The obligatory licence is $18.50 per day. A minimum 3-hr trip is recommended to give you at least a chance, especially for beginners. Bear in mind (for those who know very little about trout fishing and have visions of skewering worms on hooks) that there are a number of methods of catching trout and this, combined with learning about the natural history of the fish, can be a fascinating aspect of any trip. It is not, as some expect, a case of whipping a few to death or staring at your reflection in the water for hours on end. For full listings see the VIC (I-Site), the following are all well-established operators.
Anglers Retreat, T07-372 8830, www.anglersretreat.co.nz.
Greg Catly, T07-377 0035, www.nzflyfish.co.nz.

Mark Aspinall, T07-378 4453, www.markaspinall.com.
Paddy Clark, T07-378 3336, www.nzfly fishing.co.nz. Fly-fishing specialist.
TroutLine, T07-378 0895, www.troutline nz.com. The best value option for the casual visitor with a fully guided lake trip on board the 45-ft *MV Loloma*, 3 hrs for $80-120 depending on numbers. This trip in particular creates the perfect balance between comfort, fun and expert local knowledge and includes a light meal, free tea and coffee and/or your catch cooked on board. Given the experience of the crew you have a great chance of catching a fish but even if you do not you will gain a fascinating insight into trout fishing and the fish themselves. Overnight trips are also an option. Recommended.

Gliding

Taupo Gliding Club, Centennial Drive, T07-378 5627, bartley@reap.org.nz. Tandem flights, mainly at weekends, with more regular schedules in summer, weather permitting.

Golf

Taupo is one of the best golfing venues in the country.
Taupo Golf Club, Spa Rd, then Centennial Drive, T07-378 6933, www.taupogolf.co.nz. One of the very few 'steaming' courses in the world. Green fees from $45.
Wairakei 9 Hole Course, on SH1 adjacent to the **Wairakei Resort** (north), T07-374 8021. If you are a complete novice, this place is 'hacker friendly'. Green fees from $10.
Wairakei Golf Club, SH1 North, T07-374 8152, www.wairakigolfcourse.co.nz.

Horse trekking

Taupo Horse Treks, Karapiti Rd, Wairakei (near 'Craters of the Moon' reserve), T07-378 0356. 1- to 2-hr treks, from $45.

Kayaking

Kayaking Kiwi, T07-3787902/T0800-353435, www.kayakingkiwi.com. Excellent half-day kayak and launch eco-adventures from $95.
Kiwi River Safaris, T07-377 6597/T0800-723 8577, www.krs.co.nz. Relaxed kayak trips on the Waikato. Includes a soak in the hot pools, from $40. Departs 0900 and 1300.

Motorsport

Since hosting the Formula 1 A1 GP World Championship Grand Prix in Jan 2007 at its upgraded motorsport park, Taupo has been keen to maintain its reputation as the country's principal base for motorsport.
Formula Challenge, T07-377 0338, www.fcr.co.nz. This new company offers the chance to drive an authentic Formula Challenge racing car or V8 – the dream of many a petrol head. 10 laps from $290.

Mountain biking

There are some excellent tracks nearby, including the recommended riverside track that goes all the way to the Aratiatia Rapids from Spa Rd or the Craters of the Moon. See also Transport, below, for bike hire.
Kaimanawa Helibiking, T07-384 2816, www.kaimanawahelibiking.co.nz. The luxury option with a 4-hr trip commencing with a scenic flight to a remote 10 km track with a 2500-ft descent, from $345.
Rapid Sensations, T0800-227238, www.rapids.co.nz. Guided trips including the Craters of the Moon (1½ hrs), from $65. Freedom hire from $45.

Parasailing and jet skiing

Purefun, T0800-867272, www.purefun.co.nz. Regular flights along the waterfront from £85 (spectator ride on the boat from $20). Jet-ski hire from $85 per 30 mins.

Quad biking

Taupo Quad Adventures, T07-377 6404, www.4x4quads.com. Offer the usual thrills and spills across local farmland, also taking in native bush and forest trails. 1 hr from $70, half-day $275.

Rafting

See also Turangi, below, where many of the major companies are based.
Kiwi River Safaris, T0800-7238577, www.krs.co.nz. Raft the Rangitaiki as opposed to the more famous Tongariro (2 hrs from $95), or closer to home a leisurely 1-hr trip down the Waikato from $40.

Scenic flights

Helistar Helicopters, Huka Falls Loop Rd, T0800-435478, www.helistar.co.nz. Flights vary from a quick 5-min trip hovering near

Jumping into thin air

Taupo is now considered the premiere jump site for tandem skydiving in the North Island; given the scenery and professionalism of operations here it is not difficult to understand why. During the peak season it is not unusual for up to 300 jumps to be made over the lake in one day. That's an awful lot of angst, euphoria, swear words and telephone calls to Mum.

Walk the streets of the town centre in summer and you may notice a pre-dominance of two expressions on the transient faces; these are best labelled 'pre-jump' and 'post-jump'. Pre-jumpers have that pained expression, a sort of 'what if' look, usually accompanied with a nervous glance towards the heavens and a distinct almost audible clenching of the buttocks (especially at the mere sound of an aircraft). Though they will never admit it, most are also hoping the weather is about to take a dramatic and unseasonable turn for the worse. Post-jumpers? Well, that's easy. They do not so much walk about town as float and support a grin from ear to ear.

There are three companies that compete for business and all are based at the airport at the southern edge of the town. The only differences between them companies are the aircraft, the numbers jumping at any one time and how your jump is recorded. The rest is minor detail like the mode of transport to the airport. Some use conventional means while another use a stretch limo. Frankly, you could be on a pogo stick, it matters not, such are your levels of angst and anticipation of your impending brush with gravity.

Jump heights and prices vary little between companies and escalate depending on whether you have photos, video, a T-shirt, toilet paper and so on: a jump from 9000 ft without all the bells and whistles will cost about $200; 12,000 ft around $219; and 15,000 ft (Taupo Tandem) $314. You can even go higher, with oxygen assistance, if you have the money and prior experience. Also note the weight limit is 100 kg.

Don't go for anything less than 12,000 ft jump or it will be all over far too quicly. The recommendation must be that if you have gathered the courage to get up there at all, for goodness sake splash out and go as high as you possibly can – you won't regret it. Besides, as your mother once said, you can break your neck from 3 ft, die of scurvy if you don't eat your veggies and take someone's eye out with a pencil. So come on, get a grip of yourself. What's the big deal about hurtling towards the ground at

the falls, to several hours taking in the Tongariro National Park, from $95-600.
Taupo's Floatplane, based at Boat Harbour, T07-378 7500, www.tauposfloatplane.co.nz. Float plane trips from $70-540.
Volcanic Aeroplane Adventures, T0800-AEROPLANE, www.aeroplaneadventures.co.nz. Scenic jaunts to the finest volcanic spots, Wairakei from $95, Tongariro from $225, White Island and Tarawera from $450.

Town tours
London Double Decker Bus, T07-377 0774. 20-min tours of the town, departs from the corner of Tongariro St and Ferry Rd (behind the infamous 'Superloo'), $6, child $3.

Paradise Tours, T07-378 9955, www.paradise tours.co.nz. Twice daily 3-hr tours around town or further on request. From $85.

Walking
The much-celebrated, 1-day (16 km) **Tongariro Crossing**, across the volcanic slopes and landscapes of the Tongariro National Park, is accessible from Taupo (see page 297). There are various ways of tackling the walk, with either the independent option using local transport operators and the range of accommodation around the park, or with specialist guides. The VIC (I-Site) can also help with information and hut bookings.

around 200 kph with a complete stranger strapped on your back?

There are two recording methods used for that essential keep sake of your jump depending on the company. You have the choice of being filmed by a 'third jumper', or alternatively by your own jumpmaster with a audio-digital camera attached to his wrist. Either way, you will be presented with a fully edited video or DVD only minutes after landing as a highly entertaining (or embarrassing) record of your jump.

We recommend digital hand-held cameras operated by your own jump master with your own selection of song titles with as much embarrassing exuberance as possible. This makes the record far more personal and entertaining and your mother will be thoroughly unimpressed with your spectacular range of expletives. Regards weather? Wind speed is actually more important than cloud cover. This may come as some surprise, but it is all quite simple really. There's obviously no point jumping out of an aircraft in a 50-knot wind over Taupo only to find yourself landing in Napier.

Cancellations due to inclement weather happen regularly of course so it pays to look at the long range weather forecast before booking (see www.metservice.co.nz). In the event of cancellation all the operators are happy to re-book or book an alternative jump for you elsewhere. They also all offer transportation to and from the airport.

Oh, and one other thing – it may help. On my first jump we were accompanied by two employees who, just prior to take off, threw a pack on their backs and jumped aboard. Without words and both supporting what could only be described as a 'perma-grin' they opened the door at 9000-ft, got the green for go and as one might step lightly from an escalator flew out in to the abyss. As they became specs against the blue-green waters of the lake my jumpmaster yelled in my ear… 'Buggers, they are supposed to be mowing the lawn'. Lordy, Lordy, I wonder what they do for kicks!

The three companies are as follows and all are recommended. So, have a look at what has to offer, then put your best underwear on and make the call. **Great Lake Skydive**, T07-3784662/T0800-373 335, www.freefly.co.nz; **Skydive Taupo**, T0800-586766, www.skydive taupo.co.nz; **Taupo Tandem**, T07-377 0428/T0800-275934, www.taupotandemskydiving.com.

Tongariro Expeditions, T07-377 0435, www.thetongarirocrossing.co.nz. Recommended for 'all in' packages. See also Getting around, page 293.

Whirinaki lies just east of the **Urewera National Park** (west of Taupo) and has some of the most unspoilt rainforest in the North Island. There are numerous other walks in the area including the excellent climb to the summit of **Tauhara** (1088 m), west of the town (see page 280). The VIC can provide detailed walking information and maps.
Whirinaki Rainforest Guided Walks, T07-377 2363, www.rainforest-treks.co.nz. 1- and 3-day fully catered treks led by professional Maori guides, starting at

Rotorua and Taupo. The 3-day trek includes 2 nights at a safari-style camp in the rainforest – complete with hot showers. It also offers the opportunity of an overnight stay as part of the package at a *marae* in Te Whaiti in conjunction with a local *whanau* (extended family group). Prices range from $155 for the 1-day eco-cultural walk, to $285 for a 1-day privately guided walk, and $745 for the 3-day rainforest trek.

Orakei Korako Thermal Reserve *p283*
You can hire kayaks at the visitor centre, T07-378 3131, www.orakeikorako.co.nz.
NZ Riverjet, in the visitor centre, T07-333 7111, www.riverjet.co.nz. Interesting 3-hr

jet-boat trips taking in some lovely lake and river scenery. From $125, child $50. **Paradise Tours**, Taupo, T07-378 9955, www.paradisetours.co.nz. Offers specialist tours to the reserve.

Turangi and Tokaanu *p283*
Climbing
Extreme Backpackers, 26 Ngawaka Pl, T07-386 8949. Has an international standard climbing-wall open to the public.

Cultural and Eco-tours
Haka Trails, T07-377 6016, www.haka trails.co.nz. Local Maori-owned and operated tour company based in Turangi, offering an entertaining insight into Maori culture through organized or tailor-made tours in and around Taupo, Turangi and the Tongariro National Park. Tours include a leisurely 3-hr eco-cultural walk from $70 or, for the more adventurous, a guided Tongariro Crossing hike from $150.

Fishing
Taupo and the Tongariro River is New Zealand's premier trout-fishing region. Provided you have a licence ($18.50 a day available from the VIC or DoC) you can fish all year round, though summer is considered the best time for brown trout, and winter for the rainbow variety. There are numerous boat charters and guided trips (from $60 per hr, gear included) based in and around Turangi (consult the VIC) and tackle can be hired from tackle shops on Taupehi Rd, including **Sporting Life**, T07-386 8996; or **Greig Sports**, T07-386 7713, both in the town centre.

Mountain biking
Tongariro River Rafting, see Rafting, below. Guided trips or guidance on walking some excellent local tracks including the **42 Traverse**, considered the best track in the North Island. Independent hire available.

Rafting
The Tongariro River is up to Grade III and has over 50 rapids. Further afield, the Rangitaiki is up to Grade IV, providing a bit more action. **Rock and River**, 203 Puanga St, Tokaanu, T0800-865226, www.raftingnewzealand.com. Entertaining 3½-hr trips down the Tongariro, followed by a soak in the company's hot pools back at base, from $129. Recommended.

Tongariro River Rafting, Atirau Rd, Turangi, T0800-101024, www.trr.co.nz Tours on the Tongariro, with the choice of a relaxing scenic trip (1½ hrs) or a more exhilarating challenge down some Grade II sections.

Walking
One of the best short walks around Turangi is around **Lake Rotopounamu**, which is just off SH47, 9 km south of the intersection of SH47 and SH41 towards National Park Village. It is a pleasant 2-hr stroll through native bush around the lake. Sadly, there are no views from here south to the volcanoes. For a good view north you can climb **Mt Maunganamu** in about 25 mins. This walk starts at the Scenic Reserve along a track turning right after the Tokaanu Tailrace Bridge on SH41. The VIC in Turangi has details of other walks in the area.

⊙ Transport

Taupo *p276, maps p278 and p285*
Bicycle hire Rent-a-Bike, 11 Kereru St T025-322 729 or the YHA, corner Kaimanawa and Tamamutu sts, T07-378 3311. **Car hire** A1, corner of Tamamutu and Gascoigne sts, T07-378 3670; Avis, 61 Spa Rd, T07-378 6305; Budget, corner of Titiraupenga and Tuwharetoa sts, T07-378 9764; First Choice, 7 Nukuhau St, T07-378 0985; Rent-A-Dent, 7 Nukuhau St, T07-378 2740. **Taxi** Taupo's Top Cabs, T07-378 9250; Taupo Taxis, T07-378 5100.

⊙ Directory

Taupo *p276, maps p278 and p285*
Banks All the major banks have branches and ATMs in central Taupo. **Internet** Internet Outpost, 11 Tuwharetoa St, T07-376 9920, open daily til late; Log On, 71 Tongariro St, opposite the VIC (I-Site), T07-376 5901, until 2200. **Library** Story Pl, T07-376 0070. **Medical services** Hospital, Kotare St, T07-378 8100; Taupo Medical Centre, corner of Heu Heu and Kaimanawa sts, T07-378 4080; Main Street Open Late pharmacy, Main St, 67 Tongariro St, T07-378 2636, 0900-2030. **Police** Story Pl, T07-378 6060. **Post office** Horomatangi St, T07-378 9090, Mon-Fri 0900-1700, Sat 0900-1400. **Useful addresses** AA, 3 Tamamutu St, T07-378 6000.

Tongariro National Park

→ *Colour map 3, A3*

Tongariro National Park is New Zealand's oldest national park, and the fourth oldest in the world. In 1887 Horonuku Te Heuheu Tukino, the then paramount chief of Ngati Tuwharetoa, gave the central portion – essentially the volcanoes of Ruapehu, Ngauruhoe and Tongariro – to the nation. In more recent years the park has been substantially increased in size to cover an area of 75,250 ha, taking in the forest, tussock country and 'volcanic desert'. As well as its stunning scenery, Tongariro National Park offers some excellent walking opportunities, including the Tongariro Northern Circuit, considered one of New Zealand's great day hikes. The Tongariro Crossing (part of the circuit) is hailed as one of the best one-day walks in the country. In winter, skiing is the principal activity here. ▸▸ For Sleeping, Eating and other listings, see pages 301-306.

Ins and outs

Getting there **Tongariro Expeditions,** T07-377 0435, www.thetongarirocrossing.co.nz, offers an early bird and economy service between Taupo and Tongariro Crossing in summer; or Taupo and Whakapapa in winter. The standard service departs Taupo 0620, Turangi 0700 and returns from the mountain at 1530, arriving Turangi 1700, Taupo around 1730. this will have you on the track at around 0745. In summer, the early bird departs Taupo 0540, Turangi 0620, returning at the same time; this service will have you on the track at about 0700. The return fare is $45 Taupo, $35 Turangi.

Alpine Scenic Tours, T07-378 7412, www.alpinescenictours.co.nz, also runs between Turangi and Taupo, with additional services to the Tongariro National Park (Tongariro Crossing) and Whakapapa daily in summer departing Taupo 0545, Turangi 0630 and arriving at Mangatepopo (Crossing start) at 0730, from $45 return.

In Turangi itself **Bellbird Connections,** Bellbird Lodge Backpackers, T07-386 8281, and **Club Habitat,** T07-386 7492, also offer transport. From National Park Village, most accommodation options offer shuttles, including **Howard's Lodge,** T07-892 2827, www.howardslodge.co.nz, to Whakapapa Village $205 (return), to the start of the Tongariro Crossing $25. Beware of cowboy operators in the region and try to stick to well-publicized companies. For the latest weather conditions over Ruapehu and Ngauruhoe log on to the 'live' webcam during daylight hours, www.geo net.org.nz. See also individual village 'Getting there' sections, below.

Getting around The park is bordered along its north and western sides by the SH47, with the principal settlements of Turangi, National Park Village and Ohakune, and to the east by SH1 – the famous Desert Road. The small township of Waiouru is to the southeast. Whakapapa Village, at the northern base of Ruapehu, serves as the park's main headquarters. All the surrounding townships are served by **Intercity,** with Turangi also being served by **Newman's.** The main Auckland/Wellington **TranzScenic** rail line runs through Ohakune and the national park. A number of local shuttle bus operators provide access to Whakapapa Village and major tramping drop-off/pick-up points around the park. You can also fly direct to Tongariro National Park from Auckland with **Mountain Air,** T07-892 2812, www.mountainair.co.nz. The airfield is at the junction of SH47 and SH48.

Tourist information **DoC Whakapapa** ① *Whakapapa Village on SH48, T07-892 3729, www.doc.govt.nz, www.whakapapa.co.nz, www.ruapehunz.com, daily 0800-1700,* has a wealth of information on the park, interesting displays, maps and weather reports. It also an excellent summer programme of organized and guided walks, $10-80, which usually start from the Whakapapa VIC, see page 298.

Park hut bookings/fees are administered here. If you are planning a longer tramp or summit climb you are advised to fill in an intentions sheet at the centre. For sleeping and eating within and surrounding the park see Whakapapa Village, National Park, Turangi and Ohakune listings. DoC hut bookings can be made at all major DoC field centres and the Whakapapa Visitor Centre. Campsites have been established near each of the huts. Hut fees are from $10 for basic backcountry huts to $20 for the Great Walks (Northern Circuit or Tongariro Crossing Huts). Camping fees are from $3-10 depending on the type of site.

Background

According to local Maori legend, the volcanoes were formed back around the 14th century, when Ngatoroirangi, a navigator and priest of the Arawa canoe, came to New Zealand. Journeying inland from the Bay of Plenty, Ngatoroirangi saw the majestic peaks and decided to climb them, thus laying claim to all that he saw. As he climbed, Ngatoroirangi was hit by a violent blizzard. Close to death he cried out to the gods in his homeland of Hawaiki to send fire to warm his body and revive him. In response to his plea a great fire was issued forth, forming White Island, Rotorua and Taupo, before erupting from Tongariro and saving his life. Apparently in gratitude, Ngatoroirangi then slew his slave, Auruhoe, who had accompanied him on the climb, throwing the poor soul into the newly formed crater, which later formed Ngauruhoe. The name Tongariro means 'south wind' and 'borne away' and refers to Ngatoroirangi's pleas for help. Science, of course, offers a more boring theory. It suggests that they are in fact andesitic, single and multi-vented volcanoes of recent geological origin, dating back about two million years, reaching their greatest heights during the last ice age, when glaciers extended down the slopes of Ruapehu. Have you ever heard such nonsense?

Sights

All of the national park's sights are, of course, natural and dominated by the three majestic volcanic peaks of Ngauruhoe, Ruapehu and Tongariro. Although all three mountains are active volcanoes they are quite different in size and appearance.

Ngauruhoe → *For a live webcam of Ngauruhoe visit www.geonet.org.nz/ngauruhoe.*

The symmetrical cone of Ngauruhoe (2291 m) is the youngest of the three volcanoes. Its classic cone shape is due to its relative youth, but also because it has a single vent, unlike Ruapehu and Tongariro. Although Ruapehu and White Island (Bay of Plenty) have been far more active recently, Ngauruhoe has, over the years, been considered the most continuously active, frequently venting steam and gas and, occasionally, ash and lava in spectacular displays of pyroclastics. Its last significant eruption occurred in 1954. There is plenty of evidence of these eruptions, the most obvious being the old lava flows on its slopes. The Tongariro Crossing Track skirts the eastern flank of Ngauruhoe, while another popular three- to four-day tramp is the **Northern Circuit Track**, one of New Zealand's great walks encompassing both Ngauruhoe and Tongariro.

Ruapehu → *For a live web cam of Mount Ruapehu log on to www.geonet.org.nz/ruapehu.*

About 16 km south of Ngauruhoe is the majestic shape of Ruapehu, with its truncated cone, perpetually snow-covered **summit peaks** and **crater lake**. It is the North Island's highest mountain, at 2797 m, and over the course of the last century has seen the most violent activity of all the three volcanoes. Between 1945 and 1947, due to a number of eruptions blocking the overflow, the waters of the crater

Ruapehu n. lit: rua (pit); pehu (to explode, as in violent eruption)

It is September 1995 and a beautiful, calm summer's afternoon on the slopes of Mount Ruapehu. Excited skiers descend the slopes while others clamber for chairlifts, or sit in the café and the car park admiring the view. Meanwhile, the needle of the seismograph in the Whakapapa Village Visitor Centre, twitches. This is not unusual, but it will be noted, just like others of late. Along with a rise in the temperature and discolouration of the Crater Lake, it is enough to have a few volcanologists wondering ... just wondering mind you! Shadows lengthen across the snow as the late afternoon sun slowly falls towards Mount Taranaki to the west. Again the needle twitches, and again ... faster and faster ... then she blows.

Caught on amateur video the Crater Lake explodes like a fire hydrant full of black ash and white steam, sliced open by an axe. All eyes look upward, jaws fall downwards, and a whole lot of designer epaulettes get wet from the inside. It's a mighty sight to behold, as the mountain billows ash, steam and rock and everyone suddenly becomes a champion downhill skier. By nightfall, as the mountain continues to rage and everyone is accounted for, an exclusion zone is placed round the slopes; the nation, and the world, watches and waits. In the US a report gets filed that half of the North Island has gone – wherever that was.

The 1995 eruption was nothing too unusual for Ruapehu and thankfully and perhaps luckily no one died. For a few weeks Ruapehu billowed ash and steam that could be seen for miles around and even from space. Planes were diverted and light ash fell as far away as Whakatane in the Bay of Plenty. During the near-constant emissions of steam and ash more violent spurts of molten rock occurred. The one-time waters of the Crater Lake were displaced and poured down the mountainside forming chocolate-like lahars. And although a catastrophic eruption was possible, it didn't occur. After a few weeks the mountain settled down again and the seismic needles returned to their monotonous single line. What was unusual was that the same thing happened a year later, wiping out the possibility of a ski season for both Whakapapa and Turoa and for almost another year, the mountain still vented above average amounts of steam. Now into the new century, it is just another eruption etched in our memory, on film, or documented in the record books, and the 1995-1996 eruptions will not go down as the worst of the last century. Between 1945 and 1947, due to a number of eruptions blocking the overflow, the waters of the Crater Lake rose dramatically. On the stormy Christmas Eve of 1953, without warning, the walls of the crater collapsed and a mighty lahar rushed down the Whangaehu River, wiping out the rail bridge near Karioi. The night train to Auckland arrived moments later and 153 lives were lost.

To be around such tempestuous and unpredictable forces of nature is awesome indeed. To watch a mountain erupting is more so. You almost look at Ruapehu, Ngauruhoe, Tongariro, Taranaki and will them to 'let rip'. But then you look across the huge expanse of Lake Taupo, all 619 sq km of it in the knowledge that it is a crater and was once a volcano that did just that – and you wonder and suddenly accept, that straight monotonous lines on seismographs are in fact a good thing – and not just for your epaulettes.

lake rose dramatically. On the stormy Christmas Eve of 1953, without warning, the walls of the crater collapsed and a mighty lahar (volcanic rock and water debris) rushed down the Whangaehu River, wiping out the rail bridge near Karioi. The night train to Auckland arrived moments later and 153 lives were lost. It erupted more recently in September 1995, miraculously without loss of life, and the same thing happened a year later, wiping out the possibility of a ski season for both Whakapapa and Turoa. Ruapehu attracts thousands of visitors each year who come to ski or climb, or enjoy its numerous tramping tracks. The longest track is the **Round-the-Mountain Track** which takes five to six days with overnight stays at a number of DoC huts on the way. Ruapehu is home to three ski fields: **Whakapapa** on its northern flank (serviced by Whakapapa and Iwikau Villages), **Turoa**, on the southern flank (serviced by Ohakune); and **Tukino**, the smallest and least popular of the three on the eastern slopes.

Tongariro

Tongariro, at the northern fringe 3 km north of Ngauruhoe, is a fairly complex, flat-topped affair and the lowest at 1968 m. Of the three mountains it is the most benign with only a few mildly active craters, some hot springs, lakes, fumaroles and pools of boiling mud. From a purely aesthetic point of view its most attractive features are the aptly named **Red Crater** (which is still active) and the small **Emerald Lakes** at its base. Nearby are the contrasting **Blue Lakes** of the central crater and the **Ketetahi Springs**, which emerge on its northern slopes. All of these interesting features are included on the **Tongariro Crossing**, which can be completed in a day and is considered one of New Zealand's best one-day walks (see box, page 297).

Tongariro Crossing

⁞ Tongariro Crossing

This excellent hike is hailed as one of the best one-day hikes in the country and providing the weather is kind, there is no doubt that the views and the varied volcanic features certainly make it a memorable one. To call it a walk is really an understatement: at about 16 km in length with some steep climbs and the odd bit of scrambling, it is really a mountain hike that can take up to 10 hours. In winter it can be impassable and even in summer it can be dangerous, so despite what you may have heard, don't underestimate it. Having said that, provided you are fit, well-prepared, the weather is looking good and you have the time, you should not pass up the opportunity.

The walk can be tackled from either north or south, with a number of diversions on the way. The usual recommendation is to start from the **Mangatepopo Car Park** (off SH47 on the park's western edge), walk the 10 km north to **Ketetahi Hut**, stay the night (all part of the 'package'), then either descend from the Ketetahi Hut to SH47A (walk terminus), or return the 10 km back to Mangatepopo. There is a hut at the Mangatepopo end but it has neither the character nor the view of the Ketetahi.

From Mangatepopo the track makes a gradual ascent towards the southern slopes of Tongariro, while the steep slopes and lava flows of Ngauruhoe loom to the northwest. Sandwiched between the two mountains the track is then forced to make a steep ascent up the **Mangatepopo Saddle**. Before this ascent there is the choice of a short diversion to the **Soda Springs** – a series of cold springs which emerge from beneath an old lava flow, surrounded by an oasis of greenery. Once you have negotiated the Saddle you enter Tongariro's **South Crater**.

The views of Ngauruhoe from here are excellent (and the especially fit can take in the summit diversion from here). A short climb then leads to the aptly named **Red Crater** and the highest point on the crossing (1,886 m). Following the rim of this colourful (and, in the odd place, steaming) crater you are then treated to a full artist's palette, with the partial descent to the **Emerald Lakes**. (The minerals from Red Crater create the colours in the water.) Just beyond Emerald Lakes the track branches right to **Oturere Hut**, or continues to Ketetahi Hut across the **Central Crater** and alongside **Blue Lake**, another water-filled vent. The track then straddles the **North Crater** taking in the stunning view north across Lake Taupo, before making a gradual zigzag descent to the **Ketetahi Hut**. The hut sits alone on the slopes at an altitude of about 1,000 m, like a first-class real estate property: location, location, location and a 'real' view. (It is the busiest and most popular hut in the park. If you have booked your stay in the hut bear in mind it operates on a first come first served basis, so get there early.) The huts all have mattresses, gas cookers (summer only), water supplies and toilet facilities. In the busy seasons wardens can provide information and weather reports. The hot **Ketetahi Springs** are on private Maori land only a few hundred metres away. Until recently a soak in the pools of the stream armed with a gin and tonic was a highlight of the walk. But sadly disagreements between DOC and the local Iwi mean the springs and stream are now out of bounds.

From Ketetahi it is a two-hour descent through native bush to the SH47A access point. For more information contact the Whakapapa Visitor Centre, page 298.

Whakapapa Village → *Colour map 3, A3*

Whakapapa Village is essentially the headquarters and information base for the Tongariro National Park and the gateway to the **Whakapapa Ski Field**. It is also home to the magnificent **Bayview Chateau Hotel**, built in 1929. As well as the chateau itself there are a number of accommodation and eating options available in the Whakapapa Village. There is also a store, the DoC field centre and, believe it or not, a golf course. Don't miss the excellent displays in the Whakapapa DoC Visitor Centre, especially the seismograph, monitoring the fickle moods of the mighty Ruapehu, which, lest you forget, is an active volcano that last let rip in the mid-1990s.

Getting there and around There is only shuttle bus transportation available to Whakapapa Village. **Alpine Scenic Tours**, T07-378 7412, www.alpinescenictours.co.nz, is the principal operator with daily schedules; see also Getting there, page 289. There is a shuttle bus service to the ski fields (Top-o-the-Bruce) from outside the VIC (I-Site) at 0830 and 1230 (returning 1530 and 1630), $6 return. **Tongariro Track Transport**, T07-892 3716, runs daily shuttles to the start of the Tongariro Crossing; book at the VIC.

Tourist information The **Whakapapa DoC Visitor Centre** ⓘ *SH48, T07-892 3729, www.doc.govt.nz, www.whakapapa.co.nz, daily 0800-1800*, offers a broad range of information on the park with many displays and an audio-visual theatre for rainy days ($5). The staff are expert in advising on walks. DoC's organized walks start from here, see page 298. Note the seismograph quietly sitting in the corner, just waiting for the next major volcanic event.

National Park Village → *Colour map 3, A3*

The small, unremarkable and almost barren village of National Park is set overlooking Mount Ruapehu and Ngauruhoe, at the junction of SH4 (which links Taumaranui and Wanganui) and SH47. It is also on the main Auckland–Wellington railway line. Graced only by its convenient location to both Tongariro and Wanganui national parks, it has a number of accommodation options, amenities and tour operators and is popular in the winter ski season. Its only notable 'sight' is the impressive view across to the mountain.

Getting there The Auckland–Wellington **TranzScenic**, T0800-872467, www.tranzscenic.co.nz, 'Overlander' service stops at the station on Station Road, while buses stop in Carroll Street, the village's main street. Bus tickets can be bought from **Ski Haus**, **Pukenui** and **Howard's Lodge**, see Sleeping page 302.

Getting around Alpine Scenic Tours, T07-892 3716, www.alpinescenictours.co.nz, operates a daily shuttle to and from National Park to Whakapapa Village (and the ski field), Tongariro Crossing access points and Turangi. Its buses connect with **Intercity** and **Newman's** services at Turangi. Summer services vary but will run pretty much on demand. Most of the major accommodation establishments offer shuttle services to the park. **Tongariro Crossing Transport**, Howard's Lodge, T07-892 2827, www.howards lodge.co.nz, will get you to Whakapapa Village for $20 return, the start of the Tongariro Crossing for $25 and the 42 Traverse (popular mountain bike trail) for $25.

Tourist information There is no official VIC but the staff at the BP Station on Carroll Street (SH4) can be of assistance, T07-892 2879, www.nationalpark.co.nz.

▲ Walking

Tongariro National Park offers numerous walking tracks from a few minutes to six days. There are numerous DoC huts throughout the park. The major tramps are the famed **Tongariro Crossing** (see box, page 297), the **Northern Circuit** and the **Round-the-Mountain Track**. Most of the shorter walks are accessed from Whakapapa Village and the Ohakune Mountain Road, which connects Ohakune with the Turoa Ski Field. Note that a number of local activity operators also offer guided walks, as does the DoC in Whakapapa Village, see page 293. ▸▸ *See also Activities and tours, page 306.*

Northern Circuit The Tongariro Northern Circuit winds its way over Mount Tongariro and around Mount Ngauruhoe passing through unusual landforms and volcanic features including lakes, craters and glacial valleys. Taking three to four days to complete (with overnight accommodation provided in DoC huts), it is listed as one of New Zealand's great walks. The track officially starts from Whakapapa Village and finishes at the Mangatepopo Road just off the SH47, but can also be accessed from Ketetahi Road (north) or Desert Road (east). Detailed information can be obtained from the Whakapapa Visitor Centre (see above), where you can also arrange hut bookings and are advised to fill in an intentions form. The DoC website, www.doc.govt.nz, also provides excellent details. If you do not have your own transport, the local shuttle operators will provide transportation (see Getting there, page 293, and in the relevant towns below). If you have your own vehicle do not leave valuables in it.

Round-the-Mountain Track The Northern Circuit can be combined with the full Ruapehu Round-the-Mountain Track to create a mighty six-day tramp around all three mountains. Again comfortable accommodation is available in DoC huts along the way. The track can be accessed from Whakapapa Village or the Ohakune Mountain Road. For information and hut bookings contact the Whakapapa Visitor Centre (see below) or the DoC field centre on Ohakune Mountain Road, Ohakune (see page 300).

Ruapehu Crater Lake Both the summit and Crater Lake of Ruapehu are popular climbs in both summer and winter and are, in part, easily accessible via the Whakapapa Ski Field chairlift. The climb to the crater and back takes about seven hours (four hours if you use the chairlifts). Once you reach the snowline it is tough going and can be dangerous. Ice axes and crampons are essential kit in winter and recommended even in summer. Whatever your intentions, always obtain all the necessary information before attempting this climb and let DoC know your plans. Ruapehu has claimed many lives (a close eye is also kept on the mountain's seismic activity, and at the slightest sign of any action, an exclusion zone is placed around the crater). A few local operators offer guided walks to the crater; enquire at DoC In Whakapapa, see page 298.

Ohakune ●🍴🎵🎿⛰️☕ ▸▸ *pp301–306.*

→ *Colour map 3, A3*

The pleasant little ski resort of Ohakune (meaning 'place to be careful'), near the southern edge of Tongariro National Park, changes its mood according to the season. In winter when (and if) the snows arrive, it attracts skiers in droves. But when winter brings little snow, or when spring arrives and the snow fades, it falls silent. So pretty little Ohakune is unpredictable, but whatever the season or the weather, it is worth lingering.

The main centre of Ohakune is on Clyde Street (SH49, where you arrive into the town) and this is the base for the VIC (I-Site), the main cafés, restaurants and amenities. The other 'centre' is of the après-ski variety and is about 2 km northwest, towards the mountain, up Goldfinch Street and Mangawhero Terrace. Here the focus is the **Powderhorn Chateau** (principal après-ski base) with the railway station, the mountain access point (Ohakune Mountain Road) and the DoC field centre also here. The **Turoa Ski Field** is 17 km up the Ohakune Mountain Road.

Getting there Ohakune is served by **Intercity** buses every day except Saturday, which stop in the centre of town at the VIC (I-Site). About 2 km west of the centre, towards the mountain, is the principal après-ski and mountain access point. The train station is also here, and the daily Auckland-Wellington train stops on the way, T0800-872467, www.tranzscenic.co.nz. For all booking and ticketing contact the VIC (I-Site).

Getting around Although it has essentially two centres, and shuttling between them is awkward, everything in Ohakune is within walking distance. Shuttles operate up and down the Ohakune Mountain Road (to the Turoa Ski Field) or elsewhere within the Tongariro National Park, pretty much on demand. These include **Snowliner**, T06-385 8573, **Matai**, T06-385 9169, and **Dempsey Buses**, T06-385 4022; check with the VIC (I-Site) for latest schedules and prices. **Matai**, 1 Rata St, T06-385 9169, www.matailodge.co.nz, offers a shuttle service to the Tongariro Crossing. The **Ohakune Top Ten Motorpark** also offers a service on demand, T06-385 8561

Tourist Information Ruapehu VIC (I-Site) ① *54 Clyde St, T06-385 8427, www.oha kune.info, www.visitruapehu.com, Mon-Fri 0900-1700, Sat-Sun 0900-1530 (summer).* **DoC Ohakune field centre** ① *at the base of the Ohakune Mountain Rd, T06-385 0010, Mon-Fri 0900-1500,* has some excellent displays (including video footage of the 1995 Ruapehu eruption), up-to-date weather forecasts and maps, and can advise on any aspect of park activities including local short walks. For information on the **Turoa Ski Field**, contact T06-892 3738, www.ruapehu.com, www.snow.co.nz or www.oha kune.info. For local weather and regular snow updates in winter listen to Peak FM 95.8 FM, T07-385 4919, or Ski FM 96.6 FM, T06-385 9502; snow phone, T0832-22180

Sights All of Ohakune's 'sights' are essentially natural and revolve around **Mount Ruapehu** and its associate activities: skiing and walking being the principal pursuits. There are a number of local short walks (mainly around the DoC field centre) as well as longer options, which come under the Tongariro National Park activities. If the weather is good, no trip to Ohakune would be complete without a drive to see the magnificent views from the top of the 17-km **Ohakune Mountain Road** and the **Turoa Ski Field**. The road begins at the northwestern edge of town. **Lake Rotokura**, about 12 km south of Ohakune on SH49, is also worthy of a visit. Take the track signposted to the left. There are actually two lakes, one above the other and both reached on foot through native bush (30 minutes). Both have a lovely, tranquil atmosphere, especially the upper lake, which reflects the top of Ruapehu on a clear, still day.

Outside the park ● ➤ *pp301-306.*

Waiouru and the Desert Road → *Colour map 3, A3 Population: 2500*
Waiouru is at the junction of SH1 (Desert Road) and SH49 from Ohakune (27 km) on the southern fringe of the Tongariro National Park. It is essentially an army base and, for the traveller, a last resort for accommodation when the Desert Road is closed with snow. During the winter this can happen quite frequently and when it does (if conditions allow) all traffic is diverted to the west of the mountain via Ohakune and National Park. If this happens you can expect to add another one to two hours to your journey. The Desert Road is essentially the stretch of SH1 from Waiouru to Turangi (63 km), featuring Ruapehu and Ngauruhoe to the west and the Kaimanawa Mountains to the east. The broad, flat valley is so called because of its barren landscape, given over only to grass and ancient volcanic ash fields. It has a strange beauty spoiled only by the tracks of off-road army vehicles and rows of electricity pylons disappearing into the horizon. During eruptions, potential ash-falls on these wires substantially threaten upper North Island electricity supplies.

There are few sights in Waiouru but, if you have time or the snow has fallen, the **QEII Army Memorial Museum** ⓘ *T07-387 6911, daily 0900-1630, $10, child $7, café* is worth a look. It has a generous collection of army hardware as well as a range of displays covering New Zealand's military history since the mid-1800s. There is also a dynamic Roll of Honour to remember those who have died for this great country.

Taumarunui → *Colour map 3, A3 Population: 5000*

Taumarunui is a small agricultural service town lying at the confluence of the Ongarue and Whanganui rivers, on the western fringes of the Ruapehu District. Although nothing to write home about, it is often used as an overnight base for skiing in the Tongariro National Park, and as a base for kayak, canoe and jet-boat tours of the Whanganui River and the Whanganui National Park. For Whanganui River activity operators based in Taumarunui see Whanganui National Park section, page 381.

Getting there Taumarunui is served by **Intercity** and **Newman's** and is also on the main Auckland–Wellington rail line. The VIC (I-Site) administers bookings and tickets.

Tourist information **Taumarunui VIC (I-Site)** ⓘ *at the train station on Hakiaha St, the main drag through town, T07-895 7494, www.visitruapehu.com, www.middle-of-everywhere.co.nz, Mon-Fri 0900-1630, Sat-Sun 1000-1600*, has an interesting working scale model of the 'Raurimu Spiral' (see below).

Sights The major attraction around Taumarunui is the **Raurimu Spiral**, an impressive feat of railway engineering on the main north–south trunk line, devised by the late RW Holmes in 1908. The track falls (or rises) 213 m at an incline of one in 50, by means of a complete circle, three horseshoe curves and two tunnels, which double the distance travelled. Check it out from the lookout, 37 km south of the town on SH4, or the working model in the VIC (I-Site).

There are a number of walks around the town for which the VIC (I-Site) has details. For the very energetic there is the climb to the summit of the flat-topped **Mount Hikurangi** (770 m) behind the town. For detailed directions, and to confirm permission with the local landowner, ask at the VIC (I-Site). The 155-km **Taumarunui to Stratford Heritage Trail** (scenic drive) begins or ends here, taking you through the Wanganui and Taranaki regions to Stratford. The highlight of this trip is the tiny settlement of **Whangamomona**, which, after a run-in with regional bureaucracies in 1995, declared itself a republic. It is an unremarkable little place with a population of less than 100. The village opens its borders on the anniversary of the great uprising in October each year, when there is a weekend of celebrations. No passport control or baggage checks necessary, just a pint glass. There is also an alternative scenic route from Taumarunui, across the hills via Ohura and SH40 to SH3 and New Plymouth. This is a rugged trip over remote country so make sure you are stocked up.

😴 Sleeping

Whakapapa Village *p298*
All prices rise in winter, and opening and closing times vary. Booking ahead is necessary in winter, and advisable in summer.
LL-AL Bayview Chateau, T07-892 3809, www.chateau.co.nz. Perhaps the most famous hotel in the North Island, the Bayview provides traditional luxury in a grand location. Visible for miles around, the hotel sits like a beacon in the heart of the

national park and in the shadow of 2 of New Zealand's most famous volcanoes – Ngauruhoe and Ruapehu. Whether just relaxing and enjoying its traditional comforts or using it as a base from which to ski, or walk the world-renowned Tongariro Track (special packages available), it offers a level of elegance in keeping with its age (1929) combined with traditional modern facilities, including an excellent restaurant, a bar, café, pool and even a small golf course. Ask about special packages in summer.

AL-A Skotel Alpine Resort, T07-892 3719, www.skotel.com. A good-value establishment with modern facilities, luxury and standard hotel rooms or self-contained chalets. Restaurant and bar with great views towards Ngauruhoe. Spa, sauna, gym, internet and tramping gear hire.

C-D Discovery Lodge, on SH47, 1 km from the Whakapapa turning, T0800-122122, www.discovery.net.nz. Overlooking the mountains, with a good range of accommodation options and facilities, including a bar and restaurant. Tongariro Crossing Track transport at 0600, which allows customers to be first on the track.

C-D Whakapapa Holiday Park, T07-892 3897, www.whakapapa.net.nz. Backpacker accommodation with basic facilities but set in the heart of the village and riverside, close to all amenities.

D DoC Huts, T07-892 3729. There are 9 DoC huts in the park with foot access only. Fees $10-20.

National Park Village p298

All accommodation in National Park Village is in high demand in the winter ski season, when prices also rise. Booking is advised.

AL-D Howard's Lodge, 11 Carroll St, T07-892 2827, www.howardslodge.co.nz. A fine establishment with a wide range of comfortable rooms. Spa. Well geared up for local activities especially skiing, tramping and mountain biking. Breakfast and transport service available.

AL-D Pukenui Lodge, corner of SH4 and Miller St, T07-892 2882, www.tongariro.cc. Modern single-storey lodge. Various rooms, quad, double or single, some en suite. Motel units and camping also available. Spa.

A-B Mountain Heights Lodge, SH4, T07-892 2833, www.mountainheights.co.nz. B&B, self-contained, motorcamp and camping just south of National Park Village. Bike hire.

A-D Plateau Lodge, Carroll St, T07-892 2993, www.plateaulodge.co.nz. Self-contained units, double en suites and comfortable backpacker accommodation available. Activities and transport pick-ups.

B-D National Park Backpackers, Findlay St, T07-892 2870, www.npbp.co.nz. Modern establishment with dorms and doubles with en suite bathrooms, tent sites and internet. Climbing-wall from $9. Activities and transport to Tongariro Crossing arranged.

B-D Ski Haus, Carroll St, T07-892 2854, www.skihaus.co.nz. Family and multi-share rooms, spa pool and bar. Activities and transport arranged.

Ohakune p299

As a main ski resort, Ohakune offers a wide range of accommodation, though it operates on a seasonal basis. In winter, especially at weekends, you are advised to book well in advance. If you are stuck or want to avoid the high winter prices, the far less salubrious village of **Raetihi**, 11 km to the east, has a number of cheaper options. For information, options and bookings contact the Raetihi VIC, 46 Seddon St, T06-385 4805.

LL Whare Ora, 1 Kaha St, Rangataua, 5 km from Ohakune, T06-385 9385, www.whareoralodge.co.nz. Beautiful, renovated, 2-level wooden house originally built in 1910. One en suite with spa and sitting room, 1 attic en suite room. Luxuriously appointed with great cuisine.

AL Powderhorn Chateau, corner of Mangawhero and Thames sts, T06-385 8888, www.powderhorn.co.nz. Considered the most well-facilitated hotel in Ohakune, the Alpine-style Powderhorn Chateau has always proved popular as a social and accommodation base for skiing in winter. However, of late – like many other operations in New Zealand – it has also jumped on the film *Lord of the Rings* bandwagon, advertising itself as the place where Elijah Wood (Frodo) and other key members of the cast stayed during filming in 2001. They certainly had no complaints. To add to the undeniably warm and lively atmosphere of the bar and 2 in-house restaurants, there is a fine choice of lodge-style suites, an apartment, a heated swimming pool and a small casino. Ski and bike hire is also available with the former subject to season and snow conditions.

AL Ruapehu Homestead, SH49, Rangataua, T06-385 8799, www.ruapehuhomestead.co.nz . Well-appointed rooms. In-house restaurant. Base for horse treks.

AL-A Cairnbrae House 140 Mangawhero River Rd, 7 km southwest of Ohakune, T06-385 3002, www.cairnbraehouse.co.nz. Lovely rural homestay with immaculate

en suite rooms. Private guest lounge, Sky TV and internet, not to mention the occasional door in the garden. Dinner on request.
AL-A Tairoa Lodge, 144 Magawhero Rd, T/F06-385 4882, www.tairoalodge.co.nz. Modern, spacious single-storey farm/homestay lodge beside the Magawhero River and 30 km from the ski field. Range of en suite rooms, open fire and outdoor spa pool. Activities arranged.
AL-A Waireka B&B, 11 Tainui St, T/F06-385 8092, www.waireka.co.nz. Friendly B&B, with local photographer and qualified naturopath.
A Hobbit Motor Lodge, corner of Goldfinch and Wye sts, T06-385 8248. Good in-house restaurant.
A Peaks Motor Inn, corner of Mangawhero Terr and Shannon St, T06-385 9144, www.thepeaks.co.nz.
A-D Alpine Motel Lodge, 7 Miro St, T06-385 8758, www.alpinemotel.co.nz. A cheap, central motel with backpacker accommodation. Bistro attached. Spa pool.
B Sunbeam Motel and Lodge, 4 Foyle St, T06-385 8470, www.sunbeammotels.co.nz. Bar and restaurant, spas and tours.
C-D Matai Lodge YHA, corner of Clyde and Rata sts, T06-385 9169, www.maitai lodge.co.nz. Central location, recently renovated, good range of rooms and dorms. Bike hire. Free pick-up from Waiouru, National Park and Whakapapa and in-house transport service for the Tongariro Crossing. Open year round.
D Station Lodge, 60 Thames St, T06-385 8797, www.stationlodge.co.nz. Basic, laid-back and close to all the nightlife with in-house ski shop and rental. Spa. Winter-only.

Chalets
There are numerous self-contained chalet-style options in town.
AL-A Ruapehu Chalet Rentals, 23 Clyde St, T06-385 8149, www.ruapehu.co.nz.
A Ossie's Chalets and Apartments, corner of Tainui and Shannon St, T06-385 8088, www.ossies-ohakune.co.nz.
B Ruapehu Cabins, 107 Clyde St, T06-385 8608, www.ruapehucabins.co.nz.

B-D Rimu Park Lodge and Chalets, 27 Rimu St, T06-385 9023, www.rimupark.co.nz. Also offers backpacker accommodation.

Motorcamps and campsites
C-D Ohakune Top Ten Holiday Park, 5 Moore St, T06-385 8561, www.oha kune.net.nz. An excellent facility with spotless amenities near the town centre and next to the Mangateitei Stream. Tongariro Crossing shuttle service available. Spa.
D DoC Mangawhero Campsite, Ohakune Mountain Rd, T06-385 8578. Book with DoC. Basic facilities for purist campers.

Taumarunui p301
There is not a huge range of choice, but the VIC can advise.
B-D Taumarunui Holiday Park, near SH4 and next to the river, 4 km south of town, T07-895 9345, www.taumarunuiholiday park.co.nz. The best motorpark in town. Camp kitchen.

● Eating

Whakapapa Village p298
Whakapapa Camp Store, in the village has light snacks and sells groceries at elevated prices, so stock up before you go.
▼▼▼ Bayview Chateau, see Sleeping, above. Fine, traditional à la carte dining.
▼▼ Pihanga Café and Bar, attached to the **Bayview Chateau** (see Sleeping, above) with good coffee and the best and most varied café menu in the village. Brunch and dinner from 1030 daily.
▼▼ Skotel Resort, T07-892 3719 (see Sleeping, above). Good restaurant and bar with expansive views across to Ngauruhoe. Open to non-guests for breakfast, lunch and dinner.
▼ Fergusson's Café, opposite the chateau, 0800-1530. Great for a light, cheap snack.
▼ Knoll Ridge Café, up the Top of the Bruce Rd (take the chairlift), T07-892 3738. Chairlift $20, child $10, 0900-1600 (last lift up 1530 in summer). A good place to head if you fancy a coffee with a view.

● For an explanation of the Sleeping and Eating price codes used in this guide, see the inside
● front cover. Other relevant information is provided in the Essentials chapter, pages 44-51.
Note that prices are tive in New Zealand dollars.

There is no supermarket in the village. The **BP Station** on Carroll St, T07-892 2879, 0730-1900, stocks basic supplies.
♦ **BaseKamp**, Carroll St, T07-892 2872, daily. Excellent gourmet burgers and pizza.
♦ **Eivin's Café**, on the corner of Carroll St and SH4, T07-892 2844, daily from 0830. Pleasant enough and serves traditional pub-style fare, including pizza.
♦ **Schnapps Hotel**, Findlay St, T07-892 2788, daily from 1100.
♦ **Ski Haus**, see Sleeping, page 302. In-house restaurants offering breakfast, lunch and dinner to non-guests.
♦ **Station café**, T07-892 2881, daily 1000-late. Set in the historic National Park Railway Station, which does not see many passenger trains these days. Cosy atmosphere and friendly staff.

Ohakune *p299*

A number of motels have reputable mid-range restaurants including **The Hobbit**, corner of Goldfinch and Wye sts, T06-385 8248; and **Turoa Ski Lodge Restaurant**, 10 Thames St, T06-385 8274, licensed, open daily; cosy and great value steak.
♦♦♦ **The Matterhorn** and **Powderkeg** restaurants, in the **Powderhorn Chateau**, corner of Mangawhero and Thames St, T06-3858 888. Both very popular with a fine range of traditional dishes. The Matterhorn is open daily year round; the Powderkeg restaurant is closed in summer.
♦ **Alpine Wine Bar and Restaurant**, opposite the **Ohakune Hotel** on Clyde St, T06-385 9183. More formal dining, open year-round from 1800.
♦ **Ohakune Hotel's O Bar**, 72 Clyde St, T06-385 8268. Good traditional pub food both day and evenings throughout the year.
♦ **Sassi's Bistro**, Miro St, T06-385 8758. Open for breakfast from 0700 and dinner from 1800 every night, year round. Has an intimate, congenial atmosphere.

Cafés

♦ **The Fat Pigeon Garden Café**, on the way back up towards the mountain on Mangawhero Terr, T06-385 9423, seasonal opening hours. A good café with indoor/outdoor seating. Open fire in winter.

♦ **Utopia Café**, 47 Clyde St, T06-385 9120, 0900-1600 (extended hours in winter). Good coffee and an altogether better class of snack.

🌀 Bars and clubs

Ohakune *p299*

Suggested bars include: **Margarita's**, Thames St, popular with the locals; **O Bar** and **Mountain Rocks**, Clyde St, are good bars in the centre of town; **Powderkeg Bar**, in the Powderhorn Chateau, Thames St, is without doubt the place to go – it is spacious, nicely decked out in an Alpine style, very popular and has a great open fire.

🎭 Entertainment

Ohakune *p299*

Ohakune Cinema, 17 Goldfinch St, T06-385 8488.

⛰ Activities and tours

Whakapapa Village *p298*
Mountaineering

Whakapapa provides the most accessible routes to the Ruapehu summit(s) and the Crater Lake. You can ride 2 chairlifts 2020 m above sea level to the Knoll Ridge Chalet ($16), from where you can reach either the Crater Lake and/or the summits; 6 km, 4 hrs (9 km, 7 hrs minus chairlift). The highest summit is **Tahurangi** (2797 m) on the south-west fringe of the crater. The Dome hut, which took a pummelling during the 1990s eruptions, is easily accessible at the crater's northern fringe. As always, make sure you are well-equipped and leave details of your intentions with DoC at the visitor centre (see also Ruapehu Crater Lake Walk, page 299).

Scenic flights

Mountain Air Scenic Flights, on SH47 at the junction to Whakapapa Village and the Grand Chateau (pick-ups from Turangi), T07-892 2812, www.mountainair.co.nz. Operates excellent and affordable flights over the park and beyond. From $90-220.

Skiing

Whakapapa, T07-892 3738, www.whaka papa.co.nz, www.snow.co.nz, or Snowphone T0900-99333/T083-222182. The Whakapapa ski field, on the northwestern slopes of Mt Ruapehu, is New Zealand's largest ski area. Iwikau Village is a conglomerate of runs, ski club chalets and lodges, the main focus being the ski field amenity and reception buildings. An all-day lift pass costs from $80, child from $44. Full-day ski, boot and pole hire costs from $36, child from $25 (snowboard and boots from $50). Various day and beginner packages are available from $80: ski gear rental and lifts from $109, child $66; snowboard equivalent $119, child $73; sightseeing package (lift only) from $20. There are ski school and crèche facilities available on the mountain as well as a café at Knoll Ridge (a ridge above the village).

Walking

A number of short walks can be accessed from Whakapapa, as well as the longer tramps of the **Tongariro Crossing**, **Tama Lakes**, **Northern Circuit** and the **Round the Mountain** tracks (see Walking, page 298). The **Whakapapa Nature Walk** (1 km, 30 mins) is an easy and pleasant stroll which starts near the visitor centre; the **Taranaki Falls Walk** (6 km; 2 hrs) crosses low-lying tussock to the 20-m falls of the Wairere stream; and the **Silica Rapids Walk** (7 km; 2½ hrs), is a loop track that follows another stream through beech forest to some coloured silica terraces.

Note that a number of local activity operators also offer guided walks and the DoC runs an excellent summer programme of organized and guided walks, which usually start from the Whakapapa Village VIC, T07-892 3738, from around $75.

National Park Village *p298*

There are a number of activity operators based in the village, most connected to the various lodges and backpacker hostels. Walking equipment (including boots) can be hired from **Howard's Lodge**, **Pukenui Lodge** and the **Ski Haus** (see Sleeping, page 302).

Climbing

National Park Backpackers, Findlay St, T07-892 2870, daily 0900-2100. An 8-m climbing wall open to non-guests, $12.

Kayaking, canoeing and rafting

National Park is used as a base for Wanganui river trips, the main lodges and backpacker hostels will assist in arranging trips. For operators see Whanganui National Park, page 381.

Mountain biking

The **42 Traverse** is a 46-km (3- to 7-hr) track and the major biking attraction in the area. Companies that provide guided trips, information or independent bike hire, include:
Howard's Lodge, T07-892 2827. With transport, from $35, hire from $60 per day.
Pukenui Lodge, T07-892 2882.

Scenic flights

Mountain Air Scenic Flights, on SH47 at the junction to Whakapapa Village and the **Bayview Chateau**, T0800-922812, www.moun tainair.co.nz. Excellent and affordable flights over the park and beyond. From $90.

Skiing

For information log on to www.snow.co.nz. Equipment hire is available from **Eivin's**, SH4, T07-892 2844; **Howard's Lodge**, T07-892 2827; **Pukenui Lodge**, T07-892 2882; and **Ski Biz**, Carroll St, T07-892 2717, www.skibiz.co.nz.

Walking

Adrift Guided Outdoor Adventures, T07-892 2751, www.adriftnz.co.nz. Guided trips of the Tongariro Crossing from $135, as well as kayaking and canoe adventures.

Ohakune *p299*

Eco-tours

Kiwi Encounters, T06-385 9505. A local company offering touristy noctambulations (2045-2300) into the Waimarino Forest to learn more about the kiwi. If you are lucky you may actually see one, but if not, the screeching calls will be forever ingrained in your memory. If you do see one, count your lucky stars: they reckon in 15 years the entire mainland population may be wiped out.

Horse trekking

Ruapehu Homestead, SH49, T06-385 8799. The best company for beginners but also caters for advanced riders. 1-hr $40, child $30.

Kayaking, canoeing and rafting

Ohakune is a popular base for river activities on the Whanganui River. For tours, see page 385.

Mountain biking

The area is excellent for mountain biking of all grades of difficulty. For information on what tracks are available call into the DoC field centre or VIC (I-Site).

Scenic Cycles, 6 Tay St, T021-607294, www.sceniccycles.co.nz. Organized trips to the regions best tracks including provision of bikes and transport. Their most popular trip is a drive up to the ski field for a thrilling ride back down the mountain, from $40.

Ski Shed, 61 Clyde St, T06-385 9173. Offers half- or full-day bike hire.

Skiing

Turoa, southwestern slopes of Mt Ruapehu, www.whakapapa.co.nz. Serviced by the town of Ohakune, the ski field of Turoa is preferred by many to Whakapapa. It offers some great runs and spectacular views, and sits head and shoulders above the rest in terms of après-ski atmosphere and amenities. Although popular destinations for skiing, both Turoa and Whakapapa have suffered in recent years due to the Ruapehu eruptions in the mid-1990s and a lack of fresh winter snow. As a result, many people have gravitated to the South Island ski resorts, with disastrous economic consequences for the town. However, when conditions are right there is no doubt Turoa can offer some of the best skiing in the North Island. There are numerous ski equipment hire shops in Ohakune as well as at the base of the ski field itself. An all-day lift pass costs from $80, child from $44. Full-day ski, boot and pole hire costs from $36, child from $25 (snowboard and boots from $50). Various day and beginner packages are available from $80: ski gear rental and lifts from $109, child $66; snowboard equivalent $119, child $73. A group lesson on the mountain will cost about $30 while a private lesson will cost $80. For further information on skiing see Whakapapa and National Park Activities and tour sections, page 304. Also try to source the *Turoa 2002* booklet. For transport services up the mountain see page 300.

Walking

The Ohakune Mountain Rd provides short and long walks, some of which join the Tongariro National Park's major walking circuits.

There are 2 very pleasant short walks which depart from the DoC field centre at the edge of town. The 15-min **Rimu Track**, with its interpretative information posts, is wonderful, even in the rain, while the 1-hr **Mangawhero Forest Walk** follows the river valley up towards the mountain.

A further 12 km up the road, the 1-hr **Waitonga Falls Track** is popular, as is the longer (5-hr) **Lake Surprise** tramp, which starts about 16 km up the road. The less active can try the 10-min **Mangawhero Falls Walk**, also accessed off the Mountain Rd.

For details, maps and the latest on weather call in at the DoC field centre, T06-385 8578. The **Tongariro Crossing** is also accessible from Ohakune. For information see box, page 297. For shuttle transport see page 293.

---

❶ Directory

Ohakune *p299*

Internet Peppatree Design and Print, Cedar Mall, Goldfinch St, T06-385 9320. **The Video Shop**, 53 Clyde St. 1000-2030. **Police** 10 Clyde St, T06-385 0100. **Post office** 5 Goldfinch St, T06-385 8645. Mon-Fri 0700-1700, Sat 0800-1600.

Taranaki

⁝ **Footprint features**

Introduction

In many ways Taranaki is more mountain than region. The awesome 2518-m snow-capped volcanic cone of the same name seems to dominate everything and, even shrouded in mist, it is strangely omnipresent. Although many have enjoyed the volcano, it has also caused a number of deaths, and they say it is due for another eruption. However, whether you look at it with reverence or fear, it will always be the region's one defining feature.

The mountain has two names, Taranaki and Egmont, both official, but in a way controversial. Taranaki is the original Maori name, while Egmont is the result of Captain Cook's habit of renaming anything in sight during his explorations in 1770.

The largest town is New Plymouth, a proud, prosperous and modern centre that lies in the shadow of the great mountain on the northwest coast. Although a little bit out of the way, those who make the effort to visit the region will not be disappointed. As well as the superb scenery and range of activities on or around the mountain itself, the region boasts a fascinating history, fine parks, gardens, arts and crafts and a coastline internationally recognized for its excellent surfing.

★ Don't miss ...

1 **Govett-Brewster Gallery** Wonder at the bizarre contemporary artworks in this celebrated New Plymouth institution, page 312.
2 **Going green** Take a stroll through Pukekura and Brooklands Parks or wander round the Pukeiti Rhododendron Gardens, pages 312 and 314.
3 **Paritutu Rock** See if you can see Mount Ruapehu from above the New Plymouth Power Station, then see if you can get down again! page 313.
4 **Oakura** Learn to surf along 'Surf Highway 45', page 318.
5 **Mount Taranaki** Perhaps the most beautiful mountain in the country: climb it, ski down it, walk or drive around it, or stroll through its 'Goblin Forest', page 319.
6 **Dam-dropping** Try one of the more unusual activities from Hawera, page 322.

Taranaki Introduction

New Plymouth → Colour map 3, A1 Population: 67,000

Based on resources of rich agricultural land and natural gas and oil supplies, lively New Plymouth enjoys considerable prosperity and is the main service town and population base of the Taranaki Region. The town, and the entire district, is dominated by the mountain, which seems to dictate the general mood, like some huge meteorological barometer. On a clear day, when the mountain radiates, its sheer size and stature are mirrored proudly in the town and the region. But, when shrouded in mist and rain, the area feels dull and sombre. As well as being a fine base from which to explore the recreational delights on and around the mountain and the region as a whole, New Plymouth itself has an excellent art gallery, some interesting historic buildings and a fine marine and public park. ➤➤ *For Sleeping, Eating and other listings, see pages 315-318.*

New Plymouth

Taranaki New Plymouth

Sleeping 😴
Abode On Courtenay
  Motor Inn **6** *A6*
Arlie House **1** *C1*
Belt Road Holiday
  Park **17** *B1*
Braemar Motor Inn **2** *C1*
Brougham Heights **3** *B3*
Central Motel **11** *B6*
Copthorne Grand
  Central **5** *B3*
Cottage Mews Motel **4** *B5*
Devon **9** *A6*
Egmont Eco Leisure
  Park **13** *D2*
Hookner Park Motor
  Camp **15** *D4*
Issy Manor **10** *C4*
Nice & Restaurant **7** *B3*
Shoestring
  Backpackers **4** *B5*
Top Ten Motorcamp **12** *A6*
Waterfront Motor
  Inn **8** *A2*
YHA Egmont Eco
  Lodge **16** *D2*

Ins and outs

Getting there **New Plymouth airport** ① *12 km north of the town*, is served by **Air New Zealand Link**, T0800-737000. Shuttles to and from the airport are available with **Withers**, T06-751 1777, www.withers.co.nz, and cost about $17 one way.

By road, New Plymouth is a little out of the way: 254 km from Hamilton and 172 km from Wanganui, which is roughly halfway between Auckland and Wellington. SH3 links New Plymouth to Hamilton, is notorious for slips and is in a constant state of upgrading, while its continuation to Wanganui is a little better, but still quite slow. **Intercity, Newman's** and **Dalroy Express**, 7 Erica Place, T06-759 0197/T0508-465622 www.dalroytours.co.nz, run regular bus services to New Plymouth from Auckland and Hamilton to the north and Wanganui and Palmerston North to the south. The major operators stop on Ariki Street in the city centre. **White Star**, 25 Liardet Street, T06-758 3338, www.yellow.co.nz/site/whitestar, also has daily freight and passenger services south from Ariki Street. For bookings and information contact the VIC (I-Site) or the **Travel Centre**, 19 Ariki Street, T06-759 9039.

To ⑨ ⑫ , North, Airport & Fitzroy Pole

Woolworths Supermarket

New World Supermarket

Pukekura Park

To Brooklands Park

To South (SH 3), Mt Egmont National Park & around the Mountain Circuit

Getting around New Plymouth's central grid of streets has a very confusing one-way system, so a certain amounmt of patience is required. The local bus company is **New Plymouth City (Okato) Services**, T06-753 9646, www.okatobus.co.nz. **Wither's**, T06-751 1777, www.withers.co.nz, runs a service to hostels and the mountain.

Tourist information **New Plymouth VIC (I-Site)** ① *at the Puke Ariki Museum and Library, near the waterfront, 65 St Aubyn St, T06-759 6060, www.newplymouthnz.com or www.taranaki.co.nz, Mon, Tue, Thu, Fri 0900-1800, Wed 0900-2100, Sat-Sun 0900-1700.* The VIC can give details of a number of Heritage Trails, including an interesting two-hour walk in town starting at Puke Ariki Landing, a park with sculptures and the lofty 'wind wand' by the shoreline. **DoC** ① *220 Devon St West, T06-759 0350.*

Background

Like the mountain, New Plymouth and Taranaki as a whole has an unsettled and, at times, explosive history. Prior to the arrival of Europeans there were several Maori *pa* in the vicinity of New Plymouth, particularly around the port area and the natural fortification of Paritutu Rock. The first *Pakeha* (European) to arrive in 1828 were whalers who soon found themselves joining forces with the local Te Ati-awa to defend against marauding tribes from the Walkato. In 1841, in an area now almost deserted as a result of these skirmishes, the New Zealand Company bought up large tracts of land, and European

Eating ⊘
Agra 1 *A5*
Andre L'Escargot 6 *B3*
Blow Fish 15 *B1*
Chaos 2 *B3*
El Condor 3 *A5*
GCR & Bar 5 *B3*
India Today 13 *A4*
Mills 7 *B3*

Ozone 14 *A4*
Peggy Gordon's Celtic Bar 11 *B2*
Simply Read 8 *A1*

Bars & clubs ⊙
Crowded House 10 *A4*

Taranaki New Plymouth

settlement began in earnest. With the return of exiled Maori, disputes quickly arose surrounding the sale of their land and, after unsuccessful arbitration by the crown and fuelled by the white settlers' greed, war broke out. The Maori in the Taranaki had not signed the Treaty of Waitangi so were treated as rebels and many land claims and transactions were highly dubious. The war was to last for 10 years, and battles between the Europeans and the Maori were amongst the fiercest ever fought in the country. As a result, most settlers deserted the area leaving New Plymouth as little more than a military settlement. It was not until 1881 that formal peace was made and New Plymouth and the region as a whole settled down and began to prosper through its rich agricultural lands. New Plymouth was named after Plymouth in Devon, England, from where many of the first settlers came. Today, as well as agriculture, economic booms have been enjoyed through the discovery of natural gas and oil.

Sights

One of the town's most celebrated institutions is the **Govett-Brewster Gallery** ⓘ *corner of Queen and King sts, T06-759 6060, www.govettbrewster.com, daily 1030-1700, free*. Although it opened 35 years ago you could be forgiven for thinking the paint was still wet. The interior is on three levels and looks very modern, befitting its reputation as the premier contemporary art gallery in the country. Although perhaps not to everyone's taste, the mainly three-dimensional and highly conceptual pieces are well worth a look. The gallery doyen is Len Lye, a poet, writer and multimedia artist who specialized in pioneering animation work in the 1930s. His mainly abstract films are regularly shown.

For contemporary works by local artists, stop by for a muse at the evocatively named and snigger-inducing **Real Tart Gallery** ⓘ *62 Devon St West, T06-756 5717, daily 1100-1600, free*. Here over 100 local artists are represented and the works range from the awful to the appealing, depending entirely on your own taste.

The rather flash **Taranaki Museum and Library (Puke Ariki)** ⓘ *Egmont St, T06-759 6060, www.pukeariki.com, Mon, Thu, Fri 0900-1800, Wed 0900-2100, Sat-Sun 0900-1700, free (temporary exhibitions $6)*, is worth a visit and houses an interesting collection of Maori artifacts and displays, mixed with the usual pioneer exhibits and wildlife specimens. Obviously the great mountain features heavily and this is an opportunity to learn of its importance to the region, if not its power. The quaint little **Richmond Cottage** ⓘ *Ariki St, Sat-Sun 1100-1530*, now almost absorbed by the museum, is a furnished colonial cottage built in 1853.

There are some other notable historic buildings and sites in the city including the oldest stone church in the country, **St Mary's**, on Vivian Street. The original church was built in 1846. The interior contains some lovely Maori carvings and stained-glass windows. The cemetery echoes the military theme, with the graves of several soldiers testifying to the area's colourful and, at times, bloody past.

The **Fitzroy Pole** (Pou Tutaki) which stands proudly at the northern end of town on the corner of Devon Street East and Smart Road was erected by the Maori in 1844. It commemorates Governor Fitzroy's decision to question the legalities of white settlers and forbid their acquisition of huge tracts of land. Although not the original, the carving speaks for itself.

In distinct contrast and far more contemporary is the **'Wind Wand'** on the waterfront near the museum. Created for the 2000-millennium celebrations by local multimedia artist Len Lye it is a 45-m, 900-kg kinetic sculpture that is designed to sway gently in the breeze. The bulb at the end is lit at night to enhance this effect though watching it at any time can prove quite therapeutic. For more information log on to www.windwand.co.nz; it seems even artworks have their own websites these days.

New Plymouth is famous for its parks, the oldest and finest of which are **Pukekura** and **Brooklands**, which merge. They are best accessed at Fillis Street, just east of the town centre. Pukekura, opened in 1876, is a well-maintained 20 ha of lakes and assorted gardens, with a cricket ground, fernery and tearoom serving refreshments and light meals daily except Tuesday. From here, on a clear and calm day, you will see the reflection of Mount Taranaki across the main lake, which is crossed by a Japanese-style bridge. Brooklands has an outdoor amphitheatre, ponds studded by lily pads, English-style rhododendron gardens, an historic colonial hospital museum/gallery and a 2000-year-old puriri tree. There is also a small **children's zoo** ① *daily 0830-1700*, with all the usual inmates, including kune-kune pigs, goats and miniature horses, as well as monkeys and a fine collection of parrots and parakeets.

Near the ugly towers of the power station and the busy port is the **Sugar Loaf Island Marine Park**, with its eroded, volcanic rock islands. Designated in 1986, the park is home to New Zealand fur seals and a variety of nesting seabirds. Boat trips to visit the park and view the wildlife are available. The shoreline of the park is part of an interesting 7-km Coastal Walkway, the highlight of which is the climb up **Paritutu Rock** – if you can. The climb requires considerable effort and involves pulling yourself up by a steel cable, but the view (though spoilt slightly by the power station and oil storage tanks) is worth the effort, with the ever-present Taranaki cone to the east and the town to the north, and Ruapehu and Ngauruhoe just visible on a clear day. Then you're faced with the descent, which is not so much a scramble, as an abseil. If the climb is too daunting, a fine view can also be had from Marshland Hill, off Robe Street, which was formerly the Pukaka *pa*. ▸▸ *See Activities and tours, page 318.*

Around New Plymouth ● ▸▸ *pp315-318.*

North on SH3

There are a few attractions, walks and viewpoints along this road that are definitely worth a visit; pick a copy of the free *Scenic Highway 3* leaflet and the more detailed *Walks in north Taranaki* ($1) from the DoC or the VIC (I-Site) in New Plymouth.

Heading north past Waitara and Urenui, which have some popular beaches in themselves, is the **White Cliffs Brewing Company** ① *487 Main North Rd, Urenui, T06-752 3676, daily 1000-1800*, a boutique organic beer brewery offering tastings and sales of some fairly heady brews. The **Whitecliffs Walkway** is the most celebrated in North Taranaki. The Whitecliffs (named after the famous Dover cliffs in England), although not on the same scale or grandeur as their namesake, are nonetheless quite impressive and dominate the shore for some 7 km. The track can be accessed from the south at the Pukearuhe Historic Reserve at the end of Pukearuhe Road, north of Urenui. The total length of the track is 9.5 km, terminating at the northern access point, on Clifton Road at the mouth of the Tongaporutu River. Much of the track is along the shoreline, so make sure you check the tides.

The immediate coastline either side of the **Tongaporutu River** is scattered with rock towers, caves and arches, though they are not easily accessed (low tide only). For a superb view of them head just north of the Clifton Road, across the bridge and up the hill on the other side. Turn left onto Cemetery Road. From the end a short walk across an accessible field will take you to the headland. There is also a fine view of the Whitecliffs from there.

Just north of Tongaporutu are **Mokau** and **Awakino**. Both are popular but remote holiday spots especially good for coastal walks and fishing. For canoe trips and cruises on the Mokau River see Activities and tours, page 318.

A lengthy diversion off SH3 along SH40 will take you to the 74-m **Mount Damper Falls**, the highest waterfall in the North Island. From SH40 take the Okau Road to the Mount Damper Falls car park, which is well marked. The 15-minute walk will take you to a lookout platform. The falls are best viewed after heavy rain.

Carrington Road (off Victoria Road) heads southwest out of New Plymouth towards the mountain. It has a number of sights including **Hurworth Cottage** ① *906 Carrington Rd, T06-753 3593, Wed-Fri 1000-1400, Sat-Sun 1300-1700*, which was originally built in 1856 by young lawyer Harry Atkinson, who was also New Zealand's Prime Minister, not once, but four times. Young Harry and his family had to flee the house and the area during the Taranaki Wars in 1860. The house today is a well- renovated tribute to the family. Further along is the **Pouakai Zoo Park** ① *1296 Carrington Rd, T06-753 3788, Tue-Sun 1000-1630, $5, child $2*, a small, private, enthusiastically run zoo, exhibiting a number of native and non-native species including meerkats and gibbons. The zoo and its inhabitants were sold shortly before going to press, hopefully as a going concern, but this remains to be seen.

The highlight on the Carrington Road, however, is the **Pukeiti Rhododendron Trust Gardens** ① *2290 Carrington Rd, T06-752 4141, daily 0900-1700, winter 1000-1500, $15 ($10 in winter)*. This is a 4-sq-km garden surrounded by bush that is world renowned for its beautiful displays of 'rhodies' and azaleas, which are best viewed in the spring/summer and especially during the Rhododendron Festival in late October. There is a restaurant, and a shop selling plants and souvenirs.

If you continue on Carrington Road you will join the network of roads that surround the mountain. There is a fine walk and views of the mountain on the **Stony River** and **Blue Rata reserves**. From Carrington take a left onto the Saunders Road dirt track and follow it to the end. From there, by foot, negotiate your way through the bush following the sound of the river. You will emerge onto the Stony River boulder field. From here you can walk carefully east or west, under the shadow of the mighty mountain. The large Blue Rata, from which the reserve takes its name, is hard to find, about 100 m into the bush, on the riverside of the track, about halfway up its length.

Before rejoining SH45 and heading north or south, take a discreet peek at the memorial to the great man, prophet and Maori chief, Te Whiti, which is at **Parihaka Pa**, on Mid-Parihaka Road (signposted).

Lake Mangamahoe

There is something you simply must do on your visit to New Plymouth (weather permitting) and that is to soak up the beauty and serenity of Lake Mangamahoe. Just 10 km southeast on SH3, this scenic reserve is one of the very best places where you can see a reflection of the mighty mountain on water. After enjoying the lake itself, with its numerous swans, ducks and geese, head to the road end and take the right hand track up the steps to the lookout point. From here at sunset, or anytime when the mountain is clear, the view is magnificent. Take your camera.

'Surf Highway 45'

If you fancy doing the 175-km trip around the mountain, it involves at least a full day via the 'Surf Highway 45' and SH3. But on a clear day the mountain will be good company throughout, and there are a number of interesting places to see and visit on the way.

Heading south from New Plymouth the view of the mountain is shielded by the Kaitake and Pouakai ranges for a short while, then you arrive in **Oakura**, famous for its surf, windsurfing and swimming beach. There is also an interesting craft shop called the **Crafty Fox** in the heart of town next to the main road. Various local art and craft pieces are for sale and there is a railway wagon café next door.

While in the area you may like to visit the **Emacadamia Nut Orchard** ① *219 Surrey Hill Rd, T06-752 7793, www.emacadamia.co.nz, tours available on Sun 1330-1630, free*, where you will get a fascinating insight into the great nut and its associated products – they are also GM free.

Lucy's Gully, 3 km south of Oakura, is a pleasant picnic spot with exotic trees, including redwoods, and ferns. There are also walking tracks into the Kaitake Range.

Around the small settlement of **Okato** the mountain comes back into view and the road edges its way closer to the coast. You can satisfy your desire to see it again at the **Cape Egmont Lighthouse**, about 9 km down Cape Road. Although the lighthouse is closed to visitors it is still of interest. It seems strangely out of place, standing in a field with a huge mountain in the background. Just south of Cape Road back on SH45 is Mid-Parihaka Road. Two kilometres up is **Parihaka Pa**.

Back on SH45, you can enjoy the scenery or explore the many side roads until you reach **Opunake**, which has a fine surf and swimming beach and a 7-km walkway, starting at Opunake Lake, which takes in lake, beach and river scenery. Visit the **VIC (I-Site)** ① *in the library, Tasman St, T06-761 8663, Mon-Thu 0930-1700, Fri 0930-1830*, for accommodation options.

The next settlement south of Opunake is **Manaia** which is the place to leave SH45 if you want to get a bit more intimate with the mountain at **Dawson Falls**. There is not a lot in Manaia itself, a small settlement of about 1000, named after a Maori chief. Country and Western fans might like to pop into the **Taranaki Country Music Hall of Fame** ① *11 Surf Highway, T06-274 8442, Sat-Wed 1000-1600*.

● Sleeping

New Plymouth *p310, map p310*
For full listings contact the VIC (I-Site) or www.accommodationtaranaki.co.nz. For mountain accommodation see page 320.
L The Nice Hotel, 71 Brougham St, T06-758 6423, www.nicehotel.co.nz. A small, 2-storey, luxury boutique hotel well placed for the town centre and all amenities. Each of the 8 rooms is themed according to its outlook and reflects the town's history or contribution to the arts. Examples include the 'Redcoats' room relating to the former British army barracks near the town, or 'The Wind Wand', relating to Len Lye's kinetic sculpture on the waterfront. As well as stylish design, the rooms offer all the comforts, such as a spa bath and large comfy armchairs. The popular, in-house **Table Restaurant** is intimate and relaxed, offering excellent contemporary Pacific Rim cuisine. Also offers nice tours.
L-A Waterfront Motor Inn, 1 Egmont St, T06-769 5301, www.waterfront.co.nz. One of the newest offerings in the town centre, with a contemporary feel. The location and views are hard to beat.
AL-A Abode on Courtenay Motor Inn, 155 Courtenay St, T06-769 5465, www.abodemotor inn.co.nz. One of the newest, centrally located.
AL-A Airlie House, 161 Powerham St, T06-757 8866, www.airliehouse.co.nz. A historic villa B&B, centrally located and very tastefully renovated, with 2 en suite rooms and a self-contained studio, fast internet. Recommended.
AL-A Brougham Heights, 54 Brougham St, T06-757 9954, www.broughamheights.co.nz.

Well-located, modern and comfortable motel that seems to absorb some of the niceties from the Nice Hotel across the road.
AL-A Copthorne Grand Central Hotel, 42 Powerham St, T06-758 7495, www.grand centralhotel.co.nz. Conveniently placed standard hotel with a solid reputation, spa rooms and in-house restaurant.
AL-A Devon Hotel, 390 Devon St, T06-759 9009/T0800-843338, www.devon hotel.co.nz. The best in this range, along with **Grand Central**, above.
AL-A Issy Manor, 32 Carrington St, T06-758 2375, www.isseymanor.co.nz. Classy, contemporary boutique accommodation in a renovated former 1857 coach-house. Centrally located next to Pukekura Park. 4 good value rooms, spa, internet and off-street parking.
A Braemar Motor Inn, 152 Powerham St, T06-758 0859, www.breamarmotorinn.co.nz. Well-established 3-star motel, fairly modern with a distinct Scottish theme. Restaurant.
A Central Motel, 86 Eliot St, T06-758 6444. Excellent value studios with Sky TV.
A The Loft, 729 Frankley Rd, T06-753 2950, www.taranakiloft.com. A lovely rural self-contained option in 27 ha of farmland.
B Cottage Mews Motel, 48 Lemon St, T06-758 0403. Suites attached to **Shoestring Backpackers**, below. Immaculate, good value and run by fine folk.
B-D Shoestring Backpackers, 48 Lemon St, T06-758 0404. A large traditional villa with a range of rooms and fine facilities. Friendly folk, sauna and fast internet.

Taranaki New Plymouth *Listings*

B-D YHA Egmont Eco Lodge, 12 Clawton St, T06-753 5720, www.taranaki-bakpak.co.nz. Small, very friendly and set in a quiet location a 15-min walk from town (taxi fare refunded). Full range of rooms including motel-style en suites to tent sites. An added attraction here is the free introduction to some large and rapacious local river inhabitants.

C-D EcoInn Backpackers Hostel, 671 Kent Rd, T06-752 2765, www.ecoinn.co.nz. Eco-friendly and relaxed backpacker hostel, 3 km from the Egmont National Park. Solar, hydro and wind-powered property with doubles and share, hot tub, internet.

Motorcamps and campsites
There are several options in town.
B-D Belt Road Holiday Park, 2 Belt Rd, T06-758 0228, www.beltroad.co.nz. Near the water and well facilitated but overlooking the port.
B-D Egmont Eco Leisure Park, 12 Clawton St, T06-753 5720, www.egmont.co.nz. Set in native bush with lodge, cabins powered and tent sites, fully equipped camp kitchen. A short walk from the town centre.
B-D 'Top Ten' Motorcamp, 29 Princess St, Fitzroy, T06-758 2566, www.nptop10.co.nz. Small and central.

North on SH3 *p313*
A Mokau Motel, SH3 T06-752 9725. 4 basic, but comfortable units.
C-D Palm House, 1 Reanga St, T06-752 9081, www.egmont.co.nz/retreat/mokau. A good backpacker hostel, affiliated with the **Taranaki Experience** accommodation conglomerate, with the full range of rooms and a quiet relaxing atmosphere.

Motorcamps and campsites
C-D Seaview Motorcamp, Awakino, just before SH3 turns inland heading north, T06-752 9708. Excellent, right on the beach, with camp kitchen and a café attached.

Carrington Road *p314*
A Patuha Farm Lodge, 575 Upper Pitone Rd, Okato, T06-7524469, www.friars.co.nz/hosts/patuha.html. This 10-bedroom working farm lodge is well placed in a quiet bush setting on the edge of the Pukeiti Rhododendron Trust Gardens. En suites and in-house spa. Overall a fine relaxing retreat and guests have the opportunity to join in daily farm activities.

Motorcamps and campsites
B-D Hookner Park Motorcamp, 885 Carrington Rd, about 10 km from town, T06-753 6945. A good quiet country option. Part of a working dairy farm where you can join in with farm activities. En suite or standard cabins, powered and tent sites.

'Surf Highway 45' *p314*
L-AL Ahu Ahu Beach Villas, 321 Ahu Ahu Rd, Oakura, T06-752 7370, www.ahu.com. Rustic award-winning architecture in the form of 2 villas housing 4 fully self-contained units overlooking the ocean. Cosy and highly individual. Recommended.
A Oakura Beach B&B, 1160 SH45, Oakura, T06-752 7320, www.oakura.com. Lovely villa-style B&B belonging to a well-travelled, friendly couple.
A Oakura Beach Motel, 53 Wairau Rd, Oakura, T06-752 7680, www.oakura.co.nz. Standard self-contained units 3 mins from the beach.

Motorcamps and campsites
C-D Oakura Beach Camp, 2 Jans Terr, Oakura, T06-752 7861. Basic but has a store and is across the road from the beach.

❼ Eating

New Plymouth *p310, map p310*
There is a **Countdown** supermarket on Leach St and a **Pack-n-Save** on Gill St.
❛❛❛ Andre L'Escargot 37-43 Brougham St, T06-758 4812, Mon-Sat from 1700. This is an old favourite offering award-winning, fine French-style cuisine in a congenial setting.
❛❛❛ The Nice Hotel's Table Restaurant, 71 Brougham St. Mon-Sat from 1600. Fine à la carte with superb desserts and a good wine selection. Well it couldn't be horrible, could it?
❛❛❛ Salt Restaurant, Waterfront Hotel, 1 Egmont St, T06-769 5304, daily 0700-2200. Modern, trendy and overlooking the ocean.
❛❛ Agra, 151 Devon St, T06-758 0030, daily from 1730-late. A small, good-value Indian diner deserving of its loyal following.
❛❛ GCR Restaurant and Bar, 40 Brougham St, T06-758 7495, Mon-Fri from 0630-0930 and from 1800, Sat-Sun from 0730-1030 and from 1800. A modern restaurant and bar specializing in gourmet pizzas.

₩₩ India Today, 40 Devon St East, T06-769 9117, daily from 1730, lunch 1130-1430. A little more conventional than Agra.
₩₩ The Mills, 2 Courtney St, T06-758 1935, Mon-Sat from 1100. Pub that has joined the growing trend of serving a variety of dishes on hot slabs of stone – the 'stone-grill'.
₩₩ Peggy Gordons Celtic Bar, corner of Devon and Egmont sts, T06-758 8561, daily from 0700. Good pub grub.
₩ The Blow Fish, 406 St Aubyn St, T06-759 1314. No airs and graces. Good value.
₩ Chaos, 36 Brougham St, T06-759 8080. Popular organic café with good coffee and a wide range of snacks. Good breakfast venue.
₩ El Condor, 170 Devon St East, T06-757 5436, Tue-Sat from 1700. Good-value Argentine pizza joint.
₩ Ozone, 117 Devon St East, T06-769 9020. Good coffee and light snacks.
₩ Simply Read, 2 Dawson St, T06-757 8667. Café in a sunny spot overlooking the sea, with a small bookshop attached.

ⓕ Pubs, bars and clubs

New Plymouth *p310, map p310*
Crowded House, 93 Devon St, T06-759 4921. About the size of a football field and claims to be the official bar of the famed Taranaki rugby team supporters.
The Mill Rock, 2 Courtney St, see Eating above. A favourite, with a cosmopolitan clientele and live bands.
Peggy Gordon's, corner of Devon and Egmont sts, T06-758 8561. The town's Irish-style offering.

ⓔ Entertainment

New Plymouth *p310, map p310*
Cinema and theatre
Cinema 5, 125 Devon St East, T06-759 9077.
New Plymouth Operatic Society, 76 King St, T06-758 4958. Excellent annual shows.
TSB Showplace, 92 Devon St, T06-758 4947. Regular national and international acts.

ⓧ Festivals and events

New Plymouth *p310, map p310*
See www.taranaki.co.nz for details.
Mar Taranaki Wine and Food Festival usually held at one of the top vineyards

and with the added attraction of live music. **WOMAD**, www.womad.co.nz. A 3-day celebration of World music with over 400 artists from 21 counties.
Jul-Aug Taranaki Festival of the Arts, www.artfest.co.nz. A biennial festival (next held in 2007) of international and New Zealand artists and performers. Theatre, contemporary music, fine music, choirs, literature, dance, visual arts, film and cabaret.
Oct Taranaki Rhododendron Festival, www.rhodo.co.nz. Various events and tours take place at various major gardens.
Dec-Feb New Plymouth Festival of Lights, held in Pukekura Park, involves the illumination of trees, waterfalls and fountains with additional staged events.

ⓞ Shopping

New Plymouth *p310, map p310*
There are numerous excellent arts and crafts galleries and outlets in the region, for details see the VIC.
Rangimarie Maori Art and Craft Centre, near Paritutu Rock on Centennial Drive, T06-751 2880, Mon-Fri 0900-1500.
Real Tart Gallery, 62 Devon St West, T06-756 5717. Wide range of local contemporary art.

▲ Activities and tours

New Plymouth *p310, map p310*
For mountain activities see Mt Egmont (Taranaki) National Park, page 320. New Plymouth offers many of the usual activities, along with dam-dropping (see under Hawera, page 322) and tandem-surfing.

Fishing, scuba diving and cruising
Chaddy's Charters, Lee Breakwater Marina, Ocean View Parade, near the port, T06-758 9133. For 1-hr cruises to the Sugar Loaf Islands $30, fishing $60.
Mokau River Cruises, T06-752 9775. River cruising on the Mokau north of New Plymouth (Nov-Apr), departs 1100, 3 hrs from $35, cruise and kayak from $65.
New Plymouth Underwater, 16 Hobson St, T06-758 3348, www.newplymouth underwater.co.nz. Scuba diving.

Horse trekking

There are several operators so shop around. **Gumboot Gully Horse Treks**, 1034 Piko Rd, Okoki, T06-756 5809. From 2 hrs to 5-day hill country treks on horses that featured in the film *The Last Samurai*, from $40 **Tuahu Quarter Horses**, 641 Kaipikari Rd, Urenui (30 mins east of New Plymouth), T06-752 3400. Bush and hill treks from 2 hrs to a full-day, views of Mt Taranaki, from $40.

Kayaking

Canoe and Kayak Taranaki, 6/631 Devon Rd, T06-759 5506. Various regional whitewater and coastal options, from $40. **Chaddy's Charters**, T06-758 9133. Kayak hire. Shoreline and marine park explorations.

Mineral pools

Mineral Pool Complex, 8 Bonithon Rd, T06-759 1666, Mon-Fri 0900-2000, Tue 0900-1700, Sat-Sun 1200-2100, bookings essential. This modern complex is the result of a very tasteful renovation of the former mineral pool that has an artesian mineral well spouting 29,000-year-old water. It offers both communal and private pools (4 people) with a range of professional massages and health treatments. The pools cost $6-45 with $15 for around 30 mins. This is on a 'per pool' basis and they are freshly filled for each client. Very therapeutic.

Mountaineering and climbing

The following will see you safely up and down the mountain from around $300. Other activities include trekking and abseiling. MacAlpine Guides, T06-765 6234, www.mac alpineguides.com; and Top Guides, T0800-448433, www.topguides.co.nz.

Scenic flights

Heliview Taranaki, T06-753 0123, www.heli view.co.nz. Mountain specials from $125.

Surfing and windsurfing

The Taranaki or Egmont Coast is one of the best surfing places in the country. The so-called 'Surf Highway 45' which hugs the coastline between New Plymouth and Wanganui has some fine surf beaches, particularly at **Oakura** and **Opunake**. Particular gems also include **Ahu Ahu Road**, the **Kumara Patch** and **Stent Road**. In town, **Footsore Beach** is one of the favourites.

Companies offering trips and lessons come and go as much as the surf, for the most recent listings contact the VIC (I-Site). **Sirocco**, 605 Main St, Oakura, T06-752 1363. Private hire and wave information. **Vertigo**, Oakura, T06-752 7363. Surf board hire and also offers windsurfing lessons.

Tours

Cycletours Taranaki, T06-756 7727, www.cycle-taranaki.co.nz. Self-guided trips include a 1-day downhill 'Mountain to Sea' (38 km) and a 2-day (125 km) 'Round the Mountain' from $100. **Samurai Village Tours**, T06-752 6806, www.samuraivillagetours.com. Trips of 1½ hrs to the former film set at Uruti (50 km north of New Plymouth), with its now recreated props and displays, from $35, child $20. **Taranaki Tours**, T06-757 9888, www.taranakitours.com offer tours of the region with emphasis on the mountain with a full-day 'Round the Mountain' from $135, shuttle service from $40 return.

⊖ Transport

New Plymouth *p310, map p310*
Airlines offices Air New Zealand, 12-14 Devon St East, T06-757 3300. **Bicycle hire** Cycle Inn, 133 Devon St East, T06-758 7418. Raceway Cycles, 207 Coronation Av, T06-759 0391. **Car hire** Avis, 113 Gill St, T06-755 9600. Budget, T0800-283438. **Taxi** New Plymouth Taxis, T06-757 3000.

⊕ Directory

New Plymouth *p310, map p310*
Banks Most main branches can be found on Devon St. Currency exchange at TSB Centre, 120 Devon St East, T06-759 5375. **Internet** Computer Corner, Shop 8, Richmond Centre (Egmont St) is the cheapest. Also at: Antons, 242 Devon St East; and New Plymouth Library, Brougham St. **Medical services** Pheonix Accident and Medical Clinic, 95 Vivian St, T06-7594295, Mon-Fri 0900-1800, Sat-Sun 0900-1600. **Police** Powerham St, T06-759 5500. **Post office** Currie St, Mon-Fri 0730-1730, Sat 0900-1300. **Useful numbers** AA, 49-55 Powerham St, T06-968 7840.

Mount Egmont (Taranaki) National Park → *Colour map 3, A1*

Weather permitting, no trip to Taranaki would be complete without getting close to the mountain. At 2518 m, Mount Taranaki is not only in the heart of Egmont National Park, but metaphorically it is the heart. This classically shaped, dormant volcano was formed by the numerous eruptions of the last 12,000 years. The most recent happened 350 years ago and they say she is now 'overdue', with the potential to 'go off' at any time. Fatham's Peak, on the southern slopes, is a parasitic outcrop from the main vent, while the Pouakai and Kaitake ranges to the west are older andesite volcanoes and have eroded for much longer than Taranaki. ➤➤ *For Sleeping, Eating and other listings, see page 320.*

Ins and outs

Getting there The main access points to the park and the mountain are at North Egmont (Egmont VIC), Stratford (East Egmont) and Manaia (Dawson Falls). East Egmont is accessed via Pembroke Road, which heads 18 km towards the mountain from Stratford. Dawson Falls is at the end of Upper Manaia Road, via Kaponga on the southern slopes of the mountain, 24 km from Stratford. **Wither's**, T06-751 1777, www.withers .co.nz, and **Taranaki Tours**, T06-757 9888, www.taranakitours.com, offer shuttle services to the mountain from New Plymouth (particularly Egmont VIC), from $40 return.

Tourist information Before attempting any walks on the mountain you should read all the relevant information. The VIC (I-Site) in New Plymouth (see page 311) can provide basic information particularly about getting there, while the DoC office (both in town and on the mountain) can fill in the detail with walking information, maps and weather forecasts. **Egmont VIC (I-Site)** ① *16 km from North Egmont Village, at the end of Egmont Rd (which heads towards the mountain), T06-756 0990, nevc@oc.govt.nz, daily 0800-1630.* **Dawson Falls VIC (I-Site)** ① *T027-443 0248, Mar-Dec Wed-Sun 0800-1630, Jan-Feb daily.* **DoC Stratford Field Centre** ① *839 Pembroke Rd, T06-765 5144.*

▲▲ Walks

The 140-km of walks take from 30 minutes to four days and are well maintained by DoC. The tracks vary in difficulty, but all are easily accessible from the main access points and information centres above. The forest and vegetation is called 'goblin forest' (due to its miniature 'hobbit-style' appearance as the altitude increases) and the entire mountain is drained by myriad babbling streams. Beware that the higher you go, obviously, the more dangerous it gets. In winter the slopes are covered in snow and ice, so climbing boots, crampons and an ice axe are essential. Even in summer crampons are advised on the summit, though the main enemy underfoot is loose scree. Guides can supply crampons as part of their service, but otherwise you will need your own.

To the uninitiated, **Mount Taranaki** looks deceptively easy, however the weather is highly unpredictable and many people have lost their lives on its slopes, so you must be well prepared. DoC produces a number of leaflets: *Around the Mountain Circuit* and *Short Walks in Egmont National Park* are both excellent. The VICs around the mountain can also advise on routes, hut accommodation, prices and bookings.

The **Mountain Circuit** takes three to five days and is about 55 km in length. There are a number of huts to stay in en route, but these must be pre-booked at DoC. At Dawson Falls two of the best short-walk options include the track to the falls which can be accessed via the **Kapuni Loop Track** (one hour). This walk offers some good photo opportunities along the way, as does the **Wilkie's Pools Track** (one hour), which takes in some very pretty 'goblin forest' and a series of plunge pools, formed by

66 99 The forest and vegetation is called 'goblin forest' (due to its miniature 'hobbit-style' appearance the higher in altitude you go ... and the entire mountain is drained by myriad babbling streams ...

sand and gravel running over the lava. At North Egmont, the 45-minute walk from the park entrance to the **Waiwhakaiho River** has some beautiful base native bush, while the **Ngatoro Loop Track** (one hour) takes in some beautiful 'goblin forest', and the **Veronica Loop Track** (two hours) some excellent views. Both of these tracks start from the top of the road. If you want to go the full nine yards and climb the summit, good luck: it's quite a hard climb, but boy, is it worth it.

● Sleeping

Mount Egmont National Park *p319*
For all mountain hut bookings contact and pre-book with DoC.
L Dawson Falls Tourist Lodge, Manaia Rd, Dawson Falls, T06-765 5457, www.dawson-falls.co.nz. An Alpine-style lodge, comfortable suites, log fire and all mod cons, restaurant.
AL Stratford Mountain House, Pembroke Rd, Stratford, East Egmont T06-765 6100/T0800-668682, www.mountainhouse.co.nz. Popular hotel close to the slopes with an award-winning restaurant serving Euro-style cuisine.
AL Anderson's Alpine Lodge, 922 Pembroke Rd, East Egmont, T06-765 6620. Swiss-style chalet with 3 guestrooms.
C-D The Camphouse, North Egmont VIC, T06-756 0990, nevc@doc.govt.nz. Basic bunk-style accommodation, with cooking facilities and hot showers near the centre.
C-D Konini Lodge, Upper Manaia Rd, Kaponga, Dawson Falls, T027-4430248. A poor relation of the above, but comfortable nonetheless. DoC owned.
C-D Missing Leg Backpackers, 1082 Junction Rd, Egmont Village, North Egmont, T06-752 2570, missingleg@xtra.co.nz. Very friendly and relaxed backpacker hostel with doubles and dorms, log fire, bike hire and shuttle service up the mountain. The 'missing leg' refers to

'journey' as opposed to shark attacks or poor travel planning. Recommended.

▲ Activities and tours

Mount Egmont National Park *p319*
Mountain guides
If you want some experienced company and some great information en route then the 3 main operators below offer guided summit treks and other walks. All will see you safely up and down the mountain from around $170-300 per day. Other activities include climbing, abseiling and low-level hikes. **Adventure Dynamics**, T06-751 3589, www.adventuredynamics.co.nz. **MacAlpine Guides**, T025-417042, www.macalpine guides.co.nz. **Top Guides**, T0800-448433, www.topguides.co.nz.

Skiing
The only ski field on Taranaki is **Manganui** on the Stratford Plateau, 20 km from Stratford and 3 km past the **Mountain Lodge**, Pembroke Rd, East Egmont, T06-765 6100, from where you can hire skis. For information contact the **Stratford Mountain Club**, T027-280 0860; or call the ski field direct, T06-765 5493, www.snow.co.nz.

● *For an explanation of the Sleeping and Eating price codes used in this guide, see the inside*
● *front cover. Other relevant information is provided in the Essentials chapter, pages 44-51.*
Note that prices are tive in New Zealand dollars.

Hawera and around → Colour map 3, A2

Hawera, an interesting little town with many architecturally significant buildings, is the largest of the southern Taranaki townships and is on the coast at the confluence of SH45 and SH3. It's a good place to stop for a break and take in a few sights and attractions. From here it is about 70 km to complete the circuit around the mountain, north to New Plymouth. ▶▶ *For Sleeping, Eating and other listings, see page 322.*

Ins and outs

Hawera VIC (I-Site) ① *55 High St (just head for the water tower), T06-278 8599, visitorinfo@stdc.govt.nz, Mon-Fri 0830-1700, Sat-Sun summer 1000-1500*, also acts as travel and accommodation booking agent.

Sights

The most obvious 'sight' is the **water tower** ① *open to climb daily 1000-1400, $2, child $1,* built in 1914. Apparently, it was built at the request of insurance underwriters who were getting somewhat dismayed at the town's amazing propensity to burn down, which it did to varying degrees in 1884, 1895 and 1912. The VIC has a *Historic Hawera* heritage trail leaflet that details the major buildings. Strangely enough there is not an old fire station.

The **Tawhiti Museum** ① *401 Ohangai Rd, T06-278 6831, Fri-Mon 1000-1600, open daily in Jan, Sun only Jun-Aug, $10, child $2,* is an amazing little museum that uses realistic life-size exhibits and scale models to capture Taranaki's past. It is a private museum with an interesting history of its own. Its founders Nigel and Teresa Ogle make the models and figures on site. There is also a narrow gauge railway.

Equally unusual is the **Elvis Presley Memorial Room** ① *51 Argyle St, phone for appointment, T06-278 7624, www.digitalus.co.nz/elvis, donation*, where avid collector and fan Kevin Wasley has amassed memorabilia and 2000 of 'The King's' records.

SH3 from Hawera to New Plymouth ⊞🛈▲ ▶▶ *p322.*

Eltham

Eltham is well known for its dairy products, especially its production of cheese, but for the tourist the main attraction is its surrounding lakes. **Lake Rotokare** (Rippling Lake), 11 km southeast on Sangster Road, is in a pretty setting with a one-hour walk and picnic sites. Further afield, **Lake Rotorangi** on Glen Nui Road (via Rawhitiroa Road) is 40 km in length and was formed by the damming of the Patea River. It is popular for watersports and fishing. For information regarding other local attractions and accommodation, contact **Eltham Library** ① *High St, T06-764 8838, Mon-Fri 0930-1730.*

Stratford

A glance at the street names in Stratford will soon confirm your suspicion that this rural service centre and eastern gateway to the Egmont National Park was named after Shakespeare's birthplace in England. But there the similarity really ends. Stratford, New Zealand, is a pleasant little town but there is little to detain you beyond a meal, a coffee and perhaps a look at the **glockenspiel** (playing clock) on the clock tower in the centre of town. The five-minute performance of life-sized figures depicts a few lines and music from the story of Romeo and Juliet and takes place at 1000, 1300 and 1500. Other than that the main attraction in town is the **Taranaki Pioneer Village** ① *SH3, T06-765 5399, daily 1000-1600, $10, child $5.* It consists of 50 re-sited buildings on 4 ha, all faithfully equipped to depict the Taranaki of the early 1900s. The on-site café is deservedly popular and keeps the same opening hours.

For more information on accommodation and local attractions, contact **Stratford VIC (I-Site)** ⓘ *Broadway, T06-765 6708, www.stratfordnz.co.nz, Mon-Fri 0830-1700, Sat-Sun 1000-1400.* It also acts as a travel agent. There is a café and the **Percy Thomson Gallery** ⓘ *T06-756 0917, www.percythomsongallery.co.nz, Mon-Fri 1000-1600, Sat-Sun 1030-1500,* next door that is worth a muse to see how the great mountain inspires local artists.

If you have kids, **Inglewood**, 13 km south of New Plymouth, has the **Fun Ho! National Toy Museum** ⓘ *25 Rata St, T06-7567030, www.funho.com, Mon-Fri 0900-1700, Sat-Sun 1000-1600, $6, child $3.* It is small but may keep them occupied for a few milliseconds. To recover, head for the popular **MacFarlanes Caffe** ⓘ *corner of Kelly and Matai sts, T06-756 6665.*

● Sleeping

Hawera *p321*
L Kingfisher Cottage, 483 Skeet Rd (north, between Hawera and Eltham) T06-272 6630, www.kingfishercottage.co.nz. New, well-appointed self-contained cottage with great views and good fishing nearby.
A-B Kerry Lane Villas Motel, 2 Kerry Lane, T06-278 1918, www.kerrylanemotel.co.nz. A good modern option in a quiet rural setting 5 mins from town.
C-D Wheatly Downs Farmstay Backpackers, Ararata Rd, T06-278 6523, www.taranaki-bakpak.co.nz. Well-equipped and entertaining farmstay backpacker lodge, 2 km from town.

Motorcamps and campsites
B-D King Edward Park Motorcamp, 70 Waihi Rd, T06-278 8544. 1 km from the town centre, camp kitchen. Next door to a heated public swimming pool (from $2.50).

Stratford *p321*
Motorcamps and campsites
B-D Stratford Holiday Park, 10 Page St, T06-765 6440, stratfordholpark@hotmail.com. The closest motorcamp to the mountain.

● Eating

Hawera *p321*
The Tawhiti Museum also has café attached (see page 321).
♥ Anderson's Pies, 142 Princess St. Simple but good value.
♥ The Fuse Factory, 47 High St, T06-278 4444. A safe bet.
♥ Morrieson's Café and Bar, 58 Victoria St, T06-278 5647.

Stratford *p321*
♥♥ Urban Attitude Café and Wine Bar, Broadway, T06-765 6534. Considered one of the best eateries.

▲ Activities and tours

Hawera *p321*
Dam-dropping
This is another of those 'Kiwi unique' adrenaline offerings. This time you throw yourself down a dam outlet with only a boogie-board and some other lunatics for company. There are 2 river runs available: the 1½-hr trip involves dam-dropping only, while the extended full-river run takes in 9 rapids, from $100. Minimum age is 8 years.
Kaitiaki Adventures, based in Hawera, T0800-336376, www.damdrop.com.

East coast

⚡ Footprint features

Introduction

The east coast of the North Island is all about sun, wine and remote coastal scenery. The East Cape (the 'heel' of the 'upside-down boot') is where you can witness the day's first warming rays and a little further south, the coastal town of Gisborne prides itself on being the first place Captain Cook set foot in New Zealand in 1769.

Inland from Wairoa (south of Gisborne) and the enchanting Mahia Peninsula, are the dense forests of the Te Urewera National Park, a place of almost spiritual beauty and particularly famous for its 'Great Walk', which circumnavigates its most scenic jewel, Lake Waikaremoana. Back on the coast you enter the wine country of northern Hawke's Bay and the pretty coastal town of Napier, almost completely flattened by an earthquake in 1931 and now reborn as an international showpiece for its art deco buildings.

Further south, on the bleached cliffs that caress Hawke's Bay, is the largest gannet colony in the country, at Cape Kidnappers. Continuing southwards is one of the most stunningly beautiful and remote parts of the North Island, the Wairarapa, where, from Castlepoint to the lighthouse at Cape Palliser – the southernmost tip of the island – the peace and isolation is unsurpassed anywhere in the North Island.

★ **Don't miss ...**

1 **Motu River** Raft into the wilderness of and lose contact with civilization for days, page 328.

2 **East Cape Lighthouse** Be one of the first in the world to see the day's sunrise, page 329.

3 **Mount Hikurangi** Climb to the top and see for miles, page 329.

4 **Napier** Admire the art-deco architecture and re-visit the day of New Zealand's worst earthquake in the Hawke's Bay Museum, page 341.

5 **Cape Kidnappers** Meet the gannet colony and visit some of Hawke's Bay's premier vineyards, pages 344 and 345.

6 **Castlepoint** Appreciate the wild scenery of the Wairarapa's remote coastline, page 357.

7 **Waiohine Gorge** Cross the swing bridge, near Carterton, page 358.

8 **Cape Palliser Lighthouse** Explore the coast road to the southernmost tip of the North Island and walk into the 'chancel' of the Putangirua Pinnacles, page 359.

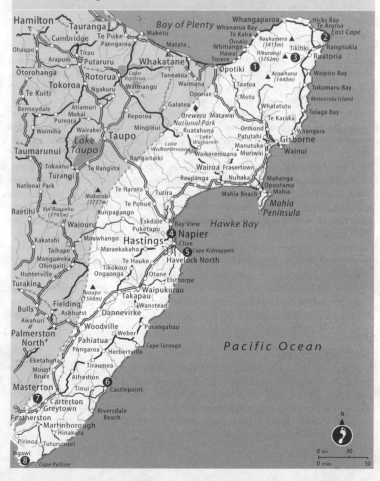

East coast Introduction

East Cape to Wairoa → *Colour map 2, B4*

Those with a healthy imagination and good sense of geography will recognize East Cape as the 'heel' of the 'upside-down boot' that is New Zealand. Along with the Wairarapa, East Cape is the least-visited area in the North Island. This is due not so much to its isolated location but its geography. Almost the entire peninsula is sparsely populated, remote and mountainous. Indeed, much of the Raukumara Range, which makes up most of its interior, remains impenetrable by road, with only wild rivers like the Motu and Mata carving their way through the wilderness. ➤➤ *For Sleeping, Eating and other listings, see pages 335-337.*

Ins and outs

Getting there
Air Gisborne airport ① *2 km west of town centre*, is served by **Air New Zealand Link**, T132476, several times daily from Wellington and Auckland. Local operator **Sunair**, T07-575 7799, www.sunair.co.nz, also offers flights from the main centres, including Hamilton, Rotorua and Tauranga. **Sun City Taxis** operates an airport shuttle, T06-867 6767, $12.

Road Gisborne is linked with all major points south to Wellington (550 km), and north to Opotiki (147 km) and Auckland (504 km) by SH2. Gisborne is a major stop on the well-signposted 'Pacific Coast Highway' which includes SH35. This 330-km trip terminates at Opotiki, where SH35 rejoins SH2.
  Both Opotiki and Gisborne are served by **Intercity** buses, T06-868 6139. Beyond those places getting around the East Cape by public transport is possible, but unpredictable. Your best bet is with **Polly's Passenger and Courier Services**, T06-864 4728, T07-315 6350, which operates a return service from Hick's Bay (at the top of the Cape) to Whakatane (via Opotiki) Monday to Friday, and a similar service from Hick's Bay to Gisborne Monday to Saturday; from $80 one way. The bus departs Whakatane VIC (I-Site) at 1230, Opotiki VIC (I-Site) for the cape at 1430, and Gisborne VIC (I-Site) at 1300. **Cook's Couriers**, T06-864 4711, T027-437 1364, cook.teararoa@xtra.co.nz, also offers a Monday to Saturday service from Gisborne to Hick's Bay and back, departing Gisborne VIC (I-Site) Monday to Friday 1400 and Saturday 1230, from $40 one way. Couriers to take you from Hick's Bay to Opotiki and Whakatane can also be arranged. Always check with the VIC (I-Site) for any changes to schedule and price. **Kiwi Trails**, T07-343 7922, www.kiwitrails.co.nz, is a culture/eco-oriented regional operator offering another transportation option with a wide range of all inclusive theme tours around the cape. National operator **Kiwi Experience**, T09-366 9830, www.kiwiexperience.com, offers backpacker-oriented four-day trips from Rotorua and Taupo departing Monday, Wednesday and Friday.

Getting around
The best way to explore the Cape is undoubtedly to drive the 334 km of SH35 from either Opotiki to Gisborne or vice versa. Although the trip can be done comfortably in two days, taking longer will allow you to soak up the laid-back atmosphere and explore the numerous bays and beaches as you go, or attempting to climb Hikurangi, the North Island's fourth highest peak. From this legendary summit, on a clear day, the entire East Cape is laid out before you.

⁞ Rise and shine

East Cape has earned the label of North Island's 'last wilderness'. People come here to get away from it all and shift down a few gears. But it is not only the remoteness that attracts visitors. They also come for the sun.

Not in the sense of soaking up the rays but to experience the joy and strange sense of pride at being the first souls on earth to witness the day's sunrise – according to human time and provided it is not cloudy, that is.

Tourist information

Gisborne VIC (I-Site) ① *209 Grey St, T06-8686139, www.gisbornenz.com, Mon-Fri 0830-1730, Sat-Sun 0900-1730*, and **Opotiki VIC (I-Site)** ① *corner St John and Elliott sts, T07-315 3031, opotiki@i-site.org, daily 0800-1700*, can both provide information for the East Cape. The latter (see page 269) has two excellent free handbooks, the *Opotiki and East Cape Holiday Guide* and the *Eastland Visitor Guide*, both essential pieces of kit for the trip. **Gisborne DoC** ① *63 Carnarvon St, T06-869 0492*, and **Wairoa VIC (I-Site)** ① *corner of SH2 and Queen St, T06-838 7440, www.wairoanz.com, Nov-Mar daily 0900-1700, Apr-Oct Mon-Fri 0900-1700*, acts as bus booking agents, can help organize transport to Waikaremoana and has internet.

East Cape

Opotiki to East Cape Lighthouse ☻ ▸▸ *pp335-337.*

→ *Colour map 2, B4/5*

The cape road, SH35, begins at Opotiki (see page 270) and you will soon begin to feel that you are entering another world. Change your watch to 'Coast Time', which really means taking the batteries out. Maori influences are also apparent in the first small settlement of **Torore** (24 km) and the beautiful carvings which adorn the gates to its school.

With the coast now your guide and the steaming volcanic White Island offshore as companion you continue past **Hawai** and make your way around the mouth of the **Motu River** (49 km). Here, when there has been little rain, the expansive boulder fields of the Motu riverbed can make it look like an insignificant trickle. But don't be deceived, at times this river can be a raging torrent spewing forth from its mountain wilderness and leaving huge piles of driftwood as evidence of its fury. On this part of the coast, there often seems to be more tangled wood on the beach than there is rock and sand. **Omaio**, the next settlement, has one such beach and is renowned for its good fishing. Just around the corner from the Motu River mouth keep your eyes open for the **Whitianga Marae** at Whitianga Bay (51 km), which is beautifully carved.

After Omaio is **Te Kaha** (70 km) with its shallow rocky coast and popular beaches. Te Kaha is pleasant and offers the first really credible place to stop for supplies or accommodation. **Whanarua Bay** (88 km), a mere 20 minutes north of Te Kaha, also offers real serenity and is another fine spot to spend your first night on the cape. As the road climbs into the tiny village take the track on the left (easily missed) that falls abruptly to the beach. This small secluded bay is stunning. Whanarua has a fine backpacker hostel and a basic camping ground about 1 km past the village.

Just before Waihau Bay, the next settlement, **Cape Runaway** and the northern sweep of the East Cape come into view, where you'll find the idyllic **Raukokore Anglican Church** (99 km) standing by the beach. **Waihau Bay** (107 km) itself offers accommodation, fuel and a well-stocked general store. From **Whangaparaoa** (118 km), where the road temporarily leaves the coast and ducks below Lottin Point, it is possible to walk to Cape Runaway, but bear in mind that this is Maori land and permission must first be sought. Contact June MacDonald at **Cape Runaway Maori Historic Walks**, Waihau Bay, T07-325 3697. **Lottin Point** (140 km), which essentially makes up the northern edge of the East Cape, is named afer an officer who sailed with French explorer Jules Sebastian Cesar Dumont d'Urville in 1827 (presumably the latter's name was too long for people to remember). Lottin Point has one of the most remote motels in the country, at the very end of Lottin Point Road, offering sanctuary and, reputedly, some fine rock fishing.

From Lottin Point the road meets the coast again at **Hick's Bay** (151 km), this time named for one of Captain Cook's sidekicks. Hick's Bay has a wild surf beach and an old wharf at its northern end. There is also a small store and a petrol stop. Around the corner from Hick's Bay is **Horseshoe Bay**, which is also impressive.

Before reaching East Cape and the lighthouse you pass through the tiny settlement of **Te Araroa** (160 km) before negotiating about 21 km of unsealed road. There are two particular points of interest in and around Te Araroa. The first is the **pohutukawa tree** which dwarfs the school grounds (it is believed to be one of the largest in the country and over 600 years old). The second is the **Manuka Oil Distillery** ① *between Te Araroa and Hick's Bay, about 4 km from the Gisborne junction, T06-864 4824, www.manuka-oil.com, Mon-Fri 0900-1630.* There is a factory shop at the distillery selling the delicious Manuka honey.

● *Te Kaha holds a sinister claim to fame as the site of New Zealand's last fatal shark attack in*
● *1976 when a local diver was attacked and killed by a bronze whaler.*

⁞ Climbing Mount Hikurangi

Hikurangi is an attractive mountain but does not look the 1,752 m that makes it the fourth highest (and highest non-volcanic mountain) in the North Island. The name Hikurangi means 'Sky Peak' and refers to the well-loved peak in Hawaiki, the ancient ancestral home of the Maori. It is relatively accessible and a delightful climb. The summit return will take at least nine hours (13 km) so give yourself plenty of time. If you follow the Tapuwaeroa River Road almost to the end you will see an iron bridge that crosses the boulder fields of the Tapuwaeroa River to several farm buildings on the hill. At the far side of the bridge a sign will remind you that you are on Maori (private) land, but once you park your car down the side road towards the river, you can still use the track that heads up and past the houses, over the hill and beyond, towards the summit. Once you reach the top of this first hill you will clearly see the climb that lies before you. Follow your nose and the stiles up a well-formed sheep station track that goes almost two thirds of the way to the summit. It terminates at Hikurangi's 'well-kept secret' – the Millennium Maori Pou (carvings). These are beautifully crafted pieces that are full of spiritual meaning and stand in a circle to greet the sunrise. From here head upwards and locate the white bunkhouse. From behind the bunkhouse things start to get difficult. Climb up the scree slope to the rock outcrops and the path that leads you through a tract of mountain bush. Keep your eyes open for Tom Tit – a native black and white bird that looks like a robin and is particularly fearless. Beyond the bush it is a hard slog to the summit – of which there are many – with the main summit reached after several almost equally high 'false summits'. On a clear day the view is spectacular. To the north the empty bush-cloaked peaks of the Raukumara Ranges dominate and offshore to the north, White Island's active crater can be seen steaming away.

For more information on the mountain, hut accommodation ($5) and guided tours ($70) contact the local Iwi (tribe), Ngati Porou, T06-8679960, www.ngatiporou.iwi.nz. You must inform Ngati Porou that you intend to climb the mountain and seek official permission. If you join a tour it will save a lot of climbing and if the weather turns nasty it is added security.

If you want to see the sunrise at East Cape, Hick's Bay and Te Araroa are your best (and only) options for accommodation. The coast road to the lighthouse and the most easterly point of New Zealand is beautiful, with numerous rock platforms, small rivers, pohutukawa trees and a long and empty stretch of beach worthy of investigation. The **Coastal Arts Gallery** ① T06-864 4890, daily, is also worth a peek.

The **lighthouse**, which only comes into view at the last minute, sits proudly on a hilltop all of its own. It can be easily accessed through a gate and via a set of seemingly never-ending steps, beyond a small group of derelict buildings.

East Cape to Gisborne ⊜▲ ›› pp335-337.

→ Colour map 2, B/C6

The eastern side of the cape is more populous than the west and for much of the time the road winds its way through countryside between coastal settlements. If you wish to access the coast this is best done at these settlements, or with short diversions using a detailed map. From Te Araroa you head south and gain the first sight of Mount Hikurangi before arriving in **Tiki Tiki**. Here, the Anglican church with some fine Maori designs is worth a visit. It was built in 1924 as a memorial to local Iwi tribesman (Ngati Porou) who died in the First World War.

Just before the Mata River crossing is the turning to **Mount Hikurangi** (see box, page 329). Even if you do not intend to climb the mountain it is worth the short diversion to enjoy the river and mountain views. The road, which flirts with the Tapuwaeroa River, is a bit of an obstacle course as you dodge stray pigs, chickens, horses, sheep and cattle. Back on SH35 it is only a short distance to **Ruatoria**, the main administrative base of the predominant East Cape Iwi, the *Te Runanga O Ngati Porou*. It has a food store and petrol station where you can have a light-hearted chat with the locals.

Turning your back on the mighty Hikurangi, the next stop is **Te Puia Springs** ① *T06-864 6755, open to non-residents but hours are seasonal*, whose eponymous hot thermal pools are behind the hotel. The village also has a store and a petrol station. A short diversion from Te Puia is scenic **Waipiro Bay** with its three *marae*. The beachside holiday resort of **Tokomaru Bay** is next, where you can find accommodation and food. Between Tokomaru and Tolaga Bay is **Anaura Bay**, a 7-km diversion from SH35, where there's a very pleasant, relatively easy two-hour coastal walk.

Tolaga Bay is the largest coastal town and resort on the east coast. Worth a visit is the 660-m-long wharf (reputed to be the longest in the southern hemisphere) which can be accessed down Wharf Road to the south of the town. Also here is **Cook's Cove** where the intrepid explorer stopped to make repairs and gather supplies; the ship's naturalists Banks and Solander were particularly interested in the coastal scenery and unusual rock formations which can now be seen on a three-hour walkway.

For decades the sleepy little settlement and beach at **Whangara**, 29 km north of Gisborne (then 5 km east), was seldom visited by tourists. All this has changed due to the success of the film *Whale Rider*, in which the location (particularly the beach), was extensively featured. There is no disputing its beauty or spirituality, but local Iwi are now worried is that its popularity may well prove to be its demise.

From Tolaga Bay the road leaves the coast for a while before reuniting at Tatapouri and Makorori, both well known as fine surfing spots. **Wainui** is essentially a beachside suburb of Gisborne with all the attendant amenities. From Wainui you have just about reached your East Cape journey's end (or beginning) and Gisborne.

Gisborne ⊖❼◑❀▲⊟◑ ≫ *pp335-337.*

➜ *Colour map 2, C5 Population: 31,000*
The busy agricultural service town, port and coastal resort of Gisborne attracts many visitors in search of the sun, eager to jump on a surfboard or explore the East Cape. Being the most easterly city in the country, Gisborne prides itself on being the first city in the world to see the sunrise. It is also the first place that Captain Cook set foot in New Zealand. On top of that, it boasts an almost subtropical climate with long hours of sunshine and rich fertile plains. You'd be forgiven for expecting the place to be brimming with pride and vitality, yet somehow Gisborne seems a little tired.

Background
The first Maori to settle were thought to be from the Horouta and Te Ikaroa-a-Rauru *waka* (canoes) that landed at the base of the Kaiti Hill in 1350. When Captain Cook made the first European landing at the same site in 1769 he was met by a threatening

● *On the fine surf beach at Wainui there is an interesting 'Sperm Whale Grave' that was the*
● *inevitable result of a mass stranding of 59 sperm whales in 1970.*

⁝ Culture clash – Cook's first landing

On 8 October 1769 a group of Maori living on a *pa* just to the east of the Turanganui River, looked out to sea and saw an enormous bird on the horizon. It was in fact Cook's ship, *The Endeavour*. The Maori dispatched a party of warriors to investigate, while Cook and his men were rowing merrily ashore in search of supplies and eager to make contact with any 'savages'. Cook disembarked and the first ever footprint of a shoe was made on New Zealand sand. He and his men took some gifts to the local *whare* (meeting house) while others guarded the longboats. As they chatted on the shore the warriors emerged and performed a *haka* (posture dance). Utterly terrified and taking this to be a sign of imminent attack, the *Pakeha* (white Europeans) fired warning shots, one of which felled a Maori warrior. Both warriors and Cook hastily retreated. That night the Maori kept a close watch on the great big bird in both fear and amazement. Next morning Cook tried a second landing. A party of warriors once again met the landing party and performed a *haka* (a traditional Maori war dance). This time, accepting the fearful dance as a bizarre 'welcome',

Cook kept his muskets at bay. For a time, warriors and *Pakeha* mixed uneasily and gifts and words were exchanged. But when a gleaming metal sword was snatched from one of Cook's party a shot was fired and another Maori was fatally wounded. Once again Maori retreated to their *pa* and Cook to his ship. Next day it was the Maori who approached Cook in their *waka*, but yet more deaths occurred when the approaching party failed to understand the ships signal volley. The Maori persisted and some were taken on board, fed, given gifts and returned to shore the following morning. After another brief sortie on shore by ship's naturalists Banks and Solander, Cook weighed anchor and the 'great big bird' took flight. On 11 October, Cook named the place 'Poverty Bay' because: 'It had afforded us not one thing we wanted'.

In the words of a respected modern day Maori "One wonders what Captain Cook expected – surely not a group of Maori uttering the words 'Oh look it's Captain Cook, at last, we've been expecting you'!" In 1995 the replica of *The Endeavour* retraced its steps around the coast of New Zealand, but its presence in Poverty Bay created uproar.

group of Maori. Cook promptly scarpered, leaving only the name 'Poverty Bay' behind. Although the area was home to a whaling station, European settlement did not occur in earnest until the 1840s with the establishment of several Christian missions. Captain G E Read, who settled in 1852, was a pivotal figure in the town's development. After a period blighted by threats and attacks by Maori, eventually things settled down in the 1860s when steady growth and development continued.

Sights

After the VIC (see page 327) your first stop should be **Cook's Landing Site and National Historic Reserve** next to the main port and the base of Titirangi (Kaiti Hill). To get there, cross to the east bank of the river, which flows through the centre of the town. The reserve marks the spot where Cook first set foot, on 9 October 1769, to a hostile response from local Maori. Above the reserve the **Titirangi Domain** or **Kaiti Hill** provides great views across the city and the second of three Cook memorial edifices. At the summit of the hill is the **Cook Observatory**ⓘ *T06-867 7901, Tue only at 1930*, which has seen better nights.

East coast East Cape to Wairoa

N

0 metres 200
0 yards 200

Sleeping 🛏
Al Fresco Motor
 Lodge **12**
Beachcomber **1**
Cedar House B&B **4**
Colonial **21**

Flying Nun
 Backpackers **6**
Gisborne YHA **7**
One Orange **3**
Portside **2**
Senator Motor Inn **13**

Tatapouri Camp
 Ground **19**
Teal Motor Lodge **5**
Waikanae Beach
 Holiday Park **11**
White Heron **9**

Eating 🍴
Café Ruba **1**
Fettucine Brothers **2**
Gordon Gecko **8**
Irish Rover **3**
Three Rivers Marina **4**

Verve Café 5
Wharf Café 6
Works 7

Set in trees at the foot of the hill to the east is the **Te Poho-O-Rawiri marae** ① T06-868 5364, which was built in 1930 and is one of the largest carved meeting houses in the country. Nearby is the **Toko Toru Tapu Church** ① T06- 867 2103.

Before re-crossing the river it is worth taking a look at the Inner Harbour Area. The Works on the Esplanade is home to the well-known **Gisborne Wine Company** ① T06-863 1285, 1000-1800, who have been producing a fine range for 35 years. There are tastings, an outlet and also a good restaurant within the renovated 1906 warehouse. Opposite the nearby **Wharf Café** is a wall colourfully adorned with children's self-portraits.

Head to the beachside reserve on the southern bank of the river to see another **Cook memorial**. A little further along is a statue of Cook's cabin boy, Young Nick, who is credited as being the first to sight land. He was rewarded by having the promontory, **Young Nick's Head** (which forms the southern edge of Poverty Bay), named in his honour. He also apparently won himself a bottle of rum, the customary reward for the first able seaman to see land. These statues are of particular interest simply because of their location with the backdrop of the port and huge steel-hulled cargo ships, which prove we have come a long way since the tall ships and crow's nests.

To learn more about Young Nick and the region's history head for the small but effective **Gisborne Museum (Tairawhiti)** ① Stout St, T06-867 3832, www.tairawhiti museum.org.nz, Mon-Fri 1000-1600 Sat 1100-1600, Sun 1330-1600, donation. It houses all the usual stuff with a particular bent towards the fascinating Maori history and, of course, that man Cook. There are also ever-changing exhibitions of national and international contemporary art. Attached to the museum (quite literally) is the wheel-house of *HMS Canada*, which foundered at the base of Kaiti Beach in 1912. It forms part of the maritime section of the museum.

East coast East Cape to Wairoa

There is one other, less remarkable museum in the city, of particular interest to transport and technology buffs, the **East Coast Museum of Technology** ① *Main Rd, Makaraka, To6-868 8254, daily 1000-1600, $5, child $1.*

There are an ever increasing number of **vineyards** around the region producing the notable vintages. Names to look out for include **Kirkpatrick Estate (KEW)** ① *Wharekopae Rd, To6-862 7722, www.kew.co.nz;* **TW Chardonnay** ① *Back Ormond Rd, To27-450 2339, www.twwines.co.nz;* **Lindaur** ① *Solander St, To6-868 2757, www.montanawines.co.nz;* **Waiohika** ① *75 Waimata Valley, To6-867 4670, www.waiohika.co.nz,* and the organic **Wrights Wines** ① *202 Wainui Rd, To6-868 0967, www.wrightswines.co.nz.* Most offer tastings. Contact the VIC (I-Site) for details or visit www.gisbornewine.co.nz.

If wine is not your tipple fear not, as usual, boutique **breweries** are also in evidence and fill the niche admirably. Try the lauded Gisborne Gold at the **Sunshine Brewing Company** ① *109 Disraeli St, To6-867 7777.*

South to Wairoa ●❼ ▸ *pp335-337.*

→ *Colour map 3, A6*
From Gisborne, SH2 climbs the **Wharereta Hills** offering great views back across Poverty Bay. On the southern slopes are the **Morere Hot Springs** ① *60 km south of Gisborne, To6-837 8856, daily summer 1000-2100, winter 1000-1700, $6, child $3,* where public and private thermal pools are set among a pleasant bush setting, with a number of good short walks. There is accommodation and a café across the road.

At the tiny junction settlement of **Nuhaka**, 8 km south of the springs, a scenic coastal road leaves SH2 towards the **Mahia Peninsula**. The Mahia is a barren, windswept peninsula, 21 km long and about 12 km wide, which marks the coastal boundary between the Pacific and Hawke's Bay. The Mahia used to be an island and is now joined to the mainland by a sandspit, or tombolo. Almost totally devoid of trees, infested by sheep and deeply rutted by eroded green valleys, the peninsula has a strange appeal. One of the great Maori migration *waka* (canoes), the *Takitimu*, made landfall here in the 14th century, after circumnavigating the northern and eastern coasts from its first landfall at Awanui near Ninety Mile Beach. Some of its crew never left and the peninsula was also home to one of the North Island's biggest whaling stations.

Today, at the neck of the peninsula, is the small holiday village of **Mahia Beach** which forms a link between two beaches: **Mahanga Beach**, lying to the east, is exposed to the elements of the open ocean and a popular surf spot; **Opoutama Beach**, on the Hawke's Bay side (west), is much more sheltered and therefore better for swimming. On the eastern edge of the peninsula are the settlements of **Oraka** and **Mahia**, connected by a rows of holiday baches which hug the shore like a string of pearls. In summer the peninsula is a very popular spot for surfing, windsurfing, swimming and fishing, but year-round it enjoys the erstwhile island atmosphere, which makes it an idyllic spot in which to get away from it all. You will need your own transport. From Mahia it is a 44-km drive to Wairoa past farmland and coastal lagoons renowned for their birdlife.

Wairoa → *Colour map 3, A5 Population: 5200*
Wairoa is the eastern gateway to the Te Urewera National Park and sits on the coast at the junction of SH2 and SH36, roughly halfway between Gisborne (98 km) and Napier (118 km). Strategically built on the banks of the Wairoa River, it was once a thriving port. These days, however, it has little to hold the visitor except perhaps a brief peek at the relocated and reconstructed 1877 **lighthouse** which once shone on the Mahia Peninsula. The town has a number of shops in which to stock up, and small takeaways to grab a snack before heading north, south or inland to **Waikaremoana** via SH36. There is limited accommodation available in town; the VIC (I-Site) has details.

⊖ Sleeping

Opotiki to East Cape Lighthouse p328

Torere, Te Kaha and Whanarua Bay

A Tui Lodge B&B, Copenhagen Rd, T07-325 2922. Spacious modern home with tidy twins and doubles, shared facilities. Excellent cuisine.

A Waiwaka B&B, 2 km north of Te Kaha and 12 km from Whanarua Bay, T07-325 2070, www.waikawa.net. 2 attractive self-contained options in a beautiful peaceful spot.

A-B Te Kaha Hotel and Motel, T07-325 2830, www.tekahahotel@xtra.co.nz. Rooms and 4 modern beachfront units overlooking a sheltered beach. Bar/restaurant serves lunch/ dinner, recommended for local seafood.

B-D Te Kaha Holiday Park, T07-325 2894. Recently upgraded with modern amenities and popular backpacker accommodation.

D Maraehako Camp Ground, 1 km past the holiday park, T07 3252047. Beachfront.

Waihau Bay and Lottin Point

AL Waihau Bay B&B, T07-325 3674, n.topia@clear.net.nz. 2 self-contained units and a double overlooking the beach. Free use of bikes and kayaks.

A Lottin Point Motel, T06-864 4455. Given its remote ocean-side location, a great sense of escape is assured. A licensed restaurant complements simple self-contained units. Activities including in-house fishing charters to some of the cape's best spots are available.

A Oceanside Apartments, far end of Oruaiti Beach, 3 km northeast of Waihau, T07-325 3699, www.waihaubay.co.nz. Excellent apartments or B&B rooms, fishing charters.

B-D Waihau Bay Holiday Park, T07-325 3844. Opposite the beach. Full range of options, camp kitchen, store and a café.

B-D Waihau Bay Lodge (Hotel), T07-325 3804. Comfortable rooms with shared facilities, licensed bar and restaurant. Backpacker beds and campsite available.

Hick's Bay and Te Araroa

B-D Hick's Bay Motel Lodge, up the hill past the village, T06-864 4880. Licensed restaurant.

B-D Te Araroa Holiday Park, at the end of the bay, west of the village, T06-864 4873. Modern facilities, store and off-licence.

C-D Mel's Place, Onepoto Beach Rd, T06-864 4694, eastcapefishing@xtra.co.nz. Cosy and friendly, next to bay. Popular with surfers.

C-D Saddle and Stay Backpackers Homestay, 4 km inland from Hicks Bay, Onepoto Beach Rd, T06-864 4634. A small, well-facilitated country backpacker hostel with doubles, singles, shared rooms and tent sites. Horse trekking and lighthouse trips.

East Cape to Gisborne p329

B Tolaga Bay Motel, corner of Cook and Monkhouse sts, Tolagoa Bay, T06 862 6888. Basic but adequate.

B-D Te Puia Springs Hotel, T06-8646755. Basic but saved by the hot thermal pools.

B-D Tolaga Bay Motor Camp, 167 Wharf Rd, Tolaga Bay, T06-862 6716. A bit tired and basic but the only one for miles.

C-D Brian's Place, Potae St, Tokomaru bay, T06-864 5870. Intimate and relaxed back-packers with friendly host. Loft rooms, fresh crayfish and horse trekking an added bonus.

C-D Waikawa Lodge, Waikawa Rd, Waipiro Bay, T06-864 6719, www.waikawalodge.co.nz. A remote and charming backpacker lodge, quite small but modern and offers a perfect getaway. Also home to **Waikawa Horse Adventures**.

Gisborne p330, map p332

Gisborne is a popular summer resort so book ahead in the high season. The VIC has full listings of B&Bs and holiday rentals, the best of which are to be found at Wainui Beach. Most of the motels are on Gladstone Av, which is the main drag (SH35), and Salisbury Rd, which is centrally located near the beach.

LL Cedar House B&B, 4 Clifford St, T06-868 1902, www.cedarhouse.co.nz. Centrally located Edwardian-style boutique B&B with 4 spacious rooms, with en suite or private bathrooms. Dinner on request.

LL-AL Portside Hotel, 2 Reads Quay, T0800-767874, www.portsidegisborne.co.nz. Gisborne's newest hotel set in centrally located waterfront position. Studio rooms and suites, broadband, pool and gym.

AL One Orange, Wainui Beach, 8 km east of Gisborne, T06-868 8062, www.oneorange .co.nz. This contemporary self-contained 'designer apartment' makes a refreshing change to the ageing hotels so prevalent in Gisborne. Accommodation comprises a studio apartment and king-size bedroom;

both are fresh, modern and minimalist and offer plenty of privacy. Set right next to the surf beach in Wainui, it is also perfectly positioned to enjoy the 'first coastline in the world to see' the sunrise. Evening meals are a specialty; breakfast included.

AL Senator Motor Inn, 2 Childers Rd, T06-868 8877, www.senatormotorinn.co.nz. New and harbourside.

AL-A Al Fresco Motor Lodge, 784 Gladstone Av, T06-863 2464, www.alfrescolodge.co.nz.

AL-A Teal Motor Lodge, 479 Gladstone Av, T06-868 4019, www.teal.co.nz.

A Beachcomber, 73 Salisbury Rd, T06-868 9349, www.nzmotels.co.nz/beachcomber.

A Colonial, 715 Gladstone Av, T06-867 9165, www.gisbornecolonial.co.nz.

A White Heron, 474 Gladstone Av, T06-867 1108.

C-D Flying Nun Backpackers, 147 Roebuck Rd, T06-868 0461, yager@xtra.co.nz. Colourful and comically ecclesiastical from the outside, and although perhaps not the best in town, the interior is modern enough and the place certainly has character. Cable TV.

C-D Gisborne YHA, near the inner harbour, 32 Harris St, T06-867 3269, yha.gis@clear.net.nz. Friendly, well-maintained and just a short walk from the town centre. Full range of rooms and all the usual facilities, including tent sites.

Motorcamps and campsites

B-D Waikanae Beach Holiday Park, Grey St, T06-867 5634. This is the best equipped and most centrally located motorcamp in town. Short walk to the beach and the VIC (I-Site).

D Tatapouri Camp Ground, 5 Innes St, T0800-828276. A good camping option 15 mins north of the town, right by the beach.

South to Wairoa p334

Booking ahead is advisable in summer.

AL The Quarters Te Au Farmstay, Te Au Farm, Nuhaka (Mahanga), T06-837 5751, www.quarters.co.nz. Modern isolated farmstay/self-contained cottage overlooking the ocean. Plenty of peace and quiet.

A Cappamore Lodge, 435 Mahia East Coast Rd, T06-837 5523, www.cottagestays.co.nz/cappamore/cottage. This is like Scandinavia by the sea. The log cabin has one double and a twin with full self-catering facilities and a great view across the ocean.

A-D Moonlight Lodge, Morere, T06-837 8824. Tidy self-contained cottage and backpacker lodge conveniently located across the road from the hot springs.

Motorcamps and campsites

B-D Mahia Beach Motel and Holiday Park, 43 Moana Drive, Mahia Beach, T06-837 5830, T0800-383262. The centre of activity on the peninsula, with café and camp store.

⊘ Eating

Gisborne p330, map p332

There are 2 supermarkets: **Woolworths**, corner of Gladstone Rd and Carnarvon St, daily 0700-2200, and **Pak-n-Save**, 274 Gladstone Rd, daily 0800-2000.

▸▸▸ Gordon Gecko Restaurant and Bar, No1 Wharf Shed, on the Esplanade, T06-868 3257, 1100-late. Relatively new and locally very popular offering a varied Pacific-Rim menu.

▸▸▸ The Wharf Café, 60 The Esplanade, The Wharf, T06-868 4876, daily 0900-late. This is not very expensive but still at the high end, very popular, with wide-ranging menu with European, Pacific Rim and Asian combinations.

▸▸ The Fettuccine Brothers Restaurant, 12 Peel St, T06-868 5700, daily 1800-late. Decor and food is Mediterranean. Locally popular.

▸▸ The Three Rivers Marina Restaurant, Vogel St, T06-868 5919. Well-established and popular eatery next to the marina. Fine international cuisine and the rather unique opportunity to sample locally grown Perigord Black Truffles – something of an obsession with the restaurant's 3 chefs. Good wine list.

▸▸ The Works, The Esplanade, Inner Harbour, T06-863 1285, 1130-late, wine-tasting 1000-1500. Home of **Longbush Wines** so no need to recommend the wine list. Good for lunch.

▸ Café Ruba, 14 Childers Rd, T06-868 6516. Chic award winner with fine coffee.

▸ The Irish Rover, Peel St, T06-867 1112. The best pub and pub grub in town.

▸ Verve Café, 121 Gladstone Rd. Value light meals and internet.

South to Wairoa p334

▸ Café Mahia, 476 Mahia East Coast Rd, Mahia Beach, T06-837 5094.

▸ Sunset Point Sports Bar and Bistro, Newcastle St, Mahia Beach, T06-837 5134.

ⓘ Pubs, bars and clubs

Gisborne *p330, map p332*
The Irish Rover, Peel St, T06-867 1112. The town's offering to the mighty leprechaun is especially good during happy hours (1700-1900) and on Fri evening. Regular live bands.
The Meetings, Gladstone Rd, T06-863 3733. The most recent pseudo-Irish offering.
Sandbar, Oneroa Rd, Wainui, T06-868 6186. The hub of nightlife north of the town, frequented by tousled surfies. Live music at weekends and free shuttles to town.

⊛ Festivals

Gisborne *p330, map p332*
Dec Rhythm and Vines, www.rhythmand vines.co.nz. New Year's Eve music festival.

▲ Activities and tours

East Cape to Gisborne *p329*
Horse trekking
Given its relative inaccessibility and grass-roots way of life, let alone its aesthetics, the East Cape lends itself to perambulations on 4 legs not wheels with horse trekking a predominant activity. Treks start from an hour for $40.
Eastender Horse Treks, Rangitukia, Tikitiki, T06-864 3033, www.eastenderhorse treks.co.nz. 2-hr bush and beach rides with memorable views and a cultural edge. Accommodation available.
Hicks Bay Horse Trekking, Hicks Bay, T06-864 4634, joycebennett@paradise.net.nz.
Maungaroa Station Horse, Maungaroa Access Rd, just north of Te Kaha, T07-325 2727, www.maungaroa.co.nz. Bush and beach rides from $40. Group accommodation available.

Rafting
The Motu River offers a memorable multi-day wilderness adventure. For information contact:
Wet'n Wild Rafting Company, T07-348 3191, www.wetnwildrafting.co.nz.

Gisborne *p330, map p332*
Surfing
Wanui Beach is a 2-km stretch open to a variety of swell from the north right around to the south. For the latest surf reports call T06-

868 1066, or listen out for radio 89 FM after 0700 news and ZG90.9 FM after 0800 news.
Chalet Surf Lodge, 62 Moana Rd, Wainui, T06-868 9612, www.chaletsurf.co.nz. Get a taste of the region's fine surf beaches, $35. Lodging and board hire are also available.
Gisborne Surf School, T06-8683484, qissurf@xtra.co.nz. Offers lessons.
Wainui Surf School, T06-863 3912, magoo140@hotmail.com. Also offers lessons.

Tour operators
Ashworth Helicopters, T06-867 7128. Everything from short scenic flights around the bay to heli-fishing.
Dive Tatapouri, T06-868 5153, www.divetata pouri.co.nz. Seal and dolphin encounters in the Te Tapuwae o Rongokaka Marine Reserve. Accommodation available.
New Zealand Safari Adventures, Tangihau Station Enterprise, Rere, T06-867 0872, www.nzsafari.co.nz. An interesting venture offering a range of Station life experiences from basic farm tours and shepherd's muster, to ATV quad bike tours and deer hunting.
Paradise Tours, T06-868 6139. Local winery tours from $35.
Surfit Charters, T06-867 2970, www.surf it.co.nz. A chance to encounter those persecuted denizens of the deep; shark cage encounters $250. Fishing half-day $150.
Whalerider Tours, T06-868 6139. Visit film locations, see the props and learn about local Maori culture with Hone Taumaunu, cultural adviser to the movie *Whale Rider*. From $50.

⊖ Transport

Gisborne *p330, map p332*
Taxi Sun City Taxis, T06-867 6767.
Gisborne Taxis, T06-867 2222, operates a bus service on weekdays.

ⓘ Directory

Gisborne *p330, map p332*
Banks All the major banks have branch offices on Gladstone Rd. **Internet** Available at Treb-Net, Shop 7, Treble Court, 17 Peel St, T06-863 3928. Verve Café, 121 Gladstone Rd. VIC (I-Site), Grey St. **Police** Corner of Childer Rd and Peel St, T06-869 0200. **Post office** Kaiti Mall, Gladstone Rd, T06-867 7100, Mon-Fri 0830-1700, Sat 0900-1200.

Te Urewera National Park

Te Urewera is daunting and mysterious; a place of almost threatening beauty. The national park encompasses the largest area of native bush in the North Island and is the fourth largest national park in the country. The main focus of the park is Lake Waikaremoana, the 'Sea of Rippling Waters', while the track, which circumnavigates it, the Lake Waikaremoana Circuit, is one of the most popular walks in the country. The vast park is home to a wealth of wildlife: some native and welcome including kiwi, kaka and kokako (one of New Zealand's rarest and most endangered birds); others introduced and very unwelcome, such as the omnipresent possum, stoats, goats, rats and feral cats. The park is also a favourite haunt for pig hunters, though, thankfully, there are few known banjo players. ▶▶ *For Sleeping, Eating and other listings, see page 340.*

Ins and outs

Getting there and around Frasertown to Waikaremona is about 50 km; From Waikaremoana to Murupara is another 75 km. Access to Lake Waikaremoana and the heart of the park is via the hardy SH38. This almost completely unsealed highway links Murupara on the western boundary of the park with Frasertown, near Wairoa to the east. It is pretty heavy going: very windy, often subject to fallen trees and, if you break down, you're on your own. The park and all the amenities of Lake Waikaremoana are best accessed from the east via Wairoa and Frasertown. This will allow you to get intimate with the park on foot from Waikaremoana before building up the strength to explore the western part. **Big Bush Holiday Park**, in Wairoa, T06-837 3777, www.lake waikaremoana.co.nz, offers a regular shuttle service to and from Wairoa ($30) depending on demand. It also runs a water taxi service on Lake Waikaremoana taking trampers to and from the trailheads, from $30 one way.

Tourist information DoC Aniwaniwa Visitor Centre ① *SH38 at Lake Waikaremoana, T06-837 3803, urewerainfo@doc.govt.nz, daily 1000-1700,* has modern displays, an audio-visual show ($2) and a gallery, which is entrusted to care for and display the controversial **Urewera Mural** by Colin McCahon. Staff can assist with the limited but surprisingly good accommodation options and also handle walk information, fees and hut bookings. If accessing the park from the west (Rotorua) contact **DoC Murupara** ① *SH38, T07-366 1080.*

Background

The Te Urewera area is home to the Tuhoe people, known as 'the children of the mist'. They have always been amongst the most determined of Maori tribes. Before the Europeans arrived the Tuhoe effectively ruled the forest. Even other Maori were fearful of their *mana* (standing, integrity) and legendary bush skills. So when the Europeans arrived to lay claim to the forest it was obvious trouble would ensue.

During the New Zealand Wars of the 1860s and 1870s the great Maori leader and rebel, Te Kooti (see page 214) took refuge in Te Urewera with the Tuhoe. From here he fought his enemies until the Tuhoe made peace and Te Kooti was forced to seek exile in the King Country of the Waikato. With the end of the wars in 1872, and after being pardoned 11 years later, Te Kooti died a free man. But although the official wars ended in the Te Urewera, the troubles and hard feeling did not. Tuhoe religious prophet and leader Rua Kenana, who headed a thriving religious community in Maungapohatu,

● *The name Urewera comes from the Maori words 'ure' meaning 'burnt' and 'wera' meaning*
● *'penis'. Legend has it that the park is named after an old and feeble local Nga Potiki chief who had the rather unfortunate accident of falling asleep next to a fire and burning his genitals.*

⁝ The Waikaremoana Circuit Track

The Circuit Track, a 46-km walk of moderate difficulty, completely circumnavigates the lake. It can usually be completed in three to four days taking in a variety of bush types, full of birdlife and rocky or sandy bays ideal for fishing and swimming. Most of the route is fairly easy going except for ascent of the 900 m Panekiri Range, which offers a spectacular view across the lake and national park. There are five modern, comfortable DoC huts and five designated campsites along the route which provide basic amenities. The walk can be tackled in either direction from the southern access point at Onepoto (which climbs Panekiri first), or from the most popular starting point, Hopuruahine, on the lake's northern shores. Although there is parking at both access points most people leave their vehicles at the Waikaremoana Motorcamp ($5) and take the water taxi to either starting point (from $25). The taxi will also pick up or drop off from various designated points along the way, which is ideal for those who only wish to walk part of the circuit. Weather can be very changeable throughout the year and downright ugly in winter, so, as always, go well equipped. The walk is very popular in summer, so late spring or early autumn is advised. Bookings is essential. The huts cost $20 per person per night, child $10. Campsites are $10. For all information, maps, and bookings contact the DoC Aniwaniwa Visitor Centre, T06-8373900 (see page 338). For web bookings and information log on to www.doc.govt.nz (Great Walks).

remained a thorn in the *Pakeha's* side until his arrest in 1916. Thereafter, leadership crumbled and so did the Tuhoe's hold on the region. The kauri fell, the land was 'acquired' and the *Pakeha* took control. Many Tuhoe still live in Te Urewera and although most would say the forest is no longer theirs, in spirit it remains so.

Sights

Beautiful Lake Waikaremoana was created 2000 years ago when the Waikaretaheke River was dammed by a huge landslide between the Ngamoko and Panekiri ranges. One section of that landslide is thought to have been 3 km long by 1 km wide. This relatively new addition to the landscape sits beautifully with the equally impressive bush that cloaks its indented shores. The main activities on the lake are trout fishing and boating, but it is most famous for the network of excellent walks around its shores.

▲ Walks

Most of the short walks radiate from the main settlement of **Waikaremoana**, which is little more than a scattering of DoC buildings and a motorcamp at the northeastern end of the lake. There are two waterfalls within 15 minutes of the DoC visitor centre. The first, the **Aniwaniwa Falls**, is less than 1 km from the centre and is accessed from a track right beside it. The slightly higher and more impressive **Papakorito Falls** are up a short track opposite the centre (or by car to within a five-minute walk). The 2-km **Black Beech Track** (30 minutes) is a pleasant track connecting the visitor centre with the motorcamp.

If you fancy something more demanding and scenic, the **Ngamoko Track** (2½ hours), south of the motorcamp, climbs the mountain through a delightful tangle of native bush before emerging at a 1099 m trig and viewpoint. Better still is the four-hour tramp to see the idyllic **Lake Waikareiti**, which is a smaller body of water formed in the same way as Lake Waikaremoana. Set 300 m above Lake Waikaremoana, it is almost like a lost world with a magical atmosphere and shores entirely cloaked by bush. The DoC **Sandy Bay Hut** is available for an overnight stay (book at the visitor centre, $20) and there is also boat hire. Most serious trampers, however, come to Lake Waikaremoana to experience the scenic **Waikaremoana Circuit Track**, a national tramping top 10 (see box, page 339).

There are numerous other walks and huts in the park including the three to five-day **Whakatane River Round Trip**, the three-day **Manuoha-Waikareiti Track** and the two-hour **Onepoto Caves Track**. For more information and bookings contact DoC or call at the Aniwaniwa Visitor Centre (see page 338).

◉ Sleeping

Te Urewera National Park *p338*
Accommodation is available at Waikaremoana or the settlements of Kaitawa and Tuai at the southeast entrance to the park. Booking is advised in summer.
A-B Big Bush Holiday Park, Onepoto (4 km from the start of the track), T06-837 3777, www.lakewaikaremoana.co.nz. Full range of accommodation at the eastern entrance to the park. Transport and water taxi services.
A-B Waikeremoana Homestay, 9 Rotten Row, Tuai, T06-837 3701, ykarestay@xtra.co.nz. Thankfully Bev's hospitality and the accommodation does not reflect the street name. Single and double, dinner $25.
A-B Whakamarino Lodge, Tuai, T06-837 3876, www.lakelodge.co.nz. Comfortable self-contained units, 5 km from Waikaremoana.
D DoC Sandy Bay Hut, booking from DoC office, SH38 at Lake Waikaremoana, T06-837 3803, urewerainfo@doc.govt.nz.

Motorcamps and campsites
B-D Waikaremoana Motorcamp, T06-837 3826, www.lake.co.nz. Well situated right next to the lake near most of the major short walks and the visitor centre. Modern range of lodges, chalets, cabins and backpacker beds, powered and non-powered tent sites, petrol and a well-stocked store. Recommended.

▲ Activities and tours

Te Urewera National Park *p338*
Fishing, boat and kayak hire
There are many activities based on and around the lake. Fishing, fishing licences, hunting trips, and cruises are available from **Big Bush**, T06-837 3777, bigbush@paradise.co.nz; and **Waikaremoana Motorcamp**, see Sleeping, above.

Napier and around → *Colour map 3, A5 Population: 55,500*

Napier is a bright, dynamic place with the pleasant vibe of a Mediterranean coastal town. On the surface it enjoys the perfect relationship with nature: the rich fertile land and the warming sun making it the wine-producing capital of the North Island. However, it paid a heavy price in 1931 when an earthquake almost razed the town. Undeterred, the proud and determined people used this to their advantage and set about its rebuilding with an internationally recognized collection of art deco buildings thought to be amongst the finest in the world. Now, well into the new millennium, Napier seems in the best of health. ▸▸ *For Sleeping, Eating and other listings, see page 347-354.*

Ins and outs

Getting there **Napier airport** ① *just north of the town on SH2*, is served by **Air New Zealand Link**, T0800-737000/T132476, with regular daily flights from Auckland, Wellington and Christchurch and other principal national destinations. **Sunair**, T07-575 7799, www.sunair.co.nz, is a small company offering flights from some main centres including Hamilton, Rotorua and Tauranga. The **Airport Shuttle**, T0800-SHUTTLE, costs around $14 one way.

By bus, Napier is served by **Intercity** and **Newmans**. Buses arrive and depart from the **Napier Travel Centre** ⓘ *train station, Munroe St, T06-835 2720, 0830-1700*. All major buses companies serve Hastings too. The VIC (I-Site) act as ticketing agents.

By car, Napier is on SH2, 321 km north of Wellington. The junction with SH5 and SH2 is about 6 km north of the town and from there it is 117 km to Taupo and 397 km to Auckland. Napier is the premier east coast destination on the 'Classic New Zealand Wine Trail', www.classicwinetrail.co.nz.

Getting around Much of the city is negotiable on foot and, given the architectural appeal, is best appreciated from the street. The local suburban bus company is **Nimons Nimbus**, T06-877 8133, www.nimons.co.nz. It operates weekdays only and offers a service to Hastings and Havelock North. For car rental companies, cycle hire and taxis, see page 354.

Tourist information Napier VIC (I-Site) ⓘ *100 Marine Parade, T06-834 1911, www.hawkesbay.nz.com, Mon-Fri 0830-1700, Sat-Sun 0900-1700*, has information and leaflets on local and regional heritage walks, food and wine, gardens and art and craft trails. **DoC** ⓘ *59 Marine Parade, T06-834 3111, napier-ao@doc.govt.nz, Mon-Fri 0900-1615*. It has information about Cape Kidnappers Gannet Colony (plus tide times), as well as Te Urewera and Ruahine national and forest parks. **Hastings VIC (I-Site)** ⓘ *Westerman's Building, corner of Russell and Heretaunga sts, T06-873 5526, www.hawkesbaynz.com and www.hastings.co.nz, Mon-Fri 0830-1700, Sat-Sun 0900-1700*, has internet access and can help with transport booking.

Background

When Captain Cook first mapped the bay in 1769, the Maori were already happily ensconced on local *pa* and harvesting the local marine resources. This harvest was expanded in the 1830s when seasonal whalers arrived from Australia to be joined a decade later by missionaries and another decade after that by the first significant group of European settlers. In 1854 the town was named after British general Charles Napier.

During the New Zealand Land Wars of the 1860s the residents, with the help of local Maori, managed to defend themselves against aggressive tribes from the north and, with the development of agriculture, the settlement flourished. But though the devastating earthquake of 1931 destroyed everything, the subsequent rebuilding led to great improvements. The land surrounding Bluff Hill had been raised several feet and huge tracts of land, previously underwater or covered in swamp, became available for use. The redesign of the city encompassed the widespread creation of earthquake-resistant concrete boxes of art deco design and within a decade the town had a new face and a new future. Although the earthquake remains a painful memory, it has, in many ways, shaped the coastal town that Napier is today.

Sights

The main attraction of Napier is its famous **art deco architecture**. On foot, the two central streets, Emerson and Tennyson, have many examples. On Emerson Street is the **ASB Bank** with its incorporated Maori designs and fine doorway, while on Tennyson Street the highlights are (from east to west) the **Daily Telegraph Building**, restored **Municipal Theatre** and the **Deco Centre** (art deco shop).

Further afield is perhaps the most attractive building of all, the façade and entrance of the 1932 **National Tobacco Company** at the corner of Bridge and Ossian streets. Although somewhat distant from the town centre (in the port area of Westshore), it is worth the diversion. The building is even more impressive at night, when it is beautifully and imaginatively lit. During the day it is possible to have a look

Napier detail

Floral Clock, Tom Parker
Fountain & Pania of
the Reef

Browning St

DoC
Hawke's Bay
Museum

Daily
Telegraph
Building

Tennyson St

Colonnade
& Sound Shell

Tower
ASB Bank

Opossum
World

Emerson St

Sunken
Gardens

AA
Dickens St

N

0 metres 200
0 yards 200

Sleeping
Anchorage 1
Apartment 14
Archies Bunker
  Backpackers 21
Art Deco Masonic 2
Beach Front 3
Bluewater 4

Cobden Villa 10
County & Churchill's Bar 5
Criterion Backpackers 6
Deco City Motor
  Lodge 19
Five May 17
Harbour View Motor
  Lodge 7
Kennedy Park Top Ten
  Motel & Holiday Park 16
Master's Lodge 8
McHardy House 9
Napier Prison
  Backpackers 18

East coast Napier & around

at the interior which hosts just as much attention to detail. For a more modern example of art deco take a wander inside the pharmacy at the southern end of Emerson Street. ▶▶ *For tours of the art deco buildings, see Activities and tours, page 352.*

▶▶ *For tours of the art deco buildings, see Activities and tours, page 352.*

Marine Parade

Marine Parade creates an impressive perspective with its long promenade lined with **Norfolk Pines** and old wooden houses (the few that survived the earthquake). The **Marine Parade Walkway and Cycleway** starts at the northern end of Marine Parade. It features a number of art deco sculptures in a beachside garden setting and links several waterfront attractions that combine to create an almost English/Mediterranean ambience. First up, at the northern end heading south is the **Ocean Spa complex** ① *T06-835 8553, Mon-Sat 0600-2200, Sun 0800-2200, $6, child $4, private spa $8, massage from $35*. It has hot pools, private spas, health and beauty therapies, and a café and gymnasium.

Almost immediately to the south of the spa complex gardens again predominate with a **floral clock**, the **Tom Parker Fountain** (no Elvis connections here) and **'Pania of the Reef'** statue. The fountain is just your average garden fountain by day but by night comes alive with a multi-coloured aquatic light show. 'Pania' is a small, attractive statue of a Maori maiden, with her legend of love described accordingly in a shower of the fountain's mist.

Heading south is the art deco **Colonnade** and **Sound Shell**. The Colonnade was once used for dancing and skating. Opposite the Sound Shell, which is occasionally used for open-air concerts, is the **Hawke's Bay Museum** ① *9 Herschell St, T06-835 7781, www.hawkesbaymuseum.co.nz, daily 1000-1700, $7.50, children free*, which offers a wide range of exhibits relating to the history and art of the region in modern surroundings. *Nga Tukemata* (The Awakening) presents the art and *taonga* of the local Maori and a rare presentation of evidence that dinosaurs once existed in New Zealand. Special attention is afforded to the earthquake of 1931. Relics from the rubble accompany audio-visual descriptions and touching memories of survivors. Recommended.

East coast Napier & around

Dominating the corner of Emerson Street and Marine Parade are the **Art Deco Tower** (The Dome), which is nicely lit at night, and the art deco **Masonic Hotel**.

Back on the seaward side of Marine Parade past the modern VIC (I-Site) and Mini Golf Park are the **Sunken Gardens**, complete with ponds of water lily and a lazy waterwheel. Further south is **Marineland** ① *T06-834 4027, www.marineland.co.nz, daily 1000-1630, shows at 1030 and 1400, $11, child $5.50; Touch the Dolphins Tour at 0900, $16, child $8; Swim with the Dolphins, daily sessions $50; Penguin Recovery Workshop at 1300, $16*, where seal and dolphin displays are combined, perhaps with a twinge of guilt, with ongoing programme of wild penguin and gannet rehabilitation. You can also touch, feed and swim with the dolphins. Thankfully, all the animals seem to be in caring as opposed to strictly commercial hands.

Opossum World ① *157 Marine Parade, T06-835 7697, www.opossumworld.co.nz, daily 0900-1700, free*, bills itself as 'creating useful products from an ecological nightmare'. If the aesthetically appealing Australian import was a native species and not the infamous pest and destroyer of native plants and animals that it is in New Zealand, such a tourist oriented shopping and educational concept would be actively frowned upon. But as it stands it is worth popping your head in here to learn just how easily man's ill-conceived ideas can cause such permanent and ongoing ecological havoc, before perhaps furnishing said head with a fetching furry hat, or taking the plunge with set of matching nipple warmers.

Continuing south you then encounter the intriguing **Millennium Sculpture** created by local artist, David Trubridge. The work is carefully lined up to where the sun rose at the dawning of the new millennium. One can only wonder if it will still be standing for the morning of 1 January 3000 and if so, what on earth will be reflected in its steel discs.

The **National Aquarium of New Zealand** ① *T06-834 1404, www.national aquarium.co.nz, 0900-1900, $14, child $7.50, behind the scenes tours $25, child $12, tank dives from $50*, hosts an eclectic mix of native and non-native water and land creatures, from the enchanting seahorse to the iconic kiwi. The design of the building is quite clever, creating the impression that one is descending into the depths. 'Izzy', a remarkably toothy Australian import, will also have any unsuspecting herpetophobe breaking into a cold sweat.

Around Napier ⬤🏍🌸🏔🎭 ➤➤ *pp347-354*.

Cape Kidnappers' gannet colony → *Colour map 3, B5*
① *All trips are subject to season and tide times. There is a shuttle between Napier and Clifton or Te Awanga, $25. Contact Kiwi Shuttles, T0800-147488, or the VIC (I-Site)*.
Cape Kidnappers is the jagged white peninsula that marks the southern boundary of Hawke Bay. It gets its name from another rather unfortunate incident involving Captain Cook and the local Maori. Believing Cook's Tahitian interpreter was being held against his will, the Maori sent a *waka* to bring him back to shore. Doubtless a little confused, the Tahitian captive escaped back to the Cook's ship, which promptly weighed anchor and left, leaving only a name behind – Cape Kidnappers.

The cape is famous for its colony of gannets. These large, elegant seabirds have lots of attitude and, weighing in at about 2 kg with deadly 6-inch beaks designed to spear fish, they have every right to it. They hunt by gliding high over the surface of the water and diving at tremendous speed with wings folded back to catch the unsuspecting fish beneath. In the summer months up to 15,000 gannets gather at Cape Kidnappers to breed, forming the biggest mainland colony in New Zealand, and one of the biggest in the world. Perhaps given their attitude and armoury, gannets are not particularly fearful of anything or anybody, which makes them very approachable, particularly when grouped together and guarding their own little breeding patch. The tourist visiting season runs from October to late April, with the best time to view being early November chicks fledging and leaving the colony for their migration to Australia during May.

There are two tours available to see the gannets. One operator negotiates the beach and the tides below the peninsula, the other goes overland. Provided the tides are right you can walk the 10 km to the colony yourself. The walk starts from the **Clifton MotorCamp** (see Sleeping, page 349) but given the time restrictions due to the tides, you are advised to join a tour. If you are determined to go it alone, you can get the latest tide times from the VIC (I-Site) or DoC.

Classic Sheepskins Tannery
① *22 Thames St, Pandora, near Napier airport, T06-835 9662, www.classicsheep skins.co.nz, Mon-Fri 0730-1700, Sat-Sun 0900-1600, free.*
Even if you have think you have seen enough sheep, the Classic Sheepskins Tannery offers tours of the premises at 1100 and 1400 to see just how those hearthrugs and car seat covers are made. Drying lines with row after row of stretched sheepskins is a bizarre sight and conjures up an image of a flock of naked, highly embarrassed sheep hiding somewhere in the fields beyond.

Hawke's Bay vineyards
Given the climate and the soil in the Hawke's Bay area, it was inevitable that it would not take long for the first grapevine to be planted by the first Europeans settlers. Since that first harvest, the vines and the industry have boomed, making Hawke's Bay second only to Marlborough as the country's top wine-producing region. The two regions combined produce a range of wines to can compare with the world's best. Hawke's Bay offers a particularly wide variety due to the composition of the land and diverse 'sub regions'. Two such established 'sub-regions' are Gimblett Gravels Ngatarawa Triangle and the Esk Valley. There are over 40 wineries in the area so, unless you are a connoisseur, knowing which to visit can be a dilemma. Thankfully the free *Hawke's Bay Winery Guide* leaflet gives details of what each vineyard offers. Some have stunning architecture, some are particularly famous or more established, others have fine restaurants or cafés. Most offer sales and tastings. You can either embark on a tour according to your own choice and itinerary, or join a number of organized tours. If you know little about wines, and New Zealand wine in particular, an organized tour is advised.

Hastings → *Colour map 3, B5   Population: 50,000*
Hastings is a lively, sprawling, mainly agricultural service centre 21 km south of Napier and, like Napier, it was devastated by the 1931 earthquake, with the loss of 93 lives. In rebuilding the town the architects echoed Napier's art deco and Spanish Mission styles, much of which can clearly be seen in the town centre. The two best examples are the **Westerman's Building** that now houses the VIC (I-Site) on Russell Street and the recently refurbished **HB Opera House** on Hastings Street. The prominent art deco **clock tower**, right in the centre of town, was erected in 1935 to house the bells from the old 1909 Post Office Tower which collapsed in the quake; architect Sydney Chaplin won 25 Guineas ($52) for its design. During the summer the town is a blaze of colour for the annual **Blossom Festival**, when row upon row of hanging baskets line the streets providing a tourist attraction in itself and winning the town much praise around the country.

Modern-day attractions in Hastings include the **Hawke's Bay Exhibition Centre** ① *201 Eastbourne St, T06-876 2077, Mon-Fri 1000-1630, Sat-Sun 1100-1600, usually free depending on exhibitions*. It is the region's premier arts venue offering a varied

● *The first grapevines were planted primarily for religious use; the Catholic Society founded a*
● *Mission Vineyard in Taradale in 1851.*

The Big Shake

The 2 February 1931 in Hawke's Bay was a day like any other, but with one notable exception: local farmers noticed that their stock were in a strange and inexplicable state of angst. Dairy cattle, usually so routine in their willingness to stroll to the milking sheds, refused to budge. Instead they wanted only to huddle in the corners of the paddock – usually something they did prior to a thunderstorm. Yet the skies were clear and all was still. It is now believed that some animals can sense the very subtle tremors that often occur before a major earthquake, several days or hours before the main shock. Alas, if only the people of Napier had known that. The following day at 1046 there was a ferocious quake measuring 7.9 on the Richter Scale. The effect was devastating. Survivors recall that the land became 'almost fluid' and to a deafening roar, buildings were toppled, trees were uprooted and over 3,600 hectares of coastline thrust upwards by several feet. The few buildings the earthquake did not destroy, fires would, and with the loss of any water supply, let alone the organized means with which to fight them, all the shocked survivors could do was watch. By the time it was all over, Napier was essentially flattened and 162 lives had been lost. In Hastings, to the south, the damage was less severe, but older buildings still collapsed and 93 people were killed. In rural areas as far away as the Wairarapa, roads and bridges were destroyed, rivers became lakes and communications were cut off. Aftershocks followed for several weeks afterwards, the biggest, 10 days later, dragging out the terror and suffering of the survivors. But although many lives were lost and the town was destroyed, the spirit and determination of those survivors was not. Despite the enormity of the task, within two years the town was rebuilt and actually benefited from the availability of new land that had previously been seabed. Undoubtedly another benefit was the manifestation of its art deco architecture. Yet the quake remains, for now, the worst in New Zealand's human history.

programme of national and international touring exhibitions. Science and history also feature and there is an in-house café.

Given the dangerous nature of some beaches in the region, **Splash Planet** ① *Grove Rd, T06-876 9856, www.splashplanet.co.nz, daily 1000-1800, from $25, child $19.50,* a modern themed water park, is proving very popular. There are hot pools and the inevitable slides and rides to keep the kids happy for hours. If wine tasting doesn't whet your appetite, the **Pernel Fruitworld** ① *1412 Pakowhai Rd (north towards Napier), T06-878 3383, www.pernel.nzliving.co.nz, daily 0900-1730, $11, child $5.50,* might. It offers an interesting orchard tour and experience, fruit tastings and small animal farm for kids. It is especially good in spring when the trees are in blossom. There's a café on site.

If your visit to the town coincides with a Sunday the weekly **Farmers Market** ① *Hawke's Bay Showgrounds, Kenilworth Rd, 0830-1230 rain or shine,* provides an ideal opportunity to meet locals and purchase fresh produce.

Havelock North → *Colour map 3, B5 Population: 9000*

Havelock North is a very pleasant little village nestled amongst vineyards and orchards towards the coast and in the shadow of the 399-m **Te Mata Peak**. The view from the summit of Te Mata on a clear day is a 'must see' and it is easily reached by car via the village and Te Mata Peak Road. Weather permitting, it is also a popular spot for paragliding.

As well as the wineries surrounding Havelock North it is also home to another one of nature's great delights, honey. **Arataki Honey Ltd** ① *66 Arataki Rd, T06-877 7300, www.aratakihoneyhb.co.nz, Mon-Sat 0830-1700, Sun 0900-1600, free*, was established in 1944 and is one of the largest bee-keeping enterprises in the southern hemisphere, with a staggering 17,000 hives. There is a guided tour daily at 1330, a shop and the spectacular 'wall', with its army of 40,000 live and very busy bees.

The **Village Growers' Market** ① *at the Black Barn (Lombard) Vineyard, every Sat in summer 0900-1200*, is worth a visit and is where the locals stock up on fresh produce and the latest gossip.

Central Hawke's Bay south to the Wairarapa → *Colour map 3, B4*

From Hastings, SH2 winds its way through Central Hawke's Bay towards the stunning region of the Wairarapa, before arriving in Wellington. On SH2 there are a number of small towns including **Waipawa, Waipukurau, Dannevirke** and **Norsewood** (the latter two having obvious Scandinavian links). Although these settlements have little to offer the visitor there are plenty of activities available in the area including ballooning and tramping. The wild **Kaweka** and **Ruahine ranges** have some fine tramping but you are advised to plan carefully and go well prepared. DoC (Napier) or the field station in the historic village of **Ongaonga**, T06-856 6808, 15 km west of Waipukurau, will provide all the necessary information and leaflets. The **VIC (I-Site)** ① *Waipukurau railway station, (southern end of town), T06-858 6488, www.centralhawkesbay.co.nz, Mon-Fri 0900-1700, Sat 0900-1300*, can assist with activity and accommodation bookings.

Before leaving Hawke's Bay region proper, there is one other place worth visiting. However, bear in mind it is on the 'alternative' route into the back country of the Wairarapa and involves a bit of a hike. For the sake of it, it is worth the trip to see the ludicrously latitudinous sign that points at a distinctly unremarkable hill called **Taumatawhakatangihangakoauauotamateaturipukakapikimaungahoronukupokaiwhenuakitanatahu** and declares it as having the longest place name in the world (85 letters). Roughly translated, it means 'The place where Tamatea, the man with the big knees, who slid, climbed and swallowed mountains (known as land eater) played his flute to his loved one'. As you carefully contemplate both sign, place and meaning, you can be sure of one thing – old Tamatea may have been a big eater but he was a lousy lover if this was his idea of a romantic spot. Tours with exclusive access to the summit (252 m) are available with **Airlie Mount Farm Walks**, T06-858 7601.

To get to the hill from Waipukurau, take the coast road towards Porangahau. After about 40 km take a right. Follow the AA 'Historic Place Sign'. From Porangahau it is possible to take the back road to Wimbledon and undertake the alternative route to the Wairarapa, re-emerging on SH2 at either Eketahuna or Masterton. This will allow you to take in the stunning Castlepoint on the way.

● Sleeping

Napier *p340, map p342*
Napier is a popular holiday spot, in summer you are advised to book ahead.
LL The Apartment, 214 Emerson St, T025-450314, www.artapartment.co.nz. Centrally located luxury establishment and a great idea. A sort of cross between a penthouse and an art gallery with numerous contemporary pieces to muse upon of mixed media and

surrounded by all the comforts. 3 themed bedrooms with one master double suite.
LL Cobden Villa, 11 Cobden Rd, T06-835 9065, www.cobdenvilla.com. Stylish and tastefully decorated art deco-style accommodation that gives a nice reminder of the local style without being over the top.
LL Master's Lodge, 10 Elizabeth Rd, Bluff Hill, T06-834 1946, www.masterslodge.co.nz.

East coast Napier & around Listings

2 luxury private suites, solarium, in-house museum and veranda with commanding views. All comes at a price however. Dinner on request.

LL McHardy House, 11 Bracken St, Hospital Hill, T06-835 0605, www.mchardyhouse.com. One of Napier's oldest estates, central, with 4 suites and 2 rooms. Luxuriously appointed with fine dining and panoramic views.

LL-L The County Hotel, 12 Browning St, T06-835 7800, www.countyhotel.co.nz. Restored art deco Edwardian hotel in the centre of town and one of the few original buildings to survive the 1931 earthquake. There are 18, spacious, individually decorated suites, named after New Zealand birds, ranging from 2 bedrooms with private lounge, spa bath and balcony, to a standard double. All have Sky TV and internet. Popular **Chambers Restaurant** and **Churchill Bar** attached. No off-street parking.

LL-L Scenic Circle Te Pania Hotel, 45 Marine Parade, T06-833 7733, www.scenic-circle.co.nz. Named after Te Pania, a legendary Maori maiden of the sea, this modern 6-storey block sits on the waterfront like a human aquarium and seems a little clinical in appearance. It is certainly far removed from the art deco theme of the city. Character aside, however, the rooms, which range from the executive to family, are quite spacious, fresh and offer sea views. There is a restaurant and bar on the ground floor with alfresco dining. An added bonus is the **Ocean Spa complex** (see page 343) which is directly opposite. Secure parking.

L Five May, 5 May Av, T06-835 0373, www.fivemay.co.nz. Nicely appointed villa offering queens and doubles and all the comforts including a modern kitchen, bathroom with claw-foot bath and a lounge with open fire. Good value and just a 10-min walk from the town centre.

AL Bluewater Hotel, 10 West Quay, Ahuriri, T06-835 8668, www.bluewaterhotel.co.nz. A modern hotel in a pleasant location overlooking the Westshore Marina. Spas, restaurant and bar.

Motels
There are many motels in Napier, especially in Auriri (Westshore) and along the promenade.
AL Deco City Motor Lodge, 308 Kennedy Rd, T06-843 4342, www.decocity.co.nz. One of the most modern and well-facilitated motels in town, especially popular during the art deco weekend.

A The Anchorage, 26 West Quay, T06-834 4318, www.anchorage.net.nz. Modern and well-appointed, overlooking the harbour and marina.

A Art Deco Masonic Hotel, 64 Tennyson St, T06-835 8689, www.masonic.co.nz. A slightly cheaper, older style option.

A The Beach Front, 373 Marine Parade, T06-835 5220. Modern and the best on this street, along with **Shoreline Motel**, below.

A Harbour View Motor Lodge, Westshore, T06-835 8077, www.harbourview.co.nz.

A The Rocks, 27 Meeanee Quay, Westshore, T06-835 9626, www.therocksmotel.co.nz. Perfect if you are hankering after an old-fashioned bath in your motel.

A Shoreline Motel, 337 Marine Parade, T06-835 5222, www.shorelinenapier.co.nz. Attractive location next to the beach and just a few mins' walk from the centre of town.

A-B Sea Breeze B&B, 281 Marine Parade, T06-835 8067, seabreeze.napier@xtra.co.nz. Tidy guesthouse with themed rooms and plenty of character, right on the promenade.

Backpacker hostels
C-D Archies Bunker Backpackers, 14 Herschell St, T06-833 7990, www.archies bunker.co.nz. A good, centrally located option set in an historic building. Full range of rooms, internet, bike hire, Sky TV and secure parking.

C-D Criterion Backpackers, 48 Emerson St, T06-8352059, www.criterionartdeco.co.nz. A former hotel with spacious rooms and above average amenities, including bike and scooter hire, café and bar.

C-D Napier Prison Backpackers, 55 Coote Rd, T06-835 9933, www.napierprison.com. Here you can 'do time' in a small hostel within the old prison complex. The

● *For an explanation of the Sleeping and Eating price codes used in this guide, see the inside*
● *front cover. Other relevant information is provided in the Essentials chapter, pages 44-51.*
Note that prices are tive in New Zealand dollars.

accommodation is comfortable enough but it is the free jail tour that is the attraction.
C-D Napier YHA, 277 Marine Parade, T06-835 7039, Comfortable and friendly, with internet.
C-D Wally's Backpackers, 7 Cathedral Lane, T06-833 7930, www.wallysbackpackers.co.nz. Napier's newest backpacker hostel, centrally located within a listed art deco building. Spotless and well facilitated with a choice of double en suite, standard double/twin, single or dorm, internet. Recommended.
C-D Waterfront Lodge, 217 Marine Parade, T06-835 3429, www.napierwaterfront.co.nz Also comfortable and friendly, with internet.

Motorcamps and campsites
AL-D Kennedy Park Top Ten Motel and Holiday Park, Storkey St, T06-843 9126, www.kennedypark.co.nz. For campervans and tents this is a popular and well-established motorpark offering a wide range of options. Recommended.

Cape Kidnappers *p344*
For self-contained options refer to www.capeaccommodation.co.nz.
C-D Gannet Cottage, 77A School Rd, Clive, T06-870 1222, gannetcottage@paradise .net.nz. Backpackers need look no further than this small and personable hostel.

Motorcamps and campsites
B-D Te Awanga Holiday Park, 52 Kuku St, Te Awanga, T06-875 0334. Can accommodate campervans and tent sites.
C-D Clifton Motor Camp, Clifton Beach (road terminus) T06-875 0263. Offer adequate beachside accommodation near the cape.

Hastings *p345*
LL Hawthorn Country House, 420 SH2, T06-878 0035, www.hawthorne.co.nz. Award-winning luxury B&B again in a country setting. Spacious rooms. Sumptuous breakfasts.
LL-L Olea Cottages, 101 Ru Collin Rd, T06-879 7674, www.oleacottages.co.nz. 2 modern purpose-built, self-contained cottages in peaceful rural setting between Hastings and Havelock North. Very nicely appointed with great attention to detail. Beds the size of football pitches and baths

the size of small swimming pools. Very friendly hosts.
A Angus Inn, Railway Rd, T06-878 8177. Large, renovated complex with on-site restaurant and pool.
A-B Aladdin Motel, 120 Maddison St, T06-8766322. Slightly cheaper motel option, centrally located.
C-D Travellers' Lodge, 608 St Aubyn St West, T06-878 7108, ask@tlodge.co.nz. One of several budget options in Hastings, locally recommended, with purpose-built facilities, spacious doubles, singles and dorms, sauna, internet, free bike hire and assistance finding seasonal fruit picking work (Feb-Apr).

Motorcamps and campsites
A-D Hastings Top Ten Holiday Park, 610 Winsor Av, T06-878 6692. Wide range of options and good facilities. Within walking distance of Splash Planet so ideal for kids.

Havelock North *p346*
There are a number of magnificent traditional and modern 'country house style' B&Bs and lodges in the area. For full listings contact the VIC (I-Site).
LL Black Barn Private Retreat, Havelock North, T06-877 7985, www.blackbarn.com. Luxury self-contained lodges set in the heart of the vineyard and a large homestead situated on Summerlee Station, which incorporates Cape Kidnappers and the Beach House at Waimarama Beach.
LL Mangapapa Petit Hotel, 466 Napier Rd, Havelock North, T06-878 3234, www.manga papa.co.nz. A world-famous small luxury hotel in 100-year-old refurbished country house. Magnificent range of accommodation and fine in-house restaurant.
L-AL Brompton Apartments, 39 Havelock Rd, T06-877 0117, www.brompton.co.nz. Modern self-contained apartment complex in the heart of the village. Classy decor and spas.
L-AL Olea Cottages, 101 Ru Collin Rd, T06-879 7674, oleacottages@xtra.co.nz. 2 excellent, modern self-contained cottages ideal for couples.
L-AL Te Mata Lodge, 21 Porter Drive, Havelock North, T06-877 4880, www.temata lodgemotel.co.nz. Comfortable, self-contained and centrally located in the village, spas.

AL-A Village Motel, corner of Te Aute Rd and Porter Drive, T06-877 5401, www.village motel.co.nz. Modern motel, centrally located with very tidy units, spas, Sky TV and internet. **C-D Peak Backpackers**, 33 Havelock Rd, T06-877 1170. Well situated right in the heart of the village. Off-street parking, internet.

Motorcamps and campsites
AL-A Havelock North Motor Lodge, 7 Havelock Rd, Havelock North, T06-877 8627, www.havelocknorthmotorlodge.co.nz. Another quality, modern motel, well located. **B-D Arataki Motel and Holiday Park**, 139 Arataki Rd, Havelock North, T06-877 7479. Peaceful location, good facilities including a heated indoor pool.

❷ Eating

Napier *p340, map p342*
Given the region's love affair with food and wine there is plenty of choice when it comes to eating out. In the town itself there are essentially 2 main areas, the CBD (especially Marine Parade) and the waterfront and wharf within the suburb of Ahuriri, 2 km to the north. Both are equally good. Beyond that, if time and funds allow, it is well worth considering the numerous vineyard restaurants and cafés. Useful websites include: www.savourhawkesbay.co.nz and www.hawkesbaywinemakers.co.nz.

There is a small foodcourt in the **Ocean Boulevard Mall**, off Dickens St.
♨♨-♨♨ Acqua Brasserie, corner of Emerson St and Marine Parade, T06-835 8689, daily from 1130. Modern, good seafood and in prime location. Get a seat by the aquariums.
♨♨-♨♨ Breakers Café and Bar, corner of Tennyson St and Marine Parade, T06-835 8689. Central location, perhaps a bit over the top on modern 'neon' aesthetics but fine food, again with an emphasis on seafood.
♨♨-♨♨ Shed 2, West Quay, Ahuriri, T06-835 2202, daily from 1830. Waterfront location, imaginative international menu including ostrich, good seafood.
♨♨ Provedore, 60 West Quay, T06-834 0189, the latest offering at West Quay. Stylish surroundings, Euro-influenced menu complemented by local fare.

♨ Take Five Jazz Bar, 189 Marine Parade, T06-835 4050, daily from 1800. Local favourite with emphasis on local organic cuisine. The works of local artists adorn the walls, there is live jazz at weekends and of course an admirable wine list.
♨ Westshore Fish Café, 112a Charles St, T06-834 0227, Tue-Sun 1130-late. The best fish and chips in town.

Cafés
♨ Café Ujazi, 28 Tennyson St, T06-835 1490, daily from 0800. Good coffee and some imaginative vegetarian dishes.
♨ Sappho and Heath, 222 Emerson St, T06-834 3933. For a reliably good caffeine fix.
♨ Soak Café, in the Ocean Spa complex, 42 Marine Parade, T06-835 7888. A good option offering an eclectic range of food and wine and of course the inevitable lure of the spas.

Cape Kidnappers *p344*
♨ Clifton Bay Café and Bar, T06-875 0096, daily in summer, Wed-Sun in winter, 1000-1600. Excellent place near the entrance to the motorcamp and overlooking the beach. Ice cream and good coffee.

Hawke's Bay vineyards *p345*
You are advised to try at least one lunch or dinner at one of the vineyards (see page 353). For more detail and a map ask at the VIC (I-Site) for the *Hawke's Bay Food Trail* leaflet. Recommended vineyards with fine restaurants include: **Sileni Estate**, **Brookfields**, **Crab Farm**, **Craggy Range**, **Mission Estate**, **Te Awa Winery** and **Vidal Estate Winery**.

Hastings *p345*
For fine dining near Hastings see **Sileni** or **Vidal** vineyards page 345 and page 353. There is a **Countdown** supermarket on Queen St, Mon-Fri 0800-2100, Sat-Sun 0800-2000.
♨ Corn Exchange, 118 Maraekakaho Rd, T06-870 8333, daily for lunch and dinner. A stylish modern café in the old corn exchange building. Gourmet pizza a speciality.
♨ Warren's Bakery, 123 Russell St, T06-878 7476, Mon-Sat 0700-1700, Sun 0900-1400. Historic bakery dating back over a century offering a wide range of delicious

light snacks, sandwiches, pies and cakes as well as good coffee. Outdoor seating.
Rush Munro's, 704 Heretaunga St West. Old and famous place serving fine ice cream.

Havelock North *p346*

Crave, 108 Market St South, Hastings, T06-8788596, open for lunch and dinner daily. Recommended.

Peak House Restaurant, Te Mata Peak Rd, T06-877 8663, www.peakhouse.co.nz, Wed- Sun 1130-1400 and from 1730 for dinner, licensed. Magnificent view, but be sure to book ahead and ask for a table by the window.

Rose and Shamrock, corner of Napier Rd and Porter Drive, T06-877 2999, daily from 1030, lunch 1200-1400 and dinner 1800-2130. A spacious and delightful Anglo/Irish-style pub in the centre of the village with fine ale and good pub food. For a good breakfast on a Sat head for the farmers' market (see page 347).

The Olive Tree, 17 Joll Rd, T06-877 0222. Serves snacks and good coffee.

The Post, in the old village post office on Havelock Rd, T06-8771714, dinner Thu-Mon from 1830. Affordable Mediterranean dishes with a good blackboard wine list.

Pubs, bars and clubs

Napier *p340, map p342*

There is the inevitable scattering of Irish pubs in Napier, including **Rosie O'Grady's** and **The Brazenhead**, both on Hastings St. Although not notable for aesthetics, they sometimes 'go off' with bands at the weekends.

Gintrap and the bar restaurant combos of **The Thirsty Whale** (no 62) and **Provedore** (no 60) all on West Quay Ahuriri, are the trendy places to be seen at the moment. The former in particular is like a cross between a wool shed and NASA's mission control centre with music that may well result in 'lift off'.

Back in the centre of town **Churchill's Bar**, below the County Hotel in Browning St is great if you want to have a bit of fun. The staff are well used to merry clients doing awful Churchill impersonations but quite rightly draw the line when it gets to… 'Never, in the field of human drinking….'

Festivals and events

Napier and Hawke's Bay *p340, map p342*

Beware: Napier and the Hawke's Bay's famous itinerary of annual events involves an awful lot of food and wine. Here, in hedonistic Napier it seems food, wine and all things convivial are the one continuum and very core of the region's lifestyle. A useful source of information is www.hawkesbaynz.com/events.

Feb Harvest Hawke's Bay Wine Festival, www.harvesthawkesbay.co.nz, is a weekend of fun and games celebrating the region's wine production. Apparently, grown men race around a park in wine barrels before dispersing for a spot of lunch – tremendous stuff. **International Mission Estate Concert**, is an outdoor concert at the Mission Estate Winery drawing increasingly large crowds, truckloads of picnickers and some famous (if ageing) performers. Over the last few years they have included Dionne Warwick, the Beach Boys and Cliff Richard. **Brebner Print Art Deco Weekend** (3rd weekend), is Napier's biggest and most popular event celebrating the art deco-style. It involves vintage cars, period costume, parades, Devonshire teas on the promenade and a spot of 'wineglass wanders'. **Weta Wine and Food Fest**, offers time to relax after a hectic month, with some more food and wine.
Mar Edible Arts Fest, is apparently a unique event and a world-first incorporating yet more food and wine with the added attraction, this time, of 'edible art exhibitions', live music and theatre performances. The event kicks off with the infamous **Great Long Lunch**, which attracts over 700 gourmands. **Horse of the Year Show**, is the largest horse show in the southern hemisphere attracting over 1000 riders and a small army of well-fed spectators.
Jun Winter Arts Festival/Winter Solstice Fire Festival, is a celebration of the arts, with theatre, restaurant theatre and vocal arts all enhanced by a spectacular fire show at the Sound Shell. **Matariki (Maori New Year) Festival**, has traditional events, performances and copious *hangis* (feasts).
Oct Kelt Capital Stakes is New Zealand's most glamourous horse races.
Nov Month of Wine and Rose is a series of private garden tours with a little music and, naturally, lots (and lots) of food and wine.

O Shopping

Napier *p340, map p342*
Art Deco Shop and Information Centre,
163 Tennyson St (old fire station building),
T06-835 0022. Good selection of quality gifts
and souvenirs related to Napier's art deco
architecture, and to the style in general.

▲ Activities and tours

Napier *p340, map p342*
Art deco or earthquake walks
There are several guided or self-guided tour
options available. The **morning walk** (1 hr,
$10) leaves daily from the VIC at 1000; the
afternoon walk (2 hrs, $15) leaves at 1400
from the Art Deco Shop, 163 Tennyson St.
All the tours are hosted by the Art Deco
Trust, an organization set up in 1985 to
help preserve and promote art deco in
the region. Included in the morning
and afternoon walks is an audio-visual
and free refreshments at the **Art Deco
Shop**, www.artdeconapier.com.

If you wish to see the buildings on your
own, or are pushed for time, pick up a copy
of the excellent *Art Deco Walk* leaflet ($4.50)
from the VIC. There are also *Art Deco Scenic
Drive* maps available. These walks encompass
the history and events surrounding that
fateful day in 1931 when an earthquake
measuring 7.8 on the Richter scale hit the
city. If on a self-guided walk, a pre-emptive
tremor musing upon the relevant exhibits
in the museum is recommended.

Swimming
The main beach in Napier is pebble, deeply
shelved and too dangerous for swimming.
However, there are more sheltered bays
namely Westshore, Waipatiki and Waimarama
(the VIC can provide directions). There is also
a small lap pool and hot pools at the **Ocean
Spa Complex**, Marine Parade. See page 343.

Tour operators
Airplay, Havelock North, T06-845 1977/T025-
512886, www.airplay.co.nz. Paragliding.
Bay Tours and Charters, T06-845 9034,
www.baytours.co.nz. Local and regional
sightseeing tours from $50.

Early Morning Balloons, T06-879 4229.
Hot air balloon rides from $260.
Grant Petherick Fly Fishing, T06-876
7467, www.flyfishingwinetours.co.nz.
Fishing trips and wine tours. Recommended.
Kiwi Adventure Company, 58 West Quay,
T06-834 3500, www.kiwi-adventure.co.nz.
Canoeing, kayaking and climbing trips
and hire. Climbing-wall open Tue-Fri
1500-2100, Sat-Sun 1000-1800, from $15.
Long Island Tours, T06-877 0977,
www.longislandtoursnz.com. Local and
regional sightseeing tours from $20.
Mountain Valley (Mohaka River),
T06-834 9756, www.mountainvalley.co.nz.
Rural adventure centre offering a range of
activities including horse treks, kayaking
and rafting, accommodation available.
Napier Prison Tours, T06-835 9933.
Visit the local prison reputed to be the
oldest in New Zealand, daily 0930 and
1500, from $15.
Out of the Blue, T06-875 0188,
www.outoftheblueboatcharters.co.nz.
Customized ocean and trout fishing trips.
Riverside Jet, T06-874 3841, www.riverside
jet.co.nz. Jet-boat tours from $30.
Whana Valley Walk, T06-874 2421,
www.whanawalkhawkesbay.co.nz.
Walk and accommodation packages
on the renowned coastal and backcountry tracks, from $80.
Wine Country Cat, West Quay, Ahuriri,
T06-877 7850/T0800WINECAT, www.hb
winecountrycat.co.nz. It was only a matter
of time before the sampling of local wine
and produce took to the high seas. Luxury
3½-hr catamaran cruises leave daily at
1100, from $50; a 6-hr smorgasbord
dinner cruise at 1830 costs from $55.

Cape Kidnappers *p344*
Gannet colony
The big attraction on the cape is the
gannet colony (the largest in the North
island). Several operators run tours.
Gannet Beach Adventures, T06-875 0898,
T0800-426638, www.gannets.com. The
oldest company. This 4-hr tour leaves
daily (Oct-May) from Clifton Beach by
tractor and allows about 1½ hrs with
the gannets, from $33, child $19.

Gannet Safaris Overland, at the Summerlee Station on the cape (near Te Awanga), T06-875 0888, www.gannetsafaris.co.nz. Go overland by shuttle bus, which involves very little walking. The 3-hr tours depart daily Sep-May at 0930 and 1330, from $65. Transport from Napier $22.

Golf

Cape Kidnappers Golf Course, 448 Clifton Rd, Te Awanga, T06-875 1900, www.cape kidnappers.com. A challenging course with stunning views – but at $400 for visitors ($300 low season) – it comes at a price.

Hawke's Bay vineyards p345
Vineyards

A useful source of information is www.hawkesbaywinemakers.co.nz.
Black Barn Vineyards, Te Mata Rd, T06-877 7985, www.blackbarn.com, daily 1000-1700. Excellent accommodation, underground cellar and host to the village growers' market every Sat morning in summer.
Church Road, 150 Church Rd, Taradale, T06-844 2053, www.churchroad.co.nz, daily 0900-1700. Formerly the McDonald Winery. Owned by the internationally famous Montana Estates. Winemaking museum and restaurant. Hosts excellent jazz concerts.
Clearview, 194 Clifton Rd, Te Awanga, Hastings, T06-875 0150, www.clearview estate.co.nz, daily 1000-1700. One not to miss if you are visiting Cape Kidnappers. Quality not quantity with a classy Mediterranean-style café.
Craggy Range, 253 Waimarama Rd, Havelock North, east of the village, T06-873 7126, www.craggyrange.com. and one of the most celebrated wineries in the region, in the shadow of Te Mata Peak. All the grandeur and self-promotion is perhaps a bit over the top. Classy restaurant that could make more of the view. Lunch from 1200 and dinner daily.
Mission Estate, end of Avenue Rd, Taradale, T06-844 2259, www.missionestate.co.nz, Mon-Sat 0900-1700, Sun 1000-1630. The oldest vineyard in New Zealand. Famous labels, restaurant and established tours.
Sileni, Maraekakaho Rd, Hastings, T06-879 8768, www.selini.co.nz, 1000-1700,

restaurant open until late. Perhaps the finest cuisine amidst stunning modern architecture and pleasant surroundings. Although 34 km from Napier on the Maraekakaho Rd (via SH50), it is worth the journey. Top-class dining at the **Mesa Alfresco Restaurant**. Book ahead.
Te Awa, 2375 SH50, T06-879 7602, www.tea wa.com, daily 0900-1700. Interesting building, fine labels and good restaurant.
Te Mata Estate, Te Mata Rd, T06-877 4399, www.temata.co.nz, Mon-Fri 0900-1700, Sat 1000, Sun 1100. Another architectural stunner. Reputable label.
Vidal Estate, 913 St Aubyn St East, T06-876 8105, www.vidal.co.nz, daily 0900-1700. Excellent restaurant for lunch and dinner daily.

Wine tour operators

Most of the tours available are flexible, and will cater for your needs.
Bay Tours, T06-843 6953, www.bay tours.co.nz. Locally recommended and good value with a flexible itinerary, from $50.
Bike About Tours, T06-845 9034, www.bikeabouttours.co.nz. Explore the vineyards by bicycle.
Bike D'Vine, T06-833 6697, www.bikede vine.com. Tours are flexible, usually self-guided and sometimes include other less libatious? destinations. Lunch is often provided as well as maps, cell phones and even pick-ups, should you get too tired or weighed down with purchases. Prices start at a very reasonable $40 per day.
Grant Petherick Wine Tours, T06-876 7467, www.flyfishingwinetours.co.nz. High quality, entertaining and informative, customized tours. Recommended.
Hawkes Bay in a Glass, T06-836 7427, www.qualityhb.co.nz. A quality operator offering flexible tours arranged to your own time schedule and tastes. Price varies.
On Yer Bike Winery Tours, Hastings, T06-879 8735, www.onyerbikehb.co.nz. The energetic option, by bike from $50 (requires supreme coordination and orientation skills towards the end of the day).
Vince's Vineyard Tours, T06-836 6705. Personalized tour with friendly, local, knowledgeable guide. In operation for 10 years. Flexible itineraries from $50.

Airplay, T025-512886, www.airplay.co.nz.
For those wishing to take to the sky,
paragliding flights and courses are
available from $180.
Grant Petherick Wine Tours, T06-876
7467, www.flyfishingwinetours.co.nz. Offers
high-quality, entertaining and informative,
customized tours.

⊕ Transport

Napier *p340, map p342*
Bicycle hire Marineland, 209 Marine
Parade, T06-834 4027. **Car hire** Hertz,
T06-835 6169; Xpress, T06-835 8818.
Taxi Napier Taxi, T06-835 7777;
Star, T06-835 5511.

❶ Directory

Napier *p340, map p342*
Internet Cybers, 98 Dickens St, Mon
0830-2100, Tue-Fri 0830-2400, Sat 0900-
2400, Sun 0900-2000. **Ocean Boulevard
Mall**, Dickens St. **Library** Station St,
T06-8344180. **Police** T06-835 4688. **Post
office** corner of Dickens and Hastings
sts, Mon-Fri 0800-1700, Sat 0930-1230.

Hastings *p345*
Internet Hectic Netway, 1/123
Heretaunga St, Hastings, open 1000-2200.
Medical services Hawke's Bay Regional
Hospital, Omahu Rd, Hastings, T06-878 8109.
Post office Hastings, corner of Market and
Heretaunga sts, Mon-Fri 0830-1800.

The Wairarapa

The Wairarapa is one of the least-visited regions in the North Island. Most visitors miss it out in their rush to reach Wellington via SH1, which lies to the west beyond the natural barrier of the Ruahine and Tararua ranges. If that simple fact is not appealing enough, the remote and stunning coastal scenery and relaxed atmosphere will, if you make the effort to visit, confirm that this is a place worth getting to know. The highlights, other than the delights of rural towns like Martinborough, which lie like a string of pearls along SH2, are the ever-increasing number of quality vineyards, a terrific range of country B&Bs and the coastal splendour of Castlepoint and Cape Palliser, the North Island's most southerly point. ➤➤ *For Sleeping, Eating and other listings, see pages 360-364.*

Ins and outs

Getting there Tranzit Coachlines, T0800-71227, T06-377 1227, www.tranzit.co.nz, runs regular bus services between Wellington and Palmerston North (including Mount Bruce) from $19. There is a weekday service between Masterton and Martinborough from $6 one way, and twice daily 'Gourmet Wine Escape' tours to Martinborough from Wellington and the Wairarapa in conjunction with TranzMetro (see below). The fare of $99 includes tasting fees at four vineyards and lunch at a local café. The 'Wairarapa Natural Discovery' takes in the Paua Shell Factory in Carterton and The Mount Bruce National Wildlife Centre, from $99. **Wairarapa Coachlines**, T0800-666355/T06-308 9352, www.yellow.co.nz/site/wairarapacoachlinesandlimousines, www.tranzit.co.nz, also offers 5 daily services between Featherston and Martinborough and one daily service between Masterton and Martinborough

By train, **TranzMetro**, T04-801 7000, www.tranzmetro.co.nz, provides regular services from Wellington to Masterton (six daily Monday to Friday, twice daily at weekends) and has the added attraction of the long Rimutaka tunnel across the ranges. There is a special day excursion fare of $15, child $8; standard fare $13 one way. There is also a concession for a group of four from $30. Masterton train station is on Perry Street, about a 15-minute walk from the town centre. **Tranzit** coaches, T0800-843596, link with **TranzMetro** rail services.

Saved by cow 569

Until the great floods of winter 2004, dairy farmer Kim Riley (45 years) of Woodville, North Island, had a fairly indifferent relationship with her charges on the farm. Perhaps it was that almost omnipresent vacant look or the incessant chewing of the cud? Perhaps it was those awfully muddy buttocks or that irksome stubborn nature at five in the morning – and that was just her husband. But all this indifference quickly changed to the warm and fuzzies when the great rains came and Kim was washed away in the rising waters of the local river.

"I thought if I was washed away in to the main river, I would be gone" she explained to the local media. "I drank a fair bit of water and it was foul muck, then I was hampered by my wet weather gear and gumboots. On the verge of panic and fearing for my life it was then that I spotted my salvation. Looking back I saw one of the cows bearing down on me and as she went by I just grabbed her by the mane, laid back, relaxed and let the big lump take me home. Eventually reaching solid ground we both sat there puffing and shaking a bit before the cow rejoined the herd now massed safely on higher ground." Mrs Riley says she knew the cow responsible and with a new-found admiration for her stock said further: "It was 569, she's an old cow, an ugly old tart, but I'll have to say thank you to her, that's for sure."

Getting around Wairarapa Coachlines offers a regular weekday and limited weekend services between Masterton, Martinborough and Featherston and connect with all **TranzMetro** train services, T0800-666355/T06-308 9352. There is no public transport to Castlepoint. However, you may be able to hook up with the holiday park or hotel staff on supply trips to Masterton.

Tourist information Masterton VIC (I-Site) ① *316 Queen St, T06-370 0900, www.wairarapanz.com, Mon-Fri 0900-1700, Sat-Sun 1000-1600*, and **Martinborough VIC (I-Site)** ① *18 Kitchener St, T06-306 9043, www.wairarapanz.com, daily 0900-1600*, are the two main accredited VIC (I-Sites) in the region. They hold comprehensive information about sights and activities, as well as the wealth of B&B beds throughout the Wairarapa region. Other non-accredited, volunteer manned VICs are to be found in **Greytown** ① *110 Main St, T06-304 9008, Fri-Sun 1000-1600*, and **Featherston** ① *in the Old Courthouse (SH2) in the village, T06-308 8051, daily 1000-1500*.

Walks information can be secured at the **DoC Masterton Field Centre** ① *South Rd (continuation of Queen St), T06-377 0700*.

Masterton → *Colour map 3, C3 Population: 18,000*

Given its relative geographical isolation (thanks to the Tararua Ranges), Masterton was not settled to any great degree until the late 1850s, but with rich fertile soils and a favourable climate, when settlement came, growth was rapid. Today, the town is the chief commercial centre for the Wairarapa Region. Masterton also gives Te Kuiti in the Waikato (the 'sheep-shearing capital of New Zealand') a run for its money in the big woolly event stakes. The **Golden Shears** is the major date in the local young farmers' calendar and offers moderate fame and fortune to the fastest clipper around. It is held at the beginning of March, lasts about four days and ends with a dinner and cabaret.

Just opposite the VIC (I-Site) is the **Aratoi Wairarapa Museum of Art and History** ① *T06-370 0001, www.aratoi.co.nz, daily 1000-1630, donation*, which admirably showcases many aspects of the area's social, cultural and natural history, as well as

Shelling out for paua

The inner shell casing of the sea-mollusc paua has to be one of the most beautiful and colourful things in nature. The paua is very closely related to the abalone, of which there are about 130 species worldwide, and both are related to snails and limpets. The Maori, as a source of both food and decoration, have long valued paua and the same is true for the masses in modern times. To protect paua as a sustainable resource, strict quotas are in place in New Zealand and no paua harvesting is allowed with compressed air. This makes their collection, with only a snorkel, often in cold southern waters over 12 m in depth, quite an art. Dives of up to two minutes are not uncommon. What comes up from those depths is not the radiant casing that you see in the souvenir shops, but a drab coralline coated shell, that once removed of its flesh, must be ground down to reveal the beautiful patterning beneath. The paua industry is well established in New Zealand, not only for seafood, but also more especially for the shell from which the polished jewellery is made. You will encounter the huge range of designs in almost every souvenir shop throughout the land. In some parts of the country the humble paua has even reached icon status. In Bluff, near Invercargill an elderly couple (in that typically eccentric New Zealand style) decided to decorate almost their entire house (in and out) with paua. Why, frankly, remains an enigma. The result is the famous 'paua house', which must feature in many a photo album all over the planet as that 'decidedly weird place' at the bottom of the world.

rapidly blossoming into the main focus for local contemporary artists. The museum also hosts visiting national exhibitions, something it was missing out on for years. There's also a good in-house café. Alongside Aratoi is the new **Shear Discovery National Shearing and Woolhandling Museum** ① *12 Dixon St, T06-378 8008, www.sheardiscovery.co.nz, daily 1000-1600, $5, child $2*. Developed in two relocated former woolsheds it offers 'a fine round-up' of the shearing and weaving process and showcases the champions of the prized annual 'Golden Shears' contest.

Also within walking distance of the VIC (I-Site) and town centre is the much-loved and celebrated **Queen Elizabeth Park**. First planted in 1878, today it boasts a lake (with boats for hire), sports grounds, a miniature railway, swing bridge, aviaries, a deer park and the usual tracts of manicured herbaceous borders. A little further out of town, on Colombo Road, is **Henley Park**, with lakes offering fishing and lakeside walks.

Masterton has a number of interesting gardens and **Heritage Trail Walks** (one to two hours) which are part of an eight-walk Regional Heritage Trail. Information and leaflets for all can be obtained from the VIC (I-Site). If you are a budget traveller, or simply a little tired from your endless travels, be sure to check out the bronze statue and charming story of **Russian Jack**, the erstwhile Wairarapa 'swag' man, on Queen Street.

For recreational walks the **Mount Holdsworth** area offers access to the Tararua Range with short and long walk options. Details are outlined at the car park. To get there take Norfolk Road just south of the town (17 km).

Mount Bruce → Colour map 3, C3
The main focus of Mount Bruce, 30 km north of Masterton on SH2, is the **Pukaha Mount Bruce National Wildlife Centre** ① *T06-375 8004, www.mtbruce.org.nz, daily 0900-1630, $8, children free*. This centre is the flagship of DoC's conservation and endangered species breeding programme. Although much of what happens at Mount Bruce takes place behind the scenes (and involves dedicated staff acting as

surrogate mothers), the public can see many species otherwise rarely seen. There is something very special about sitting on the veranda of the café, sipping a coffee and overlooking an enclosure with a takahe (a charming prehistoric-looking purple bird, not dissimilar to a large chicken) going happily about its business in the knowledge that there are only 200 or so left in the world. Likewise, taking a stroll through the native bush, to see other enclosures hiding stitchbirds and kokako, all of which you will probably never see again in your lifetime.

There is a nocturnal kiwi house that rates among the best in the country and leaves you in no doubt as to the numerous threats which this national icon faces in the modern world. Other highlights include the eel feed at 1330 and the kaka feed at 1500. The wild eels live in the stream running through the reserve and gather beneath the bridge at feeding time in a swirling mass. This particular species, native to New Zealand, is far larger than the average eel and lives up to at least 80 years. The kaka is a cheeky and at times raucous native bush parrot. There is a small colony at Mount Bruce that have been bred in captivity and now live wild in the area. They all have names and will quite happily nibble your hair or your ear before cracking open a peanut with their powerful beaks. If you go to the feeding area just before 1500 they will usually be hanging about in the trees, available for interviews and photographs. Within the main building there are some fine displays, a shop and a café.

Castlepoint → *Colour map 3, C4*
It is a major diversion to get to this remote coastal settlement (65 km from Masterton) but the trip is well worth it. Castlepoint is considered to be the highlight on the Wairarapa's wild and remote coastline and it certainly deserves the honour. At the eastern end of the main beach a stark rocky headland, from which sprouts the **Castlepoint Lighthouse**, sweeps south to enclose a large lagoon. The picturesque bay, which is itself a popular spot with surfers and swimmers, is dominated at its southern entrance by the aptly named 162-m **Castle Rock**, which can be accessed from the southern end of the bay. The lighthouse can be accessed across the sand tombolo which connects it to the mainland via a boardwalk. Just below the lighthouse there is a cave that can be explored at low tide, but beware – Maori legend has it that it is the hiding place of a huge menacing octopus. One word of warning: a small memorial stone testifies to the number of people who have drowned while exploring the offshore reef, so take care. On its eastern side, huge ocean waves can catch you unawares. While contemplating the memorial stone, look closely at the rocks that surround it and you will see hundreds of fossil shells embedded therein.

Riversdale Beach and Flat Point
The small coastal resort of Riversdale is 35 km northeast of Te Wharau which is itself east of Masterton (130 km round trip). The beach is long and sandy and as it's patrolled in summer offers safe swimming as well as surfing, fishing and diving. The Flat Point to Honeycomb Rock section of coast is wilder than Riversdale with interesting rock formations and an old shipwreck.

Carterton → *Colour map 3, C3*
Carterton acts as a secondary service town to Masterton and is famous in spring for its daffodils (first planted in 1920). Although not as aesthetically pleasing as its neighbouring settlements, it is perhaps worth a stop to see the Paua Shell Factory and use the town as an access point to the Mount Dick Viewpoint and the Tararua Forest park at Waiohine Gorge.

The **Paua Shell Factory** ① *54 Kent St, T06-379 6777, www.pauashell.co.nz, daily 0800-1700, free,* is one of the few places in the country that converts the stunningly beautiful paua (abalone) shells into jewellery and souvenirs. It is possible to see how the shell is crafted and to watch a video about the paua itself, with complimentary coffee or tea. This is all cleverly designed to get you into the shop, where there is a vast range of paua shell items on sale, some of which are painfully kitsch.

Sporting your new paua shell earrings and key rings, and provided the weather is fair, you can then go and see one of the best views in the Wairarapa, from **Mount Dick**. At the southern end of town turn into Dalefield Road which heads straight towards the hills like a never-ending runway. At the very end of the road keep going and just before its terminus look for a farm track on the left. This track, which is negotiable without a 4WD (just), goes about 3 km up to a viewpoint; 14 km total.

The trip to **Waiohine Gorge** (22 km) at the entrance to the **Tararua Forest Park** is well worth it for the scenery itself, let alone the walks on offer and the heart-stopping **swing bridge**, one of the longest in New Zealand. The road is signposted just south of the town on SH2. Eventually an unsealed road connects you with the riverbank which gradually rises high above the river gorge. At the road terminus you can embark on a number of walks from one hour to several days, almost all of which involve the initial negotiation of the swing bridge which traverses the gorge at a height of about 40 m. If you do nothing else at Waiohine, a few trips back and forth on the bridge is great fun. Although it is perfectly safe, jelly has less wobble.

Greytown → *Colour map 3, C3*

Greytown, along with Martinborough, is the prettiest of the Wairarapa settlements and is best known for its antiques, art and craft shops and roadside cafés. It's also a great spot to stop and wander around the old buildings and quaint shops. Given its historic village feel it is not surprising to learn that Greytown was one of the first places settled in the area. Settlement began in earnest in the 1850s on land purchased by Sir George Grey, one of New Zealand's first governors and after whom the town is, of course, named. The **Cobblestones Museum** ① *169 Main St, To6-304 9687, daily 0900-1630, $3, child $1,* is a collection of buildings and memorabilia from the early settler days.

Martinborough → *Colour map 3, C3*

Martinborough is located towards the coast from SH2, 16 km southeast of Greytown. It is not dissimilar to Greytown but enjoys its country location and a quiet town square more (as opposed to the bustling SH2). First settled by a nationalistic Briton, John Martin in the late 1880s, the **village square** and the streets running off it form the shape of the Union Jack. With names like Kansas, Texas and Ohio, it is clear that Martin had as much a love of the US as he did his homeland. Described as a unique 'wine village', with 20 vineyards within walking distance of the square, and blessed with as many charming B&Bs, it is a favourite romantic haunt for Wellingtonians in search of a quiet weekend followed by a savage headache on the Monday morning.

Of local historical interest is the **Colonial Museum** ① *on the square, To6-306 9736, Sat-Sun 1400-1600, donation,* which was itself the former village library built in 1894. It is furnished with all the usual early settler artifacts. The *Vintage Village Heritage Walk* leaflet available from the VIC will pinpoint other sites of historical interest like the rather grand and recently restored **Martinborough Hotel**. Again there are a number of 'open gardens' for which the VIC will point the way.

The **Patuna Chasm** ① *Patuna Farm, Ruakokopatuna Rd, book through the VIC or To6-306 9966, www.patunafarm.co.nz,* is an interesting limestone gorge featuring stalactites, fossils and waterfalls and a host of native wildlife. The chasm is on private land but guided walks are available from $15. Along a similar theme the nearby **Ruakokopatuna glow-worm caves** are also on private land but can be accessed with instruction from the VIC (I-Site); take a torch and your gumboots. About 20 km southeast of the village are the busy white propellers of the **Hau Nui Wind Farm** on White Rock Road. Although you are not free to wander amongst them there is a viewing platform provided. From there you might consider going all the way to the remote coast at **Tora** or **White Rock** which offers some great walks and coastal scenery.

The main attraction is of course the **vineyards** and most offer tastings and tours, but note that not all of them are open year-round. The most noted labels tend to be Sauvignon Blanc, Riesling and Pino Noir. The popular **wine centre** ⓘ in the heart of the village, T06-306 9040, www.martinboroughwinecentre.co.nz, is a good place to get a feel for what is available and ask about tours. *The Martinborough Wairarapa Wine Trail* leaflet, available from the VIC (I-Site), will also get your tour started. The website www.nzwine.com is useful. The **Ata Rangi Vineyard** ⓘ T06-306 9570, www.atarangi.co.nz, Sep-Mar, Mon-Fri 1300-1500, Sat-Sun 1200-1600, is one of the better known, producing a Pinot Noir, for which the village is now famous. There are a number of local tour operators who can arrange specialist wine tours, including **Wairarapa Coachlines Tours**, T0800-666355. If you are around in November, your visit may coincide with the immensely popular **Toast Martinborough** celebrations, a festival of fine wine and food.

Cape Palliser, Ngawi and Lake Ferry → *Colour map 3, C3*

The day-long drive to see the Cape Palliser Lighthouse epitomizes the region and is highly recommended. On the way you can take in the bizarre rock formations of the Putangirua Pinnacles, the charming coastal fishing village of Ngawi and a colony of enchantingly languid fur seals, before the road terminates at the steps of the lighthouse. To get there from Featherston or Martinborough make your way down Lake Ferry Road, towards Lake Ferry. Just before the village turn left for Ngawi. From here the lighthouse is about 40 km. Once the road joins the coast and if it is a clear day, you may be able to see the snow-capped Kaikoura Ranges of the South Island.

After about 15 km look out for the **Putangirua Pinnacles** car park. The pinnacle formations are a series of gravel spires and turrets. They are about an hour's walk down a stream bed, so take proper footwear. Once you reach the entrance to the pinnacles (on the left, after about 30 minutes) you have the choice of climbing a steep path through bush to a viewpoint (30 minutes), or entering the pinnacles stream bed and going into heart of the formation. Don't miss the viewpoint but both trips are worth it.

From the car park the road continues, hugging the cliffs before opening out across a wide coastal plain, with a beautiful shore of rock and sand, well known for its excellent surfing. The coastal village of **Ngawi** soon comes into view and you will be struck by the collection of old tractors and bulldozers on the beachfront with rigs supporting a raft of fishing boats of all shapes and sizes. It is worth a stop here to take a closer look and watch as one of the dearly loved machines is used to launch a boat.

From Ngawi the red and white tower of the lighthouse can be seen. On the rocks just before it is a colony of New Zealand **fur seals**, though you have to look carefully so as not to miss them. Like fat, brown barrels they doze the day away amongst the boulders. All they're missing is a TV, a can of beer and a remote control. By all means take a closer look, but do not go nearer than 10 m. If you do, their soporific attitude will evaporate in an explosion of rippling blubber as they charge towards the surf.

From the seal colony it is only a short distance to the **lighthouse**, with its steep climb of steps and rewarding views. This is the southernmost tip of the North Island. Once you return to Lake Ferry Road it is worth the short diversion to see **Lake Ferry** itself.

Featherston → *Colour map 3, C3*

Featherston is the southern gateway to the Wairarapa (or the last settlement depending on which way you came) and sits in the shadow of the Rimutaka Range that was, and continues to be, the 'great divider' between the Wairarapa and Wellington. Featherston is best known as the 1870s base of operations, in the mammoth task of connecting the Wairarapa and Wellington by rail.

The main attraction in Featherston is the **Fell Engine Museum** ⓘ *Fitzherbert St, T06-308 9379, Mon-Fri 0930-1600, Sat-Sun 1000-1600, donation.* It houses the beautifully restored Fell Engine (the only one of its type in the world) that used to climb the steep 265-m slopes of the Rimutaka Incline. The railway line now goes through a tunnel and the **Rimutaka Incline** has been opened up as a walkway, which starts at the end of Cross Creek Road, 10 km south of Featherston. It takes a whole day to reach the summit or cross the ranges to Kaitoke (17 km). There is a YHA in Kaitoke should you need a bed at the other end, T06-526 4626.

As you leave the Wairarapa by road (or indeed arrive) a fine departing (or introductory) view can be seen from the **Rimutaka Trig** (725 m) at the crest of the ranges road. The track (one hour return) starts beside the road, just below the summit café, on the Wellington side. From the top you will get a great view of **Lake Wairarapa** and the coast.

● Sleeping

Masterton p355
The Wairarapa is renowned for its ever-increasing number of B&Bs which comfortably cater for the huge numbers of Wellingtonians, who cross the hills into the Wairarapa in droves on summer weekends and during the holiday periods. Given the sheer number of beds, standards are generally high and competition is fierce. The choices around the vineyards of Martinborough are particularly good (if a little pricey).
AL Acorn Cottage, Bowlands, Bideford, T06-372 4842, www.bowlands.co.nz. Charming, well-appointed, 130-year-old cottage in a country location. Self-contained with log fire.
AL Copthorne Solway Resort, High St South, T06-370 0500, www.solway.co.nz. A standard, fairly unremarkable hotel, but with an attractive range of amenities including pools, spas, squash courts and solarium. Good for families.
AL-A Masterton Motor Lodge, 250 High St, T06-378 2585, www.masterton-motor lodge.co.nz. Wide range of top quality units, pool, spa, in-house restaurant and bar.
A-B Victoria House, 15 Victoria St, T06-377 0186. Good value, centrally located B&B in a restored Victorian villa.
B Empire Lodge, 94 Queen St, T06-377 1902. The town's main budget hotel, with basic rooms (with bathroom) and restaurant.

Motorcamps and campsites
B-D Mawley Park Motor Camp, 15 Oxford St, T06-378 6454. All the usual basic amenities (from cabins to tent sites) situated close to town and beside the river.

Castlepoint p357
There is a well-equipped motorcamp, a tidy motel, a beach store at Castlepoint.

B Whakataki Hotel, 4 km before Castlepoint, T06-372 6852. Kiwi country pub with budget rooms and cabins available.

Motorcamps and campsites
A-D Castlepoint Holiday Park and Motels, T06-372 6705, www.castlepoint.co.nz. Well off the beaten track in a stunning, wild coastal location. Old, yet well-maintained, spacious motorpark with adequate amenities right next to the beach and overlooking the lighthouse and headland. Wide range of accommodation options from tent sites to tourist flats. Additional, modern self-contained motel units are also available in the village.

Riversdale Beach and Flat Point p357
At Riversdale Beach there is a store, a motor-camp and a few accommodation options.
AL Caledonia Coastal Farmstay, Flat Point Rd, T06-372 7553, wendakerr@xtra.co.nz. 2 well-appointed self-contained cottages in prime position overlooking the beach 65 km from Masterton.

Motorcamps and campsites
C-D Riversdale Beach Holiday Park, T06-372 3889, holidaypark@inspire.net.nz. Cabins and sites.

Carterton p357
There are numerous friendly B&Bs available. For the full range contact the VIC (I-Site).
AL Carrington Cottages, T06-379 7039, www.carringtoncottages.co.nz. Nearer Carterton, an option also worth considering.
AL Galtimore, Kokotau Rd, T06-379 6757, galtimore@wise.net.nz. Excellent value, modern 1-bedroom log cabin in private and peaceful rural setting, 10 mins from Carterton, open fire, double spa bath.

A Courthouse Cottage, 16 Hilton Rd, South Carterton, T06-379 7195, www.wairarapa .co.nz/courthouse. Very pleasant self-contained option right in the heart of town. As the name suggests the cottage was the former 1860s courthouse.

B Matador Motel, 187 High St, T06-379 8058, www.matadormotel.co.nz. Not as dodgy as the name suggests and the town's only motel.

B Wairarapa Eco Adventure Retreat, Mangaterere Valley, 16 km west of Carterton, T06-370 3796, www.frenchvillage.co.nz. Spacious, peaceful Eco-oriented lodge set in the foothills of the Tararuas and with direct access to the forest park. Bunk rooms and shared facilities and a great chance to get off the beaten track. Tuition in pilates and yoga an added attraction.

Motorcamps and campsites
B-D Carterton Holiday Park, Belvedere Rd, T06-379 8267. Powered and non-powered sites, standard cabins, self-contained units and camp kitchen.

Greytown *p358*
Greytown and the immediate area has its fair share of lovely B&Bs, details of which are available at the VICs.

LL-AL White Swan Country Hotel, Main St, T06-304 8894, www.thewhiteswan.co.nz. The White Swan has an interesting history being a relocated and fully renovated former railway building from Wellington. It offers a choice of 7 tasteful luxury, individually designed rooms from the Asian 'Bombay' to the English 'George'. There are also cheaper modern suites and studios in a separate wing to the rear of the hotel. Restaurant and bar.

L-AL Briarwood, 21 Main St, T06-304 8336, www.briarwood.biz. Boutique B&B in a renovated historic homestead with 2 tidy suites with claw-foot baths, guest lounge with open fire and just about everything else a body needs to guarantee a relaxing stay. Dinner on request.

L-A Oak Estate Motor Lodge, corner Main St and Hospital Rd, T06-304 8188, www.oakestate.co.nz. Modern luxury suites with spa and Sky TV.

Motorcamps and campsites
There is a basic campsite (**D**, Kuratawhiti St, T06-304 9837), but campers and motor homes are better facilitated at Carterton or Martinborough

Martinborough *p358*
Martinborough has a huge selection of B&Bs and self-contained cottages very similar in design and focusing on the romantic weekend market, in a region becoming internationally renowned for its quality vineyards. You are advised to visit or call the VIC to choose and book.

LL Peppers Martinborough Hotel, The Square, T06-306 9350, www.peppers.co.nz. The historic 1882 Martinborough Hotel adds character and sophistication to this Wairarapa village. The elegant, luxury en suite rooms are individually designed and named after some of the region's first settlers. Attractive features include French doors, which open on to either the hotel veranda or garden, and large claw-foot baths.

LL Wharekaukau Country Estate, Western Lake Rd, Palliser Bay, T06-307 7581, www.wharekaukau.co.nz. Pronounced 'forry-coe-hoe', this is one of the country's top luxury lodges. Located in a quiet corner of the Wairarapa, part of its appeal is the surrounding land (the lodge is based in a 2000-ha working sheep station overlooking the ocean), where you can relish the feeling of getting away from it all. Accommodation is in individual, fully self-contained cottage suites, designed and decorated with natural elements including clay tiles, an open fire and New Zealand wool carpeting. The cuisine is superb with a French/Italian influence and comes with the added allure of top local wines. On-site activities include horse riding, 4WD safaris and clay pigeon shooting, which can, if you wish, be followed by professional spa treatments.

L Petit Hotel, 3 Kitchener St, T06-306 8086, www.petithotel.co.nz. Well-appointed suites with 'plump beds and rich furnishings', bound to attract any couple for a lively weekend. Very discreet hosts. There are numerous romantic self-contained cottages.

● For an explanation of the Sleeping and Eating price codes used in this guide, see the inside
● front cover. Other relevant information is provided in the Essentials chapter, pages 44-51.
Note that prices are given in New Zealand dollars.

AL Duckback Cottage, 9 Broadway St, T06-306 9933, www.duckbackcottage.co.nz. Renovated 1890s self-contained cottage with open fire, 3 bedrooms, and bathroom with claw-foot bath. Again within walking distance of all amenities.

AL The Old Manse, 19 Grey St, T06-306 8599, www.oldmanse.co.nz. Spacious and fully renovated Presbyterian manse overlooking a vineyard and within walking distance of the village centre. 6 tasteful en suites, spa pool.

AL-A La Petite Valle Carriage, T06-306 9767, www.lapetite.co.nz. Something different in the form of an authentic hand-crafted carriage with all mod cons, including en-suite and pot belly stove, set on a working sheep farm 13 km east of Martinborough. Cottage and B&B options are also available.

A The Claremont , 38 Regent St, T06-306 9162, www.claremont-motels.co.nz. One of the few places in New Zealand where a motel is hard to find! This one seems to live up to its near singular standing.

D Kate's Place, 7 Cologne St, T06-306 9935, www.katesplace.co.nz. Small, friendly backpacker-homestay with dorms and one en suite double.

Motorcamps and campsites
D Martinborough Village Camping, on the corner of Princess and Dublin sts, T06-306 8919, www.martinboroughcamping.com. Quality motorpark with all the usual facilities. Bike hire.

Cape Palliser *p359*
B-C Lake Ferry Hotel, Lake Ferry Rd, T06-307 7831. Basic, affordable, hotel accommodation, backpacker beds, good restaurant and bar attached.

Motorcamps and campsites
DoC administers a campsite at the Putangirua Pinnacles, T06-307 8230. Self registration.
B-D Lake Ferry Motorcamp, Lake Ferry Rd, T06-307 7873. Busy, waterside and within walking distance of the hotel.

Featherston *p359*
Featherston has a number of luxury and mid-range lodges, B&Bs and self-contained cottages. The VIC (I-Site) has full listings.

Motorcamps and campsites
C-D Leeway Caravan Park and Backpackers, Fitzherbert St, T06-3089811/ T0800 533 929. Standard clean motel with backpacker facilities, SKY TV and swimming pool.

⊘ Eating

Masterton *p355*
Café Cecille, in the heart of Queen Elizabeth Park (eastern end of Park Av or from Memorial Drive off Dixon St), T06-370 1166. Good choice for either lunch or dinner. Licensed.
Java House, 10 First St, T06-377 7251, Wed-Sun until late. Locally recommended licensed living room café.
Plaza India, 3 Perry St, T06-370 5177. Does an above-average curry.
Café Strada, 232 Queen St, next to the Regent Theatre, T06-3782070, daily 0800-late. Locally recommended.

Castlepoint *p357*
There are no restaurants, so the village store T06-372 6823, and the **Whakataki Hotel**, 4 km north, T06-372 6852, are your best bet.

Carterton *p357*
Buckhorn Bar and Grill, 20 Memorial Sq, T06-379 7972, dinner daily from 1800, lunch Wed-Mon. Pub grub in nice surroundings.
Wild Oates Bakery, 127 High St, T06-379 5580, open from 0630.

Greytown *p358*
Main St Deli, 88 Main St, T06-304 9022, Sun-Thu 0800-1800, Fri-Sat 2000. Considered the best café in the region it has a large outdoor eating area and offers excellent fare for breakfast, lunch and dinner along with some great snacks and coffee, good value.
Wakelin House, 123 Main St, Wed-Mon from 1100. Very congenial and a favourite throughout the region for both lunch and dinner. Recommended.
Salute, 83 Main St, T06-304 9825, Tue-Sun for lunch and dinner and weekends for brunch. Imaginative Middle Eastern/ Mediterranean cuisine with alfresco seating and a fine range of sweets.

Martinborough *p358*

As you might expect, Martinborough is not short of choice.

The French Bistro, 3 Kitchener St, T06-306 8863, Wed-Sun 1700-late. Popular French provincial bistro and wine bar owned by ex-Wellington restaurateurs. Book ahead.

Peppers Martinborough Hotel, T06-306 9350, 0800-late. Popular for breakfast, lunch and dinner.

Cafés

There are a number of good vineyard cafés.

The Old Winery Café, on the **Margrain Estate**, corner Ponatahi Rd and Huangarua Rd, T06-306 8333, summer daily for lunch in summer, Fri-Sat dinner; winter Thu-Sun for lunch, Fri-Sat dinner. One of the most popular.

Village Café, Martinborough Wine Centre, Kitchener St, T06-377 7251, Wed-Sun till late. Convenient with an eclectic range of locally grown produce and good organic coffee.

Featherston *p359*

Lady Featherston, 31 Fitzherbert St, T06-308 6565, Mon-Fri 1000-1700, Sat-Sun 0830-1800. Homemade offerings.

Tin Hut Hotel, Tauherenikau, T06-308 9697, Mon-Fri 1000-1700, Sat-Sun 0830-1800. Country pub with local produce a wine. Ask at the VIC for a map and directions.

⊛ Festivals and events

Masterton *p355*

Mar Golden Shears, www.golden shears.co.nz. See page 355. Sheep-sheering competition.

▲ Activities and tours

Masterton *p355*

Genesis Recreation Complex, Dixon St. Heated indoor and outdoor swimming pools.

The Kaiwhata Walk, Ngahape Rd, T06-372 2772, www.kaiwhatawalk.co.nz. Well-organized 3-day walk on private land towards the coast from the Ngahape Valley. Accommodation, food and transport arranged, from $130.

Mount Bruce National Wildlife Centre, RD1, Masterton, T06-375 8004, www.mt bruce.org.nz. Wildlife viewing and eco-tours in the Wairarapa.

Oasis, 2 Akura Rd, T06-378 8789, www.oasis .org.nz. Indoor climbing wall, from $7.

Tranzit Coachlines, T06-377 1227. Offer good value daily sightseeing and vineyard tours throughout the region, from $95.

Castlepoint *p357*

Legionnaires Charters, T06-372 6613, www.legionnaire-charters.co.nz. Fishing trips, competitions in summer.

Okau Wilderness Park, T06-372 6892. Offers a range of hunting trips for non-natives in their vast 'Wilderness Park', from $200. The main beach is the venue for a famous horse race in Mar.

Carterton *p357*

Ballooning NZ, T06-379 8223. Will take you up, up and away (if the weather is settled) for an early morning 2- to 3-hr flight for about $290, breakfast included.

Martinborough and Featherston *p358*

In an effort to lure the well-heeled Wellingtonians there is an increasing range of activity operators around Martinborough. Amongst other activities you have the choice of canoeing, clay-bird shooting, jet boating and of course vineyard tours (see page 359). The VIC (I-Site) will fill you in with all the details and book on your behalf.

Kahutara Canoes, Kahutara, Lake Ferry Rd, T06-308 8453, www.wairarapa.co.nz/ kahutara. Canoeing on the Ruamahunga River with 'Tuatara Ted', a Crocodile Dundee-type character. Full-day, half-day or 1½-hr trips with BBQ from $45.

Martinborough Wet n Wild, 3 Kitchener St, T06-306 8252, www.wetnwild.co.nz. 30-min adventure jet-boat trips (from $55) and 2- to 4-hr kayaking trips (sit-on-top kayaks) on the Ruamahunga River, from $45.

McLeods Adventures, Hautotara, White Rock Rd, Martinborough, T0800-494335, www.mcleodsadventures.co.nz. Entertaining 1½- to 3½-hr guided quad bike trips (with river crossings) in the hill-country surrounding Martinborough. Ideal wet weather activity, from $100-150. Also offers accommodation and clay pigeon shooting instruction, from $25.

Patuna Farm Adventures, 17 km southeast of Martinborough, T06-306 9966, www.patunafarm.co.nz. Offers a range of activities including horse trekking (from

East coast The Wairarapa *Listings*

$30), pole to pole ropes course (4 hrs, $60), and guided walks to the Patuna Chasm from $15. Accommodation available. **Tora Walks**, T06-307 8115, www.toracoastal walk.co.nz. Offers an interesting and varied 3-day coastal tramp with an equal variety of accommodation types. $330 (all inclusive).

Transport

Bicycle hire Christina Estate Vineyard, T06-306 8920, or Martinborough Village Camping, on the corner of Princess and Dublin sts, T06-306 8919. **Car hire** Graeme Jones Car Rental, 341 Queen St, Masterton, T06-378 6667, from $60 per day.

Directory

Internet Library, 50 Queen St, Masterton T06-378 9666, Mon-Tue 0900-1730, Wed 1000-1730, Thu 0900-2000, Fri 0900-1800, Sat 0930-1300. **Police** Masterton, T06-370 0300.

Wanganui and Manawatu

⁑ Footprint features

Introduction

Stretching from south of Levin to just north of Taumarunui, and from Wanganui on the west coast across to Cape Turnagain in the east, is the Wanganui/Manawatu Region, scythed almost in half by the Whanganui River, the longest navigable river in the North Island. Steeped in history, and supporting a rich watershed of remote hills adorned with native bush, much of the region is protected within the boundaries of the Whanganui National Park.

Settlement began with groups of Maori moa hunters between 1400 and 1650, who were in turn followed by the first Europeans – whalers from Kapiti Island. The rich agricultural lands have now made the region the sixth most populous in New Zealand with almost half of it contained within the urban boundaries of Palmerston North and Wanganui. Palmerston North, home to New Zealand's largest university, is an important national seat of learning. Although not blessed with the tourist bounty of other parts, the region has much to offer and provides a good base for exploring the lower North Island and surrounding national parks. The Whanganui National Park is especially popular with kayakers and trampers, who are able to leave civilization behind for days on end.

★ Don't miss ...

1 **New Zealand Rugby Museum** Pay homage to the All Blacks at the first museum of its kind, page 370.
2 **Science Centre, Museum and Art Gallery** Swot up on art, science and history in this popular interactive museum, page 370.
3 **Bulls** Roll your eyes at the 'unbelieva-bull' signs, page 372.
4 **Whanganui River Road** Take the mail-run through the historic mission settlements of Atene, Koriniti, Hiruharama (Jerusalem) and Pipiriki, page 383.
5 **Whanganui River** Explore the country's longest navigable waterway by kayak or jet boat. Take a side trip to the 'Bridge to Nowhere', page 386.

Palmerston North and around

→ *Colour map 3, B3 Population: 75,000*

On the banks of the Manawatu River and in the heart of flat, rural Manawatu, is the pleasant university and agricultural service town of Palmerston North. Although set away from SH1 and not exactly blessed with a wealth of tourist attractions, 'Palmy' can provide a good base from which to explore the southern half of the North Island and is an important gateway west, through the impressive Manawatu Gorge, to the Wairarapa and Hawkes Bay. Other than Massey University, which is the second largest in the country, the town is perhaps most famous for its rugby museum, a place of almost spiritual significance, where many New Zealand rugby fanatics come on a pilgrimage to pay homage to their All Black heroes. ▸▸ *For Sleeping, Eating and other listings, see pages 373-375.*

Ins and outs

Getting there

By air Palmerston North airport ① *4 km northwest of the city, T06-351 4415, www.pn airport.co.nz,* receives regular flights from most domestic centres with **New Zealand Link,** T0800-737000, www.airnewzealand.co.nz. **Freedom Air,** T0800-600500, www.free domair.com, has flights from eastern Australia. A taxi to the centre costs around $17.

By road Palmerston North is about 30 km west of SH1, 140 km from Wellington and 546 km from Auckland. It is the main gateway to the Wairarapa and Hawke's Bay via SH3 to SH2 at Woodville. The town is serviced by **Intercity, Newmans,** T06-355 5633; **Nakedbus.com** and **White Star,** T06-358 8777. The latter runs a regular service from Wanganui and stops at the Courthouse, Main Street, while the others run from Wellington, Auckland and Napier and stop at the **Palmerston Travel Centre** ① *corner of Main and Pitt sts, T06-355 5633.*

By train Palmerston North is on the main north south rail line. **TranzScenic,** T0800-872467, operates only one service through the region, the 'Overlander' to Auckland. This is currently the only service between Auckland and Wellington. The station is about 2½ km from the town centre off Tremaine Avenue.

Getting around

Be warned: 'Palmy' is a nightmare for getting lost because it is so flat. Stray too far from the central square and visible tall buildings without a street map and you will be lost in a world of fast food and chain retail outlets. Most of the town's sights are within walking distance. **Horizon Tranzit,** T06-355 4955, is the local bus service; standard fare $2. The VIC (I-Site) has timetables. **Madge Buses (Uzabus),** T06-356 4896, www.madge.co.nz, runs a local service to Feilding and Levin from outside Farmers on King Street.

Tourist information

Palmerston North and Destination Manawatu VIC (I-Site) ① *The Square, T06-350 1922, www.manawatunz.co.nz, daily 0900-1700.* **Palmerston North DoC** ① *717 Tremaine Av, T06-350 9700.* **Feilding and District VIC (I-Site)** ① *10 Manchester Sq, Feilding, T06-323 3318, Mon-Fri 0900-1600, Sat 1000-1300.* **Nature Coast VIC (I-Site)** ① *93 Oxford St, Levin, T06-367 8440, horowhenua.visitor@clear.net.nz, Mon-Fri 0900-1730, Sat-Sun 1000-1500,* **Rangitikei (Taihape) VIC (I-Site)** ① *Town Hall, Hautapu St, Taihape, T06-388 0604, www.rangitikei.com, daily 0900-1700.* **Bulls VIC (I-Site)** ① *113 Bridge St, T06-322 0055, www.unforgetabull.co.nz, www.rangitikei.com, daily 0900-1700.*

Palmerston North

Background

The Maori name for the river, Manawatu, is 'still breath' and relates to a lullaby of the coastal tribes from the west coast of the lower North Island. It tells the story of the journey of a cuckolded husband, Hau, to retrieve his wayward wife. Poor Hau named many rivers during his quest to win back his spouse. Sadly, when he eventually found her, she was in the arms of another lover in Wellington – probably a stockbroker. When love-sick Hau came to the Manawatu River, it was so cold it made his breath stand still hence the name, 'still breath'. The local Rangitane Iwi lived in the area for hundreds of years before the Europeans began to settle in the mid 1800s. With the rich surrounding agricultural lands, it did not take Palmerston long to develop and prosper. By 1930 the population was about a third of what it is today.

Sights

The best-known attraction in 'Palmy' is the **New Zealand Rugby Museum** ① *87 Cuba St, T06-358 6947, www.rugbymuseum.co.nz, Mon-Sat 1000-1200 and 1330-1600, Sun 1330-1600, $5, child $2.* Established in 1969, it was the first of its kind in the country and contains the largest collection of rugby memorabilia including shirts, caps, photographs and programmes. There are also videos and detailed accounts of every All Black game since 1870 available for specialist research. If you have a particular question there is a wealth of fanatics on hand to fill you in on every pass, ruck and maul.

The **Te Manawa Science Centre, Museum and Art Gallery** ① *396 Main St, T06-355 5000, www.temanawa.co.nz, daily 1000-1700, free entry to some galleries,* is a progressive and modern centre that integrates the usual social, cultural and artistic heritage with hands-on science displays. It is split into three main parts, the museum, gallery and science centre, all of which are worth visiting. There are the some interesting Maori *taonga* and a few nationally significant artworks by contemporary gurus like Colin McCahon and Ralf Hotere. The gallery often hosts important national touring exhibitions.

If you head west towards the university and the river (Fitzherbert Avenue, then Park Road) you can access the **Victoria Esplanade Gardens** ① *dawn to dusk*, a very pleasant mix of bush, lawn and gardens that grace the banks of the river. There are numerous walking tracks and a play park complete with miniature railway for the kids.

As usual there are leaflets available from the VIC (I-Site) outlining other city walks and gardens. From a historical perspective, the **Regent Theatre** is of particular note and a main feature of the city's heritage walk. Elsewhere, horticultural properties feature under the banner of 'Health, Herbs and Honey'. The **Pohangina Valley Tourist Route**, which takes in a combination of rural scenery, gardens, craft outlets and the market town of Feilding (see page 372) is also worth considering, best broken up with an overnight stay. On a rainy day, the active can head for the climbing wall at **City Rock** ① *217 Featherston St, T06-357 4552, Tue-Thu 1530-2200, Fri 1530-1830, Sat 1000-1900, Sun 1200-1900, $11,* which has a 10-m-high top rope and boulder wall.

While wandering around, you may glimpse the graceful white blades of the **Tararua Wind Farm** towers, on the hills to the west of town. This site has been lauded as one of the largest wind farms in the southern hemisphere, but with major projects about to come to fruition in the South Island (Otago and Southland) this looks as if it will become dwarfed – a great prospect and an even greater testimony to renewable energy in New Zealand. For a closer look there is a private access route from Centre and Back Roads (off Fitzherbert East Road from Massey University) and via Jackson's Farm to Hall Block Road on the east side of the Manawatu Gorge (SH3). Access is restricted, so it may be better to join a tour. ▸▸ *See Activities and tours, page 375.*

Rugby Union – sport or obsession?

Like Australia, New Zealand finds much of its national identity in sport. Paramount among these is the game of Rugby Union. It is the focus of a public devotion that verges on the obsessive. Although invented in England, New Zealand has adopted rugby as if it were its own, making it the most played and most publicly supported national sport.

Over the years the world famous national team known as the All Blacks (due to their iconic black strip) have added a particular 'Southern Hemisphere' flair and style to the game, which, to the layman, is epitomized by the fearsome *haka* (Maori dance or challenge) that is performed in front of the opposition before every match.

The New Zealand Rugby Union was formed in 1892 and the All Blacks very quickly became a dominant force on the world stage. For decades the All Blacks were practically invincible and greatly feared by any opposition.

Drawn from a rich array of national provincial teams the 15 players are considered idols, which places an inordinate amount of pressure upon them to play well. Many have done just that, becoming almost legendary household names, like Colin Meads, who played 55 tests; George Nepia, a Maori who played 32 times; Grant Fox, an awesome goal kicker; Sean Fitzpatrick, perhaps the best captain in the game's history and, of course, the unstoppable Jonah Lomu (although Jonah is in fact Tongan by nationality).

But in many ways, the All Blacks have become victims of their own success. With the creation of the Rugby World Cup in 1987 (held every four years) the All Blacks were naturally expected to win and did so, comfortably. But in 1991 they lost to Australia in the semi-finals, which was a cause of some despair, but felt to be merely an aberration. Then in 1995, in South Africa, the bough broke, when a team considered to be unbeatable lost to the South African 'Springboks' in the dying moments of the final. Back home in New Zealand there was a period of palpable national depression and anger directed upon both players and the coach. Losing was an entirely new experience.

It did not end there. Once again salt was rubbed in the wound when in the Rugby World Cup of 1999 the French (considered underdogs) in the semi-finals trounced a team still thought to be unbeatable. Australia went on to beat France. It seemed the unthinkable was happening – Australia was beginning to take over the mantle of the world's best team.

In the run up to the 2003 Rugby World Cup, the All Blacks were still struggling. For the outsider the reasons seem obvious – the focus on a loss should be one of gracious acceptance rather than a rapacious witch-hunt. The 2003 World Cup only proved this with the usual hype and pressure placed on both players and coach contributing to another humiliating defeat to the host nation and the archenemy – Australia. The coach John Mitchell was sacked and the nation mourned.

Since then, however, the team has consolidated under the wing of veteran coach Greame Henry. And after the post-World Cup hype surrounding England's win, the stage was set for a mighty contest during the Lions tour in 2005. As it happened the All Blacks took the test series 3-0 with considerable ease. For many this was a solid sign that the All Blacks are back in business and the rugby union focus firmly back on the southern hemisphere. The 'ABs' are now firm favourites to take the 2007 World Cup in France and – as no doubt, any Kiwi will tell you – take it again with ease when they host the tournament on home soil in 2011.

Around Palmerston North ⊜🍴▲ » pp373-375.

Feilding → Colour map 3, A6

Feilding sits in the heart of the Manawatu 'flatlands' on the banks of the Oroua River. Named after Colonel William Fielding (a former Director of Emigrants and Colonists Aid Corporation in Australasia), it is a pretty, relatively prosperous town, well known for its gardens. Indeed, their careful nurturing has played a key role in the town's run of success in the nation's 'Most Beautiful Small Town Awards', which it has won a remarkable 12 times. Although there is not a huge amount to see or do, Feilding is a pleasant place to stop for a wander, with a scattering of small museums (traction engines being a speciality), craft outlets and of course, gardens. Better still, take a tour by horse and cart, or watch the local farmers bidding at the stock sales on a Friday.

Levin and Foxton → Colour map 3, B3

Levin and **Foxton**, both southwest of Palmerston North, lie in the heart of the Horowhenua Region. This narrow strip of land, bordered by the Tararua Ranges to the west and the Tasman Sea to the east is, known for its rich alluvial soils and fruit and vegetable growing properties. Earlier industries included flax milling and timber exports.

The **Tokomaru Steam Engine Museum** ① *SH57, T06-329 8867, Mon-Sat 0900-1530, Sun 1030-1530, $12, child $6,* is the highlight (if not the sum total) of Tokomaru Village, 32 km north of Levin. The museum offers the enthusiast or the layperson the chance to see the country's largest collection of working steam engines. There are a number of static displays and the occasional 'steam ups'.

The **Lake Papaitonga Scenic Reserve,** 4 km southwest of Levin, offers a delightful 30-minute walk through superb native bush, before reaching two viewpoints across the lakes. The atmosphere here, particularly at sunset, is magical. The area is rich in both Maori history and birdlife, details of which are outlined at the park's entrance.

Himatangi Beach, which is off SH1 between Foxton and Sanson, is considered the region's best. The sand dunes here are up to 19 km wide and make up New Zealand's largest expanse of sand country. This sense of wilderness, together with the driftwood strewn along the tide line, make a trip well worth while.

Taihape → Colour map 3, B3 Population: 2000

North of 'Palmy' on SH1, in the odd little region of **Rangitikei**, is Taihape, a fairly nondescript town quietly serving the local dairy farming industry. At first sight, there appears to be little of interest, other than a few cafés, motels and shops, but there are some notable activities in the area with fishing leading the way and some of the major river adventure companies are based in the town. The VIC (I-Site) can provide information about a number of garden visits and heritage tours and, of course, Taihape's famous and very silly **World Gumboot Festival,** which formerly brought some life and 'sole' to the town. Given the town's love of footwear, it would be rude not to take a closer at the giant **corrugated gumboot** beside SH1 at the northern entrance to town.

Mangaweka → Colour map 3, B3

Mangaweka is best known for its **DC-3,** which sits next to SH1 and houses a café. It is also the base for **Mangaweka Adventure Company** and **River Valley,** which operate a variety of adventure packages on the river. There is a basic camping ground in the village and a number of local walks established by DoC. » See Activities and tours, page 375.

Bulls → Colour map 3, B3 Population: 3898

The small agricultural service town of Bulls stands off the junction of SH3 and SH1, midway between Wanganui and Palmerston North. Blink and you'll miss it, but take a closer look and you may be surprised to learn that the township was not named after our four-legged friends, but after James Bull, who was one of the first settlers in 1858.

By all accounts he was quite the entrepreneur and created so much of the town's infrastructure that in 1872 the government approved the replacement of the original name for the settlement – Rangitikei – with Bulls. However, our James has a lot to answer for. In the desperate effort to put Bulls on the map, the community has gone to ridiculous lengths to incorporate its name into every one of its amenities. Take a look around and you'll find the VIC (see page 368) which is 'Inform-a-Bull', the chemist which is 'Dispense-a-Bull', the fire station 'Extinguish-a-Bull', the police station 'Const-a-Bull' and the church, which is 'Forgive-a-Bull', and so it goes on. However, there are a few major omissions including, as you head out on SH3, a sign saying 'Antiques and Collectibles' – clearly owned by

> ‡ To the south of Bulls keep an eye open for fields of beautiful sunflowers which are at their best from January to March.

the black sheep of the town. Annoyingly, this is very infectious, and for days you will find yourself suffering from this 'Voca-Bull-ary' affliction. Some may find Bulls entertaining, but others may find such behaviour 'Question-a-Bull'.

Ohakea → *Colour map 3, B3*

At the RNZAF base at Ohakea, on SH1 between Sanson and Bulls, is the **Ohakea Wing RNZAF Museum** ① *T06-351 5020, daily 0930-1630. $10, child $5*, where there are historical and hands-on displays, as well as a flight simulator and a café. Great for kids.

Some 8 km north of Bulls, signposted off SH1, is the six-hectare **Amazing Maize Maze** ① *T06-32 77615, www.maze.co.nz, Dec-Apr Sun-Thu 1000-1800, Fri-Sat 1000-2200, $10, child $6*, which has over 10 km of paths to baffle your orientation skills. 'Moonlight mazing' takes place on Friday and Saturday (bring a torch). The maze takes on a different theme each year, which if viewed from the air, displays exceptional skill.

⬤ Sleeping

Palmerston North *p368, map p369*
Most of the motels are along Fitzherbert Av or the Pioneer Highway.

L-AL Fitzherbert Regency, 250 Fitzherbert Av, T06-355 5155, www.fitzherbertregency.co.nz. New, luxury motor lodge with classy suites, some with spa, broadband.

L-A Kingsgate Hotel, 110 Fitzherbert Av, T06-356 8059, www.kingsgatepalmerston.co.nz. One of 'Palmy's' few hotels, but doesn't let the side down. Restaurant, bar, spa and sauna.

AL Cornwall Motel, 101 Fitzherbert Av, T06-354 9010, www.cornwallmotorlodge.co.nz. Modern and well-located. Enjoys a good reputation.

AL Nikau Loft, 93 Monrad St, T06-354 0561, www.nikauloft.co.nz. Very classy self-contained loft, in a quiet area at the southern fringe of the city. Great value.

AL-A Coachman Motel and Suites, 134 Fitzherbert Av, T06-356 5065, www.coach man.co.nz. Pleasant and well appointed, with café, gardens and an open fire.

A Colonial Court, 305 Fitzherbert Av, T06-359 3888, www.colonialcourtmotel.co.nz. A decent option, worth considering.

A Gables B&B, 179 Fitzherbert Av, T06-358 3209, thegables.pn.nz@xtra.co.nz. Refreshing historic homestead.

A Plum Trees Lodge, 97 Russell St, T06-358 7813, www.plumtreeslodge.com. The former coach house and solid timer beams give this B&B an Old English ambience. Well-appointed and self-contained.

B Boulder Lodge, Pohangina Valley West Rd, Ashurst, T06-329 4746, www.boulder-lodge.co.nz. Some distance from Palmerston North, this is a popular and isolated self-contained wooden lodge and cabins complex sleeping 2-12. You arrive by 4WD and can have a bath outside in an open fire heated tub under the stars. It has no electricity but LPG which provides heating and hot showers. All this is part of the charm.

C-D Peppertree Backpackers, 121 Grey St, T06-355 4054. By far the best backpacker hostel in town, close to the centre. A YHA associate in an old rambling, single storey house. Excellent facilities, open fire and garden where you can view the owner's homemade racing car.

Wanganui and Manawatu Palmerston North & around Listings

C-D Palmerston North Holiday Park, 133
Dittmer Drive, T06-358 0349, www.holiday
parks.co.nz/palmerstonnorth. Rather tired
but next to the river and the Esplanade Park.

Taihape *p372*

Ask the VIC about good farmstays in the area.
AL-B Mairenui Rural Retreat, Ruahine Rd,
T06-382 5564, www.mairenui.co.nz. Good-
value B&B and self-contained options.
A Aspen Court Motel, SH1, Mataroa Rd North,
T06-388 1999, www.aspencourt.co.nz. One of
the most modern in town, with good facilities.
B Taihape Motels, Kuku and Robin sts, T06-
388 0456. An older, cheaper option with
adequate facilities and close to the centre.
C-D River Valley Lodge, Mangahoata Rd,
Pukeokahu, T06-388 1444, www.rivervalley
.co.nz. An excellent backpacker hostel in a prime
location. Full range of rooms including en suites,
tent sites. See Activities and tours, page 375.

Motorcamps and campsites

C-D Riverview Holiday Park, Old Abattoir Rd,
3 km north of town, T06-388 0718. Cabins,
campervans and tent sites. Camp kitchen.

❷ Eating

Palmerston North *p368, map p369*

'Palmy' has more restaurants and cafés per
head than anywhere else in New Zealand.
Most of the high profile eateries are on Cuba
St, Broadway Av and George St, just off the
main square. Many of the pubs offer good
affordable grub. There are various fast food
outlets in the Downtown on Broadway mall.
♦♦♦ **Bella's Café**, 2 The Square, T06-357 8616,
lunch Tue-Sat from 1100, dinner Mon-Sat
1800-late. A popular choice offering a mix
of Italian, Thai and traditional Pacific Rim
dishes. Cosy atmosphere and great service.
♦♦♦ **Dejeuner**, 159 Broadway. T06-952 5581,
www.dejeuner.co.nz, Mon-Sat 1800-late.
A small well-established restaurant offering
an imaginative blackboard menu.
♦♦♦ **Spostato**, 213 Cuba St, T06-952 3400,
daily 1800-late. Italian-style restaurant,
at the top end of the Cuba St offerings.
♦♦ **Bathhouse café and Bar**, 161 Broadway,
T06-952 5570, Mon-Sat from 1800. A fine
year-round choice with Mediterranean-style
fireplace and all-weather courtyard. The diverse

menu includes excellent lamb, venison
and salmon dishes.
♦♦ **Costa's**, 282 Cuba St, T06-952 5577, daily
from 1800. Popular Tex Mex-style restaurant.
♦♦ **Elm Café and Brasserie**, 283 Fitzherbert
St, T06-355 4418, daily 0900-1700, Wed-Sat
1830-late. Away from the centre, but worth
the effort. Traditional cuisine in rather grand
Tuscan-style surroundings.
♦♦ **India Today**, 30 George St, T06-353 7400,
from 1730. Upmarket, with a loyal following.
♦♦ **Moxies**, 81 George St, T06-355 4238, daily
from 0730. New café already established as a
popular spot for breakfast, lunch and dinner
offering an interesting blackboard menu.
♦ **Barista**, 77 George St, T06-357 2614, Mon-
Sat. Has one of the finest breakfasts and
perhaps the best coffee in town.
♦ **Murphy's Brewery**, see Pubs, bars and
clubs, below. Pub lunches in plush surrounds.
♦ **Pompeii**, 198 The Square, T06-952 5575,
daily from 1700 (deliveries available). For a
pizza you can't go far wrong here
♦ **Robert Harris**, 16b Jasper Place, T06-355
3031. Coffee shop, for a reliable cuppa.

Taihape *p372*

There are a number of eateries on Hautapu St.
♦♦ **The Brown Sugar Café**, Huia St, T06-388
1880, daily 0900-1700, Fri-Sun until 2030.
The best café in town with good coffee,
breakfasts and an open fire.
♦♦ **The Venison Kitchen**, 65b Hautapu St,
T06-388 1011. A fairly unique venison café.
♦♦-♦ **Al Centro**, 105 Hautapu St, T06-388
0593, Tue-Sun from 1700. Decent Italian fare.

❶ Pubs, bars and clubs

Palmerston North *p368, map p369*

Flying Fish, Regent Arcade, T06-354 7215. A
hip sushi and cocktail bar going off like a rocket
with discerning locals as 'the' place to be seen.
Highflyers, corner of The Square and Main St,
T06-357 5155. For trendsetters and modernists.
Murphy's Brewery, 481 Main St, T06-355
2337. The best bet for traditionalists.

❸ Entertainment

Palmerston North *p368, map p369*

For most performances in the town you can
get more information and book with Ticketek,
Convention Centre, Main St, T06-358 0000.

Abbey Theatre, 369 Church St, T06-355 4165, www.abbeymusicaltheatre.co.nz Hosts mainly musical (rock and pop) events.

Centrepoint Theatre, corner of Pitt and Church sts, T06-354 5740, www.centre point.co.nz. Established in 1974, this is one of the few North Island theatres that can boast its own full-time professional theatre company. There are regular shows, many of national importance, from comedy to classic dramas, with an emphasis on New Zealand plays.

Downtown Cinemas, Downtown Shopping Arcade, Broadway Av, T06-355 5656, www.dt cinemas.co.nz. The city's mainstream cinema.

Regent Theatre, on Broadway, T06-350 2100, www.regent.co.nz. Formerly the 'Picture Palace' built in 1929, and reinvented several times, this latest rebirth is very impressive. Officially opened in 1998 and with a seating capacity of almost 1500 it hosts events such as ballet, musicals, orchestras and comedy.

O Shopping

Palmerston North *p368, map p369*
Bruce McKenzie Bookshop, 51 George St, T06-356 9922. Makes a refreshing change from large chain bookshops.

Square Edge Creative Centre, corner of The Square and Church St, www.pncac.org.nz. Various shops and galleries offering mainly New Zealand arts and crafts.

Taylor Jensen Gallery, 39 George St, T06-355 4278, www.finearts.co.nz. For fine art.

▲ Activities and tours

Palmerston North *p368, map p369*
Hiwinui Jet Tours, Ferry Reserve, Ballance, T06-329 2838, www.hiwinui.co.nz. Manawatu Gorge River trips 30 min from $55, child $35.

Brookfields, Te Matai Rd, T06-358 0749. Golf course.

Feilding Airfield, Taonui, T06-323 8389. Local gliding club, flights at weekends.

Feilding Golf Course, Feilding, T06-323 8636. Golf course.

Go Jump, T0800-465867, www.0800 gojump.co.nz. Offers a range of tandems skydives from 10,000 ft, $260.

Helipro, T06-357 1348, www.helipro.co.nz. Offers a range of scenic flights including the City Panorama, $90, 10 mins, and the Windfarm Wizzer, $160, 20 mins.

Lido Aquatic Centre, Park Rd, T06-357 2684. Pool open Mon-Thu 0600-2000, Fri 0600-2100, Sat-Sun 0800-2000. Swimming $2.50.

Timeless Horse Treks, Gorge Rd, Ballance, T06-376 6157, www.timelesshorsetreks.co.nz. 1- to 2-hr trips including Tararua Wind Farm.

Taihape *p372*
Mokai Gravity Action, based at Mokai Bridge (off SH1) south of Taihape, T0800-802864, www.gravitycanyon.co.nz. Adrenaline-sapping operations include North Island's highest bungee (80 m, from $125), New Zealand's longest Flying Fox (1 km) from $99.

Tarata Fishaway, T06-388 0354, www.tarata.co.nz. Fly fishing trips on the Rangitikei. Accommodation available.

Mangaweka *p372*
Mangaweka Adventure Co, Main Rd, Mangaweka, T0800-655747/T03-382 5744, www.rra.co.nz. Good river trips including rafting, kayaking, overnight campouts and wilderness safaris, 1 hr from $30, half-day from $65, full day taking in the 80-m canyons of the Rangitikei (used in the *Lord of the Rings* film trilogy) from $180. Suitable for families.

River Valley, T06-388 1444, www.river valley.co.nz. A range of activities including whitewater rafting ($139), horse trekking ($75) and kayaking ($139, hire from $35). Shuttle from Taihape $15, on-site lodging.

⊖ Transport

Palmerston North *p368, map p369*
Airline offices Air NZ, 366 Church St, T06-351 8800. Car hire Rent A dent Car Centre, 61 Milson Line, T06-355 5227. Ward Hire, 445 Tremaine Av, T06-355 3043. Taxi Taxis Gold and Black, T06-355 5059.

⊕ Directory

Palmerston North *p368, map p369*
Internet Alpha Internet Café, 108 Princess St. Library, 4 The Square. Medical services City Health, 22 Victoria Av, T06-355 3300. Palmerston North Hospital, Southern Cross, 21 Carroll St, 106-356 9169. Police 400 Church St, T06-313 600. Post office 338 Church St, Mon-Fri 0800-1800, Sat 0900-1300. Useful addresses AA, 185 Broadway Av, T06-357 7039.

Wanganui → Colour map 3, B2 Population: 43,300

Wanganui lies at the mouth of the Whanganui River roughly halfway between New Plymouth and Wellington. Proud of its river and once a bustling port, Wanganui is now principally an agricultural service town and the southern gateway to the Whanganui River National Park. The town boasts a rich heritage and retains some fine buildings as well as a reputable museum and many parks and gardens. In summer the main street is ablaze with a thousand hanging baskets of flowers and throughout the year the restored steamboat Waimarie *plies the great river, reminding both locals and visitors of days gone by.* ▸▸ *For Sleeping, Eating and other listings, see pages 379-380.*

Ins and outs

Getting there Wanganui airport ① *5 km southwest of town*, is served by **Air New Zealand Link**, T0800-737000. There is an airport shuttle operated by **Ash's Transport**, T06-347 7444, or call a taxi (see page 380). By car, Wanganui is on the main SH3 coastal route 162 km southwest of New Plymouth and 196 km north of Wellington (via SH1 which joins SH3 at Bulls). SH4 from Te Kuiti (250 km) ends in Wanganui. **Newmans** and **Intercity** buses stop at 156 Ridgeway Street. **White Star**, T06-347 6677, operates a service between New Plymouth and Wellington (via Palmerston North) stopping at 161 Ingestre Street. The VIC (I-Site) facilitates all national bus bookings.

Getting around Wanganui has four looped bus routes run by **Tranzit Citylink (Horizons)**, T06-345 4433, www.horizons.govt.nz, Monday to Friday (weekends vary), standard fare $2. The routes start at Maria Place in the centre of town, off Victoria Avenue, and link the main suburbs, including Castlecliff on the coast; pick up a timetable from the VIC (I-Site). There is also a **Mail Run** service to Pipiriki and the Whanganui National Park via the Whanganui River Road (see page 383).

Tourist information **Wanganui VIC (I-Site)** ① *101 Guyton St, T06-349 0508, www.wanganuinz.com, www.destinationwanganui.com, www.rivernz.com, Mon-Fri 0830-1700, Sat-Sun 0900-1500*, has details about the Wanganui Heritage Walk and local Arts Trail. **DoC Wanganui Conservancy Office** ① *Ingestre Chambers, 74 Ingestre St, T06-348 8475.*

Background

The Whanganui River was an important focus for the Maori and provided a vital supply route. Even the great Polynesian explorer Kupe was believed to have travelled up the river in AD 800 and the first Maori settlement dates back to about AD 1000. Intertribal conflicts were common and came to a head (literally) in the 1830 when Ngati Toa, chief Te Rauparaha from Kapiti Island, sacked the local tribe and celebrated with a cannibal feast. Heads continued to roll with the arrival of the first Europeans in 1831 in the form of trader Joe Rowe, reputed to be a dealer in preserved Maori heads. Sadly for ol' Joe it was a case of what goes around comes around and in a dispute with the Maori his head was also lopped off and preserved, the rest of him providing dinner. Thankfully, in 1840, the missionaries arrived and, for a while, everyone began to keep their heads as opposed to losing them. About the same time the New Zealand Company, keen to extend land purchases beyond Wellington, made a rather dubious deal with the local Maori and 'bought' 40,000 acres. Once the Maori realized that this spurious transaction meant the permanent loss of their land, almost a decade of bitter wrangling followed. British troops were brought in, but eventually an agreed cash payment was made in 1848. The Maori went on to assist the *Pakeha* during the Taranaki Land Wars of the 1860s. With the establishment of a railway linking New Plymouth, via Wanganui to Wellington, together with the importance of the river as a communication link, the town prospered.

Sights

Queen's Park was a former British stockade site during the New Zealand Wars of the 1860s and is east of Victoria Avenue. It is essentially the cultural heart of the city and home to the Wanganui Regional Museum, the War Memorial, the Alexander and District Libraries and the Sarjeant Gallery.

The **Wanganui Regional Museum** ⓘ *T06-349 1110, www.wanganui-museum.org.nz, daily 1000-1630, $5,* is of particular note due to the rich local history and the influence of the river. There is a fine collection of Maori *taonga* (treasures) in the *Te Atihaunui-a-Paparangi* (Maori Court) including an inevitable collection of *waka* (canoes), the finest of which is the beautifully carved *Te Mata-o-Houra*. Also of interest also is the range of displays showing the ingenious methods and traps the early Maori used to catch fish on the river and birds in the bush. Upstairs there is a large, tired-looking collection of wildlife exhibits, including numerous native birds and moa bones. Temporary galleries feature a programme of changing exhibitions.

A short distance away from the museum, proudly crowning Queen's Park Hill, is the **Sarjeant Gallery** ⓘ *T06-349 0506, www.sarjeant.org.nz, daily 1030-1630, donation,* set in a grand building and reputed to be one of the best in the country. Home to over 4000 permanent artworks, there is an ever-changing programme of local and national touring exhibitions and occasional international shows.

The **Wanganui Riverboat Centre** ⓘ *on the riverbank on Taupo Quay, T06-347 1863, www.wanganui.org.nz/riverboats, Mon-Sat 0900-1600, Sun 1000-1600; The Waimarie sails Mon-Fri at 1400 (2 hrs), Sat-Sun 1400 (3 hrs); from $30, child $12, in summer there may be additional lunch and dinner cruises, from $48,* has been a hive of activity in

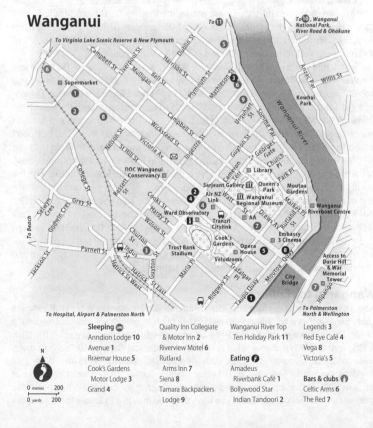

Wanganui

recent years as committed enthusiasts have been hard at work fully restoring the old paddlesteamer *The Waimarie*. This steamer worked the river for 50 years, carrying a wide variety of cargoes and tourists, before she came to grief and sank at her moorings in 1952. In 1993 she was removed from the mud and over the next seven years faithfully restored to be relaunched on the first day of the 21st century. Now, she is sailed proudly up the river daily with a loving crew and cargo of admiring tourists. Although the riverboat centre no longer houses *The Waimarie* there are displays of photographs and memorabilia from the river era. If you do go for a trip be sure to ask if you can take a look at the restored steam engine that pumps the pistons below decks. It is quite a sight and testimony to the loving care and attention that is now bestowed upon the old girl since she was pulled from the mud.

In 2006, another vessel, *The MV Wairoa*, began her second life on the Wanganui. Like *The Waimarie* she served for many years as a passenger and goods vessel back and forth from the city to Pipiriki, before sinking in 1955. Salvaged in 1987 she was lovingly restored and is now used for scheduled picnic cruises to Hipango Park 25 km upstream, from $50, child $20. Consult the centre for the latest cruise schedule.

Immediately across the road from the riverboat centre are the **Moutoa Gardens** which, though unremarkable, are famous as the spot where the deed was believed to be signed between the New Zealand Company and the Maori for the dubious land deals of 1840. This notoriety and the continued displeasure felt by Maori regarding land deals led to an occupation of these gardens in 1995. High profile court battles followed and an ugly confrontation with police was only avoided by face-to-face meetings and thankfully a peaceful end to the 83-day occupation.

Cook's Gardens, which grace the western heart of the town on St Hill Street, are home to the 1899 colonial-style **Opera House**, the modern **Trust Bank Stadium** (with its wooden cycling velodrome) and the **Ward Observatory** ① *T025-245 8066, open for public viewing Fri 2000-2130*. This observatory was originally built in 1901 and houses the largest telescope of its kind still in use in the country.

Just across the bridge from Taupo Quay is the unusual access to the **Durie Hill** and the **War Memorial Tower**. Almost immediately across the bridge, a tunnel takes you 200 m into the hillside where you can take the **Earthbound Durie Hill Elevator** ① *Mon-Fri 0730-1800, Sat 0900-1700, Sun 1000-1700, $1*. From the top you can then climb the Durie Hill War Memorial Tower, built of fossilized rock. The view from the top is rather engaging and on a clear day can include Mount Taranaki and Ruapehu, but don't expect to get any photographs of Ruapehu, unless you want a water tower in the way.

There are a number of good parks and gardens in the town and surrounding area. At the top end of Victoria Avenue up the hill is the **Virginia Lake Scenic Reserve** with the usual lake, themed gardens and aviary. There is a nice walk that goes around the lake and once completed you can celebrate by setting off the coin-operated lake fountain.

If you have kids the star attraction in Wanganui has to be the excellent **Kowhai Park** on the eastern bank of the river just across the bridge to Anzac Parade. Here you can find a wonderful array of interactive attractions including a dinosaur slide, a pirate ship, a flying fox, roller beetles and sea serpent swings, as well as the traditional bike and skateboard tracks, all of which will keep them happy for hours.

Wanganui to Hawera

About 5 km northwest of Wanganui, down Rapanui Road (towards the sea) is **Westmere Lake**. Set aside as a wildlife refuge with native bush, it provides a pleasant spot for a picnic. For the more energetic there is a 40-minute walk that circumnavigates the lake. A little further down Rapanui Road is the **Bason Botanical Gardens** ① *T06-342 9742, www.basonbotanicgardens.org.nz, daily 0800-dusk*, bequeathed to the Wanganui Regional Council in 1966 by local farmer Stanley Bason. They consist of 25 ha of gardens, with native and introduced plants, a conservatory, begonia house, camellia garden and lake with a lookout. If you have time you may like to follow the road to the

Beach, which is surrounded by cliffs but still provides a safe spot for swimming.

Back on SH3 and a further 20 km northwest is the **Bushy Park Forest** ① turn right *at the village of Kai Iwi and follow the signs (8 km), daily, small entry charge.* It's a picturesque 90-ha reserve with a rich variety of native flora and fauna. Some of the trees are magnificent and they include the great girth and twisted trunk of 'Ratanui', a Northern rata that is thought to be the largest living rata in the southern hemisphere.

Ashley Park ① *29 km northwest of Wanganui near the village of Waitotara, T06-346 5917, www.ashleypark.co.nz, daily 0900-1700, $4, child $2,* is similar to Bushy Park, but more commercial, with farm animals, pony rides, a swimming pool and a café. Even fur seals put in an occasional appearance.

● Sleeping

Wanganui *p376, map p377*
There are over 20 motels, with Victoria Av being home to some of the newest and the best. Other than motels there is not a large amount of choice in Wanganui; B&Bs are particularly thin on the ground.
AL-A Avenue Hotel, 379 Victoria Av, T06-349 0044, www.theavenuewanganui.com. Glorified modern motel with café, bar and outdoor pool, walking distance to the town.
AL-A Rutland Arms Inn, corner of Victoria Av and Ridgeway St, T06-347 7677, www.rutland-arms.co.nz. Centrally located. Well-appointed suites in the old English style. Bar, restaurant and courtyard café attached.
AL-A Siena, 355 Victoria Av, T06-345 9009, www.siena.co.nz.
AL-D Anndion Lodge, 2 km from the CBD, 143 Anzac Parade, T06-343 3593, www.anndionlodge.co.nz. Somewhere between a modern backpacker hostel and a motel this rates as one of the best establishments in the North Island. It offers modern and tidy riverside accommodation, with rooms ranging from super-king to dorms at reasonable prices. Well facilitated with spa, internet, off-street parking. Recommended.
A Cook's Gardens Motor Lodge, corner of Guyton and Purnell sts, T06-345 6003, www.cooksgardens.info.
A Quality Inn Collegiate Hotel and Motor Inn, 122 Liverpool St, T06-345 8309, www.collegiatemotorinn.co.nz.
A Riverview Motel, 14 Somme Parade, T06-345 2888.
A-B Grand Hotel, corner of St Hill and Guyton sts, T06-345 0955, www.thegrandhotel.co.nz. A 1920s hotel in the heart of town. Nothing spectacular but good value with, spa, bar and good restaurant attached. Internet.

C-D Braemar House, 2 Plymouth St, T06-348 2301, www.braemarhouse.co.nz. YHA affiliate, recently renovated and round the corner from the **Tamara**. Comfortable and more sedate, off-street parking.
C-D Tamara Backpackers Lodge, 24 Somme Parade, T06-347 6300, www.tamaralodge.co.nz. Closer to the CBD than **Braemar** and well established. Very good backpacker hostel with a locally streetwise manager, set in a large 2-storey villa overlooking the river. A range of older rooms or new units with own bathroom. Large garden, free bike hire, internet, off-street parking. River trips organized.

Motorcamps and campsites
C-D Wanganui River Top 10 Holiday Park, 460 Somme Parade, T06-343 8402, T0800-272664. A bit out of the centre but worth the drive. Quiet, modern facilities next to the river, spa, kayak hire.

Wanganui to Hawera *p378*
A-D Bushy Park Homestead, T06-342 9879, www.bushypark-homestead.co.nz. Built in 1906, this homestead provides grand B&B and budget accommodation.
B-D Ashley Park, SH3, Waitotara, T06-346 5917. Motel, B&B, farmstay and campsite.

● Eating

Wanganui *p376, map p377*
♔ **Bollywood Star Indian Tandoori Restaurant**, 88 Guyton St, T06-345 9996, lunch Tue-Sun 1100-1500, daily for dinner from 1800. Licensed. The best Indian in town.
♔ **Legends Café Restaurant**, 25 Somme Parade, T06-348 7606, Wed-Sun 0730-late.

Licensed. Popular with affordable breakfasts, lunches and à la carte evening dining.
¶¶ Vega Restaurant, overlooking the river, 49 Taupo Quay, T06-349 0078, lunch Tue-Sun, daily for dinner. Licensed. Classy establishment set in a converted warehouse that has quickly earned a reputation as the city's finest, especially for seafood. Excellent wine list.
¶¶ Victoria's, 13 Victoria Av, T06-347 7007. Tue-Fri from 1200-1400, Tue-Sun from 1800. Licensed. Also enjoys a good reputation for traditional New Zealand fare.
¶ Amadeus Riverbank Café, 69 Taupo Quay, T06-345 1538, daily 0830-1600. Licensed. Does a fine value breakfast, good coffee and outdoor seating overlooking the river.
¶ Red Eye Café, 96 Guyton St, T06-345 5646. Tue-Sat 0830-late. Live jazz 1st Sun of the month 1000-1500. Has a loyal following and serves a good coffee.

❶ Pubs, bars and clubs

Wanganui *p376, map p377*
For the inevitable Irish-style offerings try **Rosie O'Grady's**, attached to the Grand Hotel, Guyton St; and **Celtic Arms**, 437 Victoria Av, T06-3477037.
The Red, Anzac Parade. Along with the **Rutland Arms**, this is one of the main pubs in town, also offering à la carte dining.
Rutland Arms Inn, see above. Seems to attract a friendly clientele.

❻ Entertainment

Wanganui *p376, map p377*
Embassy 3 Cinema, 34 Victoria Av, T06-345 7958. For details about other up-and-coming performances contact the VIC.
Royal Wanganui Opera House, on the edge of Cooks Gardens, St Hill St, T06-349 0511, www.royaloperahouse.co.nz. Small but very grand and a regular venue for touring shows.

❀ Festivals

Wanganui *p376, map p377*
Dec-Mar Wanganui in Bloom. The streets are adorned with 1000 hanging baskets of flowers. The highlight is the festival and **Heritage Weekend** in Mar, when there are various events including a raft race, vintage car procession and street bands.

Mar Wanganui Artists Open Studios Weekend (last 2 weekends). This nationally recognized festival offers a fine opportunity to sample the (considerable) local talent in the towns fine galleries. The *Arts Trail* leaflets from the VIC provide information. **Wanganui Arts Festival** is a more high profile biennial event that takes place over the course of a week; next held end Mar 2008.

▲ Activities and tours

Wanganui *p376, map p377*
For all river activities based in or around Wanganui, see page 383. Note that there is a **Mail Run Tour** service operating to Pipiriki and the Whanganui National Park via the Whanganui River Road (see page 383).

Mountain biking
As well as being the main gateway to the national park, Wanganui is known for its excellent mountain biking. Favoured tracks include **Lismore Forest**, **Hylton Park**, **Bushy Park Loop**, **Whanganui River Road** and **Pauri Village Forest**. The VIC can provide details. **Wanganui Pro Cycle Centre**, 199 Victoria Av, T06-345 3715. Bike hire and advice.

❺ Transport

Wanganui *p376, map p377*
Airline offices Air NZ, 133 Victoria Av, T06-348 3500. **Bicycle hire** Wanganui Cycle Centre, 199 Victoria Av, T06-345 3715, from $40 per day. **Car hire** Avis, 192 Guyton St, T06-348 7528. Rent-a-Dent, 26 Churton St, T06-345 1505. **Taxi** Wanganui Taxis, T06-343 5555.

❶ Directory

Wanganui *p376, map p377*
Internet Available at the VIC (I-Site) and the library, Queen's Park, T06-349 1000, Mon-Fri 0900-2000, Sat 0900-1630. **Post office** 226 Victoria Av (between Ingestre and Plymouth sts), T06-345 4103, Mon-Fri 0830-1700. **Medical services** After Hours, 163 Wicksteed St, T06-348 0333. Wanganui Hospital, Heads Rd, T06-348 1234. **Police** Bell St, T06-349 0600. **Useful addresses** AA, 78 Victoria Av, T06-348 9160.

Whanganui National Park

→ *Colour map 3, A3*

Springing from high on the volcanic slopes of Tongariro National Park, the Whanganui River begins its 290-km journey to the sea, carving its way through some of the most remote and inaccessible country in the North Island. At its most remote mid to lower reaches, it cuts deep in to the soft, sand and mudstone and is joined by tracts of intact lowland forest, which form the heart of the Whanganui National Park. Although the river is not the longest in the North Island (that honour goes to the Waikato) it has been the longest navigable river for generations. As a result the river is rich in both Maori and European history, from the first days of early exploration and settlement through to the river's renaissance as a tourist and recreational attraction. Although the entire area is hard to access (which is undoubtedly part of its charm), there is the opportunity to explore the historical sites of the river and enjoy its atmosphere. You can do this, in part on its banks by road and walking tracks, or on the river itself by jet boat or kayak. ➤➤ *For Sleeping, Eating and other listings, see pages 385-386.*

Ins and outs

Getting there and around The three principal gateway settlements to the river are **Taumarunui** to the north, **Raetihi** to the northwest and **Wanganui** to the south. Physical access to the river and the park is from six main access points: from the north, **Ohinepane**, 21 km downriver from Taumarunui; from the east, **Whakahoro** (linked to SH4 by roads from Owhango and Raurimu), **Pipiriki** (accessible from Raetihi), and **Ohura Road** (from SH4 north of Raetihi); from the south via the **River Road** off SH4 (just north of Wanganui) to Pipiriki; and from the west via way of **Stratford/Ohura Road** (SH43) where Brewer Road and Mangaehu Road lead on to Kohi Saddle and the Matemateaonga Track. As well as the daily **Mail Run** service from Wanganui to Pipiriki, T06-347 7534, www.whanganuitours.co.nz, most tour operators will provide transport in and out of the park for about $40-50 return. Other than that you are on your own.

Note that both the backroads, tracks and the river itself is subject to slips and flooding so always consult the **DoC** before attempting a major excursion. Summer is undoubtedly the busiest and safest time to visit the park. During this time you are advised to pre-book all accommodation.

Tourist information There are **DoC** offices in Wanganui, T06-345 2402, Pipiriki, T06-385 5022, and Taumarunui, T07-895 8201. For DoC bookings also refer to their website www.doc.govt.nz. They deal with all information enquiries and hut/campsite bookings and fees. Consult the local office for latest fee structures and conditions. There are a number of good books available about the river and the park (available from main DoC offices) while DoC produces detailed leaflets, including the helpful *In and Around Whanganui National Park* and the *Whanganui Journey*. They also stock the recommended publication *Guide to the Whanganui River* ($10).

Background

Legend has it that the Whanganui was created as a result of a mighty love feud between the mountains of Tongariro and Taranaki in the central North Island. When both fell in love with the beautiful Mount Pihanga, a battle ensued. Taranaki lost the fight and, wild with grief and anger, ripped himself from his roots and tore a path towards the coast, where he now stands alone – in a mighty huff. Perhaps through indifference or appeasement, Tongariro created the waters that filled Taranaki's path of destruction and the Whanganui River was born.

Less than 300 years after the great Maori explorer Kupe first explored the healing scars of Taranaki, the descendants of the early canoes began to settle the riverbanks. In time the river became linked by a series of *pa* (Maori settlements) and on almost every bend there was a guardian controlling and protecting the life forces of the river. The 'river people' became expert at utilizing the river's resources. Sheltered terraces were cultivated and elaborate eel weirs were built and, although not necessarily at harmony with neighbouring tribes, they were certainly in harmony with the environment. The first major European influence came in the form of missionaries in 1840 who created a number of missions on the banks of the river's lower reaches.

Whanganui National Park

These mission settlements were given evocative names that were transliterated in to Maori equivalents, including Jerusalem (Hiruharama), Athens (Atene) and Corinth (Koriniti). Although only one mission remains in Jerusalem, these settlements still grace the banks of the lower reaches along the Whanganui River Road.

By the mid-1860s the steamer *Moutoa* was the first to reach Pipiriki (now located at the head of the Whanganui Road but then accessible only by boat). Soon a regular riverboat service was established that by 1891 was carrying passengers, mail and freight to the European settlers who had attempted to farm the remote banks and valleys. It is a testimony to the navigational skills and upkeep of the river that these boats could reach Taumarunui, almost 200 km upstream from Wanganui. With such a remote location and unique method of transportation, the area and the river soon began attracting tourists and by the turn of the century there were over 10,000 annual visitors. For a time the river became known as the 'Rhine of New Zealand' and the sparse, struggling settlements along the river prospered. Hotels were built, including a huge establishment at Pipiriki (since burnt down) and further inroads were made to reach the river. This included a road built from Raetihi in the 1930s of which the 'Bridge to Nowhere' is now the only lasting monument. With the creation of such roads and the main trunk railway together with the ceaseless silting up of the river the riverboat service waned, finally ceasing regular operations in the 1920s. With the improvement of communication links everywhere the tourist trade also suffered and the area went into decline with the paddles of the last steamboats ceasing to turn in the late 1950s. Now, when it comes to tourism Taranaki's old tear of destruction is enjoying its second honeymoon.

Whanganui River Road

Whanganui River Road

Due to its inaccessible nature it takes some effort, and almost certainly a trip on the river itself, to get a proper feel for the park and the river (see Activities and tours, page 385). However, if you are short of time or if you don't fancy getting your feet wet, the best way to make your acquaintance with the park is via the Whanganui River Road.

This windy scenic road branches off SH4 15 km north of Wanganui and follows the river to Pipiriki, before turning inland to Raetihi where it rejoins SH4. The entire trip is 106 km and although the road is slow and for the most part unsealed, it can be done comfortably in about four hours. As well as the scenery itself, there are a number of small historically significant settlements, specific historic sites, *marae* and some fine short- to medium-length walks along the way.

From south to north after the Aramoana Walkway and Lookout (now closed) the road joins the river proper. The first specific point of interest is the *Pungarehu Wharenui* (meeting house), just before the settlement of **Parikino**, which used to be located on the other side of the river and now occupies a former Maori village. Just after Parikino the road cuts into a series of **Oyster Shell Bluffs** (once seabed) before reaching **Atene** (Athens), the first of a number of mission settlements created in the 1840s by the Reverend Richard Taylor. Just before the village is the access point to the **Atene Skyline Track**. This recently upgraded DoC track crosses farmland before climbing to take in rewarding views of the entire region before continuing to rejoin the River Road further north (viewpoint 1½ hours return; full walk six to eight hours).

The next settlement and former mission settlement is **Koriniti** (Corinth). Formerly the Maori settlement of Otukopiri, it still retains a fine *marae* that welcomes visitors. The Anglican Church dates back to 1920. Keep your eyes open here too for flood markers, one of which is half way up a barn, providing a shocking reminder of the potential dangers of the river. The **Operiki Pa**, just north of Koriniti, was the original home of the Koriniti Maori and the site of the first Anglican Church built in 1840. About 6 km further north is the **Kawana Flour Mill**, a fully restored example from 1854, complete with miller's cottage. Both the mill and the cottage are a short walk from the main road and well worth a quick look. **Ranana** (London) is the next small settlement. Ranana was one of the largest former mission settlements first established in the 1890s and its church is still in use today.

After Ranana is **Hiruharama** (Jerusalem) the most picturesque of all the former missions. Originally a larger Maori village known as Patiarero, it was once home to famous New Zealand poet James Baxter and French Sister Mary Aubert whose Catholic mission still remains to this day. You can visit the church that was built in the late 1800s. From here the road climbs to a fine viewpoint and the **Omorehu Waterfall Lookout** before delivering you at **Pipiriki**. Pipiriki used to be the major tourist destination at the turn of the century, complete with a large hotel. These days, although not so blessed with luxurious accommodation, it is still an important settlement, serving as the main southern gateway to the heart of the national park via the river itself. Although the large hotel, Pipiriki House, that once stood here has long since burnt down, a former **Colonial House** ⓘ *summer 1000-1600, $1, child $0.50*, remains and serves as a small museum and information centre, as well as a reminder of the former glory days.

The small DoC office in Pipiriki can assist with information and also provides overnight parking. On the way you will pass the rather sorry remains of the former 1903 steamer *MV Ongarue*, which plied the river until the late 1950s. Although restored in 1983 and placed high and dry on the hill for all to see, she is clearly much in need of some attention and a new lick of paint. From Pipiriki the road then turns inland and winds its way for 27 km to the small township of Raetihi, where it rejoins SH4.

One of the major man-made 'sights' within the park is the very aptly named **'Bridge to Nowhere'**. Built in 1936 to provide access for a remote rural pioneer settlement, it never really served its intended purpose after the project was abandoned with the advent of the Second World War. Regenerating bush quickly covered the track and the bridge is all that remains. It is located about 30 km upstream from Pipiriki and can only be reached from the river by jet-boat, canoe or by a three-day walk.

▲ Tramping

Matemateaonga Walkway This track, which penetrates deep into the heart of the park and traverses an expanse of thick bush-clad hill country between Taranaki and the Whanganui River, is considered one of the North Island's great walks. It uses an old Maori trail and former settlers' dray road and for the most part follows the ridges of the Matemateaonga Range before arriving at the river and the Ramanui Lodge. The highlight is a short 1½-hour diversion up the 730-m Mount Humphries for a fine view. The track is 42 km in length, considered 'moderate' in difficulty and takes about four days. There are three DoC huts along the way for which a fee must be paid. Transport must be arranged with one of the jet boat operators either to pick you up or drop you off at the river end of the track. From the west the track is accessed from SH43 at Strathmore, near Stratford. Look for the signpost that indicates the road to Upper Mangaehu Road and the track which begins at Kohi Saddle. ▸▸ *See also Activities and tours, page 386.*

Mangapurua Track The Mangapurua Track is a similar length to the Matemateaonga Walkway and takes three to four days to complete. It starts from Whakahoro (easily accessed at the end of the Whakahoro Road) up the Kaiwhakauka Valley past the Mangapurua Trig (663 m) and then descends through the Mangapurua Valley, via the 'Bridge to Nowhere' to meet the river at the Mangapurua Landing, 30 km upstream from Pipiriki. There is only one hut at Whakahoro but a number of good campsites along the way. Again, you will need to arrange jet boat transportation back to base.

● Sleeping

Whanganui National Park
p381, map p382
Both the walking tracks and the river itself within the park are well-endowed with DoC huts and campsites.
AL-D Bridge to Nowhere Lodge, 21 km north of Pipiriki, T06-348 7122, T025-480308, www.bridgetonowhere-lodge.co.nz. In addition to the DoC facilities and the *marae*, this is a very popular option. Set in a very remote spot on the riverbank in the heart of the park, access is either by boat or on foot, which makes the place very special. There is B&B (dinner if required), cabin and campsite accommodation, along with a bar and positively exquisite home cooking. Guided tours to the 'bridge' also available.

Whanganui River Road *p383, map p383*
A Rivertime Lodge, Parikino, T06-342 5595, www.omakaholiday.co.nz. 1000-ha hill farm with self-catering homestay. One en suite and 2 twins with shared facilities. The lodge is only 4 km from the Atene Skyline Track.
B Flying Fox, Koriniti, T06-342 8160, www.theflyingfox.co.nz. The Flying Fox is on the western bank of the river and is only accessible by an exciting aerial cableway or by jet boat. The accommodation is full of character and consists of B&B, 2 self-contained cottages and campsites. There is a very cute outdoor wood-fired bath, some fine 'home brew' to sample and the home cooking is superb. Recommended.
B Kohu Cottage, 3154 Whanganui River Rd, T06-342 8178, kohu.cottage@xtra.co.nz. Renovated and peaceful riverside cottage sleeps 3-4.

B Operiki Farmstay, Operiki, T06-342 8159 operiki@whanganuiriver.co.nz. Traditional single storey house farmstay close to the river. One double and one twin, dinner on request. Friendly hosts and good value.
D Koriniti Marae, Koriniti, T06-342 8198 www.koriniti.com. An ideal opportunity to stay at an authentic *marae*. A traditional *hangi*, flax weaving lessons and *waka* (canoe) cruises under the banner of the full 'Marae Experience' is available from $190. Recommended.

Campsites
D DoC, Pipiriki, T06-385 5022.
D Kauika Campsite, near Ranana, T06-342 8061.

▲ Activities and tours

Whanganui National Park
p381, map p382
There are numerous options available for exploring the river from simple independent and self-guided canoe hire, to single- or multi-day kayak trips, jet-boat trips and multi-day tramps. The various operators can supply all the necessary equipment (including camping gear). As well as the designated DoC huts and campsites along the way there is a comfortable B&B Lodge (Ramanui) in the heart of the park. Note that if you do go it alone, especially tramping, the tracks essentially end at the river and pick-ups will have to be arranged. If you are alone this may be costly, so careful logistics are sometimes necessary to time your arrivals and departures with scheduled tour trips.

The Whanganui is very popular with kayakers and canoeists due to its sheer length – and the 239 listed rapids along the way. But it is fairly unique in this sense, in that for almost its entire length the rapids are of a grade suitable for beginners. There are a wide range of trips available from 5 days (Taumarunui to Pipiriki) to just a few hours. There are designated DoC huts and campsites with basic amenities, throughout the park for use by kayakers and trampers. Note fees apply and bookings are required. Kayaking trips can be done independently or with the various tour operators, most of whom access the river from the north. The best time to embark on a major trip is in the summer, though more experienced canoeists sometimes tackle the river after winter rains. Costs vary but standard independent canoe or kayak (Canadian) hire starts at about $60. A trip with a tour operator, which includes all equipment, will cost you about $85-110 per day. DoC charges the Great Walks Hut and Campsite Pass fee of $45 for hut and campsite use in peak season 1 Oct-30 Apr. In the off season standard backcountry hut/campsite rates apply.

Blazing Paddles, Taumarunui, T07-895 5261, T0800-252946, www.blazingpaddles.co.nz. 1- to 5-day trips. Canadian or kayak. Self-guided from $230 for full 5-day trip. Guides optional.

Bridge to Nowhere, Bridge to Nowhere Lodge, T06-348 7122, www.rivercitytours.co.nz 1- to 6-day guided or independent hire.

Canoe Safaris, Ohakune, T06-385 9237, www.canoesafaris.co.nz. Canoe and rafting trips throughout the area, fully guided and catered. Whanganui 2- to 5- day guided trips from $320, all-inclusive.

Wade's Landing Outdoors, Whakahoro, T06-895 5995/T0800-226631, www.whanganui.co.nz. Canoe, kayak and jet-boat trips (including combinations thereof), tramping drop-offs. Flexible itineraries.

Waka Tours, Raetihi, T06-385 4811, www.wakatours.net. 3-day guided Canadian canoe trip with a Maori cultural and environmental edge, including a stay and *hangi* at the Koriniti Marae from $560. Recommended.

Yeti Tours, Ohakune, T0800-322388/ T06-385 8197, www.canoe.co.nz. Luxury or economy 2- to 6-day trips, from $335. Recommended for the longer excursion.

Jet boating

Since the 1980s, jet boats have been the principal fast transport link up and down the river. There are various operators providing sightseeing trips from 15 mins to 2 days (including the drop-off for the 40-min 'Bridge to Nowhere' walk) and pick-ups from the river ends of the Matemateaonga Walkway and Mangapurua Track. Again costs vary but a 5-hr trip to the bridge will cost about $95.

Bridge to Nowhere Jetboat Tours, Pipiriki, T025-480308/T06-348 7122, www.bridgeto nowheretours.co.nz. 4 hrs, $95. All trips depart from Pipiriki (see page 384).

Wade's Landing Outdoors, Whakahoro, T06-895 5995. Canoe, kayak and jet-boat trips. Flexible itineraries.

Whanganui River Adventures, T06-385 3246/T0800-862743, www.riverspirit.co.nz. Trips from Pipiriki to Bridge to Nowhere, 45 mins, $50.

Tramping

From 1 Oct-30 Apr you must buy a hut and campsite pass from DoC (or VIC and some operators) before staring your journey. This pass costs $45 youth $22.50. In the off season standard backcountry hut/campsite rates apply. Concessions are available for some canoe and jet boat trips. Campsites provide a water supply, toilets and shelters with benches for cooking. Huts have bunks with mattresses, stoves, benches, tables and cooking facilities. In winter campsites are free of charge while hut users must have hut tickets or an annual hut pass. The **Teieke Hut** on the eastern riverbank near the Matemateaonga Landing is fairly unusual in that it is also a *marae*, (traditional protocol must be observed).

As well as the **Bridge to Nowhere** track which is accessible only by jet boat canoe or by foot there are 2 main tramps in the park: the Matemateaonga Walkway and the Mangapurua Track, see page 385.

✦ Footprint features

Introduction

Although Wellington is the nation's capital it enjoys a small-town atmosphere. And with its surrounding hills, generally compact layout and well-preserved historical buildings, it has far more character than sprawling Auckland or monotonously flat Christchurch. Wellington is a vibrant, cosmopolitan city, noted for its arts and café culture, with almost as many restaurants and cafés per capita as New York. Its most famous visitor attraction, the multi-million dollar 'Te Papa' Museum, is on the city's recently revamped and buzzing waterfront. Some of the best shopping in the country can also be found in the compact city centre. If you are heading for the South Island by ferry, you will inevitably encounter Wellington and you are advised to give it more than a cursory glance before boarding the ferry.

To the east of the city are the rather unremarkable commuter towns of Upper and Lower Hutt, from where you can reach the beautiful, off-the-beaten-track region of the Wairarapa, with its remote coastline. First, though, you must negotiate the Rimutakas (known as 'the hill'), a natural barrier that has always prevented the spread and pace of settlement and development. To the north, major rail and road links hug the scenic Kapiti coastline, with its pleasant coastal towns and their associated beaches and attractions – the most noteworthy being the nature reserve of Kapiti Island looming a short distance offshore.

★ Don't miss ...

1 **Mount Victoria** Take in the city views and, on a windy day, watch the planes make the tricky landing into Wellington Airport below you, page 392.

2 **Waterfront** Go rollerblading next to the harbour, then enjoy an alfresco lager, page 393.

3 **Museum of Wellington, City and Sea** Stand in awe at the stunning holographic displays on Maori legends, page 393.

4 **Te Papa Museum of New Zealand** Learn about all things Kiwi at the impressive national museum, but beware of sensory overload, page 395.

5 **Botanic Gardens and Cable Car** Head up the hill from the city centre to enjoy the views and smell the roses, then walk back down via the Parliamentary District, page 396.

6 **Cuba Street and Courtenay Place** Enjoy Wellington's world-class café and restaurant scene, page 402.

7 **Nga Manu Nature Reserve** View native and non-native species in a bush setting, page 408.

8 **Kapiti Island** Take a day trip off the scenic Kapiti Coast to this incredible, wildlife paradise of the old non-human New Zealand, page 408.

Wellington Introduction

Ins and outs → *For Sleeping, Eating and other listings see pages 399-406.*

Getting there

Air **Wellington airport** ① *Miramar, 6 km south of the centre, T04-385 5100, www.well ingtonairport.co.nz*, is highly modern and efficient, handling both international and domestic flights. It is perhaps the most infamous airport in the country due to its short runway, nestled precariously between populated hillsides. During southerly storms the news often shows the latest 'interesting' landing from Wellington. The fact you can practically make eye contact with the residents in the houses on the hillsides, makes arrival by air rather memorable. Although there are dozens of **Trans-Tasman** and **Pacific Island** flights per week, Wellington primarily operates a domestic schedule, with regular daily flights from most principal centres. **Air New Zealand**, T0800-737000, www.airnewzealand.co.nz, and **Qantas**, T0800-808767, www.qantas.co.nz, are the main carriers. A number of smaller operators fly from upper South Island destinations. These include **Sounds Air**, T0800-505005, www.soundsair.co.nz, which offers regular and very reasonable fares from Picton (from $79 one way) and Kaikoura ($125); and **Air2there.com**, T0800-777000, which operates from Nelson and Blenheim. The terminal has all the usual facilities including food outlets, shops, left luggage, visitor information and car rental companies. There are plenty of taxis to meet you and the fare into town is about $28. Shuttle buses can be shared for about $15, T04-939 9590. Shuttles and taxis depart from outside the baggage claim area. The **Metlink's Stagecoach Flyer**, T0800-801700, runs a regular bus service (No 91) between the airport and the city, $4.50, Monday to Friday 0545-2020, Saturday and Sunday 0555-2050.

Rail The train station is next to the quay on Bunny Street and has an information centre, T0800-692378. **TranzScenic** operates the daily 'Overlander' service from Auckland, T0800-872467, T04-495 0775, www.tranzscenic.co.nz. **TranzMetro**, T0800-801700, www.tranzmetro.co.nz, offers regular daily services from the Wairarapa including Martinborough (bus link) and Masterton direct.

Road Wellington is 658 km from Auckland. The principal route is via SH1. SH2 is the principal route to the Wairarapa and the east coast. **Intercity** and **Newmans**, T04-472 5111, are the principal bus companies and arrive and depart from the train station. **White Star**, T04-47 84734, operates services to Palmerston North, Wanganui and New Plymouth. Tickets are available from the VIC (I-Site).

Getting around

Wellington city centre is quite compact and best explored on foot. There is also a wealth of well-marked walking tracks around the city, with some interesting highlights and views (ask at the VIC for details).

Parking can be a nightmare in the city centre. It is heavily metered and mercilessly patrolled. If you struggle to find a spot in the centre, try the 'park and display' areas around the railway station, north and south of the centre, and at the 'Te Papa' Museum; you can walk from there to the centre.

Stagecoach/Metlink buses operate throughout greater Wellington daily 0700-2300. For information call T04-801 7000, www.stagecoach.co.nz/www.metlink.co.nz, and get your hands on the free *Wellington bus and train guide* from the VIC (I-Site). The yellow **City Circular Bus** runs every 15 minutes daily (1000-1645) from the railway station taking in major sites including 'Te Papa', Cuba Mall, the cable car on Lambton, and Parliament Buildings. It costs $3 (child $1). For taxi, car rental and bike hire, see page 406.

TranzMetro runs regular daily services between Wellington City and Upper Hutt, Melling and Paraparaumu. There are also services to the Wairarapa and Palmerston North. For information call **TranzMetro**, T0800-801700, www.tranzmetro.co.nz.

Wellington is easy to negotiate, unless you are in a car and swept away on its one-way systems. However, all roads lead to the centre, which is sandwiched between the hills and the waterfront, and those arriving by road will be delivered right into the heart, within a stone's throw of Lambton Quay, the main business and shopping street. Lambton then doubles back north to meet Molesworth Street, Thorndon and the Parliament District. The harbour, with its merging main roads (north to south) of Waterloo and Aotea Quay, Customhouse, Jervois, Cable Street and Oriental Parade, sweeps back south and east, encompassing the modern and highly developed waterfront, including the dominant 'Te Papa' Museum. From the heart of the waterfront south, Willis and Jervois connect with Victoria, Cuba and Courtenay places, where you'll find many restaurants and cafés. Behind the CBD are the spacious Botanical Gardens and hillside suburb of Kelburn. Dominating the view southeast is Mount Victoria, a 'must see' lookout and an ideal place to get your bearings.

Tourist information

Wellington VIC (I-Site)ⓘ *corner of Wakefield and Victoria sts, T04-802 4860, www.well ingtonnz.com, Mon-Fri 0830-1800, Sat-Sun 0930-1700.* **Upper Hutt VIC (I-Site)** ⓘ *6 Main St, Upper Hutt, T04-527 2141, www.upperhuttcity.com, Mon-Fri 0800-1700, Sat-Sun 0900-1500.* **Hutt City (Lower Hutt) VIC (I-Site)**ⓘ *The Pavilion, 25 Laings Rd, Lower Hutt, T04-560 4715, www.visithuttcity.org.nz, Mon-Fri 0900-1700, Sat-Sun 1000-1600.* **DoC** ⓘ *2 Manners St, T04-384 7770, www.doc.govt.nz, Mon-Fri 0900-1630, Sat-Sun 1000-1500.* Useful free guides include: *Wellington Visitors' Guide*, *What's On Wellington*, the *Wellington Arts Map*, *Wellington Wine Food and Shopping* and the *Wellington Fashion Map*. The weekly newspaper *Capital Times* is also designed for visitors. The main daily newspaper in the lower North Island is the *Dominion Post*.

Maps *Positively Wellington Tourism* promotes a 'four quarters' map system, which is often referred to in brochures. The four quarters run in a clockwise direction from Mount Victoria round the bay through the CBD and then north are: **Courtenay**, **Cuba**, **Lambton** and **Waterfront**. There is a specialist map shop, on the corner of Vivian and Victoria Streets (near Cuba Street), as well as the stocks available at major bookshops **Whitcoulls** and **Dymocks** (see page 404).

Background

According to Maori legend it was Kupe, the great Polynesian explorer, who first made landfall in the region in about AD 950, and his descendants, the Ngai Tara and Rangitane tribes, became the first permanent settlers. The first European ships to enter the harbour were the *Rosanna* and the *Lambton* on a preliminary exploration for the first New Zealand Company in 1826. But it was not until 1839-1840, when the first settlers arrived, that the inevitable dubious land deals with the local Maori were made. Initially the first blocks of land purchased were at the northern end of the harbour towards what are now Petone and the Hutt Valley. However, the land was found to be unsuitable for building, so the settlers moved south, to what is now Thorndon, in the heart of modern day Wellington. Along with the rest of the country, Wellington suffered three decades of Maori/*Pakeha* friction surrounding the various land deals. Despite this, and a major earthquake in 1855 (which actually had the positive effect of creating new and ideal flat land for building), Wellington prospered. By the 1860s, with the various inroads being made in to the South Island and the then capital Auckland suffering due to its geographical position, it was decided to move the seat of government and make Wellington the capital in 1865. The name Wellington was bestowed in honour of yet another British general, Arthur Wellesley (1769-1852), the first Duke of Wellington.

Sights

Mount Victoria Lookout → *Take a No 20 bus (Highbury)*

Most of Wellington's major attractions are within walking distance or a short bus ride from each other. An ideal spot to get your bearings, is the 196-m Mount Victoria Lookout. Although from a distance the wooded sides of the mount hardly seem in character with the film trilogy *Lord of the Rings*, it proved both a convenient and aesthetically suitable location for several scenes depicting 'The Shire' in the first film, the *Fellowship of the Ring*. It was also here that the four Hobbits hid from the evil Nazgul. Looking southeast from the city centre Mount Victoria is not hard to miss, but, to the uninitiated, reaching the lookout can be somewhat akin to an expedition up K2. The best ascent is by car. Head straight for the hill up Majoribanks Road at the bottom of Courtenay Place. From Majoribanks turn left on to Hawker, carry on up Moeller, Pallister, and then Thane. The entrance to the lookout is on the right, off Thane. If you get lost in the web of residential hillside streets, just keep going up and eventually you will reach the summit. You might like to investigate the **Byrd Memorial**, a rather modernist edifice pointing south towards the Antarctic, in honour of the American Admiral Richard Byrd. The view is spectacular at sunrise and after dark. If you are on foot, the summit is part of the 'Southern Walkway'; leaflets are available from the VIC.

Parliamentary District

The Parliamentary District is centred on and around Bowen Street, in the Lambton Quarter just west of the rather grand looking **railway station** building. Standing on Lambton Quay or Bowen Street you will be immediately struck by the rather odd and aptly named **Beehive**, which houses the various government offices. Designed by British architect, Sir Basil Spence, and built in 1980, it is either loved or hated. Far more pleasing is the 1922 **Old Parliament House** ① *T04-471 9503, Mon-Fri 0900-1700, Sat 0930-1600, Sun 1130-1600; tours Mon-Fri 1000-1600, Sat 1000-1500, Sun 1200-1500, 1 hr, free.* And next door to that is the **Parliamentary Library**, which is older still. There is an excellent **visitor centre** in the ground floor foyer of Parliament House. Regular tours are available and you can also see parliament in session.

While in the vicinity of Parliament House take a peek or stop for lunch in the **Backbencher Pub**, across the road on Molesworth Street facing the High Court. Adorning the walls are some superb cartoons and *Spitting Image*-style dummies of past and present prime ministers. The best has to be the less than flattering one of Rob Muldoon (perhaps New Zealand's most famous prime minister), which is particularly grotesque, looking for all the world like an alien slug – or 'Jabba the Hut' from *Star Wars*.

Just a short stroll from the **Backbencher Pub** on Lambton Quay is the historic **Old Government Buildings** ① *partially open to visitors, T04-472 7356,* built in 1876 to house the Crown Ministers and public servants of the day. It has an interesting interior with a rather grand staircase and cabinet room, but it is worthy of above average scrutiny externally as well. The building was designed to look like stone but actually constructed of wood and is the second largest wooden building in the world (the largest being the Todaiji Temple in Nara City, Japan). An expensive restoration was completed in 1996 and it now houses the Victoria University's Law Faculty. Also in the Parliamentary District is the **National Library Gallery** ① *5b-7b Molesworth St, T04-474 3000, Mon-Fri 0900-1700, Sat 0900-1300, ,* with its impressive collection of research books, colonial photographs and in-house gallery. It also has a shop and a café.

From the library, heading towards the water is the **Archives New Zealand** ① *10 Mulgrave St, Thorndon, T04-499 5595, www.archives.govt.nz, Mon-Fri 0900-1700, Sat 0900-1300, free.* Within its hallowed walls are a number of important historical documents including the original and controversial 'Treaty of Waitangi'.

Also on Mulgrave Street is the **Old St Paul's Cathedral** ① *To4-473 6722, daily* 393

1000-1700, free, an 1866 Gothic-style church adapted from traditional stone to native timbers. It is worth a look, not only to see the superb timberwork of the interior, but also the impressive stained-glass windows.

The suburb of **Thorndon**, to which the Parliamentary District essentially belongs, is the oldest and most historic in Wellington. The *Thorndon Heritage Trail* leaflet (available from the VIC) outlines other historical sites in the area. Two notable examples are the 1843 **Premier House** (still the official Prime Minister's residence) on Tinakori Road and, further north at 25 Tinakori Road, the **Katherine Mansfield Birthplace** ① *To6-473 7268, www.katherinemansfield.com, Tue-Sun 1000-1600, $5.50.* Mansfield is generally hailed as New Zealand's most famous writer, having penned many internationally well known short stories. Some of those stories (including *Prelude* and *A Birthday*) feature this house, where she lived until she was five. The house and gardens have been faithfully restored and there is an interesting video portrait of the writer.

Civic Square and the waterfront

Civic Square, just behind the VIC (I-Site), was given a major revamp in the early 1990s and is blessed with some interesting architectural features. These include the instantly striking Nikau Palm columns adorning the modernistic **Public Library** and the imaginative and beautiful silver fern orb, cleverly suspended above the centre of the square. Civic Square is often used for outdoor events and also houses the **City Gallery** ① *To4-801 3952, www.city-gallery.org.nz, daily 1000-1700, free; the Nikau café on the ground floor is recommended.* With Wellington considered the artistic heart of the nation, the gallery strives (successfully it would seem) to present a regular programme of the very best of contemporary visual arts. There is an impressive array of media on show and the gallery also hosts special events, film screenings and performances.

Also in the square is the kids' paradise of **Capital E** ① *To4-913 3720, www.capitale. org.nz, open during events and exhibitions only.* Described as 'an inner city children's events centre' it offers an ever-changing agenda of experiences, events and exhibitions. You won't be surprised to learn that there is a large and expensive toy shop attached.

From Civic Square it is a short walk across the very arty **City to Sea Bridge**, which connects the square with the waterfront. The bridge sprouts a number of interesting sculptures that celebrate the arrival of the Maori in New Zealand.

The **waterfront** has become a major focus in the city for its museums, aesthetics and recreational activities. Stretching from the modern landscaped milieu of '**Waitangi Park**' east of Te Papa to Queens Wharf, on a sunny weekend it is abuzz with tourists and locals simply relaxing, sightseeing, inline skating, kayaking or fishing.

At the heart of the waterfront and to the north of Civic Square is **Frank Kitts Park** with its impressive children's play area complete with model lighthouse and slide. Further north is the classy revamped **wharf**, with its waterfront cafés and restaurants where you can relax over a beer and watch the sightseeing helicopter come and go.

The **New Zealand Film Archive** ① *84 Taranaki St, CBD, To4-384 7647, www.film archive.org.nz, Mon-Fri 0900-1700, Sat from 1200, free, tours by appointment,* houses a collection of New Zealand and overseas film and TV materials of artistic, social and historical value dating back to 1897. It runs frequent specialist exhibitions.

Museum of Wellington City and Sea

① *To4-472 8904, www.museumofwellington.co.nz, daily 1000-1700, free.*
Housed in the former Bond Store on Queens Wharf is the recently revitalized Museum of Wellington City and Sea. Being in such close proximity to Te Papa, you might think its attempts to compete and woo visitors was an exercise in futility, but this museum is actually superb and, in its own way, competes favourably with Te Papa. The multi-levelled design of the interior is modern yet rustic, maintaining the feel of its former

Wellington Sights

Wellington

To Katherine Mansfield Birthplace
To 18
To 20

Hawkestone St

THORNDON

Premier House

Harriet St

Old St Paul's Cathedral

National Library Gallery

Westpac Trust Stadium

Pipitea St

Molesworth St

Murphy St

Thorndon Quay

Hill St

Parliamentary Library

Aitken St

Old Parliament House

Kate Sheppard

Archives New Zealand

Lewisville

Tinakori Rd

Parliament St

Beehive

Waterloo Quay

Bowen St

Old Government Buildings & DoC

Bowen St

Whitmore St

Stout St

Lady Norwood Rose Gardens

Bolton St

The Terrace

Ballance St

Bunny St

Carter Observatory

Wesley Rd

Aurora Terr

Featherston St

Botanic Gardens

Salmont

Clermont

Talavera Terr

Clifton Terr

Waring Taylor St

John St

Lambton Quay

Customhouse Quay

Brandon St

Panama St

Grey St

Queen's Wharf

Cable Car Museum

Cable Car

Everton Terr

Boulcott St

Gilmer

Hunter St

Museum of Wellington City & Sea

Lambton Harbour

Salamanca Rd

Kelburn Park

Willeston St

Jervois Quay

Frank Kitts Park

KELBURN

The Terrace

Boulcott St

Willis St

Supermarket

Victoria St

Harris St

City Gallery

Kelburn Par

Bond St

Public Library

Civic Square

City to Sea Bridge

MacDonald

Capital E

New Zealand Film Archive

Te Papa Museum of New Zealand

Ghuznee St

Wakefield St

Waitangi Park

Herd St

TE ARO

Cuba Mall

Dixon St

Manners St

Cable St

Chaffers St

Oriental Par

Map Shop

Butler St

Cuba St

Egmont St

Courtenay Central Complex

Allen St

Embassy Theatre

Supermarket

Able Smith St

Victoria St

Marion St

Taranaki St

Courtney Pl

Blair St

Majoribanks St

Palmer St

Cuba St

Tennyson St

Roxburgh St

Aro St

Wigan St

Jessie St

Tory St

Lorne St

Levy St

To Karori Wildlife Sanctuary

Ohiro Rd

Vivian St

Frederick St

College St

Elizabeth St

Haining St

Arthur St

Webb St

Brooklyn Rd

Nairn St

Thompson St

Torrens Terr

Hopper St

Taranaki St

Buckle St

Cambridge Terr

Kent Terr

Queen St

To Mount Victoria Lookout

Pirie St

Colonial Cottage Museum

MT COOK

Tasman St

Sussex St

National Cricket Museum

Basin Reserve

Brougham St

Armour

Austin St

Ellice St

Paterson St

Rugby St

Dufferin

Porritt Av

To ECNZ Wind Turbine

To Wellington Zoo

To Airport & 21 22 43

function and the modern dose of sensual bombardment it now houses is very powerful. As the name suggests, the emphasis is on local history, with a particular maritime bent. Of note is the **Wahine Disaster Gallery** and the state-of-the-art holographic display on Maori legends. *The Wahine* was a passenger ferry that came to grief at the harbour entrance in 1968 with the loss of 51 lives. Original film footage set to a suitably dramatic score documents the chilling series of events. The 3D and holographic mix of the Maori legend display is simply stunning and is a fantastic example of how technology has injected new life into museums as a whole. Recommended.

Te Papa Museum of New Zealand

① *T04-381 7000, www.tepapa.govt.nz, daily 1000-1800, Thu 1000-2100, free, (around $12 for temporary exhibitions). Allow half a day at the museum; much more and you'll suffer from sensory overload. 1-hr 'Introducing Te Papa Tours' available Nov-Apr daily on the hour 1000-1600, $10; May-Oct 1015 and 1400. Specialist tours (including a Maori Experience Tour) are available at a cost. There is an excellent shop on the ground floor but the café is less than impressive.*

To the south of Civic Square and gracing the harbour's eastern bank is the unmistakable Te Papa Museum – Wellington's biggest tourist attraction. As if the exterior was not enough, the interior is also mindbending. Heavily publicized Te Papa has tried to faithfully represent the nation's heritage since 1998, at a cost of $317 million. Since then over twice the population of the nation itself (9.3 million) have passed through its doors; not surprisingly, its most successful temporary exhibit to date is the *Lord of The Rings* exhibition, which was created in 2003. They say there is something for everybody and this does seem to hold true. As expected, there is a heavy emphasis on Maori heritage, *taonga* (treasures) and biculturalism, mixed with the inevitable early settler material, contemporary displays of all things Kiwi and, most recently 'Toi Te Papa' – an exhibition of 130 New Zealand artworks.

0 metres 200
0 yards 200

Sleeping
Apollo Lodge Motel 1 *E3*
Base Backpackers 19 *E3*
Cambridge 15 *E3*
Comfort Wellington 12 *E2*
Duxton 23 *D2*
Edgewater
  Homestay 21 *F3*
Eight Parliament St 4 *A1*
Halswell Lodge 6 *E3*
Intercontinental 7 *C2*
James Cook
  Grand Chancellor 5 *C2*
Kingsgate Millennium
  Oriental Bay 9 *D3*
Lambton Heights B&B 2 *B2*
Lighthouse 22 *F3*
Museum Hotel-Hotel
  De Wheels 8 *D3*
Rowena's City
  Lodge 10 *F3*
The Stables 17 *A1*
Top Ten Hutt Park
  Holiday Park 18 *A2*
Victoria Court
  Motor Lodge 13 *E1*
Wellesley 11 *B2*
Wellington Motel 20 *A3*
Wellington YHA 14 *E3*
Wildlife House
  Backpackers 16 *E2*
Worldwide
  Backpackers 3 *D1*

Eating
Astoria Café 1 *B2*
Backbencher 2 *A2*
Boulcott Street
  Bistro 4 *C1*
Café Istanbul 9 *E2*
Café Lido 10 *D2*
Caffe L'Affare 41 *E2*

Chocolate Fish 43 *F3*
Citron 8 *E1*
Dockside 12 *C2*
Donald's Pie
  Cart 13 *B2*
Espressoholic 15 *D2*
Fidels 40 *E2*
Floriditas 18 *E2*
Hummingbird 11 *E3*
KK Malaysia 23 *E2*
Kai 5 *E3*
Krazy Lounge 19 *E2*
Little India 3 *E3*
Logan Brown 20 *E2*
Midnight Espresso
  & Olive 21 *E2*
Molly Malone's
  Dubliner 14 *E2*
Monsoon Poon 6 *E3*
One Red Dog 35 *E3*
Parade Café 42 *D3*
Sakura 16 *B2*
Satay Kampong 25 *E3*
Satay Village 38 *F2*
Shed 5 26 *C2*
Tasting Room 7 *E3*
Tugboat on the
  Bay 37 *D2*
Tulsi 24 *E2*
Uncle Changs 27 *E3*
Wellington
  Seamarket 39 *E1*

Bars & clubs
Big Kumara 28 *D2*
Blondini's 45 *E3*
Bodega 30 *E1*
Coyote St 32 *E2*
Establishment 29 *E3*
Pound 44 *D2*
Wellington Sports
  Café 36 *E3*

Wellington Sights

The museum leaves a deep impression of the country's relative youth on the grand scale of world history and events. However, it also provides the usual high-tech sensual bombardment and you will find the hours passing happily by as you become engrossed. Since it's free, it is a good idea to have an initial quick recce and return later for a more in-depth investigation. A word of advice: go early to avoid the processions of noisy children.

Botanic Gardens, Cable Car and Cable Car Museum

① *The main entrance is on Glenmore St in Thorndon, on the No 12 bus route (Karori Park), T04-499 1400, www.wbg.co.nz, free, open dawn till dusk. The Cable Car, T04-472 2199, runs every 10 mins, Mon-Fri 0700-2200, Sat-Sun 0830-2200 , $1.80, child $1. Before going anywhere near the gardens you should pick up the free gardens map and leaflet, available from the VIC (I-Site).*

Wellington's Botanic Gardens are really quite magnificent, but excruciatingly hilly, and although well worth the visit and a stroll, almost require oxygen and a base camp support team to do so. Gracing its precarious slopes are 26 ha of specialist gardens, radiant flowerbeds, foreign trees and native bush. Its crowning glories are the **Carter Observatory** and the **Lady Norwood Rose Garden**. By far the most sensible and conventional way to visit the gardens is via the **Cable Car**, at 280 Lambton Quay, first built in 1902 and now a tourist attraction in itself. The almost completely subterranean single line has cables that haul the two lovely red carriages up and down, with four stops on the way. When your carriage glides in quietly to the summit (Kelburn) station you step out into the gardens and are immediately rewarded with a fine view across the city. The recently renovated and expanded **Cable Car Museum** ① T04-475 3578, www.cablecarmuseum.co.nz, daily 0930-1730, free, houses some lovingly restored cars, audio-visuals and interpretive displays.

Having arrived in such style you are now in the perfect position to explore the gardens. At the crest of the hill and a short walk from the summit station is the **Carter Observatory** ① T04-4728167, www.carterobservatory.org, Sun-Tue 1000-1700, Wed-Sat 1000-late (reduced in winter); shows and telescope viewing available (call for details), $12, child $5. It has static displays, planetarium shows and audio-visuals. Be sure to see another fine view over the city on the lawn, just in front of the observatory. The **Lady Norwood Rose Gardens**, with its circular display of over 300 varieties, are at the northern end of the gardens, at the base of the hill and along with the **café** ① Mon-Fri 1100-1500, Sat-Sun 1000-1600, should perhaps be your last port of call.

The **Otari Wilton's Bush** ① 160 Wilton Rd, Wilton, northwest of the Botanic Gardens, T04-499 1400, www.owb.co.nz, dawn to dusk, free, take bus No 14 (Wilton via Wadestown), is another famous garden that is the only botanical garden in the country dedicated solely to native plants.

South of the city centre

Wellington Zoo ① 200 Daniell St, Newtown, directly south of the city centre, T04-381 6750, www.wellingtonzoo.com, daily 0930-1700 (last entry 1615), $15, child $6; take bus No 10 from the city centre.

Like Auckland and Hamilton, Wellington has embraced the need for the modern-day zoo to be involved in conservation projects as well as being commercially viable. Wellington Zoo has just celebrated its centenary and offers some fine exhibits of natives, including **kiwi** (housed in a modern nocturnal house), **tuatara** and a wide variety of non-natives species, including Sumatran tigers, red panda, Malayan sun bears and troupe of chimps, the second largest in the southern hemisphere.

An exciting new addition to its activities is the 'Zoo Encounters' programme, which allows the public to go behind the scenes with keepers and get close up and personal with some of the more congenial inmates, like the giraffes, red pandas and cheetahs, from $65 to $800.

The **National Cricket Museum** ① *T04-385 6602, daily 1030-1530, weekends only*
in winter, $5, child $2, is a small but worthy attraction, particularly for the enthusiast. It is housed in the old grandstand of the Basin Reserve (a ground that has hosted some famous encounters) and displays a range of national and international memorabilia dating back to 1743. Inevitably perhaps, particular emphasis seems to be placed on the team's encounters with the arch-enemy Australia.

The **Colonial Cottage Museum** ① *68 Nairn St, Brooklyn, T04-384 9122, daily 1000-1600, May-Dec weekends only, $5, children free,* is housed in one of the city's oldest buildings dating back to 1858. Georgian in style, the faithfully restored and furnished interior takes you back to the early settler days.

While visiting the Colonial Museum you might like to supplement the trip with a city view and the starkly contrasting **ECNZ Wind Turbine**, which slices the air above Brooklyn. From Brooklyn Road turn right in to Todman Street and follow the signs.

Around Wellington

There are a number of attractions around Wellington that are worth a visit. The **Karori Wildlife Sanctuary** ① *T04-920 9200, www.sanctuary.org.nz, daily 1000-1700, from $10, child $4; guided tours daily (at night by arrangement), to view or hear nocturnal wildlife, including kiwi, from $45, child $20, pick-ups from the VIC,* is located in a valley of regenerating bush in the suburb and hills of Karori. In 1994 an area of 250 ha was set aside and protected with a predator-proof fence. Now, with the eradication of non-native pest species within the boundary of the fence, the benefits are already being seen. Reintroduced species are making a comeback and birdsong is returning to bush that once lay silent. The sanctuary has an **information centre** at the end of Waiapu Road in Karori. The area around the perimeter fence is popular for walking and mountain biking. If you don't have your own transport, **Wellington Rover Tours**, T021-426211, www.wellingtonrover.co.nz, can get you there and back (allowing over two hours to explore) as part of their hop-on hop-off Wellington Rover Day Pass, from $40.

Set in the middle of Wellington harbour is the **Matiu Somes Island Reserve** ① *T04-499 1282, www.eastbywest.co.nz, Dominion Post Ferry $18.50, child $10.* Once a quarantine station, the island is now administered by the DoC and is home to a number of protected native birds. The island can be reached by **ferry** ① *T04-499 1282, with regular departures,* from Queen's Wharf stopping off at the island on the way to Days Bay near the coastal resort of Eastbourne.

There are two New Zealand **fur seal colonies** near Wellington. The first and the most accessible is the Red Rocks colony, which can be reached on foot from Owhiro Bay (see Walks, below). **Seal Coast Safari** offers tour options, while **Wellington Rover Tours** can provide transport and point you in the right direction (see Activities and tours, page 406). The second colony, at **Turakiae Head** to the south east of Pencarrow Lighthouse, requires permission from the DoC. To get there, take the Coast Road to Baring Head via Petone (Upper Hutt) and Wainuiomata. Then walk east to the headland (it's a half- to full-day trip). There is no public transport to Pencarrow.

Good beaches in the area, suitable for sunbathing and swimming, can be found to the east of the city. From the airport follow the road round the headland to Palmer Head and **Scorching Bay** on the edge of Seatoun.

If you take a scenic drive around the bays, try to take in the eclectic metal and junk creations of **Carl Gifford's Stonewall Co** ① *287 Happy Valley Rd, T04-971 8618, www.stonewallco.net.nz.* Following a work accident, the Italian found himself with lots of spare time, which acted like a fertile growbag from which the his latent creative talent has exploded in to life. From miniature metal kiwis to squashed cars, his quirky installations now consume the valley. Call at the house for sales and permission to view at close hand.

There are a number of great walks in and around the city and details and free leaflets that cover these are available from the VIC (I-Site) or DoC. The *Heritage Trail* leaflet takes in many of the sights within the city above. There are **Northern, Southern, Eastern** and **Waterfront walkways**. These range from one or two hours covering just a few kilometres to a full day's jaunt. They take in a range of city, suburb, waterfront, coastal and country scenery with both historic, contemporary or natural sights outlined. **Mount Kaukau** (430 m), to the northwest of the city, is a good climb and offers a rewarding view of the region. It can be accessed from Simla Crescent in Khandallah (two hours). One of the most popular walks near the city is the walk to **Red Rocks** and the fur seal colony (see above), which is accessed via the quarry track at the western end of Owhiro Bay (4 km). Owhiro Bay is reached via Brooklyn and Happy Valley Road (take bus Nos 1 or 4, then 9).

Hutt Valley 🖾▲▲ ⇥ *pp399-406.*

→ *Population: 130,000*

To the east of Wellington, sitting obstinately right on a major fault-line and split by the Hutt River, are the fairly unremarkable Wellington dormitory towns of Lower and Upper Hutt, or 'Hutt City'. There isn't much to draw in the visitors, but if you can drag yourself away from Wellington or just happen to be passing, there are a few sights and activities that may appeal.

Sights

In Lower Hutt, the **Petone Settlers Museum**ⓘ *waterfront, T04-568 8373, Tue-Fri 1200-1600, Sat-Sun 1300-1700, donation,* is quite small but highlights the early historical significance of the area in an effective way. The recently renovated **Dowse Art Museum and Café** ⓘ *corner of Myrtle St and Laings Rd, T04-570 6500, www.dowse.org.nz, Mon-Fri 1000-1600, Sat-Sun 1100-1700, free,* is a nationally respected showcase of contemporary arts and crafts. The coffee in the café is reputed to be the best in the area.

In Upper Hutt, the **Silverstream Railway Museum** ⓘ *Reynold Bach Drive, Silverstream, T04-971 5747, Sun only 1100-1600, $7, child $4,* houses a large collection of steam locomotives, some of which operate on a short track on Sundays between 1100-1600. A bit of a trek but still worth it is the **Staglands Wildlife Reserve** ⓘ *Akatarawa Rd, T04-526 7529, www.staglands.co.nz, daily 1000-1700, $14, child $7,* a capable steward and advocate of native New Zealand wildlife conservation. There is a very pleasant café on site with an open fire in winter. The **Kaitoke Regional Park** (12 km north of Upper Hutt) is a popular recreational spot which, since the release of the *Lord of the Rings* trilogy, has attracted a stream of loyal fans. It was here amidst the native beautiful forest glades and alongside the riverbank that the set of 'Rivendell' was created. During filming over 300 crew were on site – hard to imagine now since, like all the other film locations, little remains except the memory, the atmosphere and little *Rivendell* signs directing you to the right spot. To get there enter the northern entrance to the park off SH2 down Waterworks Road and follow the signs.

The **Hutt River** also featured in the film as the 'Great River Anduin' that flowed through Middle Earth from the 'Misty Mountains' and 'Mirkwood'. Locations used for filming were between **Moonshine** and **Totara Park**. Access is left off SH2 across Moonshine Bridge, just beyond Poets Park.

Upper Hutt also gives access to some short and more challenging walks in the **Akatarawa Forest** and **Rimutaka Forest Park** (camping available).

⬤ *For an explanation of the Sleeping and Eating price codes used in this guide, see the inside*
⬤ *front cover. Other relevant information is provided in the Essentials chapter, pages 44-51.*
Note that prices are tive in New Zealand dollars.

Wellington p392, map p394

Although there is not as much choice as in Auckland, Wellington has the advantage that all types of accommodation are centrally located and within walking distance of most attractions. During festivals and in summer you are advised to book ahead. Upper-range hotels seem to dominate but, given the emphasis on weekday business, prices are usually halved at weekends.

LL-L Lambton Heights B&B, 20 Talavera Terr, Kelburn, T04-472 4710, www.lambton heights.co.nz. Elegant, heritage home with 2 classy king-sized en suites, garden with spa and city views, all within a short walk of the city centre. Charming hosts.

LL-L The Stables, 3 Poplar Grove, Thorndon, T04-972 4796, www.thestables.co.nz. A stylish, contemporary B&B that was originally a stable. Set in a quiet location and within walking distance of the centre it offers 2 tidy guest rooms and good café-style breakfast. Off-street parking.

LL-AL Duxton, 170 Wakefield St, T04-473 3900, www.duxton.com. Right in the heart of the city and a stone's throw from the waterfront and Te Papa, this is one of the best of the hotel chains. It has all the usual amenities including a surprisingly affordable restaurant/bar. Ask for a room on an upper floor with views across the city and harbour.

LL-AL Hotel Intercontinental, 2 Grey St, T04-472 2722, www.ichotelsgroup.com. Having recently been granted a 5-star rating by Qualmark the Intercontinental fancies itself as the city's best. Located in the heart of the action, it offers the full range of quality facilities including an indoor pool and 2 restaurants – the **Chameleon**, offering contemporary NZ cuisine and the well-established **Arizona Bar and Grill** for that quintessential Tex-Mex.

LL-AL James Cook Hotel Grand Chancellor, 147 The Terrace, T04-499 9500, www.jamescookhotel.co.nz. All mod cons, a fine piano bar and in an ideal spot to climb the steps down to Lambton Quay.

L The Lighthouse, 326 The Esplanade, Island Bay, T04-472 4177, www.the lighthouse.net.nz. Your chance to stay in a lighthouse (built in 1993). Offers suitably impressive views across the harbour entrance and oozes character. Small kitchen and bathroom, with living and sleeping areas (2 rooms with 1 main bedroom with spa) above. Breakfast included.

L-AL Museum Hotel-Hotel De Wheels, 90 Cable St, T04-802 8900, www.museum hotel.co.nz. A modern establishment ideally located across the road from Te Papa and in the heart of the café, bar and restaurant areas. It oozes class, both inside and out, and a recently added apartment complex including single studios may also prove an attractive proposition.

L-AL Wellesley Hotel, 2-8 Maginnity St, T04-474 1308, www.thewellesley.co.nz. A 1920s neo-Georgian style hotel offering tastefully appointed period furnished suites right in the heart of the Lambton Quarter. Elegant suites throughout appointed in Georgian period style. In-house facilities include a sauna and a popular English-style restaurant featuring an open fire and regular live entertainment (mainly jazz).

AL Kingsgate Millennium Hotel Oriental Bay, 73 Roxburgh St, T04-385 0279, www.millenniumhotels.com. On the water-front with wonderful views across the harbour and CBD, it's worth staying here for that reason alone. With a recent 10-million upgrade it also boasts some fine facilities including an indoor pool and popular licensed restaurant.

AL-A Eight Parliament Street, 8 Parliament St, T04-499 0808/T027-280 6739, www.boutique-bb.co.nz. A wooden villa, typical of Wellington's traditional colonial houses, offering 3 rooms (en suite or shared bathrooms) with plenty of colour and modern style. Generous breakfast.

A Apollo Lodge Motel, 49 Majoribanks St, T04-385 1849, www.apollolodge.co.nz. Standard modern unit interiors, most with kitchen facilities. Conveniently placed within walking distance of Te Papa and Courtenay Pl.

A Cambridge Hotel, corner of Alpha St and Cambridge Terr, T04-385 8829, www.cambridgehotel.co.nz. Impressive establishment on the edge of the Courtenay Quarter that feels more like a grand hotel than a mid-budget option. Full range of rooms from shared backpacker-style, to tidy doubles with en suite bathroom, standard in-house facilities, Sky TV and a quite remarkable bathroom section. Quality budget meals are also a feature. The only drawbacks are the lack of atmosphere and off-street parking. Otherwise recommended.

A Comfort Hotel Wellington, 213 Cuba St, T04-385 2153, www.hotelwellington.co.nz. Recently restored and right in the heart of the happening Cuba Quarter. Fine facilities and tidy, good-value rooms. The only drawback is it can feel a bit like a rabbit warren. In-house café and 'charge-back' arrangements with 3 local restaurants, off-street parking.

A Edgewater Homestay, 459 Karaka Bay, Karaka Bay, Seatoun, T04-388 4446, www.edge waterwellington.co.nz. Modern and classy, near the airport and best city beaches.

A Halswell Lodge, 21 Kent Terr, T04-385 0196, www.halswell.co.nz. Comfortable units to suit all budgets, sited well off the main street. Walking distance from Te Papa and Courtenay Place restaurants and cafés.

A The Victoria Court Motor Lodge, 201 Victoria St, T04-472 4297, www.victoria court.co.nz. Nicely appointed motel in a perfect location for the café/restaurant districts of Cuba and Courtenay. Standard range of rooms and apartments, some with spa and kitchen. Sky TV. Off-street parking.

A Wellington Motel, 14 Hobson St, T04-472 0334, www.nz.co.nz/Wellington. Close to the South Island ferry terminals.

C-D Base Backpackers, 21-23 Cambridge Terr, T04-801 5666, www.baseback packers.com. Part of a national chain with modern, spacious accommodation (including en suites and a girls-only level) close to the happening Cuba Quarter. In-house bar, but no off-street parking.

C-D Rowena's City Lodge, 115 Brougham St, Mt Victoria, T04-385 7872, www.wellington backpackers.co.nz. Pleasant, friendly hostel in a large rambling house, far more intimate than many of the larger backpacker hostels. Value single rooms and tent sites available.

C-D Wellington YHA, 292 Wakefield St, T04-801 7280, www.yha.org.nz. Deservedly popular with a wide range of rooms (some with en suite bathrooms and TV), excellent facilities and helpful friendly staff. All this just a stone's throw from Courtenay Quarter's cafés and restaurants, a major supermarket and Te Papa. The only drawback is the lack of off-street parking. Daily coupon ticketed parking ($5) is available 200 m away. Recommended.

C-D Wildlife House Backpackers, 58 Tory St, Courtenay Quarter, T04-381 3899, www.wildlifehouse.co.nz. Famous for its zebra-stripe exterior, the purpose-built interior is even more notable both aesthetically and functionally. Large living areas, full range of rooms from motel-style double en suites to dorms, large open-plan kitchen, Sky TV room and a 24-hr internet suite, spa, sauna. Off-street parking also available.

C-D Worldwide Backpackers, 291 The Terrace, T0508-888555/T04-802 5590, www.worldwidenz.co.nz. Proving something of a hit this new, small, homely option offers cosy shared, double and twins. Spotless throughout, with tasteful decor, it also offers attractive freebies like internet, breakfast, the occasional glass of wine and ferry pick-ups.

Hutt Valley *p398*
Motorcamps and campsites

There are no motorcamps in Wellington itself.

B-D 'Top-Ten' Hutt Park Holiday Park, 95 Hutt Park Rd, Lower Hutt, T04-568 5913, www.huttpark.co.nz. The best and closest to the centre. Standard 'Top Ten' facilities with a full range of accommodation options, from 2-bedroom motel-style units, to non-powered campsites. Camp kitchen, spa and internet.

❼ Eating

Wellington *p392, map p394*

Wellington prides itself on its thriving café and restaurant scene and is often dubbed 'the café-crazy capital'. More than 100 new establishments have opened up in the last 7 years and the choice is vast, which means you are almost guaranteed good quality. The **Courtenay Quarter** is where most are located (Blair St, off Courtenay Pl is practically wall-to-wall restaurants), with a number of classy pubs offering fine, reliable and mainly international or Pacific Rim cuisine. **Cuba St** has numerous inexpensive restaurants, funky cafés and takeaways. **Queen's Wharf** on the waterfront is also a favourite haunt. For the more expensive restaurants booking is advised.

Finally, if it is late at night, you are near the railway station and desperate, there is always the 24-hr **Donald's Pie Cart**.

♈♈♈ Boulcott Street Bistro, 99 Boulcott St, T04-499 4199, www.boulcottstreetbistro.co.nz,

Mon-Fri from 1200, Sat from 1800. A top restaurant in the historic surroundings of a period wooden villa. The cuisine is mainly French, with some international dishes.

Citron, 270 Willis St, T04-801 6263, daily from 1000, licensed. Consistently lauded as one of the best restaurant/cafés in town. Imaginative international cuisine served in 3- and 8-course set menus.

Dockside, Queen's Wharf, T04-499 9900, www.docksidenz.com, daily from 1100. Very popular eatery and fine evening venue. Alfresco dining, mainly Mediterranean or seafood lunches. A great place to watch the world go by with a cold beer.

Logan Brown, corner of Cuba and Vivian sts, T04-801 5114, www.loganbrown.co.nz, lunch Mon-Fri, dinner daily. A well-established, multi award-winning establishment, offering international cuisine in the old historic and spacious banking chambers. The spectacular interior sports a huge chandelier.

Shed 5, Queen's Wharf, T04-499 9069, www.shed5.co.nz, daily from 1100. A fine evening venue, but particularly popular during the day and at weekends. Alfresco atmosphere is great for people-watching. The menu is mainly seafood or Mediterranean.

Café Istanbul, 156 Cuba St, T04-385 4998, www.istanbul.co.nz daily from 1730. A Turkish-style restaurant with a very congenial atmosphere and a loyal following.

Floriditas, 161 Cuba St, 104-381 2212 daily from 0700. Stylish option, popular with locals, with good value, imaginative contemporary menu and great coffee. Breakfasts are highly recommended, but you won't be alone.

Hummingbird, corner of Blair St and Courtney Pl, T04-801 6336, Mon-Fri 1100-0300, Sat-Sun 1000-0300. Attracts a loyal following and is known for its great tapas.

Little India, 18 Blair St, T04-384 9989, and 115 Cuba Mall, T04-384 2535, www.little india.co.nz, lunch Mon-Fri, dinner daily from 1730. One of the city's best Indian offerings.

Kai, 21 Majoribanks St, T04-801 5006, Mon-Sat from 1730. It's about time the city hosted a truly Maori eating experience and it doesn't come much better than this. Small and friendly, the frenetic kitchen churns out a delicious range of traditional Maori dishes from kumara pies (Pacific sweet potato) to kuku (steamed green-lipped mussels) all for a reasonable price. Recommended.

Monsoon Poon, 12 Blair St, T04-803 3555, Mon-Thu 1100-2300, Fri 1100-2400, Sat 1700-2400, Sun 1700 till the chefs get sleepy. Considered the pick of the Asian restaurants, offering a wide range of dishes from Thai to Vietnamese. The chefs do their thing in full view of the spacious dining floor. Lively bar, great atmosphere.

One Red Dog, 9-11 Blair St, T04-384 9777, daily 1000-2400. A bar-cum-restaurant offering some of the best gourmet pizza in town. Fine wine list. The only drawback is its popularity as both restaurant and bar can get a little too busy at times.

Sakura, corner of Featherston and Whitmore sts, T04-499 6912, Mon-Fri 1130-1400 and Mon-Sat from 1730. In the heart of the city, for excellent traditional Japanese fare.

Tasting Room, 2 Courtenay Pl, T04-384 1159, Mon-Fri 1100-late, Sat-Sun 1000-late. Touts itself as a premium 'gastro pub'.

Tugboat on the Bay, in an old tugboat in Oriental Bay, 104-384 8884, lunch from 1130, dinner from 1730. If you prefer waterscapes to cityscapes and really want to get intimate with the harbour, this place offers the classy seafood dishes with traditional Kiwi backups.

Tulsi, 135 Cuba St, T04-802 4144, daily for lunch and dinner. An Indian restaurant with a very classy modern interior, known for its highly contemporary cuisine and friendly service. Recommended.

Uncle Changs, 72 Courtenay Pl, at the other end of Courtenay, T04-801 9568. One of the better Chinese restaurants, it specializes in Taiwanese and Szechuan.

Backbencher, 34 Molesworth St, T04-472 3065. Popular pub opposite the Beehive, famous for its 'Spitting Image'-style political 3-D caricatures. Good pub lunches.

KK Malaysia, 54 Ghuznee St. Good-value and quality Malaysian fare.

Molly Malone's Dubliner Restaurant, (upstairs), corner of Courtenay and Taranaki sts, T04-384 2896, daily from 1100. You can't go wrong with a traditional pub lunch here.

Satay Kampong, 16-24 Allen St, lunch and dinner. Basic and immensely popular Malaysian restaurant.

Satay Village, 58 Ghuznee St, T04-801 8538. Will not disappoint in either price or quality.

Wellington Seamarket, 220 Cuba St, Mon-Sat 0700-2030, Sun 0800-2000. Fine fish and chips or fresh seafood.

Cuba St is the focus of the café scene where 'funky' **Fidels** (No 234), recommended late-night **Midnight Espresso** (No 178), **Olive** (No 170) and **Krazy Lounge** (No 132), all stand out. Others include:

Astoria Café, 159 Lambton Quay, T04-473 8500, Mon-Thu 0700-1930, Fri 0700-2030, Sat-Sun 0900-1600. A modern, popular Euro-style café that fills with suits at lunchtime; it is famous for the weird water sculpture outside that looks for all the world like a stand off between a group of rival sperm – something to mull over while you drink your coffee.

Café L'Affare, 27 College St, T04-385 9748, Mon-Fri 0700-1630, Sat 0800-1600. Well worth the extra walk. It is a thriving coffee business as well as an excellent café, full of atmosphere. As you might expect the coffee (and even the smell of the place) is sublime.

Café Lido, right in the heart of town, just opposite the VIC, T04-499 6666, Mon 0730-1500, Tue-Fri 0730-late, Sat-Sun 0730-late. One of the most popular in the city and always busy. A fine place to mix with Wellingtonians and watch the world go by.

Chocolate Fish, 497A Karaka Bay Rd, Scorching Bay. Full of character and hugely popular on sunny summer afternoons.

Espressoholic, 128 Courtenay Pl, T04-384 7790, Sun-Thu 0730-late, Fri-Sat 0730-0300. Laid-back base for the serious caffeine addict.

Parade Café, 148 Oriental Parade, T04-939 3925. A popular award-winning café overlooking the harbour and CBD.

⊙ Pubs, bars and clubs

Wellington *p392, map p394*
The main hot spots in the city are **Courtenay Pl** and its off-shoots **Blair St** and **Allen St** with the odd reputable drinking hole in **Cuba St**, **Willis St** and the **Central Business District (CBD)**. With the vast range of cafés and restaurants, many of which are licensed, the main pubs tend to remain quiet until late, when they fill with young and old into the wee small hours, especially at weekends. For details see www.wellingtonnz.com.

Backbencher, 34 Molesworth St, Thorndon, T04-472 3065, is worth a look just out of interest, with the *Spitting Image* type dummies and cartoons decking the walls, keeping the country's politicians in check. It

also is a good venue to watch sports, has live bands at the weekend and is a hugely popular venue on Fri nights.

Queen's Wharf is a great daytime drinking venue with a number of fine waterfront cafés providing the ideal spot for that relaxing afternoon libation. These include **Dockside** and **Shed 5** (see Eating, page 401). **The Bodega**, 101 Ghuznee St, T04-384 8212, a laid-back, live music venue; and **Big Kumara**, 80 Cuba St, T04-803 3380, a similar venue, especially good for cheesy 1980s music.

The selection on Courtenay and its off-shoot streets of Blair and Allen are vast but the following are a few of the most popular: **Molly Malone's**, corner of Taranaki St and Courtney Pl, T04-384 2896, the city's most popular Irish offering and hosts bands both folk and rock most nights. The beer too is reliably good. **One Red Dog** and the American-style **Ponderosa**, both on Blair St, are upmarket 'bolly til you're jolly' venues.

Other names to look out for include **Matterhorn**, **Jet**, **Vivo** and **Gogo**.

Clubs

Wellington enjoys a lively club scene although the popularity of individual places waxes and wanes. As usual it always pays to talk to the locals. See www.wellingtonnz.com.

Big Kumara, 60 Dixon St, T04-384 8441. A laid-back low-key place playing lots of 1980s music. Has a loyal and friendly local clientele.

Coyote St Bar, Courtenay Pl, T04-385 6665, www.coyotebar.com. Takes itself less seriously than **The Establishment**.

The Establishment, Courtenay Pl, T04-382 8654. Rather trendy and uptight but popular dance music venue.

Good Luck Bar, 126 Cuba St. Often referred to as the 'Chinese Opium den revisited' and the best place to be in this part of town.

Phoenix, 13 Dixon St. Especially noted for hosting overseas DJs.

Other places to look out for include: **The Last Supper Club**, Blair St; **Bathhouse**, 171 Cuba St; and **Sandwiches**, 8 Kent Terr.

Gay and lesbian

The **Pound** and **Sovereign Oaks Complex**, 63 Cuba St, are popular and continue well into the night with anything from karaoke to drag performances. For more information refer to the website www.nzglta.org.nz.

🌐 Entertainment

Wellington p392, map p394

Although Aucklanders would disagree, Wellington probably has the edge when it comes to a good night out. As well as a large number of pubs and clubs, there are numerous venues including large concert halls such as the Michael Fowler Centre, offering rock and classical, and noted theatres such as the Westpac St James and Circa, offering contemporary drama, dance and comedy.

For listings ask at the VIC or check the daily newspaper *The Dominion Post*, or the tourist paper *Capital Times*. Useful websites are: www.feelinggreat.co.nz or www.wellington nz.com. Tickets for major events can be bought from Ticketek, Michael Fowler Centre, 111 Wakefield St, T04-384 3840, www.ticket ek.co.nz. The VIC sometimes offers discounts on theatre tickets.

Art galleries

Wellington is a major national venue for the visual arts and there are some fine galleries. Positively Wellington Tourism produces an excellent free guide – *The Wellington Arts Map* booklet. Dealers in contemporary New Zealand art include: The Bowen Galleries, 35 Ghuznee St, T04-381 0351, www.bowen galleries.con Mon-Fri 1000-1730, Sat 1000-1500; The Tinakori Gallery, 42 Victoria St, T04-471 2636, Mon-Fri 0930-1730, Sat 1000-1600 and Ora, 23 Allen St, T04-384 4157, Mon-Fri 0830-1800, Sat 1100-1700, Sun 1100-1600.

Cinemas

Tue night is cheap ticket night.
The Embassy Theatre, 10 Kent Terr, at the bottom of Courtenay Pl, T04-384 7657, www.deluxe.co.nz. This deserves special mention due to its giant screen (one of the largest in the southern hemisphere). It was also used to host the premieres of Kiwi director Peter Jackson's *Lord of the Rings* trilogy.
Paramount, 25 Courtenay Pl, T04-384 4080, www.paramount.co.nz. Considered the town's best, most characterful cinema. In-house bar.

Mainstream cinemas: **Reading Theatres**, in the Courtenay Central Complex, Courtenay Pl, T04-801 4600, www.readingcinemas .co.nz; **Rialto Theatres**, corner of Cable St and Jervois Quay, T04-385 1864, www.rialto .co.nz; and **Hoyts**, Manners St, T04-384 3567.

Comedy

Bathhouse, 171 Cuba St, T04-801 6797. Well known for its laid-back comedy nights.

Concert halls

The **Michael Fowler Centre**, 111 Wakefield St, T04-801 4242, and the **Wellington Town Hall**, T04-801 4231, combine to form the **Events Centre**, T04-801 4242, www.wellingtoncon ventioncentre.com. The city's largest concert venue, hosting a mix of rock and classical concerts. Tickets sold on-site by Ticketek.

Theatres

There are 4 principal theatres in Wellington, all with good reputations.
Bats Theatre, 1 Kent Terr, T04-802 4175, www.bats.co.nz. A small characterful venue offering live professional theatre focusing on alternative works and New Zealand drama.
Circa Theatre, 1 Taranaki St, T04-801 7992, www.circa.co.nz. Next to Te Papa, this well-established theatre offers lively international drama, comedy and music. In-house café.
Downstage Theatre, 12 Cambridge Terr, T04-801 6946, www.downstage.co.nz. Recently renovated and one of New Zealand's leading professional theatres presenting touring shows of classic contemporary drama, dance and comedy.
Opera House, 111 Manners St, T04-802 4060. Another favourite venue for touring shows.
Westpac St James Theatre, Courtenay Pl, T04-802 4060, stjames@stjames.co.nz. Originally built in 1912, after a multi-million dollar refurbishment in 1998 it is now considered a premier venue and a central focus to the performing arts. The James is also home to the **Royal New Zealand Ballet**.

Live music

Occasional **classical** concerts are staged at **University School of Music; Conservatorium of Music** (Polytechnic) and **St Andrews** on the Terrace. See VIC (I-Site) for further details.

For **folk music**, check out Molly Malone's, corner of Taranaki St and Courtenay Pl, T04-384 2896, which can usually get the toes tapping most nights; and Kitty O'Sheas, T04-384 7392, a few doors down, less traditional but comes a close second.

Jazz fans should head to **Blondini's Café and Bar**, at the Embassy Theatre on Kent Terr, which offers a dynamic jazz programme

Wellington Listings

at weekends from early evening till late. The **Humming Bird**, corner Blair St and Courtenay Pl, T04-801 6336, is another popular venue in winter on Sun afternoons.

There are numerous pub venues that host mainly weekend **rock** gigs including: **Bodega**, 101 Ghuznee St, T04-384 8212; **Backbencher**, 34 Molesworth St, T04-472 3065; **Indigo**, 171 Cuba St, T04-801 6797; **Matterhorn**, 106 Cuba St, T04-384 3359; **Shooters**, 69-71 Courtenay Pl, T04-801 7800; **Starlight Ballroom**, 235 Willis St, T04-802 1310; and **Wellington Sports Café**, corner of Tory St and Courtenay Pl, T04-801 5515.

✵ Festivals and events

Wellington *p392, map p394*
It seems that Wellington is happy and proud to host more 'events' than any other town or city in New Zealand and there is always something going on. The jazz and arts festivals are particularly well celebrated.
Jan Wellington Cup Carnival, T04-528 9611, www.trentham.co.nz. $10 entry. A major social and sporting event, and the region's high point on the annual racing calendar. Usually held in the last week of the month.
Feb-Mar Wellington Fringe Festival, T04-495 8015, www.fringe.org.nz. An exciting month-long event that begins in the last week of Feb and celebrates and showcases modern and contemporary theatre, music and dance.
Mar International Rugby Sevens Tournament, T04-389 0020, www.sevens.co.nz. The world's best rugby sevens teams run around like loonies at the Westpac Stadium. **New Zealand International Arts Festival**, T04-473 0149, www.nzfestival.telecom.co.nz. This is a biennial event (next in 2008) and Wellington's most celebrated. It lasts for 3 weeks and is currently the country's largest cultural event with a rich and varied pageant of music performers, drama, street theatre, traditional Maori dance, modern dance and visual arts.
May NZ International Comedy Festival. www.laugh.co.nz. A popular event open to local, national and international talent.
Jul Wellington Film Festival, T04-385 0162, www.enzedff.co.nz. A showcase of nationally and internationally celebrated films.
Sep World of Wearable Art Awards, T03-548 9299, www.worldofwearableart.com.

A unique Kiwi arts affair that has grown from strength to strength from humble beginnings in the country's arts capital, Nelson. This is your once in a lifetime chance to see models dress as a banana, or a boat, or in something made of copious sticky back plastic and toilet roll holders. Anything is possible and even PM Helen Clarke once hit the catwalk donned in a fetching kind of paua shell number. Delightful. Recommended.
Oct-Nov Wellington International Jazz Festival, www.jazzfestival.co.nz. An increasingly popular celebration of national and international jazz talent.

○ Shopping

Wellington *p392, map p394*
Wellington is a fine city for shopaholics. The main shopping areas are Lambton Quay, Willis, Cuba and Courtenay sts. For quality souvenirs try the shop at Te Papa.

Cuba St As you might expect, Cuba St's wide variety of cafés and restaurants are echoed in the nature of its shops. Whether it is 1970s clothing, 2nd-hand books, utter kitsch, a pair of skin-tight pink plastic pants or an erotic device (batteries not included), this is where to go. It is always good fun to muse even if you do not indulge yourself.

Courtenay Place A little more upmarket than Cuba but still retains a wide variety of interesting shops.

Featherston St has Robin Mathieson, 183 Featherston St. Menswear.

Lambton Quay Nicknamed 'The Golden Mile', the highlights here are the elegant boutique shops of the **Old Bank** and **Kirkcaldie and Stains**, Wellington's answer to Harrods. You can indulge, browse or simply try the huge variety of scents before re-emerging on the street like a mobile flowerbed. **Sommerfields**, 296 Lambton Quay, is a grand shop for New Zealand souvenir hunters. **Dymocks**, 366 Lambton; and **Whitcoulls**, 312 Lambton, the major bookshops, are also based here.

Willis St Well-known for its sheer variety with a number of popular clothing stores including **Starfish**, 128 Willis St; **House of Hank**, 145 Willis St, outlet of Hank Cubitt the poster boy of Wellington fashion; and **Unity Books**, 57 Willis St. An excellent bookshop specializing in New Zealand titles.

▲ Activities and tours

Cruising

Charter boats are available at Queen's Wharf, see www.wellingtonwaterfront.co.nz. **Dominion Post Ferry**, T04-499 1282, www.eastbywest.co.nz. For day trips around the harbour and the eastern harbour seaside resorts of Days Bay and Eastbourne via Somes Island ($8.50, child $4.50 one way, Somes Island return $18.50). It operates a regular sailing schedule daily from Queen's Wharf.
Wellesley Boutique Cruises, based at the Taranaki Wharf, T04-474 1308, www.wellesley cruises.co.nz. Weekend excursions (from $5) and Dinner Cruises on the harbour (from $45).

Golf

Karori Golf Club, on the outskirts, T04-476 7337. Quite a challenging course.
Miramar Links Golf Course, next to the airport, T04-801 7651. Average.
Paraparaumu Beach Golf Club, just north of Wellington, T04-902 8200. An international standard links ranked 73rd in the world and still benefiting from the fact, Tiger Woods played here in the New Zealand Open in 2001.

Horse trekking

Country Club Riding Academy, Johnsonville (Ohariu Valley), T04-478 8472. New Zealand's largest equestrian centre specializing in horse trekking and tuition.

Inline skating

Hugely popular along the waterfront.
Cheapskates, 60 Cuba St, T04-499 0455. Skate hire from $15, 1 hr.
Ferg's Kayaks, Shed 6 on Queen's Wharf, T04-499 8898, www.fergskayaks.co.nz. Blade hire $10 per hr, tuition also available.

Kayaking

Ferg's Rock 'n' Kayak, see Inline skating, above. Hugely popular at weekends hiring out a range of single or double kayaks for self-guided or organized trips on the harbour. Hire from $12 for 1 hr, Basic Skills Course (Sun mornings) from $60. There is also a climbing wall on the premises reputed to be the highest in the country, 1-hr coaching with entry and all equipment, from $30.

Mountain biking

There are a number of good tracks around Wellington including the **Karori Wildlife Sanctuary** perimeter fence (from Brooklyn Hill), **Karori Reservoir**, parts of the **Southern Walkway**, **Tinakori Hill** and **Mount Kaukau**. **Mud Cycles**, T04-476 4961, www.mud cycles.co.nz. Cycle hire and tours from $25 for a half-day, $40 full-day.

Rugby

Westpac Stadium, Waterloo Quay, T473 3881, www.westpactruststadium.co.nz. Rugby fans should try to catch a Wellington Lions game at this world-class venue.

Scenic flights

Helipro, Queen's Wharf, T04-472 1550, www.helipro.co.nz. Helicopter flights over the city, harbour or beyond, $95 for 10 mins.

Swimming

The best beaches are east of the city around the coast at Seatoun. The invitingly named **Scorching Bay**, 3 km north of Seatoun, is a favourite. If the beach holds no appeal, head for the **Freyberg Pool**, 139 Oriental Parade, T04-801 4530, daily 0600-2100.

Tour operators

There are a number of specialist sightseeing operators offering a range of city (and further afield) tours as well as specialist operators and an attractive option for the kids.
Experience Stansborough, 100 Hutt Park Road, Seaview, T04-566 5591, www.stans borough.com. Unique 1½-hr tours to look at Stansborough Greys, a very rare sheep that produce a hallmark quality grey wool. The wool has become a highly regarded fashion accessory and the fascinating tour takes in the history and successes of this local cottage industry. From $19, child $14.
Flat Earth, T0800-775805/T04-977 5805, www.flatearth.co.nz. A new tour company offering an exciting range of tours with the quintessential 'capital' edge, from a 'Wild Wellington Tour' that focuses on local native wildlife; a 'Maori Treasures Tour' that offers demonstrations of art and crafts (with an opportunity to create an artwork of your own); a 'Classic Wine Tour' to the Wairarapa and of course the

inevitable *Lord of the Rings* tour. Other options include sightseeing and a city arts tour. Tours are half- or full-day and cost around $120/$275. Recommended.
Seal Coast Safari, T04-939 7839/T0274-534880, www.sealcoast.com. Departs from the VIC at 1030 and 1330 and offers entertaining tours of the seal colony and Red Rocks often taking in the ECNZ Wind Turbine on the way, $79, child $40, 2 hrs 45 mins.
Walk Wellington, T04-802 4860, www.walk. wellington.net.nz. For informative and entertaining guided walks around the city From $20, child $10 (2 hrs). Book at least 3 days ahead if possible.
Wally Hammond's Tours, T04-472 0869, www.wellingtonsightseeingtours.com. Scheduled daily trips for the more mature traveller with a well-established and entertaining operator, 2½ hrs, $45.
Wellington Rover Tours, T021-426211, www.wellingtonrover.co.nz. Good value city tour taking in Mt Victoria, the zoo, the seal colony at Red Rocks, and a coffee stop at the Chocolate Fish Café. Additional tours and venues include the Karori Wildlife Sanctuary (from $40), Wairarapa (from $165) and a day-long *Lord of the Rings* tour taking in city and regional film locations from $150.
Wild About Wellington, T027-441 9010, www.wildaboutwellington.co.nz. A fine option for hedonists, with beer, chocolate, and shopping options. The small-group flexible tours do a fine job of combining the city's sights and culinary specialities, and a special 'Wellington for Kids Tour' is a convenient adjunct, taking the kids off your hands while you enjoy one of the other tours. From $75.
Zest, T04-479 1778, www.zestfoodtours.co.nz This operator offers an attractive package for small groups of self-confessed gourmands, whipping up the ingredients of local knowledge and fascinating ventures behind the scenes to create a fine tour experience. Walking option 0930-1330, from $195, full-day tour from $500. Recommended.

Windsurfing/surfing
Wild Winds Sail and Surf, at the Overseas Terminal near Te Papa, T04-384 1010, www.wildwinds.co.nz (summer only). Windsurf hire and tuition.

Hutt Valley *p398*
H20Xtream Aquatic Adventure Centre, corner of Blenheim and Brown sts, Upper Hutt, T04-527 2113, daily. Water slides, wave machine and all manner of water activities.
HangDog Climbing Centre, 453 Hutt Rd, Alicetown, Lower Hutt, T04-589 9181, Mon-Thu 1300-2100, Fri 1300-1800, Sat-Sun 1000-1800. From $19, child $16 (includes harness, shoes and chalk). 14-m walls with over 70 routes as well as a bouldering room, abseiling tower and climbing shop. All in all, for the vertically unchallenged, its well worth a visit.
Mount Devine Horse Treks, Russell's Rd, Upper Hutt, T04-528 9973.

Transport

Wellington *p392, map p394*
For travel to South Island, see box, page 410.
Bicycle hire Mud Cycles Karori, 1 Allington Rd, Karori, T04-476 4961. Penny Farthing, 89 Courtenay Pl, T04-385 2279. **Car hire** At the airport, also: Ace, 150 Hutt Rd, T04-471 1176; Budget, 81 Ghuznee St, T04-802 4548; Pegasus, 51 Martin Sq, T04-384 4883. **Taxi** Wellington Combined, T0800-384444/T04-384 4444.

Directory

Wellington *p392, map p394*
Embassies and consulates See Essentials (page 53). **Foreign exchange** Travelex, 358 and 120 Lambton Quay, T04-472 8346. **Internet** Available at the VIC. Otherwise, Manners, Cuba and Courtney sts are your best bet. Cyber City, 97 Courtenay Pl; Cyber Spot, Lambton Sq, 180 Lambton Quay; and IPlay, 49 Manners St. **Library** Victoria St (Civic Sq), T04-801 4040, Mon-Thu 0930-2030, Fri 0930-2100, Sat 0930-1700, Sun 1300-1600. **Medical services** Wellington Hospital, Riddiford St, T04-385 5999. A&E Centre (and After Hours Pharmacy), 17 Adelaide Rd, T04-384 4944. Urgent Pharmacies, Medical Centre Building, 729 High St, T04-939 6777. **Police** Corner of Victoria and Harris sts, T04-381 2000. **Post office** 94-98 Lambton Quay, T04-472 3301. Mon-Fri 0830-1700. Post Restante, 43 Manners St, T04-473 5922. Mon-Fri 0800-1730, Sat 1000-1330. **Useful numbers** AA, 342 Lambton Quay, T04-931 9999.

Kapiti Coast

Just north of Wellington, SH1 slices its way through the hills of a major fault-line and passes the rather dull town of Porirua before joining the picturesque Kapiti coastline. For the next 30 km the small coast and inland settlements of Paekakariki, Waikanae and Otaki are shadowed by Kapiti Island on one side and the Tararua Forest Park on the other. Kapiti Island is well worth a visit while Paekakariki, Paraparaumu and Waikanae offer a number of interesting local sights and activities. Otaki is the principal access point to the Tararua Forest Park. ▸▸ *For Sleeping, Eating and other listings, see page 409.*

Ins and outs

Getting there Paekakariki, Paraparaumu, Waikanae and Otaki are all on SH1 and the main rail line. The main bus companies and **TranzMetro** trains stop at these centres. The regional trains to and from Paraparaumu run frequent day and evening services and are relatively cheap. A day rover ticket costs $10. Contact **Metlink**, T0800-801700, for information. It is also worth considering the **Metlink Explorer Pass** which allows a day of unlimited travel on regional buses and trains along the Kapiti Coast for $15.

Tourist information **Paraparaumu VIC (I-Site)** ① *Coastlands shopping centre, off SH1, T04-298 8195, www.naturecoast.co.nz, Mon-Fri 0900-1700, Sat-Sun 1000-1500.* **DoC** ① *10 Parata St, Waikanae, T04-296 1112.* **Kapiti Coast VIC (I-Site)** ① *Centennial Park, SH1, Otaki, T06-364 7620, www.naturecoast.co.nz, Mon-Fri 0900-1700, Sat-Sun 1000-1500.*

Paekakariki → *Colour map 3, C2 Population: 1600*

Paekakariki is a tiny seaside village, popular with train enthusiasts, still recovering from some of the worst flooding in recent history, which occurred in February 2004. The first thing to do is take a 3-km diversion up to the **viewpoint** on Paekakariki Hill Road. On a clear day there are great views of Kapiti Island and the coast right up to Wanganui. At the village railway station is the **Steam Inc Engine Shed** ① *T0800-783264, Wed, Thu, Sat (evenings),* where devoted enthusiasts have restored a number of vintage trains, some of which still huff and puff along the tracks. A few kilometres further north is the **Wellington Tramway Museum** ① *Queen Elizabeth Park, T04-292 8361, weekends 1100-1630,* where historical displays look back at one of Wellington's former modes of transport. Several trams are currently in operation and rides are available.

Paraparaumu and Waikanae → *Colour map 3, C2 Population: 29,000*

Paraparaumu is the principal township on the Kapiti Coast and has close ties with Wellington both as commuter town and as a seaside resort popular during the summer months. There are two main beaches, **Raumati** to the south and **Paraparaumu Beach** to the north. All the usual facilities are here and the town also serves as the gateway to Kapiti Island. A little further north on SH1 is the small satellite town of **Waikanae**, which also prides itself on its fine beach. Paraparaumu's main claim to fame came in 2001 when Tiger Woods was lured with a rather attractive $2 million to play at the New Zealand Open golf challenge on its world-class golf course, T04-902 8200.

Other than the beach, the main attractions are scattered along SH1 just to the north of Paraparaumu and around Waikanae. The **Lindale Centre** ① *2 km north of town, T04-297 0916, daily 0900-1700,* is essentially a kitsch coffee stop for coach tours, but there is also a farm park for kids with weekend farm shows ($13, child $8).

Just a little further north still on SH1 is the **Southward Car Museum** ① *T04-297 1221, www.southward.org.nz, daily 0900-1700, $10, child $3.* It has a huge collection of 250 vehicles dating from 1895. In addition to cars there are traction engines, motorcycles, bicycles and a model railway, shop and café.

On the outskirts of the pleasant village of **Waikanae**, 5 km north of Paraparaumu is the **Nga Manu Nature Reserve** ⓘ *T04-293 4131, www.ngamanu.co.nz, daily 1000-1700, $10, child $4; it is quite hard to find but signposted from SH1.* Although mainly for educational purposes, this reserve, which is set in delightful bush, with man-made lakes and bush walks, is definitely worth the detour. Everything is well presented and this is one of the few establishments in the country that is not ashamed to display the 'enemy' – the heinous non-native pests. There is a wonderful (well enclosed) display of rats, some possums and the less well advertised mallard ducks on the lawn, eyeing up your picnic. Added to the refreshing 'pest' displays are the usual collections of native birds, geckos, tuatara and a nocturnal kiwi house. Eel feeding takes place at 1400.

At some point along the coast it is well worth taking at least a look at the beach. This can be done at a number of access points, one of which is **Te Horo Beach** just north of Waikanae. The coast is piled high with amazingly sculpted pieces of driftwood.

Kapiti Island → *Colour map 3, C2*

Ins and outs All access and landing permits must be pre-booked well in advance with DoC. Only 50 people can land per day; permits cost $9, child $4.50. No overnight stays are allowed. The useful booklet *Kapiti Island Nature Reserve*, is available from the Wellington DoC, see page 391. Private boats are not allowed to land but two principal permitted private operators run day-trips: **Kapiti Tours Ltd**, T04-237 7965, www.kapititours.co.nz, and **Kapiti Marine Charter**, T04-297 2585, www.kapitimarinecharter.co.nz; both $45, child $20. Boats depart from Paraparaumu Beach in front of the Kapiti Boating Club at 0900-0930 and return 1500-1530. **Kapiti Island Alive**, T06-362 6606, www.kapitiislandalive.co.nz, departs at 0900 or 1430 with one-hour guided walks ($20) on the island. Night-time kiwi-spotting trips are also a possibility. **Flat Earth Company**, T04-977 5805, offers transport from Wellington.

Sights Kapiti Island is a very special place; not only is it a delight to visit but it's like going back in time to when New Zealand was an unspoiled paradise. Lying 5 km offshore from Paraparaumu, it is 10 km long, 2 km wide and has a total land coverage of 1965 ha. Its highest point is Tuteremoana at 520 m. The island is now one of the most important reserves in the country and has an adjunct marine reserve, all of which is administered, protected and nurtured by DoC. It took a huge budget and six years of hunting and poisoning in the 1980s to rid the island of 22,500 possums, while further exhaustive helicopter poison drops in the 1990s have been successful in keeping rats at bay. After numerous plant and animal re-introductions, the results are the first signs of regeneration and hints of what once was. Here you are in nature's territory – not human. You can walk on a number of well-kept tracks through proper New Zealand bush. Inquisitive birds like robin, saddleback and stitchbird flit about your head, while weka and takahe poke about for insects disturbed by your feet. At night you can hear kiwi, or share the coastal path with little blue penguins that do not run in fear, but merely stick their heads in the grass and croak at you with their little white bottoms sticking in the air. And at dawn, if you are very lucky, you can hear one of the most beautiful bird songs ever to grace human ears – that of the endangered kokako.

Otaki → *Colour map 3, C2   Population: 5600*

Otaki is the last (or first) settlement within the Wellington Regional Boundary. Steeped in Maori history, there are a number of *marae* canoe including the 1910 finely carved **Te Pou O Tainui Marae** on Te Rauparaha Street. The **Rangiatea Church** was one of the finest restored Maori churches in the country, but was destroyed by fire in 1995; restoration is now complete. Otaki is the main eastern gateway to the **Tararua Forest Park**. Otaki Gorge Road, 2 km south of town, takes you 19 km to Otaki Forks where a number of tracks lead into the mountains. Information about the park, local sights and accommodation options can be obtained from the VIC (see page 407).

● Sleeping

Paekakariki p407

A Killara Homestay, 70 Ames St, T04-905 5544, www.killarahomestay.co.nz. 2 rooms (queen and twin) in a large comfortable beachfront villa within walking distance of the village. Spa and internet.

C-D Paekakariki Backpackers, 11 Wellington Rd, T04-902 5967, www.wellingtonbackpackers.co.nz. Very pleasant, comfortable wee place set on the hillside above the village. Doubles, twins, singles and dorms.

C-D Paekakariki Holiday Park, Wellington Rd, T04-292 8292. Above average rooms and amenities close to the beach.

Paraparaumu and Waikanae p407

LL Greenmantle, 214 Main Rd North, T04-298 5555, www.greenmantle.co.nz. 6 beautifully appointed private suites, outdoor hot tub, spa, pool and 'the full set of irons'. B&B or dinner.

AL Te Horo Luxury Lodge, 109 Arcus Rd, Te Horo, T06-364 3393, www.tehorolodge.co.nz. Luxuriously homestay with 4 rooms in a peaceful setting near the driftwood beach. Open fire and no shortage of wood.

AL Te Nikau Forest Retreat, Kakariki Grove, Waikanae, T04-938 7774, www.tenikau.co.nz. Contemporary house with wooden interior set in coastal forest, 2 spacious doubles, treehouse spa.

A Copperfield Seaside Motel, 13 Seaview Rd, Paraparaumu Beach, T04-902 6414, www.seasidemotel.co.nz. Modern motel, 2 mins' walk from the beach, offering a convenient stop on the Kapiti Coast. Studio units and 1- to 2-bedroom apartments (some with double spa baths), Sky TV. Licensed restaurant.

A Sand Castle, Paetawa Rd (off Peka Rd), Peka Peka, Waikanae, T04-293 6072, sandmotel@kapiti.co.nz. An aptly named motel right next to the beach.

Motorcamps and campsites

C-D Lindale Motor Park, Main Rd North, SH1, Paraparaumu, T04-298 8046. Ideally located next to all Lindale tourist amenities. Good value basic doubles with cooking facilities.

D Ngatiawa Campsite, Terrace Rd, Waikanae, T04-293 5036. A lovely quiet campsite set in bush by the Ngatiawa stream.

Otaki p408

A Byron's Resort, 20 Tasman St, Otaki Beach, T04-364 8121, www.byronsresort.co.nz. Quality motel units with all resort amenities including restaurant, pool, spa and sports facilities. Camping is also available.

● Eating

Paekakariki p407

¶¶ **Paekakariki Cafe**, Wellington Rd, T04-292 8860, Open breakfast and lunch Wed-Mon, dinner Thu-Sat. Relaxed and pleasant café with quality Kiwi cuisine and good coffee.

Paraparaumu p407

¶¶ **Aqua Vitae Wine Bar and Restaurant**, Lindale Tourist Centre just north of Paraparaumu, T04-298 9889. New Zealand and international cuisine in the heart of the tourist complex.

Otaki p408

¶ **Brown Sugar Café**, corner of SH1 and Riverbank Rd, T06-364 6359. Lots of delicious home cooking in a garden setting.

▲ Activities and tours

Paraparaumu and Waikanae p407

Ferndale Equestrian Centre, 148 Ngarara Rd, Waikanae, T04-293 6209, www.ferndalehorses.com. 2- to 3-hr horse treks over farmland and along the beach.

Kapiti 4x4 Adventures, Maungakotukutuku Rd, T04-299 0020, www.kapitifourX4.co.nz. Trailblazing bike trips near Paraparaumu. 1 hr ($70), all day ($250) and overnight trips.

Kapiti Island Alive, T06-362 6606, www.kapitiislandalive.co.nz. Day trips to the island, departing 0900 or 1430 with 1-hr guided walks ($20). Overnight kiwi spotting trips are also a possibility but book well ahead.

Kapiti Tours and Kapiti Island Nature Reserve, T0800-527484, www.kapititours.co.nz. Also runs day trips to the island, departing Paraparaumu 0900 from $45.

⁑ Getting to the South Island

The scenic 85 km journey across Cook Strait takes three hours. The service is offered by two companies: the long-established **Interislander** T0800-802802/T04-498 3302, www.interislander.co.nz, has three vessels in its fleet with the latest, the *Kaitaki*, being the most modern and well facilitated. **Bluebridge**, T0800-844844, T04-471 6188, www.blue bridge.co.nz, offers a single vessel, which is older but the best choice if you are looking for character and a more traditional ferry experience.

In adverse weather conditions the crossing can be a bit of an ordeal with one crossing in 2006 taking a nauseating 10 hours. Sailings will be cancelled if conditions are considered too dangerous, but this is rare. If you can, schedule your trip so it is daylight during the one-hour scenic approach through the 'sounds' to Picton. Advance booking in advance is advised at all times, but especially in December/January. Most major VICs (I-Sites) and travel agents can organize bookings and tickets.

Interislander vessels: Arahura, Aratere and Kaitaki

There three vehicle/passenger ferries in the Interislander fleet consist of, the newly upgraded *Arahura* (meaning 'Pathway to Dawn'), the *Aratere* (meaning 'Quick Path') and the newest acquisition the *Kaitaki* (meaning 'Challenger'). Facilities include a range of bars, food courts, cafés, a movie theatre and information point. There is also a children's play area and nursery and private work desks, although negotiating a laptop on stormy seas can prove entertaining in itself.

Club class tickets will allow you access to a private lounge, complimentary tea and coffee, magazines, newspapers and a slightly better class of sick bag.

A free shuttle bus to the terminal (2 km) is available from the Wellington railway station (Platform 9), 30 minutes before each scheduled ferry departure. At the Picton end, a free shuttle is available to the railway station connecting Picton with Christchurch.

Various day/limited-excursion, family and group fares and standard discounted fares are available but must be booked in advance and are subject to availability. Like most travel bookings these days the internet will secure the best deals. At peak periods (particularly December/January) discounts are rarely available; discounts are offered mainly in winter and for very late or early sailings. Fares for passengers range from the standard $65 (child $33), to the web saver $50 (child $23). Vehicles, including campervans, cost $180-250 including the driver and depending on time of departure. Motorcycles cost $90-$120 including passenger, bicycles $10 on top of passenger charge.

Bluebridge

The *Bluebridge* came into service in mid-2002 and has become very popular, not only because it is slightly cheaper but because it is traditional, yet modern, and has plenty of deck space for viewing and photography. This is a real ship and, unlike the modern, fast and comfortable catamarans, does not look like something straight out of a Batman movie. Facilities are adequate, the service is very efficient and the staff are amicable.

The standard fare for passengers is from $45 (child $25). Vehicles including campervans cost $150-350 including driver.

South Island

Marlborough and Nelson

Introduction

The regions of Marlborough and Nelson have all the classic New Zealand ingredients – mountains, lakes, golden beaches and great tramping tracks – all safe within the boundaries of its national parks and warmed by the sunniest climate in the country. If that weren't enough, they also have a relatively low population density.

Those who do live here are a diverse bunch: from the farmers, fruit growers and winemakers in the valleys, to the artists and writers in the quiet creative havens of the Marlborough Sounds and smaller rural towns, like Motueka or Takaka. Despite the appealing lifestyle and obvious attractions, few foreigners have heard of this 'secret region'. Most simply pass through on their way to the tourist honey pots further south, stopping only briefly in Picton, the main ferry port on the South Island.

★ Don't miss

1 **Marlborough Sounds** Explore the myriad sounds by kayak or on foot, or take a cruise, page 416.
2 **Wineries** Visit the world-class vineyards of the Marlborough Region then join the locals in a rain dance, page 422.
3 **French Pass** Take the back roads to the remote aquatic maelstrom, page 426.
4 **Nelson** Soak up the buzzing atmosphere in New Zealand's most popular coastal town, page 437.
5 **Nelson Lakes National Park** Trek up to beautiful Lake Angelus, page 444.
6 **Flightseeing** Take a scenic flight from Nelson, taking in three national parks and the Marlborough Sounds all in one day, page 449.
7 **Golden Bay** From arty Takaka, visit the crystal-clear waters of the Pupu Springs, page 461.
8 **Farewell Spit** Explore the strange and lonely sandscapes, page 463.
9 **Wharariki Beach** Discover the caves and empty bays along the spectacular coast from Cape Farewell, page 464.

Marlborough Sounds → *Colour map 4, A5*

The Marlborough Sounds is like the South Island's giant foyer. This vast, convoluted system of drowned river valleys, peninsulas and islets – often dubbed New Zealand's 'little slice of Norway' – is the picturesque introduction to the South Island where you can enjoy stunning scenery, cruising, tramping, kayaking, wildlife watching or just a few days' peaceful relaxation. The port of Picton is the gateway to the sounds. From here it is then only a short journey to Blenheim, the region's capital. Although the town itself is fairly unremarkable, the area produces some of the best wines in New Zealand. A visit to some of the top vineyards is recommended. South of Blenheim is the pretty coastal settlement of Kaikoura, famous for its whales, dolphins and seabirds (see page 499).

On the map, it may look like the Marlborough Sounds takes up a relatively small area of the South Island, but its myriad sounds (drowned river valleys as opposed to fjords, which are drowned glacial valleys) create an astonishing 1500 km of coastline. Although the endless inlets and bays are not bound by snow-capped peaks as they are in Norway, the topography is just as intriguing and very picturesque. Wildlife flourishes and the area is particularly well known for its seabirds and dolphins. The two main inlets are the Queen Charlotte and Pelorus Sounds, the former being plied several times daily by the inter-island ferry between North and South Islands. ▶▶ *For Sleeping, Eating and other listings, see pages 427-436.*

Background

The sounds exhibit evidence of Maori settlement from as early as the 14th century, but the most famous early historic association was with Captain James Cook, who visited them on each of his three voyages in 1770, 1773-1774 and again in 1777. He was particularly fond of Ship Cove near the mouth of Queen Charlotte Sound, which he visited five times; a monument in Ship Cove commemorates his visits. As you might expect, Cook is responsible for many place names in the area.

Other less celebrated visitations included those of Abel Tasman (before Cook) and French navigator Jules Dumont d'Urville in 1827. It was D'Urville who discovered the chaotic and incredibly narrow passage of water between the mainland and D'Urville Island which guards the northwestern corner of the sounds. He called this strait French Pass, or Passe des Français, and it remains as much of a threat to shipping today as it did to the early navigators. In the same year as D'Urville's visit, London whaler John Guard established Marlborough's first European settlement, and the country's first land-based whaling station at Te Awaiti Bay, on Arapawa Island in the Tory Channel. Guard went on to explore and name Pelorus Sound in search of other suitable sites for settlement. Apart from the whaling stations and some early attempts at farming, the area, due to its topography, remained sparsely populated, keeping much of its native bush intact. Sadly, much of that bush has now given way to the ubiquitous sheep.

Tramping in the sounds 🛏 ▶▶ *pp427-436.*

Although most of what the sounds has to offer is easily accessed by boat, it is also possible to explore much of it on foot. There are two popular tramping tracks, the **Queen Charlotte Track** and the **Nydia Track**.

Ins and outs

Marlborough Sounds Adventure Company, based in Picton (see Activities and tours, page 434), offers guided walks (four-day, $1220/five-day $1490) and self-guided walks (four- or five-day, including food, transport and accommodation, $530). It also offers kayaking trips and an increasingly popular three-day walk/paddle/mountain bike adventure from $495, which is recommended. **Southern Wilderness NZ**, T03-529 3095, T0800 366 366, www.southernwilderness.com, organizes a range of trips on the Queen Charlotte Track ranging from a one-day guided walk ($165) to a five-day guided ($1450) including luggage transfers and hotel-style accommodation with own facilities and à la carte restaurant dining. A two-day guided walk on the Nydia Track is also available. Packages are also offered for independent walkers.

There are plenty of water-based operators who will drop off or pick up from a number of points along the track, with most offering day-walk options. Unbiased information can be secured from the VIC (I-Site). Sea access is possible at Ship Cove, Resolution Bay, Endeavour Inlet, Camp Bay (Punga Cove), Bay of Many Coves, Torea Bay (the Portage), Lochmara Bay, Mistletoe Bay (Te Mahia) and Anakiwa. **Arrow Water Taxis**, based in Picton, T03-573 8226, www.arrowwatertaxis.co.nz, offers flexibility and will go to anywhere in Queen Charlotte Sound or Tory Channel for about the same price. A typical single fare to Anakiwa is $25. **Beachcomber Fun Cruises**, based in Picton, T03-573 6175/T0800-624526, www.beachcombercruises.co.nz, also offers a wide range of daily cruise/walk packages or simple drop-off/pick-up transport options, with a flexible 'Track and Pack' pass, costing from $88. **The Cougar Line**, based on the Waterfront in Picton, T0800-504090/T03-573 7925, www.queenchar lottetrack.co.nz, is the most modern and comfortable. It offers one way transfers from

The Marlborough Sounds

Sleeping		**Camping**
Bay of Many Coves Resort **3**	Nydia Lodge **7**	Te Mahia Bay Resort **14**
Bayview Backpackers **1**	Parklands Marina	
Driftwood Cottage **15**	Holiday Park **6**	**Camping**
D'Urville Wilderness	Portage **8**	Bay of Many Coves **1**
Resort **19**	Punga Cove Resort **9**	Black Rock **2**
French Pass Beachfront	Raetihi Lodge **10**	Camp Bay **3**
Villas & Sea Safaris **18**	Resolution Bay Cabins **11**	Cowshed **4**
Furneaux Lodge **2**	Smiths Farm Holiday	Davies Bay **5**
Hopewell **16**	Park **12**	Mistletoe Bay **6**
Lazy Fish **4**	St Omer House **13**	Ship Cove **7**
Lochmara Lodge **5**		
Ngaio Bay Homestead **20**		

$30; multi-day walk packages; mountain biking packages and a daily scheduled 'Track Pass' that will drop you off at Ship Cove (departs Picton 0800, 1000 and 1330) and pick up at Anakiwa (Tirimoana, 1430 and 1645) from $90. It can also deliver your pack to your accommodation and offers half- or full-day cruise walks from $50. **Endeavour Express**, based in both Endeavour Inlet and at the Waterfront in Picton, T03-573 5456, www.boatrides.co.nz, offers similar wide-ranging services, with drop-offs and pick-ups from various strategic points on the track (including Ship Cove and Anakiwa) as well as a scheduled daily service to Ship Cove and Endeavour Inlet (departs Picton 0900, 1000, 1315 and 1800; returns from Endeavour Inlet 1100 and 1530 from $80). Basic single drop-off fares start from $30. **West Bay Water Transport**, based near the Ferry Terminal in Picton, T03-573 5597, www.westbay.co.nz, serves the southern end of the Queen Charlotte Track, from Torea Bay to Anakiwa (single $35). It also offers half- and full-day, track-walk options (from $45). Departs Picton five times daily (seasonal variations).

There are also general road tours and options by road from Picton to Anakiwa **Beachcomber Cruise's Rural Mail Run**, T0800-624526/T03-573 6175, www.beach combercruises.co.nz, from $75, is one option. This and other road trips can be booked and pre-paid via the VIC (I-Site). If you have your own wheels, road access is also possible at Camp Bay (Punga Cove), Torea Bay (The Portage) and Mistletoe Bay (Te Mahia).

Queen Charlotte Track

ⓘ *Details of the track are outlined in DoC leaflets available from the VIC (I-Site); DoC in Picton provides information and maps. The website www.qctrack.co.nz is also useful.*
The Queen Charlotte Track is a 71-km (three- to five-day) well-formed track from **Ship Cove** (Captain Cook's New Zealand base, 1770-1777) to **Anakiwa**. It is suitable for most people of average fitness and sections of the track are also popular for mountain biking. The track makes its way around sheltered coves, over skyline ridges and through native forest fringing a vast network of sunken river valleys. Although the track can be tackled from either Anakiwa or Ship Cove, conventionally the start is at Ship Cove and all written information describes the track in this direction (east to west). The track is becoming increasingly popular, so plan and book well in advance. There are numerous DoC campsites along the route and independent accommodation establishments cater for all budgets. Boat access is also well organized and readily available. Water taxis and cruise operators regularly stop not only at Ship Cove, but also at many of the accommodation establishments or campsites en route so it is possible to do part of the track, or to stay in one place and simply chill out. For the real cheats you can also arrange to have your backpack transported on to your next accommodation or port of call.

Nydia Track

ⓘ *Details of the track are outlined in the relevant DoC leaflets. The VIC (I-Site) and DoC offices in Picton and Havelock can provide comprehensive information and maps.*
The Nydia Track is the lesser known and shorter of the two tramping tracks. It is 27 km in length and takes two days. The track, which is essentially a network of old bridle paths, begins at Kaiuma Bay (near Havelock) and traverses the Kaiuma and Nydia saddles, taking in the sheltered, historic timber-milling site at **Nydia Bay**, before ending at **Duncan Bay**. The track is particularly noted for its magnificent forest, much of which is untouched and a fine example of the native bush that once covered the region. Although the Nydia Track is more difficult than the Queen Charlotte and requires detailed planning, it offers a shorter, less busy alternative, though it is not so well served by accommodation and public transport. From Havelock it is 12 km (45 minutes) drive via SH6 to the turn-off at Dalton's Road, then another 21 km to Kaiuma car park and the start of the track. Given that, you are far better catch a water taxi (five minutes) to Shag Point from Havelock. Contact the VIC (I-Site) in Havelock or Picton for the latest operator listings, T03-520 3113.

Picton ⊟🚲▲🚌🅲 ➠ *pp427-436.*

➠ *Colour map 4, A5 Population: 4000*

Once you cross the Cook Strait and enter the 'The Sounds', you arrive in the pretty township of Picton, gateway to the Marlborough Sounds and the South Island. In summer Picton is a buzz of activity with visitors coming and going by ferry, car or train, but in winter it reverts to its more familiar role as a sleepy port.

Despite its size, Picton has an interesting history. It was once the site of an important Maori *pa* called Waitohi before the first Europeans settled and renamed it Newton. For a while Newton was the proud capital of Marlborough (before Blenheim stole the honours) and later, after being renamed Picton, became a candidate for the country's capital. In more recent times controversy has affected the town. For almost a decade the issue of relocating the ferry port south closer to Blenheim has been hotly debated. Thankfully for 'the Picts' that option was dismissed by the government, who claim it is not financially viable. So, thankfully, as the gateway to both the South Island and the sounds, pretty Picton looks set to remain.

Ins and outs

Getting there Picton airport ① *10 km south of town*, is served by **Soundsair**, T03-520 3080/T0800-505005, www.soundsair.com, eight times daily from Wellington, $79 one way. Scenic flights and a range of flight/activity combos are also available. ➠ *See Activities and tours, page 433.*

Picton

To Scenic Route to Havelock & Nelson

Sleeping 🛏
Americano Motor Inn **1**
Bayview
  Backpackers **13**
Blue Anchor Top
  Ten Holiday Park **2**
Broadway Motel **3**

Gables **4**
Harbour View **5**
Jasmine Court **6**
McCormick House **16**
Parklands Marina
  Holiday Park **14**
Picton Lodge **7**

Sequoia Lodge
  Backpackers **12**
St Catherine's B&B **8**
Tourist Court Motel **9**
Villa **10**
Waikawa Bay
  Seafront Apartments **15**

Eating 🍴
DAs **2**
Gusto Café **3**
Le Café **5**
Toot & Whistle **4**

There are numerous bus companies that network their way to Picton from the south or west: **Intercity**, T03-520 3113/T03-573 7025, www.intercitycoach.co.nz, from Nelson, Blenheim, Kaikoura and Christchurch; **Atomic Shuttles**, T03-322 8883, www.atomictravel.co.nz, throughout the South Island; and **Richies Coachlines**, T03-389 9551, www.ritchies.co.nz, from Blenheim and beyond. Other smaller companies offering a range of options include: **Kahurangi Bus (Kbus/Southern Link)**, T03-358 8355, www.kbus.co.nz, from Nelson, Abel Tasman via Blenheim and the internet-based **Nakedbus.com**, throughout the South Island. A single fare from Blenheim is $10-12, Nelson $16-20 and Christchurch around $40. Buses drop off or pick up at the railway station, ferry terminal or outside the VIC (I-Site). The main intercity coach agent is the VIC (I-Site), but the **Picton Travel Centre** ① *in the ferry terminal building, T03-573 7025*, can also assist with onward travel.

The **Interislander** and **Bluebridge** ferries dock in the rather plush **ferry terminal** ① *500 m north of town centre*. There are at least four sailings daily, see box page 410, or contact T0800-802802/T04-498 3302, www.interislander.co.nz/www.ferrytickets.co.nz.

The **train station** ① *Auckland St, T03-573 8857/T0800-872467, 0900-1700*, is the terminus for the daily **TranzCoastal** service from Christchurch, T0800-872467/T04-495 0775, www.tranzscenic.co.nz. It arrives daily at 1213 and departs at 1300, from $59-100. This trip is famous for its stunning coastal scenery.

Tourist information   Picton VIC (I-Site) ① *on the foreshore, T03-520 3113, www.destinationmarlborough.com, daily 0830-1800 (1700 winter)*, has many useful leaflets including the invaluable *What to Do In Picton* and *The Queen Charlotte Track*. **DoC** information is available in the same building, and there is a range of books and maps on sale. Useful websites include www.picton.co.nz, www.creativemarlborough.co.nz, www.marlborough4fun.co.nz and www.marlboroughweb.co.nz.

Sights

If you have arrived on the **Lynx** ferry in rough seas, with its almost comfy seats and state-of-the-art radar screens, you will be immediately thanking your lucky stars for progress when you encounter the old wooden hulk of the **Edwin Fox** ① *between the ferry terminal and the town centre, daily 0900-1700, $6*. The remains of the 1853, once fully rigged East India Trading ship is being lovingly restored to a reminder of her former glory by the Edwin Fox Society. The vessel, which is (apparently) the ninth oldest ship in the world and the only remaining example of her type, was a troop carrier in the Crimean War before being commissioned to bring immigrants to Australia and New Zealand.

Next door is **Seahorse World** ① *T03-573 6030, www.seahorseworld.co.nz, daily 0900-1700, day pass $16, child $9*. As one of the few aquariums in the country it is perhaps worth a look, but more fun for kids. A range of displays house the usual characters including an octopus called Larry, some seahorses, rays, and the obligatory sharks. Staff are always on hand to enthuse and answer any questions.

A short walk across the footbridge and the inlet to the eastern side of the waterfront to Shakespeare Bay will deliver you to the **Echo Gallery and Museum** ① *daily in summer, $3, child $1*. The *Echo* is a former 'scow' built in 1905 that has been lovingly and gradually restored after her retirement in 1965. She was formerly a trading vessel, and apparently the last commercial trader under sail in New Zealand before further services in the Second World War. By all accounts, she has led rather an unfortunate existence, having been stranded 15 times, damaged 16 times, had two new engines, propellers and shafts, had fires in 1911 and 1920, seven collisions involving 75 different vessels and was sunk twice and no doubt captained by Laurel and Hardy. Be careful not to trip going up the gangplank.

For a comprehensive guide to the walks around Picton, get hold of the excellent *Picton by Foot broadsheet, available free from the VIC (I-Site). There are a number of* options, with most traversing the narrow peninsula to the northeast of the town separating Waikawa Bay and Picton Harbour. Most are around two hours return, with the longest being the **Snout Track**, taking in the **Queen Charlotte Lookout**. Other walks taking in fine views are the **Karaka Point Lookout** (20 minutes, on the main road east of Waikawa) and the **Tirohanga Walk Lookout**, above and south of the town (start point off Newgate Street just east of the town centre, two hours return). For the numerous activities based in Picton, see page 433.

Blenheim ⊟🕐✳▲🖶🛈 ➠ pp427-436.

→ *Colour map 4 B5 Population: 27,000*

Although it is depressingly flat and unremarkable looking, Blenheim – Marlborough's largest town – is a popular tourist base, primarily for those intent on sampling the region's fine wines. Most of the wineries lie just to the west of town, on the fertile soils of the Wairau Plains. In Blenheim you can be sure a local winemaker will never be far away. Winemaking in Marlborough is big business and fiercely competitive; it brings new meaning to the phrase 'designer label'.

Ins and outs
Getting there Blenheim airport🛈 *Middle Renwick Rd, 7 km west of town*, is serviced by **Air New Zealand Link**, T0800-737000, www.airnewzealand.co.nz. Flights are met by the **Airport Super Shuttle**, T03-572 9910; or **Neal's Shuttles**, T03-577 5277, $14.

Blenheim sits on both the main road (SH1) and rail links south, via Kaikoura (129 km) to Christchurch (308 km). An interesting alternative route by car to Blenheim from Picton is via the coast road, Port Underwood and the scenic bluffs of Rarangi. There are many bus services heading south. There are also services that head northwest via SH6 to Nelson, the Abel Tasman National Park and Golden Bay and west to St Arnaud and the Nelson Lakes National Park. See Picton Ins and outs, page 419, for details.

The **TranzCoastal** train service north to Picton or south to Christchurch passes through Blenheim once a day, T0800-872467, www.tranzscenic.co.nz.

Tourist information Marlborough VIC (I-Site) 🛈 *railway station on Grove Rd (SH1), T03-577 8080, www.destinationmarlborough.com/www.winemarlborough.net.nz, daily 0830-1830; winter Mon-Fri 0830-1800, Sat-Sun 0900-1600*, has information about the town, region and, of course, the wineries. The free *Marlborough Visitor Guide* is useful.

Sights → *See map page 422.*
Being primarily a service town, Blenheim has little to offer the tourist in the way of sights, with most visitors simply joining the various winery tours based in town, or picking up the information to tour the vineyards. However, of some historical interest is the provincial museum and archives complex at the **Brayshaw Museum Park** 🛈 *New Renwick Rd, 3 km south of the town, daily 1000-1600, free entry with a small charge for some attractions*. The museum is a mainly open-air affair, featuring an interesting reconstruction of an early settlers' village along with the inevitable farm machinery and ancient vehicles. Also of some note back in town is **Pollard Park** on Parker Street – a pretty conglomerate of flowerbeds, ponds and rose gardens. Right in the centre of town is **Seymour Square** with its landmark clock tower. It also hosts the **Millennium Gallery** 🛈 *T03-579 2001, Mon-Fri 1000-1700, Sat-Sun 1200-1630, donation*, which is the main focus for the arts in the region. If you are interested in more regional detail surrounding arts and crafts pick up the free *Art and Craft Trail* leaflet from the VIC (I-Site).

Wineries

The biggest attractions around Blenheim – and arguably the entire region – are the world-class wineries. Sun-baked Marlborough is New Zealand's largest wine-growing region, with over 50 wineries producing highly acclaimed Chardonnay, Riesling, Cabernet Sauvignon, Merlot, Pinot Noir, sparkling Methode Champenoise and some of best Sauvignon Blanc in the world. Montana sowed the first seeds of success in the

Blenheim

Sleeping
Antria Boutique Lodge **10**
Blenheim Bridge Top Ten
  Holiday Park **19**
Blue Ridge Estate B&B **13**
Clovelly B&B **17**
Cranbrook Cottage **4**
d'Urville **1**
Grapevine Backpackers **15**
Honi-B Backpackers **9**

Knightsbridge Court
  Motor Lodge **5**
Koanui Backpackers **8**
Lugano Motor Lodge **2**
Marlborough **3**
Old St Mary's Convent **6**
Peppertree **18**
Phoenix Motor Inn **16**
St Leonards **12**
Timara Lodge **11**

Waterfall Lodge **7**
Watson's Way
  Backpackers **14**

Eating
Bellafico Wine Bar **1**
Paddy Barry's Irish Pub **3**
Rocco's **5**

Wineries around Blenheim

A comprehensive list of the wineries is beyond the scope of this guide, but some wineries of particular note are listed below. The best time to visit the vineyards is in April when the heavily laden vines are ripe for the picking. See also Winery tours listings, page 435.

Allan Scott Estate, Jackson's Rd, T03-572 9054, www.allanscott.com, daily 0900-1700, lunch from 0900. Established in 1973, producing fine Sauvignon, Chardonnay and Riesling wines. The Twelve Trees restaurant, is deservedly popular.

Cellier Le Brun, Terrace Rd, Renwick, T03-572 8859, www.lebrun.co.nz, daily 0900-1700 (dinner Wed, Thu and Sat). A long-established contender offering a little contrast as the producer of a fine Methode Champenoise. On-site café.

Cloudy Bay, Jackson's Rd, T03-520 9140, www.cloudybay.co.nz, tastings and tours daily 1000-1700. An internationally famous label.

Herzog, 81 Jeffries Rd, T03-572 8770, www.herzog.co.nz, daily 1100-1500. Not only fine wine (particularly Pinot Noir) but one of the best winery restaurants in the country, open Oct-mid May. Exceptional international wine list.

Highfield Estate, Brookby Rd, T03-572 9244, www.highfield.co.nz, daily 1030-1700. Fine wine, architecture and the best view of the lot from its rampart tower. Reputable indoor/outdoor restaurant open daily for lunch 1130-1530.

Hunters Wines, Rapaura Rd, T03-572 8489, www.hunters.co.nz. Another of the larger, most popular labels producing a wide variety of wines. Also home to a fine restaurant open for lunch (1130-1430) and dinner Thu-Sat, from 1800.

Johanneshof Cellars, SH1, Koromiko, 20 km north of Blenheim, T03-573 7035, www.johanneshof.co.nz, summer Tue-Sun 1000-1600. Cellar tour $8. Famous for underground 'rock cellars', lined with both barrel and bottle.

Montana Brancott Winery, Main South Rd (SH1), just to the south of Blenheim, T03-578 2099, www.montanawines.com, daily 0900-1700. It is almost rude not to visit this, the largest wine-producer in the country. The new visitor centre is very impressive and there are half-hourly tours (1000-1500), tastings, a restaurant with outdoor seating and a classy shop. This is also the venue for the now world-famous **Marlborough Food and Wine Festival** in February (see Festivals and events, page 433).

Prenzel Distillery, Sheffield St, Riverlands Estate, T03-578 2800, www.prenzel.com. New Zealand's first commercial fruit distillery producing a range of fruit liqueurs, schnapps, and brandies.

Seresin, Bedford Rd, Renwick, T03-572 9408, www.seresin.co.nz, summer daily 1000-1630, winter Mon-Fri 1000-1630. Noted not only for its wine, but also its artwork.

early 1970s and is now the largest winery in the country. Three decades on, Montana has been joined by other world-famous names and has become a major national export industry.

Like Hawke's Bay in the North Island, the wineries have been quick to take advantage of the tourist dollar, with most offering tours, tastings (free or small charge) and good restaurants. Although the competition in Marlborough is fierce, the region's vineyards lack the architectural splendour or variety of Hawke's Bay. Perhaps they just leave the wine to do the talking.

Marlborough & Nelson Marlborough Sounds

If you are a complete novice it's a good idea to join one of the many excellent tours on offer. They generally last a full- or half-day, taking in the pick of the crop and the widest variety of wine types. There is always an informative commentary, often a lunch stop and, of course, numerous tastings included in the package. If you know a bit about wines and have particular tastes, many tour operators will create a personal itinerary. If you wish to explore by yourself, there are plenty of maps and leaflets at the VIC (I-Site).

Most of the wineries are located off SH6 around the small village of **Renwick**, 10 km west of Blenheim. Should you get sick of all the wine, or pompous 'wine- speak', there are other distilleries, breweries, vineyards and orchards in the area producing everything from liqueurs and fruit wines to olive oil. There is even an English-style pub and brewery, **The Cork and Keg** ⓘ *Inkerman St, Renwick, T03-572 9328*, which produces its own beer. Add to this the many fine eating establishments and there is no doubt your visit to the area can get very expensive.

Some excellent and detailed information about the region and New Zealand wines generally can be found in the magazine *Campbell's Wine Annual*, which can be bought in most leading bookshops and magazine outlets. The VIC (I-Site) also produces *The Wines and Wineries of Marlborough – Wine Trail Map* and *The Marlborough Wine Region* broadsheet. With all of these you cannot go wrong. For web information visit www.winemarlborough.net.nz.

Havelock ⬤🏃🏛🏨 » *pp427-436.*

→ *Colour map 4, A5 Population: 500*

From Blenheim SH6 passes through the small village of Renwick before winding its way through the rolling hills of the Inner Marlborough Sounds to Nelson. About a third of the way (41 km), at the head of the expansive Pelorus Sound, is the enchanting little village of Havelock. Blink and you will miss it, but if you have time, a stop here is well worth it.

Ins and outs

Getting there and around Havelock is 41 km from Blenheim and 75 km from Nelson on SH6. By bus, **Intercity, Atomic Shuttles** and **K'Bus**, T0508-458835/T03-358 8355, www.kbus.co.nz, all service Havelock (Main Road) on their way back and forth to Nelson. For full service listings, see Picton Ins and outs, page 419.

For track transport, **West Bay Water Transport**, T03-573 5597, www.westbay.co.nz, based near the ferry terminal in Picton, serves the southern end of the Queen Charlotte Track from Torea Bay to Anakiwa (single from $25) and offers half-day track-walk options ($45). **Pelorus Water Transport**, T027-239 0000, www.peloruswt.co.nz, offers water taxis and charter services.

Tourist information There are several independent visitor centres in the main street that serve as a source of local information and local activity booking agents. Internet is also available. Try the long established **Rutherford Travel (YHA)** ⓘ *46 Main Rd, T03-574 2114, www.rutherfordtravel.co.nz*. The website www.havelocknz.com is also useful.

Sights

The village itself has little to offer except a friendly welcome, a fine café, restaurant, art and craft galleries, some rugby-playing mussel shells (honest), a small but interesting **museum** ⓘ *Main Rd, T03-574 2176, daily (seasonal) 0900-1700, entry by donation*, and a fine Scottish pub, but it is an ideal base from which to explore the glorious Pelorus and other 'outer sounds'. As the quiet neighbour to the much-hyped Queen Charlotte Sound, the Pelorus does not receive as much attention, but it is no less impressive and, in summer, provides a much quieter alternative. Havelock was once a thriving gold-mining town and also the boyhood home of one of New Zealand's most famous sons, Ernest Rutherford 'the man who split the atom'. His former home is now the busy youth hostel. Havelock was also the latter-day home of another famous New Zealander, the writer Barry Crump. 'Crumpy' was the archetypal 'Kiwi bloke' whose humorous accounts of hunting and life in the bush has had many a proud Kiwi smiling in recognition. These days Havelock's gold is the green-lipped mussel, without doubt the finest-tasting thing in a shell, and a major export industry within the sounds.

If you intend to explore the sounds by road you can do this along the **Kenepuru Road**, which starts just past Linkwater (east of Havelock on Queen Charlotte Drive), or the **Tennyson Inlet** and **French Pass** roads, just north of Rai valley, west of Havelock (see below). Maps are available at the Picton or Havelock VICs (I-Sites).

▲▲ Walks

Havelock is the principal base from which to embark on the increasingly popular **Nydia Track** (see page 418); **Rutherford Travel**, T03-574 2114, can advise. About 18 km west of Havelock is the **Pelorus Bridge Scenic Reserve**. This is a pretty little spot where the azure waters of the Rai and Pelorus rivers carve their way through the surrounding bush-clad hills. There are a number of walks from 30 minutes to three hours. A number of DoC information boards or the tearooms near the car park will keep you right. At the very least, stop and have a look at the river from the bridge.

Closer to Havelock itself is the climb to **Takorika Hill**. Located behind the town, its ascent will be rewarded by fine views. The lazy, or pushed-for-time, can reach the transmission tower by car via forest tracks (6 km). The entrance via Wilsons Road is about 5 km west of Havelock on SH6.

Tennyson Inlet, French Pass and D'Urville Island
▸▸ *pp427-436.*

→ *Colour map 4, A5*

The Ronga and Opouri roads which connect the remote corners of the outer sounds are worthy of investigation, offering some stunning coastal scenery of a type that is unsurpassed elsewhere in the country. Both roads can be accessed just beyond the small settlement of Rai Valley, 48 km east of Nelson and 27 km west of Havelock. To explore the roads properly you should stock up with food and petrol and give yourself at least two days: one to take in Opouri Road and Tennyson Inlet (40 km), then back to Ronga Road to French Pass (70 km); and the second to spend some time in French Pass before returning to SH6. From French Pass it is possible to explore the most remote and largest of the sounds' islands, D'Urville Island, named after the intrepid French explorer who discovered it in 1827. If you don't have your own transport, you could try the local **Mail Run** but times and schedules vary, or contact **Rutherford Travel**, T03-574 2114.

Tennyson Inlet

About 1 km from SH6, Opouri Road shadows the Opouri River and cuts through paddock upon paddock full of sleepy stock lying in the shade of sheds that have seen better days. Then it suddenly and dramatically straddles **Lookout Hill** (900 m) before falling like a stone to Tennyson Inlet. The view at the crest of the hill is almost as impressive as the hairpin bends which must be negotiated to reach the inlet. But once there, the peace and tranquillity seem reward enough. If you are feeling energetic you might like to walk part of the Nydia Track to **Nydia Bay** where there is camping and accommodation available (see pages 418 and 429).

Marlborough & Nelson Marlborough Sounds

⁝ Pelorus Jack

The name and tale of Pelorus Jack has been synonymous with the Marlborough Sounds, and particularly French Pass, for over a century, relating not to some old pirate or explorer, but to a dolphin. And at the time, perhaps the most famous dolphin in the world. It was also this particular dolphin that paved the way for the concept of legal protection for all sea mammals.

As long ago as the late 1800s, the Marlborough Sounds and the route from Wellington to Nelson via the treacherous waters of French Pass were regularly used and negotiated by a vast array of trading and passenger vessels. Although there is no evidence as to the exact date of the strange dolphin's first appearance, by the turn of the century the antics of the 'Great White Fish' or 'Jack' (as he was christened by the local fishermen) were becoming legendary. Almost every vessel that appeared over the horizon, east of French Pass, would be habitually escorted by 'Jack' to its entrance, where he would mysteriously disappear, only to reappear in readiness to escort the next. What was most unusual about 'Jack' (but not initially

understood) was that he was a large Risso's dolphin, a rare species which are not the classic 'dolphin' size, shape or colour, having a bumpy forehead and very pale skin. Before long, people from all over New Zealand were making the trip just to see the 'mysterious creature' and many other people, especially the regular seafarers, held 'Jack' in high regard. News quickly spread and through word of mouth, letters, postcards and newspaper articles, 'Jack' began to gain notoriety around the world. But of course not all the stories of the day got the details right and almost every aspect of 'Jack' the strange sea creature became exaggerated. Some said he was 40 ft long and others that he was in fact, a mighty whale just like Moby Dick. One article even said he was protected by an Act of Parliament. Remarkably, it was this particular piece that stirred the then tourist office, and one Daniel Bates – a junior clerk in the Government Weather Office – to lobby for 'Jack's' official protection. One must remember that at the time, any sea mammal, be it whale, seal or dolphin, was something of a mystery and an

French Pass

Back on Ronga Road, the route cuts through the paddocks of a river valley before climbing through attractive native bush to reach the first stunning views of Croisilles Harbour and out to the west coast of **D'Urville Island**. The first settlement of any consequence is **Okiwi Bay**, a secret little haunt of many a boatie Nelsonite. Okiwi provides a great base from which to go sailing or fishing in the quiet undisturbed bays of the Sounds westernmost coastline.

Just past Okiwi Bay the road passes through some beautiful tracts of beech forest before becoming unsealed. It is another 40 km to French Pass but after just a few kilometres the views of the sounds really open up and damage to your hire car will be the last thing on your mind. From **Elaine Bay** the road clings precariously to bush-clad ridges giving you a glimpse of the scenic splendour, before the trees peter out and D'Urville Island comes into view. You then head along the western side of the now bare ridge to French Pass. On the way, take the short detour to the top of the hill with the transmitters. From there you can soak up another stunning vista of Tennyson Inlet.

French Pass is really nothing more than a row of houses and a DoC campsite in a small sheltered bay at the very tip of the mainland. It takes its name from the nautical nightmare that is just around the corner. The best view of this alarmingly slim channel of water can be seen from a path that leads down to a viewing point from the road (about 1 km before the settlement). At anytime, but particularly mid-tide, the chaotic animal to be either feared or killed. And given the grandiose details being touted all over the world surrounding the mysterious 'Jack', museum curators were beginning to put a price on his head and desire his brain in a bottle! Already, he was being shot at and surreptitiously hunted for bounty. Thankfully, after much lobbying and personal determination by Bates, an official Act of Parliament – the first of its kind protecting any sea mammal – was passed in September 1904 and as a result it became illegal to hunt or harm 'Jack' or any of his ilk in New Zealand waters. Of course this only exacerbated 'Jack's' newsworthiness and social standing. Children wrote sack loads of postcards and letters addressed 'To Pelorus Jack – New Zealand' and his visitations were listed in social columns of the national papers. Visiting celebrities like Mark Twain took the Nelson voyage especially to see him and seafarers the world over gave a special toast at gatherings in respect and honour of his protection and guidance. It was the spring of 1912, some 25 years since his first 'official' documented sighting that 'Jack' mysteriously disappeared. Although at the time there was national outrage and a subsequent and unsuccessful witch-hunt to find his 'killer', it is now thought that 'Jack' most probably died of old age. It is also now known that 'Jack' was perhaps the last individual of a once thriving pod of Risso's dolphin that resided in the area and that is why perhaps he turned all his attention to seeking company in the form of shipping and human beings. But it is the Maori who have perhaps the best explanation of the whole phenomenon. To them 'Jack' the dolphin (or *tahurangi*) is said to be a *taniwha* – or a spirit sent by the gods to be our guide and helper. Because he is a spirit and therefore magic, he can never die, and has for the last century been merely asleep, resting in his ocean cave between spells of duty. What is most interesting of all are a handful of stories that swear of the appearance or sighting of a dolphin when boats have been in peril or have been lost in the sounds. So keep an eye out because it seems Pelorus Jack may still be out there.

currents can be seen forcing their way between the mainland and D'Urville Island. First discovered by D'Urville in 1827, this passage is a very important point on the nautical map because it offers an enticing short cut between Wellington and Nelson. If you are lucky you can time your visit to coincide with the passage of a ship. Some are so large you swear they will never make it and you can almost shout hello to the captain on the bridge, wave, and then tell him to watch where he is going.

French Pass is not only famous for its scenery, pass or shipping. Without doubt the most famous sight and resident was Pelorus Jack (see box, above).

Sleeping

Queen Charlotte Track *p418, map p417*
The Queen Charlotte Track is well served with accommodation options with a broad range from DoC campsites ($5) to privately owned backpacker hostels, self-contained units and luxury lodges. The VIC (I-Site) has full listings and will help you plan your itinerary and book your accommodation, but in summer you are advised to do this well in advance. There are also ample accommodation options elsewhere throughout the sounds with most offering meals and some having in-house restaurants or at the very least adequate cooking facilities. Some can be reached by water taxi, others by road, or even by air. Again the VIC (I-Site) will advise. Some of the more noteworthy establishments are listed below.

LL-LLazy Fish, about 12 km from Picton, Queen Charlotte Sound, T03-573 5291, www.lazyfish.co.nz. A superb luxury option set in its own bay, only accessible by boat. Its motto is 'Ubi Dies Omnis Festus' ('where every day is Sunday'). The homestead is beautifully appointed and renovated, only a few metres from the water with guest bungalows set in bush. Contemporary artworks and antiques dominate the decor and each bungalow has a 4-poster bed. The old UK telephone box on the jetty adds to the character and charm. Meals included. Outdoor bathtub, excellent kitchen, windsurfer/canoe/fishing tackle hire.

LL-LRaetihi Lodge, Kenepuru Sound, T03-573 4300, www.raetihi.co.nz. Modern, luxury lodge over looking Double Bay in Kenepuru Sound noted for its architecture, secluded location and cuisine. 14 themed rooms reflect a variety of topics from the colours of the Sounds, to nautical or Egyptian, stunning views, licensed à la carte restaurant. Dinner, B&B packages available. Accessible by road, boat or by air (direct from Wellington with **Soundsair**). Boat recommended.

LL-ABay of Many Coves Resort, Queen Charlotte Sound, T03-579 9771, www.bayof manycovesresort.co.nz. Comes recommended and represents the sounds at its best. Remote seclusion yet all the comforts of a modern award-winning resort. Classy studio units and apartments with memorable views across the sound, café, restaurant and a wide range of activities from kayaking to heli-fishing.

L-CPunga Cove Resort, Punga Cove, Endeavour Inlet, T0800-809697/T03-579 8561, www.pungacove.co.nz. Wide range of options from private chalets and self-contained studios to a backpacker lodge. Facilities and services include a licensed restaurant, shop, laundry, spa and canoe hire. The resort is a 500-m walk from the road. Water taxi recommended.

AL-DPortage Hotel, Kenepuru Sound, T03-573 4309, www.portage.co.nz. A wide range of accommodation from luxury spa rooms to bunkrooms. Restaurant, well-stocked shop, pool and DoC campsite nearby. Kayak and bike hire available.

A-DFurneaux Lodge, Endeavour Inlet, T03-579 8259, www.furneaux.co.nz. Historic lodge set in idyllic gardens near a waterfall. Self-contained chalets and backpacker accommodation in a lovely stone 'croft'.

Campsite available. Restaurant and bar. Ideal for a night stopover from Ship Cove.

A-DLochmara Lodge (Backpackers), Lochmara Bay, T03-573 4554, www.lochmara lodge.co.nz, closed Jun-Oct. A deservingly popular eco-oriented backpacker hostel with a great, laid-back atmosphere. Dorm and private studio chalets (some en suite). If you can remove yourself from a hammock there is a spa (in the bush where the Punga People live), open fire, free kayak and windsurf hire. Excellent in-house eco-trips to Motuara Island.

A-DResolution Bay Cabins, Resolution Bay, T03-579 9411, www.resolutionbaycabins.co.nz. Accommodation ranges from cabins to self-contained cottages. Good atmosphere and fine café. Shop on site.

A-DSt Omer House, Kenepuru Sound, T03-573 4086, www.stomerhouse.co.nz. Historic villa with rooms (some shared), units, self-contained cottages, powered sites. Lovely setting with a private beach only yards away. Restaurant on site.

A-DTe Mahia Bay Resort, Kenepuru Sound, T03-573 4089, www.temahia.co.nz. Compact and in a peaceful location. Popular new and old self-contained accommodation, backpacker hostel and tent sites available. Store but no restaurant. Kayak and dinghy hire.

B-DHopewell, Kenepuru Sound, T03-573 4341, www.hopewell.co.nz. Excellent establishment in a remote location on Kenepuru Sound, providing the perfect blend of value and comfort. Although accessible by road from Havelock North or Picton it is a tortuous drive. A water taxi is recommended and adds the overall experience, or you can fly direct from Wellington (**Soundsair**) to the local airfield from where you can be picked up. A range of options from a self-contained cottage to doubles and 4-shares. Attractive grounds right down to the water's edge. Outdoor spa overlooking the sound, internet, kayaks and plenty of water-based activities, with fishing trips a speciality. Friendly, caring hosts. One night is not enough. The secret is out so book well ahead. Recommended.

C-DSmiths Farm Holiday Park, Queen Charlotte Drive, Linkwater, T03-574 2806. Spotless self-contained motel units, cabins, powered and tent sites close to the track start at Anakiwa to which there is courtesy transport. Bike hire and lots of friendly animals. Recommended.

Campsites

D DoC campsites are available at Ship Cove, Camp Bay, Bay of Many Coves, Black Rock, Cowshed, Mistletoe Bay and Davies Bay.

Nydia Track *p418, map p417*

C-D Driftwood Cottage, Nydia Bay, T03-579 8454, www.nydiabay.co.nz. A small, excellent and 'alternative' backpacker hostel with candle and solar powered cabins. Breakfast, dinner and pack lunches available.
D Nydia Lodge, on the south coast of Nydia Bay, T03-574 2019. Sleeps 50.

Campsites

DoC campsites (from $5) available in the northwestern corner of Nydia Bay: 2 in Tennyson Inlet and 1 in Duncan Bay.

Picton *p419, maps p417 and p419*

There are few modern hotels but plenty of motels to choose from.
LL McCormick House, 21 Leicester St, T03-573 5253, www.mccormickhouse.co.nz. A modern, friendly and luxury B&B in a quiet location. 2 en suites. Courtesy car.
AL Waikawa Bay Seafront Apartments, 45 Beach Rd, T03-573 5220. A modern establishment located beside the Waikawa Bay marina complex, east of Picton. Offers luxury self-contained apartments, pool, spa, and café/restaurant/bar nearby.
AL-A The Broadway Motel, 113 High St, T03-573 6563, www.broadwaymotel.co.nz. Centrally located and handy for the ferry terminal the Broadway is one of the most modern motels in the town. Spotless standard units, some with spa and balcony.
A Americano Motor Inn, 32 High St, T0800-104104/T03-573 6398, www.americano.co.nz. Right in the heart of town this is a large motel with a popular licensed restaurant attached.
A The Jasmine Court, 78 Wellington St, T03-573 7110, www.jasminecourt.co.nz. Another good motel offering a fine range of well-appointed, modern units. Good location.
A St Catherine's B&B, 123 Wellington St, T03-573 8580, www.stcatherines.co.nz. Set in a very relaxing historic former convent it offers 2 rooms, 1 queen with shared

bathroom and 1 room (en suite bathroom) with a 4-poster bed and great views from a private balcony.
A-B The Gables, 20 Waikawa Rd, T03-573 6772, www.thegables.co.nz. Enjoys a good reputation and in an ideal location with 3 rooms and 2 self-contained cottages on site plus another cottage option in Waikawa Bay.
B The Harbour View, 30 Waikawa Rd, T03-573 6259. 12 fully self-contained studio units and fine views across the harbour.
B Tourist Court Motel, 45 High St, T03-573 6331, www.touristcourt.co.nz. One of the better, long-established budget motels, near the centre.
B-D Bayview Backpackers, 318 Waikawa Rd, T03-573 7668, bayview.backpackers@xtra.co.nz. A modern, friendly and rapidly expanding place in Waikawa Bay, just east of Picton. Good value dorm beds, single/twin and double rooms some with en suite bath and TV. It offers the peace and quiet absent at the bustling hostels in the town centre. Free pick-up/drop-off to the ferry. Free bikes, kayaks and sailing trips arranged. Internet. Recommended.
B-D Picton Lodge, 9 Auckland St, T0800-223367/T03-573 7788, www.pictonlodge.co.nz. The closest hostel to the ferry terminal and close to the VIC (I-Site) and town centre, pub next door. Singles, doubles/ twins and small dorms. Large open plan living area. Free breakfast, blankets and bike hire.
B-D Sequoia Lodge Backpackers, 3A Nelson Sq, T03-573 8399, www.sequoialodge.co.nz. Although about 500 m from the town centre and 1 km from the ferry terminal, this is an excellent hostel run by an enthusiastic manager. Modern, recently renovated facilities with secure parking. Dorms, private singles, twin and double rooms, some en suite. Log fire, free breakfast, tea and coffee and great homemade bread. Free pick-up/drop-off to ferry. Internet.
B-D The Villa, 32 Auckland St, T03-573 6598, www.thevilla.co.nz. A deservedly popular, well-established and lively backpacker hostel in a century-old villa. Dorms, twins and doubles. Fine facilities and a great outdoor area with spa. The managers are a hive of information

● For an explanation of the Sleeping and Eating price codes used in this guide, see the inside
● front cover. Other relevant information is provided in the Essentials chapter, pages 44-51.
Note that prices are given in New Zealand dollars.

on local activities and can assist with plans and bookings. Free 'all you can eat' breakfast, tea, coffee, duvets, bike hire and shuttle service. Internet. Pre-booking advisable.

Motorcamps

B-D Blue Anchor Top Ten Holiday Park, 78 Waikawa Rd, T0800-277444. An excellent award-winning holiday park and very popular. It is well located within walking distance of the town, has tidy cabins and tourist flats and great facilities. It gets a little crowded at times, especially if you are camping, so try to arrive early in the day.

B-D Parklands Marina Holiday Park, T03-573 6343 on Beach Rd, Waikawa, close to the marina. This is another large, but older less salubrious holiday park.

Blenheim *p421, map p422*

There is no shortage of beds in Blenheim with plenty of hotels, motels and backpacker hostels. The emphasis, however, is on the many excellent boutique-style lodges, B&Bs and homestays outside the town, often in the vineyards. The VIC (I-Site) has comprehensive listings and can book on your behalf. During the picking season (Apr/May) it's advisable to pre-book backpacker hostels in the region.

Blenheim Township

LL Hotel D'Urville, 52 Queen St, T03-577 9945, www.durville.co.nz. Quality boutique hotel in a former bank in the heart of the town centre. Individually themed rooms, from the 'New Zealand' or 'Merlot' room; to the African or 'Retro', ensures something for everyone. Classy restaurant attached.

L The Marlborough Hotel, 20 Nelson St, T03-577 7333, www.the-marlborough.co.nz. A modern option with a wide range of rooms and suites, heated pool, internet and the quality **Nikau** restaurant.

AL-A Lugano Motor Lodge, corner of High and Henry sts, T03-577 8808, www.lugano .co.nz. A modern and popular luxury motel, close to the centre of town. Ever tried a 'thermo-mattress'? Well, now is your chance.

AL-A Phoenix Motor Inn, 174 Middle Renwick Rd, T03-577 9002, wwwphoenixmotor inn.co.nz. Modern, with a good reputation. 12 studios and 3 luxury units with spa.

A Knightsbridge Court Motor Lodge, 112 Middle Renwick Rd, T03-578 0818, www.knightsbridgecourt.co.nz. Considered one of the better motels in town. Spa suites available. Shopping centre opposite.

A-D Blenheim Bridge Top Ten Holiday Park, 78 Grove Rd, T03-578 3667. Located to the north of the town beside SH1, the main railway line and the river. A bit noisy so close to the main road and railway line but otherwise, well equipped and functional.

B-D Grapevine Backpackers, 29 Park Terr, T03-578 6062, rob.diana@xtra.co.nz. Another large suburban single-storey villa on the riverbank. Full range of rooms, free canoe and bike hire. Assistance finding seasonal work.

B-D The Koanui Backpackers, 33 Main St, T03-578 7487, www.koanui.co.nz. A rambling single-storey refurbished villa and a purpose-built lodge close to town. The villa serves as the traditional backpacker hostel while the lodge offers studio style en suites with TV. Both offer spacious lounges and well-equipped kitchens. Internet, bike hire and off-street parking.

C-D Honi-B Backpackers, corner of Hutcheson and Parker sts, T03-577 8441, honi-b-backpackers@xtra.co.nz. Centrally located hostel that is revitalizing the town's backpacking scene. Standard modern facilities and wide range of rooms, parking and internet. Recommended.

Around Blenheim

LL Antria Boutique Lodge, 276 Old Renwick Rd, T03-579 2191, www.antria.co.nz. Described as a modern European castle, Antria is certainly aesthetically different. But don't expect ramparts or moats. This is a truly modern concept, more Mediterranean in design, with large Gothic timber doors opening up into an open-air courtyard. Stylish, well-appointed Italian-style rooms and contemporary artwork throughout adds to the overall class and atmosphere. The tariff is reasonable in comparison to many other top-range establishments.

LL Old Saint Mary's Convent, Rapaura Rd, T/F03-570 5700, www.convent.co.nz. One of the most popular places to stay in the region. A century-old, renovated and relocated 2-storey convent set in expansive gardens and surrounded by vineyards. Spacious modern en suites vary according to price, but all have great views across the vineyards, Sky TV, access to the balcony or garden. Even if you are not in the honeymoon suite ask to see it, it is positively angelic. Library, billiard room, authentic chapel and free bike hire.

LL Timara Lodge, Dog Point Rd, T03-572 8276, www.timara.co.nz. Luxury by the lake. 1920s homestead amidst 73 ha of beautiful gardens. Superb rooms, facilities and fine cuisine.

LL L The Peppertree, SH1, Riverlands, T03-520 9200, www.thepeppertree.co.nz. Historic villa with a range of luxury en suites. Fine breakfast.

L Cranbrook Cottage, Giffords Rd, T03-572 8606, www.cranbrook.co.nz. Without doubt one of the most characterful self-contained cottage B&Bs in the region. Set among the vines and fruit trees, the 135-year-old renovated cottage provides plenty of privacy and is very romantic, with breakfast delivered to the door each morning.

L-AL Waterfall Lodge, Le Grys Vineyard, Conders Bend Rd, Renwick, T03-572 9490, www.legrys.co.nz/cottage. Self-contained, beautifully appointed mud-block cottage or en suite rooms in the main house, set in the heart of the vineyard. Solar heated pool.

AL Blue Ridge Estate B&B, 50 O'Dwyers Rd, T03-5702198, www.blueridge.co.nz. Very classy purpose-designed homestay in an 8-ha rural setting, with fine views across some of the best-known vineyards. Well-appointed rooms with earthy colours and an almost minimalist feel. Good value, recommended.

AL Clovelly B&B, 2a Nelson Pl, Renwick, T03-572 9593, www.clovelly.co.nz. A more affordable B&B option in the sleepy village of Renwick 10 km west of Blenheim. Good value and only 2 mins from **The Cork and Keg** English-style country pub and brewery.

AL St Leonards, 18 St Leonards Rd, T03-577 8328, www.stleonards.co.nz. Beautifully appointed self-contained accommodation sleeping up to 6, in 3 vineyard cottages (one of which is a former stables) and a homestead annexe. Open fires, potbelly stoves and claw-foot baths add to a cosy, homely atmosphere. Great value.

B-D Watson's Way Backpackers, 56 High St, Renwick, T03-572 8228, www.watsonsway backpackers.co.nz. The most popular hostel in the Blenheim region. Lots of character, relaxed and well-equipped, and within walking distance of numerous vineyards and **The Cork and Keg** English pub and brewery.

Havelock p424

There is little in the way of accommodation in Havelock itself, most is out in the sounds.

B Havelock Garden Motel, 71 Main St, T03-574 2387, www.gardenmotels.com. Set in large gardens close to all amenities.

C-D Rutherford YHA, 46 Main Rd, T03-574 2104, www.rutherfordtravel.co.nz. Spacious YHA, the former home of world famous scientist Ernest Rutherford, run by a caring relative. Double, twin and bunks. Camping available. Internet. Activity specialists.

Motorcamps and campsites

C-D Chartridge Park, SH6 (3 km south of Havelock), T03-574 2129. A superb peaceful and low-key little motorpark with 2 great value cabins and a bunkroom. Small camp kitchen and games lounge with TV. Recommended. Book ahead.

C-D DoC campsite, Pelorus Bridge, T03-571 6019. Cabins and powered sites. Café nearby with good homemade fare.

C-D Havelock Motor Camp, 24 Inglis St, T03-574 2339. Powered/tent sites and only a few basic cabins close to the harbour.

French Pass p426

There are lots of places to stay and a surprising amount of activities in or around French Pass.

L Ngaio Bay Homestead, on the western side of the peninsula, T03-576 5287, www.ngaiobay.co.nz. Idyllic B&B with its own private beach. Home-grown organic produce a speciality.

AL French Pass Beachfront Villas and Sea Safaris, T03-576 5204, www.seasafaris.co.nz. Here in this remote and fascinating corner of the Marlborough Sounds, this is the main focus for activities and offers delightful motel accommodation. The modern 3-star units are fully self-contained and have balconies looking out across the bay. Meals provided on request. Trips are flexible, half- to multi-day adventures including diving, fishing, walking or wildlife watching, with dolphins a regular sight. Booking essential. Recommended.

A-B D'Urville Wilderness Resort, T03-576 5268, www.durvilleisland.co.nz. It doesn't get much more remote than this. Comfortable accommodation and a waterfront café and bar accessible only by boat. Ideal for that total getaway experience or for exploring D'Urville Island.

B-D**Okiwi Bay Holiday Park**, T03-576 5006, www.okiwi.co.nz. A small homestay lodge, powered and tent sites, petrol and a store.
D **DoC Campsite French Pass**. Small and basic but, not surprisingly, popular ($6).

● Eating

Picton *p419, maps p417 and p419*
Despite (or perhaps because of) competition from so many fine vineyard restaurants around Blenheim and resort restaurants in the sounds, Picton seems lacking in fine dining options. There is a supermarket, **Supervalue**, in the Mariners Mall on High St, 0730-1930.
DAs, 53 High St, T03-573 5223, daily 0900-2200. A reliable mid-range option with a café-style menu, specializing in gourmet pizza but it cannot seem to decide if it is a pokie (slot machine) parlour or a café.
Gusto Café, 33 High St, T03-573 7171, Sun-Fri 0800-1500, Thu-Sat 1700-late. Imaginative menu, good coffee and service to match.
Le Café, on London Quay, T03-573 5588, daily for breakfast, lunch and dinner. Perhaps the best bet, it has a good atmosphere and is well placed on the waterfront.
Toot and Whistle, Auckland St, near the ferry terminal, T03-573 6086, daily 0900-late. The best pub grub and beer to be found in town. A lively place that has seen no doubt seen its fair share of clients miss the ferry.

Blenheim *p421, map p422*
With the influence of the wineries and the many gourmet travellers, the choice and quality are excellent. The **New World** supermarket is on Main St, daily 0800-2100.
Hotel D'Urville, 52 Queen St, T03-577 9945, daily 0600-2400. The place for fine dining in Blenheim.
Nikau, Marlborough Hotel, 20 Nelson St, T03-577 9821. Recommended poolside dining.
Bellafico Wine Bar, 17 Maxwell Rd, T03-577 6072, www.bellafico.co.nz, Mon-Sat 1000 until late. European offerings and a huge wine list, even by Blenheim standards.
Kekerengu Store, Kekerengu (halfway between Blenheim and Kaikoura), T03-575 8600, 0700-late. Set overlooking the ocean with fine café-style cuisine. Crayfish is a speciality, but stop for a coffee at the very least. Recommended.

Paddy Barry's Irish Pub, 51 Scott St, T03-578 7470. Good for pub grub.
Rocco's, 5 Dodson St, T03-578 6940, evenings only. A fine Italian restaurant.

Wineries *p422 and p423*
Some of the larger wineries have fine restaurants or cafés offering indoor/outdoor seating and lunch and/or dinner. Some of the best can be found at: **Allan Scott**, T03-572 9054; **Cellier le Brun**, T03-572 8859; **Hunters**, T03-572 8489; **Highfield**, T03-572 9244 ; **Montana**, T03-577 5775; and **Wairau River Wines**, T03-572 9800.

Havelock *p424*
Mussel Boys Restaurant, 73 Main Rd, T03-574 2824, daily 1100-2130. A stay in Havelock would not be complete without sampling the green-lipped mussels at this award winning restaurant. A bowl of seafood chowder will cost a value $9 and steamed mussels from $15.
Clansman Scots Pub, Main Rd. Great for a pint and some fine pub grub.
Slip Inn Café and Wine Bar, by the main marina, T03-574 2345, Mon-Thu 1000-2000, Fri-Sun 1000-2300. Small but lively place worth checking out if you are planning a trip out on the sound.
Darling Dill Café, corner of Main Rd and Neil St, T03-574 2824. Good for a coffee or breakfast.

French Pass *p426*
The only place to eat is at the **D'Urville Wilderness Resort**, see Sleeping. There's also a small store and a petrol station.

● Festivals and events

For further information on other annual events and specific dates contact the VIC (I-Site) or look up the regional website www.marlborough4fun.co.nz.

Blenheim *p421, map p422*
The **Marlborough Centre**, Arthur St, T03-578 2009, is the region's principal entertainment venue with a variety of shows, exhibitions and performances on offer throughout the year. However, most of the Blenheim and Marlborough events obviously revolve around fine wines and food.

Feb **Blues, Brews and Barbecues** annual festival (1st week), T03-578 9457, entry fee. This is the breweries' answer to their wine-making neighbours, whereby tents are raised and all kinds of ales dismantled to accompanying live entertainment.

BMW-Marlborough Wine Festival (2nd Sat), T0800-000575, www.bmw-winemarlborough-festival.co.nz . The principal event of the year and now world famous, is the lively and very alcoholic celebration of the region's gourmet food and wines. Live music provided.

Apr **Easter Airshow** (end of month), www.classicfighters.co.nz. Heads are raised from wine glasses for this show which stages some mock dog fights between classic fighter planes from both world wars. Wine and food included of course.

▲ Activities and tours

Picton p419, map p419

Most activities are based around cruising, tramping (see page 416) or kayaking, with the odd bit of dolphin and birdspotting thrown in. The VIC (I-Site) in Picton has a comprehensive list of activities, which are helpfully listed by time of day, not operator, and well worth a look. It can also advise on horse trekking, winery tours (see page 435), diving, tandem paragliding, scenic flights, fishing and independent boat charters. With so many choices and choices within choices it pays to take your time and shop around.

Cruises

There are endless bays, coves and islands to explore in the sounds, with a rich variety of wildlife including dolphins and rare seabirds. As you might expect, there is a mind-boggling range of cruise options available with fiercely competitive operators. Most are based on the waterfront in Picton. It's a good idea to check at the VIC (I-Site) before parting with your cash.

Beachcomber Fun Cruises, on the waterfront, T0800-624526, T03-573 6175, www.beachcombercruises.co.nz. Offers a range of cruise options, including a popular half-day 'Mail Boat' cruise: the *Queen Charlotte Mail Boat* explores the Queen Charlotte Sound, with a stop at Ship Cove and a salmon farm, from $75. The 2-hr 'Round the Bays' cruise takes in a number of Queen Charlotte Sound bays, including

Double Cove where you stop briefly to feed tame fish; departs daily at 0900, 1130 and 1100, from $48. The 6-hr luncheon cruise to the **Portage Resort Hotel** and Torea Bay, departs daily at 1015, from $52 (transport only). There are also a range of half- or full-day cruise-and-walk options from $40, Queen Charlotte Track transfers pass (with pack transfers) from $88 and an eco-tour of Motuara Island Bird Sanctuary, from $60.

The Cougar Line, on the waterfront, T03-573 7925/T0800-504090, www.cougarlinecruises.co.nz. Offers a similar series of cruises. The most popular is the day trip to Ship Cove where you have the option of a 5-hr bush walk to **Furneaux Lodge** where you are picked up later in the afternoon. It departs at 0800 and 1000. Various short cruises are also available taking in up to 80 km of coastline in 3 hrs with an informative commentary on the way. These depart at 1000 and 1330. Cougar also offer a luncheon cruise to the **Punga Cove Resort** that leaves at 1000 and a 3-hr twilight tour that departs at 1800. Cruises cost from $53.

Endeavour Express, on the waterfront, T03-573 5456, www.boatrides.co.nz. Offers a similar range of day walking options from $45 as well as tramping track and accommodation transfers.

Water Taxis, T03-573 8229, www.arrowwatertaxis.co.nz. Flexible water taxi service.

West Bay Water Transport, T03-573 5597, www.westbay.co.nz. As above.

Day walks

Most operators offer half- or full- day walking trips. Popular trips include Ship Cove to Furneaux Lodge (with **Endeavour Express** and **Cougar**, from $60), which takes in the Captain Cook monument and some lovely native bush and views. Also popular is the eco-based trip to Motuara Island Bird Sanctuary (with **Beachcomber Cruises** and **Endeavour Express**, from $60). The VIC can advise. Cougar has the best boats and tends to offer the most modern, comfortable service, but competition is fierce.

Eco-tours

The Sounds are not only home to seals and dolphins but also some rare birdlife such as the king shag (found only in the sounds), New Zealand robins, little blue penguins and saddlebacks. Many of the land-based birds are typically fearless and will constantly check your route for disturbed insects.

Dolphin Watch Marlborough, 14 Auckland St, 200 m east of the VIC (I-Site), T03-573 8040, www.naturetours.co.nz. Offers a range of trips including dolphin swimming (when the dusky dolphins allow); an excellent jaunt to the Motuara Island bird sanctuary (departs 0830/1330, from $80) and a 'Birdwatchers' Special' (departs daily in winter and twice daily in summer at 1330, from $95).

Sea Safaris, based in French Pass, T03-576 5204, www.seasafaris.co.nz. Also offers some superb, flexible wildlife trips to see dolphins and seabirds in the outer Marlborough Sounds. Recommended.

Fishing

Sounds Connection, 10 London Quay, T0800-742866/T03-573 8843, www.sounds connection.co.nz. Scheduled half-day trips or charters with expert local guides departing daily at 1300.

Flightseeing

Soundsair, based across the road from the VIC (I-Site) in the old railway station, T0800-505005, www.soundsair.com. Offers an extraordinary number of flight combinations and options that include one night's lodging, lunch, day walks and cruises from $135-350. Standard flightseeing trips range from a 20-min flight over Kenepuru Sound from $100, 45 mins taking all the main sounds for $135 and a 1 hr 15 mins that includes both the Sounds and vineyards of the Wairau Valley from $220. The standard single fare to Wellington costs from $79, child $67.

Sailing

The VIC (I-Site) has full charter and cruise listings.

Compass Charters, T0800-101332, www.compass-charters.co.nz. Skippered and self-drive cruise and charters.

Sail Marlborough, T03-575 7312, www.sailmarlborough.co.nz. Geared up for group charter, more luxury orientated.

Scuba diving

Dive Marlborough, Beach Rd, T0800-463483, www.godive.co.nz. Given the location it is no surprise that this company specializes in wreck

diving with the 155-m *Mikhail Lermontov* (1986) the highlight, guided from $215.

Sea kayaking

Most travellers save their kayaking experience for the Abel Tasman National Park (see page 452), the most famous sea-kayaking venue in the country. However, Abel Tasman is now getting very crowded in summer and the idea of having a beautiful golden bay to yourself is a near impossibility. What the sounds can offer that the Abel Tasman often cannot, is almost guaranteed shelter and relative peace and quiet. Also note that Abel Tasman has about 50 km of coastline, whereas the sounds has 1500 km.

Marlborough Sounds Adventure Company, on the waterfront, T0800-283283/T03-573 6078, www.marlboroughsounds.co.nz. The principal operator in Picton, it offers a wide variety of highly professional trips including kayaking, walking and mountain biking. The excellent options vary from a few hours (including a twilight trip), to the 4-day paddle/ walk or 6-day specialist itineraries. It is also possible to hire mountain bikes (from $55; one-day guided trips from $120) or kayaks (from $40 per day decreasing to $35 after 3 days). The excellent and increasingly popular 3-day 'Ultimate Sounds Adventure', is a guided 1-day hiking, 1-day sea kayaking, 1-day mountain biking adventure, with an overnight stay at **Portage Resort Hotel**. The trip departs every Wed from 1 Nov-30 Apr, and costs from $495 at a backpacker rate and $695 twin share en suite. Note there is no other track in New Zealand where you can walk and mountain bike on the same track. Recommended.

Sea Kayaking Adventure Tours, based in Anakiwa, T03-574 2765, www.nzsea kayaking.com. 1- to 5-day trips on both Queen Charlotte and Pelorus Sounds from $85-480.

Wilderness Guides, Railway Station, 3 Auckland St, T0800-266266/T03-520 3095, www.wildernessguides.co.nz. Day trips from $90, independent hire from $40 and good guided kayak/walk and kayak/cycle options on the Queen Charlotte Track from $130.

Self-drive

If you are looking for an alternative method of exploring the sounds you can do so in part by road. Note, however, that the roads throughout the Sounds are tortuous, mostly unsealed and not entirely suitable for campervans, or indeed sightseeing. Perhaps this is the time to have a break from driving and take a boat? The **Queen Charlotte Drive** is (for the passenger) a scenic 35-km drive from Picton to Havelock taking in a number of sheltered bays, campsites and viewpoints on the way. From Linkwater it is possible to then traverse the ridge between Queen Charlotte and Kenepuru Sounds by road (close to the route of the Queen Charlotte Track) before the road joins the main landmass of the sounds. The intrepid explorer can reach the outermost bays from this road and combine some walking on parts of the Queen Charlotte Track, including the most popular day walk – the **Endeavour Inlet to Ship Cove Track**. On a clear day the half-day to full-day walk to the summit of **Mount Stokes** (at 1203 m the highest point in the sounds) is recommended for the view. The walk is a moderate expedition involving 500 m of ascent.

Campsites are available at Mistletoe Bay, Cowshed Bay, Punga Cove (Endeavour Inlet) and at Titirangi Bay. Note that some accommodation establishments are also accessible by road, including **Punga Cove**, **The Portage**, **Te Mahia**, **St Omer House** and **Raetihi Lodge**. For another fine and remote exploratory drive in to the sounds see the French Pass section, page 426.

Tandem skydiving
Skydive the Sounds, Picton Airport, T0800- 373264/T03-573 9101, www.skydive thesounds.com. Tandems with views of the sounds from 9000-12,000 ft, from $245-295.

Blenheim *p421, map p422*
The wilderness of the Marlborough back-country and the remote Molesworth Station (New Zealand's largest cattle station) can be explored with **Molesworth Tour Company**, T03-575 7525, www.molesworthtours.co.nz . 1- to 5-day excursions from $235.

Horse trekking
High Country Horse Treks, Ardnadam, Taylor's Pass Rd, Redwood Village, T03-577 9424, www.high-horse.co.nz. 1-4 hrs from $40.

River trips
Marlborough River Queen, T0800-266322/ T03-577 5510, www.riverqueencruise.co.nz. If you fancy a trip along the Opawa River on board a paddleboat, try this very gracious trip. Both lunch and dinner trips from Tue-Sun.

Walking
There are some fine walking venues in the region, particularly around the Richmond Ranges, the **Withers Farm Park** and on the coast road, via Rarangi, to Picton. The ascent of **Mt Richmond** (1760 m) with its memorable views is recommended. For self-guided trips consult DoC or the VIC (I-Site) for their free leaflets.

Winery tours
There is a broad range of tours and many operators available, all of whom will look after your every whim. Some offer more formal scheduled trips, while others can design a trip around your personal tastes or take in arts and crafts and garden visits. You can even go by bicycle.
Highlight Tours, T03-577 9046, www.high light-tours.co.nz. Both full-day or half-day, morning and afternoon tours. Flexibility with venues (including craft and garden venues) and lunch (extra cost) included.
Marlborough Travel Centre Winery Tours and Wine Line, T03-577 9997, T0800-990800, www.marlboroughtravel.co.nz. Quality half-day tours from $79.
Marlborough Wine Tours, T03-578 9515, www.marlboroughwinetours.co.nz. Personalized tour of up to 8 wineries. Flexible itinerary depending on taste, from $39. UK wine delivery service.
Sounds Connection, T03-5738843, www.soundsconnection.co.nz. Scheduled and private half- to full-day tours. Based in Picton. Half day from $55, full $55, gourmet (includes food and wine matching, underground cellar tour, olive grove and lunch stop at your own account), from $69.
Wine-Tours-By-Bike, T03-577 6954 www.winetoursbybike.co.nz. This is the delightfully common sense method of visiting the wineries by bike. The great attraction here is the slow pace and the greater bombardment of the senses only felt on a bike. The drawback obviously is the steady deterioration of those senses as the

day wears on and the inability to pedal in any direction after 10 glasses of wine. You can join a guided tour or hire your own bikes with accessories (a map being pivotal) and have them delivered to your door. Half day from $40, full $55, guided tour $25 per hour.

Havelock *p424*

Most of what Havelock has to offer and almost all of its services will be found on Main Rd or down at the harbour, which is a short walk from centre of the village.

Cruises

Pelorus Sound can be explored by boat or by road. There are numerous opportunities to get on the water from scheduled cruises to charter boats and kayak trips. Note that water taxis are available from Havelock and you can be flexible with your intentions and itinerary (see Ins and outs, page 422). There are also fishing and diving charters available.
Affinity Cruises, T03-572 7223, www.affinity cruises.co.nz. Day charters or overnight cruises from 2-7 days. The 63-ft vessel has 8 private cabins, all meals are included and activities range from fishing to bush walking.
All Season Cruises, based in Havelock, T0274-389866, www.allseasoncruises.co.nz. Sedate and popular range of trips on board the 58-ft launch *Foxy Lady*. A choice of morning, evening (BBQ) or overnight cruises all taking in the beautiful scenery of the sounds with an added insight in to how the famous mussels are bred and harvested.
Marlborough Travel, T03 577 9997, www.greenshellmusselcruise.co.nz. Offers the 'Greenshell Mussel Cruise': an afternoon cruise through the Pelorus and Kenepuru Sounds. Daily departures from Havelock at 1330 (Nov-Mar) including a visit to a mussel farm where you can enjoy freshly steamed mussels with a glass of Sauvignon Blanc.
Pelorus Mail Run Cruises, T03-574 1088, www.mail-boat.co.nz, leaves Havelock at 0930 on Tue, Thu and Fri, costing from $105, child free. The Mail Run delivers supplies and mail to a number of the isolated settlements and visits one of the many mussel farms before returning at about 1730.

Fishing

Captain Clays, T03-574 2911. Half- or full-day cruise/fishing charters with local guru Clayton after snapper and the feisty kingfish. Optional lunch or overnight stops.

Sea kayaking

If this is your thing or you would like to try it, the sounds provides excellent opportunities.
Sea Kayaking Adventure Tours, Anakiwa, T03-574 2765, www.nzseakayaking.com. Trips are half-day from $85, full- or multi-day $180-480. Independent hire available from $40.
Sounds Natural, Havelock Youth Hostel, 46 Main Rd, Havelock, T275-382203, www.soundsnatural.co.nz. Full or multi-day 'clothing optional' guided trips to remote private locations from $95.

☉ Transport

Picton *p419, map p419*
Car hire Lots of companies just outside the ferry terminal, with a few others on High St in the centre of town: **A2B**, T0800-222929; **Ace**, T0800-422373; **Apex**, T0800-939597; **Budget**, T03-573 6081; **Pegasus**, T03-5737759.
Petrol (24 hrs) Shell Picton, 101 High St, T03-573 7949. **Taxi** T03-573 7662.

Blenheim *p421, map p422*
Bicycle hire Spokesman Cycles, 61 Queen St, T03-578 0433. Bikes for winery tours can be hired from **Wine-Tours-By-Bike**, T03-577 6954.
Taxi Marlborough Taxis, T03-577 5511.

ⓘ Directory

Picton *p419, maps p417 and p419*
Internet United Video, corner of High and Dublin sts, 0900-2100. **Police** High St, T03-520 3120. **Post office** Mariners Mall, High St, T03-573 6900, Mon-Fri 0830-1700.
Storage Sounds Storage, 7 Market St, T021-335136, soundsstorage@xtra.co.nz. Offers secure car and boat storage.

Blenheim *p421, map p422*
Internet Travel Stop Cyber Centre, corner of Market and Alfred sts and the I-Site. **Post office** Corner of Scott and Main sts, T03-578 3904, Mon-Fri 0830-1715, Sat 0930-1230.

Havelock *p424*
Internet Available in the Rutherford Travel Information and Travel Centre and the YHA both on the Main Rd.

Nelson and around

➔ *Colour map 4, A4 Population: 50,000*

Nelson is known as the sunniest place in the country, though this label could apply to its atmosphere, its people and its surroundings, for as well as its Mediterranean climate, Nelson has a great deal more going for it. It is lively and modern, yet steeped in history. Surrounding it, all within 100 km, are some of the most beautiful coastal scenery and beaches in New Zealand, not to mention three diverse and stunning national parks, where you can experience some of the most exciting tramping tracks in the South Island, plus a host of other activities. Little wonder that Nelson is one of the top holiday destinations in the country as well being considered the best place to live in New Zealand. ▶▶ *For Sleeping, Eating and other listings, see pages 445-450.*

Ins and outs

Getting there By car Nelson is 144 km from Picton via SH6, 424 km to Christchurch via SH6, SH65 (Lewis Pass) and then SH1 and 226 km to Westport via SH6.

Nelson airport ① *6 km southwest of the town centre on SH6, in the suburb of Nayland*, is small but efficient. **Air New Zealand Link**, T0800-737000, www.airnew zealand.co.nz, offers regular scheduled flights from Auckland, Wellington and Christchurch. Also worth noting is **Abel Tasman Air**, T03-528 8290/T0800-304560, www.abeltasmanair.co.nz, which runs a good-quality service with small fixed-wing aircraft throughout the region. **Super Shuttle**, T03-547 5782, or **Airport Shuttle**, T0800-400110, both operate to and from the airport; about $14.

The following companies provide regular bus services to Nelson and the region as a whole: **Intercity**, T03-5483290/T03-5481538, www.nelsoncoaches.co.nz, runs from Christchurch via Blenheim/Picton and the west coast. **Atomic Shuttles**, T03-322 8883, www.atomictravel.co.nz, runs from Blenheim/Picton and the west coast. **K-Bus**, T03-358 8355/T0508-458835, www.kahurangi.co.nz, runs from Christchurch, Blenheim, Picton, Golden Bay, the Heaphy Track, Abel Tasman and Kaikoura.

Operators servicing Motueka and the Abel Tasman National Park include: **Atomic Shuttles**, **K'Bus** and **Abel Tasman Coachlines**, T03-548 0285, www.abeltasman travel.co.nz. **Abel Tasman Coachlines** and **K'Bus** also run further northwest to Takaka and Golden Bay.

Buses heading south to St Arnaud and the Nelson Lakes National Park and the Rainbow ski area include: **Nelson Lakes Shuttles**, T03-521 1900, www.nelsonlakes shuttles.co.nz. The VIC (I-Site) can assist with bookings.

Average fares to Christchurch are $54, Greymouth $50, Takaka $30, Heaphy Track $50 and Blenheim $28. Most of the bus services stop right outside the VIC (I-Site) on the corner of Trafalgar and Halifax streets. **Intercity** drop off at the bus terminal on Bridge Street.

Getting around The local suburban bus company is **Nelson SBL**, T03-548 3290, www.nelsoncoaches.co.nz, based at the **bus terminal** ① *Lower Bridge St*. SBL runs a 'summertime bus', which does a circuit of the city's major attractions on the hour departing the VIC (I-Site) from 1000-1600. The standard fare starts at $2.

Tourist information **Nelson VIC (I-Site)** ① *corner of Trafalgar and Halifax sts, T03-548 2304, www.nelsonnz.com, Mon-Fri 0830-1700, Sat-Sun 0900-1600* The booklet *Nelson – Live the Day* is informative and there is a range of other brochures available. **DoC** information is also held at this office. The website www.backpacknelson.com has lots of useful information.

The Nelson region has a rather bloody Maori history, with many of the early tribes who started arriving from the North Island in the 16th century being successively conquered by others migrating south. The Ngati Tumatakokiri (who gave Abel Tasman his hostile reception in 1642) were for a while the largest tribe, but they were effectively wiped out by the Ngati Apa (from Wanganui) and Ngati Tahu (also from the South Island). This transition was short-lived, however, when in the 1820s the Ngati Toa from Kapiti arrived and conquered the lot. So, when the New Zealand Company's agent, Captain Wakefield arrived about two decades later, it was with Te Rauparaha (chief of the Ngati Toa) that he negotiated land purchase. From the early 1840s Wakefield went on to effectively establish the company's largest New Zealand settlement – Nelson. However, very quickly problems arose when too many migrants arrived to too little work and not enough agriculturally viable land. To counter this, Wakefield and a survey party went in search for more land in the Wairau Valley to the southeast. Wakefield thought this land to be already his, but Te Rauparaha disputed that claim. The misunderstanding and subsequent disagreement led to what was called the **Wairau Affray** and the death of Wakefield, 21 of his party and four Maori. Understandably, this incident retarded the development of early Nelson and to make matters worse, the New Zealand Company went bankrupt in 1844 leaving many destitute and unemployed. Redemption arrived in 1857 when gold was discovered near Collingwood (Golden Bay) and a new impetus was brought to the region. By the end of the century, long after the gold had run out, the rich agricultural potential and sustainability of the region was finally being realized – a natural resource that remains the most important resource in the region to this day.

Nelson

Sleeping	Green Monkey **2**	Paradiso **3**
Boutique Motel **1**	Honest Lawyer	Richmond Motel & Top Ten
Brook Valley Holiday	Country Pub **7**	Holiday Park **9**
Park **8**		

0 metres 500
0 yards 500

Sights

Sadly the appearance of central Nelson is spoiled by one thing you cannot miss. The **Civic Tower** across the road from the VIC (I-Site), which dominates the central city skyline, is without doubt the most hideous looking building in the country. An utter mess of concrete and steel, covered with aerials and radar, it looks like something that is about to take off. Whether to the moon or Mars, it would matter not as long as the architect responsible was strapped to it. That aside, there are many more attractive sights to see in and around Nelson.

A fine place to start is a short climb (one hour return) to the **viewpoint** above the **Botanical Gardens**, which can be accessed off Milton or Maitai roads. This site is claimed as the geographical centre of New Zealand, but other than offering a fine view of the town and giving you a sense of location, it is also the regular target for some delightful expressions of daring and protest. It recently staged a flag proclaiming disgust at the use of GM (genetically modified) foodstuffs; and it is not at all unusual to see some wonderfully colourful and frilly lingerie fluttering from the flagpole. Sadly, after that, the attractive botanical gardens, though admirable, are far less remarkable. Other green havens in Nelson include the very attractive **Queens Gardens** off Bridge Street, complete with the city's fair share of ducks, and the vibrant flowerbeds of **Anzac Park** at the end of Rutherford Street. The **Miyazu Japanese Park** ① *Atawhai Drive, dawn to dusk, free,* has a traditional 'stroll' garden built to celebrate Nelson's links with sister city Miyazu in Japan. There are numerous other fine gardens to visit in the region and the VIC (I-Site) can provide further information, including the handy leaflet *Gardens of the Nelson Region*.

Related map
A Nelson centre, page 440.

Tahuna Beach Holiday Park 4	Tuscany Gardens Motor Lodge 5	Eating ⑦	Saltwater 3
Te Puna Wai 10	Warwick House 11	Applemans 4	Venice Cove 2
	Wheelhouse Inn 6	Boat Shed 1	
		Honest Lawyer 5	

The most lauded tourist attraction in the Nelson area is perhaps the **World of Wearable Art and Collectable Cars** ① *95 Quarantine Rd, Annesbrook, just north of the airport, T03-547 4573, www.wowcars.co.nz, daily 1000-1830 (1700 in winter), from $18, child $10,* set in a 1-ha site. The complex has two galleries. The first is the Wearable Art Gallery showcasing the historic Wearable Art Garment collection (now an iconic aspect of the region). There is a fully-scripted show that uses mannequins rather than live models but with all the usual elements of sound and lighting. The second gallery has an impressive collection of classic cars formerly on view in the town centre.

Although Nelson was one of New Zealand's earliest and largest settlements, there is little architectural evidence. Of obvious notoriety, but hardly historical (having being finally completed in 1965), is the **Nelson Cathedral** ① *T03-548 1008, daily in summer 0800-1900 (winter 0800-1700), tour guides are on duty most days,*

Nelson centre

N

0 metres   100
0 yards   100

Sleeping 🛏
Accents On The Park **12**
Cambria House **2**
Cathedral Inn **3**
DeLorenzo's
 Apartments **5**
Little Manor **6**
Nelson City YHA **7**
Palace Backpackers **8**
Palms Motel **9**
Rutherford & Miyazu
 Japanese Restaurant **10**
Shelbourne Villa **11**
South Street Cottages **13**

Tasman Bay
 Backpackers **4**
Trafalgar Lodge **14**
Tramper's Rest **15**

Eating 🍴
Hopgoods **2**
Lambrettas Café Bar **7**
Victorian Rose **10**

Bars & clubs 🍸
Little Rock Café **11**
Maen Fiddler **12**
Oyster Bar **1**
Phat Club **3**

Let's split

New Zealand's most eminent scientist, Ernest Rutherford, is best known for being the first person to split the atom. He was born at Spring Grove near Nelson in 1876 and after being awarded several scholarships, graduated with a Bachelor of Arts at the age of 17, and a Bachelor of Science two years later. By the age of 22 he was a professor at McGill University in Montreal and was already deeply involved in to research surrounding radioactivity. Within a decade he had discovered the natural transmutation of elements, the development of techniques that allowed the radioactive dating of geological samples and also made the first deduction of the nuclear model of the atom. All this brought him to world prominence and earned him several prestigious awards, including the Nobel Prize for Chemistry in 1908 and a knighthood in 1914. But despite all this, his best work was yet to come, and at the end of the First World War he conducted an experiment which split the atom – something which had far reaching consequences for mankind. Rutherford died in Cambridge, England at the age of 61.

entry by donation, which dominates the southern end of town. Although its exterior barely matches the view of Trafalgar Street from the steps that lead up to it, the interior contains some fine stained-glass windows.

Also worth a quick look is **Broadgreen Historic House** ① *276 Nayland Rd, Stoke, 6 km southwest of town via the coast road, T03-547 0403, summer daily 1030-1630, $3, child $0.50*. It is an 11-room 1855 Victorian 'cob' house furnished accordingly and set amongst pleasant gardens.

A far better sense of history can be found at the new **Nelson Provincial Museum: Town Acre 445** ① *corner Hardy and Trafalgar sts, T03-548 9588, www.museum np.org.nz, exhibitions Mon-Fri 1000-1700, Sat-Sun 1000-1630 and Sat-Sun 1200-1600*, which serves as the region's principal museum and contains all the usual suspects covering life from Maori settlement to the present day using an imaginative and dynamic range of well presented displays. The free leaflet *Nelson City of History – Trevor Horne Heritage Trail* is available from the VIC (I-Site).

With over 300 artists resident in the town arts and crafts feature heavily in the list of attractions. A copy of the *Nelson Regional Guide Book – Art in its Own Place* is a great guide and available from most bookshops. The Te Aratoi-o-Whakatu or **Suter Gallery** ① *208 Bridge St, T03-548 4699, www.thesuter.org.nz, daily 1030-1630, $3*, heads the list of major art galleries. Located next to Queen's Gardens, it boasts four exhibition spaces that showcase both permanent and temporary historical and contemporary collections. There is also a café, cinema and theatre on site that runs a programme of musical and theatrical performances.

There are many other galleries in the area displaying a vast array of creative talent. Of particular note is the **Höglund Art Glass** ① *Korurangi Farm, Landsdowne Rd, Richmond, T03-544 6500, www.hoglund.co.nz, daily 0900-1700, tours from $15*, home to the Hoglund Glass Blowing Studio. Here the internationally renowned pieces are created for sale and show in the gallery. There is also a café and the entire set-up is located in a pleasant park-like environment. Also worth a visit is the **South Street Gallery** ① *10 Nile St West, T03-548 8117, www.nelsonpottery.co.nz*. This is the historical home of the Nelson Pottery where 25 selected potters of national and international renown create their various wares. The street itself is also noted for its 16 working-class **historical cottages** built between 1863 and 1867.

Wineries and breweries around Nelson

Wineries

Grape Escape, McShane Rd, T03-544 4341, www.grapeescape.co.nz. Richmond incorporates a number of facets, producing two wines including a certified organic variety and housing an arts and crafts outlet; a café, a nursery and even a candlestick maker.

Greenhough Vineyard, Hope (Patons Rd) T03-542 3868.

Seifried Estate Vineyard, Redwood Rd, Appleby, T03-544 5599, www.seifried.co.nz. The largest and oldest in the region and offers tours and tastings with a fine restaurant.

Waimea Estate, 22 Appleby Highway, Hope, T03-544 6385, www.waimeaestates.co.nz. Which also has a café and is open daily from 1000-1700. Live local music Sun 1230-1530.

In the pretty locale known as Upper Moutere there are a number of fine wineries including:

Glovers Vineyard, Gardner Valley Rd, T03-543 2698, www.glovers-vineyard.co.nz. Owned by the very congenial David Glover, who is considered something of an institution when it comes to producing fine wines and sampling others. The great 'sorcerer' will be delighted to give you a taste, but best pre-book, since there may be a great tasting party raging. If you get lost, just head for the sound of classical music.

Moutere Hills, Sunrise Valley, T03-543 2288, www.mouterehills.co.nz. Noted not only for its wine but its café, open daily 1100-1800 (weekends only in winter).

Neudorf, Neudorf Rd, T03-5432643, www.neudorf.co.nz. Offers tastings.

Ruby Bay Wines, Korepo Rd, T03-540 2825. Very scenic.

Spencer Hill Estate, Best Rd, T03-543 2031. Popular and well-established.

Breweries

Founders Brewery, Founders Historic Park, 87 Atawhai Drive, T03-548 4638, www.biobrew.co.nz, open daily 1000-1630. A certified organic brewery offering a range of heady organic brews. Good café.

McCashin's Brewery, 660 Main Rd, Stoke, T03-547 0526, www.macs.co.nz. Home to the popular Mac's Ales. Open daily and tours are available at 1100 and 1400 daily, from $10.

South Pacific Distillery, 258 Wakefield Quay, T03-546 6822, www.roaringforties.co.nz, open Mon-Sat 1000-1630, tours available in season. If spirits are more your thing, this is a good one to try.

For those wishing to go one step further in their explorations of the region's creative talent you may like to consider one of the interactive workshops on offer through **Creative Tourism** ① T03-526 8812, www.creativetourism.co.nz. For $55-110 you can try your hand at a range of contemporary or traditional crafts from bone carving to organic brewing.

Around Nelson ⑦ ➤ pp445-450.

Beaches

No visit to Nelson would be complete without a trip to the beach. The most popular stretch of golden sand is to be found at the **Tahunanui Beach Reserve**, just a few kilometres southwest of the town centre. Although you will not find the same scenic beauty and certainly not the solitude of the other, more remote beaches in the region, it is a convenient place to lay back and soak up the rays, swim or fly a kite. It is a great

spot for kids with the small **Natureland Zoo** ① *T03-548 6166, 0900-1600, $5, child* 443
$2, and a large fun park nearby. Slightly further afield (20 km) towards Motueka
(SH60) are the beaches and forest swathe of **Rabbit Island**. This seemingly never-
ending beach offers a far quieter and expansive alternative. It is worth checking with
the DoC, however, to confirm that it is not closed due to fire risk. With recent droughts
this is becoming a more regular occurrence.

Wineries

Wineries around Nelson are also a big attraction. Although the region and its fine
winemakers perhaps suffer from the reputation and sheer scale of their much-hyped
neighbours in Marlborough, the wine they produce can be of a very fine quality. For
more information on Nelson Region wineries consult www.nelsonwines.co.nz. For a
list of some of the better-known wineries, which all offer (at the very least) tastings,
see box, page 442.

Breweries

Lovers of beer will be relieved to learn that some local brewing talent is hot on the
heels of the winemakers and the region now has its own Brewery Trail. The VIC (I-Site)
can provide all the detail and the major players are listed in the box on page 442.
While it is hardly on a par with Australia's legendary Bundaberg, from small seeds
great things can grow.

Nelson Lakes National Park and Murchison
🛏🍴▲ ▶ *pp445-450.*

▶ *Colour map 4, B4*
The slightly under-rated Nelson Lakes National Park protects 102,000 ha of the
northernmost Southern Alps range. The park is dominated by its long, scenic and
trout-filled lakes – **Rotoroa** and **Rotoiti** – cradled in beech-clad alpine ranges, hiding
beautiful tussock valleys and wildflower-strewn meadows. Although a quick look at
the lakes are all that most people see of this park, the ranges and river valleys offer
some superb walking. The two most noted tramps are the 80-km, four- to seven-day
Traverse-Sabine Circuit and the excellent two- to three-day **Robert Ridge/Lake
Angelus Track**. There are a number of very pleasant short walks from 20 minutes to
two hours that extend into the park from St Arnaud or Lake Rotoroa. Nelson Lakes also
plays host to the popular **Rainbow Valley** and **Mount Robert ski fields** (only
accessible in winter); the views from the chairlifts are spectacular.

The principal base for the park is pretty village of **St Arnaud**, which nestles at the
northern end of Lake Rotoiti. Almost all accommodation, services, major park access
and activities are located here. The park is also accessible from the more remote and
sparsely populated Lake Rotoroa.

Ins and outs

Getting there St Arnaud is 90 km from Nelson (via SH6), 100 km from Blenheim
(SH63) and 163 km from Westport (SH6/63). To visit Lake Rotoroa, turn off SH6 at
Gowan Bridge west of St Arnaud. An 11-km side road takes you up the Gowan Valley to
the lakes. The west coast-bound buses (including **Intercity**, T03-548 1538; **Atomic
Shuttles**, T03-322 8883, www.atomictravel.co.nz; and **K-Bus**, T0508-458835/T03-358
8355, www.kahurangi.co.nz) all stop in Murchison outside **Collins Tearooms**,
Beechwoods Restaurant or the VIC (I-Site). St Arnaud is served by **Nelson Lakes
Shuttles**, T03-521 1900, www.nelsonlakes shuttles.co.nz, and **K-Bus**, T0508-458835/
T03-358 8355, www.kahurangi.co.nz, on a year-round basis. In the ski season other
local companies also operate; consult the VIC (I-Site) in Nelson.

Water taxis on lakes Rotoroa and Rotoiti offer scenic and/or fishing trips and tramping pick-ups/drop-offs. Contact **Rotoiti Water Taxis**, To3-521 1894, or **Lake Rotoroa Water Taxi**, To3-523 9199, simpson.rotoroa@xtra.co.nz; from $30 for two people, lake's end one way.

Tourist information **DoC Nelson Lakes National Park** ① *St Arnaud, To3-521 1806, nelsonlakesvc@doc.govt.nz, daily 0800-1900 (seasonal)*. An excellent centre that provides comprehensive displays and information on the park, as well as offering advice on local accommodation and transport. **Nelson Lakes Village Centre** ① *on the main road, To3- 521 1854, 0800-1830 (seasonal hours)*. The centre serves as the main grocery store, petrol station, postal agency and has EFTPOS. Lake Rotoroa does not have a shop. **Murchison VIC** ① *on the main road through town, at 47 Wallar St (SH6), To3-523 9350, www.murchisonnz.com, 1000-1700 (seasonal)*. **Ski-ing information** ① *To3-521 1861, www.skirainbow.co.nz, www.snow.co.nz*.

▲▲ Mount Robert to Lake Angelus Basin walk → *2-3 days, 30 km*

If you are short of time this walk is touted as one of the best in the park. The destination (and highlight) is the beautiful Lake Angelus Basin and an overnight stay at the Mount Angelus Hut ($10) from which to take it all in. It is a walk that should only be considered by those of reasonable fitness, in good weather conditions. Go prepared and pre-book your hut accommodation (and fill in an intentions sheet) at the DoC visitor centre.

From the Upper Mount Robert car park (accessed from West Bay, 5 km from St Arnaud) climb the steep zigzag track up the face of Mount Robert to the bushline shelter near the summit (two hours). From there follow the marked route along the ridge and around the **Mount Robert ski field** to **Flagtop Summit** (1690 m). Then descend and continue on the saddle beneath **Julius Summit** (1794 m). The route now leaves the ridge briefly, crossing rocky ground before rejoining the ridge. At a small saddle marked by a metal pole, the route drops again to the west side and crosses a steep, rocky slope to another broad saddle at the head of **Speargrass Creek**. From here a short climb to the ridge reveals the beautiful **Angelus Basin** (five hours).

Stay the night at the Angelus Hut (book at DoC, $10) and get up for sunrise. To return you can either retrace your steps, or descend in to the **Hukere Valley** to join the **Cascade Track** to **Coldwater Hut** at the southern end of the lake. From there the Lakeside Track will deliver you back to the lower Mount Robert car park. If you have no vehicle and have been dropped off, you may consider booking a water taxi from the southern end of the lake and reward yourself with a scenic cruise back to St Arnaud.

Murchison → *Population: 750*

Murchison, 65 km further along SH6 from St Arnaud, at the head of the Buller Gorge and junction of the Matakitaki and Buller rivers, is a service centre for the local farming community and for many, the gateway to the west coast from the north. Although once an important gold mining town (and famous for being nearly wiped out by a violent earthquake in 1929), it is today a quiet place, primarily of interest to the tourist as the base for a number of interesting activities. It is also the haunt of the odd serious tramper intent on exploring the remote southern wilderness of the Kahurangi National Park. The small **Murchison Museum** ① *Fairfax St, daily 1000-1600, donation*, has interesting exhibits on gold mining and the town's somewhat shaky past.

● *For an explanation of the Sleeping and Eating price codes used in this guide, see the inside* ● *front cover. Other relevant information is provided in the Essentials chapter, pages 44-51. Note that prices are given in New Zealand dollars.*

● Sleeping

Nelson p437, maps p438 and p440

Being such a popular holiday destination there is no shortage of beds in Nelson with a few good hotels, numerous B&Bs and homestays, the usual rash of motels and more backpacker hostels than almost anywhere else in New Zealand. Despite this, mid summer is very busy and you are advised to book ahead.

LL-L Cambria House, 7 Cambria St, T03-548 4681, www.cambria.co.nz. A well-established, beautifully appointed and well-located B&B in a 130-year-old homestead.

LL-L Cathedral Inn, 369 Trafalgar St South, T03-548 7369, www.cathedralinn.co.nz. Well-located, historic option with a fine reputation.

LL-L DeLorenzo's Apartments, 43-55 Trafalgar St, T03-548 9774, www.de lorenzos.co.nz. Modern, well-appointed fully self-contained block of 5-star rated apartments in a central location.

LL-L Shelbourne Villa, 21 Shelbourne St, T03-545 9059, www shelbournevilla.co.nz. Right next to the cathedral, offering 3 king size suites and 1 loft with 2 twins. Beautiful garden.

LL-L Te Puna Wai, 24 Richardson St, Port Hills, T04-548 7621, www.tepunawai.co.nz. An immaculate villa-style B&B set overlooking the bay in the Port Hills area. 3 luxury en suite rooms, 2 of which can be combined to form a spacious apartment. Great views, open fire, classy decor and hosts that go the extra mile to ensure a truly memorable stay. Recommended.

LL-L Warwick House, 64 Brougham St, T0800-022233/T03-548 3164, www.warwick house.co.nz. Built in 1854, and used as a major venue for lavish entertainment by early New Zealand politicians and leading merchants, 'the castle' as it is affectionately known has been transformed in to an elegant boutique hotel, complete with ballroom and spiral tower staircase. There are 3 beautifully appointed Victorian heritage-style en suites replete with native Kauri and of course the obligatory claw-foot baths. Excellent cuisine, attractive gardens and a warm welcome also add to its considerable appeal. Recommended.

LL-AL The Rutherford Hotel, Trafalgar Sq, T03-548 2299, www.heritagehotels.co.nz. The principal hotel in the city, centrally located and now part of the nationwide Heritage Hotels group. It has all the usual mod cons including a pool, sauna and health centre. Rooms range from spacious standard doubles to executive suites. There are 2 restaurants and a café, one being **Miyazu** – a very good Japanese option. Secure parking.

L The Honest Lawyer Country Pub, 1 Point Rd, Monaco, T03-547 8850, www.honest lawyer.co.nz. Although out of town (near the airport) this is well worth the effort. Rustic en suite rooms above a characterful English-style pub. Cosy restaurant/bar downstairs where you are invited to relax and 'tell little white lies with the locals'. Off-street parking.

L Little Manor, 12 Nile St, T03-545 1411, the.little.manor@xtra.co.nz. A charming, 2-storey, historic self-contained cottage in the heart of town.

L South Street Cottages, 1, 3 & 12 South St, T03-540 2769, www.cottageaccommo dation.co.nz. Compact, self-contained historic cottages in Nelson's most historic street.

L-AL Palms Motel, 5 Paru Paru Rd, T03-546 7770, www.palmsnelson.co.nz. One of the best upper-range motels in the centre.

L-AL Tuscany Gardens Motor Lodge, 80 Tahunanui Drive, Tahunanui , T03-548 5522, www.tuscanygardens.co.nz. Luxury motel with a good reputation, close to the beach.

L-AL Wheelhouse Inn, 41 Whitby Rd, T03-546 8391, www.wheelhouse.nelson.co.nz. A spacious, timber-style establishment, with self-contained accommodation. Quiet bush setting with a superb view.

A Boutique Motel, 7 Bail St, Stoke, T03-547 1439, www.boutiquemotel.co.nz. A new and well-appointed establishment located in the quiet suburb of Stoke and near the airport.

A Trafalgar Lodge, 46 Trafalgar St, T03-548 3980, www.trafalgarlodge.co.nz. A fine and well-located budget option with 2 en suites and 2 shared rooms in the lodge and 4 studio motel style units.

Backpacker hostels

The choice of budget accommodation is vast with over 15 to choose from. The following are recommended.

B-D Accents on the Park, 335 Trafalgar Sq, T03-548 4335, www.trafalgaraccommodation .co.nz. In a word: exceptional. A beautifully renovated Victorian villa with a distinct air of class. A full range of well-appointed rooms from en suite to shared dorms with all the usual facilities and a lovingly constructed basement lounge bar with open fire and plenty of character.

B-D The Green Monkey, 129 Milton St, T03-545 7421, www.thegreenmonkey.co.nz. A small, modern and quiet option with great doubles and fine facilities.

B-D Nelson City YHA, 59 Rutherford St, T03-545 9988, www.yha.org.nz. A large, modern, purpose-built YHA which is popular. Mainly twin and doubles but ask to see them first as some are very small. A little lacking in atmosphere but well located right in the town centre. Internet and plenty of local advice.

B-D Palace Backpackers, 114 Rutherford St, T03-548 4691, www.thepalace.co.nz. Another popular place set in a spacious historic villa overlooking the town. Wide variety of rooms including separate en suites. Great view, free breakfast/coffee, spa and a nice friendly atmosphere. Internet.

B-D Paradiso, 42 Weka St, T03-545 7128/ T0800-269667, www.backpacker nelson.co.nz. Club-Med in Nelson. A bit of a walk from the centre of town but very popular with a pool, spa and sauna. Wide range of rooms, conservatory kitchen, Sky TV and internet. Busy so book ahead.

B-D Tasman Bay Backpackers, 10 Weka St, T03-548 7950, www.tasmanbay backpackers.co.nz. A relaxing, homely and friendly backpacker hostel with the full range of rooms and good facilities including an open fire. Free bike hire, breakfast and homemade bread. The owners also have their finger on the pulse regarding local information and activities so you will be well looked after.

B-D Tramper's Rest, 31 Alton St, T03-5457477. This is a small, homely backpacker hostel with plenty of character, set in a suburban house in a quiet location near the centre of Nelson. Accommodation is in a small dorms and double rooms with proper beds. The atmosphere is relaxed and friendly and the owner is something of a guru when it comes to tramping locally and throughout the South Island. Perfect for the single, active, independent traveller. No off-street parking. Book well ahead.

Motorcamps and holiday parks

AL-D Richmond Motel and Top Ten Holiday Park, 29 Gladstone Rd, Richmond, T03-544 5281. The pick of the bunch. 14 km from Nelson but worth it. Full facilities.

AL-D Tahuna Beach Holiday Park, 70 Beach Rd, Tahunanui, T03-548 5159, www.tahuna beach.co.nz. Close to the most popular beach in town. Shop on site.

B-D Brook Valley Holiday Park, 2 km south town centre on Brook St, T03-548 0399. The closest motorcamp to the town in a pleasant position in the valley beside the river but it is basic and the sandflies can be a menace.

Nelson Lakes National Park *p443*

LL Kikiwa Lodge, Korere, Tophouse Rd, T03-521 1020, www.kikiwalodge.co.nz. Reputable luxury B&B.

LL Lake Rotoroa Lodge, T03-523 9121, www.lakerotoroalodge.com. Exclusive fishing retreat.

AL-D Alpine Lodge and Chalet, St Arnaud, T03-521 1869, www.alpinelodge.co.nz. The mainstay of accommodation and eating in the village. A wide range of unremarkable yet convenient options from self-contained studio units in the main lodge to twin, family or dorms in the chalet. Licensed à la carte restaurant, café, bar and spa. Bike hire.

A St Arnaud Log Chalets, T03-521 1887, www.nelsonlakes.co.nz. Offers very pleasant modern self-contained log chalet-style units.

A Tophouse, Tophouse Rd, 9 km north of St Arnaud, T03-521 1848, T0800-867468, www.tophouse.co.nz. A very animal-friendly, historic farm guesthouse. It has 4 self-contained units and 5 comfortable B&B rooms all good value. At one time it also boasted New Zealand's smallest bar. Café on site, open daily to non-guests 0930-1700.

A Woodrow Cottage, Tophouse Junction (5 km), T03-521 1212. Pretty and self-contained.

C-D Yellow House, T03-521 1887, theyellow house@xtra.co.nz. YHA associate which is modern and friendly with good facilities, including a spa. They can also provide good tramping information and gear hire.

Campsites

B-D Gowan River Holiday Camp, Gowan River Valley Rd, beside the river (6 km from SH6), T03-523 9921, www.gowanriver.co.nz.

Excellent and friendly, cabins and standard facilities including camp kitchen.
D DoC campsite. Sites with power, at the edge of the lake in West and Kerr bays, T03-521 1806. Deposit fees at DoC visitor centre. Beware: the sandflies will eat you alive.

Murchison *p444*
LL Maruia River Lodge, Shenandoah, Maruia River Valley, T03-523 9323, www.maruiariverlodge.co.nz. The most luxurious option in the immediate area offering all mod cons, in a pleasant bush setting next to the river.
AL-A Murchison Lodge B&B, 15 Grey St, T03-523 9196, www.murchisonlodge.co.nz. Pretty B&B with 4 comfortable, well-appointed rooms. Fishing trips are a speciality.
C-D Lazy Cow Homestyle Accommodation 37 Walker St, T0800-5299269 / T03-523 9451, www.homepages.paradise.net.nz/lazycow. A warm welcome at this 18-bed backpacker hostel right in the heart of the village, complete with in-house spa.

Motorcamps and campsites
AL-B Kiwi Park Motel and Holiday Park, 170 Fairfax St, T/F03-523 9248, offers some tidy, modern motel units.
AL-D Riverview Holiday Park, 2 km north of town, T03-523 9591. Basic and by the river. Exorbitant charges for showers ($2).

❼ Eating

Nelson *p437, maps p438 and p440*
There are over 50 cafés and restaurants in Nelson with the centre of town or the waterfront being the prime locations. Ask for the free and comprehensive *Eat, Drink Nelson guide* from the VIC (I-Site). Supermarkets include: **Woolworths**, corner of Paru Paru Rd and Halifax St, T03-546 6466; and **Fresh Choice**, Queen St, Richmond, T03-544 8299.
♦♦♦ The Boat Shed, 350 Wakefield Quay, T03-546 9783, www.theboatshedcafe.co.nz, daily for breakfast, lunch and dinner. There is no denying the quality of the food or the location. Fresh, local seafood is a speciality.
♦♦♦ Miyazu Japanese Restaurant, Rutherford Hotel, Trafalgar Sq, T03-548 2299, Mon-Sat from 1800. An excellent but expensive Japanese restaurant with a loyal regional following.

♦♦♦ Venice Cove, Nelson Yacht Club, 322 Wakefield Quay, T03-539 1307, Tue-Sun 1200-1400, 1730-2130 (closed Tue lunch). A tad cheaper than the **Boat Shed** but has an equally imaginative menu with an Italian edge.
♦♦ Applemans, 294 Queen St, Richmond, T03-5440610. The pick of the eateries in Richmond should you be staying out in that direction. Specializes in local cuisine.
♦♦ Hopgoods Restaurant and Bar, 284 Trafalgar St, T03-545 7191. Quality handcrafted locally sourced cuisine, with much of it-including the beer and wine-proudly organic. Recommended.
♦♦ Lambrettas Café Bar, 204 Hardy St, T03-545 8555, www.lambrettascafe.co.nz, 0900-late. Another popular, good value café specializing in all things Italian, including scooters. Excellent pizzas.
♦♦ Saltwater, 272 Wakefield Quay, T03-548 3361, www.saltwatercafe.co.nz, daily 0900-late. Another restaurant within the Quay community popular for the view and with numerous excellent seafood offerings. Also a good venue for breakfast.
♦ The Honest Lawyer, 1 Point Rd, Monaco, near the airport. Another fine pub worthy of the ale and steak lover's attention.
♦ The Victorian Rose, 281 Trafalgar St, T03-548 7631. An Olde English-style pub with very expensive beer but good value food. Cheap all-you-can-eat Sun roasts a speciality.

Wineries *p443*
There are a number of winery restaurants out of town but worth the trip for a leisurely lunch. These include:
♦ Seifrieds, corner of SH60 and Redwood Rd, Appleby, Richmond, T03-544 1555, www.seifried.co.nz. A popular restaurant at the biggest winery.
♦ Waimea Estates, 22 Appleby Highway, Hope, T03-544 4963, www.waimeaestates.co.nz.

Murchison *p444*
♦♦ Commercial Hotel, next to the VIC, T03-523 9696. Ironically, a far less commercial atmosphere here than in many other places.
♦ Beechwoods Café, on SH6 where all the buses stop at SH6 southern end of town, T03-523 9571, daily 0630-2130. Highly commercial, with a wide range of light meals and snacks available.

¶ **Rivers Café**, at the Adventure Centre, 51 Fairfax St, T03-523 9009, www.rivers.co.nz. Good for a quick coffee and check of the email. But, beware, you will be hard pushed to walk out without being lured for a trip down the river. And why not?

❶ Pubs, bars and clubs

Nelson *p437, maps p438 and p440*
When it comes to nightlife, most of the action in Nelson (and it can be considerable) takes place on or around Bridge St.
Honest Lawyer, Monaco. A bit out of town, but a good venue for conversation and traditional Irish music at the weekends.
Little Rock Café, 165 Bridge St. Very 'Mad-Max', it goes off with dancing at the weekend with the young set shaking their pants into the small hours.
Maen Fiddler145 Bridge St, T03-546 8516. The obligatory Irish offering, but as the name suggests more authentic than most.
The Oyster Bar, 115 Hardy St, T03-545 8955. For something a bit more sedate.
Phat Club, 137 Bridge St, T03-548 3311. The place to go in the wee hours to shake your pants – presumably big ones?
The Shark Club, 132 Bridge St, T03-546 6630. Not, as the name suggests, a haunt for second-hand car salesmen or lawyers but perhaps the town's most popular pool parlour and backpacker hangout. Free pool 1700-1900.
Victoria Rose, Trafalgar St, the place to go if you like jazz or blues, or if you're fed up with the noise of Bridge St and just want to watch some sport on the big screen. The good stuff (Irish and English beer) is expensive.

❸ Entertainment

Nelson *p437, maps p438 and p440*
Cinema and theatre
State Cinema Centre, opposite the VIC (I-Site), T03-548 8123. Also has a café upstairs.
Suter Gallery, 208 Bridge St, T03-548 4699, www.suter.org.nz. Occasionally the focus for more cultural events including theatre, dance and non-mainstream films.

❂ Festivals and events

Nelson *p437, maps p438 and p440*
For up-to-date events listings consult the website www.nelsonnz.com/events. The most famous event in the region used to be the iconic **Wearable Arts Festival** but thanks to its resounding success it has now been relocated to the country's capital, Wellington. This has of course caused ripples of controversy among the locals but it should perhaps be seen as a tribute to the region's considerable creative talent, a talent that thankfully is, despite the loss, still showcased through many other events throughout the year.
Feb Festival of Opportunities (late Feb). Typically unusual, this festival explores and contemplates the mind, the body, the spirit and probably even your navel, www.nelsonhealthfest.co.nz.
Oct Nelson Arts Festival. The biggest event of the year, with a week-long celebration showcasing the region's many colourful forms of artistic expression.
Dec-Feb Sealord Summer Festival. Various highlights including a lantern festival and Opera in the Park all aimed mainly at families.

❍ Shopping

Nelson *p437, maps p438 and p440*
For detailed information on arts and crafts outlets get a copy of the *Nelson Regional Guide Book – Art in its Own Place*, available from most bookshops.
Bead Gallery, 18 Parere St, T03-546 7807, www.beads.co.nz. Excellent.
Höglund Art Glass Gallery, Korurangi Farm, Landsdowne Rd, Richmond, T03-544 6500.
Monty's Market, Montgomery Sq, T03-546 6454. Sun 0900-1300. Popular and has a crafts edge.
Nelson Market, Montgomery Sq, Sat 0800-1300. Local arts and crafts.
Pomeroys Coffee and Tea Co, 80 Hardy St, T03-546 6944. Stock up on filter coffee or tea.

▲ Activities and tours

Nelson *p437, maps p438 and p440*
The Nelson Region offers a wide range of activities from the crazy to the traditional.

4WD quad biking and the skywire

4WD quad biking is a speciality in the region with one of the oldest and best operators in the country based nearby. **Happy Valley Adventures**, 194 Cable Bay Rd, Hira T03-545 0304, www.happyvalley adventures.co.nz. Back-country guided rides, taking in a mighty maitai tree and some superb views. Interesting eco-based commentary. Kids' fun rides in an 8WD also available, also a café on site. An excellent wet weather option. From 1-4 hrs $70-130, standard tour $95 for 2½ hrs. Skywire is a novel addition to the adrenaline cocktail and is essentially a 4-person flying-fox that runs 1.6 km across the valley, reputedly at 120 kph. A 'Granny Run' is available for the faint-hearted, presumably with tea and scones and classical music playing in the background. From $85. Transportation available.

Arts and crafts workshops

Creative Tourism, T03-526 8812, www.creativetourism.co.nz. An excellent creative workshop programme where you can try your hand at an amazing range of contemporary or traditional crafts from bone carving to organic brewing for $80-120. Visit the website or VIC (I-Site) for more details. **Nelson Bone Carving**, 87 Green St, T03-546 4275, www.carvingbone.co.nz. Has a studio at Tahura Beach and offers a day traditional bone carving workshop from $65.

Cruising and sailing

Cat Sailing Charters, 46 Martin St, Monaco, T03-547 6666, www.sailingcharters.co.nz. Offers an excellent range of affordable sailing and launch cruise options, from evening racing, fishing or the exploration of local nautical sights, to half or full-day and overnight/multi-day trips to the Abel Tasman National Park. Recommended.

Flightseeing

Abel Tasman Air, Nelson Airport, T03-528 8290, www.abeltasmanair.co.nz. An excellent and friendly outfit offering both transportation and flightseeing options. A flight around Abel Tasman and Kahurangi national parks is recommended. **Nelson Helicopters**, T0800-450350 / T03-547 1177, www.nelsonhelicopters.co.nz.

Scenic helicopter flights. Used extensively during the filming of *Lord of the Rings* for shuttling cast and crew into the depths of the Kahurangi National Park.

Golf

Nelson is not short of quality courses, including: **Golf Range**, 453 Nayland Rd, Stoke, T03-547 2227; **Greenacres**, Richmond, T03-544 8420, from $30; and **Nelson Golf Club**, Bolt Rd, T03-548 5029. From $35.

Horse trekking

Stonehurst Farm Horse Treks, Stonehurst Farm, Clover Rd, T03-542 4121, www.stone hurstfarm.co.nz. Excellent variety of treks to suit all levels from 1-4 hrs and from $55. **Thorndale Horse Treks**, north of Nelson (near **Happy Valley Adventures**), on Cable Valley Rd, T03-545 1191. Recommended, 1 hr to overnight from $40. **Western Ranges Horse Treks**, Wakefield, T03-522 4178, www.thehorsetrek.co.nz. A good outfit well suited to both beginners and the experienced. Treks in the Kahurangi National Park and Northwest Nelson ranges from half-day to 10 days, from $90.

Rock climbing

Vertical Limits, 34 Vanguard St, T03-545 7511, www.verticallimits.co.nz. Offers some excellent half- or full-day rock climbing trips to some notable venues in Golden Bay, $65-130. It also has an indoor climbing wall for instruction or independent use, from $16. Open Mon-Thu 1200-2100, Fri-Sun 1000-1800.

Skydiving, paragliding, kiteboarding and hang-gliding

Adventure Paragliding, 18A Marybank Rd, Atawai, T0800-212359, www.skyout.co.nz. Tandem paragliding and kiteboarding from $150, courses also available. **Nelson Hang-gliding Adventures**, T03-548 9151, www.flynelson.co.nz. From $150. Tandem and solo introductory hang-gliding courses are also available. **Nelson Paragliding**, T03-544 1182, www.nelsonparagliding.co.nz. Tandem paragliding from $110, courses from $150. **Skydive Abel Tasman**, 16 College St, Mouteka, T0800-422899/T03-528 4091, www.skydive.co.nz. If the weather is in your favour you can do your obligatory tandem skydive from 9000 ft ($210) or 12,000 ft ($260).

Walking

For a short walk the viewpoint above the Botanical Gardens is recommended (see page 439), while for longer excursions and expansive views try the **Dun Mountain Walkway**, which is accessible via the Broom Valley. From Brook St take a left on to Tantragee Rd.

Water-skiing, wakeboarding and kitesurfing

Kitesurfing is huge in Nelson with the winds over Tahunanui Beach often creating the perfect conditions. **Kitescool**, based in Marahau, T021-354837, www.kitescool.co.nz. Lessons from $150.

Winery tours and sightseeing

There are numerous sightseeing and wine tour operators available. See also box page 442. Recommended operators include: **Bay Tours**, 48 Brougham St, T03-548 6486, www.baytoursnelson.co.nz. Flexible with wine tours a speciality from $69.
JJ's Quality Tours, T03-546 5470/T0800-568568, www.jjs.co.nz. A well-established operator offering a brewery tour as well as the standard vineyard tours, half- or full-day from $69.

Nelson Lakes National Park p443 Mountaineering

For all tramping and mountaineering information in the Nelson Lakes National Park contact the **DoC Nelson Lakes Visitor Centre**, View Rd, St Arnaud, T03-521 1806, www.doc.govt.nz.

Murchison p444

The principal activities in the area include fishing, whitewater rafting, kayaking, caving, mountaineering and walking. If you feel lucky and want to try **gold-panning**, the VIC hires out pans and shovels for $6 ($20 bond) and will point you in the right direction. The VIC can also provide details and directions of the numerous short and long walking options in the area. The view from the **Skyline Walk** (1½ hrs, 6 km) is recommended. If a walk seems too much, it's worth visiting the **Ariki Falls** which are located 3 km from O'Sullivan's

Bridge heading west down SH6 (turn left down the track 1 km after the statue of 3 people hugging). The pink rocks are even more attractive than the falls. But beware, take insect repellent.
Auto Engineering, 27 Grey St, T03-523 9425. Mountain bike hire.
Buller Jetboat Tours, Buller Gorge Swingbridge, T03-523 9595/T0800-802023, www.murchison.co.nz. Jet-boat trips down the Buller from $75 (hourly, Sep-Apr).
New Zealand Kayak School, 111 Waller St, T03-352 5786, www.nzkayakschool.com. Offers a 4-day introductory, intermediate, advanced and women-only whitewater kayaking courses from $695. Price includes accommodation.
Ultimate Descents Murchison Adventure Centre, 51 Fairfax St, T03-5239899, www.rivers.co.nz. An attractive range of rafting and kayaking trips, with the local Buller River (Grade 3-4) being the main focus. A 4½-hr blat down the Buller followed by a soak in the hot tub costs from $105. There is also a shop and a café on-site.

● Transport

Nelson *p437, maps p438 and p440*
Bicycle hire Coppins Great Outdoors Centre, 255 High St, Motueka, T03-528 7296, from $25 per day. **Car hire** Budget, Nelson Airport, T03-547 9586; Pegasus, 83 Haven Rd, T03-548 0884; Hardy Cars, 8 Bridge St, T03-548 1618. **Taxi** Sun City Taxis, T03-548 2666, and Nelson City Taxis, T03-54 88225.

● Directory

Nelson *p437, maps p438 and p440*
Banks You will find all the main branches in or around Trafalgar St. **Internet** Boots Off, 53 Bridge St; Aurora Tech, 161 Trafalgar St, and KiwiNet, 93 Hardy St. **Medical services** Nelson Hospital, Tipahi St, T03-546 1800. **Emergency Pharmacy**, corner of Hardy and Collingwood sts, T03-548 3897. **Police** T03-548 8309.
Post office Post Restante, corner of Trafalgar and Halifax sts, opposite the VIC (I-Site), T03-546 7818, Mon-Fri 0745-1700, Sat 0930-1230.

North of Nelson

For many international visitors (perhaps too many) Nelson and the small township of Motueka, 54 km to the north, act merely as a convenient staging post to the main focus of tourism in the region, the Abel Tasman National Park. This small stretch of coastline, with its picturesque sandy bays, well-worn coastal walking track and world-class kayaking trips, is one of the most popular natural attractions in the country. As such, it seldom disappoints, but don't expect to find much solitude here. For that you should leave the crowds behind and head further north on SH60, traversing Takaka Hill to the quieter, far more laid-back realms of Golden Bay.

Beyond the great hill, the small arty township of Takaka offers a fine introduction to the region, while the nearby Pupu springs possess an almost palpable sense of peace, and an extraordinary clarity. Then, skirting the shores of Golden Bay, via the former gold rush town of Collingwood, SH60 finally terminates at the surreal sandy sweep of Farewell Spit, with the unforgettable beauty of Wharariki Beach within walking distance. All in all, in can prove a memorable diversion and the scenery and general atmosphere of this little corner of the South Island can act like a natural tranquillizer well worth taking. ›› *For Sleeping, Eating and other listings, see pages 456-460.*

Nelson to Motueka

From Richmond, 14 km southwest of Nelson, SH60 follows the fringe of Nelson Bay west to Motueka. This route – often labelled as 'Nelson's Coastal Way' – is the realm of vineyards, orchards, arts and crafts outlets and some pleasant seaside spots. One such spot worth a look, particularly around lunch or dinnertime, is **Mapua**. A congenial little settlement at the mouth of the **Waimea Inlet** (and just a short diversion off SH60), it boasts one of the best restaurants in the region, **The Smokehouse**, see page 458.

Across the road is the fairly unremarkable **Touch the Sea Aquarium and Gift Shop** ① *T03-540 3557, daily, $6, child $4,* which is maybe worth a look if you love seahorses or have kids. Far more impressive is the quality work of local artisans showcased nextdoor in the **Cool Store Art Gallery** ① *T03-540 3778.*

Motueka ●■🚲🏔 ›› *pp456-460.*

→ *Colour map 4, A4 Population: 12,000*

Motueka itself is a rather unremarkable little place of little note, but set amidst all the sun-bathed vineyards and orchards and within a short distance from some of the most beautiful beaches in the country, it seems to radiate a sense of smug satisfaction. Once a thriving Maori settlement, the first residents were quickly displaced by the early Europeans, who were also intent on utilizing the area's rich natural resources. Today Motueka is principally a service centre for the numerous vineyards, orchards and market gardens that surround it, or for the many transitory tourists on route to the Abel Tasman National Park and Golden Bay. With such a seasonal influx of visitors Motueka is also a place of contrast, bustling in summer and sleepy in winter. One thing you will immediately notice on arrival is its almost ludicrously long main street – so long you could land a 747 on it and still have room for error. See also Abel Tasman National Park, page 452.

Ins and outs

Getting there The **Motueka airport** ① *College St, SH61, 2 km west of the town centre,* has no scheduled air services but **Abel Tasman Air,** T03-528 8290, www.abel tasmanair.co.nz, can get you there from within the region if you want to arrive in style.

By road, Motueka is 51 km from Nelson on SH60 (Coastal Highway). Several bus companies offer regular services to Mouteka and beyond including **KBus**, **Abel Tasman Coachlines** and **Atomic Shuttles**. See Nelson Ins and outs, page 437.

Tourist information **Motueka VIC (I-Site)** ① *Wallace St, in the town centre, T03-528 6543, www.abeltasmangreenrush.co.nz, daily 0800-1800 (0800-1630 winter)*, is a busy centre that prides itself on providing the best and most up-to-date information on the Abel Tasman National Park. **DoC field centre** ① *corner of King Edward and High sts, T03-528 1810,motuekaao@doc.govt.nz, Mon-Fri 0800-1630*, has maps and leaflets for the entire region and can book huts for the Abel Tasman Coastal Walkway, Kahurangi National Park and Heaphy Tracks. You could also call into **Abel Tasman Wilson's Experiences** ① *265 High St (main road into town, next to the New World supermarket), T0800-223582/T03-528 2027, www.abeltasmanco.nz*, which operates beachfront lodges, launch cruises, water taxi, guided/non-guided sea kayaking and walking; it can provide maps, tide information and help with itinerary planning.

Sights

The best beaches near Motueka (and before the national park) are in **Kaiteriteri**. For a local short walk try the Motueka Quay accessed via the waterfront west of the town centre. For other walks in the area contact the DoC. There's also the small and fairly unremarkable **Motueka Museum** ① *High St, T03-528 7660, Mon-Fri 1000-1500 (also weekends in summer), donation*. ⇥ *For activities in the Abel Tasman National Park see page 459.*

Kaiteriteri and Marahau → *Colour map 4, A4*

Kaiteriteri and Marahau are both on the dead-end road to the southern boundary of the Abel Tasman National Park, which is accessed from SH60 just north of Motueka. **Kaiteriteri** (13 km) is a very pretty village with two exquisite beaches of its own and is a popular holiday spot. The main beach is the departure point for scenic launch trips, water taxis and kayak adventures into the Abel Tasman National Park. If you do nothing else in Kaiteriteri, allow yourself time to take in the view from the **Kaka Pa Point Lookout** at the eastern end of the beach. There is a signpost with destinations and distances that will remind you how far you are from home – and how close to paradise. **Breakers Beach** below, looking east towards the park, is truly idyllic.

    Marahau, a further 6 km east of Kaiteriteri, is principally an accommodation and activity base at the main access point to the national park. There is a good range of accommodation options, a number of water taxi and activity operators and a café to satisfy the needs of exhausted, hungry trampers. There is much controversy surrounding a $15 million resort development on environmentally sensitive wetlands, right at the entrance to the national park that has been given building consent but as yet (thankfully) remains on the drawing table. Should it go ahead (which it inevitably will), sadly this sums up the fears of many conservationists that it may be the beginning of the end for the unspoilt beauty of the Abel Tasman.

Abel Tasman National Park 🖾▲ ⇥ *pp456-460.*

→ *Colour map 4, A4*

The Abel Tasman is the smallest and most popular national park in New Zealand, and one of the most beautiful, protecting 23,000 ha of some of the finest coastal scenery and beaches in the country. Rolling hills of native bush fall to azure-coloured clear waters and a 91-km coastline, indented with over 50 beaches of golden sand. It is a paradise for trampers and sea kayakers and boasts the famous and increasingly popular 51-km **Coastal Walkway**; while the **Inland Track** offers a quieter and more energetic tramp away from both the coast and the hordes of people. The park is also home to the Tonga Island Marine Reserve.

The park was opened in 1942 after the tireless efforts of conservationist and resident Perrine Moncrieff; it was named after the Dutch navigator Abel Tasman who first sighted New Zealand in 1642. Many of the place names are accredited to the explorations and subsequent mappings in 1827 by the French explorer Jules Sebastien Cesar Dumont d'Urville.

Abel Tasman National Park

Wharwharangi Hut

Anapai Bay

Tasman Bay

Pigeon Saddle

Totaranui

Inland Track

Wainui Falls

Awaroa Bay

P

Coastal Track

Awaroa Hut

Te Canaan & Harwood's Hole

Bark Bay Hut

Anchorage Hut

Torrent Bay Lodge

Tinline Bay

Marahau

To Motueka

N

0 km   1

0 miles   1

Sleeping 🏠
Awaroa Lodge **1**
Meadowbank
Homestead **3**

Torrent Bay Lodge **4**
Totaranui Beach Camp **2**

Eating 🍴
Park Café **1**

Getting there Marahau, at the park's southern entrance, is the principal gateway to the park. Access from this point is by foot, water taxi, kayak or launch. The northern (walk) gateway to the park is via Takaka (Golden Bay) at the road terminus on the eastern edge of Wainui Bay. There is access by unsealed road into the northern sector of the park terminating at Totaranui and Awaroa Bay. You can also fly into Awaroa Bay from Nelson or Motueka, with **Abel Tasman Air**, T03-528 8290.

Kaiteriteri and Marahau are served via Motueka by **Abel Tasman Coachlines**, T03-548 0285, www.abeltasmantravel.co.nz, from Nelson, and **Kahurangi Buses**, T0508-458835/T03-358 8355, www.kahurangi.co.nz. **Abel Tasman Coachlines** and **Kahurangi Buses** also serve the northern sector of the park to Totaranui.

All the major water taxi and/or water-based transportation and tour operators are based in Kaiteriteri or Marahau which are both considered the gateways to the park. Other than pure sightseeing trips the various services and schedules offer casual walkers or day-trippers the option of being dropped off at one beach to be picked up later at the same, or at another. For trampers this can also provide numerous options to walk some of the **Coastal Walkway** or to retire early in the attempt to walk its whole length. Note also that some operators will tow kayaks, giving you the option to kayak and walk or again retire early. Bags and backpacks can also be carried independently, but this tends to be in conjunction with organized trips. Alas, in the Abel Tasman these days it is actually possible to 'hail' a water taxi, or at least gesticulate wildly to catch one, even though you are not pre-booked. Also note that most water-taxi companies can pick up or help arrange bus transport from Nelson and Motueka to coincide with departures and of course they also offer a huge range of 'suggested' itineraries for a set price. In Kaiteriteri the principal operator is **Abel Tasman Sea Shuttles**, T0800-732748, www.abeltasmanseashuttles.co.nz; a return fare to Tonga Bay will cost from $55 return. In Kaiteriteri the principal beachfront operators are, again **Sea Shuttles**, www.abeltasmanseashuttles.co.nz, and **Abel Tasman Wilson's Experiences**, T0800-223582, www.abeltasman.co.nz. In Marahau **Abel Tasman Aqua Taxi**, T03-527 8083, T0800-278282, www.aquataxis.co.nz, has an office and café (where you also board your boat-n-first leg by tractor-trailer). Prices are reasonable and competitive. An average fare to Totaranui at the top end of the park will cost from $30-38 one way. Most water taxis depart between 0830 and 1030 from Motueka, Kaiteriteri and Marahau with additional sailings in the early afternoon (1200 and 1330), depending on the tides.

Tourist information VIC (I-Site) and DoC offices in Motueka (see Motueka Ins and outs, page 451) are the principal sources of information on the park. They can assist with accommodation bookings and passes, transportation and activities; they can also provide tide times. DoC can also assist with general information, hut bookings, maps, and leaflets. Unmanned DoC information stations and intentions sheets are available at Marahau and Totaranui (seasonal).

▲▲ Abel Tasman Coastal Track

This two- to five-day, 51-km walk requires medium fitness and the track itself is well maintained (and certainly well trod). The only obstacle encountered and sections that can cause difficulty are the two estuary crossings at Awaroa Inlet and Torrent Bay; these two stretches must be negotiated at low tide, otherwise it is your swimming skills that will be tested, rather than your walking.

There are a number of ways to tackle the track in whole or in part. The most popular route is from south (Marahau) to north (Wainui), or commonly from Totaranui in the north (by water taxi from Marahau) back to Marahau in the south. There are plenty of DoC campsites and huts along the way and a few other, more salubrious, independent lodges should you choose the luxury option. Detailed information about the track can

⁝ Abel Tasman Track

A rough outline of the recommended route, distances and times (from south to north) is as follows:

Marahau to Anchorage: 11½ km, four hours
Anchorage Bark Bay: 9½ km, three hours
Bark Bay to Awaroa: 11½ km, four hours
Awaroa to Totaranui: 5½ km, 1½ hours
Totaranui to Wharwharangi: 7½ km, three hours
Wharwharangi to Wainui: 5½ km, 1½ hours

be obtained from DoC in Motueka and the website www.doc.govt.nz; its leaflet *The Abel Tasman Coast Track* ($1) is invaluable and it can provide the essential tide tables. Although the walk takes in many attractive bays, inlets and beaches, it does involve a lot of bush walking, where the view of the sea, never mind beaches, are obscured for long periods of time. So if you are not a seasoned tramper a combination of water taxi/walking over part of the route is perhaps recommended. Although the whole trip is a delight, the most scenic beaches are **Torrent Bay** and the **Awaroa Inlet**. These should not be missed and have the added novelty of the tidal crossing – which will give you a mild taste of what tramping in New Zealand is all about.

There are DoC huts at Anchorage, Bark Bay, Awaroa and Wharwharangi and numerous campsites along the way (see below).

▲ Inland Track
The Inland Track is for obvious reasons less popular and links **Marahau** to **Wainui** via the **Pigeon Saddle** on the Takaka-Totaranui Road. It is a 37-km, three- to five-day effort. The main attraction here, other than the fact it is far less trodden than the coastal track, is the beautiful undisturbed and regenerating bush and occasional fine views. The track can be tackled in whole or part and one recommendation is to start at the car park at **Harwood's Hole**. This way you can take in the impressive Harwood's Hole before tackling the remaining 20-km track north over the Pigeon Saddle to Wainui. Note that the track can also be tackled in part with the access point at Pigeon Saddle (Totaranui Road via Takaka). DoC can provide information and an essential broadsheet about the track. There are four huts but no separate campsites. They are not of the same standard as those on the Coastal Track.

▲ Day walks
If you are short of time or cannot stand the sight of a paddle, the following are two-day walks that will provide a pleasant taste to what the Abel Tasman is all about. They are also not too strenuous and have the added fun of getting your feet wet and then stopping for a lovely cup of tea. The first is accessed from the southern end of the park, the other from the north.

Torrent Bay to Marahau (14 km, three to six hours) From Marahau take an early morning water taxi to **Torrent Bay**, $30-38. Although there is an alternate high tide route around Torrent Bay try to make sure your arrival at Torrent Bay coincides with low tide so you can make the direct crossing. Take in the immediate delights here, then take the Coastal Track heading south, for which you need to take off your boots and then follow the markers across the estuary. Return boots to feet and find the track again that climbs the small headland before falling to the exquisite **Anchorage Bay**

Beach. Then, from halfway up the beach, climb the hill, not forgetting to look back at the stunning view. Take the sidetrack (15 minutes) from the top of the hill down to the incredibly cute (and hopefully quiet) **Watering Cove**. Climb back up to the coastal track and continue south. If you have time check out **Stillwell Bay** and certainly walk along **Appletree Bay** (re-access to main track at far end of the beach). From there complete the walk past **Tinline Bay** to the Marahau entrance point. If the tide is in your favour, you can cross the bay directly just beyond Tinline Bay (where the path descends to beach level). Fall exhausted and happy in to the **Park Café**, reward yourself with a pint of beer, a glass of wine or the full seafood fettuccine. While there use the email facility to make friends jealous back home.

Awaroa Bay (6 km, three to six hours) From Takaka take the Totaranui Road via **Pohara**, **Wainui Inlet** and the **Pigeon Saddle**, enjoying the views on the way. From the Totaranui Road take a right on the Awaroa Road to the **Awaroa** car park. Make sure once again that your arrival coincides with an outgoing tide. Digest the view across the inlet and the walk you are about to do. Descend to the beach and remove footwear. Cross the inlet in a direct line towards the sea, ignoring the especially muddy bit for the first 100 m. Enjoy the paddle and negotiate the deepest part (should be no more than knee deep) to **Sawpit Point** and the DoC Awaroa Hut. Follow the bay around and if possible extend your walk to the tip of the sand spit. From there walk along Awaroa beach to the far end. Follow the signs to **Awaroa Lodge**. Enjoy this oasis in paradise and sample the beer, a coffee or a refreshing cup of tea. Then retrace your steps to the Awaroa car park, keeping an eye on the tide.

● Sleeping

Nelson to Motueka *p451*
LL Jester House, 15 km south of Motueka on the Coastal Highway (SH60), T03-526 6742, www.jesterhouse.co.nz. Something totally different and without doubt the most original accommodation in the region. Quite simply, this could be (and probably will be) your only opportunity to stay in a giant boot.
LL-L Bronte Lodge, Bronte Rd East, T03-540 2422, www.brontelodge.co.nz. A luxury option set in beautiful gardens. 2 suites and self-contained villas over looking the bay and with all mod cons.
LL-L Kina Colada Holiday and Health Retreat, Kina Peninsula, T03-526 6700, www.kinacolada.co.nz. Enjoy the congenial surroundings, a massage, sauna or an oxygen, hydro- and moor-mud therapy.
AL Istana Coastal Cottage, located just south of Mapua on the Coastal Highway (SH60), T03-544 1979, www.istana.co.nz. Self-contained rammed earth cottage in a superb position overlooking the coastal inlet, very peaceful and tastefully appointed with Asian antiques and modern furnishings. Swimming pool and free kayaks.

B-D Mapua Leisure Park (clothing optional), 33 Toru St, T03-540 2666, www.nelson holiday.co.nz. An excellent camp, set amidst pine trees and sheltered surroundings, at the river mouth. It has numerous pretty areas to camp in, powered sites, cabins, chalets, sauna, pool and spa. There is also a small café and bar on the beach and internet. If the holiday park is not to your taste, there are a number of good B&Bs in the area.
B-D Tipistay Backpackers, Upper Moutere Highway, T03-543 2119, www.tipistay.com. A novel rural-based backpacker hostel with double and dorm native American-style tipis, shared cooking facilities in a thatched hut, open-air showers and bath and, yes, even totem poles. All good ingredients for a memorable stay. Bike hire and pick-ups from Motueka.

Motueka *p451*
The area has many fine lodges, B&Bs and homestays, most of which are located out of town. The VIC (I-Site) has full listings. Given the proximity to the Abel Tasman National Park you are advised to book well ahead in summer.

LL **Kahurangi Estate**, Sunrise Rd, T03-543 2980, www.kahurangiwine.com. Luxury self-contained cottage set in a working vineyard.
LL **Motueka River Lodge**, Motueka Valley Highway, Ngatimoti, T03-526 8668, www.motuekalodge.co.nz. A small, luxury boutique fishing lodge designed in French provincial style and located in the picturesque Motueka River Valley. Whether you're an angling fanatic or not you will be given a warm welcome and you cannot fail to be impressed with the aesthetics. Modern, country-style decor and open fires create a warm and homely feel and cordon bleu cuisine is offered. In-house fishing guides with an intimate knowledge of the best local and regional fishing spots. Minimum 2-night stay.
AL Old Schoolhouse, Kina Beach Estate, T03-526 6252, www.kinabeach.com. Beautiful self-contained cottages set among vineyards.
AL-A Blue Moon, 57 School Rd, T03-528 6996, www.thebluemoon.co.nz. Self-contained, spacious guest room. Tastefully decorated and good value.
AL-A The Estuary B&B, 543 High St, T03-528 6391, www.hauplains.co.nz. Good value, modern with good facilities.
A **Rowan Cottage Organic B&B**, 27 Fearon St, T03-528 6492, www.rowancottage.net. Studio with good facilities and character amidst a proudly nurtured organic garden.

Motels
B **Ashley Troubadour Motels and B&B**, 430 High St, T03-528 7318. A possible exception to a rather unimpressive rule. Good value.
B-D Bakers Backpaka YHA, 4 Poole St, T03-528 0102, www.bakerslodge.co.nz. A modern and well-maintained establishment with a wide variety of rooms, purpose-built facilities and a nice atmosphere. Internet and off-street parking. Very popular so book well in advance.
B-D Hat Trick Lodge, 25 Wallace St (opposite VIC), T03-528 5353, www.hattricklodge.co.nz. Purpose-built and conveniently located.
B-D White Elephant, 55 Whakarewa St, T03-528 6208, www.whiteelephant.co.nz. Deservingly popular and spacious backpacker hostel. Try the new en suites.

Motorcamps
B-D Fernwood Holiday Park, 519 High St (SH60), T03-528 7488. Beside the roundabout at the start of the never-ending main road through the town (2 km). Usual facilities including camp kitchen.
B-D Motueka Top Ten Holiday Park, 10 Fearon St, at the other end of the town, T03-528 7189, www.motuekatop10.co.nz.

Kaiteriteri *p452*
LL-AL Kimi Ora Holiday and Health Resort, Martin Farm Rd, T03-527 8027, www.kimiora.co.nz. 20 modern chalets, pool, spa and a health centre offering a range of treatments. In-house restaurant (open to non-guests) and courtesy pick-ups also available.
AL Bayview, Kaiteriteri Heights, Little Kaiteriteri, T03-527 8090, www.kaiteriteribandb.co.nz. Offers exactly what the name suggests from 2 lovely rooms, while enjoying breakfast on the deck.
AL-A Torlesse Coastal Motels, Kotare Pl, Little Kaiteriteri Beach, T03-527 8063, www.torlessemotels.co.nz. The best motel option with a choice of studio or 2-bedroom units.

Motorcamps and campsites
C-D Kaiteriteri Motor Camp, across the road from the beach on Sandy Bay Rd, T03-527 8010, www.kaiteriteribeach.co.nz. Has tent and powered sites and cabins.

Marahau *p452*
L **Ocean View Chalets**, T03-527 8232, www.accommodationabeltasman.co.nz. Neat, self-contained 1- to 2-bedroom cottages and studio units set on the hillside overlooking the bay, about 500 m from the main village.
L-B Abel Tasman Aqua Packers, Anchorage Bay, T0800-430744, www.aquapackers.co.nz. A rather unusual option worth considering with accommodation on board a small ex-Second World War naval patrol vessel. Standard, dinner or B&B options. Private doubles or dorm-style rooms. It isn't cheap but then you can't get an ever-changing view

Marlborough & Nelson North of Nelson *Listings*

● *For an explanation of the Sleeping and Eating price codes used in this guide, see the inside*
● *front cover. Other relevant information is provided in the Essentials chapter, pages 44-51.*
Note that prices are given in New Zealand dollars.

like that very often. Plenty of activities and a good base from which to explore the park.

AL Abel Tasman Marahau Lodge, T03-527 8250, www.abeltasmanmarahaulodge.co.nz. Purpose-built establishment conveniently located between Kaiteriteri Beach and the start of the Abel Tasman Coastal Track. Modern studios and self-contained units, pool, sauna and spa. Breakfast and room service evening meals on request.

C-D Barn Backpackers, Harvey Rd, T03-527 8043, www.barn.co.nz. A smaller but similar set up to Old McDonald's, below. Can assist in park accommodation and activity bookings.

C-D Old McDonald's Farm and Holiday Park, Harvey Rd, at the entrance to the Abel Tasman Park, T03-527 8288, www.old macs.co.nz. A large but sheltered, well-facilitated holiday camp complete with various animals, including 2 friendly and extremely dozy kune pigs. There are plenty of sheltered tent and powered sites and a range of well-appointed self-contained units, cabins and a backpacker's dormitory. Small café and shop on site and internet. Within walking distance of the Park Café, see page 459.

C-D Southern Exposure Kayak Company, Moss Rd, T0800-695292/T03-527 8424, www.southern-exposure.co.nz. One of the principal kayak companies offering budget accommodation, including camp sites.

Abel Tasman National Park *p 452, map p453*

LL Meadowbank Homestead, on the beachfront at Awaroa, with Abel Tasman Wilson's Experiences (see pages 454 and 459). A replica of the original settler's home. It is a relaxed holiday home on the beachfront, providing accommodation primarily for guided walkers and kayakers. Price includes twin/double accommodation, en suite bathroom, meals and launch transfers.

LL Torrent Bay Lodge, further south, also owned and operated by Abel Tasman Wilson's Experiences, T03-528 7801, www.abeltasman.co.nz. Offers an excellent standard of modern, mid- to upper-range accommodation as part of a walks or kayaking package from 2-days/1-night to 5-days/ 4-nights. The lodge in Torrent Bay has a relaxed atmosphere, with natural wood decor reflecting a nautical theme. It is only metres from the beach and Abel Tasman coastal track. All equipment, meals and transport by water taxi are included in the package.

LL-L Awaroa Lodge, Awaroa Inlet, T03-528 8758, www.awaroalodge.co.nz. Offers a range of modern studio suites, deluxe and family rooms in a remote location in the heart of the park and along the coastal track. A licensed café and open fires adds to its appeal. Note Awaroa is accessible only by foot, water taxi, by fixed-wing plane or helicopter.

Campsites and huts

There are 4 DoC huts and 21 campsites on the Coastal Track plus a number of private B&Bs and lodges. DoC huts have heating, toilets, bunks, mattresses and a water supply (all water should be boiled). Campsites have water and toilets. From Oct-Apr, DoC huts must be booked in advance and a summer season hut pass ($10-$45 per hut per night depending on season) purchased. Campsites cost $10 per night.

D Totaranui Beach Camp, T03-5288083. Popular budget camp next to the beach. It is accessed from the north by road, or from the south by water taxi. It is basic (no power) with limited facilities and is administered by DoC ($10). Bookings are essential Oct-Apr.

❼ Eating

Nelson to Motueka *p451*

❦ Flax Restaurant, Mapua, T03-540 2280, daily for lunch and dinner, from 1100. Has plenty of class and also enjoys a fine reputation especially for its pork belly and sublime desserts.

❦ The Smokehouse Restaurant, a few doors down from Flax, Mapua, T03-540 2280, www.smokehouse.co.nz, daily for lunch and dinner. Well known for its fine smoked fish and other seafood delicacies. The restaurant is set overlooking the river with a very pleasant outdoor eating area where you can sample a glass of local wine while taking in the view. Attached is a very popular fish and chip shop.

Motueka *p451*

Gothic Gourmet Restaurant, 208 High St, T03-528 6699, daily 0730 late. Interesting concept, but lacks atmosphere and is too expensive for what it is.

Hot Mamma's Café, 105 High St, T03-528 7039. Attracts a younger crowd, great coffee.

The Moorings, 218 High St, T03-528 6103. Open daily 'atc' till late. Along with Hot Mamma's Café, above, has a loyal local following, good coffee and inviting blackboard menus.

Riverside Café, just out of town on the way to Lower Moutere (Inland Highway 7 km), T03-526 7447, Tue-Wed 0930-1730, Thu-Sun 0930-late. A fine option, especially if you have kids. Spacious grounds, great staff.

Up the Garden Path, 473 High St, T03-528 9588, daily 0900-1900 (winter 0900-1700). Also a good bet for a quality caffeine hit amidst an attractive art garden. Good vegetarian options.

Kaiteriteri and Marahau *p452*

Hooked on Marahau Café and Restaurant, Marahau Waterfront, T03-527 8576. Daily for breakfast, lunch and dinner (closed Jun-Sep). A new establishment in a prime location offering outdoor and indoor dining, licensed.

Park Café, just at the entrance to the park on Harvey Rd, T03-527 8270, daily from 0800 (closed May-Aug). Fine blackboard fare, a bar, good coffee and Internet. Great atmosphere.

Pubs, bars and clubs

Motueka *p451*

Dodgy Ref, 121 High St, T03-528 4101 The best place for a beer in town.

Hot Mamma's Café and Bar (see Eating, above). A popular spot, especially with the younger set. Regular D.J's and 'Jam' sessions.

Activities and tours

Nelson to Motueka *p451*

Mapua Adventures, opposite the wharf, T03-540 3833, www.mapuaadventures.co.nz. Very helpful with friendly staff, offering an exciting range of options centred around jet-boating the river estuary, coastline and forests, 30 mins from $59; 1 hr from $89), birdwatching trips of 20 mins to 2½ hrs from $35-150.

For other activities see Nelson, page 448, and Kaiteriteri, below.

Abel Tasman Aerobatics, T0800-360180/ T03-528 8290, www.uflyextreme.co.nz. Thrills and spills aboard a Pitts-Special Biplane. Truly a once in a lifetime sick bag experience. Recommended.

Abel Tasman Wilson's Experiences, see page 454. Offers a wide range of guided/ non-guided sea kayaking, and walking trips to the Abel Tasman National Park.

Bush and Beyond, 35 School Rd, T03-528 9054, www.naturetreks.co.nz. Offers a variety of conservation-based walks from 1-8 days, mainly in the Kahurangi National Park, from around $150 a day.

Kaiteriteri and Marahau *p452*

Cat Sailing Charters, 46 Martin St, Monaco, T03-547 6666, www.sailingcharters.co.nz. Offer an excellent range of affordable sailing and launch cruise options, from evening racing, fishing or the exploration of local nautical sights, to half or full-day and overnight/multi-day trips in the Abel Tasman. Recommended.

Marble Hills 4 Wheel Motorcycle Adventures, Moss Rd, Marahau, T0800-2623253, www.marblehills4fun.co.nz. Provides some excellent scenic trips and 4WD fun 1 hr from $55, 2 hrs from $85. Cabin accommodation available.

Abel Tasman National Park *p452, map p453*

The choice is so vast that on initial acquaintance it is all very confusing. You can tramp, walk, kayak, walk/kayak, cruise or even swim with seals, but exactly how you do it and how much you pay is a headache. The advice therefore is to give yourself plenty of time to pre-plan and not to jump at the first option with which you are presented. See also Kaiteriteri Activities and tours, above.

Organized trips and cruises

For other water taxi operators, see page 454. There are a bewildering number of organized trips on offer designed to help make the decisions for you, but they can, if you are indecisive, make it very difficult to choose. All the water taxi operators offer a range of cruises and half- to full-day trips, with combinations of cruising and walking.

Abel Tasman Seal Swim, Sandy Bay Rd, Kaiteriteri, T0800-252925, www.sealswim.com. Swim with the seals at the Tonga Island Marine Reserve (within the park boundary). It is the only operator that has a DoC concession to do so. From $149 (spectator from $70). Most water taxis depart between 0830 and 1030 from Kaiteriteri and 1200 and 1330 from Marahau. In summer wherever you are in the park it is basically a 0900-1700 operation with water taxis plying the coast and various stops constantly between those times.

Abel Tasman Wilson's Experiences, 265 High St, Motueka, T03-5287801, www.abeltasman.co.nz. A professional and reliable outfit. It offers half- to 5-day guided/non-guided options based from the only beachfront lodges in the park, including transport on water taxi or comfortable launch. A transport-only fare can be as little as $30 and a day-cruise from $60, while a 5-day guided walking/sea kayaking trip weighs in at around $1500, all inclusive.

Sea kayaking

The Abel Tasman offers a world-class sea kayaking experience and it is, without doubt, the top venue in New Zealand. But it is very busy. On a midsummer's morning the colourful flotilla of kayaks departing from Kaiteriteri and Marahau are a sight to behold and something that would probably even have had the early Maori paddling their *waka* for cover. There is an army of operators offering a wide range of options from simple independent day hire and self-guided day-trips, to multi-day, guided kayak/walking combinations. The choice is yours and the decision difficult.

If walking is not your thing, then a kayak only trip is obviously recommended. But to get the overall essence of the Abel Tasman, a guided combination of both kayaking and walking is recommended. The beauty of the Abel Tasman, other

than the scenery, crystal clear waters and the wildlife, is the layout of its myriad bays and beaches, which makes a staged trip and the logistics eminently surmountable. Even if you have never been sea kayaking before, it is relatively safe and easy. The modern day sea kayak is very stable and all the major operators provide training, guidance and have adequate safety standards. Serious sea kayakers tend to leave the Abel Tasman to the novice flotillas and are to be found hiding in the serenity of the Marlborough Sounds or Fiordland. Competition is fierce so the best advice is to shop about and research thoroughly before deciding. Prices range from about $45 independent hire per day, $85-175 for a guided day trip, to around $430 for a 3-day trip (camping) with food provided. The principal and reputable companies include the following.

Abel Tasman Kayaks, Marahau Beach, T03-5278022/T0800-732529 www.abel tasmankayaks.co.nz. Offers a range of trips from half- to multi-day. The 1-day guided 'Beaches and Islands' excursion, $99, is recommended.

Abel Tasman Sea Kayak Company, 506 High St, Motueka, T03-528 7251, www.seakayaknz.co.nz.

Abel Tasman Wilson's Experiences, 265 High St, Motueka, T03-528 2027 www.abeltasman.co.nz. Offers civilized adventures staying at the only beachfront lodges, chef-prepared meals and private rooms with en suite bathrooms. A 3-day guided kayak/walk costs around $1000.

Golden Bay Kayaks, Pohara, Golden Bay, T03-525 9095, www.goldenbaykayaks.co.nz. Popular and slightly different with trips in both the Abel Tasman National Park and Golden Bay region.

Kaiteriteri Sea Kayak, Kaiteriteri Beachfront, T0800-252925, www.seakayak.co.nz.

Ocean River Adventure Company, Motueka, T0800-732529, www.sea kayaking.co.nz. Specializes in independent freedom rentals from $69 a day.

Southern Exposure, Moss Rd, Marahau, T03-527 8424, www.southern-exposure.co.nz. Accommodation available.

Golden Bay → Colour map 4, A4

From the pretty township of Takaka SH60 continues northwest, eventually reaching the coast and the tiny village of Collingwood, the gateway to Kahurangi National Park, the Heaphy Track and Whariki Beach, one of the most beautiful beaches in the country. From the end of terra firma, 22 km north of Collingwood, the huge 35-km Farewell Spit extends like a golden rainbow out into ocean to envelop the vast mud flats of Golden Bay. ►► *For Sleeping, Eating and other listings, see pages 466-468.*

Ins and outs

Getting there Takaka airfield ① *6 km west of town on SH60*, is served by **Abel Tasman Air**, To3-528 8290, www.abeltasmanair.co.nz, from Nelson. This operator also provides excellent scenic flights and air transport from the southern end of the Heaphy Track. By road (SH60), Takaka is 109 km from Nelson and 50 km to Farewell Spit. Bus companies include **Abel Tasman Coachlines**, To3-548 0285, www.abeltasmantravel.co.nz. **Golden Bay Coachlines**, To3-525 8352, www.goldenbaycoachlines.co.nz and **K-Bus**, To508-458 835/To3-358 8355, www.kahurangi.co.nz. Buses stop outside the VIC (I-Site).

Tourist information and orientation Almost all the services the visitor requires can be found along Commercial Street, the main street through Takaka. **Golden Bay VIC** ① *Willow St, at the southern entrance to Takaka, To3-525 9136, gb.vin@nelson nz.com, www.goldenbay.net.nz, www.nelsonnz.com, daily 0900-1700*, stocks the full range of information for the entire Golden Bay area, including Collingwood and Farewell Spit. The free *Golden Bay Heart of the Parks Guide* is useful. **DoC** ① *62 Commercial St, Takaka, To3-525 8026, goldenbayao@doc.govt.nz, Mon-Fri 0800-1600*, has detailed information on both the Abel Tasman and Kahurangi national parks (including the Heaphy and Abel Tasman Coastal Tracks).

Takaka → Colour map 4, A4 Population: 1224

Takaka was founded in 1854 and is the principal business and shopping area for Golden Bay. In summer it is a bustling little place and year round the residence of a colourful and cosmopolitan palette of arts and crafts people. It is also home to a large dairy factory. There are a number of interesting attractions around the town including the intriguing 'Pupu' Springs and Rawhiti Cave. The township also serves as the gateway to the northern sector of the Abel Tasman National Park, the vast Kahurangi National Park and the remote 35-km Farewell Spit. The small seaside village of **Pohara**, about 10 km east of Takaka on the road to the northern boundary of the Abel Tasman National Park, boasts the best local beach and provides safe swimming.

In the town itself, the **Golden Bay Museum and Gallery** ① *To3-525 6268, daily 1000-1600, closed Sun in winter, $1*, displays the usual local treasures and a special feature on early explorer Abel Tasman's unfortunate first encounter with the local Maori. Of further interest is the gallery next door, which showcases the cream of local arts and crafts talent. There are many other independent galleries in the area for which the VIC's free *Arts of Golden Bay* leaflet can point you in the right direction.

The biggest attraction in the immediate area are the beautiful and crystal-clear **Te Waikoropupu or Pupu Springs** ① *administered by DoC, open daily; to get there follow SH60 north of Takaka, turning left just after the bridge over the Takaka River, follow Pupu Valley and Pupu Springs Rd to the car park*. There are well-maintained paths and the reserve can be explored thoroughly in about 45 minutes. Nearby the **Pupu Walkway**, which starts at the end of Pupu Valley Road, retraces an old gold-mining water race, taking in some interesting features and lovely bush. It is one of the best short walks in the region and takes about two to three hours.

Te Waikoropupu Springs

Borne of the Takaka Marble Aquifer, the turquoise waters of the 'Pupu Springs' bubbles out at an average rate of 13.2 cubic metres per second, creating a lake that is the clearest of any freshwater body outside Antarctica. To the scientific community they are of interest not only as an unusual landform, but also for the resident aquatic plants and animals. If these springs were in North America and Europe there would be no way casual divers would be able to enter the waters given the sheer demand and subsequent environmental impact but here in the 'clean and green' as long as you adhere to the stringent criteria you can dive casually providing the experience of a lifetime. To the Maori, the springs are considered 'taonga' – a treasure, and 'wahi tapu' – a sacred place to be revered. It is a peaceful, beautiful place that has a palpable and rare sense of purity lost in the parks and reserves in the more populous nations of the world. If you are in the area a visit is highly recommended.

Of the two limestone cave systems in the area, Te Anaroa and Rawhiti, it is the **Rawhiti Cave** that is the most impressive. It is, however, the least accessible. This ancient cave, with its enormous entrance laden with thousands of coloured stalactites, can be accessed independently, but a guided tour with **Kahurangi Walks** ① T03-525 7177, www.kahurangiwalks.co.nz, 3 hrs $25, child $15, is recommended. Closer to Takaka are the weird and wonderful limestone (karst) formations of the **Labyrinth Rocks** ① 3 km outside town, Labyrinth Lane, Three Oaks, T03-525 8434, daily 1200-dusk, $7, which will keep the kids occupied for hours.

Also of note, and accessed where Motupipi meets the Clifton Crossroads, is the **Grove Scenic Reserve**. A short 10-minute walk will bring you to an intriguing spot where massive rata trees grow out of curiously shaped karst rocks. Nearby those with green fingers and the love of a fine view will enjoy the **Begonia House and gardens** ① Richmond Rd, Pohara, T03-525 9058, daily 1000-1700, free.

While in the area, take a look at the **Abel Tasman Memorial** on the headland just beyond Tarakohe (Totaranui Road) and look, then listen, with eyes shut to the pretty **Wainui Falls** (Wainui Bay); an easy 40-minute walk. This road can also take you to the northern beaches and tramping access points of the **Abel Tasman National Park**.

Of some novelty are the famous Anatoki eels at **Bencarri Farm** ① 6 km south of Takaka, signposted off SH60 on McCallum Rd, T03-525 8261, www.bencarri.co.nz, daily 1000-1730, $12, child $6. The eels are reputed to be the oldest tame eels in the country with some individuals still enjoying a daily snack after 80 years of residence. Bencarri Farm also has a host of touchy-feely animals including llamas and some homesick Scottish 'Heelaan coos'. There is a good café on site (open 1000-late).

Collingwood → Colour map 4, A4

Collingwood was formerly known as Gibbstown and was (believe it or not) once a booming gold-mining town that was promoted as an eminently suitable capital for the nation. But that dream turned to dust when the gold reserves were laid waste and a fire almost destroyed the entire village. Rebuilt and renamed Collingwood in honour of Nelson's second-in-command, fire struck again in 1904 and yet again as recently as 1967 when the town hall, hotel and two shops were reduced to ashes. Despite its fiery past, Collingwood still retains a few historical buildings, including the characterful **courthouse**, which is now a café where you can sentence yourself to a lengthy tea break. Collingwood itself also has a small and unpretentious **museum** ① Tasman St, T03-524 8131, daily 0900-1800, donation $2, child $1.

The area has a few other notable attractions worth visiting. South of Collingwood, in the attractive **Aorere River Valley** and back on the limestone theme, are the privately owned **Te Anoroa and Rebecca Caves** ① Cave's Rd, near Rockville, T03-524 8131, 1-hr guided tours of the Te Anaroa Caves available in summer at 1030, 1230, 1430 and 1630 (in winter by arrangement); dual cave tours of 2-3 hrs are also available $15, child $6. The Te Anaroa Caves are 350 m in length and include the usual stalactite and stalagmite formations and fossilized shells, while the Rebecca Caves are best known for their glow-worms. At the end of Cave Road are two limestone rock monoliths known as the **Devil's Boots** (presumably because they are upside-down). The walks and mountain bike tracks of the **Aorere Goldfields**, which were New Zealand's first, are accessed from the road end and are of far more interest. The free DoC leaflet provides information. For something longer and more challenging, the three- to four-day hike to **Boulder Lake** is recommended.

If you have time, an exploration of the pretty **Aorere River Valley** (Heaphy Track Road) is recommended. Beyond the pleasures of the drive itself, a stop at the river **gorge** at Salisbury Bridge (Quartz Range Road) and the old **Bainham Store** will both have the camera clicking. Access down to the river is possible, to the left just beyond Salisbury Bridge, while the Bainham Store is an original, store that has changed little in decades and is still open for business.

Farewell Spit → Colour map 4, A4

① Access on the spit is restricted so an organized tour is the only way to truly experience this weird and wonderful place. You can also book and join the Farewell Spit tour en route to the spit at the visitor centre, or see tour operators, page 468.

The spit is formed entirely from countless tons of sand ejected into the northerly ocean currents from the numerous river mouths scattered all the way up the west coast. It is a dynamic, almost desert-like landscape, with sparse vegetation struggling to take root in the dry and constantly shifting sand. The majority of the spit is a DoC nature reserve and the vast mud flats that it creates along its landward edge are one of New Zealand's most important wading-bird habitats. Over 100 species have been recorded around the spit, but it is the sheer numbers of each species that are most notable. Migrating flocks of godwit and knot can run well in to the thousands, providing a memorable sight. **Black swans** use the food-rich mud flats of Golden Bay, and when the tide is in they gracefully tread the water in huge flocks. There is also a small colony of rapacious **gannets** at the very end of the spit.

Both Cape Farewell and Farewell Spit were noted by Tasman in 1642 (no doubt a little shorter than it is now) and named by Cook when he left the shores of New Zealand in 1770. The lighthouse, at the very tip of the spit, was first erected in 1870. It has an interesting history and was replaced due to rotting timber.

The spit is a remarkable and memorable landscape if only for its powerful sense of isolation, but to see it from afar and from sea level is a strangely unremarkable experience. With its vast dune system, no more than 20 m in height, its sheer length and the omnipresent coastal haze, its very presence is, to say the least, muted. At best only a small grove of pine trees near its tip can be seen, like some tiny far off island. If you cannot afford to go out on the spit or simply want to get a better impression of its scale from afar, the best place to view it is from the elevated hills around the Pillar Point Light Beacon, accessed from Wharariki Road and Puponga.

At the base of the spit and just beyond the last small settlement of Puponga is the **Farewell Spit Visitor Centre and Paddlecrab Kitchen** ① T03-524 8454, daily 0900-1700 (seasonal). It stocks a range of informative leaflets and has a number of interesting displays surrounding the spit, its wildlife and the rather sad and repetitive whale strandings in Golden Bay. The café sells a range of refreshments and snacks and has a fine deck overlooking the bay and the spit itself. Most of the established walking tracks leave directly from the centre.

❝❞ Wharariki Beach is so beautiful you almost find yourself feeling a corrupting sense of guilt at leaving your lone footprints in the sand ...

Wharariki Beach

Wharariki Beach has to be one of the most beautiful beaches in the country. Perhaps it is its very remoteness that makes it so special, but add to that its classic features – including caves, arches and dunes – and you have near perfection. It is so beautiful you almost find yourself feeling a corrupting sense of guilt at leaving your lone footprints on its swathes of golden sand. You can access the beach by road from Puponga via Wharariki Road (20-minute walk) or make it the highlight on a longer and stunning coastal walk from **Pillar Point Lighthouse** (see Activities and tours, page 468). Note that swimming here on Wharariki Beach is very dangerous.

Pillar Point to Wharariki Beach coastal walk → *13 km, 6-8 hrs*

From **Puponga**, follow Wharariki Beach Road to the turn-off (right) up to **Pillar Point Light Beacon** ('Blinking Billy'). Note this is a rough non-signposted road. Park your vehicle at the base of the hill below the light beacon. Climb the hill to Pillar Point and enjoy your first proper view of Farewell Spit before heading further north towards the **Old Man Rock** (155 m) along the crest of the hill. Take in the views of the spit and Golden Bay before retracing your steps to Pillar Point. From Pillar Point follow the sporadic orange markers south through a small tract of manuka trees. From there follow the markers and the cliffs taking in all the cliff-top views to **Cape Farewell**. Keep your eyes peeled for fur seals, whose plaintive cries will probably reach the senses first. Continue south along the cliffs before descending to Wharariki Beach. If the tide is in your favour, walk its entire length and investigate the many caves and rock corridors along its length. Once at the base of **Pilch Point** (at the very end of all the beaches) retrace your steps to Pillar Point. Now *that* is a coastal walk!

Kahurangi National Park ⊜▲ ↠ *pp466-468.*

→ *Colour map 4, A3*

Opened in 1996, Kahurangi is New Zealand's second newest national park (Stewart Island was opened in 2001) and also the second largest, after Fiordland. It is a vast and remote landscape of rugged alpine ranges and river valleys, the most notable being the Heaphy, which meets, in part, the park's most famous tramping route, the Heaphy Track. One of the most interesting features of the park is its ancient geology. It contains some of the country's oldest rock landforms, with spectacular limestone caves, plateaux, arches and outcrops. Kahurangi is home to over half of New Zealand's native plant species (over 80% of all alpine species) and over 18 native bird species, including the New Zealand falcon, the great spotted kiwi and the huge New Zealand land snail.

The **Heaphy Track** is usually the visitor's first and only acquaintance with the park but the **Cobb Valley**, **Mount Arthur** and the **Tablelands** (accessed from the Cobb River Valley, 50 km south of Takaka and from the Flora car park, 30 km south of Motueka) offer some shorter walking options. The view from Mount Arthur (four hours, 8 km), which is accessed from Motueka, is particularly recommended.

● Whale strandings

Although science has yet to confirm the exact reason why whales become stranded, it is an undeniable and sad fact that the coastline of New Zealand is highly prone to this bizarre phenomenon. Almost every year, especially in summer, strandings occur around the country's coastline, with some bays like Keri Keri Bay in Northland, the Mahia Peninsula in the Hawke's Bay and, worst of all, Golden Bay in the Nelson Region being the most notorious. Without doubt it is the geography and enclosed nature of these locations that trap the pods of herding whales, led, it is thought, by just one sick or disorientated adult. Once in shallow tidal waters they quickly become confused then ground themselves, often with fatal results. Over the years the most common species affected have been pilot whales, but many other species in fewer numbers have also been stranded. For those species small enough to be physically moved, New Zealand has led the world in the delicate art of re-floating these mammoth, intelligent leviathans. At any given stranding, large numbers of volunteers from all walks of life turn up to help in accordance with strict protocols and a national program lead by DoC and the charitable organization Marine Watch based in Christchurch. Through 'peacetime' training, many Kiwis are now well-versed in how to deal effectively with the emergency. In essence the following takes place: while beached and out of the water, the whales must all be kept upright and wet. If the individual that initiated the stranding can be identified it is usually destroyed to prevent an almost inevitable re-stranding. Then, once the tides turn, they are gently rocked to 're-set' their balance, then re-floated in unison, sometimes on specially built pontoons. As you can imagine this takes considerable skill, logistics and organization. Sadly, despite the huge effort, most whales die, but there have been some major successes, sometimes with almost every whale being returned to the sea successfully. The biggest whale stranding in recent years occurred when a staggering 385 pilot whales stranded in Golden Bay in 1991. Only 15 died, the were rest successfully re-floated. To attend a whale stranding is an incredible experience both to witness its effect on people (bringing out both the best and the worst) and to sense the almost haunting presence of these intelligent creatures. For more information contact **DoC**, T0800-362468, or **Marine Watch** in Christchurch, T025-358909. If you encounter a stranded whale or dolphin or even a freshly dead carcass, contact DoC immediately, T0800-362468.

Marlborough & Nelson Golden Bay

Ins and outs

Getting there Transport to the various trailheads is available from Nelson, Motueka, Takaka, Collingwood and Karamea (west coast). **Kahurangi Bus,** Nelson, T0800-881188, T03-525 9434, www.kahurangi.co.nz, and **Abel Tasman Coachlines**, Nelson, T03-528 8805, www.abelttasmantravel.co.nz, and **Golden Bay Coachlines**, Takaka, T03-525 8352, www.goldenbaycoachlines.co.nz, are the main inter-town operators. **Golden Bay Coachlines** and **Trek Express**, Upper Moutere, T03-525 8352, www.trek express.co.nz, can get you to the various trailheads. **Wadsworth Motors,** T03 522 4248, wadsworthmotors@xtra.co.nz, runs from Nelson to the Whangapeka Track. **Karamea Express,** west coast/Karamea, T03-782 6617, serves the Heaphy from the south (west coast). The average fare from Takaka is $28 and from Karamea $12. **Abel Tasman Air**, Nelson, T03-528 8290, offers flights to Karamea and Takaka.

Heaphy Track

The approximate walking times are as follows – west to east:
Kohaihai River Mouth to Heaphy Hut: 16 ½ km, five hours
Heaphy Hut to Lewis Hut: 8 km, 2½ hours
Lewis Hut to Mackay Hut: 13 ½ km, 3½ hours
Mackay Hut to Saxon Hut: 14 km, three hours
Saxon Hut to Gouland Downs Hut: 5 km, 1½ hours
Gouland Downs Hut to Perry Saddle Hut: 8 km, two hours
Perry Saddle Hut to Brown Hut: 17 km, five hours

Getting around They say it takes a long time and many walks to acquaint yourself properly with Kahurangi and for many this is its main appeal. One of the best ways to see the park is from the sky (see Activities and tours, page 468). The eastern Heaphy Track trailhead is accessed via Collingwood (28 km) and Bainham (Aorere River Valley) at the end of the Heaphy Track Road. The route is signposted from Collingwood. The eastern trailhead is served daily (see Getting there, above) in summer and on demand in winter.

Tourist information The DoC field centres in Nelson (see page 437), Motueka (see page 452) and Takaka (see page 461) can provide detailed information on the park, including access, walking and tramping. On longer walks or tramps you are advised to go well prepared and, in summer, book the huts and passes ahead – especially on the popular Heaphy Track. The DoC administer hut tickets and bookings.

Heaphy Track

The Heaphy Track is one of New Zealand's most popular 'Great Walks' and the most popular tramp in the Kahurangi National Park. It is a relatively low-level tramp of 82 km taking four to six days. The Heaphy is named after Major Charles Heaphy, a noted soldier, who was the first to traverse the coastal portion of the modern track in 1846. Although not famed for its mountainous vistas, the track does provide a wide range of interesting habitats and a superb coastal section. It is also noted for being 'open' for much of its length, offering a fine sense of space and wilderness. **Flannigan's Corner** (915 m), near Mount Perry (880 m), is the highest point on the track and provides memorable views. The Heaphy is usually negotiated from west to east. The western trailhead starts about 15 km north of Karamea, while the eastern, starts 28 km south of Collingwood. Take plenty of insect repellent with you.

Sleeping

Takaka *p461*
The VIC has a full list of B&Bs and homestays, most of which are near the beaches at Pohara.
LL-L Bay Vista, Pohara, T03-525 9772, www.bayvistahouse.co.nz. A single-storey, spacious and modern B&B with 2 doubles and a de luxe en suite with private lounge.
L-D The Nook Guesthouse, 8 km from Pohara on Abel Tasman Drive, T03-525 8501/ T0800-806665, www.thenookguesthouse .co.nz. Comfortable, self-contained doubles in a straw-bale cottage, or guesthouse doubles,

twins, shared rooms and tent sites.
Free bike hire, cosy log fire, organic produce.
AL Mohua Motels, Willow St, T03-525 7222, www.mohuamotels.co.nz. The newest motel in town located next to the VIC.
AL-A A1 Rose Cottage Motel and B&B, 5 km south of Takaka, Hamama Rd, T03-525 9048. Offers a 3 unit motel and a cute 2-bedroom B&B in a country setting.
A Anatoki Lodge Motel, 87 Commercial St, T0800-262333/T03-525 8047, www.anatoki motels.co.nz. Modern facilities and well located.

B Sans Souci Inn, Richmond Rd, Pohara, T03- 525 8663, www.sanssouciinn.co.nz. A mud- brick Mediterranean style establishment with lovely bedrooms and a great licensed in-house restaurant.

B-D Annie's Nirvana Lodge, 25 Motupipi St, T03-525 8766, T0800-266937, www.nirvana lodge.co.nz. Well-established and cosy backpacker lodge. Full range of rooms, spa pool, bike hire and internet.

B-D Barefoot Backpackers, 114 Commercial St, T0508-525700/T03-525 7005, www.barefoot.co.nz. Offers free trips to the Pupu Springs, has a spa and terrific homemade bread.

B-D Get Away Backpackers, 28 Motupipi St (just opposite Annie's), T03-525 6261, T0800-801 1120. Another alternative in a spacious, well-kept suburban house with caring owners, bikes and internet.

C-D River Inn, Waitapu Rd, at the other end of town, T03-525 9425, www.riverinn.co.nz. Closest to the Pupu Springs, a century-old pub-style place. Has a wide range of rooms and cheap singles. Kayak hire, free bike hire, Sky TV and internet.

Motorcamps
B-D Pohara Beach Top Ten Holiday Park and Motels, Abel Tasman Drive, Pohara, T03-525 9500, www.pohara.com/paradise. The best motorcamp with tent, powered sites, modern timber kitchen cabins and full facilities all next to the beach.

Collingwood *p462*
LL Collingwood Homestead B&B, Elizabeth St, in Collingwood itself, T03-524 8079, www.collingwoodhomestead.co.nz. It gets the vote as the best B&B in the entire region. Recommended.

A Skara Brae B&B and Motels, Elizabeth St, T03-524 8464, www.accommodation collingwood.co.nz. Quiet and peaceful, garden setting.

C-D Innlet and Cottages, Main Rd, Pakawau, on the road to Farewell Spit, T03-524 8040, www.goldenbayindex.co.nz/theinnlet. Oozes character and is in a lovely bush setting offering dorms, twins and doubles and 2 charming self-contained cottages that sleep 3-6. The owners are friendly, dedicated long-term residents. Bike hire available and excellent harbour/rainforest kayak trips, guided or self-guided from $45-85. Internet.

C-D Somerset House Backpackers, Gibbs Rd (signposted off the main road in the village), T03-524 8624, www.backpackers collingwood.co.nz. Top-quality 16-bed place with good facilities, including internet, kayak and bike hire, a very congenial deck overlooking the village. There is also hopelessly affectionate cat called 'Somerset' for the homesick. Recommended.

Motorcamps
B-D Collingwood Motor Camp, in the centre of the village at the end of William St, T03-524 8149. Unremarkable self-contained cabins, basic cabins and sites.

Heaphy Track *p466*
The 7 huts along the track are supplied with bunks, heating, water (must be boiled) and toilets. Hut passes are $20 in peak season (Oct-May), $10 non-peak. Note a pass does not guarantee a bunk. Camping is $10/$7. For more information and bookings contact DoC or the major VICs. You can also book direct with DoC greatwalksbooking@doc.govt.nz.

● Eating

Takaka *p461*
❡❡ **The Brigand Café Bar**, 90 Commercial St, T03-525 9636, daily from 1000. A good choice with an imaginative menu and pleasant outdoor eating area. Local mussels a speciality.

❡❡ **Dangerous Kitchen**, 48 Commercial St, T03-525 8686, daily 1000-late. Fine pizza.

❡❡ **Sans Souci**, Richmond Rd, Pohara, T03-525 8663. A pleasant mud-brick Mediterranean Inn with a reputable licensed restaurant, open for lunch and dinner (seasonal).

❡❡ **Wholemeal Café**, Commercial St, T03-525 9426, www.wholemealcafe.co.nz, daily 0730-late. A bit of an institution in Takaka and the main haunt for the locals. It has good coffee, breakfasts, health-conscious blackboard menu and excellent service.

❡ **Bencarri Farm** (south off SH60), T03-525 8261, daily 1000-late. For a café experience surrounded by a veritable menagerie.

Collingwood *p462*
❡❡ **Collingwood Tavern**, Tasman St, T03-524 8160. Serves pub/bistro style food.

¶¶ **Mussel Inn Bush Café**, Onekaka, half way between Takaka and Collingwood on SH60, T03-525 9241, www.musselinn.co.nz, 1100-late. Good pub grub, great value mussels, the best beer around and a toilet to remember.

¶ **Courthouse Café**, corner of Gibbs and Elizabeth sts, T03-524 8025, daily 0830-late (seasonal). The best bet in Collingwood.

¶ **Paddlecrab Kitchen**, at the very end of the road at Farewell Spit, T03-524 8454, daily 0900-1730 (seasonal). Hosts a good café with a basic blackboard menu.

▲ Activities and tours

Takaka p461
Barefoot Guided Tours, 114 Commercial St, Takaka, T03-524 8624, www.bare-foot.co.nz. For local, regional or national park guided tours from $40-200.
Bencarri Farm, T03-525 8261, www.bencarri.co.nz. Eel farm, see page 462.
Golden Bay Kayaks, Pohara, Golden Bay, T03-525 9095, www.goldenbaykayaks.co.nz. Popular operator with trips in both the Abel Tasman National Park and Golden Bay region from $60. Independent hire from $30-80.

Collingwood p462
Kahurangi Guided Walks, T03-525 7177, www.kahurangiwalks.co.nz. Offers guided half-, full- and muti-day trips from $50. 3-day Boulder Lake for $180; 5-day Wangapeka Track from $1000.

Tours to Farewell Spit
Farewell Spit Tours, 6 Tasman St, T03-524 8257, T0800-808257, www.farewellspit.com. This is, as the name suggests, the original tour operator and has been taking people out on to the spit for over 60 years.

The most popular tour is the 'Lighthouse Safari' which is a 4½-hr excursion to the end of the spit and the lighthouse. Transportation takes the form of robust but comfortable RL Bedford trucks. You will meet the spit's wildlife (which can include the occasional bleary-eyed fur seal) and allowed stops to take in the special atmosphere of the spit, before arriving at the lighthouse. There you can climb it to see the rather unremarkable view from the top, before learning a little of its interesting history over a welcome cup of tea. This tour costs a very reasonable $80, child $45.

The 'Gannet Colony Eco Tour' (6½ hrs, $110, child $50) is an extended trip that takes in the above and the gannet colony at the very end of the spit (this company are the only operators with the DoC concession to get up close).

The 'Cape Farewell Eco Tour' (6 hrs) is basically the same trip as the Lighthouse Safari with a diversion to the dramatic cliffs at Cape Farewell, the most northerly point of the South Island, from $95, child $50.

The 'Wader Watch Safari' (3-4 hrs, $80) is a specialist and fascinating trip to see the wading birds on the spit often numbering into the thousands. Although most suited to birdwatchers and somewhat seasonal (summer only), it would be of considerable interest to any nature lover, especially given the limited access to the spit.

Wharariki Beach p464
Cape Farewell Horse Treks, Puponga, T03-524 8031, www.horsetreksnz.com. Some of the most scenic routes in the region. 1 hr to overnight, from $45. Recommended.

Kahurangi National Park p464
Guided walks
Barefoot Guided Tours, also in Motueka, T0508-525700, www.bare-foot.co.nz.
Kahurangi Guided Walks, Takaka, T03-525 7177, www.kahurangiwalks.co.nz.

Rock climbing
Vertical Limits, Nelson, T03-545 7511, www.verticallimits.com. Offers some excellent rock climbing trips to Kahurangi, from $130.

Scenic flights
Tasman Bay Air Nelson, T03-528 8290. Flights across the bare mountaintops and remote valleys. A truly memorable experience.

⊖ Transport

Takaka p461
Bicycle hire The Quiet Revolution, 7 Commercial St, T03-525 9555. From $25 per day. They also offer local tours from $35.

❶ Directory

Takaka p461
Internet GBnet, 4 Commercial St, Gazebo Backpackers, 7 Haiwatha Lane.

⠿ Footprint features

Introduction

Whichever way you arrive in Canterbury, by air or by road, the Canterbury Plains dominate, giving an impression of flatness. And yet, despite appearances, much of Canterbury is mountainous and home to New Zealand's highest peak, Aoraki, or Mount Cook (3754 m). Canterbury is the largest region in the South Island, extending from the Pacific Ocean and the Canterbury Plains in the east to the Great Divide and Southern Alps to the west, and from the Marlborough Mountains and Kaikoura Ranges in the north, to the braided Waitaki River in the south.

Central Canterbury is the hub of the South Island and its capital, Christchurch, is the country's second largest city. Dubbed 'The Garden City', it also claims the title of New Zealand's favourite city, although it lacks the architecture and the remarkable friendliness of Dunedin. North Canterbury is home to the South Island's 'little piece of Rotorua' in the form of the Hanmer Springs thermal resort, providing just one of the good reasons to stop en route to the west coast via the beautiful Lewis Pass. Along with Arthur's Pass to the south, these form the region's two main portals from the east coast to the west and are also the focus for skiers in winter.

In South Canterbury the pleasant coastal port of Timaru provides a starting point from where to head west, via Fairlie and Burke's Pass to the MacKenzie Country. Here you will find the region's most stunning and diverse scenery, culminating in Pukaki Lake and Mount Cook Village.

★ Don't miss ...

1 **Christchurch** Go punting on the Avon River and stop by the Arts Centre in New Zealand's 'Garden City', page 476.

2 **Port Hills** Take a gondola to the crater rim then mountain bike back down, page 482.

3 **Hot air ballooning** Float gracefully over the Canterbury Plains at dawn, page 489.

4 **Akaroa** Explore the Banks Peninsula and find the French connection', page 494.

5 **Kaikoura Coast** Get acquainted with the oceans 'Who's Who', page 499.

6 **Hanmer** Enjoy a soak in the hot pools, page 498.

7 **Mount Hutt** Pass through some beautiful scenery en route to the ski fields, page 511.

8 **Arthur's Pass** Head to the west coast on one of the world's most scenic train journeys, page 512.

9 **Waimate** Try a wallaby pie with plum sauce, page 520.

10 **Lake Tekapo** Go star gazing, page 524.

11 **Twizel** Try to spot one of the rares: birds in the world (the black stilt), page 525.

12 **Aoraki (Mount Cook)** Take an unforgettable scenic flight around the glaciers, page 533.

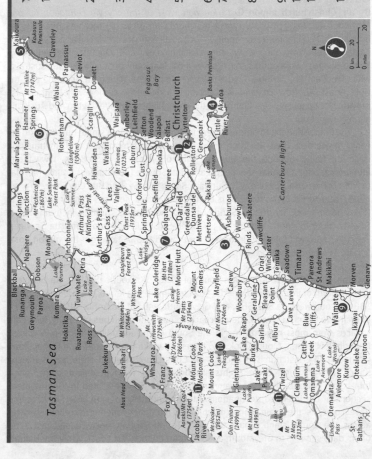

Christchurch → *Colour map 5, A/B6 Population: 350,000*

Dubbed 'The Garden City', Christchurch is known as being the most English of New Zealand's cities. Reminders of these roots are everywhere from the formal blazers and straw hats of the city's school children to the punts on the river and the distant chorus of 'howzatt' from its myriad cricket pitches on lazy summer Sunday afternoons. Without doubt the key to its charm is the immense, tree-lined Hagley Park that borders its centre and has over the decades remained remarkably intact. With the park, its trees and the pretty Avon River that threads it all together, the aesthetics of Christchurch verge on the adorable. But natural aesthetics and its obvious English colonial feel aside, Christchurch has developed its own very Kiwi-orientated atmosphere. It has the buzz and vitality of Auckland, the cosmopolitan 'town' feel of Wellington and it shares a pride in its heritage and architecture that only Dunedin can beat. ▸▸ For Sleeping, Eating and other listings, see pages 482-491.

Ins and outs

Getting there

By air Christchurch airport ① *12 km northwest of the city via Fendalton Rd and Memorial Av, T03-358 5029, www.christchurch-airport.co.nz,* receives direct flights from Australia, Singapore and Japan, as well as all national provincial airports. **Air New Zealand,** T0800-737000, www.airnewzealand.co.nz, and **Qantas,** T03-379 6504/ T0800-808767, www.qantas.co.nz, cover most long-haul destinations and Australia; while **Freedom Air,** T0800-600500, www.freedom.co.nz, flies from Brisbane and the Gold Coast. **Air New Zealand** is the principal domestic carrier with **Qantas,** also providing regional services. Combined they offer flights from Wellington and Auckland almost every hour.

The international and domestic terminals are located in a single building and are easily negotiated. There are information centres in both terminals, and city transport is to be found outside the building. **Metro buses,** T03-366 8855, www.metro info.org.nz, offer a regular service to Cathedral Square (20 minutes) hourly, Monday to Friday 0600-2300, Saturday to Sunday 0800-2300, $7. **Red Bus City Flyer,** T03-379 4260/T0800-733287, www.redbus.co.nz, also offers services hourly Monday to Friday 0600-2300, Saturday to Sunday 0730-2230. Various shuttles, including **Super Shuttle** (door to door), T03-357 9950/T0800-SHUTTLE, or **Airport Shuttle Services,** T03-356 3286, will take you into town for around $18. A taxi from the airport costs $35-40. ▸▸ *See Transport, page 491.*

By road Christchurch is 336 km south of Picton (Kaikoura 183 km) via SH1; and 579 km north of Invercargill (Dunedin 362 km/Timaru 163 km) on SH1. Queenstown is 486 km southwest via SH1/SH8, and Greymouth, 258 km via Arthur's Pass and SH73. **Intercity,** T03-365 1113, www.intercitycoach.co.nz, is the main bus company, with daily services from most major towns in the South Island including Picton (5½ hours), Dunedin (six hours), Mount Cook (5½ hours), Wanaka (nine hours) and Queenstown (10 hours). In Christchurch its agent is the **Christchurch Travel Centre,** 123 Worcester Street, T03-377 0951. **Great Sights,** T0800-744487, www.greatsights.co.nz, offers tour-based options. There are many smaller shuttle services listed in 'Getting there' sections of the intended destinations. **Atomic Shuttles,** T03-322 8883, www.atomic travel.co.nz, is the main Christchurch-based company offering excellent services across the South Island. **Coast to Coast,** T0800-800847, www.coast2coast.co.nz, offers daily services to Greymouth and Westport on the west coast; while the **Hanmer**

Shuttle, T03-366 4556, www.hanmerbus.co.nz, offers a daily service to Hanmer Springs. **The Cook Connection,** T0800-266526, www.cookconnect.co.nz, offers a daily shuttle between Tekapo, Mount Cook and Oamaru. It links with the Wanaka/ Queenstown **Intercity,** and **Atomic** services. For special deals, including the Intercity **Travelpass** which offers a combination of train, ferry and coach travel, see the Getting around section of Essentials, page 37.

Most coach companies including Newmans and Atomic Shuttles stop in or around cathedral Square. Check specific drop off or pick-up points with each company. The VIC (I-Site) has full details on national bus travel and can make bookings on your behalf. Typical return prices are: Dunedin $45, Queenstown $65, Invercargill $65, Tekapo $45, Kaikoura $29, Picton $50, and Greymouth $48.

By train Christchurch's **train station** ① *Addington St, 3 km from the city centre at the southwestern tip of Hagley Park*, is the departure point for two of New Zealand's major railway journeys. **TranzScenic,** T0800-872467, www.tranzscenic.co.nz, operates the northbound 'TranzCoastal' service (departs 0730; to Kaikoura- Blenheim-Picton, $40-100); and the deservingly popular 'TranzAlpine' (departs 0815; to Greymouth $116). For details and fares get the 'times and fares' booklet from the train station or the VIC (I-Site). The **Travelpass** offers a combination of train, ferry and coach travel (see Essentials, page 39). A shuttle from the station to the centre costs from $10; taxi $15.

Related map A Around Cathedral Square, page 477.

	Chateau on the Park **5** *B1*	Milano Motor Lodge **13** *A2*	Vagabond Backpackers
	City Centre Motel **21** *A2*	Occidental	**30** *B3*
	Colombo in the City **8** *A2*	Backpackers **28** *B3*	Weston House **24** *A2*
	Copthorne	Old Countryhouse **29** *B3*	
Sleeping	Commodore **12** *A2*	Otahuna Lodge **15** *B1*	**Eating**
Aalton Motel **1** *B1*	Dorset House **25** *A2*	Peppers Clearwater	Alexander Lawrence
Adelphi Motel **2** *A2*	Eliza's Manor **22** *A2*	Resort **17** *A2*	at Charlotte Jane
Airport Christchurch	Elm Tree House **16** *A2*	Strathern Motor Lodge **7** *A2*	Hotel **3** *A2*
Motel **14** *A2*	Foley Towers **26** *B3*	Stonehurst Apartments	Mainstreet Café **4** *A2*
Amber Park **18** *C1*	Frauenreisehaus **27** *B3*	& Backpackers **23** *B3*	Mona Vale Homestead **1** *A1*
Apollo Motel **9** *B1*	Hambledon **6** *A2*	Sudima Grand	Morworth Estate Vineyard
Avalon Motel **3** *A3*	Holiday Inn **19** *A3*	Chancellor **11** *A2*	**5** *B1*
Avenue Motor Lodge **20** *A2*	Meadow Park Top	Tuscana Motor	Sign of the Takahe **2** *C2*
Bella Vista **4** *A3*	Ten Holiday Park **10** *A2*	Lodge **22** *A2*	Tiffany's **6** *B3*

Christchurch is best explored on foot or by public transport. If you do have a car, note that the one-way road system can be confusing, and although there are plenty of parking lots and meters they are almost as tightly patrolled as Auckland and Wellington. An hour in the city centre will cost about $4. You can park for free south of Moorhouse Avenue (the Old Train Station and Hoyts 8 Cinema) and catch the free shuttle from there. Being so flat the city provides easy cycling. ▸▸ *For bike, motorcycle and car hire, see Transport, page 491.*

Christchurch has an excellent public bus system with a modern terminal, the **Bus Exchange** ① *corner of Lichfield and Colombo sts*. For all bus information contact To3-366 8855, www.metroinfo.org.nz, Monday to Friday 0630-2230, Sunday 0900-2100, or **Red Buses**, To800-733287, www.redbus.co.nz. The buses run on a two-zone system; Zone 1 costs $2.50; Zone 2 costs from $2.90. Monthly passes and **Metrocards** (electronic top-up cards from $10 minimum) are available and you can purchase cash fares from the driver as you board the bus. The electrified **Free Yellow Shuttle** takes in a north-south route from the casino, through Cathedral Square and down Colombo Street and back, every 10-15 minutes (Monday to Friday 0730-2230, Saturday 0800-2230, Sunday 1000-2000). It's worth jumping on to get your bearings.

The **Best Attractions Shuttle** To800-484485, takes in the main city attractions including the Antarctic Centre and the Gondola, departing Cathedral Square, daily 0900-1800. A day pass will cost around $15.

The **Midnight Express**, offers late selected night services to the outer suburbs departing on the hour from 0100-0500 from Oxford Terrace, $5. For shuttle services to Lyttleton and Akaroa see the Bank's Peninsula section, page 492.

Between 1905 and 1954 Christchurch had a thriving **tram system** ① *To3-366 7830, trams operate Apr-Oct 0900-1800 and Nov-Mar 0900-2100, from $12.50.* There is also a restaurant car that hosts a daily dining tour, To3-366 7511, www.tram.co.nz. Since 1995 the beautifully restored trams now follow a 2½-km loop around central Christchurch, passing various sights of interest on the way (commentary provided). The trams can be boarded at many stops including Cathedral Square.

Tourist information

Christchurch VIC (I-Site) ① *Old Post Office Building, Cathedral Sq (West), To3-379 9629, www.christchurchnz.net, www.christchurchinformation.co.nz, www.localeye.co.nz, daily Mon-Fri 0830-1700, Sat-Sun 0830-1600.* There are also VICs (I-Sites) in the international (To3-353 7783/4) and domestic (To3-353 7774/5) airport terminals.

There is a wealth of free material including the useful *Today and Tonight/ Christchurch and Canterbury*, which is a must. There are also numerous city attractions and 'drive' maps including the *Top Attractions, A Guide to Christchurch's City Centre; The Avon River Drive; The Garden Drive; The Antarctic Heritage Trail; Wine Trail;* and *Arts Trail* maps. The daily paper in the Central South Island is the *Christchurch Press*.

DoC ① *133 Victoria St, To3-371 3706, www.doc.govt.co.nz, Mon-Fri 0830-1630*, can provide local, regional and South Island walks and tramping information.

Maps For negotiating the CBD get hold of the *Christchurch Mini-map*. The major bookshops (see Shopping page 488) also stock Christchurch city map books, and **Mapworld** ① *corner of Manchester and Gloucester sts, To3-374 5399, www.map world.co.nz*, is an excellent source of city, town, provincial and national maps. See Tourist information, below, for details of free sightseeing maps.

Background

Given Christchurch's strong and outwardly obvious English links, it is perhaps ironic that the first European settlers on the Canterbury Plains were in fact Scottish. Although having originally emigrated separately to Nelson and Wellington in 1840 and 1842 in search of better living conditions, brothers William and John Deans arrived on the plains and established themselves on land the local Maori called *Putaringamotu* in 1843, calling it Riccarton after their home town in Central Scotland. Five years later the New Zealand government made a contentious land deal with the local Maori purchasing about eight million ha of land for – it would seem – little more than 'two sticks and a balloon', which paved the way for more concerted settlement.

In 1849 a prestigious 53-member organization called the Canterbury Association was founded by Irishman Robert Godley. Comprising two Archbishops (of Canterbury and Armagh), seven bishops, 14 peers, and other notables, mainly from Godley's old university college of Christchurch, in Oxford, its aim was to establish a new utopian Anglican settlement in the new colony of New Zealand. The site of this new settlement was chosen by the association's surveyor, Captain Joseph Banks, who, presumably after seeing the Deans brothers' prize 'neeps' and 'tatties' (turnips and potatoes), saw the obvious potential of the rich alluvial plains for agriculture.

In 1850 the 'first four ships' – *Charlotte Jane*, *Randolph*, *Sir George Seymour*, and *Cressy* brought 782 colonial souls to the then whaling base of Lyttleton, which had already been established on the Banks Peninsula. Even before their arrival, the Canterbury Association had already christened the great settlement-to-be, Christchurch. But perhaps, human nature being what it is, it seems little of either Christ or the church prevailed and bitter wrangling between members quickly led to the Association's disintegration in 1855 and the end of the great Anglican settlement plan.

Despite these hiccups the new colony flourished and today its roots are obvious. One only need look at the trees and cricket pitches in Hagley Park, the gardens, the street names and the punting on the river, the public school boys skipping out of Christ's College in blazers and straw hats, to realize how much of its founding English influence prevails. Indeed, in Christchurch, to be in the slightest way related to anyone on 'the first four ships' is, 'darling', to belong to the city's elite. As for the Deans boys, William drowned in 1851 on a journey to Australia to buy sheep, and John died in the cottage three years later after contracting tuberculosis.

City centre

The heart of Christchurch lies just to the west of **Hagley Park**, with **Cathedral Square** being the focus. The borders of the city centre are known as the 'Four Avenues': **Deans Avenue**, which borders the western fringe of Hagley Park, **Moorhouse Avenue** to the south, **Fitzgerald Avenue** to the east and **Bealey Avenue** to the north. One of the most attractive features of the city is the **Avon River**, which winds its way through Hagley Park and the city centre from west to east. The city is essentially flat and has a basic grid system of streets extending in all directions from Cathedral Square, with the north/south **Colombo Street** being the main shopping street. The city centre is easily negotiable by foot using the cathedral and high-rises around Cathedral Square as a reference point.

Within the **'Four Avenues'**, and easily negotiated on foot, are a number of sights and attractions that easily take up one day. Ask at the VIC (I-Site) about the **Super Pass**, which can combine entry to a number of major venues from $69, child $29.

Dominated by the Gothic-revival Anglican **Christ Church Cathedral** ① *T03-366 0046, 1-hr tours Mon-Fri 1100 and 1400, Sat 1100, Sun 1130, free*, Cathedral Square is considered the heart of the city and its main focus point, but it is not without contention. An on-going and expensive redevelopment of the square since the late 1990s has resulted in most Cantabrians feeling the development is an aesthetic disaster and a crass waste of money. Certainly, it does seem hopelessly out of character with the rest of Christchurch, with its sharp angles and dull façades of steel and concrete. And once again it seems to suffer from the scourge of the average New Zealand architect – a severe disregard for trees. However, current aesthetics aside, the main feature worth looking at in the square is of course the cathedral itself. It houses a number of interesting memorials and boasts an interior design that is an interesting and eclectic mix of Maori and European. The spire can be climbed in part, offering a panoramic and memorable view of the city. There is also an audio-visual presentation and a good café attached.

The square is also home to two notable characters: one permanent, made of bronze, a memorial and pleasantly quiet; the other now semi-retired, wearing a cloak, a pointy hat and that never stops talking. The former is the statue of **John Robert Godley**, the founder of the Canterbury Association and essentially Christchurch itself; the latter is the **Wizard**, a local eccentric who has been 'entertaining' the masses with his views on life, the universe and just about everything contentious for decades. As a wizard he apparently travels without a passport and has been known to get through customs, presumably for the sake of some peace and quiet. Perhaps to afford the good citizens of Christchurch a break (or perhaps for his own sanity) The Wizard is rumoured to have headed south to Timaru, but occasionally, just occasionally he returns to his old haunt in the old hat, no doubt berating the very concept of the great young impostor, Harry Potter.

Also in the square is the '**Four Ships Court**', a memorial to the 'first four ships' which stands outside the 1879 **Old Post Office** (which now houses the Christchurch VIC). Accessed through the VIC (I-Site) is the **Southern Encounter Aquarium and Kiwi House** ① *T03-359 0581, www.southernencounter.co.nz, daily 0900-1630, from $14, child $5; trout and salmon feeding 1300, marine tank dive and feeding 1500*, which seems remarkably out of place but is still worth a look, housing an interesting collection of local sea creatures and the obligatory kiwi exhibit.

Avon River

Heading west from Cathedral Square you immediately encounter (and not for the first time) the pretty Avon River. This is one of the city's greatest assets. The river meanders like a snake from the northwest tip of the 'four avenues' through Hagley Park and the Botanical Gardens, through the city centre, before finally continuing its journey through the city's eastern suburbs to the sea. The river is particularly attractive in autumn when poplar and weeping willows are radiant in golden hues. It offers some lovely inner-city walks, which are outlined in the free *River Walks of Christchurch* available from the VIC (I-Site). The *Avon River Drive* is another alternative. On the eastern bank of the river, just beyond Cathedral Square and beside the Worcester Street Bridge, is a base for **punting** ① *T03-379 9629, daily 0900-2100, winter 1000-1600, 30 mins, $18, child $9*, on the river. Note also the 1917 statue of **Scott of the Antarctic** beside the river – a reminder that Christchurch is a principal gateway to the Antarctic.

● Although the Wizard has officially retired, he still puts in the odd appearance in the
● Square between November and March. If he is in evidence make sure you also see his car!
For an argument or more information visit his website, www.wizard.gen.nz.

Arts centres

Across the bridge and on the right, further up Worcester Street, is the **Christchurch Art Gallery (Te Puna O Waiwhetu)** ① T03-941 7300, www.christchurchartgallery.org.nz, daily 1000-1700 (Wed 2100), free with a charge for major exhibitions. Immediately christened by some cynics as 'a warehouse in a tutu' it is actually supposed to be 'evoking the sinuous form of the koru and the River Avon that flows through Christchurch'. With over 3000 sq m of exhibition space, it is over four times the size of the Robert McDougall Gallery that for years struggled to showcase its formidable 5500 permanent works. So whether you see it as a tutu or as an impressive edifice from the outside is up to you, but what cannot be denied is the quality of its content. Many of the famous New Zealand artists are represented including Charles Goldie, Colin McCahon

Around Cathedral Square

N

0 metres 100
0 yards 100

Sleeping 🛏
Christchurch City YHA **1** B3
Copthorne **6** A2
Croydon House **2** B2
George & Pescatore
  Restaurant **8** A1
Heritage & OGB
  Restaurant **3** B3
Hotel off the Square **13** B3

Metro Suites **10** A3
Millennium & Piko
  Piko Restaurant **4** B3
Orari **5** B1
Rolleston House YHA **7** B1
Thomas's **11** C1
Windsor B&B **9** B1

Eating 🍴
Annie's Wine Bar **2** C1
Bon Bolli **3** B1
Boulevard Bakehouse **4** B1
Café Metro **5** A3
Caffe Roma **6** B2
Casino **25** A2
Coyote Street Bar **7** C2

Curator's House &
  Café **31** C1
Dux de Lux **9** C1
Hay's **10** A2
Il Felice **11** C3
Java **12** C3
Le Café **13** B1
Little India Bistro
  & Tandoori **14** B3
Oxford on Avon **16** A3
Palazzo del Marinaio **17** C2
Passport to Asia **29** C3
Retour **21** A3
Sala Sala Japanese **8** B2
Santorini **18** B2
Strawberry Fare **19** A3

Tandoori Palace **28** B3
Tap Room Bar **1** C2
Thai Smile **20** A3
Thai Tasty **30** B3
Yellow Rocket
  Bagel & Coffee
  Company **15** B2

Bars & clubs 🍸
Bailies **22** B3
Bard **23** B2
Bog **24** C2
Jolly Poacher **26** A2
Loaded Hog **27** C3

478 and Ralph Hotere, but there is also an emphasis on contemporary works and a dynamic schedule of national and international exhibitions. There is a quality retail outlet that specializes in contemporary art and crafts and the obligatory café/bistro.

The **Centre for Contemporary Art** ① *66 Gloucester St, T03-366 7261, www.co ca.org.nz, Tue-Fri 1000-1700, Sat-Sun 1200-1600, free*, is also worth visiting. There are five galleries and over 50 exhibitions per annum; much of the art is for sale.

Nearby, **The Arts Centre** ① *2 Worcester Boulevard, T03-366 0989, www.artscen tre.org.nz, tours daily from 1030-1530*, was once the site of the original University of Canterbury. The old Gothic revival buildings now house an excellent and dynamic array of arts and crafts, workshops, galleries and sales outlets, as well as theatres, cinemas, cafés, restaurants and bars. It is well worth a visit, particularly at the weekend when it hosts a lively arts and crafts market. It becomes very much the focus of attention for tourists with an international food fair and top local entertainment, from a local town crier to city buskers. There are also some notable historical features including the 'Den' of scientist Ernest Rutherford (see box, page 441), the Great Hall with its stained-glass windows and the Townsend Observatory with its working telescope. Free guided tours are available and depart from the information centre in the clocktower foyer and for the best coffee go to the **Backstage Bakery** in the heart of the complex behind the Court Theatre. The free *What's on at The Arts Centre* and *Christchurch City Arts Trail* booklets are very useful.

Hagley Park

At the western edge of The Arts Centre, Worcester Street meets Rolleston Avenue and the eastern fringe of Hagley Park. Amazingly intact after all the years of development, Hagley Park (over 200 ha) is divided in two portions by Riccarton Avenue and comprises pleasant tree-lined walkways, sports fields and, in its central reaches, the **Botanical Gardens** ① *0700-dusk, Conservatory Complex 1015-1600*, enclosed by a loop of the Avon River. Well maintained and with a huge variety of gardens from 'herb' to 'rose', these provide a great escape from the buzz of the city year round. Autumn sees the gardens at their most colourful. There is a small **information centre and café** ① *T03-941 7590, daily Sep-Apr Mon-Fri 0900-1600, Sat-Sun 1000-1400*, housed in the old Curators House off Rolleston Avenue near the Peacock Fountain, which showcases the social and natural history of the gardens.

At the entrance to the Botanical Gardens on Rolleston Avenue is the **Canterbury Museum** ① *T03-366 5000 www.cantmus.govt.nz, daily 0900-1730 (winter 1700), general entry is free but there are charges for the Exhibition Court and Discovery Centre ($2); guided tours are also available.* Housed in a grand 1870 neo-Gothic building and founded in 1867, it is well worth a visit, the undoubted highlights being its impressive Maori collection and the Hall of Antarctic Discovery. In keeping with other museums in the country, it also hosts a dynamic Discovery Centre for kids and big kids alike. The Exhibition Court displays a changing programme of travelling national and international exhibitions. There is also a fine in-house shop and a café overlooking the Botanical Gardens.

Just north of the museum is **Christ College Canterbury** ① *for information about guided tours in summer, T03-379 5570*, which is without doubt New Zealand's most famous historic school. Built in 1850 it is an aesthetic and architectural delight, and in the late afternoon spills forth suitably clad and 'proper' scholars.

At the southern end of Rolleston Avenue are the **Antigua Boat Sheds**, which were built in 1882, making them one of the oldest buildings in Christchurch. The former boat-builders' premises now host a café and are the base for **Punting in the Park**, ① *T03-366 0337 www.punting.co.nz, 30-min punting trips daily 1000-dusk, from $16.50*. You can also hire canoes, paddleboats and rowing boats ① *T03-366 5885, 0930-1730 (winter 1600)*.

Canterbury Brewery

① *Near the junction of Riccarton and Hagley Avs (Hagley Park), 36 St Asnholt St* *To 3 379 4940. Tours and tastings Mon-Thu, from $12, bookings essential.*

Founded in 1854, its long established 'CD' (Canterbury Draught) is something of a libatious institution in the Canterbury Region. The brewery has a good museum and tours are available.

City North and West

Mona Vale

① *Just beyond the northwest corner of the 'Four Avenues' at 63 Fendalton Rd, To3-348 9660, May-Sep Wed-Sun 1000-1530, Oct-Apr 1000-1900.*

Heading out towards the airport is Mona Vale, a beautiful Elizabethan-style homestead and gardens, built in 1905 on the land first settled by the Scots Dean brothers in 1843. While the Homestead itself is now a fine restaurant and café, the 5½-ha grounds are a spectacular array of features including a lily pond, rhododendrons, azaleas and exotic trees, all set in reverence to the lovely River Avon. The gardens can be reached by punt, and guided tours are available. Phone for details.

International Antarctic Centre and Hagglund Ride

① *At the airport (signposted), Orchard Rd, To3-353 7798, www.iceberg.co.nz, daily Oct-Mar 0900-2000, Apr-Sep 0900-1730; from $30, child $20. Guided tours are available from officers who have lived and worked on the ice or you can self-guide with the help of 'snow-phones' ($6). A combo visitor centre/ride costs $48, child $36. The city-airport bus (from Cathedral Sq) stops here and runs every 30 mins.*

Since the turn of the 20th century and the days of Scott and Shackleton, Christchurch has been a principal 'gateway to the Antarctic'. Today, the Antarctic Centre is a working campus and formidable array of buildings. In its entirety, it is home to **Antarctica New Zealand** (managers of New Zealand's activities in the Antarctic), the **Antarctic Heritage Trust**, the US and Italian Antarctic programmes, the **International Centre for Antarctic Information and Research**, and the Antarctic passenger terminal and aircraft hangers, where you can often see the Hercules that head off into the wild blue and very cold yonder. The **visitor centre**, which was opened in 1992, is an excellent introduction to the great white continent and a place from which would-be world travellers will emerge dreaming. Overall it is both informative and fun, with an excellent array of displays from the historical to the modern-day.

One of the first displays you will encounter are the current Antarctic weather statistics, which send a shiver down your spine and your hands plunging into your pockets. Then, to get an even better idea of the real thing, you can don jackets and overshoes and enter the **Snow and Ice Experience**, a room kept at -5°C, replete with manufactured snow and ice. The **Antarctic Storm** room promises to take you into 'another world of wind and extreme cold'; visitors must attempt to endure an indoor blizzard replete with howling wind, plummeting temperatures and a general sense of severe meteorological extremes. Naturally, if you are from warmer climes this is a new and fascinating experience, but if you are from the UK it is just liking popping out for a pint of milk. Once back to normal temperatures, you can sit in a comfy seat and be treated to a superb audio-visual presentation, which beautifully marries images from the ice with inspiring music.

The latest attraction at the Antarctic Centre is the **Penguin Encounter** a small group of mainly rehabilitated and permanently disabled little blue penguins – a species that is, ironically, far more at home around the golden beaches of Australasia than the icebergs of Antarctica. From the displays you then emerge into the well and unusually stocked Antarctic shop and the **South Café and Bar**.

⋮ The road to Edoras

For *Lord of the Rings* fans or indeed anyone who wants to see some classic Southern Alpine scenery, then the trip to **Mount Sunday** (Potts Station) in the Rangitata Valley is a great day out. Mount Sunday, which sits predominantly in the Rangitata River Valley and in stark contrast against the mountainous skyline of Southern Alps, became the perfect filming location and set for Edoras and King Theoden's grand hall in *The Two Towers*, the second film in the *Lord of the Rings* trilogy. From Mount Somers take the road west through the Ashburton Gorge towards Hakatere and **Lakes Camp and Clearwater**. At Hakatere the road splits (turn left). From here the countryside opens up in to the wide tussock valley giving an almost surreal sense of space. The lakes and their scattering of holiday baches are favourite haunts for windsurfers and waterskiers. Keep heading west towards the end of the valley. There, at the western edge of the Mount Harper Range (Harpers Knob), is a sudden and dramatic view down in to the Rangitata Valley and in the far distance, the prominent outcrop known as Mount Sunday (611 m). In geological terms Mount Sunday is known as a 'roche moutone', which roughly translated means a low, round hill shaped by a glacier. It was

(apparently) named 'Mount Sunday' by high country station boundary riders who used to meet there on Sundays. As you get ever nearer you can see why it was the perfect film location and although nothing remains of the set itself, it still has plenty of impact. The best place for photos is just past the Mount Potts Station or looking back down the valley as the road climbs the hill towards the Erewhon Station.

If you don't have your own transport you can join a day or multi-day tour with **Hassle-free Holidays**, T03-379 6377/T0800-427753, www.hasslefree.co.nz, and **Tussock and Beach Tours**, T03-303 0880, www.nature.net.nz, both based in Christchurch, (see Activities and tours, page 490) or, if you are feeling flush, even charter a light aircraft and fly in to the valley and the airstrip at Mount Potts. Mid-range accommodation is available at **Mount Potts Alpine Lodge**, T03-303 9060, www.mtpotts.co.nz.

Travel notes The road is unsealed from Hakatere, 24 km from Erewhon. The last petrol stop station on the journey is the **Mount Somers Store**, T03-303 9831, open daily till 1800. For breakdown assistance call **Methven Motor Services**, T03-302 8201. There is no cell phone coverage west of Mount Somers.

In addition to the centre's indoor activities is the **Antarctic Hagglund Ride**. The Hagglund is a tracked vehicle that was originally used by the USA and New Zealand Antarctic programmes in Scott and McMurdo bases. During the 45-minute ride you are taken to see some of the major facilities of the centre before experiencing the all-terrain abilities of the vehicle on a man-made adventure course. The centre also forms part of the interesting **'Antarctic Heritage Trail'** (free leaflet from the VIC/I-Site). Note that the Canterbury Museum (see page 478) also hosts an excellent Antarctic display.

Orana Wildlife Park and the Willowbank Wildlife Reserve

While out in the vicinity of the airport it is worth visiting one (or preferably both) of Christchurch's main wildlife attractions. **Orana Park** ① *743 McLeans Island Rd (10 mins from the airport)*, T03-359 7109, www.oranawildlifepark.co.nz, *daily 1000-1700, from $19, child $7*, is New Zealand's largest captive wildlife reserve, set in 80 ha of parkland. It has a good mix of native and international wildlife with an emphasis on African animals, All the usual suspects are there from the lofty giraffes and horny rhinos to the ever-popular, inquisitive meerkats. And, of course, amongst the many New Zealand natives you will find a nocturnal kiwi house.

Also near the airport (five minutes' drive), is the **Willowbank Wildlife Reserve** ① *60 Hussey Rd (off Gardiners Rd), T03-359 6226, www.willowbank.co.nz, daily 1000-2200, $20, child $10; for transport, book at the city VIC (I-Site) or T0800-484485*, which focuses on native wildlife and farm animals. There are daily guided tours ($2) and kiwi viewing is available by day or at night. The reserve has a very successful kiwi-breeding programme and you can also see the cheeky kea (mountain parrots) being fed.

The reserve is also base for the **Ko Tane Maori Experience** ① *daily at 1730, 1830 (1830 winter), $36, child $20 (performance only); $45, child $22.50 (performance and tour), $85, child $36.50 (performance and hangi)*, a well-regarded performance that includes the traditional 'Powhiri' (welcome), song and dance, an interactive tour of a Maori village, a wildlife tour and of course the obligatory and indulgent *hangi* (feast). *Hangis* aside, there is a good restaurant offering buffet dinners from 1830 to 2030, from $54, including a guided walk.

Riccarton Bush and Riccarton House (Putaringamotu)

① *3½ km west of the city centre on the banks of the Avon River, the main entrance to the reserve is at 16 Kahu Rd, T03-341 1018, www.riccartonhouse.co.nz. Deans cottage is open daily, the homestead is open Mon-Fri 1300-1600. Tours Sun-Fri at 1400, $10.*
Set in 12 ha of parkland, the historic Riccarton Estate was once the home of the Scots pioneers and brothers William and John Deans (the first European settlers on the Canterbury Plains). It features the faithfully restored and furnished original 1843 **Deans cottage** in which they first lived, and the grand Victorian/Edwardian **homestead** that was built by the next generation from 1856-1874. Within the house, which has been restored and redecorated in period style, you will find the detailed brochure *The Story of Riccarton House* which gives more details about the family and the lives they led. There is a café on site.

The Nga Hau E Wha Marae

① *T03-388 7685, www.nationalmarae.co.nz, daily, free. Evening performance and hangi 1845-2115, from $75, book ahead; tour only 1845-2000, from $30, child $19, includes transport from the city. To get there from the city, take Hereford St (northeast), turn right into Linwood Av then left into Buckleys Rd, continue through to 250 Pages Rd.*
The Nga Hau E Wha Marae or 'Marae of the Four Winds' is the country's largest *marae*. The meeting house (Whare Nui) is beautifully constructed and comes complete with greenstone (*pounamu*) inlaid steps (which should be rubbed for good luck). Guided tours provide an introduction to Maori culture, protocol, history and tradition. You can also extend your visit and stay to experience the evening performance and *hangi* (feast).

City East

East of the city centre the River Avon negotiates suburbia before emptying its contents into the Pacific. There is a **wildlife reserve** on the estuary that offers good birdwatching, opportunities for short walks and a number of fine beaches. **New Brighton** is the main focus of activity, with beachside cafés and a pier that attracts hopeful anglers. New Brighton can be reached from the centre of the city, via Cashel Street, then Buckleys Pages Road (8 km). South of the estuary via Ferry Rd (SH74) is the coastal resort of **Sumner** (12 km) which also has some fine beaches with safe swimming and plenty of cafés. The scenic drive to **Lyttleton** and the **Lyttleton Harbour** from Sumner (Evans Pass Road) is recommended.

City South

Airforce World

① *On the old RNZAF base at Wingram, Main South Rd (15 mins southwest), T03-343 9532, www.airforcemuseum.co.nz, daily 1000-1700, $15, child $5.*

If vintage aircraft are your thing then Airforce World will appeal. It has an impressive collection of 28 classic aircraft including a Spitfire and a Skyhawk. All of the aircraft have been faithfully restored and are theatrically displayed alongside special sections on the Second World War and the role of the modern-day RNZAF. It is worthy of a visit even if you are not a plane buff, and there is the added attraction of free flight simulators. Guided tours are available and there is a café on site.

Science Alive

① *392 Moorhouse Av (Old Train Station), T03-365 5199, www.sciencealive.co.nz. Sun-Thu 1000-1700, Fri-Sat 1000-1800, all-day pass from $12, child $8.*

Although the Discovery Centre in the museum, the Antarctic Centre and wildlife parks are all obvious draws for kids, the Science Alive centre is a great wet weather attraction. It is very much a hands-on place that could even see your kids waiting outside for you.

Christchurch (Port Hills) Gondola

① *T03-384 0700, www.gondola.co.nz, daily 1000-2130, $22, child $10. The Best Attractions Shuttle Bus leaves from the visitor centre at 1000, 1400 and 1600 ($8 all-day pass) or the No 28 bus from the Bus Exchange, from $2.*

If only for the stunning views, the Christchurch Gondola is well worth the trip. The base terminal is in the Heathcote Valley 10 km southeast of the city via Ferry Road. From there gondolas whisk you 945 m to the top of the Port Hills (1500 m) and the Summit Complex. The complex has all the expected shops and a café but also offers viewpoints from which you can gaze down to Lyttleton and across the Banks Peninsula. Northwards, the view across the city is equally stunning, and on a clear day, beyond the Canterbury Plains, is the distant line of the Southern Alps. You can embark on a number of walks from the complex that explore the crater rim, including the Bridle Path which was once used by the early pioneers as the main route to Lyttleton. An attractive way of descending is by mountain bike (see page 490).

On the way or coming back from the gondola you might like to stop off at the **Ferrymead Historic Park** ① *in the suburb of Ferrymead (Ferrymead Park Dr), T03-384 1970, www.ferrymead.org.nz, daily 1000-1630, $6, child $3 ($12/5 at weekends when trams are operating).* It's an entertaining mock-1920s' Edwardian township and a working museum with a wide array of period memorabilia including transport displays, Clydesdale horse-drawn carts and a working bakery. Trams and trains operate at weekends.

● Sleeping

As you would expect, Christchurch has plenty of accommodation catering for all tastes and budgets. Almost all the national chain hotels are in evidence in the city centre, with the majority being located in or around Victoria and Cathedral Sq. A few independent boutique-style options surround Hagley Park and overlook the River Avon. Likewise there are many B&Bs both in the city centre and a little further out, with some set in historic and spacious villas. There are literally dozens of motels, offering affordable prices, within walking distance of the city; many are northwest of the city centre along Papanui Rd and Bealey Av west (to SH1), or on Riccarton Rd heading south. Hostels abound in the city centre, from the small purpose-built, or old hotel/pub-style to the large and modern. All the motorparks are on the city fringes in all directions, but mainly close to SH1 north and south. Overall you will find prices above average for the South Island, but winter can see a drop in rates and some very reasonable deals, especially with the many competing hotels. Since Christchurch is the starting point for so many South Island travellers you are advised to pre-book in mid summer.

City centre *p475, maps p473 and p477*
LL The George Hotel, 50 Park Terr, T03-371 0256, www.thegeorge.com. Overlooking the river and handy for the Arts Centre, The George has a solid reputation with excellent, well-appointed suites, facilities and award-winning cuisine.
LL Heritage Hotel, Cathedral Sq, T03-377 9722, www.heritagehotels.co.nz. Modern, well appointed with good facilities, this is perhaps the best of the chain hotels. The restaurant and bar is popular with non-clients due to the ideal location.
LL Weston House, 62 Park Terr, T03-366 0234, www.westonhouse.co.nz. This listed neo-Georgian mansion offers luxurious suites and elegant surroundings opposite Hagley Park and the Avon River. Private guest entrance, very helpful, friendly hosts and a legendary breakfast.
LL-L Copthorne Hotel, corner of Kilmore and Durham sts, T03-365 4699/T0800-342522, www.milleniumhotels.com. A large, high-profile chain hotel conveniently located on the fringe of the CBD, alongside the Avon River and opposite the casino. Renovated rooms with standard facilities and city views.
LL-AL Hotel off the Square, 115 Worcester St, T03-374 9980, www.offthesquare.co.nz. Central and modern but a pleasant change from the standard chain hotels. Labelled as 'highly individual' with 'new-age modernism' it offers a variety of classy, character rooms from standard (yet far from it) to 'superior loft apartments', all generously adorned with contemporary art. The city trams pass through the entrance level, which adds that memorable and quintessential Christchurch touch. Recommended.
LL-AL Millennium Hotel, Cathedral Sq, T03-365 1111/T0800-227006, www.millennium hotels.co.nz. Central, modern and well

appointed with all the usual facilities. The popular restaurant is open to non-clients.
L-AL Metro Suites, above the Metro Café, corner of Kilmore and Colombo sts, T03-366 4067, www.metrosuites.co.nz. For sheer convenience these 2 stylish suites are recommended. One has a historic theme complete with claw footbath, the other has a modern minimalist feel. A light breakfast in the café downstairs is included.
L-AL Orari, 42 Gloucester St, T03-365 6569, www.orari.net.nz. Smaller, slightly cheaper with modern decor and close to the Arts Centre. Rooms have a private bathroom.
L-A City Centre Motel, 876 Colombo St T03-372 9294, www.citycentremotel.co.nz.
AL Chateau on the Park, 189 Deans Av, T03-348 8999, www.chateau-park.co.nz. Near the river and retaining that 'Garden City' feel at the northwestern edge of Hagley Park. A little further from the action but that is part of its appeal. Its gardens – complete with vineyard – are excellent and the restaurant and bar have a nice cosy atmosphere.
AL Holiday Inn, 356 Oxford Terr, T03-379 1180, www.holidayinnchristchurch.nz-hotels.com. Right next to the Avon River. Small, discreet and good value.
AL Windsor B&B Hotel, 52 Armagh St, T03-366 1503, www.windsorhotel.co.nz. A good-value B&B in the heart of the city. Although nothing remarkable, the century-old 2-storey house provides some character and the trams that pass right by the property.
AL-A Colombo in the City, 863 Colombo St, T03-366 8775, www.colombointhecity.co.nz. Convenient for the town centre.
AL-A Croydon House, 63 Armagh St, T03-366 5111, www.croydon.co.nz. A fine choice, friendly and well located. Rooms are en suite. It's a pleasant spot for watching the trams rattle past outside. Good breakfast.
A Stonehurst Apartments, 241 Gloucester St, T0508-786633/T03-379 4620, www.stonehurst.co.nz.

Backpacker hostels
B-D Stonehurst Backpackers, 241 Gloucester St, Latimer Sq, T0508-786633/ T03-379 4620, www.stonehurst.co.nz.

Without doubt one of the best backpacker hostel in the city, with the added appeal of a modern motel annexe and campervan facilities. It is centrally located and has just about everything: a wide range of good single, double, twin and dorm rooms (some are self-contained and en suite), clean facilities, a pool, pizza bar, internet, travel shop and off-street parking. It is deservedly popular so book in advance.

C Christchurch City YHA, 273 Manchester St, T03-379 9535, www.yha.org.nz. The more modern of the 2 YHA options. It is purpose-built, well located and spacious with all the usual facilities and services. Limited off-street parking is available.

C Foley Towers, 208 Kilmore St, T03-366 9720, foley.towers@backpack.co.nz. Has a great range of rooms and facilities, internet. Friendly and peaceful.

C-D Occidental Backpackers, 208 Manchester St, T03-379 9284, freebreakfast@occidental.co.nz. Pub/hotel-style lodging. A little tired but has clean, comfortable single, double, twin and dorm rooms and a lively and popular bar downstairs and great-value meals. It's definitely a social place.

C-D Old Countryhouse, 437 Gloucester St, T03-381 5504, www.oldcountryhousenz.com. 2 renovated well-equipped villas, similar in style, with doubles and shared rooms. Internet, off-street parking. Recommended.

C-D Rolleston House YHA, 5 Worcester Blvd, across the road from the Arts Centre, T03-366 6564, www.yha.org.nz. A little tired but still popular and has a good atmosphere.

C-D Thomas's Hotel, 36 Hereford St, T03-379 9536, www.thomashotel.co.nz. Ideally located (on the other side of the Arts Centre), well-equipped and spotless. Ideal for couples looking for a good-value double and some peace and quiet, but perhaps lacking atmosphere if you are alone.

C-D Vagabond Backpackers, 232 Worcester St, T03-379 9677, vagabondbackpackers@hotmail.com. Very tidy, peaceful and friendly with off-street parking.

Motorcamps and campsites

B-D Stonehurst Backpackers, see above. The only establishment in the city centre catering for campervans offering a small number of powered sites with full amenities.

City North and West *p479*

LL Elm Tree House, 236 Papanui Rd, Merivale, T03-355 9731, www.elmtreehouse.co.nz. Further out and quieter location. Characterful 1920s colonial-style homestead with 6 luxury suites and fine cuisine. Recommended.

LL Hambledon, 103 Bealey Av, T03-379 0723, www.hambledon.co.nz. A large and well-appointed 1856 mansion with 4 lovely luxury rooms (with bath), 1 self-contained apartment, 3 self-contained historic cottages (close to Hambeldon), a large collection of antiques and a peaceful garden.

LL Peppers Clearwater Resort Hotel, Clearwater Av, Harewood, T03-360 1009, www.peppers.co.nz. Home to the popular (and highly aquatic) Bob Charles 72-hole championship golf course. The hotel provides luxury lakeside villas and suites, spas and a quality restaurant. Discount B&B or golfing packages are often available.

LL-L Eliza's Manor on Bealey, 82 Bealey Av, T03-366 8584, www.themanor.co.nz. A vast, historic, well-appointed mansion with 12 rooms, 10 of which are en suite. The wooden façades and staircase of the ground floor are superb and the open fire gives a lovely atmosphere. Off-street parking.

LL-AL Copthorne Hotel Commodore, at the end of Memorial Av, 5 mins from the airport and the Antarctic Centre, T03-358 8129, www.commodore.net.nz. Set in 3 ha of land with award-winning gardens.

L-AL Sudima Hotel Grand Chancellor, end of Memorial Av, 700 m from airport, T03-358 3139, www.sudimahotel.co.nz. Comfortable and convenient for that early morning flight or late night arrival.

B-D Dorset House, 1 Dorset St, T/F03-366 8268, www.dorsethouse.co.nz. A historic, friendly place pitched somewhere between a backpacker hostel and a B&B, with good doubles, twins and singles. It also has Sky TV, wireless internet and provides pick-ups.

Motels

L-A Airport Christchurch Motel, 55 Roydvale Av, T0800-800631/T03-977 4970, www.airportchristchurch.co.nz.

AL-A Avenue Motor Lunch, 136 Bealey Av, T03-366 0582, www.avenuemotorlodge.co.nz. Standard facilities.

AL-A Bella Vista, 193 Bealey Av, T03-377 3363, www.bellavistamotel.co.nz.

AL-A Milano Motor Lodge, 67 Papanui Rd, T0800-878766/T03-3552800, www.milanomotorlodge.co.nz.

AL-A Strathern Motor Lodge, 54 Papanui Rd, T03-355 4411, www.strathern.co.nz.

AL-A Tuscana Motor Lodge, 74 Bealey Av, T03-377 4485, www.tuscana.co.nz.

A Adelphi Motel, 49 Papanui Rd, T03-355 6037, www.adelphimotel.co.nz.

A Avalon Motel, 301 Bealey Av, T03-379 9681, www.avalonmote.co.nz. Near the centre. Standard facilities.

Motorcamps and campsites

A-D Meadow Park Top Ten Holiday Park, 39 Meadow St (off Papanui Rd at the northwestern end of the city), T03-352 9176, www.meadowpark.co.nz. Has a great range of options from self- contained motels, lodges and flats to chalets, cottages and standard cabins, powered/tent sites. That said, you pay more for its location and the facilities, which include a spa pool, sauna and weight training room. Keep your eyes peeled for the sign off Papanui Rd – it is quite hard to spot.

B-D Amber Park, 308 Blenheim Rd, southwest of the city centre , T03-348 3327, www.amberpark.co.nz. Older but tidy, it offers flats, cabins, powered/tent sites in a quiet garden setting.

City East p481

D Frauenreisehaus, 272 Barbadoes St, T03-366 2585. Bohemian, health-promoting backpackers for women only. It prides itself in offering beds not bunks and has internet.

City South p482

LL Otahuna Lodge, RD2, Rhodes Rd, Tai Tapu (30 km), T03-329 6333, www.ota huna.co.nz. A characterful historic homestead with 7 immaculate luxury suites and a day spa, all set amidst spectacular century-old gardens. There is also a horse-trekking operation on site.

AL-A Apollo Motel, 288 Riccarton Rd, T03-348 8786, www.apollomotel.co.nz.

A Aalton Motel, 19 Riccarton Rd, T03-348 6700, www.aalton.co.nz. Central.

● Eating

While Christchurch can't quite match Auckland, Wellington or Queenstown in its range of fine eateries, it is by no means wanting. Generally you will find a wide range of options to suit all budgets. Most of the modern eateries are to be found along the trendy 'Strip' overlooking the river from Oxford Terr. This is a fine place for lunch and is very convenient for the city centre. Colombo St and Manchester St also offer a wide choice.

Note Christchurch has 3 rather unique dining options. For the romantic couple, you can arrive at the **Retour Restaurant** by punt. Other unusual options include the **Tramway Restaurant** and the **Willowbank Wildlife Reserve**, see below.

City centre *p475, maps p473 and p477*
A number of the better restaurants are within hotels, including **Pescatore** in the George; **The Piko Piko** in The Millennium; or the **O.G.B** in the Heritage, all are growing in popularity (see Sleeping, above).

₸₸₸ The Alexander Lawrence Restaurant, Charlotte Jane Hotel, 110 Papanui Rd, T03-355 1028, www.charlotte-jane.co.nz. Offers an intimate and congenial atmosphere with the added attraction of outdoor seating with an open fire.

₸₸₸ Bon Bolli, corner of Worcester and Montreal sts, T03-374 9444. A good French option, rather too modern in aesthetics, but more than makes up for it with the cuisine.

₸₸₸ Mona Vale Homestead, 63 Fendalton Rd, T03-348 9660. The daytime menu (0930-1530) offers the best chance to appreciate the surroundings, but it is also open for dinner.

₸₸₸ Pescatore in the George, T03-371 0278. An award-winning hotel option (see page 483) offering fine Pacific Rim cuisine in a very pleasant setting.

₸₸₸ Retour Restaurant, in the rotunda, corner of Cambridge Terr and Manchester St, T03-365 2888, lunch Wed-Fri 1130-1400, dinner daily from 1730 (Apr-Sep closed Mon). A great romantic option, it is very unusual aesthetically, offering a fine imaginative, mainly NZ menu and, most importantly perhaps, can be reached by punt from the city centre. To book a punt, see Avon River page 476 or Hagley Park, page 478.

¶¶ Annie's Wine Bar and Restaurant, corner Rolleston Av and Hereford St, T03-365 0566, daily from 1100-2300. Good for light lunches and has a good wine list.

¶¶ Coyote Street Bar and Restaurant, 126 Oxford Terr, T03-366 6055. Imaginative Kiwi/Mexican combos, from seafood to pasta. Vegetarians should try the 'Tortilla Twosome'.

¶¶ Dux de Lux, 41 Hereford St, T03-366 6919. A Christchurch institution, perhaps the best thing is its position on the fringe of the Arts Centre complex. It is busiest at the weekend when the markets are in full swing, but remains popular well after dark. Attracting a mixed crowd, a lively atmosphere is virtually guaranteed and there is a fine choice of beer.

¶¶ Hay's, 63 Victoria St, T03-379 7501, Tue-Sat from 1700 and Mon evenings in summer. Great New Zealand Lamb.

¶¶ Il Felice, 56 Lichfield St, T03-366 7535, Mon-Sat from 1800. Recommended Italian.

¶¶ The Little India Bistro and Tandoori, corner of Gloucester and New Regent sts, T03-377 7997, Mon-Fri for lunch from 1200 and daily for dinner from 1700.

¶¶ Palazzo del Marinaio, 108 Hereford St, T03-365 4640, daily for lunch and dinner. For seafood it would be rude not to mention this Italian-style restaurant. Try the 'Piatto combo'.

¶¶ The Sala Sala Japanese Restaurant, 184 Oxford Terr, T03-366 6755, daily from 1730 and Mon-Fri 1200-1400 for lunch.

¶¶ Santorini, corner of Gloucester St and Cambridge Terr, T03-379 6975. A good and very colourful Greek option with live entertainment most nights.

¶¶ Strawberry Fare Restaurant, 114 Peterborough St, T03-365 4897, Mon-Fri 0700-late, Sat-Sun 0900-late. Lovers of weight-gaining and creative desserts should throw caution to the wind here.

¶¶ Tandoori Palace 56 Cathedral Sq, T03-365 7816, www.tandooripalace.co.nz, Mon-Fri 1130-1700 for lunch and daily for dinner from 1700.

¶¶ Tap Room Bar and Restaurant, 124 Oxford Terr, T03-365 0547, breakfast, lunch and dinner. One of the best and most popular.

¶¶ Thai Smile, 818 Colombo St, T03-366 2246. Any Thai restaurant that proclaims that 'your satisfaction is our happiness' and is one of only 3 in New Zealand to be awarded the Thai Government's very own 'Thai cuisine to the World' award surely has to be tried.

¶¶ Tiffany's Restaurant, 95 Oxford Terr, T03-379 1350. A great choice for NZ cuisine.

¶¶ Tramway Restaurant, T03-366 7511, www.tram.co.nz. An unusual and romantic dining option. In the evening you can join the popular dining tour that adds a very pleasant convivial edge to the usual sightseeing trip.

¶ Casino, Victoria St (see Entertainment, page 488). Has several good-value eateries.

¶ The Oxford on Avon, 794 Colombo St, T03-379 7148. A Christchurch institution offering huge, great-value lunch and dinner from $18, or set-price meals, from 0700.

¶ Passport to Asia, 266 High St. Cheap no-nonsense Asian fare.

¶ Thai Tasty, in the Gloucester Arcade, 129 Gloucester St, T03-3797540, daily until 2200.

City North and West p479

¶¶ Willowbank Wildlife Reserve, on the city fringe, T03-359 6226 (see page 480). A unique dining option encompassing a heavy emphasis on Kiwi culture and nature. Dine next to a variety of tame native animals.

City South p482

¶¶¶ The Sign of the Takahe, 200 Hackthorne Rd, in the Port Hills (south via Colombo St then straight up Dyers Pass Rd), T03-332 4052, www.signofthetakahe.co.nz, daily from 1000. Historic country house and restaurant with award-winning cuisine. The views are better than anything in the city. Bookings essential.

¶¶ Morworth Estate Vineyard, Broadfield (7 km southwest via Main South Rd, left on Hampton's Rd, then right on Block Rd), T03-349 5014, www.morworth.com, Wed-Sun 1000-1700. A great restaurant/café providing a pleasant escape from the city.

Cafés

Boulevard Bakehouse, below the Arts Centre, T03-377 2162, daily 0800-2400. Popular, especially at lunchtime.

Café Metro, corner of Colombo and Kilmore sts, T03-374 4242. Has a loyal following and a good atmosphere.

Caffe Roma, 176 Oxford Terr, T03-379 3879. Very popular breakfast/brunch hangout, especially at the weekend.

Curator's House Restaurant and Café, 7 Rolleston Av, at the edge of the Botanical Gardens, T03-379 2252, www.curators.com,

daily 1000-late. Local cuisine with a Spanish touch. Excellent tapas, very pleasant.
Java, corner of High and Lichfield sts, T03-366 0195. Funky and a popular hangout with the younger and more alternative crowd.
Le Café, Arts Centre, Worcester St, T03-366 7722, Sun-Thu 0700-2400, Fri-Sat open 24 hrs. Based in the heart of the city, this is a popular hangout for both locals and tourists. It is especially popular at the weekends when the colourful markets and street performers provide an added attraction to the permanent arts and craft outlets, architecture, theatre and cinema. There is an extensive menu of traditional Kiwi fare; brunch is a speciality.
Mainstreet Café, corner of Colombo and Salisbury sts, T03-365 0421, daily 1000-late. Generous and imaginative vegetarian dishes.
The Yellow Rocket Bagel and Coffee Company, southwest corner of Cathedral Sq, T03-365 6061, daily from 0900. Although not one of the city's most celebrated cafés, the Yellow Rocket, tucked in the corner of Cathedral Sq and next door to the 1879 Old Post Office building (which now houses the VIC), is a very pleasant option in a fine location. It's is a great place to escape the traffic and watch the tourist world go by, particularly in fine weather. Here you can muse over your various information centre leaflets and plan your sightseeing agenda with a choice of sweet or savoury bagels and a fine cup of coffee.

❶ Pubs, bars and clubs

Christchurch p472 maps p473 and p477
Pubs and bars
Christchurch's main drinking venue is a conglomerate of modern, well-appointed and lively restaurant/bars on Oxford Terr or 'The Strip'. It is a good spot to be both in the evening and more especially during the day, when you can sup a bottle or glass of your favourite libation while watching the world (and the river) go by. Most pubs/bars stay open to at least 2300 with some on 'The Strip' remaining open at weekends until 0230.
Bailies, Cathedral Sq, T03-366 5159. Older and more spacious than many of the pubs.
The Bard, corner of Oxford and Gloucester sts, T03-377 1493. An old English favourite.

The Bog, across the road from the **Tap Room**, at the top of Cashel Mall, T03-379 7141. Will satisfy the Irish pub fans.
Dux de Lux, in the Arts Centre, corner of Hereford and Montreal sts, T03-366 6919, daily from 1100, particularly popular at weekends. A spacious long-established pub with an old English feel. It attracts a daytime clientele as well as night revellers. Also has a microbrewery on site producing a range of potent beers, and regular live music.
Jolly Poacher, Victoria St (opposite the casino), T03-379 5635. Another English-style venue with a good atmosphere and range of traditional and import beers.
Loaded Hog, corner of Manchester and Cashel sts, T03-366 6674. A mainstream chain venue. It may not be to everyone's taste but popular nonetheless and a good place to meet locals and other travellers.
Tap Room Bar and Restaurant, 124 Oxford Terr, T03-365 0547. Currently the most popular place, serving the full range of South Island brews and also serves great food.

Clubs
For listings of local gigs and visiting acts consult *The Press* newspaper. The website www.bethere.org.nz can also be useful. There are plenty of pubs hosting live music, especially at weekends, and overall there is a lively and modern dance/club scene in the city centre. The best bet, if you can stand all the mobile phones, is to gather with the city slickers in the pre-club pubs along 'The Strip' on Oxford Terr, then just tag along. Many of the late-night clubs are on Lichfield St.
Base, 92 Struthers Lane, T03-377 7149. Good venue for base and house.
Illusions, corner of Chancery Lane and Gloucester St. The best bet for 'trendy-phobics', with disco classics from the 1960s and 1980s.
Ministry, 88-90 Lichfield St. Popular and large dance venue.

❷ Entertainment

Christchurch p472, maps p473 and p477
For performance and cinema listings consult *The Press* newspaper. The free leaflet *The Package* available from the VIC (I-Site) is also useful, www.thepackage.co.nz.

Christchurch Casino, 30 Victoria St, T03-365 9999. A well-established institution and naturally a popular entertainment venue. Even if you do not get lured to the 'pokies', roulette and card tables, it can be a fascinating place to watch the desperate, cool or ecstatic go by. There are also various bars and good-value food outlets. Dress code is smart casual, the minimum age limit is 20, and it is open 24 hrs. The free yellow shuttle stops right outside, T0800-227466.

Cinema

The following are mainstream cinemas.
Cinema 3 Hornby, Hornby Mall, T03-349 2365.
Hoyts, 392 Moorhouse Av (Old Train Station), T03-366 3791.
Hoyts 6, Northlands Mall, T03-366 6367.
Regent on Worcester Cinemas, 94 Worcester St, T03-366 0140.
Rialto Level 1, 250 Moorhouse Av, T03-374 9404.

Theatre

If you missed out on the Maori performances and *hangis* (feasts) in the North Island, Christchurch provides one of the few opportunities in the South Island (see Willowbank Wildlife Reserve, page 480). A good source of information for performance dates and venues is www.artists.co.nz/concerts.html.
The Arts Centre, Worcester Blvd, is home to the **Court Theatre**, T03-963 0870, www.courttheatre.org.nz; the **University Free Theatre**, T03-374 5483; the **Southern Ballet and Dance Theatre**, T03-379 7219; and the **Academy Cinema**, T03-366 0167. There is a dynamic programme of events year-round listed at the information centre, T03-363 2836, www.artscentre.org.nz. The 'Friday Lunchtime Concert Series' featuring local, national and international musicians is held in the **Great Hall of the Arts Centre**, 1310, $8.
Theatre Royal, 145 Gloucester St, T03-363 3311/T0800-474697, www.isaactheatre royale.co.nz. The other major events venue featuring everything from rock to jazz.
Town Hall, 86 Kilmore St, T03-377 8899, www.nccnz.co.nz. Includes the in-house James Hay Theatre.

✿ Festivals and events

Christchurch *p472, maps p473 and p477*
For details on events have a look at the useful website www.bethere.org.nz and www.christchurchnz.net.

The 'Summertimes' programme, www.summertimes.org.nz, includes summer theatre and retro events, twilight concerts and even a teddy bears picnic. The culminating outdoor **Motors Classical Sparks** in Mar is the highlight, with a classical concert and fireworks in Hagley Park.

National and international rugby **Super Twelve** and **Tri-Nations** (Mar-Oct) and Test matches at Christchurch's Jade Stadium in the south of the city is a top spot and still wet with the tears of British Lions supporters after the tour of 2005.
Jan World Busker's Festival (15-24), www.worldbuskersfestival.com. A lively event attracting artists of all shapes and sizes.
Feb Coast to Coast (6-7), www.coastto coast.co.nz, a classic South Island event with a gruelling combination of running, kayaking and cycling to the west coast. **Festival of Romance**, dancing and jazz in Victoria Sq. **International Garden City Festival of Flowers**, www.festivalofflowers .co.nz, over 30 events from garden tours to floral carpet displays. This event coincides with the **Jade Wine and Food Festival**, a celebration of local produce held in Hagley Park.
Mar Festival of Asia A day of Asian celebration at The Arts Centre. **Le Race**, www.lerace.co.nz, South Island's largest cycling event.
Jul Kidsfest (3-16), www.kidsfest.org.nz. This is an annual fun festival of events, workshops and performances for children.
Jul/Aug Christchurch Arts Festival, www.artsfestival.co.nz. Includes theatre, dance, classical and jazz concerts, cabaret and exhibitions of the visual arts.

○ Shopping

Christchurch *p472, maps p473 and p477*
Arts, crafts and souvenirs
There is a rash of souvenir shops in and around Cathedral Sq selling everything from furry kiwis in rugby shirts to sheepskin slippers. **The Arts Centre**, Worcester Blvd, is an excellent place to pick up arts and crafts,

as is the weekend market. Rugby shirts are always a great buy in New Zealand and Christchurch is home to Canterbury Clothing Company (CCC), Westfield Shopping Town, Riccarton, T03-348 0144. The best label to buy. You can find a wide selection here and at **Champions of the World**, outlets at 767 Colombo St, T03-377 4100.

Bookshops and maps
Whitcoulls and **Dymocks** are in the Cashel Street Mall, just south of Cathedral Sq. **Mapworld**, corner of Manchester and Gloucester sts, T03-374 5399, www.mapworld.co.nz. **Scorpios**, 79 Hereford St, T03-379 2882. An excellent modern independent store. **Smiths Bookshop**, 133 Manchester St, T03-379 7976, www.smiths.bookshop.co.nz. A good second-hand bookshop in a mult-storey building.

Outdoor and camping equipment
Mountain Designs, 91 Cashel St, T03-377 8522.
Snowgum, 637 Colombo St, T03-365 4336.

Second-hand shops
Toffs, 141 Gloucester St, just off Cathedral Sq. An innocuous looking place that gives no indication of the marvels inside. The perfect place for shopa-phobics with all manner of second-hand clothing and accessories, from snow chains and Nikon photo jackets to Armani business shirts and silk ties. The challenge: try going in there for less than 20-mins and coming out empty handed. Quite an experience.

▲ Activities and tours

Christchurch *p472, maps p473 and p477*
There is a huge range of tours operating out of Christchurch, encompassing everything from sightseeing, activity combos, wineries, gardens, walking and motorcycling. The VIC (I-Site) has brochures and full listings.
Adventure Canterbury, T03-358 5991/T0800-847455, www.adventurecanterbury.com. One of the main activity operators in Christchurch. It offers a wide array of trips and activities including jet boating on the Waimakariri (2-2½ hrs, $75-110), horse trekking (2½-3½

hrs, $75-95), fishing (5-6 hrs $715); farm visits (3-4 hrs, $70, with lunch $110); winery tours half-day including 20 tastings, from $110. Day trips to Hanmer and Akaroa from $160.

Bone carving
The Bone Dude, 229B Fitzgerald Av, T03-379 7530, thebonedude@hotmail.com. A carving studio where you can carve your own Maori-style pendants (tiki) from $55. Excellent value.

Climbing
YMCA, 12 Hereford St, T03-366 0689. Has a climbing wall that is open to the public for casual use, from $10. Equipment hire and instruction are available at extra cost.

Cruising
For wildlife and historic/scenic cruises on the Lyttleton Harbour see page 496. For punting, see River Avon, page 476, and Hagley Park, page 478.

Eco-tours
Heritage Expeditions, 53B Montreal St, Christchurch, T03-365 3500, www.heritage-expeditions.com. Guided birdwatching trips and expeditions throughout New Zealand and the sub-Antarctic Islands.

Fishing
There are a number of operators offering half-day to full-day trips or tailor-made options from $600. The VIC (I-Site) has listings.

Horse trekking
Waimak River Horse Treks, T03-323 9064/T0800-873577, mcstay@xtra.co.nz. Offers interesting 30-min or 1½-hr horse trek/jetboat combos, or trekking-only trips from 1 hr to full-day, from $60.
Otahuna Horse Riding, based in Tai Tapu, T03-329 0160, www.otahuna.co.nz. An upmarket operation offering intensive riding lessons as well as trekking.

Hot air ballooning
Ballooning over the Canterbury Plains is perhaps Christchurch's classic activity. Both of these companies offer early morning flights of about 1 hr, with champagne breakfast from $260. Recommended.

Aoraki Balloon Safaris, Methven, T03-302 8172, www.nzballooning.com. **Up Up and Away**, T03-381 4600, www.ballooning.co.nz.

Jet boating
Both companies offer jet-boating trips on the eastern Southern Alps rivers from $75-200, including transport.
Jet Stream Tours, T03-3851478/T0800-277729, www.jetstreamtours.co.nz. Also offers a heli-jetboat option with 15-min heli and 30-min jetboat, from $210.
Waimak Alpine Jet, T03-318 4881/T0800-263626, www.waimakalpinejet.co.nz.

Mountain biking and cycling tours
There are some attractive options around Christchurch, with the Port Hills and Banks Peninsula being the main venues. See also Transport, page 491, for hire companies.
Adventure South, T03-942 1222, www.adv south.co.nz. Offers more far flung options.
Christchurch Bike Tours, T03-366 0337. An old-fashioned cycling experience touring the local parks and historical sites in typical Christchurch English fashion – on a bike with a basket and a bell. 2 hrs from $50 for 2 people (departs 1400 from the VIC/I-Site).
Mountain Bike Adventure Company, T03-339 4020/T0800-424534, www.cyclehire -tours.co.nz. Offers a good trip that goes up the Port Hills via the gondola to then descend by bike, from $50, plus longer tours from 3-5 days and independent hire from $35 per day.

Paragliding
Paragliding is big in Christchurch, with a number of companies vying for the tourist dollar. All are safe and pretty similar in price.
Nimbus, T03-389 1999/T0800-111611, www.nimbusparagliding.cjb.net. Offers a 2-hr trip and flights daily at 1000 and 1300 for $140. Introductory courses $100-1600.

Rafting
Rangitata Rafts, T03-696 3534/T0800-251251, www.rafts.co.nz. Offers day excursions down the scenic Rangitata River, south of Methven (Grade IV-V), from $174 including transport from Christchurch.

Swimming
Atlantis Pool, QEII Park, Travis Rd, New Brighton, T03-941 6849, www.qeiipark.co.nz, Mon-Fri 0600-2100, Sat-Sun 0700-2000. A modern themed attraction that has the largest wave pool in the country. It is a great place to take the kids and has spas, sauna, steam room and café, from $5, child $2.50.

Tandem skydiving
The Christchurch Parachute School, T03-343 5542, www.skydiving.co.nz. Operates out of the Wingram Airfield 15 mins south of the city, 2-hr trip 10,000 ft, from $245.

Tours
Hassle-free Holidays, T03-354 6050, www.hasslefree.co.nz, from $199, departs 0900. *Lord of the Rings* fans or indeed anyone who wants to see some classic Southern Alpine scenery could try a trip to Mt Sunday (Potts Station) in the Raingitata Valley. Day or multi-day tours available.
TranzAlpine High Country Explorer Tour, T03-377 1391/T0800-863975, www.high-country.co.nz. An interesting full-day trip that combines 1-hr transfer by coach across the Canterbury Plains, morning tea, a 15-km jet-boat trip, a 65-km 4WD safari lunch and then a 2-hr trip back to Christchurch from Arthur's Pass on the famous **TranzAlpine** railway line, from $330.
Tussock and Beach Ecotours, T03-303 0880, www.nature.net.nz. Several eco-tour options including 2 nights' accommodation, all meals and a fully guided eco-tour through a spectacular glaciated landscape, culminating in Mt Sunday with the opportunity to explore the site of 'Edoras' from *The Two Towers*. A beech forest walk along a mountain stream and a champagne lunch beside a sub-alpine lake are also included. Accommodation is in the historic Ross Cottage, a peaceful, carefully restored building registered with the New Zealand Historic Places Trust, from $315.

Walking
In town, a stroll along the River Avon is recommended, as are the 'city walks' (self-guided or guided, brochures from the VIC/I-Site). Further afield the 'Port Hills Bridle Path' and 'Crater Rim Walks' provide great views and can be tackled in part with the

gondola. The VIC (I-Site) has details,
or see page 482. The beaches of New
Brighton and Sumner offer good and
easygoing beach walks. DoC has details
and leaflets covering walks throughout
the Banks Peninsula (see Tourist
information, page 474).
Hikers Heaven, T03-377 9953. Offers 'drop-
offs' and 'pick-ups' to 9 walkways including
the crater rim walk around Godley Head.
Tuatara Tours, T03-962 3280, www.tuatara
tours.co.nz, (see Akaroa Activities, page 497).
Offers the all inclusive 3-day, 39-km
Christchurch-Akaroa walk, from $990.

⊖ Transport

Christchurch *p472, maps p473 and p477*
Airline offices
Air New Zealand, 549 Colombo St, T03-363
0600 (after hours T0800-737000). Mount
Cook, T0800-730000. Qantas, T03-374 7100
(after hours T0800-808767).

Bicycle hire
City Cycle Hire, Addington, T0800-343848.
Mountain Bike Adventure Company,
T03-339 4020/T0800-424534,
www.cyclehire-tours.co.nz.

Car hire
All the major national companies have offices
at the airport and in town. Prices average
about $60 per day with unlimited mileage.
Scotties, 189 Blenheim Rd, T03-3482002/
T0800-736825. Also has offices in Auckland,
is recommended and can offer good hire
rates and buy back sales.
  Others include: **Apex**, T0800-939597;
Hertz, T0800-654321; **KiwiCar**, T0800-
5494227; **Omega**, T0800-112121;
Pegasus, T0800-803580.
  For cheaper deals try: **Cut Price**, T03-366
3800; **Mac's**, T0800-154155; **Rent-A-Dent**,
T0800-736823; **Shoestring Rentals**,
T03-385 3647; and **Trusty**, T03-366 6329.

Motorcycle hire
Motorcycle Rentals and Tours, 32 Allen St,
T03-377 0663, www.nzbike.com.
Rental Motorcycles, 28B Byron St,
T03-372 3537, www.motorcycle-hire.co.nz.
$85-235 per day.

Motorhome hire
Adventure Kiwi, T03-366 8008,
www.adventurekiwi.co.nz; **Backpacker
Campervan Rentals**, T0800-288699; the arty
colourful vans of **Escape Independent Car
Rentals**, T0800-216171, www.escape
rentals.co.nz; **Maui**, T0800-651080; or
Tomlinson Campers, T03-374 5254.

Taxi
Blue Star, T03-353 1200/379 9799, 24 hrs.
First Direct, T03-377 5555.
Gold Band, T03-3795795.

❶ Directory

Christchurch *p472, maps p473 and p477*
Banks ANZ, ASB, BNZ, National and
Westpac are around Cathedral Sq.
Banking hours Mon-Fri 0900-1630.
Currency exchange Most of the major
bank branches offer exchange services.
Interforex, 65 Cathedral Sq, T03-377 1233.
Travelex, at the VIC or Harvey World Travel,
corner of Armagh and Colombo sts,
T03-366 2087, www.travelex.co.nz.
Disabled services Disability Information
Service, 314 Worcester St, T03-3666189,
dis@disinfo.co.nz, 0900-1630; Kiwiable,
T03-941 8774. **Internet** There are
numerous places around Cathedral Sq:
Cyber Café, 1/166 Gloucester St, T03-
365 5183, Mon-Fri 0900-2100, Sat-Sun
0900-2000; E Blah Blah, 77 Cathedral Sq
(bus info corner), T03-377 2381, daily
0800-2230. **Laundry** 21 Stanmore Rd,
T03-389 1831, 0800-1730, Sat-Sun 0800-
1400 or 247 Armagh St, T03-379 6622.
Library Gloucester St, Mon-Fri 1000-2100,
Sat 1000-1600, Sun 1300-1600. **Medical
services** 24 hr surgery corner of Bealey
Av and Colombo St, T03-365 7777;
Christchurch Hospital, Riccarton Av,
T03-364 0640; Dentist, T03-366 6644 (ext
3002); Urgent pharmacy, 931 Colombo St,
T03-366 4439, until 2300. **Police** Central
Station, corner of Hereford and Cambridge
Terr, T03-379 3999. **Post office** (Post
Restante) Cathedral Sq, T0800-501501,
Mon-Thu 0800-1800, Fri 0800-2000,
Sat-Sun 1000-1600. **Useful addresses**
AA, 210 Hereford St, T03-379 1280.
Emergencies, T111.

Banks Peninsula → Colour map 5, B6

Jutting out into the Pacific Ocean from Christchurch, like the bulb on a jigsaw piece, is the Banks Peninsula. Distinctly out of character with the (now) connected and monotonously flat alluvial Canterbury Plains, it is a refreshing and rugged landscape of hills and flooded harbours formed by two violent volcanic eruptions. The two largest harbours, which now fill the craters and shelter their namesake settlements, are Lyttleton to the north and Akaroa to the south. These settlements provide an interesting excursion from Christchurch, with Lyttleton – 12 km away via the Lyttleton Tunnel – being by far the more accessible.

Other than the refreshing hill and harbour scenery, both places offer some historic sites, and activities such as dolphin watching. The bays and waters that surround the peninsula are home to the world's smallest and rarest dolphin, the Hector's dolphin. The two- or four-day trek on the Banks Peninsula Track from Akaroa is also a popular attraction. ►► For Sleeping, Eating and other listings, see pages 495-497.

Ins and outs

Getting there If you can afford it, hiring a car is the best way to explore the peninsula (see Christchurch Transport, page 491, for hire companies). By road, Lyttelton is 12 km from the centre of Christchurch via the tunnel or about 20 km via the windy roads above Sumner. Both Sumner and Lyttelton are well signposted from Ferry Road at the southeastern corner of the city. The scenic Port Hills road is accessed via Colombo Street via the Cashmere Hills. Akaroa is 84 km southeast of Christchurch via SH75, which skirts past Lake Ellesmere, before turning inland into the heart of the peninsula. Just past the small settlement of Little River the road climbs, offering great views from the **Hilltop Hotel**, before falling to the head of Akaroa Harbour and into Akaroa itself. An alternative route is via Lyttelton but it is no shorter.

Banks Peninsula

By bus, Lyttelton is served by the No 28, which leaves regularly from the casino or Cathedral Square in Christchurch. The **Akaroa Shuttle**, T0800-500929, www.akaroashuttle.co.nz, provides day tours and shuttle services. Shuttles depart from the Christchurch VIC (I-Site) daily November to April at 0830 and 1400, returning from Akaroa at 1030, 1535 and 1630, from $30, child $20 return; in winter daily from Christchurch at 1000 returning at 1600. Day tour shuttles depart at 1000 and 1030 and return at 1535 or 1630, from $40, $95 with lunch. Similarly, **Akaroa French Connection**, T03-366 4556, T0800-800575, www.akaroabus.co.nz, offers a scenic day-tour and shuttle services to Akaroa and other places of interest on the peninsula, departing daily from the Christchurch VIC (I-Site) at 0845 (shuttle), 0930 (tour), 1300 (additional service at 1645 on Friday), with the last shuttle returning from Akaroa at 1545 (April to August) and 1615 (September to March), from $20 return, tour from $40; transport only.

Tourist information Lyttelton VIC (I-Site) ① *20 Oxford St, T03-328 9093, www.lytteltonharbour.co.nz, daily 0900-1700*, has enthusiastic staff who can provide leaflets on all the relevant walks and activities; of particular interest is the self-guided historical walks leaflet. It also has full accommodation listings and internet access. **Akaroa VIC (I-Site)** ① *Akaroa District Promotions, 80 Rue Lavaud, T03-304 8600, www.akaroa.com, daily 0900-1700*, is an independent information office, with very helpful staff, who will share their knowledge regarding the village and the peninsula's more out-of-the-way places.

Background
The first inhabitants of the peninsula were members of the Waitaha tribe who came south from the Bay of Plenty, but their claim was not to last. Around 1577 they were violently ousted by the Ngati Mamoe from Poverty Bay, who in turn fell to the onslaught of the Ngati Tahu, another east coast tribe, in around 1700. For over 100 years peace reigned before yet another violent battle ensued between the Tahu and the invading Toa from Kapiti Island.

Captain Cook was the first European to discover the peninsula, but he actually thought it was an island and charted it as such, bestowing on it the name Banks Island after his ship's naturalist Sir Joseph Banks. This confusion remained until 1809 when further surveys by Captain Stewart of the 'Pegasus' proved otherwise. Ironically, the Banks Peninsula was once an island. After the violent eruption that created it, it was eventually connected to the mainland by the advancing alluvial plains that spread east from the Southern Alps.

By 1830 the seas around the South Island were plundered for their whales and seals and the sheltered harbours and bays of the Banks were an ideal base for a number of whaling stations. Permanent European settlement began with the arrival of the French at Akaroa in 1840 and the British in Lyttelton three years later. In effect, it was this pre-emptive settlement strike by the French that spurred the British to initiate the Treaty of Waitangi and effectively place New Zealand under British sovereignty and subsequent rule. Had they not, today, the Sky Tower in Auckland would perhaps be of the Eiffel variety and its residents would say 'Bonjour', not 'G'day'.

Lyttelton → *Colour map 5, B6 Population: 3100*
Whichever way you arrive in Lyttelton, by the **Port Hills** scenic route via Sumner, or through the **road tunnel**, it is quite an exciting delivery and will, along with the deeply contrasting scenery, provide a pleasant sense of escape from the city buzz and the flat vistas of Christchurch. Lying on the northern shores of the volcanic crater that now forms the **Lyttelton Harbour**, this busy characterful port has an air of history, befitting its

stature as the place where the 'first four ships' arrived in 1850. It was also the port that Captain Scott and Lieutenant Shackleton used as their base to explore the Antarctic.

Relics from these times and its fascinating past can be found in the **Lyttelton Museum** ① *Gladstone Quay, To3-328 8972, Tue, Thu, Sat-Sun 1400-1600, donation.* Also of historical interest is the **Lyttelton Timeball Station** ① *high on the hillside off Sumner Rd, To3-328 7311, www.historic.org.nz, daily 1000-1730 (winter Wed-Sun), $7, child, free.* After years of disuse the station building, which is very grand both inside and out, was fully restored and is now open to visitors. Built in 1876, it is the only survivor of three such contraptions ever constructed in New Zealand, and was used as an essential timing device to keep mariners accurate in their calculations of longitude. From 1876 to 1934 the large ball, clearly visible at the top of a mast on the building's turret, would drop at precisely 1300 in accordance with Greenwich Mean Time.

Ripapa Island ① *To3-328 9078, www.blackcat.co.nz, trips with Black Cat depart daily at 1330 if group numbers are sufficient, from $25, child $10,* was originally a Maori *pa* before it became home to Fort Jervois, once declared 'the strongest port fortress in the Empire'. It was built originally in 1886 to repel the 'Great Russian Scare'. Jervois later held the notorious First World War prisoner of war, Count Felix Von Luckner, who sunk 14 allied vessels before being captured and imprisoned.

In contrast, **Quail Island** ① *3-hr trip, Sep-Apr daily at 1020 and 1220, May-Aug daily at 0930 and 1230, $15, child $7.50,* was a former leper colony but now, devoid of both lepers and introduced predators, it is a safe haven abounding with native birds.

Akaroa → *Colour map 5, B6 Population: 642*

Background The name Akaroa, which is a variant on the Maori word 'hakaroa'– meaning 'Long Harbour', gives no impression of Akaroa's distinctly French roots. In 1835 French whaler Jean Langlois established a whaling station in the harbour at French Bay and, seeing its potential for settlement and as an ideal shipping port, made a down payment on the land with the local Maori. Once he had secured the deal he returned to France to organize the colonization of the newly acquired territory. Knowing nothing of the Treaty of Waitangi, which had effectively placed New Zealand under British sovereignty only 13 days before, a group of French settlers set sail on board *L'Aube* on 19 February 1840. When the French arrived there was a fractious period of political 'growling, lamp post sniffing and marking' before the French eventually agreed to accept the situation, sell their claims and integrate. Thankfully, perhaps through their long association and history of dealing with such situations, this integration was successful and before long Akaroa had become a pleasant and cosmopolitan European community. They brought with them the rich culture that gives Akaroa its modern-day legacy of fine architecture, place names and, still, a wonderful sense of community and friendship.

Sights Akaroa is a very pretty little place with a lovely atmosphere, made even more intriguing by its French names. But perhaps before getting properly acquainted with the place you should take in the superb view of the locality from the hill to the south, via Rue Jolie and then Onuku Road (lighthouse road). Given the village's rich history it's worth paying a visit to **Akaroa Museum** ① *corner of Rue Lavaud and Rue Balguerie, To3-304 1013, daily Nov-Apr 1030-1630, May-Oct 1030-1600, $4, child $1.* A 20-minute film provides a fine introduction backed up with collections focusing on early Maori, whaling, the French connection and the British succession. The **Custom House** at Daly's Wharf that dates from 1852, the old **Court House** and the **Langlois-Eteveneaux House** nearby, are three fine remnants that are an adjunct to the main museum.

[[Given the fact it is little dolphins wearing smiley faces and not 'old Europeans' wearing berets that are equally (if not more) popular around these parts it is no surprise to find an attraction dedicated solely to them. In late 2005 the Blackcat Group (see page 496) opened the **Dolphin Discovery Centre** ① *Main Wharf, To3-*

is on interactive, state-of-the-art displays with, in this instance, a particular focus on the rare and endangered Hector's dolphins, which are only found around the South Island of New Zealand.

Of more convivial and contemporary interest is **Barry's Bay Cheese** ① *Main Rd, Barry's Bay (at the head of Akaroa Harbour), T03-304 5809*. This small family-owned operation makes a fine array of cheeses between October and May, and visitors are welcome to watch the process (alternate days between October and April) and sample the varieties, before purchasing their favourites in the shop.

⊜ Sleeping

Lyttelton *p193*

There are a few good B&Bs within walking distance of the town centre.

L-AL Cavendish House, 10 Ross Terr, T03-328 9505, www.cavendish.co.nz. A well-appointed Edwardian villa with doubles, an en suite with a spa and nice views.

A Lochranza, 14 Godley Quay, T03-329 6940, www.lochranza.co.nz. Historic (1892) B&B with 2 comfortable rooms, open fires and good harbour views.

C-D Tunnel Vision Backpackers, 44 London Rd, T03-328 7576. Tidy and friendly, doubles, twins and dorms, right in the heart of town.

Akaroa *p494*

There is some attractive and more remote accommodation throughout the peninsula, including plenty of B&Bs and homestays, with most boasting a historic and/or French flair. The VIC has full listings.

LL Maison de la Mer, 1 Rue Benoit, T03-304 8907, www.maisondelamer.co.nz. Elegant 5-star B&B on the waterfront.

LL Mill Cottage, Rue Grehan, T03-304 8007. Another good 5-star option. Romantic 1850s cottage with modern interior, set in a large peaceful garden.

LL-AL Oinako Lodge, 99 Beach Rd, T03-304 8787, www.oinako.co.nz. A historic B&B, built in 1865, spacious, with 6 elegant individually themed rooms all in a convenient central location. Gourmet breakfast.

LL-AL Tresori Lodge Motel, corner of Rue Jolie and Church St, T03-304 7500, www.tresori.co.nz. Offers spotless classy studios and suites, in a distinctly French style. Good value and recommended.

L Maison des Fleurs, 6 Church St, T03-304 7804/T0800-6952000, www.maisondesfleurs.co.nz. A stark contrast to the others: cute, purpose-built and self-contained.

L Wilderness House, 42 Rue Grehan T03-304 7517, www.wildernesshouse.co.nz. Historic B&B set in a beautiful garden, all 4 rooms are en suite.

L-A Akaroa Village Inn, opposite the main Wharf at 81 Beach Rd, T03-304 7421/T0800-6952000, www.akaroavillageinn.co.nz. In a central position, this French-influenced hotel offers standard rooms or self-catering luxury apartments, most with views over the harbour. Swimming pool, spa and bike hire.

AL Linton (Giant's House), 68 Rue Balguerie, T03-304 7501, www.linton.co.nz. Decorated with quirky artworks by local Josie Martin and complete with artists' garden, this residence offers 2 spacious, comfortable doubles, one with conservatory, the other with a 'boat bed'. A memorable stay is guaranteed. Recommended.

AL-A Akaroa Criterion Motel, 75 Rue Jolie, T03-3047775, www.holidayakaroa.co.nz. Spacious luxury studios and rooms close to the village centre.

A L'Hotel Motel, 75 Beach Rd (wharf end), T03-304 7559, hotel-akaroa@xtra.co.nz. Good units overlooking the harbour and a licensed restaurant downstairs.

Backpacker hostels

C-D Bon Accord Backpackers, 57 Rue Lavaud, T03-304 7782, www.bon-accord.co.nz. Tidy dorms and cosy, good-value doubles. Well located and peaceful. Ask about the house's interesting history. Bookings advised.

C-D Chez-la-Mer Backpackers, 50 Rue Lavaud, T03-304 7024, www.chezlamer.co.nz. Equally well placed and a pleasant historic house with a secluded garden. It offers dorms, doubles, twins and singles, is well facilitated throughout and has its own backpacker boat for fishing trips and 4WD tours.

C-D Pohatu Penguin Reserve Batch, Pohatu-Flea Bay, T03-304 8552, www.pohatu.co.nz. In keeping with the nature of the peninsula and owned by **Pohatu Adventure Tours**, this a self-contained bach in a sublimely peaceful setting near the beach. Recommended.

Motorcamps and campsites
B-D Akaroa Top Ten Holiday Park, off Morgan Rd at entrance to village, T03-304 7471, www.akaroaholidaypark.co.nz. It is the best-equipped motorcamp with flats, cabins, powered/tent sites and views across the harbour. The camp kitchen is very small.

● Eating

Lyttelton p493
There are plenty of places to eat in Lyttelton, with most on Norwich Quay or London Rd.
♥♥ **Volcano Café and Lava Bar**, corner of London and Canterbury sts, T03-328 7077, Brightly coloured, good traditional blackboard menu and good coffee.
♥ **Satchmos**, 8 London St, T03-328 8348, daily 1000-2100. Wide-ranging good-value menu, attractive courtyard garden and, as the name suggests, some mellow sounds. Even the pizzas are named after music legends.
♥ **She Café and Tapas Bar/Restaurant**, 8 km west, 79 Main Rd, T03-329 9825. Café open Thu-Mon 1000-1600, restaurant Fri-Sat from 1700, Overlooking the harbour and worth the trip out of town.

Akaroa p494
Given the French influence, Akaroa offers some fine restaurants and cafés, but many are subject to seasonal hours.
♥♥♥ **C'est La Vie**, 33 Rue Lavaud, T03-304 7314, daily for dinner (closed in winter). Arguably the top restaurant in Akaroa, offering great meals (especially seafood) by candlelight.
♥♥ **Harbour 71**, 71 Beach Rd, T03-304 7659, open for lunch and dinner, licensed. Traditional option with fine harbour views. Fresh fish recommended.
♥♥ **Ma Maison**, 2 Rue Jolie, T03-304 7668. Traditional food with harbour views.
♥ **Akaroa Bakery**, 51 Beach Rd, daily 0730-1600. Wonderful fresh bread.
♥ **Turenne Coffee Shop**, corner of Rue Balguerie and Rue Lavaud, T03-304 7005, daily 0700-1800. Seems to be the most popular daytime café and has good coffee, light snacks, legendary muffins and internet.

● Pubs, bars and clubs

Lyttelton p493
There is no shortage of pubs – it is a port after all. London Rd is the focus.
Wunderbar 19, T03-328 8818. Aesthetically the most memorable, it offers regular live acts and is deservingly popular.

▲ Activities and tours

Lyttelton p493
Cruises
Several cruises leave from the port from vessels both old and new.
Black Cat Group, T0800-436574, www.black cat.co.nz. Offers an interesting array of catamaran harbour trips. The 2-hr 'Wildlife Cruise' takes in both sides of the harbour and out just beyond its entrance, passes some interesting sites on the way including an old whaling station, a shipwreck and the Godley Head Lighthouse. There is usually plenty in the way of wildlife, with the highlight being the tiny and rare Hector's dolphin. Departures are from B Jetty, Lyttelton, at 1330 , from $52, child $20. Note that there is a free shuttle that departs from the Christchurch VIC (I-Site) 35 mins before departure. The 'Island Adventures Cruise' takes in either Quail or Raipara islands.
Tug Lyttelton Preservation Society, T03-322 8911, www.nzmaritime.co.nz/tug.htm. The 1907 steam tug *Lyttelton*, lovingly restored, has been taking passengers for historical cruises for 28 years. Contact the VIC for details.

Walking
As well as the historical walks around town and those up to the Christchurch (Port Hills) Gondola, the **Crater Rim Walkway** (19 km, 4 hrs) provides a longer and spectacular walk with memorable views across the Banks Peninsula and the Canterbury Plains to the Southern Alps. The VIC (I-Site) can provide directions and all the relevant leaflets.

Akaroa p494
The **Akaroa Adventure Centre** (see Kayaking, below) rents out kayaks, surf boards and mountain bikes.

If you fancy exploring the many bays of the peninsula yourself perhaps a smart scooter is another option, with hire available from the La Rochelle Motel, T03-304 8782, 2 hrs from $40, full-day $90. Mountain bikes from $15 per day.

Harbour/wildlife cruises
Akaroa Dolphins, T03-304 7866. Independent boat charter and harbour cruises.
Akaroa Harbour Cruises, T03-304 7641/ T0800-436574, www.blackcat.co.nz. Offers a 2-hr scenic/wildlife cruise. While the highlight is the probable sighting of Hector's dolphin, you can also see little blue penguins, spotted shags and fur seals. The cruise costs from $52, child $20.
Akaroa Seal Colony Safari, T03-304 7255, www.sealtours.co.nz. An interesting 2½-hr road trip via the rim of the crater to a fur seal colony on the eastern bays, from $70, child $50. Trips leave from the VIC twice daily.
Dolphin Experience, 61 Beach Rd, T03-304 7726, www.dolphinsakaroa.co.nz. Offers 3-hr dolphin-swimming trips from $98, child $80 (viewing only $48). Trips depart Nov-Apr 0600, 0830 1130 and 1330; May-Oct 0900 and 1200.
Dolphins up Close, T03-304 7641, www.swimmingwithdolphins.co.nz. Operated by **Blackcat** (see under Lyttleton), the 'Swimming with Dolphins' experience is a 3-hr excursion to encounter the rare Hector's dolphin, from $105, child $85 (viewing only $55/30). Trips depart the main wharf at 0600, 0830, 1130 and 1330.
Pohatu Adventure Tours (Shireen Helps), T03-304 8552, www.pohatu.co.nz. Offers 2 tours: a full day-tour of historical and scenic sites with a sea kayaking and snorkelling option, from $70; or a 3-hr specialist tour of the Penguin Reserve, from $55, child $25. Also offers good-value accommodation in a great setting (see Sleeping, page 496).

Kayaking
Kayak hire is available from **Akaroa Boat Hire**, T03-304 8758, and the **Akaroa Adventure Centre**, T03-304 8709, eiffelaka@xtra.co.nz, from $30. See also **Blackcat**, based in Lyttleon, see page 496.
Mafi's Kayak Trips, Onuku Farm Hostel, T027-411 0369. Entertaining trips with possible encounters of Hectors dolphin, daily from $40.

Walking
The 2- or 4-day, 35-km **Banks Peninsula Track**, T03-304 7612, www.bankstrack.co.nz, is a popular tramp across private farmland, the hills and outer bays, and is recommended. It is very much an off-the-beaten-track experience, with great huts provided for accommodation. The track is open from 31 Oct-Apr and costs from $225 for the 4-day trip and $125 for the 2-day. Cost includes an introductory talk, booklet, transport to the first hut and accommodation. You must take your own food. For other day-walk options on the peninsula contact the VIC in Akaroa.
Tuatara Tours, T03-962 3280, www.tuatara tours.co.nz. Offers a 39-km walk from Christchurch to Akaroa. The journey starts with easy taking the gondola to the crater rim, then you walk 9 km along the summit track before descending into Lyttelton to visit the Timeball Station. The first night is then spent in Diamond Harbour. Day 2 sees you negotiating 19 km of ridge trails with expansive views and another comfortable night at the private Pentrip Lodge. Day 3 takes in a further 11 km of track before you are delivered by boat to Akaroa. The 3-day/ night package costs $990 all-inclusive.
Eastern Bays Scenic Mail Run, T03-325 1334. The Eastern Bays Scenic mail run combines an authentic mail delivery with a scenic drive covering 100 km through some of the most beautiful scenery on Banks Peninsula and visiting local attractions like the Barrys Bay Cheese factory and French Farm Winery. Departs Christchurch daily at 0900 and arrives in Akaroa at 1330, from $50.

❶ Directory

Akaroa *p494*
Banks The very attractive BNZ Bank is opposite the VIC, Mon-Fri 0900-1630, and has an ATM. **Internet** Akaroa Library, 141 Rue Jolie, T03-304 8782, Mon-Fri 1030-1600, Sat 1030-1300. **Bon Email**, corner of Rue Lavaud, T03-304 7782, 0900-2000. **Turenne Coffee Shop**, corner of Rue Balguerie and Rue Lavaud, T03-304 7005. **Useful numbers** Police, T03-304 1030. Doctor, T03-304 7004.

North of Christchurch

From Christchurch SH1 heads north through the unremarkable settlement of Amberley before reaching the junction with SH7 and the Waipara Valley. From here SH7 heads northeast, through the Hurunui District to Hanmer Springs and the west coast via the Lewis Pass, while SH1 heads north to Kaikoura and eventually Blenheim. Another road, SH70, leaves SH7 just north of Culverden, offering a scenic short cut from Hanmer Springs to Kaikoura. These routes are known collectively as the (signposted) Alpine Pacific Triangle, which is designed to combine the lesser attraction of the Waipara Valley vineyards with its two star destinations, Hanmer Springs and Kaikoura. Although many people visit Kaikoura (which actually lies in Marlborough, not Canterbury) on their way to Christchurch from the north, this 'triangle' offers an attractive multi-day trip from Christchurch. There is much to see and do in both Hanmer Springs and Kaikoura, but they are very different. In landlocked Hanmer the wealth of activities includes skiing, rafting, horse trekking and, perhaps its speciality, mountain biking. All these activities of course are in addition to the more obvious and soporific attraction of its hot pools in the thermal resort. Kaikoura, in contrast, set on the spectacular northeast coastline and almost miniaturized in the shadow of the Kaikoura mountain ranges, is equally abuzz with activity. But here the emphasis is most definitely in the colder waters of the ocean and its inhabitants. At Kaikoura you can see and even swim with an impressive list of the oceans 'who's who', including albatrosses, seals, dolphins and of course Kaikoura's very own whales. ▸▸ For Sleeping, Eating and other listings, see pages 503-510.

Hanmer Springs ●❼▲❶ ▸▸ *pp503-510.*

→ *Colour map 4, B4 Population: 900*

Hanmer has long been popular with Kiwi holiday-seekers, and has only recently come into its own as a top national tourist venue. Its biggest attraction is of course its impressive **Thermal Reserve**, but it is also very popular as a base for mountain biking and walking in the **Hanmer Forest Park** nearby and, in winter, as a base for the **Hanmer** and **Mount Lyford ski fields**. When winter snows lie on the ground or spring rain plays on the puddles, the hot pools are the perfect place to be. Hanmer offers a wide range of modern accommodation, some good restaurants and numerous activities from bungee jumping to horse trekking. The town is particularly beautiful in autumn when the forest and tree-lined streets are flush with golden hues and falling leaves. The name Hanmer derives from the name of Canterbury pioneer Thomas Hanmer, often misspelt.

Ins and outs

Getting there Hanmer Springs is 136 km north of Christchurch and 214 km east of Greymouth. By bus, the **Hanmer Shuttle**, To3-366 4556, www.hanmerbus.co.nz, offers a daily service to Hanmer Springs. Springs Junction is 95 km west of Hanmer Springs via SH7. There is a service station at Springs Junction with 24-hour EFTPOS.

Tourist information **Hanmer Springs VIC (I-Site)** ① *in front of the Thermal Reserve off Amuri Av in the centre of the village, To3-315 7128/To800-442663, www.hanmer springs.co.nz, www.hurunui.com, daily 1000-1700,* has information on DoC walks.

Sights

With all the other activities on offer, a visit to the **Hanmer Springs Thermal Reserve** ① *Amuri Av, To3-315 7511/To800-442663, daily 1000-2100, $12, child $6 (return pass $15, child $7.50),* may not be high on your agenda. However, the reserve is undoubtedly the top attraction. The springs were first discovered by the Europeans in 1859 and later became a commercial venture and public attraction; in 1907, the first facilities and a hotel formed the beginnings of the resort and, subsequently, the town as a whole. The resort has enjoyed an impressive expansion and improvement in recent years, and has various pools including open and landscaped, freshwater, swimming and a children's play pool – all connected by steaming boulder streams. The mineral-rich waters range in temperature from a lukewarm 32°C to a balmy 42°C. Also on site are a massage and beauty clinic, private pools, saunas, a steam room, a licensed café and a picnic area.

Hanmer Springs to the west coast

From Hanmer Springs SH7 crosses the northern ranges of the Great Divide (Southern Alps) to the west coast via the **Lewis Pass**, **Maruia Springs**, **Springs Junction** and **Reefton**. Although not as dramatic as Arthur's Pass further to the south (see page 512), it offers some lovely scenery and a few good walking opportunities on the way. It also boasts a mountain with one of the most unusual names in the country. There are many with wonderful names, but frankly **Mons Sex Millia** has to take the prize.

At the top of the Hope River Valley from Hanmer, the road skirts the borders of the **Lake Sumner Forest Park** and begins to follow the Lewis River to its headwaters and the saddle known as Lewis Pass (864 m). In pre-European times the Ngai Tahu Maori of Canterbury used this route to access the west coast in search of greenstone (*pounamu*). Having negotiated the pass on their return, they are said to have dispensed with their slaves – alas not with a 'thanks lads, see you next year', but a brutal death followed by a feast of their various bodily parts. A valley known as **Cannibal Gorge** remains testament to this rather grim form of the early 'transport café'.

The pass itself was named in 1860 after pioneer surveyor Henry Lewis. Ironically, Henry's daughter Eleanor married Arthur Dudley Dobson who surveyed 'Arthur's' Pass. But it doesn't end there. Arthur's sister then married the geologist and surveyor Julian Von Haast who is accredited with much of the exploration, survey work and many place names on the west coast.

Lake Sumner Forest Park and the Lewis Pass offer some excellent walks, which are outlined in various DoC leaflets, including the *Lewis Pass Region* broadsheet, which is available from the Hanmer VIC (I-Site). The lichen-covered beech forests are particularly superb in this region and well worth further investigation.

The five-day **St James Walkway** that begins near the Lewis Pass summit car park (and infamous Cannibal Gorge) is particularly good. There is a network of DoC huts, and the moderate track is best negotiated in summer or autumn. Just beyond the Lewis Pass, heading west, is the oasis of **Maruia Springs**, a small thermal resort with hot pools, accommodation, a restaurant and a bar. It is a perfect stop for tired trampers. A further 21 km west is **Springs Junction**, the only significant settlement between Hanmer and Reefton, with accommodation, a café, and also a petrol station.

Kaikoura ⊕🍴▲⊕🌐 ➤ *pp503-510.*

➔ *Colour map 4, B5 Population: 4000*

So you want to see Moby Dick and friends? Well, you have certainly come to the right spot. Kaikoura is a place that is not only aesthetically stunning but one that has some of the best sea creatures in the world. They are all here: Moby, Flipper, Keiko, Jaws – you might even bump into Marine Boy having a beer in the local boozer or a mermaid on the bus. Okay, not quite. But for the wildlife enthusiast the Kaikoura Coast is second only to the Otago Peninsula for richness and accessibility to some of New Zealand's biggest and most famous wildlife icons. This is due to the topography and depth of the ocean floor: just south of Kaikoura, a trough comes unusually close to the coastline creating an upsurge of nutritious plankton soup, giving rise to the many creatures with which we are more familiar further up the food chain. At the very top of course, on the ocean throne, is the majestic and much victimized king of them all – the whale.

But even if you came to Kaikoura thinking that whales was a small and fine rugby-playing nation somewhere in Britain, or indeed that seals clap and throw beach balls to each other, you cannot fail to be impressed. From the azure waters that surround the beautiful Kaikoura Peninsula, backed by the snow-capped peaks of the Kaikoura Ranges, you can get up close and personal with them all, from whales and dolphins to seals, albatrosses and even sharks. So the place is very special and even before you arrive there is a sense of excitement.

Ins and outs

Getting there Kaikoura is 187 km north of Christchurch, 129 km south of Blenheim (154 km Picton) on SH1, and 133 km northwest of Hanmer Springs via SH70. By bus, Kaikoura is served from Christchurch-Blenheim-Picton by **Intercity**, 123 Worcester Street, T03-319 5641 (book at the VIC); **Atomic Shuttles**, T03-322 8883, www.atomic travel.co.nz, daily; and **K-Bus**, T03-358 8355, www.southernlinkbus.co.nz. The fare to Christchurch or Blenheim costs from $25.

By train, Kaikoura is served by **TranzCoastal**, T0800-872467, daily (Christchurch 1528, from $52; Blenheim-Picton 0954, from $45). The train station is on Clarence Street. For a taxi call T03-319 6214. The VIC (I-Site) caters for all transport bookings and enquiries.

Getting around Kaikoura Shuttle, T03-319 6166/T0800-766962, operates shuttles on demand to all the principal sights and offers one- or two-hour tours of the region. There are scheduled or on-demand shuttles to both the Hanmer and Lyford ski fields, for $20-30. For details contact the VIC (I-Site).

Tourist information Kaikoura VIC (I-Site) ① *West End, T03-319 5641, www.kai koura.co.nz, daily 0800-1800 (Jun-Aug 0900-1700)*, provides information and arranges bookings for accommodation and transport. There is also a 20-minute precursory audio-visual presentation about the local environment and wildlife shown every hour or on demand, $3, child $1. All DoC information is also held here.

Background

Although the peninsula was known to be heavily settled by Maori before the Europeans arrived, modern-day Kaikoura was, ironically, first established as a whaling station in the early part of the 1800s. Its most noted pioneer was George Fyffe, who succeeded his uncle as the station manager. George built Kaikoura's oldest remaining house (**Fyffe House**) in 1860, near the Old Wharf. The Fyffe name was also bestowed upon the mountain immediately behind the township. After whaling it was mainly fishing, particularly for crayfish that took over. Today of course Kaikoura is synonymous with wildlife, thankfully now hunted only by the camera lens not harpoon, and it is the resident and migratory whales that remain the focus.

Sights

Of course most of what you have probably come to see lies beneath the waves and has flippers, but Kaikoura also offers a number of land-based features worthy of investigation. Paramount is the **Kaikoura Peninsula** that juts out into the ocean like a well-weathered head. The cliff-top and shoreline walkways, which link the northern and southern settlements of Kaikoura, cross the head of the peninsula and offer superb coastal scenery (see page 509). A good spot to get an overall impression of the town, the peninsula and its mountain backdrop is from the **lookout** just off Scarborough Terrace (off SH1 between the northern and southern settlements).

Kaikoura

To 22 23

To 2 17 21 7 9, Blenheim & Picton

Kaikoura Helicopters
Whale Watch Kaikoura

To Airport, Christchurch, Hanmer Springs, Maori Leap Cave, Kaikoura Winery & 3 19 20

Kaikoura District Museum

Kodak Express

Supermarket

Dolphin Encounter

Deal St

Pacific Ocean

Scenic Reserve

South Bay Parade

Peninsula Walkway

Nga Niho Park

Scenic Reserve

South Bay

Lookout

Kaikoura Peninsula

To Point Kearn Car Park

Lower Ward

Fyffe House

Peninsula Walkway

Peninsula Walkway

N

0 metres   100
0 yards   100

Sleeping

Admiral Court Motel 16
Albatross
  Backpackers 18
Alpine Pacific
  Holiday Park 3

Anchor Inn 1
Bay Cottages 25
Blue Seas 5
Campsites 20
Clifftop Apartment 9
Cray Cottage 6
Donegal House 23
Dusky Lodge 7
Fifeshire B&B 8
Fyffe Country Lodge 19
Hapuku Lodge 2
Kaikoura (Maui) YHA 10

Kaikoura Top Ten
  Holiday Park 11
Lemon Tree Lodge 15
Lyell Creek Lodge 17
Mediterranean 21
Miharotia 24
Nikau Lodge 12
Old Convent 22
Sleepy Whale
  Backpackers 4
Topspot Backpackers 13
White Morph 14

Eating

Craypot Café & Bar 2
Green Dolphin 4
Hapuku Café 7
Hislop's Café 8
Mussel Boys 9
Pier Hotel Pub &
  Café 1
Sonic on the Rocks
  Bar & Café 5
Why Not Café 6

Modern-day whaling in Kaikoura

The whale-watching experience is a wonderful mix of expectation, unpredictability and awe. Kaikoura is home to its own pod of sperm whales – the species you are most likely to see. Although it is a complex social set up and much is still not known, it is probably one or two of the young males from these resident bachelor pods that you will see. A bull male can weigh as much as 50 tonnes and be up to 20 m in length. Other whale species that are seen regularly include humpbacks, rights and orcas. If you are exceptionally lucky you may also see the endangered and truly industrial-sized blue whale.

Your boat trip to 'hunt down' and 'encounter' the whales is a fascinating and well-orchestrated performance of hydrophonics and simple 'eye-spy'. However, before all the action takes place you are invited to watch a new and very clever state-of-the-art computer graphic that shows the incredible depths of the Kaikoura Trench and explains why the whales are so drawn to it. Once out in the bay proper, a combination of local knowledge and hydrophonics is used to locate the whales. It is very exciting and timing is all-important as they are known to surface for around three minutes. This is your big and brief chance. With such unpredictability and in such a frenzy of expectation people-watching can be as much fun as watching the whales. When the great leviathan is spotted and the word is given, everybody jumps from their seat and clambers to get that illusive *National Geographic* shot from the decks. On rough days this can be quite riotous, with copious bouts of unintentional head-butting and hair-pulling. Only a few poor souls are left strapped to their seat, their vision of a whale long lost at the bottom of a sick-bag. On calm days it is much more orderly and you will get a better view of the whale's vast bulk. Whales are a bit like icebergs: for all you can see above the surface, there is an awful lot more beneath. However, regardless of conditions, what you are guaranteed to see is the point when the whales dive, flipping their tail in the air and descending gracefully like a hot knife through butter, back into the depths. It is this vision that is so engrained in our imagination. You can expect to see up to three whales on each trip, however, there is of course no guarantee and you will receive a refund if the trip is unsuccessful.

There are three historical venues of note. The first is the **Kaikoura District Museum** ① *14 Ludstone Rd, T03-319 7440, Mon-Fri 1230-1600, Sat-Sun 1400-1600, $3, child $0.50*, was established in 1971 and offers an interesting insight into the early Maori and whaling activities. If the weather closes in and you cannot get out on to the water it can provide a good activity option and help pass the time. **Fyffe House** ① *62 Avoca St, near the Old Wharf, T03-319 5835, 30-min guided tours Thu-Mon 1000-1700, $7*, is the remnants of the Waiopuka whaling station dating from 1842, see Background page 500. The **'Maori Leap Cave'** ① *2 km south, T03-319 5023, from $12, child $5*, was only discovered this century and is a sea-formed limestone cave featuring all the usual karst scenery. It can be visited on a 40-minute guided tour.

While in the area of the cave you might like to visit the **Kaikoura Winery** ① *just south of town, T03-319 7966, www.kaikourawines.co.nz*. There are hourly tours (from $8.50), underground cellars and tastings ($20 with transport from the VIC/I-Site).

● Sleeping

Hanmer Springs p498

There is plenty of choice in Hanmer to suit all budgets, with most of the options being modern, well-appointed and within walking distance of the town centre. You are advised to book ahead in mid-summer and at weekends in the winter ski-season.

LL Braemar Lodge, T03-365 4200, www.brae marlodge.co.nz. A fine modern luxury lodge on a hillside 9 km from the town that has recently undergone a $16 million redevelopment and been labelled perhaps rather pretentiously as a 'super luxury lodge'. The result is undoubtedly impressive with beautifully appointed rooms, spa, holistic healing centre and excellent cuisine, but it all comes at a 'super inflated price'.

LL-L Cheltenham House B&B, 13 Cheltenham St, T03-315 7545, www.cheltenham.co.nz. Well-located, with 6 spacious suites from super king to queen with en suite bath.

LL-AL Heritage Hotel and Resort, 1 Conical Hill Rd, T03-315 0060, www.heritage hotels.co.nz. Modern and ideally located overlooking the town centre. Rooms range from the honeymoon suite to standard, with self-contained stand-alone villas also available. It has all the usual facilities including a good restaurant, bar and a swimming pool. 2 mins from the hot pools.

AL Hanmer View B&B, 8 Oregon Heights (very end of Conical Hill Rd), T03-315 7947, www.hanmerview.co.nz. Set high on Conical Hill above the town this place offers memorable views to complement a warm welcome and 3 tidy en suites.

AL-A Glenalvon Lodge Motels and B&B, 29 Amuri Av, T03-315 7475, www.glenalvon.com. A cheaper and friendly option. It has pleasant rooms with private bath. Self-contained modern units are also available.

Motels

Motels here are generally of a high standard.

AL Clear Ridge, corner of Chisholm Cres and Jacks Pass Rd, T03-315 5144/T0800-555596, www.clearridge.co.nz. New luxury motel offering classy spa bath suites, all a short walk from the town centre.

AL Tussock Peak Motor Lodge, corner of Amuri and Leamington sts, T03-315 5191/ T0800-8877625, www.tussockpeak.co.nz. Modern luxury option in the heart of town, a stone's throw from the thermal reserve.

AL-A Alpine Lodge, 1 Harrogate St, T03-315 7311/T0800-9933//, www.alpinelodge motel.co.nz. Modern lodge-style, well-placed.

AL-A Greenacres Chalets and Apartments, 84 Conical Hill Rd, T03-315 7125, www.green acresmotel.co.nz. Modern, with self-contained chalets/apartments overlooking the town. Spa.

AL-A Scenic Views, 10 Amuri Av, T03-315 7419, www.hanmerscenicviews.co.nz. Just at the entrance to the town, this place offers peace and quiet, and mountain views.

B-D Kakapo Lodge YHA, 14 Amuri Av, just as you come in to the village on the left, T03-315 7472, www.kakapolodge.co.nz. Modern and spacious, a fine hostel but lacking in atmosphere. It offers the full range of rooms including motel-style en suites and has good kitchen facilities, internet and off-street parking.

B-D Le Gite Backpackers, 3 Devon St, to the west off Jacks Pass Rd, T03-315 5111, www.legite.co.nz. Described as a boutique backpacker hostel, it is indeed cosy with tidy doubles in separate garden chalets, dorms, polished wood floors, TV lounge with log burner, internet and off-street parking.

C-D Hanmer Backpackers, 41 Conical Hill Rd, T03-315 7196, hanmerbackpackers@ xtra.co.nz. Well established backpacker hostel, just north of the town centre. Friendly, with dorms and good-value doubles. Open fire, high-speed internet and off-street parking.

Motorcamps and campsites

Both places have flats, cabins, powered/ tent sites and clean modern facilities.

B-D Alpine Adventure Tourist Park, 200 Jacks Pass Rd, south of the thermal resort, T03-315 7112, www.aatouristpark.co.nz. A good walk from the town centre but none the less an excellent choice with spacious sheltered sites, excellent value cabins and good facilities. Recommended.

B-D Mountain View Top Ten, at the entrance to town, T03-315 7113. All the usual Top Ten quality.

Hanmer Springs to the west coast *p499*

L-AL Maruia Springs Thermal Resort, T03-523 8840, www.maruia.co.nz. Has lovely luxury/standard studio and family units. 2 licensed restaurants, one of which is traditional/Kiwi, the other Japanese. The tariff includes unlimited access to the thermal pools. Public access to the hot pools daily 0900-2100, from $15, child $8. Private pools available 1100-1700, from $30 per hr.

A Lewis Pass Motels, SH7, 16 km from Maruia Springs Thermal Resort, T03-523 8863, www.lewis-pass.co.nz. Modern self-contained units in a pleasant country setting.

B-C Alpine Motor Inn and Café, Springs Junction, T03-523 8813, sj.alp.inn@xtra.co.nz. Offers studio units and a separate budget chalet for backpackers. Attached is a café and shop selling light snacks, daily 0800-1930. Internet.

Kaikoura *p499, map p501*

There is plenty of choice in Kaikoura, with motels being the dominant force, but there are also plenty of fine B&Bs. Local farmstays are another option often overlooked. You are advised to book ahead in mid-summer; the VIC (I-Site) has full listings.

LL-L Fyffe Country Lodge, SH1 (south), T03-319 6869, www.fyffecountrylodge.com. Luxury accommodation in mud-brick, native timber lodge surrounded by English-style gardens. There is a range of studio en suites and a romantic in-house gourmet licensed restaurant with open fire, specializing in seafood, beef, lamb and Pacific Rim cuisine.

LL-L Hapuku Lodge, Hapuku Rd (12 km north of Kaikoura), T03-319 6559, www.hapuku lodge.com. A contemporary complex offering 7 elegant en suites and an apartment with open fire and spa. The emphasis is very much on natural materials and a scattering of original New Zealand art. There is a good café.

L-A Old Convent, Mt Fyffe Rd, T03-319 6603, www.theoldconvent.co.nz. In a quiet setting and full of character. This former convent, built for French nuns in 1911, now offers an unusual B&B option. Here you can imagine yourself as Mother Superior taking up her former quarters, or try behaving yourself

in a choice of former nuns' cells. The chapel is now a cosy guest lounge with log fire. Although a French-style dinner is available you would be better to sample the eateries in town. Internet, off-street parking.

AL-A Donegal House, Schoolhouse Rd, T03-319 5083, www.donegalhouse.co.nz. Has a strong Irish influence and 13 tidy en suites. However, what makes the place special are the grounds and the Irish bar/restaurant.

AL-A Fifeshire B&B (The Point Farm), out towards the peninsula and its walkway, T03-319 5059. Has a tidy double, twin and single and is very peaceful.

B&Bs and apartments

There is a scattering of fine B&Bs and self-contained apartments on the peninsula itself, all offering spectacular views.

L-AL Lemon Tree Lodge 31 Adelphi Terr, T03-319 7464, www.lemontree.co.nz. A boutique B&B that caters especially for couples or single independent travellers. Renovated 2-storey house with 4 tidy rooms, all with private deck or balcony and good attention to detail. Outdoor hot tub. Caring, experienced and well-travelled owners.

L-AL Miharotia, 274 Scarborough St, T03-319 7497, www.miharotia.co.nz. Modern boutique B&B set overlooking the town and Kaikoura Range. There are 4 contemporary guestrooms, one king en suite with a 4-poster and 3 queen en suites all with private patios. The long-term resident owners also possess a wealth of local information especially regarding the areas fishy residents.

L-AL Nikau Lodge, 53 Deal St, T03-319 6973, www.nikaulodge.com. Has 5 en suites and a room with private bathroom. Internet, Sky TV and good views across town.

AL Clifftop Apartment 5 Dover Terr, T03-319 6649. A modern, spacious timber home with a magnificent outlook. Value twins and doubles.

B Bay Cottages, 29 South Bay Parade, South Bay, T03-319 5506, baycottages@xtra.co.nz. Tidy modern and good-value self-contained cottages sleeping up to 4.

Motels

There are almost 20 motels to choose from, with most being along the Esplanade or heading north out of town on Beach St, SH1.

LL-L White Morph, 92-94 Esplanade, T03-319 5014, www.whitemorph.co.nz.

L-AL Admiral Court Motel, 16 Avoca St, near the wharf, T03-319 5525, www.kaikoura motel.co.nz. A good choice, a short walk from the start of the coastal walk.
L-AL Anchor Inn, 208 Esplanade, T03-319 5426, www.anchor-inn.co.nz. Recommended.
AL Mediterranean, 239 Beach Rd, T03-319 6776, medmotel@xtra.co.nz. Slightly cheaper option north of the town centre.
AL-A Blue Seas, 222 Esplanade, T03-319 5441, blue.seas@xtra.co.nz.

Backpacker hostels
There is no shortage of beds in the town.
B Lyell Creek Lodge, at the northern end of town, 193 Beach Rd, T03-319 6277, lyellcreeklodge@yahoo.co.nz. A great place for couples looking for value and peace. It has 5 modern tidy rooms, a twin and double with en suite and 3 rooms with shared bathroom. All have TV and there is a cosy lounge.
C-D Cray Cottage, 190 Esplanade, T03-319 5152. Good quiet option, with decent facilities, dorm and twins. Closed Jun-Jul.
B-D Dusky Lodge, 67 Beach Rd, 3 mins to the West End, T03-319 5959, www.dusky lodge.com. Recently expanded, it is modern, spacious and friendly with dorms, twins and good-value en suite doubles with TV. Facilities include internet, spa, heated pool, sauna, open fire, off-street parking and bike hire. Another nice touch is the value, authentic Thai cuisine served alfresco beside the pool daily from 1700.
B-D Kaikoura (Maui) YHA, 270 Esplanade, T03-319 5931. The best sea and mountain views, it has dorms, twins and doubles and a good atmosphere, and is worth the 10-min walk from the West End.
B-D Sleepy Whale Backpackers, 86 West End, T03-319 7014, www.sleepywhale.co.nz. Right in the heart of the West End, aesthetically unremarkable, but handy for amenities and has a deck overlooking the action.
B-D Topspot Backpackers, 22 Deal St, T03-319 5540, topspot@xtra.co.nz. Very tidy, with dorms and doubles. It runs good-value $60 seal-swimming trips.
C-D Albatross Backpackers, 1 Torquay St, T03-319 6090, www.albatross-kaikoura.co.nz. A little further west in the old telephone exchange on a quiet suburban street. Good attention to detail and a warm welcome for guests. Wide range of spotless, themed

rooms (including a self-contained option) and good facilities, not to mention some cool music that complements a laid-back atmosphere. Internet and off-street parking.

Motorcamps and campsites
There are also a number of basic beachside campsites (**D**) on the coastal roads south of Kaikoura. For information call the local council on T03-319 5348.
AL-D Alpine Pacific Holiday Park, 69 Beach Rd, T03-319 6275, www.alpine-pacific.co.nz. If the Top Ten is full, or for a quieter option, try this very friendly place.
A-D Kaikoura Top Ten Holiday Park, 34 Beach Rd, T03-319 5362, www.kaikoura holidaypark.co.nz. The best motorpark, only 3 mins from the town centre and the beach. Modern facilities, motel units, en suite units, cabins and powered/tent sites.

● Eating

Hanmer Springs *p498*
There is a scattering of cafés along Amuri Av, Conical Hill Rd and in the Mall, all of which are quite similar in fare and value.
₹₹₹-₹₹ Heritage Hotel, see Sleeping, above, T03-315 7021, breakfast 0730, lunch 1200-1430 and dinner from 1800. A la carte and buffet breakfast, lunch and dinner in elegant surroundings.
₹₹ Alpine Village Inn, Jack's Pass Rd, T03-315 7005, Mon-Fri 1100-2130, Sat-Sun 0900-2130. The local pub. Hearty, value pub food.
₹₹ Malabar, Alpine Pacific Centre, 5 Conical Hill Rd, T03-315 7745, daily from 1800. A fine mix of Indian and Malaysian in a casual setting. Takeaway service.
₹₹ Old Post Office Restaurant, near the Thermal Resort at 2 Jack's Pass Rd, T03-315 7461, daily from 1730. Lots of character, it specializes in New Zealand cuisine.
₹₹ Wai Ariki Nature Park Cafe, 108 Rippingale Rd (off Argelins Rd that bisects the golf course) T03-315 7772, www.waiariki-naturepark.co.nz, Tue-Sat 1000-1700. While adults can indulge in a coffee or light snack the kids can come face to face with a llama or highland cow.
₹ Mumbles Café, Conical Hill Rd, T03-315 7124, daily from 0930-1700. Good coffee and value breakfasts, and is a good spot to watch the world go by.

There are plenty of affordable options for both lunch and dinner, with most specializing in seafood.

There are 2 supermarkets: **Dreaver's Four Square**, West End, T03-319 5332; and **Night and Day**, opposite the Top Ten Holiday Park on Beach Rd (SH1) open until 2300.

♥♥ **Craypot Café and Bar**, 70 West End, T03-319 6027, www.craypot.co.nz. A good place to try crayfish at an affordable price.

♥♥ **Donegal House**, Mt Fyffe Rd, T03-319 5083, daily 1100-1400 and 1800-2100. In a lovely setting, with an Irish touch.

♥♥ **Fyffe Country Lodge**, south on SH1, T03-319 6869, daily for lunch and dinner. Good seafood and a fine view (especially after a late whale-watch). Cosy evening dining.

♥♥ **The Green Dolphin**, 12 Avoca St, at the far end of the Esplanade, T03-519 6666, daily in summer lunch and dinner, Tue-Sun dinner only in winter. A firm seafood favourite serving such delights as scallops on kumara mash.

♥♥ **Hapuku Café**, 16 km north on Hapuku Rd, T03-319 6558. Set on a deer and olive farm, a fine choice for organic fare, vegetarian dishes and microbrewed beer.

♥♥ **Hislop's Café**, 33 Beach Rd, T03-319 6971, daily for lunch and dinner, closed Tue evenings in winter. The place to find wholefoods and the best vegetarian dishes.

♥♥ **Mussel Boys**, 80 Beach Rd, T03-319 7160, May-Sep from 1200, closed Mon. Superb mussels and seafood dishes.

♥♥ **Pier Hotel Pub and Café**, 1 Avoca St, T03-319 5037, daily from 1700. Combine a coastal walk to the wharf (1 km) with good pub-style grub, a fine atmosphere and views. Indoor and outdoor seating.

♥♥ **Sonic on the Rocks Bar and Café**, 93 West End, T03-319 6414, daily 1000-late. The best place for evening entertainment, with live bands; the main backpacker hostel hangout. It also serves a fine value meal.

♥ **Why Not Café**, 66 West End, T03-319 6486, 0600-2100 in summer and 0600-1800 in winter. Recommended for its coffee.

▲▲ Activities and tours

Hanmer Springs *p498*
There are plenty to choose from, with mountain biking and skiing being the most prominent.

Hanmer Springs Adventure Centre (HSAC), 20 Conical Hill Rd, T03-315 7233, www.hanmer adventure.co.nz daily. Wide range of activities, mountain-biking a speciality. Independent hire of mountain bikes, scooters, motorbikes (ATV adventures from $129), fishing tackle, rollerblades and ski equipment, also available.

Thrillseekers Adventure Centre (TAC), 9 km south of the town at the Waiau River Bridge, T03-315 7046, www.thrillseeker.co.nz. Offers a 35-m bridge bungee, which is a 'light taster' for the higher jumps in Queenstown (from $135), as well as jet boating and rafting.

Fishing
There is excellent local fishing, and the VIC (I-Site) sells licences ($18.50 per day) and lists local venues and guides. A half-day will cost about $250.

Flightseeing
Hanmer Springs Helicopters, T0800-888308, www.hanmerhelicopters.co.nz. Offers 8-min to 1-hr trips over the forest park and surrounding mountains, $155-385.

Four-wheel drive trips
Backtrax, T03-315 7684, www.backtrax.co.nz. A 2-hr trip across farmland and the hills bordering the Waiau River will cost $110 ($80 per head 2 people).

Molesworth Tours, T03-315 7181, www.molesworth.co.nz. Day trips by 4WD to the largest and one of the most remote cattle stations in New Zealand, from $139.

Horse trekking
Hanmer Forest Park and the surrounding countryside is superb horse riding country.

Alpine Horse Safaris, Hawarden, T03-314 4293, www.alpinehorse.co.nz. Standard treks and some excellent multi-day trips in the region from $155 (1 day) to $3450 (12 days).

Hanmer Horses, T03-315 7444/T0800-873546, www.hanmerhorses.co.nz. Offers 1-hr to full-day rides from $45.

Hurunui Horse Treks, T03-314 4204, www.horseback.co.nz. Entertaining 1- to 8-day options from 'Station to Station' or 'Mountain to Sea', from $150-2975, Oct-May.

Massage
If you are exhausted even reading this list, or fancy some pampering after your activities,

then a massage can be secured at the new **Hanmer Springs Thermal Reserve** therapy centre (30 mins from $50), see page 498 Wisteria Cottage Day Spa, 34 Conical Hill Rd, T03-315 7026, www.nzhotsprings.com/dayspa. Numerous treatments with a 1-hr run-in with some seaweed costing from $95.

Maze

Kids might like to lose themselves (or adults might like to lose their kids) in the fairly unremarkable **Hurunui Jones and the 'Lost Temple of Indra' Maze**, on the roadside as you come into town, 1000-1730. It's fun and great if you want to get lost, but you cannot help wondering if it was only ever a rock garden project gone horribly wrong. From $7, child $6.

Mountain biking

Mountain biking is a major reason why many come to Hanmer Springs, and the **Forest Park** offers some superb tracks from easy and moderate to the wonderfully muddy. **HSAC** (see page 506) offers bike hire from around $16 for 1 hr to $45 for a full day.

Skiing

Skiing is another major reason why many flock to Hanmer in winter. Ski equipment can be hired from **HSAC** (see page 506). Lift passes start at about $45. **Hanmer Heli-ski and Heli-board**, T0800-888308, offers half-day trips from $325, full-day $650. For ski shuttles see Getting around, page 500. For more information contact the VIC (I-Site) or visit the website, www.nzski.com, or www.snow.co.nz. The 2 ski fields are: **Hanmer Springs Ski Area**, 45 mins from town, T03-315 7201, has 2 rope tows, poma and lodge and accommodation facilities. **Mount Lyford**, off SH70 (75 mins), T03-315 6178, has some challenging runs for both intermediates and the advanced as well as a good learners area, ski hire, lodge and a restaurant.

Walking

There are plenty of good walking tracks around Hanmer, particularly in the **Forest Park** offering both short/long and easy/moderate options. The 1-hr **Conical Hill Lookout Walk**, with its views south across the town, is accessed from the top of Conical Hill Rd and

continues through the forest to link up with Jollies Pass Rd and back into town. For more walks information contact the VIC (I-Site).

Kaikoura *p499, map p501*

There are 2 things you need to bear in mind with the boat-based activities in Kaikoura. The first is simple: in mid-summer book the whale-watching and dolphin-swimming well in advance. Even the other less popular activities are worth pre-booking to avoid disappointment. The second is the notoriously fickle weather. Given its position on the Southern Ocean, Kaikoura is subject to the vagaries of wind and wave, and trips can be cancelled at a moment's notice. Again to avoid disappointment allow yourself at least 2 days, just in case your trip is rescheduled. Also be sure to request your inclusion on another trip on cancellation, since this will not be done as a matter of course.

4WD

Glenstrae Farm 4 Wheeler Adventures, T03-319 7021/T0800-004009. Offers 4WD and quad-bike adventures. Based about 25 km south of the town it offers 3-hr trips in the coastal hinterland with great views. Departs 0900, 1330 and at dusk, from $110 (Argo from $80). Courtesy pick-ups from Kaikoura.

Birdwatching

New Zealand is considered the seabird capital of the world and a remarkable 70% of its bird list are pelagic species. Kaikoura offers a world-class opportunity to see many that would otherwise involve long excursions far offshore. Of particular interest are the albatross, mollymawks, and numerous petrel species. The many notable regulars include the giant petrel, which is as big as a goose, the Westland petrel, which is endemic to New Zealand, and the cape pigeon that could not be more aptly named. The birds are attracted to the boat using a block of 'chum' (fish guts) and almost the instant it hits the water the show begins. **Albatross Encounter with Ocean Wings**, 96 Esplanade, Kaikoura, T03-319 6777, www.oceanwings.co.nz. Boat trips to see a wide variety of rare seabirds. **Ocean Wings**, 96 Esplanade, T03-319 6777, www.oceanwings.co.nz. Run by the **Dolphin Encounter** outfit, 2-3-hr trips on demand, from $80, child $40. Recommended.

Dolphin swimming/watching

The coastal waters around Kaikoura abound with dolphins, and not just 1 species. They range from the common and bottlenose dolphins to the smaller dusky and rare Hector's dolphin. It is the dusky dolphin you are most likely to encounter (or swim with), and pods running into their hundreds, even thousands, are not uncommon. The duskies are also well known for breaching, and will jump out of the water or even somersault in an almost choreographed display of 'being'. Depending on their mood they may show great interest in the boat or swimmers or, on other days, show complete indifference. **Dolphin Encounter**, 96 The Esplanade, T03-319 6777, www.dolphin.co.nz. The main operator. In summer the 3-hr trips leave from West End at 0530, 0830 and 1230, in winter 0830 and 1230, from $130, child $120 (viewing-only $65, child $55). If you swim, and provided a pod is found (which is highly likely, you'll get a refund if not), you will have plenty of time in the water frolicking around with the dolphins. You will be given a safety briefing and will be encouraged to make high-pitched bagpipe-like noises to attract them. This will keep the 'viewing-only' passengers highly entertained. Take a towel and warm clothing, and book well in advance.

Eco-tours (general)

Kaikoura Naturally, T0800-801040, kaikouranaturally@xtra.co.nz. Offers 3-hr guided coastal and bushwalks daily at 0900 and 1300, from $40 or $70 per couple.

Fishing

Top Catch, T03-319 6306, www.kaikoura fishingcharter.co.nz. 3 hrs from $90.

Flightseeing

Pilot A Plane, based at Peketa Airfield, south of town, T03-319 6579, aeroclub.kaikoura @xtra.co.nz. Offers the chance to take the controls on a 30-min scenic flight, from $100.

Horse trekking

Fyffe Horse Treks, T03-319 5069, www.kaikourahorsetrekking.com. 2 hrs, $60.

Scenic and cultural tours

Maori Tours, T03-319 5567, www.maori tours.co.nz. Offers plenty of local cultural

insight and protocol with visits to local *pa* sites and a walk amidst native bush to see how the plants were traditionally used by the Maori. Entertaining with plenty of participation, half-day from $85, child $45.

For a more conventional tour option contact **Kaikoura Shuttles**, T0800-766962.

Scuba diving

Dive Kaikoura, 94 West End, T03-319 6622/ T0800-728223, www.scubadive.co.nz. The main operator offering a wide range of options with the emphasis on seal encounters. Hire and tank fills available.

Seal watching and swimming

With whales and dolphins being the main oceanic stars, the New Zealand fur seals are often overlooked. But encounters with these inquisitive 'fat-bodies' can be a memorable experience. On land they are undisputed 'beach-bum couch-potatoes', but under water they display an ease and grace in motion that would put any ballet dancer to shame. In Kaikoura there is the choice of observing them from land, boat, kayak, or to get up close and personal in the water.
Dive Kaikoura, 94 West End, T03-319 6622, www.scubadive.co.nz. The main dive operator with an emphasis on sub-aqua seal encounters.
Kaikoura Kayaks, T021-462889/T0800-452456, www.seakayakkaikoura.co.nz.
A kayak can provide a great way to get up close and personal to the seals. This outfit has half-day guided tours taking in the lovely scenery of the peninsula, and also offers the opportunity to dive and snorkel with the seals. Trips depart from the VIC (I-Site) daily at 0830, 1230 and 1630 (winter 0900/1300), from $70, child $55. Freedom hire costs from $45 for a half-day, $65 for a full-day.
Seal Swim Kaikoura, T03-319 6182, www.sealswimkaikoura.co.nz. 2-hr shore and boat based snorkelling tours daily 0900, 1030, 1230 and 1400 (Oct-Nov, Apr-May 0900-1230), from $70, child $60.
Topspot (Backpackers) Seal Swim, T03-319 5540. Offers seal-swimming tours Nov-Apr from $70, child $50.

Star gazing

Kaikoura Night Sky, T03-319 6635, from $35, child $25. For a fine close-up of the moon and a little insight into nebulae.

Surfing

Although the peninsula itself offers few fine surf breaks, the coast to the north is excellent. **Board Silly Adventures**, T03-319 6464/ T0800-787352. Offers surf lessons from $40 per hr ($85 all inclusive), advanced coaching and independent board hire, from $40 half-day.

Tree planting

Trees for Travellers, T03-319 7148, ask for details at the VIC (I-Site), www.treesfor travellers.co.nz. A programme that allows visitors to help with local native bush restoration. You can plant your own natural memento from $20.

Walks around Kaikoura

The 2-hr return 'Peninsula Walk', which links the 2 settlements is excellent and recommended. You can either walk along the cliff-top or the shoreline (depending on the tide) and start at the Point Kean car park (at the end of Avoca St), or alternatively at the South Bay car park. You will encounter seals, lots of interesting rock pools, and some superb coastal scenery.

A much longer jaunt is the celebrated 3-day, 45-km 'Kaikoura Coast Track', which combines sights inland and along the coast. **Sally and David Handyside**, T03-319 2715, www.kaikouratrack.co.nz, offers this as a package from $150.

Mount Fyffe (1602 m), directly behind Kaikoura, offers spectacular views and can be accessed (15 km) from the end of Postman's Rd (junction Athelney Rd/ SH1 north of Beach Rd) or Grange Rd (SH1 north); 8-hr return, DoC huts en route ($5, book at the VIC/I-Site).

There is also a good lookout and short walk, 'Fyffe Palmer Track', at the end of Mount Fyffe Rd (8 km). To get there, drive out of town on Ludstone Rd (north) then turn right onto Mount Fyffe Rd and follow it to its terminus. The VIC (I-Site) has DoC broadsheets on all these walks and others.

Whale watching

The first commercial whale-watching operation in New Zealand was started in 1987 by the Maori-owned and operated **Whale Watch Kaikoura**, (see below). The company now has 4 purpose-built vessels and can accommodate about 100,000 visitors annually. You can expect to see at least one whale on your trip as well as dolphins, seals, albatrosses and other unusual seabirds. If no whales are seen at all there is an 80% refund.

A recent addition to the on-board entertainment is an excellent computer generated animation entitled 'World of the Whales' which provides an imaginative view of the geography and remarkable depth of the Kaikoura Canyon. Trips are weather-dependent and can be cancelled at any time. Note that your inclusion on a later trip is not automatic and needs to be requested.

Kaikoura Helicopters, based at the 'Whaleway Station', T03-319 6609, www.worldof whales.co.nz. Offers 30- to 40-min flights from $295-455. If you don't like the idea of a boat trip, or just fancy seeing the whales from a different (and better) perspective, then you should go whale watching from the air. This can be particularly good in calmer sea conditions when you can see the whole whale from above rather than just the tail end and flukes. At just over 150 m you can also spot dolphins and enjoy the added bonus of spectacular aerial views across the peninsula and the coast. Photographers will need a good telephoto lens, fast film and a polarizing filter.

Whale Watch Kaikoura, T03-319 6767/ T0800-655121, www.whalewatch.co.nz. Based at the 'Whaleway Station' (next to the Railway Station), accessed off Beach Rd (SH1) just beyond West End. It offers several 2- to 3½-hr trips daily (seasonal departures) from $130, child $75. The boats all leave from South Bay, 10 mins from the Whaleway Station. Recommended.

Wings Over Whales, based at the Peketa Airfield 6 km south of Kaikoura, T03-319 6580/T0800-226629, www.whales.co.nz. Entertaining and personable flightseeing trips from 30-45 mins at 0900, 1100, 1300 and 1500, from $145, child $80. Recommended.

⊖ Transport

Kaikoura p499, map p501
Bicycle hire West End Motors, 50 West End, T03-319 5056. **Taxi** T03-319 6214.

❶ Directory

Hanmer Springs *p498*
Banks There is an ATM at the Four Square foodmarket, in the main shopping centre on Conical Hill Rd. TCs are also accepted and exchanged there. **Internet** Mountain View Top Ten, at the entrance to the town, T03-315 7113. **Medical services** Medical centre, 20 Amuri Av, T03-315 7503. **Police** 39 Amuri Av, T03-315 7117.

Post office in the Four Square foodmarket, T03-315 5112.

Kaikoura *p499, map p501*
Banks BNZ, 42 West End with an ATM. **Internet** Internet Outpost, 19 West End, slower, but stays open later (until 2100). Kodak Express, on West End, daily 0900-1730. **Police** T03-319 5038. **Post office** 41 West End, T03-319 6808, Mon-Fri 0830-1700, Sat 0900-1200.

West of Christchurch

Until recently there were basically two main reasons tourists 'headed for the hills' west of Christchurch. The most obvious reason was to reach the west coast via SH73, the Craigieburn Forest Park and Arthur's Pass, while the other was to ski the popular Mount Hutt ski fields near Methven. However, since the release of the Lord of the Rings trilogy, there is now another very good reason in the surprising form of a large and conspicuous lump of rock. Mount Sunday, which sits predominantly in the Rangitata River Valley and in stark contrast against the mountainous skyline of Southern Alps, became the perfect filming location and set for Edoras and Meduseld, King Theoden's grand hall in the realm of Rohan. Although the set is long gone, it remains one of the most scenic drives in the country and, even without all the hype, was always a great place to visit. ⟫ *For Sleeping, Eating and other listings, see pages 513-515.*

Ins and outs

Getting there Methven is 90 km southwest of Christchurch via the celebrated 'Inland Scenic Route' (SH73) and SH72. **Intercity**, T03-377 0951, operates daily buses from Christchurch. For winter shuttles to Mount Hutt and Christchurch, contact **Methven Travel**, T03-302 8106, which offers Methven-Christchurch from $30. From Christchurch it is 240 km to the west coast; Arthur's Pass is 158 km. **Coast to Coast**, T0800-800847, www.coast2coast.co.nz, departs Christchurch 0800, arriving Arthur's Pass 1030 and Greymouth at 1250, from $60 return (Arthur's Pass from $25).

TranzScenic's, T0800-872467, www.tranzscenic.co.nz, daily rail service *Tranz Alpine* is touted as one of the most scenic rail journeys in the world and is a very popular way to get from Christchurch to Greymouth. The *Tranz Alpine* leaves Christchurch at 0815, arriving Arthur's Pass 1042 and the Greymouth at 1245. It makes the return journey from Greymouth at 1345, to Arthur's Pass at 1557, arriving in Christchurch at 1805. A standard return is around $180, child $90.

Getting around Methven Travel (see above) offers taxi services and a ski bus to the slopes in winter. It also provides transportation to the Mount Somers Walkway, T03-302 8106. Several companies offer shuttles to the Mount Hutt ski field from around $25 one way including: **Ride Snow Shuttles**, T0800-121414, www.ridesnowshuttles.co.nz3; **Mount Hutt Taxi and Shuttle**, T03-302 1728/T027-431 8604; **Mount Hutt Tours**, T03-302 8106, and **Leopard Coachlines**, T03-302 8707/T025-339963. Mountain bikes can be hired from **Big Al's** in The Square, T03-302 8003, from $39 per day.

Tourist information Methven VIC (I-Site) ① *121 Main St, T03-302 8955, www.meth veninfo.co.nz, daily 0900-1700 (winter 0800-1800)*, can provide free town maps and information about the ski fields. It also stocks DoC information covering regional

specific ski information and online snow reports contact the **Mount Hutt ski field**
① T03-302 8811, or www.cdbwa.■■.in(, www.nzski.com. **Arthur's Pass VIC (DoC)** ① *in
the heart of the village on the southern side of SH73, T03-318 9211, www.doc.govt.nz,
daily 0900-1600*, has various displays about the national park, a video ($1), walks
information and all local accommodation and service details. Ask for the *Village
Information* broadsheet and map. Before embarking on any long walks or tramps
check the weather forecast and ask about up to date track conditions.

Methven and Mount Hutt ⬤🚴🏇⛷🏔⛵ ‣ *pp513-515.*

→ *Colour map 5, B5 Population: 1500*

The biggest attraction to the small, but congenial agricultural town of Methven is its
location close to the **Mount Hutt ski field**. At an elevation of 2075 m and covering an
area of 365 ha, 'The Hutt' is highly regarded within the skiing fraternity. The reason for
this is not only its proximity to Christchurch, but also because of its reputation for
having some of the best snow in the country and the longest and most consistent
season in the southern hemisphere (mid-June to October). It also has modern base
lodge with brasserie, bar, cafés, shops and snowboarding facilities.

In summer, although the town is quiet, it still offers an escape from the city or the
tourist hype and various activities including balloon flights, mountain biking,
whitewater rafting or walking. The region is also noted for its farmstays.

West coast via Arthur's Pass ⬤🚴⛵ ‣ *pp513-515.*

The route to the west coast via SH73 from Christchurch across the Great Divide and
the northern ranges of the Southern Alps is one of the most celebrated scenic drives
and rail journeys in the country. It is most notable perhaps for its sheer range of
dramatic South Island landscapes from the flatlands of the Canterbury Plains to the
east, through the rugged mountain peaks and river gorges in its centre, to the lush
coastal valleys and lakes to the west. On the way, other than its aesthetics, are the
Craigieburn Forest and **Arthur's Pass National Park**, which offer some excellent
walking, tramping, rock climbing and skiing opportunities.

Sights

From Christchurch, with the almost constant sight of the mountains looming ever
larger, you pass through the small and aptly named rural settlements of **Darfield** and
Springfield to reach the foot of the Torlesse Range. Just beyond Springfield the road
climbs steeply through **Porters Pass** before falling once again into the valleys and
unusual karst landscapes that border the **Craigieburn Forest Park** (100 km). The area
offers a small flurry of ski fields including **Porter Heights**, **Mount Olympus**, **Mount
Cheeseman**, **Broken Rivers** and **Craigieburn**. All these are 'club fields', offering a wide
range of slopes and conditions. For information contact the VIC (I-Site) in Christchurch
or Methven, or consult the excellent website, www.nzski.com. There are also plenty of
walking opportunities. The DoC leaflet the *Craigieburn Forest Park Day Walks* is very
useful and available from the VICs (I-Sites) above. The rugged karst landscape of **Kura
Tawhiti** or **Castle Hill Reserve** (30 km west of Springfield) provides more interesting
walks and also some excellent rock climbing.

Six kilometres further west is the **Cave Stream Scenic Reserve** which is easily
accessible from SH73. Here you will find the rather unique opportunity of a
self-guided blackwater hike in a limestone cave system that has been created over
the millennia by the Waimakariri River and its tributaries. The cave system was used

for centuries by Maori on their transmigration west to the coast and still contains some examples of rock art and bones. The one-hour underground hike is of course more of a 'wade', but is worth the soaking. Just be sure to take a good torch and dry clothing. The DoC panels in the car park will keep you right; leaflets are available from the VICs (I-Sites).

At the northern border of the Forest Park, and just beyond the tiny settlement of Cass, both road and rail penetrate the vast open-braided **Waimakariri River Valley** before entering the Arthur's Pass National Park. From there it is only a short drive to the enveloped outpost village of **Arthur's Pass**.

Arthur's Pass → Colour map 5, A5 Population: 111

It was one Arthur Dudley Dobson, a pioneer surveyor, who first explored the route to the west coast via the east Waimakariri and west Otira River Valleys in 1864. Although at the time Arthur was merely on a routine trip, his observations became an integral part of securing road access to the west coast during the gold boom of the 1860s. Remarkably, or perhaps not, given the motivation, a basic road was built within a year, but the rail link that later served the coal and timber trade took a further 60 years to complete. Now, long after all the gold has gone, the railway remains a monument to patience, while the road continues to need constant maintenance and improvement. These modern feats of road engineering and construction become obvious just beyond Arthur's Pass in the form of the impressive, and only recently opened, **Otira Viaduct.**

Even before the rail link to Arthur's Pass was complete, the area was proving popular for tramping and skiing, and by 1930 Arthur's Pass was gazetted as a National Park. The tiny settlement of Arthur's Pass is 924 m above sea level and is used as the base for activities in the park, or as a welcome halfway stop en route to the west coast.

Arthur's Pass National Park → Colour map 5, A5

The Arthur's Pass National Park was designated in 1929 and is 114,500 ha in area. It extends from the vicinity of Harper's Pass in the northern Southern Alps to the mountains around the head of the Waimakariri and Otira rivers. The park is essentially made up of high mountain ranges, gorges and expansive braided river valleys. One of the highest and most attractive mountains is **Mount Rolleston** (2270 m), which lies just to the southwest of the Arthur's Pass. Its impressive **'Bealey Face'** can be seen from the road just west of the village.

The mountain ranges are 'alpine' in nature, containing a broad range of vegetation which varies greatly from east to west in accordance with the varying climatic conditions and rainfall. To the east the forests are almost entirely made up of mountain beech, while to the west, on the other side of the 'Great Divide', it is more complex with a variety of podocarp species, beech, kamahi and kaiakawaka. The park is rich in alpine plant species, many of which thrive above the tree line and are endemic to New Zealand. Many native birds are also present, the most notable being the notoriously inquisitive and destructive native mountain parrot, the kea. If this is your first trip across to the west coast you may also notice one other creature, one that will make its presence known in no uncertain terms: the sandfly.

The park offers a network of tramping tracks that are equipped with over 30 DoC backcountry huts. Two of the best day walks are the seven- to eight-hour ascent of **Avalanche Peak**, directly behind the village on its southern side, or, further west still, the more difficult (mainly summer) climb to the summit of **Mount Rolleston**. The Avalanche Peak track begins from behind the DoC information centre, which can offer detailed information and advice on these tracks and others. Note that braided rivers and the small tributaries that feed them are notorious for flash floods, so extra care is required. History buffs might like to negotiate the 1½-hour **Arthur's Pass Village Historic Walk**; a leaflet is available from the VIC (I-Site).

Methven and Mount Hutt *p511*

Given its popularity as a ski resort there is no shortage of beds in the town, with the majority being upper- to mid-range self-contained lodges with spas, open fires and drying rooms. There are also a good number of backpacker lodges and, again, these have a 'ski-lodge' feel with all the facilities. The VIC (I-Site) has full listings; advanced bookings are advised in winter. Prices drop dramatically in summer.

LL Terrace Downs High Country Resort, Coleridge Rd, Rakaia Gorge, Darfield, T03-318 6943/T0800-465373, www.terracedowns.co.nz. Classy golf course resort in the Canterbury foothills, offering excellent modern villas and luxury chalets and in-house restaurants, café and bar. Perfect escape for Tiger wannabes.

L Beluga, 40 Allen St, T03-302 8290, www.beluga.co.nz. Excellent high-end B&B and self-contained cottage option.

L Powderhouse Country Lodge, 3 Cameron St, T03-302 9105, www.powderhouse.co.nz. Restored villa with a glass-atrium hot tub.

AL Brinkley Village Resort, Barkers Rd, T03-302 8885, www.brinkleyvillage.co.nz. Modern option, a little lacking in atmosphere, which specializes in self-contained studios and apartments. It has a restaurant, bar, hot tubs, pool and the welcoming open fire.

AL Mount Taylor Lodge, 32 Lampard St, T03-302 9699, www.mounttaylorlodge.co.nz. Modern, well-facilitated alpine-style lodge and a good mid-range option.

AL Whitestone Cottages, 3020 Methven Hwy, T03-302 9271, www.whitestonecottages .co.nz. New 2-bedroom fully self-contained cottages near the centre of the village.

AL-A Bed Post, 177 Main St, T03-302 8508, www.mthuttbeds.com. A modern motel close to the town centre. Self-contained studios with spa and standard units.

AL-A Lodge on Chertsey, 1 Chertsey Rd, T03-303 2000, www.thelodgenz.com. Right in the heart of the town, this purpose-built lodge has some excellent luxury spa rooms, en suites, and good modern facilities including a licensed restaurant, bar and internet. Off-street parking. Often has special rates in summer.

AL-D Abisko Lodge and Campground, 74 Main St, Methven, T03-302 8875,

www.abisko.co.nz. Friendly place with modern tidy en suites, apartments (with log fires) and powered sites for campervans or tents. Restaurant, bar, spa/sauna and a comfortable lounge with obligatory open fire.

AL-D Ryton Station, on the shores of Lake Coleridge, 10800-926868, www.ryton.co.nz. The largest (14,589 ha) and best equipped, with budget lodge accommodation, en suite chalets, camping (no powered sites), a restaurant and plenty of activities from fly fishing to jet boating all in a remote setting.

A-D Pudding Hill Lodge, on the Inland Scenic Hwy, 12 km west of Methven, T03-302 9627, www.puddinghilllodge.co.nz. A 3-star rated establishment close to Mt Hutt and the ski-field. It has 1- to 2-bedroom studio units, a budget lodge rooms, powered/tent sites, sauna and spas.

C-D Alpenhorn Chalet, 44 Allen St, T03-302 8779. A cosy bungalow with new facilities, dorms and doubles and a spa. Recommended.

C-D Redwood Lodges, 5 Wayne Pl, T03-302 8964, skired@xtra.co.nz. Provides 2 good-value purpose-built self-catering lodges, one with shared facilities and one with great-value en suites. All ski facilities are provided, and it has a cosy log fire.

C-D Skiwi House, 30 Chapman St, T03-302 8772, skiwihouse@xtra.co.nz. Well-established, friendly and very comfortable with well-heated dorms and doubles. It is also good in summer with plenty of enthusiasm in arranging non-ski activities.

Motorcamps and campsites
The **Abisko Lodge and Campground**, see above, has new powered sites and is recommended.

D Methven Camping Ground, Barkers Rd, , T03-302 8005. An older option also located in town with basic but adequate facilities.

West coast via Arthur's Pass *p511*
There are a number of good places to stay before you reach Arthur's Pass. In winter these are very popular skiers, while in summer it is walking boots that sit on the steps.

LL Grasmere Lodge High Country Retreat, SH73, Cass, T03-3188407, www.grasmere.co.nz. All mod cons in luxury suites; dinner and activities as part of the package. It can also be reached on the *TranzAlpine* which stops at the edge of the property on request.

AL-D Flock Hill Lodge, a further 40 km east of Arthur's Pass, T03-318 8196, www.flockhill.co.nz. Part of the expansive Flock Hill Station, has tidy motel units, backpacker lodge and a restaurant. Activities arranged. Ideally located close to the ski fields and the Craigieburn Forest Park walks.

C-D Smylie's YHA, Springfield, on Main Rd in the centre of the village, T03-318 4740, www.smylies.co.nz. Cosy dorms and doubles, with modern facilities. The ideal base for both winter and summer activities. In winter it rents skis and arranges transport to the slopes. In summer rock climbing, horse trekking and hiking can be arranged.

Arthur's Pass *p512*

Arthur's Pass village offers a small range of accommodation options, with a B&B lodge, a motel, 2 backpacker hostels and a campsite. There is one à la carte restaurant and a café.

A Trans Alpine Lodge, at the western end of the village, T03-318 9236, www.arthurs pass.co.nz. The most expensive, with comfortable doubles, 8 of which are en suite. There is an outdoor spa, an in-house à la carte and a bistro/restaurant.

A-B Alpine Motel, just beyond the bridge on the right at the eastern end of the village, T03-318 9233. Has self-contained doubles. It also offers a 'car minding' service.

C-D Arthur's Pass Alpine YHA, T03-318 9230, yhaapass@yha.org.nz. The older of the 2 backpacker hostels. Next to the café, with dorms and doubles.

C-D Mountain View Backpackers, T03-318 9258, mountain.house@xtra.co.nz. More modern with some excellent cottages on the grounds, a spacious lodge and tent sites. Recommended.

Campsites

The **Mountain View Backpackers** is the best bet for tent sites while the **Trans Alpine Lodge** offers a few powered sites using lodge facilities. Basic camping facilities are also available at the public shelter across the road from the VIC (I-Site) in the village ($6), or free at **Klondyke Corner**, 8 km east, and **Kelly Shelter**, 17 km west.

🍴 Eating

Methven *p511*

There are 2 supermarkets: **Supervalue** and **Topnotch**, both on McMillan St. The former is open until 2100 in winter.

🍴 **The Last Post Restaurant**, Rakaia Gorge Rd, T03-3028259. Another reliable option, licensed and one of the most popular après ski venues.

🍴 **Ski Time Restaurant**, Racecourse Av, T03-302 8398, www.skitime.co.nz. Popular lodge restaurant bar with cosy atmosphere and open fire 5 mins from town by car. Courtesy vehicle available for groups.

🍴 **Steel-Worx Restaurant and Bar**, 36 Forest Drive, T03-302 9900.The 'Worx' enjoys a good reputation. It is stylish, full of character with a cosy, log-burning stove.

🍴 **Stronechrubie Restaurant**, Mt Somers, 30 km from Methven, T03-303 9814, www.stonechrubie.co.nz. One of the best fine-dining restaurants in the region.

🍴 **Café 131**, Main St, T03-302 9131, 0900-1600. Good coffee, recommended for breakfast.

🍴 **Primo Café**, McMillan St, T03-302 9060. 0730-1830. In the second-hand shop, **Secundo**, and well worth a visit

Arthur's Pass *p512*

The only other licensed restaurant is in the **Trans Alpine Lodge** (see Sleeping, above).

🍴 **Wobbly Kea Café and Bar**, T03-318 9101, in the centre of town. The best bet for a meal.

🍺 Pubs, bars and clubs

Methven *p511*

The colourful pubs, **The Blue**, on Barkers Rd, and **The Brown**, just opposite, are both traditional favourites, with the former the most popular for après-ski.

Steel-Worx Restaurant and Bar, 36 Forest Drive, T03-302 9900. Smaller and already earning a good reputation for its lively party nights in winter. All offer good pub lunches.

🎭 Entertainment

Methven *p511*

Cinema Paradiso, Main St, T03-302 1957. Specializes in art house movies.

▲ Activities and tours

Methven p511

Flightseeing and Heliskiing
Methven Heliskiing, T03-302 8108,
www.heliskiing.co.nz/methven. Spectacular
runs in the Arrowsmith Ranges from $825.
Mount Hutt Helicopters, Blackford Rd,
T03 302 8401, www.mthutthell.co.nz.
Flightseeing trips from $98 and heli-taxi
ski/board trips and service to the ski slopes,
from $155. Heliskiing runs from $155,
full day $795.

Golf
Clubs can be hired from **Big Al's** in
The Square, Methven.
Methven Golf Course, Hobbs Rd,
T03-302 8438. Quality 18-hole course
with fine mountain views.
Terrace Downs, Lake Coleridge Rd,
T0800-465373, info@terracedowns.co.nz.

Horse trekking
High Country Horse Adventures,
T0800-386336, www.horsetrek.co.nz.
Adventurous excursions from $75.
Staveley Horse Treks, Staveley, T03-303
0809. 1 hr from $35, best for beginners.

Hot air ballooning
Even outside the ski season Methven offers
a good range of activities year round.
Aoraki Hot Air Balloon Safaris, T03-302
8172, www.nzballooning.com. Relaxing flights
with a champagne breakfast, from $295.

Jet boating
Both offer scenic trips and heli-jet
options on the Rakaia River from $68.
Rakaia Gorge River Tours, T03-318
6574, www.rivertours.co.nz.
Rakaia Gorge Scenic Jet, T03-318 6515,
www.rakaiagorgescenicjet.co.nz.

Rafting
Rangitata Rafts, T03-696 3534/T0800-
251251, www.rafts.co.nz. Offers excellent day
excursions down the scenic Rangitata River,
south of Methven (Grade IV-V), from $164
($174 includes transport from Christchurch).
To keep up the adrenaline, you might also

consider a spot of mountain biking
for which the VIC (I-Site) can provide
all the details.

Skiing
Day lift passes cost $84, child under
6 free. A 3-day lift pass costs from $228,
child $117. Ski equipment hire is available
at the field itself or in various outlets in
Methven, including **Big Al's**, The Square,
T03-302 8003, www.bigals.co.nz. For more
information regarding the Mt Hutt field visit
www.nzski.com. For transport to the field
see Getting around, page 510.

Tours (Lord of the Rings 4WD tours)
The following companies offer 4WD trips
to Erewhon and Mt Sunday (Edoras); both
can be booked at the VIC.
Hassle Free Holidays, T03-354 6050,
www.hasslefree.co.nz. Trips depart
Methven at 1045, returning 1600 and
include driving on Mt Sunday. Includes a
champagne picnic lunch, from $175
Ride Snow Shuttles, T0800-121414,
www.ridesnowshuttles.co.nz. Offers
similar trips.

Walks
There are numerous walks or longer hikes
on offer in the Mt Hutt Forest (14 km west)
including 'The Foothills' and the Peel Forest
(south); the climb to the summit of Mt Somers
(1687 m) is particularly recommended.
Ask at the VIC (I-Site) for details.

❶ Directory

Methven p511
Banks BNZ (ATM), Main St. **Medical
facilities** Medical Centre, The Square,
T03-302 8105; **Pharmacy**, Main St, T03-302
8103. **Police** T03-302 8200. **Postal
agent** Gifts Galore, Main St.

Arthur's Pass p512
Internet Available at the I-Site.
Post office Main St, limited opening
hours. **Useful addresses** There is a
petrol station and a police station in the
village, T03-318 9212. For breakdown,
T03-618 9266.

South Canterbury

From Christchurch SH1 heads south through the flat heartland of the Canterbury Plains to Timaru. With so much seemingly omnipresent and stunning scenery elsewhere in New Zealand, aesthetically it is often labelled as the least exciting drive in the country; only the occasional glimpse of the distant Southern Alps far to the west and the odd wide pebble-strewn riverbed crossing, breaks the monotony of the endless roadside windbreaks and expansive fields. Even the cows look bored to death. Roughly half way between Christchurch and Timaru is the only major settlement, Ashburton.

▶▶ *For Sleeping, Eating and other listings, see pages 520-522.*

Ins and outs

Getting there Timaru airport ① *12 km north of town via SH1*, is served by **Air New Zealand Link**, T0800-737000, daily from Christchurch and Wellington. For taxi from the airport contact **Timaru Taxis**, T03-688 8899, from $15. For car hire and taxi services see page 522. The VIC (I-Site) holds local suburban bus (CRC) timetables.

Ashburton is 87 km south of Christchurch and 76 km north of Timaru on SH1. All the major bus companies heading south can stop in Ashburton and Timaru including **Intercity**, T03-688 6163, and **Atomic Shuttles**, T03-322 8883. Buses stop outside the VIC (I-Site) in Ashburton and the station in Timaru. The VIC (I-Site) can help book tickets.

Tourist information Ashburton VIC (I-Site) ① *corner of East and Burnett sts, T03-308 1050, www.ashburtontourism.co.nz, Mon-Fri 0830-1700, Sat 1000-1500, Sun 1000-1300*, has a free town map and full accommodation and local activity listings. **Timaru VIC (I-Site)** ① *in the former Landing Service Building, 2 George St, T03-688 6163, www.southisland.org.nz, Mon-Fri 0830-1700, Sat-Sun 1000-1500*, also has DoC information. **Geraldine VIC (I-Site)** ① *corner of Talbot and Cox sts, T03-693 1006, www.southisland.org.nz, Mon-Fri 0830-1700, Sat-Sun 1000-1600*, has full listings for local accommodation and DoC information. The free leaflet *Geraldine* includes comprehensive listings including the varied arts and crafts outlets. **Temuka VIC (I-Site)** ① *72-74 King St, T03-615 9537, temlibrary@xtra.co.nz*, has full accommodation listings. **Waimate VIC (I-Site)** ① *75 Queen St, T03-689 7771, www.waimate.org.nz*, has detailed accommodation and local activity listings.

Ashburton ●❼🚲▲ ▶▶ *pp520-522.*

➔ *Colour map 5, B5 Population: 13,400*

Due to its surrounding topography and perhaps its very location right on SH1, as well as being so near Christchurch and so far from the principal tourist attractions to the south, Ashburton seldom lures tourists to stop for anything other than a hurried toilet break, quick snack and cup of coffee. But having said that, it is not a bad little place and if you take a little time (especially on Sundays), it will reveal a few worthy attractions and tempting activities to complement the warm welcome offered by its friendly residents.

The main attractions are its small museums and craft outlets. The **Ashburton Art Gallery and Museum** ① *Baring Sq East, T03-308 1133, Tue-Fri 1000-1600, Sat-Sun 1300-1600, donation,* has the obvious focus on local history but is particularly noted for its displays of local and contemporary arts and crafts.

Also of note, though seldom open, is the **Plains Vintage Railway and Historical Museum**, which is just over the Manoran Road level crossing (off SH1) in the **Tinwald Domain and Recreation Park** ① *south of the town centre, T03-308 9621, www.plains*

railway.co.nz, Jul-Sep Sun only, Oct-Jun every second Sun of the month. It offers short rides on some of its fine array of restored locos and traction engines, from $6, child $2.50. Also in the Domain is the **Vintage Car Museum** ① 103-308 7025, *Sun only*, which has a collection dating back to 1905. For crafts, the **Ashford Craft Village** ① *415 West St, T03-308 9085*, is worth a look and can double as a good place for lunch.

Timaru 🏨🍴❄️⛰️🚌🌙 ⇒ *pp520-522*.

→ *Colour map 5, B4* **Population: 27,300**

The port city of Timaru, halfway between Christchurch and Dunedin, provides a refreshing stopover on SH1, or a convenient starting point from which to head west, via SH8, to the 'MacKenzie Country', Mount Cook and Queenstown. The city is pleasant, boasting the popular **Caroline Bay beach** near the town centre, a few good parks, the region's main museum, a reputable art gallery and a few unique attractions, including some ancient seventh-century **Maori rock art**.

Background

With the existence of over 500 sites featuring Maori rock art, particularly in the caves and rock overhangs of the Opihi and Opuha rivers, west of Timaru, historians have estimated that the Maori settled in the area as early as AD 1400. During the 17th century the warring Ngati Tahu, from the north of the South Island, drove the descendants of these people, the Ngati Mamoe, south into Fiordland. European settlement began in 1837 with the establishment of a whaling station at Patiti Point, close to the present town. This was followed by the purchase and creation of a

Canterbury South Canterbury

Timaru

To ④, Supermarket, DB Mainland Brewery, Christchurch, Mt Cook & Airport

Caroline Bay

Beverley Rd

Aigantighe
Art Gallery

Beverley Hill

Wai-Iti Rd

Albert

Hewling

Nelson

Seaview Terr

Jackson St

Cameron

Sefton St

Evans St

Marine Par

Pareora St

① Piazza

Bay Hill

Merefiere

Bidwill St

Elizabeth St

Grey Rd

York St

Matilda St

Brunswick St

Clyde

Dee St

Church St

Sutter

Arthur St

Hunt St

Le Cren St

Gibson St

Deal

Tasman

Theodosia St

North St

Canon

@ Computer Shop

The Terrace

Pari Loop Rd

Stafford St

Sophia St

Strathallan

Beswick

Cains

Station

Library

Perth

King George St

South Canterbury
Museum

Bank St

Butler

Later St

Woollcombe

Barnard St

Stafford St

Landing
Service Building

Turnbull

Cliff

To Oamaru (SH1 South)

To ① & Timaru Botanical Gardens

N

0 metres 200
0 yards 200

Sleeping 🛏️
1873 Wanderer
Backpackers 4
Aspen on King 1
Benvenue & Motor Inn 3

Panorama Motor
Lodge 2
Tighnafeile House 6
Timaru Top Ten
Holiday Park 8

Eating 🍴
Coq & Pullet 2
Le Monde 1
Purple Lizard Café 6
Red Rocket Café 3

Speights Ale
House 4
Stafford Mall
Foodcourt 5

sheep station known as 'The Levels' in 1852 by the influential Rhodes brothers from England. For over two decades disputes arose between the brothers and the government surrounding land ownership and development, but this was eventually settled and the two communities merged to form Timaru. With the reclamation of land in 1877 and the creation of the harbour at Caroline Bay, the town quickly developed as a major port. Today, Timaru boasts the second largest fishing port in New Zealand and is even visited by the occasional cruise liner. The name Timaru is thought to be derived from the Maori *te maru* meaning 'place of shelter'. However, some authorities dispute this and suggest the literal translation of *ti*, meaning 'cabbage tree', and *maru*, meaning 'shady' is the correct one.

Sights

At the VIC (I-Site) you are immediately confronted by the original 'bluestone' façade of the **Landing Service Building** which was built in 1870 to facilitate the export of wool and other goods from the surrounding district. This building now forms the starting point for the town's three main heritage trails.

South Canterbury Museum ① *Perth St, To3-684 2212, Tue-Fri 1000-1630, Sat-Sun 1330-1630, free,* is the main regional museum and contains some interesting exhibits on local maritime history, Maori rock art and the exploits of aviator Richard Pearse (1877-1953). In 1903 Pearse is said to have made the first manned flight, nine months before the Wright Brothers of America (see Temuka, page 519). A full replica of the impressive contraption that allowed him to do so is on display. Other relics of Pearse's various flying inventions are held at the Pleasant Point Railway Museum (see page 519).

The **Aigantighe** (pronounced 'egg and tie' and meaning 'at home' in Scots Gaelic) **Art Gallery** ① *49 Wai-iti Rd, To3-688 4424, Tue-Fri 1000-1600, Mon, Sat-Sun 1200-1600, gardens open dawn to dusk, free,* is one of the best art galleries in the country. Founded in 1956, and set in a 1908 historic home surrounded by a sculpture garden, its hallowed walls feature exhibitions from a substantial permanent exhibition dating back to the 16th century, as well as contemporary works by Colin McCahon and C F Goldie. The gallery also hosts regional and national exhibitions.

After experiencing these three-dimensional works you may like to see a very different craft in action in the form of Gareth James at the **Artisan Forge** ① *40 Fraser St, Timaru Port, To3-684 8872, www.iron.co.nz, daily 1000-1700.* Gareth is one of New Zealand's few remaining working blacksmiths and offers a fascinating 40-minute show, with all sparks flying, from $7.50.

The iconic **DB Mainland Brewery** ① *Sheffield St, 2 km north of town, To3-688 2095,* offers free weekday tours and tastings at 1030.

Timaru has some pleasant parks and beaches. The beach at **Caroline Bay**, north of the town centre, was formed as a result of land reclamation and original harbour development in 1877. Although in close proximity to the busy port, and not aesthetically remarkable, the beach still remains a popular and safe haven for swimming.

The park alongside the beach has a number of attractions including a roller-skating rink, a mini-golf course, a maze and an open-air concert soundshell. Every summer, just after Christmas, this area is the focus for the **Summer Carnival** (see Festivals and events, page 522). The **piazza** (built in 1997) leads from Bay Hill down to Caroline Bay and adds to the relaxed seaside café, restaurant and wine bar scene. More traditional are the **Timaru Botanical Gardens** ① *To3-688 6163, daily 0800-dusk,* which were established in 1864. They are especially noted for their collection of rose species and are located just south of the town centre; they are best accessed on the corner of King and Queen Streets. **Centennial Park** follows the course of the Otipua Creek and also offers a peaceful escape and a lovely 3½-km, one-hour (one way) walk that begins from the old 'bluestone' Gleniti School on Clearmont Street, west of the town centre.

Around Timaru and south to Oamaru
⊜⊘✳▲ ⊬ ᴧᴧ520 523

If you have given yourself plenty of time in the immediate area and find yourself at a loose end, the small rural communities that surround Timaru, namely, **Geraldine**, **Temuka**, **Pleasant Point** or **Waimate**, off SH1 to the south, provide some unusual attractions that may lure you off the beaten track.

Geraldine → *Colour map 5, B4 Population: 2323*

The pleasant Anglicized country town of Geraldine, nestled amidst the Four Peaks and Peel Forest Mountain ranges, is home to a thriving arts and crafts community providing an attractive, if brief, diversion off SH1 (15 km). Other than the obvious scattering of arts and craft galleries and shops, the town has two museums. The **Vintage Car Club and Machinery Museum** ① *178 Talbot St, T03-693 1006, daily 1000-1600, $5,* has a sizeable collection of cars and tractors dating back to 1900, as well some notable aircraft, including its star attraction, the unique 'Spartan'. The small but lovingly maintained **town museum** ① *Cox St, T03-693 8082, Mon-Sat 1000-1200, 1330-1530, Sun 1400-1600, donations,* is housed in the former Civic Centre (1885).

The best way to negotiate the arts and crafts outlets is with the guidance and maps available at the VIC (I-Site). Of particular note is **Barkers Berry Barn** ① *Talbot St, T03-693 9727, www.barkers.co.nz,* which offers tastings and sales from its fine range of fruity products. **The Giant Jersey** ① *10 Wilson St,* is also worth a look; it reputedly displays the largest jersey in the world.

There are a number of good walks in the vicinity, particularly in the **Talbot Forest Scenic Reserve**, next to the town, and the **Peel Forest**, 19 km northwest via SH79 (Peel Forest Road). The VIC has details or call in at the **Peel Forest Outdoor Pursuits Centre** ① *at the OPC office, T03-696 3832, www.peelforestopc.org.nz, Mon-Fri 0900-1630.*

Temuka → *Colour map 5, B4 Population: 4000*

This small agricultural service town, 19 km north of Timaru, is the former home of farmer and eccentric inventor Richard Pearse (1877-1953). In April 1903, at the tender age of 26, Pearse created history by making the first-ever powered flight in a 'heavier-than-air-man-carrying aeroplane'. His flight, though neither long nor spectacular, was a world first and was completed nine months before the better-known and much-celebrated flight by the American pioneer aviator Orville Wright of the famous Wright brothers. A **memorial** to his achievement can be seen at Waitohi (signposted off SH1), which was the site of his brief and historic flight. In 2003 – on the 100th anniversary – locals attempted to rebuild his plane and get airborne; sadly, on the day, inclement weather meant nothing except umbrellas were airborne. Pearse died an unrecognized recluse in a psychiatric hospital in Christchurch.

Besides the memory and memorial to its most famous son, Temuka is noted for its modern-day crafts outlets, particularly the **Temuka Pottery** ① *Vine St, T03-615 7719.* Its location is perhaps fitting given the fact that the town's name derived from the Maori Te-Umu-Kaha, meaning 'The Place of the Hot Ovens'.

Pleasant Point

Eighteen kilometres northwest of Timaru (SH8), Pleasant Point offers a few brief diversions including the **Pleasant Point Museum and Railway** ① *T03-686 2269, www.pleasantpointtrail.org.nz.* It is home to the world's only remaining 1925 *Model T Ford* Railcar. There are regular scheduled rides on the glistening restored loco hourly ($6, child $4), and kids will further delight at others that feature faces akin to 'Thomas the Tank Engine' and friends. Although additional rides are offered on most weekends (1030-1630) you are advised to phone for specific dates and details.

Near Pleasant Point is one of the finest examples of **Maori rock art** in the country. The weathered 14-ft drawing known as the Opihi 'Taniwha' (Maori for 'monster') is considered to be the oldest, having been created sometime in the 16th century. It is in a shallow limestone shelter on private farmland and is best viewed lying on your back. To visit the site you will need to be accompanied by a guide, which can be organized through the Timaru VIC (I-Site).

Waimate → *Colour map 5, C4 Population: 3000*

Although noted as being an atypical New Zealand rural township, Waimate, 47 km south of Timaru, is perhaps better known as a 'little bit of Aussie abroad', with its very furry resident population of cuddly marsupials. Known rather unfortunately perhaps as 'red necked' or bush **wallabies**, these appealing plump and bouncy little characters were originally introduced to the area in 1875 for fur and sport. But, like so many other intellectually wanting acts of 'wildlife familiarization', it has resulted in a resident population of rapacious native plant-eaters that are now considered a major pest. Given this, the activities surrounding the wallabies are in complete contrast with most folks taking delight in hunting them down. But it doesn't end there (Lord no!). In Waimate one eminent bright spark recently came up with the idea of making **wallaby meat pies**. Who knows, it might just prove to be a major tourist drawcard.

You can either take the indirect, sympathetic and close-range option, with copious amounts of petting and feeding, at the wallaby-friendly **EnkleDooVery Korna** ① *Bathgates Rd, T03-689 7197, www.waimate.org.nz/tamewallabies, Oct-Apr daily 1000-1700, $5, child $3,* or alternatively the more distant and direct approach, with a bullet (hunting details from the VIC). If you do take the former option you can cuddle the irresistible pouch babies. Wallabies can also be seen, petted and fed at the **Kelcey's Bush Holiday and Animal Park** ① *Mill Rd, 7 km west of the town (signposted), T03-689 8057, kelceysbush@xtra.co.nz.*

Of a more historical nature is the less cuddly but very smart **Waimate Historical Museum** ① *in the former 1879 Waimate Courthouse, 28 Shearman St, T03-689 7832, Mon-Fri 1330-1630, Sun 1400-1600, $3.* It houses a small but significant array of memorabilia and forms part of the town's 'Strawberry Heritage Trail'.

Also of historical interest, but of very different structural aesthetics, is the Te Waimate historic thatched **'cuddy'**, which is almost as cute as the wallabies. Built in 1854 from a single totara tree, it was the home of Michael Studholme, the first European settler in the town. Waimate is often used as a short cut to the Waimate River and **Benmore/Aviemore Lakes,** which are famous for their watersports and superb fishing. The huge and very uncuddly Quinnant salmon are the prime target. The VIC (I-Site) has details and listings of local guides. If you are in Waimate in February your visit may coincide with the annual **South Canterbury Busking Festival** (see Festivals and events, page 522), which although overshadowed by the annual and international Christchurch event still attracts people from far and wide.

● Sleeping

Ashburton *p516*
AL-A Ashburton Motor Lodge, 507 West St, T03-307 0399/T0800-427428, www.ashburton motorlodge.co.nz. Modern and upmarket.
AL-A Hotel Ashburton, Racecourse Rd, T03-308 3059, www.hotelash.co.nz. Modern units with in-house restaurant, bar and spas.
AL-D Coronation Park, 780 East St, T03-308 6606, www.coronationpark.co.nz. Ideally

placed with full range of accommodations and camp kitchen. Bookings advised.
A-B Taylors Lodge, 770 East St, T03-308 9119, www.taylorslodgemotel.co.nz. 11 units, standard facilities.
C-D Ashburton Holiday Park, Tinwald Domain, Moronan Rd, T03-3086805. 2 km south of town but recommended, offering 2 great value spacious cabins, powered/tent sites, and camp kitchen.

Timaru *p517, map p517*
The piazza overlooking Caroline Bay
is a fine place to be based.
LL Tighnafeile House, 02 Wai-Iti Rd, T03-
684 3333, www.tighnafeile.com. A beautiful
and historic B&B in a former run-holders
station. 5-min walk from Caroline Bay and
15 mins to the town centre. Spacious en suites
and doubles/twins with shared facilities.
AL-A Aspen on King, 51-53 King St, close
to the Botanic Gardens, T03-688 3054,
www.aspenonking.co.nz. Units with spa.
AL-A Benvenue Hotel and Motor Inn,
16-22 Evans St, T03-688 4049, www.ben
venue.co.nz. Good restaurant and heated pool.
A-B Panorama Motor Lodge, 50-52 Bay Hill,
T03-688 0097, www.panorama.net.nz. Handy
for restaurants on the piazza, and Caroline Bay.
B-D 1873 Wanderer Backpackers, 24 Evans
St, T03-688 8795, wandererbackpackers@
xtra.co.nz. All types of room, including good
spacious doubles. Homely atmosphere with
open fires, free bike hire. Pick-ups available.

Motorcamps
B-D Timaru Top Ten Holiday Park, 154a
Selwyn St, T03-684 7690, www.timaruholiday
park.co.nz. In a suburban setting, a good walk
from the centre, quiet, spacious, and modern.

Geraldine *p519*
LL Kavanagh House, SH1, Winchester,
T03-615 6150, www.kavanaghhouse.co.nz.
Luxurious boutique lodge with 3 sumptuous
en suites with spa or claw-bath and open fires.
It is also well known for its fine cuisine.
L Crossing, 124 Woodbury Rd, Geraldine,
T03-693 9689, www.thecrossingbnb.co.nz.
A former old 'gentleman's residence'
(whatever that means) in the town itself,
with sunny, spacious en suites, pleasant
gardens, open fire and in-house restaurant.
A-B Crown Hotel, 31 Talbot St, T03-693 8458,
Geraldine-crown@xtra.co.nz. Has character
and good-value en suites. Cheap pub meals.
A-B Four Peaks, 28 MacKenzie St, T03-693
8339, www.fourpeaksmotel.co.nz. Pleasant,
good value and modern.

Motorcamps
B-D Geraldine Motor Camp, 39 Hislop St,
T03-693 8147, www.geraldineholiday
park.co.nz. In a central location adjacent to
the park. Cabins and powered/tent sites.

C-D Peel Forest Motor Camp, T03-696 3567,
www.peelforest.co.nz. Basic but tidy it offers
cabins, powered/tent sites and pleasant
walks nearby. On-site café.

Waimate *p520*
B Locheil Motel and Guest House,
100 Shearman St, T03-689 7570. Offers
self-contained studios and units.
B-D Kelcey's Bush Farmyard, Mill Rd
(see page 520), T03-689 8057. Good for
campervans and has tidy cabins and flats.
C-D Hunter's Hill Lodge, Hillary St, T03-689
8726, www.huntershills.co.nz. Spacious
budget accommodation.

Eating

Ashburton *p516*
Cactus Jacks, 209 Wills St, T03-308 0495.
Open daily. Good for meat and fish mains
and lighter options like souvlaki and nachos.
Kelly's Bar and Café, 234 East St, T03-
308 881. For a good pub lunch.
Tuscany's (Somerset Tavern), across
the road from the VIC, T03-308 3389, is
good and open daily for lunch and dinner.
Ashford Café and Wine Bar, Ashford
Craft Village, 415 West St, T03-307 7664,
www.ashford.co.nz, Mon-Fri 0900-1600,
Sat-Sun 1000-1600. Great for coffee and light
snacks, with freshly baked bread a speciality.

Timaru *p517, map p517*
The piazza and Bay Hill Rd that overlook
Caroline Bay have 2 good affordable eateries:
Le Monde, T03-688 8550. A Good mix of
Euro and Pacific-rim cuisine, lunch and dinner.
Speights Ale House, George St,
T03-686 6030, As ever, a good option.
Coq and Pullet, 209 Stafford St, T03-688
6616, Mon-Fri 0730-1600, Sat 1000-1300. Great
range of light snacks, bread and huge cakes.
The Purple Lizard Café, 332 Stafford St,
T03-688 8890, Mon-Fri 0730-1700, Sat 0900-
1700, Sun 1000-1700. For homesick Scottish
people there is porridge on the breakfast
menu. It might not be as good as Granny's
but it will do and the coffee is grand.
Red Rocket Café, 4A Elizabeth St, T03-
688 8313, Mon-Sat from 1000-late, Sun from
1130. Popular café, the best coffee in town.
Stafford Mall Foodcourt, Stafford St.
Cheap takeaways.

Geraldine *p519*

♥♥♥ Kavanagh House, see Sleeping, page 521. The obvious choice for expensive fine dining. Bookings essential.

♥♥ Totara Bar and Restaurant, Crown Hotel, see Sleeping above, daily from 1100. A more affordable down-to-earth option.

♥ Barkers Berry Barn, see page 519, daily 0900-1730. Definitely the place for smoothies.

♥ Easy Way Café, next to the Barkers Berry Barn Complex, 76F Talbot St, T03-693 8090, daily for lunch and dinner. A safe bet with fine cuisine, frequent live entertainment (especially jazz) and internet.

Waimate *p520*

There is not a great deal of choice when it comes to eating, with only a handful of fairly unremarkable takeaways and tearooms.

♥♥♥ Criterion Hotel, 198 Queen St, T03-689 8069. Offers basic pub grub.

♥ Country Kitchen, also on Queen St, T03-689 8222, daily 0500-2100. Light snacks.

♥ Savoy Tearooms, 59 Queen St, T03-689 7147. The place to get your gnashers round a wallaby meat pie with plum sauce. You can also try goat, rabbit and thar (an introduced mountain goat), $5. Vegetarians had best catch the bus to Timaru.

⊛ Festivals and events

Timaru *p517*, *map p517*

Jan Summer Carnival Hugely popular amongst locals, this event attracts thousands who are entertained with organized concerts, fairground rides and sideshows.

Waimate *p520*

Feb South Canterbury Busking Festival. Buskers in all shapes and forms including acrobats, comedians, contortionists, dancers, escapologists and fire eaters do street performances.

▲ Activities and tours

Ashburton *p516*

For local activities consult the VIC. Pick-ups are provided for other activities to the west including rafting and ballooning. There are also some interesting day tours available to the Foothills and Mt Somers.

Timaru *p517*, *map p517*

Dolphin watching

Timaru Marine Cruises, T03-688 6881. Marine wildlife-watching tours that often locate the rare and tiny Hector's dolphin. The *Caroline Cat* departs daily at 1030 from No1 Wharf in the harbour (corner of Port Loop and Ritchie St), from $50.

Fishing

Timaru is noted not only for its sand and surf but also for its inland rivers, which come complete with monster trout. The VIC can advise on locations and guides.

Walking

There are plenty of good short walks in the town, with 3 heritage trails, and the 1-hr **Dashing Rocks**, the 45-min **Caroline Bay Walks**, and the **Centennial Park Walk** (see page 518). The VIC has details.

Geraldine *p519*

Geraldine is the base for activity operators. **4x4 New Zealand**, T03-693 8847, www.4x4 newzealand.co.nz. Full- or half-day excursions in a 4WD truck, including the *Lord of the Rings* tour to the stunning Erewhon Station and Mt Sunday (Edoras). **Rangitata Rafts**, T03-696 3534, T0800-251251, www.rafts.co.nz. Day excursions on the scenic Rangitata River (Grade IV-V), $164.

⊖ Transport

Timaru *p517*, *map p517*

Car hire Avis, 9 Heaton St, T03-688 6240/T0800-655111. **First Choice Rental Vehicles Ltd**, 207 Evans St, T03-688 5560. **Taxi** Timaru Taxis, T03-6888 899.

⊕ Directory

Timaru *p517*, *map p517*

Banks All the main branches have ATMs and are in the town centre around Stafford St. **Internet** The Computer Shop, 331 Stafford St, T03-684 9333, Mon-Fri 0900-1730, Sat 1000-1230. **Library** King George Pl, T03-684 8199. **Police** North St, T03-688 4199. **Post office** 21 Strathallan St, T03-686 6040, Mon-Fri 0800-1730, Sat 0900-1300. **Useful addresses** AA 31 North St, T03-688 8049.

MacKenzie Country

The area known as the MacKenzie Country refers mainly to the flat expanse of tussock grasslands that make up the watersheds of the Tekapo and Gray rivers. It is a strange barren landscape, devoid of trees and almost analogous to the plains of heartland USA. There is nowhere else like it in New Zealand and it bears little semblance to the lofty peaks that rise from around its edge. The name MacKenzie was bestowed upon it through the almost legendary activities of Scottish pioneer and sheep drover James 'Jock' MacKenzie. ➤➤ *For Sleeping, Eating and other listings, see pages 526-529.*

Ins and outs

Getting there All the daily west-east buses from Christchurch and Queenstown pass through Fairlie, Lake Tekapo and Twizel including **Intercity (Newmans)**, T03-365 1113; **Atomic Shuttles**, T03-332 8883, and **Wanaka Connextions**, T0800-244844, www.wan akaconnexions.co.nz. Out of the above only **Newmans** stops in Mount Cook. **Cook Connection**, T021-583211, www.cookconnect.co.nz, offers daily services between Mount Cook (and Tekapo) and Oamaru (via Twizel), $48 one way. Transport bookings can be made with **Kiwi Treasures**, Main Street, Tekapo, T03-680 6686 and the Twizel VIC.

Tourist information The closest you find to a VIC in Fairlie is the **Resource Centre** ① *64 Main St, T03-685 8496, www.fairlie.co.nz, daily 0900-1700.* The independent **Lake Tekapo VIC** ① *Kiwi Treasures, by the post shop on the main street, T03-680 6686, www.laketekapountouched.co.nz, daily 0800-2000,* is very small but has free town maps, information about lodging and local activities. **Twizel VIC (Events Centre)** ① *Market Place, centre of the village, T03-435 3124, www.twizel.com, daily 0900-1900 (winter Mon-Sat 1000-1600).* The free leaflet *Twizel – Town of Trees* has a detailed map and is useful. The **DoC area office** ① *Wairepo Rd, Twizel, T03-435 0802, kakivisitorhide@doc.govt.nz, Mon-Fri 0830-1730,* can provide specialist tramping and mountain bike track information. The best website is www.mtcooknz.com.

Fairlie → *Colour map 5, B4 Population: 845*

Lying relatively out on its own at the foot of the Hunter and Two Thumbs Ranges, the small rural settlement of Fairlie is often labelled as the rather dull gateway to the MacKenzie Country that lies just to the west through the portal of the **Burke's Pass**.

While it is unlikely that Fairlie will ever set the world alight, it seems perfectly happy with its pretty autumn colours and quiet existence. Quiet, that is, until winter when it is used as a base for the **Mount Dobson Ski-field** ① *T03-685 8039, www.dobson.co.nz.*

If you look a little closer you will find considerable evidence that contradicts Fairlie's reputation for being just another dull rural town. It has in fact been home to some rather innovative folk. One such resident, Rodolph Wigley, for example, drove from Timaru to Mount Cook in 1906 in a De Dion Bouton single-cylinder car, taking three days and encountering atrocious conditions (and few roads) to do so. Not satisfied with this rather impressive mechanical feat, he then went on to develop a motor-coach service and later an air transport service to Mount Cook, thereby creating the **Mount Cook Company**. Still not satisfied with this thriving enterprise, he then added a threshing mill business to his list of achievements and a traction engine that could do the work of 16 bullocks at twice the speed. And it doesn't end there. Rodolph's son, Harry, went on to design a landing gear that allowed his aircraft to land on the snow and ice of the Tasman Glacier. This gear was later to become the precursor to the landing gear used today. So, you see, it is interesting after all.

Other little insights can be procured from the two small museums in town: the **1875 Mabel Binney Cottage** and the **Vintage Machinery Museum** ① *on the main highway*

The legend of James-'Jock'-McKenzie

The MacKenzie Country, which lies west of the Burke's Pass from Fairlie, is named after the legendary Scottish sheep drover James 'Jock' McKenzie. Jock, of course, is a common label given to Scots folk, and the 'a' is optional in the 'Mac' – both Mac and Mc meaning, simply 'son of'. Anyway, the story goes that in 1855 James was caught in the Burke Pass, east of Lake Tekapo, with 1000 sheep. Nothing unusual in that (or is there?), except for the simple fact that they were not his. Said sheep actually belonged to the Rhodes brothers from the large Levels Station near Timaru. The Rhodes boys had sent out a small party to look for the flock and found James happily droving them to pastures new. Being hopelessly outnumbered, but Scottish, James managed to escape and was later recaptured in Lyttleton near Christchurch. Re-captured and suitably arraigned he was found guilty of sheep rustling and sentenced to five years in jail. But

that's where it all gets a bit hazy. Apparently, James then professed his innocence, claiming the sheep had in fact been bought and that he was taking his 'legally purchased' flock to a new claim in Otago. Initially believing this to be a load of tartan codswallop, he was jailed. But still determined, James escaped, not once, but two (some say three) times, by which time the powers that be were beginning to believe his story. Remarkably, after only nine months he was given a full pardon and released. Innocent or guilty, buried in the soils of New Zealand, or the glens back home in Scotland, we may never know. But still the stuff of legend, he is immortalized by a monument and stone cairn on the roadside, just west of the pass. On the monument you can read the immortal words:

'In this spot James MacKenzie (sic) freebooter, was captured by John Sidebottom and Maoris, Taiko and Seventeen and escaped the same night, 4th March 1855'. Go Jimmy!

west of the town centre, daily 0830-1700, seasonal, $2. Five kilometres west of here is the historic 1879 limestone **Woolshed** ① *on the privately owned Three Springs Station, T03-685 8174, daily 1000-1600, seasonal.* At its peak this station accommodated nine 'blade' shearers, which to the layman is essentially a very hard-working fella shearing with a very sharp pair of scissors – not the bionic electric clippers that are used today.

Lake Tekapo → *Colour map 5, B3 Population: 400*
Between Lake Tekapo and Twizel is the heart of the MacKenzie Country. If you have come north from the heady heights of Mount Cook there could hardly be a greater contrast in scenery. Lakes and mountains quickly give way to the vast expanse of featureless tussock grasslands of the Tekapo River basin. Suddenly it seems you have been magically transported from the Swiss Alps to Mid-West USA, and on less than a litre of petrol. From whichever direction you have approach, SH8 delivers you to the southern shores of Lake Tekapo and the settlement of the same name.

Tekapo is a pretty place, famous for its lakeside church and an ever-watchful little collie dog. However, over the last five years or so Tekapo has suffered somewhat from the rapacious development so evident throughout the central South Island. Already parts of the village are looking horribly like a Christchurch suburb, which is enough to have a little collie dog heading for the hills with its tail between its legs.

Just about everybody who visits Lake Tekapo pays homage to the **Church of the Good Shepherd**, which sits alone, in a picture-postcard position overlooking the lake. Even on closer inspection it could not look more perfect, with an open door revealing a cross on the altar backed by a large stained-glass window. It was built in 1935, primarily as a functional place of worship, but also as a memorial to the lives of the MacKenzie Country pioneers. Sadly though its midday function is almost entirely aesthetic and the minister, who is in attendance almost daily, must tend a very superficial and transitory flock (the vast majority of whom fall out of tour buses and come only to worship the Lord Digital, Kodak and Text SMS). Whatever you do, go early in the morning or late in the day to avoid the hordes.

A few pew lengths from the church is a statue of a collie **sheepdog**; a simple tribute to the shepherd's best friend. It's a lovely statue, with the dog facing the lake with an alert and loyal expression as if waiting for his master to appear from its mists. He has waited a long time, and may wait forever, his little nose covered in ice in winter, wet with rain in spring and bleached by the sun in summer.

There are plans for Tekapo to host an ambitious new project in the form of the **MacKenzie Heritage Centre**, www.themackenzie.com. At an estimated cost of around $12 million it will – we are assured – be aesthetically sympathetic with the surroundings and a state-of-the-art creation that will effectively celebrate and conserve the social and natural history of the region.

If you have time (and a rugged vehicle) the unsealed roads on either side of Lake Tekapo are well worth exploring. The road to the west passes **Lake Alexandria** and **Lake McGregor**, both of which are very peaceful (and full of trout), before winding its way north to terminate at the Godley Peak Station. On the eastern side the road travels along the lakes edge past the Mount Hay and Richmond Stations and the junction to the **Roundhill Ski Area** before continuing up in to the wilds of Macaulay and Godley River basins. On a map you will see just how far the glacier formed Godley River Basin goes before submitting inevitably to the peaks of the Mount Cook National Park and Mt D'Archiac (2865 m). This is the realm of the serious tramper and climber; without a helicopter it takes days to reach.

Dominating the scene at the western end of Tekapo Village is **Mount John**, named after one of the first European settlers in the region, a Scot named John Hay who arrived in New Zealand in 1841. Other than the superb views from its summit the mount also boasts an internationally significant observatory, which is well worth a visit. ▸▸ *See Activities and tours, page 528.*

Twizel → *Colour map 5, B3 Population: 1179*

Right in the heart of the MacKenzie Basin, near the river after which it was named, is Twizel, a former hydroelectric scheme construction town built in the 1970s. Pioneer surveyor John Thompson bestowed the name Twizel upon the town after the Twizel Bridge that crosses the River Tweed on the border between England and Scotland. Twizel's most famous residents are the critically endangered and endemic khaki, or black stilt, which, along with the village's proximity to the Mount Cook National Park and mountain biking, are its biggest tourist draw.

Twizel also presents an excellent opportunity to see cutting-edge conservation in action. The DoC's efforts to maintain the wild populations of the **black stilt** – one of the rarest wading birds in the world – have been internationally recognized. Known as 'khaki' by the Maori and considered to be a *taonga* species (living treasure), these birds were once common in the heartlands and braided-river beds throughout New Zealand. Thanks primarily to man's indirect introduction of non-native predatory species, like the weasel and stoat, numbers have been decimated and currently total less than 100 wild birds. A guided visit to the **viewing hide** ① *3 km south of the village, tours daily late Oct-mid Apr (weekdays only in winter), $12.50, child $5; contact Twizel DoC, T03-435 0802*, allows the public to see some of the stalwart survivors. The captive population of 66 are bred in enclosed aviaries and used to replenish the wild population. Bookings are essential and visits are by prior arrangement only.

Largely unbeaten by the nasty commercial stick, Lake Ohau provides a pleasant diversion off SH8 between Omarama and Twizel, and in winter a popular skiing venue. The **ski field** ① *for skiing information, T03-438 9885, www.snow.co.nz*, is best known for its scenic views, less frenzied atmosphere and the longest T-bar in New Zealand (1033 m). Most of the activity centres around **Lake Ohau Alpine Village** which is above the southern shores of Lake Ohau, just west of **Lake Middleton**, a small sub-lake separated from Lake Ohau by a narrow strip of land.

In summer the lake and its surroundings are popular for walking, fishing and mountain biking. It has six forests around its shores, with a number of tracks, access points and campsites. The best information is contained in the DoC brochure *Ohau Conservation Area*, available from the VIC in Twizel.

● Sleeping

Fairlie *p523*
AL-A Dobson Lodge, Burke's Pass, T03-685 8316, www.dobsonlodge.co.nz. Halfway between Fairlie and Tekapo (5 mins from Mt Dobson ski field), this is a charming stone B&B in a lovely quiet setting, with standard double and single en suites and a self-contained railway carriage. Dinner available.
B Fairlie Lodge, 16 School Rd, T03-685 8452. Basic but comfortable.
B Possum Cottage, McLeans Rd, Bedeshurst, T03-685 8075, possum.cottage@xtra.co.nz. Self-contained, farm-based and very cosy with an open fire.
B Rimuwhare, 53 Mt Cook Rd, T03-685 8058, rimuwhare@xtra.co.nz. Basic but comfortable motel.

Motorcamps and campsites
B-D Fairlie Gateway Top Ten Holiday Park Allandale Rd, northwest of the town centre, T03-685 8375, fairliegateway@xtra.co.nz. Also has backpacker accommodation.

Lake Tekapo *p524*
In Maori the name Tekapo means 'sleeping mat', but thankfully the village can offer far more than a bivvy beside the lake. Contact the VIC for full listings.
LL-L Tekapo Lodge, Aorangi Cres, above the main street, T03-680 6566, www.laketekapolodge.co.nz. Spacious, purpose-built B&B overlooking Lake Tekapo, a short stroll from the village centre. 4 luxury en suites, one with spa. Large guest lounge with open fire.
L-AL Godley Resort Hotel, SH8, T03-680 6848. The main hotel in town. Although getting a little tired it is in prime position in the centre of the village overlooking the

lake. It has comfortable suites with great views, and reputable Asian restaurants. It gets busy with tour groups in summer, but in winter when rates are reduced, it is worth considering.
L-A Chalet Boutique Motel, T03-680 6774. A fine lodge-style motel. By the lake (near the church) and with plenty of activities.
AL-A Lake Tekapo Scenic Resort Motel, T03-680 6808, www.laketekapo.com. In the heart of the action. Modern studio units with views and spas and also budget rooms (sleeping 4) or dorms with shared facilities.
AL-A Tekapo House, 8 O'Neill Pl, T03-680 6607, rayntek@xtra.co.nz. 10 mins from the centre of the village and has an en suite double and a twin with shared facilities.
A Pioneer Tourist Flat, overlooking the lake (near the church) on Pioneer Drive, T03-680 6755. A good self-contained option and very cosy in winter with its log fire.
B-D Tailor-Made-Tekapo Backpackers, 9-11 Aorangi Cres, T03-680 6700, tailor-made-backpackers@xtra.co.nz. Friendly and efficient. An activity-oriented place, with a good range of rooms, some good en suite.
C-D Tekapo YHA, 3 Simpson Lane, T03-680 6857, yhatekapo@yha.org.nz. Popular with backpackers, it has a lakeside location at the western end of the village, offering great views. Doubles, twins and dorms, cosy lounge with log fire, bike hire.

Motorcamps and campsites
A-D Lake Tekapo Motels and Motor Camp, western end of the village, Lakeside Drive, T03-680 6825. Spacious and peaceful in a fine lakeside spot. Self-contained motels, flats, cabins and sheltered powered/tent sites.

Twizel *p525*

L-AL MacKenzie Country Inn, corner of Ostler and Wairepo Rds, T03-435 0869, bookings@mackenzie.co.nz. Very plush, with good facilities and close to the town centre.

AL Aoraki Lodge, 32 MacKenzie Drive, T03-435 0300, www.bnb.co.nz/aorakilodge.nz. A good, reliable option.

AL Artemis B&B, 33 North West Arch, T03-435 0388, atremistwizel@para dise.net.nz. A central modern home with fine views.

AL Heartland Lodge, 19 North West Arm, T03-435 0008, www.heartland-lodge.co.nz. Has some pleasant en suite rooms and a self-contained loft, good value for up to 6.

AL-A Aspen Court Motel, 10 MacKenzie Drive, T03-435 0274, www.aspencourt.co.nz. 15 units with good facilities.

AL-A Lake Ruataniwha Homestay, 9 Max Smith Drive, T03-435 0532, robinandlester@ xtra.co.nz. A spacious modern home overlooking the lake, southwest of the centre.

A Mountain Chalets Motel, Wairepo Rd, T03-435 0785, www.mountainchalets.co.nz. Standard units, mountain chalets and a lodge with budget accommodation.

A-D High Country Holiday Lodge and Motel, 23 MacKenzie Drive, T03-435 0671, www.highcountrylodge.co.nz. A huge motel with backpacker facilities, including cheap en suites, doubles, singles and dorms. There is also a restaurant and bar on site and it is a stone's throw from Market Place.

Motorcamps

B-D Parklands Alpine Tourist Park, 122 MacKenzie Drive, T03-435 0507. In a sheltered spot and has self-contained and budget accommodation.

C-D Lake Ruataniwha Holiday Park, 4 km south of the village, T03-435 0613. In a pleasant setting near the lake.

Lake Ohau *p526*

L-AL Lake Ohau Lodge, T03-438 9885, www.ohau.co.nz. Set by the lake, it has standard self-contained studio and luxury units, a restaurant, bar and cosy open fire.

B Weatherall Motel, T03-438 9662, www.weatherallmotel.com. Self-contained and shared units (30 mins from the ski-fields).

🍴 Eating

Fairlie *p523*

🍴 **Old Library Café**, in the centre of town, T03-685 8999, daily 1000-late. Recommended, offering snacks to dinners including a great 2-course 'skiers' menu for under $15.

Lake Tekapo *p524*

There are numerous café/bars and takeaways in the main street for light meals and coffee; many have views across the lake, but the best view is to be had from the **Astro Café** at the summit of Mt John (see below). There is a **Four Square** supermarket at the service station, open daily until 2100.

🍴 **Astro Cafe**, Mt John Observatory, (follow signs west end of the village), daily 0900-1700. Once you have taken in the lakeside views this is an excellent venue for good coffee and light meals. Recommended.

🍴 **Garden Court Restaurant**, Godley Resort Hotel, T03-680 6688, daily for breakfast, lunch and dinner). Convenient with a choice of buffet or à la carte.

🍴-🍴 **Pepes Pizza and Pasta**, T03-6806677, Mon-Fri 1800-late, Sat-Sun from 1200-late.

🍴-🍴 **Reflections Restaurant**, T03-680 6234, daily from 1000. Suitable for light lunches and formal dinner, with good views across the lake.

Twizel *p525*

The limited options are centred in Market Pl.

🍴 **The Hunter's Bar and Café**, T03-435 0303. The local's choice for lunch, dinner and entertainment. It can serve up a decent coffee.

🍴 **MacKenzie Country Inn**, see above, daily from 1100. Also offers fine dining.

🍴-🍴 **The Korner Kafé**, T03-435 0501, lunch daily 0900-1430, dinner Thu-Tue from 1730. Reliable option with good veggie options.

⛰ Activities and tours

Lake Tekapo *p524*

Although Lake Tekapo is a small place there is plenty to do. Being the first major stop for the east-west tour buses and independent tourist traffic, there is an instant lure to leave the car parked and head for the skies, on an exciting scenic flight or, more recently, with the exciting new stargazing and daytime tours of the Mt John Astronomical

Observatory. Various operators also vie to offer the best deals on the hire of mountain bikes, kayaks and fishing rods. For the latest deals contact the VIC.

Astronomical observatory tours and star gazing

Earth and Sky, T03-680 6960, www.earthand sky.co.nz. Sitting discreetly atop Mt John, at the western end of the village, is the University of Canterbury's Astronomical Observatory – an internationally renowned base for astrological research and home to a new and exciting tourist operation. Daytime guided tours of Mt John Observatory are available as well as night stargazing tours at both Mt John and Mt Cook National Park. Weather permitting, the stargazing tour is fascinating and offers a great opportunity to see such 'heavenly bodies' as the Alpha-Centuri, Southern Cross, Scorpius, Kylierearendi, or indeed the Jewel Box. Even if you cannot stay for the evening the daytime observatory tour is well worth it for the memorable views. Observatory tours 1100-1500, 1 hr from $20, child $5; stargazing summer 2200 (winter 2000), 2 hrs from $58, child $25. Family tours on request. Café open 0900-1700.

Cruising and fishing

Cruise Tekapo, T027-479 7675, www.cruise tekapo.co.nz. Offers lake cruising from 20 mins to 2 hrs and half or full-day trout-fishing excursions.

Flightseeing

There are a number of flightseeing options. The airfield in Tekapo is the starting point for 2 main operators that also pick up passengers in Mt Cook, before embarking on world-class scenic flights across the Great Divide. **Air Safaris**, Main St, T0800-806880, www.airsafaris.co.nz. The popular 'Grand Traverse' is a memorable 50-min (200 km) trip that takes in Mt Cook and the glaciers on both sides of the divide. It is an unusual combination that you would be hard-pressed to find anywhere else. There will also be plenty of other options in Wanaka and Queenstown, but this trip (beyond a flight to Milford Sound) is one of the best and, at $260, child $180, is good value for money. **Tekapo Helicopters**, T03-680 6229, www.tekapohelicopters.co.nz. Helicopter

trips are a little more expensive, but provide a different kind of experience and can land on the snow. Note that the aircraft based here do not land on the snow unlike those flying from Mt Cook, but, what you lose in that experience, you will gain in flight time.

Horse trekking

McKenzie Alpine Trekking, Godley Rd (north), below Mt John, T0800-628269, www.maht.co.nz. Horse trekking from 1 hr to overnight, suitable for all levels.

Mountain climbing and trekking

Alpine Recreation, T03-680 6736, www.alpinerecreation.co.nz. Highly experienced guided mountain climbing and trekking trips from the 3-day 'Ball Pass Trek' in the Tasman Glacier Valley to the Full Monty 6-day ascent of Mt Cook, for a serious $3800.

Skiing

Roundhill Ski Area, T03-680 6977, www.roundhill.co.nz. Lift pass from $60, with gear hire from $35 per day.

Twizel *p525*

The VIC also lists over 60 things Twizel can offer in the way of activities, ranging from frisbee golf to ice skating. There are also some excellent fishing venues.
Discovery Tours, T03-435 0114, www.discoverytours.co.nz. Run by ex-park rangers, it offers a wide variety of options in Glentanner Park (see page 534) including hiking (glacier and mountain), mountain and heli-biking and even the inevitable *Lord of the Rings Tour*, start from $85. Recommended.

Climbing

Twizel Events Centre, Market Pl (just opposite the VIC), T03-435 0496, wall open Mon, Wed, Fri 1900-2100, Sat 1700-1900, Sun 1600-1800. New and impressive complex with climbing wall as well as squash courts and a gym, all open for casual use. A session on the wall costs from $12.

Eco-tours

Khaki (Black Stilt) Visitor Hide Guided Tours, Wairepo Rd, T03-435 0802, kakivisitorhide@doc.govt.nz. Guided trips to see one of the rarest waders in the world.

Flightseeing

A number of scenic heli-flightseeing trips leave from beside the MacKenzie Country Inn on Wairepo Rd, but you are advised to look at the numerous other choices available from elsewhere before parting with your cash (see Mt Cook National Park, page 533).

Mountain biking

Of particular note are the heli-biking trips to several locations including Benmore and Lake Ohau. The numerous canals and their associated tracks that connect the waterways and hydroelectric schemes provide ideal biking opportunities. For more information consult the VIC or the DoC leaflet *Ohau Conservation Area*. Bike hire is available. **Heli-bike Twizel**, T03-435 0626/T0800-435424, www.helibike.com. Rides range from 1½-3½ hrs and cost $55-200.

Mountaineering

High Country Expeditions, T03-435 0622, www.highcountry.nz.com. World-class mountain guide Shaun Norman offers climbing, mountaineering and abseiling.

● Transport

Lake Tekapo *p524*
Bicycle hire From the mini golf office behind the main shopping complex, T03-680 6961.

❶ Directory

Lake Tekapo *p524*
Banks There is only one ATM in Tekapo, next to the petrol station. **Internet** Reflections Restaurant, top end of the village and **Helicopter Flights Office** on Main St.

Mount Cook National Park

This 70,696-ha park has to be one of the most spectacular in New Zealand, and a natural 'cathedral' second only to Milford Sound. With the 3754 m peak of Mount Cook as its altar, its robust ministers include Tasman (3498 m) and Mount Sefton (3158 m), surrounded by a supportive choir of 19 peaks all over 3000 m. Rising up to this great chancel are the vast and impressive Hooker and Tasman glaciers, which not only created the long nave but once blocked the very porch. All this natural architecture makes for world-class scenery and mountaineering. Indeed, it was here that Sir Edmund Hillary first started a career that was to reach its 'peak' on the summit of Everest in 1953. The park is connected to the Westland National Park by the Great (east-west) Divide and peaks of the Liebeg Range, yet the two parks are significantly different. With such a dramatic upheaval of rock so close to the sea, the western side sees most rain and snow, creating slopes draped in dense rainforest and, higher up, huge snowfields, spawning the great Franz and Fox glaciers (to name but two). In the Mount Cook National Park, on the other hand, there is virtually no forest, with around one-third of it being permanent snow and ice. In amongst the rock beds and valley floors rare alpine plants flourish, some endemic and rare, and rummaging around in this heady garden are endemic bird species, like the mountain parrot and resident vandal – the kea.

The area is considered sacred by the Maori who see Aoraki (Mount Cook) as a powerful symbol of being, an ancestor from whom the Tangata Whenua (the Ngai Tahu people) are descended, and a link between the supernatural and natural world.
▸▸ *For Sleeping, Eating and other listings, see pages 533-534.*

Ins and outs

Getting there Mount Cook village is 63 km from Twizel. **Intercity/Newmans**, T03-365 1113 , buses offer a daily service from Christchurch (Queenstown-bound) departing at 1415 and Queenstown (Christchurch-bound) departing at 1350 from the Hermitage Hotel. Several tour buses, including **Great Sights**, T0800-744487, www.greatsights.com, also ply the Christchurch/Queenstown route daily, arriving from Christchurch at 1255 and departing early afternoon. **The Cook Connection**, T021-583211/T0800-252666, www.cookconnect.co.nz, offers a daily service between Mount Cook and Tekapo/Twizel and a service to Oamaru every Monday, Wednesday, Friday and Saturday from $42/$75 (summer only). All the bus services stop at the YHA and the Hermitage, both of which act as booking agents.

Tourist information The **DoC information centre** ① *just below the Hermitage Hotel, Bowen Drive, T03-435 1186/1818, www.mtcooknz.com, daily 0830-1800 (winter 0830-1700)*, has displays, an audio-visual presentation (good in wet weather, small charge) and information surrounding the park and its obvious attractions. There are leaflets on walks, tramping information and an up-to-date weather forecast. All hut bookings are administered here and intentions forms are provided. Of immediate use is a map of the village contained in the handy leaflet *Aoraki, Mount Cook Alpine Village*.

The road to Mount Cook

Some 8 km north of Twizel, the famed SH80 skirts the western banks and azure waters of **Lake Pukaki** to pay homage to Aoraki (Mount Cook). Before entering the chancel you are first advised to admire the cathedral from afar from the southern banks of the lake. There is a car park, information centre and **lookout point** from which, on a clear day, the mountain beckons. Unless you are really pressed for time, or the weather is foul, it really is sacrilege not to make the scenic 55-km drive to **Mount Cook Village** (see below). Located so close to the base of the mountains and Hooker and **Tasman Glacier** valleys, it is like a miniature toy-town which acts as the gateway to national park. And once here, it seems a terrible waste to move on without exploring the park from even closer quarters.

Glentanner Park → *Colour map 5, B3*

For the first 32 km towards the mountain valleys, your excitement grows in parallel with the vista before you, as the great snow-capped edifices get larger and larger and, more poignantly, you get smaller and smaller. It really is a bit like entering the gaping mouth of Moby Dick. Before reaching Mount Cook Village, and just beyond the water terminus of Lake Pukaki, you will encounter the motorpark and scenic flightseeing base of **Glentanner Park** ① *T03-435 1855, www.glentanner.co.nz*. You are strongly advised to stop here and muse at the scenic flights and other activities on offer, perhaps over a coffee, in its café overlooking the mountain. If you are in a campervan and intend to stay in the valley overnight, this will be home – there is good basic DoC campsite but no fully facilitated motorpark in the national park or Mount Cook Village.

Mount Cook Village ⬛🔰🔼📧 ›› *pp533-534.*

→ *Colour map 5 B3 Population: 300 (summer)*

From Glentanner you begin to enter the 'chancel' of the mountains and the national park proper. In Mount Cook, about 23 km further towards the mountains and 63 km from Twizel, you will find yourself climbing out of your 'dinky-toy' car feeling like a termite. It's easy to get neck ache round here.

Sights

After you have recovered from the incredible surrounding views, you will be immediately struck at how ordered and dull in colour Mount Cook Village is. This is not an accident, since the settlement comes within the boundary of the **Mount Cook National Park** and is therefore strictly controlled. The only real exception to this is the **Hermitage Hotel** ① *T03-435 1809/T0800-686800, www.mount-cook.com*, which

⦂ Sir Edmund Hillary

Sir Edmund Hillary is one of New Zealand's most famous sons, and although best known as the man who first conquered Mount Everest, he is also a noted Antarctic explorer and, in more recent times, well known for his welfare work in Nepal. Born in Auckland in 1919, he worked as an apiarist, before serving with the air force in the Pacific during the Second World War.

It was after the war that Hillary was drawn, time and again, to the mountains of the Southern Alps in New Zealand. Being a committed mountaineer and having immense stamina and ability, it was not long before his obsession took him to the Himalaya. He immediately joined expeditions in 1951 and 1952, but it was on the 29 May 1953 as a member of John Hunt's British team that Hillary and sherpa Tenzing Norgay made the first known successful ascent to the summit of Everest – a feat that brought instant fame.

After further expeditions to Nepal in 1954 and 1955, Hillary turned his attentions to another of nature's last frontiers – the Antarctic. From 1956 to 1958 he was a member of a team that completed the first tractor journey from Scott Base to the South Pole. After this successful expedition he returned once again to Everest where he led several expeditions between 1961 and 1965, before embarking on another journey to Antarctica to lead the first successful ascent of Mount Herschel.

It is refreshing perhaps that Hillary has gone well beyond the mere desire of climbing, or ego of summit-bagging, and has worked very hard to 'pay back' something to his much-loved Nepal. There is no doubt he has developed a great respect for its people and worked tirelessly over the years to help raise funds for the creation of schools and hospitals in the region. The first hospital was built in 1966 and he went on to form the Himalayan Trust. His work led to his appointment as New Zealand's High Commissioner to India in 1985.

Still drawn to both Nepal and Antarctica and with an ever-present desire to explore, Hillary served as a tour guide on commercial flights over Antarctica in the 1970s. With a love of nature added to his love of people, Hillary was also, for a time, the proud director of the World Wildlife Fund, adding conservation to his list of interests and activities. He has published several books about his expeditions and two autobiographies. As a small nation New Zealand is proud of Hillary, perhaps because he stands for much of what the country is all about: a oneness with nature and the courage to venture where others have not. Hillary is constantly in the minds of his fellow New Zealanders, not least because his face features on the nation's $5 banknote.

many claim to be the most famous in New Zealand (while others hail it merely as a blot on the landscape). Of course it is the setting that makes the hotel special, with its boast of 'mountain views' taking on far more than mere honest credibility. But although the **Hermitage** has been blessed by location it has also been cursed with misfortune. What you see today is not the original, in fact it is essentially the third. The original that was built in 1884 was located further down the valley and destroyed by flash floods in 1913. Relocated and rebuilt in its present position it was then gutted by fire 44 years later. It has now, once more, been fully renovated. From the hotel's interior, or from its well-manicured lawns, you will no doubt find yourself continuously staring up at Mount Cook. Also keep your eyes and ears open for kea, the cheeky green mountain parrots that hang about with the sole intention of harrying anything with legs and dismantling all they possess. The DoC campsite at White Horse Hill (see Sleeping, page 533) is another good place to look for them.

As well as the gargantuan vista of Mount Cook and **Mount Sefton** (3158 m), the associate glacier valleys are well worthy of investigation. Directly north of the **Hermitage** is the **Hooker Valley**, and east, over the dwarfed **Wakefield Range**, the vast **Tasman Valley** with its own massive glacier – the longest in New Zealand. Both valleys act as the watersheds, which feed Lake Pukaki and were once full of ice, hence the incredible expanse of boulder-fields that precede the lake's azure waters. It is, incidentally, the presence of fine glacial moraine ('rock flour') that gives the glacial lakes their exotic colour. There are a number of activities that focus on the glacier valleys and lakes which have already been mentioned (see Glentanner Park, page 530), but they can of course also be explored by foot (see Walking, below).

▲ Tramping

Mount Cook village is the gateway to the **Copeland Pass Track** ⓘ *given the popularity of this hike you will need to book a few days in advance, T03-435 1186,* which is a four- to five-day tramp to the west coast across the Great Divide. As attractive as this may seem, the tramp requires considerable experience and proper mountaineering experience and specialist equipment. It is also ill advised at present due to rock falls at the higher altitudes. Conditions are expected to improve, however, especially with the planned relocation of the Hooker Hut. Although you are still currently permitted to attempt the crossing you are advised to seek advice and check with up-to-date conditions with DoC.

A far more realistic option is the overnight tramp to the new **Mueller Hut**, which sits in a superb position (1768 m) on the ridge of **Mount Oliver** (1933 m) behind Mount Cook Village. Although a strenuous climb requiring a fair level of fitness, proper planning and equipment, it is a classic excursion. If you stay overnight in the vastly improved Mueller Hut, the views at sunset and sunrise over the Hooker and Mount Cook especially are simply world class. In total it is a stiff four-hour climb each way. A further one-hour return will see you at the top of Mount Oliver, which, rumour has it, was the first peak in the region that Sir Edmund Hillary climbed. For more information and bookings contact DoC and the *Mueller Hut Route* leaflet, $1.

▲ Walking

There are some very appealing walks in the vicinity that offer fine views and insights into the local hardy flora and fauna, with most beginning from the village. The shortest is the **Bowen Bush Walk**, which is only 10 minutes but takes you through some classic totara forest. It starts from behind the **Alpine Guides (Aoraki)** ⓘ *Mount Cook Village, T03-435 1834, www.alpineguides.co.nz.* A similar 30-minute walk, the **Glencoe Walk**, starts from behind the **Hermitage Hotel** and another, the one-hour **Governor's Bush Walk**, begins from the public shelter, just to the south of the Alpine Guides Centre. The latter also offers a good viewpoint. Two longer options are the two-hour **Red Tarns Track** (which again begins from the public shelter) and the two-to three-hour **Sealy Tarns Track**, which is part of the Mueller Hut ascent and begins from the Kea Point Track from the **Hermitage**. Both of these walks offer spectacular views from higher altitudes.

The **Kea Point Track** can be tackled from the **Hermitage** (two hours) or from the White Horse Hill campsite car park (one hour), which is accessed north via the Hooker Valley Road (beside the Kitchener Stream Bridge just at the entrance to the village complex). At the terminus of the Kea Walk is a lookout deck that offers memorable views of Mount Sefton, Footstool, the Hooker Valley, Mueller Glacier and of course Mount Cook. If you want to investigate the Hooker Valley you can do this from the village or from the White Horse Hill car park. In addition to the spectacular views of Mount Cook towering above, the four-hour **Hooker Valley Track** takes you all the way to the ice and melt-water features of the **Hooker Glacier terminal lake**.

The **Tasman Valley** also offers some interesting walks that take in the snout of the vast, advancing glacier. From the village you will need to travel by car or mountain bike to the end of the Tasman Glacier Road (8 km) which is accessed off SH80 south of the village. There are two walks: the three- to four-hour **Ball Shelter Walk,** which skirts the side of the glacier, and the more remarkable one-hour **Glacier Walk,** which investigates the terminal lake and head of the glacier. Both walks start from the car park.

Sleeping

Glentanner Park *p530*
A-D Glentanner Park, SH80, 15 mins' before Mt Cook, T03-435 1855, www.glen tanner.co.nz. Glentanner Park is the only motorpark in the valley, and the base for several fixed-wing and helicopter scenic flight operators. This certainly creates some noise but surrounded by such scenery it only adds to the buzz of excitement and desire to join in. The accommodation is excellent with surprisingly well-sheltered tent sites as well as self-contained cabins, bunk cabins, backpacker dorms and powered campsites. The amenities block is also very good with a fully equipped kitchen and a spacious lounge with TV, open fire and a detailed map of the region. The reception and scenic flight terminal also has a full activities booking service and a café open during the day.

Mount Cook Village *p530*
LL-AL Hermitage Hotel, T03-435 1809, www.mount-cook.com. Book ahead in high season. The Hermitage offers something for everyone, from the rather tired and expensive traditional rooms in the hotel, to a luxury wing with remarkable views and modern decor, or self-contained motel doubles, studios and chalets with basic facilities. Bear in mind that the price reflects the location, not necessarily the quality of accommodation. There is no faulting the hotel facilities, and the restaurants and bars are good. With all the tour buses lunch, however, can look a bit like a shark-feeding frenzy. Both the hotel and the motel complex have restaurants and bars and offer buffet-style lunch and dinner. The café in the hotel serves a range of light snacks and good coffee. There is also a small but expensive store and souvenir shop.

B-D Mount Cook YHA, corner of Bowen Drive and Kitchener Drive, T03-435 1820, yha.mtcook@yha.co.nz. Even if it had competition, this YHA would compete very favourably. It has tidy double, twin and shared rooms, modern ski-lodge style facilities including a log fire, sauna and internet. Book your bed well in advance in summer.

Motorcamps and campsites
Camping is also available at **Glentanner Park**, see above.
D White Horse Hill Campsite, at the end of the Hooker Valley Rd, 2 km from the village (see Walking, page 532). Basic but sheltered DoC campsite.

Eating

Mount Cook Village *p530*
₦₦₦-₦₦ Hermitage Hotel. There are 2 restaurants, the Alpine Restaurant (Buffet), and the à la carte Panorama Restaurant serving traditional New Zealand fare including seafood and game.
₦ Old Mountaineers Café Bar, just below the DoC visitor centre, T03-435 1890, daily for lunch and dinner. A fine alternative, offering a wholesome menu. It has a congenial atmosphere with open fire and a room with a pool table and internet.

Activities and tours

Glentanner Park *p530*
Flightseeing
The biggest draw at Glentanner are the fixed-wing and helicopter flightseeing trips. The choices are vast. Fixed-wing trips are also available from Lake Tekapo,

For an explanation of the Sleeping and Eating price codes used in this guide, see the inside front cover. Other relevant information is provided in the Essentials chapter, pages 44-51. Note that prices are given in New Zealand dollars.

see page 528. For all options, bookings are advised and payment is taken shortly before any flights in case of inclement weather. **Cloud 9**, T03-4351077. Offers some very appealing heli-hiking trips, from $285. **Helicopter Line**, T03-435 1801, www.heli copter.co.nz. Its Mt Cook (East) operations are based at the park, it offers 3 trips; a 20-min trip with landing to the slopes of the Mt Ohau Range ($195); a 30-min extended option over the Mt Ohau Range with a landing on the Richardson Glacier (from $290); and a 45-min 'Mountains High' adventure (from $395). If you can afford it, the 'Mountains High' trip is truly memorable: you are flown up and over the Tasman Valley Glacier, before making a snow landing at over 2000 m to sample the magnificent view of Mt Cook. Then, back in the air, you cross the Great Divide. From here you encounter the views of the west coast and the fractured bed of the upper Franz and Fox glaciers, before skirting just below Cook's awesome summit and dropping down the Hooker Valley, over Mt Cook Village and back to base. **Mount Cook Ski Planes**, at Mt Cook Airport just a few kilometres south of Mt Cook Village, T03-430 8034/T0800-800702 www.skiplanes.co.nz. This flightseeing option offers the exciting prospect of a snow-landing high up amidst the peaks on the Tasman Glacier. As if the scenery in transit is not spectacular enough, you will experience a very different world at high altitude. As you reluctantly climb back in to the aircraft after about 10 mins, you do so in the knowledge that the conditions up there are frequently very different. Trips on offer range from 25-min 'Mini Tasman' with no glacier landing (from $220) to the 40-min 'Glacier Highlights' with glacier landing (from $325), to the 55-min 'Grand Circle', with a landing and a close up of Mt Cook (from $430). Recommended.

Kayaking

Guided kayak trips exploring the ice walls of the glacier lakes, T03-435 1890, 3 hrs from $98. Kayak and hike options also available. **Glacier Explorer Trips**, T03-435 1077, glacier007@xtra.co.nz. 30-min walk to the terminus of the Tasman Lake, followed by a fascinating 2-hr boat trip to the edge of the ice. From $105, child $50. Recommended.

Other activities

Glentanner has its own horse trekking operation, T03-435 1855, from 30 mins ($40) to 3 hrs ($130). It also offers mountain bike and fishing tackle hire (fishing licence $18). See also **Discovery Tours** in Twizel (see page 528) for tours within the park.

Mount Cook Village *p530*

Note that all the activities already mentioned above (Glentanner Park) are also available from Mt Cook Village. Do not risk any climb without proper experience or equipment. Mt Cook National Park is serious business. If in doubt, don't. **Alpine Guides**, T03-435 1834, www.alpine guides.co.nz. The only resident guiding company in the park and, given the terrain, the potential challenges and hazards at hand, its presence is welcome. It offers an excellent range of multi-day mountaineering and trekking trips as well as half- to full-day (8-km) walks. In winter full-day skiing and heliskiing trips are available on the upper Tasman Glacier and other equally remote locations. Although these trips are expensive, they provide the rare opportunity to ski on virgin snow in areas simply inaccessible to the masses. For the latest details and prices visit their HQ in the village, daily 0800-1700.

❶ Directory

Mount Cook Village *p530*

The **Hermitage Hotel** forms the hub of all activity and services in the village, housing 2 restaurants, bars, a small and expensive grocery store, and a café. The hotel also offers internet, currency exchange, a post office, EFTPOS and activity bookings. The only thing it does not provide is petrol which can be purchased (24-hr credit card and EFTPOS) near the **Alpine Guides Centre** just to the south (unmanned). For breakdown assistance, T03-435 0844.

Waitaki Valley

From Oamaru you have the option of turning inland via SH83 through the picturesque Waitaki Valley to Omarama, the MacKenzie Country and Mount Cook. It is a pleasant drive, best negotiated in autumn when the poplar and lakeside weeping willows are draped in gold. Many of the orchards on the way also offer a palette of autumnal hues. The valley is best known for its lakes and the Waitaki River, which are regulated by an extensive system of hydroelectric dams that begin to dominate the waterways of the southwestern Canterbury Region. Fishing for both trout and salmon is one of the more obvious leisure activities in the area. ▸▸ *For Sleeping, Eating and other listings, see page 536.*

Ins and outs

Tourist information Oamaru VIC (I-Site) ① *1 Thames St, Oamaru, T03-434 1656, www.tourismwaitaki.co.nz, Mon-Fri 0800-1800 (1700 in winter), Sat-Sun 1000-1700 (1600 in winter)*. Although in Otago it is the main source of information for the Waitaki Valley to Omarama.

Omarama → *Colour map 5, B3*

Located at the head of the Waitaki Valley and north of the scenic **Lindis Pass** (from Wanaka and Queenstown), Omarama provides a convenient overnight stop and starting point from which to explore the MacKenzie Country (see page 523). There are a number of local activities that may detain you, including fishing and water sports on lakes Benmore and Aviemore, gliding from Omarama airfield and skiing at Lake Ohau.

Other than the obvious appeal of the local lakes, the **Clay Cliffs** between Omarama and Twizel are worthy of investigation, and echo the bizarre eroded rock and gravel formations of the Pinnacles in the Wairarapa, North Island. To reach them turn off SH8 west towards the mountains on Quailburn Road, 3 km north of the village (signposted), 15 km. There is a small charge ($6) at the gate to the cliffs. Omarama is world-renowned for gliding, with the huge expanses of thermal-rich grasslands and mountain offering world-class conditions and scenic flights that are virtually unparalleled. ▸▸ *See Activities and tours, page 536.*

Duntroon → *Colour map 5, C4*

From east to west the first settlement of any significance is Duntroon. With the discovery of gold in 1868 the town enjoyed a brief boom, before the diggings proved a failure, earning them the label of the 'poor man's field'. After a return to relative obscurity, there was more excitement with the discovery of a quartz reef between the Maerewhenua and Otekaike rivers in 1870, but once again, this was short-lived.

Now a small farming settlement, it offers a number of amenities, activities and scenic attractions. There is a petrol station, and visitor information can obtained from the **Flying Pig Café** ① *Campbell St, T03-431 2717*. The **Elephant Rocks**, accessed from Livingstone Road, near the Maerewhenua River Bridge, are an unusual set of limestone outcrops that are worth investigating and also provide good rock climbing possibilities, T03-432 6855. There are **Maori rock drawings** at Takiroa on the other side of the Maerewhenua River Valley dating back over 1000 years (ask at the café for directions).

Kurow to Omarama → *Colour map 5, B/C3*

Some 23 km west of Duntroon is **Kurow**, which nestles at the confluence of the Hakataramea and Waitaki rivers. Most of the residents work on the hydroelectric dams of lakes Benmore and Aviemore to the west, but for leisure they say there is one activity that stands head and shoulders above the rest – fishing. For insider information and guided trips contact **Waitaki Jet**, Oamaru, T027-221 1069. South of Kurow is another potential distraction in the form of the former 1871 homestead of the Hon Robert Campbell now open to the public by arrangement, To3-431 1111. West of Kurow you soon encounter **Lake Aviemore** and the higher, more extensive and truncated **Lake Benmore**. Both have dams. The Aviemore Dam has a 1-km-long fish spawning race that is used by up to 3000 adult trout at a time. The dam at the head of Benmore is the largest in New Zealand and can also be investigated though the lakeside picnic grounds. Safe swimming and water sports in both lakes may prove more attractive. For more information contact the **Benmore Power Station and Visitor Centre** ① *To3-438 9212, daily 1030-1630, tours 1100, 1300, 1500, $5.*

● Sleeping

Omarama *p535*
AL-A Heritage Gateway Hotel, T03-438 9805, heritagegateway@xtra.co.nz. 3-star hotel in a convenient location at the junction of SH8 to Wanaka and Queenstown, with SH83 to the east coast. Modern standard rooms and self-contained apartments. Bar and à la carte restaurant. Can arrange tours.
AL-D Ahuriri Motel, SH 83, T03-438 9451, www.ahuririmotels.co.nz. 14 comfortable, modern self-contained units and powered tent sites
D Buscot Station, 8 km north of the village, T03-438 9646, www.buscotstn@xtra.co.nz. Backpacker dorms, en suite rooms and tent sites on a working cattle/sheep station. Friendly hosts, good views. Quintessential kiwi experience guaranteed. Recommended.

Motorcamps and campsites
B-D Omarama Top Ten Holiday Park, T03-438 9875/T0800-662726, www.omarama top10.co.nz. Spacious and well sheltered flats, cabins and powered/tent sites. Good facilities.

Duntroon *p535*
LL-L Tokarahi Homestead, 2 km down Dip Hill Rd (47), 11 km south of Duntroon on the Dansey's Pass Rd, T03-431 2500, www.home stead.co.nz. Luxurious, beautifully appointed accommodation in 19th-century Victorian style. A perfect peaceful, historic retreat.

Motorcamps and campsites
D Dansey's Pass Holiday Camp, end of Dansey's Pass Rd, T03-431 2564. Cheaper and less salubrious but no less peaceful. Offers an interesting range of scenic tours.

Kurow *p535*
B-D Otematata Country Inn YHA 11 Rata Drive, T03-438 7797, enquiries@otematata

countryinn.co.nz. A cheery motel backpacker combo with self-contained 3 bedroom cottages and private budget rooms with shared facilities. Restaurant and bar.

Motorcamps and campsites
B-D Kurow Holiday Park, 76 Bledisloe St, T03-436 0725. If you are tired and cannot reach the **Top Ten** motorpark in Omarama then this is not a bad place.

● Eating

Omarama *p535*
There is also a restaurant in the **Heritage Gateway Hotel**, see Sleeping above.
Clay Cliffs Vineyard and Café, 500 m south of the village on SH8, T03-438 9654, www.claycliffs.co.nz, daily for lunch and dinner from 1100 (closed Jul). This café provides a bit of an escape and some fine cuisine in a peaceful setting.

Duntroon *p535*
Food is available at **Duntroon Tavern**, Main St, T03-431 2850, or the **Flying Pig Café**, Campbell St, T03-431 2717.

▲ Activities and tours

Omarama *p535*
Flightseeing
Alpine Soaring, T027-248 8800/ T0800-762746, www.soaring.co.nz. Offers a range of options from the airfield in the village, from $235 for 20-25 mins during which you can briefly take the controls.

Fishing
Recommended local guides are Doug Horton, T03-438 9808, and Max Irons, T03-438 9468.

West coast

⦂ Footprint features

Introduction

The west coast of the South Island is a land of extremes: extreme climate, extreme geography, extreme ecosystems and, above all, extreme scenery. It is a place of majestic beauty. Bounded on one side by the Tasman Sea and on the other by the heady peaks of the Southern Alps, it encompasses a narrow stretch of land that accounts for only 8% of the total landmass of New Zealand. Between these boundaries lies a quarter of all New Zealand's native forest, a lush and predominantly impenetrable landscape copiously watered by an average annual rainfall of more than 5 m. The boundaries of five of the country's 14 national parks breach the west coast region. Two of these, Paparoa National Park and the Westland National Park, it can call its very own, with the latter boasting the huge Fox and Franz Josef glaciers.

The settlements in the region, strung along the 600 km length of SH6, from Karamea in the north to Jackson's Bay in the south, are not attractive places and stand in stark contrast to the beauty surrounding them. Nature, thankfully, has never made it easy for man to live here nor plunder its resources. The modern-day west coast is sparsely populated, housing less than 1% of the country's total population. Indeed, there are less people living here now than in the late 19th century.

★ Don't miss ...

1 **Oparara Basin** Explore the ancient forests and awesome limestone features of the Kahurangi National Park, page 541.
2 **Dolomite Point** Feel the ground shake as the surf crashes down onto pancake rocks, page 545.
3 **Blackball** Go 'on strike' in this anti-capitalist town, page 553
4 **Bushman's Centre** Meet a possum and a giant sandfly in the small settlement of Pukekura, page 560.
5 **Kotukus** Visit the colony of elegant white herons by boat, from Whataroa, page 561.
6 **Okarito** Lose your watch and let time slip away, page 561.
7 **Franz Josef and Fox glaciers** Choose your favourite glacier, then take a scenic flight to land or climb upon it, page 565.
8 **Fiordland Crested Penguins** Marvel at the stunning coastal scenery of Munroe, Murphy's or Ship Creek beaches and look out for the rarest penguins in the world, page 568.
9 **Haast** Take a jet boat from coast to mountain, page 575.
10 **Jackson River Valley** Follow the river through pristine wilderness to the cascade, and then stop off at the country's most remote fish and chip shop in Jackson's Bay, page 576.
11 Enjoy REAL rain!

West coast Introduction

Westport and around

Westport, the west coast's oldest town, is not a pretty place. On first acquaintance, its long main street, fed by a flat expanse of unimaginative orderly blocks and overly wide roads, is uninspiring to say the least. Whether under clear blue skies or, more often, a veil of rain, its drabness is all the more exposed by the beautiful surroundings. But if the place lacks spirit, its people do not. They retain the proud and stoic traditions of the old pioneers and coal miners: the down-to-earth working-class attitude, the warm welcome and the humour. Westport is often used as an overnight base before heading north to Karamea and the Heaphy Track or south towards Greymouth. There, however, are a few attractions and activities that may detain you, including rafting on the Buller River and a large seal colony at Cape Foulwind. ▸▸ *For Sleeping, Eating and other listings, see pages 546-549.*

Ins and outs

Getting there Wesport airport① *8 km south*, is served daily by **Air New Zealand Link**, T0800-737000. A taxi into town costs around $15, T03-789 6900. The airstrip at Karamea is often used (from the north) for pick-ups/drop-offs for the Heaphy Track. **Karamea Village Hotel**, T03-782 6800, or **Last Resort**, T03-782 6617, act as agents. **Abel Tasman Air**, T03-528 8290, runs a quality service with fixed-wing aircraft from Nelson to Karamea.

Bus companies serving the area include: **Intercity** (from Nelson), T03-379 9020/ T03-768 7080, www.intercitycoach.co.nz; **Atomic Shuttles** (from Nelson), T03-322 8883, www.atomictravel.co.nz; **Southern Link Shuttles** (Queenstown-Christchurch-Nelson), T03-358 8355; and **Coast to Coast**, T0800-800847, www.coast 2coast.co.nz, offers daily services from Christchurch to Greymouth and Westport. Most buses stop just outside the VIC (I-Site). **Intercity** stops at Craddock's Energy Centre, Caltex, 197 Palmerston Street. For all services north to Karamea (and the Heaphy Track) call **Karamea Express**, T03-782 6757 or **Cunningham's Coaches**, 179 Palmerston Street, T03-789 7177, departs Westport 1500, Karamea 1745, from $18.

Tourist information Westport VIC (I-Site) ① *1 Brougham St, T03-789 6658, www.westport.org.nz, daily 0900-1800, winter 0900-1600*, handles DoC information and enquiries. **Karamea VIC (I-Site) and Resource Centre**① *Bridge St, just as you come into the village, T03-782 6652, www.karamea.info.co.nz, daily 0900-1700*, has helpful staff who can provide plenty of information on local attractions and all the latest on the Heaphy Track. It also has internet, can organize activities and issues DoC hut passes.

Westport 🚋🚲⛰🎭 ▸▸ *pp546-549.*

➔ *Colour map 4, B2/3 Population: 4500*

With such a tradition of gold and coal mining in the area it is almost rude not to visit the excellent **Coaltown Museum**① *Queen St South, T03-789 8204, daily 0900-1630, $8, child $4*. It has an extensive range of displays, with an emphasis on coal mining, but also gold, pioneer and maritime exhibitions. Of particular note is the interesting presentation covering the history of coal mining in the region, the simulated walk-through mine and the massive 20-ton brake drum from the Denniston Incline. Pitched at a 47° angle the brake drum creates an almost fearful sight. Even if you have little interest in mining, the sheer feats of engineering cannot fail to impress.

In contrast, yet related, is the **Miner's Brewery**① *Lyndhurst St, T03-789 6201, free tastings Mon-Sat*, where various heady brews are created to quench the thirst of the modern-day miner, including a fine pint of 'Good Bastards'. For further exploration, pick up a free copy of the *Buller Coalfields Heritage Trail* leaflet from the VIC (I-Site).

North to Karamea ⬛🅗🅕🔺🅒 ➤ pp546-549.

➤ Colour map 4, A3

From Westport, SH67 heads north to Karamea (100 km) and an eventual dead-end at the trail head of the Heaphy Track (111 km). If you have time there are a few places of interest and several good walks on offer along the way. Of particular note is the former mining township of **Denniston**. Perched high (900 m) on the Rochford Plateau and accessed via Waimangaroa (15 km north of Westport), Denniston was once the largest producer of coal in the country and the surrounding area was a hive of industrial activity. The **Denniston Walkway** (two hours, 1 km, 520 m ascent), which follows the former supply route, is the best way to explore the area and eventually leads to the former settlement. Little remains except a few rusting pieces of machinery, but there are great views of the impressive **Denniston Incline** (1878-1967) on which 20-ton brake drums brought millions of tonnes of coal down over 500 m to the railhead at terrific speeds. There is a small **museum** ① *old schoolhouse, open weekends and public holidays.*

Back on SH67 and 6 km north is the once bustling township of **Granity**. The **Drifters Café** on the main street is worth a stop and has some interesting artwork and mining remnants on display. Inland from Granity a road sweeps up the ranges to 'Porridge Hill' and two more former coal towns, **Millerton and Stockton**. Little remains of either, but again they are still worthy of some investigation. The short **Millerton Incline Walkway** (40 minutes) takes in a number of features and, as the name suggests, another incline, be it a far less impressive affair than the one at Denniston. Approximately 1 km north of Granity is the very pleasant **Charming Creek Walkway** (two hours, 4 km one way), which follows the old coal line through the Ngakawau River Gorge, taking in various old tunnels and other mining features along the way.

At the mouth of the Mokihinui River SH67 turns inland and climbs precariously around the bush-clad and scenic **Karamea Bluff**, before falling again to the coast towards Karamea.

Karamea → *Colour map 4, A3 Population: 684*

After the rather bleak nature of the former coal mining towns, encountered on its approach, you might expect Karamea to be similarly afflicted. However, this former 'frontier' settlement, perched on its namesake river mouth and overshadowed by the rising peaks of the **Kahurangi National Park**, is a far more pleasing sight and has a peaceful (as opposed to dead) atmosphere. Although most often used as a base for the famed **Heaphy Track** (which begins at the road terminus 15 km north) Karamea also has some lesser-known sights nearby that are quite simply superb, in particular the limestone caves and arches of the Oparara Basin.

Oparara Basin → *For Kahurangi National Park, see page 464.*

① *From Karamea take the main road north for 10 km, then turn right at Break Creek Bridge (signposted) and head for the hills. Access to the basin is 16 km of narrow, unsealed road. The basin is split into areas with both open and restricted public access.*

This is a magical place that offers the most interesting concentration of karst (limestone) topography in the **Kahurangi National Park**, and some of the most spectacular in the South Island. Although the karst features will keep you spellbound, the thick veil of ancient rainforest that covers it all creates a wonderful atmosphere all of its own like some 'lost world'. Some fantastical animals have been found here: ancient moa bones have been discovered in the caves along with others belonging to the now extinct New Zealand eagle with a 3-m wingspan. Today, you may still stumble across the huge carnivorous snail (*Powelliphanta*). Also of note is the wonderfully named gradungula spider, the largest in New Zealand with a leg span of 10 cm. But, even if the prospect of such creatures leaves you cold, the Oparara Basin is still a 'must see'.

⁝ Sandflies – Satan's spawn

There is no collective noun that adequately describes the family of flies known as *Psychodidae*. *Psychodidae* is the Latin family name for that nasty, insect equivalent to 'Hannibal Lector' – the New Zealand sandfly. Venture anywhere west of the main divide of the South Island and you will, without fail, not only encounter vast squadrons of them but also unconsciously enter into a state of perpetual war against them. And sadly it is a war that you cannot ever hope to win. Their staggering thirst for blood added to their tactical superiority, fighting skills and sheer numbers make them a formidable force indeed.

They say that to have the slightest chance of winning a war you should 'know thine enemy' – so here goes. There are not one, but 13 species of sandfly (or blackfly) in New Zealand. Fortunately, only two of the species actually bite, but unfortunately, you are still hopelessly outnumbered. You may not be surprised to learn that it is only the female that bites. Apparently they need a good feed of blood in order to lay their eggs.

So why is it that the moment you enter the great outdoors it takes about three milliseconds before the entire sandfly Luftwaffe are upon you? Well, apparently, you are instantly detected by a combination of breath, odour, movement, shape, colour and temperature. Biting is at its peak just after dawn or before dusk on warm, overcast, low pressure days, especially when humidity is high. Your only saviour is wind – natural as opposed to your own, even though you will find yourself trying anything to repel them – a strong breeze affects their strike rate. It is due to the high rainfall that sandflies are so prevalent on the west coast and Fiordland.

So how can you bite back? Is there anything other than a small thermo-nuclear device that is effective against the enemy? You will find a number of expensive insect repellents readily available throughout the region. Those that contain DEET (a rather strong chemical, to say the least) are the most effective. But, given that it discolours plastic and feels like it is melting your lips, prolonged use is perhaps not recommended. Antihistamines can also help to ease the swelling and allergic reaction from the bites. But, in conclusion, there is very little you can do except grin and bear them. Whatever you do, do not let them deter you from going to experience the west coast. Besides, if it was not for the sandfly, just think how much more spoilt the west coast would be by human habitation.

At the very end of the track is the access point to the main feature of the basin – the **Honeycomb Caves** ① *Oparara Tours at the VIC, T03-782 6652, 2 hrs, $70*, can only be visited on a guided tour because of their delicate nature and fragile ecosystem. They are a 15-km underground labyrinth only discovered 30-odd years ago, revealing all the usual limestone cave features plus the bones of several moa and other extinct species.

Nearby is the **Honeycomb Arch** ① *Oparara Tours at the VIC, from $70*, the first of three spectacular arches that have been formed by the age-old meanderings of the Oparara River. Although this arch is indeed impressive, access is again restricted and is by kayak only. The **Oparara Arch** ① *free public access*, is equally if not more impressive and is reached from a path (signposted) beside the road. A pleasant 20-minute (one way) walk alongside the intriguing tannin coloured river, and through beautiful forest, will bring you to the awesome arch entrance. Once you have marvelled at the main entrance it is then worth exploring the other end through the 140-m passage. This will involve getting your feet wet and crossing the river so care is required.

On a far smaller scale, but in a way more beautiful, is the **Moria (Little) Arch**,
accessed from the other side of the road. Again it is reached on a well formed track
(40 minutes). What it lacks in grandeur, the Moria makes up for in serenity. Perhaps
before or after the arches you can visit the **Crazy Paving** and **Box Canyon Caves**,
which are a five-minute walk from the road. Beyond their unnerving darkness (take
a torch), they are the least impressive of all the features. The river itself is also
beautiful and well worthy of investigation, particularly around the track to the small
and self-explanatory **Mirror Tarn**. A small map of the Oparara Basin is available free
from the VIC (I-Site).

▲ Walks
① *The VIC (I-Site) has detailed information on these walks and others.*
Karamea is a fine base for walking, particularly along the coastal stretch of the
Heaphy Track. From the Kohaihai River (trailhead), cross the swing bridge and walk
through the forest to **Scotts Beach** (1½ hours return). From there you have the option
of continuing along the coastline to **Kapito Shelter** (six hours return) or going the
whole hog with an overnight stop at the **Heaphy Hut** (five hours one way) before
retracing your steps. This stretch of coast is noted not only for its wild unspoilt
beaches but also for its nikau palms, which give it an almost tropical feel. Other tracks
and expeditions include the **Fenian Track** (three to five hours) which takes in a small
cave system and a former gold mining settlement and **Mount Stormy** (1084 m, six to
eight hours return) with its magnificent views.

South of Westport 🗐▲ ➠ *pp546-549.*

Cape Foulwind
① *11 km south of Westport; easily accessible and signposted.*
Cape Foulwind is a buttress of land, apparently named by James Cook in 1770, after
his ship was beset by gales and rain. It was formerly called Clyppygen Hoek – or Rocky
Corner – by Abel Tasman in 1642 and, before that, Tauranga by the Maori, which
meant 'a sheltered anchorage or landing place'. The main attraction on the cape is the
thriving **fur seal colony** at the very beautiful **Tauranga Bay**. You are guaranteed to see
seals here at any time of year (be it from a lookout situated quite far above the rocks)
but summer, when the pups are born, is the best time to see them with over 500 in
residence. The colony is best accessed from the Tauranga Bay car park. Before you set
off, keep your eyes open for the rather comical and cheeky **weka** around the car park
itself. Weka are a flightless, endemic, brown game-like bird about the size of a
chicken. Although you are not supposed to feed them it is hard to resist.
    From the seal colony, the **Cape Foulwind Walkway** also takes in the lighthouse
and offers great views (1½ hours, 4 km one way). At the southern end of Tauranga Bay
there is the fine **Bay House Café and Art Gallery**. It offers outdoor seating overlooking
the bay and is a great place to sup a cup of coffee, or tuck into a cooked breakfast,
while watching the surfers beyond.

Buller Gorge → *Colour map 4, B3*
There are actually two gorges on the Buller River: the Upper Gorge and the Lower Gorge.
They are separated by an area of relatively flat farmland around the small settlement of
Inangahua, which lies roughly halfway between Murchison and Westport. Following the
river is the northernmost arterial to the west coast, SH6. This 100-km road journey from
Murchison to the coast is a scenic, and at times dramatic experience, where you
descend with the river through mountains and valleys draped in an ever-increasing veil
of green. The drive to the coast is, in itself, pleasant enough but also holds a number of
interesting attractions and stops along the way.

⁞ A hard rain's a-gonna fall

The west coast of the South Island, especially Fiordland, is one of the wettest places on earth. Moist, prevailing, westerly air streams fan across the Tasman Sea and on encountering the mountain ranges of the Great Divide condense and dump rain or snow in huge quantities. At lower levels the annual rainfall is a rather aquatic 1.5 m but at higher levels this can rise to staggering 5 m. Most of the rain falls on the seaward side of the mountains in what is called the 'rain shadow'. The contrast in rainfall is echoed in the types of vegetation. On the western side of the Great Divide lush rainforests of podocarp and beech predominate, while only a few kilometres west this gives way to slopes of mainly scree and tussock. With such a gradient of rainfall and topography the rivers in Westland and Fiordland are regularly subject to flash flooding. For the uninitiated this may conjure up images of rivers merely in spate, but in reality it is an incredible thing to experience. There is such a bombardment of the senses you instantly freeze with fear. The mere sight of a vast, all encompassing wall of water – like boiling brown soup, full of boulders tossed like croutons on the surface – is bad enough but the deafening roar and the shaking of the earth beneath your feet is almost more paralysing. Many unsuspecting trampers have been killed in such circumstances, so stay away from all riverbeds and tributaries following any rain.

On a more positive note, although it frequently rains on the west coast, it often clears quickly and the sun is never too far away. Besides, west coast rain is real rain, industrial strength rain, so perhaps for once in your life get out there and enjoy it.

Just beyond the junction of SH6 and SH65 the road crosses O'Sullivan's Bridge and the **Upper Gorge** begins proper. Almost immediately you come to the **Buller Gorge Swingbridge** ① *Swingbridge Centre, next to SH6, T03-523 9809, www.buller gorge.co.nz, daily 0800-2000 (0900-1730 in winter), café*, which at 110 m is New Zealand's longest. You can walk across by foot ($5, child $2), or fly beside it, strapped to a small chair ($35/$15). The sensible can watch with great amusement from afar, the fit go for a guided walk and the hopeful go **gold panning** (guided $10, pan hire $5).

A little further on, just before **Newton Livery Hotel**, is the **Lookout** (Earthquake White Creek Fault Slip) where the violent (7.8 on the Richter scale) earthquake of 1929 was centred. Some 8 km on is the **Brunner Memorial**, which is a small metal plaque attached to the rock, commemorating the epic journeys of Thomas Brunner. The intrepid Mr Brunner took three months to negotiate the gorge in 1846.

After a long bend in the river the road then passes through the former gold mining town of **Lyell** – now very much a village. Relics of the great but brief gold rush days, including an old stamper battery, can be seen on the **Lyell Walkway** (two hours return). A further 17 km on will bring you to the rather unremarkable settlement of **Inangahua**. It has little more than a petrol pump and the rather dubious claim to fame of nearly being destroyed by an earthquake in 1968. If darkness is descending you can stay at the comfortable **Inwoods Farm Backpackers** (see page 548).

Just beyond Inangahua, the **Lower Gorge** begins its dramatic descent to the sea. At **Hawk's Crag** the rock has been gouged out to form a dramatic overhang. Its negotiation is really very interesting provided there is not a large petrol tanker coming the other way.

Punakaiki and the Paparoa National Park

🛏️🍴⛰️🅒 ➔ pp546-549

➔ *Colour map 4, B2*

From Westport SH6 begins its relentless 600-km journey south, down the length of the west coast. Once past the small and once-booming gold mining settlement of Charleston, the road hits the coast proper and then skirts the northern boundary of the Paparoa National Park. Designated in 1987, Paparoa covers a relatively small area (by New Zealand standards) of 30,000 ha and features a predominantly karst (limestone) topography. From mountain to coast, the park has everything from limestone bluffs to dramatic overhangs and caves. The most famous feature in the park are the pancake rocks and blowholes of Dolomite Point at the small coastal settlement of **Punakaiki**, which is in the main commercial centre. The park also offers some notable walks inland, including the popular Inland Pack Track.

Ins and outs

Getting there Punakaiki is 60 km south of Westport and 50 km north of Greymouth. **Intercity**, T03-379 9020, and **Atomic Shuttles** (Greymouth-Nelson), T03-322 8883, pass through the village daily and stop briefly for passengers to grab a snack and take a quick look at the pancake rocks and blowholes. There is no petrol available here.

Tourist information DoC Paparoa National Park Visitor Centre ⓘ *SH6, Punakaiki, T03-731 1895, www.doc.govt.nz, www.punakaiki.co.nz, daily 0900-1800, winter 0900-1630,* has interesting displays and information on activities and walking conditions.

Sights

Immediately across the road from the visitor centre is **Dolomite Point** with its oddly shaped **pancake rocks** and crowd-pleasing **blowholes**. The fluted vertical columns are a lime/mudstone feature known as 'karren', which develop their layered appearance as a result of erosion by rain and sea spray. The track (20 minutes return) takes the form of a loop, offering various lookout points across the rocks and blowholes, and down into the surge pools. On a high tide and especially during a strong westerly, the 'show' can be amazing, with the ground physically shaking to the thunderous pounding of the waves and the sea-spray hissing from the cracks. But note that when the tide is out, or there is little swell, the blowholes can be quiet and idle, leaving many visitors disappointed. Regardless of conditions, the rocks are certainly intriguing and the views are stunning. Keep your eye out for **dolphins**; it is not unusual to see pods or individuals mingling with surfers with the mutual intent to catch the best wave.

If you have time there is also some stunning coastal scenery, easily accessed via the **Truman Track**, which begins beside SH6, 3 km north of Punakaiki. A 15-minute walk through coastal rainforest and nikau palms delivers you on the sands and rocky outcrops of **Perpendicular Point**. The rock formations here are fascinating with fissures, holes and mosaics, and although it is quite hard going and should only be attempted at low tide, a thorough investigation of the point (northwards), is well worthwhile.

Turning your attention inland, the river valleys lead to some fine scenery and a number of other dramatic limestone features such as caves and overhangs. At **Tiromoana**, 13 km north of Punakaiki, the Fox River finds the sea, and a small car park north of the bridge acts as the northern trailhead for the **Inland Pack Track**. The entire track (which is usually walked from the southern trailhead in Punakaiki) is a 27-km, two- to three-day affair that takes in many limestone features, and inland valleys. Its

6699 On a high tide ... the 'show' can be amazing, with the ground physically shaking to the thunderous pounding of the waves and the sea-spray hissing from the cracks ...

main highlights – the **Fox River Gorge, caves** and **Ballroom Overhang** – can all be accessed from the mouth of the Fox River on an exciting four- to six-hour return walk. The track is well-formed for much of its length, but also involves crossing the river a number of times guided only by orange markers, so be prepared to get your feet wet. The Fox River caves can be accessed with a short diversion before the first major river crossing. The main cave is over 100 m in length and decorated with the usual calcite formations. Once across the river, the track follows the base of the dramatic gorge before terminating at the confluence of the Fox and Dilemma creeks. Here you can leave the Inland Pack Track, cross the river, and then continue alongside the main Fox tributary to the **Ballroom Overhang** (1 km). Sitting like half an umbrella embedded in the riverbed, its 100 m by 30 m overhang is impressive, but spoilt somewhat by graffiti.

Closer to Punakaiki are the **Bullock Creek** and **Pororari River** valleys. The Pororari acts as the southern access of the Inland Pack Track which can be walked in part to join the Bullock Creek Valley and to access **Cave Creek**, a deeply incised limestone gorge and another karst feature worthy of investigation. It is also one that now serves more as a tragic memorial than a tourist attraction: in 1995 a viewing platform set high above the cavern collapsed sending 15 students to their deaths. As a result of the incident there was a complete review of all similar DoC structures countrywide and revised safety standards and protocols were subsequently put in place. Cave Creek can also be accessed via the Bullock Creek Valley, which is generally fun to explore by car, bike, or on foot. All walks in the area are subject to flooding so check with DoC before setting off.

The area is also home to some rare wildlife. Of particular note is the **Westland black petrel** (teiko) – a gull-sized, black seabird, which nests in burrows on the bush-clad slopes of Paparoa's mountains. They do not breed anywhere else in the world. Tours are available in season (March to December); contact the VIC for details.

● Sleeping

Westport *p540*
AL Beach Haven B&B, 35 Marine Parade, Carters Beach, T03-789 8207, leslie.gary@ xtra.co.nz. A classy B&B in a beachfront location. Well- appointed en suites, a twin and a single with shared bathroom. The owners are very knowledgeable about the area.
AL-A Chelsea Gateway Motor Lodge, 330 Palmerston St, T03-789 6835/T0800-660033, www.nzmotels.co.nz. Opposite Westport Spa, also with spa units.
AL-A Westport Motor Hotel, 207 Palmerston St, T03-789 7889. Popular, well-located and well-established, with the added attraction of a good in-house restaurant and internet.

AL-A Wesport Spa Motel, 239 Palmerston St, T03-789 5273/T0800-375273, www.west portspa.co.nz. Modern and spacious spa units.
B-D Basils, T03-789 6410, bazils.backpackers@ xtra.co.nz. A vast establishment and YHA affiliate close to the town centre with a wide range of units, self-contained dorm apartments, powered/tent sites. Good facilities, internet.
C-D Berlin's, Lower Buller Gorge, T03-789 0295, www.xtremeadventures.co.nz. A good stop on the way down the Buller. Offers shared backpacker rooms and a double, café on site and excellent jet-ski trips.
C-D The Trip Inn, 72 Queen St, T03-789 7367, tripinn@clear.net.nz. A grand, spacious

villa, kept squeaky clean. Good value with a wide range of rooms and good facilities.

Motorcamps

A-D Westport Holiday Park, 37 Domett St, T03-789 7043, www.westportholiday park.co.nz. A short walk from town. Motel units, flats, en suite and standard chalets, on-site vans, powered/tent sites.

North to Karamea *p541*

AL Rough and Tumble Bush Lodge, Mokihinui River, 5 mins from Seddonville Pub, T03-732 1337, www.roughand tumble.co.nz. The epitome of a dream turned into reality. Classic and affordable bush lodge accommodation with high wooden beams and open stone fireplace overlooking the Mokihinui River and at the foot of the Glasgow Mountain Range. 5 cosy en suites some in the loft with memorable views. Furnishings of native timber abound and an outdoor campfire, swimming hole and bush bath all add to the appeal. Excellent in-house cuisine. It is remote but well worth the effort. Recommended.

B-D Gentle Annie's Coastal Enclave and Cowshed Café, on the far side of the mouth of the Mokihinui River, Gentle Annie's Beach, T03-782 1826. A great spot for food and accommodation with quiet, dorms or self-contained lodges and camping sites. The café is imaginatively housed in a former milking shed. It has information about activities including kayaking on the river nearby.

C-D Old Slaughterhouse Backpackers, 35 km north of Westport at Dean Creek, Hector, T03-7828333. A purpose-built lodge overlooking the ocean, reached by a 10-min bush walk. It offers tidy doubles and shared rooms. A good place to break the journey north to Karamea and the Heaphy Track.

Karamea *p541*

AL-A Bridge Farm Motels, Bridge St, T03-782 6955, www.karameamotels.co.nz. With a riverside location, offers 1- to 2-bedroom self-contained suites.

AL-A Karamea Lodge, 4589 Karamea Hwy, T03-782 6033, www.karamealodge.co.nz, located 4 km south of the village. Modern lodge overlooking the ocean with 3 spacious, well-appointed en suites. Shared kitchen and lounge with fireplace. The lack of TV or

internet makes a refreshing change and adds to the sense of retreat. The property is set in 3 ha of native bush with an attractive walkway. Excellent hosts. Recommended.

AL-D Last Resort, 71 Waverley St, T03-782 6617/T0800-505042, www.lastresort.co.nz. A modern and imaginatively designed complex with lodge-style accommodation and a large adjunct bar/café. Rooms include dorms, self-contained en suites and cottages. There are also tent sites with communal kitchen facilities Internet is available.

A Karamea Village Hotel, T03-782 6800, corner of Wharf Rd and Waverley St. Comfortable self-contained 1- to 2-bedroom en suites in a historic and lovingly restored building.

C-D Rongo, 130 Waverley St, T03-782 6667, www.livinginpeace.com. Colourful, cosy and laid-back hostel that lives up to its name – 'rongo' is Maori for peace. Spacious doubles and dorms, open fire, fire bath, in-house gallery, internet and fresh home-grown vegetables and free range eggs.

C-D Wangapeka Backpackers Retreat , Atawhai Farm, Wangapeka Valley (15 mins south of Karamea at the end of the Wangapeka Track, T03-782 6663, www.wangapeka.co.nz. Simple but delightful budget farmstay accommodation. Barn loft with 4 backpacker beds and a separate double. Meals by request (included with farmstay tariff). A fire-bath set in native bush offers an added attraction for trampers coming off the track. Recommended.

Motorcamps and campsites

B-D Karamea Holiday Park, Maori Point Rd, just south of the village, T03-782 6758, www.karamea.com. Offers a range of motel units, cabins and powered/tent sites.

D DoC campsite, at the mouth of the Kohaihai River (15 km north), at the trailhead of the Heaphy Track, T03-782 6652.

South of Westport *p543*

L River View Lodge, 7 km east of town, SH6, Lower Buller Gorge Rd, T03-789 6037, www.rurallodge.co.nz. A good out-of-town B&B option with 4 tidy en suites, set in pleasant gardens overlooking the Buller River.

L-AL Otaki Lake Hideaway, Virgin Flat Rd, 3 km off SH6 south of Westport, T03-789 6841, www.nzhideaway.com. One of the best B&Bs in the area. It is a lone, fully self-contained 1-bedroom chalet built over a private trout lake. Refreshingly different and peaceful. Boat provided. Recommended.

C-D Beaconstone Backpackers, 17 km south of town on SH6, T027-431 0491. An 'alternative', environmentally friendly lodge in a bush/coastal setting with solar power and futon beds. Local caving activities arranged. Recommended.

D Inwoods Farm Backpackers, Inangahua, Buller Gorge, T03-789 0205. Comfortable option if you are in the area.

Motorcamps and campsites

A-D Seal Colony Top Ten Tourist Park, Marine Parade, Carter's Beach (6 km on Cape Foulwind/Carter's Beach Rd), T03-789 8002. Popular but still 6 km from the seal colony.

Punakaiki p545

Almost all the accommodation is just off SH6. The most upmarket accommodation is at the southern end of the village.

L-AL Punakaiki Rocks Hotel and Villas, T03-731 1168, www.punakaiki-resort.co.nz. Separate but affiliated establishments both close to the beach with fine ocean views. The hotel is tidy and the individual units are very good, but have a rather clinical air. The restaurant boasts great views over the beach. Across the road, the villa complex offers luxurious options, from studio units with private decks to 12 eco-designed rooms set further back from the highway in native bush.

AL-A Paparoa Park Motel, north of the main centre, just off the main road, T03-7311883, www.paparoa.co.nz. Tidy and congenial, offering studio and family units.

A Punakaiki Tavern Accommodation and Bistro, northern sector of the village, T03-731 1188. Tidy modern en suite studio units situated near the tavern/bistro (the focus of social activity in the village) and only a short stroll from the beach.

B Hydrangea Cottages, north of the centre, T03-731 1839, www.pancake-rocks.co.nz. One of the best self-contained cottages on the coast. Very cute and reasonably priced.

C-D Punakaiki Beach Hostel, Webb St, T03-731 1852, www.punakaikibeach hostel.co.nz. 2 compact houses near the beach and pub. Outdoor spa, internet.

C-D Te Nikau Retreat, in Te Miko, just north of the Truman Track (look for homestay/ backpacker sign pointing out Hartmount Place, T03-731 1111, www.tenikauretreat.co.nz. A superb retreat with stand-alone cottages set in the bush, and a very special atmosphere. Also good for families and some units have wheelchair access. Enthusiastic manager. Excellent facilities throughout. Internet and pick-ups from the village centre also available.

Motorcamps and campsites

C-D Punakaiki Beach Camp, T03-731 1894, www.holidayparks.co.nz/punakaiki. Set next to the beach and only a short walk from the main village. It offers spacious grounds, cabins and powered/tent sites.

● Eating

Westport and around p540

There is a **Fresh Choice** supermarket at 18 Fonblanque St, T03-789 8546.

♥ **Bailies Bar**, 187 Palmerston St, T03-789 7289, from 1130. Pub grub and good beer.

♥ **Bay House Café**, southern end of Tauranga Bay, Cape Foulwind (near the seal colony), T03-789 7133, www.thebayhouse.co.nz. The best local restaurant, offering breakfast, lunch and an imaginative à la carte menu for dinner and in a superb setting overlooking the bay.

♥ **Berlin's Cafe**, Lower Buller Gorge, T03-789 0295, www.xtremeadventures.co.nz. A good stop on the way down the Buller. Besides caffeine you may will be tempted by their excellent jet-ski trips (see page 549).

♥ **Freckles**, 216 Palmerston St, 0900-1700. A daytime café with good coffee.

♥ **Serengetis Restaurant**, in the Westport Motor Hotel, Palmerston St, T03-789 7889, daily from 1800. Recommended especially for its Sun evening smørgasbord.

♥♥-♥ **Dirty Mary's Restaurant and Bar**, 198 Palmerston St, T03-7896648, Mon-Sat 1000-2100, Sun 1100-2100. A more casual daytime option.

● *For an explanation of the Sleeping and Eating price codes used in this guide, see the inside*
● *front cover. Other relevant information is provided in the Essentials chapter, pages 44-51.*
Note that prices are given in New Zealand dollars.

Karamea *p541*
The **Last Resort** and the **Karamea Village Hotel** have licensed restaurants, see Sleeping, above.
♥ **LR Bar and café**, Last Resort, daily. Cheap pub-style menu and a good atmosphere.

Punakaiki *p545*
♥♥ **Seascape Restaurant**, Punakaiki Rocks Hotel, T03-7311168, daily from 0700. For fine dining this is the best option in the village. Perfectly acceptable food and excellent views.
♥ **Punakaiki Tavern Bistro Café and Bar**, next to the motorcamp (SH6), T03-7311188. The main hub of entertainment offering palatable beer and the usual value pub grub.
♥ **Wild Coast Café**, Main Rd (across the road from Dolomite Point and the pancake rocks), T03-731 1873, daily 0800-2100 (winter 0800-1700). Good coffee and an eclectic menu. There is also a small grocery shop attached and several internet terminals at $3 per hr.

▲ Activities and tours

Westport and Buller Gorge
p540 and p543
Buller Adventures, east of Westport on SH6 (Buller Gorge Rd), T03-789 7286, www.adventuretours.co.nz. Offers rafting trips (half-day from $110); jet boating (1½ hrs from $75); 8-wheel Argo ATV tours (1½ hrs from $105) and horse trekking (2½ hrs from $65).
Out West Tours, T03-7898626/T0800-688937, www.outwest.co.nz. An interesting range of 5-hr trips by 4WD Unimog to the former Denniston coal mines, down the coast or inland to Buller Gorge. Call for latest schedules and prices.
Underworld Adventures, Charlestown, 27 km south of Westport, T03-789 6686, www.caverafting.com. Offers tours, caving and underground rafting trips to the Te Tahi and Metro limestone caves in Paparoa National Park. Trips leave twice daily from Westport and include a short trip by miniature rail (ride-only $20). 'Glowworm Cave Tour' (3 hrs from $80), 'Underworld Rafting' (4 hrs from $135), and 'Adventure Caving' with 130-ft abseil (5 hrs from $270).

Xtreme Adventures (Jetski Tours), T03-789 0295/T0800-526-405, www.xtreme adventures.co.nz. The only operation of its kind in the country Xtreme offers a thrilling and surreal perspective of the Buller River gorge by jet-ski. Good instruction, very safety conscious. Tours range from $165-185 and accommodation is also available. Recommended.

Karamea *p541*
Heli Charter Karamea, 79 Waverly St, Karamea, T03-782 6111, helicharter@ baycity.co.nz. A quality, personable company offering a flexible range of local and regional flight options, from local flightseeing, to fishing expeditions, or transportation to the track-heads of the Wangapeka or Heaphy. Recommended.

Punakaiki *p545*
Green Kiwi Tours, T03-731 1843/T0800-474733, www.greenkiwitours.co.nz. Small-group eco-tours and caving trips from $60.
Punakaiki Canoe Hire, T03-731 1870, www.riverkayaking.co.nz. 2 hrs from $30, all day from $60. Guided trips or canoe hire.
Punakaiki Horse Treks, T03-731 1839, www.pancake-rocks.co.nz. Along the beach or into Punakaiki River Valley, 2½ hrs $110.

◑ Directory

Westport *p540*
Banks Palmerston St. **Internet** Web Shed, 204 Palmerston St, Mon-Fri 1000-1800, Sat 1000-1300. **Library**, 87 Palmerston St, Mon-Thu 1000-1700, Fri 1000-1830, Sat 1030-1300. **Post office** Palmerston St.

Karamea *p541*
Banks There is no bank or ATM in the village. **Internet** VIC, see page 540. **Medical services** Doctor's surgery, Waverley St, T03-782 6737. **Postal services** Karamea Hardware Store, opposite the VIC.

Punakaiki *p545*
Banks There are no banks but EFTPOS is available in the retail and food outlets. **Internet** Wild Coast Café (see Eating, above) or both the local backpacker hostels (see Sleeping, page 548).

Greymouth and around

From Punakaiki the coast road continues its relentless route south, treating you to some fine coastal scenery, before turning inland through Runanga to meet the Grey River and the west coast's largest commercial centre – Greymouth. On initial acquaintance Greymouth seems to share the drab aesthetics of most northern west coast towns and certainly lives up to its uninspiring name. That said, the people of Greymouth are welcoming, friendly and certainly not short of heart or colour. Today, the bustling town is mostly used by tourists as a short stopover point or supply base for further investigations of the coast. It does, however, have a few local attractions and some exciting activities on offer. Inland from Greymouth, the small satellite towns of Blackball and Reefton are the main highlights along the watershed of the Grey River Valley and provide further evidence of the regions gold and coal mining past. It was in Blackball in the early 1900s that the Labour and Trade Union movements were first formed in New Zealand. Further south the peaceful surroundings of Lake Brunner are a stark contrast to the highly commercial 'Shantytown' a working replica of an 1880s gold mining settlement. ▸▸ *For Sleeping, Eating and other listings, see pages 553-556.*

Ins and outs

Getting there Greymouth is served by **Hokitika airport** ① *40 km*, with **Air New Zealand Link,** T0800-737000. The town is 258 km west of Christchurch via SH73 and Arthur's Pass; 290 km south of Nelson via SH6; and 583 km north of Queenstown, also via SH6. The major bus companies serving the Greymouth include: **Intercity,** T03-768 7080 (Nelson-Westport); **Coast to Coast,** T0800-800847, www.coast2 coast.co.nz (Christchurch-Westport); **Atomic Shuttles,** T03-322 8883, www.atomic travel.co.nz (Picton-Queenstown) and **K-Bus,** T03-358 8355, www.southernlink bus.co.nz (Nelson). Most buses stop at the VIC or at the **Travel Centre** ① *in the railway station, 164 Mackay St, T03-768 7080, greymouthtravel@snap.net.nz, Mon-Fri 0900-1700, Sat-Sun 1000- 1500.* By train, Greymouth is the western terminus of the famous **TranzAlpine,** T0800-872467, www.tranzscenic.co.nz, from Christchurch, which is considered a world-class scenic journey. The train arrives daily at Mackay Street at 1245 and departs Greymouth again at 1345 from $130 one way. Moana (on Lake Brunner) is also on the TranzAlpine line (westbound 1221, eastbound 1405).

Tourist information Greymouth VIC (I-Site) ① *corner of Mackay and Herbert sts, T03-768 5101/T0800-473966, www.greydistrict.co.nz, www.west-coast.co.nz, Mon-Fri 0830-1900, Sat 0900-1800, Sun 1000-1700,* also provides DoC information. **Reefton VIC (I-Site)** ① *67 Broadway, T03-732 8391, www.reefton.co.nz, daily 0830-1800 (1630 in winter),* has eco-based displays and lots of information on walking and tramping.

Greymouth → *Colour map 4, B2 Population: 10,000*

Greymouth enjoyed the former colonial names of Crescent City and Blaketown, before its present name (given in honour of the former New Zealand Governor, Sir George Grey) finally stuck. Not surprisingly its creation centred principally on gold prospecting and mining, but unlike so many of the other west coast settlements that diminished with its exhaustion, Greymouth continued to thrive. This was due to the coal and timber industries, sound communication links and its status as the region's principal port. But its watery affairs have not all been smooth sailing. The Grey River Valley receives some of the heaviest rainfall in the country and on more than one occasion the town has been badly flooded.

Cobden Lookout

To Rapahoe Range Scenic Reserve

To 5 10 & Punakaiki

To Reefton

Ward St
Bright St
Newcastle St
Cardwell
Taylor
Stafford
Nelson Quay
Weir
Cobden Bridge

Nimmo Park

River Grey (Mawheranui)

Travel Centre

Left Bank Art Gallery

Shades of Jade

Grey District Library

Jade Country

Customs
Waterwalk
Marian
Werita St
Mackay St
Whall St
Willis St
Chapel St
Alexander Terr
Mount St

Richmond
Johnston St
Ashton
Tarapuhi St
Albert St
Wilson
Port St
Tainui St
Puketahi
Alexander St

Gresson St
History House Museum
Boundary St
Guinness St
Herbert St
Swainson
Leonard St
William St
Abner St

Victoria Park

Preston Rd

Montieth's Brewery

Murray
O'Donnell
Thompson
Tutunamua
Hinchy
Ngahina
Elmer
Frickleton
Freyberg Terr

Lake Karoro (Tidal)

Brunner

Franklin
Cowper St
High St
Heaphy
Shakespeare St
Perotti
Winnie

To 8 9 11 12 13, Hokitika, Shanty Town & Arthur's Pass

0 metres 200
0 yards 200

Sleeping
Alpine Rose **13**
Ardwyn House **1**
Ashley **12**
Duke Backpackers **14**
Gables Motor Lodge **2**
Global Village
    Backpackers **3**
Kainga-ra YHA
    Backpackers **15**
Kapitea Ridge Country
    Luxury Lodge **9**
Kingsgate **6**
Neptune's **4**
New River Bluegums **8**
Rosewood **7**
Top Ten Greymouth
    Holiday Park **11**
Westway Homestay **5**
Willowbank
    Lodge **10**

Eating
Bonzai Pizzeria **1**
Café 124 **10**
DP: One **3**
Jone's Café & Bar **4**
Raceway Carvery **5**
Railway Hotel **6**
Smelting House Café **7**
Steamers Café & Bar **8**
West of the Border **9**

Bars & clubs
Revingtons Hotel **11**

One of Greymouth's most famous sights is the **Montieth's Brewery** ① *corner of Turamaha and Herbert sts, T03-768 4149, www.monteiths.co.nz, tours $10.* Considered locally as a place of sanctity, its brands of 'Original', 'Black' and 'Celtic Red', are considered by most Kiwis to be the country's greatest brews. Although not in the same league, nor enjoying the same reputation as Guinness or many other European beers, it is indeed a fine drop. A few years ago there was a major controversy when the powers that be decided suddenly to announce that operations were to be moved to Auckland (of all places). This act of insanity resulted in an outcry of such proportions that the owners wisely changed their minds.

If you are more culturally inclined you should head for the small, but effective, **History House Museum** ① *Gresson St, T03-768 4028, www.history-house.co.nz, Mon-Fri 1000-1600, $3, child $1.* Its emphasis is on the region's mining and nautical past with a copious collection of old photographs. Creative souls will particularly enjoy the **Jade Country** ① *1 Guinness St, T03-768 0700, daily 0830-2100, winter 1700.* It is one of the better jade galleries showcasing a range of crafted jewellery and sculptures with the added attraction of a 'Jade Discovery Walk', master sculptors at work, a huge river-polished jade boulder and a good café. **Shades of Jade** ① *16 Tainui St, T03-768 0794, www.westcoastjade.co.nz, open daily,* is a smaller gallery and shop where you can watch a jade carver fastidiously crafting the 'green gold'. Also worth a look is the **Left Bank Art Gallery** ① *Tainui St, T03-768 0038, www.leftbankart.co.nz, daily 1000-1700, small entry charge,* which displays some finely crafted examples of the west coast ancient *poanamu* (greenstone/jade) pieces.

▲ Walks around Greymouth

The **Point Elizabeth Track** (three hours return) follows an old gold-miners trail along the Rapahoe Range and provides a good local jaunt. Access is north of Greymouth via Bright Street, then Domett Esplanade and North Beach Road (6 km) or via Rapahoe, Seven Mile Road. For a longer tramp, the 18 km (eight to nine hours) **Croesus Track** from Blackball to Barrytown is recommended. It can be tackled from either end (though the Barrytown side is very steep) and takes in the grand views of the coast from above the tree line of the Paparoa Ranges and includes some notable gold-mining relics. Also, most importantly perhaps, it has good pubs at both ends: **The All Nations Tavern**, T03-731 1812, and the **'Formerly the Blackball Hilton'**, T03-732 4705, www.blackball hilton.co.nz. Both also offer accommodation. The DoC broadsheet *Central West Coast – Croesus Track* is invaluable; available from the VIC

Shantytown → *Colour map 4, B2*

① *Rutherglen Rd, just off SH6, 10 km south of Greymouth, T03-762 6634, www.shanty town.co.nz, daily 0830-1700, $18, child $10. Kea West Coast Tours, T03-768 9292, offers 3-hr guided trips from Greymouth for $60. Greymouth Taxis, T03-768 7078, offers transport at 1015, 1215 and 1415, $30, child $15, book ahead.*

Shantytown is a faithful recreation of an 1880's gold mining settlement. It comes complete with shops, a bank, saloon, goal, livery stables, fire station, working sawmill and a working steam train. Although a little commercial, it provides an interesting insight into the lives of hopeful prospectors. The steam train operates daily 0945-1600. You can also try your hand at gold panning, or even tie the knot in the original church. More traditional facilities include a café and souvenir shop.

Lake Brunner → *Colour map 4, C2*

Lake Brunner, 37 km east of Greymouth, is the west coast's largest lake and certainly one of the prettiest. Other than fine scenery, **Moana Kotuku** (or Heron Sea as it is also known) offers some great fishing, walking, swimming and other water-based activities. The settlement of **Moana** on its northern bank is the main base. One of the over the Arthur River at the western end of the village (Ahau Street). Keep your eye out for the beautiful **white heron** (Kotuku), which visit outside the summer breeding season. Guided fishing trips, tackle hire and the occasional kayak can be secured through the motorcamp, motel and hotel (see Sleeping, below).

Grey Valley and Blackball → *Colour map 4, B2*

Between Greymouth and Reefton, the Grey River heads coastward, hemmed in by the Paparoa Ranges and the northern flanks of the Southern Alps. Like much of the region, its small settlements were born during the heady days of the gold rush.

Although the small former gold mining town of **Waiuta** (21 km south of Reefton) is of interest, it is the coal mining town of **Blackball** (accessed from Stillwater, 11 km north of Greymouth), which holds most appeal. Founded on gold in 1866, but developed later on coal, it is most famous as the cradle of working-class protest and unionism in the early 1900s. In 1908 an almost inevitable clash occurred when a 30-minute lunch break was sought (as opposed to 15 minutes). This debacle led to the formation of the Federation of Miners and subsequently the Red Federation of Labour – essentially the nation's Labour Movement. Such was the anti-capitalist feeling that, for a few years after the First World War, you could attend Marxism classes in the town.

Reefton → *Colour map 4, B3   Population: 1200*

Known as the 'Gateway to the Coast', the former gold town of Reefton is a fairly unremarkable, but pleasant little place at the end (or beginning) of the Lewis Pass arterial to the coast. Famous for very little, except its claim to be the first town in the southern hemisphere to receive a public electricity supply and street lighting in 1888, it is sustained by coal, forestry, farming and gold. The nice thing about Reefton is its unpretentious atmosphere. It seems very real. Although underrated and rarely on the tourist agenda, Reefton offers some fine fishing in the local rivers as well as a wealth of walking, tramping and mountain biking opportunities, primarily in the vast and local 180,000 ha Victoria Conservation Park – the largest forest park in the country.

The two most noted walks in town are the 'Reefton Heritage Walk' and the 'Powerhouse Walk'. The Heritage Walk takes in a number of interesting historical buildings including the renovated **Courthouse**, the beautifully decorated **Masonic Lodge**, the former **School of Mines** ($2) and even the odd bearded miner. On the Strand you will find the lovingly restored, former workhorse *R28 Fairlie* locomotive, the sole survivor of its type. The Powerhouse Walk is an easy 40-minute walk across the river to see the former **powerhouse** that once proudly lit up the town. Free leaflets outlining both walks are available from the VIC (I-Site); guided tours are available by arrangement, from $8.

Blacks Point Museum ⓘ *just beside SH7 (Lewis Pass Rd) in Blacks Point, T03-732 8835, summer Wed-Fri, Sun 0900-1200, 1300-1600, $4,* has extensive displays on the region's goldfields history. For a fine view of the town and the Inangahua Valley head south on SH7, turn left after 1 km into Soldier Flat Road and left again shortly afterwards. Follow this road to the lookout point in the pine forest.

● Sleeping

Greymouth *p550, map p551*
LL-AL Kapitea Ridge Country Luxury Lodge, Chesterfield Rd (out of town, off SH6, 20 km south), T03-755 6805, www.kapitea.co.nz. Intriguing architectural aesthetics, stylish with some excellent artwork and cuisine. Well worth the journey, but comes at a price.
L-AL Hotel Ashley, 74 Tasman St, T03-768 5135/T0800-807787, www.hotel ashley.co.nz. Comfortable with good facilities and a fine restaurant.

L-AL Kingsgate Hotel, 32 Mawhera Quay, T03-768 5085, www.kingsgatehotels.co.nz. Comfortable rooms in a good location.

L-AL New River Bluegums, 985 Main South Rd (12 km south), T03-762 6678, www.bluegumsnz.com. A characterful but out of town farmstay offering B&B and luxury self-contained cabins.

L-AL Rosewood, 20 High St, T03-768 4674, www.rosewoodnz.co.nz, Charming, beautifully preserved 1920s villa built by Greymouth's 'bookie' at the time. Excellent hosts. Recommended.

AL-A Westway Homestay, Herd St, Dunollie (10 mins north of Greymouth), near Runanga, T03-762 7077, www.west way.co.nz. Well worth the effort with friendly hosts and excellent value en suite queen, twin with shared bathroom and an en suite twin with singles for families. Continental breakfast included and dinner on request.

A-B Ardwyn House, 48 Chapel St, T03-768 6107, ardwynhouse@hotmail.com. Centrally located, cheaper B&B option.

Motels

Most of the motels are on the main drag (High St/SH6) heading south out of town. The following are recommended.

L-A Alpine Rose, 139 High St, T03-768 7586/T0800-266835, www.alpinerose.co.nz.

L-A Gables Motor Lodge, 84 High St, T03-768 9991/T0800-809991, www.nzmotels.co.nz/gables.

A Willowbank Lodge, just off SH6, 3 km north of the town, T0800-668355/T03-768 5339. A quieter, cheaper option.

Backpacker hostels

B-D Kainga-ra YHA Backpackers, 15 Alexander St, T03-768 4951, yha.greymouth@yha.co.nz. A former Marist Brothers' residence, set overlooking the town, this place retains an ecclesiastical theme that certainly extends to an innately peaceful atmosphere. Full range of rooms (some en suite), well-facilitated throughout and plenty of assistance with local activities.

C-D Duke Backpackers and Bar, 27 Guinness St, T03-768 9470, dukenz@ clear.net.nz. Fully renovated, it is well located in the heart of the town and offers value doubles, twins and dorm beds with free DVD movies, tea/coffee,

an internet café (free with coffee purchase) and, of course, a bar.

C-D Global Village Backpackers, 42-54 Cowper St, T03-768 7272, www.global villagebackpackers.co.nz. The managers have a wealth of travelling experience. Good range of rooms and excellent facilities including a spa and sauna, its only downfall is its location from the centre of town. Kayaking is available in the creek that runs alongside it.

C-D Neptune's, 43 Gresson St, T03-768 4425/T0800-003768, nepts.backpackers@ actrix.co.nz. All things fishy is the emphasis this time, with the wide range of comfortable rooms and facilities (including baths) decorated accordingly, Sky TV and spa facilities in case the weather does its worst, internet and off-street parking. Neptune's is good value and particularly good for couples.

Motorcamps

A-D Top Ten Greymouth Holiday Park, 2 Chesterfield St, T03-768 6618/T0800-867104, www.top10greymouth.co.nz. A spacious, well-managed place located alongside the beach, with self-contained units, cabins and powered/tent sites with excellent facilities.

Lake Brunner *p552*

LL Lake Brunner Lodge, Mitchell's, Kumara-Inchbonnie Rd (at the southern end of the lake), T03-738 0163, www.lake brunner.com. A historic, all mod cons, fishing retreat with 11 luxury rooms and fine cuisine.

L-C Moana Hotel, 34 Ahau St, T03-738 0083, www.moanahotelmotel.co.nz. Basic but value double rooms, cabins, motel units and a restaurant.

AL-D Lake Brunner Country Motel, 2014 Arnold Valley Rd, at the outskirts of the village towards Greymouth, T03-738 0144, www.lakebrunnermotel.co.nz. Modern self-contained chalets, 1 motel unit, cabins, campervan sites and can arrange fishing and bush-walking excursions.

Blackball *p553*

B 'Formerly the Blackball Hilton', Hart St, T03-732 4705, www.blackballhilton.co.nz. Now a comfortable and friendly B&B. Can arrange a number of local activities including gold panning, horse trekking and walking.

Reefton *p553*

AL-A Historic Reef Cottage B&B and café, 51 Broadway, T03-732 8440/T0800-770440, www.reefcottage.co.nz. Cosy restored 1880's cottage, self-contained, centrally located with a café. Fine full cooked breakfast.

AL-A Lantern Court Motels, corner of Broadway and Smith St, T03-732 8574, lanterncourt@xtra.co.nz. The newest motel in town with 12 standard and fully self-contained units, Sky TV, spas.

AL-A Reefton Auto Lodge (Dawsons on Broadway), 74 Broadway, T03-732 8406, www.flyfishingparadise.co.nz. Modern self-contained studio and motel units. Spa and café/bar with a lovely open fire. Fishing trips and packages a speciality.

A Quartz Lodge B&B, 78 Sheil St, T03-732 8383, www.quartzlodge.co.nz. Perfectly comfortable with 3 tidy rooms.

B Bellbird Motel, 93 Broadway, T03-732 8444, www.nzmotel.co.nz. A cheaper motel option.

C-D The Old Bread Shop Backpackers, 157 Buller Rd, T03-7328420, breadshopback packers@gmail.com. Small, homely and colourful set in the heart of the Victoria Conservation Park. The caring owners live next door and know the best fishing spots. Doubles and a dorm. Good value.

C-D Old Nurses Home Accommodation and Backpackers, 104 Shiel St, T03-732 8881, reeftonretreat@hotmail.com. Spacious establishment offering self-contained units, family double, twin and singles with all the usual facilities. Massage therapies are an added attraction.

Motorcamps and campsites

C-D Reefton Domain Motorcamp, at the edge of town at the top of Broadway, T03-732 8477. Basic. Has powered/tent sites and cabins and a kitchen and amenities block.

Eating

Greymouth *p550, map p551*

Ashley's Hotel, 74 Tasman St, T0800-807787, daily for lunch and dinner. A la carte restaurant with a good reputation.

Bonzai Pizzeria, 31 Mackay St, T03-768 4170, 0700-late. Won't let you down.

Café 124, Mackay St, T03-768 7503, Mon-Fri 0900-late, Sat-Sun 1000-late. Classy option, popular for lunch and dinner and also for breakfast or brunch at the weekend.

DP:One, Mawhera Quay, T03-768 4005, daily 0900-2230. The best (or certainly most interesting) café in town. It is a small place but full of character, resembling something like an extrovert artist's garage. It is also the best internet venue in town.

Jone's Café and Bar, 37 Tainui St, T03-768 6468. A good alternative and open late, offers a traditional-style menu with a few good vegetarian options and has occasional live jazz and blues. Good breakfast.

Raceway Carvery, Union Hotel, 20 Herbert St, T03-768 4013. Value pub meals.

The Smelting House Café, 102 Mackay St, T03-768 0012, Mon-Sat 0800-1700. A local favourite located in a historic old bank building. It specializes in home-style food and serves good coffee.

Steamers Café and Bar, corner of Mackay and Tarapuhi sts, T03-768 4193, daily 1200-1400 and 1700-2000. Does a good Sun roast and pub grub.

West of the Border, 25 Mackay St, T03-768 5272, dinner only. Hefty Tex-Mex portions.

Railway Hotel, Mawhera Quay, T03-768 7023, daily from 1830. For the real 'fill your face' deal.

Lake Brunner *p552*

For the more budget conscious based in Moana your only eatery options are:

Moana Hotel, see Sleeping above; and

Stationhouse Café, overlooking the lake and train station, T03-738 0158, seasonal hours.

Blackball *p553*

Blackball Salami Company, Hart St, T03-732 4011, Mon-Sat. Award-winning sausages for your picnic basket.

Reefton *p553*

Alfresco, across the road from the Domain Motor Camp, 16 Broadway, T03-732 8513,

For an explanation of the Sleeping and Eating price codes used in this guide, see the inside front cover. Other relevant information is provided in the Essentials chapter, pages 44-51. Note that prices are given in New Zealand dollars.

daily in summer for lunch and dinner. Lives up to its name and serves takeaway pizza and good coffee.

¶ **Hotel Reefton**, Broadway, T03-732 8447. Traditional pub-style meals.

¶ **Reefton Auto Lodge (Dawsons)**, see Sleeping above. Pub grub, known for its roasts.

¶ **Reef Cottage Café**, 51 Broadway, T0800-770440, daily 1000-late. Cosy café serving good coffee and light snacks.

⊕ Pubs, bars and clubs

Greymouth *p550, map p551*
Greymouth has several traditional hotels which are the focus of the town's nightlife with **Revingtons Hotel**, 47 Tainui St, T03-768 7055, perhaps being the most popular and certainly a good starting point.

⊕ Entertainment

Greymouth *p550, map p551*
The cinema is the **Regent Theatre**, corner of Mackay and Herbert sts, T03-768 0920, www.regentgreymouth.co.nz.

▲ Activities and tours

Greymouth *p550, map p551*
Air West Coast, T03-738 0524, www.airwestcoast.co.nz. Scenic and charter flights, 45-min to 5-hr trips, $85-850.
Kea West Tours, T03-768 9292, www.keatours.co.nz. Range of road trips to Punakaiki, Hokitika, the Glaciers, the Grey Valley and Shantytown, from $60.
On Yer Bike, T03-762 7438/T0800-669372, www.onyerbike.co.nz. Off-road adventures with 4WD, 8WD, motorbikes and go-karts, $75-130.
Sweet As Eco Rafting Adventures, T0508-669675, www.ecorafting.co.nz. Quality half- or multi-day trips on one of the many west coast rivers from $130. Heli-option also available from $325.
Wild West Adventures, 8 Whall St, T03-768 6649/T0508-286877, www.fun-nz.com. A major activity operator in the region offering a range of trips. An exhilarating half-day blackwater rafting experience in the Taniwha cave system from $145. Jungle Boat Rainforest Cruise, on board an imaginative range of traditional Maori craft and more

conventional rafts with a distinct 'Tarzan' edge; the 3-hr trips are certainly different and offer a fine opportunity to learn more about the rich Maori culture and traditions of the west coast, from $135. 3-hr rafting trip (Grade II, suitable for families), from $135. 4-hr scenic guided tours to glow-worm caves (with some gold panning along the way), to Shantytown and to Pancake Rocks, from $95. Multi-day guided walks on application.

Reefton *p553*
Spend some time in the VIC looking at the very attractive walking, tramping and mountain biking opportunities in the highly underrated and quiet **Victoria Forest Park**. There are numerous routes and half- to multi-day walking/tramping options that take in a wealth of former gold-mining relics. An excellent 'helicopter in/mountain bike out' trip to Big River can be arranged by the VIC. Prices on application. The DoC leaflet *Reefton-Victoria Conservation Park* is useful. The local fishing is superb (information about local guides available from the VIC). **Reefton Sports Centre**, 56 Broadway, T03-732 8593. Fishing licences and tackle hire.

⊖ Transport

Greymouth *p550, map p551*
Car hire Alpine West Rentals, 11 Shelly St, T0800-257736. **Avis**, Mackay St, T03-768 0902. **NZ Rent-a-Car**, 170 Tainui St, T03-768 0379. Older, cheaper models.
Taxi Greymouth Taxis, T03-768 7078.
Hoki Airport Shuttles, T03-768 7078, airport pick-ups from $18, or transport further afield to Hokitika or Punakaiki, from about $40.

⊕ Directory

Greymouth *p550, map p551*
Banks All bank branches can be found on or around Mackay St. **Internet** DP:One Café, Mawhera Quay. Grey District Library, Mackay St. VIC (I-Site), see page 550. **Post office** Corner of Tainui and Guinness sts, Mon-Fri 0830-1700, Sat 1000-1230.

Reefton *p553*
Internet VIC (I-Site), see page 550.
Library/post office, across the road, Mon-Fri 1030-1230, 1330-1630.

Hokitika and around

Hokitika, or 'Hoki' as it is known, offers the same warm welcome and has the proud, healthy heartbeat felt all along the west coast. An important port until 1954, the town is also steeped in gold mining history; more of the precious metal passed through Hoki in the 1860s than any other town on the coast. Between 1865 and 1867, over 37,000 hopefuls arrived from Australia, America and Britain, requiring a staggering 84 hotels to put them all up in. In 1865, pioneer surveyor Julius von Haast described Hokitika as 'a scene of almost indescribable bustle and activity". In those heady days it seemed only the river itself could hold the town back. At one point during the gold rush there was at least one grounding every 10 weeks – and 21 in 1865 alone. Like everywhere else the gold ran out and old 'Hoki' slipped into decline. But today gold has been replaced by that other precious resource – tourism. It is now the craft capital of the west coast and summer sees crowds of visitors arrive by the bus load, to watch glass-blowing and greenstone carving and to browse in its numerous galleries.

South from Hokitika the influence of humanity decreases dramatically and the aesthetics begin to reflect the sheer dominance of nature. Mountain ranges climb steadily on the eastern horizon, ascending in ever-increasing beauty towards the heady peaks of the Westland National Park and to Mount Cook itself. Small villages like Ross and Hari Hari cling precariously to a history of gold mining and demonstrate in size alone how much nature rules these parts, and hopefully always will. This is where the 'real' west coast begins. ▶▶ *For Sleeping, Eating and other listings, see pages 562-564.*

Ins and outs

Getting there Hoki boasts the west coast's main **airport** ① *1 km east of the town centre*, served up to four times daily by **Air New Zealand Link**, To800-737000. By road Hoki is 40 km south of Greymouth and 429 km north of Wanaka. Principal bus services are provided by **Intercity**, To800-222145 (points south to Greymouth-Christchurch); **Atomic Shuttles**, To3-322 8883 (Queenstown/Greymouth/Christchurch, stops outside the VIC/I-Site) and **Coast to Coast**, To800-800847 (Greymouth/Christchurch, stops outside the **Travel Centre**, 60 Tancred St, To3-755 8557). If you are heading south this is also your last chance to join the **AA** ① *Council Buildings, Weld St, To800-500222.*

Tourist information **Westland VIC (I-Site)** ① *Carnegie Building, corner of Hamilton and Tancred sts, To3-755 6166, www.hokitika.org.nz, www.west-coast.co.nz.nz, daily in summer 0830-1800, winter Mon-Fri 0830-1700, Sat-Sun 1000-1600*, stocks most of what you need. **DoC** ① *Sewell St, Hokitika, To3-756 8282, www.doc.govt.nz, Mon-Fri 0800-1700.* **Ross VIC (I-Site)** ① *4 Aylmer St, To3-755 4077, www.ross.org.co.nz, daily 0900-1700 (seasonal).*

Hokitika ⊖⬤⬤⬤⬤⬤⬤⬤ ▶▶ *pp562-564.*

→ *Colour map 5, A4 Population: 4000*

Hokitika is famous for its arts and crafts, particularly **greenstone** carving and **glass-blowing**. Tancred Street is the hub of the many artisan outlets and factory shops. Not to be missed is the **Hokitika Glass Studio** ① *28 Tancred St, To3-755 7775, www.hokitikaglass.co.nz, daily 0900-1730 (longer in summer)*, where you can see the glass being blown and crafted into rather lurid ornaments and objets d'art. **Schroders Hand-blown Glass** ① *Mountain Jade Complex, 41 Weld St, To3-755 8007, www.schrodersglass.com*, echoes the Glass Studio and also houses a jade factory shop. There are a number of other factory shops including **Westland**

Greenstone ① *34 Tancred St, T03-755 8713, daily 0800-1700*, where you can see the beautiful and spiritual stone being cut and handcrafted into an array of jewellery, ornaments and traditional Maori pendants (*tiki*).

Also worthy of investigation is the **Gold Room** and **House of Wood**, both on Tancred Street. The huge natural nugget pendants in the Gold Room (at a hefty $8,000) would delight the critical eye of Jimmy Saville or even Mr T.

If you fancy a go at jade carving yourself, then try **Bonz and Stonz** ① *Hamilton St, T03-755 6504*. This outfit will give you tuition and you get to keep your masterpiece – or disaster. The full jade package costs from $85 (bone $65).

Once crafted out and replete with souvenirs, you might like to absorb some local history at the **West Coast Historical Museum** ① *Carnegie Building (accessed through the VIC), 7 Tancred St, T03-755 6898, daily 0830-1700 (seasonal), $5, child $1*. As you might expect there is a heavy emphasis on gold and jade, but the troubled history of the port and its numerous shipwrecks offshore provides some added excitement.

The **Quay**, near the museum, is worth a stroll with its centrepiece, the 1897 Custom House, now housing a small gallery. The free *Hokitika Heritage Walk* leaflet available from the VIC outlines all places of historical interest.

Far removed from both craft and history is the small, but effective, **New Zealand Kiwi Centre** ① *Tancred St, T03-755 5251, 0900-1630, $13, child $7*. It is a small complex with a variety of native and non-native species, the stars of which are the New Zealand kiwi, tuatara and eels – big eels, in fact the biggest eel species in the world. These unfeasibly large, ugly and lethargic octogenarians are fed daily at 1000, 1200, and 1500.

The town also has its very own **Glow-worm Dell** at the northern entrance to town. If you have not seen them yet and missed out on the spectacular displays in Waitomo, then this is your chance to see how amazing a glowing bottom can be.

West coast Hokitika & around

Hokitika

Sleeping ◎
Beachfront 7
Birdsong Backpackers 12
Blue Spur Lodge
  Backpackers 11
Fitzherbert Court Motel 2
Jade Court Motor
  Lodge 3
Just Jade Backpackers 5
Mountain Jade
  Backpackers 4
Rimu Lodge 13
Shining Star Log
  Chalets & Motor Camp 6
Stumpers 9
Teichelmann's B&B 8

Eating ❻
Café de Paris 2
Tasman View 3

⁝ Greenstone (Pounamu)

It would take several PhDs in geology to describe the make-up, formation and various types of greenstone (nephrite), but suffice to say it is old, uncommon and as the name suggests, coloured with almost transparent olive green shades. Greenstone, or jade – as it is better known – is precious (*taonga*) to the Maori and has been revered for centuries. The Maori called it *pounamu*. In New Zealand greenstone is found in the South Island, predominantly in Westland. The Maori called the South Island Te Wahi Pounamu (The Place of Greenstone) and they went to great lengths to find and transport the precious stone,

before carving it into a range of items, both practical and ornamental. Foremost among these was the *mere* (a flat hand-held weapon), which were highly treasured and in the hands of a warrior was lethal. *Heitiki* (pendants), were also painstakingly carved, often in the form of mythical spirits and monsters. These *tiki* were passed on from generation to generation and in doing so, increased in *mana* (prestige or spiritual power). In the modern-day, greenstone is mainly used to create ornaments and *tiki* for the tourist market. Hokitika, on the west coast of the South Island is the best place to buy it and see it being made.

Around Hokitika

Lake Kaniere → *Colour map 5, A4*
Inland from Hokitika (14 km) is the picturesque Lake Kaniere, a popular haven in summer for swimming, watersports, picnicking and walking. The lake can be explored by foot, car, boat or bicycle and has many pleasant features. At the entrance to the **Lake Kaniere Scenic Reserve** is an information kiosk outlining the options. The two best short walks, both of which include lovely beaches, are the **Kahikatea Walk**, at Sunny Bight (10 minutes), and the **Canoe Cove Walk** (15 minutes). If you are feeling energetic the **Lake Kaniere Walkway** (four hours one way), which also starts at Sunny Bight, follows the western shore of the lake to Slip Bay at its southern edge. The road on the eastern edge will give you access to the ascent of **Mount Tuhua** (1125 m, seven hours return). Further south are the **Dorothy Falls** (64 m) near Big Bay. There is a basic campsite at Hans Bay. The DoC leaflet *Central West Coast – Hokitika* outlines all the options ($1).

Hokitika Gorge → *Colour map 5, A4*
Accessed directly from Hokitika (33 km) via the settlements of Kaniere and Kokatahi (end of Kowhitirangi and Whitcombe Road) or, alternatively, via Lake Kaniere (loop road to Kokatahi) is the picturesque and moody Hokitika Gorge. Other than the impressive scenery the highlight here is the **swing-bridge**. Most of the time the river slides gracefully below, however, it can become a raging torrent after heavy rains, making the crossing an exciting prospect. Once across, you can continue through the bush for another 100 m to emerge at a rock wall that offers an even better view of the gorge.

Lake Mahinapua → *Colour map 5, A4*
Just 10 km south of Hokitika, and shielded from SH6 by a narrow tract of bush, is Lake Mahinapua and the **Mahinapua Recreation Reserve**, a popular spot for swimming, fishing, kayaking and walking. At the road terminus there is a pleasant picnic spot, a campsite and the trailheads to a number of short walks. Perched in concrete near the car park is a former 15-m paddle steamer that used to ply the route to 'Hoki' carrying both freight and passengers. A modern working model runs cruises from the outlet creek to the lake, starting 6 km south of Hokitika. ▶▶ *See Activities and tours, page 564.*

Stocked up with cash, petrol and photographic film, you can now follow the artery of SH6 into the real wild west coast. From here, the mountains rise higher and higher and become crowned with snow and impenetrable bush creeps steadily towards the road from all directions. Also, never far away, the pounding surf crashes onto lonely, driftwood-covered beaches. It all holds the promise of great things and, provided the weather is on your side, it will not disappoint. Even if you do nothing but simply gaze in wonder from the passenger seat, the 137-km journey to Franz Josef is a stunner and will ease you gently in to west coast time.

Ross → *Colour map 5, A4*

The first settlement of consequence is the tiny but pretty gold mining town of Ross, 30 km south of Hokitika. The most interesting thing about Ross is that mining still takes place here, in a very large hole at the edge of town, where the gentle chip, chip of the early pickaxe has long given way to the hum and roar of huge diggers and trucks. Even so, Ross retains the romance of its past with evidence of fond memories and many old remnants. During the great gold rush of the 1860s it was a bustling town of over 3000 hopefuls, who chipped away relentlessly at the alluvial gravels of the Totara Riverbeds in search of the 'big one'. Ironically, in 1909, towards the end of the great gold rush, one lucky miner fulfilled that dream. His find, named the **'Honourable Roddy'**, after the erstwhile Minister of Mines, was a nugget weighing in at a healthy 3.1 kg. As you might expect, the nugget immediately took on a life of its own, at first being paraded from bar to bar then sold and sold again. Then after a short stint as a doorstop (apparently true) it was bought by the government in 1911 as a coronation gift for King George V. Sadly, this act of generosity proved its demise. After a colourful life above ground, the good and the grateful Royals melted it down for use as a gold tea service at Buckingham Palace. Or that is what we are led to believe. A replica is now on view at the **Ross VIC (I-Site)** ① *4 Aylmer St, T03-755 4077, www.ross.org.co.nz, daily 0900-1700, guided walks 1000-1400.* Along with Roddy it has some interesting displays and photographs of the gold rush days and information on a number of short local walks, including the one-hour **Water Race Walk**, which takes in some former mining relics. You can also go gold panning for $8.50 (pan hire from $6). A short distance from the VIC (I-Site) is a renovated 1885 **Miner's Cottage** with a replica of the great 'Honourable Roddy' nugget.

Pukekura → *Colour map 5, A3*

About 18 km further south of Ross is the small settlement of Pukekura and the **Bushman's Centre** ① *T03-755 4144, www.pukekura.co.nz.* This place is instantly recognizable and notorious for the **giant sandfly** (*Renderus insanitus*) that hangs with menace from its walls (don't panic: despite local gossip, they could never grow that big). The Bushman's Centre is the ongoing project of local west coaster and extrovert Peter Salter and his partner Justine Giddy. As well as a fine café (with its superb 'road kill soup of the day') and shop it has a great little interactive **museum** ($4), where you can learn about bushcraft, meet live possums, stroke a pig, baulk at ugly eels, then wantonly throw sharp knives and axes at the wall. It's brilliant. Other activities based at the centre include horse trekking and gold panning.

Harihari → *Colour map 5, A3*

From Pukekura the bush continues to envelope you and you are blessed with your first occasional views of Mount Cook's snowy peak. At **Lake Lanthe** there are opportunities to stop and take in the views, enjoy a picnic on its bush-clad bank or take a leisurely 40-minute eco-cruise on board the small kauri steamboat the *Tamati*. Cruises cost around $16 and depart on demand from the Ianthe Jetty at the southern end of the lake, for details call To800-119494. From the car park you can take a short walk to visit a large **maitai tree**, the South Island's equivalent to the North Island's mighty kauri.

Harihari, 20 km south of Lake Lanthe and 80 km from Hokitika, is a small farming settlement nestled on the open alluvial plains of the Wanganui and Poerua rivers. It is famous due to the unexpected visitation by a 21-year-old Australian aviator called Guy Menzies in January 1931. Young Guy had set off unannounced and alone from Sydney in his Avro-Avian plane called the *Southern Cross* armed with little except a lot of courage and a good sense of direction. Just under 12 hours and an awful lot of sea later he crash-landed in a swamp near the town. The interesting thing is that bold Guy had not officially told anybody of his attempt to cross the ocean to New Zealand and he completed it in 2½ hours less than the much publicized success of Sir Charles Kingsford Smith, in a three-engine plane, with crew, three years earlier.

If you fancy some thorough exploration of the coastline, the **Harihari Coastal Walkway** (three hours) utilizes part of the old Wanganui River pack track and is a fine walk. It traverses kahikatea and rimu forest and essentially links the two river mouths. The car park and trailhead is accessed via La Fontaine Road at the southern end of Harihari (19 km). One of the many highlights of the walk is the lookout at the top of **Mount Doughboy** (or to use its more attractive name – Mount Oneone). Although not especially high it does afford a great view up and down the coast. The DoC leaflet *Harihari Coastal Walk* provides detailed information.

Whataroa → *Colour map 5, A3*

It is little wonder that the Maori have long revered the **white heron** (**kotuku**). Although a non-native and essentially an Australian import, its presence here on the west coast seems utterly befitting of the place. Somehow, with its colour echoing the snow of the mountaintops and its graceful unhurried flight in rhythm with west coast time, there could be no better mascot. Whataroa, 35 km south of Harihari, provides your only opportunity to see these majestic birds congregated at their sole New Zealand breeding rookery. The birds are only in residence from mid-October to mid-March.

White Heron Sanctuary Tours ① *To3-753 4120/To800-523-456, www.white herontours.co.nz, tours $110, child $60, daily at 0900, 1100, 1300 and 1500, in season*, offers a 2½-hour tour by jet boat to access the hide that overlooks the colony. All tours are guided and the colony cannot be visited independently without a permit. Outside the breeding season there is still an enjoyable 2½-hour 'Rainforest Nature Tour' available, again by jet boat, to view the ancient Kahikatea forest and whatever birdlife that decides to show (costs as above).

While in Whataroa don't miss the **Kotuku Gallery** ① *Main St, To3-753 4249, kotuku.gallery@xtra.co.nz*, Regarded as one of the best Maori galleries in the country the Kotuku showcases some superb work, including pieces carved from ancient whalebone and aotea stone, the latter of which is only found in two rivers in the world: one on the West Coast the other, surprisingly, in Germany. Poanamu (Greenstone), the signature stone of the West Coast, also features heavily.

Okarito → *Colour map 5, A3 Population: 30 (formerly 3000)*

Okarito, a small coastal settlement and former goldfields port, is 13 km off SH6 and 15 km south of Whataroa. This beautiful little paradise, set beachside next to the vast 3240-ha Okarito Lagoon backed by stunning views of the Southern Alps, is not surprisingly the favourite haunt of many a New Zealander. Thankfully most people shoot past the road junction from SH6 in their rush to see their first glacier – Franz Josef – 29 km to the south. But for those who take the time and the diversion, they will be rewarded not only with Okarito's simple do-nothing appeal, but also some excellent walking, kayaking and birdwatching opportunities. There is no public transport to Okarito and no shops in Okarito so take your own supplies.

There are few remnants of Okarito's once bustling gold mining past when the population remarkably ran into the thousands. It's hard to believe there were once 25 hotels, two banks, several stores, a busy school (now the YHA) and three theatres. Across the road from the obviously historic and incredibly cute YHA is the almost unsightly **obelisk** commemorating Abel Tasman's first sighting of New Zealand, somewhere off Okarito in 1642.

The best walk is the steady climb (1½ hours) via an old, but well-formed, pack track through native bush to the **Okarito Trig**. On a clear day it affords a stunning view across the bush-clad hills to the Southern Alps and the peak of Mount Cook and its associates. As if that weren't enough, you can then turn to take in the expansive views back towards the Okarito Lagoon and north up the coast. The **Trig Track** starts from the Strand at the southern end of the village. Once you have negotiated the Trig you can then consider carrying on along the main pack track for about an hour to reach **Three Mile Lagoon**. It is a lovely spot with a quiet beach and more coastal views. If the tide is right, you can then walk back to Okarito via the beach where huge white-veined schist rocks that have been eroded from the Kohuamarua Bluff litter the beach. Look out for dolphins playing just offshore.

The great expanse of **Okarito Lagoon** is a birdwatchers' paradise with almost every mainland bird species in New Zealand visiting at some point. Over 70 species have so far been recorded. The best way to view the birds and other fauna and flora of the lagoon is by kayak or boat tour. It's a great opportunity to go deep in to kiwi habitat to listen to (or possibly see) the great avian national icon in the wild. ▸▸ *See Activities and tours, page 564.*

● Sleeping

Hokitika *p557, map p558*
Hokitika is blessed with good accommodation but in summer, like everywhere else on the west coast, be sure to book well in advance.
LL Rimu Lodge, 33 Seddons Terr, T03-755 5255, www.rimulodge.co.nz. Purpose-built luxury lodge in a peaceful location and commanding memorable views over both river and mountain. 4 fine, spacious en suites from super-king to queen. 2-course dinner on request and full cooked breakfast included. All in all, a good-value option. Recommended.
L Teichelmann's B&B, 20 Hamilton St, T03-755 8232, www.teichelmanns.co.nz. Large heritage building, centrally located, with an arts and crafts edge. 6 en suites both double and single and a delightful cottage with spa in the garden. The hosts have a great knowledge of the town and region. Recommended.
L-AL Beachfront Hotel, 111 Revell St, T03-755 8344, www.southlandhotel.com. The most modern and high-profile hotel in town. Well-facilitated and comfortable with 53 rooms from standard to luxury, most en suite and some with ocean views. A reputable restaurant/bar overlooking the beach being its best point. Off-street parking available.

AL-A Fitzherbert Court Motel, 191 Fitzherbert St, T03-755 5342, www.fitzherbertcourt.co.nz. 1- to 2- bedroom suites (some with spa bath), studios, Sky TV.
AL-A Jade Court Motor Lodge, 85 Fitzherbert St, T03-755 8855, www.jadecourt.co.nz. Self-contained studios and 1- to 2-bedroom units in a spacious garden setting.
AL-D Shining Star Log Chalets and Motor Camp, 11 Richards Drive, T03-755 8921, www.accommodationwestcoast.co.nz. A superb motel/motorpark with tidy self-contained lodges designed and built by the owners. It is close to the beach in a quiet location and also takes campervans and tents. The facilities are excellent.
A-D Mountain Jade Backpackers, 41 Weld St, T03-755 8007/T0800-838301. Purpose-built with 2 self-contained units, doubles and shared options Also has a café downstairs. It takes the majority of the 'backpacker buses' so can get busy.
B-D Blue Spur Lodge Backpackers, Hampden St, 5 km east of town, T03-755 8445, bluespur@paradise.co.nz. Well-appointed and well-equipped, with tidy doubles, twins and shared rooms set in 3 fully self-contained buildings. It's a popular

place noted for its peace and quiet and worth the effort to get there. Kayak hire, gold panning and bush walks on site.
B-D Stumpers, 2 Weld St, T03-7556154, www.stumpers.co.nz. Pitched somewhere between a budget motel and a backpacker hostel, it offers tidy en suite and standard doubles, singles and dorms. Its central location and in house bar and café are an added attraction. In-house dining is encouraged so there are no kitchen facilities.
C-D Birdsong Backpackers, SH6 (4 km north), T03-755 7179, www.birdsong.co.nz. Small beachside backpacker hostel, just north of the town, offering dorms, doubles and a large dose of peace and quiet. Outdoor bath for navel and galaxy contemplation.
C-D Just Jade Backpackers, 197 Revell St, T03-755 7612, www.madkiwi.co.nz. Set on the beach, smaller, more homely, and offering jade carving (from $80), a pet possum (in the garden) and private beach access as added incentives to stay.

Ross *p560*
B-D Empire Hotel, Aylmer St, T03-755 4005. Basic but characterful and historic, has tent sites, backpacker cabins and en suite rooms.

Pukekura *p560*
Across the road from the **Bushman's Centre** (see page 560) there is a fine array of accommodation options (**AL-D**) from tent sites and budget dorms to motel units 'under canvas' with all facilities and even hot pools.

Harihari *p560*
AL-D Harihari Motor Inn, Main Rd, T0800-833026. Tidy en suites, backpacker rooms, powered/tent sites and a licensed restaurant.
B Tomsai Motel, T03-753 3116, across the road from **Harihari**. A basic motel option.

Whataroa *p561*
A Sanctuary Tours Motel, T03-753 4120/ T0800-523456, www.whiteherontours.co.nz. Self-contained units, studio units and cabins.
A-C Whataroa Hotel, T03-753 4076. Rooms, a motel unit, a cabin and powered sites. In-house restaurant.

Okarito *p561*
D Okarito YHA Hostel, Palmerston St, T0800-278299, www.yha.co.nz. Something

of novelty set in the former 1870's schoolhouse. Bookings can be made via the Franz Josef VIC or payment made at the warden's house close to the hostel. Coin-operated showers at the campground.

Campsites
The **DoC** campground (**D**) is opposite the hostel. A very pleasant, sheltered and basic campsite facilities are adequate. Fires are permitted. Beware of sandflies and take insect repellent. No bookings necessary.

⊘ Eating

Hokitika *p557, map p558*
There is a supermarket: **New World**, 116 Revell St, Mon-Fri until 2000, Sat 1900, Sun 1900.
Café de Paris, 19 Tancred St, T03-755 8933, daily from 0730. Award-winning restaurant with imaginative French-style à la carte dinner and changing blackboard menu for breakfast and lunch. Good coffee.
Tasman View Restaurant, attached to the **Beachfront Hotel**, Revell St, T03-755 8344, dinner daily from 1800. Popular not only for the views of the crashing waves and the sunset, but also for its seafood.
Stumpers Café & Bar, 2 Weld St, T03-755 6154, daily 0700-2200. A more conventional menu and aesthetics.

Ross *p560*
There is a supermarket on Main Rd, open until 2000.
Roddy Nugget Café, T03-755 4245, on the Main Rd, daily from 0800-1900 (seasonal).
Empire Hotel, Aylmer St, T03-755 4005. Offers pub-style breakfast, lunch and dinners.

Pukekura *p560*
Puke Pub, on the main road, T03-755 4144, www.pukekura.co.nz. Without doubt one of the finest drinking establishments on the west coast. Full of character with pub-style grub. If you are a male-only group ask to see the mock-up view into the ladies toilet – truly stunning.

Harihari *p560*
Harihari Motor Inn, see Sleeping above. Basic restaurant.
Glenalmond Tearooms, on the main road through the town.

The only eateries are both on the main road:
❧ **Whataroa Hotel**, see Sleeping, above.
❧ **White Heron Store and Tearooms**.

◐ Pubs, bars and clubs

Hokitika *p557, map p558*
Stumpers Bar, see Eating, above. The main
hub of entertainment and attracts a diverse
crowd and stages live bands most weekends.

Pukekura *p560*
Puke Pub, see Eating, above. Not to be
missed. It's pronounced 'pookie'.

◉ Festivals and events

Hokitika *p557, map p558*
Mar Hokitika Wildfoods Festival, T03-755
8321, wildfoods@westlandddc.govt.nz.
Tickets $25. Hokitika goes mad each Mar
and enjoys such a human influx that it can
jog the memories of the gold rush days. The
attraction is not gold but good food and lots
and lots of beer and wine. This is a celebration
of the west coast's unique lifestyle and
hospitality (not to mention drinking capacity).
On offer is a vast array of culinary delights
from BBQ possum, or witchetty bug to the
famed local whitebait fritter. There's even the
odd testicle – yum! A number of lesser events
over the 2- to 3-day event (which includes
diverse activities as a basketball exhibition
match and a Monteiths Beer tasting) leads
up the main festival and dance on the Sat.

▲ Activities and tours

Hokitika *p557, map p558*
Classic Car Rentals, Carnegie Building, corner
of Tancred and Hamilton sts, T03-755 6928,
www.classiccarrentals.co.nz. Always wanted
to drive a Porsche, a 1938 Alfa Romeo or a
1957 Maserati (one of only 10 in the world)?
Well, here is the opportunity to do so and
let's face it, you could hardly ask for a
better place. The car hire costs start from
$80 per hr including petrol and insurance.
But you must be over 25, not be dribbling
at the mouth and perhaps promise you
have never owned a set of furry dice.
Paddle Boat Cruises, T03-755 7239,
www.paddlecruises.com. These ply the creek

to the picturesque Mahinapua Lake just
south of the town. A 1½-hr trip costs from
$25. Departs daily at 1400 (seasonal).
Wilderness Wings, T0800-755 8118,
www.wildernesswings.co.nz. Flightseeing
trips following the Main Divide to Mt Cook
and the glaciers, then back over the wild
and remote beaches. Personable service,
45 mins-3½ hrs, from $210.

Whataroa *p561*
White Heron Sanctuary Tours, PO Box 19,
Whataroa, T0800-523456, www.white
herontours.co.nz. Guided boat trips to
New Zealand's only White heron breeding
site. See also page 561.

Okariko *p561*
For details, see page Franz Josef
Activities and tours, page 571.
Okarito Kiwi Tours, T03-753 4330,
www.okaritokiwitours.co.nz. Offers the
chance to go deep in to kiwi habitat to listen
to (or possibly see) the great avian national
icon in the wild. Low impact guiding is
backed up by good local knowledge.
2-3 hrs from $45. Recommended.
Okarito Nature Tours, T03-753 4014,
www.okarito.co.nz, offers independent kayak
rental (2 hrs, $35) and a range of excellent
guided trips to explore the scenery and
natural history of the lagoon and its many
secluded channels, from $75 (overnight
from $80). Recommended.

● Transport

Hokitika *p557, map p558*
Bicycle hire Hokitika Cycles and
Sportsworld, 33 Tancred St, T03-755 8662.
Taxi Hokitika Taxis, T03-755 5075.

⬤ Directory

Hokitika *p557, map p558*
Banks Most branches and ATMs are in
the town centre. If heading south, there are
no further banks, or ATMs until Wanaka.
Internet Kodak Shop, 15 Weld St, T03-
755 7768. **Medical services** Westland
Medical Centre, 54 Sewell St, T03-755 8180.
Post office 93 Revell St, T03-756 8034,
Mon-Fri 0830-1700. **Useful addresses**
AA, T0800-500222, breakdown services.

Glacier Region

To add to New Zealand's majestic scenery and ecological surprises, the two gigantic and dynamic monoliths of ice – Franz Josef and Fox Glaciers – provide a dramatic sight. They are the brightest jewels in the highly decorated crown of the Westland and Mount Cook national parks, joined, yet separated on the map, by the jagged summits and peaks of the Southern Alps and the Great Dividing Range. Descending from a height of 3000 m to 300 m at the remarkable speed of over 1 m a day, the glaciers create one of the best examples of glaciology in the world.

In summer there are two moods to the neighbouring villages of Franz and Fox. When the sun shines they are a frenetic buzz of activity: from the moment the sun peeks over the mountains, the skies fill with the sound of aircraft, the roads swarm with tour buses and the streets fill with expectant tourists, consumed with the desire to get to the glaciers, walk on them and photograph them. And yet, when the clouds gather (which is often) and the rain descends (or rather crashes down), the pace of everything slows, dramatically: the air hangs heavy with silence, the streets fill with puddles and the tourists' glum faces stare out from behind café windows. At Franz and Fox it's amazing just how much the weather and two multi-million ton blocks of ice can dictate. ▸▸ *For Sleeping, Eating and other listings, see pages 568-574.*

Ins and outs

Getting there There are no scheduled air services to Franz Josef. By road Franz Josef is 177 km south of Greymouth, 404 km north of Queenstown and 25 km north of Fox Glacier on SH6. Fox Glacier is 177 km north of Haast. By bus, **Intercity**, T03-365 1113, and **Atomic Shuttles**, T03-322 8883, north and southbound services all stop at Franz Josef and Fox. On Main Road in Franz Josef, **Scott Base Information**, T03-752 0288 and the **YHA**, T03-752 0754 (see Sleeping, page 569) act as the local Intercity agents.

Getting around Most of Franz Josef's amenities are on the SH6 (Main Road) with everything, except the glacier, within easy walking distance. **Glacier Valley Eco-tours**, T03-752 0699, www.glaciervalley.co.nz, provides transport to the glacier every two hours 0845-2100 (1800 in winter), $10 return. It also offers road and walking tours to Lake Matheson, Franz and Fox glaciers from $55. Hitching to the glacier and back is rarely a problem. Note that there is no petrol available between Fox Glacier and Haast.

Tourist information DoC Franz Josef Glacier VIC (I-Site) ① *southern end of town (seaward side), T03-752 0796, www.glaciercountry.co.nz, 0830-1800 (winter 0830-1630)*, has plenty of displays, information on walks and up-to-date weather forecasts. On Main Road the independent **Scott Base Information Centre**, T03-752 0288, also provides local information, arranges transport and activity bookings and has internet. **DoC Fox Glacier VIC (Area Office)** ① *SH6, at the northern end (seaward side) of the village, T03-751 0807, Mon-Fri 0900-1630*, also offers information but the Franz office is far more comprehensive. **Independent VIC** ① *Mountain Helicopters base, corner of Sullivan St and SH6 (opposite BP station), T03-751 0045, 0800-2000 (seasonal)*.

Franz Josef → *Colour map 5, A/B3 Population: 350*

Franz Josef owes its very existence and, of course its name, to the great block of ice that sits 5 km south of the village. Of the two principally tourist based settlements (Franz and Fox), Franz is the larger and better serviced. As you might expect it is very much a seasonal destination, crowded in summer, quiet in winter. Although the glacier can of course be visited in the rain and the guided glacier walks are rarely cancelled, the scenic flights, and essentially, an overall impression of the glaciers from above and

⁞ Web weather

Before booking a flight over the glaciers, it is worth looking at the detailed weather resource at www.metservice.co.nz and www.metvuw.com for the latest synopsis. **Weatherline**, T0900-99903, is also useful as is the satellite map on www.nzcity.co.nz. Although it is a bit dated you can ascertain whether a large blanket of nasty white stuff is heading your way and if rain is, once again, going to stop play.

below, are completely dependent on favourable conditions. Plan to give yourself at least two days in the area. If you have scenic flights booked, these can be forwarded if it's cloudy. While you wait there are a few things to keep you occupied, even in the rain (see Wet weather activities, page 573). The average annual rainfall in the area is 5 m over 180 rain days. In summer always book your accommodation well in advance.

Franz Josef Glacier

Franz Josef was first sighted and officially documented by both Abel Tasman in 1642 and Cook in 1770, but first properly explored and named by geologist and explorer Julius von Haast in 1865. When he first explored its lower reaches it was almost 3 km nearer the coast than it is today. The official title of 'Francis Joseph Glacier' was given in honour of the Emperor Franz Josef of Austria. The spelling was later changed to Franz Josef in accordance with the internationally accepted version – as in Franz Josef Land in the Arctic and Franz Josef Fjord in Greenland. Until 1985, and apart from a few sporadic advances last century, the glacier had actually been receding steadily since 1865. As it stands, it is unclear what it will do next. After advancing almost 1 km, at almost 1 m a day over the last 17 years, it is now slowing down. Many are worried that global warming will see the glaciers recede at an unnatural rate due to a lack of snow at the summits.

The glacier is 5 km south of town and accessed by the Glacier Access Road which runs alongside the cold, grey Waiho River, which dramatically appears from beneath its face. From the car park it is a 1½-hour return walk along the wide rocky river bed to within 500 m of the glacier. Unless properly equipped you cannot walk on the glacier itself; to do that you are strongly advised to join one of the many guided trips. By far the best way to view the glacier is from the air; there are numerous options available. From the ground, the 280 m-high viewpoint on **Sentinel Rock** (a remnant of previous glacial erosion) is perhaps the best place; it is easily accessed from near the main car park (20 minutes). ▸▸ *See Activities and tours, page 571.*

Fox Glacier → *Colour map 5, A3 Population: 300*

Many people visiting the Glacier Region only visit one of the great monoliths, with Franz Josef being the most favoured. However, if you have time, Fox Glacier (25 km south of Franz and a further 8 km southeast) is no less dramatic. The **Fox Glacier Valley** and the chilly **Fox River**, which surges from the glacier terminus, provide a significantly different atmosphere, with the precipitous, ice-carved cliffs near the car park being particularly remarkable. The Fox Glacier was originally called the Victoria Glacier and was renamed in honour of former New Zealand prime minister, Sir William Fox, on a visit in 1872. The small village of Fox Glacier is the main service centre and sits on a site that was, as recently as 5000 years ago, covered by the present glacier.

Although less commercial, Fox, like its neighbour Franz, can be explored independently at its terminus, but you will need a guide to walk or climbed on it. Once again, however, the recommendation is to admire it from the air. There are a number of interesting walks within the valley, at the coast and around the reflective **Lake Matheson**, which lies 4 km west of the village. ▸▸ *See Activities and tours, page 573.*

South to Haast ⬤🍴▲ ›› pp568-574.

From Fox Glacier you leave the great glaciers and towering peaks of the national parks behind and SH6 winds its scenic way ever southwards to Haast and to the most remote region of the west coast: South Westland. For many years Fox was as far south as any tourist ventured, the road from there becoming rough and eventually non-existent at Paringa. With the opening of the great Haast Pass Highway in 1965 the two roads were linked making the continuous journey possible. Given the terrain in South Westland, it is not hard to understand why such a link was so late in coming. Despite the intrusion, much of South Westland remains remote, unspoilt and remarkably beautiful.

Copeland Pass

The heavily forested **Copeland Valley**, 26 km south of Fox, heralds the trailhead of the **Copeland Track** ① *details on the 'Copeland Track' broadsheet from DoC*. Hut fees are $15 per night and there is a resident warden at Welcome Flat from November to April. Although the complete three- to four-day tramp makes a spectacular high-alpine crossing into the Hooker Valley and, eventually, the haven of Mount Cook Village, recent rock falls have made the route very difficult and one only suited to the experienced mountaineer. Nevertheless, the 17-km overnight tramp up the Copeland Valley to the **Welcome Flat Hut** is recommended. This tramp acquaints you with some superb forest, river and mountain scenery and includes the natural hot pools at Welcome Flat. The one-way tramp to the hut takes about six hours. From Welcome Flat you then have the option of an overnight stay and a return, or the extra (three hours one way) excursion higher up the valley to the **Douglas Rock Hut** ($5).

> ‡ *Intercity and Atomic Shuttle buses pass the Copeland Valley entrance and can drop off or pick up.*

Bruce Bay → Colour map 5, B2

From the Copeland Valley, a further 20 km will see you rejoining the coast at Bruce Bay, a quiet, scenic spot, once famous for a false gold claim made during the rush of 1865. Apparently, three miners in Hokitika initiated the story that they had secured a hundred-weight of gold in Bruce Bay and, as a result, over 2000 hopeful souls made the long and difficult journey south. Frustrated and angry after realizing it was a hoax, they then went on the rampage looting and destroying the makeshift stores and shanties. Although it is very pretty in itself, one of the most beautiful and scenic bays and beaches of the west coast lies just over the headland, to the south. The much-photographed (from the air) **Heretaniwha Bay**'s golden curve of sand and rim of windshorn rimu epitomize the west coast wilderness. With the Mahitahi River and trackless headland preventing easy access it is very difficult to reach, which is perhaps what makes it so special.

Paringa → Colour map 5, B2

Turning inland again, the SH6 continues south to cross the Paringa River before arriving at **Lake Paringa**. The river is noted as the furthest point south that the intrepid early explorer Thomas Brunner reached in his epic 18-month journey from Nelson and the Buller Gorge in 1848. Considering it would be another 100 years before the road even reached this point, his 'feat' can only be admired. A plaque by the river honours it. At Lake Paringa you will find accommodation and a café. The lake is noted for its good trout fishing and the **Jamie Creek Walkway** (15 minutes), which negotiates a fine tract of beech and rimu, 1 km south of the café near the DoC campsite.

Lake Moeraki and Munroe Beach → Colour map 5, B2

The reflective waters of **Lake Moeraki** are a further 18 km south of Lake Paringa and 30 km north of Haast. Although popular for swimming, kayaking and birdwatching most people are in an understandable rush to share the intent of its outlet river and head straight for the beach. The car park and trailhead to **Munroe Beach** is 200 m north of Moeraki River bridge. An easy, well-formed path leads through some beautiful coastal forest to the pounding surf. It is a typical west coast stunner and a place where wildlife abounds. In the breeding season (July to December), or during their moult in late summer, it is a great place to see the rare and beautiful **Fiordland crested penguin**. If you are lucky, and provided you are quiet, you can watch them fighting their way through the crashing waves to waddle uneasily up the beach before disappearing into the bush. It really is a wonderful spectator sport.

If the tide is well out try to investigate the beach and the Moeraki River mouth to the south of Munroe. It's even better. Note that there is one other species that is present in its thousands and are far less interesting or welcome – sandflies. Apply lots of repellent or you will re-emerge at the car park looking like you have had a serious road accident.

Knight Point

South of Moeraki SH6 rejoins the coast and climbs to Knight Point with its spectacular views of sea stacks and near inaccessible beaches. Just south of the viewpoint you should be able to see **fur seals** dozing on the beach. It was just south of Knight Point that the Haast Highway was officially opened in 1965, thereby connecting Otago with south Westland and the west coast proper. At the base of the hill, about 3 km south, is a small car park allowing unadvertised access to **Murphy's Beach**. This is a superb spot for a beach walk. If the tide is out you can explore this beautiful sweep of sand and the rugged coast north or south. The rock outcrops and pinnacles to the south of the beach provide some superb photo opportunities, especially at sunset.

Ship Creek

A little further south is the more popular access to the beach at Ship Creek. Here you can choose from a number of excellent short walks to explore the beach, coastal forest and a small lake held captive by the dunes. If the tide is out you can make the easy river crossing, negotiate the headland and explore the beaches heading north. In summer it is not unusual to see **Fiordland crested penguins** coming ashore to their breeding areas hidden in the coastal fringe. When it comes to an archetypal wild and remote coast it does not get much better than this. Ship Creek was named after a wreck that ironically occurred on the Australian coast at Cape Otway in Victoria in 1854. On her maiden voyage, the 2600-ton *Schomberg* ran aground and several years later, pieces of the ill-fated vessel were washed up here over 1500 km away. From Ship Creek SH6 hugs the coast and passes some spectacular examples of coastal rimu, rata and kahikatea forest on its approach to Haast and the Haast River crossing.

● Sleeping

Franz Josef *p565*
Given the amount of tourist traffic in summer and the fickle weather, you are advised to book your accommodation well in advance and add an additional night, just in case.
LL Franz Josef Glacier Country Retreat, off SH6, 6 km north of the village, T03-752 0012/T0800-FRANZJOSEF, www.glacier-retreat.co.nz. A replica of a traditional west coast homestead in a peaceful farmland setting, owned by a 4th generation west coast family. 12 beautifully appointed luxury en suite rooms with a historical edge.

4-poster beds and claw-foot or spa baths add to the appeal. In-house café and bar. Activities and massage therapies can be arranged. Recommended.
LL Westwood Lodge, SH6, 1 km north of the village, T03-752 0112, www.westwood-lodge.co.nz. A modern, well-appointed single-storey B&B, with 9 luxury en suite rooms.
LL-L Franz Josef Glacier Hotels, Main Rd, T03-752 0729, www.sceniccircle.co.nz. Catering mainly to tour groups, with a restaurant, a café and 3 bars, plus a spa. It is showing its age, but the decor is modern.

LL-L Holly Homestead B&B, off SH6, 1½ km north of the village, T03-752 0299, www.hollyhomestead.co.nz. Gracious old homestead with native timbers throughout. 4 en suites, some with wheelchair access, children welcome. Internet, full cooked breakfast included.

LL-L Punga Grove Motel and Suites, northern end of Cron St, just east of Main Rd, T03-752 0001, www.pungagrove.co.nz. Modern stylish studios and units from standard to luxury all backing on to native punga fern gardens, with premium rooms incorporating your very own 'punga grove'.

AL-A Alpine Glacier Motor Lodge, corner of Cron and Condon sts, in the village centre, T03-752 0224.

AL-A Bella Vista, northern end of Cron St, just to the east of Main Rd, T03-752 0008, www.bellavistamotels.co.nz.

AL-A The Glacier Gateway Motor Lodge, T03-752 0776. Quieter and on the southern edge of town (nearest the glacier).

L-AL Glenfern, T03-752 0054, www.glen fern.co.nz. This modern place offers self-contained and serviced apartments and in a peaceful location near the Tatare River 3 km north of the village.

AL-D Rainforest Retreat, Cron St, T0800-873346/T03-752 0220, www.rainforest retreat.co.nz. Affordable eco-based log cabins in a quiet bush setting, yet still close to the village centre. The various options include studios, self-contained suites and family units. There are also campervan facilities and tent sites, with modern facilities including a camp kitchen. Spa and internet. Recommended.

Backpacker hostels

There are many backpacker hostels available in the village, most being on Cron St.

A-D Glow Worm Cottages, 27 Cron St, T03-752 0173/T0800-151027, www.glow wormcottages.co.nz. The favourite, along with Chateau Franz, below. Both offer the best in facilities, character and atmosphere.

A-D YHA, 4 Cron St, T03-752 0754, www.yha.org.nz. Modern, spacious hostel with all the usual reliable YHA facilitation including some very tidy en suite doubles

and a heavy and refreshing emphasis on eco-awareness and recycling. Recommended. Book well ahead.

A-D Chateau Franz, 8 Cron St, T03-752 0738, www.chateaufranz.co.nz. Well facilitated and deservingly popular, with free soup, spa and video library to ease the rainfall blues.

Motorcamps and campsites

Camping (**D**) is also available at the Rainforest Retreat, see above.

L-D Mountain View Top Ten, SH6, 5 km north of the village, T0800- 467897. Great views of the mountains. Full range of options and standard Top Ten facilitation.

B-D Franz Josef Holiday Park, SH6, 1 km south of the town, T03-752 0766, www.franzjosef.co.nz.

Fox Glacier p566

LL Te Weheka Inn, opposite the DoC/VIC, Main Rd, T03-751 0730, www.teweheka.co.nz. A recent addition to the village and pitched somewhere between a motel and a boutique hotel. It has a striking design and offers modern luxury suites. Facilities include a library and internet. Tariff includes breakfast.

L Glacier Country Hotel, Main Rd, T03-751 0847, www.scenic-circle.co.nz. An old hotel that has been refurbished in recent years. It has a wide range of fairly unremarkable rooms from studio to single. Restaurant and bar with large open fire. Internet.

L-C Fox Glacier Lodge, Sullivan Rd, T03-751 0888, wwwfoxglacierlodge.co.nz. A tidy complex enjoying a recent expansion, now offering a good range of suites and units (some with spa) as well as powered sites with shared facilities.

AL-A Homestead Farm B&B, Cook Flat Rd, T03-751 0835, foxhomstd@xtra.co.nz. One of the few B&Bs in the village offering all the comforts of home in a century-old farmhouse.

A-C Fox Glacier Hotel, Cook Flat Rd, T03-751 0839, www.resorts.co.nz. Well established, popular and spacious with standard en suites, economy twins and backpacker rooms with en suites.

● *For an explanation of the Sleeping and Eating price codes used in this guide, see the inside*
● *front cover. Other relevant information is provided in the Essentials chapter, pages 44-51.*
  Note that prices are given in New Zealand dollars.

A-D Fox Glacier Inn, Sullivan's Rd, T03-751 0022, www.foxglacierinn.co.nz. Tidy family, double or shared rooms, a café, restaurant and bar. Tents also welcome.
C-D Ivory Towers, Sullivan's Rd, T03-751 0838, www.ivorytowerslodge.co.nz. An old favourite with a cosy atmosphere and great facilities, including a small cinema, sauna, bike hire and internet. Its double rooms are especially good value and the copious flowerbeds and hanging baskets are a memorable, attractive feature. Recommended.

Motels

Many motels in Fox are on Cooks Flat Rd.
L-AL Mount Cook View Motel, T03-751 0814, www.mtcookview.co.nz.
L-AL The Westhaven Motel, Main Rd, T03-751 0084/T0800-369452, www.the westhaven.co.nz. Offers a wide range of rooms, some with spa.
AL-A Lake Matheson Motel, T03-751 0830, www.lakematheson.co.nz. Recently refurbished. Recommended.
AL-A Rainforest Motel, T03-751 0140, www.rainforestmotel.co.nz.

Motorcamps

L-C Fox Glacier Holiday Park, Cooks Flat Rd, T03-7510821. The main motorpark in the village. Recently up-graded and very spacious, it has all the usual facilities including cabins, lodge rooms, flats, powered/tent sites and a backpacker dorm. Good facilities, but it can all get a bit over-crowded.

Bruce Bay *p567*

LL Mahitahi Lodge, off SH6 in Bruce Bay, T03-7510095, www.mahitahi lodge.co.nz Purpose-built luxury homestay accommodation named after the river that meets the ocean at Bruce Bay. 3 well- appointed en-suites with native timbers throughout, open fire and some fine in-house cuisine (breakfast included in tariff but dinner $50 extra). The exceptional hosts will also take you on an informative and entertaining local tour.

Lake Moeraki *p567*

LL-L Moeraki Wilderness Lodge, beside SH6 at the Moeraki River outlet, T03-750

0881, www.wildernesslodge.co.nz. An exclusive eco-based B&B establishment. The lodge has 22 rooms all with private facilities and an in-house restaurant. Guided nature/history walks and canoe trips are also available, with some being part of the package. The restaurant is open to non-guests.

🍴 Eating and drinking

Franz Josef *p565*

Grocery supplies are available from **Fern Grove Food Centre**, Main Rd, 0800-2200 (seasonal). Well-stocked but expensive.
🍴 **Alice May Bar and Restaurant**, Cron St, T03-752 0740, daily from 1500. English pub-style, with arguably more atmosphere and better value food. Noted for its fine ales.
🍴 **Beeches Café, Restaurant and Bar**, Main Rd, T03-752 0721, daily from 0800-2100 (seasonal). Standard fare for breakfast, lunch and dinner.
🍴 **The Blue Ice Café & Pub**, Main Rd, T03-752 0707. Serves up a good pizza upstairs and à la carte dining on the ground level. All-out war on the free pool table is its other speciality. Recommended.
🍴 **Franz Josef Glacier Hotel restaurants**, T03-752 0729. A la carte, but often busy with bus tours. Bookings are recommended.
🍴 **The Landing**, Main Rd, T03-752 0229, daily 1000-late, breakfast, lunch and dinner. Fine pizzas and currently the base in Franz for après-rain or after-hours entertainment.
🍴 **The Cheeky Kea Café**, Main Rd, T03-752 0139, open 0700-2100 (seasonal). A slightly cheaper option than most and is good for a no-nonsense snack or breakfast.

Fox Glacier *p566*

Grocery supplies are available at the **General Store**, Main Rd, T03-751 0829, daily 0800-2030 (1900 in winter) at in evitably elevated prices.
🍴 **Café Neve**, Main Rd, opposite the Alpine Guides Centre, T03-751 0110, open 0800-late (seasonal). Quite expensive, but still a pleasant place for breakfast, light snacks, home baking and coffee with outdoor seating that offers a good spot to watch the world go by.

¶¶ **Cook Saddle Café and Saloon**, Main Rd, T03-751 0700, open from 1200. It offers a good meat-lover's menu and has a bar.

¶¶ **Hobnail Café**, in the Alpine Guides Centre, T03-751 0005, daily 0700-1700 (seasonal). Offers a hearty, value breakfast and some fine home baking.

¶¶ **The Plateau**, Sullivan Rd, T03-751 0058, daily 0900-late (seasonal). Earning a good reputation in the village, the menu is imaginative enough but more attractive still is the open fire and the wine list.

¶¶-¶ **Fox Glacier Inn**, see Sleeping, above. Good for a beer and a chat.

¶ **Café at Lake Matheson**, T03-7510878, at the car park at the entrance to the lake, 0700-1800 (1500 in winter). A good option if you plan to go walking there, it is especially welcome after the popular sunrise photo opportunities. Cheap breakfasts.

Paringa *p567*

¶¶ **Salmon Farm Café**, just north of the Paringa River, T03-751 0837, daily 0730-1700 (winter 0830-1600). A popular 'quick-stop' eatery. Either feed the salmon in the tanks below or eat one in the café.

▲ Activities and tours

Franz Josef *p565*

There are many operators based in Franz Josef offering a range of options for acquainting yourself with the great glacier. Competition is fierce so shop around. Most people do one of 3 things: they walk to the glacier's terminal face independently, they take a guided walk on to the glacier or they take to the air. A glacier walk is both exciting and very informative, however, if you can possibly afford it, take an extended scenic flight around Mt Cook and down the face of the glacier, landing briefly on the snow at its crown. The atmosphere up there, and the silence on a calm, clear day, is simply unforgettable. When the rain shows who's boss, you might like to try a spot of indoor, all-weather ice climbing (followed by a hot bath of course) at the new and impressive **Hukawai Glacier Centre and Ice Climbing Wall** (see below). Alternatively, if ice for you is something that belongs in several small blocks deep in a gin and tonic, you can sit and watch from the comfort of the café.

Alpine Trophies, T0800-800793. Fishing on pretty Lake Mapourika, 8 km north of Franz.

Glacier Country Tours and Kayaks (Fern's Kayaks), 20 Cron St, T03-752 0230/ T0800-423262, www.glacierkayaks.com. 2½-hr kayaking trips in the area including Lake Mapourika (similar to the reflective Lake Matheson), from $60. Also offers a full-day heli-hike and kayak combo, from $400

Glacier Valley Ecotours, T03-752 0690, www.glaciervalley.co.nz. Conventional road and walking tours of both glaciers and Lake Matheson, 1-3 hrs, from $55.

Skydive Glacier Country, T0800-7510080, www.skydivingnz.co.nz. Offers 9000-12,000 ft tandem skydives amidst some of the country's most stunning scenery, from $245-285.

South Westland Horse Treks, Wahio Flat Rd, just south of Franz, T03-752 0223/ T0800-187357, www.horsetreknz.com. Offers 1- to 3-hr horse treks including some great beach rides, from $50.

Climbing (indoors)

Hukawai Glacier Centre and Ice Climbing Wall, corner of Cowan and Cron sts, T03-752 0600/T0800-485292, www.hukawai.co.nz. One of only 7 such centres in the world and one of the largest with 200 sq m of ice 10 m in height. A 1½-hr tutored session will cost around $90, child (10-15 yrs) $65. The complex also offers a memorable 'Glacier Experience' interactive walkway with high tech visuals explaining the natural and social history of the area, from $28, child $14. Combo ice-climb and walk from $105.

Flightseeing

There are 2 companies offering fixed-wing flights over the glaciers: **Air Safaris** and **Mount Cook Ski Plane Adventures** (Aoraki Mt Cook). The latter offers the only opportunity in New Zealand to land on a glacier in a fixed-wing aircraft. Both companies are based in Fox (see page 573) but can provide pick-ups from Franz.

Helicopter flightseeing is also available with all flights offering a glacier landing. Again, the companies are based in Fox: **Fox and Franz Josef Heli-services**, T03-751 0866, www.newzealandnz.co.nz/helicopters. From 20-40 mins, snow landings.

Flightseeing options

Fixed wing or helicopter? Twin engine or single? Snow landing or no landing? Weather permitting, these are the questions to ask yourself. Generally speaking fixed-wing aircraft will allow longer in the air for the price and cover more 'air', but you miss out on that unique feel of a helicopter. Helicopters have twin or single engines. Most helicopters offer 10-minute snow landings whereas most fixed-wing planes do not. All modes are intrinsically safe and all companies are accommodating regarding weather cancellations (payment takes place pre-flight and post-booking) even offering alternative flights at sister locations.

Glacier Helicopters, Main Rd, T03-752 0755/T0800-800732, www.glacier helicopters.co.nz. 10- to 40-min flights with snow landing, from $175-345.
Helicopter Line, Main Rd, T0800-807767, www.helicopter.co.nz. Flights from 20-40 mins and a 3-hr heli-hike option. Its helicopters are twin-engine.
Mountain Helicopters, T0800-369423, www.mountainhelicopters.co.nz. Flights from both Franz and Fox from 10-40 mins. It offers competitive charter prices for independent climbers.

Glacier walking and ice climbing

Glacier walking is an extraordinary experience and a magical way to explore a glacier. By climbing across the surface and descending into small crevasses you get a better feel of how they work and can witness the beautiful blue colour of the ice. The tours are also very informative. Fox is generally accepted as the better glacier for ice climbing, while Franz is steeper and more heavily crevassed which makes for better glacier walking.
Alpine Guides, see Fox Glacier, page 574. Offers ice-climbing and heli-hiking.
Franz Josef Glacier Guides, Main Rd, T03-752 0763/T0800-48433, www.franz josefglacier.com. A highly experienced and professional outfit offering 4- to 8-hr excursions as well as heli-hike and high-level alpine trips. The 8-hr trip takes you to the impressive icefalls, while the 2- to 3-hr tour takes in the lower parts of the glacier face. For tours on the glacier, the famous strap-on 'Ice-Talonz' crampons and thermal, waterproof boots make for

comfortable walking. Prices are from $55 (glacier face walk); half-day glacier trip $90 (4 hrs), full-day $140 (8 hrs); ice climbing $210 (8 hrs).
The Guiding Company, Main Rd, Alpine Adventures Centre, T03-752 0047, www.nz guides.com. Offers similar half- or full-day trips. It also offers ice climbing and heli-hiking.

Heli-hiking

For the keen tramper, being at the base of all these stunning mountains and the 2 glaciers is almost too much to bear and with time a premium you might like to consider heli-hiking. Although inevitably expensive the combination of the views and exploring the upper reaches of the glaciers makes it well worth it. All the companies listed below offer heli-hiking options from 2-3 hrs with about 10 mins in the air from $260-340.
Alpine Guides, see Fox Glacier, page 574.
Franz Josef Heli-Hike, Main South Rd, T0800-807767, www.helicopter.co.nz.
Glacier Guides, T0800-484337, www.nzguides.com.
The Guiding Company, T0800-800102.
The Helicopter Line, see Helicopter flightseeing, above.

Walking

Other than the glacier terminal walk there are a number of other walking options in the glacier valley. The wonderfully named **Lake Wombat** (after a gold miner's nickname) and another, **Alex Knob** (don't ask), can be accessed 350 m down the Glacier Access Rd.

The route, which traverses the valley wall, takes you through classic rata and kamahi forest, rich in birdlife. The 'kettle' lake Lake Wombat can be reached in 45 mins, while the stunning view of the glacier from Alex Knob will take another fairly strenuous 3 hrs.

A little further along the Glacier Access Rd is the access point to the **Douglas Walk** and Peter's Pool. Named after a young camper who set up his tent there in 1894, it is an easy walk and the lake can be reached in 10 mins. The track continues to reunite with the road further up the valley (1 hr). Located 1 km from the junction of the Glacier Access Rd and SH6 is **Canavan's Knob Walk** (40 mins return), which, like Sentinel Rock in the glacier valley, withstood the actions of the ice that completely covered it until about 10,000 years ago. Now covered only in rimu trees it offers views of the glacier and the mountains. **Glacier Valley Eco-Tours**, T03-752 0690/ T0800-999739, www.glaciervalley.co.nz. Runs regular shuttles to Franz Josef Glacier for $10 return, as well as trips to Lake Matheson and Fox Glacier.

Wet weather activities
Should the heavens open and the new ice-climbing complex not appeal, listed below are some suggested activities.
Across Country Quad Bikes, T03-7520121/ T0800-234288, www.acrosscountryquad bikes.co.nz. A good wet-weather activity, with 4 trips daily in summer, 2-3 in winter, on 2-seater ATVs from $115 (passenger $65). Safe professional outfit and of course fine scenery. Go on, take your granny!
Body Business Massage Therapy, at the Scenic Circle Hotel, Main Rd, T0800-337722, thebodybusiness@xtra.co.nz, daily 0800-2100. A great place to ease your aches and pains. Non-guests are welcome, 30-90s min from $55. Recommended.
Franz-Alpine Adventure Centre, Main Rd, T03-752 0793. Take in the 20-min *Flowing West* movie, $10, child $5.
Take Note Bookstore, Kew Building, Main Rd. The place for bookworms to find solace. It stocks a fine range of books, most with a local focus.

Fox Glacier *p566*
Flightseeing
Both companies offer pick-ips from Franz **Air Safaris**, Main Rd, T03-680 6880/T03-752 0716, www.airsafaris.co.nz. A 50-min 'Grand Traverse' flight over 10 glaciers and the upper peaks of both national parks from $260, child $180. This flight has no snow landing.
Mount Cook Ski Plane Adventures (Aoraki Mt Cook), Kew Building , Main Rd, T03-752 0714, www.mtcookskiplanes.com. Offering the only fixed-wing glacier landing in New Zealand, this company have been in business over 30 years. The 30-60 min flights offer a memorable experience and the engines are switched off once on the glacier so you can experience the silence. Should the romance of it all be overwhelming, Alex (a marriage celebrant) can oblige, anywhere from 6000-8000 ft – although the rest of the marriage is sure to be a come down! Flights start at $220.

Glacier walks
The closest short walk is the (25 mins return) **Minnehaha Walk**, which starts beside the road just south of the village. It is a pretty rainforest walk that takes in a small **glow worm dell** ($2); best viewed with a torch at night. The glacier valley walks and the glacier itself is accessed via Glacier Rd, which leaves SH6 about 1 km south of the village. The **Glacier terminus** can be accessed from the car park (1 hr return) which is about 8 km from Fox village. About 3 km down Glacier Road is a small car park on the left which is the trailhead for the River (1 km, 30 mins return) and Chalet Lookout Walk (4 km, 2 hrs return). The very pleasant **River Walk** begins with a swing bridge crossing over the cold, grey Fox River. Once across the river the track then climbs through the rainforest, offering the occasional view of the glacier, before reaching the car park and terminus of the Glacier View Rd (which runs along the southern bank of the river). From here it is a steady climb through forest and across crystal clear streams to reach the lookout point. The walk itself is as good as the view. However, do not expect to get good photographs of the glacier from here since there is too much bush in the way. The walk around **Lake Matheson** (4 km west from

Cook Flat, then Lake Matheson Rd, 1½ hrs return) and to the **seal colony** at **Gillespies Beach** (20 km west via Cook Flat Rd) are another 2 excellent options. The marked route (6 hrs return) up **Mt Fox** (1021 m), 3 km south of the village, provides great views across the higher peaks and forest.

Helicopter flightseeing

Helicopter flights cost $155-185 for 10-20 mins; $230-355 for 30-40 mins. Snow landings are offered on all flights. There are 4 helicopter companies:
Fox and Franz Josef Heli-services, Alpine Adventure Centre, T03-752 0793, T0800-800793, www.scenic-flights.co.nz. Flights from 20-40 mins. The helicopters are small but comfortable. Being perhaps the most competitive in price they better suit the budget traveller. Charters are also available.
Glacier Helicopters, Fox Glacier Guiding Building, Main Rd, T03-752 0755/T0800-800732, www.glacierhelicopters.co.nz. 10- to 40-min flights all with snow landing, from $175-$345.
The Helicopter Line, Main Rd, T03-751 0767, www.helicopter.co.nz. Flights from 20-40 mins, with snow landings and a 3-hr heli-hike option.
Mountain Helicopters, T03-751 0045, www.mountainhelicopters.co.nz. A small, local company, offering competitive prices, suitable for the budget traveller. Charters also available. Flights cost $90-180 for 10-20 mins and $225-325 for 30-40 mins.

Ice climbing

Fox is generally accepted as the better glacier for ice climbing.
Fox Glacier Guiding, Alpine Guides Building, Main Rd, T03-751 0825, T0800-111600, www.foxguides.co.nz. With 30 years of experience, this is a highly professional outfit offering 2- to 8-hr excursions as well as heli-hike, ice climbing, multi-day mountaineering and high level (overnight) alpine-hut trips. Trips leave throughout the day and include a guided excursion to the glacier terminus ($45). Heli-hike, from $330 (4 hrs)and heli-hike and Chancellor Hut experience (8 hrs), from $515-559. Ice-climbing instruction days are also a speciality ($210).

Lake Moeraki *p567*
Moeraki Wilderness Lodge, PB Bag 772, T03-750 0881, lakemoeraki@wilderness lodge.co.nz. Accommodation, guided nature walks and kayak trips in World Heritage park. See Sleeping, above.

● Transport

Franz Josef *p565*
Bicycle and scooter hire
Chateau Franz or Glow Worm Cottages (see Sleeping, page 569) both offer bikes for hire.
Glacier Country Tours and Kayaks (**Ferg's Kayaks**), 20 Cron St, T0800-423262, rents out scooters for $10 per hr.

Fox Glacier *p566*
Bicycle hire
Ivory Towers Backpackers, see Sleeping, page 570. Full day hire $25.

● Directory

Franz Josef *p565*
Banks There are no banks in the village but there is an ATM outside the **Blue Ice Pub** at the southern end of main St. The **Mobil Service Station** (Glacier Motors Ltd), T03-752 0725, open from 0800, nearby has EFTPOS. Foreign exchange is available at **Fern Grove Souvenirs**, Main Rd, (across the road from Alpine Adventures), T03-752 0731.
Internet Franz Josef Glacier Guides/ Helicopter Line the Scott Base Information Centre, both on Main Rd. Also in most backpacker hostels and **Glacier Country Tours and Kayaks (Ferg's Kayaks)**, 20 Cron St, T0800-423262. **Medical services** Doctor, Whataroa, T03-756 1080.
Police Whataroa, T03-756 1070. **Postal agent** Mobil Service station, see Banks.

Fox Glacier *p566*
Banks There are no banks or ATMs but EFTPOS is accepted in most places. Foreign currency exchange available at **Fox Glacier Guiding**, Main Rd, T03-751 0825, daily 0800-2100 (winter 0830-1730). **Internet** Glacier Country Hotel or Ivory Towers Backpackers, see Sleeping page 570. **Postal agents** Fox Glacier Guiding, Main Rd, T03-751 0825, daily 0800-2100 (winter 0830-1730).

Haast Region › Colour map 5, B1/2

The Haast Region of South Westland contains some of the most unspoiled ecosystems in New Zealand. The stunning scenery, from mountaintop to coastal plain, includes pristine streams that flow into vast river mouths fringed with dense tracts of ancient coastal (Kahikatea) forests. Within the forest lie swamps and hidden lakes and all along their fringe are endless swathes of beach covered in sculpted driftwood. Wildlife, too, abounds, from the playful keas on the mountains to the sleepy fur seals on the coast. Few tourists stop long enough in the Haast Region to truly appreciate or explore properly. But if you do, Haast itself is an ideal base and gateway to a timeless environment. ▶▶ For Sleeping, Eating and other listings, see pages 577-578.

Ins and outs

Getting there By road Haast is 120 km south of Fox Glacier and 145 km northwest of Wanaka. North and southbound **Intercity** and **Atomic Shuttle** services stop in Haast Township and/or the DoC visitor centre.

Tourist information DoC visitor centre ① *next to SH6, 300 m past the Haast River Bridge, T03-750 0809, www.haastnz.com, www.west-coast.co.nz, daily 0900-1800 (1630 in winter).* As if the sculpted water features outside were not impressive enough, the interior displays are memorable and plenty of information on local walks and natural attractions is provided. Ask to see the 20-minute *Edge of Wilderness* video, which is a fine introduction to the local landscape ($3, children free).

Haast → *Colour map 5, B2 Population: 300*

From the north, a lush corridor of coastal forest and the 750-m Haast River Bridge brings you to the rather splintered settlement of Haast. The Haast River is a fitting introduction to the village and the stunning wilderness that surrounds it. On the coastal plain the annual rainfall, at 5 m, is similar to that of much of the west coast. But above 1500 m, the average can be over three times that and, after a deluge, the great river can turn into a menacing torrent. Haast is the epitome of a west coast village: remote and unobtrusive, with residents who are full of pride and moulded by the wild, rugged and harsh environment that surrounds them.

Haast is named after the geologist/explorer/surveyor Julius von Haast who first explored the then almost inaccessible coast in 1863. He did so via the pass to the east, which now bears his name and provides the modern-day road access. Locals, however, will pull your leg and tell you the name actually derived from a misquotation by Captain James Cook on his voyage of 1770. On sailing past he was, by all accounts, so appalled at the sight and inhospitable nature of the place, he ordered all the ships flags to be flown at half-mast. Perhaps tired and, for once, short of a name, he entered 'Half-mast' in his log. A century later, when the log was reopened, the fold in the page disguised the full name and it became known as Haast.

On initial acquaintance Haast (the 'settlement') is a bit confusing. Immediately on the southern side of the bridge is a huddle of buildings that form **Haast Junction**. This is home to the DoC visitor centre, a petrol station and the **World Heritage Hotel**. A further 4 km south of Haast Junction, on the Jackson's Bay Road, is **Haast Beach**, another small conglomerate, including another petrol station, a motel, food store and some private homes. From there the road continues for 50 km before reaching a dead end and the remote village of **Jackson's Bay**. East of there an unsealed road accesses the Arawata River and the **Cascade Saddle**, a memorable day trip. The main settlement of Haast – or **Haast Township** – is 4 km inland and east of Haast Junction on SH6. Here you will find the major residential area, shops and most of the accommodation.

Other than the obvious attractions of the coast to the north, the true wilderness of the Arawata and Cascade River valleys south of Haast via the Jackson's Bay Road, is considered legendary. Though this stunning landscape is well worthy of some thorough investigation, the tiny pioneering settlement of **Jackson's Bay** is the main attraction.

From Haast Junction and Haast Beach, Jackson's Bay Road hosts the tiny settlement of **Okuru**, set on the Okuru River and principally based on whitebaiting. The road then carves a straight 20-km path through native forest to the Arawata River; on the way the covert streams crossing the road have some intriguing names including 'Dizzy', 'Dancing' and 'Dismal'. In the heart of this forest is the stubborn plug of bedrock known as **Mount McLean**, which, like Mosquito Hill near Haast, withstood the assaults of old glaciers. At the **Arawata Bridge** you are afforded a grand view up the valley before the road forks inland to the **Cascade River Valley**, or west along the coast to Jackson's Bay.

The unsealed Cascade Road follows the beautiful **Jackson River Valley** (a tributary of the Awawata). The river provides a wonderful place to go fishing or simply kick back and admire the scenery. But perhaps your first stop should be the walk to the hidden **Lake Ellery**. Beginning just beside the Ellery River Bridge, a well-disguised track follows the river to the lake edge. It is neither well signposted nor well maintained so expect to get muddy and lost. However, the beautiful reflections of the forest on the river and the tranquil atmosphere of the lake itself, makes the one-hour return walk well worthwhile. Once you reach the lake head you can go no further and must back track.

From Lake Ellery River the Cascade Road rises steadily crossing the Martyr River and the evocatively named **Monkey Puzzle Gorge**, before reaching a high point in the valley and the road terminus. From here you are afforded an expansive view down to the **Cascade Valley** and the dramatic glacial sculpted sweep of the hills to the coast. Inland the Olivine Range and Red Hills herald the boundary of the **Mount Aspiring National Park**. The **Red Hills** are a particularly interesting and noted geological feature. The colouration is caused by high concentrations of magnesium and iron in the rock that has been forced up by the actions of the Austral and Pacific tectonic plates. What makes this mountain range of special interest is that their other half (Dun Mountain) now lies in the Nelson Region.

Jackson's Bay → *Colour map 5, B1*

Fighting hard to survive its wild remoteness, is the historic little village of Jackson's Bay at the end of Jackson's Bay Road. Jackson's Bay has an interesting and troubled history. Now a small fishing settlement with about 20 registered vessels moored in what is the nearest thing to a natural harbour the length of the west coast, it was first settled by a hardy group of 400 in 1875. A cosmopolitan bunch of Scandinavians, Germans, Poles, Italians, Irish, Scots and English, they set about trying to establish agriculture and the small port. However, due to the weather, poor soils and a general lack of interest from beyond, the project was a catastrophic failure. Within weeks whole families fell ill, or simply gave up and moved out. Only three years after landing the community shrank from 400 to a mere handful. Only a few of the most prosperous survivors managed to stay by founding large cattle runs.

The iron-framed grave of pioneer settler Claude Morton Ollivier, who died of pneumonia only weeks after his arrival, is a fitting testament to the Europeans' failed attempts. It is the oldest known European grave on the west coast and is next to the main road above the beach.

Other than a wander around Jackson's Bay itself you might like to try the 1½ hour return **Smoothwater Track**. Beginning about 500 m north of the village it climbs the forested hill to take in the fine views north, before crossing a saddle and dropping down again to the Smoothwater River Valley and neighbouring Smoothwater Bay. One attraction not to miss in Jackson's Bay is the **Cray Pot Café**, on the waterfront (see Eating, page 578).

From Haast Township SH6 turns inland and follows the bank of the Haast River before being enveloped by mountains and surmounting what was, until 1960, the insurmountable. The Haast Pass at 563 m is an ancient Maori greenstone trail known as Tiori-patea, which means 'the way ahead is clear'. Ironically, being the principal water catchment of the Haast River and plagued by frequent floods and landslips, the name is one of misplaced optimism as the modern-day road can testify. However, although sometimes treacherous and difficult to negotiate, the crossing captures the mood of the place, with names such as the **Valley of Darkness** and **Mount Awful**. Even beside the road there is suggestion of this, with other evocative titles like **Solitary Creek No 2** and the first of three waterfalls, **Roaring Billy**, 28 km inland from Haast. Best viewed on a short (signposted) loop walk, Roaring Billy plunges down mountain slopes on the opposite side of the river, and although it's only a steady flow most of the time, after heavy rains it most certainly lives up to its name.

A further 25 km, just before the 'Gates of Haast', another waterfall – the competitively named **Thunder Creek Falls** – drop a vertical 28 m into the Haast River. They too can be accessed and photographed from a short loop track beside the road.

The gorge, known as the **Gates of Haast**, is just a little further on and you can see the huge boulders and precipitous rock walls that proved such a barrier to road construction for so many years. Above the Gates the road and the river level off and the mountains take on a less menacing appearance, as do the waterfalls, with **Fantail Falls** (signposted and accessed next to the road) proving far less threatening, with moderate plumes of whitewater tumbling over a series of rocky steps. From Fantail Falls it is only a short distance before the Haast Pass itself and the boundary of Westland and Otago. From here the scenery dramatically changes and you leave the west coast behind.

● Sleeping

Haast and Jackson's Bay Road
p575 and p576

L Collyer House B&B, Jackson's Bay Rd, further south on the banks of the Okuru River, T03-750 0022, www.collyerhouse.co.nz. The best in the region, owned by long-term natives of the area. It is wonderfully peaceful and offers 4 luxury en suite rooms with terrific views. Large open fire and antiques abound. Activities can also be arranged.

L-A McGuires Lodge, between Haast Junction and Haast Township, T03-750 0020, www.mcguireslodge.co.nz. Has a fine range of en suite units and the added attraction of a fine in-house restaurant/café and broadband internet.

AL-C Haast World Heritage Hotel, corner of SH6 and Jacksons Bay Rd, Haast Junction, T0800-502444/T03-750 0828, www.world-heritage-hotel.com. Long-established and recently refurbished, it has 54 en suite units from standard to family, but is best known for its restaurant and bar. The open log fire is particularly attractive and looks like some huge artistic installation. Activities arranged.

AL-D Aspiring Court Motel and Haast Lodge, T03-750 0703/T0800-500703, haast_lodge@xtra.co.nz. Has a range of units, cabins, powered/tent sites and also acts as the local YHA associate. Close to all amenities.

A-B Acacia and Erewhon Motel, Jackson's Bay Rd, 4 km from junction, Haast Beach, T03-750 0803. Modern and friendly, it has 3 elite (upper floor with coastal view), 4 studio and 5 standard units all self-contained.

A-B Heritage Park Lodge, Marks Rd, Haast Township, T03-750 0868, www.heritageparklodge.co.nz. Cheaper option with a range of modern units and en-suites.

A-C Wilderness Backpackers Motel, Pauareka Rd, T03-7500029. The favoured backpacker hostel. Spacious, single-storey building with good value en suite doubles, twins, family units and a pleasant atmosphere. Of particular note is the large conservatory, which is a fine place to listen to west coast rain! Bike and scooter hire and internet access.

Motorcamps and campsites
Camping is also available at **Haast Lodge**,
see Sleeping, above.
A-D Haast Beach Holiday Park, Okuru
(15 km south), Jackson's Bay Rd,
T03-750 0860, haastpark@xtra.co.nz.
Excellent. It offers a number of motel units,
self-contained and standard cabins, but is
mainly noted for its location, friendliness and
fine modern kitchen and lounge facilities.

● Eating

Haast *p575*
There is a supermarket on Pauareka Rd in
Haast Township. 0800-1930 (seasonal).
There's also a general store next to the
motel in Haast Beach, T03-750 0825.
♥♥ **Fantail Café and Restaurant**, Haast
Township, T03-750 0055, 0730-2200.
Basic meals served all day.
♥♥ **Haast World Heritage Hotel Café and
Bar**, Haast Junction, T0800-502444, daily
1100-1000. The best (and only) option at the
junction. Hearty, good value and quality meals
and perhaps the best open fire in the country.
♥♥ **McGuire's Lodge**, between Haast
Junction and Haast Township, T03-750 0020.
Café open 0800-1600, restaurant daily from
1830-2130. A licensed restaurant and café
that is by far the best in the region offering
fine venison, lobster and whitebait in
intimate surroundings with a log fire.
During the day lighter meals and quality
coffee are also available. Recommended.
♥♥ **Smithy's Tavern**, Marks Rd, Haast
Township, T03-750 0034, daily from 1100,
dinner from 1800. Pub grub.

Jackson's Bay *p576*
♥♥ **Cray Pot Café**, T03-750 0035, Jackson's Bay,
daily 1030-1900. A quirky cross between a rail
carriage and a barge serving average fish and
chips. You can eat in (recommended) or take
away, but beware of the sandflies.

▲▲ Activities and tours

Haast *p575*
Haast River Safaris, in the 'Red Barn'
between Haast Junction and Haast Township,

T0800-865382, www.haastriver.co.nz.
Reputedly offers a scenic river safari up the
Haast River Valley. The 1½-hr trips on its
purpose-built (covered) jet boat depart
daily at 0900 and 1400 and cost from
$120, child $50. Recommended.
Heli Ventures, Haast Township, T03-750 0866/
T0800-7500866, www.heliventures.co.nz.
Owned by the McGuires Lodge operator
and ideally located for some stunning scenic
helicopter flights, but may suffer due to the
fact many have already parted with their
scenic flight savings in Franz or Fox. If you
haven't, then Haast offers some great scenery.
Round About Haast Tours, Jackson's
Bay Rd, T03-750 0890, www.round
abouthaast.co.nz. Operated by locals
Mauryne and Bob Cannell, the tours are
an ideal way to acquaint yourself with the
area, its history and folklore. The tours last
from 3-4 hrs and cost $60-135.
Waiatoto River Safaris, also at the Red Barn,
T0800-538723, www.riversafaris.co.nz. As the
name suggests, provides an opportunity to
explore the Waiatoto River south of Haast.
The 2-hr trips depart at 0845, 1200 and
1515, from $125, child $75.
Wanna Go Fishing, T03-750 0134. Offers
guided trips from half-day $650 to full-day
at $900. There is some superb local fishing
on offer especially south of Haast on the
Arawata River.

● Directory

Haast *p575*
Internet Wilderness Backpackers,
Pauareka Rd, Haast Township and
McGuires Lodge. **Police** T03-750 0850.
Telephone There is no cell phone
coverage in Haast. **Useful addresses**
Johnston Motors (Caltex), in Haast
Junction, beside the VIC, T03-750 0846,
has EFTPOS and provides AA recovery
and an independent breakdown recovery
service (a godsend!). Petrol is available
24 hrs with EFTPOS and credit cards.
Mobil Service Centre, Haast Beach,
T03-750 0802, also provides the same
services and acts as car hire and
postal agents.

Otago

⦂ Footprint features

Introduction

If the Otago Region was a girl she would be a very engaging
sort from a good Scottish background and good-looking.
Her height and build can be likened to the towering peaks of
Fiordland and Mount Aspiring national parks in the west, to
the gently rolling hills, harbours and golden beaches of the
Otago Peninsula to the east. Her two large blue eyes would be
Lakes Wakatipu and Wanaka. And down her entire length
carves the vein of New Zealand's second longest river, the
Clutha. Her personality varies too: from the student city buzz
of Dunedin to the quiet whispers of Glenorchy or Clyde.
Otago is also down-to-earth and wears her heart on her
sleeve. She has distinct moods which change with the
seasons: cold and snowy in winter; miserable with rain
in spring; and boasting beautiful golden hues in autumn.
Otago owes her considerable pedigree to her predominantly
Scottish heritage and the discovery of gold, a resource that
was once her lifeblood. Now, though, Otago pumps fast
and furious with sheer adrenaline. Although her head is
in Dunedin, her heart is in Queenstown – the adventure
sports capital of the world. Otago is not only pretty,
she also knows how to have a good time.

★ Don't miss ...

1 **Dunedin** Check out the Scottish heritage and architecture and try rolling your R's' with the locals, page 582.
2 **Otago Peninsula** Be captivated by the grace of the albatross or the charms of the yellow-eyed penguins, page 592.
3 **Gold panning** Try your luck in the historic Central Otago goldfields, page 600.
4 **The Remarkables** Take in the 'remarkable' view from the lookout, page 609.
5 **Queenstown bungee** Find your courage and make the jump, page 616.
6 **Paradise** Visit the real Paradise just north of Glenorchy, page 625.
7 **Wanaka** Take a scenic flight to Milford or go canyoning, tandem skydiving or skiing – the possibilities are endless, page 638.
8 **Rob Roy glacier** Do the best day walk in the region, page 641.

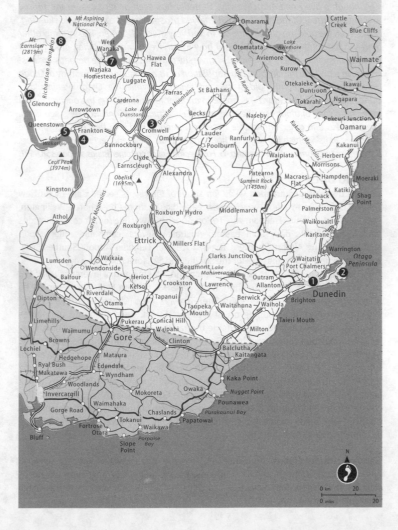

Dunedin → *Colour map 6, B6 Population: 100,000*

There is perhaps nowhere else in the world – and certainly nowhere so far from its roots – that boasts a Scottish heritage like Dunedin, the South Island's second largest city. For those who have walked the centuries-old streets of Edinburgh in Scotland, let alone lived there, a trip to Dunedin (which actually means 'Edin on the hill') is somewhat disconcerting. Immediately, you will notice the echo of Scottish architecture – grand buildings of stone, built to last, that go far beyond the merely functional and, in true Scottish tradition, defy inclement weather. The streets are blatant in their similarity, even sharing the names of Edinburgh's most famous – Princes Street, George Street and Moray Place – and presiding over the scene, in its very heart, a statue of one of Scotland's greatest sons, the poet Robert Burns. As you ponder his gentle expression of intellect, with the seemingly omnipresent seagull perched on his head, you cannot help but wonder what he would say about this pseudo-Scottish city, so very far from home.

Although a lively and attractive city, Dunedin has seen better days. In the 1860s, thanks to the great Otago gold boom, it enjoyed prosperity and considerable standing. But as ever, the gold ran out, decline set in and very quickly Dunedin, like so many other places in the South Island, had to learn how to survive. Having said that, modern-day Dunedin has many assets, of which its university and rare wildlife are perhaps the best known. In term-time the city boasts a population of 18,000 students who study at Otago University, New Zealand's oldest seat of learning. While the Otago Peninsula – Dunedin's beautiful backyard – is home to another form of wildlife: the only mainland breeding colony of albatross, the rare yellow-eyed penguins and Hooker's sea lions. There is also one other undeniable asset to Dunedin, and one that can perhaps be attributed to its Scottish heritage: without doubt it has the friendliest people and offers the warmest welcome in New Zealand. ▶▶ *For Sleeping, Eating and other listings, see pages 587-591.*

Ins and outs

Getting there Dunedin airport ① *27 km south of the city*, is served daily by **Air New Zealand Link**, T0800-737000, www.airnewzealand.co.nz, from Christchurch, Wellington, Auckland and Rotorua. **Freedom Air**, T0800-600500, www.freedomair.co.nz, provides trans-Tasman flights daily from eastern Australia. Several companies offer airport shuttles including **Airport Shuttles**, T03-473 7017, or **Dunedin Airport Shuttles**, T03-447 6611. Expect to pay from $17 for the shuttle and $45 for a taxi (one way).

Dunedin is 362 km south of Christchurch and 217 km north of Invercargill via SH1. Queenstown is 283 km south then west via SH8. By bus Dunedin is served by **Intercity/Newmans**, book at the VIC (I-Site), T03-474 3300 (Christchurch/Invercargill/Queenstown/Wanaka) stopping on St Andrews Street. Several shuttle companies offer regional services and stop outside the railway station on Anzac Avenue. They include: **Nakedbus.com** (throughout South island as far south as Dunedin); **Atomic Shuttles**, T03-322 8883, www.atomictravel.co.nz (Christchurch/Invercargill/Wanaka Queenstown); **Wanaka Connexions**, T0800-244844, www.wanakaconnexions.co.nz (Queenstown/Wanaka); **Catch-A-Bus**, T03-479 9960, www.catchabus.co.nz, which serves the direct Dunedin-Te Anau route; **Catlins Coaster**, T021-682461, www.catlins coaster.co.nz, and **Bottom Bus**, T03-434 7370, www.bottombus.co.nz, which serve the Southern Scenic Route (to Te Anau) via Catlins and Invercargill and provide pick-ups and drop-offs along the way.

Getting around Citibus, T0800-474082/T03-477 5577, www.orc.govt.nz, www.citi bus.co.nz, serves Dunedin and its surrounds. The VIC (I-Site) has timetables. City buses stop in the Octagon, the distinctive heart of the city. For bus services to the Otago Peninsula, see page 592.

Otago Dunedin

N

| 0 metres | 200 |
| 0 yards | 200 |

Sleeping 🛏
97 Motel **10** *C2*
858 George St **16** *A2*
Albatross Inn **2** *A2*
Allan Court Motel **3** *A3*
Billy Brown's
 Backpackers **15** *A3*
Commodore
 Luxury **21** *A3*
Corstorphine
 House **18** *E1*
Dunedin Holiday
 Park **19** *E1*
Elm Lodge **4** *C1*
Elm Lodge Too **20** *C1*
Fletcher Lodge **5** *D1*
Hogwartz
 Backpackers **1** *C2*
Hulmes Court **6** *C1*
Leith Valley Touring
 Park **17** *A2*
Leviathan **7** *C3*
Mandeno House **12** *A3*
Manor House **8** *E1*
Manor Motel **9** *E1*
Regal Court **11** *A3*
Southern Cross **13** *D2*
Stafford Gables
 YHA **14** *E1*

Eating 🍴
Ale House at the Speights
 Brewery **24** *D1*
Anarkali Indian Café
 & Takeaway **2** *A3*
Arc Café **3** *D1*
Bell Pepper Blues **4** *E1*
Etrusco at the Savoy **5** *C2*
Good Oil Café **6** *A3*
Governors Café **7** *A3*
High Tide **8** *E3*
Indian Summer **9** *C2*
Jizo **10** *C2*
Joseph Mellor **25** *C1*
Little India **11** *B3*
London Lounge **22** *A2*
Mazagran
 Espresso **12** *C2*

Nova **13** *C2*
Percolator **15** *C2*
Potpourri **21** *C2*
Reef Seafood
 & Bar **17** *A3*
Table Se7en **1** *A3*
Tangente **18** *C2*

Bars & clubs 🍸
Albert Arms **19** *A2*
Bath St **20** *B2*
K World Karaoke
 Bar **28** *C2*
Ra Café & Bar **16** *C2*
Woolshed &
 Grill **27** *C2*

Tourist information Dunedin VIC (I-Site) ① *Octagon, No 48, below the Municipal Chambers Building, T03-474 3300, www.dunedinnz.com, www.cityofdunedin.com, Mon-Fri 0800-1800, Sat-Sun 08450-1800*, is an efficient centre that provides free city maps and advice on local tours and activities, particularly to the Otago Peninsula; it also acts as a transport booking agent and has internet. **DoC** ① *77 Lower Stuart St, T03-477 0677, www.doc.govt.nz, Mon-Fri 0800-1700.*

Background

The largest Maori *pa* in the area was on the Otago Peninsula at Otakau, which saw its fair share of inter-tribal disputes before being ravaged by diseases brought by the early European whalers and sealers. Otakau is also the source of the name Otago that came about through a mispronunciation by the early pioneers. Scottish parliamentarian George Rennie who, concerned at the levels of poverty and unemployment in Scotland, presented a plan for Presbyterian colonization in a 'New Edinburgh' of the south sowed the first seeds of Dunedin's settlement and creation in 1842. Although this idea was initially declined, it was adapted and later accepted by a 300-strong Free Church colony that arrived in 1848, under the leadership of Captain Cargill (of Invercargill fame) and the Reverend Dr Thomas Burns. With the discovery of gold just over a decade later the population exploded (between 1861 and 1865 its population grew by 500% to 10,000) and the town developed into a cosmopolitan, commercial centre becoming the largest and most prosperous city in New Zealand by the late 1860s (it was even the first place outside the USA to have a tram system). Despite the loss of gold as a resource, Dunedin has been more successful than most in retaining a strong economic base and is now a pleasant mix of old and new.

Sights

Although they could never be as ancient or as fine as their real namesakes in Edinburgh, **Princes Street** and **George Street** combine to form the main thoroughfare through the city centre, with the **Octagon** forming its heart. The Central Business District (CBD) is easily negotiated on foot, and even by car, which makes a pleasant change to the charmless, flat streets of Auckland or Christchurch. You will find most restaurants and cafés at the northern end of George Street or around the Octagon.

The Octagon

Presiding over the Octagon, is the statue of **Robert Burns**, the Scottish poet, whose nephew, the Reverand Thomas Burns, was a religious leader of the early settlers. There are many fine examples of the city's architecture, including the grand **Municipal Chambers buildings**, which house the VIC (I-Site).

The city's churches are worth more than just a passing glance, particularly the **First Church of Otago** ① *Moray Pl, T03-477 7150, daily 0800-1800*, which is a distinctly pointed affair and one of Dunedin's famous landmarks, and **St Paul's Cathedral**, which houses the only stone-vaulted ceiling in the country. Just west of here, **St Joseph's Cathedral**, on the corner of Rattray and Smith Street, is noted for its robust architectural aesthetics.

Aside from the safe, but unintentionally wobbly, grand staircase in its foyer, the **Dunedin Public Art Gallery** ① *Octagon, T03-477 4000, www.dunedin.art.museum.co.nz, daily 1000-1700, free*, providing a grand and stable platform to display a fine collection of traditional and contemporary art. It is the oldest art gallery in the country and of special note is its collection of New Zealand works that date from 1860 to the present day. There are also some works by the more familiar iconic names like Turner, Gainsborough and Monet.

South and east of the Octagon

A five-minute walk east of the Octagon, Dunedin's **train station**, at the end of Lower Stuart Street, is a fine example of the typical Scottish desire to take architecture way beyond the purely functional. Built in 1906, its grand towered exterior cannot fail to impress, but the interior too is rather splendid complete with stained-glass windows, Royal Doulton tiles, mosaics and brass fittings. The almost omnipresent New Zealand Rail (NZR) logos are proudly displayed with more repetition than a large herd of branded, prize cattle. Upstairs, the **New Zealand Sports Hall of Fame** ① *1st floor, T03-477 7775, www.nzhalloffame.co.nz, daily 1000-1600, from $6, child $3*, celebrates the legacy of more than a century of New Zealand champions and is a worthy attraction for any avid sports fan.

Just a few hundred metres from the train station, and boasting a couple of monstrous historic steam trains, is the **Otago Settlers Museum** ① *31 Queens Gardens, T03-474 2728, www.otago.settlers.museum.co.nz, daily 1000-1700, $4, child free; guided tours daily at 1100, from $5, and 1½-hr city heritage walks departing daily at 1400, from $8*. The emphasis is placed firmly on people and transport, with many fine temporary and permanent displays. Recent additions include the 'Across the Ocean Waves' exhibit, which focuses on the ocean crossings that many of the early settlers had to endure. Various interactive elements incorporated into a recreation of the steerage quarters (including free reign to climb into bunks and sit at tables) adds some authenticity and a firm reminder of the relative luxury of modern-day travel. There are also two fine old locos including the 1872 *Josephine* and a fine collection of archives and over 20,000 photographic portraits of the early pioneers. The museum is worth a visit if only to muse at their hardy, hopeful expressions and eyes full of memories.

On Dowling Street, the **Milford Galleries** ① *18 Dowling St, T03-477 8275, www.milfordgalleries.co.nz, Mon-Fri 0830-1700, Sat 1100-1500*, are considered to be one of the country's leading dealer galleries and represent more than 130 artists.

While in the area, chocoholics should head straight to **Cadbury World** ① *280 Cumberland St, T03-467 7967/T0800-223287, www.cadburyworld.co.nz; regular tours 0900-1515, $16, child $10*, which recently opened its doors to the drooling public. Though they could never quite live up to the fantasy of *Charlie and the Chocolate Factory*, the interactive tours offer an interesting and mouth-watering insight into the production of the irresistible stuff and can even impress with mere statistics. There are, for example, 120 million chocolate bars sold in New Zealand annually, which equates to almost 40 bars per head of population or an estimated 4 kg each every year. Naturally, there is a well-stocked shop that does very well.

Although Denedin hosts many fine Scottish churches it also, not surprisingly, pays homage to that other great Scottish religion: the alcoholic beverage. The South Island's iconic **Speights Ale** is the worship of many a 'Good Southern Man' and its communion is to be found in the hallowed walls of the surprisingly small **Speights Brewery** ① *200 Rattray St, T03-477 7697, www.speights.co.nz; heritage tours and tastings Mon-Thu 1000, 1200, 1400, 1900, Fri-Sun 1000, 1200, 1400, 1600, from $17, child $6; also worth considering is the 'tour and meal' option from $55*. Unlike the churches these days, bookings are essential.

If beer is not your tipple perhaps you might like to visit the **Weston Vintage Winery** ① *out of town, 25 Forresbank, Wakari, T03-467 5544*. Although not quite in the same league as its many New Zealand counterparts it can boast of being the world's most southerly winery.

North and west of the Octagon

About 1 km north of the Octagon, is the 1906 'Edwardian time capsule' of **Olveston House** ① *42 Royal Terr, T03-477 3320, www.olveston.co.nz; guided 1-hr tours recommended, $14.50, child $5*. Bequeathed to the city in 1966 by the last surviving member of the wealthy and much-travelled Theomin family, the 35-room mansion comes complete with an impressive 'collection of collections', containing many items from the Edwardian era. It gives an interesting insight into Dunedin of old and the lives of the more prosperous pioneer.

A few minutes' east of Olveston, the **Otago Museum** ① *419 Great King St, T03-474 7474, www.otagomuseum.govt.nz, daily 1000-1700, $5 donation; 'Discovery World' $6, child $3; café on site; guided tours daily at 1530, $10,* was established in 1868 and is one of the oldest in the country, with a staggering 1.7 million items. The museum's primary themes are culture, nature and science, all housed in newly renovated surroundings and displayed in the now almost obligatory state-of-the-art fashion. The 'Southern Land – Southern People' exhibit is particularly good and has been designed to become the museum centrepiece. In essence, it is intended to reflect the unique beauty and diversity of Southern New Zealand. The traditional Maori and Pacific heritage, maritime, natural history and archaeology displays are also impressive and there is (of course) a hands-on 'Discovery World' to keep the kids engrossed for hours. There is also free internet.

A short stroll from the museum is the sprawling campus of the **University of Otago**. Founded in 1869, it was New Zealand's first university and is famous for its architecture as well as its contributions to medical science. The grand edifice of the original **Administration building and clocktower** ① *Leith St,* is perhaps the most photographed icon in the city.

Another New Zealand 'first' in Dunedin are the **Botanical Gardens** ① *north of the university campus, corner of Great King St and Opoho Rd, T03-477 4000, dawn to dusk.* Nurtured since 1914, the 28-ha site is split into upper and lower gardens that straddle Signal Hill. Combined they form an interesting topography and all the usual suspects, with a particular bent on rhododendrons (at their best in October), plants from the Americas, Asia and Australia, native species, winter and wetland gardens. If you tire of the flora there is also a modern aviary complex, housing many exotic and native birds including the 'cheeky' kea and kaka parrots. Also on site are information points, a café and a small shop, all in the Lower Garden. Access to the Lower Garden is from Cumberland Street while the Upper Garden is reached via Lovelock Lane. The **Centennial Lookout** (6-km, 1½ hours' walk) and **Lookout Point** offer grand views of the harbour and the city, and are accessed via Signal Hill Road (beyond Lovelock Avenue).

While in the north of the city, you might also like to visit the famed **Baldwin Street** ① *5 km north of the centre, head north via Great King St then veer right at the Botanical Gardens on to North Rd; Baldwin is about 1 km (10th street) on the right,* which at a gradient of nearly one in three, is reputed to be the steepest street in the world. It's worth a look, if only to work out the building methodology and what happens when the residents are eating at a table, in the bath or shooting some pool. The aptly named '**Gut-Busters**' race is held annually in February during the **Dunedin Festival** to see who can reach the top and back again in around two minutes. Doubtless the street has been the scene of much fun over the years, but in 2001 the irresistible desire to defy or master gravity turned to tragedy when a young student took a 'wheelie-bin' (used for rubbish) to the top of the street, climbed in and launched herself down the hill toboggan-style. Sadly, the result was fatal and Baldwin Street claimed its first life.

Taieri Gorge Railway and the Otago Central Rail Trail

① *Details available at the train station or T03-477 4449, www.taieri.co.nz. Trips to Pukerangi/Middlemarch depart daily Oct-Mar at 1430 (additional trip on Sun at 0930), Pukerangi $67 return; extended trip to Middlemarch $75, one child free, one way $44 (Middlemarch $49); train and coach connection to Queenstown $115. Licensed snack bar on board.*

The Taieri Gorge Railway is considered a world-class train trip encompassing the scenic splendour and history of Otago's hinterland. The former goldfields supply line was completed in 1891 and, as one negotiates the **Taieri Gorge** with the aid of 12 viaducts and numerous tunnels, it very quickly becomes apparent why it took over 12 years to build. The four-hour trip gets off to a fine start amidst the splendour of Dunedin's grand train station before heading inland to the gorge and Pukerangi. An informative commentary is provided along the way and you are allowed to disembark at certain points of interest. Also, if you ask really nicely, you may also be able to ride alongside the locomotive engineer. If you wish, you can extend the rail journey by coach across the rugged **Maniototo Plateau** to **Queenstown** (6½ hours), from $115. Another popular alternative is to take a mountain bike (no extra charge) and disembark at **Middlemarch** (only selected trains, but one-way fares available). From there you can negotiate the 150-km **Otago Central Rail Trail** (the former goldfields railway from Middlemarch to Clyde). It is a wonderful bike ride that includes over 60 bridges, viaducts and tunnels and much of Central Otago's classic scenery. The VIC (I-Site) can supply all the relevant details. Horse trekking is also an option. DoC, in conjunction with the Otago Central Rail Trail Trust, produces an excellent leaflet *Otago Central Rail Trail Middlemarch-Clyde*, available from the DoC or the VIC (I-Site).

Tunnel Beach

① *south of the city centre near Blackhead, 1 km, 1 hr return; car park seaward end of Green Island Bush Rd off Blackhead Rd.*

Tunnel Beach is a popular spot and a precursor to the splendid coastal scenery of the Otago Peninsula. A steep path through some bush delivers you to some impressive weathered sandstone cliffs and arches. For details see DoC's *Tunnel Beach Walk* broadsheet. If you do not have your own wheels take the Corstorphine bus from the city centre to Stenhope Crescent (start of Blackhead Road) and walk from there.

● Sleeping

Dunedin *p582, map p583*

Dunedin has a good range of options, but you might like to consider those available on the Otago Peninsula (see page 592). For both, pre-booking in summer is advised.

LL Corstorphine House, 23A Milburn St, Corstorphine, T03-487 1000, www.corstorphine.co.nz. A popular 1863 Edwardian luxury private hotel surrounded by 5 ha of private gardens and commanding great views across the city. The house is beautifully appointed throughout offering 7 stylish themed suites from the 'Scottish' or 'Egyptian' to the 'art deco' room and has a reputable in-house restaurant.

LL Mandeno House, 667 George St, T03-471 9595, www.mandenohouse.com. Within walking distance of the city centre its interior design has a strong hint of Glasgow's most famous architect Charles Rennie Mackintosh and as such has a distinct air of class and sophistication. 2 queen suites and a twin, Sky TV, breakfast, off-street parking.

L Fletcher Lodge, 276 High St, T03-477 5552, www.fletcherlodge.co.nz. Another fully renovated luxury establishment set in an elegant historic mansion. There are 6 en suites all richly furnished with antiques.

L-A Southern Cross, corner of Princes and High sts, T03-477 0752, www.sceniccircle.co.nz. Dunedin's premier hotel, well located in the heart of the city, with 131 rooms and 8 suites. Its history dates back to 1883 when it was the original **Grand Hotel**, but it now boasts all the mod cons of the Scenic Circle Chain with an in-house bar/restaurant.

AL Nisbet Cottage, 6A Eliffe Pl, Sheil Hill (east of the city centre), T03-454 5169, www.natureguidesotago.co.nz. At the base of the Otago Peninsula, a short drive to the city centre. A choice of 2 tidy en suites sleeping 2-3, a guest lounge with open fire and great hospitality. The German hosts also operate **Otago Nature Guides** (see Activities and tours, page 598) and organize packages that include dawn and dusk trips to see the peninsula penguin colonies, or multi-day trips to the Catlins and Stewart Island.

AL-A Hulmes Court, 52 Tennyson St, T03-477 5319, www.hulmes.co.nz. A well-established, slightly cheaper option set in an 1860s Victorian mansion close to the city centre. Comes complete with a friendly ex-stray cat called Solstice. Having expanded to include an adjoining property it now offers 8 en suites, as well as doubles, twins and singles. The caring owners have plenty of local knowledge and can offer valuable advice on activities and tours.

AL-B Leviathan Hotel, 27 Queens Gardens, T03-477 3160/T0800-773773, www.dunedin hotel.co.nz. An older and good-value establishment with character located near the train station and a short walk to the Octagon. It has a wide range of rooms from self-contained suites (with spas) to budget rooms. In-house bar/restaurant, internet, off-street parking and above average service and hospitality. Recommended.

B Albatross Inn, 770 George St, T03-477 2727, www.albatross.inn.co.nz. A pleasant and spacious budget B&B with 13 rooms, well located close to the city centre.

Motels

There are plenty of motels to choose from, with most on the main drags in and out of town, particularly George St.

AL-A 97 Motel, hidden away at 97 Moray Pl, T03-477 2050, www.97motel.co.nz. Modern motel offering a wide variety of standard and executive units that are quiet, well appointed, and all within a stone's throw of the Octagon. Off-street parking.

A 858 George St, no prizes for guessing the location, T03-474 0047, www.858george streetmotel.co.nz. Modern, and an aesthetic award winner. Recommended.

A Allan Court Motel, 590 George St, T03-477 7526, allan.court@earthlight.co.nz.

A Commodore Luxury, 932 Cumberland St, T03-477 7766, commodore.motels@xtra.co.nz.

A Regal Court, 755 George St, T03-477 7729.

B Manor Motel, 22 Manor Pl, T03-477 6729, manormotel@earthlight.co.nz.

Backpacker hostels

There is no shortage of choice when it comes to backpacker hostels and vast majority are housed in traditional suburban villas.

C-D Billy Brown's Backpackers, 423 Aramoana Rd, Hamilton Bay (across the harbour, just outside Port Chalmers, 15 mins north of Dunedin), T03-472 8323, billybrowns@ actrix.co.nz. If you fancy a day or 2 away from the city centre, you would do well to consider this small, relaxing, rural hostel with friendly owners and fine views . Also offers free bike hire. Recommended.

C-D Elm Lodge, 74 Elm Row, up the hill from the Octagon, T03-4741872, elmlodge@ xtra.co.nz. Noted not so much for its accommodation (though there is no problem there) but for its superb adjunct operation the **Elm Wildlife Tours**, run by the friendly and nature-loving owners. (See Activities and tours, page 598.) Comfortable dorms and doubles offer fine views, and there's a very congenial atmosphere. Elm also runs an overflow establishment the **Elm Lodge Too** further up the hill. Pick-ups and internet.

C-D Hogwartz Backpackers, 37 Dowling St, close to the Octagon, T03-474 1487, hogwartz@actrix.co.nz. Set in a spacious, historic villa, this is a popular choice with the log fires keeping it very cosy. Dorms, singles, twins and doubles. Open fire, internet, no TV.

C-D Manor House, 28 Manor Pl, T03-477 0484, www.manorhousebackpackers.co.nz. Another historic colonial villa, with modern kitchen and dining areas, dorms, twins and doubles. Quiet location, bike hire, off-street parking and organized wildlife tours.

C-D Stafford Gables YHA, 71 Stafford St, T03-474 1919. A rambling old villa with lots of character, offering a good range of rooms including a particularly attractive double on the top floor with a view across the harbour. Parking, rooftop garden, internet and an emphasis on recycling. Recommended.

Motorcamps and campsites

B-D Dunedin Holiday Park, 41 Victoria Rd, alongside St Kilda Beach at the southern end of town, T03-455 4690, www.dunedinholiday park.co.nz. Modern facilities, en suite units, standard cabins, flats and powered/tent sites.

B-D Leith Valley Touring Park, 103 Malvern St (towards the northern end of town), T03-467 9936. In a sheltered setting next to the Leith Stream. It has modern motel units, self-contained cabins and powered/tent sites.

❶ Eating

Dunedin *p582, map p583*

There is plenty of choice in Dunedin, with over 140 restaurants and cafés, with most being along George St or around the Octagon. On George St you will also find plenty of cheap Asian eateries and takeaways designed to keep poverty-stricken students mildly plump and chirpy, with numerous Thai and Chinese options particularly between St Andrew and Fredrick sts. You will also find 2 **Star** 24 hour shops in George St.

ⵟⵟ Bell Pepper Blues, 474 Princes St, T03-4740973, lunch Wed-Fri, dinner Mon-Sat from 1830. A few mins' walk from the Octagon but worth it. The menu is highly imaginative and the service and presentation is excellent.

ⵟⵟ Etrusco at the Savoy, 8a Moray Pl (1st floor), T03-477 3737, daily from 1730. Very grand and a fine Italian choice that is good value despite the plush surroundings.

ⵟⵟ High Tide, 29 Kitchener St, T03-477 9784. Tue-Sun from 1800. Provides a convenient escape from the city centre and overlooks the harbour. It has a mainly seafood but can cater for those looking for traditional New Zealand/European dishes.

ⵟⵟ Indian Summer, corner of Upper Stuart and Moray Pl, T03-477 8880. Affordable and enjoys a good reputation.

ⵟⵟ Little India, 308 Moray Pl, T03-477 6559. Similar to **Indian Summer**. Good reputation.

ⵟⵟ Table Se7en, 1st floor, corner of George and Hanover sts, T03-477 6877, Mon-Thu 1200-2400, Fri 1200-0300, Sat 1700-0300. A chic and well-established traditional choice.

ⵟ Ale House at the Speights Brewery, 200 Rattray St, T03-471 9050, daily from 1130. Traditional pub grub, generous in both choice and servings. Tour and meal option from $55.

ⵟ Anarkali Indian Café and Takeaway, 365 George St, T03-477 1120, Mon-Sat 1130-1430 and 1700-2100. Noted for vegetarian dishes.

ⵟ Joseph Mellor Restaurant, Tennyson St, T03-479 6172, Mar-Nov daily 1200-1400 and 1800-2130. Well worth considering with very affordable and imaginative dishes created by trainee chefs. Lunch $9.50 and dinner $19.50. Where else would you get seared Cervena Medallions Baden-Baden for that price? Recommended.

ⵟ London Lounge, above the Albert Arms, corner of George and Hanover sts, T03-177 0033, Mon-Thu 1100-2230, Fri-Sat 1100-2300, Sun 1130-2130. Recommended for traditional pub grub.

ⵟ Reef Seafood Restaurant and Bar, 333 George St, T03-471 7185. For fish and chips.

Cafés

Many of the cafés are around the Octagon. **Arc Café**, 135 High St, T03-474 1135, Mon-Sat from 1200. Getting a bit tired but remains a very popular place with local artists, 'musos' and laid-back students. It's great for a coffee and offers regular live gigs. Free email but you will have to wait. At the time of going to press it was up for sale so it remains to be seen what happens with the local icon.

Good Oil Café, 314 George St, T03-479 9900. Great for people-watching amidst a minimalist milieu, here the coffee has to be good.

Governors Café, 438 George St, T03-477 6871, daily 0800-late. No great shakes aesthetically but is very popular, with a cosmopolitan clientele, good-value meals (especially breakfasts) and an internet suite next door.

Jizo, 56 Princes St, T03-479 2692, Mon-Sat 1130-2100. A pleasant Japanese café offering standard and affordable sushi.

Mazagran Espresso, 36 Moray Pl, T03-477 9959. Recommended specialist coffee house.

The Nova, 29 The Octagon, next to the Dunedin Art Gallery, T03-479 0808, Mon-Wed 0800-late, Thu-Fri 0700-late, Sat 0900-late, Sun 1000-2300. A good place for brunch, breakfast and even sells porridge.

The Percolator, 142 Lower Stuart St, T03-477 5462, Sun-Thu 0900-2300, Fri-Sat 0900-late. Also recommended.

Potpourri, 29 The Octagon, 97 Stuart St, T03-477 9983, daily for lunch from 0630, Sat 0930; dinner Mon-Fri. Good reputation for cheap vegetarian and vegan cuisine, organic coffee and homemade bread.

Tangente, 111 Moray Pl, T03-477 0232, Mon-Tue, Sun 0800-1500, Wed-Sat 0800-late. Designer café/restaurant that is pretty faultless. Specializes in organic fare and offers a wide-ranging blackboard menu with some great vegetarian dishes and brunch options. It also has a great atmosphere, wine list and service, all making a return trip likely.

♪ Pubs, bars and clubs

Dunedin *p582, map p583*

There are a number of café/bars around the Octagon; they are especially popular at the weekends and with the mobile phone brigade.

Albert Arms, corner of George and Hanover sts. Popular drinking establishment, at the north end of George St, especially with the younger set, and it often stages live gigs at weekends.

Bath St, 1 Bath St, T03-477 6750. For the full 'shake of the pants'.

Bennu Café and Bar, 12 Moray Pl, T03-474 5055. Aesthetically one of the best and also offers good food.

Di Lusso, 12 The Octagon, T03-477 3776. One of the newest and most frequented.

K World Karaoke Bar, 142 Princes St, T03-477 2008. At the end of a good night out this place can be a riot. Take to the stage and choose from an eclectic range of pop classics such as A-Ha, Duran Duran or Tom Jones.

The Ra Café and Bar, 21, T03-477 6080. Also popular, with good food.

Woolshed Bar and Grill, 318 Moray Pl, T03-477 3246, A good all-round drinking, eating and music venue.

● Entertainment

Dunedin *p582, map p583*

There is a healthy music, arts and cultural scene in Dunedin, and the best place to view current event and gig listings is in the *Otago Daily Times* or the free weekly *Fink* magazine available free from the VIC (I-Site).

Casino

Dunedin Casino, 118 High St, T03-477 4545, www.dunedincasino.co.nz, daily 1000-0300.

Cinema

Hoyts, on the Octagon, T03-477 7019.

Metro, in the town hall, T03-471 9635, www.metrocinema.co.nz. A venue that boasts 'No raincoats, no popcorn, no dinosaurs – just the finest films'. Hosts the best in Euro-arthouse film.

Rialto, Moray Pl, T03-474 2200, www.rialto.co.nz. Mon-Tue cheap night, $8.

Theatres

Fortune Theatre Company, corner of Moray Pl and Stuart St, T03-477 1292, www.fortunetheatre.co.nz. Offers performances in both the **Mainstage** and **Studio Theatres**, Feb-Dec, Tue-Sun.

Regent Theatre, on the Octagon, T03-477 8597. Hosts the annual film festival as well as touring international and national shows.

⊛ Festivals and events

Dunedin *p582, map p583*

For more information on these or other annual events contact the VIC (I-Site) or log on to www.dunedinnz.com.

Feb Dunedin Summer Festival. Annual festival celebrating the region and its lifestyle.

Mar Dunedin Fashion Show. Dunedin fashion designers showcase their collections in the City's premier fashion show.

Jul Taste Otago, Dunedin Food and Wine Festival, Edgar Centre. Focuses on all things food and wine related.

Jul/Aug Dunedin International Film Festival. For 2 weeks international films are shown at the Regent Theatre.

Cadbury Chocolate Carnival. Events include the Choc Art Awards, a 'Bake-off' and Jaffa (iconic New Zealand, small, round orange coated chocolates). Race down the steep gradient of Baldwin St.

Sep-Nov Rhododendron Festival. With a climate and soil well suited to growing rhododendrons, the whole city blossoms during these months.

⛰ Activities and tours

Dunedin *p582, map p583*

For the highly popular attractions and tours beyond Dunedin to the Otago Peninsula see Activities and tours, page 597.

Flightseeing

Helicopters Otago, T03-489 7322, www.helicoptersotago.co.nz. A flexible flightseeing schedule locally and throughout Otago from $400.

Mainland Air, Dunedin airport, T03-486 2200, www.mainlandair.com. Flights throughout the southern South Island and off-shore to see passing icebergs.

Golf

Dunedin claims yet another first, having created the first Golf Club in the southern hemisphere in 1871.

Otago Golf Club, 125 Balmacewen Rd, T03-467 2096, www.otagogolfclub.co.nz. From humble beginnings the club was officially formed in 1892 and is regarded as one of the best 18-hole courses in the country. The clubhouse also houses an interesting collection of early memorabilia, cups and medals. Green fees from $75.

Horse trekking

Bums 'n' Saddles, Blackhead, south of the city, T03-488 0097. Negotiate a network of coastal beach tracks, 2 hrs from $40.
Hare Hill, based in Port Chalmers, north of the city, T03-472 8496, www.horseriding-dunedin.co.nz. Standard and overnight adventures with harbour views, half- or full-day from $50.

Mountain biking

Other than the obvious attraction of the Otago Central Rail Trail (see page 586), there are a number of other shorter tracks available in the area. These are outlined in *Mountain Bike Rides in Dunedin*, available free from the VIC (I-Site).

Surfing

Southern Coast Surf Clinic, T03-455 6007, www.surfcoachnz.com. Lessons available from $40 per hr, half-day from $100, full $200.

Sightseeing tours

Given the region's colourful history it is not surprising to find ghosts lurking somewhere on the heritage walks agenda and should you be interested in the alleged facts you can join 'The Hair Raiser' ghost walks, departing from the VIC (I-Site) at 1800 on Wed and Fri, from $20.

Arthur's Tours, T0800-840-729, www.arthurs tours.co.nz. Long-established operator offering a entertaining and flexible range of local tours ranging from gardens to architecture.
Dunedin Heritage Tours (Citibus), T03-477 5577. Offers a 1-hr tour around the major city sights with pick ups at the Octagon at 0900, 1015, 1300, 1415 and 1530 from $18, child $9. It also runs 2- to 4-hr tours to Larnach Castle on the Otago Peninsula departing at 1000,

from $42, child $21 and Olveston (adjunct to city tour from $33, child $16).
Passion for Fashion, T03-477 7692, www.walkthetalk.co.nz. The perfect local catalyst for shopaholics. Retail enthusiast Jeannie Hayden takes the search out of shopping. 2-hr to half-day trips, with coffee breaks and lunch included, from $40.

Walking

Other than the **Centennial Lookout** (Signal Hill) and **Tunnel Beach** (see page 587), another recommended local walk is to the summit of Mt Cargill with its wonderful views across the city and the Otago Peninsula. It can be accessed by foot (4 km, 3½ hrs return) from Bethunes Gully (Norwood St off North Rd past the Botanical Gardens), or via Cowan Rd (off Pine Hill Rd, off SH1 heading north). For details see the DoC broadsheet *Mt Cargill and Organ Pipes Walk*, available from the DoC or the VIC.

�e Transport

Dunedin *p582, map p583*
Bicycle hire Cycle Surgery, 67 Stuart St, T03-477 7473, www.cyclesurgery.co.nz. **Car hire** Jackie's Rent-a-Car, 23 Cumberland St, T03-477 7848. Pegasus, 1 King Edward St, T03-477 6296. **Affordable Rentals**, 115 Kaikorai Valley Rd, T03-477 3232. **Taxi** City Taxis, T0800-771771. Dunedin Taxis, T03-477 7777. Southern Taxis, T03-476 6300.

❶ Directory

Dunedin *p582, map p583*
Banks Represented along Princes and George sts, with many accommodating currency exchange services. Travelex, 346 George St, T03-477 3383, Mon-Fri 0830-1700, Sat 1000-1230. **Internet** Dunedin Library, Moray Pl, Mon-Fri 0930-2100, Sat 1000-1600, Sun 1400-1800. NetPlanet, 78 St Andrew St, T03-479 2424, open daily till late. **Medical services** Dunedin Hospital, 201 Great King St, T03-474 0999; Urgent doctor, Otago Peninsula, 95 Hanover St, T03-479 2900 (pharmacy next door). **Police** 25 Great King St, T03-477 6011. **Post office** 243 Princes St, T03-477 3518, Mon-Fri 0830-1730. Post restante services. **Useful addresses** AA, 450 Moray Pl, T03-477 5945.

Otago Peninsula → *Colour map 6, B6*

The beautiful Otago Peninsula, which stretches 33 km northeast from Dunedin out into the Pacific Ocean, is as synonymous with wildlife as Dunedin is with Scotland. If there were any place that could honour the title of being the wildlife capital of the country, this would be it. It is home to an array of particularly rare species including the enchanting yellow-eyed penguin and the soporific Hooker's sea lion, as well the more common New Zealand fur seals. But without doubt the peninsula's star attraction is the breeding colony of royal albatross on Taiaroa Head, at the very tip of the peninsula. This colony is the only mainland breeding albatross colony in the world and offers an extraordinary opportunity to observe these supremely beautiful masters of flight and long-haul travel. A day trip to see all these wildlife delights is highly recommended and will leave a precious and lasting memory. Besides wildlife, the principal attractions on the Otago Peninsula are historic Larnach Castle and the stunning vista of Sandfly Bay, as well as activities such as sea kayaking, cruising and walking. ▸▸ For Sleeping, Eating, and other listings, see pages 597-598.

Ins and outs

Getting there The best way to see the peninsula is by car, but if you have no wheels of your own or you are not familiar with the wildlife, an organized tour is recommended. Some of the tours on offer can take you to several wildlife sites (and sights) that are out of bounds to the general public. By road there are two main routes that penetrate the peninsula. On the western side, hugging the numerous small bays and inlets of the Otago Harbour, is the Portobello Road which serves the peninsula's main village, Portobello. From Portobello this road then continues past the small settlement of Harington Point to terminate at Taiaroa Head and the albatross colony. An alternative route to Portobello via Highcliff Road accesses two of the peninsula's major physical attractions, Larnach Castle and Sandfly Bay, and straddles the hilltops of the peninsula offering some memorable views. Note that both roads are sealed but very windy and dangerous. It is important to slow down and not maintain the pace and buzz of Dunedin's city streets. Both Highcliff Road and Portobello Road are easily accessed via Cumberland Street (city) across the railway line and then by skirting the Otago Harbour on Wharf Street and Portsmouth Drive. For a free map of the Otago Peninsula ask at the VIC (I-Site). ▸▸ *See Activities and tours, page 597.*

Tourist information One of the principal *raisons d'être* of the **Dunedin VIC (I-Site)** (see page 584) is arranging half- to full-day trips out to the peninsula. There are a number of options regarding the length of time of visit, the route and the sight itinerary, so it pays to study the options carefully before parting with your cash. The DoC office in Dunedin can provide further information on walks and wildlife.

Albatrosses

Although **Taiaroa Head** is an interesting historic site in its own right, it is the colony of royal albatross that has really put the small, rocky headland on the map. Ever since the first egg was laid in 1920, the site, which is the only mainland-breeding colony in the world, has become an almost sacred preserve of these magnificent seabirds. The colony, now numbering almost 100, is fully protected and managed by the DoC and the Otago Peninsula Trust. With the opening of the **Royal Albatross Centre** ① *T03-478 0499, www.albatross.org.nz, daily 0830-2100 (seasonal)*, in 1972, thousands of people have been given the opportunity to view the birds from an observatory and to learn about their fascinating lifestyle and the threats we place upon them. Even before you enter the centre, if the conditions are right, you can see the great birds wheeling in from the ocean on wings that span over 3 m (the largest of any bird) and with a grace that defies the effort. If there is such a thing as airborne ballet this is it.

The albatross centre has some superb exhibits that include static and audio-visual displays and even a **live close-circuit TV feed** from the occupied nests in the breeding season. It takes about eight months for the parent birds to rear one of these avian *B52s* so your chances of seeing the industrial size carpet-slipper chicks are high. The activity of the adults varies, depending on courting, mating, incubating and feeding, with the best viewing times generally being between late-November and April. Having said that you would be fairly unlucky not to see at least one on any given visit at any time of year. The centre also has a café and a shop. ▸▸ *See Activities and tours, page 598, for details of the different tours available.*

There is plenty of other wildlife to see on and around Taiaroa Head. Of particular note are the rare **Stewart Island shags**, which also breed on the headland. They are beautiful birds but when it comes to flight they are the complete antithesis of the albatross. Also known as 'the flying brick', on a very windy day, it is not completely out of the ordinary for one to 'take out' you, your child and your ice cream from the viewing area near the centre. Around the base of the headland, **fur seals** and **little blue penguins** can regularly be seen and, if you have binoculars, the ocean will reveal a plethora of petrels and other seabirds.

The coast and headlands immediately south of Taiaroa Head are private land and out of bounds to the public, however, **Nature's Wonders** offers wildlife-watching tours of the area by ATV, see page 598.

Yellow-eyed penguins

The Otago Peninsula is a haven and breeding site for the yellow-eyed penguin, one of the rarest penguin species in the world. For many, the conditioning we have of the penguin/ice relationship and their near symbiosis is shattered amidst the golden sands and grasses of the peninsula's bays and inlets. The 'yellow eyes' or *hoiho* (to give them their Maori name) have been using the peninsula and the southeast coast of the South Island for centuries as a spill over from the sub-Antarctic islands that are their traditional home. But rarity, range and biology aside, it is the mere sight of these enchanting, congenial characters' daily comings and goings that is the irresistible attraction. At a number of sites on the peninsula (almost all on private land and protected) you can watch them returning home at dusk from their daily fishing trips or leaving again at dawn – all highly entertaining. Like fat amphibious little surfboards they emerge from the surf and take a few minutes to cool off. Then, usually in small groups, they scuttle up the beach into the undergrowth.

There are a number of locations and tours on which you can experience this delight. Most people visit the award-winning **Yellow-eyed Penguin Conservation Reserve** ① *just before the Albatross Colony at Harington Point; for bookings contact the reserve direct, T03-478 0286, www.penguin-place.co.nz or the Dunedin VIC (I-Site), daily from 0800 (May-Sep from 1515), $35, child $15.* This is the most commercial operation, set on a private reserve with an expanding colony of about 200 birds, which has been carefully created and managed as a workable mix of tourism, commercialism and conservation. Once provided with an introductory talk you are then delivered by 4WD truck to the beach where an amazing network of covered tunnels and hides allows you to view the birds discreetly. The breeding season and adult moult periods (mid-October to late February and early May) are the best times to see large numbers, but you are almost guaranteed to see at least half a dozen birds all year round especially around dusk. Although Penguin Place provides a fun and informative experience, and is certainly the best location for photographs, its commercialism can, at times, let it down. In the company of so many camera-toting individuals, and in such confined spaces, it can all be a bit too busy and staged. The same outfit runs the Twilight Wildlife Conservation Tour (see page 598) and can provide backpacker-style accommodation.

Otago Otago Peninsula

For a less commercial experience see **Elm Wildlife Tours** and **Otago Nature Guides,** page 598. To see penguins independently you can visit the DoC hide at Sandfly Bay at dawn or dusk. This is pretty straightforward and unless you want an in-depth description of the birds on a guided tour you are best to go it alone.

Hooker's sea lions and New Zealand fur seals

The Otago Peninsula is also home to the endemic Hooker's sea lion, which is the rarest of the world's five species of sea lions. Fortunately these huge creatures, which can be over 3 m in length and weigh over 400 kg, are making a comeback to mainland New Zealand after being eliminated by Maori hunters centuries before the arrival of Europeans. In 1995 they bred again on the peninsula for the first time in 700 years. Encountering these ocean-going couch potatoes almost anywhere along the coast is an

Otago Peninsula

Sleeping 🛏
932 Harington Point
 Village Motel **1**
Bus Stop Backpackers **9**
Conehenge **8**
Homestead **10**
Larnach Lodge **2**
Margate-by-the-Sea **3**
McFarmer's Backpackers **4**
Nisbet Cottage **5**
Penguin Place Lodge **6**

Portobello Village
 Tourist Park **7**

Eating 🍴
1908 **4**
Glenfalloch **2**
Larnach Castle **3**
Nature's Wonders **6**
Portobello Coffee Shop **5**
Royal Albatross Centre **1**

unforgettable experience. Seemingly devoid of any fear (and who wouldn't be, given those proportions and an impressive set of dentures housed in a mouth the size of a large bucket), they haul up on beaches and even the roads to rest. Having done so, they then display an overwhelming desire to do very little, except sleep, break wind, scratch, or eye you up occasionally with an expression of complete indifference. If you are lucky enough to see one, do not go any nearer than 10 m and never get between the said 'Jabba the Hut' and the water, since they are hardly going to say 'excuse me' as they head for home. Despite their looks, they can move like a slug from a slingshot and you would certainly lose the argument. Otago also has a number of **fur seal colonies**, the most accessible of which is around Taiaroa Head. Below the main car park you can usually find one or two hauled up in an almost enviable soporific state. Again, you can take a closer look but do not approach within 10 m.

Larnach Castle

① *Signposted off Castlewood Rd (from Portobello Rd), To3-476 1616, www.larnach castle.co.nz, daily 0900-1900 (1700 in winter), $20, child $10 (gardens only $10, child $3). The castle provides some of the best accommodation and views in the region.*

Perched on the highest point of the peninsula, 16 km from Dunedin, is Larnach Castle, the former residence of Australian William Larnach (1833-1898). As a minister of the Crown, banker, financier and merchant baron of the prosperous late 1880s, there is no doubt Larnach was a man of wealth and title, but he was far more renowned for his personal life and excesses – which finally lead to his tragic suicide surrounded by the very monument of his desires. Only the best would do for Larnach, who had both the will and the wherewithal to live up to the saying 'a man's home is his castle'. He employed 200 workmen for three years to build the exterior, and another 12 years was spent by master craftsmen embellishing the interior with 32 different woods, marble from Italy, tiles from England, glass from Venice and France, and even slate from Wales. Both Larnach and his castle have a fascinating history. After his death, the castle changed hands a number of times before falling into a state of disrepair. Then in 1967 the remains were purchased by the Barker family who have since lovingly renovated the place to something very close to its former glory and opened it to the public. Both the castle and its 6 ha of gracious grounds now remain open for self-guided tours and give a fascinating insight into the period and the man. There is a licensed café on site in the very Scottish ballroom, which comes complete with stag's head and open fire. Most of the peninsula tour operators visit Larnach Castle as a matter of course.

Other sights

There are many scenic bays and walks on the peninsula, with perhaps the most dramatic and accessible being the idyllic, and at times wild, **Sandfly Bay**, on its eastern shore. From Highcliff Road take Seal Point Road to the reserve car park. From there the beach can then be accessed by foot (20 minutes). At the far end of the beach there is a small public hide overlooking the only free, or publicly accessible, **yellow-eyed penguin colony** on the peninsula (40 minutes return). The best times for viewing are just before dawn and dusk. Do not be tempted to go down to the beach when the penguins are there – remember you are looking at one of the rarest birds in the world.

Beyond Sandfly Bay, and either accessible by foot (poled route) or via Sandymount Road (also off Highcliff Road), is the **Sandymount Summit**, **Chasm** and **Lover's Leap** Walk (one hour). The Chasm and Lover's Leap are impressive coastal cliff features formed when the sea eroded the soft, lower layers of volcanic rock. For details about these walks and others on the peninsula get the *Otago Peninsula Tracks* leaflet from the Dunedin VIC (I-Site) and the peninsula walks broadsheets, available from the DoC. **Glenfalloch** (Gaelic for 'hidden valley') ① *9 km from Dunedin, 430 Portobello Rd, To3-476 1775, daily, donation*, is a pleasant wooded garden and historic estate. The gardens are particularly noted for their rhododendrons, azaleas and camellias, which are at their bloomin' best between mid-September and mid-October. There is a restaurant on site.

Near Portobello, on the shores of Otago Harbour, is the **New Zealand Marine Studies Centre** ① *Hatchery Rd, To3-479 5826, www.otago.ac.nz/marinestudies, daily 1200-1630, $18, child $9; guided tours $42, child $18.* On display are a number of aquariums and 'touch tanks', with a range of native New Zealand sea creatures from sea horses to the octopus. There is even the opportunity to taste nutritious seaweed, and knowledgeable and friendly staff are on hand to answer any questions.

● For an explanation of the Sleeping and Eating price codes used in this guide, see the inside
● front cover. Other relevant information is provided in the Essentials chapter, pages 44-51. Note that prices are given in New Zealand dollars.

💿 Sleeping

Otago Peninsula *p592, map p594*

L-A Larnach Lodge, T03-4761616, www.larn achrastle.co.nz. Accommodation at Larnach Castle is some of the best in the region. The lodge offers beautifully appointed themed rooms from the 'Scottish Room' with its tartan attire, to the 'Goldrush Room' which comes complete with a king size 'cart bed' made out of an original old cart found on the property. The views across the harbour and peninsula from every room are simply superb. Breakfast is served in the old stables; dinner is optional in the salubrious interior of the castle. Cheaper 'Stable Stay' rooms with shared bathrooms in the former coach house are also available. Book well in advance. Recommended.

AL Conehenge, High Cliff Rd, T03-478 0911, kolig@ihug.co.nz. A modern purpose-built property set above Portobello village amongst an intriguing rock sculpture garden. The well-travelled hosts ensure a warm welcome and lost of good local advice regarding sights and activities. Cosy private en suite.

A 932 Harington Point Village Motel, Harington Point, T03-478 0287, www.haringtonpointmotels.co.nz. Further out on the peninsula and conveniently placed for both the albatross and Penguin Place yellow-eyed penguin colonies. Small, modern and comfortable.

A Homestead, 238 Harington Point Rd (2 km north of Portobello), T03-478 0384, www.the-homestead.co.nz. Set in a lovely position near the water's edge overlooking Portobello Bay, 3 modern self-contained units with Sky TV. Includes breakfast.

A Margate-by-the-Sea, 5 Margate Av, Broad Bay, T03-478 0866. Cosy and self-contained with spa.

A Nisbet Cottage, 6A Eliffe Pl, T03-454 5169, www.natureguidesotago.co.nz. Located at the base of the Otago Peninsula and only a short drive to the city centre. A choice of 2 tidy en suites sleeping 2-3, a guest lounge with open fire and great hospitality. The German hosts also operate **Otago Nature Guides** (see page 598) and organize packages that include dawn and dusk trips to see the peninsula penguin colonies, or multi-day trips to the Catlins and Stewart Island.

C-D Bus Stop Backpackers, 252 Harington Point Rd, Portobello, T03-478 0330, www.bus-stop.co.nz. Peaceful waterside house close to the major wildlife attractions, with 2 rooms and additional beds in a house bus or caravan. A log fire adds to the appeal and character.

C-D McFarmer's Backpackers, 774 Portobello Rd, T03-478 0389. Homely farmstay with dorms and doubles. Close to village amenities.

C-D Penguin Place Lodge at the yellow-eyed penguin reserve, Harington Point, T03-478 0286. Offers basic, but modern budget accommodation with single, twin and doubles with shared facilities.

Motorcamps and campsites

C-D Portobello Village Tourist Park, 27 Hereweka St, Portobello, T03-478 0359, portobellotp@xtra.co.nz. Self-contained tourist flats, powered/tent sites and a bunkroom. Bike hire is available.

✪ Eating

Otago Peninsula *p592, map p594*

There are only 2 restaurants and a scattering of cafés on the peninsula. **Larnach Castle** (see Sleeping, above), **The Royal Albatross Centre** and **Natures Wonders** have cafés. There is a well-stocked general store on the main street in Portobello, T03-478 0555.

🍴 1908 Café/Restaurant, 7 Harington Point Rd, Portobello, T03-478 0801, daily for lunch and dinner. Pleasant but a little expensive. European/NZ menu with a seafood edge.

🍴 Glenfalloch Restaurant, 430 Portobello Rd, T03-476 1006, daily from 1100. A licensed café style establishment set in the pleasant Glenfalloch Gardens.

🍴 Portobello Coffee Shop, 699 Highcliff Rd, T03-478 1055, open 0900-1700. Has snacks, breakfast, acceptable coffee and internet.

▲ Activities and tours

Otago Peninsula *p592, map p594*

Cruising

Monarch Wildlife Cruises and Tours, corner of Wharf and Fryatt sts, T03-477 4276, www.wildlife.co.nz. Award-winning outfit offering a variety of trips from 1-7 hrs taking in all the main harbour and peninsula sights.

The main highlights are the Marine Studies Centre Aquarium at Portobello and the wildlife of Taiaroa Head; Larnach Castle, the Albatross and penguin reserves can also be included. For a short trip you can join the boat at the Wellers Rock Jetty near Taiaroa Head. Regular daily departures, 1-hr cruise (Wellers Rock) $35; tour combining bus tour of the peninsula and cruise half-day $75, full package including entry to main sights $180.

Sea kayaking

Otago Harbour and Taiaroa Head provide some of the best sea kayaking in the country with the added attraction of viewing and accessing wildlife in a manner simply not possible by land. Where else in the world can you kayak while viewing albatross? **Wild Earth Adventures**, T03-473 6535, www.wildearth.co.nz. Provides an excellent range of tours, some in combination with the land-based attractions, with the most popular being the 4- to 5-hr 'Taiaroa Ocean Tour' around the heads and its Albatross colony, from $95 (connections available with **Elm Wildlife Tours**). Recommended.

Wildlife

Citibus, T03-477 5577, www.transport place.co.nz. A well-established sightseeing operation by bus to the peninsula providing packages to all the major sights including Larnach Castle, the albatross centre and the Penguin Place Yellow-eyed penguin colony. It can also drop off at the Monarch Wildlife Cruise jetty. Regular daily departures from the city, From $41.

Elm Wildlife Tours, Elm Lodge, Dunedin, see page 588, T03-454 4121/T0800-356563, www.elmwildlifetours.co.nz. Provides a wide range of excellent award-winning eco-tours of the peninsula and the region. Its 5- to 6-hr peninsula trip takes in the Albatross Centre, a New Zealand fur seal colony and their its yellow-eyed penguin-breeding beach at the remote Cape Saunders. The tour is fun and informative, yet non-commercial, and gives you access to some of the most scenic private land on the peninsula. From $75 (albatross observatory and additional activities extra). Pick-ups available. Recommended.

Nature's Wonders, near Taiaroa Head, T03-478 1150/T0800-246446, www.natures wondersnaturally.com. Has expanded its operation in recent months to include a cross-country '8x8 Argo tour' and walk to the penguin colonies on private land. Albatross sightings, fur seals and occasionally sea lions are also encountered. The main tour is 1-hr minimum and costs $40, child $35. Coach transport from Dunedin $25. Café on site.

Otago Nature Guides, T03-454 5169, www.nznatureguides.com. Personalized, small group tours at dawn to see the Yellow-eyed penguin colony at the beautiful Sandfly Bay. Tours in conjunction with its fine B&B accommodation in Nisbet Cottage (see Sleeping, above) are recommended. Extended trips to the Catlins and Stewart Island are also available. German spoken.

Royal Albatross Centre, see page 592. There are a number of tours available. The 1½-hr 'Unique Taiaroa' tour includes an introductory video, a viewing of the colony from the hilltop observatory, and a look at the remains of Fort Taiaroa. This is a series of underground tunnels, fortifications and a 'disappearing gun' that were originally built in 1885 in response to a perceived threat of invasion from Tsarist Russia. From $35, child $17. Also on offer is the 1-hr 'Royal Albatross' which includes all the above except the fort. From $30, child $15. For those with an interest in forts, paranoia and guns you may like to join the 30-min 'Fort Taiaroa Tour' ($15, child $7). The 30-min 'Albatross Insight Tour' involves a guided tour of the centre and an introductory talk while viewing them on close-circuit TV, as opposed to first hand from the observatory ($10, child $5). Note that the observatory is closed 17 Sep-23 Nov each year, to allow the new season's birds to renew their pair bonds.

Sam's 4x4 Adventures, T03-4780878, www.samsoffroadtours.com. A small group oriented operation offering personalized 4WD road tours of the peninsula. 2½-hr evening tour ($50). Peninsula accommodation package also available.

Twilight Wildlife Experience Tours, T03-4743300, www.wilddunedin.co.nz. A relaxed and friendly 5- to 6-hr tour of the albatross colony (entry optional), various wildlife sites, peninsula beaches and the Penguin Place Reserve. The Monarch Wildlife Cruise (see Cruising, above) is also an optional extra. Tours depart from Dunedin Mar-Oct 1330 (Nov-Feb 1430). From $68, child $45.

Central Otago

The barren, rugged and almost treeless landscapes of Central Otago have a dramatic sense of space and loneliness. Looking at these vistas now and passing through the quiet, unassuming towns of its back roads and river valleys, it is hard to imagine the immensity of the chaotic gold boom years that once made Otago the most populous region in the land. After gold was first discovered in 1861 by Gabriel Read, an Australian prospector, near Lawrence in the Clutha River Valley, Central Otago erupted into a gold fever that spread like wildfire across its barren landscape. It was a boom and a resource that would last until the turn of the 20th century. This period saw the establishment of many towns including Alexandra, Clyde, Cromwell, Roxburgh, Ranfurly and St Bathans and the construction of the impressive Taieri Gorge Railway and what is now the Otago Central Rail Trail which both formed vital communication links with Dunedin.

With the lure of Wanaka and Queenstown to the west, Central Otago sees little but transitory tourist traffic. However, if you have a couple of days to kill, a more thorough exploration of this historic gold-mining region can be rewarding and provide some respite from the crowds elsewhere. Attractions of particular note include the Taieri Gorge Railway trips, a walk around historic St Bathans or Clyde, and the 150-km Otago Central Rail Trail. The latter is becoming increasingly popular, with its 68 bridges, and numerous tunnels and viaducts to add to the pleasant scenery. The trail also offers some of the best mountain biking in the region. Other equally less gold-orientated activities include fishing, walking and horse trekking. ▶▶ *For Sleeping, Eating and other listings, see pages 603-605.*

Ins and outs

Getting there There are three main roads into Central Otago which converge to form a loop. From Palmerston, 55 km north of Dunedin (via SH1 and the coast), SH85 turns inland to follow the 'Pig Root' to Ranfurly and Alexandra, with a small diversion to St Bathans. At Alexandra SH85 joins SH8 that follows the Clutha River Valley, south through Roxburgh, Raes Junction and Lawrence, before rejoining SH1 near Milton, 60 km south of Dunedin. At Mosgiel, 15 km south of Dunedin, SH87 follows close to the Taieri George Railway and Otago Central Rail Trail to merge with SH85 just east of Ranfurly.

One of the best ways to get a taste of Central Otago is by train via the Taieri Gorge Railway and then by mountain bike from Middlemarch to Clyde on the now disused line that forms the Otago Central Rail Trail (see page 586). Alternatively you can combine train and bus to Queenstown. Roxburgh, Alexandra, Clyde and Cromwell are all on the main highway to Queenstown (SH8) and are served by **Intercity/Newmans**, book at the VIC (I-Sites), (Christchurch/Invercargill/Queenstown/ Wanaka). Several shuttle companies offer regional services including: **Nakedbus.com** (throughout the South island as far south as Dunedin); **Atomic Shuttles**, T03-322 8883, www.atomic travel.co.nz (Christchurch/Invercargill/Queenstown/Wanaka); and **Wanaka Connexions**, T0800-244844, www.wanakaconnexions.co.nz (Queenstown/Wanaka). **Catch-a-Bus (Wanaka)**, T03-479 9960, www.catchabus.co.nz, offers the only public transport from Wanaka to Middlemarch along the Otago Central Rail Trail.

Tourist information **Alexandra VIC (I-Site)** ① *22 Centennial Av, T03-448 9515, www.centralotagonz.com, Mon-Fri 0900-1700, Sat-Sun 1000-1700 (1600 winter),* is an excellent centre almost as full of information as the staff are with enthusiasm for the region. There are free maps, leaflets and displays outlining the many historical aspects of the region and its most popular activities, including mountain biking, fishing and horse trekking. **DoC Central Otago Regional Office** ① *43 Dunstan Rd,*

To3-440 2040. **Cromwell and Districts VIC (I-Site) and Museum** ① *47 The Mall, To3-445 0212, www.cromwell.org.nz, Mon-Fri 0900-1700, Sat-Sun 1000-1600*. The staff here are very enthusiastic and helpful and will do their best to make sure you see the financial and health benefits of staying in Cromwell as opposed to Queenstown. The website is excellent and full of useful information.

For **ski information** contact: **Cardrona**, To3-443 7341; **Coronet Peak**, To3- 442 4620; **The Remarkables**, To3-442 4615; **Treble Cone**, To3-443 7443; and **Waiorau**, To3-443 7542; www.nzski.com. The *Time for Real Adventure – Cromwell and Lake Dunstan* is an excellent leaflet that is available from the VIC (I-Site) listing everything from climate statistics to local walks.

The **Otago Goldfields Heritage Trust** ① *To3-445 0111, www.nzsouth.co.nz/goldfields*, has a useful website. Many of the region's towns and goldfields heritage sites come within the boundaries of the Otago Goldfields Park administered by DoC. For the serious historian the *Otago Goldfields Heritage Trail* booklet, available free from all of the region's VICs (I-Sites), provides a solid route guide from which to explore the diverse historical sites scattered throughout the region. The websites www.centralotagonz.com and www.tco.org.nz may also prove useful. The **Otago Central Rail Trail** has its own website, www.otagocentralrailtrail.co.nz.

Alexandra → *Colour map 6, B5 Population: 5000*

At the junction of the Clutha and Manuherikia Rivers, Alexandra was one of the first gold mining towns to be established in Central Otago. Its creation was due to the first strikes made in 1862 by Horatio Hartley and Christopher Reilly in the once rich Dunstan fields, in what is now the neighbouring town of Clyde. The river junction became known as Lower Dunstan and later became the settlement of Alexandra. Once the gold ran out at the end of the 1800s the orchardists moved in, making fruit growing Alexandra's modern-day industry. The town is at its best in autumn when the riverside willows and poplars, ironically, bathe the valley in another golden hue. Alexandra serves as the principal gateway to the **Otago Central Rail** and **Dunstan gold mining heritage trails**, which are a major attraction for mountain bikers and 4WD enthusiasts.

Almost instantly noticeable and visible from almost everywhere is the 11-m diameter **clock** on part of the **Knobbies Range** to the east of Alexandra. Completed in November 1968, its creation came about through no particular reason other than the pure and simple desire of one Alexander Jaycee. After managing to get his idea endorsed by the town's residents, he then found the support and finances to build it, requiring 1264 hours of work. Although hardly ugly, it seems a little out of place, and does not reflect the general atmosphere of life in the town. One gets the feeling that if it stopped no one would be particularly bothered about going up there to give it a tap.

Besides the clock and its simple riverside aesthetics, the main attraction in town is the **Alexandra Museum** ① *Dunorling St, To3-448 6230, Mon-Fri 1000-1630, Sat-Sun 1400-1600, donation*. It concentrates naturally on gold mining, but also includes some interesting displays on the role of the early Chinese settlers and sheep farmers as well as the work of local artisans.

A short walk from the centre of town will take you to **Shaky Bridge**, which crosses the Manuherikia River on Fox Street (just below the clock). Originally built in 1879, it was once used by wagons and horses. Now purely a footbridge, although aesthetically pleasing, it does not provide the impending adrenaline rush that its name suggests, however, the smart **Shaky Bridge Vineyard Café and Restaurant** on the far side provides added incentive.

As well as orchards, the area has its fair share of vineyards including the **Black Ridge** ① *76 Conroys Rd, To3-449 2059, daily 1000-1700*, which claims to be the most southerly winery in the world. Ask the VIC (I-Site) for the free *Central Otago Wine Map*.

If you are a *Lord of the Rings* fanatic, Alexandra will no doubt provide the launching pad to visit the remote **Poolburn Reservoir,** which sits on the Rough Ridge

Range 40 minutes east of the town. There, an expansive area of rocky outcrops (tors) and tussock surrounding the reservoir, provided the perfect backdrop for the realm of **'Rohan'**. Note that the area is by no means easy to reach and you are advised to seek detailed directions from the VIC (I-Site) before venturing out independently. If you do not have a reliable vehicle of your own then you can always join one of the local tours, perhaps taking in the former gold mining village of **Ophir** on the way. Contact the VIC (I-Site) in Alexandra for the latest details.

Clyde → *Colour map 6, A5 Population 1500*

Just 10 km west of Alexandra is the pretty and historic village of Clyde. Backed by the concrete edifice of the Clyde Dam, which incarcerates **Lake Dunstan**, it offers a pleasant stop on the way to Queenstown or Wanaka. Originally called Dunstan and the hub of the rich Dunstan Goldfields, it assumed its present name in the late 1860s. Clyde in Scottish Gaelic is *Clutha* – which is the river that once flowed freely through the Cromwell Gorge and is the longest in the South Island. Amidst Clyde's very pleasant aesthetics are a number of historic old buildings including the **Town Hall** (1868), various pioneer cottages and a handful of its once 70 hotels. The **Old Courthouse** on Blyth Street is another fine example that was built in 1864. Sadly, the many interesting artefacts displayed inside, including the original courtroom dock, leg irons, handcuffs and a set of scales, are no longer open to the public. These scales, which no doubt were the focus of many an argument, are thought to have weighed over 70,000 ounces of gold. It is not surprising that during the gold boom, with so many hopefuls harbouring such a sense of greed, there were many disputes in the town. Perhaps the worst of these was the $26,000 gold and banknotes robbery that caused uproar in 1879.

Nearby, are the **Clyde Historical Museum** and **Briar Herb Factory** ① *12 Fraser St, T03-449 2092, museum $1, herb factory $2, Tue-Sun 1400-1600 or at other times by arrangement*. The herb factory originally began operations in the 1930s processing local thyme, but has since grown into a museum housing not only the original herb-processing machinery, but also a variety of exhibits illustrating the life of the early settlers. These include the workshops of blacksmith, farrier and wheelwrights, and stables with various horse-drawn vehicles.

The trilogy of historical sites is completed by the **Clyde Station Museum** ① *at the former railway station on Fraser St, T03-449 2400, Sun 1400-1600 or by appointment, donation*. It houses some lovingly restored locos.

Although perhaps a bit morbid, the **cemetery** in Clyde (Springvale Road) can be an interesting place for reflection. Having been in use since the 1850s, the headstones provide fascinating reading, particularly the ages, surnames and origins of the former settlers. Once you have enjoyed the atmosphere and historical aspects of the village, you might like to take the 30-minute walk to the **Clyde Lookout hill** (signposted) above the town and enjoy the views.

Cromwell → *Colour map 6, A5 Population: 2700*

From Clyde, SH8 negotiates the Cromwell Gorge and plays tag with a section of Lake Dunstan, which on the map looks like the antenna of a large blue sea creature. At its head, 23 km to the north, is the tidy little town of Cromwell. Cromwell is faced with five very large dilemmas: a pear, an apple, a nectarine, an apricot and its proximity to Queenstown. It is the latter of course with which it struggles the most. Just how do you stop any tourist so intent on reaching perhaps the busiest tourist town in the country? Well, it seems some bright spark (there is always one) thought a sculpture of four man-eating pieces of fruit might be a good idea; you have to wonder if this has only added to the dilemma. Sure, people stop, they stare, make the suitable ooh and ahh noises, then take the inevitable photographs, but that is often the problem – they go no further. That's Cromwell. Forever and around the globe, Cromwell has become that place with the whooping fruit, ingrained forever in a million memories with a silly photo. Having said that, Cromwell is ideally situated between Wanaka, Queenstown, the Lindis Pass to Mount Cook and SH8 to Dunedin. The accommodation here is much cheaper than Queenstown and the place is far less stressful. It is also in a great position to access five ski fields (see Tourist information, page 600). It does in fact make a lot of sense, despite the fruit, to base yourself here. What's more, it is also one of the sunniest, warmest places in the south and has to be given considerable credit for being the only place in the world that has a reserve set aside especially for beetles.

A former gold town, Cromwell was originally called 'The Junction' due to its position at the confluence of the Clutha and Kawarau rivers. These important bodies of water, which are now masked with the creation of Lake Dunstan, form an integral part of the South Island's hydropower scheme. The **museum** ① *attached to the VIC (I-Site), donation*, focuses on the early history and building of the dam and is worth a look. The decision to build the **Clyde Dam** in the 1980s, using Cromwell as the accommodation base, brought many changes to the town and gave rise to a mix of old-world charm and modern, tidy aesthetics. A wander through its very congenial Mall (almost in the shadow of the giant fruit), followed by another in its historic precinct, provides a stark and interesting contrast. With the dam now established they say Cromwell's future lies in tourism, and of course its horticultural status as the 'Fruit Bowl of the South'.

The main attraction in the town itself is the **Old Cromwell Town Precinct** ① *at the end of Melmore Terr, at the point where the 2 rivers merge, 1000-1630, free*. Since the 1980s and encouraged by the disruption of the dam work, many of the former buildings have been restored or reconstructed and now house local cafés and craft shops. The precinct boasts several restored buildings that are open for viewing and the VIC (I-Site) has various free leaflets. *In Search of the Main Street* is particularly useful.

As you might expect, there are also numerous former gold mining sites and relics surrounding Cromwell. **Bannockburn**, **Bendigo** and the **Carrick Goldfields** are of particular interest. The VIC (I-Site) has details and maps. The **Goldfields Mining Centre** ① *Kawarau Gorge (SH6 west), 6 km towards Queenstown, T03-445 1038, www.goldfieldsmining.co.nz, daily 0900-1700, $15, child $7.50; guided tours $20, child $10*, provides the opportunity to explore historic gold workings, a Chinese settlers' village, gold stamper batteries and a sluice gun. You can also pan for gold, go horse trekking or jet boating ($75, child $45).

Vineyards

As well as its many orchards, the immediate area is also home to a number of vineyards. In **Bannockburn**, just to the south of Cromwell, you will find the **Felton Road Winery** ① *Felton Rd, T03-445 0885, by appointment, May-Oct*; **Akarua** ① *Cairnmuir Rd, T03-445 0897, café/bar daily 1100-1600*; **Carrick** ① *Cairnmuir Rd, T03-445 3480, www.carrick.co.nz, daily 1100-1700*; and the **Olssen's Garden Vineyard** ① *306 Felton Rd, T03-445 1716, tastings daily 1000-1700, closed Sat and Sun May-Sep*. The intriguingly named **Mount Difficulty Vineyard** ① *Felton Rd, Bannockburn, T03-445 3445, www.mountdifficulty.com, daily 1030-1700 (1030-1600 Apr-Oct)*, is a small boutique winery that is fast contributing to the region's reputation for fine Pinot Noir, if not its expansive views.

If time is short and you have only a vague interest in wine, a visit to the **Wine Adventures Big Picture Complex** ① *corner of Sandflat Rd and SH6 (towards Queenstown), T03-445 4052, daily 0900-2000*, may spark a new interest. It offers an interactive experience through a film; an intriguing 'Aroma Room' that aims to 'maximize the sensory impact of Central Otago wines. Then there are of course tastings, which further maximize your compulsion to buy a bottle or six in the retail outlet or augment it all with a spot of lunch or dinner at the restaurant/café.

Alexandra *p600*

The VIC (I-Site) has full accommodation listings and can book on your behalf. There are a number of motels, most on the main drag north, towards Clyde.

L Rocky Range, Half Mile, T03-448 6150, www.rockyrange.co.nz. Luxury B&B with 4 well appointed en suites, excellent hosts and good views.

AL-A Iversen B&B, 47 Blackman Rd, T03-449 2520, www.otagocentral.com. For a lovely orchard stay.

A Centennial Court Motor Inn, 96 Centennial Av, T03-448 6482, www.nzsouth.co.nz/centennialcourt. A la carte restaurant and bar, luxury spa suites, fully-equipped family units.

A-B Alexandra Heights Motel, 125 Centennial Av, T03-448 6366, www.manz.co.nz/alexandra. All units have cooking facilities. Spa baths available.

B Alexandra Garden Court Motel, Manuherikia Rd, T03-448 8295. Recommended. Standard amenities and pleasant gardens.

C-D Alexandra Backpackers, 8-12 Skird St, T03-448 7170, alexandrabackpackers@hotmail.com. The main budget hostel in town, centrally located and well geared up for cyclists and advice about the Rail Trail.

C-D Ophir Lodge Backpackers, 1 McDonald St, in the historic village of Ophir (28 km north), T03-447 3339, blgaler@xtra.co.nz. A fine alternative with cabin dorms, 1 twin, a double and tent sites. The added attractions here, other than the peaceful and friendly atmosphere of the village, are the local walks, bike trails and fishing and the local pub.

Motorcamps and campsites

B-D Alexandra Holiday Camp, on the Manuherikia Rd, T03-448 8297. Has cabins, backpacker rooms, powered/tent sites, camp kitchen and hires kayaks and mountain bikes.

Clyde *p601*

LL-AL Olivers Lodge, 34 Sunderland St, T03-449 2860, www.olivers.co.nz. Equally lauded for the quality of its accommodation and its restaurant, Oliver's offers a classic mix of old world character and fine cuisine. Choose from one of 12 individually styled en suites ranging from the 'stable' and 'homestead' rooms, to the individual 'smokehouse' room with its charming old shower and sunken bath. The restaurant, which also exudes character with its cobblestone fireplace and red brick floor, has been a focus for quality fine dining in the region for years. Recommended.

A Antique Lodge Motel, 56 Sunderland St, T03-449 2709. A good motel option.

A Dunstan House, Sunderland St, T03-449 2295, www.dunstanhouse.co.nz. This historic former hotel has been well refurbished and offers elegant en suites decorated in turn-of-the-20th-century style.

C-D Hartley Arms Backpackers, Sunderland St, T03-449 2700, hartleyarms@xtra.co.nz. Friendly place set in a historic cottage right in the thick of things.

Motorcamps

C-D Clyde Holiday Complex, Whitby St, T03-449 2714, has 1 cabin, on-site vans and powered/tent sites. For other accommodation options contact the VIC (I-Site) in Alexandra.

Cromwell *p601*

There is a surprisingly good range of accommodation in Cromwell and, given its popularity as a base close to (but cheaper) than Queenstown, the number of beds is increasing. The VIC (I-Site) has a full list of options and can book on your behalf. In summer it would still be wise to book ahead.

L-AL Villa Amo, Shine Lane, Pisa Moorings on Lake Dunstan, T03-445 0788, www.villaamo.co.nz. A modern spacious villa built in neoclassical Roman-style and a good option in the upper B&B range. Located on the shores of Lake Dunstan and commanding fine views of the mountains, it offers 1 room with shared bathroom with an adjunct double if required. There is also an outdoor spa and in-house eco-experience tours of the region (see Activities and tours, below).

AL-A Carrick Lodge Motel, 10 Barry Av, T03-445 4519, www.carricklodge.co.nz. New motel with studios and units (some with spa) all with broadband internet.

AL-A Golden Gate Lodge, Barry Av, T03-445 1777, www.goldengate.co.nz. The closest thing to a hotel in town.

Smart and spacious, it is designed to reflect the region's gold-mining heritage and offers well-appointed studios, suites (some with spa) and units and restaurant. **AL-B Lake Dunstan Lodge**, Cromwell Rd, SH8, 5 km north of Cromwell, T03-445 1107, www.lakedunstanlodge.co.nz. A smart, modern home in a peaceful location on the shores of Lake Dunstan, offering tidy twin and queen rooms, with balconies, a spa pool and some great home cooking. **A-B Cottage Gardens B&B**, 3 Alpha St, T03-445 0628, eco@xtra.co.nz. A good choice. **B Anderson Park Lodge**, 9 Gair Av, T0800-220550. A cheaper option with spa pool. **B Colonial Manor** corner of Barry and Mead Aves, T03-445 0184, www.colonial manor.co.nz. Quality motel accommodation.

Motorcamps and campsites

B-D Cromwell Top Ten Holiday Park, 1 Alpha St, T03-445 0164, www.cromwell. holiday.co.nz. A wide range of modern motel, en suite/standard cabins and powered/tent sites in a quiet setting beside the golf course. **C-D Chalets and Holiday Park**, 102 Barry Av, T03-445 1260, www.thechalets.co.nz. Former revamped dam workers' residences. It has bunkrooms and cheap but comfortable singles and doubles with shared facilities.

● Eating

Alexandra p600

Clyde, see below, provides far better dining options than Alexandra.

Grumpy's Café and Bar, next door to the VIC (I-Site) at 26 Centennial Av, T03-448 9189, daily 1030-2130 (2030 in winter). A historic single-storey villa offering imaginative and affordable European/NZ lunches and dinners. **Red Brick Café**, just off Ennis St, T03-448 9174, Mon-Sat for lunch or dinner. The exception to the plethora of unremarkable cafés and takeaways in the centre of town. **The Shaky Bridge Café**, near Shaky Bridge, Graveyard Gully Rd, T03-448 5111. Sun-Thu 0900-1600, Fri-Sat 0900-1730. A fine venue for an alfresco lunch or a coffee all year and for dinner in summer.

Clyde p601

Dunstan House, 29 Sunderland St, T03-449 2295, Mon-Wed 1800-late, Thu-Sun 1200-1400 and 1800-late. Offers café-style cuisine that focuses mainly on local produce in an equally historic setting. **Oliver's Restaurant**, 34 Sunderland St (in the former 1863 general store) T03-449 2860, www.olivers.co.nz, daily for lunch and dinner (bookings advised). The award-winning food is complemented by the pleasant surroundings. **Blues Bank Café and Bar**, Sunderland St (in the former bank), T03-449 2147, Tue-Sun from 1100-late. A funky little place, with a light, imaginative menu and good coffee. **The Post Office Café and Bar**, 2 Blyth St, T03-449 2488, daily from 1000. Pleasant aesthetics and light meals.

Cromwell p601

Bannockburn Hotel, 420 Bannockburn Rd, 8 km from Cromwell, Bannockburn, T03-445 0615, daily for lunch and dinner. Boasts a pleasant setting and good selection of local wines. Recommended. **Gentle Annie's Restaurant**, in the Golden Gate Lodge, on Barry Av, T03-445 1777, daily 0700-2100. The best bet for à la carte. **Cromwell Town and Country Club**, Melmore Terr, T03-445 1169, Fri-Sat. Provides a good cheap feed. **Grain and Seed Café**, 63 Melmore Terr (in the original 1880 Grain and Seed store), T03-445 5475, daily from 1000-1630. The best coffee in town and light meals.

▲ Activities and tours

Alexandra p600

Fishing permits and a list of local guides are available from the VIC (I-Site).

Alexandra is a principal starting point for the Otago Central Rail Trail and Dunstan Trails. The VIC (I-Site) can provide information and leaflets on the methods and negotiation of both, mainly by mountain bike or 4WD. The Otago Central Rail Trail has its own website, www.otagocentralrailtrail.co.nz, which is very useful. Various transport operators provide luggage and bike pick-up or drop-offs and bike hire (and/or guided tours) for both trails. **Altitude Adventures**, 88 Centennial Av, Alexandra, T03-448 8917, www.altitude adventures.co.nz. Offers a 2- to 3-hr, fast single track ride from $69, a full-day trip locally for a very reasonable $85, various

customized multi-day 'Rail Trail' packages and a full-day backcountry biking tour to Poolburn (*Lord of the Rings* film location), from $165. Full rental service.
Dunstan Trail Rides, 118 Waikerikeri Valley Rd, Clyde, T03-449 2445. Offers horse trekking on the Dunstan Trail from $25 per hr, 2 hrs $40.
Etours, T03-471 8438, www.inmark.co.nz/e-tours, Interesting day tours ($95) of the peninsula by bike, which really allows you to get a feel for the place; departs 0900. Self-guided tours and hire available.
Trail Journeys, corner of SH8 and Springvale Rd, T03-449 2150/T0800-724587, www.trail journeys.co.nz. Offers mountain bike hire, complete 1- to 3-day guided packages, personal itineraries and transport associated with the trail.

Cromwell *p601*
There are plenty of good walks in the area, described in the *Walk Cromwell* brochure available free from the VIC (I-Site). The area also has some excellent fishing, mountain biking, motorcycle touring and 4WD opportunities, again, contact the VIC (I-Site).
Lake Dunstan Eco-experience, T03-445 1745, ecoexperience@xtra.co.nz. Offers an interesting 3- to 4-hr trip up Lake Dunstan to

the Bendigo wetlands that are home to numerous water birds and waders.
Southern Lakes Pack Horse Trekking, T03-445 1444, www.nzsouth.co.nz/kagan/packhorse. Local trekking operator.

Vineyard tours
There are also several orchard and vineyard tour operators including.
Freeway Orchards, T03-445 1500, www.freewayorchard.co.nz;
Jackson Orchards Tours, T03-445 0596, www.jacksonorchard.co.nz. From $10.

❶ Directory

Alexandra *p600*
Internet Cobblestone Café, daily in season 0830-1800. Library, Mon-Fri 0900-1700, Sat 1000-1200. Both on Tarbert St in the centre.

Cromwell *p601*
Banks BNZ and National Bank, in the Mall **Internet** At the Library, The Resource Centre and Composite Computers, all in the Mall. **Police** T03-445 1999. **Post office** 68 The Mall, Mon-Fri 0900-1730, Sat 0900-1300. **Useful addresses** Breakdown services, CR Motors, Murray Terr, T03-445 1844.

Queenstown → *Colour map 6, A4 Population: 10,000*

Ladies and gentlemen, fasten your seat belts and welcome to Queenstown – Adrenaline Central, Thrillsville, New Zealand – the adventure capital of the world. You are perhaps studying this guide in your hotel room, or perched in your hostel bunk, with a pained expression trying to decide which of the 150-odd activities to try and, more importantly, how your wallet can possibly cope? But first things first: look out of the window. Where else in the world do you have such accessible scenery? And all that is free.

Queenstown has come a long way since gold secured its destiny in the 1860s. It is now the biggest tourist draw in New Zealand and considered one of the top (and almost certainly the most scenic) adventure venues in the world. It simply has so much to offer. Amidst the stunning setting of mountain and lake, over one million visitors a year partake in a staggering range of activities from a sedate steamboat cruise to the heart-stopping bungee jump. You can do almost anything here, from a gentle round of golf to paddling down a river in what looks like a blow-up carrot. Add to that a superb range of accommodation, services, restaurants and cafés and you simply won't know where to turn. And it goes on year-round, day and night. In winter the hiking boots are simply replaced by skis, the T-shirt with a jumper and, after sunset, the activity guide with the wine glass, knife and fork. It just goes on and on.

▶▶ *For Sleeping, Eating and other listings, see pages 611-623.*

Getting there **Queenstown airport** ① *8 km east of the town in Frankton, T03-442 3505, www.queenstownairport.co.nz*, receives direct daily flights from Auckland, Christchurch, Wellington and Dunedin with **Air New Zealand**, T03-441 4870. There are also regular flights from Sydney in summer and both Sydney and Brisbane in winter. **Qantas**, T0800-0014 0014/T03-441 4352, also offers winter services out of Sydney and Brisbane. Note that the international schedules change regularly due to the stiff competition. Several small domestic operators offer flights to Milford, including **Air Fiordland**, T0800-107505/T03-442 3404, and **Milford Sound Flightseeing**, T03-442 2686, see Activities and tours, page 618. From the airport, **ConnectaBus**, T03-441 4471, costs $6 into town. **Kiwi Shuttle**, T03-442 2107 or **Super Shuttle**, T0800-748885/ T03-442 3640, serve the airport door to door. A taxi will set you back about $30.

By road, Queenstown is 486 km from Christchurch, 283 km from Dunedin, 68 km from Wanaka and 170 km from Te Anau (Milford Sound 291 km). The town is served daily by **Intercity**, T03-379 9020/T03-442 4100, www.intercitycoach.co.nz (Dunedin/ Christchurch via Mount Cook/Te Anau/Franz Josef); **Atomic Shuttles**, T03-322 8883, www.atomictravel.co.nz (Dunedin/Christchurch/Invercargill/Greymouth); **Southern Link**, T03-358 8355, www.southernlinkcoaches.co.nz (Dunedin/Christchurch); **Nakedbus.com** offers cheap internet fares to Christchurch and Dunedin; **Mount Cook Landline**, T0800-800904, serves Christchurch via Mount Cook. Fares to Dunedin start from $40, Christchurch $65. **Catch-a-Bus**, T03-479 9960, www.catchabus.co.nz, goes daily to Dunedin from $40. The backpacker-orientated **Bottom Bus**, T03-434 7370, www.bottombus.co.nz, serves Dunedin and the Southern Scenic Route to Invercargill and Te Anau, four times weekly. **Intercity**, **Atomic Shuttles**, and the recommended **Wanaka Connexions**, T0800-244844/T03-443 9122, www.wanakaconnexions.co.nz, run from Christchurch/Dunedin/Te Anau/Invercargill and are recommended for transport to Wanaka (several times daily), from $25. The smaller shuttle operators **Topline Tours**, T03-249 8059, www.toplinetours.co.nz, and **Tracknet**, T03-249 7777, www.tracknet.net, also go to Te Anau from $40. For bus trips to Milford Sound, see pages 654 and 658 .

Getting around The **Connectabus**, T03-441 4471, www.connectabus.com, stops at most major hotels and accommodation establishments. It offers a day pass for $13 , which can be a good way to negotiate the town (timetable from the VIC/I-Site).

Ski Shuttle, T03-442 8106, www.skishuttle.co.nz, and **Alpine Taxis**, T03-442 6666, are the principal ski field shuttle operators serving Cardrona, Coronet Peak, the Remarkables and Treble Cone, from $35. **Arrowtown Bus**, T03-442 1900/ T027-436 7347, runs shuttles to Arrowtown (stops outside McDonald's) five times a day from 0945, from $15 return, while **Connectabus** offers a 'Double-Decker Bus Tour' T03-441 4471, top of the Mall 0930 and 1330 to Arrowtown via several attractions, from $38 return. **Backpacker Express**, T03-442 9939, www.glenorchyinfocentre.co.nz, runs daily buses to Glenorchy. For taxis, car rental and bike hire see Transport, page 622. You are advised to book car rental well in advance in summer.

For detailed information on tramping track transport and trailhead bookings contact the **Information and Track Centre** (see Tourist information below). **Tracknet**, T03-2497 777, www.tracknet.net, are the specialist tramping track operators to Te Anau (Kepler/Milford/Dusky). For Glenorchy and beyond (Routeburn/Greenstone-Caples/Rees-Dart) contact **Backpacker Express**, T03-442 9939, info@glenorchyinfo centre.co.nz. For water taxi transport via Lake Wakatipu and up the Rees/Dart, contact **Glenorchy Cruising**, T03-442 9955, wakatipu@xtra.co.nz, or **Backpacker Express**.

Tourist information There is total information overload in Queenstown. For impartial advice head straight to the very efficient and busy **Queenstown Travel and Visitor Centre** ① *below the Clock Tower, corner of Shotover and Camp sts, T0800-668888, T03-442 4100, www.queenstown-vacation.com and www.queenstown-nz.co.nz, open*

0700-1900 (winter 1800). **DoC** ① *37 Shotover St, T03-442 7935,* queenstownvc @doc.govt.nz, is next to the **Information and Track Centre** ① *37 Shotover St, T03-442 9708, www.infotrack.co.nz, daily 0830-1000, winter Mon-Fri 0900-1700, Sat-Sun 0930-1630*, which provides up-to-date information on local walks and major tramps, and deals with transportation and hut bookings. It also offers gear hire and has the latest weather forecasts. The DoC office closes in winter. The **Real Journeys**

Queenstown

To Supermarket & 32
Queenstown Hill Walkway ▲ To 21

N

| 0 metres | 100 |
| 0 yards | 100 |

Sleeping ⬤
A-Line **1** *C3*
Alpine Sun Motel **2** *C3*
Alpine Village
  Motor Inn **23** *D3*
Blue Peaks Lodge &
  Apartments **3** *C3*
Bumbles Backpackers **4** *C1*
Chalet Queenstown
  B&B **22** *D3*
Coronation Lodge **24** *C3*
Creekside Campervan
  Park **5** *A2*
Dairy **6** *B2*
Discovery Lodge **30** *C2*

Eichardt's **31** *C2*
Glebe Luxury
  Apartments **20** *C3*
Heritage **28** *D1*
Hippo Lodge **8** *B3*
Hurleys **9** *C3*
Lakefront Apartments **18** *C1*
Lakeside Motel **10** *C1*
Lodges **11** *C1*
Matakauri Lodge **26** *D1*
Millennium **12** *C3*
Novotel Gardens **7** *C2*
Point Luxury
  Apartments **21** *A3*
Punatapu **27** *D1*
Queenstown
  House B&B **13** *B3*
Queenstown Lakeview
  Motor Park **14** *C1*
Queenstown Lodge &
  Fernhill Apartments **29** *D1*
Queenstown YHA **15** *D1*

Scallywags **16** *D1*
Sofitel **25** *C1*
Southern Laughter;
  Sir Cedrics **17** *B2*
Waterfront **19** *C1*

Eating ⬤
Bathhouse **2** *C2*
Boardwalk **3** *C2*
Brazz on the Green **1** *B2*
Coco **13** *B2*
Cow **8** *C2*
Dux de Lux & McNeill's
  Cottage Brewery **17** *C2*
Ferg's Burgers **24** *C2*
Gantley's **32** *A3*
Habebes **10** *C2*
HMS Brittannia **11** *C2*
Joe's Garage **12** *C2*
Little India **14** *B2*
Loaded Hog **15** *C1*
Minami Jujisei **18** *C2*

Naff Caff **19** *C1*
O'Connells Food
  Hall **20** *B2*
Pasta Pasta
  Cucina **21** *C2*
Pog Mahone's **23** *C2*
Skyline **27** *A1*
Tatler **29** *C2*
Vudu Café **30** *C2*

Bars & clubs ⬤
Bunker **4** *C2*
Chico's **6** *C2*
Lone Star &
  Rattlesnake **16** *B1*
Minus 5C **33** *C1*
Morrison's **22** *C2*
Red Rock **25** *B2*
Tardis **28** *C2*
World **31** *B2*

Visitors Centre ① *Steamer Wharf, Lakefront Drive, To3-249 7416/To800-656501, www.realjourneys.co.nz*, deals with a multitude of pleasures and trips to Milford and the Fiordland National Park. It also owns the *TSS Earnslaw Steamship*. ►► *For details, see Activities and tours, pages 610 and 616.*

Background

The first European known to have visited the vicinity was Scottish sheep farmer Donald Hay, who explored Lake Wakatipu in 1859, and also gave his name to Lake Hayes near Arrowtown. From this point on, several sheep drovers set up camp along the eastern shore of Lake Wakatipu at Queenstown Bay. With the discovery of gold in the Shotover River Valley by prospectors/shearers Thomas Arthur and Harry Redfern in 1862, the race was on. Within a year, over 2000 hopefuls were camped in the area and searching the Shotover and Kawarau for gold. The Shotover is known to be the richest gold-bearing river of its size in the world. Despite that, it only took about a decade before the gold was exhausted and the population declined, falling to a meagre 190 by 1900, most of whom were farmers. By the mid-1900s the town was well on its way to being a popular tourist resort. The name Queenstown is believed to have been bestowed in 1863, when at a public gathering it was agreed that the town and its location were 'fit for a Queen'. Various heads of state have since marvelled at the place.

Sights

Queenstown is compact and easily negotiable by foot. The main street for information and activity bookings is Shotover Street while the **Mall**, bordered by Camp Street to the east and Marine Parade on the waterfront, is the principal shopping and restaurant centre. The **Esplanade** (lakeside) and **Steamer Wharf** also have retail, information and activity outlets. **Queenstown Gardens**, on the southern edge of Queenstown Bay, offers sanctuary from the chaotic town centre.

Perhaps the best place to start is the **Skyline Gondola** ① *Brecon St, To3-441 0101, www.skyline.co.nz, 0900-dusk, gondola $20, child $9; gondola and luge (5 rides) $38, child $28*. Perched on **Bob's Peak**, 450 m above the town, it boasts a world-class view and has a host of activities including The Ledge Bungy, The Luge, The Sky-Swing, paragliding and helicopter flightseeing. The **Kiwi Haka Maori performance**, To3-442 7063, is also based at Skyline with 30-minute shows nightly from $47 (including gondola) and the option of an all-inclusive dinner from $95. Other on-site amenities include shops, a café (0930-2100) and a restaurant (see Eating, page 613). A good time to go up is just before sunset when the golden rays slowly creep up the **Remarkables Range** and the town's lights come on. Then you could perhaps enjoy a meal before watching the bungee jumpers and the novel 'Sky-Swing' below the main building. At night it is quite hard to believe such a place and such activities exist. You can also walk (one hour one way) up to the Skyline Complex via the **Ben Lomond Track** which starts on Lomond Crescent (via Brunswick Street off the Lake Esplanade).

While at the base of the gondola you might like to see the obligatory kiwi and friends in the **Kiwi and Birdlife Park** ① *Brecon St, To3-442 8059, www.kiwibird.co.nz, daily 0900-2100 (winter 0900-1700), $30, child $15*. Set in 8 ha of quiet(ish) pine forest it displays all the usual suspects, including kiwi, morepork (owl), parakeets, tui and of course the 'cheeky kea'. Of the 16 endangered species, the rarest is the delicate black stilt, sadly, one of only about 150 remaining. Added attractions include a free 20-minute conservation show held at 1100, 1330 and 1500 and in the evenings a Maori cultural performance held in conjunction with a traditional Kiwi dinner from $94, child $45 (includes entry to the park); bookings required.

Also in Brecon Street is **Caddy Shack City Mini-Golf** ① *To3-442 6642, 1000-dusk, $15, child $10*, where a plethora of weird and wonderful holes will keep small kids (and big kids) amused for hours on rainy days or evenings. Beside the town centre on the

⁞ The best view in Queenstown

Although it takes a rugged drive and a fair scramble (in summer) to get there, the view of Lake Wakatipu and Queenstown from the **Remarkables Lookout** is worth every rut and step of the journey. Before considering this trip make sure the weather is clear and settled, since you will be more than 2000 m above sea level. Assure that you are well prepared, with warm clothing and proper walking boots and that your car will survive the 1500-m climb up the unsealed road to the ski fields (in winter you may need chains). The ski field road is accessed off SH6 about 2 km south of Frankton. If the ski field is open you might consider taking a shuttle from Queenstown, T03-442 6534. From the Remarkables ski field buildings you are basically trying to reach the top of the Shadow Basin Chair Lift, the base of which is in the main car park. If the

lift is open you have the option of using it, but in summer (or if you fancy the climb) then follow the path that zigzags up the slopes behind the main building to the 'Mid-Station'. From the Mid-Station continue on the path in a rough line with the chairlift until you reach its terminus. The lookout is about 200 m directly behind and further up from this point. On a clear day surrounded by snow, you won't forget it!

From the lookout (2½ hours return) it is then possible to climb and scramble with care, further south along the ridge to the weather station. From here you will have even greater views including Lake Alta, the entire ski field below and north, to Mount Aspiring. On an exceptional day you may even see Mount Cook almost 200 km away.

waterfront the **Queenstown Gardens** are well worth a visit and offer some respite from the crowds. There are oaks, some stunning sequoias and 1500 roses planted in 26 named rose beds. On the way you might like to pop into the historic 1865 **Williams Cottage**, on Marine Parade, which has been restored and now serves as a shop selling quality homeware.

There are also a number of **wineries** around Queenstown that boast surprisingly fine wines (especially Pinot Noir) and claim to be the most southerly vineyards in the world. The most notable include: **The Peregrine** ① *T03-442 4000, www.peregrine wines.co.nz*; **Chard Farm** ① *T03-442 6110, www.chardfarm.co.nz*; **Amisfield Lake Hayes** ① *T03-442 0556, www.amisfield.co.nz*; and **Gibbston Valley** ① *T03-442 6910, www.gvwines.co.nz*, which are on or just off SH6 on the way in to Queenstown. The VIC (I-Site) has details and tours are available. ⟫ *See Activities and tours, page 622.*

Deer Park Heights ① *T03-442 2949, www.thedeerpark.co.nz, daily 0900-dark, 2½-hr tours depart Queenstown at 0930, 1230 and 1530, $75, child $35.* Sitting like an enchanting massive cow-pat between the second 'dog-leg' of Lake Wakatipu and the Remarkables, Range Deer Park Heights has always been a wonderful venue for walking, cycling, soaking up the surrounding views and feeding the occasional deer. But with all the hype that surrounded the *Lord of the Rings* film trilogy it is now the small tarn at the summit (used as a filming location) that is now the major draw. It is perhaps a sad reflection that it took a fictional film and a few actors to advertise its innate beauty, since the view has essentially always been there. So now, most people simply come to see the lake's perfect reflection, take a photo, tick it off as yet another *LOTR* location and completely ignore the deer. But what is perhaps most regretful was the sudden and dramatic increase in entry fees. At three times the price, you now get a guided 'safari', which can be combined with a trip to the Kiwi Birdlife Park or with jet boat and heli-trips. You can also have a champagne while watching the sun set for an extra $5 (departs 1800).

Finally, if you have run out of money or simply want a good laugh, head for the **Kawarau Bungy** (23 km east on SH6) and watch the jumpers. It is a fascinating mix of fear and fun and watching the spectators is just as entertaining.

Activities

The choice is of course vast. There are over 150 activities to choose from, with everything from the tipples of a wine tour to the ripples of jet boating. And Queenstown is not just geared up for the young and the mad. There are activities to suit all ages, from infant to octogenarian and from the able to the disabled. If a 91-year-old can do a bungee jump, surely the possibilities are endless? Of course it is the bungee that made Queenstown famous. If you are prepared to make 'the jump' and have been saving your pennies to do so, then it is here that you must finally pluck up the courage. Heights vary from 40 m to 134 m, and if there is any advice to give (other than psychological and financial counselling) it is: do it in style and go high.

The 'big four' activities in Queenstown are considered to be the **bungee**, **jet boating**, **rafting** and **flightseeing**. Try to consider a variety of pursuits according to the budget at hand. For example, consider something that costs nothing and is rather sedate, like taking a walk to appreciate the stunning views (see box, page 609), since this as just as much 'Queenstown' as anything else. Then by all means get the pulse racing with something high on the 'adren-o-meter', like a bungee, then perhaps something easy-going or an activity you can do nowhere else like a cruise on the *TSS Earnslaw* (see Cruising, page 617). Above all, don't only consider what you are 'supposed' to do, but also what most others do not. Queenstown is special and deserves far more of your attention and imagination.

The moment you arrive you will be confronted with sales and promotional outlets that can sniff your dollars in a dead calm, so be careful. Do not be swayed by reputations or the Las Vegas-style marketing. The big players are **A J Hackett** (Lord of the Bungee) and **Shotover Jet**. A J Hackett has its high-profile office in 'The Station', conveniently located right where the buses stop, at the corner of Shotover and Camp streets, with numerous others surrounding it and biting at their heels.

> **⁑** *If you are unsure about an activity, do not part with your cash. You can't expect a refund if you back out.*

Bookings can be made direct, but most accommodation establishments, especially backpacker hostels, will book on your behalf. The station is also the main pick-up and drop-off point for activities. The best advice is to head to the unbiased **Queenstown Travel and Visitor Centre** (see page 606), have a chat and avail yourself of the leaflets and information, then retire quietly to a coffee shop for a small nervous breakdown.

Activity combos There are a huge number of combo packages available from the main players like **A J Hackett** and **Shotover** to independents like **Adventure Marathon**. Most gravitate (no pun intended) between the 'big four' activities, with the odd 'luge' or movie thrown in. Others offer fishing, trekking, heli-skiing or hiking. If you are short of time a combo is probably the best way to go, and with prices ranging from about $200-500 the savings can be substantial. One of the best, but most demanding combos, is the **Awesome Foursome** ① *Queenstown Combos, T03-442 7318, www.combos.co.nz*, which includes the Nevis Bungy, Shotover jet-boat, rafting and a helicopter flight over Skippers Canyon for $495.

A slightly less demanding package is the **High Five** ① *Shotover, T03-442 5252, $215*, which includes a 3½-hour jet-boat, helicopter, skyline, movie and luge. The half-day (five-hour) helicopter-raft and jet-boat **Triple Challenge** ① *Queenstown Rafting, 35 Shotover St, T03-442 9792, www.rafting.co.nz*, is also good value at $299. If you are still intent on a bungee this could perhaps be combined with one of the Hackett multiple jumps. ⤤ For all Activities and tours, see page 616.

● Sleeping

Queenstown *p605, map p607*

Despite a healthy range of accommodation and around 8500 beds, it is essential to book 2 or 3 days in advance in mid-summer or during the height of the ski season (especially during the Winter Festival in mid-Jul). This particularly applies to backpacker accommodation. To browse the options check out www.queens townaccommodation.co.nz or visit the **Queenstown Accommodation Centre**, 30 Shotover St, T03-442 7518, www.qac.co.nz.

LL Eichardt's Private Hotel, Marine Parade, T03-441 0450, www.eichardtshotel.co.nz. Grand yet discreet, catering to the luxury boutique market, Eichardt's has accrued some lauded international awards and offers all the décor, lavish furnishings and amenities one might expect for the exorbitant price. That said, however, it does have the edge when it comes to a caring, personable service.

LL Millbrook Resort, T03-441 7000, www.millbrook.co.nz. Sumptuous out-of-town choice with a world-class golf course and luxury facilities. It has suites, villas and cottages, 2 restaurants, a bar, and a health and fitness complex.

LL Sofitel, 8 Duke St, T03-450 0045, www.sofitelqueenstown.com. One of the newest and most celebrated hotels sitting in prime position just above the town centre. Luxury rooms, suites and penthouses furnished in European style and in warm shades of beige and brown marry well with the views. The class extends to the facilities and the in-house restaurant, but perhaps, just perhaps, your abiding memory will be of its famous 'little' boy's room in the lobby (go on girls – have a peek!).

LL-L Millennium Hotel, corner of Frankton Rd and Stanley St, T03-441 8888/T0800-227006, www.millenniumhotels.co.nz. Well positioned and close to town. Also has a wide range of suites and all the usual modern well-appointed facilities.

LL-AL Heritage Hotel, 91 Fernhill Rd, T03-442 4988, www.heritagehotels.co.nz. One of the town's most popular chain hotels, located at the western edge of town in a quiet position and commanding fine views back towards the town. Luxury rooms and suites from 1-3 bedrooms with all the standard, quality facilitation. Cosy in-house

restaurant with open fire, and a health club with pool, sauna and spa. Excellent service.

LL-AL Novotel Gardens, corner of Earl St and Marine Parade, T03-442 7750, H5308-RE01@ accor-hotels.com. It wouldn't win any beauty contests from the outside, but this modern hotel is ideally situated on the waterfront by the town centre, and a stone's throw from the peace and quiet of Queenstown Gardens.

AL-A A-Line Hotel, 27 Stanley St, T03-442 7700, www.scenic-circle.co.nz. A cheaper option that offers well-appointed A-frame-style units with great views within 2 mins of the town centre.

Lodges and B&Bs

LL Matakauri Lodge, Farrycroft Row (off Glenorchy Rd), T03-441 1008, www.mata kauri.co.nz. A magnificent B&B set in private bush 5 km west of Queenstown, with uninterrupted views across Lake Wakatipu. Accommodation is in modern villas and fully self-contained suites. The spacious lodge offers a library and 4 fireplaces, while within the grounds a spa pavilion is perfect for that après-ski. A la carte dinners prepared by an in-house executive chef replete with top local wines are all part of the experience.

LL Pear Tree Cottage, 51 Mountain View Rd, T03-442 9340, www.peartree.co.nz. Enchanting B&B at the base of the Coronet Peak ski field. A quiet, tastefully restored 1870s cottage, fully self-contained with 2 bedrooms. In summer, flowers abound.

LL Punatapu, 1113 Rapid Gate (7 km from town on Glenorchy Rd), T03-4426624, www.punatapu.co.nz. A sumptuous B&B with an individually styled 'hamlet' of suites around a central courtyard. The views are stunning and there is a swimming pool, spa, sauna and the works. Contemporary New Zealand Art features heavily and in summer there is usually an artist in residence.

LL Remarkables Lodge, south along SH6, T03-4422720, www.remarkables.co.nz. A well-established renovated luxury lodge set at the base of its namesake mountain range, with a fine reputation. It offers modern facilities and great cuisine but it is the location that really appeals.

LL-L The Dairy, 10 Isle St, T03-442 5164, www.thedairy.co.nz. Central newly renovated

B&B with 13 cosy en suites in period-style house restored and modelled on a 1920s dairy.

LL-L Queenstown House B&B, 69 Hallenstein St, T03-442 9043, www.queenstown house.co.nz. A well-established modern upper-range B&B in a central location overlooking the town. Elegant en suites and new villa suites complete with fireside sitting rooms. Excellent full cooked or continental breakfast. Internet and off-street parking.

L-AL Chalet Queenstown B&B, 1 Dublin St, T03-442 7117, www.chalet.co.nz. Swiss-style chalet in a quiet location, with 5 cosy en suites and excellent hosts. Massage and specialist health therapies are an added attraction.

B-C Scallywags, 27A Lomond Cres, T03-442 7083. A cross between a budget B&B and a backpacker hostel, this is good value, friendly, slow paced and quiet. Dorms, twins and doubles.

Self-contained apartments

Like the main cities, Queenstown has realized the preference for luxury, fully self-contained and serviced apartments. Just a few of the recommended examples are:

LL-AL Glebe Luxury Apartments, corner of Stanley and Beetham sts, T03-441 0310, www.theglebe.co.nz. 5 star and central with off-street parking.

LL-AL Point Luxury Apartments, 239 Frankton Rd, T0800-222239, www.thepoint.net.nz.

L-AL Lakefront Apartments, 26 The Esplanade, T03-441 8800, www.queenstown accommodation.co.nz. Long established and waterside.

Motels

There are over 75 to choose from, so shop around. The VIC (I-Site) has full listings. Prices are generally more expensive than elsewhere, especially in mid-summer, so do not necessarily expect the value for money that you are used to. Those on the waterfront offer superb views, but this is reflected in the price.

LL-AL Coronation Lodge, 10 Coronation Drive, T03-441 0860, www.coronation lodge.nz. New with spacious rooms with natural wood abounding, well placed close to both the town centre and the sanctuary of the botanical gardens

L-AL Blue Peaks Lodge and Apartments, corner of Stanley and Sydney sts, T03-442

9224, www.bluepeaks.co.nz. In an elevated position and conveniently located a short distance from the town centre the motel complex offers standard units, while a sister property located opposite Queenstown Gardens offers very tidy self-contained apartments, again a very short distance from the town centre. Off-street parking.

L-AL Hurleys, T03-4425999/T0800-589879, www.hurleys.co.nz. Has tasteful fully self-contained studios supported with great facilities, centrally located.

L-AL Lodges, 8 Lake Esplanade, T03-442 7552, www.thelodges.co.nz. Suites and apartments on the lakefront.

AL Lakeside Motel, 18 The Esplanade, T03-442 8976, www.queenstownaccommoda tion.co.nz. 15 no-nonsense units, all with views.

AL Waterfront, 109 Beach Rd, T03-4425123/ T0800-889889, www.thewaterfront.co.nz. As the name suggests, it's in prime position.

AL-A Alpine Village Motor Inn, 633 Frankton Rd (on the way into town), T03-442 7795, alpinevillage@xtra.co.nz. A large place best noted for the views of the Remarkables from the rooms or chalets. In-house restaurant.

A Alpine Sun Motel, 18 Hallenstein St, T03-442 8482, www.alpinesun.co.nz. Basic but comfortable and well positioned.

C-D Queenstown Lakeview Motor Park, Off Brecon St, T03-442 7252, www.holiday park.net.nz. Although not a motel the modern units here are often very good value, especially for small groups. It is also centrally located and has facilities on a par with any standard mid-range motel.

Budget options/backpacker hostels

As you can imagine Queenstown is not short of backpacker hostels and with around 20 establishments both old and new, staid or funky, there is plenty to choose from. This is not the complete listing, just those that we recommend or that stand out. In summer you should book at least 5 days in advance.

AL -C Queenstown Lodge and Fernhill Apartments, Sainsbury Rd (a little further out at the west end of town), Fernhill, T03-442 7107/T0800-756343 , www.queenstown lodge.co.nz. Reasonably priced ski lodge-style property located at the western fringe of town. It is quiet, has off-street parking, a pizza restaurant, spa, sauna and most of the rooms offer excellent views across Lake

Wakatipu. The lodge also administers a new, self-contained apartment complex for which clients have full use of lodge facilities.
AL-D Discovery Lodge, 47-49 Shotover St, T03-441 1185, www.dlq.co.nz. A purpose-built affiliate of the **ACB Backpackers** in Auckland, **Pipi Patch** in Paihia and **Hot Rocks** in Rotorua. Set in the heart of town it is pitched somewhere between a budget hotel and backpacker hostel with tidy en suite doubles with TV and bath and shower to dorms with shared facilities. Well-facilitated throughout with travel and job search centre, good security, high-speed internet café and nightclub. Being right in the heart of town it is a happening place and not one for quiet sanctuary. As ever, parking is also a problem.
B-D Bumbles Backpackers, corner of Brunswick St and Lake Esplanade, T03-442 6298, www.bumblesbackpackers.co.nz. Well-established 50-bed hostel, spotlessly clean and efficient. Has a good range of well-heated dorms, singles, twins and doubles, all with modern facilities and views. Storage, drying rooms, internet and – importantly – off-street parking.
B-D Hippo Lodge, 4 Anderson Heights, T03-442 5785, www.hippolodge.co.nz. A fine place with the best backpackers' view in town. It is modern, friendly, clean and well equipped, with dorms, twins and doubles (1 en suite), making it worth every step of the climb to get there. Parking can be a problem.
B-D Queenstown YHA, 80 Lake Esplanade (at the western end of town), T03-4428413, yhaqutn@yha.org.nz. Deservedly popular and with a wide range of comfortable shared, twin and double rooms and modern facilities. Internet. Off-street parking.
B-D Southern Laughter: Sir Cedrics, 4 Isle St (towards the gondola, but still well positioned for town), T03-441 8828, www.southernlaughter.co.nz. Small, but well established, has a good atmosphere and facilities, including a spa, Sky TV, 24-internet and off-street parking. The Larsson cartoon theme will keep you chuckling on rainy days.

Motorcamps and campsites
A-D Creeksyde Campervan Park, 54 Robins Rd, T03-4429447, creeksyde@camp.co.nz. Centrally located and has modern motel units, flats, cabins, lodge rooms and good

facilities including spa. It perhaps takes too much advantage of its position with charges and gets busy in summer, so pre book. Supermarket very close by.
C-D Queenstown Lakeview Motor Park, Off Brecon St, T03-442 7252, www.holiday park.net.nz. After a complete revamp this park has increased dramatically in popularity and stature. The complex is the closest park to the town centre (2 mins) and includes tidy and good-value studio units, en suite cabins, luxury flats, as well as the standard powered/ tent sites. There is a spacious kitchen block with internet and lockable food cupboards. Note that the showers are not broken: they take 2 x 50c pieces. Also good for information and activity bookings.

Eating

Queenstown *p605, map p607*
There are over 100 eateries in Queenstown with a choice and quality to compete with any of the larger cities in New Zealand. There are Chinese, Mexican, Indian, Korean, Lebanese and Italian restaurants alongside those serving traditional New Zealand fare with many doubling as bars and nightspots. Again, although prices can be slightly elevated, there are restaurants to suit all budgets as well as 2 unique eating options in the form of the Gondola restaurant which can be combined with a Maori cultural performance and the *TSS Earnslaw*, see Activities and tours, page 617.
The Boardwalk, 1st floor, Steamer Wharf, T03-442 5630, daily from 1200. Well known for its superb seafood and great views. They are still dining out on the fact that it was Bill Clinton's choice when he visited in 1999.
Gantley's, Arthur's Point Rd, T03-442 8999, www.gantleys.co.nz, daily from 1830. A very romantic affair set in a historic stone building 7 km out of town towards Arrowtown. Award winning, the equal of the others above and its wine list, like its cuisine, is superb.
Skyline Restaurant, at the Skyline Gondola Complex, Brecon St, T03-441 0101, daily, lunch buffet 1200-1400, dinner from 1800. Offers a 6-course 'Taste of New Zealand' buffet which includes roast meats, seafood, local produce and salads followed by dessert and cheeseboard from $43 (lunch),

$67 (dinner). The views are exceptional, even at night. You can also combine your visit and meal with the Kiwi Haka Maori cultural performance from $95, child $48.

TT-TT Tatler, at the west end of the Mall, T03-442 8372, daily 1000-late. Modern, stylish and popular not only for traditional New Zealand fare including lamb but also seafood with chowder a speciality. There is also some fine and regular live jazz.

TT Bathhouse, T03-442 5625, daily from 1000. Perched on the edge of the beach, next to Queenstown Gardens is this very romantic place. With an imaginative menu, it is a lovely spot for both lunch and dinner.

TT Brazz On the Green, 1 Athol St, T03-442 4444, daily from 1100. Modern and classy, and given its open fires, especially popular with the après-ski crowd in winter. Traditional New Zealand/European menu and a fine place to watch the world go by.

TT The Cow, Cow Lane, T03-442 8588, daily 1200-2300. Also popular, though more for its exterior aesthetics and atmosphere than its food. Set in a former stone milking shed it is a little cramped but full of character. Pizza and pasta are the specialities.

TT Dux de Lux and McNeill's Cottage Brewery, 14 Church St, T03-4429 688, daily from 1130. A nice mix of heritage and atmosphere, it's another award-winner with a good selection of gourmet pizzas, open fire outside, live bands at the weekend and, of course, some fine home brewed ales.

TT HMS Britannia in The Mall, T03-442 9600. Good if you have kids or simply enjoy good seafood. It is a wee bit on the expensive side but the portions are huge and the walls are something of a museum exhibit.

TT Little India, 15 Shotover St, T03-442 5335, Good Indian food. Sit-in or takeaway.

TT Loaded Hog, Steamer Wharf, T03-441 2969. Great for pub grub and beer.

TT Minami Jujisei, 45 Beach St, T03-442 9854. Decent Japanese choice.

TT Pasta Pasta Cucina, 6 Brecon St, T03-442 6762, daily from 1800. A popular pizza place.

TT Pog Mahone's, 14 Rees St, T03-4425382. Irish pub with good food and atmosphere.

T Ferg's Burgers, Cow Lane. The late-night munchy option.

T Habebes, Wakatipu Arcade, Rees St, T03-442 9861, daily 1100-1800. Very popular café for vegetarian and Middle Eastern takeaways.

T O'Connell's Food Hall, Camp St. Daily from 0800. The usual cheap buffet lunch outlets.

Cafés

Coco, further up towards town next to the VIC (I-Site), T03-442 8542. It's small but in a perfect position for that essential caffeine hit after arriving back from all the activities based at the 'The Station'.

Joe's Garage, originally in Camp St and now it seems successfully relocated to Searle Lane nearby Joe's. is the secret hang out for locals and noted for its great coffee and light meals.

Naff Caff, 1/66 Shotover St, T03-4428211, daily from 0730. One of Queenstown's best, with light snacks, coffee and a value breakfast.

Vudu Café, Beach St, T03-4425357. Has a loyal local following and is good for breakfast.

Supermarkets

Alpine Food Centre, Upper Shotover St, Mon-Sat 0800-2000, Sun 0900-2000. Handy for groceries and tramping food supplies.

First Choice, 1 km out along Gorge Rd (Skippers and Coronet Peak Rd), T03-441 1252, Mon-Sun 0800-2100. The largest and most convenient.

New World, Franktown (6 km), T03-442 3045. This is the cheapest.

⊙ Pubs, bars and clubs

Queenstown *p605, map p607*
Pubs and bars

Queenstown is very much a party town and, particularly at New Year, it goes off like a firecracker. It can all be a lot of fun, but at its busiest don't go out looking for refined culture and conversation. With so much adrenaline and testosterone flying around it doesn't go far beyond the standard yelps about the 'awesome' bungee jumping, or the double-flip-half-hernia on the snowboard, maaaan. The well-established favourites known for a good beer and atmosphere are the **Loaded Hog**, Steamer Wharf; the Irish offerings **Pog Mahone's**, Rees St; the smaller more sedate **Morrison's**, Level 1, Stratton House, Beach St; and the quaint **McNeill's Brewery**, Church St.

That said, the latest hype surrounds the intriguing sculpted ice bar called **Minus 5C**, Steamer Wharf, T03-442 6050, daily from 1030. Of course it depends where you come from really. If you are just off the plane from Texas or Australia, or if you have had a hot day on the ski slopes or are coming down from a bungee jump, the thought of a cocktail in a beautifully sculpted ice cavern may be very appealing. But for the average European, particularly the Irish or the Scots, a bar made of ice? Big deal, try a car made of ice, a street made of ice, a toilet seat made of ice, a girlfriend made of ice – its just like being back home in mid-Feb. Besides, the pub is exactly where Europeans go to get away from the stuff. That said it is the unusual experience that counts and it is indeed impressive. Entry costs $30 includes the first drink and you are of course kitted out with warm jackets and gloves. Naturally this is more a tourist attraction than a conventional bar, so don't expect to settle in for a session or a game of darts.

More conventional and popular with the upwardly mobile is the **Boiler Room** in the Steamer Wharf; **The Tatler**; **The Mall**; and the hard to find **The Bunker**, Cow Lane. **Red Rock**, 48 Camp St, T03-442 6850, is a well-known place to 'acquaint oneself with the opposite sex' as is **The Lone Star**, Brecon St, and **Rattlesnake** (upstairs). They all provide regular live music and DJs beats and are the favoured haunts of the younger set.

Clubs
As far as late-night drinking and dancing goes, try **Chico's**, at the bottom of the Mall (open until 0230); **The Tardis**; and **The Bunker**, Cow Lane. **Sub Culture**, Church St, is a new and popular nightclub. **The World**, Shotover St, and bars on Brecon St are the most commercial, chat-up (or throw-up) venues with regular happy hours. Most stay open until about 0230.

🞄 Entertainment

Queenstown *p605, map p607*
The **Embassy Cinema** is in The Mall, T03-442 9990. There is also the **Queenstown Wharf Casino**, Steamer Wharf, T03-441 1495, 1100-0300, for those wishing to try their luck.

⊛ Festivals and events

Queenstown *p605, map p607*
Throughout the year there are many multi-sport events from triathlons to mountain traverses, peak to peaks, jet-boat races, marathons and even horse cavalcades. For more details visit www.queenstown-nz.co.nz.
Jan Glenorchy Races (1st Sat in Jan). A local affair regarded as reflecting Glenorchy's true colours as a wild west frontier town.
Feb Central Otago Wine Festival. Gourmands gather in the town's gardens to sample the delicacies produced by 15 local vineyards.
Mar Arrowtown Autumn Festival (late Mar) and the **Ben Lomond Assault** (late Mar). Colourful and exhausting race to the town's famous 1747 m lookout.
Apr Queenstown Half Marathon (mid-Apr). More strain on 2 legs. **Silverstone Race to the Sky** (mid-Apr). 4WD races in the Cardrona Valley, the highlight of which is a race to the summit to see who is 'king of the mountain'.
Jun/Jul Lindauer Queenstown Winter Festival, www.winterfestival.co.nz. Queenstown's most famous and popular event (9 days), which of course has its focus on skiing, but also involves many other forms of entertainment from live concerts, arts and fashion events to madcap races.
Sep Spring Carnival (mid-Sep). More extreme and zany ski competitions at the Remarkables Ski Area.
Oct Queenstown Jazz Festival (Labour weekend), www.queenstownjazz.co.nz.
Dec Christmas and particularly **New Year** see the town a-buzz with Kiwis and foreigners.

⊙ Shopping

Queenstown *p605, map p607*
Gallery Oceanic, 43 Beach St, T03-442 6076. One of the finest galleries in town with an eclectic range of artworks and jewellery.
Outside Sports, Shotover St, T03-442 8883, www.outdoorsports.co.nz, 0700-2200. For new sports/outdoor/ski equipment.
Small Planet Recycling Co, 17 Shotover St, T03-442 6393. For second-hand outdoor and ski equipment.
Whitcoulls, Beach St, T03-442 9739. The principal bookshop and stationer in town.

▲ Activities and tours

See also p610

Queenstown *p605, map p607*

Kingston Flyer, T03-2488848, www.kingston flyer.co.nz. The famous vintage steam train puffs along for 1¼ hrs on a 14-km track from Kingston, 47 km south of Queenstown from Sep to mid-May, daily 1000 and 1330, morning pick-ups available from Queenstown. Return ride $40, child $20, one way $30/$15 with transfer from $100, child $50.

Quirky Queenstown Historical Walking Tours, T03-4420572. In the town itself you can learn something of its interesting past on the 1-hr historical perambulation followed by a welcome libation in McNeill's Cottage Brewery. Trips depart from the west end of the Mall at 1130, 1330 and 1530. The immediate Queenstown area offers many excellent walks from 1-hr to ½-day. The DoC Visitor Centre on Shotover St has displays and can advise on the local alternatives.

Remarkable Experience, T03-4098578, www.remarkableexperience.co.nz. Operates a fully restored open-topped 1937 Chevrolet convertible bus on a 3-hr tour visiting local sights including Arrowtown (see page 624) and Lake Hayes amongst others and the alfresco factor just adds to the experience. Departs daily 0930 and 1330, $125, child $58.

Skyline (Gondola) Complex, T03-4410101, www.skyline.co.nz. Amongst the multitude of activities available at the Skyline above the town is the **Luge**, the rather tame cousin of the famous course in Rotorua. The gondola trip and 5 rides will cost $38, child $28 (0930-dusk). Also based at the Skyline, is one of the few opportunities to enjoy a **Maori Concert and Feast**. If you missed out in Rotorua this is your chance. The performance alone costs from $47, child $26 (includes gondola) while the performance and dinner costs from $95, child $48.

Sunrise Balloons, T03-442 0781, www.ballooningnz.com. Offers a 3-hr flight with champagne breakfast for $345, child $225. It is expensive, but given the scenery it is a great venue (0530 summer/0830 winter).

Bungee jumping

The first commercial bungee jump in the world was created at **Kawarau Bridge**, about 12 km east of Queenstown, by A J Hackett and

associates in 1988. Although perhaps the most famous spot and certainly the most accessible, at 43 m it is now dwarfed by most of the others. Since 1988 Hackett has created several other sites in and around Queenstown. The 47-m urban **Ledge' Bungee**, beside the Skyline complex above Queenstown is the baby of the set while the mightiest and certainly the best, is the awesome and the highest (ground based) 134-m **Nevis Highwire**. Jump prices range from $150 for the Kawarau and a cool $210 for the Nevis. This includes a T-shirt, but videos are usually extra. Given the prices and the fact you may only ever do it once the best advice is to 'go high'– the Nevis – it is simply rude not to.

A J Hackett, at 'The Station', corner of Shotover and Camp sts, T03-442 4007/ T0800-286495, www.ajhackett.com. Daily 0700-2100, winter 0800-2000. For all bungee bookings.

Bungee variations

It hasn't taken long for the Great Adrenaline Professors to realize that wetting your pants at high speed need not necessarily occur at vertical angles alone, so the fiendishly clever-and-rich chappies have now come up with various cunning 'swing' contraptions. These are also wonderful fun and accrue the same hefty dry cleaning bills.

Ledge Sky Swing, Skyline Complex, book through A J Hackett (see Bungee jumping, above). At 47 m high, this is the more sedate option, from $99 including Gondola.

Shotover Canyon Swing, T08002SWING, www.canyonswing.co.nz. This is the real monster. We won't get in to the technical details, suffice to say 109-m-high, 60-m freefall, 200-m arc using various jump styles from the 'Backwards', 'Forwards', the 'Elvis Cutaway' and even the 'Gimp Boy Goes to Hollywood'. Prices start at $159, spectators $29. Souvenir underpants extra.

Canyoning

Note, this canyoning lark is not one for the agoraphobic or the 'damn it darling, my shoes are wet' type.

Routeburn Canyoning, T03-441 4386/T0800-222696 www.gycanyoning.co.nz. Offers an attractive package that involves a part walk and canyoning session on the Routeburn Track near Glenorchy. As well as the great

30-min walk and scenery along the initial stage of the track the trip involves abseiling, scrambling, rappelling and plunging your way down a mountain river. Full day $225.
Twelve-Mile Delta, T03-441 4468, www.xiimile.co.nz. Although Wanaka is famed for its canyoning activities, this outfit offers abseiling as well as canyoning, departs twice daily 0900 and 1330, from $145.

Children's activities
If you have kids and want to do the family thing, or conversely leave them in somebody else's capable hands, try one of the companies below. A fine resource for sourcing other activities for children of families is the *Kidz Go* magazine, available free from the VIC (I-Site), www.kidzgo.co.nz.
Activekids, T03-442 1003, activekids@ xtra.co.nz. Qualified care and day trips to Arrowtown and around Queenstown for those 7 years and up.
Family Adventures, T03-442 8836, www.familyadventures.co.nz. Offers full- or half-day 'sedate' rafting trips for families from $150, child $110.

Climbing, abseiling and mountaineering
The possibilities are endless, and the Mt Aspiring National Park provides world-class venues. Most of the facilities and operators are based in Wanaka.
Queenstown Events Centre, Joe O'Connell Drive, Frankton, T03-442 3664, www.qt events.co.nz. Has a 12-m climbing wall, $12, child $6, Mon-Fri 0900-2100, Sat-Sun 0900-1700. There are also instructor supervised nights Tue and Thu.
Queenstown Mountain Guiding, corner of Shotover and Rees sts, T03-441 2300, www.mountainguiding.co.nz. Offers a wide variety of trips from glacier walks and heli-hikes to expeditions and instruction courses. It also guides on Mt Aspiring, Mt Cook and Mt Tasman. Prices range from about $550 for a full-day of rock climbing with instruction (depending on numbers) to about $21,000 for a 4-day mountain climb with 2:1 instruction.

Cruising
MV Yvalda, T027-434 5555. Offers 2-hr or overnight lake cruises aboard the lovingly restored 1936 ketch. Call for schedules/prices.

Real Journeys, beside the Steamer Wharf, T0800-656503, www.realjourneys.co.nz It won't take you long to spot the delightful **TSS Earnslaw** (TSS stands for Two Screw Steamer), plying the waters of Lake Wakatipu from the Steamer Wharf in Queenstown Bay. The **TSS Earnslaw**, named after the highest peak in the region, Mt Earnslaw (2819 m), was launched at the most southerly end of Lake Wakatipu, Kingston, in 1912 and burns 1 ton of coal per hour. Despite her propensity to belch half of New Zealand's 'Kyoto-nasty smoke quota' into the air she is a lovely sight indeed and there are a number of cruising options available. A standard 1 hr 35-min cruise heads west across the lake to its southern edge to the Walter Peak Station. It departs from the Steamer Wharf, Oct-Apr every 2 hrs from 1000-2000 (reduced winter schedule), from $40, child $15. A 3½-hr cruise, plus a farm tour of the Walter Peak Station which is designed to give an insight into typical Kiwi farming life (and to access lots of affectionate animals), costs $60, child $15. With a BBQ it's $22 extra. A 4-hr evening dinner cruise costs $99, child $49.50.
There are also 40-min horse trekking and wagon rides available at Walter Peak from $99 (all inclusive). Numerous cruise/bus and cruise/fly options on Milford and Doubtful Sounds operate out of Queenstown (see Milford and Doubtful Sound, page 657 and page 661).

Fishing
The region provides some excellent trout and salmon fishing, and there are numerous guides offering simple half-day to full-day heli-fishing trips. Prices vary from around $100 per person for a 2-hr trip, to $400-650 for the full day. Heli trips range from half-day for $800 to a full day for $3,250, both for 2 people. A compulsory fishing licence costs $18.50 per day.
Born to Fish, T03-248 8890, www.borntofish.co.nz.
Over the Top Helicopters, T03-442 2233, www.flynz.co.nz.
Queenstown Fishing Guides, T03-442 5363, www.wakatipu.co.nz.
Stu Dever, T03-442 6371, www.fishing-queenstown.co.nz.

▲ Snow business

Queenstown is as much a winter ski resort as it is a summer madhouse. From June to September the two local ski fields of Coronet Peak and the Remarkables spring into action.

Coronet Peak (1649 m) is the larger of the two and the more accessible (25 minutes via SH6 west and Lower Shotover Road). It also has a longer season, night skiing (Friday and Saturday 1600-2200), and a brasserie, bar, café and crèche. Slopes are suitable for all levels, with intermediate skiers being the best catered for. A day lift pass costs $79, youth (7-17) $41, under 7's free, T03-442 4620.

The Remarkables ski field is higher (1935 m) and accessed from SH6, south of Frankton (45 minutes). The road is steep and often requires snow chains. Shuttle buses from Queenstown are recommended. Being the highest in the region, the snow conditions are often superior, and then, of course, there are the stunning views. Slopes cater for all levels of skier and snowboarder as

well as cross-country. A day lift pass costs $74, youth (7-17) $39, under 10's, free, T03-442 4615.

Also within range of Queenstown are the **Cardrona** (45 km), T03-443 7411, www.cardrona.com, and **Treble Cone**, T03-4437443, www.treblecone.co.nz (95 km).

Getting there The standard group fares (four) to Coronet are around $35, Remarkables $85 and Cardrona $155 one way. See Ins and outs, page 600, for transport options. For detailed information on both ski fields get your hands on the *Queenstown Winter Resort Guide* from the VIC (I-Site), or visit the website www.nzski.com or www.snow.co.nz.

Rental equipment One-day ski/boots/poles rental costs $38; youth $27; one-day snowboard and boots $51, youth $40. Group lessons: 2 hrs from $47, youth $34; personal lessons from $85 per hr. For hire shops, see Directory, page 623.

Snow reports For snow reports, T0900-99766 ($0.99/min), www.met service.co.nz, or the resort websites.

Flightseeing

There are numerous options available and you are advised to shop around. If you don't have time to reach **Milford Sound** by road then a scenic flight is highly recommended. Note that there are numerous fly-cruise-fly and bus-cruise-fly options on offer to Milford. Other flightseeing options include **Mt Cook** and the glaciers, **Mt Aspiring National Park** and the **Catlins Coast**. Prices range from a 30-min local flight costing from $175 to the full 4-hr Milford Sound and Mt Cook experience, from $375; shop around. Fixed-wing operators offering flights to Milford and Fiordland are listed below. See also helicopter flights, and Lord of the Rings flights, below.
Air Fiordland, T03-442 3404, www.airfiordland.com.
Air Milford, T03-442 2351, www.airmilford .co.nz. A small personable company with lots of local knowledge and a flexible itinerary.

Air Wakatipu, T03-442 3148, www.flying.co.nz.
Milford Sound Scenic Flights, T03-442 3065, www.milfordflights.co.nz.
Queenstown Air, T03-442 2244, www.queenstownair.co.nz.

Helicopter flights

Prices range from a 20-min local flight across the Remarkables from $200, to the full 'Milford Extravaganza' from around $1000. For more information on flightseeing trips to Milford Sound and Fiordland see Milford page 652.
Actionflite, T03-442 9708/T0800-360264, www.actionflite.co.nz. If you fancy a flight with a difference try the 3-hr aerobatics 'Pitts Special'. Labelled as the 'Ferrari of the skies', it reaches speeds of up to 300 kph with 3G turns. Guaranteed to get your angst waters flowing. Trips cost from $300 for 15 mins.

Glacier Southern Lakes, T03-442 3016/
T0800-801616, www.heli-flights.co.nz.
The Helicopter Line, T03-442 3034/
T0800-500575 www.helicopter.co.nz.
Heliworks, T03-441 4011/T0800-464354,
www.heliworks.co.nz.
Over The Top Helicopters, T0800-123359/
T03-442 2233, www.flynz.co.nz . Provides
a great range of Milford, Queenstown,
heli-fishing and heli-skiing options.

Fly-by-wire
Fly-by-Wire, Rees St, T03-442 2116/
T0800-359299, www.flybywire.co.nz.
The sister operation to the original experience,
created in Paekakariki, Wellington Region,
which sadly had to cease operations due
to flooding. Nonetheless Queenstown's
operations are quite literally in full swing,
5 mins from $139.

Golf
Arrowtown (see page 624) has a nice course
at Centennial Av, T03-442 1719, from $45.
Frisbee Golf Course, Queenstown Gardens.
Of course Queenstown would have one of
these, but don't be surprised if a dog
disappears with your frisbee. Contact
Outside Sports, Shotover St, T03-442 8883,
$2, who sell frisbees, but no dog treats.
Millbrook Resort, Malaghan's Rd, Arrowtown,
T03-441 7010, proshop@millbrook.co.nz.
One of the best courses in New Zealand.
It was designed by former Kiwi ace Bob
Charles and opened in 1993. It is renowned
for its long fairways, water hazards and, of
course, its views. Green fees from $135.

Horse trekking
For other operators see Glenorchy, page 627.
Moonlight Stables, 15 mins from
Queenstown near Lake Hayes, T03-442
1240, www.moonlightcountry.co.nz.
A 1½-hr ride costs from $75, child $45. Full
day treks, fishing trips also available.
Shotover Stables, based at Arthurs
Point, T03-442 9708. Offer half- or full-
day treks from $65. Another option is to
combine a lake cruise (TSS Earnslaw) with
horse trekking and a visit to Walter Peak
from $99 (see Cruising above). Horse and
carriage rides are available in town from $25;
depart Steamer Wharf 1200-1600 and
1800-late (seasonal).

Jet boating
Such is the marketing, somehow you seem
familiar with the Shotover Jet before you
even arrive in Queenstown. That indelible
blurred image of a red boat full of smiley
faces and Captain Cool in shades at the
wheel. Jet boating is one of the 'Big 4'
activities in Queenstown and, other than the
thrills of the precipitous Shotover Gorge,
there are also other independent operations
on the Kawarau and the superb
aesthetics of the Dart River.
Shotover Jet, The Station, Shotover St,
T03-442 8570/T0800-SHOTOVER , www.shot
overjet.com. The original company, having
been in existence for over 30 years, offers the
almost 'must-do' operation on the Shotover
River – the only folks permitted to do so on
the lower reaches. An efficient, safe and
thrilling 30-min, 70-kph 'blat' down the river
will see you too with a smiley face, interrupted
only intermittently with one of shock as you
are given the impression of coming perilously
close to rock walls and jagged logs. The
highlights of all the trips are the superb 360°
turns that always soak some poor soul in the
boat. Shotover Jet picks up from town several
times a day for the 15-min ride to the
riverside. From $99, child $59.
    Other companies include: Kawarau Jet,
Marine Parade (lakeside), T03-442 6142/
T0800-529272, www.kjet.co.nz in
combination with Twin River Jet. Both zoom
out across Queenstown Bay and down the
Kawarau and up the lower reaches of the
Shotover; 1 hr from $85, child $45. Dart River
Safaris (recommended) or Dart Wilderness
Adventures in Glenorchy (see page 625)
offer one of the best scenic jet-boating trips
in the world; 3-6 hrs from $209, child $105
(includes transport).

Kayaking
Some superb day to multi-day sea kayaking
is offered on Milford (see page 658) and
Doubtful Sounds (see page 660). Locally
kayaks can usually be hired on the waterfront.
Funyak Trips, on the Dart River, see page .
Offers the very enjoyable 'blow-up carrot';
full-day costs from $285 including transport.

Lord of the Rings flights
An addition to the many local flightseeing
options is the Lord of the Rings 'Trilogy Trail'

offered by the personable owners and staff of **Glenorchy Air**, Queenstown Airport, T03-442 2207, www.glenorchy.net.nz, www.trilogytrail.com, $325, child $163. This down-to-earth company has been around for many years and were regularly utilized by the *Rings* cast and crew during extensive filming in the region. The 2½-hr Trilogy Trail takes in the mountains and valleys of Skippers Canyon and the Rees-Dart, with a landing near Paradise (quite literally), and then a journey south to Mavora Lakes with plenty of informative commentary and behind-the-scenes stories as you go. Given the aesthetics one cannot fail to be awestruck, even if such fictional location names as Isengard, Lothlorien, Amon Hen and Fanghorn Forest mean very little. Even without the complex world of Tolkien to fuel your imagination this has to be one of the most spectacular and affordable scenic flight experiences in the world. There is also an extended 5-hr Trilogy Trail offered, taking in other locations including the spectacular Rangitata Valley-Mt Sunday ('Edoras') from $720 and a 3½-hr road trip only to local filming sites from $125.

Massage
If you can simply take no more action, try a soothing massage, or beauty treatment with **Body Sanctum**, 12 Man St, T03-442 8006, www.bodysanctum.co.nz, or **Hush Spa**, Level 2, corner of Gorge and Robins Rds, T03-409 0901, www.hushspa.co.nz. Massage treatments start at 30 min from $60.

Mountain biking
There are many options, from the manic heli-bike to the low level mundane. For bike rentals see Transport, page 622. **Fat Tyre Adventures**, T0800-328897, www.fat-tyre.co.nz. Offers a range of local trips and tracks from 6-hr easy to moderate, $195, and heli-biking from $375. **Gravity Action**, T03-442 5277, www.gravity action.com. Offers half-day rides on the famous 'Skippers Pack Track', departing Queenstown at 0800, 1200 and 1600, from $129, child $109. Heli and raft combos are also available. **Vertigo Mountain Biking**, 17 Shotover St, T03-442 8378, www.heli-adventures.co.nz. Offers 3 downhill heli/bike combo adventures

taking in the Gondola Track, backcountry farm tracks and the Remarkables, $149-349.

Off-road, rallying, trial-bike and snowmobile adventures
Cardrona Adventure Park, Cardrona (Highway 89) near Wanaka, T03-443 6363, www.adventurepark.co.nz. Here you can try conventional ATV tours of 1-3hrs from $95 or choose to ride in a range of overly rubber-endowed, customized vehicles from trucks to buses. Guided tours from $150 (10 mins), self-drive from $250 (10 mins), family rides from $80 (15 mins) and humble go-carts from $45.
Nevis Snowmobile Adventures, T03-442 4250, www.snowmobilenz.co.nz. Self-drive or guided heli/snowmobile adventures available in winter. Expensive but great fun (mid Jun-Oct), 3 hrs costs from $560.
New Zealand Nomad Safaris, T03-442 6699/T0800-688222 www.nomad safaris.co.nz. Offers an excellent range of 4WD tours taking in some of the stunning scenery used in *LOTR*, including the stunning scenery around Glenorchy and the Dart River Valley, which was used as the backdrop to Isengard and Lothlorien; departs 0815 and 1330, from $130, child $65. The 'Wakatipu Tour', concentrates on local sites from the stunning vistas over Deer Park Heights (used as the dramatic backdrop to the scene depicting the escaping refugees of Rohan) and a number of other locations used in the trilogy; departs 0830 and 1330, prices from $130, child $60. The tours are very relaxed with entertaining knowledgeable guides some of whom were extras during filming. Other non-*LOTR* orientated trips include a 4-hr tour taking in the former gold-mining remnants along the 'entertaining' Skippers Canyon Rd from $130 and quad bike tours from $185.
Off Road Adventures, 61A Shotover St, T03-442 7858, www.offroad.co.nz. Conventional 4WD tours with *LOTR* options or self-drive guided tours from $139. Kids welcome. Trail bike hire also available.

Parapenting, paraflying and hang-gliding
When you arrive in Queenstown it won't be long before you see the colourful chutes of the tandem paragliders descending

▲ Walks around Queenstown

Remarkables ski field If you have half a day, reliable wheels and walking boots, the walk to the lookout above the ski field is highly recommended, see box page 609.

Queenstown Hill Accessed from York Street (look for DoC sign), this is a two- to three-hour moderate walk up to a scenic lookout above the town. The millennium gate on the way up is a nice and unusual piece of craftsmanship.

Ben Lomond (1747 m) dominates the scene above Bob's Peak and the Gondola and provides stunning views of the town and Lake Wakatipu. The full walk can be negotiated through forest from Lomond Street (from the Esplanade), but the best bet is to take the Gondola and join the track from there, six to eight hours return. Details available from DoC. **Ben Lomond Guided Walks**, T03-442 9434, www.benlomond.co.nz, offers a two-day fully guided walk to Ben Lomond with the added attraction of an exhilarating 4WD trip through Skippers Canyon, a night in a high country station lodge and meals from $495, child $395. Recommended.

Cecil Peak The peak dominates the southern shore opposite Queenstown and is another challenging option. A hike to the summit can be combined with a scenic helicopter flight and/or boat trip across Lake Wakatipu to get there and back. The ridgeline offers some fantastic views back across to Queenstown, and on the way up you can always throw in a picnic beside the rather dubiously named 'Fanny Falls'. It would be a full-day trip and you would need to organize either charter boat transportation, or better still, a boat there and helicopter pick-up, but it will be expensive. Getting a group together will reduce costs and it does present a great opportunity for a self-organized trip in a town (let's face it) that just loves to offer the opposite. Bear in mind it can get mighty cold up there and the weather can close in rapidly, so go well kitted out and if you can, take a mobile phone. For boat charter try **Fishing Boat Trips (Stu Dever)**, T03-442 6371 www.fishing-queenstown.co.nz, and for helicopter **Over the Top**, T03-442 2233, www.flynz.co.nz.

Twelve-Mile Delta to Bob's Cove Far more conventional and an easy two-hour jaunt on the shores of Lake Wakatipu It is accessed from the main Glenorchy Road (12 km).

Mount Crichton Scenic Reserve Inland and just a bit further along the road also offers good options. DoC can provide details and leaflets.

gracefully down into the town from Bob's Peak and the Skyline Complex. It's a wonderful way to see the views, but all a bit 'Queenstown' when your instructor answers his mobile phone mid-flight. Flights are also available from Coronet Peak. **Coronet Peak Tandem Paragliding**, T03-442 2988/T0800-467325, www.tandemhangliding.com. Tandems from Coronet (15 mins) from $175, hang-gliding from $175. **Paraflights Queenstown**, T03-441 2242, www.parasail.co.nz. If you would rather be alone and feel safer over water, then you might like to try paraflying across the lake, after all if a 2-year old and a 98 year old can do it? 20 mins from $95, child $80.

Queenstown Commercial Paragliders, T03-4418581/T0800-759688, www.paraglide.net.nz. From $185.

Queenstown Paragliding School, T0800-727245. If the tandem flight has you hooked you might then like to have lessons here. Day course from $295.

Sky Trek, T03-409 0625, www.skytrek.co.nz. Similar trips from $185.

There is a glut of rafting operators, all trying to lure you with their ineluctable inflatables. Shop around for the best deal.

Challenge Rafting, T03-442 7318/T0800-423836, www.raft.co.nz. Offers half-day or raft combo trips, again on the Shotover and Kawarau from $149. Minimum age 13.

Extreme Green Rafting, T03-442 8517, www.nzraft.com. Offers similar options.

Family Adventures, T03-442 8836, is a family and children's rafting adventure specialist, see Children's activities, above.

Queenstown Rafting, T03-442 9792, www.rafting.co.nz. Plies the rapids of the Shotover, Kawarau and Landsborough with such enchanting highlights as 'The Toilet' and 'The Sharks Fin'. Departs Queenstown 0815 and 1315, half- to full-day conventional, heli or in combination with other 'Big 4 Activity Combos', $159-1195.

River sledging and surfing

River surfing is the cunningly simple concept of replacing a raft with your own personal body board. It is great fun and provides a far more intimate experience with the water. River sledging involves more drifting as opposed to surfing and provides more buoyancy. Companies include:

Frogz Have More Fun, Wanaka, see page 628, T03-443 8244/T0800-437649, www.frogz.co.nz. Pick-up from Queenstown twice daily. All trips are about 4 hrs (2 hrs on the water) and cost from $135

Mad Dog, T03-442 7797, www.river boarding.co.nz.

Serious Fun, T03-442 5262/T0800-737468 , www.riversurfing.co.nz.

Tandem skydiving

Queenstown offers one of the most scenic venues on earth, for the 'bungee without the bounce' – or the elastic rope for that matter.

Nzone 35 Shotover St, T03-442 5867/T0800-727245, www.nzone.biz. This slick high-profile operator offers jumps from 9-15,000 ft from $245. Allow 3 hrs.

Tramping

Queenstown is a principal departure point for the Routeburn, Greenstone-Caples and Rees-Dart Tracks. For detailed information, hut and transportation bookings visit the

Information and Track Centre (see Tourist information, page 607). Another attractive local option is the **Ben Lomond trek** or **Cecil Peak** (see box, page 621).

Arrowtown Lodge, T03-442 1101, www.arrowtownlodge.co.nz. Is a small non-commercial outfit (with accommodation) offering a wide range of professionally guided trips of all grades with a historical, bush or Alpine edge, half- and full- to multi-day from around $100.

Guided Walks New Zealand, T03-442 7126, www.nzwalks.com. A very professional outfit, again offering a flexible range of guided options from 2hr local nature walks (from $98) to 3- to 9-hr 'samplers' of the 'Great Walks' from $215.

Ultimate Hikes (Encounter Guided Day Walks), T0800-659255, www.ultimate hikes.co.nz. A good company and offers guided walks on the Routeburn, Greenstone and Milford tracks from 1-6 days. A 3-day/2-night package on the Routeburn will cost from $1050 low season, $1190 high; Milford from $1690. It also offers a wide range of 10-hr day 'encounter' or multi-day options both locally on the Routeburn or further afield on the Milford or Mt Cook from $145, child $95.

Wine tours

Vineyard, garden and general sightseeing tours offer a more sedate diversion from the mainstream adrenaline activities.

Appellation Wine Tours, T03-442 0246, www.winetoursnz.com. Takes you to local vineyards and further afield to the Cromwell vineyards. Half- to full-day from $135.

Queenstown Wine Trail, T03-442 3799, www.queenstownwinetrail.co.nz. Visits all the main Kawarau Valley vineyards, 3-5 hrs from $99, child $65. Also offers local garden tours, from $80.

Wine Time, T0508-946384, www.wine time.co.nz. Full- or half-day lunch and dinner tours, from $115, child $70.

⊕ Transport

Queenstown *p605, map p607*

Airlines Air NZ, Queenstown Travel and Visitor Centre, Clocktower Shotover St, T03-442 4100. **Bicycle hire** Gravity Action, 37 Shotover St, T03-441 1021; **Outside Sports**, Shotover St, T03-4428883, from $45 a day, 0800-2100). **Car hire** First Choice, 48 Shotover St, T03-441 1302; **Budget**, Chester Building, corner of Shotover and Camp sts, T03-442 9274; **Hertz**, 2 Church St, T03-442 4106; **NZ Rent-A-Car**, corner of Shotover and Camp sts, T03-442 7465; **Pegasus**, The Mall, T03-442 7176; **Queenstown Car Rentals**, 26 Shotover St, T03-442 9220; **Thrifty**, Queenstown Airport, T03-442 8100.

Taxi AA Taxis, T03-441 8222; **Alpine Taxi**, T0800-442 6666; **Queenstown Taxis**, T03-442 7788; **Prestige Tourist Services**, T03-442 9803. A Mercedes complete with interpreter.

❶ Directory

Queenstown *p605, map p607*
Banks All the major banks are represented and ATMs are available in the Mall, Shotover St, Beach St, Rees St, Steamer Wharf and the O'Connell's Shopping Centre. **Currency exchange** There is a Travelex in the VIC (I-Site) and additional outlets at the BNZ, Rees St (daily 1000-2000); **Travelex**, corner of Camp St and The Mall, ANZ Postbank, Beach St. **Travelex**, at the airport, daily until 1900.

Internet The E Café, 50 Shotover St. Internet Outpost, 27 Shotover St. Most outlets open 0900-2300. **Library** 10 Gorge Rd. **Medical services** Hospital, Douglas St, Frankton, T03-442 3053. No Accident and Emergency Department. Doctor, Athol St Surgery, T03-442 7566; Queenstown Medical Centre, 9 Isle St, T03-441 0500.

Outdoor equipment hire Information and Track Centre, 37 Shotover St, T03-442 9708. **Police** Non-emergency, 11 Camp St, T03-441 1600. Emergency, T111. **Post office** Corner of Camp and Ballarat sts, T03-442 7670, Mon-Fri 0830-2000, Sat 0930-2000, Sun 1000-1800; post restante.
Ski and snowboard hire Browns , 39 Shotover St, T03-442 4003; Snow Rental, 39 Camp St, T03-442 4187; Green Toad, 7 Duke St, T03-442 5311.

Around Queenstown

With time usually so short the vast majority of visitors to Queenstown settle for the almost omnipresent and stunning aesthetics on offer from the town itself or en route to the activities, but if you have a day or two to spare – and preferably your own transport – it is well worth exploring beyond its own much hyped magnetism.

To the north, at the head of Lake Wakatipu, the small and far less developed settlement of Glenorchy is the gateway to some of the country's most impressive scenery and several of its best tramping tracks, including the Routeburn, the Greenstone, Caples and Rees-Dart. But without even needing to don boots and gaiters you can explore the immediate area or partake in several activities including jet-boat trips, canoeing or horse trekking. The Dart River Basin reached almost legendary status when it was used as a set for the Lord of the Rings trilogy, but you don't need to know your Orcs from your Nazguls to appreciate its innate natural beauty, nor muse upon the small settlement of Paradise to agree that it was indeed aptly named.

Of a more historic bent is the small former goldrush settlement of Arrowtown, which sits tucked away in the corner of the Wakatipu Basin, 23 km south of Queenstown. It has a fascinating history that is now well presented in the village museum and complemented nicely with a main street that looks almost like a Hollywood film set. But history and aesthetics aside, behind the old doors and down the alley ways you will find a surprising number of fine shops, cafés, restaurants and pubs in which you can let the infectious and exhausting mania of Queenstown quietly subside.

▶▶ *For Sleeping, Eating and other listings, see pages 625-627.*

Ins and outs

Getting there and around The Arrowtown **Double Decker Bus Tour** departs from the top of the Mall in Queenstown daily at 0930 and 1330, allowing one hour in Arrowtown and returning from outside the museum. It visits Lake Hayes and the Kawarau Bungy

Bridge on the way, T03-441 4421, $38, child $15. The **Arrow Bus** runs regularly between Queenstown and Arrowtown from outside McDonald's in Queenstown and the museum in Arrowtown, T03-442 1900, $18, child $10 return (0945-1700). It is happy to take bikes and even the occasional gold pan. **Backpacker Express**, 2 Oban Street, T03-442 9939, info@glenorchyinfocentre.co.nz, offers a comprehensive transport system between Queenstown, Glenorchy and the major tramping track trailheads by road ($18 one way) and a water taxi.

Tourist information Arrowtown VIC (I-Site) ① *49 Buckingham St, Lakes District Museum building, T03-442 1824, www.arrowtown.org.nz, daily 0900-1700.* The free brochures *Welcome to Historic Arrowtown* and *Historic Arrowtown* are comprehensive guides to the history and historic sites of the village and the surrounding area. **DoC VIC (Glenorchy)** ① *corner of Mull and Oban sts, T03-442 9937, daily 0830-1630 (closed weekends in winter),* or the independently run **Glenorchy VIC (I-Site)** ① *Oban St, T03-442 9939, www.glenorchyinfocentre.co.nz,* provide all the relevant local walks and tramping information/bookings. If your intentions are merely to pass through Glenorchy on your way to one of the major tracks, you are advised to avail yourself of the information, and secure hut bookings at the Queenstown offices. Likewise for accommodation and activities, the **Glenorchy Store** in the Holiday Park on Oban Street, can provide information. For general pre-visit information on Glenorchy, the VIC (I-Site) in Queenstown is your best bet, as well as the website, www.glenorchy.com. For information on the Routeburn, Greenstone and Caples Tracks, see Walking, page 627.

Arrowtown → *Colour map 6, A4 Population: 1800*

Arrowtown provides some respite from the stress and adrenaline highs of Queenstown. Yet another former gold mining settlement, its pleasant tree-lined streets with their old historic buildings lie nestled below the foothills of the Crown Range – an apt name given their once rich reserves of gold. The origins of Arrowtown go back to 1862 when prospector William Fox made the first rich strike in the Arrow River Valley – a find that soon brought over 7000 other hopefuls to the area. The first few weeks of mining produced 90 kg alone. Although first called Fox's, once the settlement was firmly established it was renamed Arrowtown after the river that revealed its riches. Once the gold was exhausted, the town's economy was centred first on agriculture and, in more recent years, the more lucrative resource of tourism. Looking down its quaint but almost Hollywood-style main street, one hopes this modern form of gold will not destroy its true aesthetic wealth and soul. Autumn (end of March) sees the village at its most colourful both in scenery and spirit when the hugely popular **Arrowtown Autumn Festival** takes place.

Sights The **Lakes District Museum and Gallery** ① *49 Buckingham St, T03-4421824, www.museumqueenstown.com, 0830-1700, $6, child $1,* offers plenty of insight into the 'calm before the storm', and then depicts the area's rather chaotic and feverish gold mining boom. For a small fee you can also hire out gold pans (with instruction sheet).

Outside the museum the tree-lined avenue of **Buckingham Street** reveals several old historic cottages that add to the much-photographed aesthetics. At the far end of Buckingham Street the **Chinese Settlement** offers further insight with several mud-walled huts, and a reconstruction of a general store. The Chinese were subjected to much prejudice and derision by the European miners and, much of the time, instead of seeking claims of their own, would sift through the tailings looking for fine gold undetected or simply left by the other rapacious miners.

In the hills upriver from Arrowtown, and accessed via a difficult 13-km track, is the former mining settlement of **Macetown**. Its remnants are the focus for a number of interesting tours by foot, 4WD or on horseback.

North of Queenstown (48 km) via the superb **Wakatipu Lake** scenic drive is the tiny former frontier village of Glenorchy. Perched and surrounded on both sides by the rugged peaks of the **Fiordland** and **Aspiring National Park**, the glacier-fed **Rees** and **Dart Rivers** and ancient beech forests, it is little wonder it has been labelled the 'Gateway to Paradise'. Indeed, part of the attraction here, other than the pure scenic delights or activities is a visit to **Paradise** itself – an aptly named little farming settlement 20 km further north. So stunning are the mountain backdrops around here and so lacking in any signs of human habitation that the Dart River Valley became a principal filming venue for the *Lord of the Rings* trilogy as Isengard, home of the evil wizard Saruman, and the forests of Lothlorien.

Activities available in Glenorchy include jet boating and horse trekking. The village also serves as the main access point to the **Routeburn**, **Greenstone/Caples** and **Rees-Dart** tramping tracks. Both 4WD and scenic flight tours from Queenstown explore the *Lord of the Rings* film locations (see Queenstown Activities and tours, page 616).

● Sleeping

Arrowtown *p624*

The VIC has full listings of the many charming B&Bs in the village and its surrounds.
LL-L Arrowtown House, 10 Caernarvon St, T03-442 0025, www.arrowtownhouse.co.nz. Right in the heart of town, in the original church grounds, is this very smart boutique luxury lodge with 5 well-appointed en suites.
AL Pittaway's Cottage, 69 Buckingham St, T03-442 0441, www.holidayhouses.co.nz/properties/3891.asp. A fully self-contained and refurbished 1875 miners cottage with wood fire, double spa bath. Good value and within a short walk of the village centre.
AL-A Arrowtown Lodge and Hiking Company, 7 Anglesea St, T03-442 1101, www.arrowtownlodge.co.nz. If you enjoy walking you might consider these walking or walking/accommodation packages. There are 4 cottage-style en suites all designed in keeping with the village's historic past.
AL-A Settlers Cottage Motel, 22 Hertford St, T03-4421734, www.settlerscottage motel.co.nz. Reasonably characterful units.
AL-A Viking Lodge Motel, 21 Inverness Cres, T03-442 1765, www.vikinglodge.co.nz. Self-contained A-frame units and a pool. Good for small groups.
B New Orleans Hotel, 27 Buckingham St, T03-442 1745 neworleanshotel@xtra.co.nz. 9 comfortable en suites, close to amenities.
B-D Riverdown Boutique Backpackers, 7 Bedford St, T03-409 8499. Look no further than this 6-bed hostel. It is immaculate and has the feel of a cosy B&B. Shared, doubles and twins. Off-street parking. Book ahead.

Motorcamps and campsites

B-D Arrowtown Holiday Park, Centennial Av, T03-442 7252, www.arrowtownholiday park.co.nz. Recently redeveloped and only 600 m from the town centre offering full range of accommodation including flats, cabins, shared lodge, powered/tent sites and camp kitchen.

Glenorchy *p625*

LL Blanket Bay,T03-441 0115, www.blanket bay.com. One of the most celebrated luxury lodges in the region and with undoubtedly some of the best amenities and aesthetics in the country. International celebs are said to be frequently flown in here.
AL-A Mount Earnslaw Motels, 87 Oban St, T03-442 6993, www.earnslaw.bizland.com. Glenorchy's most modern motel offers tidy en suite units.
A Hotel Glen Roydon, corner of Argyle and Mull sts, T03-442 9968, www.glenroydon.com. Offers ski lodge-style en suites or standard rooms all with a shared lounge and open fire. There is also an in-house restaurant and bar.
A-B Kinloch Lodge, T03-442 4900, www.kinlochlodge.co.nz. Historic lakeside lodge and the perfect base from which to explore the area before (and especially after) tramping the Routeburn or Greenstone tracks. Tidy doubles (the heritage doubles are very small), twins and shared dorms, all the usual facilities as well as a outdoor hot tub, a café/restaurant and a small shop. Road or water taxi transport is available from Glenorchy and local activities arranged.

Really well managed and a memorable stay is just about guaranteed.

A-D Glenorchy Hotel and Backpackers, across the road from Hotel Glen Roydon on Mull St, T03-4429902/T0800-453667, www.glenorchynz.com. Traditional New Zealand-style hotel doubles, en suites or a self-contained cottage. Also has backpacker dorms. The cheap in-house restaurant and bar is popular, with the outdoor upper-deck views proving a top spot.

Motorcamps and campsites
C-D Glenorchy Holiday Park and Backpackers, 2 Oban St, T0800-109939/T03-442 9939, www.glenorchyinfocentre.co.nz. Has a self-contained villa, standard cabins, bunkrooms and powered/tent sites. There is also a small store and information centre.

❶ Eating

Arrowtown *p624*
♦♦ **Café Mondo**, Ballarat Arcade, Buckingham St, T03-442 0227, Mon 1000-1730, Tue-Wed 0800-1730, Thu-Sun 0800-late. Popular for its traditional café-style breakfast or lunch and seems to attract a diverse crowd. The coffee is some of the best in the village and there is internet and occasional live music.
♦♦ **Saffron**, 18 Buckingham St, T03-442 0131, www.saffronrestaurant.co.nz, daily 1130-2130. A very congenial atmosphere and an excellent reputation for its Pacific-rim menu.
♦♦ **Stables Café and Restaurant**, 28 Buckingham St, T03-442 1818, daily 1100-late. Older and more historic but especially popular for alfresco dining.
♦ **Arrowtown Bakery**, 11 Ballarat Av, Buckingham St. Light snacks and especially great pies.
♦ **The Blue Door**, 18 Buckingham St. Excellent little pub in the old European style, with cosy open fire and large leather settees.
♦ **New Orleans Hotel**, Buckingham St. Recently renovated with cheap pub grub.
♦ **The Tap** , 51 Buckingham St, T03-4421860. A resurrection of the Royal Oak Hotel with contemporary cuisine and a good ambience.
♦ **Wind in the Willows Bookshop Café**, Ramshaw Lane (turn right at the top of Buckingham St), near the river, T03-442 0055, daily. For something more peaceful.

Glenorchy *p625*
♦ **Glenorchy Café**, Mull St, T03-442 9958. A funky little place that offers light snacks and a good breakfast – all of which can be enjoyed to the dulcet tones of 1980s hits, played on an ageing record-player.

⊛ Festivals and events

Arrowtown *p624*
Apr/May Autumn Festival, T03-442 1570, www.arrowtownautumnfestival.org.nz. Brings locals and visitors together to celebrate autumn with various shows, arts and events.

⊙ Shopping

Glenorchy *p625*
Made in Glenorchy Fur Products, Main St, www.glenorchy-fur.co.nz. Have you been wanting to get your dear mother or girlfriend that special homecoming present? Well, if so you have found 'ideal presents utopia'. Of particular appeal is the fine range of possum fur nipple warmers. They are the genuine article and come in a fine array of colours. And should your mother or dearest not feel the urge to accept or indeed model them on a regular basis, then they make a wonderful pair of eyeshades for the next flight back to New Zealand after the fall out. Just don't expect to make friends with the person sitting next to you.

▲ Activities and tours

Arrowtown *p624*
For walking and tramping, see **Arrowtown Lodge**, Sleeping above.
Gone Potty, 18 Buckingham St, T03-442 0890, www.gonepotty.co.nz. If it is raining you might like to consider madly colouring your own ceramic. The finished product is fired for you and can be picked up within a few days.
New Zealand Nomad Safaris, T03-442 6699, www.nomadsafaris.co.nz. An exhilarating 2-hr (4½ hrs from Queenstown) 4WD trip to Macetown. There are over 25 river crossings and a stop for a spot of gold panning in the Arrow River (summer only), from $130. Also popular 'Safari of the Rings Tours' $130 (see Queenstown Activities and tours, page 610).

Glenorchy p625
Flightseeing
Glenorchy Air, T03 442 2207, www.glen
orchy.net.nz. Flightseeing trips around both
national parks and to Milford Sound, as well as
the popular *Lord of the Rings* 'Trilogy Trail Trip'.

Horse trekking
Dart Stables, Glenorchy, T03 442 5688,
www.dartstables.com. Several attractive
options including 2-hr trek ($100), 5-hr
'Ride of the Rings' ($155), and 2-day/1-night
($495) horse-trekking trips through scenic
forest trails near the Rees and Dart rivers.
This is a great way to really experience
the *Lord of the Rings* locations.
High Country Horses, T03-442 9915,
www.high-country-horses.co.nz. Based in
the Rees Valley. Good for small groups.

Jet boating
Other than the stunning scenery and the
services on offer to the tramping fraternity,
the big attraction in Glenorchy is the jet-
boating operations that ply the **Dart River**.
Unlike the highly commercial rides of the
Shotover and Kawarau in Queenstown, the
Dart penetrates parts of the **Mt Aspiring
National Park** not accessible by road, and
provides one of the most scenic jet-boat trips
in the world. Combos are worth considering
including reductions on a Milford Sound
fly/cruise/fly; horse trekking; 3-hr guided walk
and a 4WD gold mining heritage trip to the
ghost town of Sefferton. Note there is a bad
weather refund policy on all trips.
Dart River Safaris, Mull St, T03-442 9992/
T0800-327853, www.dartriver.co.nz, transport
provided from Queenstown. There are 2
excursions on offer: the 6-hr 'Safari' involves a
wonderfully scenic ride to Glenorchy by bus,
then a 1½ hr fun-filled jet-boat trip upriver
followed by a short stroll through native
beech forest at the start of the Rees/Dart
Track. From there you transfer to 4WD to
negotiate the back roads past the settlement
of Paradise taking in the 2 main *Lord of the
Rings* film locations on the way back, from
$209, child $104 including transport
($179/$89.50 with own transport).
  The 'Wilderness Adventure Trip' is 2½ hrs
of pure jet-boating going higher up the
Dart River, from $209, child $105 including
transport from Queenstown ($188/$94 with

own transport). Departs Queenstown daily
0800 and 1200; Glenorchy 0900 and 1330.
  Also on offer is the 'Wilderness Funyak'
(www.funyaks.co.nz), which is part jet boat
(32 km, 1¼-hrs), part paddle (2 hrs) on a
blow-up carrot (actually a kayak), $285, child
$213 including transport from Queenstown.
It's a great day out and the scenery is very
memorable. Lunch is included (departs
Queenstown 0800; Glenorchy 0900).
Dart Wilderness Adventures, T03-4410303,
www.glenorchyinfocentre.co.nz. Somewhat
over-shadowed by Dart River Safaris but a fine
operator in its own right, it also offers a 70-km
3-hr trip on the Dart River taking in the *Lord
of the Rings* film locations and Maori culture.
Pick-ups are available from Queenstown.
Call for latest schedule and prices.

Walking
If you wish to explore the area under your
own steam there are several short walks on
offer immediately around Glenorchy, with
the 2-km wetlands boardwalk (**Glenorchy
Walkway**) just at the northern outskirts of
the town (accessed from Islay St) being
particularly recommended. The reflections
and views of **Mt Earnslaw** are superb and
there is an abundance of birdlife. By road you
can head north of Glenorchy and explore the
Rees or **Dart River (Routeburn) valleys**, or
better still visit **Paradise** (the surrounding
fields were the film location for Isengard and
Lothorien) and head to the western trailhead
of the **Rees-Dart Tramping Track**. From the
trailhead, you can also take a short walk
through the beech forest on the tramping
track's first section. Again the views of Mt
Earnslaw from the Paradise Rd are excellent
and you can also have some fun with silly
photos at the Paradise road sign. For more
information on walking in the area contact
the DoC visitor centre in Glenorchy.

◑ Directory

Arrowtown p624
Internet Café Mondo, see Eating, page
626. Also at the library, Buckingham St,
Mon-Fri 1000-1700, Sat 1030-1230.

Glenorchy p625
Internet Glenorchy Café, Mull St.
Postal agent Mobil Station, Mull St.

Wanaka and around

Wanaka is almost unfeasibly pleasant and has to rank as one of the most desirable places in New Zealand. With the lake of the same name lapping rhythmically at its heels and its picture-postcard mountain backdrops – bordering as it does the Mount Aspiring National Park – it is easy to understand why Wanaka is such a superb place to visit, or indeed live. In recent years Wanaka has seen a boom in both real estate sales and tourism, but it is reassuring that its manic neighbour, Queenstown, will always keep growth in check. As it is, Wanaka is just perfect: not too busy, not too quiet; developed but not spoilt, and a place for all to enjoy. Although now you would never guess it, Wanaka's history goes back to the 1860s when it played an important role as a service centre for the region's itinerant gold miners. Today, its principal resources are activities and its miners are tourists. Year-round, there is a multitude of things to do from watersports and tramping in summer to skiing in winter. But it can also be the perfect place to relax and recharge your batteries beside the lake. Wanaka is that kind of town. ▶▶ *For Sleeping, Eating and other listings, see pages 633-642.*

Ins and outs

Getting there Wanaka is accessed via Queenstown airport, which is served twice daily by **Air New Zealand Link**, T0800-737000. The airfield for the Wanaka Region is 11 km east of the town via SH6. **Aspiring Air**, T03-443 7943, www.nz-flights.com, flies between Queenstown and Wanaka.

Wanaka is 424 km southwest of Christchurch via SH1 and SH8; 276 km northwest of Dunedin via SH8; and 117 km north of Queenstown via SH8 and SH6. Alternatively, it's 70 km from Queenstown via the Cardrona Valley Road. Wanaka is served daily by **Intercity**, T03-377 0951/T03-441 1344 (Christchurch/Dunedin); **Atomic Shuttles**, T03-322 8883 (Christchurch/Dunedin/Queenstown), and **Southern Link**, T03-358 8355 (Christchurch/Dunedin/Queenstown). **Wanaka Connections**, T03-443 9122/T0800-244844, www.wanakaconnexions.co.nz, serves Christchurch, Dunedin, Te Anau, Invercargill and is recommended for transport to Wanaka (nine times daily), from $25. Typical one-way fares to Christchurch from $55; Dunedin from $45; Fox Glacier from $40; and Queenstown from $25. **Intercity** services can be booked at the VIC (I-Site).

All the major bus companies heading up or down the west coast pass through Makarora. **Cook Connection**, T021-583211, www.cookconnect.co.nz, runs between Oamaru to Mount Cook three times a week October to May, from $45 one way (Omarama $25). You can connect with this bus in Omarama.

Getting around Local shuttle services are available to Wanaka airfield ($12), the ski fields (from $30 return), local sights (Puzzling World from $3) and the Mount Aspiring trailheads (from $45). The two main companies are: **Alpine Coachlines Wanaka** (Good Sports), 17 Dunmore Street, T03-443 7966, www.alpinecoaclines.co.nz and **Mount Aspiring Express**, T03-443 8422, www.adventure.net.nz. The latter specializes in trailhead connections (Raspberry Creek, twice daily from $45 return, Mount Roy $5, Diamond Lake $10) and offers a drive up/bike back option ($5 extra). **Coastline Tours**, T03-434 7744, www.coastline-tours.co.nz and the **Penguin Express** shuttle to the penguin colony and other local attractions costs from $28 (including entry).

Tourist information Wanaka VIC (I-Site) ① *in the Log Cabin on the lakefront, 100 Ardmore St, T03-443 1233, www.lakewanaka.co.nz, daily 0830-1830 (winter 0930-1630).* This office also administers most of the local activity and adventure bookings through **Lakeland Adventures**, T03-443 7495, www.lakelandadventures.co.nz. There is also a café on site that overlooks the lake. The **DoC VIC (Wanaka)** ① *Upper Ardmore St* at the junction with McPherson St, To3-443 7660, www.doc.govt.nz, daily 0830-1630, deals with all national park/tramping hut bookings and local walks information. An up-to-date weather forecast is also available. **DoC VIC (Makarora)** ① 103-443 8365, daily 0800-1700 (closed weekends in winter), has information on the northern sector of Mount Aspiring National Park, Haast Pass, local short walks, and also issues hut passes ($5-10). Given the isolation and the potential for very wet weather conditions in the area you are advised to consult DoC before embarking on any of the major walks or tramps. Intentions sheets are provided. **Oamaru VIC (I-Site)** ① corner of Itchen and Thames Sts, To3-434 1656, www.tourismwaitaki.co.nz, Mon-Fri 0900-1800 (1700 Easter-Nov), Sat-Sun 1000-1700 (1600 Easter-Nov). The centre has town maps and a wealth of information surrounding the historical buildings, local tours and things to see and do. The leaflet Historic Oamaru is useful, and local DoC walks leaflets are available. Note the penguin colony has its own **Information Centre** ① base of MacAndrew Wharf (Waterfront Rd), To3-433 1195, www.penguins.co.nz, can supply general information after hours.

Wanaka → Colour map 5, C2 Population: 4500

One of the most immediate ways to get acquainted with the area is to make the short 45-minute climb up **Mount Iron** (240 m), just 2 km before the township on the main road. A stubborn lump of rock left by the glaciers, its 360° views are very impressive and provide an ideal way to get your bearings. The track is well marked and there is a car park by the roadside. Wanaka town centre borders the very pretty **Roy's Bay** that opens out beyond Ruby Island into the southern and indented bays of **Lake Wanaka**. The lake, which is 274 m above sea level and over 45 km long, occupies an ancient glacier bed. The aesthetics speak for themselves, but the glistening waters are also a prime attraction for boaties, water-skiers, kayakers and windsurfers. Even before you consider these activities you will find yourself simply admiring its beauty from Wanaka's attractive lakefront.

On the way into town you cannot fail to miss New Zealand's 'Leaning Tower of Wanaka', the centrepiece of **Stuart Landsborough's Puzzling World** ① To3-443 7489, www.puzzlingworld.com, 0830-1730, $10, child $7, shop and café. This is a madcap and puzzling conglomerate of mazes, illusions and holograms that is worth a muse. The toilets and 'Hall of Following Faces' are particularly engaging.

Some 8 km east on SH6, surrounding Wanaka airfield, are a couple of interesting museums. The **New Zealand Fighter Pilots Museum** ① To3-443 7010, www.nzfpm.co.nz, daily 0900-1600, $10, child $5, honours the lives (and deaths) of New Zealand fighter pilots and provides a fascinating insight into general aviation history. The museum's enviable and much-loved collection of flyable, classic Second World War fighters and trainers includes a, Hurricane and a Mustang, all of which are the star attractions of Wanaka's main biennial event, the 'Warbirds over Wanaka' which attracts thousands of spectators. Real enthusiasts will also delight in other unusual aircraft on display; the 'Polikarpovs', housed in a separate hanger, are particularly unique. Further major developments are planned for 2008 that will include an interactive theatre, a First World War diorama and an art gallery that will all join the current exhibits in a new building. Around the museum you might like to sit and watch terrified faces turn to ecstatic ones at the base of **Skydive Wanaka**. ▸▸ See Activities and tours, page 641.

Also on site is the **Wanaka Transport and Toy Museum** ① To3-443 8765, www.wanakatransportandtoymuseum.com, daily 0830-1700, $6, child $3. It provides a good wet-weather option and is the largest privately owed vehicle and toy collection in New Zealand. There are over 15,000 items on display, including a staggering 9000 toys and 200 vehicles, comprising a tank, fire engines, trucks and the obligatory tractors. There is even a collection of spark plugs. Within the museum is **Wanaka Beerworks** ① To3-443 1865, www.wanakabeerworks.co.nz, daily 0900- 1800, $5, child, free. In these such when beer and transport make uncomfortable relations, it seems unusual to find a brewery at a transport museum, but so be it. It is a craft brewery producing very palatable award-winning beers for many Central Otago outlets. There are daily tours at 1400, tastings and, of course, sales.

Near the airfield is the **Have a Shot** complex, T03-443 6656, with its range of 'smack it or shoot it' activities from clay-birds to archery to golf. Prices range from $7-30.

Hawea → *Colour map 5, B/C2*

North of Wanaka on SH6 towards the west coast is **Lake Hawea** and the small holiday settlement of Hawea. Lake Hawea, like its neighbour Lake Wanaka, occupies an ancient glacier valley, and only a narrow strip of moraine known as 'The Neck' separates the two. Lake Hawea is noted for its fishing and beautiful scenery, with mountain reflections that disappear towards its remote upper reaches, 35 km north of Hawea settlement. The lake level was raised by 18 m in 1958 as part of the Clutha River hydropower system. Hawea itself nestles on its southern shore and, although a fairly new settlement, was formerly the site of an important and strategic Maori *pa*.

Wanaka

N

0 metres 200
0 yards 200

Sleeping
Aoturoa Lodge **20**
Aspiring Campervan
  Park **1**
Aspiring Lodge Motel **2**
Brookvale Manor **3**
Cardrona **26**
Cardrona Alpine
  Resort **27**

Clearbrook **6**
Edgewater Resort **5**
Glendhu Bay Motor
  Camp **28**
Holly's **23**
Lakeside Apartments **18**
Lake Wanaka Lodge **12**
Lime Tree Lodge **24**
Minaret Lodge **19**
Moorings **7**
Mt Aspiring **15**
Oak Ridge Pool Resort **9**
Pleasant Lodge Top 10
  Holiday Park **22**
Purple Cow **10**

River Run **21**
Te Wanaka Lodge **11**
Tir Na Nog B&B **13**
Wanaka **14**
Wanaka Bakpaka **17**
Wanaka Lakeview
  Holiday Park **16**
Wanaka Stonehouse **4**

Eating
Ashrafs **6**
Bombay Palace **4**
Kai Whakapai **1**
Muzza's Bar **2**
Reef **7**

Relishes &
  Apartment One **3**
Soulfood **12**
Tuatara Pizza Co **8**
White House Café
  & Bar **4**

Bars & clubs
Finchy's Restaurant
  & Bar **5**
Paradiso Cinema
  & Café **11**
Shooters **9**
Slainte **10**

Makarora → *Colour map 5, B2*

From Lake Hawea and the narrow Neck you revisit Lake Wanaka and head north through some beautiful 'Scottish' scenery to its northern edge and the small settlement of Makarora. At about 67 km from Wanaka, and almost on the border of the Otago and west coast regions, Makarora acts as the portal to the northern tramps and activities within the **Mount Aspiring National Park**. The village itself offers little except a small conglomerate of tourist services reflecting the desires of most visitors who either pass through quickly or head for the hills.

Oamaru → *Colour map 5, C4 Population: 12,500*

Oamaru is an unusual and appealing coastal town on the South Island's east coast, somehow befitting its position gracing the shores of 'Friendly' Bay. Primarily functioning as a port and an agricultural service town, its modern-day tourist attractions lie in the strange combination of stone, architecture and penguins. Thanks to the prosperity of the 1860s-1890s, and the discovery of local limestone that could be easily carved and moulded, the early architects and stonemasons of Oamaru created a settlement rich in imposing, classic buildings, earning it the reputation of New Zealand's best-built town. Many old buildings remain, complete with Corinthian columns and gargantuan doorways, giving it a grand air. Add to that a small and congenial colony of yellow-eyed and blue penguins that waddle up to their burrows on the coast like dignified gents in 'tux and tails', and the town's appeal becomes truly unique.

Most of the historic buildings and associated attractions are in the **Tyne-Harbour Street Historic Precinct** (begins at the southern end of Thames Street), which boasts the largest and best-preserved collection of historic commercial buildings in the country. Although the *Historic Oamaru* leaflet will provide enough information for a self-guided tour, there are one-hour **guided walks** available on demand through the VIC (I-Site), from around $10, child $5. You will find that most of the buildings demonstrate a range of architectural styles from Venetian to Victorian and are now occupied with a variety of tourist lures, from antique and craft outlets to second-hand book stores, auto collections and cafés. The **Harbour and Tyne Market** ① *2 Tyne St, Sat-Sun 1000-1600 (Sun only in winter)*, specializes in local crafts, food and produce. Another interesting attraction is the **Oamaru Steam Train** ① *T03-434 7525*, which is lovingly owned and operated by the local and very enthusiastic Steam and Rail Society. The shiny engine comes complete with a proud conductor in period uniform and hisses into action from beside the VIC (I-Site) to the Harbour on Sundays, 1100-1600, from $6, child $3. As if there were not enough history on the streets, the town is also home to the **North Otago Museum** ① *58-60 Thames St, T03-434 1652, www.northotagomuseum.co.nz, Mon-Fri 1130-1630, Sat 1000-1300, Sun 1300-1630, donation,* which has a modest collection, focusing on Maori history and the early settlers. Of special interest are the information and displays about 'Oamaru Stone', the white limestone for which the town is so famous.

In one of Oamaru's original banks is the **Forrester Art Gallery** ① *9 Thames St, T03-434 1653, www.forrestergallery.com, daily 1030-1630, donation*. It features local contemporary works as well as national and international touring exhibitions. The VIC (I-Site) has listings of other notable galleries in the area.

There are a number of historic homesteads that are open to the public, including the Victorian country mansion, **Burnside** ① *T03-432 4194*; the **Tokarahi** ① *T03-431 2500*, and the Oamaru stone buildings of the **Totara Estate** ① *T03-434 7169, www.totaraestate.co.nz, daily 1000-1700, $7 child $2*. Most offer regular self guided or guided tours. Ring for details and opening times.

If you get fed up with stone then head for the very pleasant **Oamaru Public Gardens** ① *off Severn St, dawn-dusk, free*. Rated as one of the top 10 public gardens in the country, and first set aside in 1876, its 12 ha boast rose and Chinese gardens, fountains, statues and, of course, the ubiquitous duck pond. The area also has a number of private gardens open to the public; the VIC (I-Site) can provide the details.

No visit to Oamaru would be complete without visiting its penguin colonies. The town has two very different species in residence – the enchanting little blue penguin (the smallest in the world) and the rare, larger, yellow-eyed penguin. There are two colonies and observation points, one at Bushy Beach (see below), where you can watch the yellow-eyed penguins from a hide for free, or the official harbour-side **Oamaru Blue Penguin Colony** ① T03-443 1195, *www.penguins.co.nz, $17.50, child $6*, which you must pay to access. Obviously the free option is an attractive one, but if you do not know anything about penguins and were always under the impression they lived on icebergs and wore bow ties, then you are advised to join a tour, or visit the official colony before venturing out alone. The only time to view the penguins is from dusk (specific times are posted at the colony reception). There is a large covered stand from which you are given a brief talk before the penguins come ashore and waddle intently towards their burrows. During the day 'behind the scenes tours are available', which can be done in combo with the 'evening viewing' from $22.50, child $7.The colony is accessed via Waterfront Road past the Historic Precinct.

The **Bushy Beach** yellow-eyed penguin colony and viewing hide is accessed on foot via the walkway at the end of Waterfront Road (30 minutes), or alternatively by car via Bushy Beach Road (end of Tyne Street from the Historic Precinct). The best time to view the birds is an hour or so before dawn and dusk when they come and go from their fishing expeditions. If you want a closer, more informative experience you are advised to join Jim Caldwell's walking tours during the summer. Tours last 40 minutes and depart at 1800 and 1900, from $10. Book at the VIC (I-Site). The **Penguin Express**, T03-439 5265, offers transport and tours to both colonies from $28, child $12.

As well as its historical aspects and penguin-watching, Oamaru has a number of other activities on offer including fresh and salt-water fishing, kayaking, heritage and fossil trails, gold mining and farm tours, jet boating, horse trekking and glider flights. The VIC (I-Site) has all the details.

Oamaru to Dunedin → *Colour map 5, C4/3*

If you are heading south and have time, take the quiet and scenic coast road from Oamaru, through **Kakanui** to rejoin SH1 at Waianakarua. The area hosts a number of market gardens so keep your eyes open for fresh, good value produce at roadside stalls. Kayak hire is also available for the lower reaches of the **Kakanui River**, T03-439 5404. About 10 km south of Waianakarua are the **Moeraki Boulders**, a strange and much-photographed collection of spherical boulders that litter the beach. Although Maori legend has it that these boulders are *te kai hinaki*, or food baskets and sweet potatoes, science has determined that they are in fact 'septarian concretions', a rather classy name for 'darn big rock gob-stoppers' left behind from the eroded coastal cliffs. To understand exactly how they are formed requires several PhDs in geology and physics, but you will find something near a layman's explanation at the **Moeraki Boulderpark Visitor Centre and Café**, T03-439 4827, which is signposted just off SH1. The centre is, rather predictably, shaped like the boulders themselves and is open daily for lunch and dinner. The path to the boulders starts at the car park, where an interpretative panel provides information for the geologically wanting. You are requested to provide a donation of $2. **Coastline Tours**, T03-434 7744, operates from Oamaru and includes the boulders on their range of itineraries from $20-50.

There are other, smaller boulders to be seen at **Katiki Beach** and **Shag Point** a few kilometres south, beyond the village of Moeraki. Sadly, there used to be many more, with most having been pilfered as souvenirs, prompting the protection of the larger boulders at Moeraki. The small fishing village of **Moeraki**, 3 km from the boulders, can be reached along the beach by foot (three hours return) or by car via SH1. Once a whaling settlement, first settled as long ago as 1836, it now offers far more acceptable

Mount Aspiring National Park

Like most of New Zealand's majestic national parks, Mount Aspiring has an impressive list of vital statistics. First designated in 1964 the park has been extended to now cover 3500 sq km, making it New Zealand's third largest. It stretches for about 140 km from the Haast Pass to the Humbolt Range at the head of Lake Wakatipu and it is 40 km at its widest. It contains five peaks over 2600 m, including Aspiring itself – at 3027 m, the highest outside the Mount Cook range. It contains over 100 glaciers, including the Bonar, Therma and Volta. It enjoys an annual rainfall of between 1000-6000 mm a year. It is home to some unique wildlife like the New Zealand falcon, the kea and the giant weta. It is part of a World Heritage Area of international significance – the list just goes on. But, it is not figures that best describe this park. It is without doubt the names, words and phrases associated with it. How about Mount Awful, Mount Dreadful or Mount Dispute. Or Mount Chaos perhaps? Then there is the Valley of Darkness; Solitude Creek; Siberia River. How about the Pope's Nose or the mind boggling Power Knob? This is a wilderness worthy of investigation and well beyond mere imagination; a park of stunning and remote beauty. The locals call the place 'Tiger Country'. Enough said. Get in there and enjoy but go prepared. For more information contact the DoC Information Centre in Wanaka or Makarora (see page 628) or visit the website www.doc.govt.nz.

forms of fishing, as well as swimming, wildlife cruises (to try to see the rare Hector's dolphin) and some very pleasant coastal walks. The historic **lighthouse** is also worth a visit and for seafood don't miss **Fluer's Place** (see Eating, page 637). The coastline at **Shag Point**, south of Moeraki, is a good spot to observe New Zealand fur seals but do not go too close.

With the boulders still fresh in your mind your imagination can really run wild a further 20 km south on SH1 in **Palmerston**. Dominating the scene above the town is the rather spectacular phallus adorning **Puketapu Hill** (343 m). A monument to the late John McKenzie, a Scottish runholder who rose to high office and pushed through the Land Settlement Act in the 1890s; the monument and its accompanying views can be reached from the northern end of town (signposted). If you resist closer inspection perhaps you can gaze from afar while sampling the almost legendary mutton pies from the **McGregors Tearooms**, T03-465 1124. Children and budding Lepidopterists may also like to alight upon the **Palmerston Butterfly House** ① *left off SH1 (heading south), Tiverton St (SH85), T03-465 1812, daily 1000-1730, $10, child $5*. From Palmerston it is a further 55 km through gently rolling hills to Dunedin.

Sleeping

Wanaka *p628, map p630*
Although Wanaka has about 3000 beds you are advised to book at least 3 days in advance in summer (especially at New Year) and during the winter ski season. As well as hotels, there are many B&Bs and homestays available, from the luxury lodge or self-contained cottage to the basic B&B. You may also like to consider Lake Hawea, which offers a very pleasant and peaceful alternative to Wanaka and is only 15 mins away. The VIC (I-Site) has full listings.
LL Aoturoa Lodge, 17 km from Wanaka on the banks of the Clutha River, T03-443 5000, www.aoturoa.co.nz. 4 excellent, very private suites on offer amidst spacious grounds.
LL Minaret Lodge, 34 Eely Point Rd, T03-443 1856, www.minaretlodge.co.nz. Set in a

peaceful 1-ha park-like setting a short walk from the town centre. The modern mud-brick lodge has 4 en suite guest rooms in chalets behind the property and a 2-room suite. Sauna and spa.

LL River Run, Halliday Rd, T03-443 9049, www.riverrun.co.nz. Set on an escarpment with sweeping views across the mountains, this huge 120-ha property provides a perfect retreat with imaginatively appointed rooms and furnishings, often using recycled materials in traditional New Zealand style. There are 5 excellent en suites. Fine dining is offered but given the price you would be better off sampling some of the good eateries and congenial atmosphere in town.

LL Wanaka Stonehouse, 21 Sargood Drive, T03-443 1933, www.wanakastonehouse.com. A top-quality country house 'boutique' lodge within Wanaka township, a short stroll from the lake. Has 4 well-appointed double en suites, pleasant gardens, spa and sauna.

LL-AL Edgewater Resort, Sargood Drive, T03-443 8311, www.edgewater.co.nz. Set in spacious grounds overlooking Roy's Bay and within a short stroll of the town centre. Modern rooms and apartments with standard facilitation including Sky TV and internet access. Lots of activities can be arranged in-house and there is a spa, sauna and in-house à la carte restaurant.

LL-AL Oak Ridge Pool Resort, corner of Cardrona Valley and Studholme Rds, T03-443 7707, www.oakridge.co.nz. Purpose-built luxurious resort with well-appointed units (some with spa) and smart self-contained apartments that look out across spacious lawns and a swimming and spa pool complex to the mountains. Living areas are very spacious and comfortable with a large log fire. Restaurant/bar on site.

L Lime Tree Lodge, Ballantyne Rd, T03-443 7305, www.limetreelodge.co.nz. A modern, spacious, single-storey place with 8 luxury en suites, pool, spa and 5-hole golf course, set in 4 ha of farmland near Wanaka Airport. Very impressive.

L-AL Cardrona Hotel, Crown Range (Cardrona) Rd, 26 km from Wanaka, T03-443 8153, www.cardronahotel.co.nz. A little way out but well worth the journey, especially in winter when fires are lit in the gardens from dusk to welcome those coming off the ski field. The hotel is over 140 years old and still

retains much of its former character. As it is, the 16 comfortable en suite double rooms in the old stables are charming and front a beautiful enclosed garden and courtyard. There is a great rustic restaurant and bar attached and a spa. Bookings are essential.

L-A Wanaka Hotel, 71 Ardmore St, T03-443 7826, www.wanakahotel.co.nz. Not an aesthetic stunner by any means but well located and facilitated. Good value en suites (some with spa) and backpacker rooms (quads). In-house restaurant and a good restaurant/bar next door. Recommended.

AL Mt Aspiring Hotel, Mt Aspiring Rd, T03-443 8216, www.wanakanz.com. Newly refurbished and within walking distance of the town centre. A popular choice, with comfortable, good-value studios and suites, some with spa. Restaurant, bar and internet.

AL Te Wanaka Lodge, 23 Brownston St, T03-443 9224, www.tewanaka.co.nz. Excellent centrally located alpine-style lodge complex with en suites, self-contained cottage, garden spa (with in-house massage service), open fire, wine cellar and library. Internet and off-street parking.

AL-A Tir Na Nog B&B, Studholme Rd, T03-443 7111, tirnanog@xtra.co.nz. A pleasant self-contained cottage with spa.

A Lake Wanaka Lodge, 24 Tenby St, T03-443 9294, www.lakewanakalodge.co.nz. Backs on to the golf course and offers 10 quiet, well-appointed en suites.

Motels and apartments

Apartment complexes are very much an increasing feature in Wanaka.

LL Lakeside Apartments, 9 Lakeside Rd, T03-443 0188, www.lakesidewanaka.co.nz. 4- to 5-star fully serviced apartments in a central position with lake views, pool and spa.

LL-AL Clearbrook, corner of Helwick and Upton sts, T03-443 4413, www.clearbrook.co.nz. Well-appointed motel units. Right in the heart of the town centre.

LL-AL Moorings, 17 Lakeside Rd, T03-443 8479, www.themoorings.co.nz. Modern and classy boutique apartment and motel block overlooking the lake and only metres from the lakeshore and town centre. Stylish motel rooms with good views from the balconies, and spacious apartments with log burners and individual carports. Sky TV.

AL-A Aspiring Lodge Motel, corner of Dunmore and Dungarvon sts, T03-443 7816, www.aspiringlodge.co.nz. Offers good standard and executive suites and a spa.
A Brookvale Manor, 35 Brownston St, T03-443 8333, www.brookvale.co.nz. 1-bedroom and studio suites, pool, spa.
A Cardrona Alpine Resort, T03-443 7411, www.cardrona.com. Units actually within the ski field complex, sleeping 1-8 from $320.

Backpacker hostels

The hostels in Wanaka are all generally of a high standard. Three of the best are:
C-D Holly's, 71 Upton St, T03-443 8187, hollys@xtra.co.nz. Ideal if you want to avoid the crowds and heavy social scene of most of the other hostels. It is homely, well-facilitated and owned by a long-term local painter whom, along with his staff, makes you very welcome and will make sure you make the most of what the area has to offer. It has dorms, doubles and twins, internet, a good video library and is close to the town centre.
C-D Purple Cow, 94 Brownston St, T03-443 1880, www.purplecow.co.nz. A large place with stunning views across the lake. A wide range of comfortable dorms, twins and doubles all with en suites. Great facilities, Sky TV, internet, walks information and a friendly atmosphere.
C-D Wanaka Bakpaka, 117 Lakeside Rd, T03-443 7837, www.wanakabakpaka.co.nz. 5 mins' walk from the centre of town but worth it. It has great views, a good range of dorm, twins and doubles and clean, modern facilities. It is very much a tramper's retreat with great walking advice and information. Kayaks for hire and internet.

Motorcamps and campsites

There are several choices here from the convenient to the luxurious and the stylish.
AL-C Aspiring Campervan Park, Studholme Rd, T03-443 7766, www.campervanpark.co.nz. An entirely different and new concept in motorcamps. Charges a hefty $35 for a powered site, but has all mod cons including a spa (included in tariff) that looks out towards Mt Aspiring. Modern lodge, motel and tourist flats are also available.
AL-D Pleasant Lodge Top 10 Holiday Park, 217 Mt Aspiring Rd, at the western end of the town 3 km towards Glendhu, T03-443 7360. In an elevated position overlooking the lake and with all the usual facilities including spa, bike and fishing rod hire.
A-D Wanaka Lakeview Holiday Park, 212 Brownston St, T03-443 7883. Closest to town and rather unremarkable, it has adequate facilities, cabins and powered/tent sites.
C-D Glendhu Bay Motor Camp, Mt Aspiring Rd, 11 km from town, T03-443 7243, glendhucamp@xtra.co.nz. For the best aesthetics, offers lakeside sites with views up to Mt Aspiring. Facilities are really too basic given its obvious popularity and it is in need of an upgrade. However, there is no denying the superb location. Gets very busy in mid-summer and in the ski season (book ahead). It has petrol a small store and boat hire.

Hawea *p630*
AL Bellbird Cottage, 121 Noema Terr, Lake Hawea, T03-443 7056, www.bellbird cottage.co.nz. A fine and good-value self-contained option in Hawea Village offering an ideal escape from the bustle of Wanaka. Fully self-contained can sleep up to five, log burner. Minimum 2-night stay.
AL Lake Hawea Station, Rapid 22, Timaru River Rd, Lake Hawea, T03-443 1744, www.lakehaweastation.co.nz. With 2 fully self-contained former packhorse cottages sleeping 4-8. Wood burners, a peaceful setting and good value.
AL-A Lake Hawea Motor Inn, 1 Capell Av, T03-443 1224, www.lakehawea.co.nz.

Makaroa *p631*
AL-A Larrivee Homestay, near the VIC (I-Site), T03-443 9177, www.larrivee homestay.co.nz. Comfortable and offers a spacious en suite room or self-contained cottage. Dinner on request. Good value.
B-D Makarora Wilderness Resort, T03-443 8372, www.makarora.co.nz. Motel, cabin, backpacker and camping facilities.

Oamaru *p631*
There is an ever-increasing number of fine B&Bs and homestays on offer with many being in historic surroundings. Many of the motels are on Thames Highway, heading out of town. There are several hostels in and around town, all pretty comfortable, clean and friendly. The VIC (I-Site) has full listings.

LL Pen-Y-Bryn Lodge, 41 Towey St, T03-434 7939, www.penybryn.co.nz. A vast, lovely and historic Victorian villa, which is actually the largest single-storey timber dwelling in the South Island. It offers luxury en suites and a sumptuous 4-course dinner (and breakfast) included in the price.

AL Homestead 271, T03-434 2610, www.globalife.co.nz. If you fancy a break from all things Kiwi, this modern, well-appointed and good-value B&B located just outside Oamaru, is owned by a Japanese couple (ex-Christchurch chefs), who combine the conventional B&B experience with Japanese cooking (tariff includes Japanese breakfast, dinner from $50). Double, twin and single rooms with lounge and loft with open fire.

AL-A Bella Vista Motel, 206 Thames St, T03-434 2400, www.bellavistamotels.co.nz. Centrally located.

AL-A Heritage Court Motor Lodge, 346 Thames Highway, T03-437 2200, www.heritagecourtlodge.com. Tidy and modern accommodation.

AL-A Millennium Hotel Brydone, 115 Thames St, T03-434 0011, www.millennium hotels.com. Centrally located and built of the locally ubiquitous Oamaru stone in 1881, it has standard doubles or suites. The popular 'T' Bar and restaurant housed in the hotel is the biggest attraction.

A Glenhaven B&B, 5 Forth St, T03-437 0211. Very friendly and has a separate en suite and a triple room in the house. Anybody interested in cars or toys will be fascinated with the Matchbox car collection.

B Alpine Motel, 285 Thames St, T03-434 5038, www.alpineoamaru@xtra.co.nz.

C-D Empire Hotel Backpackers, 13 Thames St, T03-434 3446, www.empirebackpackerso amaru.co.nz. Cosy, centrally located, Victorian-style house that has the added attraction of free internet and even penny farthings. All room types.

C-D Red Kettle YHA, corner of Reed and Cross sts, T03-434 5008, yhaoamaru@ yha.org.nz. Traditional villa offering dorms or doubles/twins and a welcoming open fire.

C-D Swaggers, 25 Wansbeck St, T03-434 9999, swaggers@es.co.nz. A large suburban house double/twin dorm and 1 single. Small and homely.

Motorcamps and campsites
B-D Oamaru Gardens Top Ten Holiday Park, Chelmer St (signposted off Severn St, SH1), T03-434 7666, www.oamarutop10.co.nz. Backs onto the Oamaru Public Gardens and has generally overpriced flats, cabins, units, powered/tent sites and standard facilities.

Oamaru to Dunedin *p632*
AL-C Moeraki Village Holiday Park, 114 Haven St, T03-4394759. Motel units, flats, cabins and powered/tent sites. Shop on site.

A Moeraki Motels, corner of Beach and Haven sts, Moeraki, T03-4394862. Basic but comfortable self-contained units and cottages.

B-D Olive Grove Lodge, SH1, just before the settlement of Waianakarua (28 km south of Oamaru), T03-439 5830, www.olive branch.co.nz. An excellent eco-friendly organic lodge near the river offering tidy doubles, twins and dorms, spa and sauna, log fire, free local tours and plenty of resident farm animals. It is so relaxing you probably won't want to leave.

D The Hall Coastal Backpackers, south of Oamaru, T03-439 5411, www.coastal backpackers.co.nz. A popular and peaceful place within walking distance of the beach (All Day Bay). It has good-value doubles, twins and dorms, has a small licensed bar offering dinners and canoes, bodyboards and bikes can be hired. The nearest shop is 4 km away, so stock up if self-catering.

🍴 Eating

Wanaka *p628, map p630*
The New World supermarket is on Dunmore St, daily 0800-2030.

🍴🍴🍴 **White House Café and Bar**, corner of Dunmore and Dungarvon sts, T03-443 9595, daily from 1100. Deservedly popular with an imaginative Mediterranean/Middle Eastern menu with vegetarian options. Fine wine list, outdoor eating and a big fat cat that jumps on your lap.

🍴🍴 **Bombay Palace**, upstairs in Pembroke Mall, T03-443 6086. A good Indian choice.

🍴🍴 **Cardrona Hotel**, see Sleeping above, T03-443 8153, daily from 1100. Historic and cosy and well worth the 26-km journey for lunch or dinner.

🍴🍴 **Kai Whakapai**, Lakefront, T03-443 7795, daily from 0700. A good spot for daytime eating. Has freshly baked bread, pies, pastas, pizzas and a good vegetarian selection. Breakfasts are good value, the coffee is great and there is outside seating from which to watch the world go by on the waterfront.

¶¶ Reef, 145 Ardmore St, T03-443 1188, daily. Modern seafood specialists, good lake views.

¶¶ Relishes, 1/99 Ardmore St, T03-443 9018. 0800-1500 and 1800-late. A decent option with a good-value blackboard menu, outdoor dining in summer and fireside dining in winter. Good coffee and breakfasts.

¶¶-¶ Ashrafs, 2 Brownston St, T03-443 1073. Run by 2 brothers who offer great service and quality Indian and Kashmiri food. Good value. Recommended.

¶¶-¶ Soulfood, 74 Ardmore, T03-443 7885, daily from 0700. Offers an excellent range of organic produce in a relaxed and friendly atmosphere. Recommended.

¶¶ Tuatara Pizza Co, 76 Ardmore St, T03-443 8186. For gourmet pizzas.

¶ Muzza's Bar, corner of Brownston and Helwick sts, T03-443 7296. Good pub food.

Hawea *p630*

¶ Sailz, Capell Av, T03-443 1696. Serves light meals and refreshments.

Oamaru *p631*

Oamaru has a surprisingly good range of eateries offering everything from seafood to Thai. Most are on or around Thames St. The town also has quite a high Chinese population which has a noticeable influence on the standard of the Chinese restaurants.

¶¶¶ T'Bar Restaurant, Millennium Hotel, 115 Thames St, T03-434 0011. Pleasant ambience and good traditional NZ/European menu.

¶¶ Golden Dragon, 36 Ribble St, T03-434 8670. The most noted Chinese restaurant, along with **Golden Island**, below.

¶¶ Golden Island, 243 Thames Hwy, T03-434 8840.

¶¶ Last Post Bar and Restaurant, 12 Thames St, in the former Oamaru Stone-built Post Office, T03-434 8080. Casual dining at reasonable prices.

¶ Criterion Hotel, in the Tyne St precinct. Pub grub and good beer in historic hotel.

¶ Emma's Café, 30 Thames St, T03-434 1165, Tue-Sun 0900-1800. The locals' choice for light snacks, a hearty breakfast and coffee.

¶ Whitestone Cheese Factory, corner of Torridge and Humber sts, T03-434 8098, daily 0900-1700. As well as the innovative blackboard menu in the café, you can of course sample and purchase their impressive range of cheeses.

Oamaru to Dunedin *p632*

¶¶ Fluer's Place, 169 Haven St (Old Jetty), Moeraki, T03-439 5980. Excellent seafood. Recommended.

◗ Pubs, bars and clubs

Wanaka *p628, map p630*

Apartment One, above **Relishes Restaurant**, 99 Ardmore St, T03-443 4911. Especially popular for its laid-back atmosphere, balcony overlooking the lake and its cocktails, après ski and open fire in winter.

Finchy's Restaurant and Bar, 2 Dunmore St, T03-443 6262. A more sedate atmosphere.

Paradiso Cinema and Café, 1 Ardmore St, T03-443 1505, www.paradiso.net.nz. Famous for its 1-of-a-kind movie offerings, complete with easy chairs and homemade ice cream. Front man (and Scot) Calum McLeod often provides an entertaining introduction. The café is just as laid back. Recommended.

Shooters Bar. Highly commercial and seems very much aimed at the young and rapacious. Its saving grace is its fine position overlooking the lake.

Slainte Irish Bar, 21 Helwick St, T03-443 7663. Proving popular and offers live music.

Oamaru *p631*

Penguin Entertainers Club, Sea Side, Harbour St, T025-373922, www.thepenguin club.co.nz. A little-known spot for occasional visiting live acts. Check the website for dates and directions.

Armada Motor Inn Bowling Complex, 500 Thames Highway, T03-437 9040. Also popular. Serves takeaway pizzas.

✺ Festivals and events

Wanaka *p628, map p630*

Mar Warbirds Over Wanaka, T03-443 8619, www.warbirdsoverwanaka.com. New Zealand's premier air show is held biannually (next in 2008). The venue is of course the airfield, which hosts a wide variety of visiting 'birds', but also blows the dust off the New Zealand Fighter Pilots Museum's very own Spitfire. Entry is from $60, child $10 (3-day $140).

Apr Festival of Colour, www.festivalof colour.co.nz. Launched in 2005, this is a 5-day biannual arts and music festival featuring both artists from New Zealand and across the globe including sculptors, contemporary dancers, jazz musicians and photographers.

Oamaru *p631*

Nov Oamaru Victorian Heritage Celebrations. This annual event take place in the Historic Precinct on the 3rd weekend in Nov. It's all fun, top hats and penny-farthings.

▲ Activities and tours

Wanaka *p628, map p630*
Most activities can be booked at the VIC (I-Site) or the Lakeland Adventures office. There are obviously many options but if Wanaka is known for one thing it is perhaps rock climbing, especially with the opening of the new **Base Camp** complex (see climbing below). The principal operators are:
Good Sports, Dunmore St, T03-443 7966, www.good-sports.co.nz. Hires out bikes, kayaks, 'funyaks', 'sit-on kayaks', fishing rods and tackle, plus the full range of ski and snow-sports equipment.
Lakeland Adventures, T03-443 7495, www.lakelandadventures.co.nz. Offers fishing, jet boating and cruising.

Canyoning

Most of the activities available in Wanaka you can also do elsewhere, but canyoning is a local speciality and recommended. It basically involves negotiating a mountain river with the assistance of gravity and in suitable attire. Methods of descent include scrambling, abseiling or just plain jumping. All great fun. Heli and jet boat combos are also available.
Deep Canyon, T03-4437922, www.deep canyon.co.nz. 'Do' the Emerald creek, Niger Stream and others (6-7 hrs) from $215 (min age 16). Transport and lunch included.

Cruising

Lakeland Adventures, see above. Scenic cruises of varying duration explore the waters and islands of lake Wanaka from 1-3 hrs, $55-100.

Fishing

The local fishing is excellent and there are many operators and guides. Most of the companies listed below can also organize more adventurous heli-fishing trips throughout the region. Prices start at about $100 per person per hr and about $350-750 for a privately guided half-day trip. **Lakeland Adventures** and **Good Sports**, Dunmore St, offer independent rod hire from $30 per day and licences from $18.
Alpine Fishing Guides, T03-443 1023, www.driftfishingnz.com. Specializes in drift trout fishing ($425 per boat per day).
Southern Lakes Fishing Safaris, T03-443 9121, www.southernlakesfishing.co.nz. Full day $580 (1-2 people).
Wanaka Fishing Safaris, T03-443 7748, www.trout.net.nz.

Flightseeing

Wanaka is a superb base from which to reach **Milford Sound** by air, with the bonus of the stunning aesthetics of the **Mt Aspiring National Park** on the way. Most flights from Queenstown and other centres (which cost about the same) do not follow the same spectacular flight path. Given its museum it also hosts other exciting flight options.
Aspiring Air, at the airfield, T03-443 7943, www.aspiringair.com. Offers a range of flights from a 20-min local flight for $140 to its highly recommended 4-hr 'Majestic Milford Sound' flight. Leaving at 0845 or 1345 and arriving back at 1300 or 1800 this epic involves a superb flight over Wanaka, up the Matukituki River Valley, past Mt Aspiring and then out across the national park and out to sea, before flying up the chancel of Milford Sound and Milford Sound Village. Included in the trip is a 45-min cruise on the Sound. It is a truly memorable experience and well worth the $395, child $245. Other alluring options include a scenic flight over Mt Cook (from $380) or several activity combos from jet boating in the Haast Region to west coast glacier landings (from $610).

Vintage Tigermoth Flights, Wanaka Airport, T027-2209277, www.classicflights.co.nz. This offers something a little bit different. Don a leather flying helmet, goggles, silk scarf and tally ho yourself in to a bygone era aboard a 1941 Tigermoth. Several flight options $95-350 with the more adventurous involving aerobatic stunts. There is even an option for the real romantics with sunrise/sunset for 2.

Wanaka Flightseeing, at the airfield, T03-443 8787, www.flightseeing.co.nz. Offers similar trips to **Aspiring Air**, $330.

Golf

Wanaka's very scenic course is on Ballantyne Rd, just behind the town, and welcomes visitors, T03-443 7888. Green fees are a very reasonable $30, club hire full set $35.

Rippon Vineyard, T03-443 8084, www.golf cross.co.nz. Hosts Wanaka's **Golf Cross** course which uses an oval ball and goals as opposed to holes.

Horse trekking

The Wanaka region offers some superb horse-trekking possibilities.

NZ Backcountry Saddle Expeditions, near Cardrona, T03-4438151, www.ridenz.com. Offers 2-hr to 4-day treks, from $65, child $45 (full day $180).

Jet boating

Lake Wanaka and its surrounding scenic rivers would almost have to incorporate a jet-boat trip somewhere, and there are a number of operators.

Clutha River Jet (Lakeland Adventures), on the Lakefront, T03-443 7495. Offers 1-hr trips down the Clutha for $80, child $40.

Wilkin River Jets, Makarora. Plies the Makarora and Wilkin rivers.

Kayaking

Lakeland Adventures and **Good Sports** see above, offers independent kayak hire.

Alpine Kayak Guides, T03-443 9023, www.alpinekayaks.co.nz. Daily guided whitewater trips on the Clutha, Matukituki and Hawea rivers, suitable for beginners. Transport and free pick-ups included, from $250 full day, $129 half day.

Mountaineering and rock climbing

With Mt Aspiring and so many attractive mountain climbs so close to Wanaka it is not surprising to find a number of quality companies offering a range of packages.

Adventure Consultants, T03-443 8711, www.adventure.co.nz. Mt Aspiring $2450, 2:1 client-guide ratio, with flights. Very good for mountaineering and ice climbing courses.

Alpinism and Ski Ltd, 11 Rimu Lane, T03-443 6593, www.alpinismski.co.nz. Offers guided trekking excursions throughout the region, and year-round to a number of peaks including Mt Aspiring and further afield to Mt Cook and the Westland National Park. Once you have flown over Aspiring you will appreciate that having a guide makes a lot of sense! The price of a guided climb of Aspiring on a 2:1 client: Guide ratio is around $2180 (5 days without flights). Mountaineering courses, snow tours and trekking also offered.

Base Camp Wanaka, 50 Cardrona Valley Rd, T03-4431110, www.basecampwanaka.co.nz. This new camp is described as an 'all weather mountain adventure centre' boasting a sate of the art 500 sq m climbing space/wall for all levels. The complex houses a café, map room, library, shop and even a micro-brewery. They also offer organized indoor tuition and outdoor climbing trips and hire out a wide range of outdoor gear for climbing, trekking etc. Casual free-climbing from $15, child $9, gear hire (full set) from $10, 45 mins tuition from $45.

Mount Aspiring Guides, T03-443 9422, www.aspiringguides.com. Offers a range of trips and packages all year round. Mt Aspiring $2495 2:1 client-guide ration, with flights.

Wanaka Rock, at Base Camp, T03-443 6411, www.wanakarock.co.nz. A reputable company. Courses include introductory (1 day from $185), abseil (half-day from $110) and multi-day technical courses, from $450.

Mountain biking

Mountain bike hire is also available from **Lakeland Adventures**, see above.

Cardrona Alpine Resort, T03-443 7341, www.cardrona.com. Stays open in summer to allow climbers, trampers and bikers to access the mountains. The chairlift operates daily 1000-1600 and there are 2 purpose-built downhill bike tracks. Cardrona is 34 km southeast of Wanaka on the Crown Range Rd.

See also Queenstown Activities, page 620.
**Criffel Peak Safaris/Cardrona Adventure
Park**, SH89, Cardrona Valley Rd, T03-443
6363, www.criffelpeaksafaris.com. The
principal ATV 4WD quad bike specialists,
offering guided half to 3-hr trips on farm a
nd hill trails with great views, $75-260.
Also offers a 'Monster Trucks' option,
with ludicrously deformed and bouncy
vehicles from $140.
EWA Adventures, T03-443 8422,
www.adventure.net.nz. Offers 2½-hr 4WD
tours taking in some stunning views from $95.

Paragliding

Paragliding is huge around Wanaka with
the slopes of Mt Roy in particular providing
ideal terrain and conditions. On a fine day
it is not unusual to see over 20 colourful
chutes drifting across the skyline.
Wanaka Paragliding, T0274-697685/
T0800-359754, www.wanakapara
gliding.co.nz. 15-25 min tandem from
Treble Cone (800 m), $170.

River sledging

Whitewater sledging is growing in
popularity and provides a far more
intimate experience with the water
on a modified boogie board.
Frogz Have More Fun, T0800-437649,
www.frogz.co.nz. A French-owned outfit
offering 1- to 2-hr trips on the Clutha, Hawea
and Kawarau rivers, from $135 (minimum
age 10-14 years depending on the river).

Skiing

Wanaka has several great ski fields within
50 km of the town and encompassing
standard ski and board slopes, cross-country
and even a specialist snowboard freestyle
park at the new Snow Park. Cardrona, Snow
Park and Snow Farm are to the south, while
Treble Cone is to the northwest. For general
information and snow reports check out
www.snow.co.nz; www.nzski.com; www.snow
parknz.com; www.snowfarmnz.com or
www.skilakewanaka.com.
   Daily transport from Wanaka is available
with **Alpine Snow Shuttles** (transport and
lift day-packages available), T03-443 7966.
Other shuttle operators are listed in
Getting around, page 628.

Equipment can be hired from: **Base**,
corner of Helwick and Dunmore sts, T03-443
6699, www.base.net.nz; **Good Sports**,
Dunmore St, T03-4437966, also arranges
transport; and **Racer's Edge Planet Snow**, 99
Ardmore St, T03-443 7882, www.racers
edge.co.nz. Average prices are skis/boots
$34, child $17. Snowboard and boots from
$42, child $20. **Harris Mountain Heli-skiing**,
99 Ardmore St, T03-442 6722,
www.heliski.co.nz, offers 3-7 days from $725.
Cardrona, 34 km from Wanaka on the
Crown Range (Cardrona) Rd, T03-4437411,
www.cardrona.com. It has a base area at
1670 m, and ski and board runs suitable for
all levels, with the intermediates being
especially well catered for. Facilities include
bars and restaurants and, unusually,
apartment accommodation. The ski season
runs from 23 Jun-7 Oct but the resort (and
some lifts) remain open in summer for
trampers and mountain bikers. Lift passes
from $77, child (6-17) $39, with rental
ski/snowboard (day) from $110, child $70
Treble Cone Ski field, 20 km northwest of
Wanaka via Glendhu, T03-4437443,
www.treblecone.co.nz. Well known for its
good snow and interesting terrain, not to
mention its stunning views of Lake Wanaka
and Mt Aspiring. It also offers more skiable
terrain than any other ski or board area in the
South Island and has the longest vertical rise
in the Southern Lakes Region. Little wonder
it is considered one of the best fields in the
country. It is open from 0900-1600 late
Jun-early Oct (no access in summer). Lift
passes are from $89, child $37. 'First Timer'
package including lift/hire and lesson from
$100. Full clothing, ski and board hire are
available on the mountain with rental ski
(day) from $100, child $55, snowboard from
$110, child $65. There is also a café, bar,
childcare centre and ski/board schools.
Snow Farm, on the other side of the valley
to Cardrona, T03-443 0300 www.snowfarm
nz.com A base for cross-country skiing with
international standard tracks. It is open
mid-Jun to the end of Sep and a pass costs
from $30, child $15.
Snow Park, Cardrona, T03-443 0300
www.snowfarmnz.com A base for freestyle
snowboarding with international standard
'pipes'. It is open mid-Jun to the end of Sep
and a pass costs from $64-$75.

✦ The Rob Roy glacier walk

If you haven't time or the energy for any of the major tramps, there is one day-walk in the Mount Aspiring National Park that is accessible from Wanaka and quite simply a 'must do'. From Wanaka drive (or arrange transportation) to the Raspberry Creek Car Park in the West Matukituki Valley (one hour). From there follow the river, west to the footbridge over the river and up in to the **Rob Roy Valley**. From here the track gradually climbs, following the chaotic Rob Roy River, through beautiful rainforest, revealing the odd view of the glacier above. After about 1½ hours you will reach the tree line and enter a superb hidden valley rimmed with solid rock walls of **waterfall** and **ice**. It is simply stunning and well deserving of the label '**The Jewel of the Park**'. Keep your eyes (and ears) open for kea and in the forest for the tiny rifleman. After some thorough investigation of the area, you can then retrace your steps back down the valley to the Matukituki River and the car park (five hours return). **Mt Aspiring Express** can shuttle you to Raspberry Creek for $55 return, $30 one way, T03-443 8422. Departs 09330 and 14330 returning 1030 and 1530.

Tandem skydiving

The Wanaka Region is one of the most scenic in the country, which gives that added edge to any jump.
Tandem Skydive Wanaka, T03-443 7207. T0800-786877, www.skydivenz.com. Operates out of the airfield from heights of 9000 ft ($229) and 12,000 ft ($279), 15,000 ft ($389) allowing 30-60 seconds of freefall at around 200 kph, followed by a gentle and peaceful 6-min parachute ride to earth. Weight limit 100 kg/age limit 7 years. The scenery both on the way up and down are superb and many people in the business recommend Wanaka as we do. Pick-ups from Wanaka are free.

Tours

Ridgeline, T027-6886830/T0800-234000 . Offers full-day wine tours, and heli-hikes, from $170.
Wanaka Sightseeing, T03-379 1684, www.lordoftheringstours.co.nz. Offers very pleasant 2- to 5-hr sightseeing tours of the region and has added half-, full- and multi-day *Lord of the Rings* tours. The full-day takes in 18 filming locations from $290.

Walking

Other than the **Mt Iron Walk** (see page 629) and the walk to **Rob Roy Glacier** (highly recommended, see box, above), there are many other possibilities. Popular alternatives are the ascent of Mt Roy or the easier, but still quite demanding, climb to the top of **Rocky Mountain past Diamond Lake**. From lakeside, the vision of Mt Roy (1585m), which dominates the western edge of Roy's Bay, can hardly be missed, but its ascent can reward you with some tremendous views. A well-formed path zigzags its way to the summit from a car park 6 km north of Wanaka towards Glendhu Bay. The walk takes about 5 hrs return (return transfer to the car park $12).

Further up this road, past Glendhu and before the entrance to the Treble Cone Ski field, is the **Rocky Mountain and Diamond Lake Walk**. The appeal here is the view of Mt Aspiring and the Matukituki River Valley, as well as Lake Wanaka itself. The geology is also fascinating, with rocks that form unusual mounds and folds across the landscape. It is a stiff climb, but the path is marked and it is definitely worth the effort. At the end of Hospital Flat you will see the signposted car park. From there it is 20 mins to the fairly unremarkable lake before the track skirts around the slopes to the top. On the descent be careful not to stray off the path far from the lower lookout. You need to double back here to rejoin the track. The walk takes about 3 hrs return (transfer $45 return).

For detailed walks information see the numerous walks leaflets available from the

DoC Visitors Information Centre
(see information above).
Eco Wanaka Adventures, T03-443
2869, www.ecowanaka.nz and
Mount Aspiring Guides, 99 Ardmore St,
T03-443 9422, www.mountaspiring
guides.com, both offer an extensive
range of guided day and multi-day options.
The latter also offers transfers for both
of the walks detailed above.

Watersports
Lake Wanaka is the perfect place for
waterskiing and wakeboarding and big
enough for you to be able to find a quiet spot.
Sun and Snow Business, 103 Ardmore St,
T03-443 8855. Independent hire.

Makarora *p631*
Walking
Of special note in this area is the superb
3-day **Gillespie Pass Tramp** and 'The
Siberia Experience'. This evocatively named
jaunt is a combination of scenic flight,
tramp and jet boat, which gets consistently
good reviews. You are first flown (25 mins)
into the beautiful and remote Siberia Valley,
from where you tramp for about 3 hrs to
the Wilkin River to be picked up by jet boat
with a 30-min scenic ride back to Makarora.
At $245, it is good value. It also offers scenic
flights to Milford, Mt Cook or over Aspiring
National Park (Mt Aspiring) from 20 mins to
2-4 hrs ($210-680).
    Trips are run by **Southern Alps Air**,
T03-443 8666/T0800-345666, www.siberia
experience.co.nz, www.southernalps
air.co.nz, in conjunction with **Wilkin River
Jet Boats**, T03-443 8351, www.wilkinriver
jets.co.nz. The latter also offers 1-hr trips on
the scenic Wilkin from $85, child $42, as well
as water taxi services for trampers from $65.

⊖ Transport

Wanaka *p628, map p630*
Bicycle hire Good Sports, Dunmore St,
T03-443 7966, www.good-sports.co.nz,
$25-50 per day. **Lakeland Adventures**,
lakefront, T03-443 7495. **Car hire**
Aspiring, 212 Brownston St, T03-443
7883. **Adventure Rentals**, 20 Ardmore St,
T03-443 6050. **Wanaka Rent-a-car**,
T03-443 6641. **Taxi** Wanaka Taxi,
T03-443 7999; Wanataxi, T03-443 2288.

⊙ Directory

Wanaka *p628, map p630*
Banks National, T03-443 7521. Westpac,
T03-443 7857. They also have ATMs.
Internet Bits & Bytes, 48 Helwick St,
T03-443 7078, daily 1000-2200. Wanaka
Web, 3 Helwick St, T03-443 7429, daily
0900-2100. **Medical services** Aspiring
Medical Centre, 28 Dungarvon St, T03-
443 1226. Wanaka Medical Centre,
21 Russell St, T03-443 7811. **Police**
28 Helwick St, T03-443 7272. **Post
office** 39 Ardmore St, T03-443 8211,
Mon-Fri 0830-1730, Sat 0900-1200.

Oamaru *p631*
Banks Most of the major bank branches
and ATMs are on Thames St, with some
housed in grand historic buildings.
The **National Bank**, in the former 1871
Bank of Otago building, is the best example.
Internet VIC (I-Site), see page 628.
Small Bytes Computing, 187 Thames St,
T03-434 8490. Lagonda Coach Travel
tearooms, 191 Thames St, T03-434
8716. **Post office** Severn St, near the
intersection with Thames.

Southland

⁑ Footprint features

Introduction

Southland is a region of stark differences. It is one of the most spectacular yet inaccessible landscapes on earth. Even its boundaries are contrasting, stretching roughly in a straight line from the unremarkable and flat coastal town of Balclutha in the east, to the towering peaks and fiord of Milford Sound to the west. Half of its coast is mountainous, remote and inhospitable – virtually unchanged since Cook first landed (briefly) in 1770. The other half is home to Southland's largest town, Invercargill, the beautiful coastal holiday haunts of the Catlins and Riverton and an unsightly aluminium smelter. Amidst all that, knocking at its backdoor, is New Zealand's third island and newest national park: Stewart Island.

Most visitors head for the hills, and who can blame them? The Fiordland National Park, which is part of the internationally acclaimed Te Wahipounamu World Heritage Area, is a staggering 2.6 million hectares of some of the world's most magnificent scenery; it covers 10% of the country as a whole. And, although the vast majority of it is wonderfully inaccessible, it contains over 5000 km of walking tracks. But don't be fooled into thinking the less spectacular parts are not worth a look. There, too, you will find a warm welcome and some pleasant surprises. Where else on earth, for example, can you meet a 120-year-old tuatara, a reptile that has outlived the fiords themselves? Or see, unusually in daylight hours, the weird and wonderful kiwi, that flightless national icon.

★ Don't miss ...

1 **Milford Road** Drive to the magnificent Milford Sound via the unforgettable road from Te Anau, page 648.
2 **Milford Sound** Escape the crowds and head under the waterfalls by kayak or take a twilight tour, page 654.
3 **Lake Manapouri** Cruise the beautiful lake and go underground to the power station, page 659.
4 **Doubtful Sound** Take an overnight trip to experience the deafening silence, page 660.
5 **Invercargill** Meet 'Henry' the tuatara in the Southland Museum, page 667.
6 **Stewart Island** Look out for wild kiwi in New Zealand's newest national park, page 672.
7 **Catlins Coast** Take the quiet back roads and enjoy the stunning scenery, page 679.
8 **Nugget Point** Watch the rocks glow orange as the sun rises, page 682.
9 **Tramping** Put your boots on to tackle the 'moderate' Kepler, the 'challenging' Dusky or the new Hump Ridge Track, page 687.

Te Anau → *Colour map 6, B3 Population: 3500*

On the shores of New Zealand's second largest lake and at the edge of the magnificent wilderness of the Fiordland National Park is the 'walking capital of the world', Te Anau. Pretty isn't it? But, as they say...'You ain't seen nothing yet'. In summer it is like a busy gatehouse with crowds of eager trampers, intent on and excited by the prospect of visiting its enormous garden. In winter it is like an unused holiday house, with only its resident caretaker, quietly waiting and wanting to turn the heating on again. Ironically, as you drive into Te Anau, often wedged between a convoy of tour buses, it can initially seem a rather dull little town, but once you acquaint yourself with its bustling centre, spacious open areas and beautiful lake views, your desire to move on will quickly fade. And although what lies beyond the town is what you have really come to see, it is worth giving Te Anau a little time. And, given the fickle weather in these parts, you my have little choice. >> For Sleeping, Eating and other listings, see pages 650-653.

Ins and outs

Getting there By air **Te Anau airfield** ① *between Te Anau and Manapouri*, is served from Queenstown using unscheduled services with **Air Fiordland**, T03-249 7505, www.airfiordland.co.nz though the vast majority of visitors arrive by road. For airfield transport contact **Te Anau Taxis**, T03-249 7777. By car, Te Anau is 177 km southwest of Queenstown via SH6, 152 km from Invercargill via SH99 (Southern Scenic Route) and 290 km west of Dunedin via Gore and SH94. The town is served by **Intercity**, T03-249 7505 (Christchurch/Invercargill/Dunedin daily); **Atomic Shuttles**, T03-322 8883, www.atomictravel.co.nz (Wanaka/Queenstown, daily from $40); **Topline Tours**, T03-249 8059/T0508-832628, www.toplinetours.co.nz (Queenstown); **Tracknet**, T03-249 7777/T0800-483262, www.tracknet.co.nz (Queenstown daily, from $40); **Catch-a-Bus**, T03-479 9960, www.catchabus.co.nz (Dunedin daily); **Scenic Shuttle**, T03-249 7654/ T0800-277483 (Invercargill, daily November to April, Monday to Friday May to October); and the backpacker-orientated **Bottom Bus**, T03-4347370, www.bottombus.co.nz (Queenstown/Dunedin/Invercargill). All buses stop in the town centre. **Back Road Transport (Tracknet)**, T03-249 7777, offers a rather unique way to get to Te Anau via Lake Wakatipu (Queenstown) and the steamer *TSS Earnslaw*. Once ashore at the remote Walter Peak Station you can then travel by coach via the pretty Von Valley and Mavora Lakes to Te Anau, from $80.

Getting around Local fixed-wing and helicopter companies offer chartered transportation (or packages) for tramping to Milford and beyond, see Activities and tours, page 651. **Air Fiordland**, Town Centre, T03-249 7505 (Hollyford/Milford); **Wings and Water,** Lake Front (Milford/Dusky), T03-249 7405, wingsandwater@teanau.co.nz; **South-West Helicopters**, T03-249 7402, www.southwesthelicopters.co.nz, offer helicopter charters throughout the region. **Tracknet**, based at Te Anau Lake View Holiday Park, Te Anau-Manapouri Highway, T03-249 7777, www.tracknet.co.nz, offers shuttle bus services and packages to Queenstown ($40 one way); Milford-Te Anau Downs ($20); Routeburn/Greenstone/Hollyford turning ($32); Kepler control gates ($6). All shuttle services run from October to May except the Milford Track service which is year-round, T03-249 7777, www.greatwalksnz.com. **Topline Tours** (see Getting there, above) also offers shuttle services to tramping trailheads.

By boat, **Real Journeys**, based at the lakefront, T03-249 7416, www.real journeys.co.nz, offers a water shuttle service to the start of the Milford Track, from $57, child from $15. **Kepler Water Taxi**, Te Anau, T03-249 8364, stevesaunders@ xtra.co.nz, runs a water taxi service to Brod Bay and the Kepler Track daily at 0830 and 0930, from $16 one way.

Tourist information Te Anau has a disconcerting number of information centres and booking offices. The most unbiased information is available from **Fiordland VIC (I-Site)** ① *Lakefront Drive, T03-249 8900, fiordland@i-site.org, daily 0830-1800 (winter 0830-1700)*. It deals with all local information and serves as the agents for domestic air and bus bookings. **Real Journeys**① *downstairs from VIC (I-Site), daily summer 0830-2100*, deals with its own considerable scope of transport, sights and activity bookings including local sightseeing trips on Lake Te Anau (including the Te Anau Caves) and to Milford and Doubtful Sounds. **DoC Fiordland National Park Visitor Centre**① *southern end of lakefront, 103-249 8514, greatwalksbooking@doc.govt.nz, daily 0830-1800 (seasonal)*, is the principal source for track information, track bookings office and up to date weather forecasts. There is also a small museum and audio-visual theatre ($3).

Other information and booking offices: **Te Anau Travel and Information Centre** ① *Lakefront Drive, T03-249 7516, teanau.travel@xtra.co.nz*. **Tick-it Te Anau (Air Fiordland)**① *town centre, T03-249 7505, www.airfiordland.com, www.tickit.co.nz, 0800-1830 (seasonal)*, has a booking office, but places a heavy emphasis on its own trips.

Sights

Once settled in to your accommodation, without doubt the first thing to do is book a ticket to see the 35-minute film *Ata Whenua or Shadowland*, at the contemporary

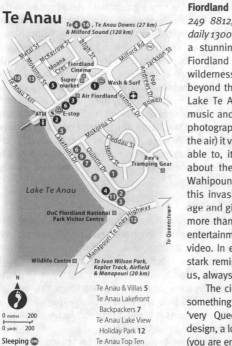

Te Anau

Sleeping 🛏
Anchorage 1
Arran 2
Cat's Whiskers B&B 3
Croft B&B 4
Fiordland Lodge 14
Lake Front Lodge 6
Lakeside Motel 8
Radfords Motel 9
Red Tussock Motel 11
Steamers Beach
 Backpackers 12
Te Anau & Villas 5
Te Anau Lakefront
 Backpackers 7
Te Anau Lake View
 Holiday Park 12
Te Anau Top Ten
 Holiday Park 10
Te Anau YHA 13

Eating 🍴
Kingsgate Hotel 4
La Toscana Pizzeria 1
Moose & Bar 2
Naturally Fiordland 6
Olive Tree Café 3
Redcliff Café & Bar 5

Fiordland Cinema ① *The Lane, T03-249 8812, www.fiordlandcinema.co.nz, daily 1300 and 1730, from $10*. The film is a stunning visual exploration of the Fiordland National Park and the vast wilderness area that extends almost beyond the imagination to the west of Lake Te Anau. Dubbed with evocative music and filmed using state-of-the-art photographic techniques (mostly from the air) it visits areas you would never be able to, it will leave you in no doubt about the purity and awe of the Te Wahipounamu World Heritage area. In this invasive and frantic technological age and given current world events it is more than a mere tonic, some fleeting entertainment or a promotional activities video. In essence it is a refreshing and stark reminder that nature will, despite us, always be 'the boss'.

The cinema itself has been causing something of a stir in the town since it is 'very Queenstown' with contemporary design, a log fire and a wine bar attached (you are encouraged to take a glass in to the film with you). It is an example and an indication of where the town is inevitably going, which in a way is exciting and welcome, but if you take a trip to the outskirts of town and see the suburban eyesore and the real estate eating away the countryside, you will also see the more insidious 'dark side'.

At 61 km long, 10 km at its widest point and a total of 344 sq km in area, Lake Te Anau is the largest lake in the South Island and second largest in New Zealand. Looking from the lakeside up its length to the Earl Mountains it certainly seems worthy of those dimensions and perhaps the label of prettiest in the country. Directly opposite Te Anau, unseen in the bush, is the meandering **Kepler Track** which begins at the southern end of the lake and skirts its southwestern edge, before climbing steadily towards the Kepler Mountains and the spectacular views from the **Luxmore Hut**. Also along the western edge between the Middle and South Fiords are the 200-m **Te Ana-au Caves**. Long revered by Maori, but only rediscovered by the Europeans in 1948, they provide the usual spectacular rock formations, fossils, whirlpools, waterfalls and glow-worms. The caves can only be accessed by boat, and 2½-hour guided trips leave from the wharf at Te Anau up to six times daily. After arriving by launch, there is a video presentation. The caves themselves are then explored by foot and on the water by punt. The 2015 (summer) or 1845 (winter) evening trips are recommended. Book with **Real Journeys**, Lakefront Drive, T03-249 7416; tours cost from $54, child $15.

On the southern shores of the lake on the road to Manapouri, is the **DoC Te Anau Wildlife Centre** ⓘ *T03-249 7921, entry by donation*, an important breeding centre for **takahe** and other rare native species. The story of the takahe is a fascinating one. Thought to be extinct for over 50 years, a small group were rediscovered in the Murchison Mountains above Lake Te Anau in 1948, by ornithologist and medical practitioner Dr Geoffrey Orbell. Although much of what goes on at the centre (in their efforts to maintain the new breeding colony in the Murchison Ranges) is off-limits, the open-air aviaries and grounds are very appealing. It is very refreshing to see such efforts being made in wildlife conservation in New Zealand and to witness unique species in such a relaxed atmosphere. There are takahe, kea, morepork and kaka to name but a few. Across the road from the wildlife centre is the 35-ha **Ivor Wilson Park** (open dawn to dusk), which offers a number of pleasant tracks and picnic spots amongst native bush and surrounding Lake Henry. For children or urbanites **Glen Monarch Farm Tours** ⓘ *off SH94 (17 km), T03-249 7041*, offers an entertaining three-hour introductory kiwi farm tour with the obligatory sheep shearing and working dog demonstrations as well as plenty of animal petting, from around $50 (vehicle transport from Te Anau extra).

Milford Road → *Colour map 6, A3*

The 119-km trip into the heart of the **Fiordland National Park** and **Milford Sound** is all part of the world-class Milford Sound experience. In essence it is a bit like walking down the aisle, past the interior walls of a great cathedral, to stand aghast at the chancel and the stunning stained-glass windows above. This may sound like an exaggeration but if nature is your religion, then the trip to Milford is really nothing short of divine. Of course much depends on the weather. Ideally it should be of either extreme – cloudless, or absolutely thumping it down. Under clear blue skies it is of course magnificent, but many say that the trip through the mountains is better during very heavy rain. It is an incredibly moody place so don't be put off by foul weather.

From Te Anau you skirt the shores and enjoy the congenial scenery of Lake Te Anau before heading inland at **Te Anau Downs** (30 minutes). This is principally a boat access point to the Milford Track; there is a motel, T0800-500706, and a hostel, T03-249 8133, www.teanau-milfordsound.co.nz. Another 30 minutes will see you through some low-lying alluvial flats and meadows as the Earl Mountains begin to loom large. After penetrating some beech forest you suddenly emerge into the expanse of the **Eglinton River Valley** with its stunning views towards the mountains. This is known as the 'Avenue of the Disappearing Mountain' and it speaks for itself.

At the northern end of the valley you then re-enter the shade of the beech forests and encounter **Mirror Lake**, a small body of water overlooking the Earl Mountain

Fiordland National Park

Fiordland National Park is 1.25 million ha and the largest of New Zealand's 14 national parks. It is twice the size of Singapore with 0.06% of the population. In 1986 it was declared a World Heritage Area on account of its outstanding natural features, exceptional beauty and its important demonstration of the world's evolutionary history. Four years later, in 1990, Fiordland National Park was further linked with three others – **Mount Aspiring**, **Westland** and **Mount Cook (Aoraki)** to form the World Heritage Area of South West New Zealand. It was given the Maori name **Te Waipounamu** (*Te* 'the'/ *Wai* 'waters'/ *Pounamu* 'greenstone' or 'jade'). Hopefully we can rest assured, that with such official labels and protection it will remain the stunning wilderness it is.

Range. The lookout point is a short walk from the road. On a clear day you can, as the name suggests, capture the mood and the scene twice in the same shot.

Several kilometres further on is **Knobs Flat** where there is a DoC shelter and information/display centre and toilet facilities. For much of the next 25 minutes you negotiate the dappled shadows on a near constant tunnel of beautiful beech forest before reaching **Lake Gunn**, which offers some fine fishing and a very pleasant 45-minute nature walk through the forest. The copious growth of mosses and lichens here provide the rather unsubtle hint that the place can get very wet, very often!

From Lake Gunn you are really beginning to enter 'tiger country' as the road climbs to **The Divide**, one of the lowest passes along the length of the Southern Alps. Here a shelter and an assortment of discarded boots marks the start of the **Routeburn** and **Greenstone/Caples Tracks**. The car park also serves as the starting point to a classic, recommended (three hours return) walk to **Key Summit** which looks over the Humboldt and Darran Ranges. Round the corner there is the **Falls Creek (Pop's View) Lookout**, which looks down the **Hollyford Valley**. Depending on the weather this will be a scene of fairly quiet serenity or one of near epic proportions as the swollen Hollyford River rips its way down to the valley fed by a million fingers of whitewater.

Following the river is the **Lower Hollyford Road** and access to **Lake Marian** (1 km), a superb (three hours return) walk up through forest and past waterfalls into a glacial hanging valley that holds the lake captive. A further 7 km on is the charming **Hollyford (Gun's) Camp,** and the Hollyford Airfield, important access and accommodation points for the **Hollyford Track** (see page 691), the trailhead for which is at the road terminus 6 km further on. The short 30-minute return walk to the **Humboldt Falls**, which again are spectacular after heavy rain, starts just before the car park.

‡ If you don't have your own transport, you'll need to rely on tour buses. About 30 make the daily pilgrimage to Milford Sound in summer, especially from 1100, so go early or late in the day.

Back on the main Milford Road the mountains begin to close in on both sides as you make the ascent up to the **Homer Tunnel**, an incredible feat of engineering, and a bizarre and exciting experience, like being swallowed by a giant drain. It seems to have changed little since the last bit of rubble was cleared and is only lit by road markers. This simply adds to the appeal as long as you are not claustrophobic, or indeed on a bike! (If you are, you'd better pedal like mad for its entire 1200 m length.)

However, keep your eyes open for **kea** (native mountain parrots) that frequent the main stopping areas at either end of the tunnel. If they are not there, it is worth stopping a while to see if they turn up. Watching these incredibly intelligent birds go about their business of creating general mayhem in the name of food and sheer vandalism is highly entertaining. There will be plenty of photo opportunities and

650 despite the obvious temptation DO NOT feed them. A parrot fed on white bread, crisps and chocolate is, obviously, a very sick parrot.

Once out of the tunnel you are now in the spectacular **Cleddau Canyon** and nearing Milford Sound. Instantly you will see the incredibly precipitous aspect of the mountains and bare valley walls. The rainfall is so high and rock and mudslides so frequent that the vegetation has little chance to establish itself. As a result the rainwater just cascades rapidly into the valleys. Note the creeks that cross under the road. There are so many they don't have names, but numbers. These all count up steadily to form the **Cleddau River**, which, at **The Chasm** (20 minutes return), is really more waterfall than river, and has, over the millennia, sculpted round shapes and basins in the rock. From The Chasm it is five minutes before you see the tip of the altar of **Mitre Peak** (1692 m) and spire of **Mount Tutoko** (2746 m), Fiordland's highest peak. It's now only five minutes before your appointment with the Minister of Awe at the Chancel of **Milford Sound**.

● Sleeping

Te Anau *p646, map p647*
Bear in mind that there are some excellent overnight cruise options on both Milford and Doubtful sounds see page 657 and page 662. There are a generous number of B&Bs and homestays, many of which are out in the country. There are also plenty of motels around town, the best and most expensive being on Lakefront Drive heading south from the centre, and the older and cheaper tending to be elsewhere, with many on Quintin Drive.

LL Te Anau Hotel and Villas, 64 Lakefront Drive, T03-249 9700, www.teanauhotel.co.nz. Lakeside, and the most high-profile hotel in town. It has had a number of name changes and renovations and offers good rooms, some with lake views, self-contained villas and 4 de luxe suites. A la carte restaurant, spa pool and sauna.

LL-L Fiordland Lodge, 472 Te Anau-Milford Highway (5 km north of Te Anau), T03-249 7832, www.fiordlandlodge.co.nz. A purpose-built luxury lodge, built in the classic lodge-style and commanding stunning views across the lake and mountains. Smart en suite guest rooms, 2 self-contained log cabins, quality restaurant and a large open fire. The high ceilings, full trunk pillars and huge windows add to the appeal and atmosphere of space. The owners also offer a wide range of guided excursions. Recommended.

L-A Lake Front Lodge, 58 Lakefront Drive, T03-249 7728, www.lakefrontlodge teanau.co.nz. Modern upmarket motel close to the lake, 13 units, some with spa bath.

AL Cat's Whiskers B&B, 2 Lakefront Drive, T03-249 8112, www.catswhiskers.co.nz. Conveniently placed town B&B.

AL Croft B&B, Milford Rd (on the edge of town, 3 km north), T03-249 7393, www.thecroft.co.nz. With 2 self-contained cottages set in private gardens on a farm with memorable views across the lake. Very peaceful and plenty of pets dying to make your acquaintance including Dolly the pet sheep (but not that 'Dolly').

AL-A Radfords Motel 56 Lakefront Drive, T03-249 9186, www.radfordslakeview motel.co.nz. Standard facilities.

A Arran, 64 Quintin Drive, T03-249 8826, www.arranmotel.co.nz.

A Lakeside Motel 36 Lakefront Drive, T03-249 7435, www.lakesideteanau.com. Set amongst pleasant gardens;

A Red Tussock Motel, 10 Lakefront Drive (at the southern end), T03-249 9110, www.redtussockmotels.co.nz.

A-B Anchorage, 47 Quintin Drive, T03-249 7256, www.teanaumotel.co.nz.

Backpacker hostels
There are lots of backpacker hostels, most of which are geared up to cater for trampers and muddy boots. There are also options on the road north to Milford or south to Manapouri.

A-D Grumpy's, Te Anau Downs (30 km north), T03-249 8133, www.teanau-milford sound.co.nz. Lakeside on SH94, 600 m from the Milford Track departure point (water taxi). 11 rooms with en suite, TV and fridge. Share kitchen, lounge and log fire.

B-D Te Anau YHA, 29 Mokonui St, T03-249 7847, yhatanau@yha.org.nz. After years out of town it was relocated and purpose-built right in the centre. It is the most popular backpacker option (deservedly so) with a wide range of rooms and a very comfortable lounge. There is also a fully self-contained cottage available. Recommended.

C-D Barnyard Backpackers, 80 Mt York Rd (south off SH95, 9 km), T03-249 8006, www.barnyardbackpackers.com. Tidy log cabins, van or campsites on a deer farm, open fire, horse trekking, internet and transport.

C-D Steamers Beach Backpackers, across the road from the DoC visitor centre, T03-249 7737, www.teanau.info.co.nz. The strangest looking backpacker hostel in town, owned and operated by the **Te Anau Lake View Holiday Park**. Perhaps looks a little over the top but you'll find perfectly comfortable and fine facilities on deck.

C-D Te Anau Lakefront Backpackers, 48-50 Lakefront Drive, T03-249 7713, www.teanaubackpackers.co.nz. A large bustling place with all the usual facilities plus some excellent double or quad ex-motel units and fully self-contained units at reasonable prices. Spa, TV theatre and internet. Bike hire. At the time of going to print the property was for sale so changes may be a foot.

Motorcamps and campsites
See also backpacker hostels, above.
AL-D Te Anau Lake View Holiday Park, 1 Te Anau-Manapouri I lighway (overlooking the lake on SH95), T03-249 7457, www.teanau.info. Spacious with a wide range of options from new motel units, to cabins, powered sites and tent sites. Internet café, sauna and spa, Sky TV. The added attraction here, other than the modern facilities is the organization of activities and ease of tramping track transportation in conjunction with the in-house 'Tracknet' company.
A-D Te Anau Top Ten Holiday Park, 128 Te Anau Terr, T03-249 7462, www.teanautop10.co.nz. A proud multi-award winner and one of the best

holiday parks in the country. The facilities are excellent and kept exceptionally clean and well maintained. You are even personally escorted to your site. It lives up to its name as having a 'bed for every budget'.

🍴 Eating

Te Anau *p646, map p647*
There are 2 supermarkets: **Super Value**, 1 The Lane, daily 0800-2000; and **Four Square**, town centre, 0830-2100, seasonal.
₩₩₩ Kingsgate Hotel (Bluestone), T03-249 7421, daily. Provides fine à la carte dining.
₩₩₩ Redcliff Café and Bar, 12 Mokonui St, T03-249 7431, daily 1800-late. Intimate and congenial, and offers some particularly good lamb and venison dishes.
₩₩₩ Te Anau Hotel and Villas (McKinnon Room), T03-249 9700, daily. Fine à la carte dining in this hotel restaurant.
₩₩ La Toscana Pizzeria, 108 Town Centre, T03-249 7756, 1730-2200. Good for pizza.
₩₩ Moose Restaurant and Bar, Lakeside Drive, T03-249 7100, daily from 1100 for lunch and dinner. It has lost a little of its former atmosphere but can still serve up a good meal and has the town's most popular bar attached.
₩₩ Naturally Fiordland, 62 Town Centre, T03-249 7111, daily 0900-2100. Good value, excellent pizza and recommended.
₩ Olive Tree Café, 52 Town Centre, T03-249 8496, daily 0800-2130. Good coffee.

⛰ Activities and tours

Te Anau *p646, map p647*
The vast majority of visitors to Te Anau use it as a portal to Milford and Doubtful sounds and the major tramping tracks. Note that there are other activity operators in Milford Sound, Manapouri and Queenstown offering a wide range of other trips in the region (see page 616 and page 661).

Cruising
Real Journeys, lakefront, T03-249 7416, www.realjourneys.co.nz. Although, as yet, no specific lake cruises are available, taking the

shuttle to the start of the Milford track is an attractive option, you can then organize your own transport back (see **Tracknet** above) from Te Anau Downs. Another option is to join their the Milford Track Guided Day Walk.

Fishing

As you might imagine the fishing in the region is superb, provided you can take your eyes off the stunning backdrops. **Fiordland Guides**, T03-249 7832, www.fiordlandguides.co.nz. More specialist services. Charges about $100 per hr or $600 for 2 people on a full day trip. Overnight camping trips are also an option. **Fish Fiordland**, T03-249 6855, www.fish fiordland.co.nz. Full-day trips from $95 per hr. **Fish and Trips**, T03-249 7656, www.fiordland-flyfishing.com. Similar trips to **Fish Fiordland**.

Flightseeing (fixed wing)

Without doubt the best way to see the Fiordland National Park is from the air. See also helicopter flightseeing, below. **Air Fiordland**, Town Centre, T03-249 7505, www.airfiordland.com. Fixed-wing flights to Milford and Doubtful sounds with numerous options and combinations with sounds cruising and coach, ex Te Anau, $150-400. Also available for private charter. **Wings and Water**, Lakefront Drive, T03-249 7405, wingsandwater@teanau.co.nz. A fixed-wing floatplane that operates from the lakeshore. Offers a range of options principally to Milford and Doubtful sounds including flight only to flight/cruise and coach in/fly out, from 1-4½ hrs, $250-450. Also offer flights with kayaking and hiking options. Can also be chartered to see some of the remote locations used for filming in the *Lord of the Rings* trilogy.

4WD

High Ride 4 Wheeler Adventures, T03-249 8591, www.highride.co.nz. Offers scenic (3-4 hr) backcountry safaris on 4WD ATVs from $145. Recommended in any weather conditions but an ideal option if you booked a more weather dependent activity that has been cancelled.

Helicopter flightseeing

All the companies below offer a dynamic range of flights and packages from 10 mins (from around $140) to 1½ hrs ($675). Again the principal locations are **Milford** and **Doubtful sounds** though a trip to see the remote wilderness of the **Dusky Sound**, a heli-hike-cruise trip to the Mt Luxmore Hut on the **Kepler Track** or a scenic flight and jet-boat combo are all available (at a price). See also Flightseeing, above. **Fiordland Helicopters**, T03-249 7575, www.fiordlandhelicopters.co.nz. **South West Helicopters**, T03-249 7402, www.southwesthelicopters.co.nz. **Southern Lakes Helicopters**, Lakefront Drive, T03-249 7167, www.southernlakes helicoptersco.nz. The principal helicopter operator in Te Anau.

Golf

Golf Fiordland, T03-249 7247. Can take care of all the arrangements, for a reasonable fee. **Te Anau Golf Club**, T03-249 7474. Green fee from $25, clubs from $15.

Horse trekking

High Ride, see 4WD, above. Horse treks with transport from Te Anau, 2½ hrs, from $80. **Westray**, 55 Ramparts Rd, T03-249 9079, www.fiordlandhorsetreks.com. 2 hrs, $75.

Jet boating

Luxmore Jet, T03-249 6951, www.luxmore jet.co.nz. Offers memorable 1-hr scenic trips with very personable guides down the Upper Waiau River, which connects Lake Te Anau and Lake Manapouri, from $85, child $40. The trip is also suitable for kids and more scenic oriented rather than the 'Queenstown style' thrills and spills. It also offers a '*Lord of the Rings*' heli/jet option (1 hr 40 mins) taking in local film locations, from $430

Kayaking

Other spectacular kayaking options are available in Milford and Doubtful sounds from Manapouri (see page 657 and page 661). **Fiordland Wilderness Experiences**, T03-249 7700/T0800-200434, www.fiordland seakayak.co.nz. Full-day excursions on Milford from $130, multi-day trips to Doubtful Sound from $310. The Milford trip is especially good, taking in the scenery of the Milford Rd.

Milford Sound Sea Kayaks, see page 658. A long-established company based in Milford Sound, offering similar trips.

Scuba diving
Tawaki Dive (Dive Milford), T03-249 9006, www.tawakidive.co.nz. Full-day diving trips to view the unique species of the fiords including the rare black coral from $199 (ex Te Anau). Open Water courses from $399.

Sightseeing tours
All the highly commercial Queenstown-based scenic day coach tours (see page 610) pass through Te Anau and you can join these to reach Milford or Doubtful sounds. The VIC (I-Site) has details and you are advised to book in advance.
Trips and Tramps, T03-249 7081, www.milfordtourswalks.co.nz. Locally orientated, personable day-trips to Milford Sound (including cruise and walking options) from $136, child $75.

Tandem skydiving
Although most will have already done the almost obligatory tandem in Taupo, Franz Josef or Wanaka, this operation in Te Anau presents another fine opportunity and is on a par with anything else around the country.
NZSkydive Fiordland, Te Anau Airport, T03-249 9116, www.simplifly.co.nz. Tandems are good value at 9000-12,000 ft, $245-295. Digital video and photography packages mixed with your own music choices from $165.

Walking
The biggest local attraction here is of course the 67-km (2- to 3-day), **Kepler Track** which can be walked in whole or part. One of the most popular day or overnight walks is to capture the view from the **Luxmore Hut**, which is the first DoC hut on the track (in the traditional anticlockwise direction). To access the hut by foot, walk along the southern edge of the lake to the control gates. From there it is a fairly strenuous 11-km (6 hrs) one-way walk along the lake edge and up above the tree line to the hut. A very appealing way to cut out much of the strain

is to get a water taxi (T03-249 8364, $35 return) or to join a walk/cruise trip (see Cruising above) from Te Anau to Brod Bay It is then a 16 km (8 hrs) return trip.
Bev's Tramping Gear, 16 Homer St, T03-249 7389, www.bevs-hire.co.nz. Rents out a range of walking, tramping and camping equipment at competitive prices.
Sportsworld, 38-40 Town Centre, T03-249 8195, www.sportsworldteanau.co.nz. Has a vast range of walking, tramping and camping equipment for hire.
Trips and Tramps, T03-249 7081, www.milfordtourswalks.co.nz. Locally orientated, personable day-trips to Milford Sound (including cruise and walking options to Lake Marian and Key Summit) from $136, child $75.

⊖ Transport

Te Anau *p646, map p647*
Bicycle and scooter hire
Fiordland Bike Hire, 7 Mokonui St, T03-249 7211, bikes and scooters.

Car hire
Hertz, T03-249 7516. Te Anau Taxi and Tours, T03-249 7777. For breakdown services contact **Mobil**, town centre, T03-249 7247 (24 hr).

Taxi
Te Anau Taxi and Tours, T03-249 7777.

❶ Directory

Te Anau *p646, map p647*
Banks There are 2 banks (Westpac/BNZ) in the town centre both have ATMs and offer currency exchange services. **Internet** Te Anau Photocentre.com, 62 Town Centre, T03-249 7620. E-stop, Jailhouse Mall, town centre, 0900-2100, seasonal. Air Fiordland (tic-it Te Anau), town centre, 0900-1900, seasonal. Mountain View Holiday Park, Te Anau Terr. Lake Te Anau Backpackers, 48 Lakefront Drive. Fiordland Electrical, 19 Luxmore Drive, (24 hr). **Laundry** Fiordland Electrical, see above, open 24 hrs. **Medical services** Doctor Luxmore Drive, T03-249 7007, Mon-Fri 0800-1800, Sat 0900-1200. **Police** Milford Rd, T03-249 7600. **Post office** 'Paper Plus', town centre.

Milford Sound → *Colour map 6, A3 Population: 300 (seasonal)*

There are simply no words in a thesaurus to describe the sight of Milford Sound; let alone its moods. Come rain or shine, calm or storm, dawn or dusk, it is ever-changing, always dramatic, and never dull. In every sense Milford Sound is quite simply New Zealand at its glorious and unparalleled best. Given the enormity (quite literally) of the attraction you will be immediately struck by how under-developed Milford Sound is. With its conservative scatter of low-key buildings it seems only the boat terminal stands out like a sore thumb. This is quite deliberate. The fact that Milford is the jewel in the crown of the Fiordland National Park and administered by the DoC, means that further development is strictly controlled, hence the lack of accommodation. How utterly refreshing it is to see a place of such outstanding natural beauty so unspoilt and not completely over-run with rapacious developers out to make a buck, or the well-heeled building their dream homes, eating up the acres and then calling in the 'Animal Control' man. In Milford only nature (and sandflies) rule and you had better respect it.

However, that said, this is still one of New Zealand's biggest tourist attractions and our physical presence there is, sadly, predominantly money-driven and places a huge burden on the environment. Despite the limits on building in Milford Sound, those that already exist are in desperate need of a facelift, if not a complete transplant. Other than the recently upgraded yet completely sterile cruise terminal, the waterfront buildings are nothing short of a national disgrace and surely an embarrassment to the image of tourism in New Zealand. Also, the big corporates that exist there are no less rapacious and profit driven as they are in money-mad Queenstown. In mid-summer the place is a hum of propeller and diesel engines, as the masses are brought in to 'take the cruise'. On any given day in the high season there are scores of coaches and campervans doing the trip from Queenstown and Te Anau which, against a backdrop of such enormity, can be a surreal sight in itself. This is one place where 'Ant Travel' or 'Humblin Coaches' would seem entirely appropriate. Without proper investigation Milford can almost be too much for the senses, so it's best to arrive independently, or indeed go in winter. By all means take a cruise, and more especially a scenic flight, but if you can linger a while, and wait until the buses have left, you can appreciate this incredible place even more. ▶▶ *For Sleeping, Eating and other listings, see pages 656-658.*

Ins and outs

Getting there You can reach Milford Sound by air, by bus, by road, or in real style by foot, via the Milford Track. But the best way to arrive, if you can afford it, is to take a scenic flight/cruise combination from Wanaka or Queenstown. Then, if you do not have your own wheels, hire a car from Queenstown or Te Anau and give yourself at least two days to explore the area properly. Your arrival by air will almost certainly be in combination with a scenic flight or tour option from Wanaka, Queenstown or Te Anau (see Flightseeing, page 658). The landing and take-off from the airfield in Milford, 1 km from the visitor centre, is a memorable experience.

‼ *Whatever you do, don't forget to bring insect repellent. The sandflies in Milford are legendary.*

There is a vast array of bus and coach operators serving Milford Sound, with an equal number of tour options, from simple bus-in/bus-out, to bus/cruise/bus or bus-in/cruise/fly-out and even bus/overnight cruise options. Most operators are based in Queenstown, from where they make the 12-hour, 291-km day trip by road, picking up passengers from Te Anau on the way. This is one of the most spectacular bus trips in the world, provided the weather is favourable. However, if dark clouds are gathering, or the forecast is for heavy rain (which it frequently is) do not despair. Even if it is pouring down this can actually add to the drama and spectacle of the Milford

Ken and the Great Naked Tunnel Race

The Homer Tunnel, which is one of the undeniable highlights of the Milford Road (SH94), is a remarkable example of engineering and a monument to human endeavour. Commenced in 1935 by workmen using simple picks and shovels and completed with the loss of three lives in 1953, it provides the essential link to the outside world with the scenic utopia that is Milford Sound.

But this is no Channel Tunnel or Sydney Harbour underpass. There are no laser-guidance systems; no tidy tollgates or hamburger stands thoughtfully placed halfway through for your convenience. When you first encounter the entrance to the Homer at the base of what can only be described as a massive face of granite, the word 'drain' springs to mind. But stunning aesthetics and principal functions aside, ol'Homey has become the venue for perhaps New Zealand's most unusual annual events – known in these parts (no pun intended) as the 'Great Annual Nude Tunnel Run'. The concept was thought up by a local based in Milford and enacted for the first time (no doubt after several beers) by a small group of wanton lunatics in 2000. But they say lunacy is a true asset in life and it certainly is in these parts (no pun intended), so as you can imagine it wasn't long before the idea caught on.

Now, attracting over 50 participants and scheduled for April Fools day each year, the competitors run completely naked from east to west (a distance of 1.2 km) carrying little except a torch, a lot of courage and an undeniable sense of *joie de vivre*.

Although there is obviously plenty of scope for spot prizes there are two officially recognized winners – the fastest male and the fastest female – both of which have their names engraved on the trophy, which for men is 'Ken' doll and for women a 'Barbie' (naked and in a running position – naturally)!

Apparently, the most exciting moment is when everyone gathers at the entrance to the tunnel and furtively takes off their clothing, before donning a towel and making their way to the starting line. Then, with whoops of joy and almost primeval chants the official foghorn is sounded and the mad dash into the great drain begins. Few hang about and, with posteriors rippling, dash like chilled dervishes towards the bottom (again, no pun intended) of the tunnel and the chance of fame, no fortune and a 'Ken' doll (and why not). They say some even practice in secret in order to win the great prize.

In recent years the event has also attracted those some with an understandable lack of desire to win such an item (or who have the collection anyway), simply pour out a glass of wine and perambulate through the tunnel at a leisurely pace talking about life, the universe and one can only presume the 'heady delights of naturism'.

One competitor (let's just call him 'Ken') says of the event: 'It's an invigorating feeling being naked and makes one realize how natural and beautiful it is to have no kit on. Group nudity is definitely non-perverse, a good way to make new friends and influence people and something we should all do more often'. Absolutely Ken! Let's all try it – starting at Auckland Airport perhaps?

Road as channels of water fall from the precipitous outcrops and in all directions like a some sort of surreal giant's car wash. In fact, the heavier the better. Many people actually prefer Milford in awful weather and quite right too – with an average of about 7 m annually it really knows how to rain here. See also Tour operators, page 658.

Tourist information If you have arrived independently and not yet pre-booked any activities you can choose from the array of options at the **Milford Sound Visitor Centre** ① *boat terminal, 0900-1700*. You are, however, advised to research the huge number of options prior to your visit. The VICs (I-Sites) in Queenstown and Te Anau will assist.

Sights

Milford Sound is in itself, of course, just one huge sight but there are individual aspects worth noting. The centrepiece of the Sound is **Mitre Peak**. At 1692 m it is not that high by New Zealand standards but, as with the entire corridor of Milford Sound, it is the sheer rate of ascent created by the actions of the glaciers that creates such an impact. Opposite Mitre Peak is **The Lion** (1302 m) and further up the ridge behind it **Mount Pembroke** (2045 m). Milford Sound itself is 15 km in length and about 290 m at its deepest. The mouth of the fiord is only about 120 m wide, due to melt action and the terminal moraines of the former glaciers. In heavy rains the fiord can seem like one great waterfall but by far the most impressive at any time are the 160-m **Bowen Falls**, which was until recently reached by a boardwalk from beside the boat terminal. Sadly, due to unstable rock conditions on the slopes above, this is now closed until further notice. Similarly, about midway along the eastern well of the fiord are the **Stirling Falls** (154 m) whose mist and rainbows can only be visited by boat or kayak.

The fiords are home to some fairly unusual and hardy wildlife. **Fur seals** are commonly seen lazing about on the rocks on almost every cruise, but it is below the water's surface that the most noted species are found. Milford Sound is home to the unusual **Milford Deep Underwater Observatory** ① *T03-441 1137/T0800-264536, www.milforddeep.co.nz*, which was no mean engineering feat. In the sheltered waters of **Harrison Cove**, about a third of the way out of the sound on its eastern edge, the observatory can be visited in combination with a Red Boats cruise from $24 on top of the cruise price. From the observatory's interesting interpretative centre you can descend 8 m into a circular viewing chamber where a wide array of sea creatures can be seen at close quarters. There are many rare species in Milford including the very rare black coral (which is actually white), a species that can live for over 300 years. Another white resident you may encounter is 'Charlie' the kotuku (white heron). Charlie has been using Milford Sound as his winter residence for over 12 years. In summer Charlie reunites with his mate in Okarito on the west coast, which is New Zealand's only breeding colony. The best place to spot Charlie is around the boat harbour or on the beach where he will probably be busy fishing or just watching the tourists go by. ▸▸ *See also Activities and tours, see page 657.*

⊜ Sleeping

Milford Sound *p654*
A-D Milford Sound Lodge, just off the Milford Rd about 1 km east of the airfield, T03-249 8071, www.milfordlodge.com. For the independent traveller this really is the only place to stay in Milford Sound and, in mid-summer outside the Milford pub opening hours, forms the hub of Milford's leisure activity. Here you can mix with all types, from the rich to locals and trampers, to the almost inevitable townie sitting all alone looking like Stan Laurel after dropping a piano on his foot because he "was never told about the sandflies and tried using my girlfriend's Ponse Mystique perfume to ward

them off". Despite those inevitable 'damned biting things', it has a comfortable range of double/twins, dorms and hard, sheltered and very pricey tent sites. Bathroom facilities are shared. All in all surrounded by such splendour it's a great place to be. The staff are good fun, there is a small, a guest kitchen, large comfortable lounge, small grocery store and satellite internet. You can also get a continental breakfast. A word of warning about the kitchen, however: in summer it can be like the last train to Rawalpindi from 1700 onwards, so get in there at 1600 and spend the rest of the evening relaxing in the lounge and feeling

smug as the tempers fray next door.
Then pay your sympathies to the poor
staff member who has to clean it all up.
Plans are also afoot for an upgrade to
better accommodate couples in modern
motel-style units. Hopefully, this will not
deflect from the rudimentary atmosphere
of the place nor attract an 'altogether more
urbanite' clientele. One other thing – the
resident keas. Several individuals regularly
visit the lodge to cause the standard
mayhem and your car and possessions
are naturally a prime target. These guys
are more switched on than you could
ever imagine. So, beware for example
the heinous photo on the rock trick. It's
simple genius really. While one grabs your
undivided attention posing for you on a
rock like Victoria Beckham another family
member will be eating your dinner, chatting
up your girlfriend or downloading the
contents of your I-pod behind you.
Marvellous stuff.
B-D Mitre Peak Lodge, T03-441 1138,
near the boat terminal. More salubrious,
yet a blot on the landscape, that caters only
for clients of Milford Track guided walks.

🍴 Eating

Milford Sound *p654*
Blue Duck Pub and Café, next to the main
car park on the waterfront T03-249 7657,
summer 0830-1700, bar 1100 till 'close' (local
jargon for when most of the punters have all
left and the local operators have had their
fill); winter 0900-1630, bar 1630 till 'close'.
Owned by Red Boats, this is your only option
for eating, other than the **Milford Lodge**.
It serves a full range of pub-style food from
generous breakfasts to toasted sandwiches.
There are also lunch options on some
cruises. When the rain is relentless, the
renovated bar, with its open fire and
widescreen TV, provides sanctuary.
Milford attracts a multifarious bunch of
characters both long-term and transitory
and you can almost be assured of an
entertaining night out. But be careful.
Drop your defences, drink too much and
partake in idle bets and you may find
yourself enlisted as 'lead runner' in the
annual naked Milford Tunnel dash (see
box, page 655). Not pretty!

⛰ Activities and tours

Milford Sound *p654*
Cruising
The majority of day cruises explore the entire
15-km length of the sound to the Tasman
Sea, taking in all the sights on the way,
including the waterfalls, precipitous rock
overhangs, seal colonies and the underwater
observatory (optional). On the overnight
cruises (see **Real Journeys**, below) you take
in all the usual sights, but can enjoy an
extended trip, meals, accommodation
and other activities including boat-based
kayaking. Given the fact you are not joined
on the water by the fleets of day cruise ships
you are more likely to see the local wildlife,
including dolphins. All prices listed are ex
Milford but there are also numerous options
that include air or bus transportation from
Wanaka, Queenstown or Te Anau.
Mitre Peak Cruises, T03-249 8110,
www.mitrepeak.com. One of the smaller
cruise operators offering a low-passenger
number (smaller boat), nature-orientated
day cruise, from $56-$64.
Milford Sound Red Boat Cruises, T0800-
264536, www.redboats.co.nz. A major
operator, offering similar cruises and rates to
Real Journeys, but they have no overnight
cruises. They also own and operate the
Underwater Observatory (see page 656),
which can only be visited as an adjunct
to their cruises.
Real Journeys, T03-249 7416/T0800-
656501, www.fiordlandtravel.co.nz. Offers
a 'Small Boat Daytime Cruise', a standard
(larger boat) 'Scenic Cruise' and a longer
'Nature Cruise'. Prices range from $55
(child $15) to $80. There is an interesting
commentary, with free tea or coffee, and you
are encouraged to ask the crew questions.
Free access is allowed all around the boat
with the most hardy souls and budding
National Geographic photographers braving
the wind on the upper decks. Additional
lunch options are also available.
    Overnight cruises are available on 3 vessels:
the *MV Friendship*, which is the smallest and
most intimate (1645-0900; multi-share
accommodation from $195); the *MV Milford
Wanderer*, which has quad-share bunk style
cabins (1645-0915; from $164, child $84); and
the top of the range *MV Milford Mariner*

Overnight Cruise (16 hrs; from $280, child $140) which has double cabins and includes dinner and breakfast. All prices are for twin share but sole occupancy is available.

Flightseeing

Flightseeing trips to Milford are readily and principally available from Wanaka, Te Anau and Queenstown. The most popular option is the combination fly/cruise trip, which combines an extended scenic flight with one of the regular daytime cruises. Expect to pay $320-375 (Queenstown/Wanaka). Note, however, that although exciting and well worth the money, this only allows about 2 hrs in Milford itself. Another popular trip, missing out the long bus journey back, is the bus-in/cruise/fly-back option, which costs from $500 (Queenstown). The flight into and around Milford Sound is right up there with the glacier and Mt Cook flights of the west coast.

The principal operators based in Milford, Queenstown and Te Anau are listed below. They offer an array of options, with some flights taking in the Sutherland Falls on the Milford Track and Doubtful Sound. **Air Fiordland**, T03-249 7505/T0800-103404, www.airfiordland.com; **Air Milford**, T03-442 2351/T0800-462252, www.airmilford.co.nz; **Fiordland Helicopters**, T03-249 7575, www.fiordland helicopters.co.nz; and **Milford Helicopters**, T03-249 8384.

Kayaking

A far more serene and atmospheric way to see the sound is by kayak, giving you an incredible sense of scale and intimacy. **Fiordland Wilderness Experiences**, Te Anau, T03-249 7700, www.fiordland seakayak.co.nz. Offers a day excursion on the Sound from $130, taking in the scenery of the Milford Rd. Summer only. **Milford Sound Sea Kayaks**, based at Deep Water Basin (just east of the airfield), T03-249 8500, www.kayakmilford.co.nz. Operated by the intrepid Rosco Gaudin and offers a range of day safaris, fly/kayak, paddle/walk (part of the Milford Track) from 4-7 hrs (flight options are also available from Queenstown). The standard paddle costs $135 from Te Anau, $105 from Milford. This is the only company that operates year round.

Scuba diving

Tawaki Dive (Milford Dive), Te Anau, T03-249 9006, www.tawakidive.co.nz. Full-day fiord diving trips to view the varied species of this unique habitat including rare black coral and the odd sea dragon, from $195 (includes equipment hire).

Tour operators

From Queenstown the principal upmarket operators serving Milford Sound can be booked through **Real Journeys**, see below. There are a few other companies operating out of Queenstown (via Te Anau) that cater for smaller groups, thereby offering a more personable experience.
BBQ Bus, T03-442 1045/T0800-421045, www.milford.net.nz. A reputable company and recommended. Its day trip from Queenstown (departs 0715, pick-ups in Te Anau, return to Queenstown at 1900), includes lunch in the Hollyford Valley, a cruise on the Sound and a visit to the native wildlife centre in Te Anau, all from $189. You can also join the tour from Te Anau (from $145) and there is also a coach/cruise and return flight option, from $480.
Kiwi Discovery, Camp St, Queenstown, T03-442 7340, www.kiwidiscovery.com; and **Kiwi Experience**, 37 Shotover St, Queenstown, T03-442 9708, www.kiwi experience.com. These backpacker-orientated outfits offer a similar coach/cruise options from $165. They will also pick up in Te Anau.
Real Journeys, 74 Shotover St, Queenstown, T03-442 7509, www.realjourneys.co.nz; or at the VIC (I-Site) in Te Anau, T0800-656501/T03-249 7416. Expect to pay around $205 for a coach/cruise day trip, from $330 for a coach/overnight cruise combo (from $228-950) and around $399 for the bus/cruise/fly option.

There are also many options available by bus from Te Anau, many linking up with the Queenstown tours. Again **Real Journeys**, above, is the principal operator. The VIC (I-Site) lists others. From Te Anau expect to pay $175 for a day coach/cruise option, or $228-544 for an overnight trip.
Trips and Tramps, T03-2497081, www.milford tourswalks.co.nz. Locally orientated, personable day-trips to Milford Sound (including cruise and walking options to Lake Marian and Key Summit) from $136, child $75.

Manapouri and Doubtful Sound

→ *Colour map 6 B3 Population: 400*

As you drive into Manapouri with its stunning vistas across the eponymous lake, you are immediately struck by how unobtrusive it is. If it were anywhere else in the developed world, it would probably be an unsightly mass of exclusive real estate and tourist developments. Thankfully it is not, though perhaps the recent history of this pretty little village, the main gateway and access point to activities on Lake Manapouri, Doubtful Sound and the incredible and challenging Dusky Track, has something to do with that. Though you would never guess it, Manapouri has been the sight of some major altercations between the advocates of economics and conservation. Hidden away at the West Arm of the lake, and smack-bang in the heart of Fiordland National Park, is the country's largest hydroelectric power station, which has, over the years, created much controversy. Yet it is the very development of the power station that allows the tourist and conservationist access to some of the most remote parts of the park. Now it is home to an uneasy mix of power station workers and eco-friendly tourist operators and service providers. ▶▶ *For Sleeping, Eating and other listings, see pages 661-662.*

Ins and outs

Getting there Manapouri is 20 km south of Te Anau via SH95. Several bus companies pass through Manapouri on their way south via SH99 to Invercargill, including **Scenic Shuttles**, T03-249 7654/T0800-277483 (Invercargill, daily November to April, Monday to Friday May to October); **Bottom Bus**, T03-442 9708; and **Topline Tours**, T03- 249 8059/T0508-832628, www.toplinetours.co.nz. **Real Journeys**, T03-249 7416, also offers regular shuttles back and forth to Te Anau.

Getting around Fiordland Explorer Charters, T03-249 6616/T0800-434673, www.explorercharters.co.nz, offers water taxi services on Lake Manapouri for trampers and mountain bikers who wish to explore the Wilmot Pass, or access the Dusky Track trailhead. **Real Journeys**, Pearl Harbour, Manapouri, T03-249 6602/T0800-656501, www.realjourneys.co.nz, offers excellent day (eight hour) and overnight (24 hour) excursions to Doubtful Sound via Lake Manapouri and the Wilmot Pass.

Tourist information There is no information centre in Manapouri, but **Real Journeys** ⓘ *on the wharf (Pearl harbour), T03-249 6602, www.realjourneys.co.nz,* is the base for all water activity on the lake and Doubtful Sound tour operations. For further information contact the **VIC (I-Site)** ⓘ *T03-249 8900,* or **DoC** ⓘ *T03-249 7924,* in Te Anau.

Lake Manapouri

Lake Manapouri is stunning not only because of its backdrop of bush and mountain but also its moods. From the beach beside the village the whole scene echoes the constant change of Milford Sound. It is of course not so dramatic in its topography, but no less dynamic. There are 35 islands which disguise its boundaries and, at a forbidding 420 m deep, is the second deepest lake in the country (the deepest is Lake Haurokö in southwestern Fiordland). To really appreciate the size and complex nature of Lake Manapouri it is necessary to get out on the water, which, thankfully, is a matter of course on the route to Doubtful Sound.

Manapouri Underground Power Station

At the terminus of West Arm, and forming the main access point via Wilmot Pass to Doubtful Sound, is the Manapouri Underground Power Station. Although an unwelcome development to the conservationist, one cannot fail to admire the environmentally sympathetic way in which this incredible feat of engineering has been achieved and is maintained. Started in 1963 and completed eight years later, now only a few unsightly pylons connected to a switchyard, a control building and water intakes, belie the mammoth constructions underground – all supplied by a fairly unobtrusive barge that goes back and forth across the lake to Supply Bay near Manapouri. A 2040 m (1:10) tunnel set in the hillside allows access to the main centre of operations – a large machine hall housing seven turbines and generators, fed by the water penstocks from 170 m above. What is most impressive is the 9.2 m diameter tailrace tunnel, which outputs the used water at the head of Doubtful Sound – an amazing 10 km from Lake Manapouri and 178 m below its surface. Started in 1964 the tailrace took four years to build. **Real Journeys** (see Activities and tours, page 661) make three-hour trips to the power station (it is also a port of call on the Doubtful Sound day-excursion, see below); the bus drives down the dank and forbidding access tunnel and makes a very tight turn at the bottom where passengers are decanted out to look at the interior of the machine hall. Even the worst luddite will be impressed.

Wilmot Pass

① *The road can be explored independently by mountain bike (provided you are fit enough) and acts as the northern trailhead to the Dusky Track.*

The 22-km road from West Arm to Doubtful Sound across the Wilmot Pass is a spectacular drive, encompassing remote mountain and beech and podocarp forest scenery, lookout points and waterfalls. The unsealed road, which took two years to complete, was built as part of the hydropower project. At a cost of nearly $5 for every 2.5 cm, it is easily the most expensive road in the country. With its numerous twists and turns and heady topography, together with an annual rainfall of over 7 m, it is also a very hard road to maintain. Like the power station, the road forms part of **Real Journeys'** Doubtful Sound day trip (see page 662).

Doubtful Sound

Doubt nothing, this fiord, like Milford Sound, is all it is cracked up to be – and more. Many who have made the trip to Milford feel it may be very similar and therefore not worthy of the time or expense to get there. But Doubtful Sound has a very different atmosphere to Milford. With the mountain topography in Fiordland getting generally lower the further south you go, and the fiords becoming longer and more indented with coves, arms and islands, Doubtful Sound offers the sense of space and wilderness that Milford does not.

Doubtful is, after Dusky, the second largest fiord and has 10 times the surface area of Milford and, at 40 km, is also more than twice as long. It is also the deepest of the fiords at 421 m. There are three distinct arms and several outstanding waterfalls including the heady 619-m **Browne Falls** near Hall Arm. This is only marginally less than the near-vertical Sutherland Falls on the famed Milford Track. At the entrance to Hall Arm is the impressive 900-m cliff of **Commander Peak** (1274 m), the only true echo of Milford's dramatic corridor.

Doubtful Sound hosts its own pod of about 60 bottlenose dolphins that are regularly seen by visitors as well as fur seals and fiordland crested penguins. It is also noted for its very lack of activity; on a calm night the silence is deafening.

Captain Cook originally named it Doubtful Harbour during his voyage of 1770. He decided not to explore past the entrance, fearful that the prevailing winds would not allow him to get back out; hence the name. It was not until 23 years later that Italian explorer Don Alessandro Malaspina, leading a Spanish expedition, dropped anchor

and sent a small crew on a whaleboat into the fiord to make observations. Although a
brief excursion it was both brave and meticulous and left a number of present-day
names in its wake. Melsnping Beach being the most obvious.

● Sleeping

Doubtful Sound *p660*
Real Journeys, T03-249 6602, www.real
journeys.co.nz, offers overnight packages in
season on Doubtful Sound, from $260
quad-share to $698 single occupancy.
LL Beechwood Lodge, 40 Cathedral Drive,
T03-249 6993, www.beechwoodlodge.com.
A modern, deservingly popular boutique B&B
that sits overlooking the lake and mountains.
Guests are accommodated on the ground
floor, which has 2 spacious en suites, a private
entrance and a guest kitchen. From the
lounge you can sit and muse upon the
ever-changing moods of the lake. Internet
and off-street parking. No children.
LL Murrell's Grand View House, 7 Murrell
Av, T03-249 6642, www.murrells.co.nz.
A rambling house near the mouth of the
outlet and surrounded by spacious gardens.
It offers 4 spacious double en suites and
fine cuisine, just a short walk from the
cruise terminal.
**A-D Manapouri Lake View Chalets and
Motor Park**, 50 Manapouri-Te Anau
Highway, T03-249 6624. Wonderfully quirky
place whose elderly (and clearly) European
owners tend a range of 'disney-esque'
cottages, old Morris Minors and even a
period costume collection. It has the
cottages of course, which are a delight plus
more conventional cabins, powered sites
and good facilities. The lakeshore is just
across the road.
A-D Manapouri Lakeview Motor Inn,
68 Manapouri-Te Anau Highway, T03-249
6652, www.manapouri.com. This older
place overlooks the lake and has serviced
units, plus 2 self-contained and 11 budget
rooms, a café and internet.
B-D Freestone Backpackers, 3 km east of
Manapouri on Hillside Rd, T03-249 6893,
freestone@xtra.co.nz. 5 tidy self-contained
timber chalets with wood burners in a 4-ha

rural setting. Singles, doubles, twins and
shared rooms. Recommended.
D-D Manapouri Glade and Possum Lodge,
at the end of Murrell Av and right on the
headland at the Waiau River mouth,
T03-249 6623, possumlodge@xtra.co.nz.
Self-contained cottages, backpacker cabins
and powered/tent sites. Peaceful place with
lovely short walks.
D Deep Cove Hostel, very remote, at the
head of Doubtful Sound, T03-249 6602.
A possibility outside school term-time
but phone first for details.

● Eating

Doubtful Sound *p660*
There are few options in Manapouri and
you would be better to head back to
Te Anau for evening dining.
¶ Beehive, in the Lakeview Motor Inn, T03-
249 6652, Mon-Sat 1100-2130 (seasonal).
Has a licensed café and bar, serving
acceptable pub-style grub into the evening.
¶ Cathedral Café, Cathedral Drive (next to
the general store and petrol station). Serves
coffee and snacks during the day.

▲▲ Activities and tours

Doubtful Sound *p660*
Eco-tours
Adventure Kayak and Cruise, Waiau St,
T03-249 6626/T0800-324966, www.fiordland
adventure.co.nz. Offers day or overnight
rental or fully equipped kayaks on Lake
Manapouri (from $45 per day) as well as
full-day guided and guided overnight trips
to Doubtful Sound, from $195 (overnight
$225, 2-day $309).
Fiordland Ecology Holidays, based on the
main road in Manapouri, T03-249 6600,
www.fiordland.gen.nz. Offers an excellent
range of holiday options from 3 days to

Southland Manapouri & Doubtful Sound *Listings*

● *For an explanation of the Sleeping and Eating price codes used in this guide, see the inside*
● *front cover. Other relevant information is provided in the Essentials chapter, pages 44-51.*
Note that prices are given in New Zealand dollars.

2 weeks on board its 12 passenger, 65-ft yacht *Breaksea Girl*. The yacht is very comfortable and well equipped and the tours offer a very sensitive insight into Fiordland's unique wildlife. Trips cost from $215 per day.

Fiordland Wilderness Experiences, based in Te Anau (see page 652). Offers 2- to 5-day trips to Doubtful, Breaksea and Dusky Sounds from $310. It also offers independent rental for the experienced, from $55 a day.

Mountain biking

The **Wilmot Pass** is a superb (but challenging 500 m ascent) road to explore by mountain bike. For bike hire see Te Anau page 653.

Tours of the sound

This trip is recommended not only because of the stunning natural scenery and the wildlife but because of the novelty of entering into the very bowels of the earth.

Deep Cove Charters, Manapouri, T03-249 6828, www.doubtful-sound.com. Offers a small-scale craft and a personalized laid-back operation. It is perfect if you want to spend a night out on the sound and avoid the big commercial operations. An overnight cruise costs from $330, child $300. Departs 0900.

Fiordland Explorer Charters, based in Pearl Harbour, T03-249 6616, www.explorer charters.co.nz. Also offers a smaller scale, personalized operation and day excursion (7½ hrs) daily at 0930, from $200, child $80.

Real Journeys Pearl Harbour, T03-249 6602, www.realjourneys.co.nz. The main commercial tour operator to the Manapouri Power Station and Doubtful Sound. It offers a Wilderness Day Cruise (10 hrs) from $230, child $55; and the popular Overnight Cruise.

'Wilderness Day Cruise' After boarding a modern launch at Manapouri you cross the lake to West Arm (interesting commentary and free tea/coffee). From West Arm you then board a bus and negotiate the Wilmot Pass, stopping at a viewpoint over Doubtful Sound before descending past rivers, waterfalls and the hydropower tailrace outlet to the Doubtful Sound wharf. From there you board another launch for a superbly scenic and informative cruise through the Sound to the Tasman Sea.

If time allows, you negotiate one or 2 of the fiords 'arms' and throughout the cruise can often see the resident dolphins. Once returned to the wharf, reunited with the bus and Lake Manapouri's West Arm, you then leave the dramatic scenery and daylight behind and negotiate the underground access tunnel to the machine hall of the hydropower station. There you stop for 30 mins to learn how it all works before re-emerging into daylight and catching the launch back to Manapouri. Trips depart daily at 0930 (Te Anau at 0815) and cost from $230 child $55 (Te Anau $248, child $64).

'Overnight Cruise' This trip involves all of the above, plus an overnight stay on the Sound, aboard the comfortable Fiordland Navigator. Designed along the lines of a traditional New Zealand trading scow, it comes complete with sails and offers private en suite cabins or quad-share bunks. There are friendly nature guides on board and also kayaks with which you can do your own scheduled exploring. Trips depart daily Nov-Apr at 1230 from $260 quad-share to $698 single occupancy. Both these trips link in with Queenstown and Te Anau departures.

Walking and tramping

The Wilmot Pass is the principal access point to the northern trailhead of the **Dusky Track** (see page 687). There are also a number of walks available around Manapouri most of which negotiate the **Garnock Burn** catchment and start on the southern bank of the Lake Manapouri outlet at Pearl Harbour. The most popular walk is the (3 hrs) **Pearl Harbour Circle Track**, which follows the riverbank, upstream, before negotiating the forest ascent to a lookout point, then descending back to Pearl Harbour. The Circle Track also allows access to the longer **Back Valley** and **Hope Arm Hut tracks** that explore Hope Arm (Lake Manapouri) and the inland **Lake Rakatu**. For details pick up the Manapouri Walks leaflet ($1) from the DoC VIC in Te Anau. For dinghy hire across the river (call at the post centre next to the petrol station and café) or contact **Adventure Kayak and Cruise**, T03-249 6626, www.fiordlandadventure.co.nz.

Southern Scenic Route

From Manapouri SH99 leaves the vast majority of tourist traffic behind, as most retrace their steps to Queenstown or cross-country east, to Dunedin. The Southern Scenic Route, which first heads south to the coast via Tuatapere and Invercargill, then north via the beautiful and underrated Catlins coast to Dunedin, provides an attractive alternative. The highlights of this trip, other than the sheer peace and quiet, are the potential stops in Tuatapere to walk the relatively new and celebrated Hump Ridge Track, an overnight stay in the pleasant seaside resort of Riverton, a day or two in Invercargill, before a trip to Stewart Island (see page 672) and then a thorough exploration of the Catlins Coast (see page 679). ▶▶ For Sleeping, Eating and other listings, see pages 669-672.

Ins and outs

Getting there and around The Southern Scenic Route which is sometimes advertised as encompassing the entire journey from Dunedin to Milford Sound is a total of 440 km. By bus, the route is served by **Scenic Shuttle**, T03-249 7654/ T0800-277483, (Invercargill, daily November to April, Monday to Friday May to October), and the backpacker orientated **Bottom Bus**, T03-434 7370, (Queenstown/ Dunedin/Invercargill). Local shuttle services and transport to and from Invercargill are listed in the places below.

Tourist information **Tuatapere VIC** ① *corner Half Mile and Clifden Rds, 31 Orawia Rd, T03-226 6739, info@humpridgetrack.co.nz, daily 0900-1700 (winter Mon-Fri 0900-1700)*, has enthusiastic and helpful staff who can provide infinite detail about the Hump Ridge Track, www.humpridgetrack.co.nz. They also administer all track bookings and have internet. **DoC** has an office in Tuatapere but you will find all the relevant administration at the VIC. **Riverton VIC (I-Site)** ① *across the river (from the west), 172 Palmerston St, T03-234 9991, www.riverton-aparima.co.nz, daily 0900-1700*. **Invercargill VIC (I-Site)** ① *next to Queen's Park and housed in the Southland Museum and Gallery Building, Victoria Av, T03-214 6243, www.southlandnz.com, daily Oct-Apr 0900-1900, May-Sep 0900-1700*, has listings of local activities, transport, accommodation and attractions. **DoC** ① *regional office, 7th floor, State Insurance Building, 33 Don St, T03-211 2400, www.doc.govt.nz, Mon-Fri 0800-1700*, can also organize hut bookings for Stewart Island tramps.

Manapouri to Tuatapere 🏠🚌🏔️ ▶▶ *pp669-672.*

Still reeling from the highs of Fiordland's stunning scenery, your journey south could include the main drag of Vegas and still seem boring, so just accept that fact and sit back and enjoy the peace and quiet of the road. SH99 has to be one of the quietest main roads in the country and between Manapouri and Milford it's unusual to pass more than half a dozen cars even in summer. Generally speaking you will encounter very little with two legs. Instead what you will see is paddock upon paddock of sheep.

Although birdwatchers can find considerable pleasure at the **Redcliffe Wetland Reserve** just north of Blackmount (38 km) there is little to justify a stop until **Clifden** (66 km). As well as its limestone caves, Clifden boasts one of the oldest and longest suspension bridges in the country (built in 1899). Though a little disappointing in global terms, it is still worth a look and makes a nice picnic spot by the river. Near Clifden (signposted off Clifden Gorge Road to Winton) are its non-commercial and undeveloped limestone caves, which can be explored carefully with a good torch.

Just south of Clifden is the 30-km unsealed road to **Lake Hauroko**, the deepest body of water in New Zealand. Its remoteness is undoubtedly appealing and there is an interesting walk up a precipitous bluff to a lookout point. The area is also known for its many Maori (Ngai Tahu) burial sites. Lake Hauroko provides jet-boat access to the **Dusky Track**, one of the country's most challenging and remote tramps. **Lake Hauroko Tours**, based in Tuatapere, T03-226 6681, www.duskytrack.co.nz, can provide access. On your way back from Lake Hauroko you may consider the short diversion north (off the Hauroko Road just before SH99) to sample the delights of **Dean Forest**. There, a pleasant short walk takes in its most famous native, a 1000-year-old totara tree. Once back on SH99 it is a further 13 km to Tuatapere, considered the gateway to the southeast corner of the Fiordland National Park (not that there are any roads).

Tuatapere → *Colour map 6, B3 Population: 800*

Tuatapere is a quiet little town that wants to start making a big noise. The reason for this and the town's intended 'raison d'être tourisme', is the 53-km **Hump Ridge Track**, New Zealand's newest 'Great Walk' and one that is advertised as being on a par with any of the others in Fiordland, or indeed the country (see page 688). The track starts at the western end of **Bluecliffs Beach**, which, in itself, is a nice spot to spend a couple of hours. Nearby, on the first section of the Hump Ridge Track is the 36-m-high, 125-m-long **Percy Burn Viaduct**, the largest wooden viaduct in the world. But even as it stood, this former saw-milling and farming town and (mysteriously) self-proclaimed 'sausage capital' of the country, had a few other notable local attractions, including some fine jet-boating operations down the **Wairaurahiri River**. Lake Hauroko Tours, T03-226 6681, offers transport and trips to and from the tracks.

Tuatapere to Invercargill ⬤🎵⬤▲ ⇥ *pp669-672.*

A further 10 km south and SH99 reaches the coast at the evocatively named **Te Waewae Bay**. Here you can stop at **McCraken's Rest** to admire the beach and the views west over southern Fiordland, or east, to **Monkey Island**. Monkey Island was the anchor site of the great Maori *waka* (canoe) Takitimu which, as legend tells, was wrecked on the bar of the Waiau River. Te Waewae Bay itself is quite a serene sight in fine weather and often the playground for Hector's dolphin and the odd whale, but in winter the wind can come sweeping in from the Antarctic with a vengeance.

This phenomenon is starkly highlighted in the next port of call – the intriguing village of **Orepuki** – where the macrocarpa trees have been sculpted into amazing, tangled shapes by the wind. Apparently, it is not in fact the wind that is directly responsible for this but the tree's aversion to sea salt in the air. The tiny former gold rush village is worth investigating, not only for its trees, but because it looks like the village that time forgot. The buildings seem to have changed little in decades. Also, 500 m north of the village is the **Orepuki Gemstone Beach**, which may reveal garnets, jasper, quartz, nephrite as well as the odd worm fossil or even sapphires.

From Orepuki the road garrotes the Wakaputa Point before rejoining the coast again at the beachside settlement of **Colac Bay**. A place rich in Maori history, it is now mainly frequented by surfers. Unless you have a board, you are best moving on to the far more ample amenities and sights of Riverton, a further 11 km east.

Riverton → *Colour map 6, C3 Population: 1900*

Riverton – or Aparima, to use its former Maori name – is the oldest permanent European settlement in Southland and one of the oldest in the country. Located on the banks of the common estuary formed by the Aparima and Purakino rivers, it was formerly a safe haven for whalers and sealers and was first established as early as the

is a fine place to stop for lunch, a short walk on the beach, or even to consider as a
quieter alternative base to Invercargill, now only 42 km to the east.

Given the rich history of the area the **Wallace Early Settlers Museum** ① *172
Palmerston St, T03-234 8520, daily 1030-1600, donation*, is worth a look. It houses
displays and photographs focusing on the early Maori, whaling and gold mining days,
with over 500 portraits of the early pioneers. It also provides genealogical research
assistance. Nearby, the **South Coast Environment Centre** ① *T03-234 8717, daily 1330-
1630*, promotes the local environment and wildlife with displays and information.

The **Riverton Rocks** and **Howell's Point**, at the southern edge of Taramea Bay,
provide safe swimming, fishing, short walks and fine views across to Stewart Island. If
you are looking for a good place for lunch then try the excellent **Beachhouse Café and
Bar** (see Eating, page 670). Other local walks are outlined in the free *Riverton Scenic
Walks* leaflet; available free from the VIC (I-Site).

Invercargill 🔲🍴🏍🏕🏛️🏔🚌🛈 ➤➤ *pp669-672.*

➔ *Colour map 6, C4 Population: 53,209.*
When it comes to aesthetics a lot has been said about Invercargill over the years and
sadly (and undeservingly) much of it has been negative. Invercargill is not pretty. Let's
be honest. Stuck at the very rear end of New Zealand and sandblasted by the worst
extremes of the southern weather, even its climate and geography are against it. This
is nothing new or unusual, after all Scotland (to which Invercargill and the region as a
whole is so closely linked) is an entire country that suffers the same affliction. But for
Invercargill there is one added problem. For most tourists the city features late on the
travel schedule and by the time they get here they are almost drunk on stunning
world-class scenery. No remedy there of course, it's an inevitable 'coming back down
to earth', but were it not for the geography and the climate one cannot help wonder if
the problem could all be addressed with one weekend of frenzied mass tree-planting.

However, that said, Invercargill has many good points, and although you will hear
different, it is certainly not the underdog it is reputed to be. For a start, it is the capital of
the richest agricultural region in the South Island and so far in to the new millennium
has had the strongest economic growth in the country. As the commercial hub of the
region the 'City of Water and Light' (as it has been labelled) often buzzes (yes buzzes!)
with the prosperity of that thriving economy, the vivacity of student life (the city is the
regional focus for further education) and of course boasts a rich and fascinating history
that marries the strong Maori and Celtic influence that pioneered the region. It is also a
fine base from which to explore the delights of Southland and the 'Southern Scenic
Route'. Within a two-hour radius are a wealth of internationally acclaimed experiences
of which Stewart Island, the Catlins Coast and southern Fiordland are the most obvious
and the most lauded. So, by all means linger for a while – you won't regret it – and
before you leave (while no one is looking) plant a tree!

Ins and outs

Getting there Invercargill airport ① *2½ km south of the city*, is served by **Air New
Zealand Link,** T0800-737000, www.airnewzealand.co.nz. There are direct flights daily
from Christchurch and Dunedin. **Stewart Island Flights** (Southern Air), T03-218 9129,
www.stewartislandflights.com, and **Southeast Air,** T03-214 5522, southeast.air@
xtra.co.nz, also serve Oban and Mason Bay on Stewart Island.

By bus, Invercargill is 579 km from Christchurch and 217 km from Dunedin via SH1;
and 187 km from Queenstown via SH6 and 168 km from Te Anau via SH99 Southern
Scenic Route. It is served by **Intercity,** T03-214 6243 (Christchurch/Dunedin); **Atomic**

Shuttles, T03-214 6243 (Queenstown/Christchurch/Dunedin); **Wanaka Connexions,** T03-216 0717/T0800-244844, www.wanakaconnexions.co.nz (Queenstown/Wanaka daily); **Knightrider** T03-342 8055, www.knightrider.co.nz (Christchurch/Dunedin, every night except Saturday); **Scenic Shuttle,** T03-214 1851/T0800-277483 (Invercargill, daily November to April, Monday to Friday May to October); and the backpacker- orientated **Bottom Bus,** T03-434 7370, www.bottombus.co.nz (Queenstown/ Dunedin). Also plying the Southern Scenic Route is the **Catlins Coaster** (Catlins/ Dunedin), T021-682461/T0800-304333, www.catlinscoaster.co.nz. Most buses arrive at and leave from the VIC (I-Site). Note there is now no train service south of Dunedin. For ferry services from Bluff (Stewart Island), see page .

Getting around Scenic Shuttle, T03-218 7381/T0800-277483, connects with Invercargill airport flights and will pick-up from your accommodation ($6). **Invercargill Passenger Transport,** 100 Leven Street, T03-218 7170, provides local suburban bus services $1.50-3.50. **Stewart Island Experience,** T03-212 7660/T0800-000511, www.stewartislandexperience.co.nz, provides shuttle services to Bluff and the Stewart Island ferry ($16, child $8 one way). For taxis, car and bike rental, see Transport, page 671. **Lynette Jack Tours,** T03-215 7741, is a noted local and regional sightseeing tour operator.

Invercargill

Queen's Park

Southland Museum & Art Gallery

Water Tower

Pall Mall Courtville

Public Library

DoC

24hr Supermarket

Cinema

Supermarket

To ⑨, Airport, Oreti Beach, Bluff & Southern Scenic Route, Catlins

To ⑧

N

| 0 metres | 200 |
| 0 yards | 200 |

Sleeping
Ascot Park **14**
Balmoral Lodge **12**

Beersheba Boutique
   Accommodation **11**
Birchwood Manor **1**
Burtonwood **2**
Coachman's
   Caravan Park **13**
Garden Grove **9**
Homestead Villa **3**
Invercargill Top 10
   Holiday Park **10**

Queen's Park Motel **4**
Southern Comfort
   Backpackers **6**
Tuatara Backpackers YHA **7**
Tudor Park Country Stay **8**

Eating
148 on Elles **8**
Fat Indian **10**
Frog & Firkin **1**

HMS Kings **2**
Lone Star Café **3**
Louie's Café &
   Tapas Bar **4**
Outpost & Cabbage
   Tree Café **9**
Tillermans **5**
Waxy O'Shea's **7**
Zookeepers Café **6**

⁏ The Tuatara

To describe the noble and endemic tuatara as the most ancient reptile on earth is impressive enough, but when you consider that these 'living fossils' are even older than the landscape itself, it seems truly remarkable that they exist at all. They belong to a very singular order of reptiles known as beakheads that once roamed the earth (be it very slowly) over 225 million years ago. Once common throughout the country, but subject to predation and a widespread loss of habitat, the tuatara, has sadly joined the long list of New Zealand creatures in decline and now exists on only 30 offshore islands. They grow to a maximum of 610 mm, live in burrows and feed mainly on ground-dwelling insects. Given their status and natural habitat, your best chance of seeing a tuatara is in one of the country's zoos or museums. The Southland Museum in Invercargill is without doubt the most famous venue, having the most successful breeding and research programme in the world. It also boasts perhaps the most famous tuatara in the land – 'Henry'. In appearance and mannerism tuatara generally (but Henry in particular), seem the very epitome of the word ancient and a true mascot of an old, far less manic world. No click-of-a-switch, press-button reactions here; no loud noises; no 'Reality TV' – 'When reptiles carry away your children' or films by Steven Spielberg; no bloodthirsty chases, hideous maulings, or perverse 'Crocodile Hunter'-induced poison bites. No, not necessary. Somehow, Henry, who is at least 120 years old, without expression or movement and in a time zone all of his own, makes a mockery of all this human nonsense. Yet he and his ilk are not like the human centenarian awaiting death in some old folks' home, most probably devoid of dignity or normal function. He looks more like a proud bronze bust, head held high and starring, waiting, waiting and waiting, his existence set to a schedule well beyond anything we adhere to. He clearly looks like he has all the time in the world to watch in utter complacency as you come and go and, one could swear, a look that even says, 'and not only you punk, but the human race, period'.

Background

Although the south coast was settled by European sealers and whalers as early as 1835, it was not until 1857, that the Chief Surveyor for Otago, John Turnbull Thompson, was ordered by Governor Sir Thomas Gore Browne, to choose a site and take responsibility for the planning of what is now the country's most southerly city. When Southland seceded from Otago in 1861 to become a separate province, Invercargill became its capital. Named in honour of Captain William Cargill (1784-1860), the first superintendent of Otago, 'Inver' is Scottish Gaelic for 'at the mouth of' and refers to the city's proximity to the Waihopai River. Note the many street names dedicated to Scottish rivers.

Sights

The main highlight in the town is the excellent **Southland Museum and Art Gallery** ① *edge of Queen's Park, Victoria Av, T03-219 9069, www.southlandmuseum.co.nz, Mon-Fri 0900-1700 Sat-Sun 1000-1700, donation*. Housed in the largest pyramid in the southern hemisphere (27 m), it boasts all the usual fine Maori Taonga and early settler exhibits and national and international art exhibitions, but is particularly noted for its 'Roaring Forties Antarctic and Sub-Antarctic Island' display and audio-visual

(25 minutes, $2) shown several times daily. Also excellent is the museum's **tuatara** display and breeding programme. The 'Tuatarium' is an utter delight and an opportunity to come face to face with a reptilian species older than the land on which you stand. Henry, the oldest resident at an estimated 120 years plus, usually sits only a foot or two away from the glass. You can try to stare the old fella out, but you will fail, because Henry has had plenty of practice.

Beyond the museum is **Queen's Park**, the city's saving grace. Its 80 ha of trees, flowerbeds and duck ponds provide a lovely setting for a walk, a picnic or a quiet doze. **Anderson Park** ① *McIvor Rd, 7 km north of the city centre (signposted off SH6), T03-215 7432; gallery open daily 1330-1700*, is another 24 ha of beautiful parkland, with an interesting public art gallery. The VIC (I-Site) has a very useful free *Parks and Gardens* and *Heritage Trail* leaflets.

If beaches and sand are your thing, then the huge 30-km expanse of **Oreti Beach**, 10 km west of the city (past the airport) will not disappoint. It has the added attraction of allowing vehicles (with sensible drivers) on the sand and safe swimming. Nearby **Sandy Point**, on Sandy Point Road, offers a range of short walks and other recreation activities. There is an unmanned information point at the entrance to the park. For a fine view of the city head for the very unusual 1889 **Water Tower** ① *corner of Gala St and Queen Drive, Sun only, 1330-1630*.

Southland Southern Scenic Route

Bluff ⬛🍴🌀 ⇥ *pp669-672*.

➜ *Colour map 6, C4 Population: 2000*

Some 27 km south of Invercargill, the small port of Bluff heralds the end of the road in the South Island. Most visitors to Bluff are either on their way or returning from Stewart Island, or come to stand and gawk at a wind blasted signpost at the terminus of SH1, which tells them they are several thousand miles from anywhere: next stop Antarctica.

The town itself is as strange as it is intriguing. As a result of a dying oyster-fishing industry and protracted general social decline, there is a very palpable sense of decay in Bluff. While the vast majority of New Zealand's other towns progress and grow at a healthy pace, here, it is as if the clocks have stopped and no-one's home. The place is like some long forgotten, withered pot plant in desperate need of a drink. Worse still, the architectural aesthetics leave a lot to be desired. Here, the tastelessness and kitsch of many of the older properties and their facades is so awful it's almost an attraction in itself – as the late and iconic Paua Shell House once proved. Up almost every street the older property designs and colour combinations leaves one in a such a state of sensory shock, that had one never indulged in recreational drugs you'd be excused for thinking you just did – and to some excess. However, human creations aside, on the southern side of the peninsula the coastal scenery is stunning. There is no shortage of wind down here and the entire peninsula is sculpted accordingly. Bare boulder-clad hills shrouded in part with stunted wind shorn bush and, on its leeward side, a surprisingly tall stand of native trees creates a fascinating mix of habitats. All well worth investigating along a network of fine walking tracks.

Ins and outs
Getting there Stewart Island Experience, T03-212 7660/T0800-000511, offers a regular daily shuttle service ($16 one way, child $8) to and from Invercargill to coincide with the Stewart Island ferries. Secure parking is available opposite the terminal from $6. For ferry services see Stewart Island National Park, page 672, or contact **Stewart Island Experience**, T03-212 7660, www.stewartislandexperience.co.nz.

Sights

The main attraction in Bluff remains the **signpost** at Stirling Point, which marks the terminus of SH1. The prickly yellow icon admirably fits that weird human compulsion to reach a certain point then take a digital snap of doing so. Note, contrary to popular belief this is not the most southerly point in New Zealand. That particular honour goes to Slope Point in the Catlins, see page 680.

Stirling Point is also the starting point for some fine coastal and bush walks, some of which climb to the top of **Bluff Hill** (Motupohue) at 270 m. From there you will be rewarded with fine panoramic views of the region and Stewart Island. The summit can also be reached by car from the centre of town (signposted). To the north the view is dominated by the monstrous **Tiwai Aluminium Smelter** ① *T03-218 5440, 2-hr tours held up to 3 times a week (week days only); bookings are essential.* Those with time on their hands and a disturbing interest in aluminium smelting can take a free guided tour. If it is raining the small **Maritime Museum** ① *Foreshore Rd, T03-212 7534, Mon-Fri 1000-1630, Sat-Sun 1300-1700, $2,* is worth a look to soak up the town's long history. Finally, if all else fails take a small tour of the town's backstreets to see just how tasteless some architects work and colour co-ordinations can be.

Bluff's biggest event of the year is the famous **Oyster and Southland Seafood Festival** usually held in April. ➤➤ *See Festivals and events, page 671.*

● Sleeping

Tuatapere *p664*

A-D Humptrack Backpackers and Motel, 6 Clifden Rd, T03-226 6418. The main backpackers, with powered and unpowered sites.
B Waiau Hotel, 47 Main St, T03-226 6409, info@waiauhotel.co.nz. Basic B&B and budget accommodation, some en suites.

Riverton *p664*

L Harbour View House Boutique B&B, 12 Dallas St, T03-234 8755, www.harbour viewhouse.co.nz. Characterful 1910 homestead overlooking the harbour. Queen and twin with private facilities.
AL-A Riverton Rock, 136 Palmerston St, T03-234 8886, www.riverton.co.nz. An excellent mid-budget establishment in a restored historic villa. It offers a range of very well appointed, themed rooms including one with a superb original Victorian bath. There is also an open fire in one room. Modern facilities and good value.
C-D The Globe Backpackers, 144 Palmerston St, T03-234 8527, www.theglobe.co.nz. Centrally located in the town's oldest hotel offering doubles, twins and dorms. Pizzas available from the bar. Also offers 2 self-contained units near the beach, $95 per unit.
C-D Riverton Caravan Park, Hamlet St, T03-234 8526. Basic with a cottage, cabins and on-site vans as well as powered tent sites, but still pleasant with good views.

Invercargill *p665, map p666*

For farmstay options contact the very helpful **Western Southland Farm Hosting Group**, T03-225 8608, www.nzcountry.co.nz/farmhost.
LL-A Ascot Park Hotel, corner of Tay St and Racecourse Rd, T03-217 6195, www.ilt.co.nz/ascot. One of the city's top hotels and a large modern establishment offering a wide range of rooms and fine facilities in a quiet setting. Spa, pool and in-house restaurant and bar.
L Beersheba Boutique Accommodation, 58 Milton Park Rd, T03-216 3677, www.beer sheba.co.nz. A modern B&B set in peaceful setting on the outskirts of the city. Designer en suites, outside fireplace and pool.
L-A Burtonwood, 177 Gala St, T03-218 8884, www.burtonwood.co.nz. Convenient 3-bedroom option with friendly, caring hosts across the road from Queen's Park.
AL Tudor Park Country Stay, 21 Lawrence Rd, Royal Bush, T03-221 7150, www.tudor park.co.nz. An affordable B&B option 15 mins' north of the city. Set in 4 ha of beautiful garden it is a neo-Tudor home with comfortable en suite rooms. Meals available.
B-D Tuatara Backpackers YHA, 30-32 Dee St, T0800-8828272, tuataralodge@xtra.co.nz. A modern hostel ideally located in the centre of town. It offers a full range of rooms with some very tidy shared standard double/

twins and a few luxurious and value double en suites. Good kitchen, popular street-side café with fast internet and value meals and breakfasts, Sky TV and off-street parking.
C-D Southern Comfort Backpackers, 30 Thomson St, T03-218 3838. An old, spacious villa near the museum and Queen's Park. It is a Southland favourite and offers dorms, doubles and free bike hire. Recommended.

Motels
There are plenty of motels, some upmarket and modern, others older and cheaper.
AL-A Birchwood Manor, 189 Tay St, T03-218 8881, www.birchwoodmanor.co.nz.
A Balmoral Lodge, 265 Tay St, T03-219 9050, www.ilt.co.nz/balmoral. Recommended.
A Homestead Villa, corner Avenal and Dee sts, T03-214 0408, www.lit.co.nz/homestead.
A Queen's Park Motel, 85 Alice St, T03-214 4504, www.queensparkmotels.co.nz. Good motel within a short walk of Queen's Park.
B Garden Grove, 161 North Rd, T03-215 9555, www.gardengrovemotel.co.nz.

Motorcamps and campsites
C-D Coachman's Caravan Park, 705 Tay St, T03-217 6046, www.coachmans.co.nz. The only reputable central option.
D Invercargill Top 10 Holiday Park, 77 McIvor Rd (northern edge of town off SH6), T03-215 9032, www.invercargilltop10.co.nz. Small, peaceful and friendly. Recommended.

Bluff p668
Bluff has a few good accommodation choices but, given the regular shuttle service and lack of general services most Stewart Island bound choose to stay in Invercargill.
AL Land's End Hotel, at the very end of SH1, T03-212 7575, www.landsend.net.nz. A boutique hotel with comfortable, well-appointed en suite rooms and a wine bar/café with open fire. Good views.
AL-A Lazy Fish, 35 Burrows St, T03-212 7245, www.thelazyfish.nz. A pleasant B&B in a traditional villa. Separate self-contained option and private room in the house, both cosy and comfortable. Good value and close to ferry terminal. Also has tent sites.
B-D Argyle Park Camping Ground Gregory St (off marine Parade), T03-212 8704. Recently redeveloped with good facilities. Units, powered and non-powered sites.

Eating

Tuatapere p664
Highway 99 Café/Bar and Takeaway, 73 Main St, T03-226 6996. Fine for a quick daytime snack. But, its biggest attraction is 'Brandy' the cockatoo, with a level of conceit so great it would make the great Mohammed Ali seem modest. As you enter the shop you will be told in no uncertain terms that 'Brandy is a very (very) pretty boy'.

Riverton p664
Beachhouse Café and Bar, 126 Rocks Highway, T03-234 8274, 1000-late. Overlooks the bay and understandably popular. Internet.

Invercargill p665, map p666
Not a huge amount of choice. There is a supermarket on the eastern fringe of the city centre on Tay St, open until 2100 or 2200.
148 On Elles, 148 Elles St, T03-216 1000. Closed Sun. Both are recommended.
Birchwoods Restaurant, Ascot Hotel, T03-2176195, lunch Mon-Sat 1200-1400, dinner Mon-Sun from 1800; and
Fat Indian, 38 Dee St, down Piccadilly Lane, T03-2189933. Backpackers from the Tuatara regularly recommend this place.
HMS Kings, 80 Tay St, T03-2183443, daily lunch and dinner. Serves up a great seafood chowder amidst the nets and anchors.
Lone Star Café, corner of Leet and Dee sts, T03-214 6225, daily from 1730. Recommended Tex-Mex.
Louie's Café and Tapas Bar, 142 Dee St, T03-214 2913, Tue-Sun from 1800. Affordable evening dining.
Tillermans, 16 Don St, T03-218 9240, Mon-Fri 1200-1400 and 1800, Sat from 1800. Pleasant arty ambience.
Frog and Firkin, Dee St, next to the cinema, T03-214 4001, lunch 1200-1400, dinner Mon-Sat from 1700. Pub grub.
Outpost and Cabbage Tree Café, 379 Dunns Rd (west, out towards Otatara and Oreti Beach), T03-213 1443, 1100-late. Lunch or dinner in a relaxed rural setting.
Waxy O'Sheas, 90 Dee St, T03-214 0313. More of the same at Invercargill's Irish pub.
Zookeeper's Café, 50 Tay St, T03-218 3373, daily from 1000-late. The best café in town with has a nice atmosphere, good coffee and good-value evening meals.

Bluff *p668*
ᵀᵀ-ᵀ Land's End (see Sleeping, above). Serves breakfast, lunch and dinner and will happily serve up the famous oysters Mar-Aug.
ᵀ Drunken Sailor, Stirling Point, T03-212 8855, Mon-Thu 1130-1600, Fri-Sat 1130-2100. A recent addition offering traditional fare and good views. Sporadic opening hours.

❶ Pubs, bars and clubs

Invercargill *p665, map p666*
The *Southland Times* is the best source of local events and entertainment information. **Zookeeper's Café**, **Tillerman's**, 16 Don St, and **Waxy O'Sheas**, see above, are popular spots and often have live gigs at the weekend. **The Globe**, Tay St, opposite the **Zookeeper's Café**, is currently the most popular (and the nation's most southerly) nightclub. **Invercargill Brewery**, 8 Wood St, T03-214 5070, Mon-Sat 1100-1800, Fri 1100-1900. While visiting Invercargill it would perhaps be rude not to sample its finest beer. The very tasty brews on offer from the including 'Pitch Black' and 'Stanley Green' are really very good, as the evening queues outside the small outlet can attest.

⊛ Entertainment

Invercargill *p665, map p666*
Reading Cinema, 29 Dee St, T03-214 1110. **Ten Pin Bowling Centre**, corner of Kelvin and Leet sts (licensed bar), T03-214 4944.

❀ Festivals and events

Bluff *p668*
Apr Oyster and Southland Seafood Festival, www.bluffoysterfest.co.nz. A celebration of the diminishing world-class Bluff oysters and other seafood delights, with lots of fine wine to wash it down and plenty of entertainment, including live bands and oyster opening and eating competitions. The festival's raucous finale is the Southern Seas Ball.

◐ Shopping

Tuatapere to Invercargill *p664*
Southland is noted for its *paua* (abalone), used both for food and decorative jewellery. The **Southern Paua** and **Pacific Shell Factory**

and **Shop**, 35 Bath Rd, T03-234 8825; and **Riverton Paua Shoppe**, 134 Palmerston St, T03-234 9043, are the main outlets.

▲ Activities and tours

Tuatapere *p664*
Jet boating
Jet boating on Lake Hauroko and the Wairaurahiri River are the big attractions. Exciting full-day jet-boat trips down a 10-km section of Lake Hauroko, before negotiating its 27-km 'outlet' river to the coast. It is a Grade III river, which to the layperson means very little, but what it does boast is the steepest lake-to-coast river fall in the country. Recommended. From $199, child $99. Heli-jet (from $299), 2-day trips (Hump Ridge Jet, from $220). Water taxi services to both Dusky and Hump Ridge Tracks are also available (from $139). There are 2 main companies, both offer a safe and personable service. **Hump Ridge Jet**, Otautau, T03-225 8174, www.humpridgejet.co.nz. **W Jet**, Clifden, T03-226 6845, www.wjet.co.nz.

Riverton *p664*
Adventure Southland, close to town, T03-235 8962, www.adventuresouthland.com. High ropes activities and course, from $50. **Kiwi Wilderness Walks**, T03-226 6739, www.nzwalk.com. A popular operator that provides guided eco-walks of Stewart Island (5 days, 4 nights, from $1495) Raikura Track (also on Stewart Island) the Hump Ridge Track and the Dusky Track. The all-inclusive guided trips are best suited to the less independent traveller but are no less exciting. The highlight of the Stewart Island trip is the chance to observe kiwi in daylight, an unforgettable experience. Recommended.

⊜ Transport

Invercargill *p665, map p666*
Bicycle hire Wensley's Cycles, corner of Tay and Nith sts, T03-218 6206. **Car hire** The airport has branches of most major players. Others include **Riverside Rentals**, corner of Bay and North Rds, T03-215 9030. **Rent-a-Dent**, T03-214 4820. **Taxi Blue Star**, T03-217 7777. **City Cabs**, T03-214 4444.

ℹ Directory

Invercargill *p665, map p666*
Banks The main banks (most of which offer currency exchange) are around Don St in the city centre. **Internet** VIC, see page 663. **Library**, Mon-Fri 0900-2000, Sat 1000-1300. **Tuatara Backpackers YHA**, 30-32 Dee St. **Com zone**, just opposite Tuatara, T03-214 0007, daily 0930-late. **Global Byte Café**, 150 Dee St, T03-214 4724, Mon-Fri 0800-1700, Sat-Sun 0900-1600. **Medical services** Doctor, 103 Don St, T03-218 8821, Mon-Fri from 1700, 24-hr Sat-Sun. **Police** Don St, T03-214 4039. **Post office** 51 Don St, T03-214 7700, Mon-Fri 0830-1700, Sat 1000-1230.

Stewart Island (Rakiura National Park) → *Colour map 6, C3 Population: 390*

Lying 20 km southwest off Bluff, across the antsy waters of Foveaux Strait, is the 'land of the glowing skies' (Rakiura) or Stewart Island. Often called New Zealand's third island (making up 10% of its total area), Stewart Island was described over a century ago by pioneer botanist Leo Cockayne, as 'having a superabundance of superlatives'. There is much truth in that. It can be considered one of the country's most unspoilt and ecologically important areas. Such are its treasures that only the country's national parks can compare, which is why it was only a matter of time before it entered the fold in 2001, with 85% of the island now enjoying the limelight as the newest of New Zealand's 14 national parks. ▸▸ For Sleeping, Eating and other listings, see pages 677-678.

Ins and outs

Getting there Stewart Island can be reached by air (20 minutes) from Invercargill to Halfmoon Bay or the western bays of Mason, Doughboy, West Ruggedy or Little Hellfire (trampers) with **Stewart Island Flights**, T03-218 9129, www.stewartisland flights.com, from $155 return ($90 one way). There are scheduled flights three times daily. Only 15 kg of personal baggage can be flown over on a full flight (additional gear can be flown over on subsequent flights). A shuttle to/from the airfield is included in the fare.

The principal ferry operator, **Stewart Island Experience**, T03-212 7660/T0800-000511, www.stewartislandexperience.co.nz, operates regular sailings from the port of Bluff. The crossing by fast catamaran takes about one hour and costs $51/$25.50 one way). The company offers a regular daily shuttle service to and from Invercargill to coincide with the Stewart Island ferries ($16, child $8 one way). Contact direct for latest schedules, bookings advised, T0800-000511. Secure outdoor vehicle storage is available at Bluff.

Getting around Once on the island you will find that most things are within walking distance, but many hotels will provide pick-ups. **Stewart Island Experience** (see above) also offers car hire (from $60 per day) and scooters from $30 per hour. **The Stewart Island Experience Terminal**, on the Wharf, T03-219 1439/T0800-000511, info@ sie.co.nz, can also arrange tours, boat trips and water taxis. **Stewart Island Flights**, has a depot on the waterfront, T03-219 1090.

There are numerous water taxi operators including **Stewart Island Water Taxi**, T03-219 1394, www.portofcall.co.nz; **Seaview Water Taxi**, T03-219 1014; **Seabuzzz**, T03-219 1282, www.seabuzzz.co.nz; and **Kaian Water Taxis**, T03-219 1013. Fares cost $25-55 one way.

artisland.co.nz, is the principal source of non-biased information on the island. For detailed walks/tramping information and bookings contact the **DoC Visitor Information and Field Centre** ⓘ *Main Rd, T03-219 0009, www.doc.govt.nz, Mon-Fri 0800-1700, Sat-Sun 0900-1600*. It also provides storage lockers, sells maps and hires personal locator beacons.

Background

According to Maori legend, Stewart Island is the anchor stone of the canoe of the mythological hero and explorer Maui and is therefore known as 'Te Puka-o-te-waka-a-Maui'. As early as the 13th century there is evidence that the island's rich natural resources were being utilized by the Maori, with the particular attraction being attributed to the vast numbers of muttonbirds (sooty shearwater) or 'Titi'. The first European visitor (no prizes for guessing), in 1770 sailed past and mistook the island to be the mainland, calling it Cape South. Thirty-nine years after Captain Cook, it took one William Stewart, the first officer aboard the whaling ship *Pegasus*, to get it right and bless the island with its modern name. In the first half of the 18th century, whalers and sealers were beginning to establish themselves in the region and they were soon followed by fishermen and saw-millers that soon settled the island permanently.

In 1864 the island was officially bought from the Maori by the British, for the standard price of £6000. Besides a brief and sudden increase in population in the late 1800s, thanks to a very unproductive gold rush, the island has remained fairly uninhabited, with the current 390 residents mainly involved in fishing or tourism.

Stewart Island

Stewart Island has an indented coastline of river inlets, bays and offshore islands not dissimilar to parts of southern Fiordland. In many ways it is equally unspoiled and its heavily bush-clad landmass is host to a wealth of ecological habitats and a rich bio-diversity. The most common species on the island are sadly, as ever, the non-natives and the introduced. The most unwelcome and destructive of these are the possums, the rats and feral cats. Also, for over a century, white-tailed deer have roamed the bush, introduced to occupy the hunting interests of humans.

The island is home to 21 threatened plant species, some of which are endemic or occur only on the island. With the absence of dominant and introduced trout, there are 15 native fish species and, when it comes to birds, the island is surrounded by a vast array of pelagic species, including **mollymawks** (a kind of albatross), **petrels** and **shearwaters** (muttonbirds), many of which breed on the offshore islets in vast numbers. Even on the main island (and fighting to survive the ravages of introduced vermin), its impressive bird breeding list includes two of the rarest and most unique in the world: a distinctly odd and enchanting, flightless parrot called a **kakapo** (of which only about 80 remain) and perhaps most famous of all – *Apteryx australis lawryi* – better known as the **Stewart Island brown kiwi,** the largest and only diurnal kiwi in New Zealand. It is to see these whimsical birds on the beach or a bush track by daylight that many visit the island. And what's more, you may see the kiwi sidestepping a **yellowed-eyed penguin**, which is one of the rarest penguins in the world. And, in turn, the penguins may get their flippers in a twist to avoid the attentions of a dosing **New Zealand sea lion**. You've probably got the picture; Rakiura is a very special place indeed.

Oban and around → *Colour map 6, C3*

The pleasant little village of Oban on Halfmoon Bay is the island's main settlement. It is connected to several smaller settlements including Golden Bay, Horseshoe Bay, Leask Bay and Butterfield Bay, by about 28 km of mainly sealed road. Almost all of Oban's amenities and (non-B&B) accommodation can be reached easily by foot from the wharf. The principal streets are Elgin Terrace (the waterfront) and Main Road.

Oban

Sleeping
Bay Motel 4
Jo & Andy's B&B 1
Pilgrim Cottage 6

Port of Call B&B & Bach 7
South Sea 8
Stewart Island
Backpackers 9

Stewart Island Lodge 10

Eating
Church Hill 1

Kai Kart 5
Charliez Pizza
Wine & Movie 3
Wharfside Café 2

two main reasons: either to bask in its tranquillity and do very little in Oban; or attempt one of its challenging, very long and very wet tramping tracks. Yes, it rains a lot here.

Sights

Perhaps the best place to start is by foot with a short, steady climb to **Observation Rock** (southern end of Oban village, up Ayr Street). From here you get a grand view of **Paterson Inlet** and the impenetrable forests that deck its southern shores and disappear beyond the horizon. This vista gives an idea of the rest of the island's wild and unspoilt make-up. In Oban itself, the **Rakiura Museum** ① *Mon-Sat 1000-1200, Sun 1200-1400, $2,* can entertain between rain showers, showcasing many aspects of the island's interesting history, including the early Maori and their continued harvesting of muttonbirds (titi), to whaling, saw-milling, gold mining and fishing. The beach on the waterfront (Elgin Terrace) is a fine place to simply sit and watch the world go by, play industrial size chess, or decide on one of the many water-based trips that are available.

You could head north of Oban towards Horseshoe Bay, which is a very pleasant walk in itself. On the way you can spend some time exploring or swimming at **Bathing Bay**, a lovely sheltered beach accessed via Kamahi Road off Horseshoe Bay Road. This walk can be extended to **Horseshoe Point** (three to four hours), accessed from the southern end of **Horseshoe Bay**. On the southern entrance to Halfmoon Bay the three-hour **Harrold Bay to Ackers Point Lighthouse Walk**, accessed at the end of the southern bay road (Elgin Terrace), is another fine alternative. Harrold Bay is the site of **Ackers cottage** (1835), one of the oldest stone cottages in New Zealand. DoC produces a very useful *Day Walks* leaflet available from the VIC ($1).

Ulva Island

Guarding the entrance of Paterson Inlet is Ulva Island, a nature reserve criss-crossed with trails and home to abundant and extremely tame and exuberant birdlife. The island's profile was further enhanced in 2006, when DoC trialled the public viewing of a Kakapo (one of the rarest birds in the world), which proved immensely popular both domestically and internationally. Hopefully it will be repeated in the future, but Kakapo or not, the island provides the most popular day or half-day trip from Golden Bay, with a number of water taxi operators offering organized trips taking in the mussel and salmon farms in **Big Glory Bay**, as well as seal and shag colonies (four-hour guided trips, from $75, T03-2191400). Most companies also offer independent transportation from $25 return. A trip to Ulva is recommended. Ulva and Paterson Inlet also provide one of the many excellent sea-kayaking venues. You could also consider a paddle/tramp option with the trip up to the DoC Freshwater Hut and access from there to Mason Bay.

▲ Tramping

With 245 km of walking tracks, Stewart Island is a popular venue for trampers. These tracks range from the many short 'warm-up' walks around Oban, to the Northwest Circuit, a mammoth 125-km, 10- to 12-day tramp around the island's northern coast. Some other, far more remote routes are sometimes negotiated, including the fascinating **'Tin Range'** route on the island's southwestern corner, but these require expert planning, logistics and a high level of fitness. Overall, tramping on Stewart Island presents its own challenges, not only because the island is so underdeveloped, remote and rugged, but also because it is particularly wet underfoot. There are numerous basic

DoC huts that vary in size and standard. Hut details and bookings, maps and detailed track information is available with the DoC and it is highly recommended that you obtain all the details and fill in an intentions form for the longer or more remote tramps. ▸▸ *For guided walk operators, see page 678.*

Mason Bay to Freshwater Landing

This is a 14-km four-hour walk with no road access. It can be approached in various ways. You can walk to Mason Bay from Oban (37 km, three days one way), taking in part of the Rakiura Track, then reach Mason Bay via Freshwater Landing. Once at Mason Bay you can then walk or fly back to Oban. Or take a water taxi or kayak to Freshwater Landing then make the return walk to Mason Bay (28 km, two days return). The recommended alternative is to fly into Mason Bay, then make the leisurely return walk to Freshwater Landing (14 km, four hours) giving yourself an extra day to explore Mason Bay (and give yourself the best chance of seeing kiwi). You can then get a water taxi from Freshwater landing to Golden Bay and Oban. The track is low-level all the way, with a pleasant mix of open flax and tussock country and intriguing corridors of enclosed manuka tree. You will not manage to negotiate this trip without getting your feet wet and it is notoriously muddy, but there are boardwalks in the worst sections. The DoC Mason Bay hut has 20 bunks but is popular and runs on a first come first served basis, so take a tent if you can.

Rakiura Track

The Rakiura is one of New Zealand's 'Great Walks' immediately accessible by foot from Oban and is a 29- to 36-km track requiring two to three days. The appeal of the Rakiura, other than ease of access, is the mainly rimu and kamahi forest scenery, and views and secluded beaches of **Paterson Inlet**. There is also an abundance of bird life. In the forest this includes kaka, tomtit, bellbirds, tui and shining cuckoo, while wading birds including New Zealand dotterel and seabirds, including shags and little blue penguins, that can be seen on the coast. The track can be negotiated clockwise or anti-clockwise from Oban. In a clockwise direction the walking distances and times are as follows: Halfmoon Bay–Port William Hut, 12 km, four to five hours; Port William Hut–North Arm Hut, 12 km, six hours; North Arm–Halfmoon Bay 12 km, four to five hours. Port William and North Arm huts are well equipped and have 24 bunks each. There are designated campsites with water and toilets at Maori Beach, Port William and Sawdust Bay. Note huts and sites come at a first come first served basis but the VIC (I-Site) can give an indication of the anticipated numbers.

Northwest Circuit

At 125 km and requiring at least 10 days, this is one of the longest tramps in the country and is not for the faint-hearted. The appeal, other than the sense of achievement and feeling of complete solitude, is the remote and rugged coastal scenery with its stunning bays and features, some with such evocative names as Hellfire Pass and West Ruggedy Beach. The side trip to climb **Mount Anglem** (980 m), the island's highest peak, is also a recommended highlight. The track is also noted for its wildlife. The track is notoriously muddy and wet at times but don't let that put you off. There are 10 DoC huts on the route with 12-20 bunks.

❖ *A Northwest Circuit Pass allowing 10 nights in any hut on the route is available from the VIC for $38.*

The track distances and minimum times are as follows: Halfmoon Bay–Port William, 12 km, four hours; Port William–Bungaree Hut, 6 km, three hours; Bungaree Hut–Christmas Village Hut, 11½ km, six hours; Mount Anglem side trip, 11 km, six hours; Christmas Village Hut–Yankee River Hut 12 km, six hours; Yankee River Hut–Long Harry Hut, 8½ km, five to six hours; Long Harry Hut–East Ruggedy Hut, 9½ km, five hours; East Ruggedy Hut–Hellfire Pass, 14 km, seven to eight hours; Hellfire Pass Hut–Mason Bay Hut, 15 km, seven hours; Mason Bay Hut–Freshwater

Southern Circuit

The Southern Circuit is a 74-km six- to seven-day tramp suitable for the experienced
and well-equipped tramper. It takes in many similar (but more remote) aspects of the
Rakiura Track and the delights of the rugged wilderness coastline from Doughboy Bay
to Mason Bay and Mason Bay itself. Access to the start and finish point of Freshwater
Landing is by water taxi. Four DoC huts and an interesting bivvy at Doughboy Bay
provide accommodation. The DoC can provide detailed information about the tramp.

🛏 Sleeping

Stewart Island *p672, maps p673 and p674*
Most of the accommodation on the
island takes the form of comfortable
upper- to mid-range B&Bs and homestays,
cottages and budget options but there is
one hotel and a handful of motels. Note
that some of the budget hostels do not
take advance bookings in summer and
beds must be secured on the day of
departure from Bluff or Invercargill airport.
Note also that there is much gossip
surrounding certain bachelor-owned/
operated hostels and the 'comfort' of single
women travellers. The best advice is ask
the VIC about the latest vacancies and
maybe check out a few places on arrival
(particularly those recommended below),
then decide for yourself.
LL Stewart Island Lodge, 14 Nichol Rd,
Halfmoon Bay, T03-219 1085, www.stewart
islandlodge.co.nz. Well established as one
of the best upper-range B&Bs on the island.
It provides 5 luxury en suites and is famous
for its good cuisine, amidst the perfect
peaceful setting.
L Port of Call B&B and Bach, Jensen Bay,
T03-219 1394, www.portofcall.co.nz. Set in
an idyllic spot overlooking the entrance
to Halfmoon Bay, very cosy and friendly.
It offers a charming en suite double and
great breakfasts and views from the deck.
There is also a fully self-contained bach
(holiday house) offering plenty of privacy.
In-house water taxi and eco-guiding
operation, including kiwi -spotting.
AL Bay Motel, 9 Dundee St, Halfmoon Bay,
T03-219 1119, www.baymotel.co.nz. Tidy

units, good facilities, views across the bay
and within a short walk of all amenities.
A Pilgrim Cottage, T03-219 1144,
philldismith@xtra.co.nz. Neat and
affordable self-contained option,
kiwi trips are a speciality.
A South Sea Hotel, corner of Elgin Terr and
Main Rd, Oban, T03-219 1059, www.stewart-
island.co.nz. A fine place to stay if you
want to mix with the locals and experience
Stewart Island life. A mix of traditional
hotel rooms (some with sea views) and
self-contained motel units on an adjacent
property. Obviously there is an in-house
bar where all the action (or lack of it) takes
place and a restaurant where you can
sample the local delicacy – muttonbird.
B-C Jo and Andy's Bed and Breakfast, Main
Rd, T03-219 1230, jariksem@clearnet.net.nz.
Small and personable, sleeping 5 and
with the added attraction of massage
therapies – ideal for tired trampers.
C-D Stewart Island Backpackers, Ayr St,
T03-219 1114, www.stewart-island.co.nz. In
town this is a sprawling but highly functional
place, with a wide range of dorms and units.

🍴 Eating

Stewart Island *p672, maps p673 and p674*
Stewart Island has only a few eateries,
with the famed muttonbird (titi) being
the speciality dish round these parts.
By all accounts it is very tasty, being a bit
like venison and certainly more oily than
chicken. But if you see these seabirds up
close, never mind the chicks (which

● *For an explanation of the Sleeping and Eating price codes used in this guide, see the inside*
● *front cover. Other relevant information is provided in the Essentials chapter, pages 44-51.*
  Note that prices are given in New Zealand dollars.

Southland Stewart Island Listings

resemble fluffy brown slippers), you'll be picketing these establishments with a placard round your neck! The only place for groceries is **Ship to Shore** general store, on the waterfront.

♥♥ **Charliez Pizza Wine and Movie**, 10 Main Rd, Oban, T03-219 1419, www.charliez.co.nz, from 1800. At last, after much talk, the great Stewart Island movie theatre and pizzeria combo is finally open and exceeding all expectations. The pizza, the wine list and the coffee are all excellent. During the day the flavour of movies is distinctly NZ with a scenic feature on the island, while the evening movie menu alters to mainly art house offerings.

♥♥ **Church Hill Café Bar and Restaurant** next to the church on the headland above the wharf, T03-219 1323, daily from 1030 (seasonal). The best bet for fine dining.

♥♥ **South Sea Hotel**, see Sleeping, above, 0800-0930, 1200-1400 and 1800-2100, seasonal. Provides fine no-nonsense lunch and dinner options including the unique muttonbird for around $23.

♥♥ **Wharfside Café**, Ferry Terminal, Oban, T03-219 1470, daily from 0900. All-day breakfasts, café style light meals, licensed.

♥ **Kai Kart**, Ayr St, T03-219 1442. Class fish and chips for lunch or dinner.

⊙ Pubs, bars and clubs

Stewart Island *p672, maps p673 and p674*
South Sea Hotel, Elgin Terr. Without doubt the place to be for a beer and unpredictable entertainment. But what kind of night you have often depends on whom you bump into and whether they are in good spirits or bad. They are a welcoming bunch most of the time, so just place your cards on the table and give as good as you get.

▲ Activities and tours

Stewart Island *p672, maps p673 and p674*
As you can imagine there is a wide range of possibilities from fishing and diving to simple daytime sightseeing, overnight or luxury multi-day adventures. The VIC (I-Site) lists all the operators and charter possibilities.
Bravo Adventure Cruises, T03-219 1144. A 4-hr twilight boat trip/bush-walk to

attempt to see kiwi, from $90. Short of Mason Bay this may be your best chance of seeing the kiwi in half-light (see page 676).
Raikura Kayaks, T03-219 1160, www.raikura.co.nz; and
Ruggedy Range Wilderness Experience, Oban, T03-219 1066, www.ruggedyrange.com, both provide a range of guided single to multi-day sea kayaking trips around Ulva and Paterson Inlet and independent hire.
Seabuzzz, T03-219 1282. Offers a 1-hr glass-bottom boat trip, from $30 as well as scenic trips to Ulva Island.
Stewart Island Experience, T03-212 7660/T0800-000511, www.stewartisland experience.co.nz. Offers a 2½-hr scenic cruise to Paterson Inlet with a stop and guided walks on Ulva Island departing daily 1230 from $67, child $15. Picnic lunch $15 extra. It also operates a semi-submersible and given the water clarity this is usually worthwhile. Tours daily (40 mins), from $35, child $15.

Walking and ecotours
There are a couple of good companies offering guided walks, including the 'kiwi experience':
Kiwi Wilderness Walks, based in Tuatapere, T03-226 6739, www.nzwalk.com; and
Ruggedy Range Wilderness Experience, Oban, T03-219 1066, www.ruggedy range.com. Both offer multi-day walking trips in which you have the unique opportunity to encounter kiwi during daylight hours. The latter also offer half- to 5-day kayaking options from $95.
Ulva's Guided Walks, T03-219 1216, www.ulva.co.nz. Offers an informative 3-hr trips to Ulva Island, from $95.

⊙ Directory

Stewart Island *p672, maps p673 and p674*
Banks Most businesses accept credit cards, New Zealand TCs and have EFTPOS. There are no banks on the island. **Internet** Stewart Island Backpackers, Ayr St and the South Sea Hotel, Main Rd. **Medical centre** Argyle St, T03-219 1098. **Police** T03-219 0020. **Postal agents** Stewart Island Flights depot, waterfront (Elgin Terr), T03-219 1090.

The Catlins → *Colour map 6, C4/5*

If you like remote and scenic coastlines you are going to love the Catlins; the added bonus here is their location. Like the Wairarapa in the southwest of the North Island, the area is generally off the beaten track and certainly underrated. You can negotiate the Catlins from the north or the south via the publicized Southern Scenic Route, encompassing a 187-km network of minor now fully sealed roads. The journey between Invercargill and Dunedin (or in reverse) is often attempted in one day, which is definitely a mistake. A more thorough, comfortable and less frustrating investigation will take at least two days, preferably three. But, if you can really only afford one day, the highlights not to be missed are – from the north – Nugget Point (for sunrise); the opportunity to see the seductively named Hookers sea lions at Cannibals Bay (morning); the Purakaunui Falls and Purakaunui Bay (for lunch); then Curio Bay and Slope Point in the afternoon.

The Catlins is also noted for its rich wildlife and vegetation. Of particular note are the pinnipeds, or seals. The Catlins is the only mainland region where you can observe New Zealand fur seals, Hookers sea lions and Southern elephant seals in the same location. The region is also within the very limited breeding range of the rarest penguin on the planet – the yellow-eyed penguin (hoiho) – and the rare and tiny Hector's dolphin. Incredibly, with a little luck, all these species can be observed quite easily, independently and at relatively close range. The tracts of dense coastal forest that still remain are made up predominately of podocarp and silver beech (but Curio Bay is home to a scattering of petrified fossil trees that are over 180 million years old) and are home to native birds like native pigeon (kereru), yellowhead (mohua) and fernbird. The forests also hide a number of attractive waterfalls. ►► *For Sleeping, Eating and other listings, see pages 684-686.*

Ins and outs

Getting there Bottom Bus, T03-442 9708, www.bottombus.co.nz, and the **Catlins Coaster,** T021-682461/T0800-304333, www.catlinscoaster.co.nz, (Catlins/Dunedin), provide transport and tour options via Queenstown, Invercargill and Te Anau. Being on SH1 Balclutha and Gore are serviced by all the major north–south or east–west bus companies. Petrol is available at Owaka and Papatowai. ►► *See also Activities and tours, page 686.*

Tourist information The VIC (I-Site) in Invercargill can also supply information about the Catlins. The free *The Catlins* booklet and the websites www.catlins.org.nz, www.catlins.co.nz and www.catlins-nz.com, are all useful. **Owaka VIC (I-Site)** ① *20 Ryley St, T03-415 8371, www.catlins-nz.com, summer Nov-Jun Mon-Fri 0830-2030, Sat 0800-2030, Sun 0900-2130.* **Waikawa VIC (I-Site)** ① *Dolphin Information Centre, T03-246 8444, dolphinmagic@xtra.co.nz, daily Oct-Apr.* **Balclutha VIC (I-Site)** ① *4 Clyde St, T03-418 0388, vin@cluthaadc.govt.nz, Mon-Fri 0830-1700, Sat-Sun 0930- 1400.* The latter can provide all the northbound information surrounding the Catlins and Southern Scenic Route. DoC information is also available here, including leaflets ($1) on Catlin's walks and ecological highlights. **Gore VIC (I-Site)** ① *Norfolk St, T03-208 9288, www.gorenz.com Mon-Fri 0830-1700 Sat-Sun 0930-1600.* Has a list of local walks including the popular 1½-hour Whisky Falls Track.

Background

The first human settlers in the region were the South Island Maori who used the abundant coastal resources and hunted the flightless moa as long ago as AD 1350. Within 200 years most of the moa had been plundered and the settlers turned their attentions to the fur seals, fish and other seafood. The thick almost impenetrable coastal forests of the region prevented easy access inland so the population waxed and waned but was never substantial. The forbidding forests were also thought by the Maori to be the home of a race of hairy giants known as *Maeroero* (a group of early Scottish settlers looking for a pub?). The Maori were joined, first by small groups of European whalers, then timber millers who began their relentless rape of the forest from the 1860s. Once depleted, as with most other parts of New Zealand, it was the farmers who moved in. Thankfully a few tracts of the original coastal forest escaped the axe.

Invercargill to Papatowai → *Colour map 6, C4/5*
From Invercargill the Southern Scenic Route (SH92) crosses the Southland Plains to join the coast and the Mataura River mouth at the former coastal whaling station of **Fortrose** (42 km). At Fortrose you leave SH92 and begin to negotiate the coastal road networks of the Catlins towards **Otara** and Waikawa. The first potential diversion is to **Waipapa Point**. From just beyond Otara take the signposted road cross-country to a car park beside the lighthouse. The gently sloping beach is backed by dunes and decked with rock pools and offshore reefs. These reefs were the cause of New Zealand's second worst shipping disaster in 1881, when the *SS Tararua* ran aground with the loss of 131 lives. It was this tragedy that prompted the erection of the **lighthouse**. Completed in 1884, it was the last wooden lighthouse built in New Zealand. Keep your eyes open for Hookers sea lions, which sometimes haul up on the beaches here for a doze.

Once back on the main route near Otara continue to Haldane and follow signs for **Slope Point**, which is actually the southernmost point in New Zealand, contrary to what most visitors believe. The real geographical point and obligatory signpost can be reached here via a short 10-minute walk from a roadside car park. From the car park there are views of the dramatic headlands that herald a distinct change from Waipapa's lowly dunescapes. Also of note are the macrocarpa trees.

From Haldane the road skirts the Haldane Estuary before delivering you at the beautiful **Porpoise Bay**, a popular spot for swimming and surfing. From the junction it is a short drive (right) to the headland and Curio Bay.

The Catlins - Invercargill to Papatowai

Sleeping
Catlins Farmstay **2**
Curio Bay Camp Ground **3**
Governors Cottage (Waikawa Cottages) **4**
Nadir Outpost **11**
Papatowai Hilltop Backpackers **5**
Papatowai Motels & Store **6**
Southern Secret Motel **7**
Tautuku Lodge **8**
Waikawa Holiday Lodge **9**

The headland overlooking both bays is a superb spot to simply admire the coastal scenery, crashing waves and try to spot the tiny **Hector's dolphins**. Some patience may be required for this but eventually, you may see a pod (especially near the rocks that protect Porpoise Bay). They are a delight to observe as they breach the surface in exuberant playfulness.

At **Curio Bay**, about 500 m west, is the fossil forest. At first glance it is difficult to make out the petrified stumps and logs that scatter the rock platform, but a more thorough investigation by foot reveals the distinct features of these Jurassic ancestors.

Although it is hard to drag yourself away from Curio Bay, the road now turns briefly inland to rejoin the Waikawa River Estuary at **Waikawa**. Here you will find a small **information centre** ① *T03-246 8444, daily Oct-Apr*, in the old church and a small café. Across the road is the **Waikawa Holiday Lodge Backpackers** (see page 684) and the small **District Museum** ① *daily 1300-1600 (seasonal)*, which contains some relics from the whaling and saw-milling years.

From Waikawa the road heads north past the former saw-milling village of **Niagara**. A few hundred metres past the village you then join the main SH92 Catlins road (from Tokanui and Fortrose) and turn right through more dramatic topography and coastal forest towards **Chaslands** and Papatowai. The **Chasland Scenic Reserve** boasts some of the best forest in the area with large rimu and kamahi. Look out for the left turn to **McLean Falls** (1 km north of the Cathedral Caves turning). The falls car park is reached via the Rewcastle Road (3 km). The picturesque three-stepped falls (often said to be the most beautiful in the Catlins) are reached easily on foot (40 minutes return).

The 30-m-high **Cathedral Caves** at the north end of Waipati Beach are accessible only at low tide (posted at the road junction or available from the local VICs). The 2-km access road will deliver you to a car park where the caves are accessed via a short (30 minutes) forest and beach walk. Although the forest is part of **Waipati Scenic Reserve**, note that part of the area is Maori owned. After several land claim disputes a small fee is now requested to access the caves.

Just before the beautiful **Tautuku Bay** is the **Lenz Reserve** and the **Traill's Tractor Historic Walk** (10 minutes). Tautuku was a prolific logging area and the walk takes you to a former milling site and an original 'Traill's Tractor' logging machine, that took over

from horse-drawn trams in the steeper country. The walk starts from the Flemming River Bridge. Nearby is the hidden delight of **Lake Wilkie**. Formed in a dune hollow and surrounded by lush bush, it can be viewed from a lookout a mere five minutes' walk from the car park. You can then complete a 30-minute circuit of the lake's scenic coastal edge. The boardwalk provides another view across the lake and comes complete with interpretative signs that outline the botanical features of the unique habitat. Note there is no access to the beach from this point.

About 1½ km south of Lake Wilkie is the new **Tautuku Estuary Walk** (30 minutes return), which offers access to the estuary and coastal forest. The beautiful beach is best accessed via the **Tautuku Dune/Forest Walk** (15 minutes) which is just opposite the Tautuku Outdoor Education Centre on SH92. A stunning view of the whole bay and its thick fringe of coastal forest can be seen from the road as you climb **Florence Hill** at its eastern edge. Just offshore are the **Rainbow Isles**, which owe their name to the effects of the sun on sea-spray, squirted skywards by a small blowhole on the main island. The Maori call it *rerekohu*, meaning 'flying mist'. From Florence Hill it is a 2-km drive to **Papatowai** – the Catlins 'mid-point' and base for services and accommodation.

Papatowai to Owaka → *Colour map 6, C5*

There are a number of notable walks around Papatowai, the most popular of which is the **Picnic Point Track** (40 minutes), which takes in both coast and forest and with a short diversion to the unusual **Kings Rock** formation. From McLennan and the river of the same name you can access both the **Maitai** (north) and **Purakaunui Falls** (east). They are both easily reached from the road (Maitai first via SH92), and significantly different and worthy of investigation.

About 4 km east of the Purakaunui Falls is the access road to **Purakaunui Bay**. This is one of the most beautiful and supremely quiet spots on the Catlins Coast and is excellent for a short walk, surfing, a picnic or an overnight stay at the basic campsite. Be careful on this road, it is very narrow and winding.

If you want a change from all the coastal scenery the **Catlins River Track** (five hours one way) provides an excellent opportunity. Access is about 3 km south of Catlins Lake via **Tawanui** where there is a DoC campsite. Follow the road to **The Wisp** (farm lease) and the picnic site trailhead. The section between Wallis Stream and Franks Creek (1½ hours) is recommended.

Back on the coast many visitors are drawn along the western bank of the Catlins Lake and the Owaka Heads to see **Jack's Bay** and blowhole. At 55 m deep, with an opening of 140 m by 70 m, it is quite an impressive sight, even when it's not stormy.

Owaka and around → *Colour map 6, C5 Population: 400*

Returning back to Catlins Lake and SH92 it is then a short drive to the Catlins' largest settlement and supply centre, Owaka, which offers a host of basic facilities including a good restaurant, petrol, a grocery store, accommodation, visitor centre and internet. But if the weather is fine and you still have time on your hands before sunset, don't hang around. Instead, head back to the coast. **Pounawea**, 4 km south of Owaka, offers a very pleasant (45 minutes) nature walk through podocarp forest and salt marsh.

Just east of Pounawea is **Surat Bay**, which is reached across other side of the Owaka River (the bridge is 2 km south of Owaka). Its golden swathes of sand and those of its neighbour, **Cannibals Bay** (access from SH92, a few kilometres north of Owaka), provide the reasonable likelihood of encountering some dozing Hookers sea lions.

Cannibals Bay was mistakenly named in the late 1800s by geologist James Hector, who took the human remains from a Maori burial site to be something far more sinister. A pleasant walk from here negotiates the length of Cannibals Bay (from the car park) to the **False Islet** headlands. Then, once you have taken in the views, from the west to Jack's Bay and then east, to the rocky outcrops of the **Nugget Point**, continue on to Surat Bay, before returning across the neck of the headland to Cannibals Bay (two hours).

Nugget Point, Roaring Bay and Kaka Point → *Colour map 6, C5*

Back on SH92 the road turns inland again towards Balclutha. About 3 km east of Owaka is **Tunnel Hill**, which is a historic reserve featuring the 246-m-long tunnel, once the most southerly railway tunnel in New Zealand. Completed in 1915 it was the most prominent feature on the Catlins branch railway line that ran between Balclutha and Tahakopa near McLennan. The line closed in 1971.

Just beyond the hill is the turn-off to Nugget Point, without doubt the highlight of the Catlins Coast. To get a proper feel for 'The Nuggets' they are best visited at sunrise, when the spectacular rock pillars and outcrops take on the orange glow of the sun. The track to the 1870 **lighthouse** starts at the terminus of a delightful road that skirts the beach and rock platforms of Molyneux Bay. It takes about 10 minutes to reach the lighthouse and its associated lookout point, but by far the best view is to be had from the hill, about 100 m short of it. Care must be taken here, but the views from the top are outstanding. The islets and rocky, inaccessible coastline offer an important haven for wildlife, and is home to seals (all three species: fur, Hookers and elephant), yellow-eyed and blue penguins, sooty shearwaters, gannets and occasionally royal spoonbills. Even below the waves life abounds and the area boasts a wide diversity of underwater habitats. Keep your ears open for the plaintive wails of fur seal pups playing in and around the rock pools below the track and look out for squadrons of shearwaters, skimming the waves in search of food. It really is a magical place.

Just inland from the Point is **Roaring Bay** that has a small public hide where yellow-eyed penguins can be seen coming ashore at dusk, or leaving again for their routine fishing trips at dawn. If you are lucky enough to see one, remember you are looking at the rarest penguin in the world so be discreet and do not approach them. Back along the edge of Molyneux Bay is **Kaka Point** (8 km), a charming little coastal settlement that, along with Owaka, provides the necessary visitor amenities and accommodation. From Kaka Point it is about 22 km to Balclutha and SH1 to Dunedin.

Balclutha → Colour map 6, B5

Balclutha (which is actually in South Otago) is 80 km southwest of Dunedin on the banks of the Clutha River, which, with its origins at Lake Wanaka, is the South Island's longest (322 km). Known as 'Big River Town' its name actually refers to the Scottish Gaelic for 'town on the Clyde' after Glasgow's great river. The town's first known white resident was Scot Jim McNeill who used to run a ferry service across the river between 1853 and 1857. The modern-day concrete bridge that provides the vital road link with Southland is not the original bridge. The first effort, which was constructed in 1866, was washed away in floods. Fishing is of course a popular local pursuit and the VIC (I-Site) has details of this and other local activities. The **South Otago Museum** ① *1 Renfrew St, T03-418 2382, Mon-Fri 1000-1600 Sun 1300-1600, free,* is particularly noted for its collection of bottles and displays surrounding the history of the local **Kaitangata Coal Mine**.

Gore → Colour map 6, B4 Population: 9000

Gore, on the banks of the Mataura River, is Southland's second largest town and most famous for its unusual mix of trout fishing, country music and formerly (we can only presume) illegal whisky distilling. So although you might think the place to be a just another quiet backwater, beware. At times, particularly during the 10-day annual **New Zealand Gold Guitar Awards** (see Festivals and events, page 686), sleepy Gore can go off like Dolly Parton in a lingerie shop. During the festival both amateur and professional artists compete, while the true fanatics get the chance to dust off their cowboy boots and line dance the night away.

Other local attractions include the **Hokonui Moonshine Museum** and the **Gore Historical Museum** ① *Hokonui Heritage Centre, next to the VIC, T03-208 7032, $5, Mon-Fri 0830-1630, Sat-Sun 0930-1530* There, the heady days of Gore district's insobriety and chaos, alongside its times of prohibition and prudence, are revealed. Just opposite the VIC (I-Site) is the recently renovated **Eastern Southland Gallery** ① *14 Hokonui Drive, T03-208 9907, Mon-Fri 1000-1630, Sun 1300-1600,* showcasing the impressive private collection of expatriate Kiwi John Money, and donated works by one of New Zealand's most well-known contemporaries Ralph Hotere. Still in the planning is a **Fishing Museum** where the monster brown trout and the fishermen that come from around the globe to catch them will be celebrated. Should you fancy a spot of fishing yourself, you'll get a licence at the VIC ($18.50 for a day). The VIC (I-Site) also has an extensive list of local guides.

Southland The Catlins

Also of note in the region is **Moth Restaurant and Bar** and the new museum complex of the **Croydon Aircraft Company** ① *SH94, Mandeville, west of Gore on SH94, T03-208 9755/T03-208 9662, www.themoth.co.nz*. Not only does it provide good food but also the opportunity to combine your visit with a look at aviation history.

If you have animal-loving children, the **Reservation** ① *at the top of Coutts Rd, T03-208 1200, Tue-Sun 1200-1630, $6, child $3*, has a small menagerie of warm, cuddly animals from windless bovines to chinchillas and Clydesdale horses, all of whom are available for copious stroking and generous feeding. Café on site.

● Sleeping

Invercargill to Papatowai
p680, map p680

L Catlins Farmstay, midway between Cathedral Caves and Curio Bay, T03-246 8843, www.catlinsfarmstay.co.nz. Set on a 400-ha working farm, offers 3 rooms one self-contained, queen and twin.

AL Fernlea Farmstay, Motokua, 20 mins from Invercargill, T03-239 5432, www.fernlea.co.nz. A lovely self-contained cottage (sleeps 4) with its own private garden on a large dairy farm. Closed for reconstruction; check website for reopening.

A Governors Cottage (Waikawa Cottages), Curio Bay, T03-368 6674, www.holiday houses.co.nz/properties/3237.asp. A fine 2-bedroom self-contained option.

A Southern Secret Motel, Papatowai, T03-415 8600, southernsecret@xtra.co.nz. A stylish modern place with 4 studio units, all with balcony. Close to amenities and coastal walks.

B Papatowai Motels and Store, T03-415 8147, b.bevin@paradise.net.nz. Has 3 spacious self-contained units.

C-D Nadir Outpost, 174 Slope Point Rd, T03-246 8544, nadir.outpost@ihug.co.nz. Peaceful and friendly this 14-bed hostel offers a fine option as a first or last night stop if taking your time and in possession of your own transport. Good standard backpackers' facilities as well as tent and van sites, shop and information centre.

C-D Papatowai Hilltop Backpackers, Papatowai, T03-415 8028, www.hilltop backpackers.co.nz. An excellent place offering doubles (with a great view) and dorm beds. Log fire, modern facilities, hot tub, bikes, canoes, internet and much more.

C-D Waikawa Holiday Lodge, Waikawa, T03-246 8552. Backpacker option with comfortable budget doubles and dorms in a spacious house. In-house shop and café across the road at **Dolphin Magic**.

D Tautuku Lodge, set in the Lenz Reserve at Tautuku, T03-415 8024, dianan@clear.net.nz. Owned by the Forest and Bird Society. The lodge sleeps 10 but there is also a smaller cabin sleeping 4. Supply your own bedding.

Motorcamps and campsites
See also **Nadir Outpost**, above.

C-D Papatowai Motor Camp, behind the motel, T03-415 8565. Holiday home, basic cabins, backpacker rooms, powered and non-powered sites, camp kitchen.

D Curio Bay Camp Ground, on the headland overlooking Porpoise Bay, T03-246 8897. Has powered/tent sites, showers and a small store.

Papatowai to Owaka *p682*

A Greenwood Farmstay, Purakaunui Falls Rd, T03-415 8259, greenwoodfarm@ xtra.co.nz. An en suite queen, twin and singles in a modern villa homestead on a 770-ha farm. Dinner on request. Ideally located near the falls and Purakaunui Bay.

C-D Falls Backpackers, Purakaunui Falls, T03-4158724, www.catlins-nz.com/fallsbprz. Offers 4 doubles and shared twin rooms. Walking distance from the falls.

Campsites

D DoC campsite, Purakaunui Bay. Basic but in a superb setting – worth buying a tent for.

Owaka and around *p682*

AL Kepplestone-by-the-sea, 9 Surat Bay Rd, T03-415 8134/T0800-105134, kepplestone@ xtra.co.nz. Tucked away near the coast and Surat Bay. A delightful B&B with a range of en suite rooms and fine cuisine.

A Catlins Area Motels, 34 Ryley St, T03-415 8821. Recommended motel option.

A Catlins Gateway Motel, corner of Main Rd and Royal Terr, T03-415 8592. Has some nice new 1 bedroom units. Recommended.

B Catlins Retreat Guesthouse, 27 Main Rd, T03-415 8830, jfperry@hotmail.com. A century-old villa located right in the heart of Owaka. It has a spa, open fire and its BBQs are a speciality.

B-D Catlins Backpackers, 24 Main Rd, T03 4128111, www.catlinsbackpackers.co.nz. Recently renovated, under new management and creating something of a hit, this conveniently located backpacker hostel offers 3 lovely cottages each with 3 rooms and containing double, twin and single beds (no bunks). All the usual facilities are on hand and there is a cosy open fire in the communal lounge. Recommended.

C-D Mohua Park Eco-Cottages, Tawanui, T03-415 8613, info@catlins-ecotours.co.nz. Self-contained cottages in a peaceful rural setting with great views . Ideal for couples and just a short drive from Owaka.

C-D Surat Bay Lodge Backpackers, Surat Bay Rd, T03-415 8099, www.suratbay.co.nz. A small, peaceful backpacker lodge a stone's throw from the beach. It also runs its own nature, farm, walking and canoe tours (2-3 hrs) from $35-65.

Motorcamps and campsites
C-D Pounawea Camp Ground, Park Lane, Pounawea, Owaka, T03-415 8483, www.catlins-nz.com/pomoca. Basic motorpark.

Nugget Point, Roaring Bay and Kaka Point p682
L-B Nugget View and Kaka Point Motels, 11 Rata St, Kaka Point, T03-412 8602, www.catlins.co.nz. 15 comfortable studio units, some with spa. Free kayak hire and also offers boat-based eco-tours to the Nuggets.

AL-A Cardno's, 8 Marine Terr, Kaka Point, T03-412 8181, www.cardnosaccommo dation.co.nz. Stylish and modern, offering a choice of a self-contained or a studio unit overlooking the beach. Excellent hosts and all round good value. Recommended.

A Nugget Lodge Motels, 2 km from Nugget Point right on the beach, T03-412 8783, www.nuggetlodge.co.nz. Run by a former honorary DoC field officer with plenty of local knowledge. On offer are 2 modern units, one overlooking the bay.

C-D Fernlea Backpackers, Moana St Kaka Point, T03-412 8834. Small, homely and well-established. Wonderful view from the balcony.

Motorcamps and campsites
C D Kaka Point Motor Park, on the edge of the town on Tarata St, T03-412 8801, kakapoint@hotmail.com. Quiet place offering 2 modern cabins. Camp kitchen.

Balclutha p683
AL-A Lesmahagow, Main Rd, Benhar, T03-418 2507, www.lesmahagow.co.nz. You will find a warm Irish welcome and all the comforts at this B&B. 2 en suites and 2 rooms with shared bathroom. It is located just north of the town in a peaceful setting.

A Highway Lodge Motel, 165 Clyde St, T03-418 2363. A modern motel option that sits at the start of the Southern Scenic Route and the Catlins coast.

A Rosebank Lodge Motor Hotel, 265 Clyde St, T03-419 0021, www.rosebanklodge.co.nz. Comfortable chalet-style units, with spa, sauna and an in-house restaurant/bistro.

Motorcamps and campsites
C-D Balclutha Motor Camp, 56 Charlotte St, T03-418 0088. The only option for camper-vans. It has a few cabins, an excellent campground and camp kitchen.

Gore p683
A Oakleigh Motel, 70 Hokonui Drive, T03-208 4863, www.oakleighmotel.co.nz. Another more upmarket motel in town.

A Scenic Circle Croydon Lodge, corner of SH94 and Waimea St, T03-208 9029, www.scenic-circle.co.nz. A large motel set in extensive grounds with a 9-hole golf course, à la carte restaurant and bar and Sky TV.

C-D Old Fire Station Backpackers, 19 Hokonui Drive (across the road from the VIC), T03-208 1925. Small backpacker hostel with double/twin, singles and dorms.

Motorcamps and campsites
B-D Gore Motor Camp, 35 Broughton St, T03-208 4919. Basic cabins, on-site vans, powered/tent sites and camp kitchen.

❼ Eating

Invercargill to Papatowai
p680, map p680

If you are not in a B&B or self-contained place then eating out in the South Catlins really takes the form of a stove or a BBQ with the sandflies. There is a general store in Papatowai, daily 0830-2200, winter Sun-Thu 0900-1800, Fri-Sat 0900-1830, which sells BBQs and basic takeaway food.
🍴 **Niagara Falls Café**, Main Rd, Niagara, T03-246 8577. Popular highway café and gift shop combo offering a good selection of light meals and a fair caffeine fix.

Owaka *p682*
🍴 **Lumber Jack Bar and Café**, Main street, T03-415 8747, daily from 1200 (1600 in winter). A fairly classy place, with a traditional Kiwi menu and good coffee.

Kaka Point *p682*
🍴-🍴 **Point Café and Bar**, on the Esplanade, T03-412 8800, www.kakapoint.co.nz, daily 0800-2000. The most popular eatery/bar in the area with the obligatory ocean views. It also has a grocery store attached.

Balclutha *p683*
🍴 **Rosebank Lodge**, see Sleeping, above, daily for breakfast, lunch and dinner. The restaurant here is recommended.

Gore *p683*
🍴 **Howl at the Moon**, 2 Main St, T03-208 3851, daily from 1200. A café/bar with a reasonable blackboard menu.
🍴 **Moth Restaurant and Bar**, see page 684. Tue-Sun from 1100-2100.
🍴 **Table Talk Café**, 70 Main St, Gore, T03-208 7110. Has a modern New Zealand menu and serves a good all-day breakfast.

❸ Festivals and events

Gore *p683*
May New Zealand Gold Guitar Awards, T03-208 5587, www.goldguitars.co.nz. A 10-day annual event on the Queen's birthday weekend (end of the month). Up to 5000 people come for the southern hospitality and country music atmosphere.

▲ Activities and tours

The Catlins *p679, map p680*
Catlins Coaster, based in Dunedin, T021-682461, www.catlinscoaster.co.nz. Regional transport provider offering packages taking in the Catlins en route from or to Dunedin, Invercargill, Queenstown and Te Anau.
Catlins Encounters is an adjunct to the already very successful **Elm Wildlife Tours** operating out of the **Elm Backpackers** in Dunedin, T0800-356563, www.elmwildlife tours.co.nz. The entertaining full-day takes in all the best sights, including a good chance to see yellow-eyed penguins and Hookers sea lions. Departs Dunedin Sat/Mon/Tue and Invercargill (via Bluff) Sun/Tue/Thu from $121. Can organize onward travel to Stewart Island.
Catlins Natural Wonders, Balclutha, T03-424 7370/T0800-304333, www.catlinsnatural.co.nz. Another eco-based tour operator offering day trips (from $130 Dunedin/$85 Balclutha return) 4 times a week (departing Dunedin 0830/Balclutha 1000), and 2-day stop over trips (from $200) from Invercargill to Dunedin on Thu, which include a choice of accommodation at extra cost.
Catlins Wildlife Trackers Eco-tours, Papatowai, T03-415 8613, www.catlins-ecotours.co.nz. Has been operating for over 12 years and offers award-winning 2- to 4-day eco-tours ($345-690), which explore the region's forest, coast, natural features and wildlife. Very informative with a range of comfortable accommodation options.
Dolphin Magic, based in Waikawa, T03-246 8444, dolphinmagic@xtra.co.nz. Trips (1½ hrs) to see general marine life with the chance of spotting the rare Hector's dolphin. Departs Waiwaka Dolphin Information Centre Oct-Apr 1000/1400 and a (2½ hrs) twilight trip at 1700.
Nugget View Charters, Kaka Point, T03-412 8602, www.catlins.co.nz. Offers water-based wildlife spotting and fishing trips around Molyneux Bay and Nugget Point.

❶ Directory

The Catlins *p679, map p680*
Banks There are no banks in the Catlins but EFTPOS is available at the general stores and petrol stations. **Internet** Hilltop Backpackers, Papatowai. VIC, Owaka. Lumberjack Café and Bar, Owaka. Table Talk Café, Gore.

Tramping in Southland and the Fiords

Fiordland National Park offers some of the best tramping (hiking) tracks in the world ranging from the relatively straightforward Kepler and Humpridge tracks to the more demanding Dusky and Hollyford. Then of course there is the Milford Track considered by many (deservingly) as the best walk in the world. All the tracks are administered by DoC, are well facilitated and must be booked well in advance. Before embarking on any trip do your homework and make sure you are well prepared. The weather in this region is notorious with the higher elevations receiving over 6 m (yes, metres) of rain a year. Of course you may strike it lucky and have a clear run with omnipresent and stunning views making it a truly memorable experience, but to avoid disappointment count on about half the trip being head down, wet and cold. ▶ For Sleeping, Eating and other listings, see pages 691-692.

Ins and outs

For information (including the DoC self-guided leaflet), the latest conditions on all the tracks listed below and hut bookings contact the **DoC** at the VIC (I-Site) in Te Anau (see page 647) and the VIC (I-Site) in Tuatapere (see page 663). The following websites are also useful: www.doc.govt.nz, www.hollyfordtrack.co.nz, www.humpridgetrack.co.nz (for online bookings). Most mainstream bookshops stock specialist guides on the Milford or Fiordland tracks. DoC also stock maps.

Dusky Track → *Colour map 6, B2 Grade of difficulty 9/10*

Now this is a track for 'real trampers': the sort with tree trunk legs, well-worn boots and facial hair. The Dusky offers the widest range of 'experiences' of any track in Fiordland from stunning glacial valley and mountain scenery, to the possibility of complete immersion in icy water. It really is magnificent and thoroughly recommended. Perhaps the true attraction, other than the relative peace, is the sense of awe at the remote **Dusky Sound**, at the very heart of the Fiordland National Park. It is a true wilderness that has changed little since Captain Cook first set foot there over 200 years ago.

The Dusky attracts less than 1000 trampers a year, which is a reflection of its remote and difficult nature. Both its location and grade of difficulty make it a true challenge and one that should only be attempted in summer. Note the track is subject to bad flooding year round. Always consult with the DoC before any attempt and fill in an intention sheet (Te Anau). Locator beacons are also recommended.

Walking times and distances The track is 84 km in total. Allow 8-10 days from Lake Hauroko to Supper Cove to West Arm (Lake Manapouri), or four days one way to Supper Cove: Hauroko (Hauroko Burn Hut)–Halfway Hut: 12 km, four to six hours. Halfway Hut–Lake Roe Hut: 7 km, three to five hours. Lake Roe Hut–Loch Maree Hut: 10 km, four to six hours. Loch Maree Hut–Supper Cove: 12 km, six to eight hours. North Access (Wilmot Pass Road Access Point to Loch Maree): Wilmot Pass Road Access Point–Upper Spey Hut, 8 km, four to five hours (add 45 minutes to West Arm Wharf and Hut). Upper Spey Hut–Kintail Hut: 7 km, six hours. Kintail Hut–Loch Maree Hut: 11 km, four to seven hours.

Trailhead transport and access The Dusky Track can be accessed from the south via Lake Hauroko (64 km west of Tuatapere) or from the Wilmot Pass Road (40 minutes from West Arm Wharf), or via boat from Lake Manapouri. By road, Lake Manapouri is reached from Manapouri (SH95), 21 km south of Te Anau. **Scenic Shuttles**, T03-249 7654, scenicshuttle@xtra.co.nz, provides transport to Manapouri and Tuatapere (departs Te Anau daily at 0815; November to May Monday to Friday only). **Lake Hauroko Tours**, Tuatapere, T03-226 6681, www.duskytrack.co.nz, offers road and jetboat access to the southern trailhead via Lake Hauroko (departs November to May Monday and Thursday at 0900, $60). **Real Journeys**, T03-249 6602, and **Fiordland Explorer Charters**, T03-249 6616, explorercharters@xtra.co.nz, both based in Pearl Harbour, Manapouri, provide daily boat transport to and from West Arm and Wilmot Pass Road. You can fly in or out of Supper Cove or Lake Hauroko by floatplane with **Wings and Water**, Te Anau, T03-249 7405, wingsandwater@teanau.co.nz. Or by helicopter with **Southern Lakes Helicopters**, T03-249 7167, www.southernlakes helicopters.co.nz, or **South West Helicopters**, Te Anau/Tuatapere, T03-249 7402, www.southwesthelicopters.co.nz. For more trailhead transport and trailhead access details, see Te Anau, Getting around, page 646.

Hump Ridge Track → *Colour map 6, B2/3 Grade of difficulty 5/10*

The Hump Ridge Track opened in late 2000 and is New Zealand's newest tramping track. It is a 53-km three-day 'moderate' circuit track at the southeastern end of the Fiordland National Park. Although it remains low-profile in relation to the excellent older tracks to the north, there is no doubt it offers an great tramping experience. As well as the mix of both coastal and podocarp/beech forest landscapes, the main attraction is the historic appeal of its four viaducts. The 125-m **Percy Burn Viaduct** is reputed to be the largest wooden viaduct in the world. Wildlife to look out for include kea and bellbirds. Fur seals and the endangered Hector's dolphins can be seen on the coast. The track is boardwalk through the areas most subject to any flooding, but you are still advised to check on track conditions before departure.

Walking times and distances The track is 53 km in full. Allow three days: Bluecliffs Beach car park–Okaka Hut: 18 km, eight to nine hours. Okaka Hut–Port Craig Village Hut: 18 km, seven hours. Port Craig Village Hut–Bluecliffs Beach: 17 km, six to seven hours.

Trailhead transport and access The Hump Ridge Track starts and finishes at the western end of Blue Cliffs Beach on Te Wae Wae Bay (signposted from Tuatapere). An anticlockwise approach is generally recommended. Road transportation to the trailhead can be arranged through **Lake Hauroko Tours**, Tuatapere, T03-226 6681, reinfo@es.co.nz, or the VIC in Tuatapere (see page 663). Independent vehicles can be left at the Tuatapere Hump Ridge Track office in Tuatapere, 31 Orawia Rd, T03-226 6739, www.humpridgetrack.co.nz, or the **Rarakau Farmstay and Lodge**, Papatotara Coast Rd, Bluecliffs Beach, T03-225 8192, www.rarakaulodge.com.

Kepler Track

→ *Colour map 6, B3 Grade of difficulty 6/10*

The Kepler Track is a 60-km, three- to four-day 'Great Walk', which is easily accessible from Te Anau, providing a convenient and viable alternative to the Milford Track. It traverses the edge of the beautiful **Lake Te Anau** before ascending to the **Luxmore Hut** – reputed to offer one of the best 'hut views' in Fiordland. From the Luxmore Hut the track negotiates the scenic, open tops of the **Luxmore Range**, before falling through forest in to the **Iris Burn Valley** and back to civilization via Shallow Bay on **Lake Manapouri**. The highlights are of course the views from the Luxmore Hut and the scenic combination of lake, mountain and river valley scenery. The forest is classic silver beech and podocarp, which at night often echoes with the cry of kiwi. New Zealand robin and blue duck are also seen occasionally. This track attracts over 10,000 trampers a year so book well in advance and expect company. The Kepler offers an excellent two-day (return) part-track walk to the Luxmore Hut and back.

Walking times and distances It's a 60 km full circuit from Te Anau. Allow four days: Control Gates–Luxmore Hut: 14 km, six hours (Brod Bay campsite 1½ hours). Luxmore Hut–Iris Burn Hut: 18½ km, five to six hours. Irish Burn Hut–Moturau Hut: 17 km; five to six hours. Moturau Hut–Rainbow Reach: 6 km, 1½ hours.

Trailhead transport and access The Kepler Track starts at the Lake Te Anau outlet control gates, 5 km south of Te Anau and finishes at **Rainbow Reach**, 11 km south of Te Anau near SH95. By road, **Tracknet**, T03-249 7777, www.tracknet.co.nz, offers transportation from Te Anau town to the control gates ($5) or Rainbow Reach ($9), departs Te Anau 0830, 0930, 1445 ($5). It also provides transport from Queenstown.

By boat, the Kepler can be accessed opposite Te Anau at Brod Bay (missing out first the 5½-km lakeside section of track), contact **Sinbad Cruises**, T03-249 7106, or **Kepler water taxi**, T03-249 8364, from $20 (one way). The Luxmore Hut can be reached by helicopter with **Southern Lakes Helicopters**, T03-249 7167, www.south ernlakeshelicopters.co.nz. For more trailhead transport details, see Te Anau, Getting around, page 646.

Southland Tramping in Southland & the Fiords

Kepler Track

Ever since the *National Geographic* magazine hailed the mighty, 53-km, four-day, Milford Track as the 'World's Greatest Walk' in the early 1980s, it has become a victim of its own reputation. Of its utter scenic splendour there is no doubt, but there is also human traffic and commercialism. That of course does not mean that it cannot be treated as a challenge. It is essentially a difficult tramp and should be tackled with enthusiasm, but more importantly, also, a sense of realism.

Highlights on the Milford are many, including the stunning vista of the **McKinnon Pass** (1073 m) and the 580-m **Sutherland Falls**. Then, of course, at the track's end is the stunning and unforgettable **Milford Sound**. The Milford Track attracts up to 20,000 trampers a year so book well in advance (at least two months) and expect company. Bookings are on a first-come-first-served basis and start on 1 July for the following summer. Trampers should be of a suitable fitness level and be able to carry a heavy pack for four days. The track is very well-maintained but is still steep and rough in places. In winter the McKinnon Pass can be impassable due to snow and ice and there can be a severe avalanche danger. In winter always consult the DoC before setting off, check weather forecasts, fill in an intentions sheet and consider taking locator beacons (can be hired from the DoC Visitor Centre).

Walking times and distances   The track is 53 km one way. Allow four days: Glade House Wharf–Clinton Hut: 5 km, 1½ hours. Clinton Hut–Mintaro Hut: 16½ km, 5½ hours. Mintaro Hut–Dumpling Hut: 14 km, six hours. Dumpling Hut–Sandfly Point: 18 km, six hours.

Trailhead transport and access   The Milford Track starts (by boat from Te Anau Downs) at Glade House (south) and finishes (by boat) at Sandfly Point near Milford Sound (north). The track can be tackled in either direction in winter (April to October) but, if you are an independent tramper, it must be negotiated from south to north in summer (October to April).

By road, Te Anau Downs (and Milford Sound) is served by a number of Te Anau operators, see Te Anau Getting around, page 646. **Tracknet**, T03-249 7777 (Te Anau Downs $16; Milford Sound, departing Te Anau 0700, 0945, 1315, from $16) is recommended. Tracknet also provides transport from Queenstown.

By boat, Glade House can be accessed from Te Anau with **Sinbad Cruises**, T03-249 7016 (1030; $68) or from Te Anau Downs with **Real Journeys**, T03-249 7416 (1030, 1400; from $54). **Wings and Water**, T03-249 7405, can deliver you to Glade House by floatplane. From Milford Sound, the **DoC**, T03-249 8514 (1400, 1515; $28) and **Rosco's Sea Kayaks** provide pick-ups and drop-offs to Sandfly Point (Te Anau, 1400; $25). **Sinbad Cruises** and **Tracknet** (see above) offer a complete road transport package deal for $50 ($135 out of season with boat transport inclusive).

Milford Track

The Hollyford Track is essentially a low-level (bush) 56-km four-day (one way) tramp that negotiates the **Hollyford River Valley** and bank of **Lake McKerrow** to the remote **Martins Bay**. It is not a tramp for those expecting spectacular high-level views, but does offer fine scenery and a superb sense of wilderness. The undeniable highlight is the **Martins Bay Hut** at the mouth of the Hollyford River. Two days at Martins Bay taking in the coast and seal colony is a fine remote west coast experience. The tramp is most often tackled in conjunction with jet-boat returns/shortcuts via Lake McKerrow and a flight out from Martins Bay Lodge to Milford or Hollyford Valley airfield is highly recommended. Note that guided walks are available. Also note that the Hollyford can be extended or combined to include the long (9-10 day) and arduous **Pyke-Big Bay Track**. Martins Bay to Big Bay Hut offers a good day trip but the route is vague.

This is not a tramp to be tackled after heavy rain. The sections between the Trailhead car park and the Hidden Falls Hut (first hut) are tricky in wet weather; some river crossings have **three-wire bridges**. The sandflies at Martins Bay Hut are legendary.

Walking times and distances The track is 56 km one way. Allow four to five days to Martins Bay Hut, one way. Road End–Hidden Falls Hut: 9 km, two to three hours. Hidden Falls Hut–Alabaster Hut: 10½ km, three to four hours. Alabaster Hut–Demon Trail Hut: 14½ km, four to five hours. Demon Trail Hut–Hokuri Hut: 9½ km, five to six hours. Hokuri Hut–Martins Bay Hut: 13½ km, four to five hours.

Trailhead transport and access For air transportation contact **Air Fiordland**, T03-249 7505, www.airfiordland.com (from $435). For jet-boat transfers contact **Hollyford Track**, T0800-832226 (T03-442 3760), www.hollyfordtrack.co.nz/charters. **Tracknet**, T03-249 7777 ($39), runs buses departing Te Anau daily 0700 and 1315. **Trips 'n' Tramps**, T03-2497081, www.milfordtourswalks.co.nz, also offers road transfers. For more trailhead transport and trailhead access details see Getting around, in the Te Anau section, page 646.

● Sleeping

Dusky Track *p687*
All 7 huts (Halfway, Lake Roe, Loch Maree, Supper Cove, Kintail, Upper Spey and West Arm Hut) are 'Category 3' ranging from 12-20 bunks with mattresses and toilet facilities. There are no gas cookers but there are potbelly stoves in each hut. Huts must be booked through DoC and cost $5, child $2.50 per night. For post-walk accommodation see Manapouri/Te Anau and Tuatapere sections. For more booking information see the DoC website, www.doc.govt.nz.

Hump Ridge Track *p688, map p688*
Both huts (Okaka and Port Craig Village) are maintained and managed by the Hump Ridge Track Trust. Wardens are seconded to each hut from Oct-Apr. The huts are very modern with 40 bunks, mattresses, lighting, cooking, heating

and toilet facilities (limited hot water). Huts must be booked through the Track Trust direct, or through the VIC in Tuatapere. They cost $40, child $20 per night. For post walk accommodation see Tuatapere sections.
B-D Rarakau Farmstay and Lodge, Papatotara Coast Rd, Bluecliffs Beach, T03-225 8192, www.rarakaulodge.com. Well placed and recommended.

Hollyford track *p691*
All the DoC huts are 'Category 3' ($5) from 12-20 bunks with wood fires but no gas cookers.
Martins Bay Lodge (between Hokuri and Martins Bay Huts, accessible by jet boat and administered by Hollyford Track as part of tramping package), much higher standard than the DoC Huts. Guided trips, fully catered and fly-in/walk-out or

walk-in/walk-out tramps available with **Hollyford Track**, T03-442 7789/ T0800-832226, www.hollyfordtrack.co.nz. From Te Anau a 3-day (fly out) adventure costs from $1550.

Kepler Track *p688, map p689*

Another of the country's premiere walks and administered as one of the DoC's 'Great Walks', www.greatwalks.co.nz. All 3 huts (Luxmore, Iris Burn and Moturau) are of a good standard ranging from 40-60 bunks with mattresses and cooking facilities. Note huts do not have heating or cooking facilities in winter (May to mid-Oct). They cost $30 per night or $75 with a 3-night discount.
D Campsite at Brod Bay, $12, child $6. All bookings should be made with the DoC in advance, especially in mid summer. For trailhead accommodation see Te Anau, page 646. For more booking information, www.doc.govt.nz.

Milford Track *p690, map p690*

The 3 DoC huts (Clinton, Mintaro and Dumpling) are of a good standard with 40 bunks with cooking, heating and toilets. Wardens are seconded to all huts in summer. The cost of the 3 nights' accommodation is $120 (14 or under, $60). In winter Apr-Oct the huts revert to backcountry hut standard/ category (no heating or cooking facilities) and cost $10, child $5. The 'Guided Walks' companies have separate huts (Glade House, Quintin Hut and Milford Lodge). Given the popularity of the Milford, as an independent tramper you cannot stay consecutive nights in one hut and must move on. No camping is allowed. All bookings should be made with

the DoC's Great Walks booking office (Te Anau), well in advance (preferably the year before), especially during mid-summer.

▲▲ Activities and tours

Hump Ridge Track *p688, map p688*

Hump Ridge Track, T0800-486774, www.humpridgetrack.co.nz. All inclusive multi-day package deals with a 4-day/3-night 'Freedom Plus' package from $395 and a 4-day/3-night guided option from $1195.

Kepler Track *p688, map p689*

The following offer guided walks on the Kepler. Prices on application.
Fiordland Guides, Te Anau, T03-249 7832, www.fiordlandguides.co.nz.
Trips 'n' Tramps, Te Anau, T03-249 7081, www.milfordtourswalks.co.nz.

Hollyford track *p691*

Hollyford Track, T03-442 7789/T0800-832226, www.hollyfordtrack.co.nz. Guided trips, fully catered and guided fly in/walk out or walk in/walk out tramps. From Te Anau a 3-day (fly out) adventure costs from $1550.

Milford Track *p690, map p690*

Koromiko Trek, Te Anau, T03-2498167, koromiko@xtra.co.nz. Offers guided day-walks and packages on the Kepler and Milford from $128 (from Te Anau).
Ultimate Hikes, T03-435 1809, www.ultimatehikes.co.nz. Offers excellent full guided walk packages, from $1490 low season and $1750 high season (Dec-Mar).
Trips 'n' Tramps, Te Anau, T03-249 7081, www.milfordtourswalks.co.nz. Offers similar trips to **Koromiko**, above.

Background

Footprint features

History

Maori legends

According to Maori legend New Zealand was created by the great Polynesian demigod **'Maui-Tikitiki-a Taranga'** who hailed from the original Polynesian homeland of **Hawaiki**. Maui was well known for his trickery and guile and through the magical powers of a magic jawbone given to him by his 'sorcerer' grandmother, he was blessed with many god-like powers, with which to confront the world around him. Once, while out fishing with his five brothers, Maui used a piece of his magic jawbone as a fishhook and his own blood as bait. Soon he caught an almighty fish and struggling to pull it to the surface placed a spell upon it to subdue it forever. This great fish became **Te-Ika-a-Maui** (the Fish of Maui) and in essence the North Island of New Zealand. The shape of the North Island is said to resemble the body of the fish with the mouth being Palliser Bay at its southernmost tip, the fins Taranaki and the East Cape and its tail Northland. The mountains and valleys were created when Maui's jealous brothers hacked hungrily at the fish with their greenstone *mere* (clubs). The South Island is **'Te-Waka-a-Maui'** (the Waka of Maui) and Stewart Island **'Te-Punga-o-te-Waka-a-Maui'** (the anchor)

Maori trace their ancestry to the homelands of 'Hawaiki' and the great Polynesian navigator **Kupe**. On a brave scouting mission, across the uncharted oceans to the southeast, Kupe made landfall on a new and as yet undiscovered land (Maui's fish) at a spot now called the Hokianga in Northland, around AD 800. Finding the new land viable for settlement, Kupe named it **Aotearoa –The Land of the Long White Cloud** . Leaving his crew to colonize, Kupe then returned to Hawaiki to encourage further emigration. A century later the first fleet of *waka* left Hawaiki on the great migration to settle Aotearoa permanently. It was the crew of these great canoes that formed the first *iwi* (tribes) of a new race of people called the **Maori**.

Early beginnings

Due to its geographic isolation New Zealand was one of the last 'viable' lands to be settled by humans. Although it is a matter of debate, most modern historians speculate that the first peoples to discover and settle permanently in New Zealand were the ancestors of early Polynesians, who gradually spread southeast to the Pacific Islands from Indonesia around AD 1000. The ancestral land called Hawaiki is thought to be Tahiti and the Society Islands. This late ocean-going migration is quite incredible if you consider that just across the Tasman, in Australia, the aborigines had already been happily ensconced for over 50,000 years. Again, exactly when and how these early Polynesians arrived and how they actually lived is in doubt. What is known is that they arrived sporadically in **double-hulled canoes** and initially struggled with the colder climate of New Zealand. Finding their traditional root crops like yam and **kumara** (sweet potato) hard to establish, they had to change their principal diet and methods of hunting. Fishing and seafood gathering took precedence over cultivation, and seals and abundant flightless land birds (mainly moa) became principal food items. With such plentiful food, for many decades the early Maori thrived, but like the first aboriginal settlers of Australia they made the fatal mistake of plundering the environment without thought for the future or sustainability. They also brought with them **dogs** and **kiore** (rats) which, in the absence of predators, and along with hunting, reaped havoc on the flightless native birds.

Before long, especially in the South Island, much of the native bush had been burnt down and the hapless moa, along with a number of other species, were hunted to extinction. This period of colonization was to become known as the **Archaic Period**. Facing starvation, many of the tribes that had ventured south returned to the warmer environment of the North Island where traditional crops could still be grown and

Maori values

To the Maori everything has a *mauri*, an essence that gives everything its special character and everything is viewed as a living entity. *Mauri* infuses everything: things living and non-living, earth and sky. Sometimes a sacred stone, which is placed at a secret location in a forest or river, represents it and sometimes it has no tangible presence at all, but always the *mauri* must be nurtured, cared for and respected. When *kia moana* (seafood) is taken from the sea, a tree is felled, or any other thing is harvested, a karakia should be said beforehand and thanks given afterwards.

The concept of *mauri* leads to a sense of unity between man and nature. The unity extends to the opposing principles that make up the cosmos, as is expressed in the creation tradition. The tradition expounds how Rangi, the sky father, and Papa, the earth mother, were once united and how Tane Mahuta, the god of the forest, tore them apart to let in the daylight. The separation brought great sorrow to Rangi and Papa. This sorrow continues in the clinging mists and falling rain, and rising of the dew.

Water is therefore fundamental to the Maori world view. It is considered a basic essence, a part of every living thing, the linking medium between individuals and their environment. The water of a *hapu* or *iwi* is a crucial source of their *mana* and plays a central role in many rituals. (Department of Conservation).

seafood could easily be gathered. By the time the first European explorers arrived the Maori had developed their own culture, based on the tight-knit family unit and a tribal system not dissimilar to the Celts and Scots. In a desire to protect family, food resources and land the Maori, like the Scots, saw their fair share of brutal inter-tribal conflict. The Maori developed a highly effective community and defence system built within fortified villages or *pa* and cannibalism was also common. By the 16th century they had developed into a successful, fairly healthy, robust race, free from European diseases or intercontinental greed and were, by this time, like the aborigines millennia before them, beginning to develop a sustainable future in tune with the environment around them. This period is known as the **Classic Period**.

However despite the Maori successes in colonization, in many ways, when the first human footprint was made on New Zealand shores, the subsequent environmental damage was inevitable and irreversible. A 'classic' dynamic of cause and effect was set in place that would compromise the land forever. The Maori had proved the nemesis of the unspoiled and isolated biodiversity of the land. Now, with the sails of European ships appearing above the horizon and the first European shoe-print – it was, effectively, to become the turn of the Maori themselves to be facing threat.

European exploration

Although there is a vicious rumour that the French or Spanish were actually the first Europeans to sight New Zealand, the first documented discovery was made in 1642 by Dutch explorer **Abel Tasman**. Commissioned by the Dutch East India Company, Tasman was sent to confirm or otherwise the existence of the hotly rumoured Great Southern Continent (**Terra Australis Incognita**) and if discovered, to investigate its viability for trade. Doubtless with great satisfaction, he first set eyes on the new continent (Aotearoa) off what is now Okarito in Westland, on 13 December 1642, before heading north and anchoring in **Golden Bay** at the northern tip of the South Island. However, the excitement quickly turned to despair when the first encounter with the Maori proved hostile, with a loss of life on both sides. Without setting foot on land Tasman turned tail and fled up the west coast of the North Island en route to Tonga and Fiji. He christened the new land 'Staten Landt' which was later renamed **'Nieuw Zeeland'**. It was Tasman's first and last encounter with the new land, but his visit led to New Zealand being put on the world map.

The next recorded European visit occurred with the arrival of the ubiquitous British explorer **Captain Cook** on board the **'Endeavour'** in 1769. It would be the first of three voyages to New Zealand. Cook's first landing, on 7 October in **Poverty Bay** was eventful to say the least, with what proved to be a classic culture clash with the resident Maori. Ignorance and fear on both sides led to a mutual loss of life, but unlike Tasman, Cook persevered with his public relations efforts and after further encounters managed to establish a 'friendly' relationship with the new people he called *tangata* Maori (the 'ordinary people').

Cook spent a further six months in New Zealand coastal waters mapping and naming the geographical features as he went. From Poverty Bay he first sailed south via the Bay of Plenty and Cape Kidnappers to Cape Turnagain (on the border of modern day Southern Hawke's Bay and the Wairarapa), before heading back north, around the North Island, then south again to the Cook Strait and **Ship Cove** in the Queen Charlotte Sound. Ship Cove was clearly a favourite of Cook's and would be revisited on every subsequent voyage. After refitting the *Endeavour* in Ship Cove, Cook returned to Cape Turnagain (via Cape Palliser), before sailing down the eastern coast of the South Island, passing Stewart Island (which he mapped as a headland), sighting the entrance to Dusky Sound in Fiordland, before returning via the west coast back to Cook Strait. Perhaps reluctantly he then left for Australia, but not before naming Cape Farewell, just south of Farewell Spit.

Cook's second voyage in 1773 on board the **'Resolution'** saw him land briefly in Dusky Sound (virtually unchanged to this day) before returning to Ship Cove via the west coast of the South Island and from there on to South America. On his third and last voyage, three years later, he returned to Ship Cove and his beloved 'Sounds', before heading for Hawaii (**Sandwich Islands**), where he was killed by the natives. Modern-day New Zealand owes a great deal to Captain Cook; not least the long list of place names that he bestowed upon what was perhaps his favourite destination. There are at least six statues around the country that now immortalize the great man.

European settlement and the clash of cultures

After news spread of the Cook voyages, and perhaps more so due to the observations of his colleague and ship's naturalist Joseph Banks, it did not take long for European **sealers** and **whalers** to reach New Zealand and rape the rich marine resources. Many set up stations around the south coast and Sub-Antarctic Islands and by the 1820s the New Zealand fur seal and numerous species of whale had been brought to the verge of extinction. As the industries subsequently declined they were quickly joined or replaced with a limited but still repetition of timber and flax **traders**. Others including adventurers, ex-convicts from Australia and some very determined (and some would say, much needed) missionaries joined the steady influx in. **Samuel Marsden** gave the first Anglican sermon in the Bay of Islands on Christmas Day, 1814.

Inevitably, perhaps, an uneasy and fractious integration occurred between the Maori and the new settlers and, in the familiar stories of colonized peoples the world over, the consequences for the native people were disastrous. Western diseases quickly ravaged over 25% of the Maori population and the trade of food, land or even preserved heads for the vastly more powerful and deadly European weapons resulted in the **Maori Musket Wars** of 1820-1835, a swift and almost genocidal era of inter-tribal warfare. With such a melting pot of divergent cultures, greed and religion simmering on a fire of lawlessness and stateless disorganization, contrary to the glowing reports being given back in Europe, New Zealand was initially an awful place to be. Crime and corruption was rife. The Maori were conned into ridiculously unfavourable land for weapons deals and, along with the spread of Christianity and disease, their culture and tribal way of life was gradually being undermined. Such were the realities of early settlement that Kororareka (now known as Russell) in the Bay of Islands, which was the largest European settlement in the 1830s, earned itself the name and reputation as the 'Hellhole of the Pacific'. Amidst all the chaos the settlers began to appeal to their governments for protection.

Treaty of Waitangi

By 1838 there were about 2,000 British subjects in New Zealand and by this time the country was under the nominal jurisdiction of New South Wales in Australia. In 1833 **James Busby** was sent to Waitangi in the Bay of Islands as the official 'British Resident'. He was given the responsibility of law and order, but without the means to enforce it. Matters were made worse with the arrival of boatloads of new British immigrants sent under the banner of the privately owned and non-government supported **New Zealand Company**. Four years after Busby's arrival British settlers petitioned William IV for protection, citing the fact that Frenchman Baron de Thierry was threatening to pre-empt any British attempt to claim sovereignty of New Zealand. Fearful of losing any possibility of control, Britain appointed **Captain William Hobson** as Lieutenant Governor to replace Busby in New Zealand. His remit was to effect the transfer of sovereignty over the land from the Maori chiefs to the British Crown. In many ways the circumstances bore an uncanny resemblance to the situation in Britain before it became a United Kingdom. In essence the fact that the Maori were, like the Scots, a culture based on family (clan or tribe) and fought ferociously to protect *that* rather than a whole nation, would undoubtedly be in their favour. The lure for the Maori would of course be material gain in return for land and 'full protection' as British citizens. For many Maori *iwi* (tribes) whose power was inferior to that of others, this would of course be an attractive proposition. With the help of Busby who was now familiar with the ways and desires of the Maori, Hobson created what was to become the most important and controversial document in New Zealand history, the Treaty of Waitangi.

In the hastily-compiled document there were three main provisions. The first was the complete cession of sovereignty by the Maori to the Queen of England. The second was the promise of full rights and possession of Maori lands and resources (but with the right to sell, of course). The third, and perhaps the greatest, attraction, given the chaotic environment, was the full rights and protection of Maori as British citizens. After two days of discussions, a few amendments and amidst much pomp and ceremony, over 40 Maori chiefs eventually signed the Treaty on 5 February 1840. With these first few signatures from the predominantly Northland tribes, Hobson went on a tour of the country to secure others.

To this day the Treaty of Waitangi remains a very contentious document. From its very inception it was inevitably going to be a fragile bridge between two very different cultures. Given the many differences in communication, translation and meaning, at best it was spurious or vague but worse still could, as a result, be easily manipulated in both actual meaning and subsequent enactment. Indeed, a modern-day lawyer would look at the Treaty and rub his little hands with glee. In essence the best politician, public relations consultant or rabid optimist could only have sold it as a 'beginning' or a 'start' on the 'difficult road to stable biculturalism', while many a realist would have (and still would) declare it an unworkable 'scam'.

By the September of 1840 Hobson had gathered over 500 signatures, all in the North Island. Feeling this was enough to claim sovereignty over New Zealand he did so, and declaring the right of discovery over the South Island, made New Zealand a Crown Colony, independent of New South Wales and Australia. But the refusal and subsequent omission of several key (and powerful) Maori chiefs paved the way for regional disharmony and eventually war.

In 1840 Hobson established Kororareka (the hell-hole of the Pacific') as the first capital of New Zealand, but given its reputation and history, he moved the seat of government to Auckland within a year. With the increased influx of settlers, all greedy for land and resources, human nature very quickly superseded the legal niceties and undermined the fragile bridge of the new bicultural colony. In a frenzy of very dubious land deals between Maori and *Pakeha* (white settlers), as well as misunderstandings in methods of land use and ownership, resentment between the two was rife. This, plus the heavy taxes that were being demanded by the new and financially strapped government, strained the bridge to breaking point. The Maori were essentially beginning to feel disenfranchised and began to rebel against British authority.

One of the first disputes was initiated by a particularly fractious and persistent chief called **Hone Heke** who was one of the original chiefs to sign the treaty in the Bay of Islands. In 1844 he protested in a way that he knew would hit hard at the British psyche by cutting down the flagpole that so proudly flew the Union Jack in Kororareka (later renamed Russell). He did this not once, but (almost admirably) four times. Hone Heke's actions led to a bloody war with the British that was to last two years. Sadly, this clash was just the beginning. In 1852 the **Constitution Act** was created and in 1853 the country was divided into six provinces, each with a Provincial Council exercising the functions of local government which included land purchases and sales.

At the same time, immigration was increasing and with the spread of disease, the Maori were becoming well outnumbered. Once again it seems, as with many native peoples around the world, they were becoming a resented minority and a displaced people. Exacerbated by the provincial administration, the continued greed of the settlers and inter-tribal conflicts, the Maori continued to lose land at an alarming rate and often in return for only meagre material gains.

Some of the more savvy Maori chiefs became reluctant to sell land and, in 1858, several Waikato tribes went a step further by electing their own Maori king. This became known as the **King Movement**. Although initially designed to preserve cultural identity and serve as a land policy maker, supporters were encouraged to resist all land sales and *Pakeha* settlement. The British reacted with complete derision, seeing the movement only as a barrier to further colonization. The Land Wars (or Maori Wars) inevitably ensued. Troops from both Britain and Australia were sent to aid the New Zealand militia in an attempt to quash the uprising, which spread outside the Waikato to Northland and Taranaki. The east coast later joined the fold with the formation of a Maori 'Hauhau' religious movement. One of the most noted Maori rebels was **Te Kooti** who for a time became the most wanted man in the land (see page).

It proved to be a bloody time in New Zealand's early history with the fierce and fearless Maori warriors putting up a determined and courageous fight. Their traditional methods of fighting from a fortified *pa*, with trenches, proved so effective (and later, so admired by the British) it became the chosen method of defence and attack in ground warfare until after the Second World War.

With far superior weaponry and organization the British quickly subdued the rebels. In return for their disobedience, and despite the treaty, they confiscated huge tracts of land. This land was then sold to new or already established settlers. By 1900 over 90% of the land was outside Maori ownership or control. They were a defeated people and, with little or no power and with continued integration, their culture was rapidly crumbling.

Natural resources, consolidation and social reform

Although development in the North Island suffered as a result of the conflicts, both timber, agriculture and gold came to the rescue. On an already solid base of productive agriculture, and with the lucrative rape of the upper North Island's **kauri forest** already in full swing, the discovery of **gold** in the Coromandel in 1852 sealed the economic boom. The South Island too, which had been a relatively peaceful haven compared to the North, joined the party, with the discovery of gold from 1857 in the Nelson, Otago and west coast regions.

With much of the economic focus being on the South Island, the seat of a new central (as opposed to provincial) government was moved to Wellington which became the capital in 1876. With gold fever the prime attraction, the *Pakeha* population grew dramatically. With so much good fortune in the south, Dunedin's headcount alone grew from 2000 in 1861 to 10,000 four years later, making it the largest town in the land. Although the gold boom lasted only a decade, the infrastructures that the boom set in place paved the way for agricultural, timber and coal industries to take over.

In the agriculture sector alone, especially through sheep and dairy cattle, New Zealand was becoming an internationally significant export nation and prosperity continued. Towards the end of the 19th century led by the enigmatic Liberal Party leader **Richard 'King Dick' Seddon**, New Zealand's colonial settlers went through a dramatic and sweeping phase of **social reforms**. Well ahead of Britain, the USA and most other Western nations, women secured the vote and pioneering legislation was enacted, introducing old-age pensions, minimum wage structures and arbitration courts.

But while the *Pakeha* prospered the Maori continued to suffer. The **Native Lands Act** of 1865 was established to investigate Maori land ownership and distribute land titles, but again, thanks mainly to Maori tribal structure and the split of land to individual as opposed to communal blocks, this only exacerbated the disintegration of the Maori culture and undermined its cohesion. Maori were given the vote in 1867 but only held four out of 95 seats in the parliamentary House of Representatives. By 1900 the Maori population had decreased to less than 50,000 and with the integration of Maori and *Pakeha* and many Maori/*Pakeha* marriages, the pure Maori were becoming even more of a minority.

Prosperity and the world wars

By 1907 New Zealand progressed to the title of **'Dominion'** of Britain rather than merely a 'colony' and by the 1920s was in control of most of its own affairs. By virtue of its close links with Britain, New Zealand and the newly formed (trans-Tasman) **Australia and New Zealand Army Corps (ANZAC)** became heavily embroiled in the Boer War of 1899-1902 and again in the First World War, at Gallipoli and the Western Front. Although noted for their steadfast loyalty, courage and bravery, the ANZACs suffered huge losses. Over 17,000 never returned with one in every three men aged between 20 and 40 being killed or wounded. Almost a century on there remains a palpable sense of pride in both Australia and New Zealand for those lives lost and quite rightly so; their First World War casualties remain the greatest of any combat nation.

New Zealand joined the Western world in the **Great Depression** of the 1920s but it recovered steadily and independently progressed in an increasing atmosphere of optimism. Again from a solid base of agricultural production it prospered and immigration, particularly from Britain, grew steadily. The population had now passed one million. In 1935 New Zealand became the fist nation to enact a social welfare system, which included free health care and low-rental council properties. These pioneering acts of social reform, along with the economy, resources and common attitude, secured one of the highest standards of living in the world and New Zealand was an envied, prime 'new-life' destination.

However, along with the rest of the world, water was temporarily thrown on the fires of progress and prosperity with the outbreak of the Second World War. Once again, New Zealand and the loyal ANZACs answered the call. This time, in both Europe and Asia, it was the turn of the **28th Maori Battalion** to earn a widespread admiration and respect for their tenacity and courage. It seemed their warrior spirit, if not their culture, was still alive and well. Like most warring nations the war effort extended to the home shores where women replaced men in the vast majority of industrial and social practices. With the spread of the conflict across the Pacific, it proved a nervous time for the nation and although many would be correct in saying it was not for the first time, the people of New Zealand were under a renewed threat of invasion. However, with the dropping of the atomic bomb in Japan the threat ceased and the war was over.

Post 1945

Shortly after the war, in 1947, New Zealand was declared an independent nation but thanks to the war and its important agricultural exports, it maintained close defence and trade links with the Great Britain, the USA and Australia. In 1945 it became one of the original member states of the **United Nations** (UN) and later joined the **ANZUS Defence Pact** with the USA and Australia. Domestically, the country again prospered but the nagging problems of race relations, land and resource disputes between Maori and *Pakeha* still had to be addressed.

By the early 1970s the vast majority of Maori had moved to urban areas in search of work but with many being unsuccessful, social problems proved inevitable. In an attempt to spawn a new sense of spirit, the government passed the **Waitangi Day Act** in 1960 making 6 February a day of thanksgiving in celebration of the treaty and the cohesive bicultural society it was supposed to have created. This was further emphasized with an official public holiday in 1973. But some Maori (and *Pakeha*) merely saw the day as an opportunity for protest and although the public holiday remains, the traditional pomp and ceremony annually enacted at Waitangi in the Bay of Islands, was scrapped for much more low-key governmental diplomatic posturing. In 1975 more significant progress was made with the formation of the **Waitangi Tribunal** which was established to legally and officially hear Maori claims against the Crown. This method of addressing the problems continues to this day, but as ever, the misinterpretations of the treaty and its translation remain a major stumbling block.

New Zealand joined most of the developed world in the economic slump of the '70s and '80s. The traditionally strong agricultural exports to Europe declined, the price of oil and manufacturing imports rose and it was hit hard by the stock market crash of 1987. In response to the economic decline, the government of the day – under **Robert Muldoon's** National Party – deregulated the country's economy, paving the way for free trade. The most important and lasting trade agreement was the **Closer Economic Relations Trade Agreement** made with Australia in 1983, but New Zealand was beginning to see itself playing a far more significant role in the Asian markets as opposed to the traditional European ones.

In 1984 the Labour government, under its charismatic leader **David Lange**, took control and made further sweeping and radical changes to the economy. These were dubbed **'Rogernomics'** after the then finance minister Roger Douglas. Although the policies of privatization, free enterprise and the deregulation of the labour market improved the situation, unemployment rose and the policies began to prove unpopular with the voting public. Fearful of losing re-election votes Lange sacked Douglas, but the party reinstated him, and this resulted in his own shock resignation in 1989, leaving the party in disarray. Subsequently, the National Party led by the far less charismatic **Jim Bolger** swept to power in 1990.

One of the most important landmark decisions made on foreign policy in the 1980s was New Zealand's staunch **anti-nuclear** stand. In 1984 Lange refused entry to any foreign nuclear-powered ships in its coastal waters. This soured its relationship with the US who reacted by suspending defence obligations to New Zealand made under the ANZUS pact in the 1950s. This anti-nuclear stance is still maintained with considerable pride and is one that was only strengthened when the French Secret Service bombed the Greenpeace vessel **Rainbow Warrior** in 1985, causing national and international outrage. Relations with France were further soured in 1995 with the rather arrogant and insensitive testing of nuclear weapons in French Polynesia.

Throughout the 1990s the National Party continued successfully to nurture the free market economic policies first initiated by Labour. In 1993 a national referendum voted unanimously in favour of a mixed-member proportional representation (**MMP**) system of government. This system, which has proved successful in Germany, gives electors two votes: one for a candidate in their own electorate and the second for their favoured political party. Maori can choose to vote in either a general or Maori electorate. There is a 120-seat parliament with 60 general electorate seats, five Maori and 55 allocated to parties according to the percentage of party votes received.

Whether this system of government has been good for the country is debatable, but what did result, through internal politics and fragile power-sharing agreements, were two women prime ministers. The first in New Zealand's history was **Jenny Shipley** of the National Party who engineered a 'coup' to seize party leadership from Jim Bolger in 1997 and currently in power is **Helen Clark** of the 1999-elected Labour Party. Her success as Prime Minister is almost unprecedented. The new system can hardly be accused of restricting a diverse representation. One Green Party MP, Nandor Tanczos, is a Rastafarian and a Labour Party MP, Georgina Beyer, is transgender.

A highly significant event outside politics in 1995 was New Zealand's win in the coveted **America's Cup** yachting race. It was the first time the cup had been won by any nation other than the US and, given the country's love of yachting, it was the cause of unprecedented national celebration and pride. Over 300,000 people lined Queen Street in Auckland to congratulate the heroic yachties' return. With the successful defence of the cup again in 2000 it seemed yachting would join – or some would say replace – rugby as the nation's world-dominating sport. Amidst much hype and after considerable amounts of money were spent to transform Auckland's waterfront into a state-of-the-art sailing arena, the Kiwi populace prepared themselves for what would surely be another convincing win in 2002/2003. But it was a dream that turned, quite dramatically, into a nightmare as amidst tactical errors, design faults and even the mast snapping, former Kiwi team member Russell Coutts led a far superior outfit in the form of the Swiss *Alinghi* team to a highly embarrassing 5-0 whitewash. In the 2007 campaign, this time in Europe, Team New Zealand fought courageously to reach the final, but again despite valiant efforts, they lost to Alinghi for a second time and once again-for now-all hopes went out with the tide.

Modern New Zealand

Given its size and isolation New Zealand enjoyed its 15 minutes of international fame on 1 January 2000 when it was the first country to see the dawn of the new millennium.

Since the infamous terrorist attacks of 11 September 2001 and more recently the US-led military interventions in Afghanistan and Iraq that were, we are told, such a fundamental part of its ongoing, self-styled global **'War Against Terrorism'**, it seems New Zealand, through its steadfast determination (unlike the Howard government of Australia) not to align itself with that US policy, will almost certainly pay a heavy price, both in recognition and the nuts and bolts of trade agreements and economics. Ask the average Kiwi what they think of all this global politicking however and they will say that for them and their country little has changed. New Zealand is a great country, easily forgotten on the world stage and too easily mocked. Most are very proud of Helen Clark's intelligent and (some say) truly democratic leadership, courageously demonstrated in her stoic stance against war in Iraq and reaction to US and UK policy and its ramifications in current world affairs. The majority of Kiwis did not want to join the campaign in Iraq and its government rightfully and steadfastly exercised that voice. Kiwis are proud of their country and by their very nature and number are traditionally more concerned about community and the environment than misguided patriotism, rhetoric ad populum, power and politics. Surely, if you look at the bigger picture, through history and to the long term, it is just as wise to be as concerned about non-native species getting through customs as explosives and drugs?

So returning to the shadows (bar the considerable and on-going hype surrounding the filming of *Lord of the Rings*) New Zealand remains largely a 'low-key' nation largely left to its own devices, blessed by an outstanding natural environment, healthy independence and the huge asset of a low and cosmopolitan population. Its current economic struggles lie in a poor exchange rate and its biggest social challenge is the continued and difficult journey down the road of biculturalism as well perhaps as some sensible long-term decisions pertaining to future levels of immigration.

But perhaps New Zealand's greatest challenge lies in the conservation and protection of its environment, for which it is most famous and much loved. Dubbed the 'Clean Green Land' it remains to be seen whether its government and people can truly embrace the reality that its relatively healthy ecological condition is mainly due to its lack of population, as opposed to the common and traditional human attitudes that have proved to be so ruinous elsewhere. One can only hope that this wise and determined attitude can blossom, even though it is very much against the international grain. Without doubt, New Zealand is a premier tourist destination with a great deal to offer. Like its much larger neighbour Australia, tourism is fast becoming the biggest and most important growth industry. Encompassed within that industry is the sensible, desirable and sustainable realm of eco-tourism, which it is hoped can assist in the country's efforts to conserve its many unique and vulnerable species. At the forefront of these conservation efforts is the ongoing programme to conserve the iconic kiwi as well as the country's impressive position on international whaling and the creation of a South Pacific Whale Sanctuary. So, from the creation of the great fish by the Maori demigod Maui, to its current efforts to protect them, the land and the people remain on an inextricable and co-dependent voyage into the new millennium.

Culture

People and population

The population of New Zealand currently stands at about four million. The population densities are unevenly spread between the two islands, with the North Island home to about three million and the South Island about one million. Greater Auckland alone is home to just over one million, almost a third of the total population. New Zealand is essentially a bicultural society made up of Maori and Europeans, and many Caucasian (*Pakeha*) nationalities are present. Maori make up about 15% of the total population, with the vast majority living in the North Island. Pacific Islanders make up the second largest non-Caucasian group at around 6% with almost all living in Greater Auckland. Asians make up 3% of the total population and are the fastest-growing minority group. Again, the vast majority of Asians choose to live in Greater Auckland. New Zealanders are famous for being 'the world's greatest travellers' and at any one time a large proportion of citizens are absent or living abroad. Over 400,000 live and work in Australia alone. Through their close trans-Tasman ties Australian and New Zealand citizens are free to live and work in both countries.

Religion

The dominant religion is **Christianity,** with Anglican, Presbyterian and Roman Catholic denominations the most prominent. Other minority religions include Hinduism, Islam, Judaism and Buddhism. The Maori developed two of their own minority Christian-based faiths; Ratana and Ringatu, both of which were formed in the late 19th to early 20th centuries. Reflecting the increasing trend in most developed nations, at least a quarter of the total population are atheists or have no religion and this number is growing.

Music

For such a small country New Zealand has a thriving **rock** scene with **Dunedin** considered the hotbed of talent. In the '70s and '80s **Split Enz** was New Zealand's best-known group, reaching international recognition. Other notable bands include **Crowded House** and the **Exponents**. In the late 1990s **OMC** (Otara Millionaires Club) shot to fame with their catchy hit 'How Bizarre', but despite their success have since broken up. Many alternative bands and singers like **Bic Runga** and **DJ Amanda**, who are fast developing a unique Kiwi or rap sound, mixed with mainly Polynesian influences, thrive within the mainstream. **Neil Finn**, formerly of Crowded House, and **Dave Dobbyn**, spearhead the most successful ageing-rocker solo careers. In the classical arena **Dame Kiri Te Kanawa** has for many years been New Zealand's most noted international opera star. Traditional domestic or world music – outside of Maori performances and Irish pubs – is quite hard to find, however the **Pacific Festival** held in Auckland in March is one notable exception.

Film

Even before Kiwi Peter Jackson, director of *Lord of the Rings* changed the face of New Zealand film making, the nation had produced a number of notable feature films and was home to internationally recognized actors and directors. Perhaps the most famous film (though an alarming and uncomfortable experience) is *Once Were Warriors* (1994) – an adaptation of Kiwi writer Alan Duff's portrayal of a highly dysfunctional urban Maori family, directed by Lee Tamahori. For those looking for a reality check of the worst social aspects of the advertised, pleasant 'clean green land' it is a must-see, superbly demonstrating that New Zealand is not immune to the death of traditional cultures, poverty, alcoholism and domestic abuse.

On a lighter note, yet still depicting harsh times, is the romantic classic *The Piano* (1993) directed by New Zealand's most noted director **Jane Campion**. Starring Holly Hunter, Sam Neill and Hollywood tough guy, Harvey Keitel, it tells the haunting story of a Scottish immigrant (Hunter) and her daughter (Anna Paquin) who are brought to New Zealand in the early 19th century in an arranged marriage to troubled colonial landowner (Neill). Finding Neill to be as romantic and warm-hearted as the mud they seem to spend all their time trudging through, she turns to the brooding, yet caring employee (Keitel) for love and affection. Part of the attraction is also his willingness to transport her prized possession – a grand piano – inland from the beach where she and her daughter were so unceremoniously off-loaded. It is a deserving multi-award winner that is well acted and has a superb musical score. However, it may leave you thinking New Zealand is a very harsh, wet place of little more than tangled bush and mud – which essentially it once was. Although actor **Sam Neill** was not born in New Zealand, he grew up in the South Island and now lives in Queenstown, so is considered by many to be an adopted son. Another actor who was born in New Zealand, but grew up in Australia, is **Russell Crowe**, who shot to fame for his macho role in *Gladiator* and has been in the public eye ever since.

But it was the creative talent and determination of North Islander **Peter Jackson** that put the country firmly on the movie-making map in 1999-2000 with the filming and release of the much lauded *Lord of the Rings* trilogy. At a cost of over $300 million it was a far cry from Jackson's other lesser-known projects, which including the New Zealand classic *Heavenly Creatures*, an intriguing tale of two troubled teenage girls. Perhaps it was his talent, his passion and his unflappability that made what was for him a childhood dream – a film version of JRR Tolkien's *Lord of the Rings* (LOTR) – into such a success, but ask any Kiwi and they will add two other essential ingredients with pride and alacrity to what was a mammoth technical and logistical filming project. The first is the very nature and variety of the Kiwi landscape, from its foreboding volcanoes to classic snow-capped mountain ranges that were so suited to Tolkien's realm of 'Middle Earth' and the collective global imagination of what it would really look like. The other essential ingredient for the film's technical success is the famed Kiwi ingenuity and down-to-earth enthusiasm – traits so obvious and refreshing in Jackson's own rather plump persona. In tune perhaps with the fictional characters he so brilliantly portrayed on film, you would not catch the boffin-like Jackson posing in tux and tails at an award ceremony or emerging from some stretch limo with a vacuous, leggy model by his side. Whether on set or in Tinsel Town he is far more likely to be discussing scenes with an equally down-to-earth actor or technician, in a pair of training shoes and munching on a ham sandwich.

There is no doubt Jackson will now be seen as the true founding father of film in New Zealand and that many more films and directors will follow suit to utilize the landscape and boundless, innate Kiwi skills. In 2002/2003 *The Last Samurai*, starring Tom Cruise, was filmed in the shadow of Mount Taranaki and in 2005/6 Jackson directed his next big project – another childhood passion – *King Kong*. In 2006 *The World's fastest Indian* starring Anthony Hopkins and directed by Roger Donaldson also received international acclaim. Based on a true life story of New Zealander Burt Munro, who spent years building a 1920 Indian motorcycle with which he set the land-speed world record at Utah's Bonneville Salt Flats in 1967.

But whether you are an avid fan of *LOTR* and are still desperately keen to pay homage to the many film locations, or don't know a *Hobbit* from an *Uruk-Hai*, one thing is for sure: despite all the hype and the massively increased profile of the New Zealand landscape, in reality and aesthetically nothing has changed and the country exists as it always has – undeniably in your face and breathtakingly beautiful.

Maori culture and traditions

The Maori are essentially a tribal race consisting of the *whanau* (family unit), extending to the **hapu** (sub-tribe) and then the **iwi** (full tribe). Together they are referred to as the **tangata whenua**, which directly translated means 'people of the land'. The Maori relationship with their ancestors (or **tipuna**) is considered to exist through their genetic inheritance, and an individual's own genealogy (or **whakapapa**) can be traced right back to the gods via one of the original migratory canoes (or **waka**). There are over 40 **iwi** in New Zealand with the largest being the **Ngapuhi** (descendants of Puhi) in Northland who have over 100,000 members, to one of the smallest, the **Ngai Tahu** (descendants of Tahu) in the South Island, who have only about 30,000 members. The Maori's family based social structure is in many ways remarkably similar to the early Scottish clan system, which developed almost in parallel on the other side of the planet. Like the Scots, the Maori culture have a love of music, song (**waiata**), dance (**haka**), oration (particularly storytelling), socializing and unfortunately, fighting amongst themselves and against outside invaders with fearless courage and determination. The word **Maori** does in itself not denote a common background but derives from a term of differentiation used between the ordinary people (natives) and the European explorers.

Traditional Maori life is bounded by the customs, concepts or conducts of **tapu** (meaning taboo, or sacred) and **noa** (meaning mundane, or the opposite of *tapu*). If something is *tapu* – whether an object, place, action or person – it must be given the accordant respect. To do otherwise can result in ostracism, bad luck or sickness. A good example would be a burial place that is forever *tapu*, or a food resource that is given seasonal *tapu* to encourage sustainability. One good example for the visiting tourist is the summit of **Moehau**, the Coromandel Peninsula's highest peak. It is currently *tapu* which means that despite the views or absence of any guard (beyond the spiritual that is) it would be very culturally insensitive to go clambering all over it. Another is **Green Lake** (Rotokakahi) near Rotorua; the island on the lake is an ancient Maori burial ground and the lake is therefore *tapu*. As such you cannot use it for any recreational activity and you must not set foot on the island.

Noa is a term heard less often, but plays an important role in the balance or cancellation of *tapu*. For example, at some point the summit of Moehau may, through ceremony, have its *tapu* rendered *noa*. Once *noa* you can clamber away to your little heart's content! Of course in the modern day your average 'Maori Joe' cannot just place a *tapu* on anything he chooses – his beer for example, or the Visa bill! If this were the case there would be social mayhem! Placing a *tapu* is a matter that requires deliberation by the *iwi* and enactment by the **elders**, very often after a meeting or **hui**. All things whether living or otherwise possess **mauri** (see next page), **wairau** (spirit) and **mana**. The meaning of *mana* goes well beyond words, but in essence means prestige, standing, integrity or respectability. It is a term that is often used by both Maori and *Pakeha*, and is even sometimes heard outside New Zealand. If a Maori warrior won a fight or a battle this would increase his *mana*, if he lost it would undermine it, and so on. Objects too have *mana*. The pendants (or *tiki*) that you buy, for others never yourself, can hold spiritual *mana* or can increase in *mana* as they are passed on to others. It is a lovely term and perhaps the one most tourists remember once they leave.

Maoritanga (the Way of the Maori)

The Maori language, lifestyle, social structure, customs, spirituality, legends, arts and crafts are all enjoying something of a revival in modern-day New Zealand. The unique Maori culture and history are all very well represented in museums throughout the country, with both **Auckland Museum** and the state-of-the-art **Museum of New Zealand (Te Papa)** in Wellington, in particular, offering a fascinating insight. Although there are thought to be no 'true' full-blooded Maori left in New Zealand, the majority of those of undisputed Maori descent remain staunchly and rightly proud of their ancestry and cultural identity. It is a sad fact that their cultural journey in the face of what many would call a 'European invasion' has been, and continues to be, a difficult and troubled one. To that end it is important for the visitor to be aware of the basics and to realize that New Zealand culture, in total, goes a lot deeper than the practice or development of a cosmopolitan mix of cultures imported from elsewhere. In a country that essentially has a very short human history and one that some critics declare as 'historically wanting', Maoritanga is, in essence, as old as it gets.

The Marae

The *marae* is essentially the sacred 'place of meeting', or of simply 'being', that exist around a **wharae tupuna** (or ancestral meetinghouse). It is traditionally used as a communal centre, meeting place or sometimes a retreat. Strict customs and protocols (or **kawa**) surrounds the *marae* and for any tourist who wishes to visit or stay it is important to be aware of these customs and the protocols. It is akin to taking your shoes off in a Japanese house, offering the correct welcome, introduction and so on. Visitors are welcomed on to the *marae* with a **powhiri** (a welcome), which is multi-faceted. First, a warrior will greet you (or all visitors – **manuhiri**) with a **haka**, which is a traditional dance that can look decidedly threatening. In essence this is a challenge (or **wero**). Do not return the gestures, unless you want to be considered uncouth, culturally ignorant or have the desire to get your head removed. At the end of the *wero* there is a peace offering (or **teka**), which is placed on the ground between you and the warrior. Once accepted, a female elder will then initiate the **karanga** (a chant), that both welcomes and addresses the visitor and their ancestors.

On moving forward you must bow to acknowledge the ancestors. At the entrance to the *whare* the chief will then offer a **whaikorero** or *mihi* (a welcoming speech). If you can, you, or traditionally the leader (chief) elect of your group, are supposed to respond accordingly. You, or your chief, then perform the **hongi** – the touching (not rubbing) of noses unique to Maori. The *hongi* is an action which is equivalent to a hug or a kiss, and is often accompanied with a handshake. The equivalent of English 'hello' is the Maori **'kiaora'**.

Once this protocol is enacted you are then a welcome guest in the *marae* and free to talk, stay or feast. The feast (or **hangi**) is a superb experience of earth-oven, steamed meat and vegetables with a very distinctive, succulent taste. A **karakia** (or prayer) is traditionally said beforehand.

The Pa

The *pa* (traditional **fortified settlements**) built by the Maori are worth special mention. Built predominantly on a headland or hill and from wood and often networked by trenches, they were used to protect against invasion by hostile tribes and also the *Pakeha* during the **Maori Land Wars**. Within the *pa* boundary are the *marae*, *whare* and food storage facilities. So effective was this system defence and so impressed were the colonial British forces, that the design was echoed in the First World War in the trenches of the Western Front. There are many subtle remains around the country with one of the best being the distinct earthworks and *kumara* (sweet potato storage) pits on **One Tree Hill** in Auckland. The volcanic plugs of the Auckland area made ideal *pa* sites.

Song and dance

Like the aborigine of Australia the Maori did not keep a written history, but rather passed down the essence of their culture and historical journey by song – **waiata** – and chants – **karakai**. The two most common song types are **waiata tangi** (songs of mourning) and **waiata aroha** (songs of love).

Maori dance is known as **haka**. The most famous form of this has been given somewhat false iconic status in the modern day by the sporting rugby legends the **All Blacks** before the start of each game. This particular form of *haka* is a war chant made as a challenge to all opposition and is quite a sight to behold. Whether you were Captain Cook or a 120-kg lock forward in the English rugby team, to be confronted with a Maori doing a *haka* is to know you're in for quite a battle!

There are other far less threatening forms of dance called **taparahi**. These include the **poi** dance, commonly seen in traditional Maori performances; the *poi* being balls of strings that are swung or twirled in harmony and synchronicity to the music. Traditional musical instruments are the flute or **putorino**. The beat is kept by the stamping of feet.

Arts and crafts

The artistic styles used by the Maori were already well developed on their arrival in New Zealand and influenced heavily by Polynesian tradition. in the absence of clay for pottery and metals with which to fashion rock or wood, they developed a unique style.

Wood or greenstone (pounamu) **carving** was the commonest form of craft both for functional purposes (like **waka**) or for decoration, on panels, **pou** (equivalent to Native American totem poles) or adorning **whare whakairo** (meeting houses). **Kauri** or **totara** were the commonest native wood types and it was fashioned into highly distinctive patterns using **greenstone (pounamu)**, shells or sharp stones. Sadly the early Christian missionaries often discouraged the Maori from producing their carvings, which they saw as containing obscene or inappropriate imagery. This is especially the case in Northland where elaborate carving is far less commonly seem on the *marae*. Other forms of carving were the creation of pendants or **tiki**, which were made predominantly from whalebone or pounamu. These pendants often depict spiritual ancestors – or **hei tiki** – as well as legendary or sacred animals. Weapons like **taiaha pouwhenua** (long clubs) and **patu** (short clubs) were fashioned from wood, while **mere** (short, close-combat clubs) were traditionally fashioned from greenstone.

One of the best places to see traditional and contemporary Maori arts and crafts in creation is at the **Maori Arts and Crafts Institute**, at the Whakarewarewa Thermal Reserve in Rotorua. Aside from carving and other three-dimensional works, Maori rock art is in evidence, particularly around Timaru in the South Island. There are also some very interesting contemporary Maori artworks showpieced in the Rotorua Museum.

Moko

The unique Maori facial tattoo (or **moko**) was traditionally applied using bone chisels, a mallet and blue pigment. The moko was predominantly the decoration of the higher classes with men covering their entire face (and sometimes their buttocks) while the women were decorated on the chin. Today, Maori (especially those in the Maori gangs like the Mongrel Mob and Black Power) still apply *moko* but this is done of course using modern tattooing techniques. To get the best idea of its design and permanence (let alone to imagine the pain), take a look at the superb realist paintings of the Maori elders done in the late 1800s by renowned New Zealand painters **Gottfried Lindauer** and **Charles F Goldie**. Examples are on display in major art galleries throughout the country, with the Auckland Art Gallery being especially good.

Language

The Maori language is still spoken throughout New Zealand and generally encouraged and spoken with pride within the *whanau* and *iwi* (Maori family and tribes), but has never been given the respect it deserves in mixed (*Pakeha*/Maori) schools over the years, hence its general decline. To the layperson who cannot understand a word, it is an intriguing language to listen to, unusually repetitive in sound and hardly melodic. There is much accentuation and repetition of vowels and the 'w' and it is wise to be aware of a few basic rules before arriving in the country. Perhaps the most important feature is the pronunciation of 'wh' as the English 'f'. For example Whanau above is not pronounced 'Wha-now' , but 'Fha-now' and Whangarei is not pronounced 'Wangarei', but 'Fhongarei'. Likewise Whakapapa, or Whakarewarewa gets similar treatment and the 'a' is pronounced more like a 'u'. Other than that it's a bit like pronouncing your vowels like the Scots twins and folk-rockers *The Proclaimers* with songs like *Letter From America* – with lots of power and opening your mouth as wide as the Homer Tunnel. A limited Maori word glossary can be found on page 722.

Land and environment

Geography

New Zealand consists of three main islands – **North Island**, **South Island** and **Stewart Island** – with a handful of other small far-flung subtropical and **sub-Antarctic islands** (the largest being a group called the **Chathams**, which lie 853 km east of South Island) completing the family. The total land area is 268,704 sq km (slightly larger than the UK).

New Zealand's boundaries extend from 33° to 53° south latitude and from 162° east longitude, to 173° west longitude, which results in a broad climatic range from north to south. It is bounded north and east by the **South Pacific Ocean**, on the west by the **Tasman Sea** and on the south by the great **Southern Ocean**. The nearest mainland is Australia, 1,600 km west, which is roughly the same distance as New Zealand is in length.

Geographical features Although compact in size, New Zealand's landscape is rich and varied: glaciers, braided rivers, lakes, fiords (flooded glacial valleys), sounds (flooded riverbeds) – found predominantly in the South Island – lowlands, alluvial plains, wetlands, large natural coastal harbours and a rash of offshore islands. Given the fact New Zealand is located at the meeting point of the Pacific and Indo-Australian Plates, it is also a distinctly 'shaky' land of frequent earthquakes and constant **volcanic activity**. The **Taupo Volcanic Zone** In central North Island is one of the most active in the world. A string of volcanoes stretches from the currently active White Island in the Bay of Plenty, to the moody Mount Ruapehu in the heart of North Island. The area also has numerous **thermal features** including geysers, mineral springs, blowholes and mud pools, most of which can be found around Rotorua and Taupo. One of the largest **volcanic eruptions** in human history occurred in New Zealand in AD 186, the remnants of which is the country's largest lake – Lake Taupo. The most recent eruption occurred in 1995 (and again in 1996), when Mount Ruapehu – North Island's highest peak – had a moderate stomach upset. The country's most dramatic **earthquake** in recent history occurred in Napier on North Island's east coast in 1931.

Due to the 'uplift' created by the clash of the two tectonic plates, the South Island has many more mountain ranges than the North Island and boasts the country's highest peak, **Mount Cook**. *Aoraki*, as the Maori call it, stands less than 40 km from the west coast at a height of 3,753 m. The country's longest river is the **Waikato**, which stretches 425 km from Lake Taupo to the Tasman Sea.

Geology

New Zealand is an ancient land that has been so isolated from any other land mass for so long that its biodiversity is described by some scientists as the closest one can get to studying life on another planet. The oldest rocks, which make up part of the New Zealand we know today, were first rafted away from the great Gondwana landmass over 100 million years ago by a process called continental drift. The modern landscape is the dramatic result of geological uplift and volcanic activity created by New Zealand's location on the boundary of the Pacific and Indo-Australian Plates. Further 'sculpturing' occurred as a result of natural erosion, particularly the glacial erosion of numerous ice ages in the last two million years. Thanks to its long isolation, much of New Zealand's biodiversity is not only ancient, but also highly unique, with such incredible oddities as the kiwi, tuatara and weta still in evidence today. A useful comparison is with the endemic biodiversity of Great Britain: having been separated from continental Europe for a mere 10,000 years it has only one endemic plant and one endemic animal species. In contrast, as a result of over 80 million years of isolation, the vast majority of New Zealand species are endemic. Around 90% of its insects and marine molluscs, 80% of its trees, ferns and flowering plants and 25% of it bird species, all 60 reptiles, four remaining frogs, two species of bat and eel are found nowhere else on earth. But on the tragic day that man arrived, a mere 1000 years ago, it was not only 'paradise found', but was to become 'paradise lost'. Our arrival has caused more devastation to this 'clean green land' than anything else in 80 million years of evolution.

Wildlife

Urban

Birds It is a tribute to the little bird itself to start with the humble, clever and ubiquitous **house sparrow**. As you emerge bleary-eyed from the airport terminal, the chances are you will see one before you do a taxi. Whether on high or at your feet, they are waiting and watching, and have your bag contents under close observation. After humans and, in essence, thanks to them, these master scavengers are one of the most successful and omnipresent species on earth. In New Zealand, the humble sparrow was introduced in 1867 and like anywhere else the land provides a happy hunting ground.

New Zealand's urban landscape is home to many introduced plants and animals and Europeans especially will notice many familiar species. In the average garden these include birds like the **song thrush**, the **blackbird**, the **starling** and the **chaffinch**. Almost all of these were, of course, introduced. One notable exception that is absent is the European **robin**. However, old habits die hard and they are still seen in two dimensions, annually, on the front of New Zealand Christmas cards.

Elsewhere, in the parks and open spaces, you will see (or more likely hear) the **Australasian magpie**, as well as the comical **pukeko**, and on the urban waterways, the obligatory **mallard duck** and **black swan**. The Australasian magpie is the size of a crow. He's dressed in black and white – like a butler – and is melodious and very intelligent. They are, as the name suggests, an Australian import and very unpopular in New Zealand. While nesting they are fiercely territorial and every year newspapers are full of Hitchcockian tales of people being attacked. The **pukeko** is a much more amicable import from Australia, where it is known as the swamphen. They look like a cross between a chicken and a spider, with outrageously long feet, with which they walk on water. They are a gorgeous blue/purple colour and sport a robust red beak. Get used to the 'pookie', as you will see them everywhere.

Often mistaken for the similar-looking pukeko, the **takahe** is much larger (and certainly much rarer). The black swan takes the place of the mute swan in Europe and is common throughout. They are smaller than the mute variety, but just as daft and just as delighted to share your sandwiches. The most common urban 'seagull' is the antsy and stern-looking **red-billed gull**. They are also encountered on the coast and will show up at your feet before your stomach even grumbles. The same applies of course to the **feral pigeon**. They too are commonplace, especially in sight of flat-whites and menus. Out and about almost anywhere in the North Island you will also see the street-wise **Indian myna**, a chestnut coloured, medium-sized passerine that, like the sparrow, is an introduced, almost human-reliant 'opportunist'. Their speciality is dodging traffic, which they can do with precision while catching dead insects on the road.

Mammals When it comes to mammals in suburbia you will find that Mrs Tiggywinkle (alias the **hedgehog**) moved in long ago. By all accounts 'she' paid a visit, liked both the climate and the menu and decided to stay. While the hedgehog at least adds slugs and other such unwelcome garden pests to its menu of native bird's eggs, the notorious **cat** is just the wanton, careless and prolific killer of old. Domestic and feral cats maul literally millions of native and non-native birds every year and next to **humans**, the **stoat**, the **possum** and the **rat**, they are native wildlife's worst enemy.

Coastal
Seabirds Of course the coast is never far away in New Zealand and it is home to some of New Zealand's 'wildlife royalty', specifically the world's only mainland colony of **royal albatross**, found only on the Otago Peninsula near Dunedin. If you are from the northern hemisphere this is simply a must-see, since without an expensive trip to Antarctica, this is perhaps your only chance. To watch them in flight or see their fat, infant chicks awaiting their next inter-continental meal (looking like large, bemused, fluffy white slippers) is simply unforgettable. It is amazing to think that said 'slippers' must grow wings that will span over 3 m and that those wings will then subsequently take them around the world more times than Michael Palin or Richard Branson.

New Zealand is actually known as the seabird capital of the world and a remarkable 70% of its total avian 'who's who' is pelagic (the world average is 3%). The list is long. Numerous types of **mollymawk**, which are similar to albatrosses, are common, especially off the southern tip of the South Island, where another family of seabirds, the **shearwaters**, also abound. If you go to **Stewart Island** you may see many of them, but you are more likely to find one boiled, next to your ketchup and chips. The prolific **sooty shearwater (or Titi)** has been hunted by the Maori for centuries and is still harvested today for food. Other seabirds include numerous species of **petrel**, including the Westland, Pycroft's and Cook's, all of which are found nowhere else in the world. One, the **taiko**, which was collected during Captain Cook's voyages, was not encountered again for nearly two centuries, when it was finally tracked down to its sole breeding site on the Chatham Islands. Most petrels and shearwaters nest in burrows and in huge numbers on the many offshore islands. They come ashore mainly at night, so your best chance to see them is offshore from boats or promontories, especially in Otago and Southland. Sometimes you will see huge rafts of petrels or shearwaters surface feeding, looking from a distance like a huge

▌ The mystical kiwi

New Zealands national symbol, the kiwi, deserves a special mention. Along with the platypus of Australia, or perhaps the peacock, it has to be one of the most curious and endearing creatures on earth – one, perhaps, that even Charles Darwin, given a party pack of recreational drugs, a bottle of vodka and a considerable bet, could still not devise. Almost half-bird half-mammal it evolved over millions of years of isolation to fill a specific niche free of any predators. Although related to the ostrich of Africa, the emu of Australia and the extinct native New Zealand moa, it is unsual in many ways and in some ways absolutely unique.

Flightless of course; they have no wings and their feathers are more like hairs. They are nocturnal and, like rabbits, live in burrows. They have long whiskers almost like those of a cat, which, along with an acute sense of hearing and smell, are its ammunition in the hunt for food. It is the only bird with nostrils at the end of its beak and its egg-to-body weight ratio is legendary. The egg of a kiwi averages 15% of the female's body weight, compared to 2% for the ostrich. Females tend to be larger than males and when it comes to the brown kiwi, the male tends to do most of the incubating. They mate for life, sleep for almost 20 hours a day and live as long as 30 years.

There are four identified species of kiwi. The brown kiwi, is the most common species and the one you are most likely to see in captivity. Although relatively widespread in central and northern North Island there is only an isolated population of 160 birds occurring in the South Island at Okarito. The little spotted kiwi is extinct on the mainland and survives only as 1000 birds on Kapiti Island and 200 on four smaller islands. The great spotted kiwi is only found on the South Island and an estimated 20,000 remain. Lastly the tokoeka is found on Stewart Island, Fiordland and around Haast. The tokoekas of Stewart Island are the only kiwi that can be seen during the day, which creates something of a tourist pilgrimage to try to see them (see box, page 672).

The best and only chance the vast majority of visitors get to observe these quirky characters in one of the many darkened 'kiwi houses' scattered around the country. Some of the best are to be found at the Whangarei Museum, 'Kiwi Encounter' in Rotorua, the DoC Wildlife Centre at Mount Bruce in the Wairarapa, Wellington Zoo, Orana Park in Christchurch and in Queenstown. Like so many New Zealand species, even the kiwi is not immune from the tragic threat of extinction and it is feared that they too will no longer be found anywhere in the wild on mainland New Zealand within two decades. For more information on kiwi and the efforts being made to conserve them, consult www.kiwirecovery.org.nz.

brown oil spill. One member of the petrel family you may bump into while out sea fishing is the **giant petrel**. He's big (about the size of a goose), uniform brown, and looks like an industrial-strength mole-grip on wings. So don't mess! Throw out your fish scraps and smile politely.

Another huge treat for any visitor from the northern hemisphere are New Zealand's **penguin**. Believe it or not, there are in fact three species perfectly at home in New Zealand and without an iceberg in sight! The **little blue** is the most common, being found all round the coast. It is also the smallest of the penguin species and probably the cutest. They come ashore to their burrows at dusk, and there are many noted sites. Some reserves, like **Tiritiri Matangi** Island near Auckland have nest boxes in which you can take a quick peek at little blues during the day. This can be highly entertaining as the enchanting little souls will merely look up at you with a pained expression as if to say 'Oh god, go away, you mustn't see me this fat'. Sometimes, if you encounter them on a path at night, by torchlight, they will look utterly bemused, stick their heads in the grass and point their bums in the air.

Almost as enchanting are the endangered **yellow-eyed penguins** of the Otago and Southland coasts. Enough is said about them in the preceding chapters, but like the albatross they are a must-see. Less easily encountered is the rarest penguin in the world, the **Fiordland crested penguin**. Your best chance to see one of these is on the west coast between Fox Glacier and Haast, as they come ashore at dusk or leave again at dawn.

Other notable seabird attractions include the colonies of greedy **gannets** at Murawai (near Auckland), Cape Kidnappers (near Napier, in Hawke's Bay) and on Farewell Spit, off the northern tip of the South Island. Several species of **shag** (cormorant) are also present in New Zealand. The most common are the large **black shag**, the black and white **pied shag** and again, as the name suggests, the petite (and again black and white) **little shag**. Some very rare, endemic and more colourful cousins include the **spotted shag**, the **Stewart Island shag** and **king shag**. Many other rare birds also inhabit the coastline including the **New Zealand dotterel** and one of the world's rarest birds, the **fairy tern**, of which tragically only around 30 remain.

Marine mammals When it comes to **whales** the word 'common' can only be used with extreme caution, with many species being more prevalent around the New Zealand coast than most countries worldwide. **Kaikoura** is, of course, synonymous with the whale and presents one of the best whale-watching opportunities in the world. As well as its resident pods of **sperm whale**, it plays host to **humpback whales**, **southern right whales**, **orca** and occasionally, even the endangered and massive **blue whale**. New Zealand is a world leader in promoting the conservation of whales and certainly does not share the view that these awesome creatures that have been around for millions of years are – as one Japanese minister at the International Whaling Commission conference recently put it – 'cockroaches of the sea'. Now there's a man who needs a shark encounter without the cage! New Zealand is also a world leader in dealing with mass **whale strandings**, which are all too common, particularly in the natural trap of **Golden Bay**, at the northern tip of the South Island.

Still in the XXL department are the three sub-Antarctic pinniped species (or seal). The **hooker's sea lion** (or New Zealand sea lion), the **leopard seal** and the **southern elephant seal**. Although actual breeding is rare on the mainland, all three regularly visit the southern coast. The best place to see these soporific barrels of bad breath and wind (gas) are the Otago and Southland coasts. Indeed, the Catlins in Southland often presents the opportunity to see all three species in one day – which is unheard of out of the sub-Antarctic Islands.

Given plenty of mention throughout the text is the **New Zealand fur seal**, which is a character of infinite charm and one that you will almost certainly encounter at close range. Out of the water, their ability to look fat and lazy, break wind and scratch their privates (all at the same time), while looking at you through one eye as if you are a complete waste of space, is frankly legendary. Quite right too – having had their brains battered to near extinction around New Zealand's waters throughout the 19th century perhaps we deserve such derision. A little word of warning: do not go within 10 m of any seal that you encounter on the beach. In the water they are even more agile and can swim faster and with more grace than anything in Speedos. Underwater or on the surface is also the best place to encounter **seals**. Whether diving independently or on an organized seal swim, they will often check you out like a dog in the park.

Dolphins are also a major feature of New Zealand's coastal wildlife, with dolphin watching and swimming being one of the country's many world-class activities. Apart from New Zealand's 'speciality' species, the tiny and endemic **Hector's dolphin** (one of the rarest in the world), and at least four others are regularly seen, including the **dusky dolphin**, **common dolphin**, **striped dolphin** and **bottlenose dolphin**.

Offshore islands

The New Zealand coast features literally thousands of offshore islands that are proving crucial to the conservation of the country's native wildlife. Many combine to form an invaluable flotilla of '**arks**'; ultimately the only hope for many species. Once the Department of Conservation has eradicated formerly introduced predators, for example cats, rats and possums, which involves an expensive and time-consuming poisoning or capture programme, the remaining small pockets of resident birds, plants and animals are encouraged to re-colonize, and captive endemic breeds can be re-released. Some of the species that are now reliant on the 'arks' include birds like the kakapo, the kokako and takahe. Other non-avian species include the precious tuatara.

The most crucial of the island's reintroduction programmes concerns the ancient flightless parrot, the **kakapo**; the flagship of New Zealand's conservation efforts. Only about 62 named individuals remain and each is closely monitored. The vast majority are kept on three island reserves, **Codfish Island** (off Stewart Island), **Maud Island** in the Marlborough Sounds and **Little Barrier Island**, near Auckland in the Hauraki Gulf. But the intense efforts being made to save the kakapo is merely plugging up the holes. Many species are often their own worst enemies, taking years and very specific environmental requirements to breed successfully. Many say it is only a matter of time.

However, to visit one of these vital reserves is to at least get a taste of the New Zealand of old and to experience the 'paradise lost'. On one of these islands you enter a world of unique and ancient wildlife that shows little fear of humans, creating a near bombardment of the senses. To encounter a kiwi at night or listen to the sublime dawn chorus of the near flightless **kokako** is one of the greatest wildlife experiences in the world. While most of the offshore islands are, understandably off-limits to visitors, New Zealand is very refreshing in its attitudes towards the education and access to its endangered wildlife for the average person. The islands of **Tiritiri Matangi** (see page 121) and **Kapiti Island** off the Wellington coast (see page 408) are just two examples.

Rivers, lakes and wetlands

New Zealand is riddled with rivers, lakes and low-lying wetlands all of which are home to both common, rare and unique species of animals and plants. From the rafts of mallard and black swan on **Lake Taupo** to the endangered **brown teal** on the quiet backwaters of **Great Barrier Island**, there is much to hold your interest. Other than the brown teal, other waterfowl of particular note include the beautiful **New Zealand shoveler** and the unique **blue duck**. A resident of remote and fast-flowing forest and mountain rivers, the blue duck uses highly specialized feeding methods to find algae and river insects and it is so unique it has no close relatives anywhere else in the world. Called the *whio* by Maori, which is an apt pronunciation of its call, they can sometimes be seen (or heard) from a kayak or raft, or even on the more remote tramps near mountain rivers. The rivers that feed **Lake Waikaremoana** in the **Te Urewera National Park** are just some good places to search.

Although not strictly confined to areas of wetland, another far more common duck you will almost certainly encounter in New Zealand is the **paradise shelduck**. Most often seen in pairs the male is relatively dark in colour, while the female is unmistakable with a predominantly chestnut plumage and a white head. In city parks and publicly utilized lakes they can often be approached with little protest, but in less urban areas they are shy and notoriously loud, often circling continuously overhead issuing a repetitive, high-pitched call until you have left their territory.

On the lower reaches of glacial rivers, where they become vast braided beds of moraine, there are two **'waders'** that are very unique and special. The first is the **black stilt**, or khaki, of which only about 80 individuals remain, making it one of the rarest waders in the world. You can see these beautiful and fragile-looking 'birds in black' on a guided tour of the DoC's captive breeding hides in **Twizel**, Canterbury. These are part of the excellent conservation programme put in place to protect them.

The black stilt's close cousin the **pied stilt** is much more common and a regular sight in the shallows of lakes, estuaries and natural harbours. Again they are very delicate in stature and boast a smart, almost formal-looking plumage of black and white. Also, like their pure black relative they have legs like busy knitting needles. Another unique wader with unusual appendages is the endemic **wrybill**, which has a bill bent to one side. This remarkable adaptation assists this small bird in its search for insects under small stones and driftwood. In winter they can be seen along with huge numbers of migratory waders at the **Miranda Naturalist's Trust Reserve** on the **Firth of Thames**, south of Auckland, while in summer they join the stilts, breeding 'incognito' and well camouflaged among the moraines of the braided rivers of the South Island.

Very common in both the urban environment and especially around water is the non-native **sacred kingfisher**. Like its European counterpart it is a shy bird but does not share quite the same bright iridescent colours. Far less prevalent is the un-mistakable **white heron** or Kokutu. Although relatively common worldwide, there is only one colony in New Zealand, near Okarito in Westland, South Island. Around 200 birds gather between September and November to breed, before scattering throughout the country during the winter months. You can see these magnificent birds on one of the tours that visit the Okarito breeding colony from Whataroa, north of Franz Josef. In winter, if you find yourself in Milford Sound, look out for 'Charlie', a famous heron that has spent the last 12 winters around the boat terminal. Little wonder the Maori have always held the white heron in such high esteem. The other far more common and smaller heron you will certainly see throughout New Zealand is the non-native **white-faced heron**.

Of course New Zealand's waterways are also home to many endemic fish and insects. Two native **eels**, the short-finned eel and the long-finned eel, have been sacred to the Maori for generations and once provided an important food source. They are huge, reaching up to 2 m in length and are thought to live up to 100 years old. You can see them in many nature reserves and animal parks where they are often fed by hand. The DoC **Mount Bruce Wildlife Centre** in the Wairarapa and **Rainbow Springs** in Rotorua are just two good examples.

Lowlands and forest

Less than 25% of New Zealand is under 200 m so, despite appearances there is not as much room as you think. When man arrived and set to with his short-sighted slash and burn policy, New Zealand's landscape was irrevocably altered and has now lost over 85% of its natural forest cover. The impact on the whole ecosystem has been immense; most of the native forest that remains is confined to inaccessible areas and mountain slopes, with almost a quarter of that being in South Island's west coast region alone.

One of the most evident yet hardly common species of the forests and low lying bush is the native **New Zealand pigeon** or kereru; a large, handsome, colourful character, with a signature plumage of almost iridescent greens, browns, purples and white, with bright red eyes. Often heard crashing about in the leaf canopies, they exhibit the congenial air of one who is over-fed and bring new meaning to the word plump. Little wonder the Maori prized the kereru as an important source of food. Today, despite being protected, their numbers are declining, mainly due to habitat loss and illegal hunting. The kereru can be seen in gardens and parks, but if it remains illusive you can see them at most animal parks. 'Pig', a rather daft Kereru residing in **Wellington Zoo,** is amenable to visitors and nearly died once after swallowing a pencil!

The stitchbird, bellbird and tui are also found in the lowland and forest habitats and are New Zealand's three representatives of the **honeyeaters**. A New Zealand endemic, the **tui** is quite common throughout the country and you are bound to see, and certainly hear them. From a distance they look a dull-black colour with a distinctive white bib (that also earned it the name of the 'parson's bird'), but on closer inspection their plumage is a superb mix of iridescent blues and greens. Their song is almost legendary, a delight to listen to, but almost impossible to describe. In essence they boast a remarkable range of audible whistles, grunts and knocks – a bit like Björk on a good night. Much of the tui's repertoire is beyond our audible range which is why they often look as if someone kept the camera rolling but momentarily pressed the 'mute' button. One of the best places to see tui in large numbers is during spring in the blooming cherry trees behind the **Wairakei Golf Club**, near Taupo. There, up to 30-odd birds can be seen in action, which is quite a sight and sound. The **stitchbird** and **bellbird** are not as common as the tui but are equally colourful and just marginally less melodic. They are best seen on the offshore island reserves.

Of all the smaller birds encountered most folk's favourite is the enchanting little **fantail**. These charming little birds are a bit like butterflies on speed and your visit to New Zealand will more than once be enhanced by their inquisitive nature. While walking down any bush or forest park they will often appear from nowhere and with manic audible 'peeps' fly about your person as if interested in making your acquaintance. They do this not once but for some time, flitting about and fanning their tails manically. In actuality, fantails are only interested in the insects you are disturbing within their individual territories, which is why, after a while, they suddenly seem to lose interest. Another little charmer, that is less common and shares this behaviour, is the **tom tit**: a small, native black-and-white character that in many ways resembles the European robin. Trampers will become familiar with the tom tit, especially in the South Island. New Zealand does also have its own robin, the dull-coloured **New Zealand robin** which can often be seen in the forests of both North, South and Stewart Islands.

The **morepork** is New Zealand's only native owl species. It is a small owl that feeds mainly on insects but is not impartial to the odd lesser-sized avian. Being very illusive and nocturnal, they are most often heard rather than seen and it is their distinctive butcher's shop request – 'more pork, more pork' – that earned them the name. The only other raptors (birds of prey) present in New Zealand are the native New Zealand falcon and the 'imported' **Australasian harrier**. Commonly seen soaring above hillsides and fields in the countryside, the harrier is often mistaken by the amateur to be an eagle. But eagles are much larger; the **Haast eagle**, which is now extinct but once ruled the skies in New Zealand, was over 26 times the harrier's weight and had a wing span of over 3 m, so large it would probably have been able to tackle a child.

Also with a curvaceous beak, the adorable **kaka** is one of New Zealand's three native parrot species. Once common throughout the country they are now confined mainly to old-growth beech and podocarp forests. Although unmistakable in both call and plumage the average visitor would be lucky to see one in the wild, making your best bet the zoos or DoC wildlife centres at **Mount Bruce** in the Wairarapa or Te Anau in Fiordland. At Mount Bruce, a small group has been successfully captive-bred and were released locally. Now, although essentially wild, they remain in the vicinity, returning to the same spot at the same time each day to be fed. This daily spectacle provides the kind of quality entertainment for which parrots can always be relied upon and also offers a superb photo opportunity.

Even tamer than the kaka but sharing its love for a free lunch is the **weka**, a sort of flightless brown rail. Again, without any predators, the weka evolved to dispense with the need for flight and focused its hunting activity entirely on the forest floor. In modern times it is not just the forest, but the human car park and campground, that offers rich pickings. If you are joined at any point by this appealing albeit uninvited guest, bear in mind they can be very persistent and notoriously quick with the steal.

Of course the lowlands and forests are also home to many non-avian species, but most of the true endemics are either reptiles or insects. Two notable exceptions are the much celebrated and impressively sounding **peripatus** and **powelliphanta**, both of which are as old as the land itself. Peripatus is like a cross between a worm and a centipede, while powelliphanta is a carnivorous land snail with a shell the size of a saucer. Both are remarkable creatures and were around millions of years before man.

Mammals It is remarkable to think that New Zealand played host to only one mammal before we arrived, a small bat, of which two species evolved. The **long-tailed bat** and the **short-tailed bat** are rarely seen by the casual observer, living in small local populations, and even then mainly on only a few remote offshore islands. Of course in New Zealand today, besides the bat, there is now a thoroughly cosmopolitan and unsavoury list of mammalian guests. This extraordinary list of reprobates includes possums (an estimated 70 million – 20 to every person), stoats, weasels, rabbits, hares, wallabies, ferrets, rats, mice, pigs, cats, horses, deer, goats and the infamous Paul Holmes (watch New Zealand television any weeknight at 1900).

Highlands
With over 75% of the country being above 200 m, this is a vast, yet inhospitable habitat. However, New Zealand's mountains and glacial valleys, like the rest of its ecosystem, boast a fair number of endemic animals and many unique plants that can often be spotted by the casual observer.

Most noted of the birds is of course, the notorious **kea** – the only alpine parrot in the world. This highly intelligent, entertaining 'avian thug' lives high above the tree line, where it nests amongst rocks and feeds on just about anything edible. Although you may only ever hear them, if lucky you may encounter them at close range. Nicknamed the 'cheeky kea' – thanks to their inherently inquisitive nature and extrovert behaviour – they are particularly fascinated by cars, rucksacks and shoelaces, or anything that can be dismantled, demolished or eaten. To have a flock descend in the middle of your picnic is a bit like an encounter with a class of unsupervised infants with severe behavioural disorders – out of control. I say children because that is truly how they behave and it certainly relates best to your subsequent reaction. They are so appalling, carefree and fun-loving that it is almost impossible not to just let them get on with it.

Another creature of the slopes and mountain valleys is the equally clever, but far less frivolous, **New Zealand falcon**. Quite elusive and capable of demolishing its prey like a surface-to-air missile you would be lucky to see one, but once spotted they are unmistakable. Nothing else in New Zealand flies with such stealth or purpose, nor when it arrests momentarily (most probably still grasping its latest victim) is so stern in looks. Even keas don't mess with a falcon's lunch!

Another bird of the mountains and remote glacial valleys is the remarkable and flightless **takahe**. They are the most appealing of birds and look like some congenial, almost 'clueless', prehistoric, purple chicken. Another ancient species once thought to be extinct, they were dramatically rediscovered deep in the Murchison Mountains of Fiordland in 1948. There is now an intensive breeding programme to attempt to secure their conservation, with only about 100 birds remaining in the wild and about the same again kept in captivity or on predator-free islands. The best place to see them is **Tiritiri Matangi** Island near Auckland, where several families (about 20 birds) are allowed to roam free. Being incredibly tame and inquisitive it is both memorable and remarkable to sit amongst them. But, as with so many of the species on the brink, you do so with perhaps a sense of guilt and the worrying question – but for how much longer?

Insects
New Zealand has an impressive range of creepy-crawlies, ranging from the noisy and the colourful to one that is the size of mouse. Although lacking in butterflies and far

more replete with moths, one large and perhaps familiar butterfly that you will see, especially in Auckland and the upper North Island, is the **monarch butterfly**. Famous the world over as a migratory species, these tawny-red and black-striped beauties, with a wingspan of 10 cm first arrived in New Zealand around 1840 (some say much earlier). It is very common in the urban and suburban habitats, but rarely seen in the bush or south of Christchurch. Although well known in the Americas for their swarming and long inter-state migrations, the butterflies found in New Zealand infrequently demonstrate these behaviours. However, like their American cousins and unlike most butterfly species, they often over-winter and live for several months.

One moth species that has a remarkable tendency to commit suicide by flying into any artificial light source at night is the large, native **puriri moth**. A beautiful lime-green colour with a wingspan of up to 15 cm, it is the country's largest moth species but is only found in the native forests of the North Island. Although the adults only live for a few days the caterpillars spend several years in tunnels bored in to trees.

By far the noisiest insect in the country is the **cicada**, which in summer and en masse can create an ear-splitting din in almost any area of bush or forest throughout the country. There are many species in New Zealand with one of the most common being the clapping cicada which was one of the first insects noted by Joseph Banks, the naturalist accompanying Captain Cook on his first new Zealand voyage in 1769-1770. They are fascinating creatures, about 30 mm in length with a wingspan up to 80 mm. The larvae of the very vocal adults can live in the ground for many years before aspiring to split eardrums. It is only the males that sing and the noise is created by the vibration of a unique ribbed structure called a 'tymbal' which resonates the sound in the almost hollow abdomen. Despite their being so many, try to take some time to focus on one song and try to locate the insect on the tree trunk branch or underside of leaves.

There are a number of spider species in New Zealand with the two most notable being the **katipo** and the **avondale**. The **katipo spider** is about 10 mm in length and, along with the average politician, is the only poisonous creature in the land. Looking the part, with a shiny black body, long legs and a red spot on its abdomen, it is a relative of the famous black widow and can deliver a nasty bite that can be incapacitating, but rarely fatal. You will doubtless be relieved to learn that they are a coastal species that frequent the undersides of logs rather than toilet seats!

The **Avondale spider** is a sub-species of the well known Australian huntsman. It is relatively harmless, but very large at over 10 cm in length. A unique, localized sub-species, found only in the suburb of Avondale in Auckland, it is an amenable easily-handled species that was bred in captivity and used in the film *Arachnophobia*.

Perhaps the most remarkable native insect in New Zealand is the **glow-worm**. Although essentially a gnat, it is the worm-like larvae that frequent the damp limestone caves and sheltered cavities on both the North and South islands that are most famous. The sight of an ethereal 'galaxy' of glow-worms (often called 'grottoes') on the roof of a cave in the darkness, particularly at Waitomo in the Waikato, is a truly memorable sight. What you are actually seeing are the shiny bottoms of the larvae, which emit a bright blue/green light. It is a clever and remarkable mechanism and a chemical reaction known as bioluminescence used to attract insect prey; the prey flies towards the light and is caught in sticky threads that the worm hangs from like a row of fishing lines from the roof of the cave. To enter a grotto at night then emerge into a clear starlit sky is a firm reminder of the incredible world in which we live.

Not to be outdone by a glowing bottom, the New Zealand **weta** is perhaps the king of all the New Zealand insects. They are an ancient creature that has been around for millions of years. A number of species are found in gardens, forests caves and rock crevices throughout the country ranging from the common tree weta to the cave weta. But without doubt the most impressive is the **giant weta**. At up to 9 cm in length and weighing up to 80 g they are about the size of a mouse and the largest insect in the world. With their huge abdomens, beady black eyes, long antenna and 'alien' like legs you will either love or hate the weta. Your best bet to see one is in the country's zoos. This will usually incite one of two reactions: an instant and impressive 100-m dash or a deep desire to make their acquaintance. Weta are not dangerous despite a fine set of mandibles used to crunch up leaves, shoots and small insects.

Of course, if you go anywhere near the west coast of the South Island you will become very intimate with the infamous New Zealand **sandfly**.

Vegetation

Like the country's animal life, much of New Zealand's plant life is very beautiful, very ancient and very unique, making it a veritable paradise for any 'budding' botanist. Over 80% of the country's flowering plants are not endemic to any other land. But like the fauna, much of the country's plant life is in a worrying state of decline, not as a result of predation, but by the clear felling and burning that has taken place since the arrival of man. Tragically, only about 15% of the New Zealand's original forest remains. Even a brief description of New Zealand's plant species is beyond the scope of this guide, but the following are some of the most notable species that you are likely to see.

Fern species

Alongside the iconic kiwi, the **ponga** or **silver fern** is New Zealand's other great national emblem and just one of a vast array of over 80 fern species. Depicted on everything from the national rugby jersey to the side of America's Cup yachts, the silver fern is a common sight in both the natural and commercial world. It is found throughout the mainly subtropical bush landscape, forming stands of almost prehistoric-looking umbrellas. A lush green colour on top, it is the silver underside that has created their notoriety, and not just in pure aesthetics. One well-known aspect of 'bush survival and rescue' is to lay out the fronds upside down in a clearing so as to capture the attention of a helicopter from above. Ferns generally have always been a very significant and sacred symbol of the Maori culture, especially in their tendency to 'unfurl' into 'being'. Often alongside the ponga, you will find the taller and more classic desert island-type **nikau palm**, the **cabbage tree**, as well as creepers, palm lilies, tree ferns and mosses.

Forest trees

The ancient New Zealand forest is traditionally one of **podocarp** and **beech trees**. Without doubt the most celebrated, yet overly utilized of the 100-odd forest tree species is the **kauri**. Occurring predominantly in the north of the North Island and a member of the podocarp family, it was once the dominant tree of the Auckland province and the Coromandel Peninsula. With vast trunks often over 15 m in diameter, and 30 m tall, free from knots and blemishes, the kauri was prized by both the Maori for canoe building and by the early Europeans for masts and other ship-building materials. The tree's resin ('kauri gum') was used as a derivative of varnishes and paint products and also as medium suitable for carving into elaborate ornaments. Sadly, over 90% of the trees were harvested and only a few ancient individuals remain. Most noted of these is the impressive 1,200-year old **'Tane Mahuta'** ('Lord of the Forest') which stands proudly in the **Waipoua Forest** in Northland. Other notable podocarp species, used for canoes and boat building, are the native **matai** (black pine), **rimu** (red pine), **totara**, **miro** and New Zealand's tallest tree – the **kahikatea** (white pine). The kahikatea can grow to 60 m.

Another plant heavily utilized by the Maori is the tough stemmed **flax** plant, found predominantly in wetlands the length and breadth of the country. It was used for everything from footwear to building.

Flowering trees

Two very colourful flowering trees, well known throughout the country, are the yellow flowering **kowhai** (New Zealand's national flower) and the red flowering **rata**, a climber that literally strangles its host tree to death. New Zealand's best known flowering tree is the beautiful **pohutukawa**; a gnarled-looking coastal evergreen that bursts into bright crimson flower for three weeks in December, earning it the affectionate label as New Zealand's Christmas tree.

Endemic flowers

Of the many endemic flowers in New Zealand a large number are found in the high alpine areas, including the **Mount Cook lily**, the largest of all the buttercups. With flowers as big as its leaves it is an impressive sight provided, that is, you can find it amongst the 60-odd species of mountain daisy!

Conservation

Describing New Zealand's rich and unusual animal and plant species is an act of celebration, but it is also a sorry tale. Although the country is often dubbed 'clean and green', many agree that it is far more a result of low population than attitude. Since the arrival of man we have had a dramatic and tragic effect on the landscape and biodiversity of New Zealand. As a result of our presence 32% of indigenous land and freshwater birds and 18% of seabirds are now extinct. The most recent extinction occurred in 1907 with the last sighting of the beautiful huia, a relative of the kakako, which is now also endangered. The loss of the huia occurred not only as a result of a decline in habitat, but man's ridiculous desire to adorn himself with its feathers. Many other unique and well-known species have also disappeared, like the legendary moa, which was hunted to extinction by the Maori. In the present day many others currently sit quietly on the brink. As it stands, with endemic bird species alone, there are only 36 fairy terns remaining, 62 kakapo, about 70 Campbell Island teal, 70 taiko, 80 black stilt and 200 takahe, to name but a few. Even the kiwi, the very emblem of the nation and its people is severely under threat and without more financing, it too is expected to be completely absent on mainland New Zealand within the next two decades. To lose the kiwi itself – the very bird after which its native humans are named – seems unimaginable. One can only hope, that given its prestige, it may stir people into action.

Government initiatives

Sterling efforts are being made in the war of conservation by governmental departments, for example the Department of Conservation, as well as independent organizations and individuals. Numerous captive breeding and predator eradication programmes have been initiated to stop, or at the very least slow down, the decline of so many species. Indeed, New Zealand is on the 'front line' of the global conservation war and thankfully there have been some fine and victorious battles. The **black robin**, an endemic little bird found only on the Chatham Islands, is one such example and one of the most famous conservation successes in human history. From a population of only nine individuals in the mid 1970s, it has essentially been saved and now numbers around 250. But these battles all defy the short-sighted, financial and technologically driven society of the modern day. Since the very act of conservation is a drain on funds rather than a source, the DoC is always under-funded and under-researched and it seems , tragically, a war that can perhaps never be won. Eco-tourism offers a viable path in some areas but it is just part of a long and difficult climb towards salvation.

Paradise lost

In the New Zealand of today, the great clean, green land – the paradise, but really the paradise lost – it almost makes the heart cry to experience the deathly hush of forests once alive to the sound of birds. At times it really is like standing in an

National parks & Forest parks

National park ◆

Abel Tasman **1**	Fiordland **4**	**Forest park ◆**	Northland **24**
Arthur's Pass **2**	Kahurangi **5**	Catlins **14**	Raukumara **25**
Egmont **3**	Mt Aspiring **6**	Coromandel **15**	Pirongia **26**
	Mt Cook **7**	Craigieburn **16**	Pureora **27**
	Nelson Lakes **8**	Hanmer **17**	Rimutaka **28**
	Paparoa **9**	Haurangi **18**	Ruahine **29**
	Stewart Island **33**	Kaimai Mamaku **19**	Tararua **30**
	Tongariro **10**	Kaimanawa **20**	Victoria **31**
	Urewera **11**	Kaweka **21**	Whirinaki **32**
	Westland **12**	Lake Sumner **22**	
	Whanganui **13**	Mt Richmond **23**	

ancient church that has been sacked of all its contents and robbed of both congregation and choir. Instead of a heads held high in celebration, the whispers of prayer and beautiful arias of worship, the pose is one of despair, the atmosphere one of remorseful reflection and the sound, one of eternal silence. To lose the kakapo, the kokako or the kiwi itself, all species that have been around for millions of years is too tragic to contemplate.

Books

For detailed and excellent information on the full range of New Zealand titles, subjects and authors contact the **Book Publishers' Association of New Zealand**, T09-4802711, www.bpanz.org.nz. For general titles and worldwide availability try www.amazon.com.

Non-fiction, pictorial, natural history and environment

There is a vast array of pictorial books celebrating New Zealand's stunning scenery. The best known photographers are **Craig Potton**, **Andris Apse** and **Robin Morrison**. Their books are of a very high quality and contain some exquisite photographs. There are a few good wildlife guidebooks and field guides. **Geoff Moon's** *New Zealand Birds* is an old favourite while the new *Field Guide to New Zealand Wildlife* by **Rod Morris** and **Terence Linsey** (Collins) is recommended. From afar the pictorial websites of www.photonewzealand.com; www.andrisapse.co.nz; and www.craigpotton.co.nz, are all excellent.

History, politics and culture

The History of New Zealand by **Keith Sinclair** is a dated but celebrated historical work, starting from before the arrival of Europeans. *Maori: A Photographic and Social Study* and *Being Pakeha*, both by **Michael King**; *The Old-Time Maori* by **Makereti**; *The Treaty of Waitangi* by **Claudia Orange**; and *The New Zealand Land Wars* by **James Belich** are all equally celebrated works covering the often contentious historical issues of the Maori and *Pakeha*. For an overall insight *The New Zealand Historical Atlas: Ko Papatuanuku e Takoto Nei* is highly visual, easy to read and generally recommended.

Biographies and travelogues

For tramping, the *Moirs Guides* (NZ Alpine Club) and *New Zealand's Great Walks* by **Pearl Hewson** (Hodders) are recommended. Also check out titles by **Craig Potton**, www.craigpotton.co.nz. For cycling, **Bruce Ringer's** *New Zealand by Bike* (Mountaineers) is excellent. For skiing try the annual *Ski and Snowboard Guide* available free from Brown Bear Publications, www.brownbear.co.nz.

Guidebooks and reference

The Mobil New Zealand Travel Guide by **Diana** and **Jeremy Pope** offers a general place-orientated guide, with interesting background reading and historical insights. *Wise's New Zealand Guide*, available in most second-hand bookshops, is excellent. For B&B guides the *New Zealand Bed and Breakfast Guide* by **J Thomas** (Moonshine) and the *Friar's B&B Guide* are recommended. For fans, *The Lord of the Rings Location Guidebook* by **Ian Brodie**, ($50), provides details the film locations around the country and how to get there (with GPS references). The book is only available in New Zealand, www.harpercollins.co.nz.

Fiction

The **New Zealand Book Council**, PO Box 11-377, Wellington, T04-4991596, www.bookcouncil.org.nz. Excellent source of listings of books, places of literary interest and events. When **Keri Hulme** won the Booker Prize in 1985 for *The Bone People*, and children's writer **Margaret Mahy** won the Carnegie Medal twice for *The Haunting* and *The Changeover*, New Zealand writing was put on the map. Previously, only the celebrated short stories by **Katherine Mansfield** (1888-1923) received international acclaim. *The Collected Stories of Katherine Mansfield* is her best-known title. Other works of note include: **Maurice Shadbolt's** *Season of the Jew*, a story about dispossessed Maori identifying with the Jews of ancient Israel; **Maurice Gee's** *Going West*, a story of unravelling relationships amidst the backdrop of Auckland and Wellington; **Witi Ihimaera's** *Bulibasha*, an affectionate look at Maori sheep shearing gangs in Eastland; and **Alan Duff's** much acclaimed *Once Were Warriors*, a disturbing and powerful insight into Maori domestic life. The film of it provides a reality check and is the complete antithesis of New Zealand's clean green, peaceful image.

Footnotes

Maori words and phrases

Aotearoa New Zealand
Ariki tribal leader
Atua spiritual Being
Harakeke flax plant, leaves
Hawaiki ancestral Polynesian homeland
Hapu sub-tribe/ to be pregnant
He Ao a land or a world
He tangata the people
Iwi tribe
Kaikaiawaro a dolphin (Pelorus Jack) who cruised the Sounds and became a guardian for iwi
Kaitiaki protector, caretaker
Kapa haka group of Maori performers
Kiaora welcome
Kaumatua elders
Kawa protocols
Kete basket
Kowhaiwhai rafter patterns
Mana integrity, prestige, control
Manawhenua people with tribal affiliations with the area
Maoritanga Maori 'ness'
Marae sacred courtyard or plaza
Mauri life essence
Moana large body of water, sea
Moko tattoo

Muka flax fibre
Ngati people of
Pa a fortified residential area
Paheka white European
Poi ball attached to flax string
Pounamu sacred greenstone
Rangatira Tribal leader
Taiaha A fighting staff
Tangata people/person
Tangihanga death ritual
Taonga treasure, prized object (often passed down by ancestors)
Tapu sacred, out of bounds
Te Ika-a-Maui North Island
Tipuna ancestor
Tukutuku wall panels
Utu cost
Wahakatauki proverb or saying
Waiata song, flute music
Wairua soul
Waka canoe
Whakairo carvings
Whakapapa origins of genealogy
Whanau extended family/to give birth
Whare house
Whenua land

Notes

Notes

Notes

Complete title listing

Footprint publishes travel guides to over 150 destinations worldwide. Each guide is packed with practical, concise and colourful information for everybody from first-time travellers to travel aficionados. The list is growing fast and current titles are noted below.

(P) denotes pocket guide

Latin America & Caribbean
Antigua & Leeward Islands (P)
Argentina
Barbados (P)
Bolivia
Brazil
Caribbean Islands
Chile
Costa Rica
Cuba
Cuzco & the Inca heartland
Discover Belize, Guatemala & Southern Mexico
Discover Patagonia
Discover Peru, Bolivia & Ecuador
Dominican Republic (P)
Ecuador & Galápagos
Mexico & Central America
Nicaragua
Peru
South American Handbook

North America
Discover Western Canada
Vancouver (P)

Africa
Cape Town (P)
Egypt
Kenya
Morocco
Namibia
South Africa
Tanzania

Middle East
Dubai (P)
Jordan

Australasia
Australia
Discover East Coast Australia
New Zealand
Sydney (P)

Footprint guides are available from all good bookshops and online at www.footprintbooks.com

Advertisers' index

Index → *Entries in **bold** refer to maps.*

Acknowledgements

Thanks once again to all the staff and representatives of the many regional visitor information centres and regional tourism offices who provided invaluable advice and assistance for this up-date. Gratitude stupendicus goes to Lachlan Sutherland who did the physical research of much of the South Island, spreading good vibes and music as he went. Lynda and Darren Davidson for looking after Johnny FP the van. Also thanks to Adam, Jo and the crew in Milford and Tony and Brigitte Robinson in Australia for their valued friendship and for providing support and sanctuary from the rigours of the road. Thanks, too, to all the team at Footprint and Nicola Gibbs in particular for her much appreciated patience and hard work. Finally a special thanks, as ever, to Grace and Rebecca for their steadfast encouragement and support.

Credits

Footprint credits

Text editor: Nicola Gibbs
Map editor: Sarah Sorensen
Picture editor: Robert Lunn

Publisher: Patrick Dawson
Editorial: Sophie Blacksell, Alan Murphy, Felicity Laughton, Jo Williams,
Cartography: Robert Lunn, Kevin Feeney, John Higgins
Sales and marketing: Andy Riddle, Hannah Bonnell
Advertising: Debbie Wylde
Finance and administration: Elizabeth Taylor

Photography credits

Front cover: Darroch Donald
Back cover: Darroch Donald
Inside colour section: Darroch Donald

Print

Manufactured by Nutech Photolithographers, Delhi, India
Pulp from sustainable forests

Footprint feedback

We try as hard as we can to make each Footprint guide as up to date as possible but, of course, things always change. If you want to let us know about your experiences – good, bad or ugly – then don't delay, go to www.footprintbooks.com and send in your comments.

Publishing information

Footprint New Zealand
4th edition
© Footprint Handbooks Ltd
October 2007

ISBN: 978 1 906098 04 9
CIP DATA: A catalogue record for this book is available from the British Library

® Footprint Handbooks and the Footprint mark are a registered trademark of Footprint Handbooks Ltd

Published by Footprint

6 Riverside Court
Lower Bristol Road
Bath BA2 3DZ, UK
T +44 (0)1225 469141
F +44 (0)1225 469461
discover@footprintbooks.com
www.footprintbooks.com

Every effort has been made to ensure that the facts in this guidebook are accurate. However, travellers should still obtain advice from consulates, airlines etc about travel and visa requirements before travelling. The authors and publishers cannot accept responsibility for any loss, injury or inconvenience however caused.